San Francisco. Ghirardelli introduces a baking chip called Flickettes to compete with Nestlé's chocolate chip, but the tactic weakens the company's reputation for high-quality products. The Ghirardelli family continues to draw preferred stock dividends, which weakens the firm's financial position. Financially drained, Ghirardelli sells its land and buildings in 1962 to a real estate developer who builds a shopping complex — Ghirardelli Square — on the property to cater to the city's growing tourist trade. In 1963, Golden Grain Macaroni Company, maker of Rice-A-Roni, purchases the remaining assets of Ghirardelli.

Half a million people a year visit historic Ghirardelli Square, one of San Francisco's most popular tourist attractions.
© Larry Lee / Westlight.

1964 – 1977

In 1965, chocolate production moves to a new 80,000-square-foot plant in San Leandro, California. The plant is equipped with over $3 million of new processing equipment. The Ghirardelli Chocolate Shop and Soda Fountain opens in Ghirardelli Square. Sales are less than $2 million, but the company slowly begins to re-emerge. Growing industrial sales to dairies, bakeries, and food processors support the new plant's production capacity. Consumer sales of chocolate bars and specialty chocolates also increase. New packaging is introduced. By 1976, sales reach $9 million.

1978 – 1989

Ghirardelli becomes revitalized. A new product, Chocolate Squares, is successfully launched in 1978. Product formulas are revised to reflect the growing demand for high-quality chocolates. Packaging revisions modernize the company's image. Investments in new equipment introduce new processing technology and triple production output. Sales to eastern markets double in volume each year. Ghirardelli's milk and dark chocolate eating and baking bars receive national attention by winning a taste-test competition over all other American and European chocolate bars. Sales reach $36 million. In 1986, Quaker Oats Company acquires Golden Grain and Ghirardelli. The buyout results in a corporate restructuring. Ghirardelli enhances its production, sales, and marketing staffs and establishes greater internal control of operations. In 1988, the company introduces The Premium Collection of five bar chocolates with upscale packaging.

Ghirardelli's quality assurance staff uses state-of-the-art equipment to test raw materials and finished products.

© 1988 HARUKO as appeared in Candy Industry Magazine.

Ghirardelli's product line includes chocolates for baking (top) and chocolates for eating (bottom).

CONTEMPORARY
BUSINESS

Sixth Edition

CONTEMPORARY
BUSINESS

Sixth Edition

Louis E. Boone
Ernest G. Cleverdon Chair of Business and Management
University of South Alabama

David L. Kurtz
The R.A. and Vivian Young Chair of Business Administration
University of Arkansas

THE DRYDEN PRESS
Chicago   Fort Worth   San Francisco   Philadelphia
Montreal   Toronto   London   Sydney   Tokyo

Acquisitions Editor: Robert Gemin
Project Editor: Karen Steib
Design Director: Alan Wendt
Production Manager: Barb Bahnsen
Permissions Editor: Doris Milligan
Director of Editing, Design, and Production: Jane Perkins

Copy Editor: Nancy J. Dietz
Indexer: Sheila Ary
Compositor: York Graphic Services
Text Type: 10/12 ITC Garamond Light

Library of Congress Cataloging-in-Publication Data

Boone, Louis E.
    Contemporary business/Louis E. Boone, David L. Kurtz. — 6th ed.
      p.   cm.
    Bibliography: p.
    Includes index.
    ISBN 0-03-027559-8
    1. Business.   2. Management.   I. Kurtz, David L.   II. Title.
HF5351.B653   1990   89-1224
658 — dc19   CIP

Printed in the United States of America
901-041-987654321

Address orders:
The Dryden Press
Orlando, Florida   32887

Address editorial correspondence:
The Dryden Press
908 N. Elm St.
Hinsdale, IL   60521

The Dryden Press
Holt, Rinehart and Winston
Saunders College Publishing

Cover Source: © 1980 Larry Lee Photography/Westlight.

To Bill Schoof

an institution in business publishing,
who provided invaluable advice and counsel
during the preparation of the sixth edition,

and
To the memory of Dawn Schoof

The Dryden Press Series in Management

About the Authors

Louis E. Boone (Ph.D.) holds the Ernest G. Cleverdon Chair of Business and Management at the University of South Alabama. He formerly chaired the Division of Management and Marketing at the University of Tulsa. Dr. Boone has also taught courses in management and marketing in Greece and the United Kingdom.

Dr. Boone's research on chief executive officers, conducted with coauthor David L. Kurtz and C. Patrick Fleenor of Seattle University, has resulted in the publication of a book, *CEO: Who Gets to the Top in America* (Michigan State University Press, 1989). In addition, he has published in such journals as *Journal of Business of the University of Chicago, International Journal of Management, Journal of Marketing, Health Marketing Quarterly, Journal of Psychology, American Demographics,* and *MSU Business Topics.* He is the current recipient of the Phi Kappa Phi Outstanding Scholar Award at his university and is listed in *Who's Who in America.*

David L. Kurtz (Ph.D.) holds the R. A. and Vivian Young Chair of Business Administration at the University of Arkansas. He previously held the Thomas F. Gleed Chair in Business and Finance at Seattle University and has also served as head of the Marketing Department at Eastern Michigan University. In addition, he has served as the Ian Potter Distinguished Professor at Chisholm Institute of Technology in Melbourne University.

Dr. Kurtz has served as president of the Western Marketing Educators Association and as Vice-President for Development of the Academy of Marketing Science. He currently is a member of the editorial review boards of the *Journal of the Academy of Marketing Science* and the *Journal of Marketing Education.* He is also a section editor for the *Journal of Personal Selling & Sales Management.*

With coauthor Louis E. Boone, Dr. Kurtz has written a number of texts, including *Contemporary Marketing,* Sixth Edition (The Dryden Press, 1989), the most widely used introductory marketing text in the United States. Their text *Contemporary Business* is ranked as the most widely used introductory business text in the world.

Preface

One day in early 1992, a significant event will take place. In an introductory business class in one of the nation's colleges or universities, the two-millionth student will begin the study of business administration using *Contemporary Business.* In the past 14 years, more students have studied business using *Contemporary Business* than any other textbook published. It has become the standard against which other texts are measured.

If imitation is truly the sincerest form of flattery, *Contemporary Business* has received a host of accolades. The text model established in previous editions has been closely followed by a growing number of business texts with virtually an identical listing of chapters and an instructor's manual housed in a box patterned after the pioneering *Organizer. Contemporary Business* was the first, for example, to use learning aids such as opening vignettes and boxed items to show an actual individual or firm applying concepts discussed in the chapters. It was the first to include an annotated summary of learning objectives at the end of each chapter and marginal glossary items to assist students in studying each chapter. In the fifth edition, *Contemporary Business* introduced computer applications following each chapter.

Innovation is a hallmark of each new edition of the text. Each edition's new features are typically imitated in subsequent years by other texts. Consequently, teachers of the basic business course have grown accustomed to previews of emerging trends in business texts with each new edition of *Contemporary Business.* The new sixth edition continues this tradition.

Integrating Print and Video Technologies

Technological advances are having a profound effect on college and university teaching. In recent years, publishers have been barraged with increased requests from professors for integrated video materials that are closely aligned with business concepts discussed in the textbook. *Contemporary Business* is the first text to truly answer these requests by providing integrated video cases and an extensive video package. This video package includes the new, highly acclaimed *Growing A Business* series, now airing on PBS stations. Each of these videos presents basic concepts by utilizing real-world case studies, on-location footage, special effects, and state-of-the-art graphics. Text chapters feature a *video case* that focuses on themes developed in the related video. The result is an integrated approach to blending high-quality videos with text concepts.

The end-of-chapter video cases and the accompanying videos feature a variety of small- and medium-size organizations. Examples include

◆ *Companies Founded and Managed by Female Entrepreneurs*
　　Chapter 1　　Cocolat
　　Chapter 3　　3D Distribution Systems
　　Chapter 5　　Esprit

◆ *Companies Founded and Managed by Black Entrepreneurs*
  Chapter 6   Famous Amos Chocolate Chip Cookie Co.
  Chapter 7   Henderson Industries
◆ *Small Companies*
  Chapter 8   Lundberg Family Farms
  Chapter 17   White Flower Farm
  Chapter 19   Old New York Brewing Co.
◆ *Medium-Size Companies*
  Chapter 10   Patagonia
  Chapter 11   Quad Graphics
  Chapter 18   Springfield Remanufacturing Corp.
◆ *Nonprofit Organizations*
  Chapter 2   Trust for Public Land
◆ *International Firms*
  Chapter 4   Fluor Corp.
  Chapter 14   Ben & Jerry's Homemade
  Chapter 15   L. L. Bean
◆ *Service Firms*
  Chapter 13   University National Bank & Trust
  Chapter 16   Stew Leonard's

In addition, videos are available to supplement end-of-chapter cases for Chapters 20 to 24. These cases feature such well-known firms as Tyson Foods, Mack Trucks, and Delta Air Lines.

A video case complete with student homework assignments appears at the end of each chapter. In addition, a separate manual, *Video Case Instructor's Manual,* provides the following materials for each video case: teaching objectives; a listing of chapter concepts illustrated in the video; video warm-up questions and exercises; a detailed outline of the video; answers to video case questions in the text; video recap; experiential activities with student handouts; and a multiple-choice quiz. With these videos, we believe we have succeeded in integrating print and video technologies.

Eliminating Text Clutter

The instructor who has used a previous edition of *Contemporary Business* in an introductory business course will notice a strikingly different look to each chapter. The dozens of boxed inserts — a fixture in almost every basic business text — have been eliminated and all examples are fully integrated within the text as examples of *applications* of business concepts.

The decision to remove the clutter of boxed examples is in response to numerous criticisms of their use. Students and professors alike complained that the boxes interrupted the flow of the text discussion, making it difficult to separate important concepts from long discussions of relatively unimportant material. The attempt by many authors to add examples to their texts by including information in the form of boxed items proved to be more of a distraction than an improvement.

Elimination of these boxes was accompanied by a conscious effort to integrate hundreds of examples directly into the text materials. Real-world examples are included in almost every paragraph to illustrate the application of fundamental business concepts. Also, the use of full-color photos and content-driven captions has been greatly expanded in this edition. The captions further integrate examples into the text.

Emphasizing Small Business

Too often, students are introduced to businesses of only one size — large. *Contemporary Business* recognizes students' growing interest in small business and the many career opportunities found in organizations other than corporate giants. Every video case in the first 19 chapters focuses on a small or medium-size company. In addition, a balanced presentation of applications and examples from both small and big business is maintained throughout the text. Discussions of business careers at the end of each part and in Chapter 24 focus on career opportunities in small businesses as well as in larger organizations. In addition, an entire chapter (Chapter 6) is devoted to entrepreneurship, small business, and franchising.

Highlighting Entry-Level Management

Another problem closely related to the overemphasis on big business is the tendency of textbooks to focus on top management decisions, activities, and problems and to neglect discussion of first-line supervisory management. But, as numerous business professors have pointed out, most business students will be employed at the supervisory management level. *Contemporary Business* provides more detailed coverage of first-line management in Chapter 7 and includes examples of supervisory management activities and problems throughout the text.

Focusing on Business Ethics and Societal Concerns

Recognition of the importance of ethical and societal/environmental concerns is reflected by the inclusion of *Social Responsibility and Business Ethics* as the second chapter in the text. These issues impact every aspect of modern business; consequently, they are examined throughout the text. The following illustrate the societal/ethical issues discussed in the text:

employee drug testing	1989 ban on life detectors as
insider trading	employee screening devices
sexual harassment	AIDS and the employment decision
production and pollution	no-smoking policies
AIDS and insurance	child care

Two of the video cases, Patagonia and Ben & Jerry's, focus on firms renowned for their emphasis on societal concerns. In addition, the video case for Chapter 2, "Trust for Public Land," examines the operations of an organization dedicated to preserving the environment.

Computer Problems

The sixth edition of *Contemporary Business* accomplishes the dual objectives of increasing the student's level of analytical thinking in the basic business course and integrating the use of microcomputers in the business curriculum. A special supplement, *Computer Cases for Contemporary Business,* is available at no charge to instructors. The supplement contains 120 problems (at least five business problems for each chapter) that can be assigned to students as homework requirements.

Instructors at colleges with easy access to microcomputers can use these problems as computer assignments. The supplement includes a detailed description of the quantitative technique used to solve each problem, together with a worked-out sample problem. The *Boone and Kurtz Business Disk,* a software supplement free to adopters for use with the IBM ®PC and the Apple-®II systems, can be obtained by contacting your sales representative or a Dryden Press regional sales office. The *Disk* includes the following 16 programs, presented in a user-friendly, menu-driven format, for use in solving business problems:

1. Forecasting
2. Decision Tree Analysis
3. Supply and Demand
4. Performance Analysis
5. Competitive Bidding
6. Evaluation of Alternatives
7. Economic Order Quantity (EOQ)
8. Employee Turnover
9. Engel's Laws
10. Breakeven Analysis
11. Markups
12. Advertising Effectiveness
13. Mean, Median, and Mode
14. Financial Statements and Ratios
15. Return on Investment
16. Evaluation of Investment Alternatives

Instructors can use these computer problems in a variety of formats. If students have ready access to microcomputers, problem assignments can be used as daily exercises. If students do not have easy access to computers, the problems can be solved by using a hand calculator. When microcomputer access is difficult, instructors can integrate computer usage in their classes by making one or two assignments during the term and/or by spacing computer assignments for different groups of students throughout the course to relieve demand for computer access in the microcomputer lab. Each of these alternatives will succeed in providing homework assignments involving quantitative problems for every chapter in the text.

Pedagogical Soundness

Contemporary Business has been written to help students learn about business. Students are challenged to apply business concepts rather than just memorize lists and definitions. The following features are designed to make this new edition even more effective as a teaching/learning tool.

Increased Coverage of Important Topics

Every chapter in the new edition has been extensively revised and updated. More emphasis has been given to topics such as productivity, job switching, women returning to the work force, computers, international business, and growth of the service sector. The growing importance of international business is emphasized through increased coverage of the topic in Chapter 3 and the inclusion of a separate chapter on global dimensions of business in the opening section of the text.

Emphasizing Chapter Learning Goals

To aid students in using learning goals as a study framework, the goals are listed at the beginning of each chapter and are restated at the end of the chapter in summary form. In addition, both the *Test Bank* questions and the *Learning Guide* are keyed to specific learning goals.

Using Chapter Overviews for Continuity

Each *Contemporary Business* chapter begins with an overview that relates the material to be studied to concepts discussed in preceding chapters. This enables students to view business in a complete and unified context.

Stressing Vocabulary Building

Vocabulary building — a critical concern in the first business course — is stressed by the inclusion of definitions in the margins adjacent to the introduction and discussion of the term in the text. In addition, key terms are listed at the end of each chapter, and all terms are listed and defined in an alphabetical glossary at the end of the book.

Focusing on Student Application of Business Concepts

Although business is a rigorous subject of study with a strong theoretical basis, it can often be taught best by focusing on applications of concepts being studied. Today's business students are pragmatic individuals who most often retain those class materials they have been asked to apply to a real-world context. The video cases in each chapter and the hundreds of in-text examples serve to motivate students to apply subjects discussed in the text.

Coverage of Current Concepts

Adopters of *Contemporary Business* expect it to be, above all, current. Among the new materials included in the sixth edition are

- the likely impact on U.S. business of the Soviet policies of *perestroika* and *glasnost*
- impact on business of such recent technological advances as fax machines, laptop computers, cellular telephones, voice message systems, and electronic mail
- Plant-Closing Notification Act of 1988
- the savings & loan crisis: its causes and the federal government bail-out

◆ impact on U.S. business of European Community integration in 1992
◆ computer viruses
◆ worker ownership of companies
◆ the Stock Market Crash of 1987
◆ computer networks and the contributions of computerized expert systems
◆ the portable office and telecommuting.

In addition, the sixth edition includes expanded and updated discussions of such topics as

◆ corporate culture
◆ intrapreneuring
◆ flexible manufacturing systems
◆ burnout
◆ mergers, acquisitions, and leveraged buyouts
◆ growth in the Japanese Stock Exchange.

Highlighting Business Careers

In addition to conveying to students the excitement and challenges of business and to developing a foundation in the basic concepts and terminology of business, *Contemporary Business* provides detailed, current information on various business careers. Chapter 24, "Your Career in Business," is devoted exclusively to helping students evaluate possible careers and guiding them through each step in the career search process. In addition, each of the eight parts in *Contemporary Business* begins with a real-life profile of an individual currently pursuing a career in one of the functional areas described in that part. Each of the eight parts concludes with a description of business careers relating to that section of the text.

Instructional Resource Package

The sixth edition of *Contemporary Business* is a comprehensive teaching/learning package unparalleled in its completeness. The textbook is undoubtedly the most critical element in the package, but it is only one part. Because of extensive research and careful coordination, the complete package is uniquely suited to the needs of business professors. The *Instructional Resource Package* is designed to assist the introductory business professor, who so often has large classes and a heavy teaching load.

The *Instructional Resource Package* consists of the following supplementary teaching aids.

Integrated Resource Manual

The two bound volumes contain the following sections for each chapter:

◆ Changes from the Previous Edition
◆ Annotated Learning Goals

- ◆ Key Terms
- ◆ Opening Quotations
- ◆ Lecture Outline
- ◆ Lecture Illustration File
- ◆ Answers to Review Questions
- ◆ Answers to Discussion Questions
- ◆ Answers to Video Case Questions
- ◆ Supplemental Case
- ◆ Teaching Notes for Supplemental Case
- ◆ Controversial Issues
- ◆ Experiential Exercises
- ◆ Guest Speaker Suggestions
- ◆ Term Paper Suggestions
- ◆ Solutions to Computer Cases
- ◆ *Learning Guide* Solutions

Test Bank

The completely revised 3,500-question *Test Bank* is available in both a printed and a computerized format. Questions are keyed to chapter learning goals, text page number, and type of question — knowledge or application. The *Test Bank* was prepared by Professor Sonya K. Brett of Macomb Community College, and James McGowen and Dennis Shannon of Belleville Area College.

Numerous adopter requests have led to the inclusion of a variety of types of questions in the *Test Bank*. In addition to 2,200 multiple-choice questions, the *Test Bank* also enhances test flexibility by including approximately 1,000 true/false questions and approximately 200 short essay questions. A separate essay question is included for every learning goal in the text. The latter questions may be used for daily quizzes or as part of regularly scheduled examinations. Mini-cases with accompanying multiple-choice questions offer additional application-oriented questions.

Contemporary Business Videos and Video Instructor's Manual

The 19 videos that accompany *Contemporary Business* are available at no cost to professors using the text in their classes. The videos are available only in one-half-inch VHS format.

A separate *Video Instructor's Manual* accompanies the sixth edition of *Contemporary Business*. This manual provides complete teaching support for each video segment and includes teaching objectives; a detailed listing of chapter concepts covered in the video, with text page references; video "warm-up" questions; a detailed outline of the video; "Video recap" discussion questions; answers to video case questions in the text; two student handout exercises; and a multiple-choice video quiz.

Learning Guide

The *Guide* is a completely revised learning supplement designed to further student understanding and to provide them with additional practice in applying concepts presented in the text. Each chapter includes Key Concepts; Business Vocabulary and Applications; Analysis of Learning Goals; Self-Review; Application Exercises; and a crossword puzzle or word search that uses business terms from the text. The *Learning Guide* was prepared by Professor Joan Sepic-Mizis of St. Louis Community College at Florissant Valley.

Business Simulation Game

The QSC Pizza Shoppe Simulation game, written by Professor Tom Ness of the University of South Florida, challenges students to develop and experience the business concepts presented in the text. It gives students an opportunity to utilize some of business's major decision-making tools. The game is accompanied by an *Instructor's Manual,* which includes complete instructions for the use of the game, and a *Student Manual,* which provides game instructions and student worksheets. The simulation game is available on disk for use with IBM® PC or Apple® II microcomputers.

Computer Cases Supplement and the Boone & Kurtz Business Disk

These innovative components of the *Instructional Resource Package* are designed to assist business professors who want to include analytical problems as homework assignments and/or to use such tools as the microcomputer in the basic business course. The *Computer Cases* supplement includes at least five worked-out business problems that focus on concepts discussed in each chapter. Full descriptions of each technique used, text-page references, and sample problems with solutions are included in the manual, which is provided at no cost to professors using *Contemporary Business* in their classes. Solutions to each case are included in the *Integrated Resource Manual.*

A second component is the *Boone & Kurtz Business Disk,* which is available free to adopters. It contains complete programs for computer cases and is available to adopters for use with Apple II or IBM PC microcomputers.

Portfolio of Business Papers

A portfolio of business papers has been assembled to help students understand the variety of papers and official forms required in a modern business organization. Authentic business papers are available with complete teaching notes for professors who use *Contemporary Business* in their classes.

Full-Color Overhead Transparencies

This innovative component includes a set of approximately 150 full-color transparency acetates. Without duplicating the presentation of material in the text, each transparency is a striking graphic illustration of a concept discussed in

Contemporary Business or advertisements illustrating business concepts. The set includes teaching notes for each transparency.

A number of adopters of the previous edition have requested that transparency masters of the actual figures in the text be prepared for classroom use. These masters are available, with teaching notes, in addition to the 150 full-color transparency acetates.

Acknowledgments

Many people have made a significant contribution to *Contemporary Business.* The text has been strengthened over the years as a result of the invaluable critiques, questions, and advice of a strong cadre of academicians and practitioners who are constantly seeking to improve the quality of teaching materials in the business discipline. For their reviews of all or part of the manuscript or assistance in developing text materials, we would especially like to thank the following dedicated business professionals:

James Agresta
Prince George's Community College

Margaret Alexander
North Harris County College

Jolene T. Anders
Northwestern State University of Louisiana

Charles Armstrong
Kansas City Kansas Community College

Jim Armstrong
John Tyler Community College

Edwin C. Aronson, Jr.
Golden West College

B. Toby Atkinson
Brevard Community College

Raymond F. Attner
Brookhaven College

Carlson D. Austin
South Carolina State College

Hal Babson
Columbus State Community College

W. Gary Bacon
North Lake College

Francis Byron Ballard
Florida Junior College

William Grady Barnhart
El Centro College

Robert L. Bartholomew
College of Boca Raton

James Baylor
Riverside City College

Alec Beaudoin
Triton College

John R. Beem
College of DuPage

Kay Berry
Kansas City Kansas Community College

Leonard Bethards
Miami-Dade Community College, North Campus

Mervel Blakesley
North Dakota State University

Robert H. Boatsman
Seattle Central Community College

Anthony Boratta
Laney College

Edward Borgens
San Diego Community College District

Robert W. Braid
Atlantic Community College

Stephen C. Branz
Triton College

Sonya K. Brett
Macomb Community College

Vera Brooks
Motlow State Community College

Don R. Brown
Antelope Valley College

J. G. Bryson
West Georgia College

Thomas Buchl
Northern Michigan University

John J. Buckley
Orange County Community College

Clara Buitenbos
Pan American University

Walter Bunnell
Sinclair Community College

Carroll Burrell
San Jacinto College

Thomas Calabrese
Sacred Heart University

Joseph A. M. Camardo
Cayuga Community College

Donald Cappa
Chabot College

Hugo Carlson
Northern State College

Lou Cisneros
Austin Community College

James Cockrell
Chemeketa Community College

Jerry Cohen
Somerset County College

Terry Comingore
Brazosport College

Curt Cremean
Jackson Community College

Linda Culicetto
Prince George's Community College

D. Dexter Dalton
St. Louis Community College at Meramec

Toby F. Deal
Patrick Henry Community College

Ted Dedowitz
State University of New York Agricultural and Technical College at Farmingdale

C. Frederick DeKay
Seattle University

Jack Howard Denson
Fullerton College

Toni Denton
Norfolk State University

Gordon Di Paolo
College of Staten Island

Les Dlabay
Lake Forest College

Carol J. Doll
Rock Valley College

Michael Dougherty
Milwaukee Area Technical College

Sam Dunbar
Delgado Community College

Gervase A. Eckenrod
Fresno City College

Gil Eckern
American River College

Walter O. Einstein
*State University of New York at
   Binghamton*

John J. Elliott
San Joaquin Delta College

Ted Erickson
Normandale Community College

Ruben C. Estrada
Pima Community College DTC

Jack Evans
New Hampshire College

Robert Fishco
Middlesex County College

George Fitchett
Bridgewater College

Ray Fleig
Clark Technical College

Fred E. Folkman
Queensborough Community College

Roger Fremier
Monterey Peninsula College

William M. Friedman
Fontbonne College

Barbara J. Frizzell
Macon Junior College

Judith Furrer
Inver Hills Community College

Marlin Gerber
Kalamazoo Valley Community College

Robert L. Goldberg
Northeastern University, Boston

Robert Googins
Shasta College

Donald J. Green
Chabot College

Roberta Greene
Central Piedmont Community College

B. B. Griffith
Odessa College

Darwin K. Grimm
Iowa Lakes Community College

Joe Grissom
Tarrant County Junior College

John W. Hagen
California State University-Fresno

Louis T. Harding
University of the District of Columbia

Arthur L. Hardy
San Jacinto College

James W. Hariston
South Carolina State College

John Harrington
New Hampshire College

Robert W. Harris
Mercer County Community College

Susan Harrison
Parkersburg Community College

J. Dennis Hart
Marion Technical College

Larry Helderth
Danville Community College

Larry Henderson
National College

Shirley Hendrick
Pennsylvania State University

Joyce Henrion
St. Petersburg Community College

Russell Heritage
Treasure Valley Community College

Fred E. Hild
Valencia Community College

Harald Hillmer
Riverside City Community College

Nathan Himelstein
Essex County College

Larry Hollar
Catawba Valley Technical College

J. S. Hoy
Humboldt State University

Thomas Huddleston
*Northern Virginia Community College-
   Manassas*

Ed Huneke
Lewis and Clark Community College

David A. Hunt
Blackhawk Technical Institute

Jane Jackson
Eastern New Mexico State University

Paul F. Jenner
Missouri Western State College

Dana J. Johnson
*Virginia Polytechnic Institute and State
   University*

Edwin D. Johnson
Parkersburg Community College

Chad Jones
National College

Francis L. Jones
Cypress College

Frazier Jones
Brevard Community College

John Kaelber
St. Petersburg Community College

Frank Kahl
Ohlone College

Bernard M. Kaplan
J. Sargeant Reynolds Community College

Bernard Karne
Laney College

Bernard V. Katz
Oakton Community College

Marvin S. Katzman
George Washington University

Louis C. Kaufman
Fordham University

Warren Keller
Grossmont College

David Kelmar
Santa Monica College

Fred Kiesner
Loyola Marymount University

Stanlee Kissel
Somerset County College

Derwin Koleada
Menershe State University

Carl Kovelowski
Mercer County College

John Krane
Community College of Denver

David Krohn
Kirkwood Community College

Fran Kubicek
Kalamazoo Valley Community College

Jerry Lancio
Florida Keys Community College

John Leahy
Palomar College

James Lentz
Moraine Valley Community College

Edwin C. Leonard, Jr.
Indiana-Purdue University at Fort Wayne

Chad Lewis
Everett Community College

David Lewis
Allan Hancock College

Robert J. Lewis
*Indiana-Purdue University at
   Indianapolis*

John Lloyd
Monroe Community College

Paul Londrigan
C. S. Mott Community College

Paul N. Loveday
University of Nevada-Las Vegas

William P. Lovell
Cayuga Community College

Charles Lowery
Technical College of Alamance

Robert J. Lucas
Metropolitan State College

Marshall D. McCollum, Jr.
Portland Community College

Bates McGregor
Southwest Missouri State University

James M. McHugh
*St. Louis Community College at Forest
   Park*

Martin McKell
College of the Desert

John McMillan
Point Loma College

James MacNamara
Brevard Community College

Marie Madison
Truman College

Edward G. Magruder
Virginia Western Community College

Donald D. Manning
Colorado Northwestern Community College

Joel Mansfield
Central Missouri State University

Martin K. Marsh
Humboldt State University

Frank D. Mason
California State University, Northridge

Noel Matthews
Front Range Community College

Sylvia Mays
Kirkwood Community College

Edward Menge, Jr.
Franklin University

Sherry Mercer
Santa Fe Community College

James Meszaros
Community College of Morris

Thomas Bradford Metcalf
University of Houston College of Technology

Henry Metzner
University of Missouri-Rolla

William Middleton
Ventura College

Richard Miller
Harford Community College

Emerson Milligam
Carlow College

Keith Mills
Chemeketa Community College

Edwin Miner
Phoenix College

Robert Moore
Imperial Valley College

Ed Mosher
Laramie County Community College

William F. Motz
Lansing Community College

Robert Mueller
Olive Harvey College

W. G. Mueller
Spokane Community College

Dick Mulkey
Eastern New Mexico University Roswell Campus

A. Murphy
Hillsborough Community College

William Murray
University of San Francisco

Helen Nabors
Shelby State Community College

James Nestor
Daytona Beach Community College

Joyce E. Newton
Jackson Community College

La Jean Nichols
Alabama Christian College

Robert O. Nixon
Pima Community College

Gerald O'Boyle
St. John's University

Frank O'Rourke
Atlantic Community College

George Otto
Truman College

G. Dean Palmer
University of Northern Colorado

Dennis D. Pappas
Columbus Technical Institute

Ken Pappenfuss
Ricks College

Clarissa Patterson
Bryant College

Merle Peper
Southeastern Louisiana University

Gus Petrides
Borough of Manhattan Community College

James B. Pettijohn
Southwest Missouri State University

Norman Petty
Central Piedmont College

Stanley Phillips
Tennessee Technological University

Arnold Pisani
Berkshire Community College

Johnette Plantz
College of the Mainland

Noel G. Powell
West Georgia College

Roderick D. Powers
Iowa State University

Lorraine E. Pratt
Prince George's Community College

James R. Prucnal
Gadsden State Junior College

Richard W. Przybylski
Mission College

Elaine Rankin
Austin Community College

Robert A. Redick
Lincoln Land Community College

W. J. Regan
University of San Francisco

James Reinemann
College of Lake County

William Rice
California State University, Fresno

Robert Rizzo
Indian River Community College

Jim Robinson
University of Wyoming

Durell Rochester
Tri-County Technical College

Buck Rogers
North Harris County Community College

Bernice B. Rollins
Prairie View A&M University

Walter Richard Rooney
University of Houston Downtown Campus

James J. Runnalls
University of Wisconsin-Stout

Celene Sanders
Radford College

Fernando Santamaria
Fiorello La Guardia Community College

Nick Sarantakes
Austin Community College

Jean M. Saunders
Virginia Western Community College

Thomas C. Schaber
Miami University

S. Alan Schlact
Kennesaw College

Dennis E. Schmitt
Emporia State University

Scott Schroeder
DeVry Institute of Technology

Bill Schwartz
Temple University

Arnold H. Scolnick
Borough of Manhattan Community College, City University of New York

Jon E. Seely
Tulsa Junior College

John Seitz
Oakton Community College

Joan Sepic-Mizis
St. Louis Community College at Florissant Valley

Myron G. Sessions
Spokane Falls Community College

Barry Shane
Oregon State University

Steven L. Shapiro
Queensboro Community College

David E. Shepard
Virginia Western Community College

Thomas Shockney
Ashland College

Celeste Sichenze
Northern Virginia Community College Annandale

Bill Simpson
South DeKalb Community College

James Simpson
College of the Mainland

Clay Sink
University of Rhode Island

Michele Slagle
George Washington University

Glenn Smith
Marshall University

W. Nye Smith
Clarkson College of Technology

Carl Sonntag
Pikes Peak Community College

J. Wayne Spence
North Texas State University

Richard J. Stanish
Tulsa Junior College-Metro Campus

Herbert Stuart Stegenga
Housatonic Community College

Randy Stegner
Jefferson Community College

Harold Sternbach
University of Rhode Island

C. Strain
Ocean Community College

Joseph T. Straub
Valencia Community College

David Streifford
St. Louis Community College at Forest Park

Rhosan Stryker
Delta College

William Sidney Sugg, Jr.
Lakeland Community College

A. Kenneth Swanson
Nova Community College

Robert Tansky
St. Clair County Community College

Bill Tapp
College of the Mainland

Merle E. Taylor
Santa Barbara City College

Ray Tewell
American River College

Lula Thomas
Southern University A&M College

B. Jerry Thornton
Albany Junior College

Frank G. Titlow
St. Petersburg Junior College

Richard Trower
Danville Junior College

John Turner
Manatee Community College

William C. Tustin
Jackson State Community College

Charles E. Tychsen
Northern Virginia Community College

Al Tyson
Passaic County Community College

Pablo Ulloa, Jr.
El Paso Community College

John Vacek
Triton College

Richard Van Beek
Northern State College

Robert H. Vaughn
Lakeland Community College

Percy O. Vera
Sinclair Community College

Michael Vijuk
William Rainey Harper College

C. Thomas Vogt
Allan Hancock College

Robert Wagley
Wright State University

Larry Waldorf
Boise State University

John F. Warner
University of New Mexico

Jack Warren
Jackson State Community College

Irving Wechsler
Borough of Manhattan Community College, City University of New York

Bernard W. Weinrich
St. Louis Community College at Forest Park

Gerry Welch
St. Louis Community College, Meramec

William A. Weller
Modesto Junior College

Floyd Went
St. Louis Community College at Florissant Valley

Susan Wessels
Meredith College

Stephen L. West
Daytona Beach Community College

Clark W. Wheeler
Santa Fe Community College

Charles A. White
Edison Community College

Eugene White
Community College of Denver

Mildred M. Whitted
St. Louis Community College at Forest Park

Sally Sue Whitten
West Virginia State College

Stan Wilkinson
Appalachian State University

Jonnie L. Williams
Grand Rapids Junior College

Terrell Williams
Utah State University

Wayne Roy Wilson
Cameron University

Wallace Wirth
Thornton Community College

Paul J. Wolff
Dundalk Community College

Charles Womer
DeAnza College

Charles E. Woodfill
Franklin University

Gregory J. Worosz
Schoolcraft College

H. R. Worrell
Rose State College

Ken Wright
Passaic County Community College

William Wright
Mt. Hood Community College

Jacqueline Wyatt
Ashland College

Edward Yost
Franklin University

Robert Youngquist
Mesa College

Our work in preparing the sixth edition was enhanced greatly by the following reviewers who made numerous suggestions. In preparing the sixth edition, we sought out the advice of business specialists who reviewed text components that matched their specialized research and teaching areas. In many instances, they included their students in the review process and a number of their suggestions were implemented in the new edition. We would particularly like to thank the following individuals:

James Agresta, *Prince George's College*

Gary E. Carlson, *DeVry Institute of Technology*

Debra E. Clingerman, *California University of Pennsylvania*

Robert E. Cox, *Salt Lake Community College*

Bob Graw, *Cuyahoga Community College*

Steven Huntley, *Florida Junior College*

Lowell Lambert, *Central Oregon Community College*

Bruce Leppian, *Delta College*

Nikki Paahana, *DeVry Institute of Technology*

Richard Randall, *Nassau Community College*

We would also like to thank the professors who appear in the text itself:

Rick Gorno, *Cypress Community College*

John Lloyd, *Monroe Community College*

Paul Londrigan, *Mott Community College*

Don Ryktarsyk, *Schoolcraft Community College*

David Steenstra, *Davenport Business College*

Ron Young, *Kalamazoo Valley Community College*

We are especially indebted to Joan Sepic-Mizis for preparing the *Learning Guide.* Our special thanks go to Tom Ness of the University of South Florida for preparing the business simulation game, to Spencer Mehl of Coastal Carolina Community College for editing the *Business Papers,* and to Sonya K. Brett of Macomb Community College and Jim McGowen and Dennis Shannon of Belleville Area College for their preparation of the *Test Bank.* We would also like to thank Kathy J. Daruty for the excellent materials in the *Video Instructor's Manual.* We can never fully express our appreciation to our research associate, Nancy Moudry, for her many contributions. We would also like to thank our capable secretaries and research associates, Carol Stamps, Ruby Gardner, Jeanne Lowe, and Gary Prish for their invaluable assistance.

Finally, we gratefully acknowledge the many contributions of the professionals at The Dryden Press. We would particularly like to thank our publisher, Bill Schoof, and our editor, Robert Gemin, for their insights and suggestions for the new edition. Our project editor, Karen Steib, was a continuing source of good advice. Barb Bahnsen, Eric Elvekrog, Mary Jarvis, Doris Milligan, Jane Perkins, and Alan Wendt proved on numerous occasions their ability to eliminate seemingly unsurmountable obstacles. And our marketing manager, Patti Arneson, was a constant source of creative suggestions for improving the new edition. The revision was truly a team effort, and we are in their debt.

Louis E. Boone   David L. Kurtz
October 1989

Brief Contents

Contents

Part Two
The Structure of American Business 109

Chapter 5
Forms of Business Ownership 110

Chapter 8
Internal Organization 196

Chapter 9
Production and Operations Management 220

Part Five
Marketing Management

Chapter 13
Marketing Strategy

Part Seven
Financing the Enterprise   553

Chapter 19
Money, the Banking System, and Other Financial Institutions   554

Chapter 20
Financial Management   592

Chapter 21
The Securities Market   618

Chapter 22
Risk Management and Insurance   652

Notes

Dictionary of Business Terms

Index

Chapter 1
The Foundations of Business

Chapter 2
Social Responsibility and Business Ethics

Chapter 3
Economic Challenges Facing America

Chapter 4
Global Dimensions of Business

Contemporary Business and Its Environment

Career Profile: *Richard Shen*

Richard Shen's success story illustrates how much effort it takes to transform a good idea into a successful business. Shen is one of those rare entrepreneurs who has the skills to manage and expand his business venture. Shen started his company at 18 by selling his truck and using the $1,200 to open Audio Chamber International, which specializes in installing high-quality stereo systems in vehicles that range from VW bugs and Cadillacs to helicopters and boats.

Audio Chamber's one store has annual sales of between $1 million and $2 million. The 5-year-old company has increased sales approximately 300 percent each year. In fact, Audio Chamber has done so well that Shen has used its profits to start two other businesses, ACI Cellular Phones and Shensyn Development and Management Co., a real-estate development firm.

Shen is matter-of-fact about his success. He says he can't understand why so many new businesses fail. "What I do is not that big of a deal — I'm simple, savvy, and I work hard," he says. Working hard for Shen means putting in as many as 18 hours a day.

Rick Gorno, one of Shen's professors at Cypress Community College, Cypress, California, has a slightly different perspective on Shen. "He has what they call the entrepreneurial spirit — he wanted to go into business and had this interest at an early age," says Gorno. "In addition, he had a vision of what he wanted to do. He went into an area, car stereos, he liked and knew quite well. One other thing he did that many young people don't do is he actually set goals. And when he met them, he set new ones."

Shen stresses being frugal and listening. "You have to listen to your market," says Shen. "This means customers *and* personnel. You must be aware."

Each Audio Chamber customer receives personalized attention, and Shen emphasizes the customer's tastes, not his. Each sales representative is trained in the company's philosophy and in particular procedures. Shen stresses simplicity in sales. Once the customer's musical tastes are determined, the sales rep helps the customer select a stereo.

Shen has worked at improving his communications skills. He also has fostered a progressive workplace environment.

For instance, Shen's number one rule is "to never have employees." For his enterprises, Shen handles the management, marketing and sales tactics, and he coordinates the advertising. Everyone else who works for Shen acts as an independent contractor, even the sales manager, who's worked there since the company started. Most of the 50 or so people who work for Shen sell or install the stereo equipment, his main business.

Selling stereo equipment is not Shen's only goal. "Since I do hold responsibility and am an example, I have to be responsible and show others the correct way of making a life," Shen says. "Business is not just about making money — your most successful businesses give back the most to their people."

Shen's philosophy may have come from the slum in which he grew up. The man who says his earliest memory is of being beaten by gang members now inspires confidence in a number of people who work for him and in former professors.

Photo source: Courtesy of Richard Shen.

1 *The Foundations of Business*

Learning Goals

1. To explain what a business is and how it operates within the private enterprise system.

2. To define the roles of competition and the entrepreneur in a private enterprise system.

3. To outline the basic rights of the private enterprise system.

4. To discuss the factors of production and their factor payments.

5. To explain the concepts of gross national product and productivity.

6. To identify the degrees of competition that can exist in a private enterprise system.

7. To analyze how the historical development of the U.S. economy influences contemporary business.

8. To identify the different types of economic systems.

9. To explain how to study business and why.

One Saturday morning, Wayne Smith, the president of Emerald Technology, was about to leave his home for a weekend trip when his answering service called. A customer needed a certain product by Monday. So Smith put his personal plans on hold, went to his Bothell, Washington, office, got the needed item, and sent it to the customer via Federal Express for Monday delivery. Stories like this are common at Emerald Technology, where customer service is used to differentiate the firm from its competition.

Located just outside of Seattle, Emerald Technology is a classical example of a small firm that is competing successfully in our private enterprise system against one of the nation's largest corporations, IBM. Emerald Technology's 65 employees make computer hardware and software that allow other computers to be connected to various IBM midrange computers. In just four years, the company has grown to $10.5 million in sales and a pretax profit of over $1 million.

The key to Emerald Technology's success is its competitive strategy based upon the best possible customer service. All orders go out via Federal Express, and the customers are charged for the speedy service. The firm also, if necessary, will fly support personnel to a customer's location to fix a $895 product. Smith explains the strategy this way: "If a customer has any problem, we'll help them. We have a high caliber of people in customer support. We pay them higher salaries, and that's where we put the best people in the business."

Emerald Technology identified a specific market niche for which it provides excellent service. Smith

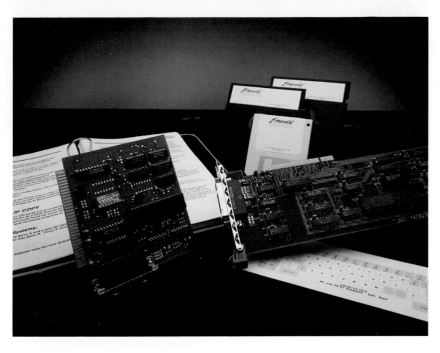

originally targeted the minicomputer features that IBM considered too small to spend resources on promoting. Smith says IBM's basic policy is not to enter a market unless it has the potential to generate $1 billion or more in revenue. But sometimes Big Blue, as IBM is known, changes its mind.

Emerald Technology's first product connected personal computers to minicomputers and was an instant success. Three weeks later, IBM announced it was entering this market. Smith described IBM's decision this way: "The effect was like sprinkling holy water on the market." The market expanded rapidly; IBM captured half of it. But there is still a lot of business for Emerald and other competitors.

Effective customer service is a major plus for Emerald Technology. But Wayne Smith also realizes he must continue to develop new products as IBM launches its new computer series. He says: "We're very close to IBM. We work in their niches. It's like walking in the footprints of the elephant."[1]

Chapter 1 points out that a firm's future depends on how well it matches and counters the offerings of competitors. On this score, Emerald Technology is clearly successful. This opening chapter also provides a preview of contemporary business systems here and elsewhere.

Chapter Overview

Mention the word business and people think of various things. Some people think of their jobs; others of the individual merchants they deal with as consumers; and still others of the thousands of firms that make up this nation's economy. This broad all-inclusive term can be applied to many kinds of enterprise. Business provides the bulk of our employment as well as the goods and services we seek.

business
All profit-seeking activities and enterprises that provide goods and services necessary to an economic system.

Business consists of all profit-seeking activities and enterprises that provide goods and services necessary to an economic system. Some businesses produce tangible products, such as automobiles, breakfast cereals, and computer chips. Others provide services, such as insurance, car rentals, and lodging. The nonstop flights to Asian cities promoted in the advertisement in Figure 1.1 are an example of a service provided by Northwest Airlines. Business is the economic pulse of a nation, the means through which society's standard of living improves. Profits are a primary mechanism for accomplishing these goals. Accountants and businesspeople define **profits** as the difference between a company's revenues (receipts) and expenses (expenditures). Profits are rewards received by successful businesspeople who take the risks involved in business.

profits
Difference between a company's revenues (receipts) and expenses (expenditures).

Besides earning profits, successful businesses also seek to meet their social and ethical responsibilities. This means businesses must be responsible in their dealings with employees, consumers, suppliers, competitors, government, and the general public if they are to succeed in the long run. More than 50 years ago, General Robert Wood, former chairman of Sears, Roebuck and Co., stated: "Business must account for its stewardship, not only on the balance sheet, but also in matters of social responsibility."[2] By conducting its business in a fair and ethical manner and working for the betterment of society, Sears has earned a reputation of integrity, a competitive strength that has enabled it to succeed as the nation's largest retailer. Social responsibility and business ethics are discussed fully in Chapter 2.

We begin our study of business by describing the private enterprise system of the United States, giving a history of U.S. business, and then presenting alternative economic systems.

The Private Enterprise System

private enterprise system
Economic system in which success or failure is determined by how well firms match and counter the offerings of competitors.

Most U.S. businesses, large or small, belong to what is called the **private enterprise system**, in which success or failure is determined by how well they match and counter the offerings of competitors. **Competition** is the battle among businesses for consumer acceptance. Sales and profits are the yardsticks by which such acceptance is measured.

competition
Battle among businesses for consumer acceptance.

The business world can provide numerous examples of firms that were once successful but failed to continue satisfying consumer demands. Competition assures that, over the long run, firms that satisfy consumer demands will be successful and those that do not will be replaced.

In the private enterprise system, firms must continually adjust their strategies, product offerings, service standards, and operating procedures or else competitors may gain larger shares of the industry's sales and profits. Consider the following cases. Although A & P was for many years the largest supermarket

Figure 1.1   A Service-Producing Business

Source: Courtesy of Northwest Airlines, Inc.

chain in the United States, Safeway has overtaken it in size and sales volume. Ford once led all automakers in production. Today, however, it ranks second to General Motors among domestic producers. At one time, Montgomery Ward competed head to head with Sears. Now, however, Ward lags far behind K mart, Wal-Mart, and J. C. Penney as Sears' nearest competitor. These events suggest the dynamic environment of the private enterprise system.

Competition is a critical mechanism for guaranteeing that the private enterprise system will continue to offer the goods and services that provide high living standards and sophisticated life-styles. Few business organizations escape the influence of competition. Nonprofit organizations such as the American Cancer Society also compete for contributions with such groups as the local symphony, your own college, and other enterprises. Similarly, the armed forces compete in the labor market with private employers.

The Role of the Entrepreneur

An **entrepreneur** is a risk taker in the private enterprise system, a person who seeks a profitable opportunity and then devises a plan and forms an organization to achieve the objective. Some entrepreneurs set up new companies and ventures; others revitalize established concerns. The entrepreneurial spirit lies at the heart of the American economic system. Without the willingness to take risks, there would be no successful businesses, and the private enterprise system could not exist. The stories that introduce each chapter in this book illustrate the entrepreneurial spirit of U.S. business. The role of the entrepreneur is discussed in more detail in Chapter 6.

entrepreneur
A risk taker in the private enterprise system.

How the Private Enterprise System Works

The private enterprise system, or **capitalism**, is founded on the principle that competition among business firms best serves the needs of society. Adam Smith, often called the father of capitalism, first described this process in his book

capitalism
Economic system founded on the principle that competition among businesses best serves society.

invisible hand of competition
Adam Smith's description of how competition regulates the private enterprise system.

Wealth of Nations, published in 1776. Smith said an economy is best regulated by the **invisible hand of competition**. By this he meant competition among firms would assure that consumers received the best possible products and price because the less-efficient producers would gradually be eliminated from the marketplace.

The "invisible hand" concept is the basic premise of the private enterprise system, competition being the primary regulator of our economic life. Sometimes, however, the public, through its elected representatives, has passed laws designed to strengthen the role of competition. These laws, called **antitrust laws**, prohibit attempts to monopolize, or dominate, a particular market. Two antitrust laws, the Sherman Antitrust Act (1890) and the Clayton Act (1914), are outlined in Chapter 23. Antitrust legislation prohibits efforts to monopolize markets and preserves the advantages of competition for society. Business is also subject to an array of government regulations that influence the way firms operate.

antitrust laws
Laws that prohibit attempts to monopolize or dominate a particular market.

Basic Rights of the Private Enterprise System

Certain rights critical to the operation of capitalism are available to citizens living in a private enterprise economy. They include rights to private property, to profits, to freedom of choice, and to competition. These rights are depicted in Figure 1.2.

Private Property   The private enterprise system guarantees people the right to own, use, buy, sell, and bequeath most forms of property, including land, buildings, machinery, equipment, inventions, and various intangible properties. The right to **private property** is the most fundamental of all rights under the private enterprise system. Most people in American society believe they should have the right to any property they work to acquire and to all benefits resulting from such ownership.

private property
Property that can be owned, used, bought, sold, and bequeathed under the private enterprise system.

Profits   The private enterprise system also guarantees the risk taker the right to all profits (after taxes) earned by the business. There is no guarantee the business will earn a profit, but if it does, the entrepreneur has a legal and ethical right to it.

Freedom of Choice   Under a private enterprise system, citizens have the maximum amount of freedom of choice in employment, purchases, and investments. This means people can go into or out of business with a minimum of government interference. They can change jobs, negotiate compensation levels, join labor unions, and quit if they so desire. Consumers can choose among different breads, furniture, television programs, magazines, and other goods and services.

Americans are so accustomed to this freedom of choice that they sometimes forget its importance: that the private enterprise economy tries to maximize human welfare and happiness by providing alternatives. Other systems sometimes limit freedom of choice in order to accomplish governmental goals, such as production increases.

Competition   The private enterprise system also guarantees the public the right to set ground rules for competitive activity. Speaking for the public, the U.S. government has passed laws to prohibit "cutthroat" competition—

Figure 1.2   Basic Rights of the Private Enterprise System

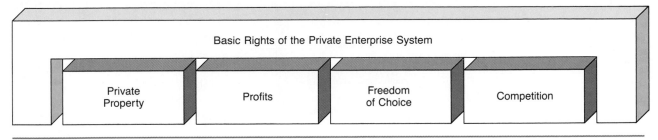

excessively competitive practices designed eventually to eliminate competition. It has also established ground rules that prohibit price discrimination, fraudulent dealings in financial markets, and deceptive practices in advertising and packaging.

Factors of Production

The private enterprise system requires certain inputs if it is to operate effectively. Economists call these inputs the **factors of production**. Not all enterprises require exactly the same combination of elements. Each business has its own mix of the four factors of production: natural resources, labor, capital, and entrepreneurship.

    Natural resources refer to everything useful as a productive input in its natural state, including agricultural land, building sites, forests, and mineral deposits. Natural resources are basic resources required in any economic system.[3]

    Labor is a critical input to the private enterprise system. The term refers to anyone who works for a business, from the company president to the production manager, the sales representative, and the assembly-line worker.

    Capital is defined as the funds necessary to finance the operation of a business. These funds can be provided in the form of investments, profits, or loans. They are used to build factories, buy raw materials, and hire workers.

    Entrepreneurship is the taking of risks to create and operate a business. As defined earlier, the entrepreneur is the risk taker in the private enterprise system. In some situations, the entrepreneur actively manages the business; in others, this responsibility is delegated to an employee, such as a salaried manager.

    All four factors of production must receive a financial return if they are to be used in the private enterprise system. As shown in Figure 1.3, these payments are in the form of rent, wages, profit, and interest. The specific factor payment received varies among industries, but all factors of production are required in some degree for all businesses.

Productivity and the U.S. Economic System

The output of its economic system is crucial to the American standard of living. In fact, this output determines the economic well-being of the nation. The overall measure of national output is called the **gross national product (GNP)**, the

factors of production
Basic inputs into the private enterprise system, including natural resources, labor, capital, and entrepreneurship.

natural resources
Everything useful as a production input in its natural state.

labor
The human resources of businesses.

capital
Funds that finance the operation of a business.

entrepreneurship
Taking risks to set up and operate a business.

gross national product (GNP)
The sum of all goods and services produced in an economy during a year.

Figure 1.3   The Factors of Production and Their Factor Payments

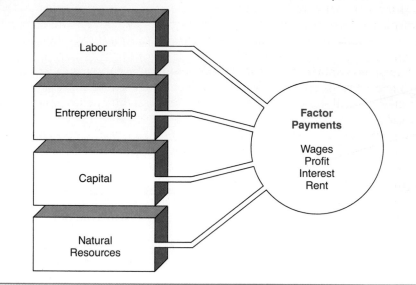

sum of all goods and services produced in the economy during a year. In a recent year the gross national product was $5.1 trillion. This concept allows year-to-year comparisons that check the current status of the economy.

But such comparisons are not easily accomplished. Inflation, or a rising price level, complicates the measurement process. Accurate comparisons of annual gross national figures must allow for inflation. Economists use the term **real gross national product** to describe inflation-discounted GNP figures. For example, the Rand Corp. projects the U.S. GNP in 2010 will be $7.9 trillion in 1986 dollars. This amounts to a 2.6 percent real annual growth rate.[4] The subject of inflation is further examined in Chapter 3.

Most economic assessments are concerned with changes in real gross national product, which leads to the concept of productivity. **Productivity** is a measure of efficiency of production. It relates to the amount of goods or services produced in a given period.

Productivity gains are important because they result in higher living standards and improved international competitiveness. Productivity growth was slow in the 1970s, rising 0.5 percent a year. Business productivity improved in the 1980s, with annual increases averaging 1.3 percent.[5] Improving productivity is one of the major challenges facing U.S. businesses. The subject is discussed in more detail in Chapter 3.

real gross national product
Inflation-discounted gross national product data.

productivity
A measure of the efficiency of production.

Types of Competition

Four basic degrees of competition exist in a private enterprise system: pure competition, monopolistic competition, oligopoly, and monopoly. Firms are classified on the basis of the relative competitiveness of their particular industry.

Pure Competition

In **pure competition**, the firms in an industry are so small that none can individually influence the price charged in the marketplace. Pure competition involves similar products, ones that cannot be differentiated from those of a competitor. Agriculture is probably the closest example of pure competition (although government price-support programs make it somewhat less competitive) and wheat is an example of a product that is similar from farm to farm. Finally, the small size of the firms involved in a purely competitive market makes it relatively easy for any firm to enter or leave that market. Price is thus set by total market demand and total market supply — the law of supply and demand.

A basic principle of economics, the **law of supply and demand** states that market prices are set by the intersection of the supply and demand curves. **Supply** is a schedule of what sellers will offer in the market at various price levels. **Demand** is a schedule showing what consumers will buy at various price levels. The intersection of the supply and demand curves marks the prevailing price level.

This price, however, will not remain constant. The law of supply and demand is a dynamic concept, so the market price — or equilibrium price, as it is also known — will change as supply and demand schedules change. Gasoline prices over the past decade are an example of this variability. The law of supply and demand is discussed in detail in Chapter 3.

pure competition
Situation in which the firms in an industry are so small that none individually influences market prices.

law of supply and demand
Economic law stating that market price is determined by the intersection of the supply and demand curves.

supply
A schedule of what sellers will offer in the market at various price levels.

demand
A schedule showing what consumers will buy at various price levels.

Monopolistic Competition

Monopolistic competition arises in an industry in which somewhat fewer firms than would exist in pure competition produce and sell products that are different from those of their competitors. Monopolistic competition gives a firm some power over the price it charges. A good example is retail stores, where prices can vary among different brands of aspirin, toothpaste, or gasoline. The relatively small size of these retailers also makes it easy for any firm to enter or leave the industry. In monopolistic competition, firms attempt to differentiate their products from those of competitors. For example, in the advertisement in Figure 1.4, Reebok explains how its shoes differ from other athletic shoes.

monopolistic competition
Situation in which a large number of competing firms sell goods and services that can be distinguished from each other.

Oligopoly

Oligopoly is a market in which there are few sellers. In some oligopolies, such as steel, the product is similar; in others, such as automobiles, it is different. The huge investment required for market entry restricts the entry of new competitors. But the primary difference between oligopoly and the previously mentioned markets is that the limited number of sellers gives the oligopolist substantial control over the product's price. In an oligopoly, the prices of competitive products are usually quite similar because substantial price competition would lessen every firm's profits. Price cuts by one firm in the industry are typically met by all competitors.

oligopoly
Market having few sellers and substantial entry restrictions.

Monopoly

Monopoly is a market situation in which there are no competitors. Since the Sherman and Clayton acts prohibit attempts to monopolize markets, nearly all

monopoly
Market situation in which there are no direct competitors.

Figure 1.4   Product Differentiation in Monopolistic Competition

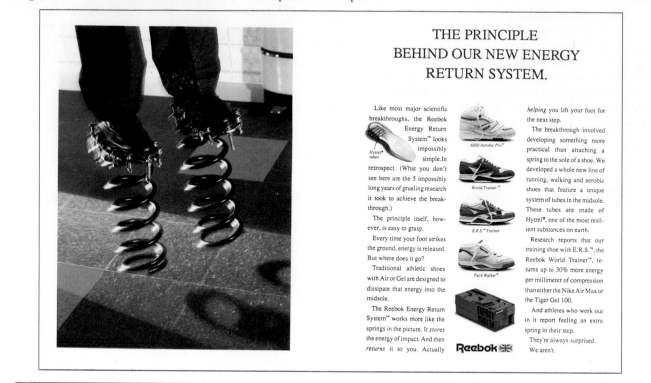

the monopolies in existence are regulated monopolies, such as the public utilities. Firms selling electricity, natural gas, and telephone service are usually regulated by agencies of the state government. These agencies administer many aspects of the regulated monopolies, including pricing and profits. In a pure monopoly, a firm would have substantial control over pricing, but in a regulated monopoly, pricing is subject to rules imposed by the regulatory body. There are few directly competitive products in a regulated monopoly, and entry into the industry is restricted by the government. In fact, in some states, a public utility must periodically seek voter approval to continue its service. Table 1.1 presents the features of each type of competition.

The Economic Development of the United States

The United States has a fascinating business history. Business significantly influenced customs, politics, and even family living. The historical development of the U.S. economy continues to affect the way business operates today.

Table 1.1   Types of Competition

Characteristics	Type of Competition			
	Pure Competition	Monopolistic Competition	Oligopoly	Monopoly
Number of competitors	Many	Few to many	Few	No direct competitors
Ease of entry into industry by new firms	Easy	Somewhat difficult	Difficult	Regulated by government
Similarity of goods or services offered by competing firms	Similar	Different	Can be similar or different	No directly competing goods or services
Control over price by individual firms	None	Some	Some	Considerable
Examples	Small-scale farmer	Blockbuster Video rental outlet	Alcoa	Local electric utility

Colonial Society

Colonial society was primarily agricultural, built on the products of its farms and plantations. The young nation's prosperity depended on the success of its crops, and most people lived in rural areas. The cities — small in comparison to those of Europe — were the marketplaces and residences of craft workers, traders, bankers, and government officials.

But the real economic and political power of the nation was centered in rural areas. The populace was tied to the land socially as well as economically. The colonies looked to England for manufactured products and capital with which to finance infant industries.

Even after the Revolutionary War (1776–1783), the United States maintained close economic relations with England. British investors provided much of the money needed to finance the developing business system. This financial influence continued well into the nineteenth century.

The Industrial Revolution

The *Industrial Revolution* occurred in England around 1750. The traditional manufacturing system of independent skilled workers individually pursuing their specialties was replaced by a factory system that mass-produced items by bringing together large numbers of semiskilled workers.

The factory system profited from savings created by large-scale production. For example, raw materials could often be purchased more cheaply in large lots. Another savings came from the specialization of labor; each worker concentrated on one specific task or job. Production efficiency improved substantially, and the factory system revolutionized business.

Influenced by the events occurring in England, the United States soon began its march toward industrialization. Agriculture became mechanized, and factories sprang up everywhere. But most business historians agree that real progress did not occur until railroads provided a fast, economical method of transporting the goods produced by businesses.

The American Industrial Revolution was highlighted by the rapid construction of railroad systems during the 1840s and 1850s. Not only did railroads provide the necessary transportation system, but they also created the need for greater quantities of lumber, steel, and real estate.

The Age of the Entrepreneur

During the nineteenth century, business made sizable advances in the United States. Eli Whitney introduced the concept of interchangeable parts, an idea that would later facilitate mass production. Peddlers, the salespeople of the day, operated throughout the country. Financiers became less dependent upon England, and the banking system became better established after some early problems. Inventors created a virtually endless array of commercially usable products.

People were encouraged to take risks and to become entrepreneurs. Cornelius Vanderbilt, John D. Rockefeller, J. P. Morgan, and Andrew Carnegie all became wealthy because of their willingness to take business risks during this period. Admittedly, some people were hurt by the speculation that characterized the economy during the 1800s, but, on balance, the entrepreneurial spirit of the age did much to advance the business system and raise the standard of living.

The Production Era

The early part of the twentieth century — the *production era* — was a period when business managers concentrated almost solely on the firm's production tasks. Industry was under considerable pressure to produce more and more to satisfy growing consumer demand and to correct product shortages.

Work assignments became increasingly specialized. Assembly lines, such as the one introduced by Henry Ford, became common. Owners turned over management responsibilities to a new class of managers who specialized in operating established businesses rather than in starting new ones.

Marketing tended to be viewed strictly as selling. Business did not yet accept disciplines like consumer research. In other words, marketers were those individuals responsible for distribution after the production function had been performed. Business was internally oriented rather than consumer oriented.

The Marketing Concept

The post-World War II era was influenced by an important new concept in management. The *marketing concept,* which became the prevalent business philosophy, advocated that all activities and functions of the organization be directed toward the identification and satisfaction of consumer wants. A consumer orientation became the principal goal of companies.

Business organizations throughout the United States formed marketing research departments to analyze what the consumer would buy before the company produced the item. This concept stood in marked contrast to the earlier

In 1916, workers on Ford Motor Company's first assembly line at the Highland Park, Michigan, plant performed specialized tasks. During the production era, the moving assembly line helped Ford management realize its goal of moving a finished Model T off the line every ten seconds. Ford has since adopted the marketing concept. Today, the company uses consumer research to produce cars that satisfy the needs and wants of different buyers. This consumer orientation has helped Ford become the world's most profitable car company.

Photo source: Courtesy of Ford Motor Company.

philosophy of producing a product, then trying to sell it to the consumer. Advertising reached ever-larger numbers of consumers and increased the efficiency of firms' promotional efforts. Today, firms must have a strong consumer orientation if they are to remain competitive in the marketplace.

The Current Business Era

Challenge after challenge has confronted business in recent years. Foreign buyers acquired many U.S. firms and real-estate landmarks. Insider trading scandals shocked Wall Street and Main Street. A host of environmental issues such as ozone depletion, acid rain, and toxic waste disposal cry out for a solution. A Pentagon procurement scandal raised questions about the status of business ethics in our society.

These challenges resulted in certain trends in the business world. First, executives now recognize the distinct role of public opinion in contemporary business. Public perceptions are critically important in today's decision-making process. Second, business has had to become more socially responsible. The societal impact of a business decision is now weighed in most management actions. Third, business managers must become global thinkers. To remain competitive at home and abroad, U.S. firms must view business from an international perspective. The issue of international competitiveness is a major topic of Chapter 3. The ever-changing business environment may mean that writers will someday describe the current era as the most challenging for the private enterprise system.

Goodyear Tire & Rubber Company managers are global thinkers. A new corporate flag showing a Goodyear "G" floating in a stylized globe symbolizes the firm's determination to be globally competitive in productivity, quality, uniformity, product cost, and value. The "World Class Competitor" flag is awarded to the employees of manufacturing plants in recognition of their ability to make products that meet and beat both U.S. and foreign competition. The Lawton, Oklahoma, plant was the first to earn the award. In this photo, Lawton employees watch as the flag is raised in honor of their reaching globally competitive status.

Photo source: Courtesy of The Goodyear Tire & Rubber Company.

Alternative Economic Systems

Many people fail to realize that a large part of the world lives under economic systems other than capitalism. The number of countries with communist and socialist systems makes it important to learn the primary features of these alternative economies. This text does not concern itself with political questions, but rather with the economic aspects of socialism and communism. Table 1.2 outlines the major features of the various systems.

Communism

communism
Economic theory, developed by Karl Marx, under which private property is eliminated and goods are owned in common.

Communist theory was the product of Karl Marx, a nineteenth-century economist. Marx believed that the laboring classes were being exploited by capitalists (entrepreneurs and managers). He predicted that a class struggle would make way for a new form of society to emerge. Marx labeled this new order **communism**. He believed the people should own all of a nation's productive capacity but conceded the government would have to operate businesses until a classless society could evolve. He also adhered to the principle that people should receive according to their needs and give according to their abilities. Despite

Table 1.2 A Comparison of Economic Systems

System Features	Capitalism	Communism	Socialism	Mixed Economy
Ownership of enterprises	Businesses are owned privately, often by a large number of people. Government ownership is minimal.	The government owns the means of production with few exceptions, like small plots of land.	Basic industries are owned by government, but small-scale enterprises can be privately owned.	A strong private sector exists along with public enterprises in a mixed economy. The private sector is significantly larger than that under socialism.
Rights to profits	Entrepreneurs and investors are entitled to all profits (less taxes) that they earn.	Profits are not officially recognized under communism.	Profits officially exist only in the private sector of socialist economies.	Entrepreneurs and investors are entitled to private-sector profits, although taxes are often quite high. State enterprises are also typically expected to break even or provide a return to the government.
Management of enterprises	Each enterprise is managed separately, either by its owners or by people who represent the interests of the owners. Government interference is minimal.	Centralized management of all state enterprises is a traditional feature of communism. Under the current policy of *perestroika,* some planning is now being decentralized.	A significant degree of government planning exists in socialist nations. State enterprises are managed directly by government bureaucrats.	The management of the private sector is similar to that under capitalism. Professional managers are also common in state enterprises.
Rights of employees	The rights to choose one's occupation and to join a labor union have long been recognized.	Employee rights are limited. The government plays a major role in one's work life. However, *perestroika* is introducing many changes.	Workers have the right to choose their occupations and to join labor unions. However, the government influences career decisions for many people.	Workers have the right of job choice and labor union membership. Unions in these countries are often quite strong.
Worker incentives	Considerable incentives exist to motivate people to perform at their highest levels.	Incentives are emerging as part of *perestroika* and similar changes in other communist economies.	Incentives are usually limited in state enterprises, but do exist in the private sector.	Capitalist-like incentives exist in the private sector. Incentives in the public sector are more limited.

Marx's prediction of a classless society, managerial and professional classes have evolved as the "privileged" groups in all communist societies.

Under communism, the government owns the means of production and the people, in turn, work for government enterprises. There traditionally has been little or no freedom of choice in terms of employment, purchases, or investments. For example, the government determines what people can buy because it dictates what will be produced, and consumer goods are generally rated as a low priority.

Many communist economies are now undergoing profound changes. For example, Mikhail Gorbachev is trying to restructure the Soviet economy through a policy known as *perestroika.* Gorbachev wants to increase the productivity of the Soviet economic system by decentralizing planning and providing more incentives for managers and other workers. In the process, he hopes to make consumer goods more readily available than they have been.

A closely related Gorbachev policy is that of *glasnost,* or open communication in the Soviet Union. News is now reported promptly and more honestly.

Features of capitalism —
competition and private enterprise — are part of reform
measures initiated in the Soviet Union to improve the
country's economy. Families
can now compete with state-
owned stores by selling part
of their harvest at free-market
prices, such as the farmer in
this photo selling produce in
a Moscow street stall. A new
law allows families to start
small, private businesses ranging from restaurants to auto-
repair shops and beauty salons. In the Soviet Union
today, it is not uncommon to
hail a cab operated by a citizen who competes with state-
owned fleets.

Photo source: © Ricki Rosen/Picture Group.

Glasnost has also affected the Soviet economy. For example, *Izvestia,* the government newspaper, now carries advertising by foreign firms in the Moscow and
overseas editions. However, advertisements for scarce consumer goods such as
toothpaste and panty hose are still banned.[6]

Gorbachev's reforms, along with similar ones in the People's Republic of
China, have spread to other communist states. While centralized planning remains a cornerstone of communist economies, it is clear that classical communist economic theory is now being rewritten to include some features that have
long characterized capitalism.

Socialism

socialism
Economic system that advocates government ownership
and operation of all basic
industries.

Socialism is an economic system that exists in countries where the government
owns and operates all the basic industries such as banking, transportation, and
large-scale manufacturing. Private ownership still exists in such smaller businesses as shops and restaurants. Socialists believe major industries are too important to be left in private hands. They assert that government-owned industries are more efficient and serve the public better. Capitalists argue that
state-run industries become massive bureaucracies that are insensitive to consumer needs.

Socialist economies usually follow some master plan for the use of the
nation's resources. Workers are free to choose their employment, but the state
often encourages people to pursue careers in areas where need is greatest. As a
result, most citizens work for government enterprises, which are often rather

Figure 1.5   The Trend of Privatization

Source: Courtesy of British Department of Energy and Young & Rubicam, Ltd., London.

inefficient and lacking in leadership. People in leadership positions usually change jobs when new politicians take office. Also, many leadership positions are awarded through political patronage, not on the basis of ability. Finally, socialist economies are characterized by extensive public welfare programs supported by high taxes often approaching confiscatory levels.

Mixed Economies

The term **mixed economy** describes an economy with a combination of government ownership and private ownership. Advocates of private enterprise often classify mixed economies as socialist if there is a high degree of public ownership. But such countries still have far more private ownership than is found in socialist nations. Japan is an example of a mixed economy.

The proportions of private and public enterprise vary widely in mixed economies. The mixes are also changing. In the United Kingdom and France, many government entities are now operated as private enterprises. This trend toward converting government enterprises into private held companies is referred to as **privatization**.

Countries are selling state-owned industries to improve their economy, believing private corporations can manage them more cheaply and efficiently than government units can. Great Britain has been the leader in the business trend of privatization. The government raised more than $23 billion by selling all or part of state-owned businesses such as British Airways, aircraft manufacturer British Aerospace, aircraft-engine manufacturer Rolls-Royce, and utility British Telecom. The recent sale of British Gas for $7.9 billion was the largest stock offering in Great Britain's history. Advertisements such as the one in Figure 1.5 publicized the sale, which drew 4.5 million buyers. The ad shows a cricket player and a

mixed economy
Economic system having a mix of government ownership and private enterprise.

privatization
The trend to substitute private ownership for public ownership in a mixed economy.

beekeeper to emphasize that anyone could buy a share of stock in the private company.[7]

A Comparative Note

Private enterprise has proved to be a very effective economic system for the United States and other countries, such as Japan. It has provided a high degree of economic freedom, a low cost of living, substantial product choice, high earnings, considerable public welfare, and many other economic benefits. The United States became a world power because of the private enterprise system and the businesses that operate within its framework.

Major U.S. corporations are among the world's leading firms. Industry in the United States is extremely diversified. Thousands of business enterprises exist in nearly every conceivable commercial activity. Figure 1.6 shows the number of firms in each major industry.

Other economic systems aspire to the high levels achieved by the U.S. business system. This is not to say that other systems are always wrong, but the vast majority of Americans are proud of U.S. business accomplishments and thoroughly support the continuation of the private enterprise system.

Studying the U.S. Business System

Many people study the U.S. business system. Senior business executives are constantly learning how to become more effective managers. Many consumers are examining how business decisions affect their daily lives. Many students are enrolled in business administration courses. With this much activity, it is fitting that attention be given to why and how people study business.

Why Study Business?

People study business for a number of reasons. Some plan a business career. Others want to learn how the business system affects them in their role of wage earner or consumer. Still others are curious about what business actually means. Certainly, business affects all of us in some manner; and the more we know about the subject, the better able we will be to cope with some of our most common, everyday problems. Some specific reasons for studying business are given below.

Career Selection   Most students do not spend adequate time in selecting a career. Many drift from one curriculum to another and then from one kind of job to another. The study of business allows a student to consider various occupational possibilities. The bulk of career possibilities are in private industry, but many similar possibilities are available in government employment and in nonprofit organizations.

The study of business allows the student to consider various kinds of jobs — the work required, the available rewards, the necessary training, and the relative advantages and disadvantages of each. This text includes sections describing jobs

Figure 1.6 The Number of Firms in Major U.S. Industries

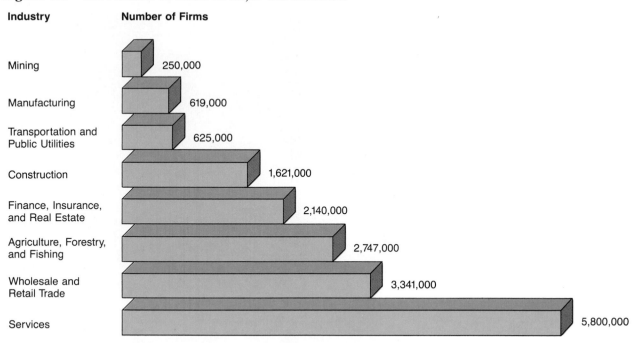

Industry   **Number of Firms**

Mining — 250,000

Manufacturing — 619,000

Transportation and Public Utilities — 625,000

Construction — 1,621,000

Finance, Insurance, and Real Estate — 2,140,000

Agriculture, Forestry, and Fishing — 2,747,000

Wholesale and Retail Trade — 3,341,000

Services — 5,800,000

Source: Statistical Abstract of the United States: 1988 (Washington, D.C.: U.S. Government Printing Office, 1987), pp. 280, 388, 540.

that can be found in each major area of business. Chapter 24 is devoted to careers in business. Employment trends, job sources, employment search strategies, resume preparation, and other useful topics are explored.

Self-Employment   Some students will decide to establish their own businesses and work for themselves. Since most business concepts and principles are the same regardless of the size of the firm, studying business can be an invaluable first step in setting up a company.

Self-employed persons are actively and personally involved in business. A knowledge of successful business practices becomes even more crucial for those who risk their own funds. The solution — study business!

Tackling the Problems of Society   Business puts people on the firing line for most of today's pressing social problems. Child care, toxic waste disposal, resource conservation, affirmative action programs, consumerism, and industrial safety are issues a businessperson encounters on a daily basis. As the advertisement in Figure 1.7 illustrates, Anheuser-Busch is concerned not only with producing quality beers but also with the safe consumption of alcoholic beverages. The company developed special programs to educate consumers about responsible drinking and supports scientific research into the causes and possible cures of alcoholism and alcohol abuse.

A business career is likely to place an individual in a position of responsibility earlier than most occupations. Many experts believe business careers are an excellent choice for people who want to improve society.

Figure 1.7   Tackling the Social Problem of Alcohol Abuse

Source: Courtesy of Anheuser-Busch Companies, Inc.

Better Consumer Decisions   Business decisions create consumer decisions. A personal computer might offer three options for accessory equipment. An executive decides to pass on a recent union wage increase to the consumer by raising a product's price. These are typical business decisions that call for related decision making by consumers.

The study of business provides an appreciation of the background for many consumer decisions. Consumer advocates often point out that an informed consumer is a better consumer.

The study of business is the study of what is happening today. It is probably one of the most relevant and fascinating subjects you will ever study.

How to Study Business

Business can be studied through formal programs of instruction such as those offered at various colleges. These programs teach the basic concepts, methods, principles, and practices used in modern business. The formal study of business provides the framework for later experiences; together they build toward a well-rounded management education.

The study of business — or business administration, as it is often called — has grown more formalized and systematic over the years. In the past, many managers achieved their positions on the basis of practical experience in a given area rather than through formal study. But times have changed, and formal education in business has become a recognized first step toward a business career. Business leaders of earlier decades would be amazed to see the modern classrooms and instructional methods used by contemporary business students.

The study of business has become one of the most popular curricula at colleges and universities. Business programs are usually organized around functional areas. Courses are offered in such subjects as accounting, computer science, finance, management, and marketing. Most business programs require students to take at least one course in each major area of study.

This book, combined with an introductory business course, will give you a broad overview of the field of business. The information acquired here will allow you to better select further business courses.

Although students can learn the basics of business in a classroom setting, they need other experiences outside the classroom for a well-rounded business education. Informal study — reading and various job-related experiences — can further a business education. Meaningful part-time and summer work experiences can be invaluable. Internships, study tours, and visits to manufacturers are also vital. Serious business students should further their knowledge by regularly reading business publications such as *The Wall Street Journal, INC., Forbes, Business Week,* and *Fortune*.

Summary of Learning Goals

1. Explain what a business is and how it operates within the private enterprise system. Business provides the bulk of our employment as well as the goods and services necessary to support a society. Although the United States is a capitalist country, a large portion of the world operates under other economic systems — primarily communism, socialism, or mixed economies. Business comprises all profit-seeking activities and enterprises that provide goods and services necessary to an economic system. U.S. businesses are part of a private enterprise system in which success is determined by competition among firms.

2. Define the roles of competition and the entrepreneur in a private enterprise system. Competition is the battle among businesses for consumer acceptance. It is a critical aspect of the private enterprise system. An entrepreneur is the risk taker in this type of economic system. Profits are the rewards for a successful entrepreneur.

3. Outline the basic rights of the private enterprise system. Certain basic rights are available to citizens living in a private enterprise economy: the right to private property; the legal and ethical right to any profits that might result from an enterprise; the freedom of choice in purchases, employment, and investments; and the right to set ground rules for competitive activity.

4. Discuss the factors of production and their factor payments. Four factors of production provide the necessary inputs for the operation of private enterprise: natural resources, labor, capital, and entrepreneurship. Each factor receives a payment, such as rent, wages, interest, or profits.

5. Explain the concepts of gross national product and productivity.
Gross national product — the sum of all goods and services produced in the economy during a year — is an overall measure of national output. By contrast, productivity is a measure of the efficiency of production. It relates to the amount of goods and services a worker provides in a given period.

6. Identify the degrees of competition that can exist in a private enterprise system.   The four basic degrees of competition in a private enterprise system are pure competition, monopolistic competition, oligopoly, and monopoly.

7. Analyze how the historical development of the U.S. economy influences contemporary business.   The development of the current U.S. economy has been influenced by colonial society, the Industrial Revolution, the age of the entrepreneur, the production era, and the post-World War II marketing concept.

8. Identify the different types of economic systems.   Many Americans fail to realize that a large part of the world lives under economic systems other than capitalism, primarily communism, socialism, and mixed economies. Communism, as proposed by Karl Marx, is a classless economic system in which private property is eliminated and goods are owned in common. A perfect communist state does not exist today.

Socialism is an economic system in which the basic industries are owned and operated by the government. Private ownership of some smaller businesses is permitted. A mixed economy is one in which businesses and industries are publicly and privately owned in various combinations.

9. Explain how to study business and why.   There are several reasons why the study of business is important. It assists in career selection. It provides opportunities for self-employment. It tackles the problems of society. It leads to better consumer decisions. The study of business often begins in a classroom and continues in a less formal manner in the world of business.

Key Terms

business

profits

private enterprise system

competition

entrepreneur

capitalism

invisible hand of competition

antitrust laws

private property

factors of production

natural resources

labor

capital

entrepreneurship

gross national product (GNP)

real gross national product

productivity

pure competition

law of supply and demand

supply

demand

monopolistic competition

oligopoly

monopoly

communism

socialism

mixed economy

privatization

Review Questions

1. Explain the role of competition in the private enterprise system.

2. What is the role of entrepreneurs in the private enterprise system? What type of people become entrepreneurs?

3. Why is Adam Smith called the father of capitalism?

4. Discuss the basic rights upon which the private enterprise system is based.

5. Identify and describe the inputs required by the private enterprise system. What payments are made to each of these inputs? Discuss.

6. How does *real GNP* differ from *GNP*?

7. Why is productivity an important public issue today?

8. The four basic degrees of competition are perfect competition, monopolistic competition, oligopoly, and monopoly. Match these types with the businesses listed below:
   a. Texaco
   b. Detroit Edison Company
   c. Wal-Mart
   d. Sid Olsen's 640-acre farm in southern Minnesota

9. Trace the historical development of the American economy. What were the major turning points in this development?

10. Differentiate among private enterprise, communism, socialism, and mixed economies. Identify examples of each of these economic systems.

Discussion Questions

1. Many U.S. companies responded to the Armenian earthquake by offering a variety of aid. Johnson & Johnson sent medical supplies and equipment. Merck, Eli Lilly, and Whitehall sent drugs and other needed items. PepsiCo, Bankers Trust, R. H. Macy's and Occidental Petroleum sent cash donations. Free transportation of relief supplies was provided by Pan Aviation and Flying Tigers. Relate these relief efforts to the concept of social responsibility and the changes that are occurring in the Soviet economy.

2. Comment on this statement: "All organizations must serve their customers or clients in some way if they are to survive."

3. List all the businesses that serve students on your campus. Discuss how effectively they serve their customers.

4. Profit has sometimes been described as the regulator of the private enterprise system. Discuss the meaning of this comment.

5. In recent years, there have been proposals to sell government entities such as Dulles Airport and the Bonneville Power Administration. Discuss how these proposals relate to the trend toward privatization.

Video Case

Cocolat

America's craving for the sensuous pleasures of chocolate has grown steadily in recent years. The average person will consume approximately 10 pounds this year and will spend about $20 satisfying this desire. Luxury chocolates, which commonly sell for between $12 and $35 a pound, make up 15 percent of all chocolate sales — double the percentage of a decade ago. The Rolls-Royce of U.S. luxury chocolate makers is Cocolat (pronounced coke'-uh-la), a Berkeley, California–based company. It produces about 3 million chocolate truffles a year and approximately 50,000 cakes and pastries. Its truffles, which have made the company famous, sell for about $1.70 each; its top-selling dessert is a chocolate torte made with almonds and cognac called *reine de saba*. A single torte serves up to 14 people and costs $18.50.

Cocolat's truffles — rich, dense mixtures of heavy cream and chocolate, flavored with brandy, liqueurs, fruits, and nuts — are shipped by refrigerated airfreight to 400 outlets across the United States. They can be purchased at locations ranging from Zabar's in New York City to Jacquisine in Houston. Cocolat operates seven of its own retail stores in the San Francisco Bay area; its chocolates are also sold to California consumers in Macy's department store. The privately-held company generates annual sales of about $5.5 million.

When asked to explain the necessary ingredients for business success, one authority offered a simple six-word answer: "Find a need and fill it." Ideas for new businesses come from a variety of sources. Some budding entrepreneurs have lifelong dreams of starting a particular business. Others get an idea for making a better product after using one they find inadequate. For Alice Medrich, the founder of Cocolat, the idea of starting a business was partly a result of her love of chocolates and partly a lark.

In 1972, Alice and her husband, Elliott (now company vice president), were living in Paris where he was on the staff of the Organization for Economic Co-

operation and Development. One day, their landlady brought them some of her home-made chocolate truffles, which the Medriches found seductive and delicious. At that time, truffles were virtually unheard of in the United States, where Hershey and Milky Way bars were more representative of the popular taste in chocolate. But Alice adored the truffles. "I had never tasted anything . . . that was as good as that," she recalled years later, "and I had always loved chocolate."

When the Medriches returned to California the following year, Alice tried making truffles at home. Just before Christmas, she took a handful to a local specialty-food shop and asked if the owner would like to buy some. The owner sampled one and immediately ordered 25 dozen. The next day, he ordered another 25 dozen, and Cocolat was under way.

Alice admits that the first two years of operating her own business were "a tremendous period of trial and error." Developing desserts other than truffles was one challenge she met by committing herself to creating one new dessert each week. She often had to perfect the new creations between Monday night and Thursday night so they would be ready for sale on Friday morning. "I was learning in the best way I knew how — that was by doing it."

In 1974, Alice enrolled in the prestigious graduate school of business at the University of California at Berkeley, hoping to learn more about running her own business. She quit two years later because, in her words, "more and more, I realized that the business school was preparing me for something I didn't want to do — and that was work for the Bank of America or a large corporation." To increase her product knowledge, Medrich took an intensive one-week course in dessert making at a renowned cooking school in a Paris suburb. With added baking experience, she was ready to open her own store and bakery. But she needed money, and no bank would lend her the $14,000 to launch the venture. In desperation, the Medriches tapped personal sources: $5,000 from their savings account and a $9,000 personal loan from Elliott's mother.

If anything, Alice underestimated her business's potential for success in those early days. On opening day, the entire stock of truffles sold out within three hours. In the weeks and months that followed, local

Notes: "Oh, Chocolate," *U.S. News & World Report,* February 27, 1989, p. 75; Katie Brown, "At Cocolat, Truffles Move Like Hotcakes," *San Francisco Examiner,* November 16, 1987, pp. 1, 32; Cheryll Aimee Barron, "Madam Cocolat," *The New York Times Magazine,* September 25, 1988, pp. 31ff; and personal correspondence, February 28, 1989.

teachers, college students, and young professionals became devoted customers. For several years thereafter, the company struggled to meet the demand for its products. By 1981, Cocolat had become so successful that a bank agreed to lend it $275,000 to finance a move to a 10,000-square-foot plant and the purchase of additional ovens and other equipment.

Unfortunately, the new premises, which the company leased, proved to be too expensive for Cocolat's level of business. This, in effect, forced the company to expand. Up to that time, it had survived on its reputation for producing some of the finest chocolates and desserts in the country. Critics in food journals, such as *Gourmet* and *Cuisine,* and in major newspapers supplemented word-of-mouth knowledge about the company by raving about Cocolat's concoctions in their reviews. The Medriches had done nothing in the way of market research and very little in the way of advertising. Now they had to figure out how to make the company larger in order to pay bills.

In the years since Cocolat's founding, America has evolved from a place relatively unaware of European-style luxuries to one suddenly flooded with everything from Perrier to Häagen-Dazs. A new interest in upscale eating contributed to Cocolat's expansion. It also promoted competition. Suddenly, Godiva, Perugina, and other luxury candies flooded the market, and American candies like Fanny Farmer, Fanny Mae, and Russell Stover began marketing campaigns to improve their images so as to compete more directly with pricey imports. Faced with a growing need for funds to make mortgage and lease payments, and with increased competition, Cocolat began losing money and taking out more and more loans. Also, the rapid growth of the firm had stretched its already thin management ranks even more. It was time to bring in professional management.

The Medriches were fortunate in attracting Morton Miller, a former president of Castle and Cooke Merchandising Corporation and a veteran of 22 years' experience in retailing, as their new president. Since Miller joined the company, it has expanded its whole-sale business, developed new products, and shown a profit. Over the next few years, Miller wants to expand wholesale business further and sell products through upscale department stores and by mail order, doubling the percentage of wholesale business to about 50 percent of total revenues. In addition, Cocolat is negotiating with a large Japanese food company to take advantage of that country's desire for anything Western by producing the firm's products in Japan.

Cocolat is a company that began as one person's pet project and gradually developed into a thriving business with a highly respected line of products. Currently, the company has reached a crossroads of sorts: Until recently, its size has made it dependent almost entirely on the Medriches. As the company continues to grow, it will need to become more financially sound and more professionally managed. It may become less dependent on the Medriches for nearly every aspect of its business, but it will spread the glories of the finest chocolate to ever-increasing numbers of people across the country and around the world.

Questions

1. Most organizations have two types of competitors: those who compete directly and those who offer products that can be substituted for another product.

a. Identify the major direct competitors for Cocolat.

b. Describe the types of people who are likely to purchase Cocolat products. Which firms and/or products are likely to offer indirect competition for the company?

2. Relate each of the factors of production to Cocolat. Explain how each factor receives a payment for its contribution to the firm's success.

3. Refer to the discussion of productivity on pages 7 and 8. How could Cocolat's productivity be measured? Recommend some methods by which the firm might increase its productivity.

4. Refer to Table 1.1 on page 11. Categorize Cocolat as either pure competition, monopolistic competition, oligopoly, or monopoly. Use each of the characteristics listed in the first column to support your choice.

2 Social Responsibility and Business Ethics

Learning Goals

1. To explain the concept of social responsibility as an accepted business policy.

2. To outline the concept of business ethics and explain how management makes ethical decisions.

3. To describe the relationship between self-regulation and government regulation.

4. To discuss how social performance can be evaluated.

5. To outline business's responsibilities to the general public.

6. To identify business's responsibilities to customers.

7. To describe business's responsibilities to company personnel.

8. To explain business's responsibilities to investors and the financial communities.

January was traditionally a bad time of year for the office staff at Nyloncraft Inc., a Mishawaka, Indiana–based plastics-molding firm. One January, Nyloncraft issued 900 W-2 tax reports to employees and former employees, yet its payroll at the time numbered only 250 people. Turnover was clearly a major problem for Nyloncraft. It hurt productivity, and with training costs of up to $2,000 per hire, it was threatening the long-term viability of the company.

Nyloncraft operates two molding plants in Mishawaka and one in nearby South Bend. Other plants are located in Hickory, North Carolina, and Bowling Green, Kentucky. Eighty-five percent of the firm's employees are women, many of whom are single mothers. Employee surveys found that child-care problems were the main cause of Nyloncraft's high turnover and absenteeism.

Management first considered subsidizing outside day care, but eventually concluded reliability of day care, not its cost, was the root of its employees' concerns. Nyloncraft decided it would run its own day-care center. Still, hurdles remained.

Most of Nyloncraft's younger female employees worked the night shift because they lacked seniority in the unionized shop. Therefore, the company's children's center would have to operate 24 hours a day. But state regulations effectively limited Indiana day-care facilities to an eight-hour schedule. For example, state regulations said cleaning was not allowed while children were on the premises. The company eventually prevailed over the bureaucracy, and the state's first 24-hour, on-site child-care center opened in 1981.

The Excel-Nyloncraft Learning Center, as the unit is now called, is praised as a state-of-the-art child-care program. The center is open to the community as well as Nyloncraft employees, who pay about half the $63 per week cost. Child care is free to Nyloncraft employees working overtime.

The children learn about the work world by punching a time clock just like their parents. A typical evening for a three-year-old whose mother works the 4 p.m. to midnight shift includes horseback riding, dinner, a toothbrushing session, and a nap until the evening shift ends. A van delivers the child back to his or her parent's plant.

Nyloncraft's learning center has been a major factor in cutting the company's once sky-high attrition rate to less than the national average of 14 percent. In a recent year, Nyloncraft lost only 26 people out of a work force of 500. Absenteeism also dropped to less than 3 percent. Furthermore, when Excel Indus-

tries Inc. bought Nyloncraft for $15 million in 1988, its board chairman called the learning centers "a heck of an asset to the company."[1]

Contemporary business must deal with a variety of social responsibility and ethical issues. Child care is just one of them. Chapter 2 will explain the full range of such issues confronting today's management.

Photo source: Charlie Archambault, U.S. News & World Report.

Chapter Overview

social responsibility
A management philosophy that highlights the social and economic effects of managerial decisions.

Social responsibility, management's consideration of the social and economic effects of its decision making, has gradually become one of the most important aspects of American business. In recent decades, our society called on private enterprise, regardless of size, location, or industry, to take a broader look at the impact its decisions will have on communities and society as a whole. In fact, companies such as Kraft, Dow Chemical, General Mills, and Cooper Industries use the term *corporate citizenship* interchangeably with *social responsibility*.

What it means to be socially responsible varies from industry to industry and company to company. There is no set standard for businesses to follow, so numerous inconsistencies between policy and practice exist in the business world.

Ethical business operation extends through all segments of business. Practicing social responsibility might mean asking production supervisors to make assembly-line jobs more meaningful; having personnel officers revise many of their procedures; and requiring credit departments to answer charges concerning invasions of personal privacy.

It also includes checking products closely for user safety. Environmental considerations in particular are becoming more important. While high-quality products are still in demand, many consumers now judge companies by what they do and how they act, as well as the quality of what they make. This chapter discusses the challenges businesses face in operating in an ethically and socially responsible manner.

The Concept of Social Responsibility

Most companies agree in principle with the concept of social responsibility; however, the actual practice of it varies widely throughout the business world. Defining social responsibility is one step toward a coherent policy. An increasing number of companies have specific statements on social responsibility. The one for Memorex-Telex Corporation is shown in Figure 2.1.

Memorex-Telex has an extensive statement on social responsibility. Still, what does it mean specifically to provide "for the best interests of customers, vendors, and employees"? The answer is likely to vary widely and to frequently be a judgment call — what seems to be the best policy may often prove incorrect, in retrospect. So even among companies with a clearly stated policy, policy and practice may commonly diverge.

The Concept of Business Ethics

Ethics in business covers a broad range of topics, none of them easy to define. The concept of ethics comes from a sense of responsibility — to a community, to employees, to shareholders, to society — and what is ethical, or what is right, can vary depending on which group management chooses to be responsible to.

Figure 2.1   Telex's Statement on Social Responsibility

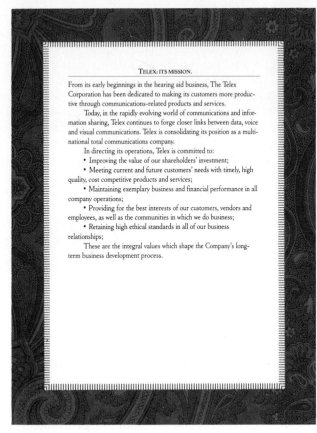

TELEX: ITS MISSION.

From its early beginnings in the hearing aid business, The Telex Corporation has been dedicated to making its customers more productive through communications-related products and services.

Today, in the rapidly evolving world of communications and information sharing, Telex continues to forge closer links between data, voice and visual communications. Telex is consolidating its position as a multi-national total communications company.

In directing its operations, Telex is committed to:
• Improving the value of our shareholders' investment;
• Meeting current and future customers' needs with timely, high quality, cost competitive products and services;
• Maintaining exemplary business and financial performance in all company operations;
• Providing for the best interests of our customers, vendors and employees, as well as the communities in which we do business;
• Retaining high ethical standards in all of our business relationships;

These are the integral values which shape the Company's long-term business development process.

Source: Telex Corporation 1987 Annual Report, p. 2.

What Are Business Ethics?

Management is required to resolve specific ethical questions. **Business ethics** deals with the right and wrong actions that arise in any work environment. Sometimes a conflict exists between an ideal decision and one that is practical under certain conditions, but it is important that companies evaluate their ethical responsibilities in decision making. One study found that 73 percent of the firms examined had developed written codes of ethics.[2] Examples include Caterpillar Tractor, Allis Chalmers, Johnson & Johnson, and Rexnord.[3]

How businesspeople deal with ethical questions was the subject of a classic study outlined in the *Harvard Business Review*. Businesspeople were presented with hypothetical situations in which some actions would normally be right and others wrong. Half the sample was asked, "What would you do?" while the other half was asked, "What would the average businessperson do?" The answers to the second question indicated more unethical behavior than did responses to the first question. Businesspeople apparently think their peers are less ethical than they are.[4]

business ethics
The businessperson's standards of conduct and moral values.

Unocal conducts fire training for its operating personnel from its refineries. The company values the safety of its operations in order to protect its employees, visitors, customers, and neighbors in the community. Unocal set up a new department of safety and risk management to implement a companywide safety program, including safety audits to ensure the program works effectively in every facility.

Photo source: Courtesy of Unocal/Larry Lee.

How Does a Manager Make Ethical Decisions?

Ethics teachers and consultants say that making an ethical decision is not so much a matter of knowing right from wrong as it is one of knowing what pressures will be faced in specific situations. Employees and managers are more likely to make decisions they consider ethical when they are aware of their values and their corporation's values.[5] Many companies have set up workshops where employees can simulate their responses to specific situations and determine what they can do to make more ethical decisions.[6]

Self-Regulation or Government Regulation?

Ethics statements, like any general code, can be interpreted in a number of ways. This does not mean certain types of behavior cannot be regulated; the 8-hour workday and the minimum wage are examples of regulated business behavior. The public outcry for increased social responsibility will not dissipate. Intelligent managers realize that self-regulation has become a prerequisite for corporate survival.

Corporations frequently have difficulties with self-regulation. Consider the case of Beech-Nut Corporation. The firm was under financial pressure to cut costs in the mid-1970s. As a result, it purchased a cheap concentrate for one of its best-selling products, apple juice for babies. Several company scientists advised against the purchase, arguing the concentrate was likely artificial, whereas Beech-Nut advertised a 100 percent natural product. When its supplier was shown to be selling adulterated apple juice, Beech-Nut cancelled its contracts but continued to sell juice made from the adulterated concentrate.

The Justice Department prosecuted, generating bad publicity for Beech-Nut. The firm's market share dropped by 20 percent, and the company posted near-record losses in 1987.[7]

The Beech-Nut case shows that when industry fails to respond to the ethical challenges posed by society, the public will is typically enforced through other means, specifically, government. The price of government intervention can be high as Beech-Nut's decline in market share and financial losses illustrate.

The Current Status of Social Responsibility and Ethics in American Industry

Ethics statements will not solve problems such as the Beech-Nut case. A recent study of 202 *Fortune* 500 companies' ethics codes showed that 75 percent failed to mention some social issue, such as the firm's role in civic and community affairs, product safety, or environmental safety.[8] As proof that putting it in writing does not make it so, a study of some 350 corporations found that those with written ethics policies were more often charged with wrongdoing than those without such policies.[9]

A recent survey of 1,082 corporate directors and officers, business school deans, and members of Congress found that 94 percent of them believe American business has an ethics problem. While only 20 percent of the respondents felt legislation would improve business ethics, and almost all believed the United States has higher business ethics than any other country, the survey also found that the industries considered the most ethical, such as commercial banking and utilities, are also the most regulated.[10]

Is Government Regulation the Answer?

Government regulation is not a panacea for ethical problems in business. Both corporate and private citizens recall the abuses of Watergate and Vietnam and see lesser offenses regularly, creating an atmosphere where a Touche Ross report noted: "The American public's confidence in its leaders and institutions is so shaken that our entire system of government has been undermined."[11] For instance, no coherent laws exist for the information sector, which makes it difficult to prosecute information thieves. Most observers argue that current laws work in favor of information thieves. Businesses would like to see an effective federal law. While some corporations, such as IBM, have managed to successfully attack information thieves through the courts, most have failed to protect themselves and their trade secrets.[12]

How Can You Evaluate Social Performance?

While the public demands higher levels of social responsibility for business, management faces the dual problems of implementation and evaluation. Implementation of socially oriented objectives requires careful analysis to determine whether the benefits derived from the action exceed the cost. One public debate centers on whether the United States should strive for completely safe work

To create a better working environment for its employees, U.S. Shoe replaced its assembly production lines with modular work units, where employees perform several steps in the production process rather than one tedious task. The modular system creates a greater feeling of camaraderie, teamwork, and pride in workmanship. Under the modular system, employees participate in daily decision making, problem solving, and new-idea development. The company invested heavily in cross-training for modular work areas and in training managers and employees in the skills of communication and group dynamics.

Photo source: Courtesy U.S. Shoe Corporation.

and living environments. Many argue that such goals are unattainable and cost prohibitive.

Business also faces the question of how to evaluate a firm's social performance. Critics readily point out that the private enterprise system is oriented toward quantity, not quality. In other words, Americans tend to confuse material goods, such as bigger and better homes, BMWs, vacation cottages, and the like, with the true quality of life.

Historically, social performance was usually evaluated by the firm's contribution to national output and provision of employment opportunities. Items such as weekly wage payments were often used as measures of social performance. Profit and employment are still of prime concern today. But now we also look at other areas of business responsibility: industrial safety, assembly-line drudgery, product safety, equal employment opportunity, and pollution. Industry has traditionally been unable to respond because it lacked adequate measures of social performance.

Conducting a Social Audit

social audit
Formal examination of a firm's social responsibility programs.

Some firms measure social performance with a **social audit**, a formal procedure that identifies and evaluates all company activities relating to social issues such as employment practices, environmental protection, conservation, and philanthropy.

The social audit provides management with information on what the company is doing and how well it is doing. Based on this information, management may take steps to revise current programs or develop new ones.

Many companies are now developing means of assessing social responsibility. General Motors, for example, publishes an annual *Public Interest Report* that outlines the corporation's accomplishments in such areas as minority contracting, research on alternative fuels, quality of work life, and industrial pollution control. Environmental, church, and public-interest groups are also attempting to create measures of corporate performance. It is important that this development continue. Lack of an adequate evaluation system for corporate social responsibility may delay accomplishing social goals.

Some consumer groups are evaluating business themselves. The Council of Economic Priorities produced *Rating America's Corporate Conscience,* which rates consumer goods companies according to their positions on national defense, involvement in South Africa, the number of female and minority executives, charitable contributions, and "social disclosure."[13]

Other Signs of Social Responsibility

Investment in socially responsible mutual funds is also increasing (mutual funds are discussed in Chapter 21). Some $400 billion is invested in such funds, some of which outperform the average general equity fund.[14] Credit card companies also are paying attention to ethics. Members of the Sierra Club can get a special low-interest credit card, and the Working Assets Visa card, which gives five cents to nonprofit organizations for each transaction, has attracted more than 90,000 cardholders.

Ethics is taking hold of consumers in stores as well. Nestlé was boycotted for its sales of milk formula in third world countries, and products as diverse as tuna and makeup can come under fire for ethical reasons. Still, there is no clear-cut way to define what is ethical and what is not, and what is the dividing line between a corporation making a profit and being sensitive to societal concerns.

Business's Social Responsibility

Because business decisions have a major impact on the daily lives of everyone in society, business leaders and politicians must weigh their decisions against a number of societal and ethical issues. Many of these issues are interrelated. The energy crisis, for example, led to concern over the use of petroleum resources, and it also raised important consumer and ecological issues.

Smoking is an example of a current social responsibility issue. Fewer than 30 percent of Americans smoke, down from a high of 42 percent in 1967, and governmental limits on smokers have become common. Nonsmokers are becoming increasingly intolerant of smokers, particularly at work, but smoking remains legal, which puts businesses in an awkward position: ban smoking and risk offending valuable employees who smoke or do nothing and ignore the complaints of the generally larger population of nonsmokers in the workplace. Fully 30 percent of America's corporations now restrict on-the-job smoking.[15]

Examples of smoking restrictions are plentiful. Turner Broadcasting System refuses to hire smokers; U.S. Gypsum has banned smoking on and off the job for all workers except those in its corporate headquarters; and Northwest Airlines

Smoking as a social responsibility issue extends beyond the workplace. For 35 years, Hasbro Inc.'s popular Mr. Potato Head had a pipe. But in 1988, the toymaker began marketing the toy without a pipe so children would not make any association with smoking.

Photo source: Courtesy of Playskool, Inc.

banned smoking on all flights after it found that 90 percent of its frequent flyers do not smoke.[16] Some employees challenge the right of companies to restrict their right to smoke, but many approve of the measures.

Business's social responsibilities can be classified in regard to its relationship to the general public, customers, company personnel, business associates, and investors and the financial community. These categories provide the outline for the sections that follow.

Responsibilities to the General Public

A number of issues such as smoking affect the general public. AIDS is perhaps the most prominent of these issues. Businesses are increasingly finding themselves in the position of educating employees about AIDS. For instance, a recent survey showed that out of 2,000 workers, 35 percent did not believe acquired immune deficiency syndrome (AIDS) could be transmitted only by sexual contact or blood contamination. A number of major employers, among them IBM and AT&T, have endorsed a ten-point bill of rights on AIDS, including general education and not testing for AIDS when hiring.[17] Other major issues affecting the general public include protection of the environment, caring for the elderly, solving the hard-core unemployment problem, and conserving and developing energy resources.

Protecting the Environment

Ecology and environmental issues continue to become more important to the public, particularly as the industrial sector of the economy becomes less visible. **Ecology** — the relationship between people and their environment — is now a legal as well as a societal issue for managers to consider.

    Nearly everyone accepts the premise that we should maintain an ecologically sound environment, but achieving this goal requires trade-offs that we are not always willing to make. For example, although we fear the danger of oil spills from supertankers, we insist upon readily available supplies of gasoline at reasonable prices. And coal-burning boilers, once converted to oil-burning furnaces in order to cut air pollution, are being used again because coal is relatively plentiful in the United States. Ecological goals are important; however, it is essential that we coordinate these goals with other societal and economic objectives. On this, no clear consensus has emerged.

    Pollution — the tainting or destroying of a natural environment — is the major ecological problem today. Water and air pollution are significant problems and they have a growing impact on businesses. Changes in environmental law require major industrial companies to suddenly spend $100 billion to clean up long-standing toxic waste dumps that are leaking hazardous chemicals into the environment. For instance, Champion International Corp. operates a paper mill on North Carolina's Pigeon River. The mill has been dumping wastewater into the river for 80 years, and the Pigeon is now sludgy and smelly. There is a growing demand from downriver that Champion clean it up, but Champion claims a clean-up would be so expensive it would close the mill instead, with a direct cost of some 2,200 jobs.[18]

    This highlights the two major pollution questions society faces: Are the benefits of cleaning up pollution worth the costs? Are we willing to pay now for a future ecological benefit? While most of us recognize the current pollution problems, our willingness to pay for corrections is sometimes doubtful. A classic case of this conflict occurred several years ago when Gulf had to withdraw one of the first unleaded gasolines because of low sales.

The Recycling Solution   Disposable packaging, such as the throwaway plastic bottle, has created a major ecological problem. Trash of this type proliferates, showing an amazing resistance to decomposition. Some states are acting to reduce such accumulations of trash. Several, like Michigan and Oregon, passed legislation requiring deposits on all soft-drink and beer bottles and cans. But the most logical approach, recycling, remains underutilized. **Recycling** — the reprocessing of used materials for reuse — could provide a substantial portion of the materials required in our manufacturing sector. Some businesses have taken the lead. AT&T and Warner-Lambert recycle their wastepaper, and some drinking establishments have added bottle busters behind the bar.

    Although the recycling concept has received considerable public support, a comprehensive system has yet to be implemented in most communities. How-

ecology
Relationship between people and their environment.

pollution
The tainting or destroying of a natural environment.

recycling
Reprocessing of used materials for reuse.

Through its Recycle America program, of which this can recycling line in San Jose, California, is part, Waste Management Inc. has taken a leadership role in recycling. The company recycled more than 250,000 tons of metal, glass, newsprint, and other materials in a recent year. It also has a consulting service to assist customers in identifying how wastes can be avoided, reduced, or recycled. More than 600,000 U.S. and Canadian families participate in the firm's curbside recycling program.

Photo source: Courtesy of Waste Management, Inc.

ever, New Jersey took a significant step toward implementing recycling by mandating that trash be sorted into different categories before collection.

The Greenhouse Effect and Acid Rain   The *greenhouse effect,* where the Earth's temperature warms as carbon dioxide collects in the atmosphere, is widely believed to be caused by carbon dioxide emissions due to fossil fuel consumption. Along similar lines, *acid rain,* or rain with high levels of acid that many blame for the death of forests and lakes, has become a source of tension between the United States and Canada. Canadians blame the U.S. industrial base for producing the nitrogen-oxide emissions widely believed to cause acid rain. The Environmental Defense Fund produced a report that stated 25 percent of the nitrogen contaminating heavily polluted Chesapeake Bay is the result of acid rain. The Environmental Protection Agency has disputed the impact of acid rain, and scientists for other agencies have also downplayed its role. So far, the United States has rejected Canadian proposals that nitrogen-oxide emissions be limited.[19]

Caring for the Elderly

Preventing pollutants is not the only realm where businesses are now expected to contribute for the good of society. Care for the elderly is becoming something that employees, and society, look to employers to handle. IBM, American Express, Bristol-Meyers, and Mobil are among corporations with programs for elder care. Generally, companies that provide care for the elderly parents of employees offer referral services, educational seminars, and support groups. Approximately 100 U.S. companies provide ongoing programs for elderly care.

As Americans live longer, demand for elderly care may increase. Many companies, though, are looking for ways to lower the cost of their fringe benefits, which may discourage such programs.[20]

Solving the Hard-Core Unemployment Problem

Dealing with the hard-core unemployed is an old issue, and one that can seem fruitless. Hard-core unemployment is also known as *structural unemployment,* which is defined as people who lack the necessary skills for employment or whose skills are no longer demanded by the industry. (See Chapter 3.)

Since the early 1950s, blue-collar employment has fallen dramatically in almost all heavy industries. Many of these workers are incapable of being employed elsewhere because they do not have the education or skills demanded by an information-based economy.

The federal government has had numerous programs to increase the skills of the hard-core unemployed, most recently the *Job Training Partnership Act.* The JTPA trains some 80,000 low-income people a year and finds jobs for approximately 60 percent of them. Critics claim the program trains people who could get jobs anyway and does nothing for the chronically unemployed — 26 percent of the program's participants are high school dropouts compared to 47 percent of the population the JTPA is intended to benefit. Also, the program lasts for an average of only four months, and the average placement wage as of 1989 is $4.63 an hour.[21]

In light of governmental inability to solve the hard-core unemployment problem, many businesses have become involved in the battle. Their success has been mixed. While some, such as IBM, Digital Equipment Corporation, and Lockheed, have battled against long odds to create successful plants in low-income areas, the efforts required have left them unwilling to invest in similar areas.[22]

Corporations find that almost all employees in such areas must be trained before they can perform useful functions. As a result, General Electric and Procter & Gamble went straight into the schools to improve the education of children from poverty-stricken neighborhoods.

Sparked by the special report "A Nation At Risk," business has shown increased interest in improving education, particularly at the primary and secondary school levels, which traditionally garner less than 10 percent of corporate donations to education. Somber statistics indicate the depth of the problem: 30 percent of all U.S. high school students drop out each year. Motorola, which had generally been able to employ eight of ten applicants for entry-level positions, finds that as many as 15 now have to be screened to hire just one.[23]

Corporations have made a variety of efforts to encourage the lower-income population to stay in school. Adopt-a-school programs, money for preschools, and active involvement in issues such as tax increases for the benefit of schools are among the programs businesses have used to improve the odds for children who traditionally have grown up to become hard-core unemployed.

Conserving and Developing Energy Resources

The term **energy crisis** refers to the world's diminished ability to provide for its current and future energy needs. The oil embargo of the 1970s made American industry and consumers rethink their energy usage. As a result, energy use

energy crisis
The world's diminished ability to provide for future energy needs.

To encourage students to stay in school and earn good grades, BP America, the leading domestic producer of crude oil, teamed up with the school system in Cleveland, Ohio, to design and underwrite a program in which students earn credits for their grades. Higher grades earn higher credits, which students can redeem later to pay for college or professional training. In this photo, a Cleveland schoolteacher explains the program to students.

Photo source: Courtesy of BP America Inc.

declined significantly in many areas and industries. Prices then declined and energy supplies grew as oil-producing nations sought to maintain their exports. Still, most experts are quick to point out that energy usage is expected to increase in the future, and current resources are not being replaced.

conservation

Preservation of declining energy resources.

Components of the Energy Problem   The complex issue of energy can be divided into its short-run and long-run components. In the short run, the problem is one of **conservation** — the preservation of declining energy resources. Many conservation programs have been proposed or implemented, but their success has been mixed. Some programs have not been as effective as people had hoped; others have been ignored by the public. For example, the 55-mile-per-hour speed limit was abandoned partially because of public displeasure with the law in western states.

Another oil embargo could bring conservation measures to the forefront again. But the emphasis for now has shifted to seeking long-term solutions to the nation's energy dilemma. The long-run problem can be divided into two critical questions:

1. How can we best discover and develop alternative energy resources?
2. How do we coordinate our need for energy resources with other societal goals?

The United States and other nations will need to develop alternative energy resources. Nuclear power, wind, sun, synthetic fuels, coal, and even garbage and other waste products have been suggested as possible substitutes for oil and natural gas. While the search for new energy sources generates considerable public interest, the basic question of how to discover and develop them in a cost-efficient manner remains unresolved. For example, the production cost of synthetic fuels is now considerably higher than the market price for oil.

The second question — how to coordinate our need for energy resources with other societal needs — is also important. Sometimes national energy needs clash with ecological and environmental objectives. One such situation arose in the early 1980s with the proposed construction of a pipeline beneath Puget Sound in Washington state to carry Alaskan oil to the East. The governor of Washington eventually vetoed the proposal because of environmental concerns.

Responsibilities to Customers

Consumer demands are another social responsibility issue facing business. **Consumerism** — the demand that business give proper consideration to consumer wants and needs in making its decisions — is a major social and economic movement within the United States and in other industrialized nations. Ralph Nader is a leading force in this movement.

Since the emergence of consumerism more than two decades ago, consumer groups have sprung up throughout the country. Some concentrate on an isolated situation, such as rate hikes by a local public utility, while others are more broadly based. The net effect has been passage of consumer-protection laws covering everything from unethical sales practices to the licensing of persons in the repair business. There is little doubt that more consumer-protection laws will be enacted in the years ahead, and business is well advised to heed the warnings of the consumerism movement.

consumerism
The public demand for business to consider consumer wants and needs in making its decisions.

President Kennedy's Statement of Consumer Rights

An excellent description of the consumer's rights was put forth by President John F. Kennedy in a 1962 speech to Congress. He outlined four specific consumer rights:

1. The consumer has the right to safety.
2. The consumer has the right to be informed.
3. The consumer has the right to choose.
4. The consumer has the right to be heard.

Much of the post-1962 consumer legislation is based on these rights. In fact, many companies go to considerable effort to assure that consumer complaints receive a full hearing. Ford Motor Company, for example, set up a consumer appeals board to resolve service complaints.

The Pentagon Scandal

The recent multibillion-dollar purchasing scandal at the Pentagon points out the importance of social responsibility and ethical decisions in dealing with customers — in this case the U.S. government. Many major military contractors had

Coors Brewing Company respects consumers' rights to be heard and to be informed. The brewer opened a Consumer Information Center (CIC) and toll-free telephone hotline to respond to consumer questions, comments, and requests. Specially trained consumer assistants take all calls, respond to letters, and analyze the content of CIC contacts. In this photo, President Jeff Coors (left), Chairman Bill Coors, and assistant Vivian Taylor retrieve examples of consumer letters on the computer.

Photo source: Courtesy of Coors Brewing Company.

previously been accused of excesses in billings or other wrongdoing, but this time the charges were sweeping accusations of widespread bribery and fraud. The Pentagon situation was viewed by many people as the most sweeping scandal in the U.S. government since the Teapot Dome oil leasing scandal in the 1920s.[24]

McDonnell Douglas, United Technologies Corp., Unisys, Teledyne, and Northrop were linked to paying Pentagon officials and consultants for information to improve their contract bids. The size of the contracts at issue fueled the situation. When Grumman lost out to a McDonnell Douglas–General Dynamics team on a bid for an advanced tactical fighter, it lost the opportunity to make some $40 billion.

The sheer size of the Pentagon also contributes to possible corruption. It spends $160 billion a year on weapons systems and employs 50,000 workers simply to buy things.[25] This Byzantine structure increases the importance of contact between a potential client and a consultant, who frequently has worked in the armed services.

Some observers argue that the current system of close contact between consultants and clients and buyers is the most effective way to conduct Pentagon business, and the information given out is not proprietary. Therefore, no harm is done. The 1988 Pentagon scandal illustrates another area of social responsibility for business.

Responsibilities to Company Personnel

While the Hawthorne studies of 1927–1933 showed the value of paying attention to employees, businesses are finding that workers — and communities — increasingly look to them to handle a number of needs such as child care. The increased role for businesses is evolving as the workplace becomes a center of life for many people, replacing more traditional institutions such as church, social groups, and school.

Business's responsibilities to its employees are far ranging. Issues include child care, equal employment opportunity, sexual harassment, sexism, and comparable worth.

The Child-Care Issue

Child care is perhaps the biggest issue. The number of families with two working parents is up dramatically — more than 10 million working mothers have children under six — and businesses are being asked to establish care for children. Some 3,300 companies have set up full or partial child-care programs in response to employee demands. America West Airlines opened a round-the-clock, seven-day-a-week day-care center near its Phoenix hub. Similarly, the Washington, D.C.–based law firm of Wilmer, Cutler & Pickering expanded its offices to include a day-care center when attorneys of both sexes had child-care crises that could have upset major cases. Finally, Paramount Pictures operates its day-care center until 3 a.m. when filming is under way.

Broadcaster Ted Koppel is perhaps the most famous father to take paternity leave, but a number of companies now offer their male employees the right to time off from work to care for a newborn. However, most companies find that men rarely will claim such a leave. Hallmark Cards Inc. has yet to have an employee use more than a week of its monthlong unpaid paternity leave. Ryder Corp. has had one man use its paternity leave policy, and Southern New England Telephone has had seven men — compared with 592 women — take leave over the last three years.[26] Loss of salary is probably the main reason men generally refuse to take advantage of such programs, particularly in families where both parents work.

Ensuring Equal Employment Opportunity

The Civil Rights Act (1964) ruled that discriminatory practices are illegal. Title VII of the act prohibits discrimination in employment. To police this part of the act, the ***Equal Employment Opportunity Commission (EEOC)*** was established. This federal commission was created to increase job opportunities for women and minorities and to assist in ending job discrimination based on race, color, religion, sex, or national origin in any personnel action. Minorities defined by the EEOC include:

◆   Black (not of Hispanic origin)

◆   Hispanic

◆   Asian or Pacific Islander

◆   American Indian or Alaskan Native

Equal Employment Opportunity Commission (EEOC)
Federal commission created to increase job opportunities for women and minorities and help eliminate job discrimination.

The goals of the EEOC have been strengthened by passage of the Equal Pay Act (1963), the Age Discrimination in Employment Act (1967), the Equal Employment Opportunity Act (1972), the Pregnancy Discrimination Act (1978), and numerous executive orders. Two additional pieces of legislation are designed to provide equal employment opportunities for handicapped workers and Vietnam-era veterans. Section 503 of the Vocational Rehabilitation Act (1973) requires all firms having U.S. government contracts of $2,500 or more to establish programs to promote career advancement for handicapped workers and to provide physical access for them.

Vietnam Veterans   The Vietnam Era Veterans Readjustment Assistance Act (1974) provides similar requirements for employers with federal government contracts of $10,000 or more. Such employers are required to protect and promote employment for disabled veterans as well as Vietnam-era veterans by taking affirmative action in recruiting and advancing qualified disabled and other Vietnam-era veterans. In addition, these firms are required to list job openings with local state employment services.

affirmative action program
Program set up by businesses to increase opportunities for women and minorities.

Affirmative Action Programs   The EEOC assists an employer in setting up an **affirmative action program** to increase job opportunities for women, minorities, and other protected categories. Such programs include analyzing the present work force and setting specific hiring and promotion goals, with target dates in areas where women, minorities, and others are underutilized. Penalties for violations can also be imposed.[27]

In many cases, legal actions are not necessary to provide increased job opportunities for women, minorities, and other protected categories of employees. A few years ago, General Motors Corporation agreed to spend $42.5 million over five years to hire additional women and minorities, to provide scholarships, and to offer special employee and supervisory training programs. These actions, in response to an EEOC complaint, were aimed at increasing the number of women and minority employees at General Motors and expanding GM's apprenticeship programs, employee training, and promotion opportunities for women and minority workers.

Even in the enlightened 1990s, America's 36 million handicapped citizens find life more difficult than it should be. Only one-third of 15 million working-age handicapped people are employed, many below their capabilities. About 6 million survive largely on Social Security and disability insurance. However, a growing number of firms are discovering that the handicapped worker is frequently the most reliable, hardworking member of the work force. Jonah Kaufman, owner of 13 Long Island, New York, McDonald's outlets, is delighted with the performance of over 35 handicapped workers on his payroll: "These people never come in late and are rarely sick." Marriott Corporation human resource department managers agree. The hotel and restaurant giant has been hiring the mentally handicapped for more than a decade and currently employs about 1,000.[28]

Removing Employment Barriers for Women   Equal employment opportunity legislation also prohibits use of job specifications that limit employment to men. Employers are not allowed to exclude women from job consideration

These market analysts at Sears, Roebuck and Company reflect the retailer's commitment to hiring female and minority employees. The Sears Merchandise Group gives support to women in business by helping sponsor an annual award that honors women who have overcome serious disabilities to achieve major success in the executive and professional ranks. The company also has set up special programs to recruit and develop supplier companies owned by minorities and women, does business with 52 women- or minority-owned banks, and invests in minority enterprises.

Photo source: 1987 annual report. Courtesy of Sears, Roebuck and Co.

unless they can demonstrate the job requires physical skills that women applicants do not have.

Until the mid-1960s, the classified advertisement sections of virtually every daily newspaper in the United States contained two categories: "Jobs — Male" and "Jobs — Female." One result of equal employment opportunity laws was elimination of these sex distinctions. A second result was a change in job titles. When the U.S. Department of Labor revised its five-pound *Dictionary of Occupational Titles,* many of the 15,000 entries reflected the removal of sexist job titles. Table 2.1 shows some of the revisions.

Table 2.1   Changes in Job Titles

Former Job Title	New Job Title
Fireman	Fire fighter
Policeman	Police officer
Mailman	Mail carrier
Salesman	Sales person
Foreman	Supervisor
Bus boy	Dining room attendant
Housewife	Homemaker
Congressman	Member of Congress/Representative
Bat boy	Bat handler
Cameraman	Camera operator
Stewardess	Flight attendant
Headmaster	Principal
Cleaning lady/maid	Housekeeper
Draftsman	Drafter
Song and dance man	Song and dance person

Source: U.S. Department of Labor, Employment and Training Administration, *Dictionary of Occupational Titles* (Washington, D.C., Government Printing Office, various years).

Among the most dramatic examples of the success of women in business are those in the traditionally male-dominated field of sales. Since 1981, the proportion of women in sales has nearly tripled, from 7 percent to 18 percent. Today's professional saleswoman is involved in industries ranging from the installation of multimillion-dollar computer systems to supplying oil-derrick parts at drilling sites. Compensation can be outstanding. Terry Casey, a sales representative and vice president of New York's AIM Telephones, earns over $100,000 a year.

Ironically, many of the so-called "inherent female traits" — empathy, intuition, and the ability to nurture long-term relationships — that once allowed sexist employers to dismiss females as too sensitive to thrive in the business world are considered crucial to successful selling. As one expert put it, "Studies show that women listen and speak better and can be more service-oriented than men."[29]

Eliminating Discrimination against Older Workers   In the past, many large firms required employees to retire at age 65. The arbitrary choice of 65 as the retirement age appears to have been based on tradition. It was first proposed by nineteenth-century German leader Otto von Bismarck. Also, 65 was named as the eligibility age for benefits when the Social Security Act was passed in 1935. As a result, many private pension plans incorporated 65 as the age for retirement.

Mandatory retirement ages were criticized for years as being unfair to older workers. Critics often pointed out that Galileo, Sigmund Freud, and Thomas Edison made some of their most notable contributions to society when they were past age 60. These protests eventually led to the passage of the Age Discrimination in Employment Act, which prohibits employers from using age as a basis for employment decisions (hiring, promotions, or separations). The original law was designed to protect workers aged 40 to 65, but in 1986 the law was amended to apply to all persons aged 40 and older. By the year 2010, people aged 40 and older are expected to make up 50 percent of the nation's work force.

A few exceptions exist. For example, under certain circumstances, senior executives can be subject to mandatory retirement at 65. Also, some firefighters, police officers, and tenured university faculty are still subject to mandatory retirement ages specified by their employer until 1994.

Sexual Harassment

Women have battled sexual harassment in the workplace since they started working. Major legal advances have been made against this type of personal abuse. Legally, there are two categories of sexual harassment: (1) unwelcome advances and requests for sexual favors that affect promotions and raises, and (2) a hostile work environment, in which a woman feels hassled or degraded because of unwelcome flirtation, lewd comments, or obscene joking. In a sexual harassment case against Chemlawn, a federal district court judge ruled that sexual material, such as pinup calendars and pornographic magazines and films, may create an atmosphere that could affect a reasonable woman's psychological well-being and interfere with her ability to perform her job.

According to a 1987 federal study, 42 percent of female government employees reported they had suffered some form of sexual harassment in the preceding 24 months. This is the same figure as in 1980. Despite improved legal options, only 5 percent of the women who claimed they had been abused filed a formal complaint.

The difficulty of winning cases is part of the reason women are reluctant to attack the system. While the laws against sexual harassment are well-defined, winning legal cases exacts a price that many women are unwilling to pay. Catherine Broderick, a lawyer with the Securities and Exchange Commission who was refused promotions and then transferred after she refused to have sex with her superior, went to court and won a promotion with back pay, but she spent nine years doing it.

Many firms, including Du Pont, Merck & Company, and American Federal Bank, have established anti-harassment policies and employee-education programs. Effective harassment prevention programs include (1) issuing a specific policy prohibiting sexual harassment, (2) developing an internal complaint procedure, (3) creating an atmosphere that encourages sexually harassed employees to come forward, and (4) taking immediate action to investigate and resolve complaints, and enforcing disciplinary action against the harassers.[30]

Sexism

While sexual harassment remains widespread, an even larger problem seems to be subtle sexism. As women make up a large percentage of the work force and become members of professions traditionally dominated by males, harassment based upon deeply rooted stereotypes is evident. Women are passed over for promotions and frequently receive less pay than their male counterparts for no other reason than being born female. Many women report instances of men ignoring them in favor of speaking to less knowledgeable male associates or having their knowledge doubted. Some also report they are excluded from social and even business meetings because men are uncomfortable with women around.

Blatant and subtle sexism are deeply entrenched in the corporate world. Both female and male professionals say the best way to erase the stereotypes is for women to continue to advance in their professions. Barbara Corday, former president of Columbia Pictures Television, remarked: "When . . . you reach a point where you become one of those people that cannot be left out, it's in [the men's] interest to talk to you."[31]

Firms can also help erase the stereotypes of women by designing advertising that portrays them in a respectful manner. American Express received many awards for its "Interesting Lives" advertising campaign, which shows women in various active and positive roles. An example is shown in Figure 2.2.

Comparable Worth

Studies by the State of Washington and the Illinois and Minnesota Commissions on the Status of Women focused on a number of generally comparable jobs, some of which are primarily held by men and others that tend to be female-dominated. The salaries paid to holders of these roughly comparable jobs varied

Figure 2.2   Erasing Sexual Stereotypes

Source: Courtesy of American Express.

considerably. Here are a few examples of monthly salaries paid at the time of the studies:

Predominantly Male Jobs		Comparable Predominantly Female Jobs	
Accountant	$2,740	Nurse	$1,794
Conservation officer	1,808	Behavioral analyst	1,590
Highway worker	1,816	Clerk typist	1,075
Delivery driver	1,382	Pharmacy assistant	1,202
Mechanic	1,462	Medical records analyst	892
Security officer	1,114	Telephone operator	808

These disparities led a number of women's rights advocates to argue that American women are being systematically and illegally underpaid for work that is different from but just as demanding as that performed by men. They advocate the concept of **comparable worth** — a philosophy seeking equal pay for jobs requiring similar levels of education, training, and skills. In some instances, they are proving their point in court. Although a federal appeals court ruling struck down a judge's order that Washington state pay hundreds of millions of dollars to women who had accused the state of wage bias, similar lawsuits on a smaller scale have been won by female workers in California, Hawaii, and Nassau County, New York.[32] Laws have been enacted in California, Idaho, Iowa, Minnesota, New Mexico, South Dakota, and Washington requiring pay equity for com-

comparable worth
Equal pay for jobs requiring similar levels of education, training, and skills.

parable work in state jobs. The Minnesota law resulted in wage increases for 9,000 of the state's 29,000 employees.

Opponents of the comparable-worth philosophy point to several potential problems, such as the difficulty of objectively defining job worth. Others contend the wage disparity exists because women have chosen jobs on which the free market has placed a lesser value. To increase the salaries of such female-dominated occupations as secretaries and nurses, opponents argue, would simply encourage women to remain in these positions rather than seeking other, higher-paying occupations. Finally, critics of the comparable-worth philosophy fear the increased control that would result from government boards making arbitrary rulings on the value of every job, should this approach to salary determinations become law.

Nancy Reder of the Washington, D.C.–based National Committee on Pay Equity summarizes the position of comparable-worth advocates as follows: "Employers evaluate jobs and set salary levels all the time. All we're asking is that they do so in a sex-neutral manner."[33]

Responsibilities to Investors and the Financial Communities

There is probably no place where the public expects a higher level of business ethics than in the arena of financial transactions. Public attention goes beyond the illegitimate activities identified by statutes. Executives are expected to exhibit the highest standards of ethical behavior concerning financial practices in order to justify the public trust placed in them.

Recent cases have heightened public concern in this area. Victims of fraudulent tax-shelter schemes reportedly range from pensioners to celebrities. A major brokerage firm is penalized for banking practices. Bank executives are sentenced to jail. Numerous other situations are not illegal but raise ethical questions. Greenmail is such an issue.

Greenmail

Greenmail refers to a situation in which wealthy investors buy a significant portion of a cash-rich but minimally profitable (or unprofitable) firm.[34] They then hint to the firm's board of directors that they are going to attempt a takeover and oust current management. In many instances, the result is an offer to buy back the greenmailer's stock at a price well above its current market value.

In a classic case, Saul P. Steinberg threatened a hostile takeover of Walt Disney Productions and walked away with almost $32 million in profit and an additional $28 million to cover his out-of-pocket expenses. Steinberg's threat to Disney began after he accumulated 11 percent of Disney stock.

Disney's board took a number of steps to ward off Steinberg's attack. It issued a new stock offering worth more than $537 million and purchased another company, Arvida, a resort and home community developer. These moves were intended to dilute the relative value of Steinberg's holdings.

However, these defensive moves produced a weakened financial position for Disney that penalized all its stockholders. Company debt more than doubled. The market value of Disney stock dropped by 22 percent in two days. Stock value declined more than $500 million during the takeover attempt.

In the end, the only way the firm could prevent the takeover was to buy back the stock held by Steinberg's firm, Reliance Financial Services Group. In exchange for his $32 million profit, Steinberg pledged not to buy Disney stock for the next ten years. Many Disney shareholders were enraged that they could not sell their shares for the premium price paid to Steinberg and that the firm's market price actually dropped after the payoff was made public.

As a result of cases such as this, companies now erect elaborate financial and legal barriers to greenmail. These defenses are described in detail in Chapter 5.

Insider Trading

"Isn't everybody doing it?" was the word from Wall Street as reported in one newsmagazine after Dennis Levine's debacle led to the Ivan Boesky case and a rash of SEC subpoenas. In one sense, everybody on Wall Street does trade on inside information — few people outside the brokerage community are aware of the rumors and other information traders regularly use to make decisions. However, most of this is accessible to those who want to find it; the inside trades that Levine, Boesky, and others made were based on information not generally available even on the "Street" (business jargon for the securities industries).[35]

The Securities and Exchange Commission moved quickly against all those it could find, and some of those involved have had their lives ruined. Some people have gone to jail and/or paid fines, as high as $100 million in the case of Ivan Boesky. Whether this punishment will prevent future insider excesses depends less on the threat of the SEC than on how badly members of certain financial communities want money, for millions — and hundreds of millions — can be made in today's active stock market.

Excessive Executive Compensation

As workers get promoted to higher positions, their pay level also increases. Executive salaries from 1977 to 1987 rose at a 12.2 percent compounded annual clip, compared to a 6.1 percent rise for others. It is no longer shocking to see top executives earning more than $1 million a year in salary along with special stock options and other perks that can bring them much higher compensation. Chrysler's Lee Iacocca, for instance, started at Chrysler on a $1 annual salary, plus stock options. Now, with a base salary over $2 million, he has gathered enough stock options to take in more than $15 million in actual income in recent years. Iacocca is small game compared to chief executives such as Lotus's Jim Manz, who earned a record $26 million-plus in total income in a recent year. In the same year, the average pay of chief executive officers rose 48 percent, compared to a 4.4 percent inflation rate. Much of the increases came when an executive exercised stock options — real salaries rose, but only by 8 percent.[36]

The apparent randomness of executive earnings adds to public confusion about executive salaries. At IBM, for instance, CEO John Akers earns less than a number of executives who run far smaller companies. A special *Fortune* study found that a number of factors influence executive compensation. Company size, performance, and risk, as well as the level of government regulation, job tenure (longer generally means less pay), and location (executives in New York City and Los Angeles average 7 to 10 percent more than executives elsewhere) can make a difference in salary. Still, according to *Fortune's* study, statistical analysis could rationalize only 39 percent of the variance in executive salaries.[37]

Corporate responsibility — being sensitive to the needs of employees and the community — was the philosophy on which Ben Cohen (left) and Jerry Greenfield founded their ice cream company, Ben & Jerry's Homemade Inc. Believing that too many firms pay their top executives too much money, Ben and Jerry established a five-to-one salary ratio policy that limits the top salary to five times that of the lowest-paid employee. The policy recognizes the important role of the workers who actually make the ice cream. Managers who want to make more money (top salary is about $85,000) must raise the salary of the lowest-paid employee to maintain the five-to-one ratio.

Photo source: © Seth Resnick/Picture Group.

Logically, the better a company performs, the more its executives make. But some executives tend to do well even if the company loses money. Many people think such scenarios should be eliminated because they endanger the earnings of shareholders. Since exercising stock options frequently provides executives with most of their compensation, some have proposed forcing companies to charge such transactions against earnings. Others suggest full and uniform earnings disclosure, and the specter of government regulation is not discounted.

Summary of Learning Goals

1.   Explain the concept of social responsibility as an accepted business policy.   Social responsibility refers to management's consideration of the social as well as the economic effects of its decisions. It is accepted policy in contemporary business affairs. Several firms now use the term *corporate citizenship* interchangeably with *social responsibility.*

2.   Outline the concept of business ethics and explain how management makes ethical decisions.   Business ethics refers to a businessperson's standards of conduct and moral values. It involves the right and wrong actions that arise in any work environment, as well as a knowledge of the institutional parameters within which the decision must be made. Some firms spell out their ethical parameters in formal codes of conduct. Other organizations allow managers to explore the ethical dimensions of decision making through workshops and seminars.

3. Describe the relationship between self-regulation and government regulation. History shows that when business fails to respond to social or ethical issues, government is quick to enter with regulatory actions. Therefore, self-regulation is in the best interest of the business community.

4. Discuss how social performance can be evaluated. Social performance was traditionally measured by such factors as the firm's contribution to national output and employment opportunities. Today, social performance is measured on a broader basis. While no generally accepted format has emerged, many companies and industries have developed their own measures of social responsibility.

5. Outline business's responsibilities to the general public. It is important for managers to appreciate that they have responsibilities to the general public as well as their duties to their employers. Currently, these public responsibilities include such areas as AIDS education, protecting the environment, elder care, solving the hard-core unemployment problems, and conserving and developing energy resources.

6. Identify business's responsibilities to customers. Business's most readily identifiable responsibilities are related to its customers. These responsibilities have been heightened by the consumerism movement, which originated in the 1960s. Most industry and legislative response to this movement has followed John F. Kennedy's statement of consumer rights. These consumer rights were that of safety, to be informed, to choose, and to be heard.

7. Describe business's responsibilities to company personnel. Relations with company personnel are some of the most significant social responsibility and ethical issues facing contemporary business. Issues include child care, equal employment opportunity, sexual harassment, sexism, and comparable worth.

8. Explain business's responsibilities to investors and the financial communities. There has been considerable publicity in recent years about business's social and ethical responsibilities to investors and the financial communities. Topics such as greenmail, insider trading, and executive compensation are now reported and analyzed in the media as well as in business circles.

Key Terms

social responsibility	recycling	Equal Employment Opportunity Commission (EEOC)
business ethics	energy crisis	affirmative action program
social audit	conservation	comparable worth
ecology	consumerism	
pollution		

Review Questions

1. Relate the concept of *corporate citizenship* to the material presented in Chapter 2.

2. Suggest a framework for improving ethical decision making within a firm.

3. Is self-regulation a deterrent to government regulation in matters of social responsibility and business ethics?

4. What is the current status of social responsibility and ethics in American industry?

5. Explain the need for social performance measures in business.

6. What are business's responsibilities to the general public?

7. What basic consumer rights were suggested by President Kennedy? How have these suggestions improved the contemporary business environment?

8. Explain business's responsibilities in regard to its employees.

9. Outline the comparable worth argument.

10. Are top executives overpaid?

Discussion Questions

1. Speaking to Seattle University's Albers School of Business, President George Bush told the students: "I don't have to tell you the image that many Americans, and many in the press, have of business students. Instead of recognizing that you're learning to help make our economy run better, they've painted a picture of a generation only concerned about quick and easy money. I know that's not true." How can business students prove the president is correct, that they are socially responsible and interested in more than just money? Discuss.

2. Stride Rite Corp. plans to open a unique child-care/elder-care center. The center will care for 60 children and 30 elderly persons. The two groups will share activities such as games and cooking. Relate Stride Rite's socially responsible effort to the material presented in Chapter 2 on child care and elder care.

3. One middle manager at U.S. West Communications in Seattle works at home in an office equipped with a computer, printer, fax machine, and three telephone lines. While many people work at home now, this manager's position is different: he has AIDS. The unusual work arrangement, which includes a half day a week in the firm's downtown office, is part of U.S. West's policy of encouraging employees with AIDS to remain on the job as much as possible. Six other AIDS victims still work in a regular office setting. The company also offers AIDS education seminars to its employees. Discuss U.S. West's policies regarding the AIDS crisis.

4. Describe the major societal and ethical issues facing the following:
   a. Automobile manufacturers
   b. Real estate developers
   c. Detergent manufacturers

    d. Drug companies selling products used in the treatment of AIDS

    e. Defense contractors

5. The Roman Catholic bishops in the United States issued a pastoral letter titled "Catholic Social Teaching and the U.S. Economy." In it, the bishops said more had to be done to combat poverty, unemployment, and income inequities. The bishops advocated greater government involvement to resolve these problems.

    Prepare a report on this publication. With what aspects do you agree? Disagree? What social responsibilities does it suggest for individual businesspersons?

Video Case

Trust for Public Land

In the past few years, the issue of social responsibility and concerns about protecting the environment have been front-page news. The 1987 incident at Chernobyl and then the tragic Alaskan oil spill in 1989 produced worldwide concerns about the devastating impact humanity was having on the world environment. Increasingly, the general public evaluates business not only on its ability to give stockholders the greatest profits, but also on its efforts to enrich the lives of those it comes in contact with. One such company is Trust for Public Land (TPL), a nonprofit organization whose goals are to save land for the use of future generations by buying and holding it until it can be turned over to a local, state, or federal government agency that can preserve it.

Author and entrepreneur Paul Hawken describes TPL as a nonprofit institution that illustrates a quality found in many entrepreneurial businesses: People who are in business to find and create meaning in their lives do far better than those with purely monetary goals. According to Hawken, "Whether a donation or a purchase, money follows ideas. Ideas never follow money."

TPL uses basic business skills to try to create a better society for everyone. Since its founding in 1983, the organization has protected more than 430,000 acres of urban, rural, and wilderness land for scenic and recreational purposes. In 34 states and Canada, TPL has purchased 529 parcels of land valued at $410 million. Because land sold to the organization is tax deductible, TPL's managers can often make purchases at below-market prices. It covers its operating costs by eventually reselling the land to a government agency for an average 8 percent profit. The organization saves taxpayers money by returning land cheaply to public use and provides positive public relations to many of the large corporations, such as AT&T and RCA, that have sold land to TPL.

President Martin J. Rosen explains how TPL got started: "What we saw was a series of tradeoffs — a

series of notions of progress — that always meant that the land got less respect and less attention; . . . we saw the shopping malls, we saw the freeways, we saw the highrises. And we always remembered afterward, if we had a memory, that those used to be peach orchards or . . . creeks or . . . waterways or . . . parks and open spaces — or even vacant lands that are simply no longer there." Concerned individuals then determined to try to save some of America's remaining lands for future use.

When TPL began, its founders realized that solving problems in real estate involves surveys, appraisals, lawyers, travel expenses, and down payments — things that take money. Lots of money. Again, Rosen says, "We chose to make the Trust for Public Land an entrepreneurial organization because risk is inherent, we think, in land acquisition, land protection, and land preservation. If you are going to be involved in business, you must understand the complexities of transactions, the diversity of motivations, and the uncertainty of results. You have to spend a lot of time listening and then be willing to take some risks. You have to be willing to put your money where your mouth is." TPL's founders went to the Bank of America and presented their proposed business plan. They managed to convince the bank that they did not intend to function as a charity but would, in fact, be a business. With this understanding, the bank agreed to lend TPL up to $10 million to begin work. Since that time, the bank has made money and its shareholders regard TPL not as some questionable, flaky, or financially uncertain organization, but as a profitable enterprise.

Among TPL's projects is Lemmon Lake in the heart of Dallas — 255 acres that were bought by the city of Dallas to serve as a municipal park. The lake sits in a poor section of the city, where the people who use it have few other recreational facilities. In New York City, TPL has saved and ultimately sold Tudor City Park and Clinton Square. The latter, in what used to be called Hell's Kitchen, was owned by the city. Perennially short of money, the city planned to sell it to developers as the site of a planned highrise, but TPL persuaded the city to let them lease the property, with all responsibility for maintaining it to be assumed by community members. Today, it is a permanently protected open space in a part of New York City with few

Notes: Sterling North, "For Some New England Residents, Natural Beauty Comes before Development," *New England Business,* May 4, 1987, pp. 52–54; Kate Ballen, "People to Watch," *Fortune,* July 6, 1987, p. 96; *Land & People,* Vol. 11, No. 1, Winter 1989; personal correspondence May 4, 1989.

such areas. It contains plots for flowers, fruits, and vegetables, and even has a barbecue pit for neighborhood residents to use.

One of TPL's recent projects illustrates how the organization works with communities. For years, an area of Telegraph Hill in San Francisco had been used as a dump and was covered with old tires, auto bodies, and even chemical waste. A resident of the neighborhood voluntarily took on the task of removing the debris and transforming the space into a lush and beautiful garden. When the developer who owned a large part of the property decided to tear down the small structure on it and build a larger one, community residents asked TPL to do something to preserve the garden. TPL went to the developer and secured an option to buy the land. It then contacted local corporations, national institutions, and private citizens, and raised money to buy the land by selling deeds to one-inch lots for $5 each. Enough money was left over for a modest maintenance and endowment fund for the garden.

One of TPL's most ambitious projects was Cascade Ranch. Set in Northern California, the ranch consists of 4,000 acres of scenic virgin redwoods, an untouched coastline, and a working farm. The area was embroiled in many conflicts — political, financial, and various development schemes — but TPL nonetheless sought to save the land for the permanent enjoyment of the general public. It made a substantial payment to the developer for exclusive rights to buy the property, even though the state of California gave TPL no guarantee that the funds needed to purchase the land would be forthcoming. But TPL's board of directors voted to borrow $7 million. The organization managed to bring together diverse interests to find a use for the land and preserve it for the future.

Trust for Public Land demonstrates that the best businesses are not necessarily those that make the biggest profits. TPL employs all the skills used by successful businesses to ensure their profits and directs these skills toward accomplishing something for the public good. Our society is coming to regard good businesses as those that do something to improve all our lives.

Questions

1. Even though Trust for Public Land is a nonprofit organization, it has most of the same concerns of any business (other than profitability). Refer to the factors of production described in Chapter 1 and show how TPL employs each of them in its operations. How would you summarize TPL's overall objectives?

2. Explain how TPL has managed to meet its responsibilities to its customers, its investors, its employees, and the general public.

3. Explain why a developer or other business that owns land would agree to sell it at a below-market price to an organization like TPL.

4. Why does Trust for Public Land, a nonprofit organization, refer to itself as an entrepreneurial organization?

5. "Acting socially responsible is good for business." Give two examples you are familiar with that support the accuracy of this statement. Give two examples of how firms have been penalized by consumers when they failed to operate in a socially responsible manner.

3 *Economic Challenges Facing America*

Learning Goals

1. To differentiate between macroeconomics and microeconomics.

2. To discuss inflation and unemployment and how monetary and fiscal policy are used to combat them.

3. To show how supply and demand determine the equilibrium price.

4. To describe how the federal deficit affects business.

5. To explain the rise of the service economy.

6. To illustrate how American business can retain its leadership position in worldwide competition.

Computer workstations — systems of desktop computers connected to a powerful central brain — didn't seem like the most promising market segment for a startup firm in 1982. The field was dominated by one firm — Apollo Computer — and the typical business purchaser of workstations was wary of dealing with unproven competitors. But that did not stop Vinod Khosla and Scott McNealy, founders of Sun Microsystems. With McNealy building the first 25 workstations by hand, the pair developed a firm that reached *Fortune's* list of the nation's top 500 companies in just six years. By 1988, worldwide sales had grown to $900 million. Khosla and McNealy accomplished their feat while running such a loose outfit that McNealy's office was turned into a miniature golf course for April Fool's Day.

How did they do it? The first key was their ability to turn the firm's weaknesses into strengths. On the one hand, they dealt with customers' fear of doing business with small, startup suppliers by making products that were compatible with their competitors'. On the other hand, they realized their inability to make custom parts would not be a problem because such components were becoming obsolete months after delivery. They used readily available parts, substituting newer ones for older ones as more powerful components became available.

The second key ingredient of this competitive strategy was quality. According to quality consultant A. Blanchard Godfrey, Sun's workstations are "definitely the best

workstations in the world. Even the Japanese use them." If imitation is the sincerest form of flattery, use by the Japanese is the highest honor for quality.

While Sun Microsystems is no longer small compared to most firms, it is still a midget in a field dominated by such giants as IBM and Texas Instruments. As McNealy commented: "There are only going to be a few major computer companies. A billion dollars in sales isn't big enough. We have to get bigger."

At the same time, Sun tries to retain its small business approach. For example, in order to finish a big project that was going nowhere, Sun engineers were ordered to go somewhere outside the headquarters to figure it out. Later, when Sun started building a lower-cost workstation, it set up a new division all

the way across the country. McNealy believes strongly in giving subordinates autonomy: "You have to firewall product development groups to give them enough authority to do their jobs." Then there are the traditions that keep everyone contented and feeling that they still work for a small firm: weekly dress-down days, beer bashes every month, and wearing gorilla suits on Halloween.[1]

Sun Microsystems is an excellent example of a firm that has developed an effective strategy for competing in the world marketplace. This type of competition is one of the major economic challenges facing the United States today.

Photo source: Courtesy of San Jose Mercury News.

Chapter Overview

Chapter 1 introduced economic concepts such as competition, factors of production and their corresponding factor payments, gross national product, productivity, degrees of competition, and comparative economic systems. These concepts provide us with some of the basic foundations of contemporary business.

This chapter will describe the two major divisions of economic theory, then examine three major challenges facing American business. These are (1) the federal budget deficit, (2) the shift to a service economy, and (3) international competitiveness, or how to keep America number one in the world marketplace.

In particular, we will discuss how improved quality and customer service can improve American competitiveness; how new technology is used to increase productivity and develop new products; and why it is important to improve the job skills of the American work force. Finally, we will discuss the kind of management changes needed to help our nation prosper in the international economy.

An Economics Primer

Economics has been defined as the science of allocating scarce resources. It is concerned with how resources are used to produce and market goods in both the private and public sectors. There are two sides to the study of economics: macroeconomics and microeconomics. **Macroeconomics** refers to the overall operation of an economy and its various parts. **Microeconomics** studies the economic activities of an individual or firm. Both topics are covered in economics classes, but they are introduced here to enhance the reader's understanding of the material that follows.

Macroeconomics

All economies face the twin dangers of inflation and unemployment. **Inflation** is a situation where there are rising prices or a decline in purchasing power of the nation's currency. One traditional cause of inflation is too much money in circulation relative to the goods and services available for sale. This is known as **demand-pull inflation**. In contrast, **cost-push inflation** results from a significant increase in a product cost (as with the major oil price hikes of the 1970s) that is then passed on to consumers. The last major surge of inflation in the United States came in the late 1970s. Prices increased at an annual rate of 13.5 percent in 1980. Since then, inflation has been much less of a problem.

Unemployment is the other major economic danger. **Unemployment** is defined as the joblessness of people actively looking for work. Publicized unemployment figures do not include people who are not seeking outside employment, such as students or homemakers, or those who have given up their attempts to find work — sometimes called **discouraged workers**.

There are four types of unemployment: frictional, seasonal, cyclical, and structural. **Frictional unemployment** refers to the 2 and 3 percent of the

economics
The science of allocating scarce resources.

macroeconomics
Study of the overall operation of an economy.

microeconomics
Study of a firm's economic activities.

inflation
Situation in which there are rising prices or decreased purchasing power of the nation's currency.

demand-pull inflation
Inflation resulting from too much money in circulation relative to the goods and services available.

cost-push inflation
Inflation resulting from a significant increase in a production cost passed on to consumers.

unemployment
Joblessness of people who are looking for work.

discouraged workers
People who give up searching for jobs.

frictional unemployment
People who are temporarily not working but are searching for jobs.

The Travelers Companies Foundation, the charity arm of the Hartford, Connecticut–based insurance organization, developed an early educational program in an effort to combat structural unemployment. The program focuses on teaching basic skills to pre-kindergarten children in the Hartford public schools that will make them successful in the workplace.

Photo source: Courtesy of The Travelers/Mitch Booth.

labor force who are temporarily not working but are looking for jobs. This includes people leaving school and just entering the work force and those who have left one job and are searching for another. **Seasonal unemployment** refers to the joblessness of workers in a seasonal industry. Construction workers, farm workers, and retail clerks often suffer seasonal unemployment. **Cyclical unemployment** involves people who are out of work due to reduced economic activity. Much of the unemployment statistics during a recession result from workers who are laid off as a result of a stagnant economy. **Structural unemployment** applies to people who lack the necessary skills for available jobs or those whose skills are no longer in demand.

Little can be done about frictional and seasonal unemployment. Various economic policy tools can be used to combat cyclical unemployment, as discussed next. Structural unemployment is an important concern related to America's competitiveness in the world economy.

seasonal unemployment
Joblessness of workers due to the seasonal hiring practices of their industry.

cyclical unemployment
Joblessness because of reduced economic activity.

structural unemployment
Joblessness of people who lack necessary skills for employment or whose skills are no longer demanded.

Monetary and Fiscal Policy

The government can use monetary or fiscal policy, or both, to combat inflation and unemployment. Both have a significant impact on business. **Monetary policy** refers to government policy to control the size of the nation's money supply. An expansionary monetary policy puts more money into circulation. Business borrowing becomes easier and often less expensive; as businesses expand, unemployment is reduced. By contrast, restrictive monetary policy reduces the money supply and helps reduce inflation. The specific methods used in monetary policy are discussed in Chapter 19.

Fiscal policy concerns government revenues and expenditures. Increased government spending can increase economic activity and reduce unemployment. A tax increase pulls money out of circulation if government spending does not also increase. This can be used to lessen inflation.

monetary policy
Governmental policies and actions concerning regulation of the nation's money supply.

fiscal policy
Governmental actions concerning revenues and expenditures.

Microeconomics

As noted earlier, microeconomics refers to the economic activities of an individual or firm. The interaction of people in markets determines both the price of goods and services and the amount sold. This information is vital for businesses because their survival depends on selling enough of their product at a high enough price to pay their expenses and return a profit. Consumers are also interested in this information because their well-being depends upon whether or not goods and services will be available and how much they will cost.

Businesses would also like to predict the future behavior of prices and amounts sold so they can be where large numbers of people want to purchase their products at a sufficiently high price for the firm to make a profit. This requires understanding the behavior of the two participants in a market: demanders and suppliers. Let's assume you are opening a doughnut shop near campus. How many doughnuts should you produce and what price can you expect to charge your customers? What quantity will be needed and what price should you charge next year?

demand curve
Schedule that shows the relationship between different prices and the quantity demanded at each price.

The Demand Curve   Demanders are people who are willing to pay for doughnuts. Their behavior in the market is called *demand*. The demand schedule shows exactly how much of a good or service people will buy at different prices. The quantity of doughnuts demanded will be affected by many things: the price of doughnuts, the price of substitute goods (such as cookies), the price of complementary goods consumed with doughnuts (such as coffee), the income of demanders, people's preferences (tastes), and the number of demanders in the market. The graph of different prices and quantities of doughnuts demanded is called the **demand curve**.

Figure 3.1 shows the demand curve, a graphical representation of the number of doughnuts demanders would buy at a specific time at different prices per doughnut. It shows the basic law of demand: As the price falls, people are willing to buy larger quantities. In this example, at $.80 per doughnut, 200 doughnuts would be demanded per week. If the price were reduced to $.50 a doughnut, more people would buy doughnuts (and some would buy more than one). The total number demanded would be 600 per week. Should the price fall even farther, say to $.20 per doughnut, 1,500 would be purchased weekly.

supply curve
Schedule that shows the relationship between different prices and the quantity supplied at each price.

The Supply Curve   Knowing the behavior only of people willing to buy doughnuts is not enough to determine how many doughnuts will be sold. Of equal importance is the behavior of people who supply doughnuts.

The quantity of doughnuts suppliers are willing to supply each week depends on a number of factors, including the price of the doughnuts, the price of the inputs used in making the doughnuts, technology, taxes, and the number of suppliers. The **supply curve** is a schedule that shows the relationship between different prices and the quantity of doughnuts that would be supplied at each price. Figure 3.1 also shows the supply curve, which reveals the basic law of supply: The quantity of doughnuts supplied rises with higher prices.

The Equilibrium Price   To find out how many doughnuts will actually be sold in the market each week, neither the demand curve nor the supply curve by itself is sufficient. The two must be combined, as in Figure 3.1, which shows the

Figure 3.1 Equilibrium in the Doughnut Market

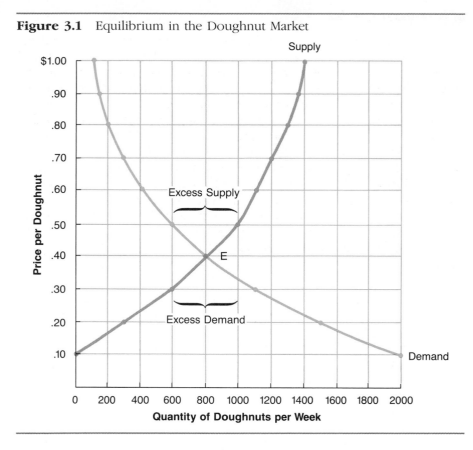

interaction of demanders' behavior and suppliers' behavior. The result is a single equilibrium price paid by the demanders and accepted by the suppliers. The **equilibrium price** is the price at which the quantity supplied by the suppliers is equal to the quantity demanded by the demanders. In Figure 3.1, the intersection of the demand and supply curves shows the equilibrium price. At the price of $.40 per doughnut, suppliers will offer 800 doughnuts for sale each week and demanders will purchase all 800 doughnuts. Both groups are satisfied at the equilibrium price.

equilibrium price
Price at which quantity supplied is equal to quantity demanded.

If the actual price in the market is different from the equilibrium price, people's behavior generates forces that return the prevailing price to the equilibrium price. How does this work? Assume that in Figure 3.1 the price of doughnuts is $.30 rather than $.40 apiece. At $.30, demanders want to buy 1,100 doughnuts a week, but suppliers will only offer 600. If each person buys only one doughnut, the first 600 will be able to complete their purchases, but there will be 500 willing to buy doughnuts at that price who cannot do so. Some of them are likely to offer a higher price to guarantee that they can get doughnuts the following week. This price competition among demanders will drive the price back up to the equilibrium price.

If the actual price temporarily is above the equilibrium price, not all the doughnuts produced will be sold. For example, at $.60 per doughnut, suppliers will produce 1,100 doughnuts, but demanders will buy only 400. As a result,

Figure 3.2   Shifts in Doughnut Demand

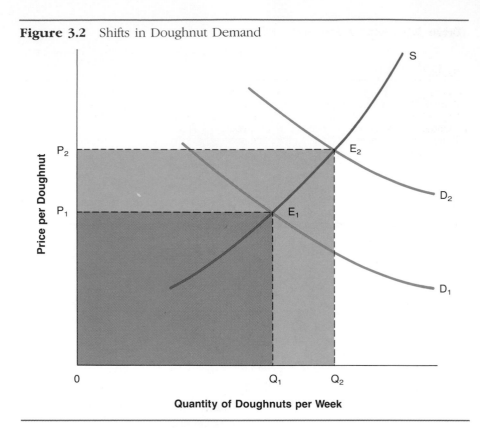

suppliers will try to take business from their competitors by lowering their prices. This will push the price back down to the equilibrium price. At this price, no frustrated demanders or suppliers pressure for the price to change.

Changes in Demand versus Changes in Quantity Demanded   Demand curves are drawn assuming that the determinants of demand — income, tastes, number of demanders, prices of substitute and complementary goods, and consumer expectations about the future — have specific values. When these values change, the demand curve shifts.

When the price of doughnuts changes, there is movement along the demand curve. When the determinants of demand change, such as an increase in demanders' income, we expect a larger number of doughnuts to be sold at every price. This means a whole new demand curve, one that has shifted to the right of the old one. In fact, a whole family of demand curves exists, one for each level of income. Every time the demand shifts, there is a new intersection with the supply curve and a new equilibrium price. As Figure 3.2 shows, when demand increases, the demand curve shifts to the right. The new equilibrium point is higher and to the right, indicating a higher price and a larger quantity than before.

Changes in the price of substitutes and complements shift the demand curve, as do changes in the number of demanders or changes in consumer preferences. Table 3.1 summarizes the shifts in the demand curve caused by these changes.

Table 3.1   Shifts in Demand Curves

Factor	The Demand Curve Shifts to the RIGHT if:	The Demand Curve Shifts to the LEFT if:
Income	Increases	Decreases
Price of substitute goods	Increases	Decreases
Price of complementary goods	Decreases	Increases
Number of demanders	Increases	Decreases
Tastes or preferences	Increase	Decrease

Changes in Supply versus Changes in Quantity Supplied   Shifts in the supply curve can be caused by changes in the prices of labor, flour, sugar, or other inputs into doughnut production. For example, if the price of labor increases, some suppliers will cut back the hours they are open or otherwise reduce production. This shifts the supply curve to the left, with a higher equilibrium price and lower equilibrium quantity, as shown in Figure 3.3.

A technological breakthrough has the opposite effect. For example, if suppliers find a way to fry doughnuts with less oil, they will produce more doughnuts at each price than they did when frying cost more. The supply curve will shift to the right, with a lower price and higher quantity at the new equilibrium point. Table 3.2 summarizes the changes in the supply curve resulting from changes in the determinants of supply.

Figure 3.3   Shifts in Supply Due to an Increase in the Price of Inputs

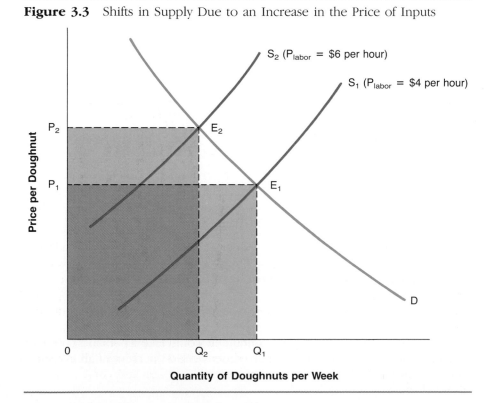

Table 3.2   Shifts in Supply Curves

Factor	The Supply Curve Shifts to the RIGHT if:	The Supply Curve Shifts to the LEFT if:
Price of inputs	Decreases	Increases
Technology	Increases	Decreases
Taxes	Decrease	Increase
Number of suppliers	Increases	Decreases

Individual shifts in supply or demand have obvious effects on prices and quantities. But in the real world, changes affecting supply and demand do not take turns. Several factors often change at once, causing contradictory pressures on prices and quantities. In other cases, the strongest effect determines the final direction of price and quantity movements.

Contemporary Economic Challenges

Now let us shift attention to three pressing economic challenges that profoundly affect contemporary business: the federal budget deficit, the shift to the service economy, and America's international competitiveness. While many other economic issues could be identified, there is almost universal agreement that these three are significant challenges to the U.S. economy.

The federal budget deficit is over $2 trillion and growing.[2] For example, in fiscal 1988 the deficit grew by $150 billion.[3] The federal deficit puts upward pressure on interest rates, attracting foreign capital to the United States and driving up the value of the dollar, which makes it more difficult to sell U.S. products overseas.

While manufacturing industries such as steel, autos, and textiles have reduced their employment in recent years, services such as health care, accounting, financial services, and retail are on the rise. Some analysts claim this means low-paying jobs replace high-paying ones, creating an economy of burger-flippers. Others point to evidence that skill requirements and salaries are rising in the service sector.

Most crucial of all, however, is the international competitiveness of the American economy. Imports now dominate many sectors of the economy. As a result, it is more important than ever for U.S. companies to be able to meet their foreign competitors' challenge in both domestic and overseas markets.

The Challenge of the Federal Budget Deficit

The amount of money the U.S. government owes its creditors — over $2 trillion — is beyond most people's comprehension. To understand the vastness of the sum, consider this: at $1,900 per minute, it would take a person 2,000 years to spend this amount.[4] This figure represents some 23 percent of all indebtedness by individuals, firms, and all governments.[5]

How the Federal Debt Affects Interest Rates

Money is a commodity just like doughnuts, and its price is known as the rate of interest. Individual consumers, businesses, and government (federal, state, and local) all compete to borrow money at the lowest possible interest rate. Because the federal government must borrow so much every year to finance its operation, it plays a big role in driving up interest rates. The federal government borrowed approximately $135 billion in fiscal 1989 because of the gap between tax revenues and spending.[6]

Business fears rising interest rates because they make expansion more expensive, result in reduced consumer spending, and threaten economic recession. Many economists believe rising interest rates could make it more difficult for the government to reduce the deficit. Thus, the deficit and high interest rates would breed a self-perpetuating cycle.

Other factors sometimes act to keep interest rates from rising, despite the high federal deficit. For example, money from abroad helped keep interest rates relatively low during the early and mid-1980s. The combination of low inflation and high interest rates made the United States a perfect place for foreigners to safely invest their money. Foreigners now own $500 billion of U.S. debt.[7]

Interest rates would have been even lower without the massive federal deficit. Allen Sinai, chief economist for Shearson Lehman Hutton, noted, "Long-term rates are two to three percentage points higher than they would be without the deficits."[8] Businesses that want to borrow money for expansion or replacement of plant and equipment face higher interest rates than would otherwise be the case. This raises their expenses, and they are under pressure to pass these higher costs on to consumers by raising prices.

A Stronger Dollar and a Growing Trade Deficit

When deficits and tight money policy put upward pressure on interest rates and lured capital from abroad, the value of the dollar jumped in comparison to the value of other currencies in the early and mid-1980s.

As a result, American goods cost more abroad and foreign goods were much less expensive for U.S. consumers to buy. Americans benefited from the dollar's strength when they bought Japanese cars and electronic equipment, Reeboks and other shoes from South Korea, and wine from France. But U.S. businesses watched their products be priced out of both foreign and domestic markets. In industries as diverse as textiles and apparel, steel, electronics, telecommunications, farm products, aeronautics, heavy machinery, and automobiles, U.S. firms found it difficult to compete with foreign companies. Many responded by moving some or all of their production overseas, a process known as **outsourcing**. Up to 1.5 million manufacturing jobs have been lost due to the U.S. trade deficit.[9]

As a result of the strong dollar, many U.S. firms and labor unions in the hardest-hit industries called for protectionist legislation. Instead, the U.S. government began talks with our major trading partners in an effort to bring down the value of the dollar. These negotiations had the desired effect. By 1988, the U.S. dollar was worth 125 Japanese yen, half of what it was worth in 1985. American goods were now cheaper in foreign markets, and foreign goods were more expensive in U.S. markets. As a result, the U.S. trade deficit began to improve by 1988.[10]

outsourcing
Contracting all or part of a firm's production to overseas suppliers.

Concern over the current trade deficit and the loss of U.S. manufacturing jobs due to competition from imported goods motivated Sam Walton, founder and chairman of Wal-Mart Stores Inc., to initiate a "Buy American" program, whereby as much merchandise as possible is purchased from American manufacturers. Signs within stores promote the program, which has created and retained more than 19,000 U.S. production jobs since it was established in 1985.

Photo source: Courtesy of Wal-Mart Stores, Inc.

Even with this improvement, experts still predict the trade deficit will continue to plague the country for many years. A further measure to improve the trade deficit came in the form of the Omnibus Trade Competitiveness Act of 1988. This 1,128-page law mandates government action against countries that do not open their markets to U.S. goods. It also makes it easier to protect patented goods from copycat products made abroad.[11]

The Gramm-Rudman Act

To counter the problem of the budget deficit head-on, Congress in 1985 passed the Gramm-Rudman-Hollings Balanced Budget and Emergency Deficit Control Act (popularly called the Gramm-Rudman Act). This law set specific limits on the allowable size of the federal budget deficit and procedures to be followed when they would be exceeded. The limits would be lower each year, until a balanced budget was achieved, originally projected in 1991. While parts of the law were later ruled unconstitutional and the deficit targets made less stringent, the goal of an eventual balanced budget remained in place.

The Shift to a Service Economy

services
Intangible tasks that satisfy both business and consumer needs.

Services are intangible tasks that satisfy consumer and industrial user needs. They differ from products in five important ways. Their intangibility is one: They cannot be seen, heard, tasted, touched, or smelled. Second, they are inseparable from the provider. Consumers are essentially buying a promise when they purchase a service, and their choice obviously depends on who is doing the promising. Third, services are perishable; their utility is time-specific. If a plane flies with empty seats or a hotel has empty rooms for the night, there is no getting back the revenue lost. Fourth, services are hard to standardize — how they are performed depends on both the particular provider and the particular consumer. Last, consumers are often involved in service development and distribution. Hairstylists must take their clients' suggestions and overall desires as the basis to work from, and patrons of restaurant salad bars put together their own meals (restaurants provide both services and goods). These are just two examples of the close interaction of customer and service provider.

In a service economy, services make up an increasingly larger share of economic activity, while manufacturing becomes less important. Many analysts see the United States developing in this direction as important manufacturing sectors lose out to foreign competitors, while the U.S. lead in such areas as financial and information services seems more secure. As noted earlier, as many as 1.5 million jobs may have been lost in manufacturing due to the trade deficit. At the same time, unemployment has fallen to its lowest level since 1974, in large part because of increased jobs in the service sector.[12]

The Service Sector Work Force Is Changing

Besides the shift in employment from manufacturing, there is another change in the nature of the American work force. As the baby boomers born from 1946 to 1964 mature, fewer new workers enter the U.S. work force. These young workers traditionally staff fast-food restaurants, retail stores, gas stations, and other service firms. For instance, the fast-food market faces the prospect that there will be 5 million fewer 15 to 24-year-olds to staff restaurants by the middle of the next decade, at the same time that preteen customers will increase by 4 million. One response has been more efforts to keep workers, such as Burger King's tuition assistance program allowing employees to earn up to $2,000 of education aid in two years. Participants had a turnover rate of only 22 percent per year, compared with the normal 97 percent rate for employees, whose average stay is only four months. But the most important response to the shortage of workers has been to raise productivity, just as in the manufacturing sector. The most farsighted approach may be that of the Two Panda Robot Restaurant in Pasadena, California, where the waiters are robots.[13]

The Challenge of Keeping America Number One

With foreign trade now accounting for 20 percent of the U.S. gross national product, it has become increasingly obvious that American firms no longer compete only with each other. To be successful, they need to be able to win out in global competition. This requires efforts in six main areas: quality, customer service, productivity, job skills, technology development, and management practice.

Intensive training designed to train, motivate, and retain employees is one way Friendly Ice Cream Corporation, a division of Hershey Foods, is addressing the shortage of service workers. The restaurant chain's Video-Based Crew Training program teaches new employees basic skills quickly and effectively, focuses on customer service, and provides a standard message to all employees. Friendly also raised pay scales, expanded employee benefits, and increased its recruiting efforts among working mothers, senior citizens, and other nonteenage populations.

Photo source: Friendly Ice Cream Corporation, a division of Hershey Foods Corporation.

The Quest for Quality

One major problem some American products have had is a well-deserved reputation for poor quality. According to TRW, American cars require an average of 3.5 repairs per year, while Japanese cars only need 1.1.[14] A poll of West German consumers found that only 6 percent thought "Made in USA" was a mark of quality.[15]

The reasons for past inattention to quality are complex, but an important element was the pent-up consumer demand after World War II. Goods were turned out as fast as possible to meet this demand, and products were often less than top quality so consumers would have to buy them again. As Alexander Trowbridge, president of the National Association of Manufacturers, remarked: "We were operating to some degree on a philosophy of planned obsolescence. In that sort of world, quality takes a back seat. Ultimately we got hurt by it."[16]

Not only did foreign consumers view American quality as low, but so did better educated U.S. consumers.[17] Today, American producers are fighting to improve the image of U.S. products. One company winning the quality battle head-to-head with the Japanese is Goodyear Tire & Rubber. Its 20 percent of the world tire market includes 500,000 tires shipped to Japan each year for installation on U.S.–bound Japanese cars. Cracking this market took Goodyear two years. One of the most important aspects of Goodyear's strategy was its emphasis on quality. Goodyear does not sell any blemished seconds at a discount. Its policy is "first-class or scrap." Machines invented by Goodyear work teams have also cut the average time to make each tire to only 10 minutes, twice as fast as the world average.[18]

Photo source: Courtesy of GTE Corporation.

GTE Corporation adopted a formal approach to setting and meeting high performance standards by adding a course to its management development curriculum called "Quality: The Competitive Edge." Managers of all GTE units are given the course. Because quality has emerged as the most important factor influencing customer buying decisions, GTE's senior management believes the course is a key element in achieving the company's goal of maintaining a quality level that equals or exceeds the performance of its competitors at home and abroad.

A. T. Cross, the pen and pencil maker, also gives its employees wide latitude. If they think a pen or mechanical pencil is defective, they are supposed to throw it off the assembly line. Quality needs to be absolute when you give a lifetime guarantee, as Cross does. It works, too — less than 2 percent of its products are returned for repairs, which the company does free.[19]

Improving Customer Service

Customer service, or the manner in which businesses deal with their customers, is another important part of a worldwide competitive strategy. Service standards in many American businesses have been declining, according to studies by the Yankelovich Monitor and the Technical Assistance Research Programs Institute.[20] Firms that provide poor service find recovery of a lost reputation can take a long time, since customers with horror stories tell 10 to 20 friends about it, while those whose problems are solved tell only five on average.[21] For example, Continental Airlines, which turned in poor records for on-time performance and lost baggage after acquiring People Express, had to spend millions of dollars on advertising and training to convince passengers it was overcoming its problems.

Some American companies are making top-notch customer service pay off in international competition. Auto parts maker and distributor Echlin Inc. produces 150,000 different parts, giving it a flexibility foreign competitors cannot match. While they may beat Echlin on the price of some products, foreign competitors do not offer the one-stop shopping that wholesalers value from Echlin.

customer service
An aspect of competitive strategy that refers to how a firm treats its customers.

Aid Association for Lutherans, a provider of life, health, and disability insurance, produced a 20 percent increase in productivity by focusing on labor. It reorganized its 500 employees into 17 work teams, such as the one shown here. Each team performs all of the 167 tasks formerly split among three functional divisions: life insurance, health insurance, and support services. AAL switched to the team approach to provide better service to its district representatives (DRs) and policyholders. Team members participate in decision making, schedule their own hours, assign tasks, rotate jobs, and celebrate when they achieve production and quality goals.

Photo source: © Buck Miller.

Speed is important in the auto repair business, so single-source service makes Echlin a $1 billion-a-year concern.[22]

American Express turned around customer service performance after problems arose during its international expansion in the early 1970s. The company's first attempt to improve matters let the various card operations departments set their own standards and measure their performance. This approach did not work. As Ray Larkin, then a senior vice president overseeing the program, says, "Each department was doing great according to its own standards, but service wasn't improving." Instead, a single group of performance standards was set up for the card division (the service tracking report), and American Express is now able to charge both its cardholders and the businesses accepting the card higher prices than its competitors — primarily because of its reputation for quality.[23]

Increasing Productivity

productivity
A measure of the efficiency of production.

A central element of international competitiveness is **productivity**, which is a measure of the efficiency of production. It is expressed as the amount of goods or services a worker produces in a given period of time. Productivity is a significant factor in America's competitiveness in world markets because U.S. wages are higher relative to the rest of the world; if its goods are to cost less than foreign competitors', American manufacturers must have higher productivity than the competition.

Determinants of the Level of Productivity   Although productivity is usually reported on a per-worker basis, more than just labor goes into productivity. Four other factors are also important (some may be more important): technology, management, education, and government action.

Why Productivity Gains Are Important   Productivity gains are what allow people to receive higher real wages — wages that are increasing faster than the rate of inflation. For example, if wages increase 6 percent in a year while productivity goes up only 2 percent, prices will rise about 4 percent. Thus, the real wage increase is only about 2 percent.

Improving U.S. Productivity   Various factors must be considered in attempts to increase U.S. productivity. American industry must continue to introduce and use the newest technology available. Labor must also be involved. For example, Ford Motor Company's program to improve product quality, illustrated best by the success of the Ford Taurus and the Mercury Sable, required extensive labor participation. Workers' suggestions were incorporated even at the design phase, such as the decision to have all bolt heads the same size so workers would not need to change wrenches.[24] Education is yet another factor. Some states have promoted their community and technical colleges in an effort to attract further development. Education's importance can also be seen by considering how many high-tech centers are located near major universities; Research Triangle, North Carolina; Route 128 in Boston; and Austin, Texas, are examples. Finally, management effectiveness is essential because managers coordinate the efforts of other workers. Contemporary management must be as effective as the latest technology if a nation is to experience future gains in productivity.

Automation, the replacement of people by machines in the work environment, is an essential element to increasing productivity. Many industries have had to automate to survive global competition. In doing so, they caused the loss of many unskilled and semiskilled jobs. American manufacturing, which employed 21 million workers in 1979, now employs only 19.5 million.[25]

automation
Replacement of a person by a machine in a work environment.

At Bethlehem Steel, automation was the key to making its Burns Harbor, Indiana, plant the most efficient in the world. The plant requires only 3 man-hours to produce one ton of steel, compared to the world average of 5 to 7 man-hours per ton. Bethlehem's primary investment was in two $240 million casters that shape and cut the steel without having to make steel ingots, which use a lot of high-wage labor. As a result, Bethlehem reduced its cost of production by $40 per ton and scaled back its Burns Habor work force from 8,800 to 5,900.[26]

But not all attempts to automate are successful. According to Stephen G. Payne, chief executive of the PA Consulting Group, General Motors spent "more on automation than the gross national product of many countries," but got little return on its investment. The service sector, despite widespread investment in computers and other equipment, showed no growth in productivity from 1977 to 1987.[27] Some economists criticize much of the productivity gains of the 1980s, resulting from closing inefficient plants, as illusory. "If productivity goes up because industrial capacity was driven out, is that good?" asks Brookings Institution economist Edward F. Denison.[28]

An example of the right way to automate comes from Cone Drive Operations Inc., a maker of the gears used for such applications as cement mixers and rotating rooftop restaurants. In the late 1970s, the firm faced declining profits as its deliveries were constantly late, causing mounting customer dissatisfaction. In 1980, it switched to a computer-integrated manufacturing system at a cost of $2 million — a hefty price for a firm with only $26 million in sales each year. There was no significant labor savings, but automation benefited Cone in other ways. Delivery on-time rate is now 95 percent, while the time to develop new products and special orders fell 85 percent. Moreover, the company reduced the amount of its assets tied up in inventory by 60 percent.[29]

Figure 3.4   The Looming Mismatch between Workers and Jobs

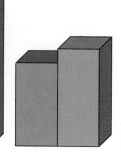

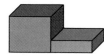
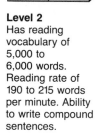

■ **Actual Skill Levels of New Workers**
Percent of 21- to 25-year-olds
entering the labor market from
1985 to 2000

■ **Skill Levels Needed for New Jobs**
Percent of new jobs created from
1985 to 2000

Level 1
Has limited reading
vocabulary of
2,500 words.
Reading rate of 95
to 125 words per
minute. Ability to
write simple
sentences.

Level 2
Has reading
vocabulary of
5,000 to
6,000 words.
Reading rate of
190 to 215 words
per minute. Ability
to write compound
sentences.

Level 3
Can read safety
rules and
equipment
instructions,
and write simple
reports.

Level 4
Can read journals
and manuals, and
write business
letters and
reports.

Level 5
Can read
scientific/
technical journals
and financial
reports, and write
journal articles
and speeches.

Level 6
Has same skills as
Level 5, but more
advanced.

Source: Aaron Bernstein, "Where the Jobs Are and Where the Skills Aren't." Reprinted from September 19, 1988 issue of *Business Week*, pp. 104–105, by special permission, copyright © 1988 by McGraw-Hill, Inc.

Improving Job Skills

A continuing economic problem for the United States is the poor job skills of many American workers. The problem begins in grade school. Math scores of our elementary and high school students are among the lowest in the industrialized world.[30] Such basic skills are needed for even the lowest of clerical positions, and people without them are often condemned to the lowest of wages. Over 500,000 high school students drop out annually, and another 700,000 who graduate are virtually illiterate. Figure 3.4 shows the mismatch of work skills and jobs that will occur by 2000.

Another problem is the preceived decline in the quality of our colleges. According to John Potempa, vice president for employee relations at Frito-Lay, top schools are not affected, but the reduction of college-age students might cause some institutions to lower their standards. The PepsiCo subsidiary reduced the number of colleges where it recruits.[31]

For people already in the work force, skill questions are of two types. The first concerns people laid off in one industry whose skills are no longer needed and who do not have the skills for other jobs. The second issue is the question of continuing training for those who do have jobs, because advanced skills for all workers is necessary for the U.S. economy to remain competitive in the world environment.

Both business and government have made efforts to improve the nation's job skills. According to one study by the Rand Corporation, 40 percent of all U.S. workers have been in training programs since starting their current jobs. The nation's annual bill for training away from the job is estimated at $30 billion by the American Society for Training and Development.[32]

One firm making a different contribution is Chrysler Corporation and its president, Lee Iacocca. Iacocca contributed $1 million to Lehigh University in Bethlehem, Pennsylvania, to help it buy a research park from the Bethlehem Steel Corp. Chrysler, like many other firms, matches employee contributions to higher education and is giving $1.5 million to help finance the $40 million Lehigh project, which will also include the Iacocca Institute for Economic Competitiveness.[33]

Motorola devotes about 2.6 percent of its payroll to training its workers, a necessity in the highly competitive semiconductor business. Two main goals of this training are: using automation well and making defect-free products. The company spends about $90 million per year on training, including the cost of wages and benefits. But the money is well spent, according to training director Bill Wiggenhorn: "We've documented the savings from the statistical process control methods and problem-solving methods we've trained our people in. We're running a rate of return of about 30 times the dollars invested — which is why we've gotten pretty good support from senior management."[34]

One government effort that has had great success is in California, where the state Employment Training Panel finances training programs for companies with unemployed workers or workers in danger of losing their jobs as their skills become outdated. The state pays only when the trainee gets and keeps his or her job. The program, funded through the unemployment insurance program, has reduced the duration of unemployment for trainees and increased their wages an average of 55 percent, according to state training head Steve Duscha.[35]

The Importance of New Technology

Possibly the most important factor in keeping America number one in the world marketplace is **research and development**, discovering new scientific knowledge and turning it into commercially useful products. R&D, as it is often called, makes possible totally new industries (such as automobiles and airplanes in an earlier day) and dramatic improvements in productivity. The United States has long been the undisputed world leader in research, with some firms, such as 3M, depending on products it has introduced in just the last five years for 25 percent of all sales.[36]

But now even America's research lead is being challenged. In a recent year, 47 percent of patents granted in the United States went to foreigners, up 13 percent from a decade earlier. Moreover, several countries, notably Japan, West Germany, and France, were recording spectacular growth in patents. Japan's 17,288 patents gave it the most for a foreign country, a phenomenal 25 percent

research and development
The scientific process of developing new commercial products.

3M stays ahead of its competition by developing new technologies and applying them commercially. The microporous membrane depicted in this photo is one of 20 new technologies 3M developed in the past five years. The membrane allows vapor to escape but not water. The technology was first applied to 3M's Thintech brand waterproof, breathable fabric for jogging suits and other sportswear. Other 3M divisions are working on applications ranging from wound dressings that promote faster healing to drug packages that indicate tampering. 3M's R&D spending totaled more than $2.5 billion over the past five years.

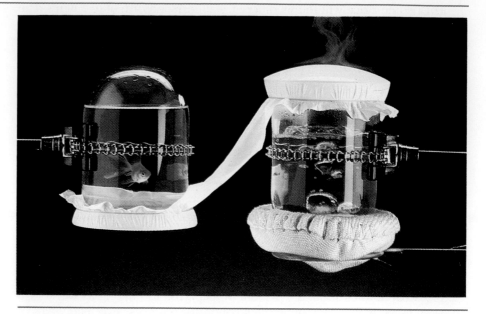

Photo source: © Steve Niedorf 1988 for 3M Company.

increase from a year earlier. Second-place Germany was up 15 percent in a year, and France recorded a 19 percent one-year increase.[37]

Moreover, even this data overstates the U.S. lead in commercially usable research, as a large percentage of American R&D goes into military research, which often remains off-limits to commercial users for an extended time. If defense-related R&D is excluded, the United States spends only 1.6 percent of its GNP on R&D, while Germany and Japan both spend 2.4 percent of their GNP for it.[38]

Even when U.S. firms do make innovations with commercial uses, they often fail to exploit the technology. The videocassette recorder is a perfect example. Invented by California-based Ampex and later improved by RCA, the two firms did little with the item. Instead, two Japanese companies, Sony and JVC, bought the right to the VCR, patented over 10,000 improvements on it, and turned it into one of the hottest-selling new entertainment products of the decade. As a result, today there is not one American producer of VCRs.[39]

The situation is not entirely gloomy. American scientists are still winning more Nobel Prizes than the Europeans and Japanese combined, and U.S. research universities are the best in the world.[40] But the country needs to widen its basic research lead and do a better job of commercializing its inventions to remain number one.

Short-Term Profits versus Long-Term Success

A final problem facing American firms in global competition is that they often focus only on the short term, trying to cut a profit every quarter even if it means not making needed improvements or investments in research. Foreign firms, Japanese in particular, take a longer-term approach to business and worry less about short-term profits. They focus their attention on building market share.

R&D is one place where this difference appears. According to Patents and Trademarks Commissioner Donald Quigg, "Stockholders demand more and more immediate results, but research and development does not occur overnight."[41] Japanese firms are much less vulnerable to this pressure. The short-run/long-run difference also shows itself in firms' response to the recent decline of the dollar. Japanese and European firms generally limited their price increases, even taking losses, in order to hold their share of the U.S. market. By contrast, many American firms increased prices in order to increase their profits, rather than lowering prices to try to take back market share.[42] U.S. management clearly needs to look less at the short-term bottom line if American is to stay number one.

Summary of Learning Goals

1.   **Differentiate between macroeconomics and microeconomics.**   Economics, the science of allocating scarce resources, can be divided into two parts: macroeconomics and microeconomics. Macroeconomics looks at the whole economy and the way it operates. Microeconomics is concerned with the economic activities of an individual or a firm.

2.   **Discuss inflation and unemployment and how monetary and fiscal policy are used to combat them.**   Inflation refers to a situation in which there are rising prices or decreased purchasing power of a nation's currency. Inflation can result from too much money in circulation relative to the goods and services available for sale or from a significant increase in production costs that are passed on to consumers. Unemployment is defined as the joblessness of people who are actively looking for work. There are four types of unemployment. Frictional unemployment refers to people who are temporarily not working, but are searching for jobs. Seasonal unemployment occurs when people are unemployed because of seasonal hiring patterns in their industry. Cyclical unemployment results from reduced economic activity. Structural unemployment refers to people who lack job skills or whose skills are no longer wanted.
Monetary and fiscal policy can be used to combat inflation and unemployment. Monetary policy refers to a government's policies and actions in regard to the regulation of the nation's money supply. Fiscal policy refers to actions affecting the government's revenues and spending.

3.   **Show how supply and demand determine the equilibrium price.**
The demand curve is a schedule that shows the relationship between different prices and the quantity that would be demanded at each price. The supply curve is a schedule that shows the relationship between different prices and the quantity that would be supplied at each price. The interaction of demand and supply curves sets the equilibrium price, the price at which the quantity supplied is equal to the quantity demanded.

4.   **Describe how the federal deficit affects business.**   The federal deficit can have a significant impact on business. The deficit means the federal government must borrow money to sustain its operations, so the government is competing with business firms for capital. This competition drives interest rates

higher than would otherwise be the case. This might dampen economic growth and employment. It also means raising the value of the dollar above what it would otherwise be, pricing American goods out of some export markets and making imports more attractive to U.S. consumers. The Omnibus Trade and Competitiveness Act of 1988 was passed to end foreign trade barriers that intensify this effect, and the Gramm-Rudman Act was passed in 1985 to reduce and eventually eliminate the deficit.

5.   Explain the rise of the service economy.   While many basic manufacturing industries are declining (often because they are no longer internationally competitive), the service sector continues to expand. The service sector's need for workers is increasing so rapidly that many experts predict a shortage of employees in the 1990s. The problem is best illustrated by the inability of franchisers to keep their restaurants staffed.

6.   Illustrate how American business can retain its leadership position in worldwide competition.   There are six key factors in keeping America number one. Businesses must turn out top-quality products and provide superb customer service. More resources must be devoted to research and the development of new technology, and this must be combined with other methods for improving American productivity. Business and government both must take responsibility for ensuring that workers have top-notch job skills. Finally, American management styles must become more long-term oriented than they currently are.

Key Terms

economics	frictional unemployment	equilibrium price
macroeconomics	seasonal unemployment	outsourcing
microeconomics	cyclical unemployment	services
inflation	structural unemployment	customer service
demand-pull inflation	monetary policy	productivity
cost-push inflation	fiscal policy	automation
unemployment	demand curve	research and development
discouraged workers	supply curve	

Review Questions

1. Match the following types of unemployment — (a) frictional, (b) seasonal, (c) cyclical, (d) structural — with the people described below:
   _____ a factory worker on temporary layoff because of slow sales
   _____ a steelworker whose job was lost when a mill was closed permanently
   _____ an unemployed agricultural worker between crops
   _____ a recent graduate who is looking for employment

2. What will happen to the equilibrium price and quantity if consumer preferences for doughnuts increase?

3. What will happen to the equilibrium price and quantity if a tax is imposed on the production of doughnuts?

4. What will happen to the equilibrium price and quantity if the following occur simultaneously?
   a. Income of consumers declines
   b. Price of flour is reduced

5. Discuss how the federal deficit might affect:
   a. Interest rates   c. Foreign trade
   b. The value of the dollar d. Employment

6. How has the growth of the service sector affected the U.S. economy? What challenges face service firms today and tomorrow?

7. What contributions can American business make to the job skills of the work force?

8. Explain the importance of R&D in keeping America number one.

9. Why is increasing productivity important?

10. Contrast the typical Japanese and American firm's management philosophy in regard to profits and market share.

Discussion Questions

1. The policies used to lower inflation tend to increase employment and vice versa. Can anything be done about this dilemma? If not, which problems do you think should be solved first? Defend your answer.

2. Wal-Mart has a "Buy American" plan whereby the firm offers to work with U.S. manufacturers to produce goods that are competitive with foreign goods that the Bentonville, Arkansas, retail giant would otherwise purchase for its stores. Sam Walton commented: "Wal-Mart believes American workers can make the difference if management provides the leadership." Discuss Wal-Mart's "Buy America" plan. How does it relate to the text's discussion about keeping America number one in the world marketplace?

3. Jan Carlzon of Scandinavian Airline System says that when dealing with customers, there are "50 million moments of truth" each year. What do you think Carlzon meant by his remark?

4. Iowa, among other states, has reported a "brain drain" in recent years as many of the state's college students leave the state after graduation. Discuss this economic challenge. What can be done to overcome the problem?

5. New York's Chemical Bank reports it must interview 40 applicants to find a single person trainable for a teller's position. Similarly, IBM invested in expensive computers for its Burlington, Vermont, plants only to learn it had to teach basic algebra to its employees before they could operate the machines. Relate these experiences to the content of Chapter 3.

Video Case

3D Distribution Systems

Two concepts emphasized throughout this chapter are (1) the rise of the service economy and (2) how U.S. business can retain its leadership in worldwide competition by emphasizing quality, improved levels of customer service, and increased productivity. Few contemporary executives exemplify the business success that can be achieved by focusing on these concepts as well as Carolyn Draper of 3D Distribution Systems.

The entrepreneurial spirit that drives business-people to start and operate firms aimed at offering superior customer service to specialized market niches led Draper and her partner, David Markel, to form a company aimed at providing one-day delivery service to firms in the Dallas area.

In the package delivery industry, many of the larger companies, such as Federal Express and Purolator Courier, require packages to be ready for pickup within specified time limits in order to guarantee overnight delivery service. But until recently no company offered same-day delivery for packages from firms with unusual or special time requirements. That niche is where Draper positioned 3D Distribution Systems.

Based in Dallas, 3D Distribution had been a long-time goal for Carolyn Draper. "From the time that I was very young, I had wanted to be the president of a company. . . . As I worked and tried to go up the corporate ladder, I realized that this was just not going to happen. And one day, I was in an argument with my boss and I was telling him how he ought to be doing it . . . he told me that I ought to think about going out and starting my own business and then I could run it any way I wanted to." At that point, the Blue, Oklahoma, native decided to abandon the corporate ladder at Polaroid and become an entrepreneur.

In the first two years of operations, Draper did almost everything herself, from handling accounts and customer service to unloading airplanes. "When we started . . . my partner loaded airplanes in the morning and I unloaded them every night." As the company gradually took on more employees, they all became more specialized. But it was $2\frac{1}{2}$ years before Draper felt comfortable enough to leave the company even long enough to go on vacation. "I really did not like to take risk that much," she recalls. "When I first started talking about this company, I had a daughter to support. It was my only source of income and I had to look long and hard at our numbers before I felt for certain that it was going to work." Her commitment to success was supported by a constant concern for customer service — the basis of 3D Distribution System's operation. When she finally did take a vacation, she was happily surprised to return to find the company had run beautifully in her absence. She knew then that 3D Distribution would survive.

3D Distribution offers same-day pickup and delivery for firms that have packages that can't be ready for pickup by 6:00 p.m. Its customers include medical testing laboratories, companies that process payroll accounts, photo finishing businesses, and data processing centers. 3D offers these customers specialized pickup anytime before 8:00 a.m. with guaranteed delivery that same night.

In 1987, 3D Distribution relocated in Dallas to a 42,000-square-foot corporate office and terminal space at Love Field Airport. This move provided added convenience to customers, since it reduced transfer time between scheduled airlines and 3D's exclusive air charter flights. The company currently offers pickup services in seven states and delivers packages on commercial and chartered airlines to any city in the United States.

Customer service has always been the watchword at 3D. Says Draper, "I think that the service in America had reached an all-time low a few years ago." But economic predictions indicate that the service sector demand is increasing and Draper is determined not only to fill a void in a specific market, but also to do so with the best customer service she can manage. As Draper puts it, "Our motto is fix the problem first, then worry about whether the customer is billed."

At 3D, a customer service department keeps a daily log of all problems or complaints phoned in by customers. These are reviewed by high-level management personnel who help in finding solutions to problems. This sort of personal attention creates a special

Notes: Heidi Waldrop, "How to Manage a Growing Company," *Working Woman,* April 1987, pp. 39–42; telephone interview, May 4, 1989.

bond with each customer, and since all businesses are in some way service oriented, those that serve their customers best are the ones that succeed.

3D Distribution's revenues are growing by about $1 million a year and Draper estimated 1989 figures at over $7 million. The number of employees has stabilized recently, with approximately 50 employees and 250 contract drivers. 3D is structuring itself a little differently now, and rather than hiring more employees, some of the distribution is being given to smaller companies. "If you've got a little bitty vision, you'll have a little bitty company. And if you have a big vision, you've got a lot of room to grow and expand." This kind of thinking is what keeps Draper constantly looking for other markets for her distribution services. Currently, new route structures are planned for implementation in Chicago, Atlanta, and Los Angeles.

Questions

1. What advantages does a small business like 3D Distribution Systems have over a large corporation in terms of customer service? What disadvantages does it have?

2. Identify other firms whose needs for same-day delivery service throughout the United States might make them potential customers for Draper's firm.

3. "The reason so many small businesses have been successful is that they can specialize." What does this statement mean?

4. "The degree of success achieved by a business is determined by the quality of its service." Do you agree with this statement? Can you think of exceptions?

4 *Global Dimensions of Business*

Learning Goals

1. To evaluate the importance of international business.

2. To define the concept of international business and analyze why countries tend to specialize in certain goods.

3. To describe the different levels of involvement in international business.

4. To assess the importance of countertrade in international business.

5. To discuss the role of the multinational corporation in world business.

6. To identify the main obstacles confronting international business.

7. To explain multinational economic integration.

8. To describe the United States as a foreign market.

Though cultural sensitivity is a must for doing business in foreign settings, it may be enough to just leave your cowboy hat at home while keeping your boots on. At least, that is what Tom Carpenter of Woodinville, Washington-based Spectrum Glass, discovered.

Carpenter once owned a successful stained glass business in Arkansas. He traveled overseas frequently and sold a lot of his glass abroad. Despite his success, Carpenter eventually sold the business and retired. Later, he attended a trade show in Florida to renew old friendships in the industry. During the meeting, Carpenter met people from Spectrum, a 120-employee specialty sheet glass maker. The retiree was soon hired as a vice-president and was assigned to develop Spectrum's international business.

Spectrum was founded in 1976 by three entrepreneurs who developed a new production process combining modern glass making techniques with aspects of the traditional, high-labor and high-capital approach employed in the industry for a century. This new process was patented in 1979 and remains the only system of its kind in the world.

Most of Spectrum's glass goes to two markets: (1) art glass wholesalers who distribute to retailers, studios, and small manufacturers; and (2) lighting fixture manufacturers in such countries as Mexico, Taiwan, the Philipines, and Korea, as well as Malaysia, Thailand, and the People's Republic of China. Most of these fixtures are re-sold in the United States.

Carpenter has a simple system for export success: "Just get on a plane and get over there and meet the people." In fact, Carpenter made three trips to Asia before deciding how to best handle Spectrum's overseas distribution. Carpenter continues to travel six months out of every year, but he is now an independent sales representative for the Pacific Rim countries. He emphasizes that foreign business takes time to develop: "It's not going to be done in a hurry overseas unless you have some unusual item that the whole world is going to beat a path to your door."

At 6 feet tall, Carpenter can look a little out of place in Asia, especially wearing his favored attire of jeans and cowboy boots. But he argues that is not what is important: "What people need to know is how real you are, and that's the thing they're looking for." His concession to cultural sensitivity is leaving his cowboy hat at home, so his Asian hosts will not feel even shorter.

Spectrum is quite pleased with the results. The company's sales went from $3.2 million to $8.5 million three years later, largely as a result of Asian exports. Spectrum is now the largest manufacturer of its kind in the world. The moral of the story is that you do not have to be big to be a successful exporter — or even follow all the rules.[1]

This chapter explores the global dimensions of contemporary business. It looks at the current importance of foreign markets and the trends that are occurring in them.

Photo source: Courtesy of Spectrum Glass.

Chapter Overview

exporting
Selling domestic goods abroad.

importing
Buying foreign goods and raw materials.

International business can be divided into **exporting** (selling goods and services abroad), **importing** (purchasing foreign goods and services), and foreign production (making goods and supplying services in a foreign country for sales there or in other countries). The United States leads the world in all three categories, but it is not as dependent on foreign trade and production as other countries, such as Great Britain and the Netherlands.

At one time, the international aspects of business mattered only to a few American firms that needed to import raw materials. A number of companies were interested in exports, but hardly any cared about producing abroad. For most, the U.S. domestic market was all they needed. Today, the various national economies of the world have grown so close that businesses can no longer afford to ignore the global marketplace. Foreign markets represent an increasingly attractive target for U.S. companies. Moreover, the domestic American market shows little consumer resistance to foreign products. In many instances, foreign products are favored by U.S. consumers.

Besides these strategic considerations, world business is important for other reasons as well. Production for larger markets means there is more opportunity for achieving economies of scale in production or marketing. Production for export also means jobs: $1 billion in exports supports about 25,000 jobs.[2] Finally, there is the bottom line to consider: 13 of the top 100 U.S. multinational firms derive more than half of their sales from foreign markets (led by Exxon with 75.1 percent), while many others earn over half of their profits abroad. For example, Control Data derived 84.2 percent of its profits from abroad. Dresser Industries and TWA both had foreign profits exceeding their domestic losses, achieving over 100 percent of their total profits overseas.[3]

Concepts of International Business

The main patterns of international business result from a combination of economic and political factors. To understand trade and world business, it is essential to become familiar with such concepts as balance of trade, balance of payments, and exchange rates.

Balance of Trade

balance of trade
Relationship between a country's exports and imports.

A country's **balance of trade** is the difference between its exports and imports. If a country exports more than it imports, it has a favorable balance of trade, called a *trade surplus*. If it imports more than it exports, it has an unfavorable balance of trade, or a *trade deficit*. In 1988, the United States had a trade deficit of $130 billion.[4]

Chemicals were the United States' leading export in a recent year, while automobiles were the leading import. Interestingly, automobiles were also the second-leading American export. Table 4.1 outlines the top five exports and imports.

Photo source: Courtesy of United Technologies.

Conducting business on a worldwide basis generates a large portion of United Technologies Corporation's total sales and profits. UTC derives 29.5 percent of its total revenues and 49.7 percent of its total operating profits from international operations. The firm provides products and services to customers in the aerospace and defense, building, and automotive industries. Its Otis elevators, escalators, and moving walkways and shuttle systems move one billion people every day in more than 160 countries. The Hong Kong and Shanghai Banking Corporation, an Otis customer for over 50 years, purchased 28 Otis elevators and 62 escalators for its new headquarters building in Hong Kong shown here.

Balance of Payments

A nation's balance of trade plays a central role in determining its **balance of payments** — the overall flow of money into or out of a country. Other factors affecting the balance of payments are overseas loans and borrowing, international investment and the remittance of profits from such investments, and foreign aid. A favorable balance of payments, or *balance of payments surplus,* means a net inflow of money from abroad. An unfavorable balance of payments, or a *balance of payments deficit* means a net outflow of money from the country. The effect of the other components on a country's balance of payments can offset or intensify the deficit or surplus resulting from its balance of trade.

balance of payments
Flow of money into or out of a country.

Table 4.1   Leading U.S. Exports and Imports

	Value (in billions)
Top Exports	
1. Chemicals and related products	$22.8
2. Automobiles, motor vehicles	18.6
3. Office machinery and computers	15.5
4. Aircraft and parts	15.1
5. Electrical machinery	13.6
Top Imports	
1. Automobiles	$45.3
2. Petroleum and petroleum products	34.1
3. Telecommunications equipment	20.7
4. Electrical machinery	20.2
5. Clothing	17.3

Source: Statistical Abstract of the United States: 1988, p. 769.

Nations with a balance of payments deficit normally try to solve this problem by some combination of reducing their dependence on foreign goods, reducing investments abroad, devaluing their currency, and increasing their exports. Often this requires politically unpopular moves that slow economic activity and the demand for foreign goods but produce increased unemployment and/or higher prices as a result.

The Exchange Rate

exchange rate
Rate at which a country's currency can be exchanged for other currencies or gold.

The value of a nation's currency in relation to that of other nations or to a fixed standard such as gold is called its **exchange rate**. A currency's exchange rate is usually quoted in terms of other important currencies. For example, in early 1989, the U.S. dollar bought about 119 Japanese yen and 1.7 German marks, while the Canadian dollar was worth about 87 U.S. cents.[5]

devaluation
Reduction in value of a country's currency.

Both market conditions and governmental action can change a country's exchange rate. **Devaluation** is the reduction of a currency's value in relation to other currencies or to gold. Devaluation of the dollar makes U.S. goods sell for less abroad and reduces costs for visiting foreigners. On the other hand, devaluation increases the price U.S. consumers pay for imported goods and makes foreign vacations more expensive as well. Finally, it would make it more expensive for U.S. firms to buy assets abroad and less expensive for foreign firms to purchase U.S. assets.

revaluation
Upward adjustment in the value of a nation's currency.

Revaluation is the upward movement of a currency's value in relation to other countries or to gold. Revaluation of the dollar would make U.S. goods more expensive abroad and make it more expensive for foreigners to visit the United States. At the same time, it would make foreign goods less expensive for American consumers and make overseas vacations more affordable. Finally, it would make it less expensive for U.S. firms to buy assets abroad and make domestic U.S. assets more expensive for foreign firms.

Changes in exchange rates can quickly wipe out or create a competitive advantage as well as affect considerations on whether or not to invest abroad. For example, in early 1985, the dollar was very high in relation to foreign currencies (250 yen and 3.1 marks).[6] U.S. goods were pushed out of many markets, both domestic and foreign. At the same time, expansion of overseas production was more attractive because foreign supplies and labor cost less in terms of U.S. dollars.

fixed exchange rates
Exchange rates fixed by government policy.

Fixed and Floating Exchange Rates   Toward the end of World War II, the representatives of the major Allied powers met at Bretton Woods, New Hampshire, to plan the postwar monetary system. They established a system of **fixed exchange rates** where the relative value of currencies was determined by government policy and was supposed to change only when a country could not keep a stable balance of payments at a particular exchange rate. Fixed exchange rates were thought to provide a predictability and stability that would help the growth of world trade. This system was undermined, however, by persistent balance of payments deficits by the United States (and to a less important extent, the United Kingdom), forcing devaluation of the dollar in 1971 and 1973 and an eventual decision in 1973 to let the market set the dollar's value. This began the system of **floating exchange rates**, where currency traders create a market for the world's currencies based on the countries' trade and investment prospects.

floating exchange rates
Exchange rates that vary according to market conditions.

Figure 4.1   Colombian Coffee: An Example of Specialization

You can always tell a Colombian Coffee party
by the way the crowd is dressed.

The richest coffee in the world."

Source: Courtesy of National Federation of Coffee Growers of Columbia.

Specialization among Nations

Nations usually benefit if they specialize in certain products or commercial activities. By doing what they do best, they are able to exchange surplus domestic products for foreign-made goods that are needed. This allows a higher standard of living than would be possible if the country tried to produce everything itself. For example, Colombia, South America, has a fertile soil and a favorable climate that enables it to specialize as a producer of coffee, the nation's leading export. Through advertisements such as the one in Figure 4.1, Colombian coffee is promoted in the United States, which imports 99.9 percent of its coffee.

However, specialization has its dangers if taken too far. Many less-developed countries depend on one or two primary commodities, such as grain and copper to earn foreign currency to pay for imported goods. If the price of their main good declines, it becomes much more difficult to import needed goods and services. Other problems can occur when a country depends on foreign nations for materials critical to its national defense. For example, the United States currently purchases all its high-grade silicon for missile guidance systems from a West German plant just 30 miles from Czechoslovakia. This source would be highly vulnerable during a European war, when obtaining the silicon would be difficult if not impossible.[7]

Specialization also produces some odd situations. Allied Mineral Products, a $22 million firm in Columbus, Ohio, exports sand to countries like Saudi Arabia. The sand is used to line foundry furnaces. Italy is nearly synonymous with footwear, yet New Hampshire–based Timberland introduced its boots and shoes in Italy before expanding throughout Europe. Finally, Lakewood Industries of Hibbling, Minnesota, rang up $14 million in sales in its first year. Lakewood's product? Chopsticks exported to Japan![8]

Absolute Advantage

absolute advantage
Situation in which a country has a monopolistic position in the marketing of a good or produces it at the lowest cost.

A country has an **absolute advantage** in the marketing of a product if it has a monopolistic position or it produces the good at the lowest cost. Examples of absolute advantage are rare because few countries are sole suppliers and because rapidly changing economic conditions can wipe out advantages in production costs.

Consider the case of Honda. As the dollar has declined in value against the yen, Honda's production costs in Marysville, Ohio, went down. In fact, some coupe versions of the Accord now use an engine made in Wako, Japan, but the model is assembled in Marysville, then loaded on a ship in Portland, Oregon, and sent to Japan for sale.[9] While other factors played a role in Honda's decisions, this example suggests absolute advantage is becoming an obsolete concept in a modern economy.

Comparative Advantage

comparative advantage
A country's ability to supply a particular item more efficiently and at a lower cost than it can supply other products.

A more practical approach to international specialization is that of comparative advantage. A country has a **comparative advantage** in an item if it can supply that item more efficiently and at a lower cost than it can supply other goods, compared to other nations. For example, if country A can produce a certain good three times as efficiently as country B, and it produces a second good only twice as efficiently as country B does, then country A has a comparative advantage in the first good. Country B, even though it produces the second good less efficiently than country A does, has a comparative advantage in this item because that is the good it is relatively more efficient at producing. The greatest supply of both goods will occur when each country specializes in producing the good where it has a comparative advantage, that is, country A producing the first good and country B producing the second good.

Countries do tend to follow this pattern of specialization. For example, American exports tend to be in those goods in which the United States has a comparative advantage over its trading partners. Being a highly industrialized country with good natural and agricultural resources, the United States tends to export manufactured items (aircraft parts and accessories), food products (grain, soybeans, and wheat), and some natural resources (coal). By contrast, countries with abundant low-cost labor often specialize in products that require a significant amount of labor, such as shoes and clothing.

The Self-Sufficiency Argument

While free trade and specialization in the products in which countries have comparative advantage can lead to higher levels of goods production worldwide, some countries prefer to be self-sufficient and avoid specialization. Most communist countries have followed this pattern at one time or another. Other countries only seek self-sufficiency in commodities they regard as strategic to their long-run development, such as energy in the United States.

In most cases, countries that seek to be self-sufficient do so for reasons of military preparedness, fear of economic reprisal from other countries, or nationalism. They see noneconomic advantages as being more important to the national welfare than the economic advantages of specialization. Israel and South Africa are two countries that try to be self-sufficient in regard to many national defense items. In other cases, a country may devote its resources to a product it does not produce efficiently in order to become an important producer in the future. Brazil's attempts to develop its computer industry illustrate this reason for avoiding specialization. If successful, Brazil would then graduate to specializing in computers for standard reasons of comparative advantage.

Levels of International Business Involvement

International business involvement is an evolving process for many firms. For example, a small company might start exporting on a limited scale, then expand its overseas efforts as management gains experience and confidence in its ability to operate effectively abroad. The company may then move to greater degrees of international involvement.

Four levels of involvement in world business are: direct and indirect exporting, foreign licensing, overseas marketing, and international production. As a firm becomes more active internationally, both the risks and the degree of control over marketing increase.

Direct and Indirect Exporting

Exporting firms produce goods at home and sell them abroad. Many companies engage in *indirect exporting,* often without realizing it, when their products are part of another good that is exported. Electronic components are a common example. When a firm commits to seeking export business, it engages in *direct exporting,* the most common form of international business. The company must devote both capital and managerial resources to this effort. Frequently, a firm will coordinate its export operation with an in-house "export manager," or may hire an outside company specializing in export promotion. Table 4.2 shows the top ten U.S. exporters.

Foreign Licensing

A one-ounce jar of "Ai Fang" facial cream sells for the equivalent of an average day's pay in China. It is produced by a local Chinese firm under license from Avon. Avon provides raw materials, plant equipment, and production assistance in exchange for 7.5 percent of the profits.[10]

The China-Avon agreement is an example of foreign licensing. Companies often select this approach because of high shipping costs, tariff barriers and other trade restrictions, or restrictions on foreign investment. For example, many U.S. firms license their technologies to Japanese companies because Japan has often made it difficult or impossible for American corporations to invest there.

Table 4.2   The Top Ten U.S. Exporters

Firm	Export Sales (in billions)
1. General Motors	$8.7
2. Ford Motor	$7.6
3. Boeing	$6.3
4. General Electric	$4.8
5. IBM	$4.0
6. E.I. du Pont de Nemours	$3.5
7. McDonnell Douglas	$3.2
8. Chrysler	$3.1
9. Eastman Kodak	$2.3
10. Caterpillar	$2.2

Source: Edward C. Baig, "Fifty Leading Exporters," *Fortune,* July 18, 1988, p. 71.

Overseas Marketing

Foreign marketing is controlled directly by the parent company, even though the goods and services may come from a variety of sources, such as domestic plants, licensees, or subcontractors. When a firm becomes involved in overseas marketing, a foreign sales office is established. For example, Square D, a Palatine, Illinois, electronics manufacturer, uses overseas sales offices in countries, such as the Netherlands, where it does not have manufacturing facilities. Milwaukee-based Belaris Machinery Inc., another sales organization, markets Soviet-made Belaris Tractors through a network of 120 U.S. dealers.[11]

International Production

Total international business involvement occurs when a company produces as well as markets its products abroad. A firm enters foreign markets in this way either by starting a subsidiary or acquiring an existing firm in the country where it is expanding. Square D set up subsidiaries in Canada and other countries, while acquiring a going concern in Germany. Sometimes, too, a company will enter into a **joint venture** with a local firm or government, sharing the operation's costs, risks, management, and profits with its local partner. The Chevrolet Prizm is produced by a joint venture between General Motors and Toyota, called New United Motors Manufacturing Inc., at a plant in Fremont, California. Chrysler and Mitsubishi Motors opened a joint venture in Bloomington–Normal, Illinois, to produce a sporty new car.

As we mentioned in Chapter 3, contracting production to firms outside the United States is known as **outsourcing**. Ford's Probe illustrates the extent of this trend. The Probe is the product of a Ford-Mazda joint venture. The car was designed in Detroit, engineered in Hiroshima, and assembled in Flat Rock, Michigan. Sixty percent of the Probe's parts were made overseas.[12]

Countertrade

Sometimes it is difficult to tell who is selling and who is buying in international trade. The primary culprit of this dilemma is **countertrade**, or international bartering agreements. Instead of simply selling its product, an exporter must also buy something as well. Some degree of countertrade is involved in an

joint venture
Sharing of a foreign operation's costs, risks, and management with a foreign firm or government.

outsourcing
Contracting of production to foreign firms.

countertrade
International bartering agreement.

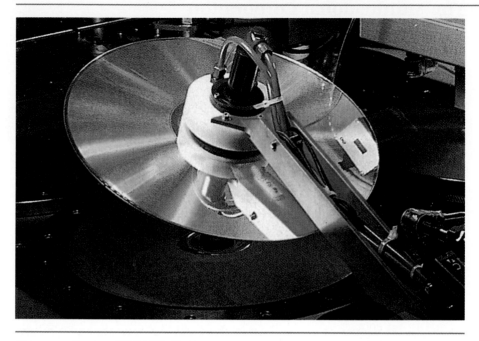

Photo source: Courtesy of N. V. Philips/Du Pont.

Du Pont is forming joint ventures with foreign firms to develop products for worldwide markets. A joint venture with the Dutch electronics firm N. V. Philips develops and produces optical-storage discs, such as the disc shown in this photo, which are made in a North Carolina plant. The joint venture is the world's largest producer of audio compact discs and involves research to perfect video and data discs used in the computer and data-processing industries.

estimated 20 to 30 percent of all international trade, and the figure is expected to climb.[13]

Countertrade is usually used when the buyer has limited foreign exchange, so payment is made in terms of other goods. On occasion, however, the buyer pays for the goods and the seller agrees to purchase other merchandise from the buyer or find a customer for his products. In an effort to head off protectionist legislation in the United States, many Japanese companies are starting to import American products. Once Honda unloads its ships in the United States, it reloads them for the return trip to Japan with American soybeans, hay, small airplanes, aluminum scrap, and cattle. Honda is now the United States' leading exporter of live cattle.[14]

Monsanto Company has two offices coordinating countertrade worldwide, with countertrade specialists in seven other offices. It sold more than $100 million using countertrade in a recent year.[15] The company's use of countertrade is almost exclusively with customers that lack foreign exchange, in particular with Eastern European countries and Latin American debtor nations such as Brazil and Argentina.

One typical countertrade agreement involved the sale of rubber chemicals to Brazil. The Brazilian government insisted it would not issue an import permit unless something were exported, so Monsanto bought $3 million worth of tin and sold it on the world market. In Monsanto's trade with Eastern Europe, countertrade is involved in a phenomenal 60 percent of its sales. Although countertrade is just a small fraction of its $7.6 billion annual sales, Carl R. Heerman, director of operations and administration for Monsanto Europe-Africa, says, "We are talking about the future." Citing the huge potential of such markets, he points out, "It takes years to build relationships in these countries, and Monsanto intends to be there when the doors open wider for more of our sophisticated products."

The Multinational Corporation

multinational corporation
Corporation that operates production and marketing facilities on an international level.

It is important to distinguish between an international firm and a multinational corporation. An international firm is limited to the first two levels of international business — selling abroad either through exports or overseas marketing. A **multinational corporation**, by contrast, operates both production and marketing facilities on an international level. The multinational corporation considers the world its market.

Who Are the Multinationals and How Do They Operate?

As Table 4.3 shows, oil, auto, and chemical companies dominate the list of the largest U.S. multinational corporations in terms of foreign revenues. All the firms on this list have increased the percent of their revenue derived from abroad during the past five years.

AMP Inc. is a good example of how a multinational firm should be operated. The U.S. company controls 15 to 20 percent of the worldwide market for electrical connectors by regularly opening plants in new countries as soon as the market is big enough. AMP insists each operation be staffed and managed by nationals of that country. The company also devotes 9 percent of sales revenue to research and development and engineering, allowing its sales to increase by an average of 15 percent annually.[16]

Global Strategies versus Multinational Strategies

Multinational corporations can use either a global or multinational strategy. A global strategy uses a standardized product and marketing strategy worldwide. The same product is sold in essentially the same manner throughout the world. Coca-Cola is the world's best-known trademark, and the product, available in more than 155 countries, has universal appeal. The advertisement in Figure 4.2, launched in Canada during the Calgary Olympics, appeals to consumers from many nations.

Table 4.3   The Ten Largest U.S. Multinational Corporations

Rank	Company	Foreign Revenue (in billions)	Percent of Total Revenue
1.	Exxon	$57.4	75.1%
2.	Mobil	31.6	60.5
3.	IBM	29.3	54.0
4.	General Motors	24.1	23.7
5.	Ford Motor	24.0	32.8
6.	Texaco	17.1	49.8
7.	Citicorp	13.3	48.4
8.	Du Pont	11.7	38.2
9.	Dow Chemical	7.4	55.6
10.	Chevron	5.9	22.7

Source: "The 100 Largest U.S. Multinationals," *Forbes,* July 25, 1988, p. 248.

Figure 4.2   Example of a Global Marketing Strategy

Source: Courtesy of The Coca-Cola Company.

Under a multinational strategy, each national market is treated differently. Firms develop products and marketing strategies that appeal to the customs, tastes, and buying habits of particular national markets. CPC International, a consumer food company producing more than 2,000 products, uses a multinational strategy. For example, CPC recently developed a new product — Flavored Maizena — for consumers in Mexico. Flavored Maizena is a base used in the preparation of *atole,* a traditional Mexican drink made from cornstarch, milk, and flavorings. *Atole* has been part of Mexico's strongly corn-linked culture for thousands of years. CPC's new product simplifies the preparation of *atole* and is marketed primarily to young people who value the tradition of drinking *atole* but desire an easy way to prepare it.[17]

Public Attitudes toward Multinationals

Multinational corporations have become so dominant in some markets, such as Chile and Canada, that they are the object of political and economic scrutiny. These firms have been criticized for their profit margins, investment policies, employment practices, and dominance of local markets.

It seems likely that the multinational corporation will continue to be criticized in these areas, sometimes justifiably, sometimes not. Companies operating abroad must be sure they behave as fairly and responsibly overseas as they do at home.

Obstacles to International Business

Various barriers to effective world business exist. Some are minor and easily overcome; others are nearly impossible to bridge. In any case, business executives must expect and learn to handle a multitude of problems in attempting to reach international markets.

Cultural Barriers

To succeed in foreign markets, firms must understand cultural factors such as language, education, social values, religious attitudes, and consumer habits. Procter & Gamble succeeds in many foreign markets by studying a nation's culture and then tailoring products and marketing to meet consumer needs. For example, P&G learned that people in the Philippines wash clothes with a laundry bar and then squeeze the juice of a local fruit, kalamansi, into the wash water. The fruit gives clothes a fresh scent and acts as a stain remover. P&G used this information to develop two laundry bars, Mr. Clean Kalamansi and Perla Kalamansi, for the Philippine market. When P&G wanted to market its Crest Tartar Control toothpaste in Latin America, the prospects looked dim because there was no recognized Spanish translation for *dental tartar*. By conducting consumer research, P&G marketers learned that Latin Americans think of tartar as an ugly, cement-like substance, expressed in their language by the word *sarro*. So P&G named the toothpaste Anti-Sarro to help consumers understand the product's cosmetic and therapeutic benefits.[18]

Mister Donut sidestepped cultural land mines in Japan by carefully modifying its product and marketing while maintaining an American image. For example, it downsized the doughnuts, lowered the counter, and used lighter weight coffee cups. Most important, it did not challenge traditional Japanese breakfast habits but instead positioned doughnuts and coffee as snack food, not breakfast. It also took advantage of the large number of rail commuters by locating many outlets near train stations.[19]

Foreign goods sometimes fail by ignoring cultural factors in the U.S. market. The German-made men's cologne 4711 was a flop in the United States because of its sharp scent and the fact that the scent disappeared quickly.

Physical Barriers

A variety of physical barriers can hurt international trade. The United States and Burma are the only countries in the world that have not adopted the metric system.[20] Now, most U.S. firms have switched to metric-measured components for both foreign and domestic sales.

Another example of a physical barrier to trade is that American electrical products are engineered for a different electric current than that used in most of the rest of the world. When Americans take their hair driers and electric shavers abroad, they need voltage adapters to use them.

American-made cars often face physical barriers because they are made for roads that are wide by foreign standards. Many streets in Europe and Asia, for instance, were built before the United States was even colonized, so automakers there have always built small cars.

Tariffs and Trade Restrictions

International business is also affected by tariffs and related trade restrictions such as import quotas, embargoes, and exchange control. While these factors have played a pronounced role in world business, there has been a general worldwide movement toward free trade. A recent example of this is the United States–Canada free trade requirement, which took effect in 1989. It should be

Photo source: Courtesy of The Procter & Gamble Company. Used with permission.

Key to Procter & Gamble's success in selling more than 160 brands in 140 countries is the firm's ability to adapt marketing and technology to different cultures. Households in Europe have front-loading washing machines that are not suitable for dispensing liquid laundry detergents. So P&G developed a "dosing ball," a plastic sphere that consumers fill with detergent and place among the clothes in the machine. The washer's agitation releases the detergent into the wash water. The dispensing innovation has helped P&G capture more than half of Europe's liquid laundry detergent market.

noted, however, that economic downturns always bring calls for economic protection of domestic industries.

Tariffs   A **tariff** is a tax levied on products imported from abroad. Some are a set amount per pound, gallon, or other unit; others are figured on the value of the good. Tariffs can be classified as either revenue or protective. A *revenue tariff* is designed to raise funds for the government. Revenue tariffs were a major source of U.S. government revenue until the early twentieth century. A *protective tariff,* which is usually higher than a revenue tariff, is designed to raise the retail price of imported products and improve the competitiveness of domestically made goods. It has often been argued that a country should protect its "infant industries" by using tariffs to bar foreign-made products. On many occasions, it has been argued that protective tariffs should be used to protect American jobs from foreign competition.

tariff
Tax levied against imported products.

Trade Restrictions   There are other ways of restricting trade besides the use of tariffs. An **import quota** sets a limit on the number of products that can be imported in certain categories. The objective of such quotas is to protect domestic industries and their employees or to preserve foreign exchange. The ultimate quota is the **embargo**, a ban on imported or exported products. Embargoes typically are used for political rather than economic purposes. For example, it is illegal to import Cuban cigars into the United States. There are also various trade restrictions pertaining to such countries as South Africa and Nicaragua.

import quota
Limitation on the number of products in certain categories that can be imported.

embargo
Ban on certain imported or exported products.

The problem with import quotas and embargoes is that they may lead to a *trade war* in which the other nation retaliates with trade restrictions, as occurred during the Great Depression. A more recent example of how a trade war gets started occurred when the Europeans refused to accept American beef that had been treated with hormones. The United States responded by slapping trade restrictions on various European agricultural products.

Most nations prefer an *orderly marketing agreement* or *managed trade agreement,* establishing negotiated, but voluntary, limits on trade. The United States and Japan have had a voluntary export agreement governing automobile

Until the late 1980s, Japan imposed strict import restrictions on tobacco products. As a result, U.S. cigarettes represented less than 3 percent of the Japanese market. After Japan lifted the trade restrictions, U.S. brand volume tripled. The opening of the Japanese market benefited Brown & Williamson Tobacco Corporation, the third-largest U.S. cigarette manufacturer. The firm's exports to Japan, including Lucky Strike and other brands, now account for about 25 percent of U.S. cigarette brand share in the country, up from 6 percent in 1986.

imports from Japan. As a result of the quantitative limit on their exports to the United States, Japanese auto firms have concentrated more and more on the high-price part of the market, leaving the low end of the market to such firms as Hyundai (South Korea). Other trade limits have been placed on machine tools, carbon steel, and semiconductors.[21]

The **General Agreement on Tariffs and Trade (GATT)** is an international trade accord that has sponsored a series of agreements on tariffs and trade restrictions. The current round of trade talks, called the *Uruguay Round,* is centered in Montreal. The GATT has led to a cut in the overall level of trade barriers faced by international business. Its 96 members include all the major industrial countries; many third world countries; several socialist countries, including Poland, Hungary, and Romania; and The People's Republic of China has observer status. The U.S.S.R., however, is a notable nonmember.[22]

Exchange Control   Foreign trade can also be regulated by exchange control through a central bank or government agency. Under **exchange control**, firms must buy and sell foreign exchange only through the central bank or other designated agency. The government can then allocate, expand, or restrict access to foreign exchange in accord with national policy.

In the summer of 1982, the Mexican peso was devalued by 45 percent to help stabilize Mexico's balance of payments. Declining oil prices and produc-

General Agreement on Tariffs and Trade (GATT)
International trade accord that has sponsored a series of negotiations on tariffs and trade restrictions.

exchange control
Allocation, expansion, or restriction of foreign exchange according to existing national policy.

Porta-Bote International of Mountainview, California, learned how tough Japanese import requirements are when the firm decided to market its recreational boat (photo at left), which folds to 4 inches flat, in Japan. The Japanese Small Vessel Association filled the boat with 610 pounds of concrete weights, raised it 20 feet above the water, then dropped it three times to see if it would sink. Porta-Bote passed the rigorous quality test with flying colors.

Photo source: Porta-Bote International, Mountainview, CA.

tion, combined with increasing interest rates on the money the government owed to foreign banks, threatened to disrupt the Mexican economy.

Alarmed at the resulting outflow of capital, the Mexican president nationalized the country's banks and imposed strict currency controls. This meant most American dollars in Mexican banks were frozen and not allowed to leave the country. If account holders wanted to make withdrawals from these accounts, they would have to convert the dollar into highly devalued pesos, drastically reducing their purchasing power.

Americans doing business with Mexicans suddenly found that their customers could no longer afford their products. Particularly hard hit were merchants in American border towns. Business was estimated to be off by as much as 80 percent because Mexican citizens could no longer afford to purchase American goods with the devalued pesos.[23]

Exchange control is not restricted to less-developed countries. Britain, for example, had exchange controls, though increasingly less comprehensive, from World War II until Margaret Thatcher came to power in 1979.

Political and Legal Factors

Many nations try to achieve political objectives through international business activities. Firms operating abroad often end up involved in or influenced by international relations.

Dresser Industries certainly appreciates how political factors influence international business. The firm intended to sell some equipment to the Soviet Union for a gas pipeline to transport natural gas from Siberia and sell it to Western Europe. The United States government disallowed the transfer of American technology to the U.S.S.R. However, the Soviets eventually purchased the equipment they needed from a French subsidiary of Dresser.

Legal requirements also complicate international business. Liquor sales in Sweden are a government monopoly. The Netherlands requires tooth-decay warnings in television candy commercials. Japan has stringent health and quality restrictions. Many nations have laws specifying the portion of a product that must come from domestic sources. The United States has considered similar legislation. These examples suggest that managers involved in international business must be well versed in legislation affecting their industry if they want to compete in today's world marketplace.

The Legal Framework for International Business

The legal environment for American firms operating abroad has three dimensions: U.S. law, host-country law, and international requirements. Firms in the United States are subject to comprehensive business legislation. International operations are also subject to various trade regulations, tax laws, and import-export requirements.

Major U.S. Legislation

Webb-Pomerene Export Act (1918)
Exemption from antitrust laws for U.S. firms acting together to develop export markets.

cartel
Monopolistic organization of foreign firms.

Export Trading Companies Act (1982)
Legislation designed to encourage export trading companies.

Foreign Corrupt Practices Act (1978)
Legislation that prohibits bribery of foreigners by American firms to secure sales.

The **Webb-Pomerene Export Act (1918)** exempts from antitrust laws certain combinations of U.S. firms acting together to develop export markets. The intent was to give U.S. industry economic power equal to that possessed by a **cartel**, a monopolistic organization of foreign firms. This is important because foreign firms frequently cooperate with each other in ways that would be illegal for U.S. firms under domestic antitrust law. Companies operating under Webb-Pomerene must not reduce competition within the United States and must not use unfair methods of competition.

The **Export Trading Companies Act (1982)** was designed to encourage formation of export trading companies by eliminating some antitrust barriers and allowing banks to participate in such enterprises. An *export trading company* is any type of organization that seeks to expand exports.

Another important U.S. law is the **Foreign Corrupt Practices Act (1978)**, which forbids American firms from bribing foreigners to buy their goods and services. Enacted in the wake of numerous reports of companies doing just that, the law also requires businesses to set up adequate accounting controls to monitor internal compliance. The law provides for penalties against both the company and the official involved. Firms can be fined up to $1 million for violations, while the individuals involved face $10,000 fines and up to five years in jail.

International Trade Requirements

friendship, commerce, and navigation (FCN) treaties
Agreements with other nations that include many aspects of international business relations.

International requirements can be seen in the various agreements existing among nations. The United States has many **friendship, commerce, and navigation (FCN) treaties** with other nations. Such treaties include many aspects of international business relations including the right to conduct business in the treaty partner's domestic market. Other international business agreements concern standards for products, patents, trademarks, reciprocal tax treaties, export control, international air travel, and international communications.

Originally set up to coordinate international financial relations, the **International Monetary Fund (IMF)** lends money to countries that require short-term assistance in conducting international trade. Since the onset of the Latin American debt crisis, the IMF has played a major role in overseeing agreements between the debtor countries and their lenders to renew their loans while ensuring repayment. The **World Bank** was established to make long-term loans for economic development projects. Both financial institutions help to facilitate international business activity.

The legal requirements of host nations strongly affect international marketers. Japan, for example, is often cited as having complex import requirements. Other nations, such as Mexico, put various restrictions on foreign ownership of their business sectors. The majority of international businesspeople realize the importance of obeying the laws and regulations of the countries within which they operate. Violations of these legal requirements constitute setbacks for international business as a whole and should be carefully avoided.

Dumping

The problem of dumping is sometimes a threat to firms engaged in international business. **Dumping**, selling goods abroad at a price lower than that charged in the domestic market, is prohibited in many countries. U.S. law requires that imported items be sold for at least production costs, plus 10 percent overhead and a minimum 8 percent profit margin. If dumping is proved, punitive trade restrictions may be assigned to the dumped products.

Firms dump products for a variety of reasons, but the most important reason recently has been to increase market share. This is similar to predatory pricing in the domestic market to undersell rivals and force them out of business. American semiconductor manufacturers accused Japanese rivals of dumping to increase their market share. Another motivation for dumping comes when a country's domestic market is too small to support an efficient level of production. In this case, the U.S. market becomes a tempting target. Alternatively, a firm might dump surplus goods or technologically obsolete products overseas.

Multinational Economic Communities

Several multinational economic communities were formed after World War II. The European Community (EC), also known as the *Common Market,* is the best known of them. Others include the European Free Trade Area in Northern Europe and the Andean Pact in South America. Countries in such regional associations often have strong political as well as economic ties.

Three basic formats for economic integration exist: the free trade area, the customs union, and the common market. Within a **free trade area**, participants trade freely among themselves without tariffs or trade restrictions. However, each maintains its own tariffs for goods from outside the area. In a **customs union**, the member nations impose a common tariff on the goods from outside their membership. In a **common market**, the member nations go beyond a customs union to try to bring all government trade rules into agreement.

International Monetary Fund (IMF)
Organization that lends foreign exchange to countries requiring assistance in international trade.

World Bank
Organization that funds long-term economic development projects.

dumping
Selling goods abroad at a price lower than that charged in the domestic market.

free trade area
Form of economic integration within which participants agree to trade among themselves without tariffs or trade restrictions.

customs union
Form of economic integration within which a free trade area is established for member nations and a uniform tariff is imposed on trade with nonmember nations.

common market
Form of economic integration that maintains a customs union and seeks to bring other trade rules into agreement.

The EC and U.S.–Canadian Free Trade Pact

In the EC, some harmonization of economic regulations has occurred in such areas as antitrust laws and government subsidies. But now, the community is moving toward complete integration of the EC member states' market, which would encompass 323 million people with a GNP of $4.2 trillion.[24] Scheduled to take place by the end of 1992, the reforms would remove remaining trade barriers between member states while harmonizing economic regulations. Among other things, it would allow the free movement of both capital and people, allowing a French firm to own or acquire a British firm with no more scrutiny than would be given a British citizen. It requires that all 12 member countries recognize licenses to practice medicine or law issued in other member nations; and harmonize taxes such as the value-added tax.[25]

Similarly important results could come out of the recently approved U.S.–Canada free trade agreement. While the two countries are already each other's largest trading partner, the pact started removing tariffs and other barriers on trade over a ten-year period as of January 1, 1989. The creation of the free trade area is estimated to create 750,000 jobs in the United States and 150,000 in Canada.[26]

Regardless of their approach, multinational economic communities play an important role in international business. American firms invested heavily in EC countries in the 1960s to take advantage of the huge, protected market there. With 1992 looming, there has been another spurt of foreign investment in the EC.[27] For instance, Richard Electronics, a medium-sized manufacturer located in LaFox, Illinois, recently bought a plant in France. CEO Edward Richardson explained: "We feel it would be much better to be in place when it all happens than to try to get in after 1992."[28]

The United States as a Foreign Market

The United States is a foreign market to firms headquartered in other countries. The importation of oil highlights the importance of foreign sources for the U.S. economy. Foreign oil accounts for 44 percent of all U.S. consumption.[29] The United States also depends on overseas firms for a variety of other goods and services. The Japanese, for example, have achieved a considerable share of the U.S. electronics and automobile markets. Particularly in consumer electronics, U.S. producers are taking a beating, with only 15 percent of the market being supplied domestically.[30]

Foreign sellers can employ any of the four levels of international business involvement noted earlier. Some sellers, such as the Japanese, have become major forces in a variety of markets. Fearing the potential of U.S. protectionism as industries such as textiles, steel, autos, and electronics are hurt by foreign competition, the Japanese are investing heavily in U.S. production facilities. One recent estimate concluded that 640 Japanese-owned factories employed 160,000 American workers. Not surprisingly, the Pacific states lead the way, but there is also substantial Japanese investment in the industrialized Northeast and Midwest.[31] Many well-known firms with American names are currently controlled by foreign interests, including Joseph E. Seagram & Sons, CBS Records, and Carnation.

Figure 4.3   Quality Import Preferred by American Car Buyers

One ride and you'll understand why most rocket scientists are German.

There is nothing else like it. Nothing.

As the intercooled, turbocharged engine spins past 3000 rpm, the raspy, throaty 282 hp flat six makes mechanical music unlike anything you've heard.

The surge of power that follows is simply astonishing. You are literally pressed back and held fast by the deep leather sports seats. Like Al Holbert, Hans Stuck and Derek Bell before you, you feel the breathtaking thrust of legendary performance.

This, after all, is the engine that conquered Le Mans and Sebring more times than any other engine in automotive history.

This is the car that *Car and Driver* tested from 0 to 60 in 4.6 seconds, and in 13.1 seconds for the quarter mile—records still unbroken by any other production car in the world in the past 20 years.

This is the car that David E. Davis, Jr., Editor/Publisher of *Automobile Magazine*, called the most likely car to become a classic in the future.

And this is the car that stands as the epitome of 40 years of uncompromised, racing-bred Porsche engineering heritage.

If you think it's a remarkable car to look at, wait until you get behind the wheel.

It may be true that German engineers have produced vehicles capable of more prodigious performance. But you won't find them on this planet.

PORSCHE

Source: Courtesy of Porsche Cars North America, Inc.

Americans often prefer foreign products to domestic ones. Imports account for over 30 percent of the automobile market, almost 55 percent of textiles and clothing, and 85 percent of consumer electronics.[32] Some foreign products, such as the Hyundai Excel, sell because of their price advantage over domestic competitors. Other foreign products, such as the German-made sports car shown in the advertisement in Figure 4.3, sell well in the United States because of their quality advantages. T. W. Kutter Inc. of Avon, Massachusetts, is a $40 million assembler of food processing and packaging machinery. Most of Kutter's volume comes from sausage processing equipment. Kutter imports its parts from Germany, which is known for both its quality standards and its consumption of sausage.[33]

It is likely that imported goods will continue to increase in importance in the American market. During the last half of the twentieth century, the long-run trend has been toward increased international trade. Apparently, the Soviets have also come to realize the benefits of increased trade. In 1989, they eliminated a rule restricting Western companies to minority ownership of joint ventures. In addition, the official Soviet daily, *Izvestia,* carries a regular Tuesday supplement offering Western advertising to its 10.5 million readers at $50,000 per page. Among the most recent entrants in the Soviet market is Ben & Jerry's

Homemade in a non-profit venture promoting world peace and designed to expand the number of available flavors from one (vanilla).[34] Today, there is talk of the Soviet Union joining GATT.

Summary of Learning Goals

1.   Evaluate the importance of international business.   Since most national economies are closely linked today, international business is growing in importance. The United States is both the largest exporter and largest importer in the world. For many U.S. companies, international business provides a sizable part of their revenue.

2.   Define the concept of international business and analyze why countries tend to specialize in certain goods.   The concept of international business includes the balance of trade (the difference between exports and imports) and balance of payments (the difference between inward and outward cash flows). Countries usually benefit if they specialize in certain products or commercial activities. A country has an absolute advantage in making a product if it holds a monopoly or produces the good at lowest cost. It has a comparative advantage if it can supply the product more efficiently or at lower cost than it can supply other products. Some countries refrain from specializing because they want to be self-sufficient, particularly in certain strategic areas.

3.   Describe the different levels of involvement in international business.   The four levels of involvement in world business are direct and indirect exporting, foreign licensing, overseas marketing, and combined foreign production and marketing.

4.   Assess the importance of countertrade on international business.   Countertrade refers to negotiated bartering agreements to facilitate exports and imports. The importance of countertrade is expected to grow in the future. Countertrade is often used when a buyer has limited foreign exchange. In other instances, a seller agrees to buy certain products from the purchaser in order to expedite the original sale.

5.   Discuss the role of multinational corporations in world business.   Multinational corporations, those that produce and market their goods internationally, have become so dominant in some markets that in several countries they are now the object of political and economic scrutiny. Consequently, companies operating abroad should act reasonably and fairly.

6.   Identify the main obstacles confronting international business.   A wide variety of obstacles face world business. Examples include cultural and physical barriers, tariffs and trade restrictions, and political and legal obstacles.

7.   Explain multinational economic integration.   Multinational economic integration is the removal of barriers to the movement of goods, capital, and people. Three formats, with increasing levels of integration, exist: the free trade area (United States and Canada), the customs union (EC today), and the common market or economic union (EC's goal in 1992).

8. Describe the United States as a foreign market. The United States is an important foreign market for many countries. Americans often show a preference for foreign goods over their domestic competitors. Some foreign products sell well because of a reputation for quality, others because they cost less than similar domestic products.

Key Terms

exporting

importing

balance of trade

balance of payments

exchange rate

devaluation

revaluation

fixed exchange rates

floating exchange rates

absolute advantage

comparative advantage

joint venture

countertrade

outsourcing

multinational corporation

tariff

import quota

embargo

General Agreement on Tariffs and Trade (GATT)

exchange control

Webb-Pomerene Export Act (1918)

cartel

Export Trading Companies Act (1982)

Foreign Corrupt Practices Act (1978)

friendship, commerce, and navigation (FCN) treaties

International Monetary Fund (IMF)

World Bank

dumping

free trade area

customs union

common market

Review Questions

1. Is it possible for a nation to have a favorable balance of trade and an unfavorable balance of payments? Defend your answer.

2. Differentiate between fixed and floating exchange rates.

3. Distinguish between the concepts of absolute advantage and comparative advantage.

4. Identify the levels of involvement in international business and give an example of each.

5. What is meant by countertrade? Why do you think this has become such an important part of international business?

6. Explain what is meant by outsourcing.

7. How do multinational corporations operate in the global marketplace?

8. Explain the difference between a revenue tariff and a protective tariff. What type is the United States most concerned with today? Why?

9. How does a trade war get started?

10. Describe the three basic formats for multinational economic integration.

Discussion Questions

1. Keep a diary of your purchases for a week. How many of the items you bought were foreign made? Discuss what you have learned from this exercise.

2. Should the United States resume trade with Cuba? Discuss.

3. The Japanese, who account for 20 percent of Hawaii's visitors, have bought $6.5 million of real estate in the state, including two-thirds of the hotels. Is this trend good for Hawaii? What if anything should be done about it? Discuss.

4. The People's Republic of China takes over Kong Kong in 1997. China has promised to keep a capitalistic economy in Hong Kong for 50 years. Still, many Hong Kong businesspeople (and their families) have emigrated to other nations such as Canada and Australia. Discuss the impact of this situation on international business.

5. Japanese marketers are known for their patience in developing foreign markets. Now Japan's Suntory is buying U.S. bottled water companies such as Polar Water in Pittsburgh. Shiro Yosumo, the president of Suntory International, explains: "I think bottled water is the most promising industry in the U.S. Your tap water is getting worse and worse, your aquifers are polluted by toxic waste, and your government doesn't have any money to clean it up." Discuss Yosumo's observation relating it to the Japanese approach to market development.

Video Case

Fluor Corp.

The added complications of conducting business on an international scale were evident to anyone viewing the daily news reports from China during 1989. The unprecedented mass demonstrations for democratic political reform were centered in Beijing's Tiananmen Square in the shadow of Mao Tse-Tung's tomb. News watchers occasionally glimpsed a smaller, and ultimately American, landmark across the square: a 500-seat Kentucky Fried Chicken restaurant. The People's Army martial law decree temporarily forced the largest single retail outlet in the firm's chain to shut down for several hours a day, substantially reducing business below its $3 million sales level of the previous year.

But the People's Republic of China represents promise as well as problems. After all, China is home for 1.1 billion people. Moreover, it is rapidly changing from an abacus technology to a computer one. As a result, U.S.–China trade passed the $10 billion level by 1988.

Income as well as people are required to create a market, however, and the average annual income of a Chinese household is only about $500. In poor sections of cities, 70 percent of household income goes for food. Even though China ranks as one of the top ten countries in film sales for Eastman Kodak, only a small number of relatively affluent Chinese even own cameras. However, "a small percentage of 1.1 billion is a pretty big chunk," says Ed Hoppe, a Kodak general manager.

Among the U.S. firms sizing up the Chinese market is Irvine, California–based Fluor Corp. But Fluor is not interested in selling consumer products abroad. The firm is one of the world's largest international engineering, construction, and industrial service companies. Its 50 offices scattered throughout the world allow Fluor to provide a broad range of services to clients in five business sectors: industrial, process, power, hydrocarbon, and government. Typical projects include complex jobs like the $4 billion Aramco

Notes: Stuart Elliott, "Protests Hurt Kentucky Fried's Sales," *USA Today,* May 24, 1989, p. 2B; Fluor Corporation 1988 Report to Shareholders; John Hillkirk, "Cautious U.S. Firms Still Bullish on China," *USA Today,* May 24, 1989, p. 2B; and Edward F. Cone, "Off the Hot Seat," *Forbes,* November 14, 1988, p. 12.

Gas Program in Saudi Arabia and the Alaska Pipeline. The firm's plan to increase the proportion of revenues generated abroad has been successful. During 1988, the percentage of new Fluor contracts outside the U.S. rose to 24 percent (from 7 percent the previous year), tangible evidence that its globalization efforts have taken hold.

Fluor's specialization in providing industrial services has caused problems in its negotiations with socialist countries such as China and the Soviet Union. In China, for example, the firm usually deals directly with government officials rather than with private businesses. The tendency of the Chinese is to view service negotiations in the same way as the purchase of equipment and to insist on a lump-sum total payment. For projects where the scope of Fluor's involvement is not well defined, the company may lose money if more work is required than was originally planned.

A second problem involves exchange rates. During times when the U.S. dollar is relatively high in relation to another nation's currency, it becomes difficult for Fluor executives to compete with firms based in other nations such as Japan. To offset this problem, Fluor takes full advantage of its offices in various countries. The exchange rate barrier can be overcome by using the currencies of Saudi Arabia, West Germany, England, Canada, or Australia — just five of the 50 nations in which Fluor operates. The firm's broad international base is an important tool in such instances.

The Chinese government's determination to improve its infrastructure, beef up its technology, and increase productivity has placed severe strains on its international currency reserves. Fluor negotiators have sought to improve their competitive position in China by accepting countertrade for many of their projects. Trade agreements for products instead of cash are negotiated. Fluor then gets its money back by selling these products in the world market.

Credibility is a necessary characteristic for any business, large or small and, in a global context, it is often the key to success or failure. David Tappan, Fluor's CEO, has a favorite saying: "Don't promise anything you can't deliver and deliver what you promise." Tappan, like one person in four, was born in China. His firm was one of the first U.S.–based companies to enter the Chinese market, establishing a marketing team there in 1978. The duration of Fluor's presence, combined with evidence of its ability to offer first-class performance and reputable service, is especially important in China with its centuries of experience with traders who appeared . . . and then disappeared without a trace.

But credibility is also built by paying attention to and respecting a country's people, customs, and culture. Since many of Fluor's clients are located in technologically less-developed countries, it is important that the firm not only provide this technology, but also involve the host country's people in its development through educational and employment opportunities. When Fluor completes a project, there must be trained, competent workers to perform maintenance and operating functions. This requires a deep understanding of the people and their customs to overcome the typical barriers of language and habits as well as intangible cultural differences. Fluor has a training program to increase its employees' abilities to interact with clients in foreign countries.

The Chinese government realizes that it needs the expertise of foreign firms to position itself in the rapidly-growing international business sector. Fluor is involved in many projects that will ultimately offer such expertise to China, simultaneously presenting more opportunities for Fluor. In fact, Fluor has invited Chinese engineers to train in the United States, which also provides an opportunity for Fluor employees to share in the cross-culturization effort.

Today, Fluor is the most diversified and broadly-based engineering and construction firm operating anywhere in the world and was recently ranked Number 1 among the top 400 U.S. contractors by *Engineer-*

ing News-Record Magazine. Fluor subsidies also enhance the parent firm's globalization efforts. The Mining and Metals Division, for example, provided many of the services for the La Escondida copper project in Chile in 1989. As the industrial and commercial building climate becomes more viable as a potential market, Fluor will already have positioned itself globally to meet the demands of the worldwide construction industry.

Questions

1. The major Chinese export to the U.S. is clothing — accounting for one-third of total exports — followed by petroleum, tin, and stuffed dolls and toy animals. The five leading U.S. exports to China are commercial aircraft, Douglas fir logs, oil and gas drilling machinery, polyester yarns, and wheat. Relate this information to the concepts of absolute advantage and comparative advantage.

2. Total Chinese exports to the U.S. exceeded purchases of U.S. goods and services by $3.5 billion in a recent year.

a. Does the U.S. enjoy a balance of trade surplus or a balance of trade deficit with China?

b. Can a determination of balance payments surplus or deficit be made from this information? Explain.

3. Relate Fluor's current operations in China to the levels of international business involvement. Why is countertrade such an important component of the firm's Chinese operations?

4. Identify the major obstacles in international business and relate each to Fluor's current operations in China.

Careers in Business

Contemporary Business introduces the reader to a range of business careers. A career section featuring employment opportunities in that particular field follows each major part of the text. In many cases, Bureau of Labor Statistics employment projections to the year 2000 are also included. Readers may use these sections as a starting point in evaluating their career plans. *Contemporary Business* also devotes Chapter 24 to making career decisions.

Some specific jobs related to Part One of the text are listed below. The Bureau of Labor Statistics estimates that demand for managers and statisticians will grow about as fast as the average for all occupations, while the demand for economists of all kinds will grow faster than average, primarily in business, rather than in academic settings.

Statistician

Statisticians analyze statistical data in order to provide managers with information for making better decisions. They work in both private and public sectors. There were 18,000 statisticians in the United States in a recent year.

Job Description. Statisticians work in all phases of business and marketing research. They study the problems related to these issues, supervise the data-collection phase, and analyze the results. The statistician's conclusions are then presented to management for action.

Career Path. Entry-level personnel are often assigned to collect data or other basic tasks under the supervision of experienced statisticians. Experienced statisticians supervise them. Senior-level personnel have increased responsibilities and may eventually be selected for supervisory or management positions.

Salary. Beginning salaries in a recent year for someone with a B.A. and no experience ranged from $14,800 to $18,400; with a master's degree, from $22,500 to $27,200; with a Ph.D., $27,200 to $32,600. Median salary for a statistician with a Ph.D. was $43,700. Statisticians in the government sector averaged $39,400.

Economist

Economists often conduct research that will assist management decision making. They are employed in the private, public, and nonprofit sectors. Academic preparation in economic theory and research methodology is necessary. Recent employment was 37,000.

Job Description. Economists research subjects such as comparative wage rates, energy costs, the impact of employment and inflation on consumer demand, and the balance of trade. Their findings are reported to the management of corporations, banks, trade associations, labor unions, government departments, and others.

Career Path. Junior-level economists assist senior-level personnel in their research. Advancement to the ranks of top management is possible.

Salary. The range of starting salaries in private business for someone with a B.A. in economics is $19,300 to $22,400. The median base salary for a business economist is $54,000. The average salary in the federal government is $40,700.

Health and Regulatory Inspectors

As government employees, health and regulatory inspectors are responsible for implementing the rules and regulations established by Congress, federal agencies, or state and local governments. Recently, 125,000 people were employed as health and regulatory inspectors.

Job Description. Health inspectors work in the area of consumer safety, food, agricultural quarantine, and environmental health. Regulatory inspectors work in the areas of immigration; customs; postal service; aviation safety; railroads; motor vehicles; occupational safety and health; mines; wage-hour compliance; and alcohol, tobacco, and firearms. Agricultural quarantine officers inspect shipments and people entering the country in order to protect U.S. farming industries. Immigration inspectors examine those seeking to enter the United States. Customs inspectors enforce the various laws and taxes dealing with exports and imports.

Career Path. A qualifying civil-service exam administered by federal, state, or local authorities is required. Successful candidates receive on-the-job training. A career ladder with regular promotions is available to all employees.

Salary. Entry-level salaries vary according to the activity involved. For federal employees, the average entry-level salary was $14,800. The national median salary is $25,200; the federal average, $30,400.

Industrial Development Specialist

Most industrial development specialists are state government employees, but a few industrial development specialists also work for utility companies. Industrial development means more jobs for a state's citizens. Tax revenue also increases when businesses locate within state lines.

Job Description. These specialists work with businesses in an attempt to persuade them to locate within a state. They work with the state's tax department to provide corporate tax incentives and with other government agencies to provide adequate facilities for offices and plants. Industrial development specialists, especially in high-tech companies, also seek the cooperation of educational institutions, which can offer businesses qualified employees.

Career Path. Industrial development specialists often gain experience working in state commerce department offices. They must have a strong background in finance as well as strong negotiating skills.

Salary. Salaries vary from state to state and with levels of experience.

International Trade Economist

International trade economists study the various economic aspects of trade with foreign nations. They can be found in the private, public, and educational sectors.

Job Description. International trade economists must meet all the job requirements of other economists. In addition, they must be experts in international trade.

Career Path. The career path depends upon whether the person is employed in the private, public, or educational sector.

Salary. Salaries for international trade economists vary according to whether the person is employed in the private, public, or educational sector.

International Banking Officer

International banking officers must be knowledgeable in foreign financial systems and the trade relations between nations. They are the bank's representatives in all of its international dealings.

Job Description. International banking officers are involved in decision-making roles in international banking divisions. They monitor existing business and accounts, and must be experts in foreign banking practices and procedures.

Career Path. Entry-level persons are usually assistants to an experienced international banking executive. Promotion to a senior position is possible. An eventual goal of many in this field is the top-level position of international banking officer.

Salary. Middle-level international banking officers earn between $60,000 and $80,000 a year.

Import-Export Manager

Import-export managers plan and supervise the flow of goods to and from other nations. They are important contributors to international business.

Job Description. These executives administer shipping, receiving, and billing activities. The import-export manager deals with domestic customers and shippers and international freight haulers. These managers are also responsible for compliance with the various legal requirements of international trade.

Career Path. Entry-level employees assist import-export managers in performing their functions. Import-export managers are usually middle-management positions reporting to an international manager.

Salary. Salaries for import-export managers vary according to the responsibilities of the specific position. They also vary between companies and industries. An average for import-export managers was between $23,000 and $35,000.

International Manager

Companies typically set up a separate international unit to handle overseas affairs. The international manager is the chief executive for this unit and has overall responsibility for its operations.

Job Description. The exact job requirements for an international management position vary from firm to firm. These people perform all the tasks expected of other managers at their particular level.

Career Path. International managers can be drawn from any department in an organization. They must be knowledgeable in international marketing, finance, law, and production. There are various levels of international management, usually ranging from middle management to top management. Some companies believe all candidates for top-management slots should have international experience.

Salary. Salaries of international managers vary by company and industry.

Chapter 5
Forms of Business
Ownership

Chapter 6
Entrepreneurship,
Small Business,
and Franchising

The Structure of American Business

Career Profile: Ron Targanski

After managing a retail store and running his own wholesale food business, Ron Targanski decided to do something different. Thus, he became an independent dealer for Kenosha, Wisconsin–based Snap-On Tools Co., the world's largest tool maker with more than $854 million in annual sales. Snap-On has more than 5,000 dealers operating as independent business owners who represent Snap-On exclusively.

It was the chance to remain an independent business owner that made Snap-On so attractive to Targanski. He was influenced by his high school dream of owning and operating his own business, as well as by the freedom he had enjoyed while running his own route. "I wanted to expand out of wholesale foods. I looked around at a number of things and found that Snap-On was the closest thing to my wholesale food business, in terms of the independence it offered," said Targanski. "Then I checked into the competition and I found that Snap-On was top of the line in the tool business."

Targanski considered franchising during his job search, but did not like the idea of paying a franchise fee. As an independent dealer for Snap-On, he pays no franchise or future fees. He works a route and deals individually with all his customers. He can also react to changes in the marketplace that might affect him negatively if he were a franchise operator, particularly in the food business. Targanski is able to keep a constant watch on his market while benefiting from Snap-On's reputation.

After researching Snap-On and its competitors, he applied for, and was granted, a dealership in the Detroit area. As a dealer, Targanski had to purchase an inventory of tools from Snap-On. The amount of inventory the company requires its new dealers to purchase depends on the routes they have. For the Novi route, the Detroit suburb in which Targanski operates, the market is shifting from the construction industry and other heavy tool users to auto repair shops and the like, so he had to purchase $55,000 worth of tools and equipment.

Snap-On arranged for him to lease a large step-up van built to company specifications and, for his first three weeks, the area field manager rode with Targanski on the route and helped him adjust to his new business. "He introduced me to the customers; . . . talked to me about financing programs; showed me how the tools work, how to report sales and place orders; and, in general, the way to approach the customers," said Targanski. To provide support, the field manager rides with dealers an average of once a month, is available to demonstrate products for customers, and can be called on to answer questions at any time.

Targanski has worked the Novi route since 1986. He meets with the field manager every other week to learn about additions to Snap-On's line of more than 10,000 tools, and to discuss new promotions or any problems he may be having. Besides price promotions, Snap-On provides dealers with catalogs to distribute to customers and national advertising in various forms.

Targanski received an associate's degree in marketing and applied management from Schoolcraft Community College. The course work gave him a good base of knowledge for business in general, and the self-discipline needed to operate a business independently. Marketing and sales classes have been the most helpful to him in running his business. "My sales class helped me to develop personally, with attitude development and personal management habits," said Targanski. "Sales abilities are very important: A product is never bought and a profit is never generated without a sale. Marketing really helped me to see business broken down into its separate functions and to see how those individual functions can be integrated to create different kinds of businesses."

Targanski spends five days a week on his route, working between eight and twelve hours a day. He does his paperwork and cleans his truck on Saturdays. He also takes courses and seminars on various topics that interest him, such as financial management or sales-related topics. This has been a key to Targanski's success, according to Don Ryktarsyk, who was one of his professors at Schoolcraft. "Ron did not stop his learning process upon the completion of his academic degree: He has developed for himself a process of discovery which has benefited him . . . and more than anything else, he has learned the habit of applying what he was taught."

Photo source: Courtesy of Ron Targanski and Jack Kausch Photography.

Forms of Business Ownership

Learning Goals

1. To identify and explain the three basic forms of business ownership.

2. To outline the advantages and disadvantages of sole proprietorships.

3. To compare the advantages and disadvantages of partnerships.

4. To differentiate between general partnerships and limited partnerships.

5. To outline the advantages and disadvantages of corporations.

6. To discuss how a corporation is organized and operated.

7. To differentiate among vertical, horizontal, and conglomerate mergers.

8. To identify the recent trends influencing corporate organizations.

9. To explain the differences among private ownership, public ownership, and collective ownership (cooperatives).

As advertising agency employees, Charles Hanley and George Schubert each received a 7 percent ownership share of the firm. But since each of five other key employees also held 7 percent of the equity and the agency's founder retained a controlling 51 percent, Hanley and Schubert's minority ownership gave them little clout in company decisions.

One day during a meeting, Hanley noticed the founder's teenage son cutting the grass outside. With several other minority owners present, Hanley observed: "We're going to end up working for the kid cutting the grass." This comment helped end Hanley and Schubert's careers with the agency.

The duo then decided to set up Light & Power Productions Inc., a Scotia, New York–based events-management and audiovisual service firm. Hanley and Schubert established their company as a corporation, a form of business organization whose assets and liabilities are differentiated from those of its owners. Remembering their experiences as minority owners, the pair realized the importance of keeping good employees. So in 1977, even before they launched their firm, Hanley and Schubert signed an agreement called the "Plan of '88," which gave their employees the option to buy the company as of October 1, 1988.

The price was set at two times the corporation's retained earnings with a $300,000 limit on the retained earnings. (Retained earnings are the undistributed profits of a business.) The purchase could be handled with a 50 percent down payment, with the balance financed over seven years. Hanley and Schu-

bert set up an employee pension and profit-sharing plan that could be used to finance the takeover and agreed not to start a competitive enterprise.

The new firm's business plan complemented the founders' personal financial plans by providing college educations for their children. But the plan was also designed to attract good people. Hanley put it this way: "We wanted a dedicated cadre of employees who would think long term, so we decided not just to hire employees, but to put them in business."

The plan proved to be a success. The five original employees were still working for Light & Power Productions on October 1, 1988. Over the 11-year period, only one employee quit. The firm's labor force is so dedicated it once recommended a 10 percent pay cut for itself.

Light & Power Productions is now a $2.5 million company with

16 employees. Its retained earnings as of fiscal 1987 were $300,000. While the Tax Reform Act of 1986 gave the employees a few anxious moments regarding their ability to borrow against pension and profit-sharing funds, once these issues were resolved the company was sold to its employees on the schedule originally specified in the "Plan of '88."

The case of Light & Power Productions illustrates the importance of determining the form of business ownership both today and in the future. In this instance, the corporate format proved a suitable vehicle for accomplishing the founders' objectives for their company.[1] Selecting an appropriate type of ownership is a key business decision. This topic is expanded in the chapter that follows.

Photo source: Courtesy of Light & Power Productions, Inc.

Chapter Overview

Selecting a legal form of business ownership is a complex and critical decision for the owners of any organization. Every business, be it Apple Computer Inc. or the neighborhood pizza restaurant, must choose the legal form of business ownership that best meets its needs.

Various factors must be considered when choosing a form of business ownership. Some of these varibles include ease of formation, financial liability, availability of financial resources and management skills, taxes, the ability to raise capital, and the personal interests of those involved.

This chapter describes the advantages and disadvantages of the three major forms of private business ownership — sole proprietorships, partnerships, and corporations — and discusses alternative forms of public and collective ownership. It also explains how corporations are organized and operated and discusses trends in corporate ownership.

Forms of Private Ownership

The most widely used form of private ownership in the United States is the sole proprietorship, an organization owned and usually operated by a single individual. The 11 million sole proprietorships account for 70 percent of all businesses. Corporations — legal entities separate from the owners — rank second, with 20 percent using this form of ownership. The smallest segment, used by 10 percent of businesses, is partnerships, organizations operated by two or more people as owners. Figure 5.1 shows the ownership structure of U.S. business. Each form of private ownership has unique advantages and disadvantages.

Sole Proprietorships

sole proprietorship
Ownership (and usually operation) of an organization by one person.

The original form of business ownership is the **sole proprietorship**, an organization owned and usually operated by a single individual. It is also the simplest type of ownership because there is no legal distinction between the sole proprietor as an individual and as a business owner. The business's assets, earnings, and debts are those of the owner. Although sole proprietorships are used in a variety of industries, they are concentrated primarily among small businesses such as repair shops, small retail outlets, and service organizations.

Advantages of Sole Proprietorships Sole proprietorships offer advantages not found in other forms of business ownership — namely, retention of all profits, ease of formation and dissolution, and ownership flexibility. All profits (and losses) of a sole proprietorship belong to the owner (except that part going to the government for personal income taxes). If the firm is very profitable, this can be an important advantage. Retention of all profits and responsibility for all losses provide sole proprietors with the incentive to operate the business as efficiently as possible.

A minimum of legal requirements make it easy to go into and out of business. Usually the only legal requirements for starting a sole proprietorship are registering the business or trade name at the county courthouse (this guarantees that two firms do not use the same names) and taking out any necessary licenses (restaurants, motels, retail stores, and many repair shops require certain kinds

Figure 5.1   The Ownership Structure of U.S. Business

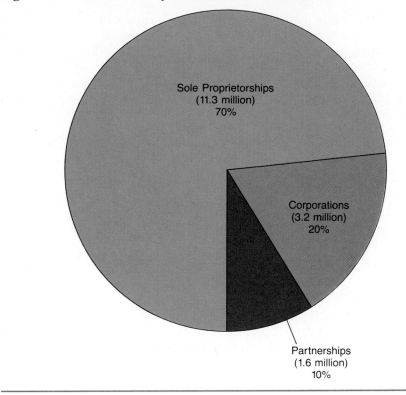

Source: U.S. Department of Commerce, Bureau of the Census, *Statistical Abstract of the United States, 1988,* 108th edition (Washington, D.C.: U.S. Government Printing Office, 1987), p. 495.

of licenses). Some occupational licenses require a firm to carry specific types of insurance, such as liability coverage.

The ease of discontinuing a business set up as a sole proprietorship is an attractive feature for certain types of enterprises. This is particularly true for businesses that are set up for a limited time period and are involved in a minimum of transactions — for example, the business created by an individual to organize a rock concert at a local sports arena.

Ownership flexibility is another advantage of sole proprietorships. The owner can make management decisions without consulting others. He or she can take prompt action when needed and can preserve trade secrets where appropriate. Such flexibility can also contribute to the proprietor's personal satisfaction, as exemplified by the common saying, "I like being my own boss."

Disadvantages of Sole Proprietorships   Some disadvantages include unlimited financial liability (except in cases of bankruptcy), limitations of financing, management deficiencies, and lack of continuity. Because there is no legal distinction between the business and its owner, the sole proprietor is financially liable for all debts of the business. If the firm's assets cannot cover its debts, the owner is required to pay them from personal funds. A sole proprietor may even be forced to sell personal property — home, furniture, and automobile — to pay business debts. The unlimited liability of a sole proprietorship can mean financial ruin to an owner if the business fails.

Chris Weber, owner of Plant Interiors by Weber in Dayton, Ohio, is one of many self-employed people who operate businesses from their homes as sole proprietorships. Weber maintains many of the plants he sells and leases to local businesses at a greenhouse in his home.

Photo source: Courtesy of Chris Weber.

The financial resources of a sole proprietorship are limited to the owner's personal funds and money that can be borrowed. Sole proprietors usually do not have access to large amounts of capital, because they are typically small businesspeople with limited personal wealth. Banks and other financial institutions are sometimes reluctant to risk giving loans to such small organizations. Financing limitations can, in turn, retard expansion of the sole proprietor's business.

The manager of the sole proprietorship is usually the owner. This person must be able to handle a wide range of managerial and operations activities. As the firm grows, the owner may be unable to perform all duties with equal effectiveness and may find it difficult to attract managerial personnel. Sole proprietorships often offer little hope of promotion (except for the owner's offspring), fewer fringe benefits than can be found in other organizations, and less employment security. But they do offer employees an excellent chance to learn about a particular type of enterprise.

Finally, sole proprietorships lack long-term continuity. Death, bankruptcy, retirement, or change in personal interests can terminate a business organized as a sole proprietorship.

Partnerships

partnership
Two or more persons who operate a business as co-owners.

A partnership is another form of private business ownership. The *Uniform Partnership Act,* which regulates this form of business ownership in most states, defines a **partnership** as an association of two or more persons who operate a business as co-owners by voluntary legal agreement. Partnerships have been a traditional form of ownership for professionals offering a service, such as doctors, lawyers, and dentists. Because most states have liberalized the requirement that professional service groups be partnerships, some professionals have incorporated, using the designations P.C. (professional corporation), S.C. (service corporation), and P.S. (public service).

A **general partnership** is one in which all partners carry on the business as co-owners and are liable for the business's debts. Some states also permit a **limited partnership** composed of one or more general partners and one or more limited partners. A limited partner's liability is limited to the amount of capital contributed to the partnership, provided the person plays no active role in the business. The sale of limited partnership shares is a common way of financing businesses today. Many professional sports teams are organized as limited partnerships. The Milwaukee Brewers, for example, is a limited partnership, with 17 partners owning the club.

A relatively new — and controversial — form of business ownership is the **master limited partnership**. Firms set up as master limited partnerships function like corporations and publicly trade stock on the major exchanges. But in some master limited partnerships, the earnings are taxed only once, to the partners. This form of ownership, which dates to 1981, was concentrated in the oil and real estate industries until passage of the Tax Reform Act of 1986, which increased the corporate tax burden. Since then, these partnerships spread to other industries and are used by both large and small firms. The Boston Celtics basketball team, Burger King, Angell Care (a nursing home company), and UDC-Universal Development (a home-building firm) are examples of master limited partnerships.[2]

A **joint venture**, another type of partnership, involves two or more parties forming a temporary business for a specific undertaking — for example, a group of investors who import a shipment of high-quality wine from France and then resell it to wine dealers in the United States. Joint ventures are often used in real estate investments. As we discussed in Chapter 4, this type of partnership is often used in international business ventures.

Advantages of Partnerships

Partnerships offer ease of formation, complementary management skills, and expanded financial capability. It is relatively easy to establish a partnership. As with sole proprietorships, the legal requirements usually involve registering the business name and taking out the required licenses. Limited partnerships must also comply with state legislation based on the *Uniform Limited Partnership Act,* which spells out the requirements for this type of business organization.

It is usually wise to establish written articles of partnership specifying the details of the partners' agreement. This clarifies the relationship within the firm and protects the original agreement upon which the partnership is based.

In some cases, however, partnerships are formed — and survive — on the basis of mutual trust. In 1962, for example, Frankie Valli, a barber, and Bob Gaudio, a printing plant employee, formed the Four Seasons Partnership on nothing more than a handshake. At the time, their musical group, the Four Seasons, performed on weekends in small clubs and bowling alleys. Since then, the partners have earned more than $50 million, including profits from hit songs such as "Sherry" and "Short Shorts." The partners continue to split their profits down the middle, even though their careers have taken off in different directions. Valli continues to perform as the lead singer in the group, while Gaudio

general partnership
Partnership in which all partners are liable for the business's debts.

limited partnership
Partnership composed of one or more general partners and one or more partners with limited liability.

master limited partnership
A limited partnership that is publicly traded and functions like a corporation.

joint venture
Partnership formed for a specific undertaking.

Complementary skills, mutual trust, and the lack of interpersonal conflicts have helped sustain the Four Seasons Partnership between singer Frankie Valli (left) and composer-producer Bob Gaudio for almost three decades.

Photo source: © Bill Nation/Picture Group.

stopped performing with the group in the early 1970s to pursue a career as a composer, pianist, arranger, and producer.[3]

A common reason for setting up a partnership is the availability of complementary managerial skills. If the people involved were to operate as sole proprietors, their firms might lack some managerial skills, but by combining as a partnership, each person can offer his or her own unique managerial ability. For example, a general partnership might be formed by an engineer, an accountant, and a marketer who plan to produce and sell a product or service. If additional managerial talent is needed, it may be easier to attract people as partners than as employees.

Partnerships offer expanded financial capability through money invested by each of the partners. They also usually have greater access to borrowed funds than do sole proprietorships. Because each general partner is subject to unlimited financial liability, financial institutions are often willing to advance loans to partnerships. Involvement of additional owners may also make available additional sources of loans.

Disadvantages of Partnerships   Like other forms of business ownership, partnerships have some disadvantages, including unlimited financial liability (except in cases of limited partners), interpersonal conflicts, lack of continuity, and complexity of dissolution. Each general partner is responsible for the debts of the firm, and each is legally liable for the actions of the others. This holds true not only for debts in the name of the partnership but also for lawsuits resulting from any partner's malpractice. As with sole proprietorships, general partners are required to pay the total debts of a partnership from private sources if necessary. In other words, if the debts of a partnership exceed its assets, the creditors will turn to the personal wealth of the general partners. When Finley, Kumble, Wagner, Heine, Underberg, Manley, Myerson & Casey — the seventh-largest law firm in the United States — went bankrupt in 1988, the more than 200 law partners in the firm were held personally liable for the firm's $83 million in bank debt, and four banks filed suit to collect the money from the partners' personal funds.[4] If only one general partner has any personal wealth, that person may be required to pay all the debts of the partnership. Limited partners lose only the amount of capital they invested in the firm.

Interpersonal conflicts may also plague partnerships. All partnerships, from law firms to rock groups, face the problem of personal and business disagreements among the participants. If these conflicts cannot be resolved, it is sometimes best to dissolve the partnership.

Continuity of a partnership is disrupted when a partner is no longer able or willing to continue in the business. The partnership agreement is then terminated and a final settlement is made.

It is not as easy to dissolve a partnership as it is to dissolve a sole proprietorship. Instead of simply withdrawing the business's funds, the partner who wants to leave must find someone (perhaps an existing partner or an outsider acceptable to the remaining partners) to buy his or her interest in the firm. Sometimes it is difficult to transfer a partnership investment to another party.

Corporations   John Marshall

A **corporation** is a legal organization whose assets and liabilities are separate from those of its owner(s). A corporation can be formed only with the approval of the appropriate government agency. Corporate ownership is represented by shares of stock in the firm. (Types of stock and their issuance are discussed later in this chapter.) Anyone who holds one or more shares of a corporation's stock is considered a part-owner of the business. Shares can usually be bought and sold readily on the open market. Figure 5.2 shows a common stock certificate.

corporation
A legal entity with authority to act and have liability separate and apart from its owners.

Artificial Beings existing only in Contemplation of law

Most Corporations Are Small   Not all corporations are large-scale enterprises. The corporate form is used by many small companies. In fact, almost 75 percent of all active corporations in the United States have under $500,000 in business receipts.[5] The corporate form is becoming increasingly popular among smaller firms. The cost of incorporating, including legal fees, is now only about $600 in most states.[6]

Advantages of Corporations   Corporate ownership offers considerable advantages, including limited financial risk, specialized management skills, expanded financial capability, and economies of larger-scale operation.

Because corporations are considered separate legal entities, the stockholders (owners) have limited financial risk. If the firm fails, they can lose only the amount they have invested. Owners' personal funds cannot be touched by creditors of the corporation. The limited risk of corporate ownership is clearly designated in the names used by firms throughout the world. U.S. corporations often use the designation "Incorporated" or "Inc." Corporate enterprises in Canada and the United Kingdom use "Limited" or "Ltd." In Australia, limited risk is

Figure 5.2   Example of a Stock Certificate

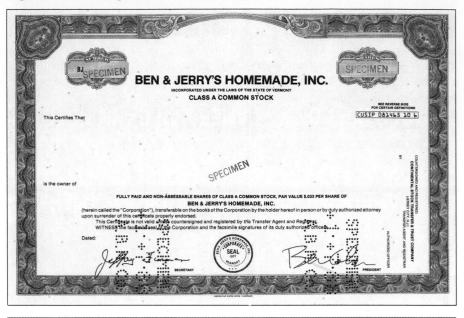

Source: Courtesy of Ben & Jerry's Homemade, Inc.

shown by "Proprietary Limited" or "Pty. Ltd." "Aktie Bolag," or "stock company," is the designation used throughout Scandinavia. This limited risk is the most significant advantage of corporate ownership over other forms of ownership.

The managerial skills of sole proprietorships and partnerships are usually confined to the abilities of the owners. By contrast, corporations can offer longer-term career opportunities for qualified people with specialized managerial skills. Employees may be able to concentrate their efforts in some specialized activity or functional area because corporations are sometimes larger than partnerships or sole proprietorships.

Expanded financial capability, another advantage, allows a corporation to grow and become more efficient than it would be if the business had been set up as a sole proprietorship or partnership. Because corporate ownership is divided into many small units (shares), it is usually easier for a firm to attract capital. People with large or relatively small resources can invest their savings in a corporation by buying shares of stock. Corporate size and stability may make it easier for corporations to borrow additional funds. Large, financially strong corporations can often borrow money at lower interest rates than can smaller businesses.

The larger-scale operation permitted by corporate ownership has several advantages. Employees can specialize in the work activities they perform best. Many projects can be internally financed by transferring money from one part of the corporation to another. Longer manufacturing runs usually mean more efficient production and lower prices, thus attracting more customers. Table 5.1 lists the largest U.S. industrial corporations.

Disadvantages of Corporations   Some disadvantages are also inherent in corporate ownership. Corporations are usually at a tax disadvantage, and they often face a multitude of legal restrictions.

Table 5.1   The 10 Largest U.S. Industrial Corporations by Sales and Profits

Ranking	Company	Sales (in billions)	Ranking	Company	Profits (in billions)
1	General Motors	$101.8	1	IBM	$5.3
2	Exxon	76.4	2	Exxon	4.8
3	Ford Motor	71.6	3	Ford Motor	4.6
4	IBM	54.2	4	General Motors	3.6
5	Mobil	51.2	5	General Electric	2.9
6	General Electric	39.3	6	AT&T	2.0
7	Texaco	34.4	7	Philip Morris	1.8
8	AT&T	33.6	8	Du Pont	1.8
9	Du Pont	30.5	9	Amoco	1.4
10	Chrysler	26.3	10	Chrysler	1.3

Source: "The Fortune 500 Largest U.S. Industrial Corporations," *Fortune,* April 25, 1988, p. D11.

As separate legal entities, corporations are subject to federal and state income taxes. Corporate earnings are taxed, and then any **dividends** — payments to stockholders from earnings — are also taxed on an individual basis. From the viewpoint of the stockholder who receives dividends, this constitutes double taxation of corporate earnings. By contrast, the earnings of sole proprietorships and partnerships are taxed only once because they are treated as personal income of the firm's owner or owners. Some states provide tax relief to corporations meeting certain size and stock ownership requirements by recognizing them as **S corporations** (formerly called *Subchapter S corporations*). These corporations can elect to be taxed for federal purposes as partnerships while maintaining the advantages of corporations. The *Subchapter S Revision Act of 1982* set the maximum number of corporate shareholders at 35. The act also required that a shareholder must hold at least 50 percent of the stock to change the company's corporate status.

Corporate ownership faces a multitude of legal problems not encountered by sole proprietorships. Corporate charters restrict the type of business activity in which the corporation can engage. Corporations must also file various reports about their operations. The number of laws and regulations affecting corporations has increased dramatically in recent years.

Table 5.2 summarizes the advantages and disadvantages of sole proprietorships, partnerships, and corporations.

dividends
Payments to stockholders from a corporation's earnings.

S corporations
Corporations that are taxed as a partnership while maintaining the advantages of a corporation.

Organizing and Operating a Corporation

Suppose you decide to start a business and you believe the corporation is the best form of ownership for your enterprise. How should you set up this corporation?

Your first step should be to consult an attorney. While it may be possible to incorporate the business by yourself, most people hire a lawyer so they can be assured that all necessary requirements are met.

The second step is to select a state in which to incorporate. This is an extremely important decision because regulations, incorporation costs, and other fees, taxes, and ownership rights vary widely among the 50 states. If you intend to operate primarily within the Commonwealth of Pennsylvania, for example, you should probably incorporate in that state. But if your principal business will be in Burlington County, New Jersey, you should probably become a

Table 5.2   Advantages and Disadvantages of Each Form of Private Ownership

Form of Ownership	Advantages	Disadvantages
Sole Proprietorship	1. Retention of all profits 2. Ease of formation and dissolution 3. Ownership flexibility	1. Unlimited financial liability 2. Financing limitations 3. Management deficiencies 4. Lack of continuity
Partnership	1. Ease of formation 2. Complementary management skills 3. Expanded financial capacity	1. Unlimited financial liability 2. Interpersonal conflicts 3. Lack of continuity 4. Complex dissolution
Corporation	1. Limited financial liability 2. Specialized management skills 3. Expanded financial capacity 4. Economies of larger-scale operation	1. Difficult and costly ownership form to establish and dissolve 2. Tax disadvantage 3. Legal restrictions

New Jersey corporation. In addition to the convenience of incorporating in your home state, it may be advisable if the business involves state-awarded contracts, since many state governments favor local firms. The selection of a state in which to incorporate should be made only after careful research.

Classifying Corporations

domestic corporation
Firm doing business in the state in which it is incorporated.

foreign corporation
Firm doing business in a state other than the one in which it is incorporated.

alien corporation
Firm organized in one country but operating in another.

Corporations can be classified as domestic, foreign, or alien. A firm is considered a **domestic corporation** in the state in which it is incorporated. If it expects to do business in states other than the state of incorporation, it registers as a **foreign corporation** in those states. A firm incorporated in one nation but operating in another is known as an **alien corporation** in the operating nation.

Johnson Products Inc., the well-known maker of personal-care products for African-Americans, operates as a domestic, foreign, and alien corporation. The company is incorporated in Delaware (domestic corporation), but its headquarters are in Chicago, where it operates a large plant (foreign corporation). The firm also operates overseas (alien corporation), with a sales and distribution center in Great Britain and a 40 percent-owned plant in Nigeria.

Incorporating the Business

Most states designate a certain official or state agency, usually the secretary of state, to administer corporations. Blank articles of incorporation, corporation charters, or incorporation certificates (depending on the terminology used in a particular state) can be obtained from this official or agency. These forms must be filed with the appropriate state agency.

Corporate charters of the various states usually include similar information. Michigan articles of incorporation show the corporate name, corporate purpose, authorized capital stock, registered office and agent, and name of the incorporator. New York's certificate of incorporation shows the name of the proposed corporation, its purposes, its location, the number of shares of stock it will have the authority to issue, the address to which any process against the corporation

These are some of the stockholders attending the annual meeting of H. J. Heinz Company. During the meeting, stockholders elected 15 members to the board of directors, elected Coopers & Lybrand as auditors for Heinz, and approved a company stock option plan.

Photo source: Courtesy of H. J. Heinz Company.

should be sent, and the incorporator's name. Similarly, Missouri requires the corporate name; address and name of initial agents; number, class, and par value of the stock; limitations and special rights; name and address of incorporator; board of directors information; corporate duration; and corporate purposes.

Stockholders

Stockholders are those people who acquire the shares of the corporation; they are its owners. Some corporations, such as family businesses, are owned by relatively few stockholders. In such a firm — known as a **close corporation** — the stockholders also control and manage the corporation's activities. But in a larger corporation, the ownership is diversified.

General Motors, for example, has over 1 million stockholders. These people obviously have little individual control over this giant corporation, but there is a ready market for their shares if they decide to sell. Adequate markets are available for the stock of large corporations, so the individual stockholder can sell the stock more easily than if the firm were a small corporation with no public market for its stock.

Corporations usually hold an annual stockholders' meeting during which management presents reports on the firm's activities. Any decisions requiring stockholder approval are put to a vote at this time. The election of certain direc-

stockholders
People who acquire the shares of, and therefore own, a corporation.

close corporation
Corporation owned by relatively few stockholders who control and manage its activities.

preferred stock
Stock that has the first claim to the corporation's assets after all debts have been paid.

common stock
Stock whose owners have only a residual claim to the firm's assets but who have voting rights in the corporation.

proxy
Authorization by stockholders for someone else to vote their shares.

cumulative voting
Practice of enabling stockholders to combine their votes in electing directors.

tors and the choice of an independent public accountant are two matters that must be voted on at nearly all stockholders' meetings.

Stock is usually classified as common or preferred. Owners of **preferred stock** have the first claim to the corporation's assets after all debts have been paid, but they usually do not have voting rights at the stockholders' meetings. Owners of **common stock** have only a residual claim on the firm's assets (after everyone else has been paid), but they do have voting rights in the corporate system. When a vote is taken, each share of common stock is worth one vote. For example, a person with 225 shares has 225 votes. If people cannot attend the stockholders' meetings, they can give their **proxy** authorization to vote the shares to someone who will attend. Many corporate boards can vote as they choose if the proxies are not returned, thus perpetuating the board of directors' positions.

Small stockholders generally have little influence on corporate management. A holder of 200,000 shares has 200,000 votes for each director, while the holder of 50 shares has only 50 votes for each director. As a result, the issue of cumulative voting has come before many stockholders' meetings. **Cumulative voting** allows smaller stockholders to have more influence on the selection of directors by enabling them to combine their votes. If, say, three director positions are to be filled, cumulative voting allows the holder of 50 shares the option of casting 150 votes (50 × 3) for one person rather than 50 votes apiece for all three positions.

Board of Directors — *approve / disapprove major expenditures*

board of directors
Governing body of a corporation elected by the stockholders.

The stockholders elect a **board of directors**, which becomes the governing authority for the corporation. The board elects its own officers — usually a chairperson, a vice-chairperson, and a secretary. Most states require a minimum of three directors and at least one annual meeting of the board. Most corporations, other than small or closely held ones, have large boards of directors that meet at least quarterly.

The board of directors must authorize major transactions involving the corporation and must set overall corporate policy. It is concerned with changes in areas such as the firm's stock, financing arrangements, dividends, and major shifts in corporate holdings. But its most important role is that of hiring the corporation's chief executive officer (CEO). This person then hires other top executives. The selection of other managers is left to those executives.

In some corporations, particularly smaller ones, the board of directors plays an active role in the management of the organization, but in most corporations it acts more as a review panel for management decisions. Most boards are composed of both corporation executives and **outside directors**, people not employed by the organization. Sometimes the corporation president is also the chairman of the board.

outside directors
Members of the board who are not employed by the organization.

Outside directors benefit firms in several ways. They bring to the board a diversity in professional backgrounds and personal qualifications, which provides a balance of perspectives in governing the corporation. Because outside directors are independent of day-to-day managerial operations, they can question, challenge, and stimulate management. For these reasons, some firms choose to have their boards made up primarily of outside directors. Retailer Dayton Hudson Corporation, for example, has a 12-member board, and 10 of the members are outside directors, including people from such diverse organi-

Figure 5.3 How a Corporation Works

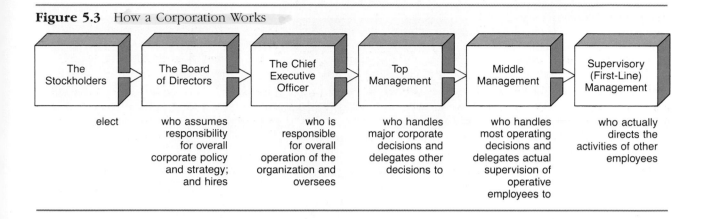

The Stockholders	The Board of Directors	The Chief Executive Officer	Top Management	Middle Management	Supervisory (First-Line) Management
elect	who assumes responsibility for overall corporate policy and strategy; and hires	who is responsible for overall operation of the organization and oversees	who handles major corporate decisions and delegates other decisions to	who handles most operating decisions and delegates actual supervision of operative employees to	who actually directs the activities of other employees

zations as 3M Company, Xerox Corporation, Cray Research Inc. (developer and marketer of supercomputers), The Aspen Institute for Humanistic Services, and Hallmark Cards Inc. Kenneth Macke, chief executive officer of Dayton Hudson, also serves as chairman of the board.[7]

Management

Top management, including the chief executive officer, is responsible for the actual operation of the corporation, subject to board approval. It makes most of the major corporate decisions and delegates other tasks to middle management, which in turn delegates to supervisory management. Top management is responsible to the board of directors and often sits on the board. State legislation usually defines the duties of major corporate officers. Other executive posts are created by the board. The corporate organization and its operation, as outlined in Figure 5.3, show the types of decisions and activities at each level in the organization.

Subsidiary Corporations

When all or a majority of a corporation's stock is owned by another corporation, it is a **subsidiary** of that corporation. The owner is usually called the **parent company**. Typically, management of the subsidiary is appointed by the chief executive of the parent company, subject to the approval of the parent's board.

Many well-known corporations are actually subsidiaries of other corporations. Weight Watchers International, Star-Kist Foods, and Ore-Ida Foods are subsidiaries of H. J. Heinz Company. The Dryden Press, publisher of this textbook, is a division of Holt, Rinehart and Winston, which is a subsidiary of the parent firm, Harcourt Brace Jovanovich Inc.

subsidiary
Corporation with all or a majority of its stock owned by another corporation.

parent company
Corporation that owns all or a majority of another corporation's stock (called a subsidiary).

Trends in Corporate Ownership

Corporate ownership has been in a state of flux in recent years. Many well-known firms have become parts of other corporations, or have been split into smaller units. One major trend has been the increased number of mergers and

The Coca-Cola Company's acquisition of the worldwide marketing and distribution rights for BreakMate is an example of a forward vertical merger. Designed for installation in smaller offices and other workplaces, BreakMate is a compact fountain dispensing system made by Siemens, a West German consumer appliance manufacturer. With BreakMate, Coca-Cola USA has tapped a major new market for the distribution of its soft drink syrups.

Photo source: Courtesy of Coca-Cola USA. "Coca-Cola" and "Coke" are trademarks of The Coca-Cola Company and used with permission.

acquisitions among U.S. companies. In 1985, for example, there were 3,428 mergers and acquisitions; in 1986, 4,314; and in 1987, 3,469. For 1987, that translates into 13 mergers and acquisitions for each U.S. working day.[8]

merger
Two or more firms that combine to form one company.

A **merger** refers to two or more firms that combine to form one company. For example, Tenneco's JI Case division merged with the agricultural division of International Harvester to form Case IH. The new company is the second largest farm equipment manufacturer in the United States and a leading maker of construction equipment.

acquisition
One firm acquiring the property and assuming the obligations of another firm.

An **acquisition** occurs when one firm purchases the property and assumes the obligations of another company. Examples are Chrysler Corporation's acquisition of American Motors and USAir's purchase of Piedmont Aviation. In recent years, the purchase of U.S. firms by foreign buyers has escalated. In fact, the largest acquisition in 1987 was British Petroleum's $7.6 billion purchase of Standard Oil Company. In another major transaction, Blue Arrow, Britain's largest employment agency group, bought American-owned Manpower, the world's largest temporary-help service.[9]

Types of Mergers

The three categories of corporate mergers are vertical, horizontal, and conglomerate. A **vertical merger** occurs between firms at different levels in the production-marketing process. Backward vertical mergers occur when a firm acquires a supplier. The purchase of Gulf Printing Company by Southwestern Bell Corporation provides backward vertical integration of the telephone company's directory publishing business. Forward vertical integration occurs when a producer acquires a firm involved in the distribution channel for its particular industry. To complement its cable television distribution, the Home Shopping Network Inc. broadened its audience reach by acquiring broadcast television stations in major U.S. television markets. The primary purposes of vertical mergers are to assure either adequate raw materials and supplies or distribution outlets.

vertical merger
Merger that occurs between firms at different levels in the production and marketing process.

Genee(Harold)ITT (handwritten)

Crystler buying ford (handwritten)

A **horizontal merger** occurs between firms in the same industry that wish to diversify and offer a complete product line. Reebok International, for example, acquired Rockport, Avia Group International, John A. Frye Company, and Ellesse North America to broaden its offerings in athletic footwear and sports apparel.

McDonalds / Mtgomery ward / Chrystler (handwritten)

A **conglomerate merger** is a merger of unrelated firms. An example is Eastman Kodak's purchase of Sterling Drug, a pharmaceutical firm. The primary purposes of most conglomerate mergers are diversification, rapid sales growth, and attempts to profitably use a cash surplus, which might otherwise make the holder a tempting target for a takeover effort.

diversified (handwritten)

Although conglomerate mergers were popular in the 1960s and 1970s, fewer corporations are using this growth strategy today. Some firms that formed conglomerate mergers did not have the management skills needed to operate firms in unrelated industries. An example is Mobil Corporation's attempt to diversify beyond its oil operations by buying retailer Montgomery Ward & Company in 1976. In 1988, Mobil sold the retailing firm. Current acquisition patterns indicate firms are focusing more on vertical and horizontal mergers.[10]

Friendly and Unfriendly Mergers

Most mergers can be classified as friendly in that both parties agree to the revised organization. However, in some instances the merger offer is unsolicited and unwanted: the so-called *unfriendly merger*. Carl Icahn's move to take over TWA Airlines is an example.

Unfriendly takeovers typically begin with a **tender offer**, in which a party (usually called the "raider") offers to buy all or a portion of a firm's stock at a premium over its current price. Management of the targeted company usually counters with a variety of defensive actions ranging from pleas to stockholders not to sell to the filing of legal challenges. One method designed to make a firm a less desirable target to a raider is referred to as taking a **poison pill**, whereby management allows stockholders to buy shares of stock well below the market value. Another protective strategy is referred to as **shark repellent**, whereby management requires a large majority of stockholders to approve the takeover. Still another strategy is to look for a friendly merger with another firm (the so-called **white knight**) that will retain current management and probably allow the acquired firm to operate as an independent unit. Finally, some firms ward off raiders by paying out company capital to stockholders and replacing it with borrowed money. By increasing its debt burden, a firm becomes a much less attractive takeover target. This method, referred to as a *leveraged recapitalization,* is discussed in more detail in Chapter 20.

Corporate managements also seek to protect their own interests with elaborate severance packages that are available if top executives lose their jobs through an acquisition or merger. Such a severance package is called a **golden parachute**. Terrence Elkes, chief executive officer of Viacom, received an estimated $25 million golden parachute after Sumner Redstone acquired his firm.[11]

Sometimes, the outside party solicits proxies in an attempt to take over a firm's board of directors. Management, of course, also works at soliciting proxies from stockholders. These rival efforts are known as a **proxy fight**.

There are arguments on both sides of unfriendly takeover attempts. Management often argues that corporate raiders are more concerned with short-term stock gains than they are with actually running the company. The outside group,

horizontal merger
Merger between firms in the same industry.

conglomerate merger
Merger of unrelated firms.

tender offer
When someone offers to buy all or a portion of a firm's stock at a premium over its current price.

poison pill
A takeover deterrent whereby stockholders are allowed to buy additional shares below market value.

shark repellent
A provision that requires that a large majority of stockholders approve any takeover.

white knight
A friendly takeover whereby the acquired firm remains independent and keeps its existing management.

golden parachute
An executive severance package available to those who lose their jobs through acquisition or merger.

proxy fight
A situation where both management and an outside party seek control of a firm through solicitation of proxies.

by contrast, suggests that management is more concerned with protecting its own jobs than with benefiting the stockholders. Raiders point out that they offer more than the market price for the firm's stock.

Some raiders believe many corporations are poorly managed and their take-over attempts are forcing corporate managers to operate more efficiently and profitably. When Carl Icahn took over TWA in 1986 and became its chief executive officer, the airline had lost $62 million. By the end of 1987, TWA showed a profit of $240 million, the best reported earnings in TWA's history. Icahn says of the turnaround, "At TWA I went in and did some productive cost cutting. Everybody was at a kind of party for years. I saved $6 million on insurance while keeping the same coverage. I saved another $30 million on advertising without hurting our visibility. We cut out 24 nonprofitable routes and introduced 31 profitable ones. We bought Ozark to build our domestic business."[12]

Alternatives to Mergers

Contradictory trends are also evident in today's corporate environment. Some of the most significant are divestiture, taking a firm private, leveraged buyouts, and employee ownership. Many of these trends are related.

divestiture
The selling off of a corporation's divisions or units.

Divestiture   The selling off of a corporation's divisions or units is known as **divestiture**. In 1985, CBS Inc. embarked on a divestiture program in an effort to refocus the firm's resources on its core business of radio and television broadcasting. In 1986, CBS sold its music, educational, and professional book publishing operations to other firms. A year later, CBS sold its Magazine Division to a purchasing group made up of the division's top management. The worldwide operations of the CBS/Record Group was sold to Sony Corporation in 1988.[13]

Corporations divest for a variety of reasons: to raise cash, to remove units that are not closely matched to the firm's other businesses, and to cut operating losses. Sometimes these units are converted into private firms, purchased via a leveraged buyout arrangement, or acquired by their employees.

Taking a Firm Private   Sometimes management or a group of major stockholders offer to buy or otherwise acquire all of a firm's stock. If the bid is successful, all of the firm's stock is then privately held and no longer publicly traded. This scenario is known as "taking a firm private."

More than 1,550 companies have gone private since 1981. Seven Up Company, for example, went private in 1986 when John Albers, the soft-drink manufacturer's chief executive officer, and an investor group bought the firm from Philip Morris.[14]

leveraged buyout (LBO)
The use of borrowed money to purchase a company or division.

Leveraged Buyouts   In a **leveraged buyout (LBO)**, a group of investors uses money borrowed from banks, investment companies, pension funds, and insurance firms to buy a company or division. The unit's assets are typically used as collateral for the loan, which can sometimes amount to 90 to 95 percent of the buyout price. Leveraged buyouts can be initiated by the organization's management or an outside party.

Leveraged buyouts have increased in recent years, many of them being initiated by leveraged buyout firms such as Kohlberg Kravis Roberts & Company, which has acquired more than 20 companies, including RJR Nabisco, Owens-

Figure 5.4   Advertisement of Avis's Employee Ownership

Illinois, Beatrice, Safeway, Motel 6, Red Lion Inns, Stop & Shop, and Duracell, Kraft's battery division. Its $25 billion purchase of RJR Nabisco in 1989 was the largest acquisition in the nation's history. Although KKR is a general partnership, each of its leveraged buyout deals is made through a limited partnership formed specifically for that deal.[15]

Most LBOs involve small firms. Of the 15 million U.S. businesses with yearly sales under $1 million, an estimated 1 in 5 changed hands in 1989. When Suellen and Daniel Kajdasz acquired a wholesale pizza-supply business in East Syracuse, New York, they put up only about 15 percent of the $275,000 purchase price. The rest of the funds were supplied by a local bank, with the firm's assets used as collateral.[16]

Employee Ownership   Employees of a plant or division sometimes buy a unit in order to preserve their jobs. A leveraged buyout is common in these situations. The corporate organization format is retained, but now the stockholders are also employees.

Many well-known firms, such as United Parcel Service, are employee owned. A recent example of a firm purchased by its employees is Avis Inc. The company featured some of the 11,000 employees who bought the car-rental agency in the advertisement in Figure 5.4. Employee ownership can give a firm a competitive edge because it motivates employees to higher levels of productivity. Avis Chairman Joseph Vittoria says employee ownership "is an absolute home run for a service business like ours."[17]

Public and Collective Ownership

While most business organizations are owned privately by individuals or groups of individuals, some are owned by either municipal, state, or federal governments, and some are owned collectively by a number of people.

Public Ownership

public ownership
An enterprise owned and operated by a governmental unit.

One alternative to private ownership is some form of **public ownership**, in which a government unit or its agency owns and operates an organization. Although public ownership is more common abroad, it is also used in the United States. For example, local governments own parking structures and water systems. The Pennsylvania Turnpike Authority operates a vital highway link across its state. The federal government established the Tennessee Valley Authority to provide electricity in that region, and the Federal Deposit Insurance Corporation insures bank savings accounts.

Sometimes public ownership comes about when private investors are unwilling to make investments because they believe the possibility of failure is too high. An example of this situation is the 1930s rural electrification program that significantly expanded utility lines in sparsely populated areas. At other times, public ownership replaces privately owned organizations that fail. Certain activities, such as municipal water systems, are considered so important to public welfare that they should not be entrusted to private ownership. Finally, some nations have used public ownership to foster competition by operating public companies as competitive business enterprises.

The Trend toward Privatization　In recent years, the move has clearly been away from public ownership. The prevailing trend has been toward *privatization,* or the performance of public functions by privately owned firms. Today, some public services like prisons and fire protection are provided by private companies. In addition, there have been proposals to turn publicly owned enterprises such as Washington's Dulles Airport and the Bonneville Power Administration over to private investors. As we discussed in Chapter 1, the privatization trend has also been evident outside the United States in countries such as the United Kingdom, France, and Canada.

Cooperatives

cooperative
Organization that is operated collectively by the owners.

Another alternative to private ownership is collective ownership of production, storage, transportation, and/or marketing activities. A **cooperative** is an organization whose owners band together to collectively operate all or part of their industries. They are often created by large numbers of small producers that want to be more competitive in the marketplace.

Figure 5.5 shows a segment of a television commercial featuring some owners of Blue Diamond Growers, an agricultural cooperative of 5,100 California almond growers. In the commercial, the owners are waist deep in 2.5 billion

Figure 5.5   Advertisement Featuring a Cooperative's Owners

Source: Courtesy of Blue Diamond Growers.

almond kernels. Their message — urging consumers to buy "A can a week, that's all we ask" — is designed to increase the consumption of Blue Diamond brand snack almonds in the United States. Other well-known cooperatives are Sunkist Growers, Associated Mills Producers, Gold Kist, CF Industries, Group Terminal Association, and Recreational Equipment Inc., the nation's largest consumer cooperative.

In most cooperatives, owners control their organization by electing a board of directors from the cooperative's members. The board then hires a team of professional managers to handle the business functions of the cooperative. The funds needed to operate cooperatives come from the owners, who usually pay an annual membership fee. Unlike stockholders who invest funds in a corporation to receive dividends, the owners of a cooperative invest funds to assure themselves of markets for their products or sources of supplies and services.[18]

The owners of Blue Diamond Growers, for example, support the cooperative's Almond Research Center, where food scientists develop new products and search for new ways other food manufacturers, such as candy and cereal makers, can use almonds in more of their products. Owners' funds also help promote Blue Diamond almonds in this country, such as the nationwide television advertising campaign, and in other countries. Blue Diamond almond exports to more than 90 countries account for more than half of the cooperative's sales. Owners' financial support of these product development and promotional efforts is important in developing new markets and expanding existing ones.[19]

The goal of cooperatives is to give members the maximum return on their investment. Most cooperatives with major-branded products, such as Ocean Spray Cranberries, pay their members from 5 percent to 10 percent more than the market price for their crops.[20]

Summary of Learning Goals

1.   Identify and explain the three basic forms of business ownership.
The three forms of business ownership are sole proprietorship, partnership, and corporation. The most widely used ownership form is the sole proprietorship, a business owned and operated by a single person. A partnership is operated by two or more people as co-owners. A corporation is a legal entity separate from its owners.

2.   Outline the advantages and disadvantages of sole proprietorships.
The advantages of sole proprietorships are retention of all profits, ease of formation and dissolution, and ownership flexibility. The disadvantages are unlimited financial liability, financing limitations, management deficiencies, and lack of continuity.

3.   Compare the advantages and disadvantages of partnerships.   The advantages of partnerships are ease of formation, complementary management skills, and expanded financial capability. The disadvantages are unlimited financial liability, possible interpersonal conflicts, lack of continuity, and complex dissolution.

4.   Differentiate between general partnerships and limited partnerships.   General partnerships are those in which all partners carry on the business as co-owners and are liable for the debts of the business. Limited partnerships are those composed of one or more general partners and one or more limited partners. Limited partners are not active in the operation of the partnership, and their possible losses are limited to the amount of their investment.

5.   Outline the advantages and disadvantages of corporations.   The advantage of corporations are limited financial liability, specialized management skills, expanded financial capability, and economies of larger-scale operation. The disadvantages are high taxes and legal restrictions.

6.   Discuss how a corporation is organized and operated.   In organizing a corporation, consideration should be given to hiring an attorney, selecting the state in which to incorporate, and following the correct legal procedures for incorporating. Registration as a domestic, foreign, or alien corporation is also important. Stockholders own the corporation, the board of directors governs it, and top management is responsible for its actual operation. Subsidiaries are corporations owned by other corporations, or so-called parent corporations.

7.   Differentiate among vertical, horizontal, and conglomerate mergers.   Vertical mergers occur between firms at different levels in the production-marketing process, such as a producer and a large retailer. Vertical mergers provide firms with expanded distribution outlets (forward vertical merger) and raw materials and supplies (backward vertical merger). Horizontal mergers involve firms in the same industry. They help firms diversify and expand product lines. Conglomerates are mergers of unrelated firms. They facilitate diversification into new business areas, rapidly increase sales growth, and profitably use cash surpluses.

8. Identify the recent trends influencing corporate organizations.
One recent trend is an increased number of unfriendly takeovers, in which the merger offer is unsolicited and unwanted. Contradictory trends are also evident in contemporary business. Some corporations are selling divisions or units, a process known as divestiture. These units may be converted into private firms, purchased via a leveraged buyout where investors use borrowed funds to acquire the business, or acquired by the unit's employees.

9. Explain the differences among private ownership, public ownership, and collective ownership (cooperatives).   Private ownership refers to an organization owned by an individual or individuals, regardless of whether it was set up as a sole proprietorship, partnership, or corporation. One alternative to private ownership is public ownership, in which a government unit or its agency owns and operates an organization on behalf of the population served by the unit. Another alternative is the cooperative, in which there is collective ownership of production, storage, transportation, and/or marketing activities.

Key Terms

sole proprietorship	close corporation	horizontal merger
partnership	preferred stock	conglomerate merger
general partnership	common stock	tender offer
limited partnership	proxy	poison pill
master limited partnership	cumulative voting	shark repellent
joint venture	board of directors	white knight
corporation	outside directors	golden parachute
dividends	subsidiary	proxy fight
S corporations	parent company	divestiture
domestic corporation	merger	leveraged buyout (LBO)
foreign corporation	acquisition	public ownership
alien corporation	vertical merger	cooperative
stockholders		

Review Questions

1. Outline the ownership structure of American business.

2. What is meant by a *sole proprietorship*? Why is it the most popular form of business ownership? Are there any negatives to this form of business ownership?

3. How does the Uniform Partnership Act define a partnership? What are the benefits and disadvantages of this form of business ownership?

4. Distinguish between a general partner and a limited partner. Explain why this distinction exists and how it is used in different types of enterprises.

5. Explain the concept of a master limited partnership.

6. Describe the features and operations of a corporation.

7. What is the primary advantage of the corporate form of business ownership?

8. Differentiate among a domestic corporation, foreign corporation, and alien corporation.

9. The business section of today's newspapers are full of terms like poison pill, shark repellent, white knight, and golden parachute. Explain what these terms mean as well as the current business trend from which they are derived.

10. How are cooperatives different from other forms of business enterprises?

Discussion Questions

1. What factors would be important to you if you were selecting a form of business ownership for a new enterprise?

2. Assume you are involved in establishing the following businesses. What forms of business ownership would you use?
   a. Roadside fruit stand (assume you own an orchard)
   b. Hairstyling salon
   c. Management consulting firm
   d. Small foundry

3. Look at the listing of the largest U.S. industrial corporations in Table 5.1. Compare this list to similar ones published in the last ten years. What changes have occurred? Can you develop any generalizations about these changes?

4. What steps are necessary to set up a corporation in your particular state or locality? Do these differ from what is required elsewhere? If so, how?

5. Secure announcements of future stockholders' meetings of corporations located in your area. Analyze the types of issues scheduled for debate at these meetings. Can you make any generalizations about them?

Video Case

Esprit de Corps

One of the best contemporary examples of a fledgling, entrepreneurial business that blossomed into an international corporation is Doug and Susie Tompkin's Esprit de Corps. The company actually traces its birth to 1968 when general partners and good friends Susie Tompkins and Jane Tise began producing clothing designs in their kitchen and marketing them under the label The Plain Jane Dress Company. Three years later, Doug Tompkins became a partner, contributing much-needed experience in owning and operating a business. Doug (who four years earlier had sold his 1953 MG sports car for $5,000 and started his own mountain-climbing equipment company, North Face) sold his firm for $50,000 and plunged full-time into launching the clothing firm on a grander scale.

With Doug's input and drive, the company quickly changed from a trendy dress company to a wholesale apparel business featuring high-quality, moderately-priced junior sportswear. In 1971, the partners also decided to change the name of their company because they liked the sound of the French phrase *esprit de corps* and its meaning: a sense of union and of common interests and responsibilities among a group of persons associated together.

In the early 1970s, Tise and the Tompkins were self-taught entrepreneurs. They did not follow trends in high fashion or do any market research. Susie, as design director, worked with a small group of designers to produce loose-fitting, clean-lined clothes that she described as "timeless." Doug masterminded the company's ad campaigns and developed its image. As co-founders and owners of the business, they could shape it and control every phase of its development.

Their early approach was anything but typical. Instead of trying to entice retailers to carry the Esprit line, Tompkins mailed 850,000 catalogs directly to upper-income households across the country to generate sales and brand recognition. Consumer response to the catalogs was phenomenal and retail buyers began contacting Esprit after their customers requested the merchandise. This kind of consumer demand gave Esprit considerable marketing clout when they decided to market their clothing through retail stores in addition to catalog sales. Department stores handling the Esprit line were required to utilize sales personnel who had undergone specialized training. In addition, they had to install specially designed stores-within-stores to display Esprit: high-tech displays found in well-known outlets such as Bloomingdale's, Neiman Marcus, and Macy's. Esprit also refused to follow the common industry practice of reimbursing retailers for markdowns on slow-selling merchandise. They were able to follow this plan because demand was so high for Esprit clothing.

Although Jane Tise left the company in 1978, Esprit continued its rapid growth under the leadership of Susie and Doug Tompkins. In 1984, the Tompkins decided to make Esprit a retailer as well as a clothing designer/manufacturer. Fifteen stores were opened in eight cities at a cost conservatively estimated at a whopping $50 million. One extravagant store in West Hollywood — a 30,000-square-foot showplace — cost $16 million alone. In 1985, Doug launched Esprit's famous *real people* advertising which solidly defined the company's image in consumers' minds. The ads provided almost instant recognition, featuring customers and employees in natural poses and stark surroundings, foregoing professional models and the typical fashion photo layouts.

By 1985, Esprit was generating annual sales of approximately $800 million in women's and children's apparel to customers in 23 countries. The company also moved to franchising to conserve capital and, by 1988, 38 Esprit franchise stores were operating in the U.S. and such foreign countries as Australia, Great Britain, Hong Kong, Singapore, and West Germany. Doug believes that franchisees benefit from the fact that seemingly competitive outlets are often operating in department stores within the same cities. "We have total proof that when we put an Esprit store in a market where a department store is carrying Esprit, it enhances our name," he states.

As the original partnership structure became more cumbersome, the company began to restructure itself as a close corporation to take on added growth and to enter new markets. Esprit began to resemble a federation of companies as its expansion took it into international markets, its top two components being

Notes: Nadine Joseph, "Patching It Up at Esprit," *Newsweek,* May 23, 1988, p. 49; Anne Ferguson, "Esprit: The Spirit Moves," *Management Today,* July 1987, pp. 59–61; Ralph King, Jr., "How Esprit de Corps Lost Its Esprit," *Forbes,* March 21, 1988, pp. 91–94; and personal correspondence, February 27, 1989.

(1) Esprit International, headed by Doug, and (2) Esprit U.S., with Susie as design consultant. Much of the actual manufacturing was contracted to foreign firms in such countries as Italy, Mexico, New Zealand, Hong Kong, and Taiwan, that relied on Esprit designs and quality specifications. Licensing agreements with other companies expanded the Esprit product line to include bed and bath products, eyewear, and socks and tights.

Rapid growth is a double-edged sword, and a start-up company frequently faces the common problems of ever-increasing sales: lack of control, inadequate distribution outlets, continual pressures for additional funds to finance further growth, and a thin layer of management for making important business decisions. Esprit was no exception.

By 1987, sales had begun to sour — both for Esprit and other sportswear firms as well. Costs were rising, especially in the Far East, where 70 percent of Esprit's product line is made. Fashion-oriented shoppers also turned fickle, balking at the rapid price increases, and sales for Benetton, The Gap, and Banana Republic, along with Esprit, all dropped. For Esprit, though, the timing was particularly bad, coming at a period when the company was in the midst of a major — and expensive — expansion.

Of that period, Doug Tompkins says, "The rapid expansion . . . created an infrastructure that wasn't really being supported by enough sales yet. A combination of many events really caused us to tighten our belts and change our focus from expansion and sales to really reevaluating every department in the company — where our expenses were going and how we could keep spiraling expenses from just getting completely out of hand." Although the closely-held corporation proved capable of managing the firm's early growth, problems grew when sales slowed and funds were lacking to cover expenses.

Esprit changed greatly in 1987. The company's San Francisco headquarters, dubbed "Little Utopia" by the young, enthusiastic workforce, was the pride of the organization. There, employees felt like part of a team, a family. There were sushi lunches, subsidized theater tickets, foreign language classes, and adventure travel. Esprit's recruitment brochure boasted of a "revolution in the workplace," where employees "have a meaningful job relationship." With the sales slowdown, employees began to notice that they were not receiving their accustomed regimen of regular raises and bonuses. Company-subsidized pasta lunches and free coffee were phased out.

To make matters worse, at about the same time, the Tompkins went through a highly-publicized and demoralizing separation. The split was none too amicable, and it left employees and buyers wondering about the direction of the company. Susie resigned as design director to become a design consultant; Doug resigned as president, but stayed on as head of Esprit International. Cost-cutting efforts resulted in layoffs for almost one-third of the Esprit staff and plans for a $120 million corporate campus were postponed indefinitely.

The inevitable decline in employee morale was also accompanied by a crisis of company image. Doug wanted to continue to produce and market the junior sportswear that had made the company famous; Susie wanted to start designing for an older clientele that was becoming the growth segment of the U.S. consumer market: aging baby boomers. This lack of clear purpose and direction left buyers confused. A company that had found success with a well-defined public image seemed to be floundering over that image.

Esprit's recent experiences have been positive. An Italian-designed menswear line, introduced in late 1988, has been successful and sales for 1989 improved to an estimated $1.2 billion. Even though direct sales through Esprit catalogs ended in 1984, the firm currently mails catalogs at least twice a year to 800,000 consumers for store purchases. Even with its problems, Esprit's success in a little over 20 years is an admirable accomplishment for Doug, a former treetopper, and Susie, once an employee of a Nevada gambling casino.

Questions

1. Why do you feel that Esprit de Corps was originally organized as a partnership? Were the original owners general partners or limited partners? What factors are likely to have resulted in the firm's restructuring as a corporation?

2. Relate the following text concepts to Esprit de Corps.

a. domestic corporation, foreign corporation, and alien corporation

b. parent company and subsidiary

3. Why did Esprit choose to organize as a close corporation? What would be the primary advantages and disadvantages of the firm becoming an open corporation?

4. Relate the concepts of vertical mergers, horizontal mergers, and conglomerate mergers to the possible acquisition by Esprit of another company.

6

Entrepreneurship, Small Business, and Franchising

Learning Goals

1. To explain the vital role played by entrepreneurs and small businesses in the U.S. economy.

2. To define *entrepreneurship* and describe how entrepreneurs are different from other businesspeople.

3. To define *small business* and to identify the industries in which most small firms are established.

4. To compare the advantages and disadvantages of small business.

5. To analyze the small-business opportunities for women and minorities and the special problems faced by these entrepreneurs.

6. To describe how the Small Business Administration functions.

7. To outline the role of franchising in the U.S. economy.

8. To list the advantages and disadvantages of franchising.

Fowler's Toys, in downtown Sacramento, is a typical small business started by two energetic entrepreneurs. Its owners, Diane Fowler and her husband, John Stoll, conceived the idea after an earlier venture that manufactured and sold to area toy stores a silk-screened city map designed for children.

Fowler and Stoll decided to open a toy store with an educational orientation. The couple believes all toys teach something, so they described their ideal product as one with "the potential for nonviolent, cooperative, imaginative learning." John Stoll described their business goal as follows: "We wanted to work together doing something we both enjoy and that could involve our two children." Fowler's Toys was legally organized as an S corporation in March 1988.

Fowler and Stoll knew such a venture needed a lot of planning. They did extensive research in the California State University, Sacramento library. They explored the possibility of buying an existing store and considered lease proposals from various shopping centers. This effort led Fowler and Stoll to conclude that most toys are bought at stores near home and that toys bought at regional malls were "spot treats" for children.

Fowler continued the investigation by spending about two hours in each of nine toy stores. This effort produced another conclusion: Independent stores could compete against major stores by concentrating on hobby or educational products. Her observations also convinced her that she should let children explore the store's offerings by playing with the toys as much as they wanted. The only question was how to proceed.

Small-business experts point out that all commercial ventures should be based on a sound business plan. Banks and other financial institutions also require such plans as part

of the loan process. Fowler and Stoll recognized that an effective plan would be an important instrument in avoiding the problems encountered by most small firms. They used their personal computer to revise the plan three times before being sure it was accurate. Fowler described their approach this way: "The most important thing about a business plan is that it always needs to be revised. It has to be a good working document."

Fowler and her husband used personal savings to finance the store. They put $20,000 into inventory and spent $5,000 on miscellaneous items such as incorporation, licenses, shelving, and a cash register. They decided a bank loan was not needed at this time.

The couple considered eight shopping centers but eventually decided on 2504 J Street, in downtown Sacramento. Several factors led to this decision: strong traffic flow, good parking, a bus stop, and nearby medical complexes.

Merchandise was the next problem the entrepreneurs faced. Fowler went to a trade show in San Francisco and was amazed at the diversity of items available, but it was just the beginning. She recalls,

"I thought the products were a fair selection, but I found it was only the tip of the iceberg — in new toys only."

Later, the couple attended a second trade show in Los Angeles. Fowler also wrote and telephoned various toy producers. Finally, she met with a manufacturer's representative for six hours. Fowler says her toughest dilemma was finding a reasonably priced doll.

Promotion was another important aspect of getting the new business off the ground. Fowler decided to have a joint grand opening with two other new stores on J Street — an apparel store and a gift shop. She also advertised in *Parents Monthly,* a newspaper distributed free in the area. Another advertisement was placed in a community news weekly inserted in the *Sacramento Bee.*

In addition to the advertising, notices were posted in schools and elsewhere inviting children to paint the tiles that would form the entryway for Fowler's Toys. So many children signed up that Fowler and Stoll had to switch to 9-inch-square tiles from 12-inch ones.

The 1,800-square-foot store was readied by Stoll and his sons. They built the shelves and checkout counter, and the boxes of merchandise that had been shipped to the couple's house were moved to the store. Fowler's Toys was ready to open its doors.

The big day was August 1, 1988. The couple and their youngest children along with Fowler's mother arrived at 9:20 for the scheduled 10 a.m. opening. It was a good thing

they came early because Fowler had forgotten the change for the store. Later in the day, it was discovered that the air conditioner had been put in backward. The store also ran out of price tags.

The first sale was to the son of one of Diane's friends. He picked out a stuffed boa constrictor, priced at about $13. Fowler's Toys took in $288 the first day; $9,000 the first

month; and $50,000 during the store's first December (when most toys are purchased). Another small business had been successfully launched.[1]

This chapter discusses entrepreneurs like Fowler and Stoll. It also looks at small businesses in general and franchises specifically.

Photo source: The Sacramento Bee, Public Relations Department.

Chapter Overview

Americans have long advocated entrepreneurship and a strong small-business sector as the backbone of the private enterprise system. Start-up operations and existing small businesses provide much of the competitive zeal that keeps the system effective. Numerous actions have been taken to encourage the development and continuity of these firms. Antitrust legislation, for example, was designed to maintain the competitive environment in which such companies thrive. A federal agency, the Small Business Administration, was set up in 1953 to assist small firms.

Small business is a vital segment of the U.S. economy. It creates two-thirds of our domestic gross national product and accounts for half the U.S. work force. Some 700,000 new firms open each year. Firms with fewer than 100 employees created 2.4 million jobs in the U.S. labor force in a recent year. These small firms provide nearly two-thirds of all new jobs in our economy.[2]

These statistics suggest the vital role that entrepreneurs and small-business owners play in contemporary business. Aside from the many services they provide to consumers, these organizations also help large businesses function efficiently. Many suppliers to large manufacturers are small firms attempting to offer a product or service superior to that of their competitors.

business incubator
A common facility that houses start-up firms.

Business incubators are an excellent illustration of the importance attached to small business in today's economy. A **business incubator** is an organization that provides low-cost, common facilities to small, start-up ventures. A typical incubator might be an abandoned plant that is sectioned off and rented to various small firms. Secretarial and other services are often shared by the tenants. Business incubators have been set up by government units such as industrial development authorities, nonprofit organizations, colleges and universities, and private investors. Regardless of their ownership or purpose, business incubators are vital breeding grounds for the small-business sector.

The U.S. private enterprise system began with the small shops and workrooms of colonial times, and Americans still depend on such independent entrepreneurs today. They are the very heart of the private enterprise system.

Entrepreneurship Not the same as Small Business

entrepreneur
A risk taker in the private enterprise system.

Chapter 1 defined the **entrepreneur** as the risk taker in the private enterprise system, a person who seeks a profitable opportunity and then devises a plan and forms an organization to achieve the objective. Entrepreneurship is not synony-

Photo source: Alan Tao, photographer for *Entrepreneur.*

Entrepreneurs Mike Thorton (left) and Peter Schworer translated their love of surfing into a profitable business venture — Surf Foto. They built a giant wave — a 3-D replica of the Banzai Pipeline in Oahu, Hawaii — placed a surfboard "in the tube," and charge would-be surfers $5 to have their photo taken in the curl of the wave. The wave is mounted on a trailer and transported to outdoor fairs and special events in Southern California. The innovation has caught the attention of large firms in the United States, Japan, and other overseas markets, so Surf Foto is now building waves for sale to other businesses.

mous with small-business management. Instead, it refers to the creation of new business.[3]

Jon Prouty, a Boulder, Colorado, lawyer, is an entrepreneur. Prouty combined his interest in sailing and hang gliding with the principles of kite flying and invented the Skynasaur, a two-stringed flying toy. Prouty and some friends made the first Skynasaurs in a rented garage. As sales increased, Skynasaur Inc. moved to a larger building. When sales hit 100,000 units a year, Prouty hired a management consultant to operate the business.[4]

Entrepreneurship is one of the hottest courses on college campuses. Twenty years ago, only four colleges taught the subject. Today, at least 250 institutions of higher education have majors or at least classes in entrepreneurship. Successful entrepreneurs all over the country have poured millions of dollars into college endowments to fund professorships in entrepreneurship.[5]

What drives entrepreneurs? The satisfaction of establishing and profiting from one's own business is the catalyst. Entrepreneurship prospered in the United States during the past decade. Some experts argue it has been the first such growth decade in 100 years.

Forms of Entrepreneurship

The Center for Entrepreneurial Leadership in the School of Management at the State University of New York in Buffalo offers a distinct categorization of entrepreneurship. The center identifies three general groupings of entrepreneurs: classic entrepreneurs, intrapreneurs, and change agents.[6]

Classic entrepreneurs are those who identify a business opportunity and allocate their available resources to tap that market. *Intrapreneurs* are entrepreneurially oriented people who seek to develop new products, ideas, and commercial ventures within the context of a large organization. (Intrapreneurs are discussed further in Chapter 8.) By contrast, *change agents* are managers who seek to revitalize established concerns in order to keep their competitiveness in the modern marketplace. These individuals are described in various sections throughout this text.

Are Entrepreneurs a Different Breed?

Research on the entrepreneurial personality suggests that such individuals possess greater tendencies for risk taking and exhibit greater needs for achievement, independence, leadership, and recognition than the average person. One study examined literature dealing with the personality differences between successful and unsuccessful entrepreneurs. The study found that unsuccessful entrepreneurs might lack the necessary management skills required beyond the creating stage. The skills needed to operate a business differ from those needed to launch the business. Consequently, some entrepreneurs gain more satisfaction from launching a business than from its day-to-day management. Once the business begins to function, some entrepreneurs lose interest.[7]

Differences between Entrepreneurs and Small Businesspeople   The Cincinnati Small Business Development Center once compared the personalities of the entrepreneurs leading *Inc.* magazine's top 500 small growth companies with the personalities of respondents in an earlier study of small, but stable Texas firms. The center, using a popular personality test, concluded there was a distinct difference between the two groups.

On the sensing/intuition category, 86 percent of the small-business leaders favored sensing, or concentrating on the here and now. By comparison, 60 percent of the entrepreneurs of the *Inc.* companies favored focusing on long-term plans and opportunities.[8] Maybe Tom Golisano, the CEO of $80 million Paychex Inc., expressed it best: "Entrepreneurs should be realists, not optimists. Optimists always look for the light at the end of the tunnel; realists look for the next tunnel."[9]

Other Ways Entrepreneurs Differ   A survey by the Gallup organization and *The Wall Street Journal* compared entrepreneurs to executives in large corporations and to executives in smaller established firms. While the three groups had some similarities, the entrepreneurs were characterized as being more independent, exhibiting an early need to take charge, possessing a strong work drive, and often keeping their own counsel.

Most entrepreneurs exhibit an independent nature; they are more likely to have been fired from a job or suspended from school, or to have worked for four or more companies, than other businesspeople. Entrepreneurs were also self-starters early in life. The Gallup survey indicated the entrepreneurial group was even more likely than the others to have operated a business while in school. While all businesspeople are work motivated, the entrepreneur takes even less vacation time than do executives of both large and small established firms. Entrepreneurs, who are more ethnically diverse than other groups, are less likely to join civic organizations and political groups. In school, they were less likely to have played varsity sports or to have served as class officers.[10]

TAKEOUT TAXI of Herndon, Virginia, is a typical small business. It is independently owned and operated by (from left in photo) Jim DeRocher, Jonathan Krasner, and Kevin Abt. The delivery firm serves the food of 40 local restaurants, such as Chilis and Chi Chi's Tex-Mex, to area residents. TAKEOUT TAXI contracts with restaurants to buy prepared food at a discount and charges customers standard menu prices plus a delivery fee. Delivery services such as TAKEOUT TAXI are sprouting up across the country. Restaurants rely on them to keep as customers the growing number of Americans who not only prefer eating at home but also want a prepared meal brought to their doorstep.

Photo source: Anthony Tribby, photographer, for TAKEOUT TAXI.

What Is a Small Business?

Any conception of a small business is dependent on comparisons with other businesses. Sales, number of employees, assets, net worth, market share, and relationship to competitors have all been used to make this determination. There are probably as many ways to define small business as there are people wanting to do so.

The Small Business Administration says a **small business** is one that is independently owned and operated, is not dominant in its field, and meets a variety of size standards.[11] Some standards apply only for loan programs, others for procurement, and still others for various special programs.

A White House conference on small business added another dimension to the definition by setting up different classes of small businesses according to the number of people employed: class A firms employ 0–9 people; class B, 10–49; C, 50–249; and class D, 250–400 persons.[12] From still another perspective, management characteristics are what set small businesses apart from larger ones.

Probably the most workable concept of small business is the one suggested some years ago by the Committee for Economic Development. To qualify as a small firm under its definition, a business must have at least two of the following characteristics: (1) independent management with the managers often owning the firm, (2) capital contribution from a limited number of individuals — perhaps only one, (3) the firm operates in a local area, and (4) the firm represents a small part of the overall industry.[13]

In general, a small business has the following characteristics:

◆ Independently owned

◆ Independently operated and managed

◆ Only a minor factor in its industry

small business
Business that is independently owned and operated, does not dominate its field, and meets a variety of size standards.

◆   Fewer than 400 employees
◆   Limited capital sources.

Typical Small-Business Ventures

Small businesses are found in nearly every industry in the United States. They often compete against some of the nation's largest organizations as well as against a multitude of other small companies. Retailing and service establishments are the most common nonfarm small businesses, and new-technology companies often start as small organizations.

Farming   For the most part, farming is still small business. The family farm is a classic example of a small-business operation. These farms are independently owned and are operated with relatively few employees but with a substantial amount of unpaid family labor. While farm failures and the emergence of corporate farming make the headlines, hundreds of thousands of independent farms have adapted to a changing competitive environment and prospered.

One excellent example of this transformation is the Rominger ranch 80 miles north of San Francisco. Since Albert Rominger bought the first small parcel during the Depression of the 1930s, the property has grown to 6,000 acres of fertile farmland. Rominger made the ranch a family affair. Until he died in 1985 at the age of 87, he was still working the land with his 2 sons and 17 grandchildren. The ranch has continued to adjust to modern farming and business practices, and is still a family operation.[14]

Retailing   While general merchandise giants like Sears, Wal-Mart, and K mart are the most significant retailing firms, they are far out numbered by small, privately owned retail enterprises. Small business, in fact, characterizes the retailing of shoes, jewelry, office supplies and stationary, apparel, flowers, drugs, convenience foods, and thousands of other products.

A frozen yogurt shop is an example of a small retail business. But sometimes these small shops do not stay small. Consider the case of TCBY. In 1981, Frank Hickingbotham decided to open a small yogurt shop in a suburban Little Rock, Arkansas, shopping center. He only wanted one store, which he named "This Can't Be Yogurt" and later shortened to TCBY. Hickingbotham's small store was an instant hit; he now has 1,200 franchises and has changed the definition of TCBY to "The Country's Best Yogurt."[15]

Service Firms   Service-oriented industries and individuals — such as restaurants, funeral homes, banking establishments, movie theaters, dry cleaners, carpet cleaners, shoe repairers, attorneys, insurance agents, automobile repair specialists, public accountants, dentists, and physicians — also abound in the U.S. private enterprise economy. There are relatively few national sellers of services, except in the case of insurance. Approximately 68 percent of all nongovernment jobs are in service-producing industries.[16] This figure is expected to jump to 86 percent by the year 2000.[17]

San Francisco's Grocery Express is a typical example of a service-oriented business. The $2.7 million firm delivers groceries, flowers, meals, and gift baskets that customers select from a catalogue. In addition to placing orders by phone, customers can order via facsimile machines or personal computers. The

For these members of the Rominger family, the "good life" is working together to run the family farm. Their goal is success of the family rather than monetary gain. They share a love of the land and the traditional value of working hard, which often means putting in 15-hour workdays. The family operates the 6,000-acre wheat and produce farm without the help of hired hands.

Photo source: © Burt Glinn/Magnum Photos, Inc.

firm charges $4.25 per delivery of orders less than $100, and products are priced about 15 percent higher than a large supermarket. Grocery Express's clientele consists of businesses, the elderly, homebound persons, two-income couples, professional singles, and couples with young children.[18]

High-Tech Firms   Many new-technology firms — those striving to produce and market a scientific innovation — typically start as small businesses, and many great inventors and technical geniuses have begun their businesses in barns, garages, warehouses, and attics. Small business is often the best (or only) option available to a scientist seeking to transform an idea into commercial reality.

Although most new businesses, including a variety of retail and service enterprises, are in industries with limited capital requirements, some technical firms require substantial capital to get off the ground. Initial capital requirements of $1 million or more are not uncommon in such industries. The high entry cost is primarily due to the long time lag between start-up and receipt of sales revenue.

The capital problems described above are illustrated by Space Industries Inc., a Houston firm that will launch the first private space station in 1991. When CEO James Caloway conceived the idea of an industrial space research station in 1981, he and two associates each invested $15,000 into the venture. Space Industries later raised $30 million from private sources, mostly wealthy individuals. But this did not approach the $700 million needed to actually build, launch, and operate the station. The breakthrough came when the federal government announced plans to lease part of a private orbiting space station for $700 million.[19]

Advantages of a Small Business

Small businesses are not simply smaller versions of large corporations. Their legal organization, market position, staff capability, managerial style and organization, and financial resources generally differ from bigger companies, which gives them unique advantages over larger-scale competitors. Innovative behavior, lower costs, and the filling of isolated market niches are some of the most important of these advantages.

Innovative Behavior

Small firms are often the companies that first offer innovations, new concepts, and new products in the marketplace. Genentech, Federal Express, and Apple Computer are classic success stories. But scientific innovation is not the only concept offered by small-business entrepreneurs. Sometimes the innovative behavior comes from the entrepreneur herself or himself.

Consider the case of Larry Adler of Potomac, Maryland. His venture netted only $100,000 during its first five years in business. But this is an amazing record if you consider that Larry Adler is only 14 years old.

Young Adler started with a lemonade stand at age 5, and went on to a magic show at age 7. Before he was 9, Adler formed a lawn service called Rent-A-Kid that now employs 60 people. Adler also works as a manufacturer's representative for 50 children's products firms. These two businesses and Kidcorp, a consulting service for young entrepreneurs, are part of Adler's parent organization, Larry Adler & Associates/The Kid Rep.

Adler works 25 hours a week out of a basement office in the family home. A Tron video game is part of the office decor. Adler studies at home with a tutor and hopes to major in business administration in college. He assesses his unique situation this way: "I like to do anything a regular kid likes to do. There's the kid side of me and then there's the business side." But Adler goes on to add: "There is no kid who does what I do."[20]

Lower Costs

Small firms can often provide a product or service more cheaply than large firms. They usually have fewer overhead costs — those not directly related to providing the goods and services — than do large firms. As a result, they may be able to earn a profit on a lower price than a large company can offer.

Small businesses have lean organizations with small staffs and few support personnel. The lower overhead costs resulting from a smaller permanent staff can provide a distinct advantage to small businesses. Small businesses tend to hire outside consultants or specialists, such as attorneys and certified public accountants, only when their assistance is needed. As a rule, all growing organizations add staff personnel faster than line (or management) personnel. Larger organizations tend to maintain such specialists on their permanent staffs.

Small businesses typically cannot afford to have internal expertise, so they seek help from outside specialists. Quality Croutons Inc. is a black-owned Chicago firm that supplies croutons for salads in 80 percent of the McDonald's restaurants in the United States. When the company had problems with packaging the croutons, it contacted Mead Corporation, a large paper and packaging products firm. Mead packaging specialists designed a more functional and better-looking package that ran smoothly on Quality Crouton's equipment and saved the company money as well.

Photo source: Courtesy of Mead Corporation.

Small businesses also often have the benefit of much unpaid labor. Entrepreneurs themselves are usually willing to work long hours, and no one pays them for overtime or holidays. In addition, family members contribute a significant amount of unpaid labor as bookkeepers, laborers, receptionists, delivery personnel, and the like.

Massachusetts-based Yumico International illustrates how small businesses hold costs down. The firm produces Frulait, a drink that blends yogurt and fruit juices. The product is distributed in New England. President Patti Tackeff and Vice-President Deborah Baye run the firm out of Tackeff's apartment. They have to step over pet cats to answer phones and work on their computers. With only six full-time employees, Yumico International tries to save money wherever possible. Before the company could afford a delivery truck, the pair went through several cars. Tackeff recalls: "140 cases of Frulait in the back of a Toyota will really burn it out."[21]

Filling Isolated Niches

Big businesses are excluded from some commercial activities because of their size. High overhead costs force them to set minimum targets at which to direct their competitive efforts. Some large publishers, for example, identify minimum acceptable sales figures that consider their overhead costs. Editorial and production expenses for a certain type of book may not be justified unless the publisher can sell, say, 7,000 copies. This situation allows substantial opportunities for smaller publishers with lower overhead costs.

In addition, certain types of businesses lend themselves better to smaller firms. Many services illustrate this point. Finally, economic and organizational factors may dictate that an industry consists essentially of small firms.

Susan Asplund got the idea for her small business while attending her 20-year high school reunion. She and her husband, David, both quit their executive posts with Pizza Haven Inc. and set up The Class Reunion in Bellevue, Washington. The Asplunds' small business organizes and runs class reunions for well-intentioned reunion committees that lack the time to do the job right. High school reunions have proved to be an isolated but profitable market niche for the Asplunds.[22]

Disadvantages of Small Business

Small firms have a variety of disadvantages, including poor management, inadequate financing, and government regulation. While these problems often can be overcome, they should be considered by anyone contemplating a small-business venture.

Poor Management

Hundreds of thousands of small businesses are begun each year. Three out of five fail within the first six years of operation. Many people who start small businesses are ill-prepared as managers.

In fact, 61,000 small businesses filed for bankruptcy in a recent year, and nearly 60 percent of those filing for bankruptcy were retailers or service firms.[23]

Since *poor management* is a vague term, it is important to look at the types of management shortcomings that characterize small business. Often, people go into business with little, if any, training or education in running a small business. They have an idea for a product or service and assume they will learn about business matters as they carry on the enterprise. Bankruptcy is often the result. A word of caution is in order: Any would-be entrepreneur is advised to acquire a sound foundation in basic business principles before initiating any small-business venture.

Another cause of failure is that small-business people sometimes let their entrepreneurial optimism run wild. They are excited about their projects and their potential, but their optimism should be tempered with caution.

A related reason for failure is entrepreneurs' not "doing their homework" before starting the small business. They may believe others will see their product or service as unique or better than that of the competition, but this should be verified by marketing research. Does a market exist for the proposed product or service? This information can be obtained through published sources, surveys, in-depth interviews, competitive analyses, observation, or a number of other research techniques.

Inadequate Financing

Inadequate financing is generally listed as a leading cause of small-business problems. Many businesses start with inadequate capital and soon experience a shortage of funds. They often lack the resources to carry them over rough spots or to expand if they are successful.

As shown in Figure 6.1, 60 percent of the financing of a typical small business comes from the entrepreneur's personal resources. Friends and relatives contribute an average of 9 percent. Banks, private investors, and the Small Busi-

Figure 6.1   Sources of Capital for New Businesses

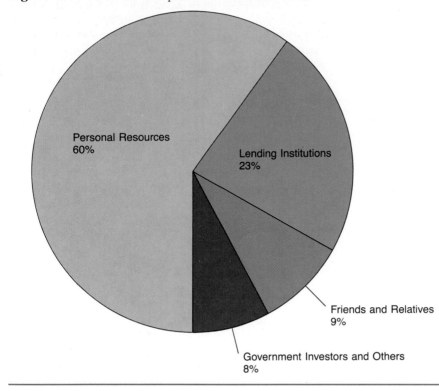

Source: The National Federation of Independent Business, *CPA Client Bulletin,* September 1982, p. 2.

ness Administration are other sources of funding. Banks are often reluctant to make loans to small businesses because of their high failure rate and will require detailed information to justify such loans.

According to the findings of a government study on small-business financing, the most frequent reason bankers reject small-business loan applications is insufficient owner equity in the business. Insufficient collateral is the second most-often-cited reason for rejection. A poor earning record ranks third, followed by no established earnings record.[24]

A **venture capitalist** is a business organization or group of private individuals that invest in promising new businesses. Sometimes venture capitalists lend the business money; other times they become part owners of the new or struggling firm. Venture capital is an important source of funds, particularly for firms offering a creative new concept or product.

venture capitalist
Private individual or business organization that invests in promising new businesses.

The Small Business Administration offers a variety of loans for small businesses, primarily through banks. These loans are used for business construction, conversion, or expansion; for purchasing equipment, facilities, machinery, materials, or supplies; and for operating funds.

Government Regulation

Small-business people complain bitterly of excessive government regulation and red tape. The Small Business Administration estimates government paperwork costs small firms billions of dollars each year. Larger firms with substantial staffs can usually cope with the blizzard of required forms and reports, but for many small-business owners it can force them to look for salaried positions. Many experts within and outside government believe a major effort must be made to reduce the paperwork required of small businesses since they are simply not equipped to handle the load.

Small-Business Opportunities for Women and Minorities

Nona Brazier of Maple Valley, Washington, reflects the trend toward increased involvement of women and minorities in small businesses. Recently named "Woman Entrepreneur of the Year" by a local group, Brazier runs Northwest Recovery Systems, a recycling enterprise, and Necessary Luxuries, a professional home-cleaning service, from a home office. She is active in public affairs, participating in a White House conference on small business and helping organize a governor's conference on small business. She is on the board of the Association of Washington Business and has led a committee for the Small Business Improvement Council. Brazier and her husband have seven children, and because she operates her businesses from home, the children are learning about managing a small business.[25]

Women-Owned Businesses

Government statistics indicate that although women are making enormous strides in many aspects of business, they still lag behind men in several important areas. On a positive note, the number of women-owned businesses in the United States has reached 3.7 million, over five times the level of a decade earlier, and women are now founding companies at a faster rate than men. Most new women-owned firms are in the service sector. In fact, women now own 75 percent of all service firms and half of all retail businesses.

Nonstore retailing is the most common type of business owned by women. It is followed by real estate, beauty shops, schools, accountants and bookkeepers, doctors and dentists, restaurants and bars, insurance, building maintenance, orchestra and entertainment, clothing stores, photographic studios, antique and secondhand shops, lawyers, and grocery stores.

Despite the gains, female entrepreneurs still lag in the critical areas of business receipts and income. Although the share of business receipts of women-operated sole proprietorships is increasing, these receipts do not compare to male-operated firms. The average woman-owned business has receipts of about $34,000, less than half the typical male-owned enterprise.[26]

While more women are setting up their own firms, these advances are not without major problems for the people involved. Some small-business problems affect women in particular. Prejudice, in varying degrees, is often a factor for women-owned firms. In the past, prospective female entrepreneurs often lacked business training or experience. Today, many of these people are retraining themselves through programs offered by colleges, universities, and other groups interested in furthering female entrepreneurship. Future generations of small-business people should include better-prepared women, judging by the greater number of women now studying business administration. Women also

Nona Brazier started her recycling business with a half-time employee and one truck to haul cardboard for grocery stores that wanted to recycle. Today, the firm has 11 employees and operates commercial, federal, and municipal recycling and garbage routes serving 16,000 homes. Like many entrepreneurs, Brazier is involved in community and professional organizations. She received an entrepreneurship award in recognition of her active support for the role of small business in state government.

Photo source: Courtesy of Puget Sound Business Journal.

encounter all the problems faced by their male counterparts. Like their male counterparts, the competent female entrepreneurs usually survive; and those who cannot adjust or satisfy their markets eventually fail.

New Legislation Designed to Help Women-Owned Businesses   The survival rate of women-owned businesses may be improved by passage of the *Women's Business Ownership Act of 1988*. The bill amended the Equal Credit Opportunity Act of 1974 to ban discrimination in business loans, as well as the previously covered personal loans. The law also established a three-year, $10 million training and assistance program for women business owners. Finally, the act set up a nine-member National Women's Business Council that will address long-term solutions to the problems faced by women-owned firms.[27]

Minority-Owned Businesses

Black-owned enterprises are a significant segment of all minority-owned businesses. This growth illustrates the surge in minority firms nationwide. During a recent five-year reporting period, the Census Bureau says black-owned businesses grew 47 percent. There are now over 339,000 such firms in the United States. Nearly a third of these enterprises are owned by black women.[28]

All small businesses face a high failure rate in their first year of operation, but minority-owned firms exceed even these high averages. Minority businesspeople have a variety of problems, starting with a frequent lack of training or education in business-related fields. Often, they are the first in their family to enter the business world. This disadvantage is being countered by training programs sponsored by the government, industry, professional business groups,

Figure 6.2   Assisting Minority-Owned Businesses

Source: Courtesy of The Stroh Brewery Company.

colleges, and others. Like women, a growing number of younger members of minority groups are beginning to study business administration.

But even the most enterprising and innovative of minority-owned firms cannot thrive on know-how and determination alone. When confronted with the difficulty of raising capital for salaries and for the purchase of equipment and inventory, many minority-owned firms do not survive. To help remove this obstacle, the government, in cooperation with minority banks and private corporations, established short-term loan funds, which make inexpensive financing available to minority businesses unable to obtain loans through conventional sources. These loans, and other forms of debt and equity financing, provide incentives for minorities to enter such nontraditional areas as construction, manufacturing, and wholesale trade. Research shows that minority firms in these areas are as profitable as nonminority firms but are more vulnerable to downswings in the business climate.[29]

In addition to the federal efforts designed to encourage minority-owned businesses, most states offer programs to assist minority businesspeople. Maryland's Small Business Development Financing Authority, for example, can acquire up to 40 percent of a start-up firm's equity. The minority owner can then buy back the state's share over a five-year period.[30] Many private corporations have created special programs to assist minority-owned businesses. The advertisement in Figure 6.2 describes Stroh's Minority Enterprise Business Program.

No one expects our society to reverse overnight the historic problems of too few women and minority entrepreneurs. However, thanks to the progress that has been made, it is not unrealistic for women and minorities to seek career opportunities in the small-business sector.

The Small Business Administration

The **Small Business Administration (SBA)** is the principal government agency concerned with small U.S. firms. The Small Business Act clearly stated Congress's intentions regarding this vital sector of the private enterprise system:

It is the declared policy of the Congress that the Government should aid, counsel, assist, and protect, insofar as is possible, the interests of small business concerns in order to preserve free competitive enterprise . . . to maintain and strengthen the overall economy of the Nation.

Founded in 1953, the SBA is small business's advocate within the federal government. A relatively small agency in the government bureaucracy, it has fewer than 4,800 employees in its Washington headquarters and its various regional and field offices. The primary operating functions of the SBA are providing financial assistance, aid in government procurement matters, and management training and consulting.

SBA Loans

The SBA has two basic types of loan programs to help small business: loans made by private lenders and those made directly by the SBA. Loans made by private lenders, banks, or other institutions are guaranteed up to 90 percent by the SBA. The current maximum for such loans is $750,000. Loans made directly by the SBA are available only to those applicants unable to obtain private financing from an SBA-guaranteed or participation loan. The maximum direct loan is $150,000.

The SBA also offers loans to special groups such as disadvantaged or handicapped business people, businesspersons involved in some type of energy conservation endeavor, and development companies involved in helping small businesses in urban and rural communities.

Qualified businesses wishing to apply for a loan must take the following steps. They must submit a financial statement listing all assets and liabilities of the business. They must prepare financial statements showing current earnings, property owned or leased, and financial obligations. The owner, each partner, or each significant stockholder must submit a current personal financial statement. Also, the firm must compile a list of collateral to be offered as security for the loan, with an estimate of the current market value of each item. The business must indicate the amount of the loan requested and the exact purposes for which the loan will be used. An SBA loan officer then processes the application.

Persons who need a loan to start a new business follow these procedures. First, they must state what type of business is planned, indicating the experience and management capabilities of principal owners. Next, they must provide a current financial statement listing all personal assets and liabilities. Applicants must estimate how much they can invest in the business and how much they will need to borrow. In addition, applicants must submit a detailed projection of earnings. Finally, they must provide a list of collateral that can be offered as security with an estimate of the present market value of each item.

Small Business Administration (SBA) Principal government agency concerned with small U.S. firms.

Loans for Small Exporting Businesses

Small businesses used to largely ignore overseas markets. Today, however, more than half of all U.S. exporters have less than 100 employees.[31] In an attempt to further stimulate small-business exports, the *Small Business Export Expansion Act* provided for SBA loan guarantees for up to 90 percent of bank loans of less than $500,000 to assist small businesses in developing international markets. Another law designed to assist the small-business exporter and other firms hurt by foreign trade is the *Small Business Trade and Competitiveness Act.* Construction and renovation guarantees are available up to $1 million and working capital used to increase exports can be guaranteed up to $250,000.

SBIC Funding

Small Business Investment Company (SBIC)
Federally funded investment group that makes loans to small businesses.

A **Small Business Investment Company (SBIC)** is an investment group that funds small businesses under an SBA license. An SBIC is set up with private monies. If the Small Business Administration licenses an SBIC, it can borrow up to 400 percent of its capitalization from the government. SBICs provide equity capital as well as fixed-rate loans of three- to ten-year durations.

Help with Procurement Contracts

Small firms can also obtain assistance in receiving a share of government contracts. Current legislation requires that small businesses receive a share of government procurement contracts.

set-aside program
Legislation that specifies only small businesses are eligible for certain government contracts.

This requirement is met by the **set-aside program** that allows only small businesses to bid for selected government contracts. Any federal agency with buying authority must have an Office of Small and Disadvantaged Business Utilization to assure that these firms receive a reasonable portion of their procurement contracts.[32]

In addition to the regular set-aside program for small firms, the SBA's *8 (a) Program* allows companies owned by "socially and economically disadvantaged individuals" to negotiate government contracts outside the standard competitive bidding procedure. Over 3,000 minority-owned firms participate in this program; slightly over 200 are female owned. Companies can remain in this program seven years.[33]

Management Training and Consulting

Service Corps of Retired Executives (SCORE)
SBA program using retired executives as consultants to assist small businesses.

Active Corps of Executives (ACE)
SBA program using volunteer consultants who assist people in small business.

Small Business Institute (SBI)
SBA program that uses business students as consultants to small businesses.

The SBA provides management advice through various publications and programs. It maintains an "Answer Desk" to receive phone calls from small-business people and others. The toll-free number is 1-800-368-5855. The SBA established a special outreach program to alert female entrepreneurs to its activities. Its hundreds of business publications can be ordered for little or no cost, and its conferences and seminars are widely available. Management counseling is conducted through a variety of programs. The **Service Corps of Retired Executives (SCORE)** and the **Active Corps of Executives (ACE)** both offer volunteer management consultants who assist people with small-business problems. There are now over 400 SCORE chapters in the United States. The **Small Business Institute (SBI)** sends out senior and graduate students as consultants on small-business problems at no cost to the firm requesting help. The SBI program operates under faculty supervision at hundreds of colleges and universities in the United States. **Small Business Development Centers** assist small businesses through research and consulting activities. Fees are charged to offset the costs.

Franchising

backbone

Domino's, McDonald's, Kentucky Fried Chicken, and Holiday Inn are some of the nation's best-known franchises. The franchising concept has played a major role in the growth of small business. **Franchising** is actually a business arrangement involving a contract between a manufacturer or another supplier and a dealer that specifies the methods to be used in marketing a product or service.

Franchising has made a difference for Jack Grist of Neenah, Wisconsin. Grist has operated an office-products store there for 25 years. While Grist ran a successful business, he was never able to stock the major computer brands. His account was too small for the large suppliers to handle profitably.

The breakthrough came when Grist read about Today's Computer Business Centers, a franchise offered by Intelligent Electronics Inc., of Exton, Pennsylvania. For an initial fee and an agreement to set aside a corner of his store, Grist became a TCBC franchisee with the ability to offer IBM and Compaq computers.

Intelligent Electronics, which also offers Hewlett-Packard and Epson products, was created to serve the 5,600 small, independent office-products stores that dot the countryside. So far, approximately 200 have signed up as TCBC franchisees. The TCBC formula has worked for Jack Grist. Over 40 percent of his store's volume now comes from computers and peripherals.[34]

The Franchising Sector

Franchising started just after the Civil War when the Singer Company began to set up sewing-machine outlet franchises. The concept became increasingly popular after 1900 within the automobile industry. Automobile travel led to demands for gasoline, oil, and tires, all commodities that employed franchising. Soft drinks and lodging became other popular franchises.

Today, franchising accounts for $640 billion in annual sales. The nation's 509,000 franchises employ over 7.3 million people. By the year 2000, it is projected that half of all retail sales in the United States will come from the franchising sector.[35]

Franchising is also growing rapidly abroad. Some 354 U.S. franchisors operate nearly 32,000 units overseas. Canada is the biggest market for U.S. franchises. It is followed by Japan, Australia, and the United Kingdom.[36] The most common franchises abroad are Kentucky Fried Chicken (54 nations), Holiday Inn (51 nations), and McDonald's (44 nations).[37]

In addition, a few franchises popular in the United States started in another country. For example, Molly Maid started in Canada in 1980 and came to the United States four years later. There are now 163 franchises.[38]

Currently, the fastest-growing franchise is Subway Sandwiches & Salads, which has been opening a new unit every seven hours. Subway positions itself to appeal to young professionals who want speed but who are health conscious.

Small Business Development Centers (SBDC) Centers using college faculty and others to assist small businesses through research and consulting activities.

franchising Contractual agreement that sets the methods a dealer can use to produce and market a supplier's goods or service.

Table 6.1   The 10 Hottest Franchises

Name/Headquarters	Average Annual Stores Opened	Type of Business
1. Subway Sandwich & Salads Milford, CT	617	Fast-food restaurants
2. Domino's Pizza Ann Arbor, MI	534	Pizza restaurants
3. Chem-Dry Cameron Park, CA	482	Maintenance, cleaning
4. Little Caeser's Pizza Farmington Hills, MI	330	Pizza restaurants
5. Coverall San Diego, CA	321	Maintenance, cleaning
6. Novus Windshield Repair Minneapolis, MN	272	Auto maintenance
7. TCBY Little Rock, AR	263	Yogurt shops
8. Jani-King Dallas, TX	257	Maintenance, cleaning
9. United Package Mailing Service Richmond, VA	245	Packaging, shipping
10. McDonald's Oak Brook, IL	224	Fast-food restaurants

Source: Reprinted from *USA Today,* December 9, 1988, p. 9B. The original source is *Venture,* December 1988.

The firm expects to have 5,000 units by 1994.[39] Table 6.1 shows the ten fastest-growing franchises in the United States. Over the next decade, the franchises that will grow the most rapidly are expected to fall in the following areas: business services, maid services, weight-control centers, hair salons, temporary help services, printing and copying, home furnishings, and automotive lube and oil change centers.[40]

The Franchising Agreement

franchisee
A small-business person who is allowed to sell the goods or services of a supplier in exchange for some payment.

franchisor
Supplier of a franchise that provides various services in exchange for a payment by the franchisee.

The two principals in a franchising agreement are the franchisee and the franchisor. The dealer, or **franchisee**, is a small-business person who is allowed to sell a good or service of a supplier, or **franchisor**, in exchange for some payment (usually a flat fee plus future royalties or commissions). The franchisor typically provides building plans, site selection research, managerial and accounting procedures, and other services to assist the franchisee. The franchisor also provides name recognition for the small-business person who becomes a franchisee. This image is created by national or regional advertising campaigns to which the franchisee typically contributes. But a word of caution is in order here: A well-known name is not enough. The franchisee must satisfy consumer needs and operate efficiently. Several celebrities (such as Tony Bennett, Joe Namath, and Minnie Pearl) have lent their names to franchise systems that failed.[41]

The franchisee purchases tangible and intangible items from the franchisor. Some franchisors charge management fees in addition to their initial franchise fee and a percentage of sales or profits. Still others require contributions to a promotional fund. Total costs can vary widely. The nation's fastest-growing fran-

Photo source: Courtesy of McDonald's Corporation.

McDonald's attributes franchising as a key factor in the growth of its restaurant system. The company granted its first franchise in 1955; today, it has about 7,913 franchises worldwide. About 75 percent of McDonald's restaurants are locally owned and operated by independent entrepreneurs. A McDonald's franchise requires an investment of about $450,000, but franchisees benefit from McDonald's worldwide name recognition, capital and employee resources, and advertising and research. The company insists franchisees be on-premise owner/operators, not simply investors, to ensure consistent delivery of the company's motto — Quality, Service, Cleanliness, Value — to customers.

chise, Subway Sandwiches & Salads, costs about $50,000. Similarly, a Spring Crest Drapery Center can be opened for about $60,000. By comparison, a Maaco Auto Painting and Bodyworks shop will cost $155,000.[42]

The Benefits and Problems of Franchising

The U.S. Commerce Department says franchisors have a failure rate only one-tenth that of other new businesses.[43] But a franchise is like any other business property: It is the buyer's responsibility to know what he or she is buying. Poorly financed or poorly managed franchise systems are no better than poorly financed or poorly managed nonfranchise businesses. Potential investors also need to be reminded that 3.5 percent of the nation's franchisors went bankrupt in a recent year.[44]

Purchasing a good franchise requires a careful study of the concept's advantages and disadvantages. The correct decision in one set of circumstances may be wrong under different circumstances. The franchising concept does not eliminate the risks for someone considering small business investment; it merely adds alternatives.

Advantages of Franchises Existing franchises have a performance record on which the small-business person can make comparisons and judgments. The likelihood of success in the proposed ventures can be assessed by looking at earlier results. This requires careful study and hard work on the part of the franchisee. In addition, a widely recognized name gives the franchisee a tremendous advantage. Car dealers, for instance, know their brand-name products will attract a given clientele. A franchise also gives the small-business person a tested management system. The prospective franchisee usually does not have to worry about setting up an accounting system, establishing quality control standards, or designing employment application forms. These items are typically provided for in the franchise agreement.

Disadvantages of Franchises   On the negative side, franchise fees and future payments can be very expensive. Good franchises with tested management systems, proven performance records, and widely recognized names usually sell for more than those lacking these characteristics. The prospective franchisee must determine whether the expenses involved are fair compensation for what will be received. Another potentially negative factor is that a successful franchise unit can lose customers if other units of the same franchise fail. An inherent disadvantage of the franchise system is that the franchisee is judged by what his or her peers do. A strong, effective program of managerial control is essential to offset any bad impressions created by unsuccessful franchises. Finally, the franchisor's management system may restrict many decisions. The franchisee may not have the independence that most entrepreneurs seek.

Entrepreneurship and small business, whether or not it involves a franchise, has long been an integral part of the private enterprise system. It remains a vital mechanism for the release of competitive energy. People who see a chance for personal achievement are usually more productive than those who see their work as being boring or routine with no chance of improvement. Business ownership offers the opportunity for personal achievement. It always has offered this opportunity, and it probably always will.

Summary of Learning Goals

1.   Explain the vital role played by entrepreneurs and small businesses in the U.S. economy.   Entrepreneurs and small businesses play an important part in the private enterprise system. They provide independence and bring competitive fervor to the U.S. economy. Small firms account for the bulk of all U.S. commercial enterprises and provide a major portion of national output and employment.

2.   Define *entrepreneurship* and describe how entrepreneurs are different from other businesspeople.   Entrepreneurship refers to the risk-taking aspect of the private enterprise system. An entrepreneur is a person who seeks a profitable opportunity and then devises a plan and forms an organization to achieve the objective.

Research shows that entrepreneurs have different personalities from other people. They are willing to take risks and they seek independence. They are also more achievement oriented than the average person. Entrepreneurs also tend to focus on the future.

3.   Define *small business* and identify the industries in which most small firms are established.   A small business is one that is independently owned and operated and does not dominate its market. In addition to farming, most small businesses are concentrated in the retailing and service sectors of the economy, although many new-technology firms also begin as small firms. Most new companies have formed in industries with low entry-level capital requirements.

4. Compare the advantages and disadvantages of small business. Small businesses have some distinct advantages over larger competitors, including innovative behavior, lower costs, and the filling of isolated niches. They also have disadvantages, including poor management, inadequate financing, and government regulation.

5. Analyze the small-business opportunities for women and minorities and the special problems faced by these entrepreneurs. The number of women-owned and minority-owned businesses has increased substantially in recent years. While both groups still face special business problems such as prejudice, lack of business training, and inadequate experience, the situation is changing rapidly. A number of government programs are available to help expand small-business opportunities for women and minorities.

6. Describe how the Small Business Administration functions. The Small Business Administration (SBA) was established in 1953 to assist small firms. The SBA is the chief advocate for small business in government. Its primary functions are to provide financial assistance, help with government procurement matters, and offer management training and consulting to small business.

7. Outline the role of franchising in the U.S. economy. Franchising is a contract between a supplier and a dealer that sets the methods to be used in producing and marketing a product. There are now 509,000 franchises in the United States, employing 7.3 million people. It is estimated that, by the year 2000, franchising will account for half of all retail sales in the United States.

8. List the advantages and disadvantages of franchising. The advantages of the franchising approach to small business are performance records on which to make comparisons and judgments, a widely recognized name, and tested management systems. The disadvantages include the high cost of obtaining some franchises, consumer judgment of the business on the basis of other similar franchises, and restrictions on business decisions.

Key Terms

business incubator

entrepreneur

small business

venture capitalist

Small Business Administration (SBA)

Small Business Investment Company (SBIC)

set-aside program

Service Corps of Retired Executives (SCORE)

Active Corps of Executives (ACE)

Small Business Institute (SBI)

Small Business Development Centers (SBDC)

franchising

franchisee

franchisor

Review Questions

1. Why is entrepreneurship and small business so important to the U.S. economy?

2. How does entrepreneurship differ from small-business management?

3. Describe the entrepreneurial personality.

4. In what sectors of the economy is small business most important? To what do you credit its strength in these areas?

5. Outline the advantages small firms have over larger organizations.

6. Why is financing such a problem for small business? Explain.

7. Describe the current status of women in small business and the reasons for it. Explain the current status of minorities in small business.

8. Discuss the various government agencies that serve the small business sector.

9. Explain the three primary functions of the Small Business Administration and how the SBA performs them.

10. Explain why franchising is such a vital element of today's small-business sector.

Discussion Questions

1. The Australian government implemented a program designed to lure entrepreneurs "down under." The Business Migration Program provides a permanent-residence visa, business counseling, financial incentives, and tax breaks to foreign entrepreneurs willing to invest in a new business in Australia. The program is credited with increasing foreign investment in the Australian economy. Discuss Australia's approach to increasing the entrepreneurial sector. What do you anticipate will be the benefits and disadvantages of the Business Migration Program?

2. Nearly 40 years after it was formed, the Small Business Administration has still not settled on one definition of small business. Discuss.

3. When oil prices collapsed during the early 1980s, Houma, Louisiana–based Bilco Tools, an oil-field equipment manufacturer, had only $18,000 in receivables to offset $1 million of debt. In desperation, the firm's president, William E. Coyle, bought an around-the-world ticket and flew off to find new business. Coyle's effort was successful, and overseas sales now account for a third of Bilco's $2 million annual revenue. Discuss why more small businesses do not seek foreign sales.

4. Senator Dale Bumpers of Arkansas, chairman of the Senate's Small Business Committee, commented: "Women-owned business is the fastest-growing segment of the economy and its success or failure can drastically affect our nation's economic future." Discuss Senator Bumpers' remark.

5. A survey by *Inc.* magazine and the Hay Group Inc. reported that employees of small businesses were more satisfied with their jobs than those who worked for large organizations. John C. Gardner, the CEO of Milwaukee's Aircraft Industries Corp., puts it this way: "Most workers in small firms are satisfied because everyone knows everyone else and you have a great sense of comradeship, of working together as a team for the good of the organization." Discuss how small-business people like Gardner can maintain employee job satisfaction.

Video Case

Famous Amos Chocolate Chip Cookie Company

If, by *entrepreneurship,* we mean a conscious, planned effort to start and develop a business, Wally Amos may not comfortably fit the definition. Although his company has become well known and highly profitable, Amos claims that he never had big dreams for his venture. When he opened his first Famous Amos cookie store in 1975 — the first chocolate chip cookie store in the world — his only goal was survival. "I just wanted to make a living," he modestly claims.

Amos, who had been a Hollywood agent for years, possessed two important characteristics that would ultimately serve him in his new venture: an engaging personality that communicated itself in person and in television interviews, and the ability to bake outstanding cookies. Clients and friends who received his fresh homemade cookies raved about them, and he was bombarded by suggestions that he go into business producing and selling them. Amos knew that he had at least one thing in common with many would-be small business operators: a lack of funds. So he decided to test his friends' conviction regarding his cookies by inviting them to invest in his venture. This way he raised a grand total of $25,000 and the first store was opened.

The store proved to be a huge success and, within five years, total sales had reached the $7 million mark. By 1985, they had increased another 50 percent to more than $10 million.

But growth proved to be a difficult undertaking for Amos. He simply did not have the funds to expand his retail outlet into a large chain, and he did not want to take on the risks associated with borrowed funds to finance this growth.

In addition, he did not have the millions needed to create a national advertising campaign. He decided to use himself as the focus for all of the Famous Amos promotional efforts. Wally became both the firm's spokesperson and trademark (his picture appears on

Notes: Kate Bulkley, "Three Baers Gobble Cookie Maker," *Denver Business Journal,* April 25, 1988, pp. 1, 2; Michael King, "To Sell or Not to Sell . . ." *Black Enterprise,* June 1987, pp. 287–290; and Gail Buchetter, "Happy Cookie," *Forbes,* March 10, 1986, pp. 176–178.

all of his products). "What I did was pattern the promotion of the cookie after the promotion of individuals that I worked with during my fourteen years in show business," Wally explained. The promotional method worked, and the company developed an enviable position in mass-market recognition and appeal. Such recognition was invaluable in overcoming established competitors like Pepperidge Farm and newcomers, such as Mrs. Fields, in the highly-competitive cookie market.

Famous Amos did not have the funds to contact retail buyers and convince them to stock its products, so Amos used the opposite approach. The firm was able to use the "pull through" style of distribution because customers began demanding that retailers stock the cookies, thereby "pulling" the product into the stores. Soon demand was so great that the company was able to adopt mass production systems for the homemade cookies. But the small business still had major problems, the most important one being how to find additional outlets for the cookies and how to convert sales made to retailers and distributors into quick cash. The solution was to distribute Famous Amos cookies through intermediaries who would buy them directly from the company and make immediate payment.

Amos realized that poor management is a potential danger for every business — large or small — and an experienced executive named Sid Ross was persuaded to join the growing company as president. Ross worked to create a network of distributors who could get the products onto shelves in supermarkets and other retail stores and would pay for the products on a timely basis. Ross explained the system this way: "We have 232 distributors who are called *store-door* distributors. And what they do is they have a route man . . . every Tuesday that route man, at 10 a.m. is going to be in a certain store. You can set your watch by it. And these route men are valuable to us because we have a limited shelf-life. We have to rotate that product. . . . We have to be handled correctly to get the proper attention the product needs. So our network of distributors does this for us."

Rick Royce, one of the independent distributors handling the Famous Amos line, explains how the arrangement works: "We buy our product directly from

Famous Amos. We go over twice a week and fill up a truck and bring it over here, unload, and then our drivers come in and take our product from us. Not only *our* drivers, by the way. I also have a sub-distributor network . . . that actually comes in and buys products from me and takes it into areas I can't. They're too far away or have better access to the market than I do."

The more than 40,000 U.S. supermarkets represent one important channel of distribution for Famous Amos cookies. The company provides attractive displays amid fresh-baked products in surroundings that enhance the cookies' positive image. Another outlet for Famous Amos cookies are convenience stores. Because these stores cater to impulse buyers who tend to buy for immediate consumption, Famous Amos produces smaller, individual-size bags of cookies for these outlets.

Wally Amos recognized customers' additional cookie preferences aside from chocolate chip and expanded the product line to include large, soft cookies and a variety of flavors, such as cinnamon raisin oatmeal cookies. Famous Amos bakeries now carry ice cream to balance seasonal sales variations. The company is also developing a variety of frozen products that can be distributed through the same channels that send out its frozen cookie batter.

As the company continued to grow and add more management talent to oversee operations and plan for the future, the financing issue continued to loom large as an obstacle to further growth. The firm's policy of dependence on plowing back earnings to finance continued growth made the dream of a Famous Amos retail outlet chain an almost impossible one. Each new store represented a significant investment. Moreover, each retail outlet would be a business in itself, requiring management, personnel, and other resources. Then the idea dawned — just as it had for McDonald's Ray Kroc two decades earlier: franchising.

According to company vice-president of domestic franchising, Ken Wolf, "It takes an awful lot of money to develop your own string of company-owned stores, and the fastest way of expanding is by utilizing other people's money, so to speak, and that's the route of franchising." These stores are known as "hot-bake" stores because the cookies are not prepackaged but are sold warm and fresh from the in-store ovens. The franchises are carefully controlled by Famous Amos; approval is required for everything from leaflets and other advertising to packaging. The uniformity helps ease training and management procedures and presents a unified image for Famous Amos, both in the U.S. and in the growing number of foreign countries where the firm's cookies are now sold.

By 1988, the success of Famous Amos had become so well known that the firm was an acquisition target for established businesses and wealthy individual investors. The small business, whose founder really became so famous that his Panama hat and brightly-patterned Indian gauze shirt are now housed in the Smithsonian's Collection of Advertising History, found a new owner when it was acquired by the Baer family. Even though Amos benefitted financially by selling the business he had founded, he is in no way forgotten. In fact, part of the sales agreement required that Famous Amos promotions continue to rely on Wally.

Questions
1. Three forms of entrepreneurship are described in the chapter. Which form best describes Wally Amos?

2. Relate the formation and growth of Famous Amos to the advantages and disadvantages of small business described in the chapter. Which advantage(s) proved most important to Amos' success? Which disadvantage(s) proved to be the greatest problem?

3. How did the "pull-through" marketing approach work to Amos' advantage in expanding distribution of his firm's products?

4. Explain why franchising rather than company ownership was chosen by Famous Amos as a means of expanding the firm's retail store network.

Careers in Business

More than half of the nation's work force is employed in small businesses, according to the Small Business Administration. Retail stores, service firms, and high-technology companies are among the most common small businesses. Franchising, an important aspect of small business, employs millions of people working in businesses that range from muffler repair shops to dental offices and from fast-food restaurants to employment agencies.

This section investigates some specific jobs in small business and franchising, including small-business owner, small-business consultant, franchise director, franchisee, venture capitalists, corporate attorneys, and legal assistants.

Small-Business Owner

Small-business owners may be involved in the conception, financing, and day-to-day operation of their enterprises.

Job Description. Many small-business owners see a consumer need for a specific good or service and decide to go into business to fill that need. Judging the marketability of a good or service involves conducting market research into such areas as location and pricing. Small-business owners must also finance their enterprises, which often involves working with banks, setting up partnerships, and submitting loan requests to the SBA. The day-to-day operation of a business entails keeping records, managing employees, advertising, and dealing with customers.

Career Path. Many owners gain experience working in other small businesses. Others work for large corporations and decide they would rather work for themselves.

Salary. The earnings of small-business owners vary widely from firm to firm.

Small-Business Consultant

Many small-business owners employ consultants to help them put their business on a sound footing.

Job Description. Small-business consultants help firms set up a financial plan to attract investors or secure business loans. They develop a marketing plan or an accounting system to meet a firm's day-to-day financial needs. They also work with owners to establish employee benefit packages or provide needed advice on management techniques.

Career Path. Many people in this field are employed by large consulting firms, while others operate their own consulting firms. Most business consultants have degrees in business. Many gain experience and develop a network of business contacts working for an established firm before becoming consultants.

Salary. Earnings vary widely, depending upon personal efforts and level of experience and contacts.

Franchise Director

Franchise directors, also known as franchisors, operate franchise operations on a local, state, or national level. They work with franchisees, who sell their product or service to the public.

Job Description. Franchisors provide the franchisee with a proven product or service, management and marketing know-how, training, ongoing assistance, standardized operating procedures, and a common identity. Franchise directors need a sound background in finance and marketing. They must also be able to work with state and local governments to ensure that the franchise operation complies with applicable disclosure requirements.

Career Path. Many franchise directors gain experience in the franchise field by first working for other franchisors. Others start successful small businesses that have the potential for growth. They believe the best way to achieve this growth is through franchising.

Salary. The earnings of franchise directors are often tied to the up-front fees collected from franchisees when the franchisees buy into the operation, ongoing royalties, and fees for many authorized parts and services. Their incomes typically depend on the number of franchises in operation and their business success.

Franchisee

Franchisees buy into ongoing franchise operations, which become their own small businesses.

Job Description. Franchisees are independent businesspeople who finance and manage their own businesses. Because buying into an established franchise chain is often costly, franchisees must be prepared to work with banks and financiers to raise funds. Once the business is in operation, they face the same responsibilities as other small-business owners. They must also establish an effective working relationship with a franchisor.

Career Path.   Franchisees share similar backgrounds to those engaged in other small businesses. One major difference is that the franchisee buys into an established business whose products and services are often already known to the public, while the small-business owner goes into business without this support.

Salary.   Earnings vary depending on the success of the franchise.

Venture Capitalist

Venture capitalists often provide an essential financing service to small-business owners.

Job Description.   Entrepreneurs in need of start-up money often turn to venture capitalists for funds. Venture capitalists see ideas that might turn into profitable businesses and decide to back the entrepreneur with needed financing in exchange for a percentage of the business. Venture capitalists work closely with banks and other financing sources. They also work closely with entrepreneurs, who present financial and business plans for review.

Career Path.   Venture capitalists must have a strong background in finance. Many have worked in the finance function of large corporations.

Salary.   Earnings depend on the number of businesses venture capitalists finance and the success of these enterprises.

Travel Agent

Travel agencies are a rapidly growing type of small business. These firms make travel arrangements for both business and individual clients. The Bureau of Labor Statistics expects faster than average growth in this employment field in the years ahead.

Job Description.   Travel agents provide an important service to their clients, saving them both time and money in planning and arranging their trips. Travel agents must be very detail oriented and able to work on a number of projects at once. Travel agencies use computer reservation systems to obtain airline tickets and hotel rooms. Agents also take phone calls from clients to determine their needs and contact vendors to work on special arrangements.

Career Path.   Beginning travel agents often work directly for airlines as reservation agents or in travel agencies handling relatively uncomplicated bookings. Their responsibility increases with experience and ability. At the top of the ladder, travel agents set up their own agencies.

Salary.   In a recent year, travel agents earned, on average, $21,000. The average starting salary was $12,000.

Corporate Attorney

Businesses have many legal needs that are primarily filled by in-house or hired attorneys specializing in corporate law. In a recent year, 527,000 lawyers were in the work force, with much faster than average growth forecast until the year 2000.

Job Description.   Depending on the size of the firm, the corporate attorney may be a generalist or a specialist in a particular type of law, such as tax law or labor law. The corporate attorney meets with top officials of the firm to discuss strategy and give them legal advice. Much time is spent preparing for negotiations or trials.

Career Path.   New law school graduates do research for experienced attorneys and handle small cases. As they gain experience, they take on increased responsibility. With a firm, advancement into top management is sometimes the final career step.

Salary.   Size of the company and location play a role in determining salaries. A corporate attorney with three years experience in Atlanta could make as little as $26,000 in a recent year, while a counterpart in San Francisco made as much as $58,000. General counsels for large corporations can make more than three times as much as the average private sector salary in a law firm. The average salary for a corporate attorney in a recent year was $101,000.

Legal Assistant

Legal assistants, or paralegals, work with attorneys in providing legal services to individuals and businesses, including many small businesses. Currently, about 45,000 people are employed as legal assistants throughout the United States.

Job Description.   Paralegals are supervised by an attorney. Most of their work involves legal research, but they also file court papers, help develop legal arguments, and assist with affidavits. Legal assistants working directly for firms assist attorneys with their specific areas of responsibility, such as financing.

Career Path.   Beginning paralegals are given routine tasks and are closely monitored. As they acquire experience, they are assigned more challenging responsibilities. Opportunity for advancement is limited; however, some paralegals achieve management positions.

Salary.   The average starting salary for legal assistants in a recent year was $17,200. The average salary was $22,200.

Chapter 7
The Process of Management

Chapter 8
Internal Organization

Chapter 9
Production and Operations Management

Management and Organization

Career Profile: Steve Minock

Family businesses often aren't connected to the family in anything but name by the third generation. But at Grand Blanc Cement, the Minock family has run the operation for 63 years, and 33-year-old Steve Minock is ready to take over when the time comes.

Minock is one of three principal owners in the family business, which sells cement blocks. It does most of its business in Michigan, with some sales coming from new operations in Pennsylvania and Ohio.

At age 18, Minock started working at the company in the yard — the area where trucks unload materials and are loaded with finished brick. He worked there part-time while he took courses in concrete technology processes at Alpena Community College. He continued his business education at Mott Community College.

Minock became vice-president of Grand Blanc Cement at age 25. But by then, Minock had already earned the respect of his peers. The year before, he had been elected president of the Michigan Builders Supply Association at the unheard-of age of 24.

His major responsibilities as vice-president include handling the company's finances, managing its four sales representatives, and taking care of the daily administrative duties involved in running a company with some 50 employees. To solve problems that arise, "I either draw from something we learned in class, or I can look it up in my textbooks and handle the situation," Minock says.

He has also learned his lessons about how to sell a product. In a recent year, Grand Blanc Cement sold a record $6 million worth of blocks and bricks to a variety of wholesalers and retailers, the largest being K mart. Minock reports that this year's sales are ahead of last year's and the new operations in Pennsylvania and Ohio are also picking up steam.

Says Paul Londrigan, Minock's professor at Mott Community College, "Steve took an intensive selection of marketing and management classes and was able to combine the skills he learned from each to let people know he had a proven, successful product. He now has a knack for knowing what to say and he also understands the basic usage of his product."

Since he read at school about technology and how changes can help a business, Minock has revamped the company's approach to doing business through the use of various technological improvements, including a computer system.

"We try to keep as up to date as possible," says Minock. "We went to computers to run our billing and operations, and we even do cost analysis to see if what we're doing is affordable, and how it could be made more so."

Photo source: Courtesy of Grand Blanc Cement Co. and Nick Beccia.

7

The Process of Management

Learning Goals

1. To identify the levels of management.

2. To explain the skills required for managerial success.

3. To outline the functions of organizational objectives.

4. To list the functions of management.

5. To distinguish among strategic planning, tactical planning, and operational planning.

6. To explain the concept of corporate culture.

7. To explain the concept of leadership and the three basic leadership styles.

8. To list the steps in the decision-making process and contrast programmed and nonprogrammed decisions.

9. To outline the importance of time management.

The small computer start-up was similar to a lot of other high-tech firms in Palo Alto, California. The founder started the company with his own money, some $7 million. The firm confidently set becoming a $1 billion corporation as its goal. The new company sought to produce a low-cost, superefficient computer.

The organization's founder and CEO had a mixed managerial background. He was highly regarded in the industry as an innovator and visionary, but he was also known as indecisive and lacking in human relations skills. He often threw tantrums and verbally attacked his staff. In fact, his former employer had eased him into a position that lacked any responsibility or authority.

Steve Jobs, the founder of Apple Computer, had a lot to prove when he started NeXT Inc. in 1985. He wanted to show the industry and his former colleagues at Apple that he could once again develop a major computer innovation like the Macintosh.

Jobs started his new venture by recruiting five of his Apple colleagues. In exchange for a pay cut, each of these key people got 2 percent of the start-up's stock. When he needed more capital, he invested an additional $5 million of his own money. He also attracted a major investor, Ross Perot, who invested $20 million. Jobs also built the support of the universities that he originally saw as his marketplace. Academic computer experts were recruited to an unpaid advisory board. Carnegie Mellon and Stanford Universities each bought 1 percent of NeXT's stock. In 1989, Jobs decided to also sell his units through Businessland, Inc., when the computer store chain agreed to

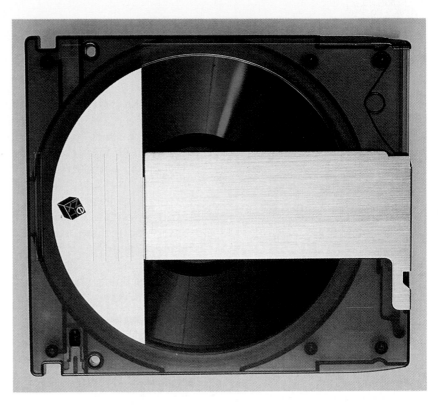

buy $100 million worth of NeXT computers during the first 12 months of their contract.

When NeXT's $6,500 computer was introduced on October 12, 1988, many people marveled at Jobs' innovative technology and his flair for marketing. A largely untold story was how Jobs had adapted as a manager. While he had always been able to inspire his employees, Jobs usually kept his own counsel on most decisions. At NeXT, he became more open to suggestions from his 150 employees and his advisory board. For example, the advisory board persuaded the strong-willed CEO to sell his computer and high-resolution laser printer as separate items. Also at the advisory board's suggestion, NeXT's internal memory was increased from the four

megabytes Jobs originally planned to eight. (Megabytes are explained in Chapter 17.)

Jobs also spent $2 million to set up an automated factory in Fremont, California. A robotic system assembles NeXT's circuit boards. This manufacturing process is capable of high levels of production, which will allow Jobs to cut prices as sales volume builds.

Can Steve Jobs become as successful a manager as he is an entrepreneur? When *Business Week* asked Jobs this question, he simply replied: "We'll see."[1] But one thing is for certain: The evolution of Steve Jobs as a manager illustrates many of the concepts introduced in the chapter that follows.

Photo source: Courtesy of NeXT, Inc.

Chapter Overview

Kay Orr, Pat Riley, and Sam Walton are all managers. Orr is the governor of Nebraska, Pat Riley is the head coach of the Los Angeles Lakers, and Sam Walton is the CEO of Wal-Mart. Other managers preside over organizations as diverse as Eastern Illinois University, Henry Ford Hospital, and a nearby Burger King.

The importance of effective management to organizational success cannot be overestimated. Analyses of small-business failures usually list "poor management" as one of the leading causes. When asked about their career objectives, many students in an introductory business course will reply, "I want to be a manager."

This chapter examines the meaning of management and its universal applications. The three levels of management in a typical organization are identified; and supervisory, or first-line, management is discussed in detail because most students entering management will be employed at this level. The role of objectives is analyzed, and the process of decision making is discussed. The managerial functions of planning, organizing, directing, and controlling are described, and the crucial subjects of leadership and time management are explored.

What Is Management?

autocratic way

System Compliance

management

Achievement of organizational objectives through people and other resources.

Leadership - object

Management skills are transferable

Management is the achievement of organizational objectives through people and other resources. The manager's job is to combine human and technical resources in the best way possible to achieve these objectives. Managers are not directly involved in production; they do not produce a finished product. Instead, they direct the efforts of others toward the company's goals. The recent actions of Gary Sasser, chief executive officer of Averitt Express, illustrates what a manager does. Sasser wanted to improve the productivity of the Cookeville, Tennessee, trucking company, so he divided his 1,400 employees into productivity-improvement groups consisting of three to ten people. This action led to a sales increase of 38 percent and an earnings increase of 48 percent. Sasser describes his approach to management this way: "We just take the coach approach. Lots of feedback, lots of encouragement; our people do the rest."[2]

Similarly, when Beth Pritchard took over S. C. Johnson Wax's insect control division, she knew she had industry-leading products such as Raid and Off. Still, Pritchard believed further gains were possible by regionalizing her product development and marketing efforts. Pritchard changed product formulas and packaging and reorganized her personnel. She attributes her accomplishments to the people who work for her: "My philosophy is that you can't do anything yourself. Your people have to do it."[3] Both Sasser and Pritchard illustrate how a manager achieves organizational objectives through people and other resources.

Management Principles Are Universal

The management principles and concepts presented in this chapter are applicable — even fundamental — not only to profit-seeking firms but also to non-profit organizations. The local hospital administrator, the head of the United

Figure 7.1   The Management Pyramid

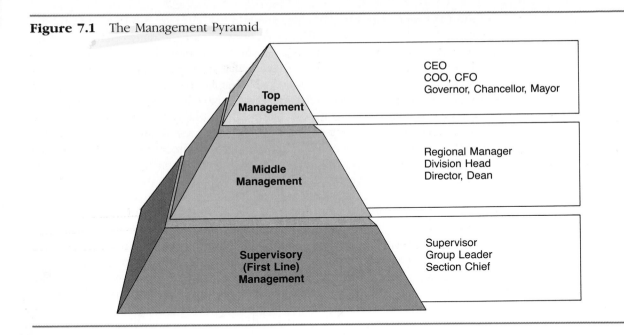

Fund, and the PTA president all perform managerial functions similar to those performed by their counterparts in industry.

Businesses are only one form of enterprise, distinguished from others in terms of objectives. Businesses are profit-oriented, while nonprofit organizations such as museums, colleges, city governments, and charitable agencies are service-oriented. But both benefit from effective management.

The Management Pyramid

The local Taco Bell franchise has a very simple organization—an owner/manager and an assistant manager or two. By contrast, large organizations have a complex managerial structure. Sherwin-Williams, for example, has a board of directors consisting of 11 people including the chairman and president. The Cleveland-based paint company also has two group presidents, seven vice-presidents, an assistant secretary and corporate director of taxes, and hundreds of other executives. Are all of these people managers? The answer is yes, since they are all engaged in combining human and other resources to achieve company objectives.

The various levels of management form a **management pyramid**, or hierarchy, in an organization. As Figure 7.1 indicates, a firm's management can be divided into three categories: top management, middle management, and supervisory management. Although all three categories contain managers, each level of the pyramid stresses different activities.

Top management is the highest level of the management hierarchy. The top position is the **chief executive officer (CEO)**. This person is responsible for the overall direction of the firm and its relations with its various policies. The CEO also typically serves as the chairman of the board of directors. The executive positions immediately below the CEO are usually the **chief operating officer (COO)** and the **chief financial officer (CFO)**. In most organizations,

management pyramid
The managerial hierarchy of an organization.

top management
Managers who develop long-range plans and interact with the government and the community.

chief executive officer (CEO)
Top position in the managerial hierarchy; responsible for overall direction of the firm.

chief operating officer (COO)
The person responsible for the daily operations of the firm.

chief financial officer (CFO)
Top executive responsible for the financial affairs of the firm.

the CFO reports to the COO; but sometimes the COO and CFO are of equal rank. The chief operating officer is responsible for the daily operations of the organization. Vice-presidents of production, engineering, marketing, and human resources report to this individual. In many companies, the COO also carries the title of president. The chief financial officer is responsible for the financial affairs of the organization. The corporate controller reports to this person. At Sherwin-Williams, the CFO's official title is senior vice-president — finance and chief financial officer. Below these top spots are other top management positions such as vice-president and group presidents.

middle management
Managers responsible for developing detailed plans and procedures to implement plans of top management.

Middle management, the second level of the management pyramid, includes regional managers, division heads, district sales managers, production superintendents, the director of research and development, and plant managers. Middle management is more involved than top management in specific operations within the organization. Middle managers are responsible for developing detailed plans and procedures to implement the general plans of top management. They may, for example, determine the number of salespeople for a particular district, operate a branch of a department store chain, select equipment for a new facility, or develop techniques for evaluating employee performance.

supervisory management
People directly responsible for details of assigning workers to specific jobs and evaluating performance.

Supervisory management, or first-line management, includes people who are directly responsible for the details of assigning workers to specific jobs and evaluating daily — even hourly — performance. This first level of the pyramid has direct and continuing contact with operative personnel and is responsible for implementing the plans developed by middle management.

Effective communication links must exist among and between all levels of management. It is also important that each level be responsible for the decisions that should be legitimately made at that point in the organization. In fact, in the advertisement shown in Figure 7.2, AIG suggests the management pyramid be turned upside down.

At any level, managers need certain skills to succeed, including the ability to work in a team, the ability to formulate and carry out long-range plans, the courage to take risks, and the ability to relate to others. The lack of some of these abilities often prevents people from moving up the managerial ladder.

First-Line Management

Supervisory management is emphasized here because it is the level at which most students will obtain their first managerial experience. Supervisory managers may have such job titles as supervisor, chairperson, department head, group leader, or section chief. In each case, the position involves coordinating the work of operative employees in accomplishing tasks assigned by middle management. Because the first-line manager interacts continuously with members of the work team, effective human relations skills are extremely important.

The first-line manager can be more of a teacher, expediter, and assistant than a supervisor. For example, at the Korean-owned Samsung television plant in New Jersey, supervisors and workers regularly swap suggestions in the cafeteria or on the plant floor. There are also monthly meetings where, among other things, supervisors check on their employees' personal needs such as an attorney for a divorce or a house closing.[4] While Samsung may be different from most American-owned firms, this example points out the need for first-line managers to have effective human relations skills.

Figure 7.2   A Different Approach to the Management Pyramid

Source: Courtesy of American International Group, Inc./Agency: Bozell, Jacobs, Kenyon & Eckhardt.

Skills Required for Managerial Success

Every manager, regardless of level in the organization, must possess three basic managerial skills: technical skills, human relations skills, and conceptual skills. Although the importance of each skill varies at different levels, managers use all three types at some time during their careers.

Technical Skills Supervisory

Technical skills refer to the manager's ability to understand and use techniques, knowledge, and tools of a specific discipline or department. Technical skills are particularly important for first-line managers who are frequently involved with production employees who operate machinery, with salespersons who must explain technical details of their firm's products, or with computer programmers working on a complicated assignment. These skills become relatively less important as the manager moves up the managerial hierarchy.

Dave Pall founded Pall Corp of Glen Cove, New York, in 1946. While he is no longer active in the operational management of the $386 million maker of high-tech industrial filters, Board Chairman Pall is a good example of someone who possesses the technical skills needed to manage such a company. Pall still works

technical skills
Ability to understand and use techniques, knowledge, and tools of a specific discipline or department.

in the firm's research and development laboratory. He also holds over 100 patents for filtration devices.[5] In short, Pall is able to manage effectively because people respect his technical expertise in the area.

Human Relations Skills

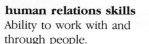

human relations skills
Ability to work with and through people.

Human relations skills are "people" skills. They involve the manager's ability to work effectively with and through people. They involve communicating, leading, and motivating workers to accomplish assigned activities. In addition, they involve the ability to interact with superiors and others outside the immediate department or work area. The ability to create a work environment in which organizational members will contribute their best efforts to achieve objectives is a crucial managerial skill at every level.

Herb Kelleher, the CEO of Southwest Airlines, clearly possesses the human relations skills necessary to run the nation's tenth-largest airline. Kelleher is often on both ends of practical jokes with his employees. He also occasionally works the ticket counter and serves cocktails. Kelleher believes the positive working environment he fosters is the major reason why Southwest's personnel are considered the most productive in the airline industry. The CEO explains it this way: "Robert Frost says that it's a shame that all of our minds work furiously until we get to work. If you come into an environment that's stimulating, your mind will keep working."[6]

Conceptual Skills

conceptual skills
Ability to view the organization as a unified whole and to understand how each part relates to other parts.

Conceptual skills refer to the ability of the manager to see the organization as a unified whole and understand how each part of the overall organization interacts with other parts. These skills involve a manager's ability to "see the big picture" by acquiring, analyzing, and interpreting information. Such skills are especially important for top managers, who must develop imaginative and analytical plans for the future direction of the organization. Even though a manager may have been promoted several times from different positions in a single functional area (such as engineering), his or her ability to be a successful top manager is greatly affected by the ability to understand the contributions of other departments, such as finance, marketing, human resources, industrial relations, and public relations.

After 20 years with Highgate Picture Learning Corp., Senior Vice-President Linda Gottlieb knew what it took to produce winning television and educational films. However, Highgate moved into feature films, and the conceptual skills Gottlieb possessed no longer fit the management profile. She was more entrepreneurial and less concerned with managing a corporate staff. Eventually, Gottlieb was fired.

At first Gottlieb blamed her former boss for her failure as a manager. Later, she assessed her own conceptual skills and realized her most effective contribution to an organization was her creative ability. Gottlieb decided she was really better at creating film projects than she was at managing people. She even wrote a book — *When Smart People Fail* — about her self-assessment.

Gottlieb soon started a new career as a feature film producer. One of her projects was rejected repeatedly by movie companies. Finally, Vestron Pictures accepted "Dirty Dancing," a movie that went on to gross $140 million while costing only $5 million to produce.[7] Gottlieb had correctly assessed where her conceptual skills fit in the movie industry.

Figure 7.3   Types of Skills Needed at Each Level of Management

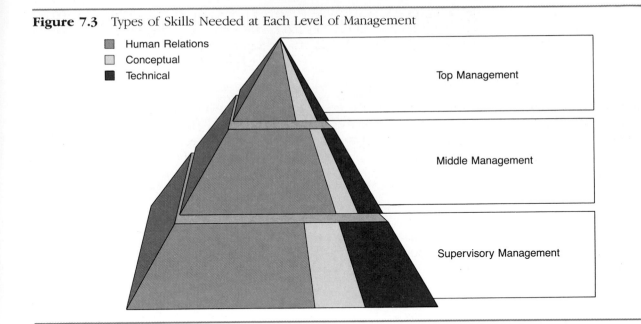

Conceptual and human relations skills may be transferred from one department, company, or industry to another. A number of major government officials have successfully switched from careers in the private sector. In addition, it is now common for top managers to have held previous managerial positions at other companies. On the other hand, technical skills are more difficult to transfer from one industry to another due to the unique characteristics and requirements of many such skills.

Although all three types of skills are needed by managers at every level in the organization, the relative importance of each differs at each level. Figure 7.3 demonstrates how the relative importance of each managerial skill varies from supervisory positions to top management positions.

The Importance of Setting Objectives

The old maxim, "If you don't know where you are going, any road will get you there," applies to business as well as to individuals. Both need definite objectives in order to be successful. **Objectives** are guideposts used by managers to define standards of what the organization should accomplish in such areas as profitability, customer service, and social responsibility. Managers can continually evaluate performance in terms of how well the organization is moving toward its objectives.

objectives
Guideposts in defining what the organization should achieve in areas such as profitability, customer service, and social responsibility.

Functions of Objectives

The activities and decisions of managers at all levels are greatly influenced by the objectives of the organization. These objectives perform three important functions.

Figure 7.4   The Johnson & Johnson Credo

Our Credo

We believe our first responsibility is to the doctors, nurses and patients,
to mothers and all others who use our products and services.
In meeting their needs everything we do must be of high quality.
We must constantly strive to reduce our costs
in order to maintain reasonable prices.
Customers' orders must be serviced promptly and accurately.
Our suppliers and distributors must have an opportunity
to make a fair profit.

We are responsible to our employees,
the men and women who work with us throughout the world.
Everyone must be considered as an individual.
We must respect their dignity and recognize their merit.
They must have a sense of security in their jobs.
Compensation must be fair and adequate,
and working conditions clean, orderly and safe.
Employees must feel free to make suggestions and complaints.
There must be equal opportunity for employment, development
and advancement for those qualified.
We must provide competent management,
and their actions must be just and ethical.

We are responsible to the communities in which we live and work
and to the world community as well.
We must be good citizens — support good works and charities
and bear our fair share of taxes.
We must encourage civic improvements and better health and education.
We must maintain in good order
the property we are privileged to use,
protecting the environment and natural resources.

Our final responsibility is to our stockholders.
Business must make a sound profit.
We must experiment with new ideas.
Research must be carried on, innovative programs developed
and mistakes paid for.
New equipment must be purchased, new facilities provided
and new products launched.
Reserves must be created to provide for adverse times.
When we operate according to these principles,
the stockholders should realize a fair return.

Johnson & Johnson

Source: Courtesy of Johnson & Johnson.

*Objectives have to be
1) measurable/definable
2) challenging but not impossible
3) achievable*

Objectives Provide Direction   By specifying an end goal for the organization, objectives direct the efforts of managers in its pursuit. For example, the "quality, service, cleanliness" credo specified by the founder, the late Ray Kroc, still guides McDonald's today. CEO Mike Quilan commented: "If there's one reason for our success, it's that Ray Kroc instilled in the company basic principles. Standards of excellence. Don't compromise. Use the best ingredients. Use the best equipment."[8] Figure 7.4 shows Johnson & Johnson's Credo, which provides overall direction to the management and employees.

Objectives Serve as Standards   Objectives function as standards for the manager since they offer concrete benchmarks for evaluating organizational performance. Without such standards, the manager possesses no tools for evaluating performance — no means of deciding whether work is good or bad. If performance appears unsatisfactory, management can take corrective action, refocusing the organization in the direction of its objectives. Moore Financial Group, a regional bank holding company headquartered in Boise, Idaho, defined its current objective as follows:

"In the next three to five years, our goal is to become a $5 billion financial service corporation with a strong presence in the western states — an aggressive, innovative, quality service provider with a sales-oriented culture."

This objective serves as an effective standard by which to judge organizational performance. At the time the above objective was announced, Moore had total assets of $3.5 billion.[9]

Objectives Serve as Motivators   Finally, objectives perform a motivational role in encouraging managers and operative workers to contribute their best efforts. Organizational members may be motivated to increase the percentage of defect-free output, for example, if they understand the objective of 99 percent defect-free products and if bonuses, profit sharing, or other incentives are linked to accomplishing this objective. The late James E. Casey founded United Parcel Service on the premise that the firm be "owned by its managers and managed by the owners." Today, UPS's 15,000 managers and first-line supervisors own virtually all of the company's stock as a result of a bonus plan. They are required to sell the stock back to UPS upon retirement, a transaction that has made former clerks and drivers millionaires.[10]

Examples of Objectives

Most people, whether they are defenders or critics of business, believe that the purpose of a business is to make a profit. Newspaper accounts of the success of firms such as American Airlines or Levi Strauss are typically stated in terms of annual earnings, which is the most straightforward measure of business performance.

But profits are not the only objective of business. Nonprofit organizations, by definition, seek to accomplish objectives other than profitability. Profits are obviously necessary for the survival of profit-seeking firms. A company must be profitable in order to attract additional capital and to satisfy its owners with an adequate return for their invested funds. But other objectives are equally important. The firm must, for example, provide its customers or clients with needed goods and services, or it will not earn any profits.

In a study of U.S. business objectives, Professor Y. K. Shetty reported that most firms had a variety of social and employee objectives in addition to objectives focusing upon profits and growth. Figure 7.5 shows the results of the study.

The Functions of Management

Management has been defined as the achievement of objectives through people and other resources. This definition implies that it is a process, a series of actions that result in a certain end. A manufacturer converts a series of inputs in the form of raw materials, machinery, workers, and other ingredients into finished products designed to satisfy the firm's customers. Completion of this process allows the firm to achieve its objectives.

Figure 7.5   The Objectives of Business

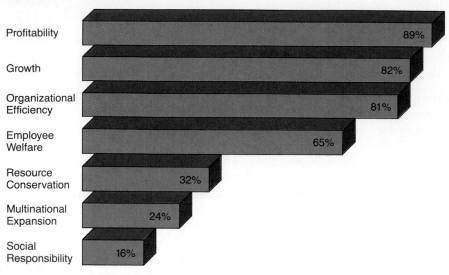

Profitability	89%
Growth	82%
Organizational Efficiency	81%
Employee Welfare	65%
Resource Conservation	32%
Multinational Expansion	24%
Social Responsibility	16%

Source: Adapted from Y. K. Shetty, "New Look at Corporate Goals," *California Management Review* (Winter, 1979), p. 73. Used by permission.

Managers at every level in the organization perform four basic functions — planning, organizing, directing, and controlling — and they must be skillful in performing them if they are to accomplish their goals. Management writers differ on both the number of management functions and the specific lists of them. Writers who define them narrowly include such functions as staffing, communicating, motivating, innovating, coordinating, and evaluating — all of which must be accomplished by managers. The four functions listed above are broadly conceived and are assumed to include these more specific functions.

Although Figure 7.6 shows the four management functions as separate, they actually are interdependent, and it is up to the manager to coordinate them. Since management is a continual process, managers must consider how each function affects and interacts with others in order to accomplish organizational objectives.

Planning

planning

Anticipating the future and determining the best courses of action to achieve organizational objectives.

Planning is the management function of anticipating the future and determining the best action to achieve company objectives. It encompasses decisions about the activities the organization should perform; how big it should be; the production, marketing, and financial strategies it should use in reaching its objectives; and the resources needed to accomplish its goals. Planning involves determining courses of action to answer the questions of what should be done, by whom, where, when, and how. In the same way that an architect designs a blueprint, a manager constructs a plan for the organizational activities necessary to reach objectives.

Planning is a continual process. The statement "The only thing constant is change" is undeniably true in today's business world. Business conditions

Figure 7.6 The Functions of Management

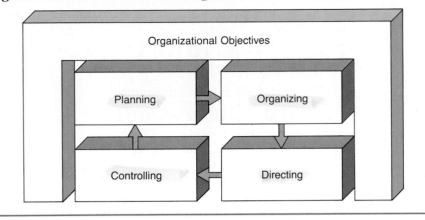

change, laws change, organizations change. Managers must continually monitor their own operations and make necessary adjustments to their plans. Shell's planning groups studied 30 companies that had existed for more than 75 years. Shell's planners concluded the common characteristic among these firms was the ability to adjust to a changing business environment.[11]

This ongoing analysis and comparison of actual performance with company objectives allows the manager to adjust plans before problems become crises. Accomplishing other managerial functions is unlikely without sound and continual planning.

Strategic, Tactical, and Operational Plans

Planning can be classified on the basis of scope or breadth. **Strategic planning** is the process of determining the primary objectives of an organization and adopting courses of action and allocating resources necessary to achieve those objectives. The strategic planning process is reflected in the Gerber Products Company mission statement shown in Figure 7.7. Strategic plans tend to be both broad and long range, focusing on those organizational objectives that will have a major impact on the organization over several years. *more meaningful*

Bush Industries, Jamestown, New York, is now a $93 million producer of ready-to-assemble furniture. But it wasn't always that way. When Paul Bush took over the family firm, it manufactured bathroom towel bars and rings, towel stands, and knockdown bathroom hampers.

The new CEO observed that the production system for manufacturing hampers was similar to that for other ready-to-assemble furniture, a concept that accounts for up to 40 percent of the European furniture market. So Bush made the strategic decision to shift his firm's operations to a ready-to-assemble furniture manufacturer just in time to catch the electronics craze that created the demand for microwave carts, TV carts, and audio racks.[12]

Tactical planning focuses on the implementation of activities specified by the strategic plans. Tactical planning tends to be shorter term than strategic planning and focuses more on current and near-term activities required to implement overall strategies. Although the two types of planning are different, both

strategic planning
Process of setting organizational objectives, then determining overall strategy and resource allocations necessary to reach the objectives.
obtaining degree

tactical planning
Planning for the short-term implementation of current activities and the resource allocation for these activities.
finish my Class

Figure 7.7   Linkage of Gerber's Strategic Planning to its Corporate Mission

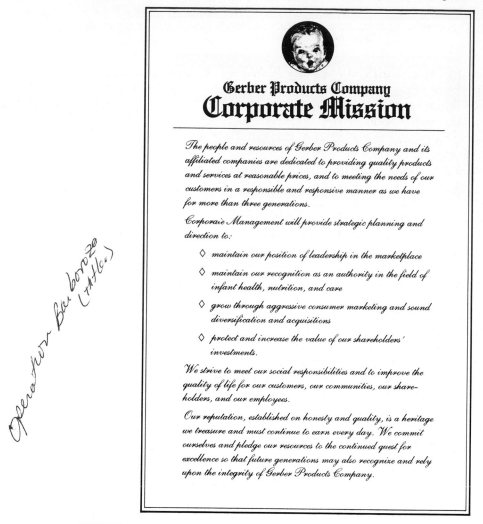

Source: Courtesy of Gerber Products Company.

must be integrated into an overall system designed to achieve organizational objectives.

Paul Bush followed his strategic decision to move into ready-to-assemble furniture with a series of tactical decisions. He installed an automated, flexible manufacturing system using European technology. Japanese management techniques were introduced. These actions cut production costs and improved quality. Later, Bush decided to produce household furniture with the introduction of ready-to-assemble bedroom furniture.

operational plans
The work standards that implement tactical plans.

The final step in the planning hierarchy is the setting of **operational plans**, the specific targets to aim toward, and the proper individuals to carry out the plans. Operational plans are the means for implementing tactical plans. They are often stated in terms of quotas, standards, or schedules such as those outlined in the section on controlling that follows.

The management of a major publishing house expects its sales representatives to make 20 customer contacts per day with the first one beginning at 8 a.m. or earlier. This type of goal illustrates operational planning by the firm's management.

The Crisis Manager and Contingency Planning   One of the more contemporary aspects of planning is contingency planning to deal with crises such as fires, explosions, product tamperings, gas leaks, and product failure. *Contingency planning* can be divided into two components: business continuation and public communication. The objectives of contingency planning are to resume operation as quickly and as smoothly as possible while fully communicating what happened to the public. For example, CEO James Burke of Johnson & Johnson is widely credited with an effective response to the Tylenol poisonings of 1982 and 1986. Burke took immediate steps to protect Johnson & Johnson's customers and the firm's valuable brand. Much of his success was due to prompt and honest communication with the press and the American public.[13]

Many firms have appointed a *crisis manager* to direct their contingency planning for such events. To understand what such a person does, consider the situation Cole Emerson faced the night of May 4, 1988. Emerson, the vice-president for communications at First Interstate, was notified that the parent company's 62-floor headquarters in downtown Los Angeles was on fire. Eventually, the late-night inferno burned $4\frac{1}{2}$ floors and killed a maintenance man. California's largest building was closed indefinitely.

Emerson, also in charge of contingency planning and computer security, was prepared because he had already devised a plan to deal with a massive earthquake—and the fires that usually accompany one. Emerson's "business resumption group" (a related group that deals with employee security) moved into the bank's emergency center seven blocks away. Emerson's team quickly took the following actions:

1. Securities traders carrying home computer disks according to First Interstate's contingency plan were dispersed to New York, Hong Kong, and other locations in Los Angeles.
2. Hundreds of telephones were rented, numbers and lines switched, and over 100,000 pieces of daily mail were handled.
3. The 1,500 people who worked in the closed building were shifted to other facilities.

The only First Interstate bank that was closed was the office on the ground floor of the headquarters building. Emerson proudly points out: "Because of the planning process, because of the group of people that was there, the team, and our instant communications with our customers, we didn't miss a beat."[14]

Organizing   *Top & middle Managers*

Once plans have been developed, the next step typically is organizing. **Organizing** is the means by which management blends human and material resources through the design of a formal structure of tasks and authority. It involves classifying and dividing work into manageable units by the following steps:

1. Determining specific work activities necessary to accomplish the organizational objectives.

organizing
Process of blending human and material resources through the design of a formal structure of tasks and authority.

Figure 7.8 Management's Role in Restructuring Greyhound Corporation

Source: Courtesy of The Greyhound Corporation.

2. Grouping work activities into a logical pattern or structure.
3. Assigning the activities to specific positions and people.

John Teet's restructuring of the Greyhound Corporation reflects the importance of organizing to achieving the strategic plan. As noted in Figure 7.8, Teets even had to sell the unit for which Greyhound was best known — its bus line.

Included in the organizing function are the important steps of staffing the organization with competent employees capable of performing the necessary activities and assigning authority and responsibility to these individuals. Organizing is discussed in more detail in Chapter 8, and staffing is dealt with in Chapter 11.

J. William Grimes, the CEO of the ESPN cable sports network, is credited with building an effective organization by hiring competent personnel and then letting them make decisions. For example, a few years ago, Grimes was looking for a blockbuster series that would confirm ESPN as the premier sports network. The CEO thought only the National Football League could provide the audience he sought.

So what did Steve Bornstein, ESPN's head of programming and production, propose? To spend $2 million for the right to broadcast the America's Cup live from Perth, Australia, at midnight for many American viewers. Grimes remembers, "I thought it was a bad idea. I felt it cost too much money and no one would watch at that hour." But the CEO stayed true to his philosophy of staffing the company with "people who can't wait to get something done, and do it in new ways." The America's Cup proved to be an instant success and produced a $2 million profit for ESPN. Grimes later got his cherished NFL rights, but he first allowed his organization to function the way it was designed.[15]

Directing *Supervisor*

Once plans have been formulated and an organization has been created and staffed, the task becomes that of directing people toward the achievement of organizational goals. **Directing** is the accomplishment of organizational objectives by guiding and motivating subordinates. It includes explaining procedures, issuing orders, and seeing that mistakes are corrected.

The directing function is particularly important at the supervisory level. If supervisors are to accomplish the task of "getting things done through people," they must be effective leaders. Directing — sometimes referred to as motivating, leading, guiding, or human relations — is the "people" function of management. It is discussed at length in Chapter 10.

Anthony O'Reilly, CEO of Pittsburgh-based H. J. Heinz, uses a unique approach to the directing function. The former Irish rugby star keeps a telescope in his office on the 60th floor of the U.S. Steel Building. The telescope is aimed at Heinz U.S.A's 17-acre plant across the Allegheny River. While he admits he cannot see much of what goes on in the five-story facility, O'Reilly likes to convey the message that he is always watching.[16]

directing
Guiding and motivating subordinates to accomplish organizational objectives.

Controlling *Supervisors*

Controlling is the function of evaluating the organization's performance to determine whether it is accomplishing its objectives. Controlling is linked closely to planning; in fact, the basic purpose of controlling is the determination of how successful the planning function has been. The four basic steps in controlling are:

1. Establish performance standards.
2. Monitor actual performance.
3. Compare actual performance with established standards to determine deviation or variation.
4. Should deviations or variations occur, determine their cause and take corrective action.

controlling
Evaluating the organization's performance to determine whether it is accomplishing its objectives.

The control function is well illustrated by the standards established for UPS employees. UPS employees are well rewarded (drivers average nearly $16 per hour), but they are expected to meet rigid performance standards. Sorters at the Addison, Illinois, hub must load delivery vans at a pace of 500 to 650 packages per hour. The standard for unloading is twice as fast. Drivers are so tightly timed that their supervisors know within six minutes how long it will take to complete the route.[17] These standards demonstrate that control is a vital managerial function at UPS. It is also an important contributor to the firm's success.

Corporate Culture

corporate culture
An organization's inner values, beliefs, rituals, norms, and philosophies.

The function of management must be performed within the context of a corporate culture. A firm's **corporate culture** is the predominant value system for the organization. It consists of the norms, beliefs, attitudes, and philosophies of the organization. This complicated and often vague concept is what gives each organization a special "feel" in terms of how employees dress, how rigid work schedules are, whether managers are separated by offices or mingle with managers in other departments, company traditions, and even rituals that influence how organization members think and act.

The corporate culture is typically shaped by the leaders who developed the company and by those who succeed them. Terrence E. Deal and Allan A. Kennedy, authors of *Corporate Cultures: The Rites and Rituals of Corporate Life,* stress the major impact corporate culture has on the success of an organization. In organizations having strong cultures, everyone knows and supports the organization's objectives; in those with weak cultures, no clear sense of purpose exists. The authors of the best-selling book, *In Search of Excellence,* concluded the presence of a strong corporate culture was the single common thread among such diverse but highly successful companies as General Electric, IBM, and McDonald's.

Four types of corporate culture have been identified:

1. The *tough-guy macho culture* is typical of high-risk industries such as construction, cosmetics, and entertainment. Such a culture demands immediate results and rewards aggressive, individualistic members.

2. The *work hard/play hard culture* is common in such sales-oriented firms as computer companies, door-to-door sales operations, and real estate companies. Sales rallies, contests, and special promotions are frequently used in such firms.

3. The *bet-your-company culture* is characteristic of a high-stakes firm in such industries as aerospace, petroleum, and capital goods manufacturing. The high risks faced by such companies are combined with relatively slow feedback concerning success.

4. The *process culture* involves relatively low-risk, slow feedback firms such as banks, insurance companies, utilities, and numerous government agencies. Members of such organizations emphasize procedures — following the rules, achieving technical perfection, and observing all procedures.[18]

Corporate cultures are passed on from one generation of employees to the next. The corporate culture of McDonald's is passed on to managers through their attendance at Hamburger University, the firm's management training facility. General Electric's corporate culture is part of the training people receive at the company's Crotonville Educational Institute for Management Development.[19]

Sometimes, management deliberately tries to change the firm's corporate culture. The recent history of Exxon provides such an example. The oil giant had long been known for its emphasis on consensus decision making. This philosophy was fostered by a bureaucratic maze of corporate staff personnel, committees, and task forces originally set up to control the corporation's far-flung activities.

When Lawrence G. Rawl took over as CEO in 1987, he decided to change Exxon's corporate culture to make the firm more efficient. He quickly reduced

Creating a positive and stimulating work environment is an important element in the corporate culture of The Progressive Corporation, an insurance holding company. The colorful print shown here is part of the firm's contemporary art collection, which decorates employees' offices. For Progressive, such art reflects respect for employees, stimulates their creativity, and amuses them. Progressive's management believes motivating employees to think creatively and develop strong leadership traits is essential in enabling the company to compete successfully and achieve its ambitious growth strategies.

Source: Courtesy of John Weber Gallery, N.Y. Barbara Kasten, "Architectural Site No. 8, December 21, 1986," cibachrome 30 × 40.

the labor force by 30 percent, cut its office automation unit, reduced the layers of management, and consolidated regional subsidiaries and various worldwide operations. While morale suffered from the shake up, Rawl clearly changed Exxon's corporate culture to a leaner, more cost-effective operation.[20]

Once the corporate culture is understood, managers can be selected whose personal styles are consistent with the corporate culture. In instances where changes in a corporate culture are required to make the firm more competitive, to adjust to corporate growth, or when the firm's environment is changing, the appropriate leadership style may be different from that used in less dynamic situations.

Leadership

Managers achieve organizational objectives by being effective leaders and motivating people to high levels of achievement. **Leadership**, the most visible component of a manager's responsibilities, is the act of motivating or causing others to perform activities designed to achieve specific objectives. Because of the importance of effective leadership in organizational success, it is not surprising that research into the characteristics of a good leader has gone on for generations.

Early leadership concepts concentrated on the **great man theory**, which held that remarkable individuals — such as George Washington, Simon Bolivar,

leadership
Motivating or causing others to perform activities designed to achieve specific objectives.

great man theory
Leadership theory that says only an exceptional person will achieve a prominent leadership position.

and Mohandas K. Gandhi — emerged and were prepared to play important leadership roles. As a result, early research focused on the traits of a good leader. Although the various listings differ, three traits were often mentioned: empathy (the ability to place oneself in another's position), self-awareness, and objectivity in dealing with others.

Obviously, these traits do not fit all leaders. Some lists mention extrovertism, but General George Marshall, author of the Marshall Plan, which transformed most of the nations of post-World War II Europe, was an introvert. Height may be characteristic of such leaders as Abraham Lincoln and Charles de Gaulle, but what about Napoleon Bonaparte? Leadership is often associated with the experience that comes with age, but Alexander the Great won some of his most important victories at the age of 18. Today, many of the nation's most successful entrepreneurs are relatively young. For instance, Andrew Ham is the 28-year-old president of Olympic Auto Sales and Leasing in Los Angeles. Ham, who works ten-hour days at his $30 million auto dealership, describes his work and approach to leadership simply: "You must know the details."[21]

Gradually, leadership research began to focus on different styles of leadership and circumstances under which each style might prove successful. By considering both alternative styles and a given set of circumstances, it is possible to determine the optimum type of leadership for a particular situation. This approach to leadership is known as the **contingency theory**. This viewpoint argues that management should adjust its leadership style in accordance with the situation at hand. Specific approaches to leadership style are examined in the section that follows.

contingency theory
Leadership styles should reflect the specific details of the managerial situation.

Leadership Styles

Leadership involves the exercise of power in an organization. **Power** is the ability of one person to influence the behavior of another. This power may result from one or more sources. Leaders secure some power from their position in the organization. As managers, they are responsible for directing the activities of their subordinates. In other cases, their power comes from their expertise and experience. First-line supervisors who were once expert carpenters are likely to be respected by the members of their crew of carpenters. Other leaders secure power from the force of their personalities. Followers of such charismatic leaders may grant them power due to a desire to please them or to be more like them.

power
Ability of one person to influence the behavior of another.

The way in which a leader uses available power in order to lead others is referred to as **leadership style**. Different styles have been used throughout history, ranging from coercing, threatening, and demanding to cajoling, pleading, bribing, and begging. A continuum of leadership styles exists, ranging from totally autocratic behavior to a completely democratic style. Within this continuum, three basic styles can be identified.

Autocratic leaders make decisions on their own, without consulting others. The autocratic leader reaches a decision, communicates it to subordinates, and requires them to implement it. *Democratic leaders,* the second type, involve their subordinates in making decisions. A democratic sales manager, for example, allows sales personnel to participate in setting sales quotas, while an autocratic sales manager simply assigns quotas for each salesperson. *Free-rein leaders* believe in minimal supervision, leaving most decisions to their subordinates.

leadership style
Way in which a leader uses available power to direct others.

This leadership style is sometimes called laissez-faire leadership, from the French expression, "Leave them alone."

Which Leadership Style Is Best?

The results of hundreds of studies of leaders — both effective and ineffective — and of various corporate cultures lead to the conclusion that the answer to this question is not nearly as simple as it appears. As researchers were forced to discard the simpler approaches, they began to realize that a number of factors affect a manager's choice of the most appropriate leadership style. The choice can be expressed as follows:

Appropriate leadership style is a function of the leader, the subordinates, and the situation.

The best leadership style is one that varies with the circumstances, changing according to three elements: the leader, the followers, and the situation. Some leaders are simply unable to encourage or even allow subordinates to participate in decision making. Some followers do not have the ability or the desire to assume such responsibility. Furthermore, the specific corporate culture or a particular situation helps determine which style will be most effective. Problems requiring immediate solutions may have to be handled without consulting subordinates. With less time pressure, participative decision making may be desirable.

In many instances, democratic leaders will ask for advice from others but will make the final decisions themselves. As Chrysler Corporation Chief Executive Lee Iacocca puts it, "Despite what the textbooks say, most important decisions in corporate life are made by individuals, not by committees. My policy has always been to be democratic all the way to the point of decision. Then I become the ruthless commander. 'Okay, I've heard everybody,' I say. 'Now here's what we're going to do.'"[22]

An almost totally democratic leader may be forced by circumstance to be autocratic in making a particular decision. For example, if there is to be a 10 percent reduction in staff, those subject to being fired are not likely to be consulted on who should go.

After devoting many years to research into the best types of leaders, Professor Fred Fiedler concluded no single best style of leadership exists. Fiedler believes the most effective leadership style depends on the power held by the leader, the difficulty of the tasks involved, and the characteristics of the workers. He argues that extremely easy and extremely difficult situations are best handled by leaders who emphasize task accomplishment. Moderately difficult situations are best handled by leaders who emphasize participation and good working relations with subordinates.

Managerial Decision Making

The most important task of a leader is decision making. Managers earn their salaries by making decisions that enable their firms to solve problems as they arise. In addition, managers are continually involved with anticipating and preventing problems. The decision-making process can be described in five steps.

Figure 7.9 Steps in the Decision-Making Process

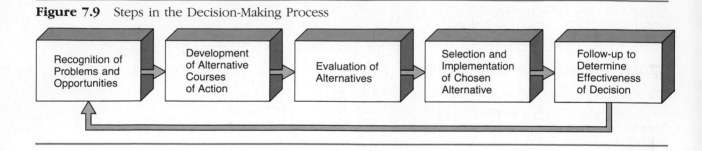

Figure 7.9 outlines how the manager systematically progresses through each step to ultimately reach a decision aimed at solving a specific problem or taking advantage of a particular business opportunity. In a narrow sense, **decision making** is choosing among two or more alternatives — the chosen alternative being the decision. But in a broader sense, decision making involves problem recognition, identification, and evaluation of alternatives, selection and implementation of an alternative, and follow-up (in the form of feedback) on the effectiveness of the decision. Whether the decision to be made is routine or unique (such as a decision to construct a major new manufacturing facility), the systematic step-by-step approach will be effective.

decision making
The process of choosing among alternatives.

Types of Decisions

Decisions may be classified by their relative uniqueness. A **programmed decision** involves simple, common, frequently occurring problems for which solutions have been determined. Examples of programmed decisions include the starting salary for a word-processing specialist; determination of reorder points for raw materials used in production; and price discounts offered to customers who make large-quantity purchases. Organizations develop rules, policies, and detailed procedures for such situations so decisions can be made consistently, quickly, and inexpensively. Since such solutions eliminate the time-consuming process of identifying and evaluating alternatives and making new decisions each time the situation occurs, they free managers to devote time to more unique problems.

programmed decision
Decision involving routine, recurring problems for which well-established solutions exist.

A **nonprogrammed decision** involves complex, important, and nonroutine problems or opportunities. These types of decisions have not been made before — the identification of alternatives, their evaluation, and the implementation of the most appropriate courses of action are critical tasks. Management effectiveness is frequently evaluated by the ability to make nonprogrammed decisions. ~~usually comes one dic table~~

nonprogrammed decision
Decision involving complex, important, and nonroutine problems or opportunities.

When John J. Nevin was brought in as Firestone's CEO a decade ago, the Akron tire manufacturer was in poor financial condition. The company lost $122 million in 1980. Firestone had high labor costs and outdated factories. To further complicate things, U.S.-produced automobiles were selling poorly.

The situation facing Nevin required a series of nonprogrammed decisions in order to save Firestone. The new CEO moved quickly. Nevin sold several diversified units such as beer kegs and plastics. He shut down 11 of the 17 Firestone plants in North America and consolidated the operations of others. The work force shrank from 107,000 to 55,000.

Nevin also diversified the company into the auto-service business. The value of Firestone's stock increased nearly ten times over an eight-year period thanks

Table 7.1 The Value of Time for Some Hypothetical Managers

Annual Salary	Benefits and Bonuses	Total Compensation	Time Value per Hour	Time Value per Minute
Supervisory Management				
Telemarketing Supervisor $25,000	$ 6,250	$ 31,250	$ 15.63	$0.26
Production Supervisor $35,000	8,750	43,750	21.88	0.36
Middle Management				
Credit Manager $50,000	17,500	67,500	33.75	.56
Regional Sales Manager $70,000	24,500	94,500	47.25	.79
Top Management				
Vice-President for Human Resources $200,000	90,000	290,000	145.00	2.42
Senior Vice-President and CFO $300,000	135,000	435,000	217.50	3.63

The calculations assume:

1. A 40-hour week, 50-week year
2. Fringe benefits are 25% of salary
3. A 10 percent bonus is available to middle management
4. Top management's bonus is 20 percent of salary

[handwritten margin note: unprogram desicion are high]

to Nevin's nonprogrammed decisions. Even a competitor, Patrick C. Ross, CEO of Uniroyal Goodrich, remarked about Nevin's ability to make tough decisions: "I give John Nevin a great deal of credit. He made the hard decisions required to get a bad situation turned around in a relatively short time." Firestone was later acquired by Japan's Bridgestone Corp., and the new owner retained Nevin.[23]

Time Management

Managers are busy people who are expected to accomplish a myriad of goals in a limited amount of time. Therefore, it is essential for managers to allocate their time efficiently. **Time management**, or the effective allocation of one's time among different tasks, is regarded as a key element of managerial success today.

time management
Process of allocating one's time effectively.

The Value of Time

The starting point for improving one's allocation of time is to appreciate what your working time is worth. In other words, what does your time cost the organization? Once you know the value of your time, you can quickly identify the activities where it is cost effective for you to spend your time.

While everyone does not have complete control over his or her daily schedule, this calculation can provide a rough yardstick for measuring whether you are using your time effectively. Table 7.1 shows the approximate value of time for people at different levels of management.

Figure 7.10   How Managers at Different Levels Spend Their Day

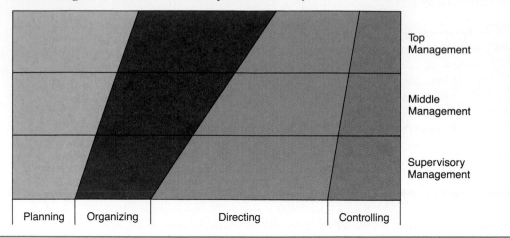

Allocating Management Time by Function

Earlier in the chapter, it was pointed out that all four management functions — planning, organizing, directing, and controlling — are performed at all levels of management. But as Figure 7.10 indicates, the amount of time devoted to each function varies by management level. Top management performs more planning than does supervisory management, while supervisors at the first rung of the management pyramid devote more of their time to directing and controlling.

Time Management Guidelines

Numerous time management guidelines have been suggested over the years. Here are some generally accepted time management ideas with examples of how some successful top executives accomplish them.[24]

Establish Your Goals and Set Priorities   Make a list of your long- and short-term projects. Look at the list regularly and revise it as needed. Arrange the items on the list in order of their importance and then divide items into specific tasks. Then start at the top of the list and get to work. Don't get upset if your priorities change by the hour. Just revise your list and get on with the work. Schedule your daily activities on an hour-by-hour appointment calendar.

Charles Exley, the CEO of NCR, schedules about 70 percent of his time up to a year in advance. This practice assures him of enough time to accomplish his priority items.

Learn to Delegate Work   Then follow this procedure to make sure you get the results you want: Give clear instructions on what you want done, make sure your instructions are understood, set a deadline, and allow enough time to correct mistakes.

For example, Allen Rosenshine, the CEO of Omnicom Group, an advertising agency holding company, said: "For me, the first decision is, do I handle it or do I delegate it to somebody else and forget about it . . . I have spent an awful lot of time screwing up in terms of time management by not realizing that you either commit to something 99 and 44/100th percent or you don't bother with it at all."

Spend Your Time on Activities that Will Yield the Most Results The Pareto Principle of time management states that 80 percent of your goals can be achieved in 20 percent of your time if you work on those tasks critical to the completion of the overall project and avoid those that contribute little to the outcome.

Barry Sullivan, the CEO of First Chicago, once hired consultant Booz, Allen & Hamilton to study how he spent his workday. The consultants concluded Sullivan was managing his time in an ad hoc manner. As a result, Sullivan now allocates blocks of time to his priorities such as meeting with customers for 25 percent of the time he has available. Like Charles Exley of NCR, Sullivan now books his time up to a year in advance.

Do Your Most Important Work when You Are at Your Best Work on high-priority items when you are mentally alert and on low-priority items when your energy has ebbed. For example, Donald Schienke, CEO of Northwestern Mutual Life Insurance, arises at 5:15 a.m. so he can spend some time working before office meetings begin at 8.

Group Your Activities By reading all your mail and making all your phone calls at once, you will make the most efficient use of your time. For example, Stanley Pace, the CEO of General Dynamics, allocates 7:30–10 a.m. every morning to return phone calls and handle his correspondence. Pace schedules no meeting before 10 a.m. or late in the afternoon, so he can wrap up his day.

Learn How to Handle Interruptions Incoming phone calls, unscheduled visitors, and even the mail can play havoc with your schedule. You can control these by having your secretary handle all but essential calls when you are working on an important task, by working in another office (no one will be able to find you), by setting times when your subordinates can talk to you and times when they cannot (except for emergencies), and by learning how to deal with long-winded callers. Interrupting yourself also wastes time. Instead of getting yet another cup of coffee or walking down the hall to chat with a friend, try to finish what you are doing, even if the job is difficult or unpleasant.

Juergen Bartels, who heads Carlson Cos.' hospitality division (Radisson Hotels), makes sure subordinates do not waste his time. "You can abuse my time once and I will caution you; twice, and you're going to get something more than a caution; but the third time, I will think you incurable." In other words, people who waste Bartels' time usually find their careers with Carlson cut short.

Summary of Learning Goals _____

1. Identify the levels of the management pyramid. There are three levels of management in most organizations. Top management includes the chief executive officer, chief operating officer, and chief financial officer, the governor of a state, a city mayor, or the chancellor of a university. Middle management includes plant managers, key division heads, branch managers, and college deans. Supervisory management includes such first-line managers as supervisors, department heads, and section leaders.

2.   Explain the skills required for managerial success.   The three basic managerial skills are technical, human relations, and conceptual. Technical skills, which involve the manager's ability to understand and use techniques, tools, and knowledge of a specific discipline or department, are most important for first-level managers. Human relations skills, which involve working effectively with and through people in the accomplishment of assignments, are important for managers at every level. Conceptual skills, which involve the manager's ability to see the "big picture" of the organization as a whole and how each part contributes to its overall functioning, are relatively more important for top management.

3.   Outline the functions of organizational objectives.   Organizational objectives perform three important functions: (1) they provide direction by specifying an end goal for the organization, thereby directing the efforts of organizational members in its pursuit, (2) they serve as standards by offering concrete benchmarks for evaluating organizational performance, and (3) they serve as motivators by encouraging managers and employees to contribute their best efforts.

4.   List the functions of management.   Managers perform four basic functions in attempting to achieve company objectives: planning, organizing, directing, and controlling. Planning involves creating blueprints for future action. Organizing involves grouping work into logical patterns and assigning tasks to specific workers. Directing involves matching performance with organizational goals. Controlling deals with evaluating actual performance to determine whether the organization is accomplishing its objectives.

5.   Distinguish among strategic planning, tactical planning, and operational planning.   Strategic planning involves determining the primary objectives of an organization and adopting courses of action and resource allocations necessary to accomplish those objectives. Tactical planning, on the other hand, focuses more on the development of activities specified by the strategic plans. It tends to be more short term in scope than strategic planning. Finally, operational planning sets the specific targets or standards for work groups or individuals. It is the final stage of implementation in the overall planning process.

6.   Explain the concept of a corporate culture.   A corporate culture is the organization's predominant value system. It is the norms, beliefs, attitudes, philosophies, traditions, and rituals of a company. For example, some firms have an open, highly communicative culture where ideas are readily exchanged. Other companies might be characterized by a more rigid style with an emphasis on tightly configured organizations.

7.   Explain the concept of leadership and the three basic leadership styles.   Leadership is the act of motivating or causing others to perform activities designed to achieve specific objectives. The three basic leadership styles are autocratic, democratic, and free-rein. The best leadership style depends on three elements: the leader, the followers, and the situation. The general trend is toward greater participation of subordinates in decisions that affect them.

8.   List the steps in the decision-making process and contrast programmed and nonprogrammed decisions.   The decision-making process consists of five steps:

1.   Recognition of problems and opportunities.
2.   Development of alternative courses of action.
3.   Evaluation of alternatives.
4.   Selection and implementation of chosen alternative.
5.   Follow-up to determine effectiveness of decision.

Programmed decisions involve simple, frequently occurring problems or opportunities for which solutions have been determined previously. Such decisions are made quickly by reference to a rule or procedure, and managers spend little time in identifying and evaluating alternatives. By contrast, nonprogrammed decisions involve more complex, relatively unique situations. Their solution requires considerable management involvement in identifying and evaluating alternatives.

9.   Outline the importance of time management.   Time management refers to the process of allocating one's time among different activities. Given the variety of goals management is expected to accomplish and a limited amount of time, it has become evident in recent years that time management is a major ingredient in managerial needs. The starting point is to know what one's time is worth and then allocate it in a cost-effective fashion.

Key Terms

management	conceptual skills	leadership
management pyramid	objectives	great man theory
top management	planning	contingency theory
chief executive officer (CEO)	strategic planning	power
chief operating officer (COO)	tactical planning	leadership style
chief financial officer (CFO)	operational plans	decision making
middle management	organizing	programmed decision
supervisory management	directing	nonprogrammed decision
technical skills	controlling	time management
human relations skills	corporate culture	

Review Questions

1. Explain the statement, "Management principles are universal." Do you agree or disagree with the statement?

2. On what level of the management pyramid would each of the following persons be listed?
   a. Department head   **d.** Branch manager
   b. Chief operating officer   **e.** Mayor
   c. Supervisor   **f.** Dean

3. Identify and briefly explain the three skills required for managerial success. Which skills are relatively more important for top management? Which is more important to first-line managers?

4. What are the functions performed by organizational objectives? Give an example of how these might be accomplished.

5. Briefly explain the four functions of management. Compare the relative importance of each function at each level of the management pyramid.

6. Give an example of strategic planning, tactical planning, and operational planning for each of the following:
   a. Off-campus bookstore
   b. *National Lampoon* magazine
   c. Local apartment complex
   d. Retail yogurt outlet
   e. Local U.S. Army recruiting office

7. What is meant by a corporate culture? Identify and explain the corporate culture of a local company. How would you classify this firm's culture?

8. Murphy Industrial Distributors has long observed St. Patrick's Day as a paid holiday for its employees. Sean Murphy, company president, noticed that St. Patrick's Day will fall on Wednesday during the next year. He wonders whether the Monday of that week should be declared a company holiday instead. Using each of the steps in the decision-making process, describe how you would make this decision.

9. Classify each of the following as either programmed or nonprogrammed decisions. Defend your answers.
   a. Registrar's office system for processing student requests for dropping and adding courses
   b. Retail store manager's decision about the number of men's dress shirts to order
   c. Hospital's procedure for admitting new patients
   d. Management's decision to relocate corporate headquarters from Chicago to Atlanta

10. Relate the three basic leadership styles to the four types of corporate culture. Identify a specific firm that matches each cultural description.

Discussion Questions

1. Don Tyson of Tyson Foods in Springdale, Arkansas, does not dress like the CEO of a $1.8 billion company. The head of the nation's largest poultry processor wears a tan uniform at work just like his employees. The uniform carries the firm's orange and yellow logo and Tyson's name. Relate Don Tyson's dress to the material presented in Chapter 7.

2. Rupert Murdoch, owner of newspapers and magazines in the United States, Europe, and Australia, observed: "I try to keep in touch with the details — you can't keep in touch with them all, but you've got to have a feel for what's going on. I also look at the product daily. That doesn't mean you interfere, but it's important occasionally to show the ability to be involved. It shows you understand what's happening." Relate Murdoch's comment to the skills required for managerial success.

3. John La Sage, an executive vice-president of Burson-Marsteller, the nation's leading public relations firm, made the following observation about crisis management: "Generally, the most important time in a crisis is in the first two to three days. If an organization has not acted within that time frame, it will be playing 'catch up' and, in fact, it may be a long time in recovering, at least in the eyes of the public." Identify recent crises that were handled correctly and incorrectly according to La Sage's premise. What can be learned from these situations?

4. Wendy's has tested a 30-second drive-up window guarantee in the Southeast. If a customer has to wait more than 30 seconds at a drive-up window, he or she receives the next meal free. Discuss this guarantee in the context of management's control function.

5. Napoleon always refused to reply to letters for six months because he believed that most of the problems raised in the correspondence would go away in that time. Comment on Napoleon's unique approach to time management.

Video Case

Henderson Industries

Henry (Hank) Henderson is the embodiment of the managerial skills required to achieve organizational objectives. He has successfully combined human and technical resources during the 35-year history of his company, Henderson Industries, and has adapted its organizational structure in relation to its growth needs. Henderson's success is illustrated by the fact that his firm was named company of the year in 1984 by *Black Enterprise* magazine.

Founded in 1954, Henderson Industries (HI) was a sub-contractor of industrial scales operating out of Hank Henderson's garage in West Caldwell, New Jersey. For over 10 years, Henderson worked for Richardson Scale Company during the day and worked for himself at night and on weekends. During this period, HI expanded its product line to include instrumentation and control panels, and in 1967 Henderson quit working for Richardson Scale in order to devote more time to his rapidly-growing business. "I now had a business that needed full-time direction and a technical person at its head," says Henderson, a university graduate with a major in electrical technology.

It wasn't long before his transition to control panels paid off. The universality of panel use in most manufacturing processes provided a very large market. "You name the process and I'll show you a use for panels," says Henderson. Like most small manufacturers, he began marketing his panels through independent agents called manufacturer's reps. Since their compensation was based entirely on sales, this approach helped keep fixed costs down while providing necessary channels of distribution.

But it soon became evident that Henderson Industries' products were technical enough to require a specialized salesforce. In response, a trained, in-house salesforce was created which streamlined the entire marketing process. More recently, competitive bidding has become a major business component through which HI has obtained many of their contracts.

Notes: "The B.E. 100s: The Nation's Largest Black Businesses," *Black Enterprise,* June 1989, p. 199; Mark Fortune, "Divide and Conquer," *Black Enterprise,* June 1988, pp. 169–175; and personal correspondence, February 28, 1989.

The number of Henderson employees grew with the company, which continues to create and fill needed positions as they appear. Since 1983, when HI had 75 employees and, with approximate sales of $10 million, was ranked No. 78 on the *Black Enterprise* list of the top 100 industrial/service companies, it has grown to over 160 employees, No. 22 on the *BE* list, and has sales of over $23 million. Being a minority owned and operated company has not influenced its hiring practices. Only about a quarter of the workers are minorities. The company has implemented an aggressive affirmative action program and has participated in a county-wide training program. It has recruited a number of minorities in its engineering and production sections, increasing the number of black professionals in the field. "The knowledge that we have gained in the manufacture of weighing systems and control panels has led to the development of some crucial ancillary skills," notes HI administration vice-president Gabe Panepinto. "We have acquired higher-level computer languages and a staff skilled in software development." As HI moves into a lucrative new field, robotics, skilled workers are becoming a major factor in the company's human resource requirements. Henderson believes that his decision to hire experienced engineers with diversified backgrounds has given the firm much insight into the best ideas and production setups of other leading companies.

In 1979, HI accepted a contract from the Federal Aviation Authority to manufacture equipment that eliminates signal interference in aircraft. "It was equipment we could build relatively easily once the design was done," recalls Henderson. But that was the hitch. The firm's equipment design partner, Edo Aire Avionics, decided to move and Henderson was worried that project design engineers would be lost. The answer, he felt, was to purchase the product line of ground navigational aids from Edo Aire and rename it Systems Control Corp., bringing the entire design group under his control.

In January 1986, the 60-year-old founder and president of Henderson Industries convened a strategy session attended by his top management with the intention of improving the company's market position. He proposed a fundamental reorganization. HI would be divided into two separate units — commercial and government. This strategy was intended to reap the benefits of specialization, recognizing each unit as a separate profit center with authority and responsibility for performing its own administrative, marketing, and management functions. Henderson's greatest doubt was that the reorganization could be accomplished quickly and effectively.

Henderson's first course of action was to determine which tasks were being performed by whom and then evaluate the company's current orders with an eye toward assigning each project to the appropriate division. Kurt Huff, 45, was appointed general manager of the government division, and Ken Henderson, 35, one of Henderson's sons, was assigned the position of general manager of the commercial division. Henderson says he allowed his two general managers to "pick and choose" from HI's pool of engineers. He admits there was some pulling and tugging as each general manager made his pitch to favored personnel. When the teams were selected, the commercial group had a majority of the design people. This was appropriate, Henderson says, because "the commercial group, unlike the government group, does not have a defined product, but rather, each job is different, requiring customer design and creativity."

HI's reorganization was based on sound business judgment. The decision to split the organization into two divisions was aimed at attacking two markets rather than one. Separating the government and commercial markets enabled HI to focus on the specific requirements of each market. The government division and high-quality manufacturing facility are designed with all the controls found in a larger government facility. There are signing-in procedures, environmental controls, and quality-assurance programs. This has proven to be a distinct selling advantage. As Henderson notes, "We're a miniature them, but I think we are better." The commercial group exclusively handles large custom systems. These one-of-a-kind contracts are often based on fixed-price agreements, meaning that HI has to pay for any unforeseen expenses. In many ways, this reorganization has provided specialized attention for each market and has allowed individualized customer service and company accounting.

Even though his is the last word on all major decisions affecting the company, Henderson describes his management style as "democratic," always involving managers in the decision-making process. Daily activities on a particular project do not always involve him. Every project has a group that meets for periodic reviews and a group leader takes charge of meeting objectives and specifications. "At the end of a project, I expect the leadership to have completely satisfied those specifications," Henderson states.

Part of Henderson's management philosophy is that nothing is written in stone. In spite of the recent division of HI, exchanges of personnel and information between the divisions is not uncommon. If one group needs the expertise of someone from the other division, the person can, in effect, be borrowed.

The success of Henderson Industries and the impressive position they hold can be directly attributed to the strategic decisions taken by Hank Henderson. His willingness to expand the company product lines by using government contracts to enter new markets has been a major source of growth for the company. He believes HI's future revenues are dependent on export markets, as is evidenced by his success in China despite German and British competition. With the foresight to lead his company in high-growth industries such as robotic and defense contracts, Henderson may play a dominant role in the industries of tomorrow.

Questions

1. The three types of skills required for management success are described in the chapter. Relate each skill to HI founder Hank Henderson's management style.

2. How would you describe Henderson's leadership style?

3. Give examples of how each of the managerial functions listed in Figure 7.6 are performed at Henderson Industries.

4. Relate the following managerial concepts to Henderson Industries.

a. corporate culture

b. programmed and nonprogrammed decisions

c. management pyramid

d. strategic, tactical, and operational plans

8 *Internal Organization*

Learning Goals

1. To explain the steps involved in the organizing process.

2. To identify the major forms of departmentalization.

3. To explain the relationship between authority, responsibility, and accountability.

4. To identify the strengths and weaknesses of organization charts.

5. To list the determinants of the span of management.

6. To describe Parkinson's law and how to avoid its effects.

7. To evaluate each of the four basic forms of organization.

8. To explain the function of the informal organization in a firm.

9. To describe the role of intrapreneurship in modern organizations.

Professional sports teams used to exist so that wealthy individuals could have unique toys. Today, they are likely to be treated much more as a business than as a sport. The shift toward professionalism has meant some changes in the way sports teams are run. For example, when the Chicago Tribune Company purchased the Chicago Cubs from the William Wrigley family in 1981, it marked the start of a series of changes for the baseball team.

Under the Wrigleys, the family was much involved, and most decisions were made by the club president after consulting family members. The Tribune Co. introduced a more professional, decentralized style of management, and took the president out of most day-to-day decision making.

"Most of the time the president isn't involved in decision making," said Wendy Lewis, director of human resources for the club. "He usually gets involved for things like contract negotiations, or if something comes in from the commissioner — anything major that comes up. He also has to handle our corporate reporting responsibilities."

The president acts as an overseer for two distinct divisions — baseball operations and business operations. Each division is headed by a team vice-president, who reports directly to the president, although each has a great deal of autonomy in running his division. General Manager Jim Frey heads up baseball operations — the team and the minor league affiliates. The team manager and the coaches report to Frey. He also is responsible for the traveling secretary, for hiring a team doctor, and for player personnel. Business Operations Vice-President Mark McGwire man-

ages the departments of marketing, finance, stadium operations, and ticket operations.

All of the separate divisions, from marketing to minor leagues, have a great deal of autonomy. In general, each branch of the organization operates independently, with top management performing a coordinating role.

The arrangement is fairly standard for a major league team. But the Cubs would not be the Cubs without their quirks; and even in corporate structure, they have quirks. Unlike most major league

teams, the Cubs' media relations and publications department and the director of human resources report directly to the club president.[1]

Whether the Tribune's changes in management have improved the Cubs' organization is open to debate. The team was an error away from winning a pennant in 1984, but they have been less fortunate in recent years.

Photo source: © Cathlyn Melloan/Tony Stone Worldwide.

Chapter Overview

We are constantly confronted with organization in a bewildering variety of activities. Sports teams, social organizations, religious groups, and work activities all create organizations. Even groups of animals — bees, ants, baboons, beavers — have organization.

An organizational structure is the result of the organizing process. In the previous chapter, we defined the verb *organizing* as the means by which management blends human and material resources by designing a formal structure of tasks and authority. It is the process of arranging work, dividing it among employees, and coordinating it so plans can be carried out and objectives can be accomplished.

The steps involved in the organizing process are shown in Figure 8.1. For a small business, these steps are relatively simple. The owner-manager of the local dry-cleaning firm employs a few people to sell, to launder and dry-clean clothing, and to make deliveries. The owner usually handles purchases of detergents, plastic wrappers, and other materials; assigns jobs to employees; and personally directs the operation of the business in pursuit of profits and growth. Coordinating work schedules of the employees and training new employees is relatively uncomplicated. Should one employee prove less effective in operating the cash register, he or she can be reassigned to one of the cleaning tasks.

But as a company grows, the need for organization increases. With increased size come specialization and a larger number of employees. Rather than a single salesperson, the manager employs a larger sales force; rather than one bookkeeper, the firm has a sizable accounting department. The large number of personnel and accompanying specialization make it impossible for one person to supervise all operations. Some formal organization is necessary because the manager faces a larger number of specialized employees to supervise.

organization
Structured grouping of people working together to accomplish objectives.

Organization, however, is the result of the organizing process. It can be defined as a structured grouping of people working together to achieve organizational objectives. Three key elements are present in an organization: human interaction, goal-directed activities, and structure. This chapter discusses the organizing process used to implement plans and achieve overall objectives. It examines alternative forms of organizational structure and discusses the informal organizational networks that frequently develop from the interactions of people.

Building the Organizational Structure

Although a small dry-cleaning firm experiences fewer organizational problems than a larger company, both have a formal structure to ensure that people perform tasks designed to accomplish company objectives. In the dry-cleaning company, for example, specific duties are assigned to wrappers, pressers, and other personnel.

The starting point in designing the appropriate organizational structure is to focus on the activities necessary to reach goals. Management analyzes the jobs to be performed. Then, people are employed who are both interested in and qualified for performing the jobs. Coordination of the activities of each worker is another important responsibility of management, because employees must "pull together" if the firm is to operate smoothly.

Figure 8.1   Steps in the Organizing Process

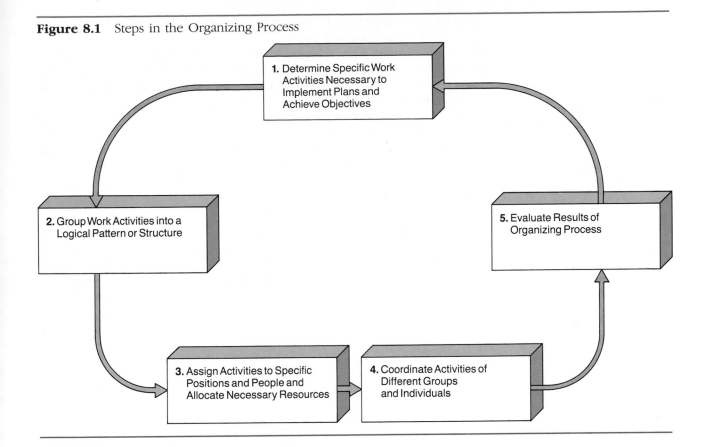

The problems resulting from a lack of coordination were all too apparent to Lee Iacocca when he took the helm of a tottering Chrysler Corporation:

Nobody at Chrysler seemed to understand that interaction among the differ- ent functions in a company is absolutely critical. People in engineering and manufacturing almost have to be sleeping together. These guys weren't even flirting!

Another example: sales and manufacturing were under the same vice- president. This was inconceivable to me because these were huge and pri- marily separate functions. To make matters worse, there was virtually no contact between the two areas. The manufacturing guys would build cars without ever checking with the sales guys. They just built them, stuck them in a yard, and then hoped that somebody would take them out of there. We ended up with a huge inventory and a financial nightmare.[2]

A well-defined organizational structure should also contribute to employee morale. Employees who know what is expected on the job, who the supervisor is, and how the work fits into the total organizational structure are likely to form a harmonious, loyal work force.

The structure of the formal organization is based on an analysis of the three key elements of any organization: human interaction, goal-directed activities, and structure. Management must coordinate the activities of workers to accom- plish organizational objectives.

A company objective of "providing our customers with quality products at competitive prices" does not specifically spell out to the mechanic that production machinery should be regularly inspected and defects repaired. Company objectives are often broad in nature and do not specify individual work activities. Consequently, they must be broken into specific goals for each employee in the organization.

Hierarchy of Objectives

hierarchy of organizational objectives
Levels of objectives that progress from the overall objectives to the specific objectives for each employee.

A **hierarchy of organizational objectives** extends from the overall objectives of the firm to specific objectives established for each employee. The broader goals of profitability, sales, market share, and service are broken into objectives for each division, each factory, each department, each work group, and each employee. Once this has been accomplished, each person can see his or her contribution to the total organizational goals. The number of levels in the hierarchy depends on the size and complexity of the firm. Smaller firms usually have fewer levels than larger ones.

Departmentalization

Building an organizational structure begins with an analysis of the major activities of the organization. In most firms, these activities consist of production, marketing, and finance. Each activity is assigned to separate departments in the firm, to both managers and employees.

departmentalization
Subdivision of work activities into units within the organization.

Departmentalization is the subdivision of work activities into units within the organization. This subdivision allows individuals to specialize in certain jobs and to become efficient in them. A marketing department may be headed by a marketing vice-president and may include sales, advertising, and marketing research. A human resources department may include recruitment, training, employee benefits, and industrial relations.

Five major forms of departmentalization exist: product, geography, customer, function, and process. As Figure 8.2 indicates, a number of these bases may be used in the same company. Deciding which bases to use involves balancing the advantages and disadvantages of each. The experience and judgment of top management come into play in such decisions.

Product Departmentalization   Procter & Gamble, the Cincinnati-based manufacturer of household products, divides its organizational structure on the basis of product departmentalization. Each of the firm's divisions — food products, toilet goods, paper products, packaged soaps and detergents, coffee, and industrial foods — is headed by a vice-president.

Geographic Departmentalization   Sears, Roebuck and Co. uses geographic departmentalization based on regions of the country, as do railroads, gas and oil distributors, and other chain stores.

Customer Departmentalization   Many sporting-goods stores subdivide using customer departmentalization, with a wholesale operation serving school systems and retail divisions serving other customers.

Figure 8.2   Various Forms of Departmentalization Used in One Company

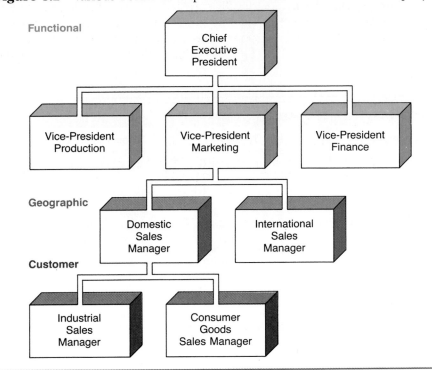

Functional Departmentalization   Oil companies are sometimes divided on the basis of functional departmentalization, with exploration, production, refining, marketing, and finance departments.

Process Departmentalization   Machinery and shoe manufacturers utilize process departmentalization. Manufacturing a product may include cutting the material, heat-treating it, forming it into its final shape, and painting it — all these activities being included in one or more departments.

Delegation

As the organization grows, the manager must assign part of his or her activities to subordinates in order to have time to devote to managerial functions. The act of assigning activities to subordinates is called **delegation**.

In delegating activities, the manager assigns to subordinates the responsibility to perform the assigned tasks. **Responsibility** is thus the obligation of a subordinate to perform assigned duties. Along with responsibility goes **authority**, the power to act and make decisions in carrying out assignments. Authority and responsibility must be balanced so subordinates are capable of carrying out their assigned tasks. Delegation of sufficient authority to fulfill the subordinate's responsibility in turn makes the subordinate accountable to the supervisor for results. **Accountability** is the act of holding a person liable for carrying out activities for which he or she has the necessary authority and responsibility.

delegation
Act of assigning part of a manager's activities to subordinates.

responsibility
Obligation of a subordinate to perform assigned duties.

authority
Power to act and make decisions in carrying out assignments.

accountability
Liability of subordinates to accomplish duties for which they have the necessary authority and responsibility.

Figure 8.3   The Organization of Apple Computer with Divisional Responsibilities

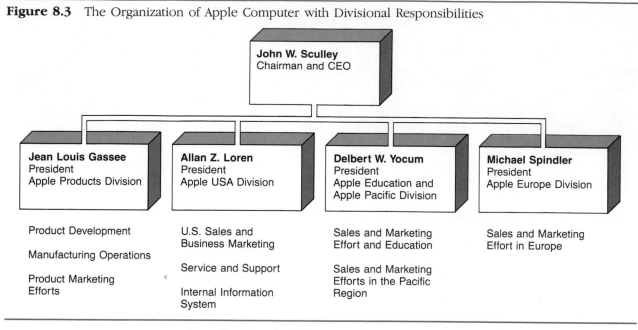

Source: Chart drawn from information in Brenton R. Schlender, "Apple Sets Plan to Reorganize into 4 Divisions." *The Wall Street Journal,* August 23, 1988, p. 2.

Even though authority is delegated to subordinates, the final responsibility rests with the manager. Therefore, that person must select qualified subordinates who are capable of performing the tasks.

In 1988, IBM announced a plan to reorganize into five product groups: personal computer systems, midrange systems, mainframes, communications, and building-block technology. Each division is headed by a general manager who has been delegated the responsibility and authority to act in this product area. CEO John Akers described his decision to delegate this way: "There's no way that one small set of managers at the top should think they are close enough to the action to make decisions in all these areas."[3]

Organization Charts

organization chart
Diagram showing the division of work, chain of command, and departmentalization of an organization.

Most companies use an organization chart as their formal outline of authority and responsibility relationships. Such charts provide all employees with a visual statement of these relationships, enabling them to see how their work relates to the overall operation of the company and to whom they report. The **organization chart** is the blueprint of the organization, indicating formal channels of communication and lines of authority. Apple Computer, like IBM, also recently reorganized. Figure 8.3 shows a simplified organization chart for Apple and the specific responsibilities of each division.

Because the organization chart specifies each area of responsibility and authority, it can also help managers coordinate activities. However, since the organization chart reflects the organization at only one point in time, it should be updated periodically to reflect changing conditions.

Organization charts were originated by Daniel McCallum in 1854. McCallum was the general superintendent of the world's largest railroad line at the time, the New York and Erie. McCallum developed an organization chart patterned after a tree. The roots were the president and the board of directors. The branches were the operating divisions and passenger and freight departments. The leaves represented the various agents, crews, and foremen.

Authority and accountability were very much a part of McCallum's organization chart. In 1856, he commented: "Obedience cannot be enforced when the foreman in immediate charge is interfered with by a superior officer giving orders directly to his subordinates."

McCallum's organization chart was widely distributed (for $1 per copy), so by 1910 these charts were a standard feature of American firms. The charts were used for a variety of purposes. Du Pont used them to study and restructure the company's operations. A major rubber company distributed them to the sales force, so its personnel could understand where they were positioned in the firm.

But not everyone agreed with the use of organization charts during the early decades of this century. Henry Ford said the charts looked like a family tree with berries (or positions) hanging on it. He criticized organization charts because a person's duties were "limited by the circumference of his [or her] berry." Ford also remarked: "It takes about six weeks for the message of [someone] living in a berry on the lower left hand corner of the chart . . . [to get to the CEO]."[4]

How Many Subordinates Can a Manager Supervise?

One reason for departmentalization is that managers are limited in the number of activities they can perform and the number of subordinates they can effectively supervise. The **span of management** (or span of control) is the optimal number of subordinates a manager can directly supervise.

span of management
Optimal number of subordinates a manager can directly supervise.

Although the optimal number varies from one firm to the next, the conventional wisdom is that top management should directly supervise no more than four to eight people. Supervisory managers who direct employees performing relatively routine tasks are capable of effectively managing a much larger number. Advanced information technology such as computer mailboxes and message systems are changing management's definition of the span of control. J. Brian Quinn of the Tuck Business School at Dartmouth argues that the span of control is being replaced by the "span of communications" that an executive possesses. Quinn believes computerized information systems may eventually allow a manager to have up to 200 people reporting to him or her.

While U.S. firms have not yet reached the spans that Quinn believes are possible, a number of organizations have been successful with broader spans of control. Franklin Mint doubled its sales in three years while cutting two of its six layers of management. Franklin Mint's CEO now has 12 people reporting directly to him, double the span that existed before.[5]

The critical factors in determining the optimal span of management are the type of work performed, the employees' training, the amount of paperwork involved, the manager's ability, and the effectiveness of communication. An experienced supervisor who manages trained personnel performing routine tasks

To ensure effective communication, New York Life Insurance Company produces video
programs to educate and inform its employees and
agents. The programs give
managers the opportunity to
field questions and discuss
company events and policies.
New York Life also publishes
a monthly employee newspaper, a newsletter for managers, and a marketing magazine
for agents.

Photo source: Photography: Enrico Ferorelli/DOT for New York Life Insurance Company.

with clear guidelines as to what is expected of them can effectively manage a
much larger number of subordinates than can the vice-president of marketing
or production.

Ensuring Effective Communication

Communication is a relatively simple task for small organizations. Because it is
often face to face, unclear instructions can be remedied by further conversation.
But communication problems increase with the growth of the organization.
Messages, many of which are transmitted in writing, pass through several layers
in the formal organization. The sender of the message must be continually
aware of the recipient and make certain the message is both clearly written and
likely to be interpreted correctly.

At the federal government level, attempts have been made to simplify written communications in order to improve understanding. But bureaucratic language continues, and readers are forced to interpret complex phrases and jargon. *U.S. News & World Report* recently translated some of this bureaucratic
babble. Among its choices: a Department of the Interior expression "directly
impact the visual quality of the present environment" means "spoil the view."
The expression, "negative saver," is a backward label for "a household that
spends more than it earns." The House Committee on Aging's "budgeting restraints and the socioeconomic climate must also be considered in evaluating
recommendations and deciding how they should be prioritized" translates into
"If there's no money, don't spend." And the Food and Drug Administration
tongue twister "innovative processes should be considered to better integrate
informed societal judgments and values into the regulatory mechanism" means
"think"![6]

Table 8.1   Basic Rules for Running a Meeting

1. Don't call a meeting to decide something you could and should decide yourself.

2. Never get people together if a series of phone calls would serve your purpose.

3. Never invite anyone who is not vital to the discussion, but make sure that everyone who would be of value is included.

4. Insist on punctuality.

5. Draft an agenda that breaks all subjects down into their simplest components. A lengthy agenda, if well constructed, often means a short meeting.

6. Circulate the agenda in sufficient time for people to read it before they come, but not so far ahead they forget it when the meeting time arrives.

7. Set time limits for each phase of the discussion and make sure everyone can see the clock. Discussion, like work, expands to fill the time available.

8. The chairperson must state the issues, keep to the agenda, let everyone have a fair crack at the subject but cut them short if they wander, and sum up succinctly as soon as all have their say.

Sources: United Technologies; Deborah Churchman, "Making Effective Use of Business Meetings," *Christian Science Monitor,* August 9, 1983, p. 14; Andrew S. Grove, "How (and Why) to Run a Meeting," *Fortune,* July 11, 1983, pp. 132–140; Eugene Raudsepp, "How to Make the Most of Meetings," *Computer Decisions,* July 1982, p. 167; Hugh O'Neill, "How to Run Meetings — and How Not To," *Management Today,* March 1982, pp. 41–44; and Robert Townsend, *Up the Organization* (New York: Fawcett-Crest, 1970).

Business Meetings   One of the most common forms of communication in organizations is the group meeting. While meetings can be informative and significantly contribute to the decision-making process, meetings should not become a strain on management's time. Management guru Peter Drucker pointed out that any manager spending more than 25 percent of his or her time in meetings is guilty of what Drucker calls "malorganization." Table 8.1 lists some of the ways to set up and run an effective meeting.

Centralization versus Decentralization

How much authority are managers willing to disperse throughout the organization? Managers who emphasize **centralization** disperse only the smallest possible amount of authority. Proponents of centralized management feel they can most effectively control and coordinate company activities by retaining most of the authority.

Managers who emphasize **decentralization** disperse great amounts of authority to subordinates. Decentralization allows middle and supervisory management more leeway in making decisions than does centralization. For example, middle managers in a decentralized operation are likely to make many financial, production, and personnel decisions rather than obtain approval from their superiors. When such decisions are made by subordinates, higher-level managers can devote their time to other problems. Decentralization also allows decision making to occur where the decisions will actually be implemented.

When Burlington Northern changed from an integrated railroad and material resource firm to a holding company, management decided it did not want its corporate staff interfering in operational decisions at the St. Paul headquarters. Management's solution was to move the corporate staff to Seattle, half of a continent away. The decision to decentralize achieved the results management sought. Burlington Northern is now a far leaner organization than it was before. Total employment is down 38 percent, and management employment has dropped 42 percent.[7]

centralization
Managerial practice of dispersing little authority to subordinates.

decentralization
Decisions to disperse substantial amounts of authority to subordinates.

While most management experts favor decentralized over centralized organization, some firms have had to centralize operations. For example, Hewlett-Packard operated as a decentralized organization from 1959 until the mid-1980s. Each Hewlett-Packard unit had its own production, marketing, finance, and personnel divisions. As a result, three divisions produced different computers for the professional and office markets. None were compatible with each other. Similarly, various divisions built circuit boards. Although the boards were often interchangeable, the decentralized approach was costly. Today, Hewlett-Packard's computers are compatible with each other, and they are produced by a single corporate group. Furthermore, circuit board manufacturing has been consolidated and costs reduced.[8]

Avoiding Unnecessary Organizational Growth

As a firm grows larger and more complex, the number of supervisory personnel and specialists increases. This tendency is natural as decentralization occurs and managers recognize their limited span of control. However, the organizational planner should be certain that the new layers of managers and the dozens of technical advisers are really needed or there will be little increase in production output or efficiency.

Parkinson's law
Theory stating that work expands to fill the time available to complete it.

Parkinson's law, as set forth by British historian-philosopher C. Northcote Parkinson in his book of the same title, can be explained as follows: "Work expands so as to fill the time available for its completion." Parkinson applied his law to organizations by illustrating how the number of employees in a firm increases over time regardless of the amount of work to be done. He pointed out, for example, that in 1914 the British navy, the most powerful in the world, contained 2,000 admiralty officials. In 1938, the number had increased to 3,569. By 1954, the British navy was managed by 33,788 members of the admiralty staff. As the British Empire shrank in the period from 1935 to 1954, the number of officials in the British Colonial Office grew from 372 to 1,661 — an average annual increase of nearly 6 percent.[9]

Why is there a tendency to add employees faster than the work is increasing? According to Parkinson, it can be blamed on (1) the selfish desire of managers to build empires by adding subordinates and (2) the paperwork created by the employment of additional workers. Preventing (or minimizing) the occurrence of Parkinson's law requires top management to be vigilant and to give honest appraisals of the need for new positions.

General Foods provides a classic illustration of Parkinson's law in operation. The firm built a temple-like headquarters overlooking a pond in Rye Brook, New York. The magnificent structure eventually housed 2,000 corporate staffers. When Philip Morris acquired General Foods, it cut most of the headquarters positions. The new owner moved an operating president into some of the vacant space and hired back part of the corporate staff. The headquarters now houses mainly operating employees.[10]

Forms of Organizational Structure

Business organizations can be classified according to the nature of their internal authority relationships. The four forms of organizational structure are line, line-and-staff, committee, and matrix. All four forms are in common use today in different sized organizations.

Figure 8.4   Organization of the Roman Legion

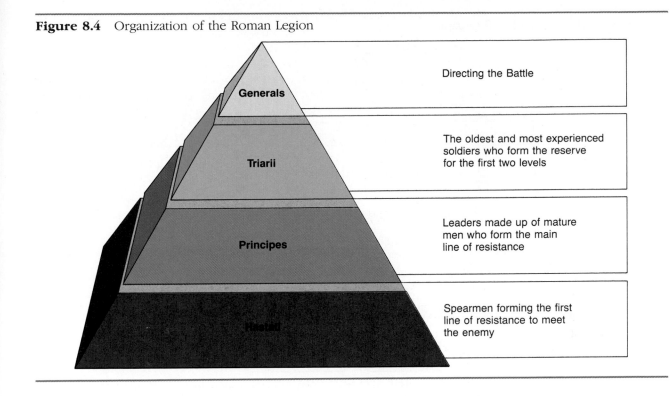

Line Organization

Line organization is the organization structure based on a direct flow of authority from the chief executive to subordinates. It is illustrated by the familiar story of the general who informs the colonel, who tells the major, who instructs the captain, who orders the lieutenant, who yells at the sergeant, who makes an unprintable request of the private, who carries out the order — or else.

The line form of organization is the oldest and simplest form of organizational structure. Caesar's legions used this form; so does the Roman Catholic Church. Figure 8.4 illustrates line organization.

The line organization is simple. The **chain of command** — the set of relationships that indicates who gives directions to whom and who reports to whom — is clear, and "buck-passing" is extremely difficult. Decisions can be made quickly because the manager can act without consulting anyone other than an immediate superior. But an obvious defect exists within line organizations. Each manager has complete responsibility for a number of activities and cannot possibly be an expert in all of them.

This defect is very apparent in medium- and large-sized firms, where the pure line form fails to provide the specialized skills so vital to modern industry. Executives are overburdened with administrative details and paperwork and have little time for planning.

In evaluating the strengths and weaknesses of the line form, the obvious conclusion is that this structure is ineffective in all but the smallest organizations. Beauty shops, cleaning plants, "mom-and-pop" grocery stores, and small law firms can operate effectively with a simple line structure. Ford, General Electic, and Boeing cannot.

line organization
Organizational structure based on a direct flow of authority from the chief executive to subordinates.

chain of command
Established authority and responsibility relationships.

Figure 8.5   The Line-and-Staff Organization

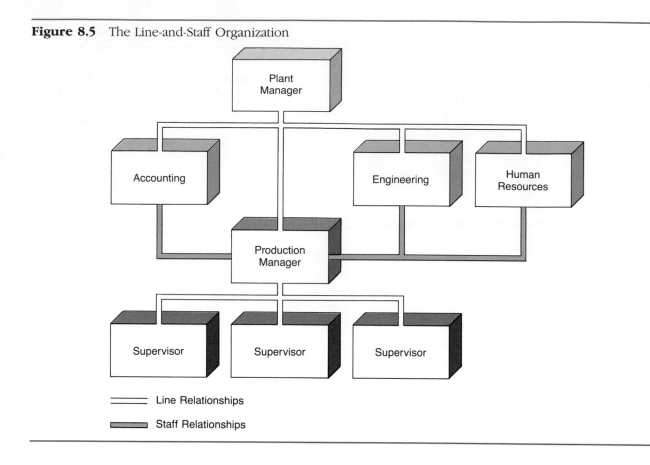

Line Relationships

Staff Relationships

Line-and-Staff Organization

line-and-staff organization
Organizational structure that combines the direct flow of authority with staff departments that support the line departments.

The **line-and-staff organization** combines the direct flow of authority present in the line organization with staff departments that serve, advise, and support the line departments. Line departments are involved directly in decisions affecting the operation of the organization. Staff departments lend specialized technical support. As Figure 8.5 shows, employees receive daily supervision from a line manager and specialized advice and suggestions from staff personnel.

For all practical purposes, the line-and-staff and the newer matrix structures are the only forms of organization capable of meeting the requirements of modern businesses. They combine the line organization's rapid decision making and effective, direct communication with the staff specialists' expert knowledge needed to direct diverse and widespread activities. The line-and-staff form is commonly used in medium- and large-sized firms.

line manager
Manager of such functions as production, marketing, and finance.

staff manager
Manager who provides information, advice, or technical assistance to the line managers.

The major difference between a line manager and a staff manager is in authority relationships. A **line manager** is directly involved with the critical functions of production, financing, or marketing. Line managers form a part of the main line of authority that flows throughout the organization. Staff members perform important functions, but their roles are advisory and service-providing for line managers. A **staff manager** provides information, advice, or technical assistance to aid line managers. Staff managers are expected to make recommendations and to advise line managers. They do not possess the authority to give

Photo source: Courtesy of Campbell Soup Company.

These men are members of a management committee formed by Campbell Soup Company in 1987. The committee advises Campbell's president, R. Gordon McGovern, on strategies for achieving corporate objectives and helps evaluate the company's progress in reaching those goals. The committee includes executives from finance, international, sales and marketing, and strategic planning.

orders or to compel line managers to take action, although they do have the necessary line authority to supervise their own departments. Examples of staff managers in medium- and large-sized organizations include the director of research, the advertising manager, the legal counsel, and the director of engineering.

Committee Organization

Committee organization is the organization structure in which authority and responsibility are jointly held by a group of individuals rather than by a single manager. It is typically used as part of the regular line-and-staff structure.

Examples of the committee structure exist throughout the organization. For example, firms such as Ford and K mart have used the *Office of the CEO concept.* The Office of the CEO refers to an organizational arrangement whereby the duties of the chief executive are shared among two or more executives. Typically, the responsibilities are split along functional lines with one person handling manufacturing, another marketing, and so on. At a lower level in the firm, committees are often used in other areas such as new-product development. The new product committee may include managers from such areas as accounting, engineering, finance, manufacturing, marketing, and research. In major corporations, the inclusion of representatives from all areas involved in developing new products generally improves planning because diverse perspectives — production, marketing, finance — are considered. Company morale is also usually strengthened when all areas participate in decision making.

But committees tend to be slow and conservative, and decisions are often made through compromise based on conflicting interests rather than by choos-

committee organization
Organizational structure wherein authority and responsibility are jointly held by a group of individuals.

ing the best alternative. The definition of a camel as "a horse designed by a committee" provides an apt description of some committee decisions.

The Matrix Organization

matrix organization
Structure in which specialists from different parts of the organization are brought together to work on specific projects.

A growing number of organizations have utilized a new approach in adjusting their existing structures to changing requirements, particularly in the areas of research and development and new-product development. This new form, the **matrix organization**, or project management organization, is a structure in which specialists from different parts of the organization are brought together to work on specific projects. Like the committee form, the matrix organization is typically used as a subform within the line-and-staff structure.

The matrix organization is built around specific projects or problems in which employees with different areas of expertise gather to focus on specific major problems or unique technical issues. An identifying feature of such organizations is that some members of the organization report to two superiors instead of one. This type of organization has been used in such organizations as Dow Chemical, Chase Manhattan Bank, Procter & Gamble, Lockheed Aircraft, and the Harvard Business School.

The matrix form received wide publicity during the 1960s, when the National Aeronautics and Space Administration used the project structure to mount Mercury and Apollo space missions. Lockheed turned to this approach when it was awarded a multibillion-dollar contract to build 58 huge C-5A military transports. In all, Lockheed temporarily assigned 11,000 employees to the project and used more than 120,000 parts from 6,000 outside suppliers to complete it.

As Figure 8.6 indicates, the matrix organization produces a combination of dual authority. Project members receive instructions from the project manager (horizontal authority), but maintain membership in their permanent functional departments (vertical authority). In order to reduce the potential problems of two bosses, the project manager is typically granted considerable authority for the project and usually reports to the general manager. The term matrix is derived from the cross-hatching of the horizontal authority-responsibility flow of the project team over the vertical flows of the traditional line-and-staff organization.

The major benefits of the matrix structure lie in its flexibility and the ability to focus resources on major problems or projects. However, it requires the project manager to mold individuals from diverse parts of the organization into an integrated team. Team members must be comfortable in working for more than one boss. To offset the temporary nature of the matrix team, the project manager is sometimes granted the authority to make salary decisions and promotion recommendations and to take other personnel actions involving team members for the duration of the project.

Comparing the Four Forms of Organization

Although most large companies are organized on a line-and-staff basis, the line organization is usually the best form for smaller businesses. The committee form is used to a limited extent in major corporations. The matrix approach is increasingly used by large, multiproduct firms to focus diverse organizational

Figure 8.6   The Matrix Organization

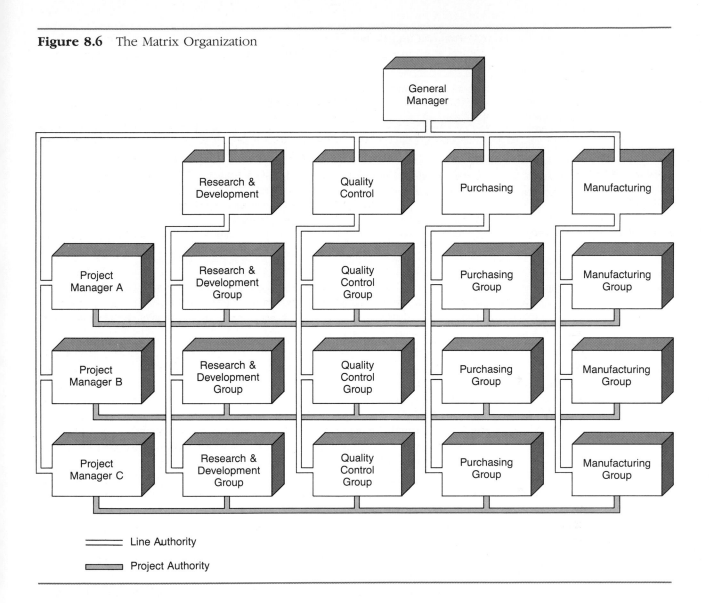

resources on specific problems or projects. Table 8.2 compares the strengths and weaknesses of the four forms of organization.

The Informal Organization

In addition to the lines of authority and responsibility in the formal organization, informal channels of communication and contact also exist. The **informal organization** is a self-grouping of employees in the organization who possess unofficial channels of communication and contact. This type of organization is not formally planned; it develops out of the interactions of people.

Formal organization is created by management; informal organization is the result of social and communication relationships. Groups of workers often cut

informal organization
A self-grouping of employees who possess informal communication channels.

Table 8.2   Comparing the Four Forms of Organization

Form of Organization	Advantages	Disadvantages
Line	Simple and easy for both workers and managers to understand Clear delegation of authority and responsibility for each area Quick decisions Direct communication	No specialization Overburdening of top executives with administrative details
Line-and-staff	Specialists to advise line managers Employees reporting to one superior	Conflict between line and staff unless relationships are clear Staff managers making only recommendations to line managers
Committee	Combined judgment of several executives in diverse areas Improved morale through participation in decision making	Committees slow in making decisions Decisions are the result of compromises rather than a choice of the best alternative
Matrix	Flexibility Provides method for focusing strongly on specific major problems or unique technical issues Provides means of innovation without disrupting regular organizational structure	Problems may result from employees being accountable to more than one boss Project manager may encounter difficulty in developing a cohesive team from diverse individuals recruited from various parts of the organization Conflict may arise between project managers and other department managers

grapevine
Informal network of communication found in most organizations.

across the formal organization structure, and informal relationships exist at both managerial and lower levels. Supervisors from a number of departments may take coffee breaks together. The conversation may range from company business to mutual interests to problems of a business or personal nature. Two machinists, a drill press operator, a receiving clerk, and a supervisor may be teammates on the company basketball team. As part of this regular interaction, they may discuss company operations and communicate the results of their talks to other workers in their areas.

Even though the informal organization is not shown on the organization chart, managers should be aware of its existence. It may even be possible to make use of some aspects of the informal organization in accomplishing organizational objectives — such as through the use of the **grapevine**, the informal network of communication found in most organizations. In his studies of the grapevine, author Keith Davis found it to be 80 to 90 percent accurate in transmitting noncontroversial information. Because this information travels by word of mouth, the grapevine is faster than formal communications.[11] The grapevine is less than accurate when it transmits rumors or other more controversial information. Although many managers use the grapevine as a supplement to formal communication channels in dispersing information and in minimizing rumors, most attempt to develop open and honest formal communication channels.

The following examples illustrate how the grapevine can work for or against management. When Bell & Howell was the target of a three-way takeover battle, the company's grapevine spewed out so many tales of impending layoffs that little work was accomplished until the takeover was concluded. For example, sales representatives were reported to have spent half their time calling Bell & Howell's Chicago headquarters for an update on the latest rumors. Bell & How-

Employees sharing a common interest interact in the informal organization. This photo shows some Minneapolis employees of General Mills serving as helpers and cheerleaders at a festival for disabled sports enthusiasts. General Mills encourages its employees to participate in such community activities although they are outside the firm's formal organization.

Photo source: © Steve Niedorf 1988 for General Mills.

ell management later estimated these rumors were responsible for a drop in productivity that caused the firm's profits to decline $2.1 million during the six-month period. By contrast, when Bethlehem Steel downsized its work force, management provided a continually updated electronic newsletter to every computer station in the company. In this instance, management replaced potential rumors with factual, open communication.[12]

Intrapreneuring

The strengths of an effective organization result from the structured groupings of people who work together to accomplish objectives. The chain of command is clear, and organizational members understand who gives directions to whom and who reports to whom. But a growing number of corporate leaders have become concerned that this structure may stifle innovation. They point to such innovative approaches to organizing as the matrix structure as evidence of the need to remain flexible enough to move in new directions.

Traditionally, major innovations have been the domain of small business, formed by forward-thinking, risk-taking entrepreneurs. From Thomas Edison's development of the phonograph to the birth of the Apple personal computer in Steven P. Jobs' garage, the U.S. entrepreneurial sector is the birthplace of dozens of major industries and is the envy of the world. Entrepreneurs have given the

intrapreneur
Entrepreneurial type manager operating within a corporate structure.

world such popular consumer products as ball-point pens, fiberglass skis, Velcro fasteners, and Big Mac hamburgers.

Today, a growing number of major corporations are attempting to incorporate the strengths of the entrepreneur within the corporate structure by creating a novel approach called intrapreneuring. Management writer Gifford Pinchot, who coined the term, defines **intrapreneurs** as "dreamers who do . . . those who take hands-on responsibility for creating innovation of any kind within an organization. The intrapreneur may be the creator or inventor, but is always the dreamer who figures out how to turn an idea into a profitable reality."[13] His intrapreneurs' Hall of Fame includes, among others, the individuals responsible for the development of 3M's Post-it note pads.

Although the intrapreneur may begin by assembling a special task force and/or working within the confines of a matrix structure, the frequent result of a successful project is an entirely new subsidiary of the corporation. In some cases, a separate company is formed at the outset. While the disadvantages of this approach are identical to those described earlier in the matrix organization, the advantages lie in the available financing and necessary manufacturing and marketing expertise already in place in a large company. In addition, the intrapreneuring option permits many firms to retain valuable entrepreneurially oriented executives who might otherwise leave the company and start their own businesses.

Several examples illustrate how large corporations are attempting to match the entrepreneurial spirit of successful small businesses. Scott Paper Company set up a venture unit to market products to the handyman market. S. C. Johnson and Son set aside $250,000 to provide initial support for new-product ideas generated within the company.[14] One of the most innovative approaches to intrapreneurship comes from SEI Corporation, a financial-services firm headquartered in Wayne, Pennsylvania. SEI is dividing its 1,100 employees into entrepreneurial units. The employees will own 20 percent of the unit. If the unit is successful, SEI will pay the unit members for their 20 percent share. If the unit fails, its members will receive only their base salaries.[15]

Summary of Learning Goals ————————————

1. Explain the steps involved in the organizing process. The organizing process and the resultant organizational structure form the basis for the implementation of plans designed to accomplish organizational objectives. The need for structure increases as organizations grow in size. As the number of subordinates increases, the responsibility for coordinating their activities through a formal structure also increases.

The act of organizing involves the blending of human and material resources through the design of a formal structure of tasks and authority. Once organizational objectives and plans have been developed, organizing involves the following five steps:

a. Determine specific work activities necessary to implement those plans and accomplish objectives.
b. Group work activities into a logical pattern or structure.
c. Assign activities to specific positions and people together with the necessary resources and authority to carry them out.

d. Coordinate activities of different groups and individuals.

e. Evaluate the results of the organizing process.

2. Identify the major forms of departmentalization. Departmentaliza-tion is the subdivision of work activities into units within the organization. This subdivision may be based on one of five major alternatives: products, geogra-phy, customers, functions, or processes. In addition, the same organization may use more than one basis for departmentalization.

3. Explain the relationship between authority, responsibility, and accountability. Developing a formal organizational structure means top man-agement must delegate to subordinates the authority and responsibility to ac-complish assignments. Responsibility is the obligation of a subordinate to per-form those assigned duties. When subordinates are delegated such responsibilities, they must also be granted the necessary authority — the power to act and to make decisions in carrying out assignments. The individual who is granted such authority is also held accountable for carrying out these assigned tasks.

4. Identify the strengths and weaknesses of organization charts. The organization chart is a blueprint of the authority relationships within the organi-zation. It shows functions, formal channels of communication, and line-and-staff relationships. It also indicates responsibility, authority, and accountability rela-tionships within the firm.

Due to the dynamic nature of organizations, organization charts can become outdated quickly and must be revised periodically. In addition, they do not reflect the informal groups or lines of communication that exist.

5. List the determinants of the span of management. Determining the optimal number of subordinates a manager can directly supervise involves a number of elements: the type of work performed, the workers' training, the amount of paperwork involved, the manager's ability, and the effectiveness of communication.

6. Describe Parkinson's law and how to avoid its effects. Parkinson's law describes the unnecessary growth that frequently occurs over time in orga-nizations. The law states, "Work expands so as to fill the time available for its completion." Such growth can usually be blamed on the selfish desires of some managers to build empires by adding subordinates and by the paperwork cre-ated by the employment of additional workers. Auditing paperwork flows and requiring managers to justify additional employees can often minimize the oc-currence of this phenomenon.

7. Evaluate each of the four basic forms of organization. Four forms of organizational structure have been used: line, line-and-staff, committee, and matrix. The line organization is the simplest form but it suffers from a lack of specialization by management. The line-and-staff form assigns authority to line managers and adds staff specialists to provide information and advice. However, conflict can arise between line and staff members if their relationship is unclear.

The committee form of organization is rarely used as the sole organization structure, but it is often incorporated to some extent within the line-and-staff structure. Because committees can be composed of representatives of a number of areas in the organization, they ensure that each area is represented in the decision-making process. However, they are relatively slow in making decisions, which often end up being compromises among conflicting interests. The matrix form of organization, another subform of the line-and-staff structure, permits large, multiproduct firms to focus organizational resources on specific problems or projects. Because of its "team" approach and the fact that team members are accountable to more than one manager, conflict can occur.

8. Explain the function of the informal organization in a firm. The informal organization is a self-grouping of employees in a firm who possess informal channels of communication and contact. It grows out of social interactions and extracurricular relationships. Such informal contacts may serve as additional sources of information and may supplement the formal organization in serving the needs of its members.

9. Describe the role of intrapreneurship in modern organizations. The term *intrapreneurship* refers to various attempts to make large organizations more entrepreneurial. Intrapreneurship units are established outside the normal organization chart in order to achieve the innovative dynamics of a smaller firm. These units are given free rein (and sometimes financial incentives) to accomplish their assigned objectives.

Key Terms

organization

hierarchy of organizational
  objectives

departmentalization

delegation

responsibility

authority

accountability

organization chart

span of management

centralization

decentralization

Parkinson's law

line organization

chain of command

line-and-staff organization

line manager

staff manager

committee organization

matrix organization

informal organization

grapevine

intrapreneur

Review Questions

1. Contrast the terms *organizing* and *organizational structure*. What are the purposes of a formal structure?

2. How are organizational objectives and organizational structure related?

3. What is departmentalization? What are its major forms?

4. Why is it important that authority and responsibility be balanced in an organization?

5. Trace the development of organization charts. What are their major purposes? Compare their strengths and weaknesses.

6. Identify the determinants of the optimal span of management.

7. Distinguish between centralization and decentralization. Under what circumstances might each be preferred?

8. Suggest some ways in which the occurrence of Parkinson's law might be prevented.

9. Summarize the major strengths and weaknesses of each type of formal organizational structure.

10. The committee structure is rarely used as a separate structure for an entire organization. Suggest several specific ways of improving the committee form of organizational structure.

Discussion Questions

1. U.S. firms have cut over a million management and professional jobs in the last five years. This trend has been labeled the "middle-management malaise" or the "leaner-and-meaner blues." Why have so many U.S. firms decided to downsize their organizations? Discuss.

2. Give an example of a firm in your state that should use the following forms of departmentalization. Defend your answers.
   a. Product   **d.** Functional
   b. Geographic   **e.** Process
   c. Customer

3. The typical professional sports team is owned by wealthy individuals who enjoy being involved with a particular sport. The owners usually make the major policy decisions, but a hired general manager handles other managerial duties. The general manager oversees facilities, equipment, vendors, and personnel matters. He or she usually also has responsibility for player personnel decisions such as trades, new-player drafts, and assignment of players to minor leagues. The field manager, or head coach, is in charge of the team's actual performance. This person assists the general manager in matters concerning players. Other personnel employed by professional teams include team physicians, assistant coaches, trainers, equipment managers, secretaries, scouts, and ticket sales personnel. Draw an organization chart for a professional sports team. Discuss the strengths of this organizational structure.

4. Management expert Peter Drucker has described how the British managed the subcontinent of India for two centuries. The Indian civil service assigned just one officer to each of the nearly 1,000 districts. These district officers reported to the provincial political secretary through a monthly report, which the political secretary responded to in detail. Each political secretary had a span of control of at least 100 district officers. Why do you think this organization structure worked so well for so long given the immense span of control involved? Discuss.

5. Ford Motor operates an in-house television network that broadcasts the latest company news as well as remarks by CEO Donald Petersen. Relate Ford's internal communication effort to the material in Chapter 8.

Video Case

Lundberg Family Farms

Some companies do not have to hold elaborate planning meetings to decide how they will organize and structure their businesses; their organization arises naturally, from within. Such is the case for Lundberg Family Farms, a Richvale, California, enterprise started by four brothers. For this producer of natural brown rice and related products, business meetings are family gatherings, and an alarming number of employees at these meetings share the same last name.

The four Lundberg brothers — Wendell, Harlan, Eldon, and Homer — came to the rice-growing business naturally: Their father, Albert, started rice farming in Nebraska in the 1930s. But the drought that resulted in the decimation of the Dust Bowl and the economic hardships of the Great Depression drove Albert and his family west to seek better opportunities. The Lundberg family was blessed by the fact that Albert chose one of America's most productive agricultural areas, the Sacramento Valley of Northern California, to settle in.

The elder Lundberg's experience with severe Nebraska dust storms led to a personal philosophy of "leaving the soil better than we found it." He taught his sons that soil is a precious resource which requires care and protection. He was also wary of the agricultural chemicals that farmers began to use in the years following World War II. That caution was passed along to his sons, and it ultimately became the key to the growth of Lundberg Family Farms.

The first crop of short-grain organic rice was planted in 1969. Today, 250 acres of Lundberg Family Farms are strictly organic crops; the remaining 2,500 acres grow "premium" quality rices which rely minimally on chemical intervention.

The Lundberg family began their California farming operations on an extremely small scale. In the early years, totally natural brown rice production frequently amounted to as little as two or three cases a week. During this period, rice was hauled to dryers at the local agricultural cooperative, where it was dumped in with crops of other area rice growers. Drying to an appropriate moisture level allows the rice to be stored for long periods until the best possible price is offered. As Barry Stice, Lundberg's general manager, explains, "Millions of bags of rice are in storage in the U.S., some of it three and four years old. Japan carries a five-year supply."

But the Lundbergs paid a price for following the traditional practice of selling agricultural products to co-ops that combined them with those of other producers, processed them, and resold them in large quantities. Such an approach meant that Lundberg rice became a commodity, indistinguishable from other rice. All of the time and effort, all of the care and concern they lavished on growing a high-quality, organic rice was lost because buyers could not tell the difference.

Wendell, Harlan, Eldon, and Homer Lundberg developed a consensus management style that called for agreement among all family members and non-family managers before making a major decision. They met as an informal committee to discuss the issue of product identity and to seek a solution. First, they asked the co-ops to process and package their rice separately, but their request was quickly rejected when the co-op owners realized the small quantities involved.

Finally, Lundberg's management agreed to make a major change in their product and marketing philosophies: (1) They would seek out the market that demanded a naturally-grown product; (2) they would control their growth as demand dictated; and (3) they would control every phase of the process "from seedline to shelf." Their desire to produce and market the best-quality product possible forced them to create a new processing/distribution system. This *vertical integration* approach meant that Lundberg Family Farms would not only own the means of producing the rice, but would also process, package, store, and ship it, as well as have sales specialists who would call on the retail stores that offered the products to consumers.

They also agreed that they would get big by thinking small. Patience was a great aid to the Lundberg brothers — that and a solid, unshakeable belief in their product. In 1969, Richvale was a town four blocks long and three blocks wide — hardly a promising

Notes: Peggy Rossoff, "Rebel Farmers, Stalking the Way of Organic Rice," *Macromuse Magazine,* Summer 1987, pp. 26–31; personal correspondence, April 3, 1989.

place to start a revolutionary new approach to rice farming. The starting point on the road to vertical integration was to build a mill there. It was certainly small enough, capable of handling one truckload of rice at a time.

The distribution system evolved from direct sales to passers-by and word-of-mouth communication to other buyers. In the early days, a substantial percentage of total sales came from California hippies who drove to the farm and loaded their vans and station wagons with rice. The sales door was finally opened as a result of a developing trend in the United States that led people to want "all natural" and "organically grown" foods. That health food movement lifted sales off the ground. Lundberg began exhibiting its product offerings at regional natural foods conventions and nearby health food stores began carrying their products. This growing distribution, however slow at first, forced the Lundbergs to consider business matters they had not previously addressed, such as packaging. Their first product offerings came in 100-pound bags with the Lundberg name stenciled across them. Such sizes proved to be slow-movers to individual food shoppers as did the subsequent 25- and 50-pound sizes. Finally, they realized that they were offering a premium-price, premium-quality, specialty product and they began producing 2-pound packages for this segment of the food-buying market.

The Lundberg product line was gradually expanded from brown rice to such items as rice pilaf, various blends of rice, hot and cold cereals, snacks, and sweeteners. Most can be purchased in health food stores across the country. The family has also expanded their operations to include the output of other California farmers who agree to use their organic growing methods and adhere to Lundberg quality specifications. These products are also marketed under the Lundberg label.

Lundberg products cost more because of the care that goes into production, but people are willing to pay more for a superior rice. Packaging products under their own name has also strengthened the family's relationship with their customers. People know who they are.

Today, Lundberg family members work in sales, marketing, and farming — in every aspect of the business. To ensure that the needed expertise is available in all operations, they have brought in non-family

managers, such as Peter Milbury, the new-product development manager, who have an equal voice in the operation. Decisions are made in a participatory manner. For example, new products are sampled and evaluated by managers and family members and will not be marketed unless they gain the approval of everyone. While the new-product efforts have generated hundreds of varieties of rice products, Lundberg rarely brings out more than two or three items a year.

The presence of four brothers with equal claims to the operation might be viewed by some as a potential problem. However, the Lundbergs consider the fact that all four brothers think for themselves and may have differing opinions as a strength, not a weakness. The organization gets four different ideas on problem solutions this way. While they try to look at a problem a little differently, they eventually reach a consensus in a spirit of family cooperation.

This unified approach comes from a sense of commitment — not just to the quality of the product, but more importantly to each other. In an industry like agriculture, troubled in recent years by the low prices and high interest rates that have driven many out of the business entirely, Lundberg Family Farms has managed to create its own specialized niche.

Questions

1. How has the growth of Lundberg Family Farms affected its organization? Incorporate the steps shown in Figure 8.1 in your answer.

2. What is the most likely form of departmentalization used by Lundberg Family Farms? Defend your answer.

3. Based on information supplied in the case, how would you categorize the form of organizational structure used by Lundberg Family Farms? What are the major merits and shortcomings of this structure?

4. In what ways might Lundberg's chain of command be difficult to understand for a newly-hired middle manager? How can this potential problem be overcome?

5. Relate the following concepts to Lundberg Family farms.

a. line managers and staff managers
b. hierarchy of organizational objectives
c. authority and responsibility
d. matrix organizational structure

9

Production and Operations Management

Learning Goals

1. To identify the roles of specialization, mechanization, and standardization in mass production.

2. To describe the contributions and problems associated with the use of assembly lines, automation, and robots in producing products and services.

3. To list the three components of production and operations management.

4. To outline the major factors involved in deciding plant locations.

5. To compare the alternative designs for production facilities.

6. To list the steps involved in the purchasing process.

7. To compare the advantages and disadvantages of maintaining large amounts of inventory.

8. To identify the steps in the production control process.

9. To explain the contributions of quality circles in improving quality control.

An expensive steak lunch at a Tokyo hotel has so relaxed a Japanese electronics executive that he gives a rare glimpse of his *honne,* his innermost feelings, to an American guest. He chats about the problems at his U.S. subsidiary, which manufactures television sets and video equipment. Finally, he leans conspiratorially over his $5 cup of coffee and asks: "Do *you* know a U.S. company that makes good parts?"

America's widespread reputation for poor production quality may be labelled a trade barrier. Even though hundreds of American products set world standards, U.S. industry's negative reputation abroad persists — often overshadowing the progress being made.

For the 250 production workers at radar-detector manufacturer Whistler, improved quality was a matter of survival. By 1985, demand had grown so fast that shoddy products had become common. Fully 25 percent of the detectors coming off Whistler's assembly line failed inspection, and over 100 of the firm's 250 production workers spent their time fixing defective units. "We were fat, dumb, and happy," recalls Production Manager Patrick Driscoll. But Whistler's parent, Burlington, Massachusetts-based Dynatech, was already testing alternative production sources, and its tests revealed the same models could be made in South Korea for less cost. Finally, Whistler's managers received the ultimatum: get costs down to within 10 percent of Korea's or the U.S. plants would be shut down. Dynatech also made managerial moves, promoting a manufacturing executive to president of Whistler and hiring production expert Richard Packer as the new vice-president for manufacturing.

Packer immediately formed a team of Whistler employees from planning, testing, manufacturing, and engineering and set to work designing and testing a model pro-

duction line. Every job in the factory was redefined by the quality team, and training programs were devised for every worker. Perhaps the most controversial move was eliminating the quality-acceptance department based on the rationale that quality was everyone's responsibility, not just the concern of a single department. As Packer put it, "We wanted to take quality and disperse it to everyone's job. We were saying to the workers, 'If you want to ship garbage, that's what we are going to ship.'"

Today, any worker can halt the assembly line to fix a problem or return defective units. Production goals are agreed to in advance by both management and workers, and workers can leave early if they have met their quotas. Whistler's president, Charles Stott, shown in the accompanying photo, and other

top executives work on the production line once every 90 days to keep in touch with quality efforts.

The results have been outstanding. The pass rate of products coming off the Whistler assembly line has jumped from 75 percent to 99 percent. The virtual elimination of defective units permitted a reduction of the production work force from 250 to 120 without lowering output. Finally, U.S. manufacturing costs are now within 7 percent of the South Korean subcontractor's. Whistler's Packer insists quality improvements such as these are not unreasonable: "It just takes recognition of the need and a couple of maniacs to go do it."[1]

Photo source: © 1988 Rob Kinmonth.

Chapter Overview

utility
Want-satisfying power of a product or service.

Society allows businesses to operate only as long as they make a contribution. By producing and marketing desired goods and services, businesses satisfy this commitment. They create what economists call **utility** — the want-satisfying power of a good or service. Four basic kinds of utility are: time, place, ownership, and form. Time, place, and ownership utility are created by marketing — by having goods and services available to consumers at convenient locations when they want to buy them and at facilities where title to them can be transferred at the time of purchase.

form utility
Utility created through the conversion of raw materials and other inputs into finished goods and services.

Form utility is created through the conversion of raw materials and other inputs into finished goods or services. For example, fabric, thread, and zippers are converted into Levi's jeans. The creation of form utility is the responsibility of the firm's production function.

production
Use of people and machinery to convert materials into finished products or services.

Production is the use of people and machinery to convert materials into finished goods or services. Although the term *production* is sometimes used interchangeably with *manufacturing,* production is a broader term and includes a number of nonmanufacturing processes. For example, production encompasses such extractive industries as fishing, lumber, and mining. Production also applies to the creation of services. Services are intangible outputs of the production system. They include outputs as diverse as trash hauling, education, haircuts, tax accounting, health delivery systems, mail services, transportation, and lodging. Table 9.1 lists five examples of production systems for a variety of goods and services.

Whether the production process results in a tangible good or an intangible service, both are created by the conversion of inputs into outputs. The conversion process may involve major changes in raw materials or a simple combining of finished parts. The butcher performs a production function by reducing a side of beef to ground beef, steaks, chuck roasts, and other cuts of meat. General Motors combines tires, spark plugs, a battery, and thousands of other components to complete a new Beretta. These processes result in the creation of form utility.

This chapter describes the process of producing goods and services. We begin by explaining how production techniques, technology, and the concept of quality increase productivity. Then we identify the tasks of the production and operations manager in planning for production, implementing the plan, and controlling the production process. Finally, we discuss the impact of production on the environment.

Mass Production and the Assembly Line

mass production
Manufacture of products in large quantities as a result of standardization, specialized labor, and mechanization.

The United States began as a colonial supplier of raw materials to Europe and evolved into an industrial giant. A major factor in this remarkable change has been the application of the concept of mass production. **Mass production** is the manufacture of products in large amounts through the effective combination of three factors: specialized labor, mechanization, and standardization. The result of mass production is the availability of large quantities of products produced efficiently and sold at lower prices than could be dreamed of if such products were individually crafted.

Table 9.1   Some Typical Production Systems

Example	Primary Inputs	Transformation	Outputs
Pet food factory	Grain, water, fish meal, personnel, tools, machines, paper bags, cans, buildings, utilities	Converts raw materials into finished goods	Pet food products
Trucking firm	Trucks, personnel, buildings, fuel, goods to be shipped, packaging supplies, truck parts, utilities	Packages and transports goods from sources to destinations	Delivered goods
Department store	Buildings, displays, shopping carts, machines, stock goods, personnel, supplies, utilities	Attracts customers, stores goods, sells products	Marketed goods
Automobile body shop	Damaged autos, paints, supplies, machines, tools, buildings, personnel, utilities	Transforms damaged auto bodies into facsimiles of the originals	Repaired automobile bodies
County sheriff's department	Supplies, personnel, equipment, automobiles, office furniture, buildings, utilities	Detects crimes, brings criminals to justice, keeps the peace	Acceptable crime rates and peaceful communities

Source: *Production and Operations Management: A Problem Solving and Decision Making Approach, Third Edition* by Norman Gaither, copyright © 1990 by The Dryden Press, reprinted by permission of the publisher.

Specialization

A key factor in making mass production possible is **specialization**, the dividing of work into its simplest components so workers can concentrate on performing each task. The father of this approach was Frederick W. Taylor, whose efforts in the late nineteenth and early twentieth centuries were devoted to achieving industrial efficiency by reducing and simplifying jobs.

Taylor's contemporary, Frank B. Gilbreth, carried this reduction of tasks to the ultimate. Gilbreth called the smallest possible time-and-motion unit for a given task a *therblig,* a term that comes from reversing the letters in his last name. He applied many of these production concepts to operating his household and became famous to later generations in the book and film *Cheaper by the Dozen,* written by 2 of his 12 children.

Firms conduct time-and-motion studies to increase worker productivity. The studies help determine the rate at which a job should be done and the most efficient sequence and number of motions needed to accomplish a specific task. The industrial engineers at United Parcel Service used time-and-motion studies to improve the sorting and delivery of packages.[2]

specialization
Dividing work into its simplest components to permit concentration in performing each task.

Mechanization

Once jobs were separated into smaller tasks, managers could consider the possibility of **mechanization**, the use of machines to perform work previously performed by people. Before the Industrial Revolution, work was performed pri-

mechanization
Use of machines to perform work previously performed by humans.

marily by people and animals. In 1850, the typical worker spent 70 hours per week on the job and produced an average of 25 cents' worth of goods per hour. Today, the average person works a 40-hour week and, with machines, produces goods having 39 times the value of his or her counterpart of the mid-nineteenth century.

Standardization

standardization
Production of uniform and interchangeable goods and parts.

The third component of a mass production system — **standardization** — involves the production of uniform, interchangeable goods and parts. Although production of virtually identical products is taken for granted today, this was not always the case. Before 1798, for example, each part of an army rifle was manufactured by hand. The result was that each part fit only one gun. That year, inventor Eli Whitney introduced a new method of forging and stamping out "standard" interchangeable parts. These parts were produced in quantity and then assembled into a finished rifle at a later stage of production. Availability of standardized parts makes possible the replacement of defective and worn-out components. Repairs of such products as automobiles are facilitated by the simple purchase of replacement parts at a local auto supply store. Without such standardization, each needed replacement would involve special machining at unacceptable expense.

Assembly Lines

assembly line
Manufacturing technique wherein the product passes through several workstations, each with a specific task.

In a logical extension of the factors of worker specialization, mechanization, and standardization, Henry Ford revolutionized the factory by using what he called the **assembly line** to assemble his automobiles. This manufacturing technique involves placing the product upon a conveyor belt that travels past a number of workstations where workers perform certain tasks such as welding, painting, installing a part, or tightening a bolt. The results were phenomenal. Before adding the assembly line, Ford's Model Ts were being assembled at the rate of one for each 12-hour workday. The assembly-line technique slashed the number of work hours required to 1.5. Not surprisingly, dozens of other industries whose production consisted of assembling complex products quickly adopted the assembly-line technique.

Although the assembly line continues to be a fixture in many manufacturing operations, the trend toward worker specialization and repetitive performance of minute tasks has been reversed. As Harvard University professor Richard Walton points out, "[The Industrial Revolution] taught that jobs should be fragmented and de-skilled and that mental functions, like planning, should be separated from physical work. Now, after six decades, we are unraveling that logic."[3] This opinion is shared by Donald F. Ephlin, vice-president of the United Automobile Workers: "We overdid the old principle that work should be broken down into the smallest operations on the basis that the workers are stupid. Thank goodness, we are beginning to reverse that."[4]

General Motors changed its attitude toward assembly-line workers. GM is creating a work environment that considers the dignity and worth of each worker. With the help of its employees, GM developed a new assembly-line approach — the craft station concept — to assemble the Buick Reatta. The car moves down the assembly line to 24 separate craft stations, where a small team of workers performs tasks at its own pace. Each team must be satisfied with the quality of its tasks before it moves the vehicle to the next craft station.[5]

This small team of employees is one of 24 craft stations that assemble General Motors' Buick Reatta. GM's goal of using this approach to assembly-line production is to create a work atmosphere that provides all GM workers the opportunity to make a worthwhile contribution in producing a top-quality product.

Photo source: Courtesy of General Motors Corporation.

Classifying Production Processes

The methods used in producing goods and services can be classified by the means and the time used to create them. The good or service results from the use of either an analytic or a synthetic system by either a continuing or an intermittent process.

An **analytic system** is one in which a raw material is reduced to its component parts in order to extract one or more products. In petroleum refining, crude oil is broken down and gasoline, wax, fuel oil, kerosene, tar, and other products are obtained. A meat-packing plant slaughters cattle and produces various cuts of meat, glue from the horns and hooves, and leather from the hides.

A **synthetic system** is the reverse of an analytic system. It combines a number of raw materials or parts into a finished product or changes raw materials into completely different finished products. On the assembly line, an automobile is produced from the combination of thousands of individual parts. Drugs and chemicals are produced by a synthetic system, as is stainless steel.

Production by **continuous process** describes a manufacturing operation in which long production runs turn out finished products over a period of days, months, or even years. The steel industry provides a classic example; its blast furnaces never completely shut down unless a malfunction occurs. Petroleum refineries, chemical plants, and nuclear power plants also represent continuous-process production. A shutdown can ruin equipment and prove extremely

analytic system
System of reducing raw materials into component parts.

synthetic system
System that combines raw materials or parts into a finished product or changes them into completely different products.

continuous process
Manufacturing operation with long production runs lasting months or years.

intermittent process
Manufacturing operation with short production runs allowing machines to be shut down or changed to make different products.

costly. The shutdown of a nuclear power plant, for example, can cost the utility an estimated $500,000 a day to replace the lost electricity.[6]

Production by **intermittent process** describes a manufacturing operation in which the production run is short and machines are shut down frequently or changed in order to produce different products. When intermittent production occurs in response to a specific customer order, it is called *job-order production*. When it is used for inventory, it is called *lot-order production*.

Most services use an intermittent production system. Standardization of services provided by accountants, plumbers, electricians, and dentists has traditionally been considered unworkable because the problems each service provider confronts are different and each of them requires a different approach or production system. This thinking has been challenged in recent years, however, as service providers seek to enhance productivity. The move to industrialize the service sector in a fashion similar to what occurred in the production of tangible goods is illustrated by Jiffy Lube auto service, giant vision retailers such as Lens Crafters, Midas's specialized muffler service, Terminix pest control services, home cleaning providers such as The Maids, and the growing number of dental chains located in regional shopping centers. Movement in the direction of the continuous-flow production system, once thought impossible for services, is revolutionizing the service sector.

Automating the Production Process

Continuous-process production systems are typically highly mechanized and frequently utilize assembly lines. As Chapter 3 pointed out, a logical extension of mechanization is *automation* — the replacement of people with machines that perform production processes with little or no help from humans.

Once jobs are divided into specific tasks, it is often possible to design machines to perform such tasks, freeing humans from the repetitive, boring work that characterizes many production operations. In an automated factory, people design the systems and occasionally monitor their operations and inspect the final outputs, but the actual work is performed by machines. At Unisys Corporation, for example, workers feed electronic parts to a robot. The robot inserts electronic chips into circuit boards. Workers then check the robot's work. Human inspection is important because the circuit boards are the core of the computer terminals and workstations that Unisys manufactures. At the end of the production process, other workers pack the finished products into corrugated cartons.[7]

In other cases, machines handle all the functions of the production process. IBM's PC Convertible laptop computer, for example, is built entirely by robots, which assemble, test, pack, and ship the computers without the assistance of human hands.[8]

The following sections describe production technologies that American businesses are using to achieve higher productivity.

Robots

In their attempts to increase factory productivity and to free humans from routine assembly-line tasks and potentially dangerous assignments, such as handling hazardous materials, many production managers are replacing blue-collar workers with "steel-collar" workers in the form of robots. A **robot** is a reprogrammable machine capable of performing a variety of tasks requiring programmed manipulations of materials and tools.[9]

Today's industrial robots look nothing like the androids of *Star Wars* fame, and they vary considerably in complexity and versatility. A pick-and-place robot is the simplest version; its freedom of movement is usually limited to two or three directions as it picks something from one spot and places it in another. The most common industrial robot is the servo robot. The name comes from the servomechanisms that permit the arm and gripper to alter direction in midair without having to trip a mechanical switch. It can be taught a sequence of arm-and-gripper movements, which are repeated indefinitely. A computerized servo robot can be taught new tasks through instructions transmitted electronically. In addition, some computerized robots have one or more artificial senses, typically sight or touch.

The usefulness of robots in the factory has been demonstrated throughout the industrialized world. Robots don't take coffee breaks, call in sick, or experience lowered productivity as a result of attitude problems or fatigue. As technology has reduced their cost and increased their flexibility, robots have become increasingly common in American industry. Initially used primarily in the automotive and electronics industries, robots are moving into other fields. For example, a class-ring manufacturer uses a robot to position and hold the rings while they are engraved by a laser. A robot at a novelties maker stretches balloons flat so they can be printed with slogans. A custom upholstering firm uses a robot to cut carpeting for vans.[10]

Advances in robotic technology in such areas as vision, sensing, and mobility are making robots especially useful in many service industries. In health care, robots that drill precisely into the skull assist surgeons in performing delicate brain operations. Some hospitals use robots to deliver meal trays to patients; others use voice-controlled robots with versatile hand movements to feed, shave, and brush the teeth of paralyzed patients. Businesses are installing surveillance robots rather than hiring human guards. With microwave vision, the robots can outperform humans by seeing through walls, in the dark, and at distances up to 130 feet.

Service robots, like their industrial counterparts, are well suited to perform jobs that are dangerous to humans. Maintenance and repair work at nuclear power plants requires hundreds of employees working in short relays to minimize their exposure to radiation. Robots can do the same work faster without suffering the risk of radiation exposure. Offshore oil and gas firms are replacing deep-sea divers — more than 50 of whom have lost their lives in the North Sea in the past two decades — with robots to build and maintain drilling rigs. The U.S. Navy is using robots instead of divers to cut the mooring cables of stationary mines. Service robots designed to fly are used to inspect high-tension electric wires and spot forest fires.[11]

Applications for robots in producing goods and services will expand as technology improves. Scientists are adapting the technology of microelectronics in developing very small motors and gears for a new generation of robots dubbed *gnat robots,* so called because they will be no larger than the size of a gnat. Researchers envision numerous applications for these microrobots. Surgeons, for example, could use microrobots to perform "closed-heart" surgery. A microrobot on a catheter could be inserted into a patient's blood vessel, travel through the vascular system to the heart where, by remote control, a surgeon could direct the tiny machine to correct a heart defect.[12]

robot
Reprogrammable machine capable of performing numerous programmed tasks by manipulating materials and tools.

Computers

The growing importance of robots and automation in the modern factory has been accompanied by the integration of new computer technologies. Computer-aided design (CAD), computer-aided manufacturing (CAM), flexible manufacturing systems (FMS), and computer simulations are revolutionizing the way American industry designs and manufactures products and are giving U.S. companies the edge they need to compete effectively with foreign manufacturers.

computer-aided design (CAD)
Interaction between a designer and a computer resulting in a product, building, or part that meets predetermined specifications.

Computer-Aided Design   A process called **computer-aided design (CAD)** enables engineers to design parts and buildings on computer screens faster and with fewer mistakes than on paper. Using a special electronic pen, engineers can sketch three-dimensional designs on a tablet connected to the computer. Some systems allow the design to be sketched directly on the computer screen. The computer can then be used to make major and minor design changes. When engineers are satisfied with their sketches, they instruct the computer to analyze the design for certain characteristics or problems. Automobile designers can then put the structural components of a new car design through the paces of a simulated road test. If they find a problem with weight distribution, for example, they can make the necessary changes on their computer terminal. Only when they are satisfied with all the structural characteristics of their design will they manufacture an actual car model. In a similar manner, aircraft designers can analyze the shape and strength of a proposed aircraft fuselage and wings under various conditions.

In recent years, many firms have installed CAD systems as part of their cost-control programs. CAD is used extensively by designers at Johnson & Johnson in an effort to shorten the development cycle, improve the efficiency, and reduce the cost of surgical staplers and other wound closure products. CAD has helped reduce the total product cost of Gillette Company's Braun coffeemakers. Computer-aided design also benefits service firms. CAD is a key tool used by engineers at Browning-Ferris Industries, a waste-disposal services firm, in the design and analysis of landfill sites.

computer-aided manufacturing (CAM)
Computer analysis of a CAD to determine steps in producing the design, and electronic transmission of instructions to production equipment used in producing the part or product.

Computer-Aided Manufacturing   The process of **computer-aided manufacturing (CAM)** picks up where CAD leaves off. It enables manufacturers to use special-design computers to analyze the necessary steps that a machine must make to produce a needed product or part. Electronic signals are then transmitted to the production processing equipment instructing it to perform the appropriate production steps in the correct order.

The Vanity Fair division of VF Corporation uses a CAD/CAM system in designing and manufacturing women's intimate apparel. Computers are used to design new styles and then transform them into patterns for different sizes. The dimensions of the garments are recorded, and patterns are laid out to minimize fabric waste. This design data is then transferred to computers on the factory floor that direct the fabric-cutting machines. The process involves several weeks of labor when performed manually, but with CAD/CAM, the process now takes only several days. By adopting the new computer technology, apparel makers such as VF are becoming more competitive with Asian firms with low wage rates.[13]

flexible manufacturing system (FMS)
State-of-the-art facility that allows production methods to be modified quickly when different products are manufactured.

Flexible Manufacturing Systems   The state of the art in industry is a **flexible manufacturing system (FMS)** that can be modified quickly to manufacture different products. The typical system consists of computer-controlled ma-

Engineers at Campbell Soup Company use the technology of computer-aided design to develop food packaging that gives consumers such benefits as added convenience and portion control. In this photo, an engineer uses CAD in designing a new frozen dinner tray.

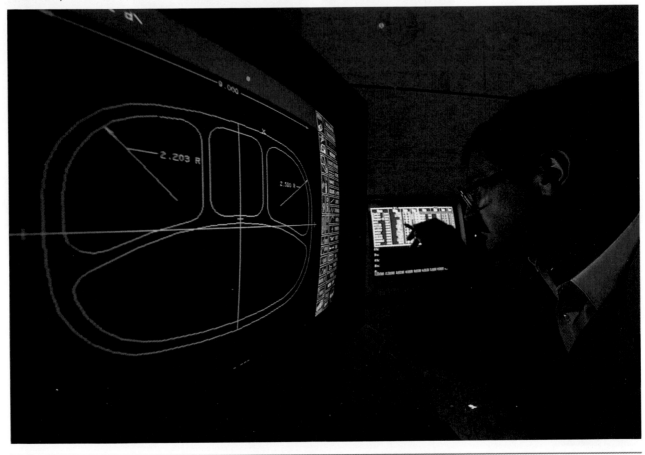

Photo source: Courtesy of Campbell Soup Company.

chining centers to produce metal parts, robots to handle the parts, and remote-controlled carts to deliver materials. All components are linked by electronic controls that dictate what will happen at each stage of the manufacturing sequence, even automatically replacing broken or worn-out drill bits and other implements.

Flexible manufacturing systems also enable manufacturers to produce different versions of a product in small batches at mass-production speeds. An FMS at one General Electric plant can be programmed to produce 2,000 variations of 40 basic models of electric motors. Such flexibility allows GE, Lockheed, Caterpillar, and other firms using FMS technology to adapt quickly to changing market needs.[14]

Computer Simulation   As automation and robots increase the complexity of the production process, more and more production managers use computer simulations to analyze the efficiency of their operations. By constructing a computer model of the production process, which is graphically displayed on a

This flexible manufacturing system at the Westinghouse plant in Sumter, South Carolina, produces sheet metal components for panelboard and switchboard enclosures. The system dramatically reduced work-in-process, storeroom inventories, and production cycle time for these parts. The FMS was developed by Westinghouse's Productivity and Quality Center and its automation division.

Photo source: Courtesy of Westinghouse Electric Corporation.

computer screen, managers can determine the best way to produce their products from the input to output stages. Some firms use computer simulations to schedule the delivery and handling of component parts. Others use it for production-line planning. Ingersoll-Rand, for example, developed a production system for making ball bearings that would utilize 77 machine tools that performed 16 functions. A computer simulation of the plan indicated it could be improved and run more efficiently by eliminating four of the machine tools, thus saving the company $750,000 in equipment costs.[15]

The Tasks of Production Managers

production and operations management
Managing people and machinery used in converting materials and resources into finished products and services.

Obviously, the process of converting inputs into finished goods and services must be managed. This is the task of **production and operations management** — to manage the use of people and machinery in converting materials and resources into finished goods and services.

Managers of the production function are responsible for three major activities. First, production managers must make plans for production inputs. This involves determining the inputs required in the firm's operations and includes such decisions as product planning, plant location, and provision for adequate supplies of raw materials, labor, power, and machinery. These plans must be completed before the conversion process from raw material to finished product or service can begin.

Second, production managers must make decisions about the installation of the necessary inputs. These include the actual design of the plant, the best types of machines to be used, the arrangement of the production machinery, and the determination of the most efficient flow of work in the plant.

Third, production managers must coordinate the production processes: the routing of material to the right places, the development of work schedules, and the assignment of work to specific employees. The objective is to promote efficiency.

Planning the Production Process

When Richard Dauch joined Chrysler Corporation in 1980 as executive vice-president of manufacturing, he faced a formidable challenge. At the time, Chrysler had the highest production costs and lowest-quality products in the automobile industry. Dauch's job was to devise a production plan that would boost the firm's productivity and improve product quality to make the firm more competitive with domestic and foreign carmakers. The plan he developed extended from product design to relationships with suppliers and workers to assembly-line layout.

Dauch's first planning step was aimed at satisfying customers who had complained that Chrysler cars rattled and squeaked and had uneven paint jobs. Dauch planned to correct these problems by automating production plants. Robots would build cars according to precise specifications, and computers would control the robots and inspect their work. New paint shops, complete with ostrich feathers that removed dust from car bodies, and the application of a clear top coating would result in better paint jobs. A new assembly-line setup would eliminate costly and inefficient repair work. Regular meetings and open communications would heighten workers' consciousness to build quality products. Suppliers would have to meet strict specifications for quality, costs, and delivery. A new product-design procedure would take manufacturing problems into account during the product planning stage. Simpler car designs and fewer options would further reduce product costs.

Dauch's production plan worked. By 1987, Chrysler was building 8,000 vehicles a day, compared to 4,500 in 1981. Today, it takes 102 worker-hours to build a vehicle, compared to 175 in 1981. Defects per 100 vehicles have decreased 42 percent. Production planning is, however, an ongoing process. By adding more robots to its flexible manufacturing system and shortening the development time for a car from four to three years, Dauch plans to reduce production costs by 30 percent and defects by 56 percent by 1991.[16]

Product Planning

A firm's total planning process begins with the choice of goods and services it wants to offer its customers. Plant location, machinery purchases, pricing decisions, and selection of retail outlets are all based on product planning. In a sense, the sole economic justification for the firm's existence is the production and marketing of want-satisfying products.

Because a product must be designed to satisfy consumer needs, marketing research studies are used to obtain consumer reactions to proposed products, to test prototypes of new products, and to estimate the potential sales and profitability of new products. The production department is primarily concerned with (1) converting the original product concept into the final product and (2) designing production facilities to produce this new product as efficiently as possible. The new product must not only be accepted by consumers, it must also be produced economically to assure an acceptable return on company funds invested in the project.

Traditionally, product planning was the joint responsibility of the production and marketing departments. But today, innovative firms such as Xerox, Procter & Gamble, Polaroid, and Corning Glass Works involve other company personnel in product design and development. For example, Xerox included manufacturing experts, marketers, product planners, systems engineers, customers, and potential suppliers in planning a new line of copier machines.[17]

The team approach to planning helps firms shorten the product development cycle, enabling them to bring products to market faster. Xerox, whose world market share dropped from 82 percent to 41 percent in six years, adopted the team approach after learning that its Japanese competitors developed new copier models in two years, while it took Xerox four to five years. Now Xerox can produce copiers in two years.[18]

Facility Location

One of the major production decisions is the choice of plant location. This decision requires careful planning and typically represents a long-term commitment and a substantial investment. A poor location poses severe problems for a firm attempting to compete with better-located competitors.

Consider the case of Lionel Trains. The firm's management based a location decision primarily on low-cost labor. In the early 1980s, Lionel executives decided to manufacture toy trains, tracks, and collector trains in Tijuana, Mexico, to take advantage of 55-cent-per-hour wages. Lionel closed its plant in Chesterfield Township, Michigan, and fired all but 5 of its 350 employees. Inadequate planning almost brought Lionel to financial ruin. Soon after the move, it encountered unanticipated communications, supply, and labor problems. The Tijuana telephone company could give Lionel only two telephone lines, not nearly the number the firm needed to conduct business. Lionel managers also realized there were no Mexican firms to do plating work, and they were forced to send parts to contractors in California. They also assumed they could hire and train local managers, but, unable to find managerial talent they needed in Tijuana, they had to bring engineers from Michigan to Mexico, which cost the firm thousands of dollars in airfare and housing. Because of these and other problems, the company was able to fill only one-third of its orders, resulting in complaints from dealers and customers. Lionel products lost shelf space in retail stores and market share to competitors. After three years in Tijuana, Lionel moved back to Michigan, leased the plant it had sold, rehired many former workers, and started recovering its financial losses.[19]

What Constitutes a Good Location?

Choosing a location typically involves two decisions: (1) selecting a community in which the facility will be located and (2) choosing a specific site within the community. The choice of a location should be made after considering such factors as proximity to raw materials and markets; availability of labor, transportation, and energy; state and local taxes; and community living conditions.

Facility location is an important element in McDonald's growth strategy. It started with restaurants in suburban locations but has broadened its business base by opening restaurants in urban areas, airports, commercial buildings, zoos, shopping malls, train stations, casinos, hospitals, and military bases. McDonald's targets the trucker and long-distance traveler market by locating restaurants near interstate highways, such as the one in this photo in Litchfield, Illinois.

Proximity to Raw Materials   When raw materials are large and heavy, manufacturing firms often locate their plants near the source of these inputs. Production facilities for sheetrock are usually close to where the major ingredient, gypsum, is mined. (Mined gypsum must be dehydrated immediately in order to avoid transporting the water in it.) Trees are processed into wood products near forests, eliminating the cost of transporting those parts of the log that become waste materials. Because 32,000 gallons of water are required to produce one ton of paper, paper mills also must be located in areas where large quantities of clean, low-cost water are available.

Proximity to Markets   If transportation costs for raw materials are not a significant part of total production costs, the plant is likely to be located near markets where the final products are to be sold. A nearby location allows the manufacturer to provide fast, convenient service for customers. Many manufacturers of automobile components are located in the metropolitan Detroit area so as to provide quick service for auto assembly plants.

Some foreign firms with large U.S. markets set up production and service facilities in the United States. They include the Industrial Bank of Japan (New York), Mitsubishi (Bloomington, Illinois), Nissan (Smyrna, Tennessee), Honda (Columbus, Ohio), and Volvo (Norfolk, Virginia).

Facilities that provide services, such as dry cleaners, laundromats, banks, hotels, local government offices, and hospitals, must be located near the largest concentrations of their target customers. If, for example, a dry cleaner were located too far from where people live, no one would patronize the business.

Availability of Personnel   A third consideration in the location of production or service facilities is the availability of a qualified labor force. One early problem faced by the developers of a giant shipbuilding complex in the little

Gulf Coast town of Pascagoula, Mississippi, was the lack of sufficient numbers of skilled workers. Many electronics firms are located in the San Jose, California, and Boston areas, which have high concentrations of skilled technicians. The same is true for Hartford (insurance), Pittsburgh (steel), and Seattle (aircraft).

When unskilled workers can be used, the manufacturer can choose from a much greater number of alternative locations. Many manufacturing plants employing unskilled labor have located in the South, where wage rates have historically been below those in the North. In the worldwide search for inexpensive labor, a number of electrical equipment manufacturers have begun to manufacture parts in the United States, ship them in unassembled form to the island of Taiwan, have them assembled there by inexpensive labor, and then ship them back to the United States for inclusion in a finished product.

Transportation   Most manufacturing plants use transportation facilities to ship raw materials to the plant and finished products to customers. At most locations, the producer can choose among several alternatives such as trucks, railroads, ships, and airplanes. Availability of numerous alternatives can result in increased competition and lower rates for transportation users.

Service facilities also must consider available transportation. Customers must be able to get to them by either public transportation or private automobile. If cars are the primary method of transportation, then adequate parking must also be provided.

Energy   While all production facilities are affected by both the availability of adequate energy resources and their costs, factories producing goods tend to be more affected than service industries.

The aluminum industry began in the Tennessee Valley because the manufacture of aluminum requires great amounts of electrical power. The cheap electricity provided by the Tennessee Valley Authority allows aluminum manufacturers to produce their product at lower costs than they could in Baltimore or Philadelphia, where electricity rates are substantially higher. The availability of inexpensive power supplies is a major consideration in plant location for certain industries.

Taxes   Another factor to consider in facility location is local and state taxes. Local and state governments typically impose real estate taxes on factories, equipment, and inventories. Sales taxes and income taxes may also be imposed. These taxes, which vary considerably from state to state and city to city, should be considered in making the location decision. Some states and cities attempt to entice manufacturers or service businesses into their areas by granting low taxes or temporary exemptions from taxation. However, low taxes may also mean inadequate municipal services. Taxes must be considered together with the availability and quality of needed city services.

Some governments attempt to influence a firm's location decision by offering other incentives in addition to low taxes. Kentucky, for example, agreed to pay half the cost of preparing the plant site and installing sewers and utilities for Toyota Motor Corporation's new auto-assembly plant near Georgetown. The state also funded construction of new local highways, built an employee training center where 3,000 American employees learn Toyota's techniques of producing vehicles, and agreed to provide English-language classes for Toyota's Japanese employees and their families for ten years.[20]

Table 9.2 Factors in the Facility Location Decision

Location Factor	Examples of Affected Businesses
Transportation	
Proximity to markets	Baking companies or manufacturers of other perishable products, dry cleaners and hotels or other services for profit
Proximity to raw materials	Mining companies
Availability of transportation alternatives	Brick manufacturers, retail stores
Human Factors	
Labor supply	Auto manufacturers, hotels
Local regulations	Explosives manufacturers, welding shops
Community living conditions	All businesses
Physical Factors	
Water supply	Paper mills
Energy	Aluminum, chemical, and fertilizer manufacturers

An increasingly common requirement for firms desiring to locate a production facility in a particular area is an **environmental impact study**. It analyzes the impact of a proposed plant on the quality of life in an area. Regulatory agencies typically require the study to cover such topics as impact on transportation facilities; energy requirements; water and sewage treatment needs; effect on natural plant life and wildlife; and water, air, and noise pollution.

Both community and state pressure in Maine and New Hampshire prevented construction of oil refineries in New England. Construction of a Miami jetport located in part on the edge of the Everglades was blocked by environmentalists. The Delaware Coastal Zone Act prevents heavy manufacturing industry from locating within two miles of the state's 115-mile coastline. State and community attitudes, thus, often play a role in the facility location decision.

Community Living Conditions A final consideration in choosing a location is the quality of the community, as measured by its school system, colleges, cultural programs, fire and police protection, climate, income levels of its residents, and community attitudes toward the new facility.

Factors affecting the decision on plant location are summarized in Table 9.2. The final decision is likely to result from careful evaluation of all the factors. Since no one location is likely to be superior in every factor, the ultimate choice is likely to involve trade-offs.

Choosing a Site

Once a community has been selected, a specific site must be chosen. Before this can be done, a number of factors must be considered: zoning regulations; availability of sufficient land; cost of the land; existence of shipping facilities, such as railroad sidings, roads, and dock facilities; and construction costs.

Most cities have at least one **industrial park**, a planned site location that provides necessary zoning, land, shipping facilities, and waste disposal outlets. These sites are created to entice manufacturers to locate new plants in the area by providing maximum cooperation between the firm and the local governing bodies.

environmental impact study
Analysis of the impact of a proposed plant location on the quality of life in a specific area.

industrial park
Planned commercial site that provides necessary zoning, land, shipping facilities, and waste disposal outlets.

Proximity to customers or clients is often the determining factor in the location of service facilities. Such service-oriented organizations as government services, health and emergency services, retailers, and profit-seeking service firms attempt to locate near their customers or clients. Locating near population concentrations allows such facilities as hospitals, fire stations, and ambulance services to provide fast service and minimize loss of life and loss of property.

Layout of Production Facilities

process layout
Manufacturing facility design suited to the production of a variety of nonstandard products in relatively small batches.

product layout
Manufacturing facility design that accommodates a few products in relatively large quantities.

fixed-position layout
Manufacturing facility design that locates the product in a fixed position, with workers, materials, and machines transported to and from it.

customer-oriented layout
Service facility design that promotes interaction between the organization's services and the customers.

An efficient production facility is the result of careful consideration of all phases of production and the necessary inputs at each step of the process. As Figure 9.1 indicates, a number of alternatives are available in selecting the most appropriate layout. The first three designs are common in manufacturing facilities, and the last layout is often used in service facilities.

A **process layout** is designed to accommodate a variety of nonstandard products in relatively small batches. In this layout, workers and equipment performing the same activity, or process, are grouped in one department or location. Custom machine shops are typically organized in this fashion.

When a firm produces large quantities of the same or similar products, an efficient design is a **product layout**. This layout accommodates only a few product variations. Product layouts are frequently used in assembly-line operations, such as those in the automobile industry.

In a **fixed-position layout**, the product stays in one place and workers, materials, and machines are transported to and from that position. This approach is common in such operations as missile assembly, ship construction, large aircraft assembly, and bridge construction, where the product is very bulky, large, heavy, or fragile.

A **customer-oriented layout** is common in service facilities where the facility must be arranged to enhance the interactions of customers and the organization's services. The example of a hospital layout in Figure 9.1 illustrates this approach.

Implementing the Production Plan

Once the product or service decisions have been made, the production facilities developed, the necessary machinery purchased, and the most efficient facility layout determined, management must implement the production plan. Raw materials, component parts, and all other goods and services that will serve as production ingredients must be purchased, from paper clips to steel bars and computers. Inventory levels must be determined and controlled, and production schedules must be put into operation. Each of these activities has to be performed efficiently if the production plan is to succeed.

make, buy, or lease decision
Whether to manufacture, purchase, or lease a needed product, component, or material.

The Make, Buy, or Lease Decision

One of the fundamental issues facing every producer is the **make, buy, or lease decision**: whether to manufacture a needed product or component, to purchase it from an outside supplier, or to lease it. Rolls-Royce provides the

Figure 9.1   Basic Types of Facility Layouts

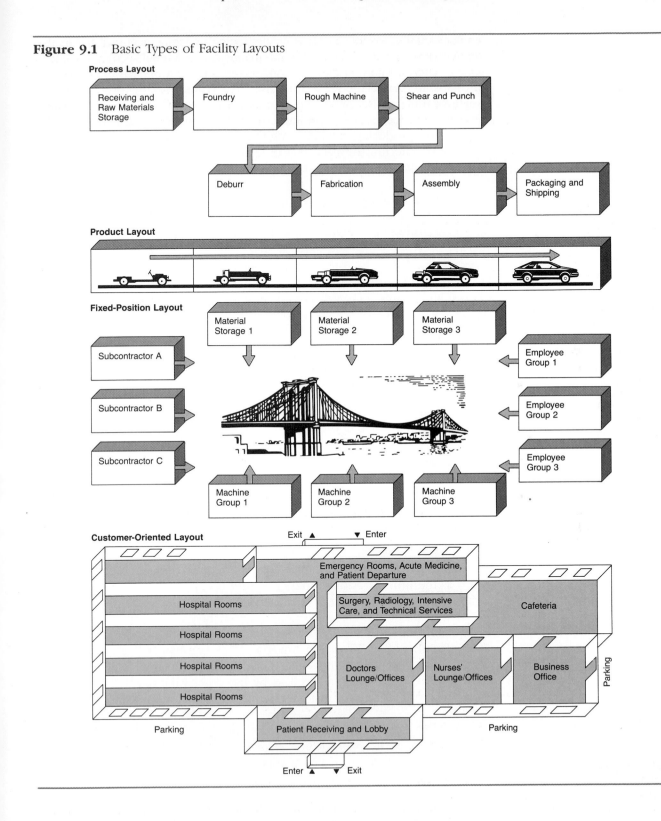

engines for the Boeing 757 plane, while Boeing's Wichita plant builds the nose, and another outside supplier, Vought, manufactures the tail section. Like other auto companies, Ford Motor Company depends upon hundreds of suppliers to produce over half of the 12,000 parts used in a typical Ford. By contrast, brewers such as Anheuser-Busch and Coors manufacture their own cans at company-owned subsidiaries. Many commercial airlines, however, lease their aircraft rather than producing or purchasing them.

Factors affecting the make, buy, or lease decision include the costs of leasing or purchasing parts from outside suppliers as compared with the cost of producing them in-house; the availability of outside suppliers and dependability of their shipments in the quality and quantity needed; the need for confidentiality; and whether the need for the commodity in question is short or long term. Because airlines often experience equipment shortages, they arrange for short-term leases of engines and other aircraft components required for immediate operating needs.

Even when the decision is made to purchase from outside suppliers, managers should maintain more than one supply source. An alternative supplier assures the availability of needed materials in the event of strikes, quality assurance problems, or other situations preventing a supplier from meeting its delivery commitments.

Purchasing Decisions

The objective of purchasing is to buy the right materials in the right amounts at the right time for the right price. To achieve this goal, the purchasing department must (1) precisely determine the correct materials to purchase, (2) select the best supplier, and (3) develop an efficient ordering system.

Selecting the Right Supplier

The choice of a supplier is usually made by comparing the quality, prices, availability, and services offered by competing companies. In many cases, quality and price are virtually identical among suppliers, and the choice is based on factors such as the firm's previous experience with each supplier, speed of delivery, warranties on purchases, and other services.

For major purchases, negotiations between the purchaser and potential suppliers may take several weeks or even months, and the buying decision may rest with a number of persons in the firm. The choice of a supplier for industrial drill presses, for example, may be made jointly by the production, engineering, and maintenance departments as well as by the purchasing agent. These departments have different views that must be reconciled before purchasing decisions are made.

Raw materials and component parts are often purchased on a long-term contractual basis. If a manufacturer requires a continuous supply of materials, a one- or two-year contract with a supplier ensures they will be available as needed.

Improving Buyer-Seller Relationships   Businesses' emphasis on quality improvement in recent years has affected the buyer-supplier relationship. Many firms are drastically reducing their number of suppliers, keeping only those that deliver defect-free parts on time. Xerox, for example, purchased parts and components from 5,000 suppliers in 1980. Today, it buys from 400 suppliers and plans to reduce that number to 250 by the mid-1990s. Xerox now receives 99 percent of its parts defect-free, compared to 92 percent in the early 1980s.[21]

Firms are also building better and longer-term relationships with their suppliers. Boeing sponsors seminars to teach its suppliers about quality improvement techniques. Harley-Davidson offers its suppliers courses in statistical process control and assists them in improving their product design. General Motors rewards suppliers by giving them long-term contracts.

Suppliers, in turn, are improving their relationships with their customers. AMP, a manufacturer of electrical and electronic connectors and terminals, guarantees the quality of its parts so customers do not have to inspect them. AMP engineers become involved in the early design stages of customers' new-product development. Walter Raab, AMP's chairman and CEO, says such involvement "allows us to enhance our customers' products, not only in terms of performance, but in making the final product easier to manufacture."[22] Some suppliers are offering to produce parts-making systems or do parts-assembly work rather than supply individual components. A division of Dana Corporation now supplies Ford with subassemblies of an entire power system (axles, drive shafts, and transfer cases); in the past, it simply supplied Ford with axles. To serve its customers better, Johnson Controls has located ten automobile seating and trim plants near its major customers, including Ford, Honda, General Motors, Toyota, and Chrysler.

Inventory Control

Inventory control balances the need to have inventory on hand to meet demand with the costs involved in carrying the inventory. The financial costs of carrying inventory are the funds tied up in it that cannot be used in other activities of the business. Among the expenses involved in storing inventory are warehousing, taxes, insurance, and maintenance. Too much inventory represents wasted expenditures.

inventory control
Balancing costs of holding raw materials, work in progress, and inventory with costs involved in ordering them.

But a shortage of raw materials, parts, goods, or sales often means lost production — and delays in production mean unhappy customers if the delays result in late delivery of promised merchandise. Firms lose business when they are consistently unable to meet promised delivery dates or when their shelves are empty. These two costs must be balanced to produce acceptable inventory levels.

A commonly used technique for monitoring the amount and location of inventory is the maintenance of a **perpetual inventory**. This inventory control system continuously updates all major inventory systems. The system is typically computerized and frequently will automatically determine orders to be made and print purchase orders at the appropriate times. The scanning devices used in many supermarkets are typically linked to perpetual inventory systems used in reordering needed merchandise. As a shopper's purchase is recorded, each item is subtracted from the inventory data stored in the computer. Once inventory on hand drops to a predetermined level, the merchandise is automatically reordered.

perpetual inventory
Continuously updated listing of items in inventory.

Just-in-Time Inventory System   Just ten years ago, you could walk into a typical American factory and see several weeks' worth of parts and supplies piled high throughout the plant. Walk into a similar factory in Japan and you would have noticed no such inventory backlog. The Japanese plant then and now may

just-in-time (JIT) inventory system

System designed to minimize inventory at production facilities.

have only enough supplies on hand to keep it going for a day. This shortage is hardly accidental. It is an essential ingredient of the **just-in-time (JIT) inventory system** used by major Japanese corporations for years and gaining acceptance in American firms.

The JIT system does what its name implies: It supplies needed parts to the production line on a last-minute basis. As a result, factory inventory levels are as low as possible and production costs are held down. Just-in-time delivery makes it easy to spot and expose production problems before they are built into the system, and it shifts responsibility for the problems from the consumer to the suppliers. If a part is defective, the assembly line shuts down and the supplier risks losing the firm's business. Often, when a slightly defective part is found in a U.S. plant, it is made to fit rather than shipped back to the supplier. With weeks of inventory on hand, companies are forced into this decision to avoid a production slowdown.

The just-in-time system also enables firms to respond rapidly to changes in the market, to maintain high standards, and to strip the production system of all but essential personnel. In addition, it forces them to keep their machinery in perfect running order at all times — a practice that has saved firms considerable time and money. Just-in-time production at an AT&T plant cut the production time for some products from three-and-one-half weeks to two-and-one-half days.

The advantages of JIT are helping many U.S. corporations, both large and small, become more competitive. By switching to a JIT system, Fireplace Manufacturers Inc., a California firm that makes prefabricated metal fireplaces, reduced its inventory of raw materials and work in progress from $1.1 million to $750,000. Just-in-time helped Huffy Corporation become the most productive bicycle maker in the world. Huffy executives measure the results of the changeover to JIT in terms of the number of tubs the firm uses to store and move parts. Before JIT, parts filled 3,000 tubs, but now only 700 are needed.[23]

Materials Requirement Planning

In order to implement the production plan, an adequate amount of the raw materials, components, and operating supplies must be available when needed. For relatively simple products with few components provided by numerous suppliers in the immediate vicinity, this is a relatively simple process. A telephone call may be sufficient to secure overnight delivery of needed materials, and management enjoys the luxury of minimal investments in inventory and little risk of production downtime resulting from lack of needed materials.

This process of ensuring adequate amounts of materials and parts in the right amounts at the right times becomes much more complicated when complex products are involved. For a firm such as Ford Motor Company, determining the efficient sequencing of precisely the exact amounts of materials at exactly the right times can be a nightmare. If the components are received too early, they must be stored until needed. If they arrive late, production is disrupted until they are available. In his book *American Made,* Harold Livesay describes a group of Chrysler Corporation workers using acetylene torches to cut holes in a locked railway car filled with bolts. Stopping the production line while assembly-line workers waited for the car to be unlocked would have cost Chrysler $40,000 per hour, so the plant manager instead opted to pay for the damaged rail car.[24]

Photo source: © 1987 Richard Alcorn.

To ensure the short delivery times required by its just-in-time inventory system, Colgate-Palmolive Company formed partner-like relationships with its valued suppliers. Here, Colgate's JIT coordinator works with employees from a Venezuelan packaging supplier to reduce changeover and make-ready time on the production line for Banner soap, a family deodorant bar similar to Irish Spring. Such meetings are held regularly between managers and workers from both companies to improve package design, increase production efficiencies, solve problems, and better understand each others' operations.

Materials requirement planning (MRP) is a production planning system designed to ensure that a firm has the parts and materials needed to produce its products and services at the right time and place and in the right amounts. Production managers use special computer programs to create schedules that identify the specific parts and materials required to produce an item, the exact quantities required of each, and the dates when orders should be released to suppliers and should be received for best timing within the production cycle.[25]

MRP is invaluable in systems involving complex products assembled with parts and materials secured from outside suppliers. It is even more important in major products such as the B-1 bomber, where entire subassemblies of the plane are produced by dozens of firms scattered throughout the nation (in every state except Alaska and Hawaii). MRP's computer program coordinates the deadlines for each subassembly in addition to deadlines for the overall assembly.

materials requirement planning (MRP)
Computer-based production planning system for ensuring needed parts and materials are available at the right time and place in the correct amounts.

Manufacturing Resource Planning

While MRP is used to control inventory, a more advanced computer-based system is designed to control all of a firm's resources. Called **MRP II**, for **manufacturing resource planning**, the system integrates planning data from individual departments — marketing, production, engineering, and finance — and produces a master business plan for the entire organization. MRP II then translates the business plan into marketing forecasts; requirements for inventory, materials handling, and personnel; and production schedules. All managers have access to this information. With MRP II, a change in a marketing forecast will automatically produce an adjustment in production scheduling. Some

manufacturing resource planning (MRP II)
Integration of planning data from individual departments resulting in a master business plan.

MRP II software programs can even give managers advice on ways to solve manufacturing and other production problems.

Control of the Production Process

Throughout this chapter, production has been viewed as a process of converting inputs into finished products and services. First, plans are made for production inputs — the goods to be produced, the location of facilities, and the sources of raw materials, consumers, labor, energy, and machinery. Next, the production plans are implemented through the purchase of materials and equipment and the employment of a trained work force to convert the inputs into salable products and services. The final step in the production process is control. **Production control** is a well-defined set of procedures for coordinating people, materials, and machinery to provide maximum production efficiency.

production control
Well-defined set of procedures for coordinating people, materials, and machinery to provide maximum production efficiency.

Suppose a watch factory has been assigned the production of 800,000 watches during October. Production control executives break this down into a daily production assignment of 40,000 for each of 20 working days. The next step is to determine the number of workers, raw materials, parts, and machines needed to meet this production schedule.

Similarly, in a service business such as a restaurant it is necessary to estimate how many meals will be served each day and then determine the number of people needed to prepare and serve the food, as well as how much food must be purchased and how often. For example, meat, fish, and fresh vegetables might have to be bought every day or every other day to ensure freshness, while canned and frozen foods might be bought less often, depending on storage space.

The Five Steps in Production Control

Production control can be thought of as a five-step sequence: planning, routing, scheduling, dispatching, and follow-up.

production planning
Phase of production control that determines the amount of resources needed to produce a certain amount of goods or services.

bill of materials
Detailed listing of all parts and materials needed to produce a product or service.

Production Planning   The phase of production control called **production planning** determines the amount of resources (including raw materials and other components) needed to produce a certain amount of goods or services. During the production planning process, a **bill of materials** is developed, listing all parts and materials needed to produce a good or service. Comparison of the needed parts and materials with the firm's perpetual inventory allows the purchasing department to determine the additional purchases required to ensure availability of needed amounts. The MRP system establishes delivery schedules so the needed parts and materials will arrive at regular intervals as required during the production process. Similar determinations are made to ensure that the necessary machines and workers are available when needed. Although material inputs contribute to service-producing systems, such systems tend to depend more on personnel than on materials.

routing
Phase of production control that determines the sequence of work throughout the facility.

Routing   The phase of production control that determines the sequence of work throughout the facility is called **routing**. It specifies where and by whom each aspect of production will be performed. Routing is determined by two

Table 9.3   Information Needed to Construct a PERT Diagram

Activity Number	Activity Completed	Time Required (in weeks)
1	Build exterior brick walls	2.0
2	Build roof supports	1.5
3	Insulate attic	0.5
4	Install roofing	1.0
5	Build room partitions	3.5
6	Install insulation in walls	1.5
7	Install electrical wiring	2.0
8	Install plasterboard	3.0
9	Install air conditioning	0.5
10	Paint interior and exterior	3.0
11	Final cleanup of house	0.5

factors: the nature of the good or service and the facility layouts discussed earlier — product, process, fixed-position, and customer-oriented.

Scheduling   Another phase of production control, **scheduling**, involves developing timetables that specify how long each operation in the production process takes and when it should be performed. Efficient scheduling ensures that delivery schedules are met and productive resources are efficiently used.

Scheduling is extremely important for manufacturers of complex products with large numbers of parts or production stages. A watch contains dozens of component parts, and each of them must be available in the right place, at the right time, and in the right amounts if the production process is to function smoothly.

Scheduling practices vary considerably in service-related organizations. Small services such as local trucking companies or doctors' offices may use relatively unsophisticated scheduling systems and resort to such devices as "first come, first served" rules, appointment schedules, or take-a-number systems. Part-time workers and standby equipment may be used in handling demand fluctuations. On the other hand, hospitals typically use sophisticated scheduling systems similar to those used by manufacturers.

A number of methods have been devised for effective scheduling of complex products. A commonly used scheduling technique for such complex products as ships and new airplane designs is **PERT (Program Evaluation and Review Technique)**. First developed for the military, PERT was used to produce guided missiles for the Polaris nuclear submarine before being modified for use by industry.

PERT is designed to minimize production delays by coordinating all aspects of the production task. Consider, for example, the construction of a house. Table 9.3 shows the various activities involved and an estimate of the time required for the completion of each activity.

Figure 9.2 shows a simplified PERT diagram. The red line indicates the **critical path** — the sequence of operations that requires the longest time for completion. The operations that can be completed before they are needed by operations on the critical path have some slack time and are therefore not critical. These operations can be performed earlier or delayed until later in the production process. Some workers and machinery can be assigned to critical path tasks early in the process, then reassigned to noncritical operations as they are needed.

scheduling
Phase of production control that develops timetables specifying how long each operation in the production process takes.

PERT (Program Evaluation and Review Technique)
Scheduling technique for minimizing production delays by coordinating all aspects of the process.

critical path
Sequence of operations in PERT diagram requiring the longest time for completion.

Figure 9.2   PERT Diagram for Building a Home

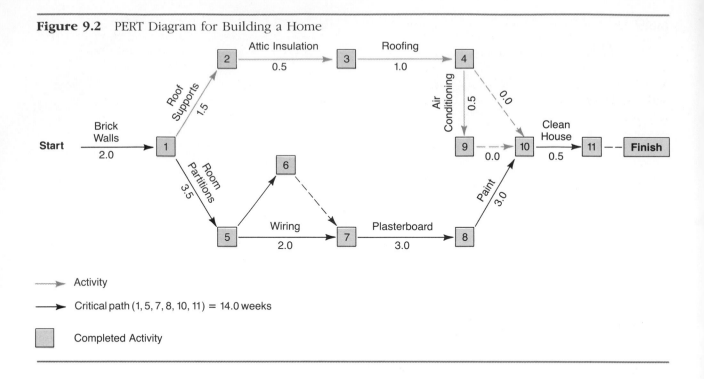

→ Activity

→ Critical path (1, 5, 7, 8, 10, 11) = 14.0 weeks

☐ Completed Activity

In practice, a PERT network may consist of thousands of events and cover months of time. Complex computer programs are used in developing the network and in finding the critical path among the maze of events and activities.

Dispatching   The phase of production control that instructs each department on what work is to be done and the time allowed for its completion is called **dispatching**. The dispatcher authorizes performance, provides instructions, and lists priorities for each job.

Follow-up   Because even the best plans sometimes go awry, some means must be available to keep management aware of problems as they arise. **Follow-up** is the phase of production control that spots problems in the production process and informs management of needed adjustments. Problems come in many forms. Machinery malfunctions, delays in shipment of vital materials or in arrival of goods or supplies, and employee absenteeism can all result in production delays. These delays must be reported to production control so adjustments in production schedules can be made. A delay in the delivery of a particular component may require new assignments to be made by the dispatcher to work areas affected by this delay.

dispatching
Phase of production control that instructs each department on what work is to be done and the time allowed for its completion.

follow-up
Phase of production control that spots production problems and informs management of needed adjustments.

The Quest for Quality

Quality begins with product and service design. Performance standards are necessary prerequisites for the development of quality controls. Once these standards are set, various types of inspections can be made to provide quality assurance.

Quality control involves measuring products and services against established quality standards. Such checks are necessary to spot defective products and to see that they are not shipped to customers. Devices for monitoring quality levels of the firm's output include visual inspection, electronic sensors, and X rays. Robots are particularly suited for many types of inspections since fatigue and inattention do not present problems. A high rate of rejected products can lead to changes in equipment or raw materials or to additional training for workers.

Few subjects have been more popular among U.S. organizations in recent years than that of quality. American firms have long held a reputation for making products of outstanding quality. Examples include Boeing's 747 family of jet aircraft, A. T. Cross ballpoint pens, Reynolds Metals aluminum foil, General Electric dishwashers, Levi Strauss 501 jeans, Honeywell heating controls, Polaroid instant camera films, Du Pont fibers, 3M tape, and Deere tractors.

But at the same time U.S. factories were improving quality, their Japanese counterparts were leapfrogging ahead by applying concepts developed in the United States. The success of their efforts in developing a reputation for outstanding quality is evident by the inroads Japanese products have made in U.S. and world markets. Japan now holds the lead in worldwide sales of steel, automobiles, machine tools, textiles, and consumer electronics — industries once dominated by U.S. manufacturers.

Japan's most coveted industrial award is the Deming Prize, given to the company and the individual who achieve the most significant gains in quality. The annual award is broadcast on national television in Japan. The prize is named in honor of W. Edwards Deming, an American statistician whose lectures on quality control were largely ignored by American managers during the competition-free, post-World War II years but were listened to by Japanese managers.

Deming suggests that building quality into the entire production process leads to improved productivity. Rather than inspect products for flaws after they are made, he emphasizes that products must be made correctly the first time to avoid wasting time and money in rework. To accomplish this, Deming taught Japanese managers and employees how to implement **statistical process control (SPC)**, a process of gathering, plotting, and analyzing data to pinpoint problem areas. SPC allows firms to spot quality problems, whether they are caused by poor employee work, poor supervision, or faulty machinery, and then install controls to ensure the problems are corrected.

Deming stresses that the commitment to quality must be a companywide philosophy and a continuous process. Top managers must be totally committed to the quality concept and serve as flexible advisors and coaches. Employees must be trained and involved as partners in the drive to produce on-time, error-free products.

Many U.S. firms, eager to restore their long-held images as producers of high-quality products, have embraced Deming's quality methods during the 1980s. Five years ago, Monsanto Company began a companywide "Total Quality" process that was saving the firm an estimated $50 million to $60 million a year by 1990. Ford Motor Company hired Deming as a consultant in 1981, and his influence has helped Ford become the most profitable domestic automobile manufacturer.

Deming's quality principles also apply to service firms. When P.I.E., a trucking company, discovered 60 percent of its shipping contracts had errors, it used SPC and employee suggestions to locate the cause of the problem. P.I.E. learned

quality control
Measurement of products and services against established quality standards.

statistical process control (SPC)
Process of gathering, plotting, and analyzing data to pinpoint problem areas.

Computers that monitor preset quality control parameters are part of Engelhard Corporation's statistical process quality control system. The system enables Engelhard to
produce coating pigments and additives that consistently match the exact specifications and standards of its customers in the paper, paint, plastics, and other industries.
Engelhard employs statistical methods to control quality throughout the entire manufacturing process, including the consistency of raw materials.

Photo source: Courtesy of Engelhard Corporation.

that 56 percent of the errors resulted from the misidentification of crates and
boxes used to ship products. The problem was corrected within 30 days, resulting in cost savings of $250,000 a year.[26]

In 1988, the U.S. government began awarding its own version of Japan's
Deming Prize. The Malcolm Baldrige National Quality Award, named after the
late secretary of the U.S. Department of Commerce and administered by the
National Bureau of Standards, is an attempt to create a prestigious national
award to communicate to the nation and the world the importance of quality in
U.S. production efforts. The first three recipients of the award were two giant
U.S. corporations — Motorola Inc. and Westinghouse Electric — and Globe Met-
allurgical of Beverly, Ohio, a 210-employee firm that makes alloys and metals for
use in such products as autos, farm equipment, and silicon chips. Prize-winning
companies such as these are likely to be adhering to the ten commandments of
quality listed in Table 9.4.

Table 9.4   Ten Commandments of Quality

1. There is no such thing as acceptable quality. It can always get better.	6. Analyze jobs to identify their elements and set quality standards for each step.
2. From the corner office to the shop floor, quality is everybody's business.	7. Take control of your process: You must know why something goes wrong.
3. Keep your ears open. Some of the best ideas will come from the most unexpected sources.	8. Be patient. Don't expect gains to show up next quarter.
4. Develop a detailed implementation plan. Talking about quality isn't enough.	9. Make extraordinary efforts in unusual situations. Customers will remember those best.
5. Help departments work together. The territorial imperative is your biggest obstacle.	10. Think beyond cutting costs. The benefits of improved quality should reach every part of the organization.

Source: Joel Dreyfuss, "Victories in the Quality Crusade," *Fortune* (October 10, 1988), p. 82.

Quality Circles

Researchers seeking to compare U.S. and Japanese firms discovered a widely used Japanese concept based upon the philosophy that the firm's work force is often the group most qualified to identify and solve work-related problems. A survey of 1,566 Japanese firms revealed that 91 percent used quality circles. A **quality circle** is a group of employees from the same work area who define, analyze, and solve quality and related problems in their area. Groups usually number seven to ten people. They meet voluntarily and on a regular basis, typically once a week. A first-line supervisor or one of the workers usually serves as team leader to facilitate discussions and to keep management informed of the issues being addressed and the group's progress.

quality circle
Group of employees from the same work area who meet regularly to define, analyze, and solve quality and related problems in their area.

Because the quality-circle concept represents a means of increasing productivity, raising quality levels, reducing costs, and improving the quality of work life through employee participation, many U.S. firms have implemented the concept. Among the first U.S. corporations to establish quality circles were Lockheed Aircraft and Honeywell. Thousands of these voluntary groups have since been formed in the auto, aircraft, electronics, steel, and other industries. Their use has also expanded to the government sector. A quality circle operating in the Hayward, California, police department modified the police headquarters' layout to create a private area for use by police detectives in conducting interviews. A streamlined method for reviewing job applications was devised by a ten-member quality circle made up of Michigan state civil service employees.

The problems tackled by quality circles vary considerably in scope. They may include methods for reducing defects, scrap, rejected products, and equipment downtime. At a Corning Glass Works plant, a quality circle composed of machine operators, mechanics, technicians, and electricians figured out a way to reduce the changeover time on their machinery by replacing threaded couplings with easy-to-use snap-on couplings, a procedure that is saving the firm $106,000 each year.[27] In other instances, quality circles may focus on employee training, working conditions, and morale problems. Another Corning Glass quality circle noticed production-line crew performance dropped when new employees joined the crew because they lacked proper training. The employees designed a training program, complete with an instruction book, video, on-the-job training, and certification test.

Gary Schuler (center), president and general manager of Stanley-Bostitch, a division of The Stanley Works, listens as three quality circle members (at right) explain reductions in set-up time they recommend for computer-controlled machining operations that produce components for the division's products. Richard Cotoia, foreman, and Deborah Pannulo, director of productivity improvements, evaluate all QC suggestions and look for applications to other manufacturing processes. Management has approved about 50 cost-reduction and over 35 quality-improvement projects recommended by QCs in the past few years. A poll revealed that over 90 percent of company employees find the QC concept meaningful and valuable.

Photo source: Courtesy of The Stanley Works.

Sometimes the quality circle produces spectacular results. At Northrop Corporation's Aircraft Division near Los Angeles, 55 separate blue- and white-collar quality circles helped reduce the cost of producing Boeing 747 parts by 50 percent in two years, even though the size of the work force quadrupled. Worker recommendations included a redesigned, break-resistant drill bit that saved the company $28,000 a year, a metal stretcher used to prevent loud popping sounds in a 747's belly at high altitudes, and special stools that enable workers to roll from one workstation to another.

At one of Chrysler's X-car plants, a quality circle discovered car-door leaks could be prevented by heating rubber gaskets before installing them on the doors — a process that made the gaskets more malleable and easier to install.

A study of organizations with quality-circle programs concluded circles have the potential to increase worker self-respect, improve capabilities of individual workers, and develop workers' supervisory potential. A major problem on the part of some managers is expecting too much too soon from these voluntary, cooperative efforts. "You have to allow time for people to adjust to new relationships," points out Gene Kofke, director of work relationships at AT&T. The problem's "worst enemy . . . is the impatience for quick and finite results. You measure the success of these things in years."[28]

Production and Pollution

An undesirable output of many production processes is pollution, which takes many forms, including air pollution, water pollution, and noise pollution. Activities such as strip mining have produced extensive damage in Illinois, Kentucky,

West Virginia, and other ore-producing states. Major oil spills along the Pacific and Gulf coasts have killed thousands of fish and birds and damaged beaches. Discharges from chemical plants have closed recreational areas and killed fish. Atmospheric discharges by lead smelters have endangered the health of nearby residents. Acid rain has become an international problem, involving the United States, Canada, and many European countries. An estimated 165 tons of hazardous materials are produced each year by American factories.

In its most extreme form, pollution can — and does — kill people. The 1984 gas leak at Union Carbide's pesticide plant in Bhopal, India, killed more than 2,000 people and caused serious, permanent disabilities to many times that number.

Antipollution Regulations

These undesirable outputs have resulted in enactment of numerous state and federal laws designed to protect the environment. Since its establishment in 1970, the Environmental Protection Agency (EPA) has been the federal agency with primary authority for dealing with various types of pollution. During the 1980s, the EPA's power was strengthened by the Resource Conservation and Recovery Act. Manufacturers are now required to adopt programs to reduce the volume and toxicity of hazardous materials. Moreover, the regulations also limit the use of landfills, traditionally the least expensive disposal solution. A recent law mandates that firms inform the communities in which they operate about the types and amounts of hazardous chemicals at their facilities and the amounts of chemicals they release into the environment.

Waste-Reduction Methods

Efforts by manufacturers to stop pollution have resulted in the investment of billions of dollars in equipment. Over $24 billion is being spent each year to control air pollution. Buyers of new cars currently pay from $250 to $450 for air pollution abatement devices. Waste-reduction programs are tailored to fit a specific industry or plant. Most companies concentrate on four areas: raw materials, processes, equipment, and reuse.

By pursuing all these alternatives, USX Corporation estimates it reduced its hazardous waste generation by almost 50 percent in four years and slashed its use of landfill sites by 80 percent in five years. For example, the steel company substituted nonleaded greases and oils for leaded lubricants in its rolling mills. In its coke plants, heavy sludge residues that were discarded are now mixed with tars and converted into fuel.

One sure way to minimize waste is to squeeze more finished products from less raw material. Minnesota Mining and Manufacturing (3M) credits a savings of $845,000 a year to a process change in its sandpaper manufacturing operation. Previously, abrasive resins used to coat sandpaper were dumped into large kettles at the beginning of the manufacturing process. The leftover resins were flushed out of the vats, creating a hazardous-waste stream. 3M redesigned its equipment to feed resins continuously into the process in the precise amount needed. The reduction in hazardous wastes: 400 tons a year.

Some firms are reducing waste by developing reuse methods. The Goodyear Tire & Rubber Company is building facilities that shred scrap tires to produce a high-energy supplemental fuel used by paper, cement, and lime manufacturers.

Chevron built a laboratory at its Richmond refinery to monitor the quality of the effluent released into San Francisco Bay. In this photo, a lab technician uses environmentally sensitive trout to test the algae-tinged effluents' compliance with regulations. Going a step beyond complying with regulations, Chevron also launched a voluntary program to reduce industrial waste generation by more than 60 percent by 1992.

Photo source: Dennis Harding, Chevron Corporation.

Consolidated Papers Inc. spent $13.8 million in 1988 on environmental improvements, mostly on air emission control equipment at a plant that produces chemical pulp for its four paper mills. Chevron spent $45 million on a project at its Richmond, California, refinery to improve the treatment of the effluent it discharges into San Francisco Bay.

A strong commitment to protection of the environment, coupled with investments in pollution control, will be an increasingly important component of production decisions during the remaining years of the twentieth century.

Summary of Learning Goals

1.   Identify the roles of specialization, mechanization, and standardization in mass production.   Mass production in manufacturing is accomplished by effectively combining (1) specialization, the division of work into its simplest components; (2) mechanization, the use of machines to perform work; and (3) standardization, the production of uniform, interchangeable goods and parts.

2.   Describe the contributions and problems associated with the use of assembly lines, automation, and robots in producing products and services.   The use of assembly lines in manufacturing increases the speed of production as employees utilize the concepts of specialization, mechanization, and standardization. A logical extension of mechanization is automation, including the use of robots. Technological developments reduced the costs of automated equipment. Robots can be assigned to perform boring, routine, repetitive, and sometimes dangerous work, thereby freeing humans for more challenging assignments. However, automation often results in unemployment, making retraining of displaced workers necessary.

3. List the three components of production and operations management. Production and operations management is responsible for (1) developing plans for production inputs, (2) installing necessary production inputs and implementing production plans, and (3) coordinating and controlling the production process.

4. Outline the major factors involved in deciding plant locations. Among the factors to be considered in selecting a plant location are proximity to raw materials and to markets; availability of labor, transportation, and energy; local regulation; and community living conditions. Regulatory authorities may require an environmental impact study to assess the impact on the quality of life of locating the plant in a particular area.

5. Compare the alternative designs for production facilities. Process layouts are used for nonstandard products produced in relatively small batches. Product layout facilitates production of a few designs in relatively large quantities. A fixed-position layout is common when production involves very large, heavy, or fragile products. A customer-oriented layout is typically used for service facilities where interaction between the customer and the service facility are important factors.

6. List the steps involved in the purchasing process. The make, buy, or lease decision results in the determination of whether needed inputs will be manufactured in-house, purchased, or leased from an outside supplier. Those responsible for purchasing determine the correct materials to purchase, select appropriate suppliers, and develop an efficient ordering system, with the objective being to buy the right materials in the right amounts at the right time for the right place.

7. Compare the advantages and disadvantages of maintaining large amounts of inventory. The task of inventory control is to balance the need to maintain adequate supplies and the need to minimize funds invested in inventory. Excessive inventory results in increased expenditures for warehousing, taxes, insurance, and maintenance. Inadequate inventory may mean production delays, lost sales, and inefficient operations.

8. Identify the steps in the production control process. The production control process consists of five steps: planning, routing, scheduling, dispatching, and follow-up, as well as quality control. Coordination of each of these phases should result in improved production efficiency and lower production costs.

9. Explain the contributions of quality circles in improving quality control. Quality control involves the measurement of products and services against quality standards through devices ranging from visual inspections to electronic sensors and X rays. One technique is the use of quality circles, groups of seven to ten people from the same work area who regularly meet to define, analyze, and solve various problems in that area. In addition to developing methods of reducing waste and improving quality, such groups have the potential to increase worker self-respect, improve individual capabilities, and develop supervisory personnel.

Key Terms

utility

form utility

production

mass production

specialization

mechanization

standardization

assembly line

analytic system

synthetic system

continuous process

intermittent process

robot

computer-aided design (CAD)

computer-aided manufacturing (CAM)

flexible manufacturing system (FMS)

production and operations management

environmental impact study

industrial park

process layout

product layout

fixed-position layout

customer-oriented layout

make, buy, or lease decision

inventory control

perpetual inventory

just-in-time (JIT) inventory system

materials requirement planning (MRP)

manufacturing resource planning (MRP II)

production control

production planning

bill of materials

routing

scheduling

PERT (Program Evaluation and Review Technique)

critical path

dispatching

follow-up

quality control

statistical process control (SPC)

quality circle

Review Questions

1. Give two examples of production facilities in your city or region that use each of the following manufacturing methods:
   a. Analytic process
   b. Synthetic process
   c. Continuous process
   d. Intermittent process

2. Suggest types of form utility that the following firms might produce:
   a. Delivery service
   b. Sugar refinery
   c. Commercial airline
   d. Family counseling center

3. Explain how specialization, mechanization, standardization, and assembly lines have contributed to the development of mass production systems and how they continue to influence the work environment.

4. Relate computer-aided design to computer-aided manufacturing.

5. Explain the concept of a flexible manufacturing system.

6. Assign a facility layout to each of the businesses listed and explain the reasons behind your selection.

_____ Automotive service center	**a.** Process layout
_____ Surgical operating room	**b.** Production layout
_____ Theater or stage production	**c.** Fixed-position layout
_____ One-hour eyeglass store	**d.** Customer-oriented layout
_____ Retail florist	
_____ Winery or brewery	

7. Discuss the concepts behind materials requirement planning (MRP) and manufacturing resource planning (MRP II).

8. What factors are likely to be most important in the make, buy, or lease decision? List instances when make, buy, or lease decisions might be made for the following firms:

   a. Lawn and garden center **c.** Party supply house
   b. Asphalt company **d.** Upholstery shop

9. Relate the three components of production and operations management to each of the following. Give specific examples of each component.
   a. Major league sports facility in the Tampa Bay area
   b. Convenience food store
   c. Fish processing facility
   d. Color television assembly plant

10. What are the chief methods of ensuring quality control? Suggest appropriate quality control techniques for use in the following firms:
    a. Local bank
    b. City hospital
    c. Amusement park
    d. Furniture factory
    e. Bottling plant

Discussion Questions _____

1. Evaluate your city or county as a prospective industrial site and suggest organizations that would be well suited to the location.

2. Name five factories and five service firms located in your community or a nearby city. Identify the factors likely to have led to the location of each. Explain your choices.

3. A successful production plan provides sufficient materials (manufactured, purchased, or leased), efficient production schedules, and a controlled inventory. Draw up a proposed production plan, including make, buy, or lease decisions, for a small business in your area.

4. Assess the effect on inventory control resulting from the various inventory systems discussed in the chapter.

5. Draw a PERT diagram for the product described below. Make any necessary assumptions.

In order to become a Vlasic fresh-packed pickle, the cucumber undergoes a series of operations. Once the cucumbers arrive at the plant, they are sized, sorted, washed, sliced, and packed into jars. Specially prepared brine containing spices is added to the sliced product, and the jars are closed. The pickles next undergo a pasteurizing process, after which labels are affixed to the jars. The individual jars are then packaged into protective cases. The cases are finally combined on shipping pallets and moved to a warehouse to await shipment to customers.

Video Case

Kirk Stieff

Changing public tastes, shifting life styles, and an inconsistent financial market have eroded the demand for silverware and other silver products over the past forty years. The number of silversmiths in the U.S. has declined dramatically and major firms such as the Kirk Stieff Company have had to merge with competitors and develop new, more efficient methods of production in order to survive.

During the post-Revolutionary period when our young country was setting its course as an independent nation, Samuel Kirk went to Baltimore and opened his first silver shop in 1815. Five years later, he introduced America to what would become known as the world-famous Repoussé style, an ornate hammered relief design of flowers and foliage. The superb quality and beauty of his products won him the acclaim of such clients as the Marquis de Lafayette, Robert E. Lee, Jefferson Davis, the Astors, and the Roosevelts. Many of their highly treasured pieces are now part of the Kirk Collection that has been exhibited in museums throughout the United States.

Another silversmith, Charles Stieff, joined the more than 200 silver craft workers operating in Baltimore by opening a sterling flatware manufacturing facility in 1892. Perhaps his greatest contribution to the silver industry was his successful drive to have the quality and authenticity of sterling silver assured by law. Stieff's efforts led to the passage of federal legislation permitting only those items with at least 92.5 percent fine silver to be marked "sterling." Stieff's company broadened its market considerably when it was selected as the exclusive reproducer of Colonial Williamsburg® Foundation Reproductions. Its reputation for high quality and exacting standards continues to win approval from such historic organizations as the Smithsonian Institution, Historic Newport, the Boston Museum of Fine Arts, the Thomas Jefferson Memorial Foundation, and Historic Charleston. Over time, the firm's pewter line was expanded and it has become the world leader in authentic reproductions.

By the end of the nineteenth century, Baltimore's silversmiths had all but disappeared, and only the Kirk Company and the newly-founded Stieff Company were still producing silver products there. Stieff's firm had made a successful market introduction with a novel offer to silverware purchasers: It offered to sell silverware and other products by the piece rather than only in sets.

The silver business prospered in the years prior to World War II. During the war years, silver production for the consumer market halted and silver was diverted to the war effort. Most U.S. households of the early twentieth century considered fine silver pieces valued possessions and the ownership of such pieces a major status symbol. Nearly every family with any social pretensions owned a set of sterling flatware. At the war's end, pent-up demand was impressive. As one Kirk Stieff official recalls, "We had lines in front of our store and we'd have to give out numbers to the people because there was such a demand. . . . We finally got caught up, but it took quite a few years."

Although the silversmiths did not know it then, these years marked the peak of sterling flatware demand. Tastes changed and, in the decades that followed, fewer people felt the need or desire for silver products in their homes. Silver companies were slow to realize this major market change and declines in overall industry sales were partially offset by reduced competition as more and more businesses closed. For many of the existing companies, merger seemed the only way to survive and, in 1979, the Stieff Company acquired the Kirk Company and Kirk Stieff was born.

It would have been difficult for the firms to have chosen a worse year for the merger. Due to wide fluctuations in silver prices that year, the acquisition price was $1 million more than originally anticipated and the new company was heavily in debt. To make matters worse, sales dropped 22 percent from the previous year and layoffs of 100 company workers were necessary.

By 1984, the sterling flatware market had dropped another 45 percent; an ominous sign since flatware constituted one-half Kirk Stieff's total sales and profits. In a desperate move to save the company, the firm brought in Pierce Dunn as president. Admits Dunn, "We were in a crisis in 1984 when I took over as

Notes: Kirk Stieff: A Great American Story, 1989; Laurie Schneider, "Group Launches Drive to Spur Pewter Demand," *American Metal Market,* February 13, 1988; and personal correspondence, March 8, 1989.

president." Several internal and industry problems plagued the company. Interest expenses and debt re-payment costs were continuing to drain company revenues. Almost no cost-control mechanisms were included in the firm's cost accounting systems. Changing lifestyles meant that more and more would-be sterling flatware purchasers began purchasing other luxury items such as vacations and VCRs.

An early — and costly — mistake was the decision to offer Kirk Stieff products at steep discounts. The highly-discounted products frequently were viewed by shoppers as commodities instead of unique quality items, and the prestige of the Kirk Stieff name suffered. Pierce Dunn quickly changed this strategy, ensuring that the firm designed products that could not be easily imitated and marketed them on the basis of craftsmanship and quality, rather than price. The firm's product line was cut 15 percent and new innovative products were developed. Instead of the specialized process departmentalization typically found in mass production and assembly-line forms of production, Kirk Stieff moved into the most costly specialty market, producing not just standard items like flatware, but also one-of-a-kind silver pieces.

The firm's manufacturing system was also restructured into what it calls *production cells*. The old Kirk Stieff system called for mass-produced products such as flatware to pass through various specialized departments such as polishing, welding, engraving, and stamping. But the firm's new emphasis on the production of unique artistic silver pieces required a more independent, self-contained production system. In a production cell, a small group of skilled Kirk Stieff craft workers are completely responsible for every aspect of the manufacture of a specific product or group of related products. They are also responsible for maintaining the required quality levels for those products.

The production cell method proved efficient in terms of time, labor, and inventory cost savings. In effect, this new system has taken many of the manufac-turing decisions out of management's hands since the craft workers have complete authority and responsibility for all production decisions — from design to quality — for each piece produced.

The new production system is a major component of the firm's ability to survive: It makes it possible to avoid direct competition by focusing on the creation of unique products of the highest quality. Today, Kirk Stieff designs are not easily copied. Designers create what they would like to buy themselves. Dunn believes that the craft workers, through the production cell system, will discover the best and most efficient means of making their products. The production cells serve as quality circles where the group meets to discuss problems and possible solutions. The cells also serve as their own quality-control centers. Rather than maintain a separate inspection department, Kirk Stieff expects craft workers to judge the quality of their own output. As entrepreneur-author Paul Hawken says, "Being in business is not about making money. It is a way to become who you are." In the case of Kirk Stieff, it was a matter of getting back to who they were.

Questions

1. The concept of mass production is described in the chapter as a major reason for the growth of the U.S. economy. Explain why Kirk Stieff chose a radically different production system for its products.

2. Relate the Kirk Stieff production system to the three components of a typical production system listed in Table 9.1. Classify the firm's production system as either

a. analytic system or synthetic system.

b. continuous process or intermittent process.

3. What type of production layout appears most appropriate for Kirk Stieff?

4. Relate each of the five steps in production control to Kirk Stieff. Make any assumptions necessary.

5. Explain the reasons for quality circles. How are they used at Kirk Stieff? Critically evaluate the firm's quality control system.

Careers in Business

Management careers are available in all types of organizations: business firms, government, and nonprofit organizations. Managers plan, organize, direct, and control tasks performed by other people to accomplish organizational objectives.

The managerial hierarchy includes top, middle, and supervisory-level management positions. Top management is concerned with overall policy/strategies and decisions. Middle management deals with the implementation of policy and makes tactical decisions within each of the functional areas. Supervisory management directs the activities of such operative employees as production and clerical workers. Production managers are involved in all phases of the production process, including product planning, plant and equipment design and purchase, and work scheduling.

Some specific jobs in management and production are city manager, hotel manager, health-service administrator, retail manager, urban planner, accounting manager, sales manager, purchasing agent, and first-line supervisor.

The Bureau of Labor Statistics' outlook through the mid-1990s forecasts that job opportunities for hotel managers, health-service administrators, and accounting managers will grow faster than the average for all occupations, and that opportunities for purchasing agents and first-line supervisors will grow as fast as the average.

City Manager

City managers are executives who oversee the operation of a city or other governmental unit such as a county. They report to the elected representatives of the community they serve.

Job Description. City managers provide overall direction for the various departments of city government. The heads of such departments as planning, water and sewers, streets, recreation, and public safety report to these executives. One of the biggest tasks city managers face is preparing periodic budget requests for the city council. A background in governmental accounting and public finance is desirable. In addition, city managers must be actively involved in the community and must keep in close contact with the public.

Career Path. The starting point in this career path is a job as an assistant city manager. Once the person acquires sufficient expertise in municipal management, he or she may apply for a city manager position. This usually necessitates a move to another city. Only 3,300 city managers exist in the United States.

Salary. Salaries vary according to city: City managers for larger cities generally earned much more than those in smaller cities. In a recent year, the salaries of city managers for cities with populations between 50,000 and 99,999 averaged $61,200; for cities with populations between 250,000 and 499,999, the average salary was $90,600. The average salary of city managers from 1,262 cities was $51,027.

Hotel Manager

Hotel managers work at the executive level of the hotel and motel industry. They make the daily decisions required to keep a hotel operating efficiently. More than 78,000 hotel managers are employed in the United States.

Job Description. Hotel managers and assistants supervise the various activities necessary to a lodging establishment: registration, cash handling, housekeeping, accounting, maintenance, food service, entertainment, and security. Hotel managers report to higher-level management or to the hotel's owners or board of directors. They are responsible for the overall profitable operation of their units.

Career Path. Many motel and hotel chains and large city hotels have management training programs. Successful completion of such a program may result in promotion to a department head in a large hotel or to manager of a motel. The next step is a general management position.

Salary. Salaries vary widely. General managers in large, prestigious hotels may earn much more than a resident manager of a small hotel. The average salary of hotel managers in a recent year was $63,900. Both resident and general managers may have housing provided on the premises, and their income is sometimes supplemented with bonuses based on profitability.

Health-Service Administrator

Health-service administrators are the business management level of the health-care industry. They work in hospitals, health maintenance organizations, clinics, public health departments, nursing homes, and other health-oriented units. The chief administrator typically reports to the board of directors or trustees of the unit. Currently, 274,000 health service administrators are employed in the United States.

Job Description.   Health-service administrators direct the full range of activities of a health-care facility. The professional medical staff makes treatment decisions concerning patients, but most of the operational decisions for the facility are made by its administrator. Health-service administrators are also extensively involved in budgeting, fund-raising, planning, and interacting with the public served by the unit. It should also be noted that individuals in the fields of long-term care or nursing homes must pass a licensing examination.

Career Path.   Trainee and assistant administrator positions are available. Promotion comes with experience and effective performance.

Salary.   In a recent year, the average starting salary for a health-service administrator with a master's degree was $30,000. For experienced administrators, salaries ranged from $51,000 to $132,000.

Retail Manager

Retail stores, particularly large ones, have a number of important management needs.

Job Description.   Store managers must perform a variety of tasks. They supervise personnel, plan the work schedule, oversee inventory and purchasing, handle pricing policy, and decide on promotions. They often work long hours and sometimes have to make sensitive decisions in matters such as personnel.

Career Path.   Retail managers often begin as assistant managers, handling one department in a larger store. They can move up into specialized areas such as purchasing or into managing an entire store or a number of stores.

Salary.   Retail salaries vary widely, depending on the size of the store and the responsibilities held. In a recent year, beginning salaries ranged from $13,000 to $17,000.

Urban Planner

Also called city or regional planners, urban planners promote the economic, social, and cultural growth of cities.

Job Description.   Urban planners evaluate the uses of city services and facilities to determine their present and future adequacy. They use information on population and economic growth, for example, to estimate needs for various kinds of city services. They must work closely with city officials and often meet with public groups.

Career Path.   Urban planners usually begin with a master's degree in planning, working under the supervision of more experienced planners. With experience, they can expect to be put in charge of large projects and make important recommendations for city policy.

Salary.   In a recent year, urban planners had a median salary of $34,100, with somewhat higher salaries in the private sector than in government or the nonprofit sector. The average starting salary for a planner with a master's degree, in the federal sector, was $22,500.

Accounting Manager

Accounting managers, sometimes called chief accountants, are experienced accountants or auditors who have been promoted to supervisory and managerial positions in this functional area. They are key members of the organization's management team.

Job Description.   Accounting managers direct the activities of accounting and related clerical personnel. They analyze and approve the information and reports generated by the accounting unit. Accounting managers interact with other functional executives and top management.

Career Path.   Accounting managers are promoted from within the accounting department, so the entry-level position is filled by an accounting trainee. Advancement to senior-level positions is possible with experience. Continued progress may lead to a position as an accounting manager.

Salary.   An accounting manager's salary, in a recent year, ranged from $40,000 to $80,000 and averaged $54,700.

Sales Manager

Sales managers supervise all or part of a company's sales force. Sales managers exist in every industry that requires a sales force and at all levels in the distribution channel: producer, wholesale, and retail.

Job Description.   Sales managers recruit, hire, train, organize, supervise, and control sales organizations. They report to the top marketing executives or to general management. Their job is to produce the company's revenue. Effective interaction with sales personnel and customers is an important aspect of the job.

Career Path. Sales managers begin as sales representatives. Successful experience may lead to being designated a senior salesperson or sales supervisor. Upon promotion to district or division manager, the individual breaks away from selling per se and becomes an executive. It is possible to be promoted to even higher levels of sales management with additional responsibilities. A vice-president of sales, or national sales manager, heads the entire sales organization.

Salary. Sales managers' salaries, in a recent year, ranged from $17,700 to $52,500 with a median salary of $35,400.

Purchasing Agent

The purchasing agent, sometimes called an industrial buyer or procurement manager, secures the raw materials, component parts, and supplies needed by the firm. Purchasing agents are employed in the private, public, and nonprofit sectors. More than 418,000 purchasing agents are employed in the United States.

Job Description. Purchasing agents must be knowledgeable about the various suppliers and their offerings. They must acquire the best possible deal for their employer in terms of price, quality, delivery, and payment. Agents in large enterprises sometimes specialize in certain types of purchases.

Career Path. Once a person understands an organization's operations, he or she is given purchasing responsibilities. An assistant purchasing manager usually oversees the work of several agents. Career advancements include the position of director of procurement, director of purchasing, vice-president for purchasing, or vice-president for materials management.

Salary. In a recent year, the average beginning salary in the private sector was $21,200; in government, $19,800.

First-Line Supervisor

Supervisory positions are the first level of management. First-line supervisors direct operative employees in manufacturing, construction, transportation, and distribution. Currently, more than 1.8 million first-line supervisors are at work in the United States.

Job Description. The primary task of first-line supervisors is to meet goals and schedules. They are responsible for motivating and leading operative employees to accomplish organizational objectives. They also deal with interpersonal relations and conflicts, labor-management issues, and on-the-job health and safety matters.

Career Path. Some trainee positions are available. A first-line supervisor may be promoted to department head and to general manager.

Salary. Earnings vary greatly depending on the industry. Recently, the median income for all first-line supervisors was $24,000.

Chapter 10
Human Relations

Chapter 11
Human Resource Management

Chapter 12
Labor-Management Relations

The Human Resource

Career Profile: *John Parsons*

John Parsons has spent nearly his entire career in human resources management, either as an executive or a consultant. Parsons, 42, is now a principal in his own firm, Cole & Parsons, Ltd., which he started two years ago.

He majored in communications in college and earned a master's degree in management from Northwestern's Kellogg School of Management.

His first job after college had little to do with the front office. He was hired by Florida Tile Co., a subsidiary of Lakeland, Florida–based Sikes Corp. Sikes Corp. hired him to work in personnel, but company policy dictated that everyone must work in production before moving on to other positions. So Parsons started as a production supervisor at Florida Tile. He spent a year and a half on the production line learning about the company and its employees before moving into the personnel office. "I really learned a lot about people on that job . . . I'm glad I didn't start out in a staff position," said Parsons.

After leaving Sikes Corp., he had several other positions prior to starting his own firm: director of corporate training and development for Braden Industries; personnel director for Combustion Engineering, which took him to Chicago ten years ago; consultant for Modern Management, a Chicago–based consulting firm; and director of human resources for McLean-Fogg.

At McLean-Fogg, a Chicago-area manufacturer, he started as the director of human resources. McLean-Fogg planned to make a number of acquisitions, and hired

Parsons to manage the human resource problems this growth would cause. "When I came in, there was no set policy on personnel — departments made their own policies on things like hiring, firing, layoffs, compensation and reward systems," said Parsons. "I put together a personnel policy manual and worked out what would go in it. . . ."

As the company grew from $50 million to $120 million in sales, Parsons coordinated the benefit plans of acquired companies to match McLean-Fogg's. Parsons also focused on negotiating new contracts with workers at the acquired plants.

Parsons also dealt with difficult personnel issues such as cases of sexual harassment, which he considers a prevalent problem in the workplace. "This is a legitimate problem — there is a standard of conduct that is changing, and things you could do or say ten years ago you can't do now, which is for the good."

After being promoted to Vice-President of Human Resources, Parsons oversaw all of the company's human resource programs, including recruitment and hiring, training, management development, performance appraisal, and affirmative action programs. Then, three and a half years after starting with McLean-Fogg, Parsons decided to start his own human resources consulting business.

Cole & Parsons specializes in consulting for manufacturers and health services and also works with financial services companies. The company focuses on such issues as the wages/salary side of compensation (as opposed to the benefits

side), the improvement of relations between management and labor, and the general quality-of-life issues that are becoming increasingly important in the workplace. The firm also solves more "traditional" problems such as whether workers should join a union or how management's leadership skills could be improved. To solve these problems, Parsons interviews key workers and managers (and union officials, if applicable) to determine the important issues for each group, the remedies they would like to see implemented, and their overall aims for the company. He will then frequently bring the groups together and work through specific situations, such as how an employee grievance has been handled in the past, to get each side to work together more closely.

One client was faced with a number of poor employee performance problems. Parsons explained, "We wanted to improve people's performance, not fire them for bad performance." To meet this goal, he designed a progressive counseling program that enabled managers and problem employees to sit down and discuss what was expected and what was actually being produced. Then the employee could look for ways to improve.

Parsons now works with many programs and issues that have little or no precedent, such as whether to implement drug-testing programs and the proper ways to do so. He enjoys dealing with these problems which keep his work challenging.

Photo source: Courtesy of John Parsons and Rustam Tahir.

Human Relations

Learning Goals

Compare/contrast

1. To trace the development of the human relations movement in the United States.

2. To identify the different needs in Maslow's hierarchy. ✓

3. To distinguish between Theory X and Theory Y managers.

4. To contrast the Theory Z organization with the typical U.S. firm.

5. To describe and differentiate a job's motivational factors and maintenance factors.

6. To outline the steps involved in a management by objectives (MBO) program.

7. To explain the quality of work life concept and identify the major categories of QWL programs.

8. To differentiate job enrichment and job enlargement.

9. To identify the alternative forms of flexible work schedules.

It started with Employee Days. Keith Dunn, president of McGuffey's Restaurants Inc., had been reading books by Tom Peters [*In Search of Excellence* and *Thriving on Chaos*] and others encouraging companies to adopt an organizational structure in which workers are on top, with middle managers acting as facilitators. Last year Dunn decided to experiment by letting employees run the restaurants — planning the menu and drink specials, handling scheduling, choosing uniforms — for two days every six months.

Employees Days have boosted morale and have "been a wash, financially," says Dunn. Labor costs usually soar during the two days, but sales increase because employees tell friends and customers to stop by.

Last fall Dunn couldn't find anyone to manage the kitchen at his Asheville, North Carolina, restaurant. He decided to make *every day* Employee Day; he turned Asheville into a "self-managing store" for a three-month trial. It works just the same as Employee Days, except that employees are handed certain monthly financial goals. If they beat those goals, they receive half the difference in cash. "You don't dry your hands with a napkin anymore because you know how much these things are costing you," says Lori Emory, a bartender.

In October 1988 management handed dining-room employees two goals: keep labor costs below 6.5 percent (they came in at 6.48 percent), and hit sales of at least $221,000 (they reached nearly $222,000). As a result, employees

earned a bonus of $184.70, which amounted to only about $8 per person. "They still wanted to stick with it," Dunn says. Bar employees earned about $30 apiece, based on meeting goals for labor costs and pouring costs. The kitchen crew earned $45 per person.

Aside from flying a Jolly Roger flag out front, employees have responded tamely. Servers voted to wear black T-shirts and pants instead of the McGuffey's uniform of white oxford shirt, tie, and green apron. The dining-room staff gave the lunch crew a raise from $2.01 per hour to $3.35 per hour to make that shift — when tips are lower — more attractive. The dining-room staff now has a say in hiring decisions. And they may get to help write an entirely new menu.

Instead of leaving right after their shifts, some employees are staying around to serve on committees, such as the one that is revamping the complicated Service Excellence recognition program.

Dunn has already eliminated two assistant kitchen manager positions, saving at least $3,000 a month. Soon, he hopes to eliminate at least two more, and he may try self-management at one of the other McGuffey's. The new system has changed employees "in motivational terms, in feeling like they are more involved," says Dunn. "It's not earth-shattering. But it's the next step so that someday — three to five years out — McGuffey's will be a truly employee-involved company."[1]

Photo source: © 1989 Herb Snitzer.

Chapter Overview

Keith Dunn knows that people are the critical ingredients in the success of his four-restaurant company. To ensure employee commitment and to enhance morale, McGuffey's promotes almost entirely from within. But, in an industry with an annual turnover rate averaging a dismal 250 percent, his solution was to provide his company's employees with the needed hands-on experience by sending his managers home and letting McGuffey's employees — waiters, waitresses, cooks, and bartenders — assume total responsibility for running the business.

The importance of *people* to the success of any organization is stressed in the very definition of management: the use of people and other resources in accomplishing organizational objectives. Management involves getting things done through and with people. In the advertisement in Figure 10.1, American Airlines emphasizes the important role its 60,000 dedicated employees play in providing on-time service. But how does the organization recruit, train, and motivate highly qualified people? As this chapter will describe, recruitment and training practices may vary from organization to organization, but they are based on understood and accepted principles of human resources management. Motivation is another matter.

human relations
Study of how organizations manage and interact with employees to improve effectiveness of the firm and the employees.

Human relations refers to the study of how organizations manage and interact with their employees in their efforts to improve employee and organizational effectiveness. Human relations is a broad term that includes such previously discussed subjects as leadership, organizational design, extent of decentralization, and willingness to delegate authority and responsibility. In addition, it involves such fundamental issues as individual, group, and organizational needs; motivation; and attempts to improve the quality of work life.

The Scientific Management Movement

During the early part of the twentieth century, management experts such as Frederick Taylor, Frank and Lillian Gilbreth, and Henry L. Gantt devoted considerable efforts to improving the efficiency of individual workers. Their application of scientific principles to the management of workers and work activities became known as **scientific management**. The starting point was a scientific analysis of jobs in which each work task was simplified and narrowed to its most elementary function. This simplification process was based upon the concept of specialization: a worker could be trained to perform a specific task and, through constant repetition, would become highly productive. Dividing the overall production process into small tasks and training workers to perform each small task would result in increased output. Worker performance standards were then established and incentive wages used to encourage individual workers to meet — or exceed — the standards.

scientific management
Management approach to increase efficiency through scientific analysis of the jobs of individual workers, careful selection and training, and improved supervision.

United Parcel Service founder James E. Casey applied the time study research of Frank Gilbreth and others in developing methods of measuring the time consumed each day by each UPS driver in order to improve efficiency. The concept of maximizing worker effort has also led to a more efficient design for equipment, vehicles, and package-loading techniques.

Figure 10.1   The Importance of People to an Organization's Success

Source: Courtesy of American Airlines, Inc.

UPS, with 152,000 employees, has the highest company work standards in the industry. As one driver put it, "They squeeze every ounce out of you. You're always in a hurry, and you can't work relaxed." At UPS, over 1,000 industrial engineers use time study to set standards for almost every task. Drivers are instructed to walk quickly — 3 feet per second — to the customer's door and to knock first so they don't lose seconds looking for a doorbell.

UPS pushes its drivers hard but pays them well. The company's drivers, all of them members of the Teamsters union, earn about $1 more per hour than the best-paid drivers at other trucking companies earn.[2]

The Human Relations Movement

Even though many managers continue to use money as a primary motivator, a number of changes have occurred, both in the assumptions made by managers about their employees and in the approaches used by managers to motivate employee excellence. The origin of many of these changes can be traced to a series of experiments that later became known as the Hawthorne studies.

In 1927, Elton Mayo and a group of Harvard University researchers met in Cicero, Illinois, at Western Electric Company's Hawthorne plant to begin a study on the relationship between changes in physical working conditions and employee productivity. These investigations, known as the **Hawthorne studies**, revealed that money and job security are not the only sources of employee motivation and led to the development of the human relations approach to motivation.

By performing controlled experiments in the relay assembly section of the plant, the researchers sought answers to such questions as, "What is the effect of different intensities of light on employee output?" and "How will varying noise levels change worker productivity?" In one experiment, sufficient lighting was provided to a group of six female workers; later the amount of light was reduced. Mayo and his colleagues were baffled to discover that reducing the amount of light has almost no effect on productivity. In some cases, output actually rose. The light intensity was then reduced to about that of moonlight, and again production increased! The researchers began looking for the reason behind this phenomenon.

The research staff pulled themselves together and began looking for it. They conferred, argued, studied, and presently found it. It wasn't in the physical production end of the factory at all. It was in the women themselves. It was an attitude, the way the women now felt about their work and their group. By segregating them into a little world of their own, by asking their help and cooperation, the investigators had given the young women a new sense of their own value. Their whole attitude changed from that of separate cogs in a machine to that of a congenial team helping the company solve a significant problem.

They found stability, a place where they belonged, and work whose purpose they could clearly see. And so they worked faster and better than they ever had in their lives. The two functions of a factory had joined into one harmonious whole.[3]

The phenomenon discovered by the researchers became known as the **Hawthorne effect**. Employees who are chosen as subjects for scientific studies may become more productive as a result of the interest the researchers have in them. Because they feel important and appreciated, they have greater incentive to excel in their work

How Needs Motivate People

The Hawthorne studies revolutionized management's approach to direction (or motivation) of employees. Before the Hawthorne investigation, most organizations had used money as the primary means of motivating workers. The importance of the Hawthorne findings lies not in denying the effect of money as a motivator, but in emphasizing the presence of a number of other sources of employee motivation.

Each individual is motivated to take action designed to satisfy needs. A **need** is simply the lack of something useful. It reflects a gap between an individual's actual state and his or her desired state. A **motive** is the inner state that directs

---

Hawthorne studies
Investigations that revealed money and job security are not the only sources of employee motivation; led to human relations approach to employee motivation.

Hawthorne effect
Phenomenon in which subjects become more productive because they feel important and appreciated.

How people react when they are being observed

need
Lack of something useful; discrepancy between a desired state and the actual state.

motive
Inner state that directs individuals toward the goal of satisfying a felt need.

Figure 10.2   The Process of Motivation

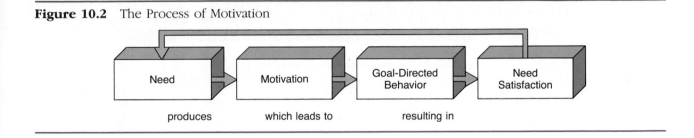

the individual toward the goal of satisfying a felt need. The individual is moved (the root word for *motive*) to act to reduce a state of tension and return to a condition of equilibrium.

The relationship between needs and motives can be explained by example. For the student who has attended classes or worked until 1 p.m., the need may be food. The lack of lunch is reflected in the motive hunger. A short walk to a nearby restaurant results in the purchase and consumption of the $2.59 special — a hamburger, french fries, and choice of beverage. By 1:30, the individual's need for food has been satisfied and he is ready for the 2 o'clock class. This process is depicted in Figure 10.2.

The Needs Hierarchy

Psychologist Abraham H. Maslow developed a widely accepted list of human needs based on these important assumptions:

◆ People are wanting animals whose needs depend on what they already possess.

◆ A satisfied need is not a motivator; only those needs that have not been satisfied can influence behavior.

◆ People's needs are arranged in a hierarchy of importance. Once one need has been at least partially satisfied, another emerges and demands satisfaction.[4]

unless a subordinate need is not satisfied the other needs will not be accomplish

Figure 10.3 depicts the hierarchy of needs with the levels arranged in order of importance to the individual. Priority is assigned to the basic physiological needs.

Physiological Needs

Physiological needs are the primary needs for food, shelter, and clothing. They are present in all people and must be satisfied before higher-order needs can be considered. A hungry person is possessed by the need to obtain food; other needs are ignored. But once the physiological need to eat is at least partially satisfied, other needs enter the picture. Since most families today can afford to satisfy their basic needs, the higher-order needs are likely to play a greater role in worker motivation.

physiological needs
Primary human needs for food, shelter, and clothing that must be satisfied before higher-order needs can be considered.

Figure 10.3   Maslow's Hierarchy of Human Needs

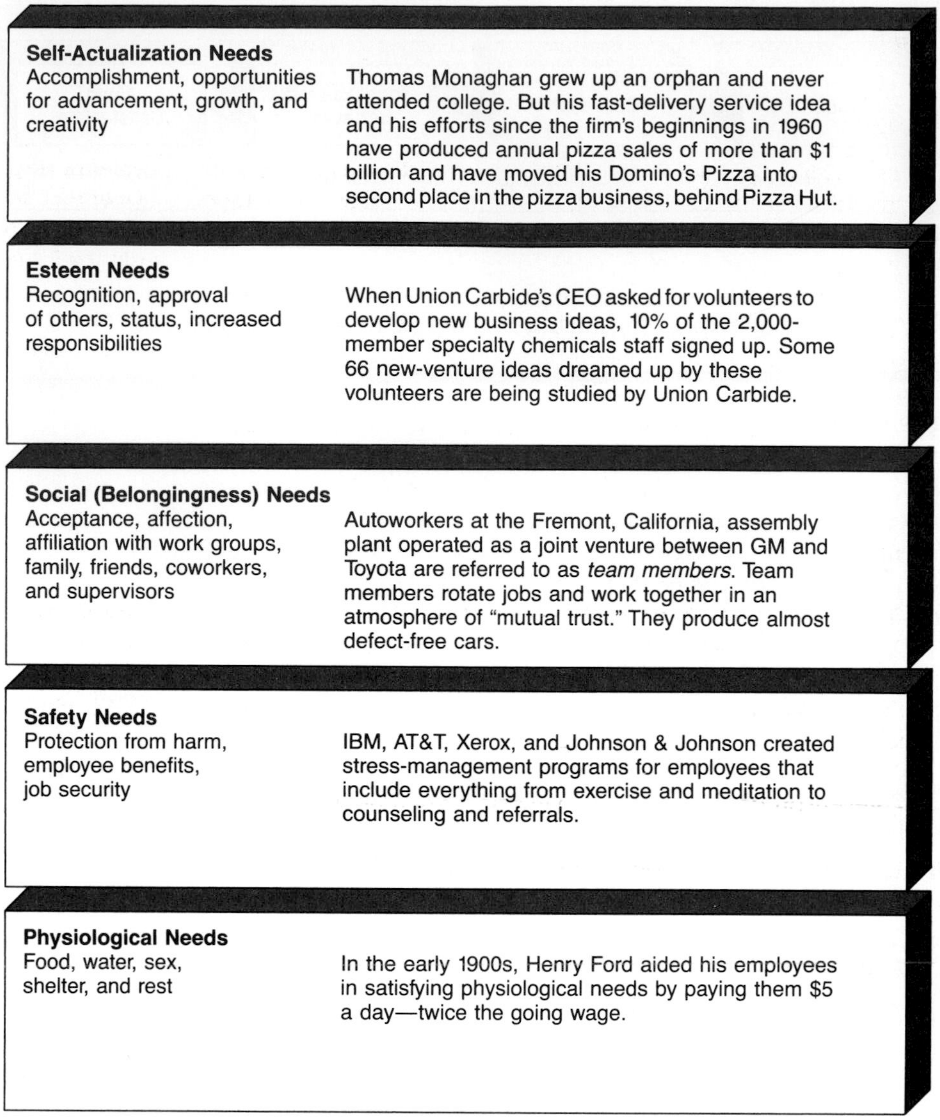

Self-Actualization Needs
Accomplishment, opportunities for advancement, growth, and creativity

Thomas Monaghan grew up an orphan and never attended college. But his fast-delivery service idea and his efforts since the firm's beginnings in 1960 have produced annual pizza sales of more than $1 billion and have moved his Domino's Pizza into second place in the pizza business, behind Pizza Hut.

Esteem Needs
Recognition, approval of others, status, increased responsibilities

When Union Carbide's CEO asked for volunteers to develop new business ideas, 10% of the 2,000-member specialty chemicals staff signed up. Some 66 new-venture ideas dreamed up by these volunteers are being studied by Union Carbide.

Social (Belongingness) Needs
Acceptance, affection, affiliation with work groups, family, friends, coworkers, and supervisors

Autoworkers at the Fremont, California, assembly plant operated as a joint venture between GM and Toyota are referred to as *team members*. Team members rotate jobs and work together in an atmosphere of "mutual trust." They produce almost defect-free cars.

Safety Needs
Protection from harm, employee benefits, job security

IBM, AT&T, Xerox, and Johnson & Johnson created stress-management programs for employees that include everything from exercise and meditation to counseling and referrals.

Physiological Needs
Food, water, sex, shelter, and rest

In the early 1900s, Henry Ford aided his employees in satisfying physiological needs by paying them $5 a day—twice the going wage.

Safety Needs

safety needs
Second level of human needs including job security, protection from physical harm, and avoidance of the unexpected.

The second-level **safety needs** include job security, protection from physical harm, and avoidance of the unexpected. Gratification of these needs may take such forms as guaranteed annual wages, life insurance, the purchase of radial tires, the obeying of job safety rules, or membership in the company health club.

Social Needs

social (belongingness) needs
Desire to be accepted by members of the family, other individuals, and groups.

Satisfaction of physiological and safety needs leads to consideration of **social needs** (also known as belongingness needs) — the desire to be accepted by members of the family and other individuals and groups. A person may be motivated to join various groups at the factory and conform to the standards established and accepted by the informal organization in order to fulfill social needs.

Esteem Needs

The higher-order **esteem needs** are more difficult to satisfy. These are the needs to feel a sense of accomplishment, achievement, and respect from others. The competitive need to excel — to better the performance of others — is an almost universal human trait.

The esteem needs are closely related to belongingness needs. However, at this level, not only does the individual want acceptance but also recognition and respect — the desire to stand out from the crowd in some area. Organizations seek to satisfy employee esteem needs through such techniques as performance recognition awards, added responsibility, and involvement in departmental goal setting and decision making.

esteem needs
Desire for accomplishment, a feeling of achievement, and the respect of others.

Self-Actualization Needs

At the top of the hierarchy are **self-actualization needs** — the needs for fulfillment, for realizing one's own potential, for using totally one's talents and capabilities.

Maslow defines *self-actualization* this way: "A healthy man is primarily motivated by his needs to develop and actualize his fullest potentialities and capacities. . . . What man *can* be, he *must* be."[5]

Robert Louis Stevenson described self-actualization when he wrote, "To be what we are, and to become what we are capable of becoming, is the only end of life."[6] For John Candy, self-actualization may mean being acclaimed the most popular comedian. For others, it may mean being named in the *Guinness Book of World Records*. Organizations seek to satisfy employee self-actualization needs through challenging and creative work assignments and opportunities for advancement based on individual merit.

self-actualization needs
Needs for fulfillment, for realizing one's potential, and for totally using one's talents and capabilities.

Applying the Needs Concept

Maslow points out that a satisfied need is no longer a motivator. Once the physiological needs are satisfied, the individual becomes concerned with higher-order needs. There will obviously be periods when an individual is motivated by the need to relieve thirst or hunger, but interest is most often directed toward the satisfaction of safety, belongingness, and the other needs on the ladder.

Business organizations have been extremely successful in satisfying the lower-order physiological and safety needs. The traditional view of workers as ingredients in the productive process — as machines like lathes, drill presses, and other equipment — led management to motivate them with money. The Hawthorne studies showed that people are not like machines, and that social and psychological needs motivate as effectively as money. Managers were forced to reconsider their assumptions about employees and how best to motivate them.

GLENFED, Inc., a financial and real estate services corporation, motivates employees by satisfying the higher-order esteem and self-actualization needs. Incentive programs reward superior customer service performance and stimulate employees' personal and professional growth. Each month, GLENFED honors more than 240 employees with awards for excellence and internal recognition at sales rallies and other events.

Photo source: Courtesy GLENFED, Inc. 1987 Annual Report.

Theory X
Managerial assumption that employees dislike work and must be coerced, controlled, or threatened to motivate them to work.

Evaluating Theory X

Psychologist Douglas McGregor, a student of Maslow, proposed the concepts of Theory X and Theory Y as labels for the assumptions that different managers make about worker behavior. **Theory X** is the traditional managerial assumption that employees dislike work and must be coerced, controlled, or threatened to be motivated to work. According to McGregor, Theory X involves the following assumptions:

1. The average human being has an inherent dislike of work and will avoid it if possible.
2. Because of this characteristic, most people must be coerced, controlled, directed, or threatened with punishment to get them to put forth adequate effort toward the achievement of organization objectives.
3. The average human being prefers to be directed, wishes to avoid responsibility, has relatively little ambition, and wants security above all.

If true, this traditional view of workers is a depressing indictment of human nature. Managers who accept the view may direct their subordinates through close and constant observation, continually holding over them the threat of disciplinary action, and demanding that they closely follow company policies and procedures. High-technology monitoring systems include daily analysis of telephone calls made by almost 10 million employees in 63,000 companies. At American Express, the call-accounting system sends instant reports to supervisors on the frequency and length of calls, as well as how quickly the phones are answered. Former Vice-President of Operations Edwin Sherin sums up the advantages: "Telecommunications monitoring provides hard data with which to prod workers to produce at a higher level."[7]

Another means of nonhuman monitoring is the activity evaluation of two-thirds of the 15 million workers in such industries as banking, hospitals, and airline companies who use video-display terminals. These electronic monitors record when an operator is off a VDT, count keystrokes by the second, time customer service actions, and track errors. An airline spokesperson defends the use of these systems in monitoring the work of the airline's reservations employees: "We have to do this. When you're in a competitive business and pay the salaries we do, we have got to set standards."[8]

The Theory X manager's underlying set of attitudes and beliefs concerning employee behavior typically results in the use of traditional economic incentives designed to satisfy lower-order physiological and safety needs. Even though close supervision and continual employee monitoring can significantly increase productivity in the short run, concerns are frequently expressed about the Big Brother aspects of electronic systems and the long-term results of all types of intense monitoring activities. As Harley Shaiken, technology professor at the University of California in San Diego, points out, "In the short term, you can squeeze more out of people. But in the long term, it destroys creativity and the initiative and desire to do a good job."[9]

Theory Y as a Replacement for Theory X

Theory X appears to have a critical deficiency. It focuses strictly on physiological and safety needs while ignoring the higher-order needs. If people behave in the manner described by Theory X, the reason for their behavior may be that the organization only partially satisfies their needs. If, instead, the organization enables them to satisfy their social, esteem, and self-actualization needs, new behavior patterns should develop — and different assumptions should be made.

Theory Y offers a new managerial assumption: workers do not dislike work and, under proper conditions, they accept and seek out responsibilities in order to fulfill their social, esteem, and self-actualization needs. Under Theory Y, McGregor points out:

Theory Y
Managerial assumption that workers like work and, under proper conditions, accept and seek out responsibilities to fulfill their social, esteem, and self-actualization needs.

1. Workers do not inherently dislike work. The expenditure of physical and mental effort in work is as natural as play or rest.
2. Employees do not want to be rigidly controlled and threatened with punishment.
3. The average worker will, under proper conditions, not only accept but also actually seek responsibility.
4. Employees desire to satisfy social, esteem, and self-actualization needs in addition to security needs.[10]

Unlike the traditional management philosophy that relies on external control and constant supervision, Theory Y emphasizes self-control and direction. Its implementation requires a different managerial strategy.

Use of Participative Management in Theory Z

During the past 15 years, the United States has imported more than automobiles, television sets, and videocassette players from Japan. In an attempt to explain the rapid strides of Japanese industry since World War II, a number of management

Table 10.1   Characteristics of Theory Z Management

Typical U.S. Organization	Theory Z Organization	Typical Japanese Organization
Short-term employment	Long-term employment	Lifetime employment
Rapid evaluation and promotion	Slow evaluation and promotion	Slow evaluation and promotion
Specialized career paths	Moderately specialized career paths	Nonspecialized career paths
Explicit control mechanisms	Implicit, informal control with explicit, formalized measures	Implicit control mechanisms
Individual decision making	Collective decision making	Collective decision making
Individual responsibility	Individual responsibility	Collective responsibility

Source: Adapted from William G. Ouchi and Alfred M. Jaeger, "Type Z Organizations: Stability in the Midst of Mobility," *Academy of Management Review* 3 (1978), pp. 308–311.

writers paid particular attention to the relationships between Japanese workers and their employers. UCLA business professor William G. Ouchi argues that part of the reason for Japan's extraordinary industrial success is not technology, but the Japanese corporations' special way of managing people — a style that focuses on employee involvement in every phase of corporate life. Table 10.1 shows the contrasts between the typical Japanese organization and the typical U.S. organization.

The Japanese approach involves lifetime employment, worker participation in decision making, and nonspecialized career paths. Unlike the high turnover in many U.S. corporations, large Japanese companies hire workers for life. About 35 percent of all workers in Japan will work for only one company during their lives. Although lifetime employment provisions are rare in the United States, a growing number of firms are adopting a no-layoff philosophy. Eli Lilly, for example, has not laid off an employee in its 110-year history. Both IBM and Hewlett-Packard are well known for their no-layoffs policies. Delta Air Lines has not laid off anyone since the 1950s.[11]

Although there is a tendency to recommend implementing the Japanese approach to management as a "quick fix," Ouchi warns that the cultural differences of the two nations require modifications in the new approach. This modified approach has been labeled **Theory Z**. Theory Z views involved workers as the key to increased productivity and an improved quality of work life. Theory Z organizations provide long-term employment for employees and a sharing of responsibility for making and implementing decisions. Evaluations and promotions are relatively slow and promotions are tied to individual progress rather than to the calendar. Employees receive varied and nonspecialized experience to broaden their career paths. The result of this approach, according to Ouchi, is increased productivity and improved worker satisfaction.

The move toward participative management is dramatically reshaping U.S. corporations. The new methods are based on asking workers how to improve their jobs and then letting them do it. Instead of relying on a bureaucracy of departments such as personnel and maintenance, Union Carbide welders now have a voice in their stand-alone operations. Consequently, they reduced the

Theory Z

Management approach emphasizing employee participation as the key to increased productivity and improved quality of work life.

These managers and employees of Stone Container Corporation participate in regularly scheduled employee involvement meetings. They discuss what could be done to make products better, easier to use, or more cost-effective. They also discuss ways to better service the customer, innovative methods to improve that service, and improvements for internal operations. The meetings are part of a company-wide process called IQS — Innovation, Quality, and Service — which has helped boost sales from $427 million to $3.2 billion during a recent five-year period.

Photo source: Courtesy Stone Container Corporation, Charlie Westerman, Photographer.

number of costly back injuries by implementing 20 minutes of exercise on the shop floor each morning before work.[12] Tandem Computers bids for worker loyalty by giving employees a voice in every new hire, including senior managers. General Electric is a participative management pioneer; its experiments with this philosophy began in the late 1960s. Productivity increased 25 percent within three years following the installation of a participative management program at GE's Ravenna, Ohio, production facility.[13]

"The problem with participative management," says Raymond E. Miles, dean of the University of California's business school at Berkeley, "is that it works." A number of companies with participative management programs report reluctance on the part of middle- and supervisory-level management to support the programs. But successful implementation typically produced dramatic results. A study of 101 industrial companies found that those practicing participative management outscored the others on 13 of 14 financial measures of company excellence.[14]

The Theory Z approach does not require adoption of all Japanese management practices. Since highly qualified young managers in the United States are likely to have numerous job alternatives with different firms, rigid adherence to the Japanese practice of slow evaluations and promotions is likely to result in the loss of an American firm's brightest talents. In addition, the Japanese practice of excluding most women from top management positions is both a waste of human resources and illegal in the United States.

Maintenance versus Motivational Factors

Over 25 years ago, psychologist Frederick Herzberg conducted a study in human motivation of various job factors as sources of satisfaction and dissatisfaction. Based on his research, Herzberg reached two conclusions:

maintenance factors
Job-related factors (job security, salary) that are not strong motivators, but must be present to prevent worker dissatisfaction.

1. Certain characteristics of a job, called **maintenance factors**, are necessary to maintain a desired level of satisfaction. They include such job-related factors as salary, working conditions, and job security. They must be present to prevent worker dissatisfaction, but they are not strong motivators. If they are absent or inadequate, they are likely to serve as *dissatisfiers*. Since most industrial firms make free parking available for their employees, a large employee parking lot is not a strong motivator. But a General Motors Corporation decision to encourage employee purchases of GM cars by banning Fords, Hondas, Toyotas, and other competitive models from salaried employees' parking lots proved to be a major dissatisfier. The move set GM employees to sniping at each other, and a number of complaints were registered before the restrictions could be removed by a chagrined GM management.[15]

motivational factors
Job-centered factors (recognition, responsibility) that are strong sources of employee motivation.

2. Other job-centered characteristics are **motivational factors**, such as the work itself, recognition, responsibility, advancement, and growth potential — the key sources of employee motivation.

Thus, although maintenance factors such as money are extremely important and will lead to job dissatisfaction when they are lacking, they are of low motivational value as long as they are present in adequate amounts. The key motivational factors are related to the job itself. The supervisor motivates the worker not with an additional coffee break but with greater job involvement.[16]

The Three Rs of Employee Motivation

From his examination of 20 top American firms, Robert Levering, author of *A Great Place to Work*, concludes any boss can turn a bad workplace into a good one through what he calls the three Rs. The first of these is granting workers more and more *responsibility* for their jobs. Preston Trucking, on Maryland's eastern shore, has been transformed from an organization characterized by frequent labor disputes over work rules to one where the unofficial slogan is "the person doing the job knows more about it than anyone else." Management's new approach involved establishing a partnership with employees rather than acting as adversaries. Supervisors were told to find and praise four acts that an employee does right for every one action that they criticize. Management demonstrated its commitment to the new approach by distributing a statement of mission spelling out the philosophy.[17]

The second R involves sharing the *rewards* of the enterprise as equitably as possible. Employees at Perfusion Services Inc. (PSI) receive a raise in every

New York Life Insurance Company provides the three Rs of employee motivation. During weekly "Ask Me" sessions, members of the Human Resources Department, such as Walter Weissinger (center) and Carl Williams (left), answer any employee questions about the company. Employees are given responsibility by participating in defining their job activities, setting goals, and decision making. They are rewarded according to their performance in meeting goals.

Photo source: Courtesy of New York Life Insurance Company.

paycheck. Every two weeks, workers of the Brighton, Michigan, firm, which provides equipment and personnel to hospitals for open-heart surgery, find that their paychecks have increased by at least a few dollars, sometimes much more. The firm's president believes the "constant reward" pay structure better motivates employees and lets them know they're doing a good job than does a system of annual performance reviews. "A year is an interminably long period of time between raises, especially for short-term-oriented people like ours. Make them wait that long and their eyes glaze over." The firm's sales and profit performance support this approach. PSI is one of the fastest-growing companies in the country, with an annual sales growth of 60 percent and an after-tax profit of greater than 7 percent. By combining salary increases with an implicit performance review, PSI keeps its employees happy — and motivated.[18]

The third R is ensuring that employees have *rights*. These include some kind of grievance procedure, access to corporate records, and the right to confront those in authority without fearing reprisals. In addition to an annual meeting of corporate shareholders, Stamford, Connecticut-based Pitney Bowes holds annual jobholders' meetings at which employees can ask top executives anything. Not only does Federal Express have a no-layoff policy and employee profit sharing, but it also has one of the best grievance procedures in America where the individual can request a trial by his or her peers. In addition, employees have a right to information. Any Federal Express employee wanting to know how pay scales are set can find out.[19]

Table 10.2   What Contributes to High Morale?

Relative Importance	Manager Rankings	Employee Rankings
Most important	Good wages Job security Promotion and growth with company	Full appreciation for work done Feeling "in" on things Sympathetic understanding of personal problems
Less Important	Good working conditions Interesting work Management loyalty to workers	Job security Good wages Interesting work
Least important	Tactful disciplining Full appreciation for work done Sympathetic understanding of personal problems Feeling "in" on things	Promotion and growth with company Management loyalty to workers Good working conditions Tactful disciplining

Source: Adapted from Paul Hersey and Kenneth H. Blanchard, *Management of Organizational Behavior* (Englewood Cliffs, N.J.: Prentice-Hall, 1977), p. 47.

Much similarity exists between Herzberg's two factors and Maslow's hierarchy of human needs. Herzberg's message is that the lower-level needs have already been satisfied for most workers, and the manager must focus on the higher-level needs — the primary motivators.

What Factors Influence Employee Morale?

morale

Mental attitude of employees toward their employer and/or job.

Morale is the mental attitude of employees toward their employer and/or their job. It involves a sense of common purpose with respect to the other members of the work group and to the organization as a whole. High morale is a sign of a well-managed organization, because workers' attitudes toward their jobs affect the quality of the work done.

One of the most obvious signs of poor manager-worker relations is poor morale. It lurks behind absenteeism, employee turnover, slowdowns, and wildcat strikes; it shows up in lower productivity, employee grievances, and transfers.

Burnout, a byword in business today, has no exact medical definition, but low morale and fatigue are two common symptoms. The most likely burnout candidates are those who care most about their jobs and the company, and they are more likely to experience burnout when they feel a sense of futility and a lack of accomplishment. Kenneth Pelletier, a stress management consultant and psychiatrist, believes a manager can inspire workers by showing appreciation for effort. Appreciation is, according to Pelletier, "the most underestimated benefit" he knows.[20]

Management's view of what leads to high employee morale is often incorrect. One research study compared how managers and workers ranked the importance of various morale factors. As Table 10.2 indicates, managers chiefly emphasized the lower-order needs of money and job security. But employees gave a quite different ranking. Opinions varied significantly on the importance of such items as job security and appreciation for work done. Other differences included the importance of fair pay, promotion, and understanding of personal problems.

The maintenance of high morale means more than keeping employees happy. A two-day workweek, longer vacations, or almost continual coffee breaks could easily produce happy employees. But high morale results from an environment in which workers obtain satisfaction from their work and are motivated to excel in their assigned duties, which should lead to greater productivity. Management, therefore, should create a work environment that will result in high employee morale.

Management by Objectives

A widely used management technique aimed at improving the overall motivation and performance of workers is **management by objectives (MBO)**. MBO is designed to improve employees' motivation by having them participate in setting their own goals, letting them know in advance how they will be evaluated, and basing their performance appraisals upon periodic analyses of their progress toward agreed-upon goals.

management by objectives (MBO)
Program designed to improve employee motivation through participation in goal setting and by informing them in advance of the factors used in performance evaluations.

The MBO approach was proposed almost 50 years ago. It was popularized in the early 1950s by management writer and consultant Peter Drucker, who described it this way:

The objectives of the district manager's job should be clearly defined by the contribution he and his district sales force have to make to the sales department, the objectives of the project engineer's job by the contribution he, his engineers and draftsmen make to the engineering department. . . . This requires each manager to develop and set the objectives of his unit himself. Higher management must, of course, reserve the power to approve or disapprove his objectives. But their development is part of a manager's responsibility; indeed, it is his first responsibility.[21]

An estimated 200 of the 500 largest industrial firms in the United States are currently using some form of MBO.

Steps in an MBO Program

Figure 10.4 illustrates the following five-step sequence used by most MBO programs:

1. Each subordinate discusses the job description with the manager.
2. Short-term performance goals are established.
3. The subordinate meets regularly with the manager to discuss progress toward the goals.
4. Intermediate checkpoints are established to measure progress toward the goals.
5. At the end of a defined period, both the manager and subordinate evaluate the results of the subordinate's efforts.

Management by objectives involves mutual goal setting by manager and subordinate. Both must reach an understanding about the subordinate's major area of

Figure 10.4   Steps in the Management by Objectives Process

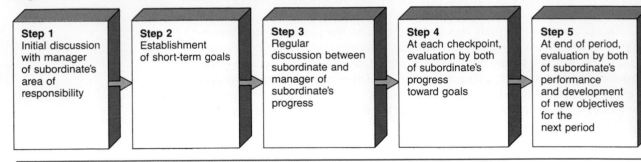

Step 1	Step 2	Step 3	Step 4	Step 5
Initial discussion with manager of subordinate's area of responsibility	Establishment of short-term goals	Regular discussion between subordinate and manager of subordinate's progress	At each checkpoint, evaluation by both of subordinate's progress toward goals	At end of period, evaluation by both of subordinate's performance and development of new objectives for the next period

responsibility and the acceptable level of performance. These understandings form the basis of the subordinate's goals for the next planning period (usually in about six months).

Goals should be in numerical terms whenever possible — for example, reducing scrap losses by 5 percent or increasing sales of pocket calculators by 15 percent. Once these goals are established and agreed upon, the subordinate is responsible for achieving them.

Meanwhile, the subordinate may check often with the manager. At the end of the period, a formal progress review is conducted. Both the subordinate and the manager discuss performance and determine whether the goals were achieved. Unmet goals are analyzed, and corrective measures may be devised for improving future performance. New goals are then established for the next period.

[handwritten margin note: Subordinates participate in setting objectives]

[handwritten note: ✓ goals have to be achieveable]

Benefits of an MBO Program

The chief purpose of management by objectives is to improve employees' motivation through their participation in setting their own goals. Workers thus know both the job to be done and precisely how they will be evaluated.

An MBO program should improve morale by improving communication between individual employees and their managers. It should also enable workers to relate their performance to overall organizational goals. Finally, it should serve as a basis for decisions about salary increases and promotions.

MBO is not limited to any single level in the organization. Ideally, it begins with the president, who should set some personal job objectives in consultation with the board of directors. The process then proceeds throughout the organization, extending to every employee.

Overcoming Potential Problems with MBO

[handwritten margin note: I don't see the benefits in most MBO programs]

MBO programs have merit if used with judgment and a great deal of planning. Their success is greatly affected by the degree of top management support and involvement in its implementation. In addition, management must make a conscious effort to avoid overburdening the MBO system with too much paperwork and recordkeeping.

Another potential problem with an MBO program is the difficulty some managers have in communicating with individual employees and in formulating short-term performance goals. When such goals are assigned rather than agreed to by both parties, the result is typically resentment and lack of commitment on the part of the employee.

Because changes may have to be made in such areas as the degree of communication between managers and subordinates, MBO will succeed only where both managers and subordinates feel comfortable with it and are willing to participate in it. Management must also recognize that in many organizations, workers' goals are constantly changing. In such situations, it is much more difficult to measure results accurately.

Improving the Quality of Work Life

Employee participation in setting performance goals in an MBO program is a major step in improving the quality of work life. However, the typical worker with an assembly-line job faces the same work conditions as do millions of others. These conditions can be traced to the investigations of the scientific management thinkers of the early part of the twentieth century. In their efforts to generate greater productivity from subdividing work activities and assigning them to specialized workers, they produced jobs with common characteristics: mechanically controlled work pace, repetitiveness, minimum skill requirements, predetermined tools and techniques, and minute subdivision of the product that requires only surface mental attention.[22] In short, such jobs lead to boredom, popularly called "the blue-collar blues." When workers cannot control their pace or use judgment and are not challenged to improve their skills above a minimal level, they are likely to be poorly motivated and will possibly suffer from alienation.

In addition, the simplifying and narrowing of tasks is becoming less applicable with technological changes and increased automation. Millions of manufacturing jobs — especially in such industries as automobile, steel, and rubber — are disappearing because of foreign competition and automation. The newly created jobs frequently require more broadly trained employees with the knowledge and flexibility to adapt to an evolving workplace.[23]

In recent years, the term **quality of work life (QWL)** has been used to describe a number of techniques currently used to reshape the workplace. QWL is a process wherein all members of the organization, through appropriate channels of communication, have some say about the design of their particular jobs and the general work environment. It involves recognition on the part of management that employees are unique, adult individuals and that their inputs are valuable and should be encouraged. As Byron P. Crane, General Motors' directors of labor relations, puts it, "There are many fancy definitions of QWL, but really they all boil down to treating people as adults when they are at work."[24] In addition to Theory Z participative management discussed earlier, two major categories of QWL programs are restructuring work to provide job enrichment and offering flexible work schedules to employees.

quality of work life (QWL) Program permitting employee participation in job design and the overall work environment decisions, includes job enrichment, flexible work schedules, and Theory Z management.

Job Enrichment

In their search for ways to improve employee productivity and morale, a growing number of firms are focusing upon the motivational aspects of the job itself. Rather than simplifying the tasks involved in a job, they seek to enrich the job by

job enrichment
Redesigning work, giving employees more authority in planning their work, deciding how it is to be done, and allowing them to learn related skills or to trade jobs.

job enlargement
Increasing the number of tasks a worker performs; may or may not be job enriching.

making it more satisfying and meaningful. **Job enrichment** involves redesigning the work to give workers more authority to plan their activities and to decide how the work is to be accomplished, allowing them to learn related skills or to trade jobs with others. Building on Herzberg's idea, it focuses on motivational factors by designing work that will satisfy individual as well as company needs.

Although the terms *job enrichment* and *job enlargement* are sometimes used interchangeably, they are not the same. **Job enlargement** is a simple expansion of a worker's assignments to include additional, but similar, tasks. Rather than performing two tasks, a worker might be given four similar tasks. Enlarging a job might lead to job enrichment, but this is not necessarily so. Job enrichment occurs only when the added tasks increase the worker's feelings of accomplishment and responsibility for the finished products and services. It is also likely to occur if the enlarged jobs enable workers to set their own pace within the constraints of the production schedule.

How Jobs Can Be Enriched

A number of companies are using job enrichment with excellent results. Two Swedish automobile manufacturers, Volvo and Saab, began a program of job enrichment more than two decades ago. Rather than station each worker on an assembly line to perform one task or a few monotonous operations on each car as it passed by, they have parts brought to the cars and installed by semiautonomous groups of workers. Today, at General Motors' Pontiac plant, a worker can stop the line when there is a problem. His or her work unit determines the problem and repairs it before starting again. At Nissan's Tennessee auto and truck assembly plant, the assembly line stops at lunch and at the morning and afternoon rest breaks for all employees.

An important application of job enrichment occurred at the Anderson, Clayton, & Co. manufacturing facility in Topeka, Kansas. The plant, built to process and package Gaines dog food products, was designed with job enrichment in mind. Workers are free to schedule their own hours for starting and stopping work. Production is built around three teams: one processes products, one packages and ships them, and one handles supporting office services. The members rotate jobs within their team. A worker on the packaging and shipping team may operate the forklift truck one day and bag Gravy Train the next. Undesirable jobs must be rotated so each worker does them periodically. Executive parking spaces do not exist. Team members screen job applicants, make employment decisions, and draw up work rules. Because team members are expected to perform numerous functions normally expected of managers, a strong need for training exists. For instance, those team members making personnel decisions must know federal, state, and local regulations concerning hiring practices. Top management at the Topeka facility recognizes the need to provide continual training and to maintain communications systems to keep up the enthusiasm workers bring to their jobs.

Is Job Enrichment for Everyone?

Like MBO programs, attempts at job enrichment have not always been successful. In an early experiment, AT&T introduced job enrichment programs in 19 areas. Management reported that nine of the programs were outstandingly suc-

Job enrichment is one way Tektronix improved productivity in manufacturing electronic measurement, design, display, and control instruments and systems. The inkjet printer assembly group shown here designed its own work area and employees cross-trained on all jobs. The group cut its inventory by two-thirds in two years, reduced its failure rate to 1.3 percent from 8 percent, and set a company record for six months in a row without a single product failure. Management recognized these employees' achievements by featuring them on the front cover of a recent annual report.

cessful, one was a complete flop, and the remaining nine were moderately successful. A series of interviews with assembly-line workers in an "unenriched" television plant revealed they did not view their jobs as either frustrating or dissatisfying. Some studies even discovered some workers prefer routine jobs because such jobs give them more time to daydream or talk with their fellow employees without affecting their productivity.

Flexible Work Schedules

At Transamerica Occidental Life Insurance Company in Los Angeles, employees may report to work as early as 7 a.m. or as late as 9 a.m., instead of the conventional 8 a.m. starting time. They may leave any time after 3:15 p.m. Except for their lunch break, workers are expected to be on the job between 9 a.m. and 3:15 p.m.

This flexible work-scheduling plan in which employees set their own arrival and departure times within specified limits is called **flextime**. An estimated 40 percent of the work force in Switzerland and 25 percent in West Germany use flextime.

The use of flexible workday schedules in U.S. companies has doubled in the last ten years. Currently, about one employee in six works on a flextime sched-

flextime
Work-scheduling system that allows employees to set work hours within constraints specified by the firm.

Figure 10.5   Use of Flextime Working Schedules

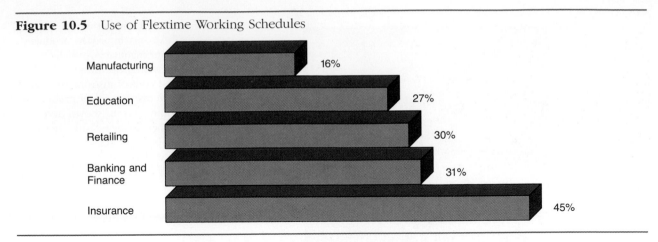

Source: 1987 *Administrative Management Society* survey data reported in Julie Stacey, "Flexible Schedules Catch On," *USA Today*, June 10, 1987, p. B1.

ule. Although the insurance, finance, and retailing industries and the federal government use flextime more than manufacturing companies, all major industry groups are at least experimenting with flexible working hours. Figure 10.5 identifies the industries where flextime is most common.

Core Hours and Fringe Hours

Most organizations designate certain core hours, such as 9:30 a.m. to 3:30 p.m., when employees are required to be on the job. Workers can adjust their schedule to suit themselves by working additional hours during fringe periods before and after the core hours. Meetings are typically scheduled during core hours when all employees are available.

Faced with a national shortage of nurses, hospitals have begun to use highly flexible work schedules to attract qualified nurses. About 90 percent of the 200 nurses at Children's Hospital in Stanford, California, work anything but a 40-hour week. The can set their own schedules, working 16 to 40 hours weekly. One even works nine months a year at the hospital, then spends three months as a cruise-ship nurse.[25]

Strengths and Weaknesses of the Flextime Concept

Proponents of flextime cite its numerous merits. Prime Computer Corporation hails flexible scheduling because it "treats people as adults." With flextime, declares Wells Fargo Bank, "productivity increases and tardiness goes down." Pharmaceutical giant SmithKline Beckman acclaims its 14-year-old program as "a big success," especially during the summer, when most headquarters' workers elect to leave at 3 p.m.[26] Bill Blatt, a labor management specialist with the National Center on Productivity, sums up its strengths: "Flextime gives people much more freedom to organize their lives, reduces pressure on transportation systems, and improves productivity. It just makes good sense. It would be my recommendation that more companies should try this."[27]

Flexible work schedules have limited applicability in continuous-production operations and in assembly-line settings where worker presence at prescribed times is essential. In addition, flexible schedules may result in increased energy use and problems when key people are not available at crucial times.

Other Forms of Flexible Work Schedules

Three additional work-scheduling practices are compressed workweeks, job sharing, and working at home. A **compressed workweek** is one in which employees work the same number of hours in fewer than the typical five days. For example, the 95 production employees at Olin Ski Company are among the 3.3 percent of all full-time employees who work a four-day, 40-hour week. The 1,600 employees at Ball Corporation's five U.S. metal-container plants are on a "4-3" schedule (4 days on and 3 days off, followed by 3 days on and 4 days off). Each shift runs 12 hours, making it possible to schedule the plant for nonstop operation.[28] For noncontinuous production facilities, compressed workweeks often result in energy savings for the firm and added time for personal pursuits by employees.

Job sharing is the division of a single job assignment among two or more persons. This approach, which basically involves the regular use of part-time employees, is relatively rare in industrial settings. According to a recent survey by the American Society for Personnel Administration, formal job-sharing programs are offered by only 16 percent of U.S. companies, from large traditional corporations such as Quaker Oats to progressive firms like Levi Strauss. It is most frequently used in clerical and retailing positions. Cindy Keech, a receptionist at Steelcase Inc., splits her time with another worker. Cindy earns half-pay working every other week at the office-furniture company's Grand Rapids, Michigan, headquarters. Before she leaves the office on Fridays, she writes a detailed note briefing her partner.[29]

While job sharing and compressed workweeks improve the quality of work life for some employees by allowing them to strike a balance between work and family or other interests, the result in not likely to be universal. Although some employees may experience increased productivity by working 10-hour days, others may experience fatigue. Still others may be prompted to "moonlight" with a second job. Persons considering job sharing may worry that such a request may communicate a lack of commitment to the firm and cause them to lose their place on the fast track.

Even though an estimated 24 million people do some of their work at home, working at home full time is relatively rare for salaried employees. **Telecommuting** — working at home on a terminal hooked to a central computer — would seem to be a likely work style of the future, given increased access to personal computers, facsimile machines, overnight mail service, and telecommunications advances. However, just one major U.S. company — Pacific Telesis Group's Pacific Bell unit — has a large-scale formal program allowing salaried employees to telecommute full time. Other companies, such as Hartford Insurance Group, tried it on a smaller scale, only to reject it after managers complained they couldn't supervise — much less get to know — employees they couldn't see. In addition, computer-to-computer transmission via telephone lines is slow and isn't always reliable.[30] Telecommuting seems to work best for self-employed executives and for free-lance workers. The latter group is huge, representing about 25 percent of the U.S. labor force.[31]

The accomplishments of formal QWL programs in a growing number of industries and firms of varying size are indications of the merits of such pro-

compressed workweek
Scheduling work so workers spend fewer days on the job, but work approximately the same number of hours.

job sharing
Division of one job assignment between two or more employees.

telecommuting
Working at home on a terminal hooked to a central computer.

grams. Even though some QWL programs are not equally applicable in every industry, the numbers of such programs will undoubtedly grow during the final decade of the twentieth century. More and more managers are recognizing that QWL programs allow integration of individual and organizational goals.

Summary of Learning Goals

1.   Trace the development of the human relations movement in the United States.   The scientific management writers and researchers of the late 1800s and early 1900s studied individual workers and groups in an attempt to increase their productivity. Jobs were divided into minute tasks to determine the most efficient means of performing them, and motivation took the form of incentive wages for meeting and exceeding quotas. The birth of the human relations movement and the emphasis on employee motivation began with the Hawthorne studies of the 1920s, which revealed that employee attitudes and interpersonal relations are important sources of motivation. In recent years, technological advances have freed workers from the boredom resulting from specialization. Various programs aimed at improving the quality of work life are being implemented by a growing number of organizations.

2.   Identify the different needs in Maslow's hierarchy.   Psychologist Abraham Maslow proposed a hierarchy of needs consisting of physiological needs (food, shelter, clothing), safety needs, social (belongingness) needs, esteem needs, and self-actualization needs. Maslow pointed out that satisfied needs are not motivators.

3.   Distinguish between Theory X and Theory Y managers.   The traditional Theory X manager views workers as being lazy, disliking work, and requiring close and constant supervision. Theory Y assumes employees want to satisfy social, esteem and self-actualization needs through work as well as through other activities. Theory Y managers emphasize employee self-control and self-direction.

4.   Contrast the Theory Z organization with the typical U.S. firm.   The typical U.S. firm is characterized by individual responsibility and decision making, specialized career paths, short-term employment, and rapid evaluation and promotion. By contrast, a Theory Z organization is more likely to include long-term employment, shared decision making, relatively slow promotions and evaluations, and varied and nonspecialized job assignments. The Theory Z approach emphasizes involved workers as the key to increased productivity and improved quality of work life.

5.   Describe and differentiate a job's motivational factors and maintenance factors.   Certain job-related factors, such as salary, working conditions, and job security, have been called maintenance factors. Although they do not serve as strong motivators, they must be present to prevent worker dissatisfaction. The key to employee motivation and positive morale appears to lie in such factors as the work itself and the potential for achievement, recognition, responsibility, advancement, and growth.

FRIEDRICH PULVER
FRIEDBERGER LANDSTRASSE 300
6000 FRANKFURT AM MAIN 60
069/5971877   TAG UND NACHT

ERICAN EXPRESS
L: 3724 147804 6100 3

K R E D I T V E R K A U F

UPER PLUS.   *
07 36,42 l DM   52,77 *
BENSMITTEL   3,60
SAMT   DM   56,37

ST   14,00%   6,48
ST   07,00%   0,24

TERSCHRIFT: ....

79 5149 23/04/92   1(
   AUF WIEDERSEHEN UND
     GUTE FAHRT

6.   Outline the steps involved in a management by objectives (MBO) program.   Management by objectives allows employees to know exactly what is expected of them and on what basis they will be evaluated. The sequence in an MBO program is:

a.   Each subordinate discusses the job description with the manager.
b.   Short-term performance goals are established.
c.   Subordinate and manager meet regularly to discuss progress toward goals.
d.   Intermediate checkpoints are established to measure progress toward goals.
e.   Subordinate and manager meet at end of predetermined period to evaluate results of the subordinate's efforts.

7.   Explain the "quality of work life" concept and identify the major categories of QWL programs.   Quality of work life is a concept that gives all employees some say about their particular job design and the general work environment. It involves management's acceptance of its employees as unique, adult individuals who should be encouraged to make meaningful inputs into the operation of the organization. The major categories of contemporary QWL programs are restructuring work to provide job enrichment, flexible work schedules, and Theory Z participative management.

8.   Differentiate job enrichment and job enlargement.   Job enrichment involves redesigning the work itself to give workers more authority to plan their activities, to decide how the work is to be accomplished, and to learn related skills or trade jobs with others. Job enlargement does not necessarily result in job enrichment.

9.   Identify the alternative forms of flexible work schedules.   Four forms of flexible work schedules are (1) flextime, a work-scheduling plan in which employees set their own work times within specified limits; (2) compressed workweeks, allowing the employee to work the same number of hours in less than the typical five-day workweek; (3) job sharing, which divides a single job assignment among two or more employees; and (4) telecommuting, where people work at home and are linked to their employers by terminals hooked to a central computer.

Key Terms

human relations	esteem needs	management by objectives (MBO)
scientific management	self-actualization needs	quality of work life (QWL)
Hawthorne studies	Theory X	job enrichment
Hawthorne effect	Theory Y	job enlargement
need	Theory Z	flextime
motive	maintenance factors	compressed workweek
physiological needs	motivational factors	job sharing
safety needs	morale	telecommuting
social (belongingness) needs		

Review Questions _____

1. Contrast the scientific management movement with the human relations movement. How did the Hawthorne studies revolutionize management's approach to employee motivation?

2. What are the three basic assumptions behind Maslow's hierarchy of human needs?

3. Based upon Maslow's hierarchy of human needs, which needs are being referred to in the following statement?
   a. "The new General Motors labor agreement will guarantee the jobs of at least 80 percent of all GM workers through 1995."
   b. "This is an entry-level job here at Marx Clothiers, and we pay minimum wage for the first six months."
   c. "We have just organized a company basketball team. Why don't you try out Thursday afternoon after work?"
   d. "Judy won our Employee of the Month award this month due to her exceptional performance."
   e. "We pay a 20 percent bonus for employees who work the midnight shift."

4. What does Frederick Herzberg mean by *dissatisfiers*? How do they relate to Maslow's hierarchy of human needs?

5. Write brief job scenarios of three people employed in an organization implementing Theory X, Theory Y, and Theory Z management. Relate each of these employees to Maslow's needs hierarchy and list factors that might be used by managers in motivating each employee.

6. Identify and give an example of each of the three Rs of employee motivation.

7. Contrast management and employee rankings of factors contributing to high morale. Relate your conclusions to Herzberg's research findings.

8. Identify the major strengths and weaknesses in the use of compressed work-weeks, job sharing, and telecommuting in the typical organization.

9. Identify several methods of work structuring that should result in job enrichment. Can you think of situations where job enrichment programs would not be effective? List them and explain your reasoning.

10. What are the strengths of the flextime schedule? What are its major limitations? How do you account for the high percentage of employees using flextime in European countries, as compared with the United States?

Discussion Questions _____

1. Relate the process of motivation shown in Figure 10.2 to the following situation. Make any assumptions necessary.

   Gordon Chenowits narrowly escaped injury yesterday when a 20-pound crate fell across his left foot. Gordon's supervisor reminded him of the requirement that all warehouse employees wear steel-toed safety shoes and warned him that he could lose his job if he were injured without wearing required safety clothing. On his way home from work, Gordon stopped at a store and purchased a pair of safety shoes.

2. Consider your most recent (or current) job supervisor. Would you describe this person as a Theory X or Theory Y manager? Why do you think your boss has adopted this management approach?

3. Outline the five steps in an MBO program. Use these steps to design an MBO program for the successful completion of a course you are now taking.

4. A survey of 2,010 workers performing 23 different jobs conducted by the Institute of Social Research of the University of Michigan gave the following "Most Boring" awards: assembly-line worker, forklift-truck driver, machine tender, and monitor of continuous flow goods. By contrast, these jobs were ranked at the bottom of the boredom scale: physician, professor, air traffic controller, and police officer. Identify some common characteristics of each group of jobs that appear to explain their rankings.

5. In a *Business Horizons* article, J. Clayton Lafferty, president of Human Synergistics, made the following statement: When a three-engine Boeing 727 flying at 40,000 feet loses all three engines at once (under normal circumstances the plane could glide for over 130 miles), the captain has ample time for quickly consulting with his copilot and flight engineer to get their ideas about the cause and remedy and to discuss emergency procedures with the flight attendants. However, if a similar power loss occurred at 500 feet during a takeoff climb, the captain would be ill-advised to practice such participative techniques.

   Relate this statement to the Theory Z approach to management and point out the perceived strengths and possible problems with this approach.

Video Case

Patagonia

Yvon Chouinard is one of those fortunate entrepreneurs who have built businesses around what they like to do. The youngest of four children, Chouinard lived in the French-speaking town of Lisbon, Maine, until he was 8, when his father moved the family to Burbank, California. A rock-climbing enthusiast, Chouinard is founder and chairman of Ventura, California–based Lost Arrow Corp., a firm best known for its rugged and colorful Patagonia line of outdoor gear. He has created a truly people-oriented company and, in the process, has remained true to his own guiding set of business goals: (1) make money, (2) give money away, (3) be creative, (4) have pride, (5) eliminate hassles, and (6) have fun.

But it did not all start that way. Chouinard's company traces its origins to one of his own mountain-climbing needs: He had been unable to buy an adequate molly, the spikes used in scaling cliffs. Consequently, he designed his own version made from chromium and, once he discovered that demand existed for the product, he found himself in the mountaineering hardware business from 1957 until 1970. In the early years, he distributed his climbing gear through retail stores such as those owned by his friend — and fellow climber — Doug Tompkins of Esprit de Corps (see video case for Chapter 5). But climbing equipment represents a tiny market and total sales amounted to only about $300,000 a year. When he first started out, Chouinard picked up extra money by working as a private detective for Howard Hughes. Then, in 1974, fate intervened on a trip to Scotland where he purchased a supply of rugby shirts and decided to expand his business to sport clothing. The clothing was of the highest quality, covering activities such as climbing, skiing, sailing, flyfishing, and kayaking. Within a year, sales had more than tripled to $1 million.

Chouinard discovered that it was easy to make money by offering high-quality products to exclusive,

but avid, customers. What became more difficult was controlling the growth of the company.

The $800 invested in Chouinard Equipment back in 1957 grew into today's Patagonia, Inc. (named after an area on the southern tip of South America). Its mail-order catalog has made the company famous. Often called the best such catalog in the United States, it features a personal, familiar tone, little anecdotes and essays that are often unrelated to the products the catalog features, real-life photographs, and a lavish, *Life* magazine-size format. About 60 percent of the firm's annual revenue comes from sales to 650 retail accounts (including such retailers as EMS, L. L. Bean, and REI). Another 20 percent is generated from mail-order sales, with the remainder coming from the equipment business and the firm's retail stores in both the U.S. and France. All of these divisions are part of the parent company, Lost Arrow Corp.

Of course, all this operational growth has been supported by increases in human resources. Over 400 people are employed in the various departments of the company, and each one was hired with one question in mind: "Would I want to have dinner with this person?" There is a strong commitment to the company's culture that is entrenched not only in the workforce but also in the customer base.

Talking with some of Patagonia's employees reveals a lack of concern for many of the standard aspects of business. Such worldly matters as sales, earnings, and inventory seem unimportant to workers, who appear concerned only with producing the highest-quality product they can. It is important that employees fit into this strong, decidedly outdoorsy, corporate culture. At the spacious company headquarters, employees do not wear ties or suits; many, in fact, wear Patagonia clothes. Most are in their mid-thirties, are health conscious, stay in good shape, eat lots of yogurt and granola, and are exercise-oriented. During the day, employees can often be found outside, roller skating around the office compound or getting into their cars for the two-minute drive to the ocean.

Chouinard has a long-term attitude toward his company and its employees: He wants them to stay and tries to ensure that they do. Part of achieving that goal is involvement. "We try to get the most intelligent people we can. . . . But in the end, you really end up

Notes: Fleming Meeks, "The Man Is the Message," *Forbes,* April 17, 1988, pp. 148–152; Gary Strauss, "Patagonia's Rugged Wear Leads the Pack," *USA Today,* January 11, 1989, pp. B1, B2; Paul Brown, "The Anti-Marketers," *Inc.,* March 1988, pp. 62–72; and personal correspondence, February 27, 1989.

with fairly average people," Chouinard explains. "The secret is to try to get average people to do above-average work." He believes this is accomplished by giving each employee a sense of responsibility, letting him or her see the direct result of the work done and the effect it has on the whole organization.

Among the many benefits offered to employees is the excellent on-premise child-care facility, Great Pacific Child Development Center, which further emphasizes Patagonia's family-like concerns. The firm recognizes that in dealing with employees' parental responsibilities, child care is everyone's concern. The Center helps integrate children and their parents' workplace into an everyday environment, relieving anxiety and frustration in both children and adults. Work satisfaction and productivity also increases. The benefit is total and mutual. Each staff member at the Center meets or exceeds all qualifications required by the State of California. The child-adult ratio allows individualized care and enhances the learning environment for the children. The child development center is one of only 150 such company-sponsored child care facilities in the U.S.

Patagonia also provides excellent cafeteria facilities for its employees, specializing in healthful and nutritious foods. Rather than going out to lunch and taking an hour and a half, employees eat in the cafeteria. They can actually conduct business there or take food back to their offices, thus remaining more productive throughout the day.

Keeping employees satisfied is important, but so is keeping customers happy, and at Patagonia this means keeping everyone involved. The customer relations established by Patagonia are unique in today's typical business world and envied by others. Says one company official for L. L. Bean, "Their customers are different." In addition to ordering at twice the rate of a typical L. L. Bean customer, these purchasers write to Patagonia. They even send pictures — about 25,000 a year. And how does Patagonia respond to its customers' communications? From about 1,000 new product suggestions received in 1987, approximately 60 percent were used, and their stories and pictures were included in Patagonia's biannual catalogs. The catalog is at the heart of Patagonia's corporate culture. While employees talk of quality, utility, and performance throughout the text and in charts and diagrams inside

the catalog, there are also essays ment with words and pictures that b or rushing white-water rapids to the f minds of readers. The Patagonia catalog is fo devoted sports enthusiasts.

But Patagonia does not stop with achievements personnel benefits and customer relations — it is a company committed to keeping the environment in its natural state for future generations. It far exceeds its corporate responsibilities in this area by donating 10 percent of its net profit to worthy charitable causes. Patagonia also donates clothing and equipment to scientists, athletes, and astronauts, as well as native American orphanages and needy families throughout the U.S. and Central America. Some of the more than 150 non-profit organizations supported by Patagonia include Greenpeace, Audubon, and the Cousteau Society. Marketing benefits also result from this corporate generosity. "You give a few thousand dollars to a group with 50 volunteers," says Chouinard, "and you create 50 customers."

As a growing corporation (since 1981, Lost Arrow sales have increased from $5 million to $76 million in 1989), Patagonia is likely to be used as an example of the new face of contemporary business: a company concerned with its employees, its customers, other people and families, and the environment of the world in which we all live.

Questions

1. Relate the work environment at Patagonia to Maslow's hierarchy of needs described in Figure 10.3. How is it related to Herzberg's concept of maintenance factors and motivational factors?

2. Patagonia is characterized as a firm blessed by high employee morale. Refer to Table 10.2 and then suggest which factors are present in the firm that contribute to high morale.

3. Three major categories of quality of work life (QWL) programs are described in the chapter. Identify each and explain how they are present in the Patagonia culture (or how they could be included).

4. What types of employees might not do well at a company like Patagonia?

5. If replacing employees is so costly for companies, why don't more firms use similar human resource practices to retain their workers? Explain your answer.

Human Resource Management

Learning Goals

1. To explain the functions of a specialized human resource department and the continuing responsibilities of all departments for the effective use of human resources.

2. To describe the concept of human resource planning and to outline the major steps involved in the process.

3. To explain how each step in the recruitment and selection process contributes to finding the right person for the job.

4. To identify the categories of employees covered by equal employment opportunity laws and to discuss the major laws affecting human resource decisions in this area.

5. To describe the different methods of training operative employees and present and potential managers.

6. To relate performance appraisal to effective human resource management.

7. To outline the different forms of compensation and to explain when each form should be used.

8. To enumerate the different types of employee benefits and the likely changes in future employee benefit programs.

9. To explain the role of OSHA in protecting employee health and safety.

In company after company, the key word today is *competitiveness.* In the worldwide battle for sales and profits, progressive firms — large and small — know the value of highly-trained, highly motivated personnel in producing a successful operation. For the employer, compensation is both a cost of doing business and a tool that holds the promise of generating productivity gains. This explains the growing popularity of hundreds of *pay for performance* incentive compensation programs installed over the past five years. The linkage of pay to output, sales, or profits not only has the possibility of inducing workers to produce more, but it also holds down wages and wage-related benefits as a percentage of sales or profits. Yet, probably half of all incentive plans simply don't work, victims of poor design and administration.

Managers seeking the right way to create an incentive pay system that will produce spectacular productivity gains are likely to travel to Lincoln Electric in Cleveland, the holy shrine of incentive pay. This 95-year-old manufacturer of welding machines and motors is a relatively small component of its industry, yet it attracts 800 visitors a year from giant firms such as Motorola, TRW, 3M, Ford, and McDonnell Douglas. Both company and union leaders make the trek to Cleveland to learn how a medium-size company can be so successful in such a cyclical industry without paying its employees a base salary. Lincoln Electric's 42-year-old no-layoff policy is gratifying, they reason, but the company's 1,800 nonunion employees have to eat.

Lincoln Electric is strictly a no-frills firm. There are no paid holidays, no sick days, no dental insurance, and the employees work in a facility with neither windows nor air-conditioning. (They do get paid vacations.) Their earnings are based on their individual output and on

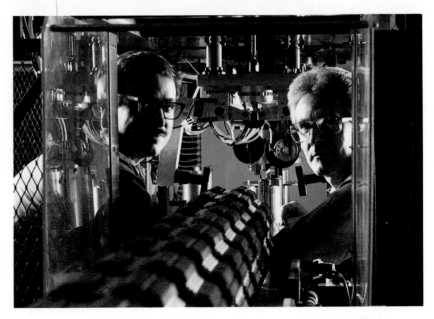

bonuses from the company's profits. (A few professional people, such as engineers, are on salary, but except for the chairman, vice chairman, and president, they all participate in the bonus plan.)

Rewards are made on a piecework basis: For each acceptable piece produced, the worker receives so many dollars. Unacceptable output must be corrected on the employee's own time, quickly adding a concern for quality to the equation. In addition, each employee is evaluated every six months in four distinct areas: output, quality, dependability, and idea generation and cooperation. These evaluations serve as the basis for a year-end discretionary bonus that has averaged 90 percent of total pay.

The underlying objective of this approach to employee motivation and compensation is to give non-management employees direct and powerful incentives to manage their work as efficiently as possible and to be on the lookout for opportunities to do more. These potential rewards, combined with job security, have worked well for both the

employees and the firm. Hard workers, who don't mind overtime, have been known to earn more than $80,000 in a single year.

Turnover rates are high — about 25 percent — during the first few months as new employees are exposed to hard work and see employees competing with their peers for bonus money. After that, they become attached to the pay-for-performance philosophy. Donald F. Hastings, company president, sums up their attitudes: "An employee has to *want* to be in a system like this."

The payoff is equally attractive to the corporation. Lincoln Electric has now gone 54 years without a losing quarter, 40 years with no layoffs, and has a work force that is up to three times more productive than their counterparts — American or Japanese — in similar manufacturing settings.[1]

Photo source: Courtesy of The Lincoln Electric Co.

Chapter Overview

The emphasis of this chapter is on people — the human element — and their importance in accomplishing an organization's goals. The acquisition, training, motivation, and retention of qualified personnel is a critical factor in determining the success or failure of a business firm or a nonprofit organization. As a consequence, most organizations devote considerable attention to the management of human resources.

human resource management
Process of acquiring, training, developing, motivating, and appraising a sufficient quantity of qualified employees to perform necessary activities; and developing activities and an organizational climate conducive to maximum efficiency and worker satisfaction.

Human resource management can be defined as the process of acquiring, training, developing, motivating, and appraising a sufficient quantity of qualified employees to perform the activities necessary to accomplish organizational objectives; and developing specific activities and an overall organizational climate to generate maximum worker satisfaction and employee efficiency. While the owner-manager of a small organization is likely to assume complete responsibility for human resource management, larger organizations use company specialists called *human resource managers* to perform these activities in a systematic manner. The position is becoming increasingly important because of increased competition, emphasis on cost control, complex wage and benefit programs, and a changing work force.[2] These human resource, or personnel, managers assume primary responsibility for forecasting personnel needs and recruiting and aiding in selecting new employees. They also assist in training and evaluation, and administer compensation, employee benefits, and safety programs.

This chapter analyzes the critical process of human resources management. It examines the steps of the employee selection process and techniques used to ensure recruitment of qualified individuals. The chapter also discusses employee training, development, and counseling; and promotions, transfers, and separations. Finally, employee compensation, benefits, and safety are analyzed.

Human Resource Management as an Emerging Managerial Function

A hundred years ago, companies hired workers by posting a notice outside the gate, stating that a certain number of workers would be hired the following day. The notice might have listed skills, such as welding or carpentry; or it might simply have listed the number of workers needed. The next morning people would appear at the front gate — a small number in prosperous times, large crowds in periods of unemployment — and the workers would be selected. The choices were often arbitrary; the company might hire the first four in line or the four people who looked the strongest or the healthiest. Workers operated under a precise set of strict rules. A whimsical example of one such list is shown in Figure 11.1.

Two Perspectives on Human Resource Management

Human resource management can be viewed in two ways. In a narrow sense, it refers to the functions and operations of a single department in a firm: the human resource or personnel department. Most firms with 200 or more em-

Figure 11.1   Rules for Clerks, 1890

1.   This store must be opened at sunrise. No mistake. Open at 6:00 a.m. summer and winter. Close about 8:30 or 9 p.m. the year round.

2.   Store must be swept and dusted, doors and windows opened, lamps filled and trimmed, chimneys cleaned, counters, base shelves, and showcases dusted, pens made, a pail of water and the coal must be brought in before breakfast, if there is time to do it and attend to all the customers who call.

3.   The store is not to be opened on the Sabbath day unless absolutely necessary and then only for a few minutes.

4.   Should the store be opened on Sunday the clerks must go in alone and get tobacco for customers in need.

5.   The clerk who is in the habit of smoking Spanish cigars, being shaved at the barber's, going to dancing parties and other places of amusement, and being out late at night will assuredly give his employer reason to be over suspicious of his integrity and honesty.

6.   Clerks are allowed to smoke in the store provided they do not wait on women while smoking a "stogie."

7.   Each store clerk must pay not less than $5.00 per year to the church and must attend Sunday school regularly.

8.   Men clerks are given one evening a week off for courting and two if they go to prayer meeting.

9.   After the 14 hours in the store, leisure hours should be spent mostly in reading.

Source: Delbert J. Duncan, Charles F. Phillips, and Stanley C. Hollander, *Modern Retailing Management* (Homewood, IL: Richard D. Irwin, 1972).

ployees establish a separate department with the responsibility and authority for selecting and training personnel.

In a broader sense, human resource management involves the entire organization. Even though a special staff department exists, general management is also involved in training and developing workers, evaluating their performance, and motivating them to perform as efficiently as possible.

The core responsibilities of human resource management are the following:

◆   Human resource planning

◆   Recruitment and selection

◆   Training/management development

◆   Performance appraisal

◆   Compensation and employee benefits.

Trained specialists from the human resource department are typically involved in carrying out each of these responsibilities. However, the responsibilities are typically shared with line managers, ranging from the company president (who is involved in overall planning) to first-line supervisors (who may be involved in preliminary interviews with applicants and in employee training). By accomplishing these critical tasks, the human resource management department achieves its overall objectives of (1) providing qualified, well-trained employees; (2) maximizing employee effectiveness in the organization; and (3) satisfying individual employee needs through monetary compensation, employee benefits, advancement opportunities, and job satisfaction.

Human Resource Planning

human resource planning
Developing a comprehensive strategy for meeting future human resource needs.

The formulation of organizational objectives results in clear guideposts for evaluating performance, but resources — human and other — are necessary for their achievement. **Human resource planning** is the development of a comprehensive strategy for meeting the organization's future human resource needs. It is the process by which management makes certain it has the right number of people with the appropriate skills in the right place at the necessary time.

Human resource planning involves three steps. First, present human resources must be assessed. At this stage, management determines whether the present work force is appropriate for the firm's current needs and whether it is being used properly. Second, the **human resource forecast** of future personnel needs must be conducted. This forecast compares current employee skills and their projected skills at some future date with the expected organizational needs at that date. Finally, a program must be developed for meeting future human resource needs. The forecast serves as a blueprint for training current employees and recruiting new employees to meet organizational needs as they occur. Figure 11.2 identifies the steps involved in the development of the human resource planning sequence.

human resource forecast
Determining personnel needs in terms of numbers of individuals and their required skills.

Job Analysis, Job Description, and Job Specification

job analysis
Identification of job characteristics and requirements of personnel for that particular job.

Human resource planning cannot be accomplished without a clear picture of current and potential employees' skills and qualifications. Three techniques are useful in providing this information: job analysis, job description, and job specification.

Job analysis is the systematic, detailed study of a job; it identifies and examines the elements and characteristics of a job and the requirements of the person assigned to the job. From the job analysis, the human resource department develops a **job description**, a document specifying the objectives of a job, the work to be performed, the responsibilities involved, the skills needed, the relationship of the job to other jobs, and the working conditions. Next, the **job specification** — the written description of the special qualifications required of a worker who fills a particular job — is prepared. The specification lists experience, education, special skills, and other requirements. For example, the Delta Air Lines job specification for flight attendants lists such minimum qualifications

job description
Defines job objectives, work to be performed, responsibilities involved, skill requirements, working conditions, and the relationship of the job to other jobs.

job specification
Written description of the qualifications required for a particular job.

Figure 11.2   Steps in the Human Resource Planning Process

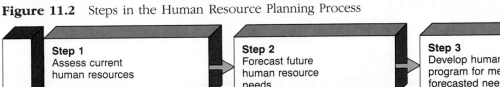

Step 1
Assess current
human resources

Step 2
Forecast future
human resource
needs

Step 3
Develop human resource
program for meeting
forecasted needs

Evaluate and Revise Periodically

as at least 20 years of age, two years of college, and good vision that must be correctable to 20/20.

As Figure 11.3 illustrates, the job specification is typically included as a section of the job description. This type of document is invaluable to human resource departments seeking qualified applicants for job openings. For example, a Windsurfer Inc. recruiter hiring an associate programmer for the position described in Figure 11.3 must ensure that the applicant has a bachelor's degree related to computer science or equivalent experience and several skills and abilities essential to job performance. The document also lists qualifications that are desirable but not essential at the time of employment. They may be used by the recruiter or the department manager in evaluating a large number of applicants and selecting a few finalists. First used in factory jobs, detailed job descriptions are common today in retail stores, offices, banks, and almost all large organizations.

Employee Recruitment and Selection

The human resource manager plays an important role in selecting employees. The recruitment and selection process results from human resource planning and is based on the philosophy, "Don't try to fit a square peg into a round hole!" Adding new employees is expensive, and recruitment costs alone are very high. Interviews and tests are often conducted before selecting new employees. Medical examinations (at company expense) are often required for applicants. Training new people is also costly, and an inefficient worker wastes money. An employee who doesn't make the grade and leaves the firm after a few months can cost a company up to $75,000 in lost productivity, money spent on training, and employee morale. A poor employee who stays with the company can cost even more.[3] The human resource manager must ensure that potential employees have the necessary qualifications for the job and that they either possess future skill needs or are capable of learning them. Figure 11.4 shows the steps in the recruitment and selection process.

Recruitment

After the job description and job specification are prepared, the next step in the selection process is the recruitment of qualified employees. Human resource departments use both internal and external sources to find candidates for specific jobs.

Figure 11.3   Sample Job Description

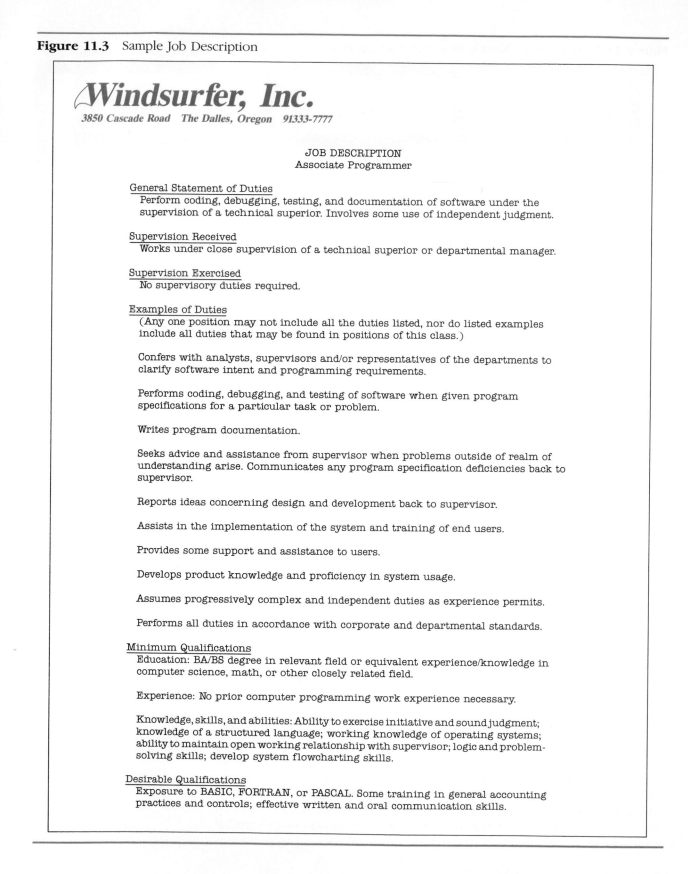

Windsurfer, Inc.
3850 Cascade Road   The Dalles, Oregon   91333-7777

JOB DESCRIPTION
Associate Programmer

General Statement of Duties
Perform coding, debugging, testing, and documentation of software under the supervision of a technical superior. Involves some use of independent judgment.

Supervision Received
Works under close supervision of a technical superior or departmental manager.

Supervision Exercised
No supervisory duties required.

Examples of Duties
(Any one position may not include all the duties listed, nor do listed examples include all duties that may be found in positions of this class.)

Confers with analysts, supervisors and/or representatives of the departments to clarify software intent and programming requirements.

Performs coding, debugging, and testing of software when given program specifications for a particular task or problem.

Writes program documentation.

Seeks advice and assistance from supervisor when problems outside of realm of understanding arise. Communicates any program specification deficiencies back to supervisor.

Reports ideas concerning design and development back to supervisor.

Assists in the implementation of the system and training of end users.

Provides some support and assistance to users.

Develops product knowledge and proficiency in system usage.

Assumes progressively complex and independent duties as experience permits.

Performs all duties in accordance with corporate and departmental standards.

Minimum Qualifications
Education: BA/BS degree in relevant field or equivalent experience/knowledge in computer science, math, or other closely related field.

Experience: No prior computer programming work experience necessary.

Knowledge, skills, and abilities: Ability to exercise initiative and sound judgment; knowledge of a structured language; working knowledge of operating systems; ability to maintain open working relationship with supervisor; logic and problem-solving skills; develop system flowcharting skills.

Desirable Qualifications
Exposure to BASIC, FORTRAN, or PASCAL. Some training in general accounting practices and controls; effective written and oral communication skills.

Figure 11.4 Steps in the Recruitment and Selection Process

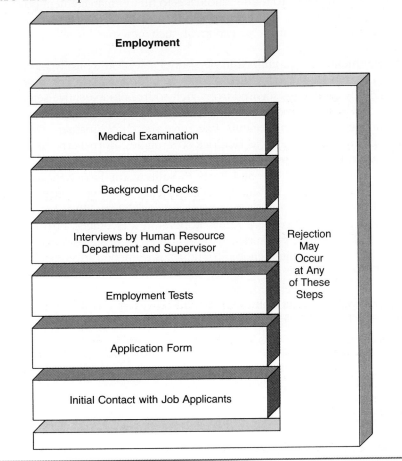

Most firms have a policy of **hiring from within** — that is, considering their own employees first for job openings. Since the human resource department maintains a file describing the special skills and other qualifications of all employees, its records can be quickly screened to determine whether any employees are qualified for a job opening.

The use of current employees to fill job vacancies is a relatively inexpensive method of recruitment that also contributes to employee morale. The railroad industry has long been known for its policy of filling job vacancies with existing workers whenever possible. As one railroad personnel manager summarized this policy, "When a president retires or dies, we hire a new office boy."

All firms must utilize external sources to some extent in filling vacancies or in adding new employees for newly created jobs. A company may not have qualified employees to fill a certain position, or better qualified people may be available from outside the firm. Sources for potential job applicants outside the company include colleges, advertisements in newspapers and professional journals, public employment agencies (such as state employment services), private employment agencies, vocational schools, labor unions, unsolicited applications, and recommendations by current employees. Baxter International em-

hiring from within
Organizational policy of first considering its own employees to fill job vacancies.

ployees recommending job candidates who are eventually hired receive cash awards of $350 to $500. To locate candidates to fill top management positions, a firm may use specialized executive recruiting agencies or advertise in *The Wall Street Journal* or the business section of such newspapers as the *New York Times.*

Recruitment sources utilized in personnel selection typically vary depending upon the type of job to be filled. Middle- and top-management vacancies are often filled by candidates secured from such sources as executive search firms, colleges and universities, former managerial employees, professional associations, and business advertisements. Executive search companies, the so-called corporate *headhunters,* such as Heidrick & Struggles, Korn/Ferry, and Spencer Stuart were responsible for finding such CEOs as Harold E. Geneen for ITT, John Sculley for Apple Computer, and Barry F. Sullivan for First National Bank of Chicago. In 1989, Spencer Stuart President Thomas J. Neff received a half-million-dollar fee for his efforts in locating a new CEO for RJR Nabisco after the firm was acquired by Kohlberg Kravis Roberts in a leveraged buyout.[4]

Relatively unskilled workers may be recruited from such sources as public employment agencies, high schools, friends of present employees, and walk-ins. Unions, vocational/technical institutes, recommendations from present employees, and newspaper advertisements may be used in recruiting craftworkers and employees with technical skills. Clerical and other white-collar employees may be recruited from such sources as private employment agencies and temporary help agencies, present employees, friends of present employees, newspaper advertisements, walk-ins, and educational institutes such as high schools and vocational/technical institutes. Community agencies are effective sources for locating and recruiting handicapped workers.

Selection

Once job applicants are located, the next step is screening them to determine which candidate is best suited for the job. First, candidates complete an application form that is used to determine whether they meet the general qualifications for the position. The form requests information such as name, address, type of work desired, education, experience, and personal references.

Federal law prohibits job application forms from including direct or indirect questions that could be construed as discriminatory. However, a recent survey of job applications used by Ohio employers revealed that 73 percent of them contained at least one illegal question. Illegal questions include those having to do with the applicant's ancestry, age, racial or ethnic background, religious affiliation, marital status, children, or sex. Although some of these questions may not be specifically unlawful by statue, they may provide evidence of an intention to discriminate unless the employer can prove that they are a legitimate occupational qualification. Employers should ask applicants for only that information directly related to their ability to perform the job.[5]

The major federal and state laws aimed at prohibiting discrimination on the basis of race, color, sex, or national origin were examined in detail in Chapter 2. Table 11.1 summarizes these statutes. Enactment of similar legislation in more than 20 states broadened the impact of many of the original laws. For example, even though the Vocational Rehabilitation Act and the Vietnam Era Veterans Readjustment Assistance Act apply only to federal government contractors and subcontractors, over 50 percent of U.S. employers are required to comply with

Table 11.1 Ensuring Equal Opportunity

Law	Key Provisions
Title VII of the Civil Rights Act of 1964 (as amended by the Equal Employment Opportunity Act of 1972)	Prohibits discrimination in hiring, promotion, compensation, training, or dismissal on the basis of race, color, religion, sex, or national origin.
Age Discrimination in Employment Act of 1968 (as amended)	Prohibits discrimination in employment against anyone aged 40 or over in hiring, promotion, compensation, training, or dismissal.
Equal Pay Act of 1963	Requires equal pay for men and women who work at a firm and whose jobs require equal skill, effort, and responsibility.
Vocational Rehabilitation Act of 1973	Requires government contractors and subcontractors to take affirmative action to employ and promote qualified handicapped workers. Coverage now extends to all federal employees. In addition, coverage has been broadened by the passage of similar laws in over 20 states. The act has also been broadened through court rulings to include persons with communicable diseases, including AIDS.
Vietnam Era Veterans Readjustment Assistance Act of 1974	Requires government contractors and subcontractors to take affirmative action to employ and retain disabled veterans. Coverage now extends to all federal employees. In addition, coverage has been broadened by the passage of similar laws in over 20 states.
Pregnancy Discrimination Act of 1978	Requires employers to treat pregnant women and new mothers the same as other employees for all employment-related purposes, including receipt of benefits under company benefit programs.

the statutes as a result of the passage of similar laws at the state level. Every year the number of states enacting similar requirements grows.

Failure to follow these requirements will result in penalties and adverse publicity for wrongdoers. In 1989, Harris Trust and Savings Bank of Chicago agreed to pay a record $14 million to settle a sex and race bias case. Even though management refused to concede it discriminated, management did agree to revise the firm's affirmative action policies. The federal government charged that Harris discriminated by promoting white men at a significantly higher rate than women and minorities with comparable skills and paid the white men more for comparable work.[6]

Rejection of Unqualified Applicants Even though applicants may be eliminated from further consideration at any stage in the selection process, a large percentage are rejected at the first stage. Frequently, a comparison of a completed application form with the job description is enough to determine the applicant does not possess the qualifications needed for the position. A letter or telephone call from the company human resource department informs the applicant of this decision.

In most instances, the letter writer thanks the applicant for contacting the company and seeks to maintain a positive image of the firm for the rejected job-seeker. But a few letters fail miserably. The student body of an Arizona university assembled a collection of such letters. The following excerpts were extracted from these letters:

After most careful consideration of your qualifications and background, we are unable to identify anything you can do for us. . . .

Unfortunately, we have to be selective. . . .

We're certain you could be more useful some place else. . . .

. . . but we're sure you will find something you can do.

I am sorry, but because of the nature of our work, we have to be more careful than others in our hiring. . . .[7]

Employee Testing

Employee testing makes the selection process more efficient. Careful studies determine the tests to be used in measuring the aptitude and abilities required for each job. Some companies with testing programs also administer personality tests.

Testing serves two main purposes. It helps eliminate those applicants who are not suited for a particular job, and it helps predict which candidates are likely to be productive employees. At Toyota's auto assembly plant in Kentucky, teams of four applicants spend $4\frac{1}{2}$ hours in a simulation of the actual job environment. They are given a series of assignments aimed at determining each candidate's ability to solve problems, follow instructions, and work in a team. Over 90 percent of the applicants who pass the tests turn out to be well qualified for the job.[8]

Employee testing became controversial after a number of courts ruled that some intelligence tests are culturally biased and do not predict job success. Because the Civil Rights Act of 1964 prohibits the use of discriminatory tests in hiring workers, efforts are being made to evaluate the objectivity of tests currently being used and to design bias-free tests.

Banning Lie Detectors as Employee Screening Devices   During 1988, an estimated 2 million U.S. workers took polygraph tests. In many instances, a lie detector test was required of persons applying for work. In other cases, they were used by firms investigating the possibility of theft or other employee misconduct. The banking industry was a particularly heavy user. One survey of 160 large banks revealed that 78 percent used polygraph testing.

By 1989, the number of lie detector tests given annually had decreased by 80 percent as a result of a federal law banning their use in almost all pre-hiring decisions and in random testing of employees. Only federal, state, and county governments; firms doing sensitive work under contract to the Defense Department, FBI, and CIA; pharmaceutical companies handling controlled substances; and security guard services are exempt from the new law.

The use of polygraph tests, which Senator Edward Kennedy once labeled twentieth-century witchcraft, has been strongly criticized on two counts. First, the tests are widely recognized as inaccurate. Even the American Polygraph

Association concedes the tests are incorrect or inconclusive about 10 percent of the time, and some studies have come up with figures as high as 50 percent.

The second issue involves the potential of such devices to invade individual privacy. Over the years, a number of companies have been accused of asking extremely personal questions during exams. Striking brewery workers once complained that Coors polygraph examiners routinely asked questions about their sex life, drug use, and political beliefs. The new law requires that any polygraph examination be conducted under strict conditions, with no questions about personal beliefs and sexual behavior, and the exam results alone cannot be used as a basis for discipline or a refusal to hire.[9]

Interviewing

The job applicant's first formal contact with a company is usually an interview with a company representative. This face-to-face contact is another step in the screening of candidates for a job. Trained interviewers are able to obtain considerable insight into the prospective employee's goals, attitudes, and motivations.

The line manager for whom the prospective employee is to work may also interview the candidate at this stage. Because the line manager will make the ultimate hiring decision (or at least participate with the human resource department in making the decision), it is sound practice to involve that person in the screening process.

The typical interviewer begins with some small talk to size up the candidate, followed by previously prepared questions. First impressions are frequently crucial in the hiring decision. A recent survey revealed that 62 percent of interviewers make a hiring decision in the first 15 minutes of a job candidate's interview.[10] Most interviewers used a *structured interview* approach in which a prepared set of questions is asked. Frequently used questions include:

◆   Why should I hire you?

◆   What interests you most about this job?

◆   What kinds of decisions are most difficult for you?

◆   Why do you want to change jobs?

◆   What causes you to lose your temper?

◆   What are your greatest accomplishments?

Job applicants increase their chances of receiving an employment offer through careful preparations before the interview. Answers to anticipated questions should be prepared in advance, and applicants should learn as much about the company and the position as possible. As one experienced interviewer points out, "The glibbest person on earth, even the most skilled debator, cannot answer questions off the cuff without damaging his or her chances of success."[11]

The Smoking Issue   The interviewer can also secure information about the job applicant's smoking habits, either through personal observation at the interview or through questions raised. Less than one-third of the adult U.S. population currently smokes, and this group is being subjected to increasing social and legal pressures. Most of them will tell you they feel like outcasts at work and in many social settings and that others look at them as lacking self-discipline, weak, unproductive, and even less intelligent than nonsmokers.[12]

When these government office workers want to smoke, they must go to a designated smoking area. An increasing number of businesses, including large corporations such as General Motors, Heinz USA, and Texas Instruments, are creating smoke-free work environments by banning smoking. Employers say smokers are expensive: they cost money in sick leave, insurance premiums, legal liability, and building maintenance.

Photo source: Insight magazine/Jon A. Rembold.

Employers are concerned about the direct costs of smoking to their organization. One study reported it costs a firm over $4,600 more per year on average to employ a smoker over a nonsmoker. The increased costs result from the fact that smokers suffer substantially greater rates of absenteeism, disability, industrial accidents, and working-age mortality. In addition, smoke in a work area can cause damage to sensitive equipment and increase routine cleaning and maintenance costs.[13]

Over half of the managers surveyed in a recent study indicated they chose nonsmokers over smokers when faced with a choice between otherwise equally qualified applicants. Missouri's Wentzville Community Hospital is one of the 3 percent of all U.S. hospitals refusing to hire smokers. Chicago-based USG Corporation went even further, telling its 1,300 employees at nine plants that they either stop smoking or lose their jobs. This company ban applied both at home and on the job. Periodic lung tests are conducted to monitor employee health.[14]

Background Checks

Even though most job applicants are asked to furnish the names of references, securing written letters of reference is done less frequently now, in part because applicants select references most likely to make positive recommendations and also because references are reluctant to include candid evaluations in written correspondence. Consequently, verification of work histories and other relevant information is frequently conducted by telephone because of its speed and, possibly, greater accuracy than the use of letters.

Reference checks are effective means of verifying information, previous job responsibilities, and the reason an applicant left a former job. A survey of 501 executives revealed one recently hired employee in six had misrepresented job qualifications.[15] Five percent of the 773 doctors who applied to Humana Inc. for jobs in outpatient clinics lied about their medical credentials.[16] The most frequent misrepresentations on job applications involve college degrees earned and grades.

The Physical Examination

Most firms include a medical examination as part of the employee selection process for certain jobs. The examination determines whether the applicant is physically capable of performing the job; it also helps protect the company against future claims for disabilities that were already present at the time of employment and, therefore did not happen on the job. Moreover, the physicals often show what employees can and cannot do. For instance, after one physical turned up a weak back, doctors warned managers at J. V. Lowney & Associates, a Palo Alto, California-based environmental studies company, to keep the new employee from lifting heavy objects.

Preventive Plus, a medical group that does physical examinations for many smaller firms, charges $70 to $106 for most pre-employment physicals. The firm's medical director says, "Small companies find their liability insurance and benefits packages are getting so expensive that they are looking for any way to cut costs."[17] Not only are health insurance premiums increasing at the rate of 20 percent or more a year, but small concerns also have found that a single serious employee illness one year can make rates double the next year.

Drug Testing   The nationwide publicity resulting from a 1987 train wreck near Baltimore, involving a Conrail engineer and brakeman who smoked marijuana before a fatal collision with an Amtrak train, focused the eyes of the nation on the problem of drug use in the workplace. It also resulted in a Department of Transportation plan to require random tests of 4 million railroad, trucking, and airline workers.

Sixty-nine percent of all major U.S. companies, including IBM, Kodak, AT&T, Lockheed, 3M, and Westinghouse, require pre-employment physicals and drug screens for some or all job applicants. Over 55 percent of companies with fewer than 500 employees have similar requirements. Approximately 10 million drug tests will be administered to current and prospective employees this year as employers attempt to provide a safe, healthy, and productive environment for their workers and to minimize potential problems. Total business spending on drug testing in 1991 is estimated at $500 million.

Although substance abuse is found at every level in the organization and among all income groups, drug use is highest among men 18 to 35 years old without college degrees. Attorney Jerry Glassman, a partner in a New York City management-labor law firm, reports that a government agency in the Northeast, which he will not identify, recently gave drug tests to 1,000 applicants for security guards; 980 failed.[18] Primex Plastics management found that just requiring drug tests for all job applicants became a screening device. The 140-employee Garfield, New Jersey, company discovered that nearly half of all would-be employees disqualified themselves by failing to appear for their drug test appointments.[19]

Other employers oppose drug testing. Some are concerned with statistics from the U.S. Centers for Disease Control that indicate two-thirds of the positive test results from 13 randomly chosen private labs were false.[20] Others worry about invasion of individual privacy and the possibility of switching or tampering with urine samples. Still others are aware that the U.S. Navy, which performs more drug tests than any other American institution, has found only a low correlation between smoking marijuana, by far the most popular illicit drug, and job performance. At least seven states have passed laws restricting drug tests.

AIDS and the Employment Decision   In Anchorage, Alaska, an employee of a 20-person business carries the AIDS virus but has no symptoms. After learning of the worker's status, the company's health insurer raises premiums 400 percent. "That's $10,000 per month, and it means the business will go under within one quarter," says Morgan Christen, an attorney hired to fight the increase.[21]

An estimated 1.5 million Americans have the disease or carry the virus. Insurance companies state that treating a person with AIDS can total well over $100,000, and this cost was a major factor in the 40 percent average increase in premiums for small businesses in the Cleveland area during 1988. But the employer who decides to ignore ethical considerations in favor of controlling insurance costs is likely to encounter legal problems if he or she decides to disqualify an otherwise qualified job candidate who carries the AIDS virus or dismiss a current employee with AIDS.

Section 504 of the Vocational Rehabilitation Act of 1973 states:

No otherwise qualified individual with handicaps . . . shall, solely by reason of his handicap, be excluded from the participation in . . . or be subjected to discrimination under any program or activity receiving Federal financial assistance.

A number of recent court cases have resulted in rulings that persons with a contagious disease such as AIDS may be considered handicapped within the meaning of the act and, if so, may be employed or continue employment if otherwise qualified.[22] Since medical evidence has documented that AIDS is not transmitted by casual contact, employers covered by the Vocational Rehabilitation Act cannot discriminate against persons carrying the AIDS virus in hiring and other employment decisions. The intent of these rulings and others aimed at guaranteeing equal rights is to protect persons capable of doing their jobs from discrimination.

Employee Orientation

Once hired, the employee completes an orientation program, which is the joint responsibility of the human resource department and the department in which the employee will work. The human resource department provides the new worker with a copy of the employee manual, which discusses employee benefits and explains company policy on vacations, absenteeism, rest periods, lunch breaks, and so on. The supervisor is responsible for introducing the new employee to fellow workers, explaining the operations of the department, and detailing how the job fits into these operations.

A new employee in a large firm should be put at ease by the supervisor and shown that he or she is welcome. The feelings of loneliness and isolation that often accompany the first days on a new job may lead to frustration, negative attitudes, and poor job performance. The orientation program is designed to convey a sense of belonging and a feeling of personal worth. Although the human resource department provides information about company history, products, and benefits, the responsibility for developing a new employee's

Employees of First Colony Life Insurance Company and its general agencies learn about the life insurance business during three-day educational sessions. The orientation program is topped off by a graduation ceremony that gives employees a feeling of personal accomplishment and a sense of belonging.

Photo source: Courtesy Ethyl Corporation.

sense of importance and involvement is primarily that of the immediate supervisor and the other employees in the department.

Employee Training, Evaluation, and Counseling

A second major function of the human resource department is the development and maintenance of a well-trained, productive labor force. Employee training should be viewed as an ongoing process throughout an employee's tenure with the company. "A person entering the work force today can expect to be retrained five times in his work life," declares John Young, president of Hewlett-Packard Co. The computer giant spends about $250 million, or 5 percent of revenue, to train its 87,000 workers each year.[23]

Training is a major factor in Motorola's plan to achieve competitive superiority in the world semiconductor market and in other electronic products ranging from cellular phones to modems. Rather than face the prospect of ridding the firm of employees with outmoded skills, about 2.4 percent of the firm's payroll is being invested in teaching new skills to the Motorola work force.[24]

First-line supervisors in the typical firm with 50 or more employees will receive 40 hours of training annually. By contrast, middle managers receive an average of 44 hours a year.[25] Two types of training programs are common:

on-the-job training and off-the-job training. In addition, specialized management development programs are frequently used to improve the skills and broaden the knowledge of present and potential managers.

On-the-Job Training

on-the-job training
Training employees for job tasks by allowing them to perform them under the guidance of an experienced employee.

For relatively simple jobs, **on-the-job training** is most often used so workers can learn by doing. In this kind of training, the new employee actually performs the work under the guidance of an experienced worker. The experienced worker, through advice and suggestions, teaches the new worker efficient methods for handling the job. La-Z-Boy Chair Co. continually retrains its 6,000 furniture makers on the company's machines.

apprenticeship training
Program wherein an employee learns job tasks by serving as an assistant to a trained worker for a relatively long time.

A variation of on-the-job training is **apprenticeship training**, which is used in jobs requiring long periods of training and high levels of skill, such as carpentry, welding, or plumbing. In apprenticeship training programs, the new worker serves as an assistant to a trained worker for a relatively long period. Employers often use apprenticeship in cooperation with trade unions to ensure that skill standards are maintained in these trades.

Off-the-Job Training

In more difficult jobs, some form of classroom training is used. In this kind of training, employees can acquire the necessary skills at their own pace, without the pressures of the actual job environment. This prior training also minimizes the possibility of wasting materials and time on the job.

classroom training
Program that uses classroom techniques to teach employees difficult, high-skill jobs.

Classroom training programs use classroom techniques to teach employees difficult jobs requiring high levels of skill. The training may involve lectures, conferences, films and other audiovisual aids, programmed instruction, or special machines.

Interactive video (IAV) is rapidly becoming one of the most popular methods for employee training. IAV, which lets the employee communicate with the computer display screen, is capable of decreasing learning time as much as 50 percent while increasing retention by 80 percent. The $8,500 price of a basic system has limited IAV system use to only about one-fourth of the nation's 500 largest corporations. However, firms such as Ford and Xerox are already replacing classroom training programs with IAV systems. Chrysler managers estimate they saved $1.3 million when 83,000 workers recently received hazardous substance training through IAV programs. IAV training costs are estimated at $6.67 per hour as compared with $10 per hour for traditional classroom training.[26]

vestibule school
Facsimiles of actual work areas where employees learn jobs using equipment similar to that on the job.

Some companies establish a **vestibule school**, where workers are instructed on the operation of equipment similar to that used in their new jobs. Vestibule schools are the facsimiles of actual work areas: They duplicate the jobs and machinery found in the plant. New employees are trained in the proper methods of performing a particular job and have an opportunity to become accustomed to the work before actually entering the department.

Management Development Programs

While job training is at least as old as recorded history, most management development programs have been established only within the last 35 years. These programs are designed to improve the skills of present managers and to

Newly hired flight attendants receive vestibule school training at American Airlines' Dallas/Fort Worth Learning Center. In an aircraft cabin mockup, trainees learn safety procedures and customer service techniques. The school enables instructors to give trainees a true-to-life setting for hands-on experience.

Photo source: Courtesy of American Airlines, Inc.

broaden their knowledge; they also provide training for employees who have management potential.

A **management development program**, which usually includes formal courses of study, is often conducted off the company premises. General Motors and Holiday Inn, for example, have established collegelike institutes that offer specific programs for current and potential managers. Probably the largest program is Xerox's Learning Center in Leesburg, Virginia. Restaurant management for McDonald's Corporation is required to complete an intensive two-week program at Hamburger University, the McDonald's training facility in a Chicago suburb. The curriculum covers a variety of subjects, with emphasis on equipment, controls, human relations skills, and management skills.

IBM and General Electric are acclaimed for developing outstanding managers. Don Laidlaw, IBM's director of executive resources, is responsible for "having the right people at the right place at the right time, properly prepared." New managers come to GE's Management Development Institute in Crotonville, New York, six months after their promotion. A special four-week program is designed to make GE managers more action, risk, and people oriented. It is intended to develop leaders, not just managers.[27] Both of these companies:

◆ Identify high-potential people.

◆ Give them challenging experiences on the job.

◆ Integrate job assignments and education.

◆ Fill top positions internally.

management development program
Training designed to improve skills and broaden the knowledge of managers and potential managers.

◆ Have formal development and succession plans.

◆ Have special management staff to oversee executive development.

Two other forms of management development programs are job rotation and mentoring. **Job rotation**, through temporary assignments in various departments, familiarizes junior executives with the various operations of the firm and the contributions of each department.

Another approach to management development, called *mentoring,* combines the energy and commitment of less experienced employees with the wisdom and experience of senior members of the organization. A **mentor** is a senior employee who coaches and counsels a less experienced employee for periods typically lasting between two and five years. The mentor serves as a friend, counselor, and source of support for less-experienced employees. A mentor relationship benefits career development; two-thirds of today's top executives had a mentor at some point in their careers.[28] Jim Poure, owner of General Alum & Chemical Corp., a small producer of chemicals used in water-treatment plants, gives most of the credit for his firm's sales growth from $350,000 in 1978 to $7 million a decade later to mentoring. Younger employees got the benefit of the mentors' experience, with the result that young managers today are "two or three years ahead of their time."[29] Mentoring has proven extremely successful in aiding promotion and advancement for women and minorities in the organization.

Assessment Centers

One method for training managers and identifying employees with management potential — the **assessment center** — traces its roots to the shadowy world of World War II espionage. The U.S. Office of Strategic Services, a forerunner of the Central Intelligence Agency, used this technique to screen and select undercover agents. Assessment centers have since been used by business firms to identify employees with management potential.

The typical assessment center is actually a program, not a place. It uses a variety of simulation techniques, leaderless discussions, and group problem-solving exercises to measure an individual's ability to perform job-related assignments. One such technique, the "in-basket simulation," places management candidates in the role of manager and asks for responses to such scenarios as a customer complaint letter, a telephone call from a superior, or a problem facing the department. Trained evaluators, or "assessors," observe the candidate's responses and judge the candidate.

Empirical research studies indicate assessment centers are highly effective in predicting job performance. Firms currently using assessment centers include AT&T (which pioneered their use in private industry in 1959), General Electric, J. C. Penney, Boise Cascade, American Airlines, Sears, and IBM. In addition to identifying management candidates, assessment centers are used as recruiting tools for firms hiring sales personnel and by such brokerage firms as Merrill Lynch.

Performance Appraisal

Performance appraisal is the evaluation of an individual's job performance by comparing actual performance against desired performance for the purpose of making objective decisions about compensation, promotion, additional training

---

job rotation
Familiarization of junior executives with the various operations and contributions of each department through temporary assignments in those departments.

mentor
A senior employee who acts as a sponsor and teacher to a younger, less-experienced employee.

assessment center
Method for training managers and identifying employees with management potential.

performance appraisal
Defining acceptable employee performance levels, evaluating them, then comparing actual and desired performance to aid in determining training, compensation, promotion, transfers, or terminations.

needs, transfers, or terminations. Such appraisals are not confined to business in today's era of evaluation. State driver's license departments evaluate the written and physical capabilities of potential drivers. Professors appraise student performance through homework assignments, quizzes, and examinations. Students, in turn, appraise instructors by completing written evaluations of instructional effectiveness.

In 1800, Robert Owen implemented a performance appraisal system in a Scottish factory through the use of "character" books and "character" blocks. Daily worker output was recorded in Owen's character books, and the following day Owen placed different-colored wooden character blocks at each worker's station to inform fellow workers of performance. Different colors represented different levels of performance, ranging from poor to excellent.

Performance appraisal serves three important purposes:

◆ *Information for employees.* By providing employees with information about their relative level of performance, appraisals enable them to learn about their strengths, weaknesses, and areas needing improvement.

◆ *Information for management.* Managers use such information to make decisions concerning compensation, promotion, additional training needs, transfers, and terminations.

◆ *Employee motivation.* Performance appraisals permit managers to identify superior employees and to reward them with promotions, praise, and pay increases.

It is important to devise objective systems to accomplish these objectives. While appraisals are the responsibility of the line supervisor, specialists from the human resource department may be able to help in devising special forms and rating instruments and comparing appraisals in individual departments with overall organizational scores.

Programs using the management by objectives technique include performance appraisal as a critical component.[30] One of the chief advantages of such programs is that they provide the employee with specific information about how performance will be evaluated. Because the employee participates in goal setting, there is little uncertainty about what constitutes satisfactory performance.

Employee Counseling

Employees with personal problems that may hurt job performance will often discuss them with their immediate supervisor. But personnel departments are now adding trained specialists to assist workers in solving certain problems, typically family or financial problems.

Tandem Computers uses an outside counseling firm for employee counseling, offering workers a toll-free number to call. A special counseling program operated by Exxon Corporation's human resource department was used by 5 percent of the firm's employees in a recent year. The most common problems cited by such programs are alcohol and drug abuse, followed by stress, family, and relationship woes.[31]

Commonwealth Edison reports 25 percent to 30 percent lower absenteeism after six years with a drug program for its employees. Georgia Power encourages workers to go to its employee assistance program if they have a drug problem. If they do not come forward and managers suspect them of drug use, the company will order a drug test and dismiss them with no second chance if they fail. A company spokesperson explains the reason for this unusual approach this way: "Since the price of detection is so high, it encourages employees to seek assistance before they're caught."[32] The company has fired 75 to 100 employees who resisted the encouragement; 527 came forward for help. Sick days have fallen 23 percent, and serious accidents have decreased from 39 during the year before the program started to 9 in 1987.

Company programs also aid employees in their efforts to stop smoking. Over 50 percent of U.S. firms have policies regulating smoking at work, and one firm in seven prohibits smoking in all areas.[33]

Promotions, Transfers, and Separations

Although three out of every four employees in the U.S. Postal Service are still in their entry positions, most business organizations experience greater employee movement. This movement involves promotions, transfers, and separations.

A **promotion** is an upward movement in an organization to a position of greater authority and responsibility and a higher salary. While most promotions are based on employee performance, some companies and many labor unions prefer to base them on **seniority** — the length of time an employee has worked at the company or in a particular job or department. Managers generally agree, however, that seniority should be the basis for promotion only when two candidates possess equal qualifications.

A **transfer** is a horizontal movement in an organization at about the same wage and level. Transfers may involve shifting workers into new, more interesting jobs or into departments where the workers' skills are required.

A **separation** can be due to resignation, retirement, layoff, or termination. Resignations result, for example, when employees find more attractive or better-paying jobs or move to other cities.

A **layoff** differs from a termination in that it is considered only a temporary separation due to businsss slowdowns. Most employers lay off workers on a seniority basis, releasing more recently hired employees first. When business conditions improve, workers are rehired, also on a seniority basis. Those with the most seniority are called back first.

A **termination**, or discharge, is a permanent separation resulting from poor job performance, repeated violations of work rules, excessive absenteeism, elimination of jobs, or the closing of work facilities. Well-managed human resource departments have specific employee disciplinary policies that are explained to all workers. The violation of work rules typically results in an oral reprimand for a first offense. Further violations lead to written reprimands and, ultimately, to discharge.

Employment at Will

Job security in the United States is recognized as a fundamental human need. It has been, and continues to be, a fundamental objective of labor unions. Laws enacted over the past half-century make it illegal to dismiss workers because of race, religion, sex, or age. Also forbidden is the dismissal of workers involved in union organizing, reporting unlawful behavior on the part of the company (whistle-blowing), or filing job safety complaints.

promotion
Increase in authority, responsibility, and salary.

seniority
Length of employment in a particular job, department, or company.

transfer
Lateral change of position with about the same authority, responsibility, and salary.

separation
Resignation, retirement, layoff, or termination of an employee.

layoff
Temporary separation due to business decline.

termination
Permanent separation resulting from poor job performance, repeated rule violations, excessive absenteeism, elimination of job, or company closing.

While most companies support these laws and strive to recruit and train qualified personnel, they also insist it is their right to fire employees who do not work out. The courts have long upheld the concept of **employment at will**, the right of an employer to retain or dismiss personnel as it wishes.

In recent years, however, this employer right has been weakened by court rulings aimed at ensuring that fair treatment procedures have been created and applied uniformly. Corporations like IBM, McGraw-Hill, Atlantic Richfield, American Airlines, and Federated Department Stores all learned that an unfair dismissal case can cost hundreds of thousands of dollars in legal fees, back wages, and punitive damages.[34] In general, the courts define this fairness standard in three basic ways:

◆ A firing cannot override a corporation's responsibility to treat its workers "fairly and in good faith." A Massachusetts court ruled, for example, that NCR Corporation was wrong in firing a salesperson just before signing a major sales contract in order to avoid paying his substantial commission.

◆ A firing cannot go against promises made in the employee handbook or during the job interview. Some courts have said that any reference to the employee's "permanent" status following a probationary period implies a promise of some degree of job security.

◆ A firing cannot conflict with public policy. An employee who is fired for refusing to lie to a grand jury, for example, is protected by the courts.

Even though dismissing an employee is one of the most unpleasant tasks most managers encounter, the situation can be eased for both parties by following a few guidelines. First, the manager must be convinced dismissal is in the best interest of both the employee and the company. Second, the setting is important. A meeting held at the end of the day in the employee's work area provides control over the length of the meeting. The manager should get to the point and end the meeting as quickly as reasonable, encouraging the employee to leave the company quickly. The individual handling the dismissal should take responsibility for the decision and, whenever possible, offer to serve as a reference to the employee's good qualities for future employers.[35]

Employee Compensation

One of the most difficult functions of human resource management is the development and operation of an equitable compensation system. Because labor costs represent a sizable percentage of total product costs, wages that are too high may result in products that are too expensive to compete effectively in the marketplace. But inadequate wages lead to excessive employee turnover, poor morale, and inefficient production. The worst possible compensation management results in a company that pays its employees just enough so they will not quit and they work just enough so they won't get fired.

A satisfactory compensation program should attract well-qualified workers, keep them satisfied in their jobs, and inspire them to produce. Consequently, **wage and salary administration** — the development and implementation of a system for compensating employees for their work — is a vital function of human resource management.

The terms *wages* and *salary* are often used interchangeably, but they do have slightly different meanings. **Wages** are an employee compensation based

employment at will
Right of employers to retain or dismiss personnel as they wish.

wage and salary administration
Development and implementation of an employee compensation system.

wages
Employee compensation based on hours worked or on productivity.

Employees of Central Fidelity Banks Inc. are eligible for cash bonuses at year-end based on individual and company performance. The compensation policy rewards high-performing individuals through a "bottoms up" bonus program. The bonus pool is funded from the bottom up, with the lowest-level employee pool funded first, then supervisors and middle managers, and finally senior management. In this photo, bank employees demonstrate their commitment to Virginia, a market in which Central Fidelity concentrates all of its efforts and resources.

Photo source: Courtesy of Central Fidelity Banks, Inc.

salary
Employee compensation calculated weekly, monthly, or annually.

on the number of hours worked or on the amount of output produced. They generally are paid to production employees, retail salespeople, and maintenance workers. **Salary** is employee compensation calculated on a weekly, monthly, or annual basis. It is usually paid to white-collar workers such as office personnel, executives, and professional employees.

The compensation policy of most companies is based on five factors: (1) salaries and wages paid by other companies in the area that compete for the same personnel, (2) government legislation, (3) the cost of living, (4) the ability of the company to pay, and (5) the workers' productivity.

Job Evaluations

job evaluation
Determination of wage level for a job based on skill requirements, education requirements, responsibilities, and physical requirements.

In developing a compensation program, the human resource department conducts a **job evaluation** — a method of determining salary and wage levels for different jobs by comparing each job on the bases of skill requirements, education requirements, responsibilities, and physical requirements. A monetary scale is then determined for each job. This process attempts to eliminate compensation inequalities among jobs. Although the human resource department does not set the specific compensation of employees, it does recommend wages and salaries paid by other firms in the area.

Alternative Compensation Plans

piece wage
Employee compensation based on productivity.

time wage
Employee compensation based on hours worked.

Employee compensation may be based on the amount of output produced by the worker (a **piece wage**), the amount of time spent on the job (a **time wage**), or may include some incentive added to a salary or to a time wage or piece wage to reward the employee with extras (such as time off or bonus money) for exceptional performance.

Time wages traditionally have been paid to assembly-line workers, clerks, and maintenance personnel. These wages are easy to compute, quickly understood, and simple to administer. Time wage plans assume a satisfactory performance level but include no incentive for outstanding performance by the employee.

Skilled craftworkers are often paid on a piece-rate basis for each unit of output produced. Their wage may be based on individual output or on the production of an entire department. The practice of compensating salespeople with commissions based on sales is an example of the piece-wage form of compensation. This kind of payment plan not only includes an incentive for increased output, but also encourages workers to supervise their own activities. It operates well in departments where the work is standardized and the output of each employee or department can be accurately measured.

Pay for Performance

For most companies, the traditional approach to employee compensation was predictable: wage earners were paid by the hour. Salary earners got paid by the month or the year. And executives — only executives — got bonuses. But this simple, seemingly logical system has been largely overturned in the past five years as company after company searched for a better way to reward past performance and motivate employees to excel. The American Productivity and Quality Center reports that 75 percent of U.S. employers now use at least one version of the incentive pay plan shown in Table 11.2 — and roughly 80 percent of the plans have been adopted in the past five years.[36]

Incentive compensation is designed to reward salaried employees and wage earners for superior performance. A new pay system at Merrill Lynch has been structured so its 11,000 brokers will spend more time with larger, more active customers. The new pay system, which has cut commissions for most small trades, was introduced because the previous plan did not adequately differentiate between large trades and less profitable ones. Major retailers such as Dayton Hudson, R. H. Macy, The May Department Stores Co., Federated, and Carter Hawley Hale Stores are replacing their traditional hourly or weekly wage structure with a commission system in which retail salespeople earn an average of 6 to 8 percent of sales.[37]

incentive compensation
An addition to a salary or wage given for exceptional performance.

In some instances, incentives are added to a traditional base wage or salary. Aetna Life & Casualty's "Superior Pay for Superior Performance" program awards bonuses in varying amounts to 2,500 top-performing employees. In other cases, such as the Lincoln Electric system described earlier in the chapter, most of the employee's pay is at risk under compensation systems linking pay directly to performance. The major types of incentive pay plans include profit sharing, gain sharing, lump-sum bonuses, and pay for knowledge.

Profit sharing — a type of incentive compensation program in which a percentage of company profits is distributed to employees involved in producing those profits — is the most widely used form of incentive pay plans. More than 20 percent of U.S. companies currently use profit sharing to increase company loyalty by creating a feeling of belongingness for employees. Hewlett-Packard's program demonstrates that this approach can prove a powerful incentive for middle managers and other white-collar staff, as well as top management, to watch the bottom line. Almost everyone at HP receives incen-

profit sharing
Percentage of company profits distributed to employees involved in producing those profits.

Table 11.2   Pay for Performance Compensation Plans

Plan Type	How It Works	What It Requires to Be Effective	Advantages	Disadvantages
Profit sharing	Employees receive a varying annual bonus based on corporate profits. Payments can be made in cash or deferred into a retirement fund.	Participating employees collectively must be able to influence profits. Owners must value employees' contributions enough to be willing to share profits.	The incentive formula is simple and easy to communicate. The plan is guaranteed to be affordable. It pays only when the firm is sufficiently profitable. It unites the financial interests of owners and employees.	Annual payments may lead employees to ignore long-term performance. Factors beyond the employee's control can influence profits. The plan forces private companies to open their books.
Gain sharing	When a unit beats predetermined performance targets, all members get bonuses. Objectives often include better productivity, quality, and customer service.	Objectives must be measurable. Management must encourage employee involvement. Employees must have a high degree of trust in management.	The plan enhances coordination and teamwork. Employees learn more about the business and focus on objectives. Employees work harder and smarter.	Plans that focus only on productivity may lead employees to ignore other important objectives, such as quality. The company may have to pay bonuses even when unprofitable.
Lump-sum bonus	Instead of a wage or salary increase, employees get a one-time cash payment based on performance or a union contract. The bonus does not become part of base pay.	Employees must have a sense that their prosperity mirrors the company's. Management must have a good relationship with employees.	The plan lets companies control fixed costs by limiting pay raises and attendant benefit increases.	Management sometimes awards bonuses subjectively, so employees may resent awards they consider unfair.
Pay for knowledge	An employee's salary or wage rises with the number of tasks he can do, regardless of the job he performs.	Skills must be identified and assigned a pay grade. The company must have well-developed employee assessment and training procedures.	By increasing flexibility, the plan lets the company operate with a leaner staff. The plan gives workers a broader perspective, making them more adept at problem solving.	Most employees will learn all applicable skills, raising labor costs. Training costs are high.

Source: Reprinted from Nancy J. Perry, "Here Come Richer, Riskier Pay Plans," *Fortune,* December 19, 1988, p. 52. Copyright © 1988 Time Inc. All rights reserved.

tive compensation every year that profitability goals are met. Dozens of major companies have adopted such plans recently, including General Motors, Ford, and USX Corporation. They expect profit sharing to build teamwork among employees and help them see how their productivity relates to overall company profitability.[38]

The primary problem with profit sharing is that factors beyond the control of employees may affect company profits. As one industry expert put it, "Many things that affect profits, such as pricing policy, the market environment, and taxes, are unrelated to workers' performance. One financial decision, such as taking on a lot of debt or making an acquisition, can wipe out anything the workers can do."[39] These problems with profit sharing have led many firms to implement a compensation plan called **gain sharing**. This approach is aimed at linking employee pay to productivity. Employees are rewarded for results they

gain sharing
Incentive compensation program in which employee pay is based on predetermined productivity increases.

can directly influence: for instance, producing more garments per hour, attracting more depositors, or collecting more delinquent accounts. Productivity at Carrier's heating and air conditioning equipment plants in Syracuse, New York, increased by 24 percent in a two-year period following installation of a gain-sharing plan in 1986. The savings in labor costs are split 50-50 between the company and its employees. Although gain-sharing plans have been around for 50 years, 75 percent of them have been adopted since 1980.

A difficult aspect of most incentive pay programs involves deciding who deserves the reward and in what amount. It is particularly difficult in many factory and office settings to get a true picture of superior performance. Frequently, everyone is simply rated above average, resulting in inflated performance evaluations. One widely reported performance appraisal system in the military resulted in 80 percent of all officers being ranked in the top 5 percent!

Gain-sharing systems are typically designed to reflect the contribution of groups rather than individuals. Gains are shared by all unit members according to a predetermined formula. When designed correctly, such programs result in reduced labor costs, absenteeism and turnover, and improved quality and service.[40] Not surprisingly, they represent the fastest-growing form of incentives in the 1980s.

A third type of incentive compensation, the **bonus**, is a one-time performance-based payment that does not get built into salaries or wages. Intended as an incentive for increased productivity, bonuses reward employees for exceptional performance. Steelworkers for Nucor Corp, a Charlotte, North Carolina, company that is the nation's eighth-largest steel producer, earn weekly bonuses based on the number of tons of acceptable quality steel their production team produces. While their base wages are only about half those of workers at bigger mills, bonuses boost their total pay to an average of $32,000 a year, with some workers getting as much as $40,000. (The industry average is about $27,000.) Bonuses are based on production for hourly workers and overall profitability for salaried employees. Workers who are late lose their bonus for the day; workers who are more than 30 minutes late lose their bonus for the week.

In 1988, General Motors Corporation set up a recognition award fund that is given in lump sums to high performers. In addition, GM managers are encouraged to give spontaneous rewards — such as theater tickets or trips — to employees for an outstanding report or a money-saving suggestion. Publisher Marie Peterson of Clapper Publishing in Park Ridge, Illinois, supports this approach: "You can give employees cash, but they can't brag about it." Bonuses at Clapper Publishing have included jewelry, paid shopping sprees, and a one-week vacation in Hawaii. WordPerfect Corporation took the approach one step further by offering every one of its 607 employees a weeklong trip for two to Hawaii if the company grossed $100 million in sales for the year. It worked.[41]

The final form of incentive compensation is **pay for knowledge**, a system in which employee salaries or wages increase with the number of tasks they are capable of performing, regardless of their current work assignment. The objective of this approach to employee pay is increased flexibility in operations as a result of a more broadly trained work force. In addition, broadly trained employees may also be employees with a broader perspective. In 1988, Northern Telecom dropped its automatic annual pay increase in favor of a pay-for-knowledge system, which awards raises to workers only when they learn new "skill blocks," such as circuitboard preparation or system testing. Although both employee pay and company training costs typically increase under this system, the result is a team of workers who are expected to understand the whole manu-

bonus
An addition to a salary or wage based on productivity or for exceptional performance.

pay for knowledge
Incentive compensation system in which employee salaries or wages increase with the number of tasks they are capable of performing.

facturing process. Says Dick Dauphinais, a compensation director at Northern Telecom, "To have flexible manufacturing, you must have flexible compensation."[42]

Closing the Compensation Gap

Although discrimination in compensation for men and women performing comparable jobs violates federal and state laws, the 30 million women who work full time earn, on average, less than men. The most recent Census Bureau survey reported women earn about $.70 for every $1 earned by male workers. The gap has been shrinking a penny a year for the past decade. At this rate, pay equity for men and women won't be reached until 2020.

The reasons for the compensation gap are many. First, women still are concentrated in relatively low-paying clerical jobs, even when they work full time. Overall, women do not have as many years of formal education as working men. Among college graduates, women are concentrated in teaching and nursing professions, while men were more frequently employed in higher-paying fields. In addition, women interrupt employment more often than men (for childbearing, among other things), undermining seniority and availability for promotion. A final possible — though illegal — reason for the male-female wage gap is sex discrimination.

The movement of women into higher-paying occupations is expected to reduce the overall compensation inequity. Today, one attorney in five is a woman, as compared with only one in 20 in 1970. Women comprise 28 percent of the nation's computer scientists today, double the percentage in 1970. In addition, the decision of many women to work without interruptions in building a career in high-compensation fields such as these will continue to close the pay gap during the 1990s.

comparable worth
Philosophy seeking compensation equity for men and women in positions requiring similar levels of education, training, and skills.

Comparable worth, a controversial issue facing human resource managers, was examined in Chapter 2. The idea that jobs requiring equal amounts of skill and responsibility are of equal value to the employer and therefore should receive equal pay has both supporters and detractors. Most businesses oppose this philosophy, pointing out the difficulty involved in calculating the worth of different jobs, the subjectivity of such attempts, and the fact that such an approach ignores the realities of the marketplace. Advocates of comparable worth view it as a means of ensuring equitable pay for different jobs requiring a similar degree of responsibility. Although comparable worth has been implemented in a few states and local government agencies, such as the city of Colorado Springs, its widest application to date is in Ontario, Canada. All public-sector (government) organizations and private companies with ten or more employees in Ontario must restructure pay rates so women and men are compensated equally for comparable work. The law has implications for Canada's neighbor to the south because the large number of U.S. companies operating in Ontario must comply with the regulations in their Canadian operations.

When Warner-Lambert's Canadian division of the Morris Plains, New Jersey, pharmaceutical company analyzed its compensation system to comply with the new law, it used the following weights: responsibility, 50 percent; skill, 28 percent; effort, 13 percent; and working conditions, 9 percent. Most salaries were within a few percentage points of those determined by the calculations. The major beneficiaries of this pay equity system appear to be nonunion clerical workers in companies with a large number of highly paid union workers in plants and distribution operations.[43]

Photo source: © 1987 George B. Frye III for Tandem Computers Inc.

Tandem Computers Incorporated has a Public Service Sabbatical program that enables employees to combine public service with the regular six-week, fully paid leave employees earn every four years. Tandem extends the sabbatical and helps pay expenses. Martha Jennings, a project leader in Tandem's strategic planning/new ventures group, took a sabbatical in Senegal, where she taught rural women how to make money from projects such as cattle raising. Jennings developed an interest in the role of women in Third World countries while working at Tandem locations throughout Asia.

Employee Benefits

The typical organization furnishes many benefits to employees and their families besides wages and salaries. **Employee benefits** are rewards provided indirectly to employees, consisting primarily of services (such as child care or insurance) paid for by employers and reimbursement of employee expenses (such as tuition costs) by employers. Many large companies employ doctors and nurses to investigate working conditions and treat minor illnesses and job-related accidents. Some companies sponsor recreation programs including hobby groups and golf, baseball, and bowling teams, all with separate recreational areas. Colgate-Palmolive Co. helps any salaried employee buy or refinance a primary residence. An estimated one-tenth of all major U.S. corporations — ranging from McDonald's to IBM — offer paid sabbaticals for long-term employees. David Rutherford, a Xerox Corp. product manager, used his nine-month sabbatical to teach auto repair, his hobby, to inner-city youths in Los Angeles. Apple Computer CEO John Sculley used his nine-week sabbatical to jog, philosophize, and think about Apple in the twenty-first century. These extended-leave programs are designed to attract and retain highly qualified employees, deal with job stress, broaden professional skills, and provide an opportunity for personal growth.[44]

    Some benefits are required by law. For example, most employers must contribute to each employee's federal social security account. In addition, they

employee benefits
Employee rewards such as pension plans, insurance, sick-leave pay, and tuition reimbursement given at all or part of the expense of the company.

must contribute to state employment insurance programs designed to assist laid-off workers and to workers' compensation programs that provide compensation to persons suffering job-related injuries or illnesses. These programs are described in detail in Chapter 22.

The major categories of benefits programs provided voluntarily by employers include insurance, pensions and retirement programs, paid vacations and leave time, and employee services such as tuition-reimbursement plans, child care, credit unions, and various recreational facilities. Ice-cream maker Ben & Jerry's offers a unique benefit: each employee is allowed to take home three pints of ice cream a day. The latest figures from the U.S. Chamber of Commerce show that wages account for only 63 percent of a worker's earnings; the other 37 percent takes the form of employee benefits. The typical person earning $20,000 annually in 1990 receives an additional $11,746 in employee benefits.

Protecting Retirement Benefits

Employee Retirement Income Security Act (ERISA)
Federal law establishing minimum standards for employee participation in private pension plans and providing protection for participants in the event of failure of a private pension plan.

Pension programs designed to provide employees with income for their retirement years represent an important component of most employee benefit programs. About 60 percent of the nation's labor force is covered by private pension plans paid for completely or in part by employers.

Since 1974, these benefits have been protected by the **Employee Retirement Income Security Act (ERISA)**. This federal law is designed to provide protection against the failure of a private pension plan. The law establishes minimum standards for eligibility to participate in private plans, encourages adequate financial funding of such plans, and insures retirement benefits in the event of a plan's failure through a government corporation operating within the U.S. Department of Labor.

Flexible Benefit Plans

flexible benefit plans
System of flexible benefits in which employees are provided with specific dollar amounts of benefits and are allowed to select areas of coverage.

The changing U.S. labor force prompted many firms to offer **flexible benefit plans** for their employees. This type of program is typically referred to as a flex plan, since it offers flexible benefits that each employee can tailor to meet his or her individual needs.

At companies such as Steelcase, the Grand Rapids, Michigan, office-furniture company, workers are allotted "benefit dollars" and allowed to select from a menu of choices. There are eight medical plans, three dental options (including no coverage at all), and various forms of long- and short-term disability and life insurance. Employees who have money left can put it in tax-free accounts to cover out-of-pocket health care or off-site day care. Unused benefit dollars can also be added to retirement contributions — or taken home in cash.[45]

Traditional benefit programs were usually devised to serve single-income households in which husbands worked and wives tended the children. But five important trends have made these programs increasingly dated.

1. Fewer male employees are now the sole support of their families. Statistically, today's married man is more likely to have a wife in the labor force than one whose primary occupation is homemaking.

James E. Jefferson, a product manager for NCR communications processors, uses the NCR-EstiMATE II software program in planning his financial future. NCR employees use the program to assess their future income through various options offered in the firm's flexible benefits program.

Photo source: Courtesy of NCR Corporation.

2. More couples are remaining childless, and those who do become parents have considerably smaller families than did their predecessors. The number of families having a fourth child has been cut in half in a decade.
3. Marriage is not the overwhelming norm it once was. At the beginning of the 1970s, 71 percent of all households were maintained by married couples. With growing numbers of Americans living alone or living together without marriage, the figure is expected to drop to 52 percent by 1995.
4. Work spans have become more discontinuous, especially among women. Working women are likely to take sabbaticals during their children's younger years.
5. Because almost all mandatory retirement programs are illegal, retirement age is no longer pegged at 65. Today, it may range 45 to 70 and older.

Flex plans are well suited for two-income households wanting to avoid duplicate coverage and for single people who don't need a more expensive family plan. Also, their flexible nature permits employees to adjust their benefits package through various stages of their life cycles. A married person with young children might select additional life insurance. Employees at Comerica, a major Michigan bank, can tailor their benefit package to help pay for child care. Employees at Exxon can add unused holidays and sick leave to their vacations and take extra paid time off. The number of such plans in firms with 1,000 employees or more has doubled in the past two years. Not only do they give employees control of how their benefit dollars are spent, but they also aid employers in controlling steep increases in the cost of such benefits as health care. Instead of giving employees a set package of benefits, the employer provides a specified dollar amount for the employee to allocate. Should health costs soar, the employee decides whether to pay more or take less coverage.

Industrial Safety

A vital employee benefit for all workers is safe working conditions. This year, an estimated 1.8 million American workers will suffer crippling injuries on the job and another 6,000 will die. Others will suffer illnesses brought on by exposure at work to chemicals, dust, and other dangerous materials, which cause their deaths many years later. Employees in the following occupations face the highest fatality risk on the job: timber cutters and loggers, airplane pilots, asbestos and insulation workers, structural metal workers, electric power line and cable installers and repairers, and firefighters.[46]

Industrial accidents result in both suffering for the injured worker and major costs for the employer through loss of experienced employees, increased insurance premiums, and poor morale. Recognition of the importance of a safe work environment led to passage in 1970 of the Occupational Safety and Health Act.

Occupational Safety and Health Administration (OSHA)

Federal agency created to assure safe and healthy working conditions.

This act created the **Occupational Safety and Health Administration (OSHA)**, a federal agency whose purpose is to assure safe and healthful working conditions for the labor force. Almost all employers are covered by OSHA; excluded are government bodies and firms covered by specific employment acts (such as the Coal Mine Health and Safety Act). Employers are responsible for knowing and complying with all OSHA standards that apply to their workplace. Employees must be informed of their rights and responsibilities under the law.

OSHA's 1,000 field inspectors examine about 60,000 workplaces annually, concentrating on the most hazardous industries and sites. About half the agency's inspections are devoted to construction — the industry with the highest lost-workday case rate of those covered by OSHA. Under a targeting system begun in the early 1980s, OSHA focuses walk-around safety inspections on the most hazardous plants in the manufacturing sector. First, OSHA prepares lists of firms in the most hazardous industries and then conducts unannounced inspections of companies on the lists. During the inspection, if a manufacturer's records show its lost-workday case rate is below the national average for manufacturing, the inspectors conduct only a records inspection. In this way, time-consuming walk-around inspections are reserved for the more dangerous workplaces.

OSHA typically conducts inspections during normal working hours, but a 1978 Supreme Court ruling requires OSHA inspectors to obtain a search warrant before conducting an inspection if the employer denies them entry. The inspections cover both work facilities and records and are followed by a department briefing that outlines violations and recommended corrective actions. Fines may also be levied. IBP Inc., the meat-packing subsidiary of Occidental Petroleum Corporation, was fined $2.6 million recently for doctoring accident and illness records.[47]

During the 1970s, OSHA was severely criticized by businesses for its blizzard of required forms and the numerous petty regulations that appeared to have little impact on either safety or health. In recent years, OSHA has eliminated many of the inconsequential rules and has redirected its efforts toward major health and safety hazards.

Concern for the welfare of its employees and the rising costs of workers' compensation insurance and claims prompted Wetterau Inc. to develop a new safety program used throughout its distribution and manufacturing operations. The program combines achievement incentives, such as the logo cap and jacket worn by the warehouse forklift operator in this photo; rehabilitative physical therapy; and work conditioning and education. During the first two months, the safety program reduced chargeable lost-time accidents by 60 percent from historical rates.

Photo source: Courtesy of Wetterau, Incorporated.

Human Resource Concerns in the 1990s

Two issues will continue to grow in importance during the final decade of the twentieth century: encouraging employees to remain on the job rather than retiring early and corporate responses to the needs of two-career couples.

Encouraging Late Retirement

Less than two decades ago, concerns about age discrimination in employment led to the passage of laws ending mandatory employment for most workers. Today, many firms use financial incentives to encourage voluntary retirement by workers nearing the traditional retirement age. The **worker buyout** plans grew out of the recession of the early 1980s as firms attempted to reduce their payroll expenses, while avoiding morale-stunting layoffs. A financial package including a cash bonus, continuation of such employee benefits as insurance coverage, and higher-than-normal monthly retirement benefits (to cover the gap between retirement and the onset of social security payments) prompted thousands of employees at such companies as Monsanto and Eastman Kodak to retire early.

Worker buyouts reduced company payrolls by eliminating the typically above-average wages and salaries of older, more experienced workers. Also, they contributed to the morale of remaining workers who saw tangible evidence

worker buyout
Financial incentive designed to encourage older employees to voluntarily retire.

of management's attempts to maintain job security by resorting to a buyout rather than a layoff. Finally, unclogging job and promotion opportunities improved the upward mobility of younger employees. The programs were extremely successful: only 32 percent of workers age 55 and older hold jobs today, compared with 45 percent in 1930. And the median retirement age for men keeps sinking — to about 62 today, from 65 in 1963.

As the ranks of younger employees thin, and shortages of workers and skills increase, astute companies are bending over backward to keep older employees. By the end of the century, only 39 percent of the work force will be under age 35, compared with 49 percent now. The number of people age 50 to 65 will increase at more than twice the rate of the overall population. Firms such as Corning Glass Works are beginning to create so-called *platinum handcuffs* in the form of shorter hours, company-paid vacation trips, and bonus plans that reward employees for staying on past a certain age or period of service.

By redesigning the job of store clerk to eliminate heavy lifting, Builders Emporium, a chain of 121 home improvement centers, was able to attract older workers as store clerks. Today, 15 percent of these 5,000 jobs are performed by employees age 55 or older. In general, the older staff knows the merchandise better and has more experience in dealing with people.[48]

Two-Career Couples

By the year 2000, 62 of every 100 women will hold jobs outside the home. Already, 73 percent of all mothers with school-age children are employed. Two-career households have specific job-related needs that must be addressed by employers. These issues frequently arise when a manager, professional staff member, or highly skilled employee is hired from another geographic area. Relocation services for the spouse are often required to attract the new employee. For example, IBM reimburses spouses for up to $500 in job-search expenses. Other firms aid by providing employment leads and financial assistance until the spouse locates a job in the new city.

Flexible work arrangements may be important for two-career couples, especially those with children. Child-care facilities and parental leave programs for both mothers and fathers may be determinants in retaining highly qualified employees. For example, Colgate-Palmolive's 12-week unpaid leave program allows salaried women or men to take time off for birth, adoption, family illness, or elderly care. Shoe manufacturer Stride Rite Corporation became the first large corporation to provide intergenerational day care in 1989 when it opened its elder-care facility.[49]

A look into the crystal ball might produce the following scenario regarding your workday in the 21st century:

It's Wednesday, September 4, 2008, and another day at the office. You drop off your daughter, 12 years old, and your father-in-law, 80, at the first-floor Family Care Center. In your office, you look over yesterday's mail (you aren't working Tuesdays this summer), and find a message from the company's School Services: They've received the tuition bill for your son's freshman year in college and have paid it. You write a memo to your boss, outlining your plan for a three-month unpaid sabbatical to work with homeless children.[50]

Although the scene may seem farfetched, the date is less than two decades from now.

Summary of Learning Goals

1.   Explain the functions of a specialized human resource department and the continuing responsibilities of all departments for the effective use of human resources.   The human resource management department is responsible for handling human resource planning, developing job descriptions and job specifications, screening job applicants, developing and administering testing programs, interviewing prospective employees, training new employees, and administering employee compensation, benefits, and safety programs.

More completely, however, is the recognition that effective human resource management is the responsibility of every line manager. The ultimate responsibility for selection, motivation, appraisal, and retention of qualified workers remains with the line managers.

2.   Describe the concept of human resource planning and outline the major steps involved in the process.   Human resource planning ensures that a sufficient number of people with the necessary skills are available at the appropriate place at the appropriate time. It involves an assessment of currently employed resources and the development of a program for meeting forecasted human resource needs.

3.   Explain how each step in the recruitment and selection process contributes to finding the right person for the job.   Specialists in the human resource department are involved with all aspects of employee selection, training, and development. The recruitment and selection process involves locating potential employees, evaluating each application, administering employment tests, arranging for medical examinations, and interviewing. Orientation is at least partly the responsibility of most human resource departments.

4.   Identify the categories of employees covered by equal employment opportunity laws and discuss the major laws affecting human resource decisions in this area.   During the past 30 years, a number of laws have been passed designed to end discrimination in hiring, promotion, firing, compensation, and other terms of employment based upon race, religion, age, sex, or national origin. Groups covered by these laws include women, minorities, handicapped workers, and Vietnam era veterans. Major legislation includes Title VII of the Civil Rights Act of 1964 (which established the EEOC), the Equal Pay Act (1963), the Age Discrimination in Employment Act (1967), the Equal Employment Opportunity Act (1972), the Vocational Rehabilitation Act (1973), and the Vietnam Era Veterans Readjustment Assistance Act (1974), in addition to various executive orders.

5.   Describe the different methods of training operative employees and present and potential managers.   On-the-job training by an experienced worker is typically used for jobs that are relatively simple, while more complex jobs may be taught off the job, through formal classroom training programs or vestibule schools. Human resource management also involves creating and administering various management development programs for current and potential executives, including job rotation, coaching, specialized courses, and assessment centers.

6.   Relate performance appraisal to effective human resource management.   Performance appraisal is the evaluation of individual job performance by comparing actual and desired employee performance to determine compensation, promotion, training, transfers, or terminations. Performance appraisal (1) provides information to employees concerning their relative strengths and weaknesses and suggests areas for improvement, (2) provides management with information for making decisions on compensation, promotions, training, transfer, or termination, and (3) serves as a source of employee motivation by permitting managers to identify superior employees and to reward them with promotions, praise, and pay increases.

7.   Outline the different forms of compensation and explain when each form should be used.   Employee compensation can be classified as *wages,* based on productivity (piece wage) or on hours worked (time wage) and usually paid to production or maintenance workers, and *salaries,* calculated weekly, monthly, or annually and usually paid to white-collar workers. Incentive compensation programs, such as profit sharing, gain sharing, bonuses, or pay for knowledge plans, are often added to a salary or wage to reward superior performance and boost employee morale.

8.   Enumerate the different types of employee benefits and the likely changes in future employee benefit programs.   Employee benefit programs, such as pension plans, insurance programs, health and safety programs, credit unions, and sick-leave pay, are typically administered by the human resource department. A growing trend is the offering of flex plans — flexible "cafeteria-style" benefits — which permit employees to match company benefits to their individual needs. Portable benefit programs that can be transferred from one firm to another, enticements to retain older workers, and programs addressing the needs of two-career households are employee benefits likely to be received by future American workers.

9.   Explain the role of OSHA in protecting employee health and safety.   Safe working conditions are a concern of employees, management, and government. OSHA, a federal agency created in 1970, seeks to assure safe and healthful working conditions by establishing workplace standards, inspecting workplaces, and requiring corrective actions when dangers are discovered.

Key Terms

human resource management	apprenticeship training	performance appraisal
human resource planning	classroom training	promotion
human resource forecast	vestibule school	seniority
job analysis	management development program	transfer
job description		separation
job specification	job rotation	layoff
hiring from within	mentor	termination
on-the-job training	assessment center	employment at will

wage and salary administration

wages

salary

job evaluation

piece wage

time wage

incentive compensation

profit sharing

gain sharing

bonus

pay for knowledge

comparable worth

employee benefits

Employee Retirement Income
   Security Act (ERISA)

flexible benefit plans

Occupational Safety and Health
   Administration (OSHA)

worker buyout

Review Questions

1. Explain the primary functions of a human resource department. Which of these responsibilities are most likely to be shared with line departments?

2. Explain the concept of human resource planning. What are the major steps involved?

3. Identify the steps in the employee recruitment and selection process.

4. Why do many firms follow the policy of hiring from within? What are the problems involved in following such a policy?

5. Compare and contrast the various types of employee training programs. What are some major differences between training programs and management development programs?

6. Distinguish between job analysis, job description, and job specification.

7. Explain the primary reasons for conducting a performance appraisal.

8. Distinguish among promotions, transfers, layoffs, and separations.

9. Distinguish between the major pay for performance compensation plans.

10. Discuss the merits and shortcomings of the comparable worth philosophy of employee compensation.

Discussion Questions

1. Give an example of a job in which each of the following employee compensation alternatives would be most appropriate:
   a. Piece wage
   b. Incentive wage
   c. Salary
   d. Time wage

2. Discuss the type of compensation plan you would recommend for each of the following:
   a. Watch repairer
   b. Retail salesperson
   c. Assembly-line worker in a home air-conditioner factory
   d. Professional athlete

3. Describe the typical benefits offered to employees in a large company. What unique types of benefits might each of the following companies offer their employees and what are the problems connected with each type?
    a. Manufacturing firms
    b. Airlines
    c. Retail stores
    d. Telephone companies
    e. Banks

4. Compare the advantages and disadvantages of hiring older workers. Why do you think firms such as Wal-Mart and McDonald's have hiring policies aimed at attracting this group?

5. To what extent do you feel employee counseling should be provided to employees? Should it be limited to issues directly involved with the company or extended to personal matters as well? Defend your answer.

Video Case

Quad Graphics (A)

Not many company presidents describe their firms as party companies. But travel to the Milwaukee suburb of Pewaukee, Wisconsin, and you will find Harry Quadracci and his 3,300 employees using precisely that term to describe Quad Graphics. "Business is the world's largest competitive sport," states Quadracci. Winning is the name of the game, and he admits that only the best team will win. Yet he also believes that the players who go on the field with smiles on their faces, ready to play and have fun, are likely to win more often. "Fun is a necessary ingredient to a successful business," he says. "It is not just a thrill or a perk. We have three simple guidelines at Quad Graphics: Make money, have fun, and don't do business with people we don't like."

Quadracci's father owned a printing company plagued with union-labor disputes. Harry, who at one time served as corporate attorney for his father's firm, left in 1971 to start his own company. His experiences with hard-nosed management decisions made him determined to develop an entirely new and radically different human resource management philosophy. In his words, "If you are a technology company, then you are a research and development company. If you are a research and development company, then you must be a knowledge company; and if you are a knowledge company, you must be a people company because that's the only place where your ideas are going to come from."

But it takes money to build a capital-intensive company in the printing industry, and money was difficult to raise at first. Quadracci and his wife launched the firm in 1971 by taking out a $35,000 loan, pledging their home as equity. They bought a single, not very reliable, printing press that they housed in a modest 20,000-square-foot plant and hired 12 employees. Today, the firm has 3,300 employees on the payroll and annual sales of one-half billion dollars. The firm currently prints over 150 different magazines and cata-

logs. Among its clients are such well-known weekly publications as *Time, Newsweek,* and *U.S. News & World Report.* Mail-order businesses like James River Traders and Lillian Vernon, seeking high quality and service satisfaction, go to Quad Graphics with their catalog printing needs.

Quadracci and his employees are particularly proud of the fact that their firm is included in the recently-published book, *The 100 Best Companies to Work for in America.* It is not a company with time clocks. No tightly-fixed job classifications or work rules restrict employees to one tiny niche in the firm. In fact, it is quite the opposite. Quadracci insists that Quad employees can be "more than they ever hoped to be." Employees have a vested interest in the company's performance for two reasons: (1) They own 40 percent of the company, and (2) a profit-sharing compensation program is aimed at linking efficiency to their take-home pay. In addition, decision making is kept on the plant floor whenever possible in the belief that the best ideas come from the hands-on workers.

Since Quad Graphics is a continuously-operating plant, work scheduling is important. Each employee works three 12-hour shifts a week and every other Sunday (at double salary). On the job, the corporate culture involves teaching and learning. Because education and training are both voluntary, employees are not *paid* to learn or teach, but rather are *expected* to do so. The underlying principle is that if you make the job easier, you can do more, with the final result that you make more money. Most of Quad's employees are high school graduates at best, and the key to corporate growth, according to Quadracci, is individual growth. Employees must not only be happy and satisfied in their work, they must also be challenged.

Quad education classes, held in a revamped elementary school, greatly affect every Quad Graphics employee. Nearly 1,000 people go through one of the various training courses each week — in almost every instance on their own time. The only exception is the required basic orientation course. In addition to job training, employees focus on "people skills" and learn to trust and depend on each other.

Once the orientation program is completed, employees are expected to begin learning more than one job. This way they can contribute to improving their

Notes: Beverly Geber, "Not Just Another Printing Shop," *Training,* May 1988, pp. 65–69; "Coming of Age," *Inc.,* April 1989, pp. 110–111; Corey Rosen, Katherine J. Klein, and Karen M. Young, "Where Employees Share the Profits," *Psychology Today,* January 1986, pp. 30–36; and Robert H. Waterman, Jr., *The Renewal Factor,* New York: Bantam Books, 1987, p. 194.

firm's management and productivity. This sense of shared purpose and individual responsibility provides a work environment that promotes individual effort and creative thinking. Passing on knowledge to fellow workers makes their own jobs easier and allows employees to grow in various directions.

The Quad Graphics motto is "Get big by thinking small." Getting better is the result of detailed day-to-day improvements through the participation of all employees. Quad's employees have not only developed improvements in production equipment, but new business ideas as well. Newly-established operating branches conceived by employees include ink manufacturing, equipment repair, and Quad Tech, a high-tech division that develops new printing technologies and sells them to other printers. In a recent year, this division had 150 employees and $20 million in sales.

Physical environment is an important tool in promoting employee creativity, voluntarism, and having fun at work. For example, most Quad employees no longer run machines — they run the machines that run machines. This usually means monitoring computers that have been specially developed to take over many of the mechanical tasks once performed by people. Even the appearance of the factory imparts a special kind of excitement and fun. The overhead pipes and various machines throughout the factory are painted in a rainbow of colors ranging from purple to green and yellow to red. The popcorn machine on the shop floor is always available. The intent is to make the environment pleasing and comfortable.

Employees not only participate in developing new and improved techniques within the plant, but also help create facilities and programs that directly benefit themselves. They have set up child-care facilities and have excellent food services available for both work-ers and company clients. Their physical-fitness programs are designed to encourage teamwork and a sense of comradeship among employees. They plan company picnics and special events, including an annual Christmas pageant put on by the Quad employees.

Quad Graphics' state-of-the-art printing plants, phenomenal growth, and unique philosophy of management help give employees a sense of shared purpose. In addition, technology is used to create a better, happier, more satisfying work environment for Quad workers. This combination of personal vision and technical development have made the company, in less than 20 years, one of the most successful and respected in U.S. industry. It is an idealized partnership of ideas and employees, where anything seems possible.

Questions

1. How does employee compensation at Quad Graphics differ from most other firms? What alternative compensation plans do they use? Relate your answer to Table 11.2 on page 314.

2. What are some of the benefit programs offered to Quad Graphics employees? In what respects are their programs different from those of a typical firm?

3. Explain the concept of *voluntarism* at Quad Graphics. Are there other ways to encourage off-the-job training?

4. Explain how Quad's management style and unique employee-company philosophy is likely to help it attract and retain self-directed individuals as employees.

5. What impact is the fact that Quad Graphics is an employee-owned firm likely to have on its performance appraisal system?

12 *Labor-Management Relations*

Learning Goals

1. To explain why labor unions were organized and to list the primary goals of organized labor.

2. To identify the major federal laws affecting labor unions and to explain the key provisions of each law.

3. To explain how collective bargaining agreements are established and the roles played by arbitrators and mediators.

4. To outline the sources of power, or "weapons," of labor and management.

5. To identify the sources of future union membership growth.

The competitive battles among Philadelphia area supermarkets during the late 1970s and early 1980s were about to claim a casualty: The A & P stores were about to close their doors permanently. Such a move would hardly have surprised shoppers who had been deserting A & P, and worker morale had reached an all-time low. The company was referred to by competitors as one of the worst-run supermarkets in the business.

A cynic once defined hard times this way: "A *recession* is a situation when large numbers of people cannot find employment. A *depression* is when you are out of a job." Back in 1982, *panic* might have been a better label for the feelings of the members of United Food & Commercial Workers (UFCW) Local 1357, the union representing A & P's Philadelphia-area employees. Closing these stores would cost the workers their jobs.

Job security is one of the primary motivations for workers to band together. Company and union officials, working together, came up with a novel idea to save these jobs. The employees would share in the business risks involved in operating the supermarkets in exchange for a share of profits. In exchange for a pay cut, union members would receive a cash bonus equal to 1 percent of store sales if total labor costs were held at 10 percent of sales. If labor costs were 11 percent of sales, employees would receive a 0.5 percent bonus; at 9 percent of sales, they would earn a bonus of 1.5 percent. These savings could be accomplished in two ways: by working more efficiently and by increasing weekly sales.

Even though profits in the supermarket industry average only about

1 percent of sales, the chain's management agreed to the proposal. Overall labor costs at A & P were 13 percent, while the industry average was 12 percent.

The gamble paid off. A & P's Philadelphia stores, now called Super Fresh, once again became profitable operations. Worker morale is high. In a recent year, the Philadelphia-area workers earned an average of $11.25 an hour in wages and bonuses. By comparison, the average food store wage in the area that year was $10.60.

With a vested interest in improving their stores' operations, A & P employees have made several useful suggestions at their bimonthly meetings with the store managers. In one black and Italian neighborhood, for example, employees suggested adding large sections of popular ethnic food. Previously, all of the stores had been stocked with virtually identical inventories. The result of such suggestions was a 24 percent increase in per-store sales in the two years following the new arrangement.

Even though the "Philadelphia experiment" has proved highly successful, many union officials have mixed feelings about any plan that puts part of employee wages at risk. However, the increased competition in the retail food business, combined with a flurry of mergers, has already made this incentive-sharing model an industry standard.[1]

Photo source: Courtesy of A&P.

labor union
Group of workers united by common goals such as wages, hours, and working conditions.

craft union
Labor union consisting of skilled workers in a specific craft or trade.

industrial union
Labor union consisting of all workers in a specific industry, regardless of occupation or skill level.

Chapter Overview

For more than 200 years, individual workers have sought methods of improving their living standards, working conditions, and job security. Gradually they learned that, by uniting, their collective strength was often sufficient to elicit responses to their demands. And so labor unions were born. A **labor union** is a group of workers who have banded together to achieve common goals in the key areas of wages, hours, and working conditions. Two types of labor unions exist in the United States: craft and industrial. A **craft union** consists of skilled workers in a specific craft or trade, such as carpenters, painters, machinists, and printers. An **industrial union** is made up of all the workers in a given industry, regardless of their occupation or skill level. Industrial unions include the United Steelworkers, the United Auto Workers, and the Amalgamated Clothing Workers.

Why Are Labor Unions Needed?

The Industrial Revolution brought the advantages of specialization and division of labor. These factors increased efficiency because each worker could specialize in some aspect of the production process and become proficient at the work. Bringing together numerous workers also resulted in increased output over the individual handicraft methods of production. The factory system converted the jack-of-all-trades into a specialist.

But industrial workers of the nineteenth and the early twentieth centuries discovered that the Industrial Revolution produced a more sinister impact on their lives. Specialization resulted in dependence on the factory for their livelihood. In prosperous times, they were assured of employment. But when depressions came, they were out of work. Unemployment insurance was a subject for dreamers, and "the poorhouse" represented reality for unemployed workers.

Working conditions were often bad. In many factories, workdays were long and safety standards nonexistent. At the beginning of the nineteenth century, young boys and girls were pressed into the work force to earn a few pennies to help their families. In Boston in 1830, children comprised two-fifths of the labor force. The entire cotton and woolen industries were based on the labor of young women. Work hours were from daybreak to dark, and wages were low. In the spinning and weaving mills of New Jersey, children earned an average of a little more than $1 a week. Imprisonment for debt was common.

By the end of the century, the workweek was typically 60 hours, but in some industries, such as steel, it was 72 or even 84 hours — seven 12-hour days a week. Working conditions were still frequently unsafe, and child labor was still common.

Workers gradually learned that through bargaining as a unified group they could obtain improvements in job security and better wages and working conditions. The organized efforts of Philadelphia printers in 1786 resulted in the first U.S. minimum wage — $1 a day. One hundred years later, New York City streetcar conductors banded together in successful negotiations that reduced their workday from 17 to 12 hours. The sweeping changes in labor-management relations that occurred during the past century produced profound changes in wages, hours of work, and working conditions. Visible signs of success of the labor movement are the presence of United Auto Workers President Owen F.

Photo source: National Archives, Records of the Children's Bureau.

In 1910, 12-year-old Addie Laird worked long hours for little pay as a spinner in a Vermont cotton mill. Addie was one of thousands of children who entered the work force in the early 1900s, a period characterized by unsafe working conditions. Note that Addie, like many other children, worked barefoot. It would be another 28 years before legislation was passed outlawing child labor.

Bieber on the board of directors of Chrysler Corporation and employee-designated board members at Kaiser Aluminum, CF&I Steel, Pan American, Transcon, and Wheeling-Pittsburgh.[2]

The History of U.S. Labor Unions

Although the history of trade unionism in the United States can be traced back to before the Declaration of Independence, early unions were loose-knit local organizations that served primarily as friendship groups or benevolent societies to help fellow workers in need. Such unions were typically short-lived, growing during prosperous times and suffering severely during depressions.

The first truly national union was the Knights of Labor, founded in 1869. By 1886, its membership exceeded 700,000 workers, but it soon split into factions. One faction had revolutionary aims, wanting the government to take over production. The second faction wanted the union to continue focusing on the improvement of the economic well-being of union members and opposed the socialist tendencies of some members. This faction merged with a group of unaffiliated craft unions in 1886 to form the **American Federation of Labor (AFL)**, which became a national union made up of affiliated individual craft unions.

American Federation of Labor (AFL)
National union made up of affiliated individual craft unions.

The AFL's first president was Samuel Gompers, a dynamic man who believed labor unions should operate within the framework of the economic system and who was totally opposed to socialism. In 1903, he stated:

I want to tell you, Socialists, that I have studied your philosophy; read your works on economics. . . . I have heard your orators and watched the work of your movement the world over. I have kept close watch upon your doctrines for thirty years; have been closely associated with many of you, and know how you think and what you propose. I know, too, what you have up your sleeve. And I want to say that I am entirely at variance with your philosophy. I declare it to you, I am not only at variance with your doctrines, but with your philosophy. Economically, you are unsound; socially, you are wrong; industrially, you are an impossibility.[3]

Gompers' bread-and-butter concept of unionism kept the labor movement focused on the critical objectives of wages, hours, and working conditions. The AFL grew rapidly, and by 1920 three out of four organized workers were AFL members.

Union growth between 1920 and 1935 was slow. The philosophy of organizing labor along craft lines that had accounted for the AFL's 40-year growth record led to difficulties because there were few nonunion skilled craft workers left to organize. One union formed during this period was the Brotherhood of Sleeping Car Porters. Asa Philip Randolph organized the union in 1925 to ensure fair wages for black railway workers. The U.S. Postal Service honored Randolph with a commemorative stamp, shown in the advertisement in Figure 12.1.

Several unions in the AFL began to organize workers in mass-production automobile and steel industries. Successes in organizing the communications, mining, newspaper, steel, rubber, and automobile industries resulted in the formation of a new group, the **Congress of Industrial Organizations (CIO)** — a national union made up of affiliated individual industrial unions. This new technique of organizing entire industries rather than individual crafts was so successful that the CIO soon rivaled the AFL in size.

Congress of Industrial Organizations (CIO)
National union made up of affiliated individual industrial unions.

In 1955, the two groups united under the presidency of George Meany. The only major national union not affiliated with the AFL-CIO is the National Education Association. Today, more than 200 separate unions exist in the United States, approximately half of which are affiliated with the AFL-CIO.

Currently, almost 17 million U.S. workers — 17 percent of the nation's full-time labor force — belong to labor unions. Although the traditional strength of unions has been in blue-collar industries and trades, during the past decade, the organized sector has become increasingly white-collar and female. White-collar workers now make up 38 percent of all organized labor, and 50 percent of all state and local government employees are organized. In addition, women account for more than 34 percent of all union members. New York is the most organized state; South Carolina is the least.[4]

Local, National, and International Unions

national union
Labor organization comprised of numerous local chapters.

local union
Branch of a national union representing members in a specific area.

A **national union** has as its base many local unions, which form the entire union organizational structure. The **local union** is a branch of a national union, representing union members in a given geographical area. After receiving approval from United Auto Workers national headquarters, representatives of UAW Local 969 in Columbus, Ohio, recently signed an agreement with a General

Figure 12.1 Honoring a Union Organizer

Source: Courtesy of U.S. Postal Service.

Motors plant that changed certain seniority and wage provisions, cutting production costs by $17 million a year and saving about 770 jobs in the aluminum moldings department.[5]

Local craft unions represent workers such as carpenters or plumbers. The local union receives its charter from the national union and operates under the national union's constitution, bylaws, and rules. Most workers identify closely with their local union and are acquainted with local union officers, even though they are unlikely to attend regular union meetings except for important issues such as contract negotiations, strike votes, or union elections. (An estimated 5 to 10 percent of the unionized work force regularly attends local union meetings.)

The six largest national and international unions in the United States are shown in Figure 12.2. Almost one in every two union members belongs to one of these giant organizations. The 2 million-member Teamsters union ranks as the largest union, followed by the National Education Association, with 1.7 million members. The Service Employees International; United Steelworkers, Machinists and Aerospace Workers; and Communications Workers round out the nation's ten largest unions.

The giant unions shown in Figure 12.2 occupy the chief positions in organized labor due to membership size and their influence over the locals. In such industries as automobiles, steel, and electrical, collective bargaining over major issues occurs at the national level with representatives of various local unions present. An **international union** is a national union with membership outside

international union
National union with membership outside the United States.

Figure 12.2   The Six Largest Unions in the United States

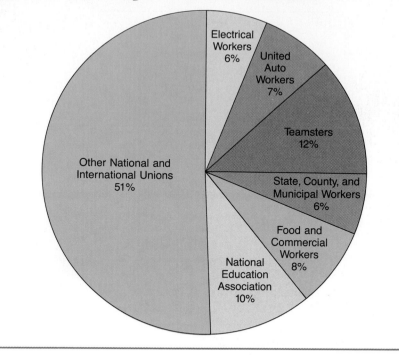

Source: Data reported in *1988 World Almanac and Information Book,* pp. 91–92.

the United States, usually in Canada. In some instances, the union chooses a name, such as the Service Employees International, to reflect its international status.

While local unions form the base of the union structure, at the top are federations such as the AFL-CIO. A **federation** is comprised of many national unions and serves a mediation and political function. However, some unions, such as the National Education Association, do not belong to the AFL-CIO. In 1989, the International Brotherhood of Teamsters was readmitted, 30 years after the union was expelled for refusing to answer charges of corruption.[6] In addition to representing national unions, other federations are usually present in large cities to represent various local unions as political and municipal spokespersons.

A major function of federations is mediation of disputes between affiliated unions. In addition, they perform a political function in representing organized labor in public issues. Their officers represent U.S. labor in world affairs and in contacts with unions in other nations. They frequently speak before Congress and other branches of government, and they assist in coordinating efforts to organize nonunion workers.

federation

Association comprised of numerous national unions; serves a mediation and political function.

Labor Legislation

Government attitudes toward unionism have varied considerably during the past century. These shifting attitudes can be seen in major pieces of legislation enacted during this period.

Carrying giant-size pencils and a banner, members of the Writers Guild of America picketed in front of the Manhattan, New York, offices of Orion and Columbia Pictures during a strike against the Alliance of Motion Picture and Television Producers. Another 3,000 WGA strikers picketed Walt Disney studios while a plane flew overhead carrying a banner saying "Stop Mickey Mousing around with our WGA." Strikers can stage such peaceful demonstrations as a result of the Norris-La Guardia Act, which limited management's ability to obtain federal injunctions stopping lawful union activities.

Photo source: S. Ferry/Gamma Liaison.

The Norris-La Guardia Act

The **Norris-La Guardia Act** (1932) is early federal legislation aimed at protecting unions through greatly reducing management's ability to obtain injunctions halting union activities. Before this time, employers found it easy to obtain court decrees forbidding strikes, peaceful picketing, and even membership drives — activities vital to union effectiveness. Once obtained, such injunctions automatically made the union a wrongdoer in the eyes of the law if it continued the activities.

Norris-La Guardia Act
Federal legislation that protects unions by reducing management's ability to obtain injunctions halting union activities.

The Wagner Act

In 1935, Congress passed the National Labor Relations Act, or **Wagner Act**, which legalized collective bargaining and required employers to negotiate with elected representatives of their employees. This legislation has been called organized labor's Magna Carta. Before this time, union activities were often ruled violations of the Sherman Act, which prohibited attempts to monopolize.

The Wagner Act not only legalized collective bargaining, but it also ordered employers to bargain with their workers' agents if a majority of those workers chose to be represented by a union. The act set up the **National Labor Relations Board (NLRB)** to supervise union elections and prohibited such unfair labor practices as firing workers for joining a union, refusing to hire union sympathizers, threatening to close the firm if workers unionized, interfering with or dominating the administration of a union, and refusing to bargain with a union.

Wagner Act
Federal law legalizing collective bargaining and requiring employers to bargain with the elected representatives of their employees; also known as the National Labor Relations Act.

National Labor Relations Board (NLRB)
Federal agency that supervises union elections and prohibits unfair labor practices on the part of management.

The Fair Labor Standards Act

The **Fair Labor Standards Act** (1938) continued the wave of pro-union legislation. It set a federal minimum wage and maximum basic hours for workers employed in industries engaged in interstate commerce. It also outlawed the

Fair Labor Standards Act
Federal law that sets a minimum wage and maximum basic hours for workers employed in industries engaged in interstate commerce.

use of child labor. The first minimum wage was set at $.25 an hour, with exceptions for farm workers and retail employees.

The recent increase in the minimum wage was the first change since it was set at $3.35 per hour in 1981. The new minimum wage results in minimum annual pay for full-time workers of less than four-fifths of the federal government's official poverty floor for a family of four. But the typical holder of a minimum-wage job does not match the profile many people think of. He or she is not from a poor family, not a household head, and not destined to remain at this wage rate for a long period. A recent study by the Congressional Budget Office revealed that about 70 percent of minimum-wage workers came from families with incomes at least 50 percent above the poverty line. Also, minimum-wage jobs are not usually held by heads of families. About two-thirds are held by young (24 and under) and single workers. Approximately one in three is a teenager. The typical minimum-wage worker is a teenager from a nonpoor family working as a waiter or waitress. One-third of all minimum-wage jobs are in restaurants. Most workers do not remain at minimum wage. Some employers pay the minimum wage to entry-level employees but quickly give raises to those they want to keep. Other jobs that permanently pay the minimum wage typically have high turnover rates.[7]

The Fair Labor Standards Act set a maximum basic week of 40 hours. Workers are allowed to stay on the job longer than 40 hours a week, but only on the basis of overtime pay.

The Taft-Hartley Act

Government support of organized labor produced a generation of growth for the unions. One by one the industrial giants — Ford, General Motors, U.S. Steel — were unionized. For the first time in history, they recognized a CIO union as their workers' bargaining agent. Union membership jumped from under 3 million in 1933 to almost 15 million by 1945. Union members in 1945 represented 36 percent of all nonagricultural employees, an all-time high.

The Wagner Act focused on unfair labor practices by employers; it said nothing about unfair practices by labor. These became the subject of the **Taft-Hartley Act** (1947), passed by Congress over the veto of President Harry Truman. The legislation was designed to balance the power of unions and management by prohibiting a number of unfair union practices. It was passed against the background of a postwar wave of strikes, as the now-giant unions for the first time made full use of their strength. Paralyzing strikes in steel, coal, and shipping alarmed the public. So did **jurisdictional strikes** — those resulting not from disputes with employers but from two unions fighting each other for jurisdiction over a group of workers. Labor, it was argued, had been given an overdose of power, and the new act was designed to curb it.

Union Security Provisions

A **closed shop** is a business having an employment agreement under which management cannot hire nonunion workers. Before being hired by such a firm, workers must join the union and remain union members, as a condition of employment. Unions considered the closed shop an essential ingredient of security. If all workers were union members, they reasoned, the employer would have to recognize the union. The closed shop also gave unions unquestionable power in the areas of wages and working conditions. Finally, because all em-

Taft-Hartley Act
Federal law designed to balance the power of unions and management by prohibiting a number of unfair union practices.

jurisdictional strikes
Strikes resulting from disputes between two unions seeking jurisdiction over a group of workers.

closed shop
Illegal employment policy of refusing to hire nonunion workers.

Figure 12.3   States with Right-to-Work Laws

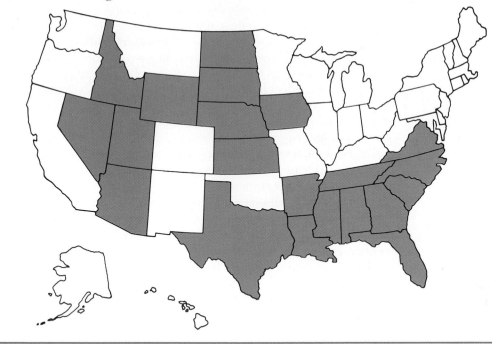

ployees enjoyed the benefits of union contracts, it was believed all should support the union.

Employers argued that a fundamental principle of freedom was violated if people were forced to join an organization as a condition of employment. If an employer could hire only union members, they argued, the best, most qualified workers might not be hired. Finally, employers claimed that, with a guaranteed membership, union leaders were likely to become irresponsible and to deal dishonestly with their members. Congress showed its support for these arguments by passing the Taft-Hartley Act, which prohibits the closed shop.

The **union shop** is a modification of the closed shop. Under such an agreement, all current employees must join the union as soon as it is certified as their legitimate bargaining agent. New employees must join the union within a specified period, normally 30 days. The majority of all union contracts in 1990 specified union shop requirements.

An **agency shop** is a business having an employment agreement whereby all qualified employees can be hired, but nonunion workers must pay the union a fee equal to union dues. This agreement eliminates what the unions have labeled "free riders," who might benefit from union negotiations without supporting the union financially. (Some nonunion members in agency shops have referred to themselves as "captive passengers" rather than free riders.)

The **open shop** is the opposite of the closed shop, making union membership voluntary for all existing and new employees. Individuals who choose not to join a union are not required to pay union dues or a fee.

The Taft-Hartley Act permits states to pass **right-to-work laws** that prohibit the union shop and make compulsory union membership illegal. Located mainly in the South and in the Great Plains areas, the 21 right-to-work states are shown in Figure 12.3.

union shop
Employment policy requiring nonunion workers to join the union within a specified period.

agency shop
Employment policy not requiring union membership, but nonunion members pay a fee equal to union dues.

open shop
Employment policy making union membership voluntary for all employees.

right-to-work laws
State laws prohibiting compulsory union membership.

Other Unfair Union Practices

featherbedding
Paying workers for work not done.

Other unfair union practices outlawed by the Taft-Hartley Act include refusal of the union to bargain with the employer, striking without 60 days' notice, featherbedding, and most secondary boycotts. **Featherbedding** is a situation in which workers are paid for work not done. Most writers cite the railroad fireman on diesel locomotives as the best current example of featherbedding. Author and former Avis President Robert Townsend cites an English example of the practice: The British created a civil service job in 1803 calling for a man to stand on the Cliffs of Dover with a spyglass. He was supposed to ring a bell if he saw Napoleon coming. The job was abolished in 1945.[8]

boycott
An attempt to keep people from purchasing goods or services from a company.

primary boycott
Boycott in which union members are told not to patronize a specific firm.

A **boycott** is an attempt to prevent people from purchasing a firm's goods or services. There are two kinds of boycotts: primary and secondary. In a **primary boycott**, union members are told not to patronize a firm directly involved in a labor dispute. Even though 90 percent of U.S. brewery industry employees are union members (in most cases, the Teamsters), Adolph Coors Co. has been nonunion since 1978. In 1988, the AFL-CIO called off a ten-year boycott against the firm's products in exchange for management's promise to hold a union vote supervised by a neutral third party, the American Arbitration Association.[9]

secondary boycott
Boycott or work stoppage intended to force an employer to cease dealing in the product of another firm.

By contrast, a **secondary boycott** is a boycott or work stoppage intended to force an employer to stop dealing with another firm involved in a labor dispute. Under the Taft-Hartley Act, secondary boycotts deemed by the courts to be coercive are illegal.

Also under Taft-Hartley, employers can sue unions for breach of contract and can engage in antiunion activities as long as coercion is not involved. Unions must make financial reports to their members and disclose their officers' salaries; they cannot use dues for political contributions or charge excessive initiation fees. The act also allows the president of the United States to ask the courts for a **cooling-off period** — an 80-day suspension of threatened strikes that "imperil the national health and safety." At the end of the cooling-off period, union members must vote by secret ballot on the latest company offer.

cooling-off period
Government-enforced 80-day suspension of a threatened strike.

The Landrum-Griffin Act

Landrum-Griffin Act
Federal law requiring regularly scheduled elections of union officers by secret ballot and increased regulation of the handling of union funds.

The Taft-Hartley Act was amended in 1959 by the **Landrum-Griffin Act**, which requires regularly scheduled elections of union officers by secret ballot and places added controls on the handling of union funds. Officials handling such funds must be bonded, and federal penalties are imposed for embezzlement. The act was passed against a background of hearings by the McClellan Senate committee investigating labor racketeering. The committee had exposed "gangsterism, bribery, and hoodlumism" in the affairs of some unions. Several union leaders had taken union funds for personal use, had accepted payoffs from employers for union protection, and were even involved in blackmail, arson, and murder.

The Plant-Closing Notification Act

During the 1980s, increased competition on a global scale threatened the jobs of U.S. workers in a growing number of industries. American firms, determined to remain competitive, often turned to foreign production facilities in their at-

One of the major labor-management disputes of the past decade involved the AFL-CIO nationwide boycott against Adolph Coors Co. The National Education Association joined the boycott even though it is not affiliated with the federation. The boycott caused Coors to lose market share and company profits. After the AFL-CIO agreed to end the boycott, Coors added 2,000 new accounts that were out of its reach because of the boycott. Union organizers now hope they can persuade Coors workers to vote in favor of being unionized.

Photo source: © Eric Lars Bakke 1989.

tempts to hold the line on costs. Concerns about plant closings and resultant unemployment led to passage of the **Plant-Closing Notification Act of 1988**. The law requires employers with more than 100 employees to give workers and local elected officials 60 days' warning of a shutdown or mass layoff. Businesses must provide advance notice if 50 or more workers in a single site of employment are to lose their jobs. In addition, a $1 billion Worker Readjustment Program was created to assist workers displaced because of plant closings or mass layoffs by providing job search, placement and counseling services, educational opportunities, and where necessary, child care, commuting assistance, and personal financial counseling.

Both organized labor and the National League of Cities supported the act. The new law gives cities more time to plan for the loss of a major employer. It also means more rapid response time to assist in retraining and finding jobs in the community for displaced workers. Even though the nation's largest corporations have traditionally given advance notice of closings, the new law makes this practice mandatory on the part of all medium- and large-size companies.[10]

Plant-Closing Notification Act of 1988
Federal legislation aimed at assisting employees and cities by requiring employers to give 60 days' notice before a plant closing or mass layoff.

The Collective Bargaining Process

The primary objective of labor unions is the improvement of wages, hours, and working conditions for its members. This goal is achieved primarily through **collective bargaining**, a process of negotiation between management and union representatives for the purpose of arriving at mutually acceptable wages and working conditions for employees.

collective bargaining
Negotiation between management and union representatives concerning wages and working conditions.

Once a majority of the workers in a firm accept a union, it is certified by the National Labor Relations Board and must be recognized by the firm's management as the legal collective bargaining agent for all employees. The stage is then set for representatives of the union and management to meet formally at the bargaining table to work out a collective bargaining agreement or contract.

Bargaining Patterns

Bargaining patterns — and the number of unions and employers involved — vary for different industries and occupational categories. Most collective bargaining involves *single-plant single-employer agreements.* On the other hand, *multiplant single-employer agreements* apply to all plants of the employer. For example, terms and conditions approved in the bargaining agreement between Westinghouse Electric and the International Brotherhood of Electrical Workers apply to all Westinghouse plants. *Coalition bargaining* involves negotiations between a coalition of several unions representing the employees of one company. In the case of *industrywide bargaining,* a single national union engages in collective bargaining with several employers in a particular industry.

In general, manufacturers prefer to bargain with each local union representing its various employee groups on an individual basis rather than deal with a coalition of several unions. The influence and power of smaller, separate unions are likely to be less than that of a coalition.

The Bargaining Zone

Issues covered in bargaining agreements include wages, work hours, benefits, union activities and responsibilities, grievance handling and arbitration, and employee rights and seniority. As is the case in all types of negotiations, the collective bargaining process is one of demands, proposals, and counterproposals that ultimately result in compromise and agreement. Figure 12.4 illustrates a contract negotiation by focusing upon a single wage issue and two security issues — a union-shop provision and a seniority rule. The horizontal lines represent a continuum of outcomes for union and management. The union's initial demand — and the best outcome — will be a 10 percent wage increase (based upon productivity increases and increases in the cost of living) and the addition of a union-shop provision. Management's initial offer will be a 2 percent wage increase and elimination of current security rules. The initial demands merely represent a starting point in the negotiations; they are rarely, if ever, accepted by the other party. As the figure reveals, each party has a final offer, beyond which it will not bargain. If the union does not accept management's final offer of a 4 percent pay increase and no union shop, the union will go on strike. Likewise, if management rejects the union's final offer of an 8 percent increase and retention of the seniority rule, management will be forced to close the plant, move its operations, or bring new employees into its existing facility rather than agree to a settlement that would make it unable to remain profitable. Between each party's initial and final offers, however, is the **bargaining zone**, a "gray area" of possibility within which both parties will likely come to agreement. The final agreement depends on the negotiating skills and relative power of management and union representatives.

bargaining zone
The range of collective bargaining before a union will strike or before management will close the plant.

Figure 12.4   The Bargaining Zone

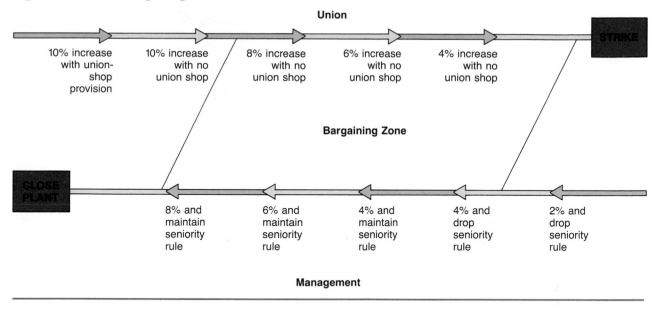

The Union Contract

Union contracts, which typically cover a two- or three-year period, are often the result of days and even weeks of discussion, disagreement, compromise, and eventual agreement. Once agreement is reached, union members must vote to accept or reject the contract. If the contract is rejected, union representatives may resume the bargaining process with management representatives, or the union members may strike to obtain their demands.

Once ratified by the union membership, the contract becomes the legally binding agreement for all labor-management relations during the period specified. Contracts typically include such areas as wages, industrial relations, and methods of settling labor-management disputes. Some are only a few pages in length, while others run more than 200 pages. Figure 12.5 indicates topics typically included in a union contract.

COLAs and Givebacks

Forty percent of all organized workers are currently covered by contracts with a **cost-of-living escalator clause (COLA)**. Such clauses are designed to protect the real income of workers during periods of inflation. They allow wages to increase in proportion to increases in the Bureau of Labor Statistics' consumer price index (CPI). A recent United Steelworkers contract with aluminum workers is typical: It calls for a one-cent-per-hour wage increase for each 0.3 percent rise in the CPI. During the three-year period ending in 1989, this COLA clause yielded average wage increases of $1.05 an hour. United Steelworkers officials expect the same clause to generate an additional $1 an hour by 1992. Increased inflation during the past few years has increased the importance of COLA clauses

cost-of-living escalator clause (COLA)
Clause in a bargaining agreement that protects real income by adjusting wages to reflect consumer price index changes.

Figure 12.5   Items Typically Included in a Union Contract

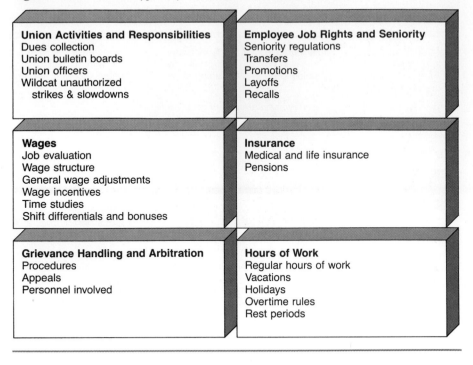

Union Activities and Responsibilities
Dues collection
Union bulletin boards
Union officers
Wildcat unauthorized
    strikes & slowdowns

Employee Job Rights and Seniority
Seniority regulations
Transfers
Promotions
Layoffs
Recalls

Wages
Job evaluation
Wage structure
General wage adjustments
Wage incentives
Time studies
Shift differentials and bonuses

Insurance
Medical and life insurance
Pensions

Grievance Handling and Arbitration
Procedures
Appeals
Personnel involved

Hours of Work
Regular hours of work
Vacations
Holidays
Overtime rules
Rest periods

givebacks

Wage and fringe benefit concessions by union members to assist employer in remaining competitive.

in labor contracts. During 1989, payouts under COLAs made up 30 percent of overall union wage increases.

A major concern of employees — union and nonunion — in recent years is the nation's balance of trade deficit and the ability of U.S. companies to compete in world markets. One tangible response of unions in many major industries has been **givebacks** — wage and fringe benefit concessions to assist employers in remaining competitive and continuing to provide jobs for union members. When the automobile industry was hurt by foreign imports and Chrysler faced the prospect of financial bankruptcy, United Auto Workers there accepted wage reductions to assist the automaker. By the 1980s, Chrysler had returned to profitability. The turnaround was so successful that the firm acquired American Motors Corporation, adding the highly profitable Jeep line of utility vehicles to its existing product line.

Givebacks have been common in industries fighting off competition from abroad — including auto, rubber, steel, mining, cement, agricultural and construction equipment, and meatpacking — and in such industries as airlines, trucking, and telecommunications where deregulation forced firms to become more cost-conscious to remain competitive. In the steel industry, union members at Wheeling-Pittsburgh agreed to eliminate six paid holidays, one week of vacation, and the cost-of-living adjustment (COLA). Meatpacking giant Wilson Foods reached agreement with its union to tie pay increases solely to company profitability, and American Airlines persuaded its unions to permit a longer probation period with no medical coverage for first-year machinists and ground workers. As one industry analyst put it, "It's competition that is forcing these

Top Banana.

New Wrangler
Islander.

Only in a Jeep.

Union givebacks, government loan guarantees, and continuing commitments from company employees and managers made possible the Chrysler Corporation turnaround. One of the firm's most profitable product offerings is the Jeep, acquired in a merger with AMC. The Jeep, descended from the World War II all-purpose utility vehicle, has never been more popular among auto purchasers.

Photo source: Courtesy of Chrysler Corporation.

issues — competition that's come from abroad and from deregulation and from new nonunion businesses in the United States."[11]

Settling Union-Management Disputes

Although strikes make newspaper headlines, 95 percent of all union-management negotiations result in a signed agreement without a work stoppage. Approximately 140,000 union contracts are currently in force in the United States. Of these, 133,000 were the result of successful negotiations with no work stoppage.

Mediation

When negotiations do break down, disagreements between union and management representatives may be settled by **mediation** — the process of bringing in a third party, called a *mediator,* to make recommendations for the settlement of differences.

The Taft-Hartley Act requires labor and management to notify each other of desired changes in union contracts 60 days before the contracts expire. They must also notify a special agency, the Federal Mediation and Conciliation Service, within 30 days after that time if a new contract has not been accepted. The agency's staff of several hundred mediators assists in settling union-management disagreements that affect interstate commerce. In addition, some states — for example, New York, Pennsylvania, and California — have their own mediation agencies.

mediation
Process of settling union-management disputes through recommendations of an impartial third party.

Although the mediator does not serve as a decision maker, union and management representatives can be assisted in reaching an agreement by the mediator's suggestions, advice, and compromise solutions. Because both sides must give their confidence and trust to the mediator, that person's impartiality is essential. Mediators are often selected from the ranks of community social or political leaders, attorneys, professors, and distinguished national figures.

Arbitration

arbitration
Process of bringing an impartial third party into a union-management dispute to render a legally binding decision.

The final step in settling union-management differences is **arbitration** — the process of bringing in an impartial third party, called an *arbitrator,* who renders a binding decision in the dispute. The impartial third party must be acceptable to the union and to management, and his or her decision is legally enforceable. In essence, the arbitrator acts as a judge, making a decision after listening to both sides of the argument. **Voluntary arbitration** occurs when both union and management representatives decide to present their unresolved issues to an impartial third party. Ninety percent of all union contracts call for the use of arbitration, if union and management representatives fail to reach an agreement.

voluntary arbitration
Arbitration in which both union and management representatives decide to present their unresolved issues to an impartial third party.

compulsory arbitration
Arbitration to which both union and management representatives must submit as required by a third party.

Occasionally a third party, usually the federal government, will require management and labor to submit to **compulsory arbitration**. Although it is rarely used in the United States, there is considerable interest in compulsory arbitration as a means of eliminating prolonged strikes affecting major industries and threatening to disrupt the economy.

Grievance Procedures

The union contract serves as a guide to relations between the firm's management and its employees. The rights of each party are stated in the agreement. But no contract, regardless of how detailed it is, will eliminate the possibility of disagreement.

Differences of opinion may arise on how to interpret a particular clause in the contract. Management may interpret the layoff policy of the contract as based on seniority for each work shift. The union may see it as based on the seniority of all employees. Such differences can be the beginning of a grievance.

grievance
Employee or union complaint that management is violating some provision of the union contract.

A **grievance** — whether by a single worker or by the entire union — is a complaint that management is violating some provision of the union contract. Because grievance handling is the primary source of contact between union officials and management from the signing of one contract to the next, the resolving of grievances plays a major role in the relationship between the employer and the union. Since grievances are likely to arise over such matters as transfers, work assignments, and seniority, almost all union contracts require that these complaints be submitted to a formal grievance procedure. Figure 12.6 shows the five steps involved in a typical grievance procedure. As this figure indicates, the employee's grievance is first submitted to the immediate supervisor by the **shop steward**, the union's representative in the organization. If the problem is solved, it goes no further. But if no satisfactory agreement is reached, a higher union official may take the grievance to a higher manager. If the highest company officer cannot settle the grievance, it is submitted to an outside arbitrator for a final and binding decision.

shop steward
Local union member responsible for representing other union members on the job on a daily basis.

Figure 12.6   Steps in the Grievance Procedure

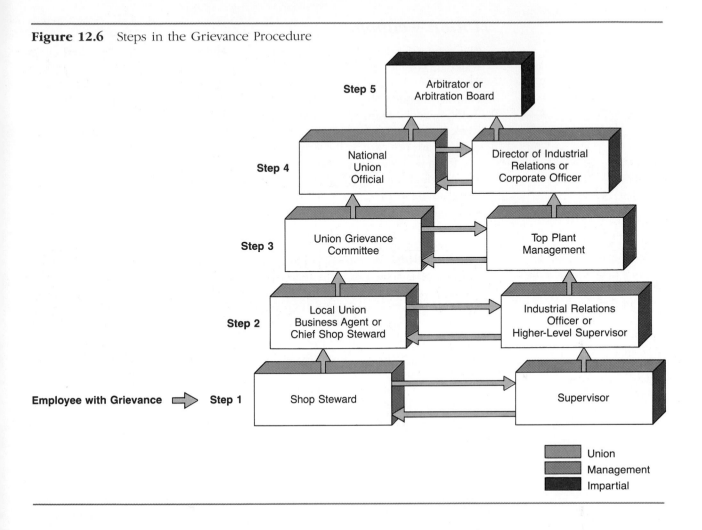

Complex cases that pass through the various steps in the grievance procedure and end up in arbitration can cost the company or the union $5,000 or
more. In addition, such cases are time consuming. Alan Moseley, shop steward
for United Steelworkers Local 1010 at Inland Steel's Indian Harbor, Indiana,
production facility, has one pending case that has dragged on since 1983. When
such delays occur, shop stewards are caught in the middle and are likely to be
attacked by both management and fellow union members. "You've got to have a
leather hide in this business," Moseley points out.[12]

Weapons of Unions and Management

Although most differences between labor and management are settled through
the collective bargaining process or through a formal grievance procedure, both
unions and management occasionally resort to weapons of power to make their
demands known.

Union Weapons

strike
Employees' temporary work stoppage until a dispute is settled or contract signed.

The chief weapons of unions are strikes, picketing, and boycotts. The **strike**, or walkout, is one of the most effective tools of the labor union. It involves a temporary work stoppage by employees until a dispute has been settled or a contract signed. The 1989 strike against Eastern Airlines by the machinists' union — representing mechanics, baggage handlers, and ground crew — halted work for 31,000 Eastern employees in 80 U.S. and 38 foreign cities. Since striking workers are not paid by the company, unions generally establish strike funds to pay them so they can continue striking.

Although the power to strike is the ultimate union weapon, it is not used lightly. In many cases, the threat of a strike is almost as effective as an actual work stoppage. The number of worker-days lost due to strikes represents slightly more than 1 percent of all lost time — less than the amount of time lost from work due to the common cold.

picketing
Workers marching at a plant entrance protesting against some management practice.

Picketing — workers marching at the entrances of the employer's plant as a public protest against some management practice — is another effective form of union pressure. As long as picketing does not involve violence or intimidation, it is protected under the U.S. Constitution as freedom of speech. Picketing can take place for a number of reasons; it may accompany a strike or it may be a protest against alleged unfair labor practices. Because union workers usually refuse to cross picket lines, the firm may be unable to obtain deliveries and other services.

As defined earlier, a boycott is an organized attempt to keep the public from purchasing the goods or services of a firm. Some unions have been quite successful in organizing boycotts. A primary boycott involves only union members who are not to patronize the specified firm. Some unions even fine members who defy a primary boycott.

Although the Taft-Hartley Act outlaws coercive secondary boycotts, a 1988 Supreme Court ruling significantly expanded the rights of unions to use this weapon. Although picketing a firm to force it to stop dealing with another company involved in a labor dispute is illegal, the court ruled that other forms of expression, such as distributing handbills at the site of the first firm, are not. This approach has been used recently by the United Paperworkers International Union in its strike against International Paper Company. In addition to secondary boycotts against two IP lenders, Bank of Boston and Provident National Bank, the paperworkers have also called for a nationwide boycott of Avon Products. Stanley Gault, an Avon board member, is also on the board of directors of International Paper.[13]

Management Weapons

lockout
Management's closing of a firm to bring pressure on union members.

Management also has weapons for dealing with organized labor. In the past, it used the **lockout** — in effect, a management strike to bring pressure on union members by closing the firm. The lockout is rarely used today, unless a union strike has partially shut down a plant.

strikebreaker
Nonunion worker hired to replace a striking worker.

In recent years, management at organizations ranging from International Paper Company to the National Football League has resorted to replacing striking workers with strikebreakers. A **strikebreaker** is a nonunion worker who crosses picket lines to fill the job of a striking worker. When 1,200 members of

To continue operations during a strike against NBC, parent firm General Electric set up special strike schools to train executives in putting on a show. In this photo, the signs carried by striking members of the National Association of Broadcasting Employees and Technicians, which represents 2,800 news writers, camera operators, and engineers, protest GE management's strikebreaking tactic. GE's efforts in keeping the number one television network operating with only 700 executive substitutes actually saved the company money.

Photo source: © 1989 Andrew Popper.

Local 14 of the United Paperworkers International Union went on strike at International Paper's giant Jay, Maine, plant — the largest paper mill in the world — they were replaced by other workers willing to accept the condemnation of striking workers in return for average annual wages of $37,000, more than twice the $15,000 median for hourly workers in western Maine.[14] A 24-day walkout by NFL players resulted in three weeks of scab football played by 1,600 eager substitutes. The games went on as scheduled, and the regular players returned, minus 4 of their 16 paychecks that year.[15]

Even though strikebreakers are less difficult to recruit in high-status fields such as professional football and in high-pay industries located in areas of high unemployment, management frequently encounters difficulties in securing a sufficient number of replacement workers with the required skills. In some instances, employers have resorted to using supervisory personnel and other nonunion employees to continue operations during a strike.

Management sometimes obtains an **injunction** — a court order prohibiting some practice — to prevent excessive picketing or certain unfair union practices. Before passage of the Norris-La Guardia Act, injunctions were frequently used to prohibit all types of strikes. Since then, their use has been limited to restraint of violence, restriction of picketing, and prevention of damage to company property.

Some employers have formed an **employers' association**, a cooperative effort to present a united front in dealing with labor unions. Employers' associations may even act as negotiators for individual employers who want to reach agreements with labor unions. In industries characterized by many small firms and a single large union, there is an increasing tendency for industry-wide bargaining between the union and a single representative of the industry employers. Building contractors may bargain as a group with construction unions. Although they do not negotiate contracts, the National Association of

injunction
Court order prohibiting some practice.

employers' associations
Cooperative efforts by employers to present a united front in dealing with labor unions.

Manufacturers and the United States Chamber of Commerce are examples of employers' associations. Both groups present the views of their members on key issues.

Labor-Management Relations in Nonunionized Organizations

Although unionization is almost an implicit assumption in any discussion of labor-management relations, more than four of five workers in the United States are not union members. In some instances, very small businesses employing only a handful of employees are involved. Another portion of the nonunionized segment of the U.S. labor force consists of managerial employees. In other instances, nonunion employees are working in industries where unions have been relatively unimportant. In still other cases, nonunion employees have simply rejected attempts to establish unions in their place of employment.

In many cases, management has chosen to offer a compensation and benefit structure comparable to those of unionized firms in the area. Provision of comparable wages and working conditions coupled with effective communications, emphasis on promotions from within, and employee participation in goal-setting and grievance handling may be effective in avoiding unionization if the workers believe they would receive few additional benefits from the union dues they would have to pay. In fact, many argue that the threat of unionization is an effective tool in securing wages, benefits, and working conditions for nonunionized employees.

Handling Employee Grievances in Nonunion Firms

peer-review boards
Committees consisting of peer workers and management representatives with the power to make binding resolutions of disputes involving promotion decisions, dismissals, and other disciplinary actions.

Employee grievance systems in nonunion companies typically follow the step-by-step approach used in unionized firms. To ensure that employees are treated fairly in disputes over firings, promotions, and disciplinary actions, a growing number of firms are instituting **peer-review boards** to resolve these disputes. Major companies such as Federal Express, Digital Equipment, General Electric, Citicorp, and Borg-Warner use peer boards, typically consisting of three peers and two management representatives. When Leesa Story claimed she was unfairly passed over for a job as a power-plant control-room operator at Salt Lake City's Deseret Generation & Transmission Cooperative, she unsuccessfully appealed the decision to her boss and to his superiors. She then turned to the peer board, which, after studying documentation by Ms. Story and her superintendent, awarded the job to her. Only seven days passed between her first conversation with her supervisor and the board's ruling.

Peer-review boards side with management's decision in an estimated 60 percent to 70 percent of all cases. They are valuable in building an open, trusting atmosphere; helping management deter union organizing; and, perhaps most importantly, stemming the rising number of costly lawsuits claiming wrongful discharge and discrimination.[16]

The need for protection provided by labor unions is considerably less in those firms where management and employees are cooperating to install Theory Z organizations. IBM is an excellent example of the about 100 major U.S. corporations that have worked to cement good labor-management relations by eliminating layoffs. Other well-known firms with programs protecting employees against layoffs include Delta Air Lines and Digital Equipment.

Job Security in Nonunion Companies

Security has always been one of the primary motivations for the formation of labor unions. Security clauses are common in bargaining agreements; seniority rights are protected; pension programs are important benefits of union affiliation.

Computer giant IBM holds the enviable record of not having laid off a single employee for economic reasons in over 40 years. Instead, IBM reassigns and retrains workers who are no longer needed in one area. Since 1970, it has retrained and relocated thousands of employees as part of the most extensive corporate education program in the United States. The following is an illustration:

Karyl Nichols worked a routine eight-hour day as a secretary in an office of International Business Machines Corporation in Westchester County, New York. Then she went through a "career bend," as IBM calls it, and became a sales representative in New York City. Today, instead of pounding a typewriter, she sells IBM typewriters and other office equipment. Eager to advance — and to make her sales quota — she voluntarily puts in ten-hour days, or "whatever it takes," and loves it.

The 24-year-old Nichols does not go so far as to sing company songs at lunchtime, but her loyalty and hard work are typical of the benefits that IBM gets for offering near-total job security to its employees.[17]

IBM believes that if people are not worried about being laid off, they will be willing to cooperate with the firm in working toward company objectives. This cooperation is reflected in company profits.

In addition to its concerns for employee job security, IBM's human resources department provides employees with career and retirement counseling; monitors health, safety, and parental leave programs; and offers special assistance to the disabled and employees with drug and alcohol problems.

In effect, these policies and procedures do what unions alone used to do — represent employees in their relationships with the employer. "Our agenda is almost identical to what a union agenda might be," says Walton Burdick, IBM vice-president in charge of personnel, one of only six executives who report directly to Chairman John Akers.[18]

On the other hand, IBM is quick to point out that it has no place for nonproducers, particularly salespeople and managers. Its president has noted that the company will not tolerate unproductive people, yet recognizes the effect job security can have on the morale of the work force. Therefore, an attempt is always made to keep people, based on the belief that if you make an employee happy with a new job, when you fill the old job you make someone else happy. To make room for these moves, the company fires nonproducers and encourages older employees to choose early retirement by offering incentive plans. As one IBM spokesperson commented:

IBM's way of dealing with its employees does not produce a regimented work force. While protective job security can produce stagnation, IBM insists that it enables employees to be more individualistic and willing to try new ideas. "If you operate in high job security without demanding performance . . . there would be a problem. But we demand performance."[19]

Worker Ownership of Companies

The ultimate step in convincing individual employees that they have a stake in the continuing prosperity of the firm is to give them a share of the business. During the past decade, more than 9,000 employee stock ownership plans (ESOPs) have sprung up across the nation. ESOPs have been used to save failing businesses and to motivate employees in healthy times to increase their productivity. Their popularity is due, in part, to the 1974 federal law that permitted a company to allocate some of its stock to workers who then feel as if they have a stake in the firm's success. ESOP programs have been set up by such corporate giants as AT&T, Atlantic Richfield, and Mobil and by thousands of smaller companies.

In some cases, successful new companies have begun operations with an employee ownership plan in place. O&O Stores ("We own it; we operate it") in the Philadelphia area is about 70 percent owned by employees who paid $5,000 each for an ownership share. Sales are up, and a key to success appears to be employees' daily involvement. Workers vote on all major business decisions involving investment, recruiting, marketing, and operations.[20]

ESOPs have been used extensively in recent years as a means of preventing plant closings and saving worker jobs. Faced with the promise by the National Steel Corporation that it would gradually reduce the operation of its Weirton, West Virginia, facility, workers at the plant decided to buy it for a price of $66 million, even though the takeover required workers to assume substantial pay cuts. As an independent, employee-owned company, Weirton Works is one of America's largest steel companies and among the 400 largest American corporations.

In recent years, ESOPs have been created following mergers of large diversified corporations. Perhaps the best-known employee-owned firm is Avis, the nation's No. 2 auto rental company. The Garden City, New York–based company, once a subsidiary of Beatrice Cos., is owned by its 12,500 employees. Since the ESOP was created in 1987, all internal measures of service quality are setting records. Service-related customer complaints declined 35 percent within a year, and on-time arrivals of airport buses have risen from 93 percent to 96 percent. Operating profits have also jumped by 35 percent, and the firm's market share continues to grow while market leader Hertz experiences erosion of its market share.[21]

According to a University of Michigan study, the increases in productivity and decreases in absenteeism and waste found in employee-owned firms can translate into profits one and one-half times as great as those in traditionally owned firms. However, success is not guaranteed when workers take over. Workers often make poor managers, and when outside managers are brought in, there is often a great deal of tension and mistrust. At South Bend Lathe Inc., the tension erupted into a strike, with employees picketing their own company.[22]

These supermarket workers are some of the employees who own 70 percent of O&O Stores in the Philadelphia area. They each invested $5,000 for an ownership share. Under most ESOPs, employees own stock but have no voice in major company operations. At O&O, employees have full voting rights in decisions ranging from marketing to recruiting, reflected in the firm's slogan — "We own it; we operate it."

Photo source: © Steven M. Falk 1987.

The Future of Organized Labor

The past decade has witnessed the steepest decline in union membership in the twentieth century. From a peak membership of 36 percent of the nonfarm labor force in 1945, U.S. union members now represent only 17 percent of total full-time employment. Should these trends continue, organized workers will represent only 13 percent of the nonfarm work force by the year 2000. In addition, the prospect for increasing union membership from traditional blue-collar occupations and industries is bleak for two reasons.

First, most blue-collar workers have already been organized. Almost every employee of the automobile, steel, aerospace, paper, rubber, and brewing industries belongs to a union. In such industrial cities as Pittsburgh, Seattle, and Detroit, nine out of ten manufacturing workers are currently union members. The days of masses of unorganized blue-collar workers are gone. Union organizers must look elsewhere for additional members.

Second, job-growth projections indicate that blue-collar ranks — the source of union membership strength in the past — will be less important in the future. In many cases, U.S. companies have relocated their manufacturing facilities to relatively low-wage nations in Latin America and Asia. Also, factories, in the United States and throughout the world, have become more automated, further reducing the demand for blue-collar workers. In the steel industry, for example, membership in the United Steelworkers declined by more than 45 percent over a four-year period at the beginning of the 1980s. One result of this decline is that labor unions are refocusing their organizing efforts on public (government) employees and white-collar workers.

Federal employees have been permitted to join unions and bargain collectively since 1962. However, they are not allowed to go on strike. Each federal civilian employee takes a no-strike pledge when hired. In the early 1980s, when the nation's air-traffic controllers went on strike to reinforce their contract de-

---

Table 12.1   Should Public Employees Have the Right to Strike?

Arguments Supporting the Right to Strike	**Arguments Opposing the Right to Strike**
1. There is no difference between workers in government and those in private industry. For example, food deliveries and utilities are as vital to the public as are the police.	1. The functions of public employees — police, fire, the military — are too vital to be disrupted by a strike.
2. Because government employees face the same high prices, rising taxes, job security uncertainties, and other increases in the cost of living as do workers in the private sectors, they should have similar bargaining tools.	2. In the case of public workers, the employer — a government body — has fewer economic weapons with which to bargain. It cannot close its plant, shift its product line, or move to another location. It can cover added costs only by raising taxes. The consequence is to shift the burden to the citizens.
3. The right to strike must be present, otherwise labor's basic weapon is nullified. The consequence is that public workers have no strength at the bargaining table.	3. Strikes by public employees simply are not in the public interest.

---

mands, they were dismissed by President Ronald Reagan. His decision was based on arguments shown on the right side of Table 12.1. By contrast, those who believe the right to strike should be extended to all employees voice the arguments shown on the left side of the table.

State and municipal employees have been other targets for union organizing attempts. Strikes have spread to police officers and firefighters, sanitation workers, doctors and hospital employees, zookeepers, and even prison guards, as these workers seek a dramatic means of obtaining higher wages and other benefits. When strikes are prohibited by law, workers go on strike by "calling in sick." Hence, police strikes have come to be known as the "blue flu."

Public school teachers have also used strikes as a means of exerting pressure on state and local officials to meet their demands. The most powerful teachers' association is the National Education Association (NEA), with more than 1.7 million members. Another 500,000 belong to the American Federation of Teachers (AFT). Besides being a professional association, the NEA often functions as a labor union, calling for strikes and pickets to enforce teacher demands and acting as a bargaining agent for public school teachers and some college faculties.

Faculty unionization on college campuses has been hindered in more than half the states by the lack of legislation that would enable employees of public colleges to organize collective bargaining chapters. In addition, many individual faculty members express concern about independence and academic freedom and question the compatibility of organized labor with their profession. More than 500 two- and four-year colleges have already been unionized, including such well-known institutions as the State University of New York, Boston University, the University of Wisconsin, and the 20,000-member California Faculty Association. In 1988, the American Federation of State, County and Municipal Employees succeeded in a ten-year effort to organize 3,700 clerical and technical workers at Harvard University.

Organizing attempts have also focused on agricultural workers and white-collar employees. Fewer than 40,000 agricultural and fishing workers are union members. By contrast, white-collar union membership is estimated to comprise approximately 20 percent of all unionized workers in the United States. Half of all full-time and local government employees are currently organized.

The success of organizing attempts in these areas — public employees, agricultural workers, and white-collar employees — may ultimately determine whether U.S. labor unions can continue to grow or whether they have reached their membership peak.

A New Generation of Workers

A major change required of U.S. labor leaders is the recognition that the work force of today is increasingly the product of the baby-boom years — a generation that has no memory of the Great Depression or of economic hardship. These workers grew up in the affluent and permissive 1960s and 1970s. They often bring to the workplace a demand for challenging work and a dislike for both union and management bureaucracies.

Over the past half-century, cartoonists portrayed the typical American worker as a Dagwood Bumstead-like figure: an inept, middle-aged man with a tyrannical boss, a stack of unpaid bills, a wife, and two children. But Dagwood Bumstead now represents a vanishing breed. Compared with those of 20 years ago, today's workers are very different. They are:

◆ *More diverse.* A record 44 percent are women, 11 percent black, and 5 percent Hispanic. Union membership is weakest among women, minorities, and immigrants, who will fill 85 percent of the new jobs created between now and the year 2000.

◆ *More affluent.* Despite inflation and unemployment, an average worker's real spendable earnings have risen 9 percent since 1960. Working spouses have pushed median family incomes above $25,000. Seven of every ten families depend on two wage earners, an increase of 16 percent since 1970.

◆ *Enjoying more fringe benefits.* These extras go beyond the wildest dreams of previous generations and include everything from dental care to health club dues.

◆ *Better educated.* In 1959, 30 percent of the work force had an elementary education or less. That group has fallen to 13 percent. Meanwhile, high school graduates rose from 30 percent to 37 percent of the work force and college graduates from 10 percent to 16 percent.

◆ *More likely to work in offices than factories.* More than half of all workers now hold white-collar jobs.

◆ *Basking in more leisure time.* Work hours have declined. Vacations are more generous. The average office worker enjoys 10 paid holidays per year, versus 7.8 in 1960.

◆ *More mobile.* The typical worker in 1963 kept a job for 4.6 years. Now he or she changes jobs every 3.6 years.

As employment in goods-producing industries continues to decline, the stereotype of the blue-collar industrial worker becomes less valid. For nearly half a century, the dominant pattern of bargaining over wages, hours, and working conditions has been set by blue-collar unions such as the United Steelworkers

Figure 12.7   Addressing the Challenges of the Modern Work Force

Source: Courtesy of United Food and Commercial Workers International Union.

and the United Auto Workers. But seven out of ten U.S. workers are currently employed in service industries. This is expected to rise to more than eight in ten by the year 2000. Jobs in information-processing industries such as finance, education, and communications will experience enormous growth.

Union Responses

Even though unions have been losing ground in recent years in collective bargaining and union membership is at a 50-year low, organized labor is beginning to respond to the labor force of the 1990s. In 1988, the AFL-CIO launched a two-year, $13 million "Union Yes" advertising campaign aimed primarily at young people joining the work force and featuring celebrity union members such as Jack Lemmon, Howard Hesseman, and Tyne Daly.[23] In addition, lobbying efforts are focusing on such broad, pro-worker issues as child care, parental leave, and guaranteed health insurance. The United Food & Commercial Workers International Union has a women's affairs department that addresses issues such as sexual harassment and child care. In the advertisement in Figure 12.7, the UFCW describes its efforts to achieve equal pay for women. Even though 73 percent of all working women are of childbearing age and 60 percent of all school-age children have mothers in the work force, only 5 percent of U.S. companies help their employees with child care.[24]

Some union organizing campaigns aimed at white-collar workers in service and high-technology jobs appear to be paying off. Union membership among health-care workers increased 6 percent between 1980 and 1985 and now stands at 20 percent. In 1987, union membership among blacks and women increased by 9,000 and 40,000, respectively, even though the percentage of nonunion workers in both groups also rose.[25]

The new workers are better educated than their predecessors. Their concerns are often broader than those of their parents and grandparents. Moreover, they are likely to be more militant on the issues of environmental concerns, flexible working patterns, and shared decision making. The future of organized labor will be greatly affected by its responses to these workers.

Summary of Learning Goals _____

1. Explain why labor unions were organized and list the primary goals of organized labor.   Although labor unions existed even before the Declaration of Independence, they were typically small, weak, and usually short-lived. Serious attempts to form national unions to protect workers' rights in the late 1800s and early 1900s were met with fierce resistance by both management and government.

Development of the American Federation of Labor (AFL) under the leadership of Samuel Gompers focused union goals on the issues of wages, hours, and working conditions. The AFL grew rapidly until 1920, when its growth slowed until 1935. Meanwhile, the Congress of Industrial Organizations (CIO) was experiencing considerable success in unionizing the automobile, mining, and steel industries. Unions experienced their greatest period of growth in the two decades following 1935, and in 1955 the AFL and CIO merged their 18 million members under the presidency of George Meany.

2. Identify the major federal laws affecting labor unions and explain the key provisions of each law.   The Norris-La Guardia Act of 1932 protects unions by reducing management's ability to stop union activities. The Wagner Act of 1935 requires management to bargain collectively with duly elected employee representatives and outlaws a number of unfair management practices. In efforts to balance power between labor and management, the Taft-Hartley Act (1947) and the Landrum-Griffin Act (1959) were passed to outlaw a number of unfair labor practices. The Fair Labor Standards Act of 1938 set a federal minimum wage and maximum basic hours and outlawed child labor. The Plant-Closing Notification Act of 1988 requires employers with more than 100 employees to give 60 days' notice before a plant shutdown or mass layoff.

3. Explain how collective bargaining agreements are established and the roles played by arbitrators and mediators.   A collective bargaining agreement specifies such things as wages, hours of work, employee rights, and grievance handling. The contract is the result of negotiations between management and labor representatives. The bargaining zone is the limits within which management and labor will negotiate. Many union contracts contain a cost-of-living escalator clause, and in some industries, contracts have permitted wage and fringe benefit reductions called givebacks.

Occasionally, a mediator or an arbitrator will assist negotiations to reach an agreement. The mediator offers advice and makes recommendations. The arbitrator, however, listens to both sides and then makes a decision that becomes binding on both parties.

4. Outline the sources of power, or "weapons," of labor and management. Although most differences between labor and management are settled through the collective bargaining process or formal grievance procedures, both unions and management have other ways of making their demands known. The chief weapons of unions are the strike, picketing, and boycotts. Management's weapons are the hiring of strikebreakers, injunctions, lockouts, and employers' associations.

5. Identify the sources of future union membership growth. Future union growth will result primarily from organizing attempts among public employees, agricultural workers, and white-collar employees. In these occupational groupings, women, minorities, and immigrants are less likely to be union members. These relatively unorganized groups of workers represent the greatest source of future union members.

Key Terms

labor union

craft union

industrial union

American Federation of Labor (AFL)

Congress of Industrial Organizations (CIO)

national union

local union

international union

federation

Norris-La Guardia Act

Wagner Act

National Labor Relations Board (NLRB)

Fair Labor Standards Act

Taft-Hartley Act

jurisdictional strikes

closed shop

union shop

agency shop

open shop

right-to-work laws

featherbedding

boycott

primary boycott

secondary boycott

cooling-off period

Landrum-Griffin Act

Plant-Closing Notification Act of 1988

collective bargaining

bargaining zone

cost-of-living escalator clause (COLA)

givebacks

mediation

arbitration

voluntary arbitration

compulsory arbitration

grievance

shop steward

strike

picketing

lockout

strikebreaker

injunction

employers' associations

peer-review boards

Review Questions

1. Trace the development of labor unions in industrialized society. Briefly outline the history of the union movement in the United States.

2. Distinguish among local unions, national unions, international unions, and federations. Categorize the AFL-CIO and identify its primary function.

3. Trace the development of labor legislation in the United States.

4. Discuss right-to-work laws and their impact on business and labor.

5. Describe the collective bargaining process and relate it to the concept of bargaining zones.

6. Differentiate between a closed shop, union shop, agency shop, and open shop. Which of these is directly affected by the Taft-Hartley Act?

7. Distinguish between mediation and arbitration.

8. Outline the steps in the grievance procedure. What role does the shop steward play in a typical grievance?

9. Explain the major weapons of unions and management. Describe instances in which each might be used.

10. Explain why so many ESOPs have been formed in recent years. What are the major advantages and disadvantages of worker ownership?

Discussion Questions _____

1. In 1977, the American Federation of Government Employees revised its constitution to permit membership of military personnel. To date, however, it has made no attempt to organize the 2 million men and women in the U.S. Armed Forces. A survey of union members showed general opposition to seeking new members from the uniformed military. Prepare a list of the advantages and disadvantages to the military of allowing soldiers to join labor unions.

2. What is the purpose of the cooling-off period that the president of the United States may order under the Taft-Hartley Act? Which party is likely to benefit more from this provision of the act?

3. Explain why major firms such as IBM, Sears, Eastman Kodak, and Texas Instruments operate without unions. Does the provision of job security eliminate the need for unions? Explain your answer.

4. Secure a collective bargaining agreement from a firm. Develop a scenario of a management-labor bargaining session for the next contract.

5. Discuss the likely changes in union operations and objectives that may result from the entry of the baby-boom generation into the labor force.

Video Case

Quad Graphics (B)

Begun in 1971 with a $35,000 home mortgage by founder and president Harry Quadracci, Quad Graphics has blossomed into a $500 million printing company. The Peewaukee, Wisconsin–based company prints such magazines as *Inc., Time,* and *Black Enterprise,* as well as many catalogs for well-known mail-order firms — over 150 magazines and catalogs in all. In addition, Quad Graphics runs an ink manufacturing company and a trucking business, and has a division that develops, manufactures, and sells advanced printing equipment to customers including the firm's competitors. Found Quadracci was inducted into the Printing Hall of Fame in 1986.

Quad Graphics is admired in the business world not only for its phenomenal financial success, but also for its efforts to provide its employees with an ideal work environment. Quad employees are attracted to the firm and motivated by the many training and personal improvement programs offered. In 1987, for example, 1,700 of the firm's 3,300 employees participated voluntarily in formal training programs offered by Quad. The workplace is designed to give employees a sense of contributing directly and tangibly to the success of the entire operation. And they care about success because — to a considerable extent — Quad is *their* company; they own it. In 1987, $2.5 million was designated for Quad's employee stock ownership program.

An essential part of the positive work environment is the company's management structure, which is virtually unique in American industry. Relations between managers and workers are so relaxed that most employees refer to their charismatic leader, Harry Quadracci, by his nickname, Larry.

Harry Quadracci tells a story about his first day in class in law school, when his professor asked the class what the term *justice* meant. After listening while students offered their opinions, the instructor said, "You're all wrong. Justice is what the judge says it is."

Years later, Quadracci still applies this philosophy to running a business. As he says, "You run a business according to good sound business principles. But what are good sound business principles? Good sound business principles are what the president says they are." He further adds that the president is the "value setter." He believes that a business in which strong values are articulated will be more unified as it grows because everyone knows what the rules are. If everyone has the same goals, the results will be understood and each employee will know how much — or how little — he or she contributed to achieving them.

Quad Graphics employs a bottom-up organizational structure. Rather than using the typical top-down approach, where middle managers and supervisory personnel tell employees what to do, Quad pushes responsibility to individual employees and small work units in every possible instance. Quad employees are given no chance to feel that their work is meaningless or that they are replaceable mechanical drones. Instead, they are motivated by a knowledge that their work and ideas are valuable and that they affect the overall performance of the company.

Quad Graphics has been accused of using Japanese management methods, but Quadracci disagrees. He admits that the Japanese system works because of the intense sense of corporate purpose shared by all members of the organization. "We may have borrowed from the Japanese the concept of intense communal purpose . . . and the idea that these shared expectations should be indoctrinated into the employee, but that does not mean that we preach the Japanese style of conformity." To the contrary, Quad Graphics is dependent on employees' individuality, creativity, and ability to make decisions on their own. In fact, Quad employees are promoted according to their individual abilities not according to seniority. Quadracci adds, "Individual freedom does not mean lack of structure. We are very structured — from the bottom up." He believes that it is essential to verbalize company values and indoctrinate employees accordingly.

As Quadracci informs employees in one of the training sessions, "We expect very little back from you. All we expect you to do is eat, sleep, dream, and think Quad Graphics." Although, as one employee puts it, all this indoctrination to Quad culture is "hard to swallow

Notes: "Coming of Age," *Inc.,* April 1989, pp. 110–111; Corey Rosen, Katherine J. Klein, and Karen M. Young, "Where Employees Share the Profits," *Psychology Today,* January 1986, pp. 30–36; Robert H. Waterman, Jr., *The Renewal Factor* (New York: Bantam Books, 1987), p. 194; and personal correspondence, February 27, 1989.

at first, after repeated exposure to it, it just becomes part of something, just like in your blood, just like ink." Some employees take offense at being referred to as Quadicized, but they seem to agree that people progress faster from the training offered to them. Each person is trained and tested on his or her understanding of the machine and the job *before* working on the floor. Quadracci feels that the idea of enlightened management is actually a major problem in American management. He argues, "Enlightened management only works on enlightened employees — and they're not born that way." Quad's emphasis on being an education company means that employees are expected to complete four steps: (1) learn the job, (2) know the job, (3) improve the job, and (4) teach the job to the next person. The process repeats itself as everyone participates at every level.

Quad's organizational structure contains no supervisory positions. Employees help one another, and each performs a variety of tasks. No seniority exists: Workers are promoted not according to how long they have been on the job, but by how well they do their job. They feel no need to protect their jobs or guard information, because they know that as soon as they master one job and take the necessary training classes, they can go on to another.

Management of each Quad Graphics division seemingly consists of — in Quadracci's phrase — "management by walking away." Rather than being told what to do, the members of each division are left to develop and implement their own ideas. For example, Quadracci once asked the firm's truckers to investigate the possibility of generating additional revenues by carrying loads for other companies on their return trips. They did, and in a few years the truckers were able to create their own subsidiary called DuPlainville Transport, which generates considerable revenues from making such "back-haul" deliveries for clients they contact themselves.

Labor-management relations are bettered by eliminating many of the more mundane aspects of human resource management. For instance, time clocks do not exist in the firm's plants; employees are trusted to perform their work to the best of their ability without such external controls. Early in Quad's development, managers found that 12-hour shifts and 3-day workweeks made workers happier and improved productivity by 20 percent over the standard 8-hour-day production rate. Quad employees have also been allowed to develop their own day-care centers, food service programs, and various fitness programs, which in Peewaukee are held in the $3 million gym recently built by the company. Employees are made to feel that they can "control our environment in terms of how we treat our customers and how we treat ourselves," according to one Quad employee.

Perhaps the ultimate symbol of the unique bond between individual and organizational objectives at Quad Graphics is the annual Christmas variety show. The show is written, choreographed, and performed by Quad employees — no professional artists — and is the result of 10 to 12 weeks of practice, often four hours a night, two nights a week. Though amateurish, the extravaganza nonetheless provides an opportunity for employees and managers to work closely together for fun and entertainment, just as they work together the rest of the year for mutual profit and esteem.

Questions

1. Labor pioneer Samuel Gompers once provided a five-word explanation for the objectives of labor unions: wages, hours, and working conditions. How are each of these objectives addressed at Quad Graphics?

2. Most union-management agreements place considerable emphasis on seniority when evaluating and rewarding people with similar performance records. Why is seniority not considered important in employee evaluations and promotion decisions at Quad Graphics? Does this reflect concern for the employee, the company, or both? Defend your answer.

3. How does Quad's philosophy of sharing responsibilities conflict with strict job classifications found in most unions?

4. Discuss the likely impact of the Quad Graphics employee stock ownership plan on employee interests in unionization.

5. Do you think it would be possible to unionize a company like Quad Graphics? Why or why not?

Careers in Business

Many readers will eventually select careers in human relations, human resource management, and labor relations. Jobs available in these fields include arbitrator, labor relations specialist, employee benefits specialist, training specialist, college recruiter, industrial psychologist, and employment counselor.

The Bureau of Labor Statistics, which has projected the employment outlook through the year 2000, forecasts that job opportunities for psychologists will grow faster than the average for all occupations and that opportunities for personnel and labor relations workers will grow about as fast as the average. Some 381,000 people worked in personnel positions in a recent year.

Arbitrator

Arbitrators use their knowledge of the law and common sense to mediate and settle a variety of disputed issues.

Job Description.   Many arbitrators specialize in labor relations, providing an alternative to costly lawsuits as a means of solving disputes for business, unions, and other parties. They analyze the information submitted to them by their clients (both parties to a dispute) and render a judgment on the proper settlement.

Career Path.   Arbitrators need a background in law to make determinations. They generally begin with simple cases and graduate to more complicated ones with experience.

Salary.   Earnings vary with experience and the type of cases handled.

Labor Relations Specialist

These specialists deal with all aspects of labor-management relations. They assist operating management in contract negotiations with labor organizations.

Job Description.   Labor relations specialists must be knowledgeable in labor law, collective bargaining, and administration of collective bargaining contracts. They assist managers in conducting negotiations and are responsible for administering the organization's labor contracts.

Career Path.   Beginning labor relations specialists deal with routine matters such as grievances. Their duties expand as they broaden their experience in the field. The director of labor relations, who often heads management teams during labor negotiations, holds the top position in this field.

Salary.   In a recent year, beginning salaries for a labor relations specialist with an undergraduate degree ranged from $14,800 to $18,400; with a master's degree, the average was $22,500; with a doctorate, $27,200. Labor relations specialists as a group had a median salary of $27,000.

Employee Benefits Specialist

Employee benefits specialists play a key role in the human resources department. They are responsible for designing and administering the company's employee benefits package, which includes insurance and pension plans.

Job Description.   Employee benefits specialists develop and administer various programs for employees, such as life, health, dental, and disability insurance; pension coverage; profit sharing; and stock options. The job of the specialist in designing and administering these programs has become increasingly complex because of government regulations and the desire of most firms to reduce the cost of employee benefits.

Career Path.   Beginning employee benefits specialists must familiarize themselves with the details of their company's benefits package. Until they gain experience, their work is closely supervised by senior staff members. With experience, workers take on more design and planning responsibilities.

Salary.   In a recent year, employee benefits specialists earned a median salary of $26,700. Managers earned salaries from $34,200 to $43,300 annually.

Training Specialist

Training specialists are in charge of the various training and employee education programs the company offers.

Job Description.   Training specialists are involved in all phases of company training programs, from assessing the need for these programs to creating and implementing them, to determining their effectiveness. Much of their work involves conducting orientation and on-the-job training sessions for new employees. They also help experienced employees polish their existing skills and learn new ones.

Career Path. To learn required skills, training specialists often rotate from department to department within the company or assess training techniques used by other employers. A background in education, instructional technology, or psychology is useful.

Salary. In a recent year, training specialists earned a median salary of nearly $39,700.

College Recruiter

College recruiters visit college campuses to search for qualified job applicants.

Job Description. Recruiters travel to colleges and universities with a list of job openings in their companies and the qualifications needed for each job. Recruiters talk with students about job openings, analyze their resumes, interview those who seem qualified, and arrange for further interviews at the company's home office for promising candidates.

Salary. Salaries vary widely depending on the size and location of the firm and its type of business. The median salary in a recent year was $26,500.

Industrial Psychologist

Approximately 15 percent of the nation's psychologists with doctoral degrees work in management and administration.

Job Description. Industrial psychologists require comprehensive education in the field of psychology. A psychologist's assistance can be useful in a variety of business situations, including personnel administration, employee counseling, organizational development, training, testing, and consumer behavior. The work of an industrial psychologist varies in accordance with the assigned activity.

Career Path. Educational attainment is very important in this career. At least a master's degree is needed for career progress, and often only those with a Ph.D. are eligible for top-level jobs.

Salary. The median annual income of doctoral-level psychologists working in business is approximately $48,000.

Employment Counselor

State employment offices employ the bulk of the nation's employment counselors. These people evaluate and attempt to place job applicants.

Job Description. Employment counselors use interviews and various tests to assess a person's capabilities for the job market. They then try to match these people to available jobs. Sometimes employment counselors get involved in career planning/counseling. They may also work with other agencies or educational institutions to improve a person's job skills.

Career Path. Most beginning counselors undergo a training period before taking on a caseload of job applicants. Supervisory and management positions are also available.

Salary. In a recent year, employment counselors with a state agency earned an average $17,000 while those in private industry earned an average $20,000.

Chapter 13
Marketing Strategy

Chapter 14
Product and Pricing Strategies

Chapter 15
Distribution Strategy

Chapter 16
Promotional Strategy

Marketing Management

Career Profile: *Debra McPhee*

Debra McPhee didn't start school with the intent of pursuing a career in retailing, but now she's the public relations director for McCurdy & Co., a six-store chain of department stores in Rochester, New York. McCurdy's, one of the few privately held department store groups remaining in the United States (there's even a Mr. McCurdy), has annual sales of between $50 million and $100 million. In 1988, McCurdy's 87th year in business, the company enjoyed a double-digit percent increase in sales, despite intense competition in the Rochester area from two larger operations — Sibley's, which is part of the May chain, and Forman's.

McPhee actually worked for the competition first. At age 16, she started her retail career as a sales assistant for Sibley's. Later, she was an assistant manager for a Lerner's, and then she managed a store that had $1 million in sales for that chain. While working for these two stores, she started school at Monroe Community College, Rochester, New York. At the time, she had no intention of remaining in retailing.

"I started school in 1976, intending to get an associate's degree in liberal arts, so I could transfer to a four-year school and get a degree in physical therapy," says McPhee. She abandoned the goal of being a physical therapist after she realized one of her weak points, science, was essential to being a therapist.

Instead, she capitalized on her experience and switched to the retailing program, earning an associate's degree. In 1980, she started in McCurdy's purchasing department, and, in two months, she moved to public relations, where she has advanced to her current position as director.

Her responsibilities are extensive. In a typical day, she may help plan strategies for a holiday sale, meet with product buyers to discuss what will sell in the market, solve problems with a catalogue mailing or production, arrange a fashion show at a local high school, book models for other shows, prepare her department's employees for upcoming events, and select the merchandise that will appear in store windows. In addition, she serves as the fashion buyer consultant, which means she spends about one week every month in New York City. And she also coordinates McCurdy's special events.

The position of public relations director is virtually tailor-made for McPhee, according to one of her former professors. "Debbie has personality plus, which makes her particularly suited for her job," said John Lloyd, a business professor at Monroe. "With what she does, you have to be able to fit in well with all types of people, and she does."

In reviewing her experience at Monroe, McPhee singles out courses in art appreciation, marketing, buying, and a general business class as being particularly valuable to her. McPhee is sharing some of that value with her old college. Monroe is starting a public relations program, and McPhee has been invited to help design the courses. Lloyd reports that she is, at age 30, the youngest person on the planning committee.

In addition to her responsibilities on that committee, McPhee serves on two community groups, including the Rochester Conventions and Visitors Bureau. She also is on planning committees for a number of special events the city conducts.

"You have to be able to network," she says. "I am very visible and serve on a lot of committees outside the store. It's very important that I am aware of the city, who's in it, what they're like."

She has a busy schedule, but McPhee thrives on it. "I get to do something different every day, and I get to meet lots of people," she says. "I'm very lucky."

Photo source: Courtesy of McCurdy & Company and Walid Raad.

13

Marketing Strategy

Learning Goals

1. To discuss how marketing's role in the exchange process creates utility.

2. To list the major functions of marketing.

3. To explain the marketing concept.

4. To outline how a marketing strategy is developed.

5. To describe the five environmental forces that influence marketing decision making.

6. To explain the concept of a market.

7. To discuss why the study of consumer behavior is important to marketing.

8. To describe the marketing research function.

9. To list and explain the bases used to segment markets.

Mary Anne Jackson was worried. The year was 1985 and she had just gone back to work as director of operations and planning at the Swift/Eckrich Division of Beatrice Co. after the birth of her daughter. Jackson was concerned about what to feed the child after she advanced beyond prepared baby food. By studying cookbooks and nutrition guides, Jackson came up with some meals that could be reheated by the babysitter for lunch or if she was on a business trip or otherwise delayed.

Her experience as a concerned mother had an interesting parallel in Jackson's work life. One of her job activities involved evaluating retort packaging, where food is put in a plastic bag and then cooked in a pressure cooker. The resulting airtight package allows the contents to remain fresh without refrigeration.

A leveraged buyout suddenly ended Jackson's career with Beatrice in 1986. Now unemployed, the former executive turned her attention to developing a line of meals for children the same age as her own. Jackson surveyed 2,000 women in a marketing research project designed to determine what mothers wanted their children to eat. She then hired a food development firm and a nutritionist to develop 24 meals that were then taste tested in focus groups by 100 children and in about 1,500 in-home use tests.

The top five kids' picks became "My Own Meals," a line of shelf-

stable microwavable meals targeted at the 2- to 8-year-old market. The five selections were: Chicken, Please™, My Meatballs & Shells™, My Favorite Pasta™, My Turkey Meatballs™, and My Kind of Chicken™. My Own Meal® products can be microwaved in 90 seconds or heated in boiling water in 4 minutes. They are retail priced at $2.39 to $2.99. A plant in South Carolina, SoPakCo, packs the meals under contract with My Own Meals, Inc. of Deerfield, Illinois.

Jackson spent only $200,000 during the two-year development process and product launch. The meals are currently available through mail order and in selected Chicago-area supermarkets. Initial reports indicate Jackson has hit on a viable target market — the 57 percent of married women who work and

have children under 6 and the additional group of homemakers who lead active lives outside the home. Why was Jackson successful with a product category ignored by the major food companies? She explains it this way: "How many of those people who run those companies or divisions are men? They don't deal with the problem of what to feed their kids, and they don't care."[1]

Effective marketing research and market segmentation proved to be the key to Mary Anne Jackson's success. These are just two of the topics discussed in Chapter 13.

Photo source: Courtesy of My Own Meals/Rob Anderson Photography, Chicago.

delivery system for a Standard of living ↑

Chapter Overview

Marketing is the link between the organization and the consumer. All organizations — profit-oriented or nonprofit — must serve consumer needs if they are to succeed. Perhaps J. C. Penney expressed it best when he told his store managers: "Either you or your replacement will greet the customer within the first 60 seconds."

But marketing is also used to advocate ideas or viewpoints. An example is the public service advertisement in Figure 13.1. The American Marketing Association defines **marketing** as the process of planning and executing the conception, pricing, promotion, and distribution of ideas, goods, and services to create exchanges that satisfy individual and organizational objectives.

This chapter examines the role of marketing in organizations. It describes how organizations develop a marketing strategy and the environmental factors that influence marketing planning. It also explains why marketers study consumer behavior and conduct marketing research. We begin by showing how marketing's role in the exchange process creates values that satisfy customer needs.

marketing
Planning and executing the conception, pricing, promotion, and distribution of ideas, goods, and services to create exchanges that satisfy individual and organizational objectives.

The Exchange Process

Marketing activity begins when the exchange process becomes important to society. **Exchange** is the process by which two or more parties give something of value to one another to satisfy felt needs.[2] For example, a consumer writes a check to Sears for $599.99 to purchase a new color TV. But where does marketing fit in?

Consider a primitive society consisting of two family units who each produce their own food, clothing, and shelter. One of the families is an expert at producing clothing; the others are skilled farmers. Without exchange, each family must satisfy all of its own food, clothing, and shelter needs, even though the members excel in only one of these areas.

The exchange process allows the families to concentrate on their strongest areas and to trade clothing for food and vice versa. This specialization and division of labor leads to increased total production and a higher standard of living for both families. The exchange process would not occur unless each family marketed its outputs. Thus, marketing is a prime determinant of society's overall standard of living. In fact, in advanced societies, marketing costs range between 40 and 60 percent of selling prices.

exchange
Process by which two or more parties give something of value to one another to satisfy felt needs.

Creating Utility

In Chapter 9, *utility* was defined as the want-satisfying power of a good or service. The production function is responsible for creating *form utility* by converting raw materials and other inputs into finished goods and services. The marketing function creates the three other types of utility: time, place, and ownership.

Marketing is a value-creating function in any organization. **Time utility** is created by having a good or service available when the consumer wants to purchase it. A community college's offering of Saturday morning courses is an

time utility
Utility created by making goods and services available when the consumer wants to purchase them.

Figure 13.1   Using Marketing to Advocate a Viewpoint

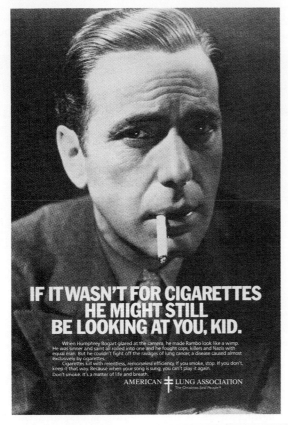

Source: Courtesy of American Lung Association.

example. Moto Photo Inc. creates time utility by providing one-hour film processing and a video studio in which customers can prepare a video message in just 30 minutes.

Place utility is created by having a good or service available in the right place when the consumer wants to purchase it. A symphony performance in a park illustrates this utility. McDonald's, Wendy's, and other fast-food restaurants create place utility by opening franchises in locations convenient to their customers.

Arranging for an orderly transfer of ownership creates **ownership utility**. A toll-free telephone order system is an example. Retailers create ownership utility by accepting currency or credit-card payments. Marketing adds to the want-satisfying power of goods and services by performing eight basic functions.

place utility
Utility created by making goods and services available where the consumer wants to purchase them.

ownership utility
Utility created by arranging for transfer of ownership at the time of purchase.

The Functions of Marketing

Marketing is more than just selling. It is a complex activity that reaches into many aspects of an organization and its dealings with consumers. As Figure 13.2 shows, marketing involves eight functions: buying, selling, transporting, storing, standardization and grading, financing, risk taking, and market information. All

Figure 13.2   The Functions of Marketing

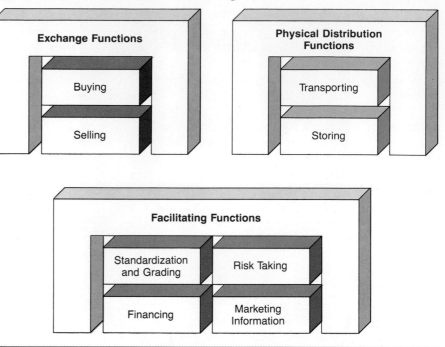

Marketing
authority
exchange
consumers

of these functions add to the utility created by marketing. Some functions are performed by manufacturers, some by wholesalers, and others by retailers.

Exchange Functions   Buying and selling are the exchange functions of marketing. <u>*Buying* is</u> important to marketing on several levels. Marketers must study how and why consumers buy certain goods and services. The study of consumer or buyer behavior is critical to the firm's overall success. For example, industrial marketers must purchase component parts and raw materials to complete their products, and retail buyers have to choose the styles and designs they believe will sell the next season. Marketers must be knowledgeable about what consumers are buying in order to make their own purchase decisions. All organizations must "sell" their goods or services to someone if they are to succeed. *Selling* is usually done through the organization's promotional strategy. Advertising, personal selling, and sales promotion are the standard sales tools.

Physical Distribution Functions   Transporting and storing are physical distribution functions. *Transporting* involves the physical movement of the product from the seller to the buyer. *Storing* involves the warehousing of goods until they are needed for sale. Manufacturers, wholesalers, and retailers can all perform these functions.

Facilitating Functions   Standardization and grading, financing, risk taking, and securing market information are referred to as facilitating functions because they assist the marketer in performing the exchange and physical distribution functions.

Standardization and grading deals with standardizing the description of goods. Many industries, like the tire industry, set up grading standards for their goods. The government also requires grading of various agricultural products.

The *financing* function involves extending credit to consumers, wholesalers, and retailers. When a wholesaler buys goods from a producer, the manufacturer receives funds needed to produce additional output. Retailers increase total sales by financing the purchases of consumers through credit arrangements.

Risk taking involves dealing with uncertainties about future consumer behavior. Marketers are entrepreneurial risk takers in many instances. Wholesalers and retailers acquire inventory for resale on the basis of their predictions of what consumers will buy. This action removes the manufacturer's risk and gives it to marketing intermediaries. Manufacturers also accept risk when they schedule speculative production of a product before consumers have entered orders.

Marketers collect and analyze *market information* to determine what will sell and who will buy it. Marketers are also concerned with the behavior of buyers and how they buy. Organizations that focus on discovering consumer needs and then developing goods and services to fill those needs have adopted a managerial approach referred to as the marketing concept, a business philosophy we discussed briefly in Chapter 1.

The Marketing Concept — *Group of ideas, attitudes*

The **marketing concept** can be defined as an organizationwide consumer orientation with the objective of achieving long-run success. Both profit-oriented and nonprofit organizations have adopted the marketing concept as a guide to operating their enterprises. The basic goal is to target all of the organization's efforts by satisfying consumer needs.

How did the marketing concept evolve? Originally, most organizations are production oriented; their primary concern is just being able to supply their product or service. This situation is known as a **seller's market**: one characterized by shortages. Later, when production problems are solved, a **buyer's market** evolves; this situation is characterized by adequate or even excess supplies. Marketing is then required to implement the exchange process.

The shift from a seller's market to a buyer's market is illustrated by the immediate post-World War II era. Industry shifted from wartime production to consumer goods. This required a change in the way firms conducted their business. The marketing concept had started to evolve.

The year 1952 can be assigned as the birthdate of the marketing concept. General Electric's annual report of that year gave one of the clearest statements of the new approach to management:

(The concept) introduces the marketing man at the beginning rather than at the end of the production cycle, and integrates marketing into each phase of the business. Thus, marketing, through its studies and research, will establish for the engineer, the design and manufacturing man, what the consumer wants in a given product, what price he is willing to pay, and where and when it will be wanted. Marketing will have authority in product planning, production, scheduling, and inventory control, as well as in sales, distribution, and servicing of the product.[3]

marketing concept
Organizationwide consumer orientation with the objective of achieving long-run success.

seller's market
Market situation characterized by shortages.

buyer's market
Market situation characterized by adequate or even excess supplies.

Figure 13.3   The Marketing Concept as a Managerial Philosophy

Source: Courtesy of ALPS America and Tycer Fultz Bellack, Ltd.

ALPS America, a computer printer firm, is an excellent example of a business that directs all its efforts to satisfying consumer needs and wants. Rather than producing a printer and then trying to sell it, ALPS uses a design process it calls "Giving the Customers What They Want." The dot matrix printer shown in the advertisement in Figure 13.3 incorporates functional features and sells at a price asked for by consumers. The firm's consumer orientation extends to its customer service and promotional strategies. Consumers are encouraged to use a toll-free telephone number to ask questions and suggest product improvements. One promotion invited consumers to design a printer that would be named after the winner. Advertisements carrying the tag line "Built by popular demand" project an image of a customer-driven company. "It's how we want to be seen," says Lori Salcido, an ALPS marketing manager. "We're a very responsive company."[4]

Marketing in Nonprofit Organizations

Adopting the marketing concept has become as important to nonprofit organizations as it has to profit-seeking businesses. Increased competition and cutbacks in government funding prompt many nonprofit groups to conduct marketing research and study consumer behavior. Fund-raising groups such as United Way of America have studied the giving habits of baby boomers, people born between 1946 and 1964, because this group represents a source of significant growth in charitable giving in the next two decades. Research indicates baby boomers prefer to support causes related to individual needs, such as homelessness and battered women, and want to know specific information about how their contributions are spent. To gain the support of this group, United Way is funding more agencies that deal with homelessness, day care, and women's centers. United Way also prepares newspaper stories that give detailed information about how funds are allocated and benefit specific agencies.[5]

The nonprofit sector consists of some 900,000 organizations. They include museums, colleges and universities, symphony orchestras, religious and human services organizations, government agencies, political parties, and labor unions. Nonprofit groups can be classified as either public or private. San Francisco State University is a public, nonprofit organization, while the University of San Francisco, a Jesuit institution, is a private, nonprofit organization that is open to the public.

Like profit-seeking firms, nonprofit organizations may market a tangible good or an intangible service. The U.S. Postal Service, for example, offers stamps (a tangible good) and mail delivery (an intangible service). Four types of nonprofit marketing are person marketing, place marketing, idea marketing, and organization marketing.

Person marketing refers to efforts designed to cultivate the attention, interest, and preference of a target market toward a person.[6] The marketing of a political candidate is an example. Campaign managers conduct marketing research to identify voters and financial supporters and then design promotions such as advertising, fund-raising dinners, and political rallies to reach the voters and donors.

person marketing
Marketing efforts designed to cultivate the attention, interest, and preference of a target market toward a person.

Place marketing refers to attempts to attract people to a particular area such as a city, state, or country. Several states, for example, have developed marketing campaigns to attract foreign tourists. Illinois launched a television advertising campaign in Great Britain with the theme "America's best kept secret: Chicago" and developed a fly-and-drive package to attract British tourists to the state. Florida spent $1 million on television advertising campaigns in Argentina, Mexico, and Venezuela to attract Spanish-speaking tourists.[7]

place marketing
Marketing efforts designed to attract people to a particular geographical area.

Idea marketing refers to the marketing of a cause or social issue. Idea marketing covers a wide range of issues, including gun control, birth defects, child abuse, physical fitness, overeating, and drunken driving. The Women's Sports Foundation is a nonprofit group that promotes the participation of young girls in sports and physical activities. The group advocates that such participation teaches girls discipline and determination, qualities that will give them the confidence they need to succeed in school and in a career.

idea marketing
Marketing efforts designed to promote a cause or social issue.

Organization marketing attempts to influence others to accept the goals of, receive the services of, or contribute in some way to an organization. For example, through advertisements such as the one in Figure 13.4, the United Performing Arts Fund of Milwaukee tries to persuade people to contribute funds to several performing-arts groups.

organization marketing
Marketing efforts designed to influence others to accept the goals of, receive the services of, or contribute in some way to an organization.

Developing a Marketing Strategy

All organizations, whether profit-oriented or nonprofit, need to develop a marketing strategy to effectively reach consumers. This two-step process involves:

1. Studying, analyzing, and eventually selecting a firm's *target market*.
2. Developing a *marketing mix* to satisfy the chosen target market.

Figure 13.4   Organization Marketing

Source: Courtesy of the United Performing Arts Fund of Milwaukee, and Kloppenburg, Switzer & Teich, Inc.

Selecting a Target Market

Consumer needs and wants vary considerably, and no single organization has the resources to satisfy the desires of all consumers. So the first decision marketers must make in developing a marketing strategy is to select a target market. A **target market** is a group of consumers toward which a firm decides to direct its marketing efforts. Consider the following examples:

target market
Group of consumers toward which a firm decides to direct its marketing efforts.

◆   Nestle targets its Oh Henry! candy bar at teens and young adults 12 to 24 years old, but its Alpine White brand is targeted at upscale men and women 18 to 34 years old.

◆   Pier 1 Imports, a retailer of wicker furniture and home furnishings, targets 25- to 44-year-old women who are well traveled, have some college education, and have an annual income of $35,000.

◆   The Saab target market consists of well-educated, 30- to 40-year-old professionals and managers with household incomes of $50,000 to $100,000.

Sometimes an organization chooses several target markets for a given good or service. A college or university might select several target markets for its $10 million fund-raising campaign: alumni, wealthy individuals, foundations, and local businesses. Target marketing requires considerable research and analysis. These activities will be discussed later in the chapter.

Developing a Marketing Mix

marketing mix
Combination of a firm's product, pricing, distribution, and promotional strategies focused on selected consumer segments.

The second step in the development of a marketing strategy is creating a marketing mix to satisfy the needs of the organization's target market. The **marketing mix** is a combination of the firm's product, pricing, distribution, and promotion strategies. Marketers focus all of these strategies on the selected consumer segments.

Product strategy includes decisions about package, design, brand name, trademark, warranty, guarantee, product life cycle, and new-product developments. It is examined in Chapter 14. **Pricing strategy**, which is also discussed in the following chapter, is one of the most difficult parts of marketing decision making. It deals with the methods of setting profitable and justifiable prices. Both government regulations and public opinion must be considered in pricing decisions. **Distribution strategy** involves the physical distribution of goods and the selection of distribution channels, the organization of wholesaling intermediaries and/or retailers who handle the product's distribution. It is discussed in Chapter 15. **Promotional strategy** involves personal selling, advertising, and sales promotion tools. These elements must be skillfully blended to produce effective communication between the firm and the marketplace. Promotional strategy is the topic of Chapter 16.

The marketing mix is the mechanism that allows organizations to match consumer needs with product offerings. To illustrate how the marketing mix elements are combined to satisfy the needs of the target market, consider the marketing strategy developed by Chuck Bennett, president and founder of Zymol Car Care Products. Four years ago, Bennett introduced the world's most expensive car wax, a product targeted at "lovers of cars and fanatics." The wax is a natural, nonabrasive compound containing expensive oils and a coconut scent. It is produced in small batches and packaged in a high-tech container imported from Sweden. The price — $22.95 for a 9-ounce container — reflects the product's prestige image and expensive ingredients. Zymol is sold at automobile supply stores and through direct-response advertisements placed in publications read by target customers, such as BMW's *Roundel,* Mercedes' *Star,* and Porsche's *Panorama,* as well as *Autoweek* and *Import Parts & Accessories.* Advertisements are designed to appeal to owners of expensive cars. In one ad, headlined "Not for the masses," the Zymol container rests in a brandy warmer next to a mound of caviar on a crystal plate. The advertising copy communicates a simple message — "Collected and enjoyed by the owners of the best loved automobiles in the world."[8]

The Marketing Environment

In selecting a target market and developing a marketing mix, marketers must consider certain environmental forces. The five dimensions of the marketing environment are competitive, political/legal, economic, technological, and social/cultural. As Figure 13.5 illustrates, these external forces provide the framework within which marketers plan product, pricing, distribution, and promotion strategies aimed at the target market.

The Competitive Environment   Marketers must continually monitor the marketing activities of competing organizations. Analyzing the competition enables an organization to devise a strategy that will give it a competitive edge. When Roadway Package Service decided to enter the small-package delivery field in the mid-1980s, the firm's marketers studied the system used by United Parcel Service, the leader in national small-package delivery. As a result, RPS invested $43 million in high-technology equipment that would provide customers with services not offered by UPS, such as itemized computer billing, bar code scanners for package tracing, and a toll-free telephone number for package

product strategy
Element of marketing decision making that deals with developing goods and services, package design, trademarks, warranties, and product life cycles.

pricing strategy
Element of marketing decision making that deals with methods of setting profitable and justifiable prices.

distribution strategy
Element of marketing decision making involving the physical distribution of goods and the selection of distribution channels.

promotional strategy
Element of marketing decision making involving the blending of personal selling, advertising, and sales promotion tools to produce effective communication between the firm and the marketplace.

Figure 13.5   The Marketing Environment

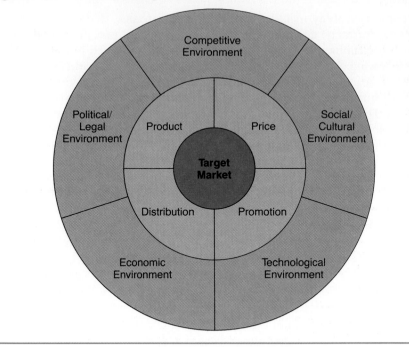

tracking and claims processing. RPS set prices similar to those of UPS, but offered a volume discount of up to 8 percent to attract new business, something the competition had never done. Bram Johnson, the marketing vice-president of RPS, said, "We thought that if we could put together a better product, we had a chance to compete."[9]

The Political/Legal Environment   Governments at the federal, state, and local levels have enacted laws that regulate many marketing activities, ranging from package labeling to product safety. Most laws are designed to maintain a competitive environment and protect consumers. Marketers must not only be aware of the many laws, but they must also comply with them. Noncompliance could result in fines, negative publicity, and expensive civil damage suits. Two telemarketing firms were assessed fines and also barred from doing business in the state of New York because they violated a federal law that prohibits deceptive trade practices and misleading advertising. Consumers complained that the firms misled them by promising expensive prizes, such as a Mercedes-Benz car or a fur coat, in return for vitamin purchases, but that the telemarketers never delivered the promised prizes.[10]

The Economic Environment   Economic factors such as inflation, unemployment, and business cycles influence how much consumers are willing and able to spend and what they buy. Marketers' understanding of how economic factors influence consumer buying behavior allows them to adjust their marketing mix strategies. For example, during a recession, consumers are more apt to buy basic products with low prices. Marketers might respond by lowering prices and increasing promotional spending to stimulate demand. Different strategies apply during times of prosperity, when consumers are willing to purchase higher-priced goods and services. Marketers might then consider raising prices, expanding distribution, and expanding product lines.

The Technological Environment   Changes in technology have a significant impact on how marketers design, produce, price, distribute, and promote their goods and services. New technology can make a product obsolete; for example, calculators wiped out the market for slide rules. Adapting new technology can give an organization a competitive advantage and create new marketing opportunities. The new technology of interactive television, which allows viewers to alter programs, gives marketers the chance to advertise to very specific market segments.[11]

The Social/Cultural Environment   Because consumer values change, marketers must keep abreast of these changes to ensure that their marketing strategies are effective. The line of exercise clothing shown in the advertisement in Figure 13.6 reflects a current social trend — Americans' concern with health and fitness. Like Puma, many other organizations have developed goods and services for our health- and fitness-conscious society. Supermarket shelves are lined with low-salt, low-cholesterol, and vitamin-fortified products. Weight-loss centers and aerobics classes have sprouted up across the country, and many offer special programs for all ages, ranging from tots to seniors. Some firms target busy professionals by marketing exercise equipment for the home.

To some extent, all organizations are affected by the external forces in the marketing environment. And in many cases marketing managers have little or no control over them. But marketers must still monitor the forces and assess the impact they have on their goods and services and marketing practices. In the following sections, we will discuss how marketers assess consumer needs and segment consumer and industrial markets.

What Is a Market?

Markets consist of buyers and sellers, but for the most part they are defined in terms of those who purchase goods and services. A market consists of people; whether they are consumers, procurement officers for local, state, or federal governments, or the purchasing department of a nearby plant. But people do not make a market. Many college students may desire a new Porsche 944 Turbo, but few have the funds needed to complete this transaction.

A **market** consists of people with purchasing power and the authority to buy. One of the first rules the successful salesperson learns is to determine which person in a firm has the authority to make purchase decisions. Salespeople have wasted hours convincing the director of purchasing about the merits of a particular product or group of products, only to discover that the ultimate buying decision actually rests with the design engineer.

market
People with the authority, financial ability, and willingness to purchase goods and services.

Consumer and Industrial Markets

Markets can be classified by the types of products they handle. The two major categories of products are consumer and industrial goods. **Consumer goods** are those goods and services purchased by the ultimate consumer for his or her own use. Most of the products you buy — toothpaste, shoes, and cassette tapes — are consumer goods.

consumer goods
Goods and services purchased by the ultimate consumer for his or her own use.

Figure 13.6   Advertisement Appealing to a Current Social Trend

We accept full responsibility for the way these people look.

Physical Culture. Sports. XTG. Clothes and shoes you can wear to exercise your body. Or just your imagination.

PUMA.
Anything but tame.

industrial goods
Goods purchased to be used directly or indirectly in the production of other goods for resale.

Industrial goods are products purchased to be used, either directly or indirectly, in the production of other goods for resale. Steel is an industrial product. Hercules Inc. is a firm that markets a variety of industrial goods that other firms purchase to make their own products. The advertisement in Figure 13.7 points out how firms that make adhesives can benefit by using a Hercules resin. Services can be classified as either consumer or industrial.

Sometimes the same product has different uses, creating a classification dilemma. The bottle of ketchup purchased by a supermarket shopper clearly is classified as a consumer good; yet ketchup bought by McDonald's is considered an industrial good. Proper classification of products should be based on the purchaser and the reasons for buying the item. A calculator purchased as a back-to-school gift is a consumer good, but a calculator used by the manager of a nearby dry cleaning store is an industrial good.

Marketers must be familiar with a market's buying patterns and the purchasing behavior of those involved. This knowledge is critical when marketers deal with consumer and industrial goods and services.

Consumer Behavior

consumer behavior
The acts of individuals in obtaining and using economic goods and services, including the decision processes that precede and determine these acts.

Consumer behavior can be defined as "those acts of individuals directly involved in obtaining, using, and disposing of economic goods and services, including the decision processes that precede and determine these acts."[12] Both consumers and industrial purchasers are included in this definition.

Figure 13.7   Marketing an Industrial Good

Source: Courtesy of Hercules Incorporated.

The study of consumer behavior allows marketers to identify the critical segments in their marketplace and to develop appropriate marketing strategies for reaching these people. Canada Dry Corporation studied the behavior of people age 30 and older, the target market for its ginger ale, because this segment is crucial to the soft drink's sales growth. The studies revealed that adults stay home more, are less interested in appearances, do not follow fads, value family life, and search for things that are simple and uncomplicated. The analysis helped Canada Dry marketers develop advertising that appeals to these values. One television commercial features a woman who admits she sought excitement as a youth but now enjoys quiet evenings at home. Another showed a couple in their thirties turning down a night on the town for a relaxing at-home dinner of Chinese take-out food and ginger ale. The campaign reversed a declining sales trend and increased the ginger ale's market share. The study of consumer behavior also prompted Canada Dry to reformulate its diet ginger ale, making it less sweet and more gingery, because older drinkers prefer a drier, less sweet flavor.[13]

Influences on Consumer Buying Behavior

Both personal and interpersonal factors influence consumer behavior. The personal influences on consumer behavior are needs and motives, perceptions, attitudes, learned experiences, and self-concept. Marketers frequently use psychological techniques to understand what motivates people to buy and to study consumers' emotional reactions to goods and services. McCann-Erickson, the advertising agency for the American Express Gold Card account, wanted to find out how consumers' perceptions of gold-card users and green-card users differed. Consumers were asked to draw stick figures of each type of cardholder. One set of sketches showed the gold-card user as a person with broad shoulders in an active stance and the green-card user as a "couch potato" watching televi-

Figure 13.8   Social and Family Influences on Buying Behavior

Source: Courtesy of Polaroid Corporation.

sion. Based on these drawings and other research, the agency decided to market the premium gold card as "a symbol of responsibility for people who have control over their lives and finances."[14]

The interpersonal determinants of consumer behavior include cultural influences, social influences, and family influences. The marketing approach used by Polaroid Corporation in promoting its Cool Cam instant camera for children age 9 and older recognizes how both social and family influences affect buying decisions. The advertisement in Figure 13.8 explains that children would want the Cool Cam for social reasons, because it "will make them the envy of all their friends" and "help them look cool." Parents, however, would buy the camera because they see it as "a learning tool that can help children view their surroundings in ways they never thought of." Cultural characteristics also affect buying decisions. Many marketers are aware of the important role the family plays in the cultures of Hispanics and Asian-Americans and use family-oriented themes in targeting these groups. For example, American Telephone & Telegraph commercials using the theme "This close — only with AT&T" show Hispanics longing for their relatives in their homeland and then picking up the phone and calling them.[15]

Industrial purchasers also face a variety of organizational influences. Many people play a role in an industrial purchase. A design engineer may be instru-

Figure 13.9   Steps in the Consumer Decision-Making Process

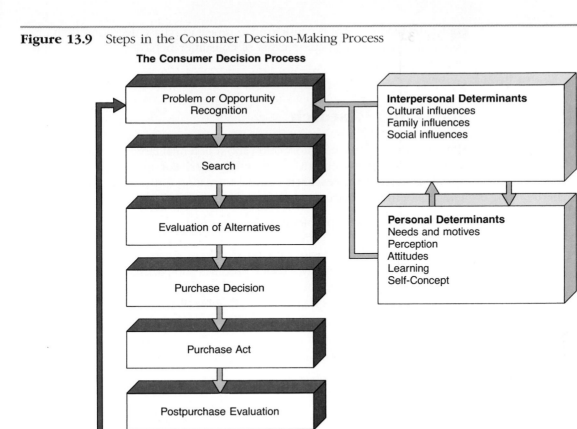

The Consumer Decision Process

Problem or Opportunity Recognition

Search

Evaluation of Alternatives

Purchase Decision

Purchase Act

Postpurchase Evaluation

Feedback

Interpersonal Determinants
Cultural influences
Family influences
Social influences

Personal Determinants
Needs and motives
Perception
Attitudes
Learning
Self-Concept

Source: James F. Engel, Roger D. Blackwell, and Paul W. Miniard, *Consumer Behavior,* 6th ed. (Hinsdale, Ill.: The Dryden Press, 1990).

mental in setting the specifications that potential vendors must satisfy. A purchasing manager invites selected companies to bid on the purchase. A production supervisor is responsible for evaluating the operational aspects of the proposals that are received. And the vice-president of manufacturing makes the final purchase.

Consumer Decision Making

Consumer decision making follows a sequential process, shown in Figure 13.9. The sequence begins with the recognition that a consumer behavior problem or opportunity exists. Examples would include a consumer who needs a new pair of shoes, or one who just won $500 in the state lottery.

The second step is search, during which the consumer seeks out information about the contemplated purchase. The alternatives (such as different brands) are delineated and evaluated. The consumer attempts to get the best response to his or her perceived problem or opportunity.

Finally a decision is reached and the transaction is completed. Later, consumers evaluate their experience with the purchase. This postmortem then becomes the feedback that is considered in repeat purchase decisions. Both interpersonal and personal determinants of consumer behavior affect the various steps in the sequence.

Marketing Research

marketing research
The information function that links the marketer to the marketplace.

How should a firm collect information about potential target markets that could be used in designing effective marketing mixes? For most organizations, the answer is **marketing research** — the information function that links the marketer to the marketplace. Marketers conduct research to:

1. identify marketing problems and opportunities
2. analyze competitors' strategies
3. assess consumer behavior
4. gauge the performance of existing products and package designs and assess the potential of new ones
5. develop price, promotion, and distribution plans

Marketing research involves more than just collecting information. Researchers must decide how to collect the information, interpret the results of research findings, and communicate the results to managers for their use in decision making.

Obtaining Marketing Research Data

internal data
Data generated within the organization.

Marketing researchers are concerned with both internal and external data. **Internal data** is generated within the organization. A tremendous amount of useful information is available from financial records. Data can be obtained on changes in accounts receivable, inventory levels, customers, product lines, profitability of particular divisions, or comparisons of sales by territories, salespeople, customers, or product lines.

external data
Data generated outside the organization.

External data is generated outside the firm and can be obtained from previously published data. Trade associations, for example, publish reports on activities in particular industries. Advertising agencies collect information on the audiences reached by various media. National marketing research firms offer information to organizations on a subscription basis. For example, Information Resources Inc. offers a national scanning service that tracks consumer purchases of every supermarket product sold with a Universal Product Code. The service integrates store sales and household purchase data, giving marketers information on their brand's buyers, store loyalty, and general shopping behavior.

Federal, state, and local government publications are the marketing researcher's most important data source. The most frequently used government statistics are census data. Data is available on population characteristics such as age, sex, race, education levels, household size and composition, occupation, employment status, and income. Such data enables marketers to assess certain segments of the population, anticipate changes in their markets, and identify markets with growth potential.

In addition to using published data, marketing researchers also gather information by conducting observational studies and surveys. In observational stud-

Janet Patterson, the research director of WBZ-TV in Boston, conducts a focus group interview on the set of *Rap-Around,* a talk show for teenagers. Such interviews help the station develop news, entertainment, and public service programming that responds to viewers' interests and needs.

Photo source: Courtesy of Westinghouse Electric Corporation.

ies, researchers actually view the actions of the respondents, either directly or through mechanical devices. Traffic counts can be used to determine the best location for a new fast-food restaurant. Researchers use people meters to observe television audience viewership. People meters are electronic, remote-control devices that record the viewing habits of each household member. The viewer information is used to measure a program's success and to set advertising rates.

Some information cannot be obtained through observation. When information is needed about attitudes, opinions, and motives, the researchers must ask questions by conducting a survey. Survey methods include telephone interviews, mail surveys, personal interviews, and focus group interviews. In a focus group interview, 8 to 12 individuals are brought together in one location to discuss a subject of interest. Focus groups are an important research tool because they provide marketers with insights into why consumers buy or do not buy their goods and services. Ideas generated during focus group interviews are especially helpful to marketers in developing new products, improving existing products, and creating effective advertising campaigns.

Applying Marketing Research Data

The information collected by researchers is valuable only when it can be used to make decisions that conform to an overall corporate plan. All marketing research should be done within the framework of the organization's strategic plan. The marketing research activities of General Motors, for example, are directed toward implementing a new corporate strategy of designing cars for specific market segments rather than for the mass market. To determine which features and accessories each targeted segment desires, GM conducts focus group interviews with consumers and dealers and mail and telephone surveys with GM car owners and owners of competing models. GM uses the information it collects by creating a market-research model that enables its engineers to apply the research findings to the design of new cars. GM's research efforts resulted in about 75 improvements in its GM10 line of midsize cars. One improvement came from a focus group session that showed consumers wanted a device more convenient than a small lever to adjust the front seats of a car. GM engineers responded to this desire by designing a long metal bar that permits simple access for seat movement.[16]

Market Segmentation

It is important to be able to clearly define who one's customers are or are intended to be. Market segmentation allows marketers to determine how and why people buy products and services.

market segmentation
Process of dividing the total market into several relatively homogeneous groups.

Market segmentation is the process of dividing the total market into several relatively homogeneous groups. Both profit-oriented and nonprofit organizations use market segmentation to help define their target markets.

Figure 13.10 shows that markets can be segmented on a variety of bases. Consumer marketers can use demographic, geographic, psychographic, and benefit segmentation. By contrast, industrial marketers use geographic segmentation, product segmentation, and segmentation by end-use application.

Segmenting Consumer Markets

Factors like age, income, place of residence, life-style, and relative product use have all been used to segment consumer markets. The most common basis for segmenting consumer markets is the demographic approach. Geographic segmentation has been used for centuries, but more recently marketers have turned to psychographic and benefit segmentation.

Demographic Segmentation   Demographic segmentation divides markets on the basis of demographic, or socioeconomic, characteristics. Sex, income, age, occupation, household size, education, and family life-cycle stage have all been used in demographic segmentation. A great amount of data is available for assisting marketers in segmenting potential markets on a demographic basis.

Recent studies indicate children are expanding their roles as consumers. About 32 million consumers are children with an estimated purchasing power of $4.2 billion for 5- to 12-year-olds and $30.5 billion for 13- to 18-year-olds. Children's influence on their parents' buying decisions has also increased. The rise in the number of working couples and single-parent households gives children more responsibility in purchasing groceries. Firms in many industries are

Figure 13.10   Bases for Market Segmentation

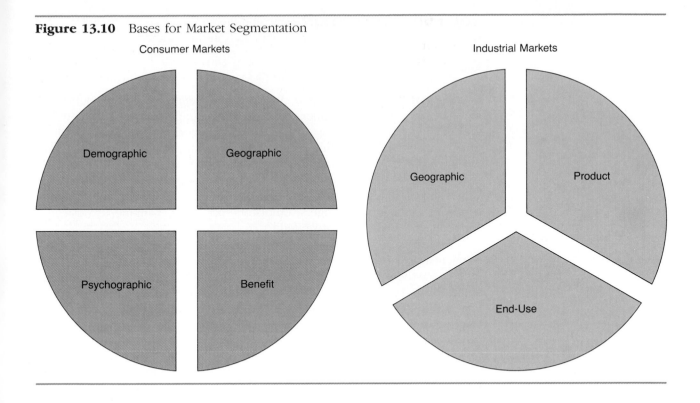

creating products and developing promotions targeted at this demographic group. K mart launched WaldenKids, a chain of bookstores for children in pre-school to age 12. Oral-B Laboratories targets its Muppets and Sesame Street line of toothpastes at 2- to 8-year-olds and creates television commercials aimed at this age group. Marketing aimed at children not only emphasizes their current roles as consumers, but is also intended to build loyalty. First Women's Bank in New York opened a bank for children in the F.A.O. Schwartz toy store. The president of First Women's says, "What better way to build loyalty to a bank than to get them while they are young." A similar strategy inspired the U.S. Army, Marines, and Air Force to place ads in children's magazines such as *Boys' Life* and *Scholastic*.[17]

Geographic Segmentation   Marketers often study population data in their efforts to segment markets. In fact, geographic segmentation is one of the oldest segmentation bases available. It can be extremely useful when consumer prefer-ences and purchase patterns for a product or service differ along regional lines. But one of the problems marketers face is that marketplaces keep shifting. For instance, there has been a decided movement in the U.S. population to the Sunbelt and coastal areas and westward.

Campbell Soup Company is an example of a consumer products firm that segments markets by geographic location. Campbell divides the country into 22 geographic regions and develops products and promotions targeted at each defined area. Region-specific products include creole soup, which is sold only in the South, and red-bean soup, which is marketed in areas with large populations of Hispanics. Because beer drinkers' tastes vary considerably in different parts of the country, G. Heileman Brewing Company markets a number of regional brands and develops advertising for each region. In Pittsburgh, Heileman promotes its Iron City beer with the campaign theme "You Can't Keep an Iron Man Down." Heileman takes a different approach in the southern half of Texas, an area hard-hit by recession, by using the theme "The Lone Star Is on the Rise Again" to promote its Lone Star brand.[18]

Psychographic Segmentation   Psychographic segmentation uses behavioral and life-style profiles to segment markets. Psychographic analysis seeks to further define the various groups of individuals in American society. This enables firms to tailor their marketing approach to a carefully chosen market segment. SRI International, a marketing research firm, conducted a study to identify life-style categories that would be useful in market segmentation. The resulting Values and Lifestyles Program (VALS) categorizes individuals into nine life-styles: survivors, sustainers, belongers, emulators, achievers, I-am-me, experiential, societally conscious, and integrated.[19]

St. Rose Hospital of Hayward, California, decided to use the VALS concept of segmentation when consumer research indicated advertisements for its new emergency-room services were ineffective. The hospital learned that the ads, which focused on the speed and cost of service, meant little to potential customers. St. Rose's market is dominated by "belongers," people who have traditional values and are intensely patriotic and sentimental. They respond to ads that soothe their anxiety and emphasize the predictability of health-care service. Armed with this knowledge, St. Rose developed a direct-mail advertising campaign that emphasized how many years the hospital had been in business and used the reassuring theme of the hospital's ability to keep "small worries from growing into big ones." The new campaign appealed to the target audience and quickly improved the hospital's business and enhanced its image.[20]

Benefit Segmentation   Market segments may also be identified by the benefits buyers may expect to derive from a good or service. In recent years, socks have become a fashion item, and many sock makers now market their goods as a fashion accessory. But Foot-Joy's brand of JoyWalker Socks offers a benefit that targets a market segment more concerned about foot comfort than fashion. In the advertisement in Figure 13.11, the company admits its socks are ugly but explains how they are designed to improve circulation, thus promising consumers the benefit of foot comfort.

When differences among competing goods or services are slight, firms may tailor their promotions to highlight benefits that appeal to a certain market segment. Advertising by U.S. airlines takes this approach. In targeting business travelers, American Airlines created advertisements promoting its dependable, on-time performance. In the ads, American refers to itself as the "on-time machine" and reports it has the fewest delayed flights of all major airlines. By contrast, United Air Lines targets business travelers with a campaign theme focusing on customer service — "Rededicated to giving you the service you deserve." The benefit that USAir offers to business travelers is frequent scheduling of flights to key destinations.[21]

Segmenting Industrial Markets

It is also possible to use market segmentation in industrial markets. The procedure is similar to that employed in consumer markets, where the bulk of the research has been conducted.

Figure 13.11   Segmenting Markets by Product Benefits

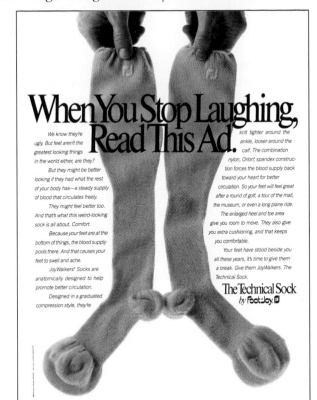

The three approaches to industrial market segmentation are geographic segmentation, product segmentation, and segmentation by end-use application. Geographic segmentation would be useful in geographically concentrated industries like aircraft manufacturing. Product segmentation refers to developing products to meet specific buyer requirements, such as the purchase of police cars. Segmentation by end-use application considers how the buyer will use the product or service. For instance, Northrop's F-20 was designed for export to nations that wanted a low-cost, general-purpose fighter aircraft. Unfortunately for the manufacturer, the F-20 did not find any overseas customers. Segmentation is a market tool of growing importance in industrial markets.

Summary of Learning Goals

1.   Discuss how marketing's role in the exchange process creates utility. Exchange is the process by which two or more parties give something of value to one another to satisfy felt needs. Marketing is closely linked with the exchange process. It creates utility—the want-satisfying power of a good or service—by having the product available when and where the consumer wants to buy it and by arranging for an orderly transfer of ownership. While production creates form utility, marketing creates time, place, and ownership utility.

2.   List the major functions of marketing.   Marketing is more than just selling. In fact, there are eight basic functions of marketing: buying, selling, transporting, storing, standardization and grading, financing, risk taking, and acquiring market information.

3.   Explain the marketing concept.   The marketing concept is a managerial philosophy that requires an organizationwide consumer orientation with the objective of achieving long-run success. Both profit-oriented and nonprofit organizations use the marketing concept.

4.   Outline how a marketing strategy is developed.   The development of a marketing strategy is a two-step process: (1) studying, analyzing, and eventually selecting the organization's target market—the group of customers toward which a firm decides to direct its marketing efforts, and (2) developing a marketing mix that will reach the organization's target market. The marketing mix is a combination of the firm's product, pricing, distribution, and promotional strategies.

5.   Describe the five environmental forces that influence marketing decision making.   The five environmental forces influencing marketing decision making are competitive, political/legal, economic, technological, and social/cultural. Marketers must monitor these forces and assess the impact they may have on their goods and services and marketing practices.

6.   Explain the concept of a market.   A market consists of people with purchasing power and the authority to buy. Markets can be classified on the basis of the types of products they handle. Consumers goods are those goods and services purchased by the ultimate consumer for his or her own use. Industrial goods are products purchased to be used, directly or indirectly, in the production of other goods for resale.

7.   Discuss why the study of consumer behavior is important to marketing.   Consumer behavior deals with why and how people buy things. This information is crucial to marketers if they are to successfully market a product or service. Marketers must understand the personal and interpersonal influences on consumer behavior as well as the organizational influences that affect industrial purchasers. It is also important that marketers understand the steps involved in consumer decision making: problem or opportunity recognition, search, evaluation, buying decision, transaction, and feedback.

8.   Describe the marketing research function.   Marketing research is the information function that links the marketers to the marketplace. It involves collecting information, interpreting the results of research findings, and communicating the results to managers for their use in decision making. Information can be obtained from internal data, such as financial records, and external data published by the government, trade associations, and research firms. Researchers also gather information by conducting observational studies, telephone interviews, mail surveys, personal interviews, and focus group interviews. Marketing research enables organizations to identify marketing problems and opportunities, to assess competitors' strategies, to understand consumer buying behavior, and to develop effective marketing mixes.

9. List and explain the bases used to segment markets. Consumer markets may be divided on four bases: demographic, geographic, psychographic, or benefit segmentation. Demographic segmentation divides the market into groups based on characteristics such as sex, age, income, occupation, and household composition. Geographic segmentation divides the overall market into groups on the basis of population location. Psychographic segmentation uses behavioral and life-style profiles to segment markets. Benefit segmentation divides a market on the basis of benefits consumers expect to derive from a good or service. Bases for segmenting industrial markets include geographic segmentation, product segmentation, and segmentation by end-use application.

Key Terms

marketing	place marketing	market
exchange	idea marketing	consumer goods
time utility	organization marketing	industrial goods
place utility	target market	consumer behavior
ownership utility	marketing mix	marketing research
marketing concept	product strategy	internal data
seller's market	pricing strategy	external data
buyer's market	distribution strategy	market segmentation
person marketing	promotional strategy	

Review Questions

1. What type of utility is created by the following?
   a. Emery Air Freight's shipment of a fast-selling fad item
   b. A Giant supermarket
   c. The finishing department of a furniture factory
   d. An escrow company that handles the details of a property transfer

2. List various examples of marketers who are performing each of the eight basic functions of marketing. What, if anything, does this list suggest?

3. How successfully do you think the following organizations have adopted the marketing concept?
   a. Procter & Gamble
   b. The college you are attending
   c. Texaco
   d. Florida Power & Light

4. Identify the likely target markets of each of the following:
   a. Washington Redskins
   b. Midas Muffler
   c. H&R Block tax service
   d. Chrysler New Yorker
   e. Supercuts hair salons

5. Develop a marketing strategy for a Chinese restaurant in your community. Defend your marketing strategy decisions.

6. Explain how the competitive, political/legal, economic, technological, and social/cultural environments influence marketing strategy.

7. What is meant by a market? Distinguish between consumer and industrial markets.

8. Outline the steps in the consumer decision-making process.

9. Describe the various methods of gathering survey data.

10. Match the four bases of consumer market segmentation — (1) geographic segmentation, (2) demographic segmentation, (3) psychographic segmentation, and (4) benefit segmentation — with the following segmentation variables:
    _____ **a.** Life-style
    _____ **b.** Sex
    _____ **c.** Urban/suburban/rural
    _____ **d.** The social contacts provided by a private country club

Discussion Questions

1. Chicago-based Information Resources Inc. has tested shopping carts with video displays in Chicago, Atlanta, and Los Angeles. Shoppers can locate items they are looking for by punching a few buttons on the cart. The video-display screens also flash up daily specials, advertisements, recipes, local news and weather, and even trivia games. Advertisers pay for the carts. Relate these unique shopping carts to the discussion of utility that appears in Chapter 13.

2. One resident in six is under 5 years old in Unita, Wyoming, giving that community the youngest population in the nation. By contrast, Pasco County, Florida, holds the oldest population title with almost one-third of its residents at 65 or older. What goods and services would be in strongest demand in each area? Defend your answer.

3. Some state legislators have argued that colleges and universities should not be allowed to spend public funds to promote their course offerings. What are your views on this issue? Defend your position.

4. Swanson's Le Menu frozen food line is targeted at 25- to 54-year-olds with a salary of $30,000 or more in one- or two-person households. What type of segmentation strategy is being employed for this product? Discuss.

5. Apple Computer now targets its products at the business and education markets. Senior Vice-President Charles Bosenberg explains the strategy this way: "We're not selling a computer box any longer. We're selling specific solutions to individuals in business or education." What type of segmentation strategy has Apple adopted? Discuss.

Video Case

University National Bank & Trust

If there is one thing California bankers know about Carl Schmitt, it is his never-ending criticism of the customer service offered by most banks. In 1975, during his term as superintendent of state banks in California, Schmitt began encouraging financial institutions to target smaller communities with better services aimed at their specific needs. He realized that the typical banking customer considers service at banks to be — in his words — "lousy," and that a fundamental factor in bank selection is personal attention, a service that the big-bank mentality frequently neglected.

Schmitt's philosophy of providing high-quality, tailored service to smaller, segmented markets led him to resign his state government post and open University National Bank & Trust Company (UNB) in 1980 in Palo Alto, California. UNB's target market consists of well-educated, relatively young, high-income professionals working in Palo Alto's high-tech industries or at Stanford University. The bank is highly selective, requiring a thorough credit check or a strong reference from an existing customer before it will open a checking account or provide a loan to a prospective banking client. Such selectivity is aimed at allowing the bank to focus on the needs of a specific group of people. In Schmitt's words, "I want people to seek out this bank for a long-term relationship. I want the bank to be held out as something special in the community."

Schmitt is well aware of the fact that banks provide financial *services,* not tangible products. Since bank personnel are responsible for both creating and dispensing these services, UNB places great emphasis on hiring competent people and making them feel like professionals who can see their career future within this one bank. Employees are well-paid by industry standards. In fact, UNB has the highest expense-per-employee ratio of all similar-size banks in the United States. "You get what you pay for," says Schmitt. "It's a big investment, but they're worth it."

Notes: "Dressing for Success," *Inc.,* April 1988, p. 129; Ruth Hamel and Tim Schreiner, "A Real Nice Bank," *American Demographics,* September 1988, p. 54; Lisa McCann, "Boutique Banking in California," *United States Banker,* April 1984, pp. 46–48; and Cris Oppenheimer, "The Funniest Act in Banking," *California Business,* September 1987, pp. 84–86.

When banking was deregulated in the early 1980s, many predicted that small banks would become dinosaurs, unable to compete with large banks and doomed to either close their doors or to become branches of Citibank, Bank of America, or one of the other banking giants. But just the opposite has occurred in many communities where small, service-oriented banks, attuned to the specific needs of the market, have prospered. UNB's Schmitt argues that banking customers want value, not size. "'Small is beautiful' is the right philosophy," he believes. UNB has no plans for future expansion of branches, further emphasizing management's intention of targeting a small market. The bank's success is keyed to the care and coddling of customers, tailoring its services to the needs of the Palo Alto market.

A recent Beta Research Corporation survey of Californians with annual household incomes of $50,000 or more provides Schmitt with the type of information needed for customer segmentation and targeting. Adults under the age of 45 (40 percent) are not as loyal to their banks as adults 45 and older (53 percent). One-third of the younger adults agree that "institutions just want my money and don't really care about my needs;" less than one-fourth of the older adults have this view. "In order to be successful, a specialty bank must not only know the demographics of its market but also understand its unique style," Schmitt explains, and this unique style is very much a part of UNB operations.

Banking hours are longer than normal, and customers who cannot make it to the bank during regular hours can phone for special appointments. Standard customer service includes everything from a free shoeshine in the lobby to a fleet of four vans that pick up deposits from business owners, sparing them a trip to the bank. This is neither a typical banking service nor a typical bank van: The van windows are painted with scenes of bank robbers being captured and counterfeiters at work. Teller service is outstanding; stamps are sold at cost and if more than three people are waiting at a teller window, the nearest available bank employee — who might be Schmitt — opens a window to minimize the time it takes for customer banking transactions.

UNB does not charge the multitude of fees found

at larger banks. For example, traveler's checks and cashier's checks are free, as are stop-payment orders and notary services. Bounced checks are rare, since customers are first given a chance to make deposits to cover the amount.

Even with these services, UNB is, above all, a profitable bank. It avoids long-term loans, as well as construction loans, although exceptions are made on occasion. Moreover, interest payments are based on floating rates that adjust to the bank's cost of funds. Very few fixed-rate loans are made.

Perhaps the most visible example of UNB's uniqueness is its advertising. Initially, Schmitt tried to emphasize tangible products — interest-paying checking accounts — in his advertisements. After three such ads brought virtually no response, he changed his tactics and launched a humorous assault on the banking industry in general and, occasionally, on one of UNB's giant competitors such as Wells Fargo and Bank of America. The ads are designed to position UNB as a bank so different as to be called alien. (In fact, one of the bank's exterior walls is painted with a huge mural of a spaceship crashing through the wall, with a little green alien climbing out.) To drive home the personal-service feature of UNB, one of its ads shows a man pinning the tail on a donkey with the caption, "Ever wonder how big banks set policy?" Another ad shows a small, square, wooden doll being hammered into a round hole with the headline, "Is this the personal touch your bank delivers?" The humor worked; by 1989, UNB had attracted over 3,500 customers.

A one-page listing of banking services is included in UNB's annual report. Many of these are common to other banks, but some are unique:

Smiles: "Our staff looks forward to greeting you with a smile," the report states.

Loans: Three specific types are mentioned: "Mansion expansion," "Motor cars," and "Other adult toys financed."

Other UNB services include a folksy monthly newsletter that recommends area restaurants and announces such events as upcoming grape-picking parties at local vineyards. Even the bank's boardroom is used as a marketing tool. Once a week, it is converted into an elegant private lunch room. Perhaps UNB's best-known marketing service is to offer Walla Walla sweet onions free to bank customers every summer. In a typical year, customers will come to the bank lobby and collect over six tons of onions in five- to fifty-pound bags.

The success of UNB's unique blend of customer service indicates that Schmitt has been successful in marketing his bank's services to his chosen target market. The high-tech professionals from California's Silicon Valley and academics/researchers from Stanford University appreciate UNB's unique combination of service, humor, and conservative business practices. UNB offers its customers a different experience in banking, and it has proven to be the experience people in the Palo Alto community have been looking for. In 1982, the bank's total assets amounted to only $37.5 million. By 1988, they had grown to $162 million. Its ads bring in new customers and its high service standards help to create a valuable reputation spread by word-of-mouth from established, satisfied customers to their friends and relatives. As UNB's marketing vice-president Ann Sonnenberg says, "Being nice is neither difficult nor expensive." And it gets results.

Questions

1. Relate the marketing of University National Bank & Trust services to the concept of the consumer and the elements of the marketing mix. Describe the target market and compare the product UNB is marketing with other products. Discuss how each of the other marketing mix elements is employed in UNB's marketing strategy.

2. Relate the materials in this case to each of the environmental factors affecting marketing decisions at UNB.

3. Explain the concept of utility and describe how UNB creates three different types of utility.

4. Eight marketing functions are described in the chapter. Describe how each function is performed by University National Bank & Trust Co.

5. Explain how each of the bases for segmenting consumer markets might be employed by marketers at UNB.

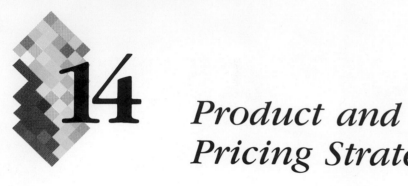

14

Product and Pricing Strategies

Learning Goals

1. To list the components of the total product concept.

2. To identify the types of consumer goods, industrial goods, and services.

3. To describe the product mix and product lines.

4. To identify and describe the stages of the product life cycle.

5. To list the stages in the new-product development process.

6. To explain how products are identified.

7. To outline the different types of pricing objectives.

8. To discuss how prices are set in the marketplace.

9. To show how breakeven analysis can be used in pricing strategy.

10. To differentiate between skimming and penetration pricing strategies.

Wayne Wilson's shopping expedition for a greeting card for a relative was disappointing. The Los Angeles native realized there were few creative or imaginative greeting cards aimed at blacks. "Most are just photographic images, and that is because it's the easiest thing to do," he said. Wilson decided to correct the situation. He invested $3,000 and set up L'Image Graphics in Culver City, California. His partner in the new venture was Taylor Barnes, a former free-lance designer. She remembers the origins of their business: "We researched the market for two years before we launched our first seven cards, which a friend of my father's agreed to print for free. We knew we were on to something when 10,000 sold immediately."

Wilson and Barnes knew they needed more seed money for their fledgling venture. Wilson approached actor Sidney Poitier with an investment proposal. After four months of negotiations, Poitier decided to invest $100,000 in L'Image. Poitier also persuaded Barry Gordy of Motown Records fame to invest a similar amount. Wilson and Barnes later bought out their investors' shares.

While Wilson and Barnes wanted to produce greeting cards for black consumers, they also wanted their collection to be innovative enough to appeal to everyone. Wilson describes their strategy this way:

We wanted to fill the void, yet we didn't want to limit ourselves. To do so, we decided that each collection would have crossover potential, that all races would buy it purely because they like the card and the message. From the outset, we felt a need to revolutionize the industry. When we started, manufacturers thought if you put a photograph of a black person on a card, the card would automatically sell. We believe that people are people regardless of race and

that everyone deserves to select from a collection that appeals to them artistically and emotionally.

L'Image now offers over 200 designs in nine original collections. Its first gift items, a mug collection based on the L'Astrology greeting card series, appeared in 1988. The L'Image line is sold in nearly 2,000 stores in the United States, Canada, Puerto Rico, and England, with recent annual sales over $500,000.[1]

The growth of L'Image Graphics shows the importance of an effective product strategy. That and pricing strategy are the topics of Chapter 14.

Photo source: Courtesy of L'Image Graphics.

Chapter Overview

product
Bundle of physical, service, and symbolic attributes designed to satisfy consumer wants.

This chapter deals with the first two components of a marketing mix: product strategy and pricing strategy. Marketers broadly define a **product** as a bundle of physical, service, and symbolic attributes designed to satisfy consumer wants. Therefore, product strategy involves considerably more than producing a physical good or service. It is a total product concept that includes decisions about package design, brand name, trademarks, warranties, guarantees, product image, and new-product development. The Sears advertisement in Figure 14.1 illustrates the total product concept. In the ad, Sears points out that consumers buy its Kenmore appliances for reasons other than the products' functional characteristics. Rather, the main reason consumers choose Kenmore is because of the retailer's satisfaction-guaranteed-or-money-back policy.

price
Exchange value of a good or service.

The second element of the marketing mix is pricing strategy. **Price** is the exchange value of a good or service. An item is worth only what someone else is willing to pay for it. In a primitive society, the exchange value may be determined by trading a good for some other commodity. A horse may be worth ten coins; twelve apples may be worth two loaves of bread. More advanced societies use money for exchange. But in either case, the price of a good or service is its exchange value. Pricing strategy deals with the multitude of factors that influence the setting of a price.

This chapter begins by describing the classification of goods and services, the product mix, and the product life cycle. We then discuss how products are developed, identified, and packaged and the service attributes of products. The second part of the chapter focuses on the pricing of goods and services, including pricing objectives, how prices are set, and different types of pricing strategies.

Classifying Goods and Services

Marketers have found it useful to classify goods and services because each type requires a different competitive strategy. Goods and services are classified as either consumer or industrial, depending on the purchasers of the particular item. Consumer and industrial product classifications can also be subdivided.

Classifying Consumer Goods

A variety of classifications have been suggested for consumer goods, but the system most typically used has three subcategories: convenience goods, shopping goods, and specialty goods. This system, based on consumer buying habits, has been used for about 70 years.

convenience goods
Products that consumers seek to purchase frequently, immediately, and with a minimum of effort.

Convenience goods are products the consumer seeks to purchase frequently, immediately, and with a minimum of effort. Items stocked in 24-hour convenience stores, vending machines, and local newsstands are usually convenience goods. Newspapers, chewing gum, magazines, milk, beer, bread, and cigarettes are all convenience goods.

shopping goods
Products purchased only after the consumer has compared competing goods in competing stores.

Shopping goods are products purchased only after the consumer has compared competing goods in competing stores on bases such as price, quality,

Figure 14.1   The Total Product Concept

Source: Courtesy of Sears Roebuck.

style, and color. A young couple intent on buying a new television may visit many stores, examine perhaps dozens of TV sets, and spend days making the final decision. The couple follows a regular routine from store to store in surveying competing offerings and ultimately selects the most appealing set.

Specialty goods are particular products desired by a purchaser who is familiar with the item sought and is willing to make a special effort to obtain it. A specialty good has no reasonable substitute in the mind of the buyer. The nearest Mercedes dealer may be 40 miles away, but a buyer might go there to obtain what he or she considers one of the world's best-engineered cars.

This classification of consumer goods may differ among buyers. A shopping good for one person may be a convenience good for another. Majority buying patterns determine the item's product classification.

Marketing Strategy Implications   The consumer goods classification is a useful tool in marketing strategy. For example, once a new lawn edger has been classified as a shopping good, insights are gained about its marketing needs in promotion, pricing, and distribution methods. The impact of the consumer goods classification on various aspects of marketing strategy is shown in Table 14.1.

specialty goods
Products perceived to be so desirable that the buyer is willing to make a special effort to obtain them.

Table 14.1   The Relationship between the Consumer Goods
Classification and Marketing Strategy

Marketing Strategy Factor	Convenience Good	Shopping Good	Specialty Good
Store image	Unimportant	Very important	Important
Price	Low	Relatively high	High
Promotion	By manufacturer	By manufacturer and retailer	By manufacturer and retailer
Channel length	Many wholesalers and retailers	Relatively few wholesalers and retailers	Very few wholesalers and retailers
Number of retail outlets	Many	Few	Very small number; often one per market area

Classifying Industrial Goods

The five main categories of industrial goods are installations, accessory equipment, component parts and materials, raw materials, and supplies. While consumer goods are classified by buying habits, classification of industrial goods is based on how products are used and product characteristics. Goods that are long-lived and usually involve large sums of money are called *capital items*. Less costly goods that are consumed within a year are referred to as *expense items*.

installations
Expensive and long-lived major capital items such as a new factory or heavy machinery.

Installations are major capital items such as new factories, heavy equipment and machinery, and custom-made equipment. Installations are typically used for the production of other items. For example, General Motors purchased an automated monorail system from Litton Industries to transport cars on the GM assembly line. Installations are expensive and often involve buyer/seller negotiations that may last several years before a purchase decision is made.

accessory equipment
Capital item, such as a typewriter, that is less expensive and shorter-lived than an installation.

Accessory equipment includes capital items that are usually less expensive and shorter-lived than installations. Examples are hand tools and word processors. Some accessory equipment, such as a portable drill, is used to produce other goods and services, while other equipment, such as a desk calculator, is used in administrative and operating functions.

component parts and materials
Finished industrial goods that become part of a final product.

Component parts and materials are industrial goods that become part of a final product. Seagate Technology, for example, makes magnetic disk drives that are sold as a component part to manufacturers of small computers. In some cases, component parts are visible in the finished good, such as the Pirelli tires used on the Ferrari and other luxury automobiles. In other cases, component parts and materials are not readily seen. American Fructose Corporation manufactures corn syrup used by other manufacturers to produce soft drinks, jams, ice cream, and canned fruit. The advertisement in Figure 14.2 illustrates how wheels and brakes made by BFGoodrich are used as component parts by aircraft manufacturers.

raw materials
Farm and natural products used in producing final goods.

Raw materials are similar to component parts and materials because they are used in the production of a final good. Raw materials include farm products such as cotton, wheat, cattle, and milk, and natural materials such as iron ore, lumber, and coal. Because most raw materials are graded, buyers are assured of standardized products of uniform quality.

Figure 14.2   Example of an Installation

Source: Courtesy of The BFGoodrich Company.

Supplies are expense items used in a firm's daily operation, but they do not become part of the final product. Supplies include products such as paper clips, cleaning compounds, light bulbs, and stationery. These items are purchased regularly and little time is spent on the purchase decision.

supplies
Expense items needed in the firm's daily operation but not part of the final product.

Marketing Strategy Implications   Each group of industrial goods requires a different marketing strategy. Because most installations and many component parts are marketed directly from the manufacturer to the buyer, the promotional emphasis is on personal selling rather than on advertising. By contrast, marketers of supplies and accessory equipment rely more on advertising to promote their goods, which are frequently sold through an intermediary such as a wholesaler. Producers of installations and component parts may involve their customers in new-product development, especially when the industrial good is custom made. Finally, firms marketing supplies and accessory equipment place greater emphasis on competitive pricing strategies than do other industrial goods marketers, who concentrate on product quality and servicing.

Classifying Services

Services can be classified as either consumer or industrial. Hair salons, child-care centers, and shoe repair shops provide services for consumers. The Pinkerton security patrol at a factory and Kelly Services' temporary clerical workers are examples of industrial services. In some cases, a service can accommodate both consumer and industrial markets. For example, when ServiceMaster employees clean the upholstery in a home, it is a consumer service. When a ServiceMaster crew cleans the painting system and robotics in a manufacturing plant, it is an industrial service.

Figure 14.3   A Product Line

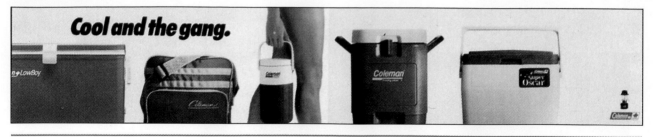

Source: Courtesy of The Coleman Company, Inc.

The Product Mix

product mix
Assortment of products offered by a firm.

A **product mix** is the assortment of goods and/or services a firm offers consumers and industrial users. Although Borden Inc. is best known for marketing dairy products, the firm's product mix also includes pasta, snack items, niche grocery products (Campfire marshmallows and ReaLemon juice), nonfood consumer goods (Rain Dance car-care products, Elmer's glue, wallpaper), and specialty industrial chemicals (adhesives, forest product resins, food-wrap items).

product line
Series of related goods offered by a firm.

The product mix is a combination of product lines and individual offerings that make up the product line. A **product line** is a series of related products. The advertisement in Figure 14.3 shows some of the individual products in one of Coleman Company's product lines — coolers. Coleman's product mix includes other lines of outdoor recreational equipment, such as canoes, sleeping bags, cookers, tents, and camping trailers.

Marketers must continually assess their product mix to ensure company growth, to satisfy changing consumer needs and wants, and to adjust to competitors' offerings. Consider how these factors have influenced the product mix of Bic Corporation.

Most of Bic's sales come from three product lines: disposable lighters, shavers, and pens. Lighters account for about 40 percent of Bic's $290 million in sales. But Bic marketers realized the growth prospects for lighters are dim, given the dwindling number of smokers and the public's increasing antismoking sentiment. They expanded the lighter line by adding a smaller version, the Mini Bic, to increase the firm's share of the market. But to build overall company sales, they broadened their product mix by adding a new product line — quarter-ounce bottles of perfume. With the new line, Bic marketers hope to capture part of the huge $3 billion fragrance market. In response to new products from foreign and domestic competitors, Bic expanded its line of pens and shavers. Bic added a roller pen after Mitsubishi Pencil Company introduced metal-point roller pens to the United States and gained 10 percent of the pen market. Bic's shaver sales dropped 5 percent after Gillette introduced the Microtrac razor. In an effort to recapture lost sales, Bic developed a similar shaver designed to reduce nicking.[2]

Product mixes and product lines undergo constant change. To remain competitive, marketers look for gaps in their assortment and fill them with new products or modified versions of existing ones. A useful tool used by marketers in making product decisions is the product life cycle.

Figure 14.4   Stages in the Product Life Cycle

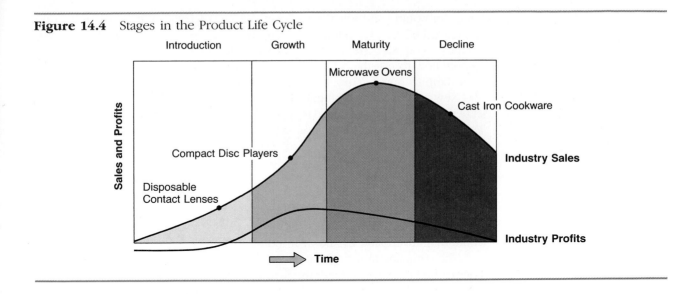

The Product Life Cycle

Successful goods and services, like people, pass through a series of stages from their initial appearance to death; this progression is known as the **product life cycle**. Humans grow from infants into children; they eventually become adults and gradually move to retirement age and, finally, death. The four stages through which successful products pass are introduction, growth, maturity, and decline. Figure 14.4 depicts these steps and shows current examples of products at the various life cycle stages.

    Both industry sales and profits at each life cycle stage are shown in the figure. Although the horizontal axis reflects time periods, the overall length of the product life cycle and each of its stages varies considerably. A new fad item such as Little Miss Makeup dolls may have a total life span of two or three years or less, with an introductory stage of 90 days. By contrast, the automobile has been in the maturity stage for over a quarter-century.

    The product life cycle concept provides important insights for the marketing planner in anticipating developments throughout the various stages of a product's life. Knowledge that profits assume a predictable pattern through the stages and that promotional emphasis must shift from product information in the early stages to heavy promotion of competing brands in the later ones should improve product planning decisions. Since marketing programs will be modified at each stage in the life cycle, an understanding of the characteristics of all four product life cycle stages is critical in formulating successful strategies.

product life cycle
Four stages through which a successful product passes: introduction, growth, maturity, and decline.

Introduction

In the early stages of the product life cycle, the firm attempts to promote demand for its new market offering. Because neither consumers nor distributors may be aware of the product, marketers must use promotional programs to inform the market of the item's availability and explain its features, uses, and benefits. When Lea & Perrins introduced its new White Wine Worcestershire

Sauce for poultry and fish, the company created advertisements, such as the one in Figure 14.5, that included easy-to-use recipes. "We knew that we had to have recipes," said Rick Heller, the firm's director of marketing. "Without telling people how to use the White Wine Worcestershire we wouldn't be able to expect them to buy it. They wouldn't know what to do with it."[3]

New-product development and introductory promotional campaigns are expensive and commonly lead to losses in the first stage of the product life cycle. Yet these expenditures are necessary if the firm is to profit later.

Growth

Sales climb quickly during the product's growth stage as new customers join the early users who are now repurchasing the item. Person-to-person referrals and continued advertising by the firm induce others to make trial purchases.

The company also begins to earn profits on the new product. But this encourages competitors to enter the field with similar offerings. For example, after the successful introduction of Lea & Perrins' sauce, H. J. Heinz and French's began marketing similar fish and poultry sauces. Price competition appears in the growth stage, and total industry profits peak in the later part of this stage.

To gain a larger share of a growing market, firms may develop different versions of a product to target specific segments. Thomas J. Lipton added two variations — no-sugar Homestyle and chunky vegetable Gardenstyle — of its original-recipe Ragu spaghetti sauce.

Maturity

As shown in Figure 14.4, industry sales at first increase in the maturity stage, but eventually reach a saturation level at which further expansion is difficult. Competition also intensifies, increasing the availability of the product. Firms concentrate on capturing competitors' customers, often dropping prices to further their appeal. Sales volume fades late in the maturity stage, and some of the weaker competitors leave the market.

Firms spend heavily on promoting mature products to protect their market share and to distinguish their products from those of competitors. For example, Goodyear Tire & Rubber Company spends between $20 million and $25 million each year on tire and service center advertising to hold its market leadership position in replacement tires for cars and light trucks. Its "Nobody fits you like Goodyear" campaign focuses on serving customer needs rather than on product features and benefits. The approach is intended to distinguish Goodyear from Firestone, Goodrich, Armstrong Rubber, and other competitors.[4]

Decline

Sales continue to fall in the decline stage of the product life cycle. Profits also decline and may become losses as further price cutting occurs in the reduced market for the item. The decline stage is usually caused by a product innovation or a shift in consumer preferences. The decline stage of an old product can also be the growth stage for a new product. In the recording industry, for example,

Figure 14.5 Advertisement Introducing a New Product

Photo source: Courtesy of Castle & Cooke Inc.

long-playing 33 rpm records and 45 rpm records are in the decline stage while compact discs are in the growth stage. *eight tracks*

Extending the Product Life Cycle

Sometimes it is possible to extend a product's life cycle considerably beyond what it would otherwise be. Some useful strategies include the following:[5]

◆ Increase the frequency of use. For example, persuading consumers that they need to have additional smoke alarms and flashlights may result in increased purchases by each household. Some watchmakers are attempting to increase customers' purchase frequency by promoting watches as a fashion accessory rather than merely a time-keeping device. An example is the Timex Watercolors advertisement in Figure 14.6.

◆ Add new users. Introducing the product abroad might accomplish this. Gerber Products increased the size of its baby-food market by creating specialty foods for foreign consumers, such as strained sushi for Japanese and strained lamb brains for Australian babies. To increase the number of users in the United States, Gerber developed special versions such as guava and mango for the growing Hispanic market.

◆ Find new uses for the product. Arm & Hammer baking soda is a classic example. Its original use in baking has been augmented by its newer uses as a refrigerator freshener, flame extinguisher, first-aid remedy, denture cleaner, cleaning agent, and pool pH adjuster.

◆ Change package sizes, labels, and product quality. Offering smaller portable color televisions led to many households' acquiring two or more models. Many food marketers are offering smaller-size packages that appeal to one-person households.

The marketer's objective is to extend the product life cycle as long as the item is profitable. Some products can be highly profitable during the later stages of

Figure 14.6   Extending the Product Life Cycle

Source: Reprint permission granted by Timex Corporation.

their life cycle, since all of the initial development costs have already been recovered.

Marketing Strategy Implications of the Product Life Cycle

The product life cycle concept is a useful tool in designing a marketing strategy that is flexible enough to match the varying marketplace characteristics at different life cycle stages. For instance, knowledge that advertising emphasis will change from informative to persuasive as the product faces new competitors during the growth stage permits the marketer to anticipate competitive actions and make necessary adjustments. These competitive moves may involve price (the significant reduction in the price of VCRs), distribution (the significant increase in the number of Japanese retail stores handling Kodak film to compete with Fuji film in its home base), product variations (Honda's introduction of the Acura Legend, an executive luxury car, to compete with Mercedes-Benz and BMW in the United States), or promotion (AT&T's shift from informative product advertising to persuasive advertising in its competition with MCI and Sprint for long-distance customers). Table 14.2 compares marketing characteristics at each life cycle stage.

Table 14.2   Characteristics of Stages in the Product Life Cycle

	Life Cycle Stage			
Characteristic	**Introduction**	**Growth**	**Maturity**	**Decline**
Marketing objective	Attract innovators and opinion leaders to new product	Expand distribution and product line	Maintain differential advantage	Cut back, revive, terminate
Industry sales	Increasing	Rapidly increasing	Stable	Decreasing
Competition	None or small	Some	Much	Little
Industry profits	Negative	Increasing	Decreasing	Decreasing
Profit margins	Low	High	Decreasing	Decreasing
Customers	Innovators	Affluent mass market	Mass market	Laggards
Product mix	One basic model	Expanding line	Full product line	Best sellers
Distribution	Depends on product	Expanding number of outlets	Expanding number of outlets	Decreasing number of outlets
Pricing	Depends on product	Expanding to match product mix	Full line	Selected prices
Promotion	Informative	Persuasive	Competitive	Reminder

Source: Adapted with permission of Macmillan Publishing Company from *Marketing,* 3/e by Joel R. Evans and Barry Berman, p. 255. Copyright © 1987 by Macmillan Publishing Company.

New-Product Development

The creation of new products is the lifeblood of an organization. Products do not remain economically viable forever, so new ones must be developed to assure the survival of an organization. For many firms, new products account for a sizable part of growth in sales and profits. The 260 new products General Mills introduced in the past five years account for nearly one-third of the firm's U.S. food sales.[6]

Each year, thousands of new products are introduced. Some new products, such as the compact disc, represent major technological breakthroughs, while others are improvements or variations of existing products. The compact disc with graphics is a product improvement. Marketers made use of the unused space that exists on all compact discs by adding song lyrics and artist biographies that can be displayed on a television screen.

New-product development is expensive, time consuming, and risky. Only about one-third of new products become marketplace successes. Products fail for a number of reasons. Some are not properly developed and tested, some are poorly packaged, and some have inadequate promotional support or distribution. Other products fail because they do not satisfy a consumer need or want. In the 1970s, Canfield Company, a regional soft-drink maker, created what the company thought would be a hit product — a banana-flavored drink. Canfield marketers gave the product a catchy name — Anna Banana — hired an artist to create an original painting for the can, and developed a coordinated marketing campaign to support the product. To publicize the drink, they sent key supermarket buyers 100 pounds of bananas and flew airplanes with advertising banners over local highways, beaches, and football stadiums. But at the supermarket, no one bought Anna Banana. Consumers had no desire for a banana-flavored drink. By contrast, Canfield's Diet Chocolate Fudge succeeded because of its wide appeal to dieters who love the taste of chocolate.[7]

Most newly developed products today are aimed at satisfying specific customer needs or wants. New-product development has become more efficient and cost-effective than it was in the past because marketers use a systematic approach in developing new products.

Stages in New-Product Development

The new-product development process has six stages: (1) new-product ideas, (2) screening, (3) business analysis, (4) product development, (5) test marketing, and (6) commercialization. Each stage requires a "go/no go" decision by management.

New-Product Ideas   The starting point in the new-product development process is the generation of ideas for new offerings. Ideas come from many sources, including customers, suppliers, employees, research scientists, marketing research, inventors outside the firm, and competitive products. The most successful ideas are directly related to satisfying a customer need. A recent new-product success is Certified Stainmaster Carpet by E.I. du Pont de Nemours & Company. Du Pont's marketing research indicated consumers wanted carpets that were more stain resistant, and the company developed a product to fill that need.[8]

Screening   This stage deals with the elimination of ideas that do not mesh with overall company objectives or cannot be developed given the company's resources. Some firms hold open discussions of new-product ideas among representatives of different functional areas in the organization. Spectrum Control Inc., a producer of electronic filters and other specialty electronic products, holds meetings once every three months during which product managers, company scientists, and other managers evaluate new-product ideas.[9]

Business Analysis   Further screening is done in this stage. Does the idea fit with the company's product, distribution, and promotional resources? The analysis also involves assessing the new product's potential sales, profits, growth rate, and competitive strengths.

Sometimes concept testing is used at this stage. *Concept testing* refers to marketing research designed to solicit initial consumer reaction to a new-product idea before the product is developed. Seven-Up Company marketers used concept testing to measure consumer attitudes and perceptions about a new soft-drink idea. They added maraschino cherry juice to 7Up and served the drink to consumers, who liked both the flavor and the drink's pale pink color. These positive responses led to development of Cherry 7Up, one of the most successful new products in recent years.[10]

Product Development   An actual product is created at this stage. It is then subjected to a series of tests and revised. Both the product's actual features and its consumer perceptions are studied.

Inadequate testing during the development stage can doom a product—and even a company—to failure. Such was the fate of an all-natural shampoo and conditioner marketed by Nature's Organics Plus Inc. The firm previously had launched a line of hair-care products that brought in annual sales of $23 million. Several years later, it introduced the all-natural shampoo and condi-

Part of the product development process for toymaker Hasbro Inc. includes observing children playing with new products before they are launched. In this photo, Milton Bradley (a division of Hasbro Inc.) marketing researchers watch children play Pass the Trash™ to ensure that they understand the object of the game and can work the levers that shoot marbles from chutes into trucks.

Photo source: Courtesy of Hasbro, Inc.

tioner without fully testing them. Retailers bought $11 million worth of the products, but, without preservatives, the shampoo and conditioner self-destructed on store shelves and turned an unappealing yellow-green color. The company had to buy back most of the products from retailers. To avoid bankruptcy, the owner sold the company's assets and personally lost more than $1 million.[11]

Testing The product is actually sold in a limited area during the **test marketing** phase. The company is examining both the product and the marketing effort they are using to support it. Cities or television coverage areas that are typical of the targeted market segments are selected for such tests. Test-market results help managers determine the product's likely performance in a full-scale introduction.

Kraft test marketed its spicy Bull's-Eye barbecue sauce to determine whether it could capture 5 percent of the sauce market and to explore a premium pricing strategy and two levels of national advertising spending ($9 million and $5 million). Test results indicated Kraft would get the market share it desired, could put a high price on the product, and could use the lower advertis-

test marketing
Stage in the new-product development process in which the product is sold in a limited area.

ing spending level. Not all products, however, are test marketed. Colgate-Palmolive introduced two major new products — Fab 1 Shot, an all-in-one laundry product, and Palmolive Automatic, a liquid dishwasher detergent — without test marketing them in order to beat competitors to the marketplace.[12]

Commercialization   This is the stage at which the product is made generally available in the marketplace. Sometimes it is referred to as a *product launch*. Considerable planning goes into this stage. The firm's promotional, distribution, and pricing strategies must all be geared to support the new-product offering.

Product Identification

brand
Name, term, sign, symbol, or design used to identify the goods or services of a firm.

Product identification is another important aspect of marketing strategy. Products are identified by brands, brand names, and trademarks. A **brand** is a name, term, sign, symbol, design, or some combination thereof used to identify the products of one firm and to differentiate them from competitive offerings. Wolverine World Wide identifies its brand of footwear with the symbol of a bassett hound and the name Hush Puppies. The well-known symbol and name are prominently displayed in the firm's advertisements, such as the one in Figure 14.7.

brand name
Words or letters that identify the firm's offerings.

A **brand name** is that part of the brand consisting of words or letters included in a name used to identify and distinguish the firm's offerings from those of competitors. The brand name is the part of the brand that can be vocalized. A recent survey revealed the most recognizable brand names in the United States are Coca-Cola, Campbell's, Pepsi-Cola, AT&T, McDonald's, American Express, Kellogg's, IBM, Levi's, and Sears.[13]

trademark
Brand that has been given legal protection exclusive to its owner.

A **trademark** is a brand that has been given legal protection. The protection is granted solely to the brand's owner. Trademark protection includes not only the brand name, but also pictorial designs, slogans, packaging elements, and product features such as color and shape. Rolls-Royce Motor Cars Inc. has received trademark protection not only on the Rolls-Royce brand name, mascot, and badge, but also for the automobile's radiator grille.

Brands are important in developing a product's image. If consumers are aware of a particular brand, its appearance becomes advertising for the firm. The RCA trademark of the dog at the phonograph, for example, is instant advertising to shoppers who spot it in a store. Successful branding is also a means of escaping some price competition. Well-known brands often sell at a considerable price premium over their competition.

Selecting an Effective Brand Name

Good brand names are easy to pronounce, recognize, and remember. Short names like Gulf, Crest, Kodak, Visa, and Avis meet these requirements. Multinational marketing firms face a real problem in selecting brand names in that an excellent brand name in one country may prove disastrous in another. Every language has a short "*a*," so *Coca-Cola* and *Texaco* are pronounceable in any tongue. But an advertising campaign for E-Z washing machines failed in the United Kingdom because the British pronounce z as "zed." 'Bimbo" is an effective brand name for a line of high-quality bakery products marketed by An-

Figure 14.7   Advertising a Well-Known Brand

Source: Courtesy of Wolverine World Wide, Inc.

heuser-Busch in Spain. But the name would be less effective in the United States, where Anheuser-Busch uses the Earth Grains brand name for its premium bakery goods.

Brand names should give the right image to the buyer. *Accutron* suggests the quality of the high-priced and accurate Bulova timepiece. Lite beer by Miller creates an image of a beer with reduced calories and carbohydrates. Federal Express suggests a fast delivery service that covers a broad geographic reach. Dep Corporation marketers recently changed the brand name of Ayds diet candy to Diet Ayds because they were concerned that the single word *Ayds* would project a negative image to consumers who might associate it with the similar-sounding AIDS virus.[14]

Brand names must also be legally protectable. Trademark law, discussed in Chapter 23, states that brand names cannot contain words in general use, such as *television* or *automobile*. Generic words — words that describe a type of product — cannot be used exclusively by any organization.

The task of selecting an effective and legally protectable brand name is becoming more difficult as the number of new-product introductions increases each year. In 1988, about 70,000 new-product names were registered with the U.S. Patent and Trademark Office, double the number of 20 years ago. Many firms hire professional namesmith consultants to create new-product names. By using computers to link word fragments into new combinations, one such firm, NameLab, generated *Compaq* computers and Honda's *Acura*.[15]

Brand Categories

A brand offered and promoted by a manufacturer is known as a **national brand**, or a manufacturer's brand. Examples are Tide, Jockey, Gatorade, Swatch, and DoveBar. But not all brand names belong to manufacturers. Some are the property of retailers or distributors.

A **private brand** (often known as a house, distributor, or retailer label) identifies a product that is not identified as to manufacturer but instead carries the retailer's label. The Sears line of DieHard batteries and The Limited's Forenza label are examples.

Many retailers offer a third option to manufacturers' and private brands: the **generic product**. These items have plain packaging, minimal labeling, and little if any advertising, and meet minimum quality standards. Generic products sell at a considerable discount from manufacturers' and private brands. Generics were developed in Europe and first appeared in the United States in 1977. Sales of generic products peaked in the early 1980s when inflation was high but have declined steadily since then as the economy has improved.[16]

Stages of Brand Loyalty

Although branding is very important, the degree of brand loyalty varies widely from product to product. In some categories, consumers insist on a specific brand. A tennis player, for example, may insist on buying a Prince racquet. For other purchases, such as paper towels, they might readily accept a generic product. Brand recognition, brand preference, and brand insistence are three stages used to measure brand loyalty.

Brand recognition simply means that the consumer is familiar with the product or service. Free samples and discount coupons are often used to build this familiarity. A recognized brand is more likely to be purchased than an unknown one.

Brand preference is the stage of brand loyalty at which the consumer will be loyal if the brand is available. Many consumer products like beer and soft drinks fall into this category. A considerable portion of all marketing expenditures are intended to build brand preference.

Brand insistence is the stage of brand loyalty at which consumers will accept no substitute for their preferred brand. If it is not readily available locally, the consumer will special-order it from a store, or turn to mail-order or telephone buying. Brand insistence is the ultimate degree of brand loyalty, and few brands obtain it.

Family Brands and Individual Brands

Another branding decision marketers must make is whether to use a family branding strategy or an individual branding strategy.

A **family brand** is a single brand name used for several related products. KitchenAid, Johnson & Johnson, Xerox, and Dole Food Company use a family brand name for their entire line of products. When a firm using family branding

The Dole Food Company uses a family branding strategy in marketing its canned pineapple products, fruit juices, and frozen desserts. The respected and well-known Dole brand name is also used for the firm's line of fresh fruits and vegetables.

Photo source: Courtesy of Dole Food Company.

introduces a new product, both customers and retailers recognize the familiar brand name. The promotion of individual products within a line benefit all the products because the family brand is well known.

Some firms utilize an **individual branding** strategy by giving products within a line different brand names. For example, Procter & Gamble has individual brand names for its different laundry detergent products — Tide, Cheer, Dash, and Oxydol. Each brand targets a unique market segment. Consumers who want a cold-water detergent can buy Cheer rather than Tide or Oxydol instead of purchasing a competitor's brand. Individual branding stimulates competition within a firm and enables the company to increase overall sales.

individual branding
Giving each product in a line its own brand name.

The Package and Label

Except for generic products, packaging also plays an important role in product strategy. The original purpose of packaging was protection against risks like damage, spoilage, and theft. But over the years, packaging also acquired a marketing objective.

Because the package must help sell the product, packages were made more attractive and appealing to consumers. Marketers are now very concerned about how a package will be perceived in the marketplace. For instance, when the sales and market share of Gillette Company's Soft & Dri female deodorant began declining, the firm held focus group interviews to determine the cause. Gillette marketers learned the product was well received by women under 30, the product's target market, but the packaging was outdated and not in keeping with the image the young women wanted to project. After studying 60 package designs and soliciting retailers' opinions, Gillette relaunched Soft & Dri with contemporary packaging that appealed to its target audience.[17]

Marketers' emphasis on targeting specific market segments and satisfying consumers' desire for convenience have increased the importance of packaging as an effective way to promote products. When Mott USA wanted to build the sales of its applesauce, the firm's marketers developed Fruit Paks, a six-pack of applesauce in 4-ounce portable containers. In six months, Fruit Paks sales increased 600 percent, with about three-fourths of consumption coming from children under age 12. "The size of the package drove the sales," said Mott's product manager.[18]

Packaging is responsible for one of the biggest costs in many consumer products. As a result, marketers are now devoting more attention to it. Cost-effective packaging is one of industry's greatest needs.

Labeling is often an integral part of the packaging process. Soft drinks, frozen vegetables, milk, and snack foods are examples. Labeling must meet federal requirements as set forth in the *Fair Packaging and Labeling Act (1966)*. The intent is to provide adequate information about the package contents so consumers can make value comparisons among competitive products. Other requirements — like the Food and Drug Administration's rule on nutritional content listing — may also apply.

Universal Product Code (UPC)

The bar code read by optical scanners, which print the item and the price on a receipt.

Another important aspect of packaging and labeling is the **Universal Product Code (UPC)**, the bar code read by optical scanners that print the name of the item and the price on a receipt. First introduced in 1974, the UPC is a labor-saving innovation that has improved inventory control, improved checkout time, and cut pricing errors. It has also become a major asset in collecting marketing research data.[19]

Customer Service

The customer service components of product strategy include warranty and repair service programs. Consumers want to know that an adequate service program is available if something goes wrong with the product. Products with inadequate service backing quickly disappear from the market as a result of word-of-mouth criticism.

warranty

Firm's promise to repair, replace, or refund the purchase price of a good or service if it proves unsatisfactory.

Warranties are also important. A **warranty** is simply a promise to repair, refund money paid or replace a product if it proves unsatisfactory. The *Magnuson-Moss Warranty Act (1975)* authorized the Federal Trade Commission to establish warranty rules for any product covered by a written warranty and costing $15 or more. This legislation does not require warranties, but it does say they must be understandable and that a consumer complaint procedure must be in place.

A growing number of service marketers, such as airlines and hotels, and producers of goods are making warranties an important element of their competitive strategy. Federal Express guarantees next-day package delivery by 10:30 a.m. in most major metropolitan areas, and L. L. Bean, a retailer and mail-order house, guarantees customers can return a product at any time and receive either a replacement, refund, or credit.[20]

To promote good customer relations, many firms operate a consumer hotline. Complaints from users of goods and services often prompt firms to make improvements. Oscar Mayer Company responded to consumer complaints that meat packages leaked by developing resealable hot dog packages.[21]

Pricing Strategy

After a good or service has been developed, identified, and packaged, it must be priced. This is the second aspect of the marketing mix. As noted earlier, price is the exchange value of a good or service. Pricing strategy has become one of the most important features of modern marketing.

Figure 14.8 Advertisement That May Influence an Allocation Decision

Source: Courtesy of Los Angeles Zoo and Poindexter/Osaki/Nissman, Inc.

All goods and services offer some utility, or want-satisfying power. Individual preferences determine how much utility a consumer will associate with a particular good or service. One person may value leisure-time pursuits while another assigns a higher priority to acquiring property, automobiles, and household furnishings.

Consumers face an allocation problem: They have a limited amount of money and a variety of possible uses for it. The price system helps them make allocation decisions. A person may prefer a new personal computer to a vacation, but if the price of the computer rises, he or she may reconsider and allocate funds to the vacation instead. The emphasis on low prices in the Los Angeles Zoo advertisement in Figure 14.8 may influence how a family decides to allocate leisure funds. Low admission prices make a day at the zoo a bargain compared to the high cost of, say, an amusement park outing.

Prices help direct the overall economic system. A firm uses various factors of production, such as natural resources, labor, and capital, based on their relative prices. High wage rates may cause a firm to install labor-saving machinery. Similarly, high interest rates may lead management to decide against a new capital expenditure. Prices and volume sold determine the revenue received by the firm and influence its profits.

Pricing Objectives

Marketing attempts to accomplish certain objectives through its pricing decisions. Research has shown that multiple pricing objectives are common among many firms. Pricing objectives vary from firm to firm. Some companies try to maximize their profits by pricing their offerings very high. Others use low prices to attract new business. The three basic categories of pricing objectives are (1) profitability objectives, (2) volume objectives, and (3) other objectives, including social and ethical considerations, status quo objectives, and image goals.

Profitability Objectives

Most firms have some type of profitability objective for their pricing strategy. Management knows that

$$\text{Profit} = \text{Revenue} - \text{Expenses}$$

and that revenue is a result of the selling price times the quantity sold:

$$\text{Total Revenue} = \text{Price} \times \text{Quantity Sold}.$$

Some firms try to maximize profits by increasing their prices to the point where a disproportionate decrease appears in the number of units sold. A 10 percent price hike that results in only an 8 percent volume decline increases profitability. But a 5 percent price increase that reduces the number of units sold by 6 percent is unprofitable.

profit maximization
Pricing strategy whereby management sets increasing levels of profitability as its objective.

target return goal
Pricing strategy whereby the desired profitability is stated in terms of particular goals, such as a 10 percent return on sales.

Profit maximization is the basis of much of economic theory. Yet, it is often difficult to apply in practice, and many firms have turned to a simpler profitability objective — the **target return goal**. For example, a firm might specify the goal of a 9 percent return on sales or a 20 percent return on investment. Most target return pricing goals state the desired profitability in terms of a return on either sales or investment.

Volume Objectives

sales maximization
Strategy under which management sets an acceptable minimum level of profitability and then tries to maximize sales.

market share
Percentage of a market controlled by a certain company, good, or service.

Another example of pricing strategy is **sales maximization**, under which management sets an acceptable minimum level of profitability and then tries to maximize sales. Sales expansion is viewed as being more important than short-run profits to the firm's long-term competitive position.

A second volume objective is **market share** — the percentage of a market controlled by a certain company, product, or service. One firm may seek to achieve a 25 percent market share in a certain industry. Another may want to maintain or expand its market share for particular products or product lines.

In an attempt to gain a larger share of the $51 billion-a-year lodging industry market, national hotel and motel firms that previously concentrated on moderate and high-priced lodging are now developing products that appeal to budget-conscious business and pleasure travelers, a segment with significant growth potential. Marriott Corporation, a market leader in the quality, full-service lodging segment, entered the low-priced market by offering Fairfield Inns, with room rates under $40. By moving into the economy segment, Marriott hopes to increase its overall share of the lodging market.[22]

Market share objectives have become popular for several reasons. One of the most important is the ease with which market share statistics can be used as a yardstick for measuring managerial and corporate performance. Another is that increased sales may lead to lower production costs and higher profits. On a per-unit basis, it is cheaper to produce 100,000 pens than it is to manufacture just a few dozen.

Figure 14.9   Enhancing the Image of a High-Priced Good

Source: Courtesy of Waterford Wedgwood USA Inc.

Other Objectives

Objectives not related to profitability or sales volume — social and ethical considerations, status quo objectives, and image goals — are often used in pricing decisions. Social and ethical considerations play an important role in some pricing situations. For example, the price of some goods and services is based on the intended consumer's ability to pay. For example, some union dues are related to the income of the members.

Many firms have status quo pricing objectives: That is, they are inclined to follow the leader. These companies seek stable prices that will allow them to put their competitive efforts into other areas such as product design or promotion. This situation is most common in oligopolistic markets.

Image goals are often used in pricing strategy. The price structures of major department stores, for example, are set to reflect the high quality of the merchandise. Discount houses, however, may seek an image of good value at low prices. So a firm's pricing strategy may be an integral part of the overall image it wishes to convey. The advertisement for Waterford crystal in Figure 14.9 projects the product's quality image and suggests why a piece of Waterford stemware costs $50 more than that of competitors: It is handcrafted with handmade tools, unlike "the soulless way other crystal is churned out by industrial robots."

Price Determination

While pricing is usually regarded as a function of marketing, it also requires considerable inputs from other areas in the company. Accounting and financial managers have always played a major role in the pricing task by providing the sales and cost data necessary for good decision making. Production and industrial engineering personnel play similarly important roles. Computer analysts, for example, are in charge of the firm's computer-based marketing information system, which provides up-to-date information needed in pricing. It is essential for managers at all levels to realize the importance of pricing and the contribution that can be made to correct pricing by various areas in the organization. Price determination can be viewed from two perspectives. Economic theory provides an overall viewpoint, while cost-based pricing looks at it from a practical, "hands-on" approach.

Economic Theory

Economic theory, which was discussed in detail in Chapter 3, assumes a profit maximization objective. It says market price will be set at the point at which the amount of a product desired at a given price is equal to the amount suppliers will provide at that price: where the amount demanded and the amount supplied are in equilibrium. In other words, the demand curve is a schedule of amounts that will be demanded at different price levels. At $3 per pound, 5,000 pounds of an industrial chemical might be sold. A price increase to $4 per pound might reduce sales to 3,200 pounds, and a $5 per pound price might result in sales of only 2,000 pounds, as some would-be customers decide to accept less expensive substitutes or to wait for the price to be reduced. Correspondingly, the supply curve is a schedule that shows the amounts that will be offered in the market at certain prices. The intersection of these schedules is the equilibrium price that will exist in the marketplace for a particular good or service.

Cost-Based Pricing

Although this economic analysis is correct in regard to the overall market for a product, managers face the problem of setting the price of individual brands based on limited information. Anticipating the amount of a product that will be bought at a certain price is difficult, so businesses tend to adopt cost-based pricing formulas. Although these are simpler and easier to use, executives have to be flexible in applying them to each situation. Marketers begin the process of cost-based pricing by totaling all costs associated with offering an item in the market, including production, transportation, distribution, and marketing expenses. They then add an amount to cover profit and expenses not previously considered. The total becomes the price.

Apple Computer's pricing of the Macintosh SE illustrates the cost-based approach. The computer sells at retail for $3,698, but dealers pay Apple about $2,137 for each unit. Each computer contains $588 worth of component parts and materials. Another $760 pays for equipment, production, labor, testing, and other factory-related expenses; $464 pays for marketing, distribution, and general and administrative expenses; and $108 pays for research and development

Figure 14.10   Breakeven Analysis

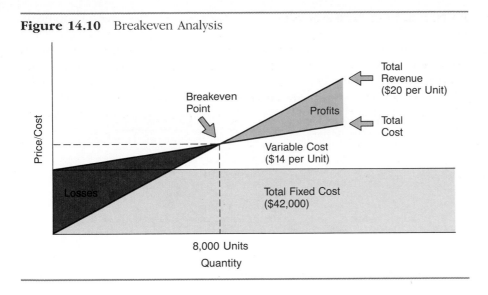

costs. Apple adds to those costs $217 per computer to cover operating expenses and profits.[23]

Breakeven Analysis: A Tool in Cost-Based Pricing

Marketers often use **breakeven analysis** as a method of determining the minimum sales volume needed at a certain price level to cover all costs. It involves a consideration of various costs and total revenue. Total cost *(TC)* is composed of total variable costs *(TVC)* and total fixed costs *(TFC)*. **Variable costs** are those that change with the level of production (such as labor and raw materials costs), while **fixed costs** are those that remain stable regardless of the production level achieved (such as the firm's insurance costs). Total revenue is determined by multiplying price by the number of units sold.

Figure 14.10 shows the calculation of the **breakeven point** — the level of sales that will cover all of the company's costs (both fixed and variable). It is the point at which total revenue just equals total cost. Sales beyond the breakeven point will generate profits; sales volume below the breakeven amount will result in losses. Breakeven points in units can also be found by using the following formula:

$$\text{Breakeven Point (in units)} = \frac{\text{Total Fixed Costs}}{\text{Per-Unit Contribution to Fixed Costs}}.$$

A product selling for $20 with a variable cost of $14 per item produces a $6 per-unit contribution to fixed costs. If total fixed costs are $42,000, then the firm must sell 7,000 units to break even. The calculation of the breakeven point in units is:

$$\frac{\$42,000}{\$20 - \$14} = \frac{\$42,000}{\$6} = 7,000 \text{ units.}$$

Marketers can use breakeven analysis to determine the profits or losses that would result from several different proposed prices. Since different prices will

breakeven analysis
Method of determining the minimum sales volume needed to cover all costs at a certain price level.

variable costs
Costs that change with the level of production, such as labor and raw materials.

fixed costs
Costs that remain stable regardless of the production level achieved.

breakeven point
Level of sales that will cover all the company's costs, both fixed and variable.

produce different breakeven points, the calculations of sales necessary to break even could be compared with estimated sales obtained from marketing research studies. This comparison can then be used to identify the most appropriate price, one that would attract sufficient customers to exceed the breakeven point and earn profits for the firm.

Breakeven points in dollars can also be calculated. The formula is:

$$\text{Breakeven Point (in dollars)} = \frac{\text{Total Fixed Cost}}{1 - \dfrac{\text{Variable Cost per Unit}}{\text{Price}}}$$

Using the data from above, the breakeven point in dollars would be:

$$\frac{\$42{,}000}{1 - \dfrac{\$14}{\$20}} = \frac{\$42{,}000}{1 - .7} = \frac{\$42{,}000}{.3} = \$140{,}000.$$

The breakeven point in dollars ($140,000) equals the number of breakeven points in units (7,000) multiplied by the selling price ($20).

Pricing Strategies

Pampers disposable diapers failed in the original market test because of pricing. Pampers were introduced when most people resisted the idea of using a noncloth material to diaper a baby. Pampers also sold for more than the per-use cost of buying a cloth diaper and washing it, and so the product failed in the marketplace. P&G redesigned production equipment and reduced production costs to the extent that Pampers' per-unit retail price could be slashed 40 percent. This reduced price brought the product's cost more into line with the cost of cloth diapers, and the convenience of using disposables soon found favor among American families.

Procter & Gamble's experience with Pampers shows how difficult it is to select a price for a product line. Because pricing decisions are risky, it is usually best to field-test alternative prices with sample groups of consumers. Once the product is launched, it is difficult to modify its price during the introductory period.

Pricing involves important decisions for the firm. One option is to price the product competitively — that is, to match the competitor's price. A marketer that selects a competitive pricing strategy is attempting to use nonprice competition. In other words, the marketer seeks to compete on the basis of advertising, distribution superiority, and the like rather than pricing. Pricing can be based on either of two strategies: the skimming price policy or the penetration price strategy.

Skimming Pricing

skimming pricing
Strategy of setting the price of a new product relatively high compared to similar goods and then gradually lowering it.

Skimming pricing involves setting the price of the product relatively high compared to similar goods and then gradually lowering it. This strategy is used when the market is segmented on a price basis, that is, where some people may buy the product if it is priced at $10, a larger group may buy it at $7.50, and a still larger group may buy it at $6. It is effective in situations where a firm has a substantial lead on competition with a new product. The skimming strategy has been used effectively on such products as color televisions, pocket calculators, personal computers, and VCRs.

A skimming strategy allows the firm to recover its cost rapidly by maximizing the revenue it receives. But the disadvantage is that early profits tend to attract competition, thus putting eventual pressure on prices. For example, most ball-point pens now sell for less than $1, but when the product was first introduced after World War II, it sold for about $20.

Some firms continue to use skimming pricing throughout the product's life cycle. For example, Bausch & Lomb's Ray-Ban sunglasses range in price from $50 to $140. The company plans to continue the high-price strategy, even though "knock-off" imitations of Ray-Ban products sell for as low as $15. Lower-priced products do not pose a threat to Ray-Ban because Ray-Ban customers are brand loyal. The firm's marketing research indicates 90 percent of Ray-Ban customers would buy the brand again.[24]

Penetration Pricing

The second strategy, **penetration pricing**, involves pricing the product relatively low compared to similar goods in the hope that it will secure wide market acceptance that will allow the company to raise its price. Soaps and toothpastes are often introduced this way. Penetration pricing discourages competition because of its low profits. It is often used when the firm expects competition with similar products within a short time and when large-scale production and marketing will produce substantial reductions in overall costs.

penetration pricing
Strategy of pricing a new product relatively low compared to similar goods in the hope that it will secure wide market acceptance that will allow the company to raise the price.

Product Line Pricing

Under **product line pricing**, a seller offers merchandise at a limited number of prices rather than having individual prices for each item. For instance, a boutique might offer lines of women's sportswear priced at $120, $150, and $200. Product line pricing is a common marketing practice among retailers. The original five-and-ten-cent stores are an example of its early use.

product line pricing
Offering merchandise at a limited number of prices instead of pricing each item individually.

As a pricing strategy, product line pricing prevents the confusion common in situations where all items are priced individually. It makes the pricing function easier. But marketers must clearly identify the market segments to which they are appealing. Three high-priced lines might not be appropriate for a store located in a low-to-middle-income area.

A disadvantage of product line pricing is that it is sometimes difficult to alter the price ranges once they have been set. If costs go up, the firm must either raise the price of the line or reduce its quality. Consumers may resist these alternatives. While product line pricing can be useful, its implementation must be considered carefully.

Consumer Perception of Prices

Marketers must be concerned with the way consumers perceive prices. If a buyer views a price as too high or too low, the marketer must correct the situation. Price-quality relationships and psychological pricing are important in this regard.

The Price-Quality Relationship

Research shows that the consumer's perception of product quality is related closely to the item's price. The higher the price of the product, the better its perceived quality.

Most marketers believe the perceived price-quality relationship exists over a relatively wide range of prices, although extreme prices may be viewed as either too expensive or too cheap. Marketing managers need to study and experiment with prices because the price-quality relationship can be of key importance to a firm's pricing strategy.

Jerome Rowitch, a California restaurateur, conducted an interesting experiment that substantiates the price-quality relationship. When Rowitch opened his Sculpture Gardens restaurant in an unfashionable section of Venice, he devised a promotion designed to attract the affluent residents of nearby suburbs. He mailed a promotional flier to households with incomes of $50,000 or more, a segment that would appreciate the restaurant's fare, which includes black spaghettini in roasted red pepper and New Zealand cockles in white wine. The flier made this offer: Patrons could pay whatever price they thought their meal was worth. On average, those who took advantage of the promotion paid about $7.50 more for their meal than the price listed on the standard menu.[25]

Psychological Pricing

Psychological pricing is used throughout the world. Many marketers believe certain prices are more appealing than others to buyers. The image pricing goals mentioned earlier are an example of psychological pricing.

odd pricing
Practice of using uneven prices, such as $1.11, in the belief that odd prices are psychologically more attractive to consumers than even ones.

Have you ever wondered why retailers use prices like $39.95, $19.98, or $9.99 instead of $40, $20, or $10? Before the age of cash registers and sales taxes, this practice of **odd pricing** was employed to force clerks to make the correct change, thereby serving as a cash-control technique for retailers. It is now a common practice in retail pricing because many retailers believe that consumers are more attracted to odd prices than to ordinary ones. In fact, some stores use prices ending in 1, 2, 3, 4, 6, or 7 to avoid the look of ordinary prices like $5.95, $10.98, and $19.99. Their prices are more likely to be $1.11, $3.22, $4.53, $5.74, $3.86, or $9.97.

Summary of Learning Goals

1.   List the components of the total product concept.   A product is defined as a bundle of physical, service, and symbolic attributes designed to satisfy consumer wants. The total product concept includes the brand, product image, warranty and service, and package and label, in addition to the physical or functional characteristics of the good or service.

2.   Identify the types of consumer goods, industrial goods, and services.   Goods and services can be classified as consumer or industrial. Consumer goods are purchased by ultimate consumers for their own use. Industrial goods are those purchased for use, either directly or indirectly, in the production of other goods for resale.

Consumer goods can be classified as either convenience goods, shopping goods, or specialty goods. This classification is based on consumer buying habits. Industrial goods can be classified as installations, accessory equipment, component parts and materials, raw materials, and supplies. This classification is based on how the products are used and product characteristics. Services can be classified as either consumer or industrial services.

3. Describe the product mix and product lines. The product mix is the assortment of goods and/or services a firm offers consumers and industrial users. A product line is a series of related products. The product mix is a combination of product lines and individual offerings that make up the product line.

4. Identify and describe the stages of the product life cycle. The four stages all products pass through in their product life cycle are introductory, growth, maturity, and decline. In the introductory stage, the firm attempts to secure demand for the product. In the product's growth stage, sales climb and the company earns profits on the product. In the maturity stage, sales reach a saturation level. In the decline stage, both sales and profits decline. Marketers can sometimes employ strategies that will extend the length of the product life cycle. These strategies include increasing the frequency of use, adding new users, finding new uses for the product, and changing package size, label, or product quality.

5. List the stages in the new-product development process. The stages in the new-product development process are (1) new-product ideas, (2) screening, (3) business analysis, (4) product development, (5) test marketing, and (6) commercialization. At each stage, marketers face "go/no go" decisions as to whether to continue to the next stage, modify the new product, or discontinue the development process.

6. Explain how products are identified. Products are identified by brands, brand names, and trademarks, which are important in developing the products' image. Good brand names are easy to pronounce, recognize, and remember, and they project the right image to buyers. Brand names cannot contain generic words; conversely, under certain circumstances, companies lose exclusive rights to their brand name if it is ruled generic. Some brand names belong to retailers or distributors rather than to manufacturers. Many retailers now offer a third option: no-brand generic products. Brand loyalty is measured in three stages: brand recognition, brand preference, and brand insistence. Some marketers use a family brand to identify several related product lines. Others employ an individual branding strategy by giving products within a line different brand names.

7. Outline the different types of pricing objectives. Pricing objectives can be classified as profitability objectives, volume objectives, and a third category of other objectives such as social and ethical considerations, status quo objectives, and image goals. Profitability objectives involve profit maximization, where management requires increasing levels of profitability, and target return goals, which are usually set as a return in either investment or sales. Volume objectives include sales maximization, a strategy whereby management sets an acceptable minimum level of profitability and then tries to maximize sales, and market share goals, which are specified as a percentage of certain markets.

8.   Discuss how prices are set in the marketplace.   Pricing is an important function of marketing. Price determination can be viewed from two perspectives. The overall view is that demand and supply determine prices. This approach was discussed in Chapter 3. The second view is the practical approach to pricing. Businesses use cost-based pricing. Costs are totaled, then an amount is added for profit and expenses not previously considered.

9.   Show how breakeven analysis can be used in pricing strategy. Breakeven analysis is an aid in making pricing decisions. It uses total costs and total revenues. The breakeven point in units is determined by dividing total fixed costs by the per unit contribution to fixed costs. Sales beyond the breakeven point result in profit.

Breakeven points can be calculated for various prices. The resulting breakeven volumes can then be compared to marketing research estimates of likely sales volume in determining a final price based upon both consumer needs and the firm's need for a satisfactory return on the investment.

Breakeven points in dollars can also be calculated by using this formula:

$$\text{Breakeven Point (in dollars)} = \frac{\text{Total Fixed Costs}}{1 - \dfrac{\text{Variable Cost per Unit}}{\text{Price}}}$$

10.   Differentiate between skimming and penetration pricing strategies.   A skimming strategy sets a relatively high price compared to similar goods and then gradually lowers it. Penetration pricing sets a price lower than similar goods and eventually raises it after the product gains wide market acceptance.

Key Terms

product	test marketing	warranty
price	brand	profit maximization
convenience goods	brand name	target return goal
shopping goods	trademark	sales maximization
specialty goods	national brand	market share
installations	private brand	breakeven analysis
accessory equipment	generic product	variable costs
component parts and materials	brand recognition	fixed costs
raw materials	brand preference	breakeven point
supplies	brand insistence	skimming pricing
product mix	family brand	penetration pricing
product line	individual branding	product line pricing
product life cycle	Universal Product Code (UPC)	odd pricing

Review Questions

1. How do marketers define the term *product*? What is meant by the total product concept?

2. Differentiate among the following categories of consumer goods, industrial goods, and services:
   a. Convenience, shopping, and specialty goods
   b. Installations, accessory equipment, component parts and materials, raw materials, and supplies
   c. Consumer and industrial services

3. What is meant by a product mix? Identify its primary components.

4. Suggest current products for each of the product life cycle stages. Why did you classify these products as you did? Explain.

5. Identify and explain the stages in the product development process.

6. Differentiate among brand, brand name, and trademark.

7. List and identify the various pricing objectives used by companies. Which ones do you think are most important to marketers? Why?

8. Assume a product selling for $10 has a variable cost of $6 per unit. If total fixed costs for this product are $38,000, how many units must the firm sell to break even?

9. Assume a product selling for $25 has a variable cost of $15 per unit. If fixed costs for the product are $180,000, what is the breakeven point in dollars?

10. Contrast the skimming and penetration pricing policies. What types of products or market situations are most suitable to each strategy?

Discussion Questions

1. Mountain Valley Spring Water Co. bottles drinking water from a spring 10 miles north of Hot Springs, Arkansas. The water, highly regarded for its purity, is consumed by the king of Saudi Arabia and has been served in the White House since the administration of Calvin Coolidge. Classify Mountain Valley Spring Water as a consumer good. Discuss why you classified it as you did.

2. Cardiologist Marvin Wayne developed his perfect cookie while experimenting in a military mess in Vietnam. Now marketed as Dr. Cookie, the cookies are high in fiber and complex carbohydrates, low in salt and cholesterol, and contain no sulfites, preservatives, or artificial ingredients. The Bothell, Washington, firm sells Dr. Cookie to consumers via mail-order and direct to airlines such as United, Horizon, and American Eagle for use as a snack. The firm is also experimenting with selling Dr. Cookie dough through local supermarkets in the Seattle area. How would you classify Dr. Cookie?

3. Quicksilver Inc., the $30 million Costa Mesa, California, producer of surfer outfits, now offers a complete activewear line. Its sales breakdowns are as follows: boardshirts (18 percent), T-shirts (15 percent), shirts (11 percent),

pants (12 percent), fleece wear (9 percent), walking shorts (27 percent), jackets (4 percent), and surfing accessories (4 percent). Quicksilver is also now moving into skiwear. Relate the above discussion to the material covered in Chapter 14. Discuss.

4. Suggest a brand name for each of the following new products, and explain why you chose each name:
   a. A development of exclusive homesites
   b. A low-price term life-insurance policy sold by mail
   c. An extra-durable, single-edge razor blade
   d. A portable drill that is considerably faster than its competition

5. Collect five advertisements illustrating the concept of psychological pricing. What generalizations are evident as a result of this exercise? Discuss.

Video Case

Ben & Jerry's Homemade

Ben Cohen and Jerry Greenfield have always had a lot in common. Born about a week apart, they met in the seventh grade, when by their own mutual admission they were always the slowest and fattest boys lumbering around the school track. They were in their twenties when they learned how to make ice cream from taking a $5 correspondence course from Pennsylvania State University. It was then that they decided to go into business for themselves making ice cream — *great* ice cream. "When we decided to make ice cream, making money was not a consideration," recalls Greenfield. "We wanted to just make the best product we could."

Launching a new business is difficult with limited funds, and Ben and Jerry had little to recommend them as entrepreneurs, especially to the financial institutions who might lend them needed money. Neither of them owned a suit and their only asset was a broken-down car. But they pulled together $12,000, much of it borrowed from family and friends, and in 1978 opened their first store in a converted gas station in Burlington, Vermont. At first, they depended totally on walk-in business. Then they moved into wholesaling by selling to area restaurants and grocery stores. A decade later their ice cream could be purchased in supermarkets throughout 35 states across the country and in more than 40 Ben & Jerry's franchised retail outlets. Plans are being finalized to open outlets in the Soviet Union. The $12,000 investment has turned into a major business with annual sales of more than $45 million.

Cohen and Greenfield admit that they entered the ice cream business at a most opportune time. A good market in superpremium ice cream had already been created by brand names such as Pillsbury's Häagen-Dazs and Kraft's Frusen Glädjē. The high-quality sweets differ from regular ice cream in several ways. Ben & Jerry's ice cream has almost twice as much butter fat as the ordinary supermarket variety, has less air,

Notes: Jonathan Adolph and Florence Graves, "Ben & Jerry: Two Real Guys," *New Age Journal,* March-April 1988, p. 32ff; Keith Hammonds, "Is Häagen-Dazs Trying to Freeze Out Ben & Jerry's?" *Business Week,* December 7, 1987, p. 65; and "Vermont Ice Cream Makers Try Marketing World Peace," *Mobile Press Register,* February 5, 1989, p. 16A.

is thicker, and is made entirely from natural ingredients. All this extra quality allows the specialty product to be priced accordingly; a pint of Ben & Jerry's sells for over $2. But customers, particularly in the U.S., have become quality-conscious, health-minded, and are willing to pay premium prices for these attributes in a product.

This was the market that Ben & Jerry's targeted. Promotional expenses were held to a relatively low 5 to 10 percent of sales. The ads have become a part of the Ben & Jerry's mystique, quickly recognizable for their cartoon simplicity, bright pastel colors, and off-beat humor. Special promotions are a major component of the firm's marketing communications. The Cowmobile, for instance, is a 17-year-old motor home painted like a dairy cow that travels to special events and dispenses ice cream at a rate of up to 1,000 scoops a day. A holdover from the early years when profits were not sufficient to permit contributions are special ice cream giveaways. On Mother's Day, moms get free ice cream cones; on store anniversaries, all customers get free cones; and at many events and festivals, the two founders are responsible for providing free entertainment in the form of sideshow-type performances.

Behind all the concern for a quality product with a specific target market lies one reason for Ben & Jerry's success — the belief that a business has an obligation to give something back to the people who support it. Consumers of Ben & Jerry's Homemade not only enjoy the fine quality and wide range of flavors offered; they can feel good about eating ice cream and knowing that a record 7.5 percent of the company's pretax profits are directed to nonprofit organizations and individuals working for social improvement. This accomplishment, compared with the 1 or 2 percent most companies contribute to charitable groups, won Ben & Jerry's the 1988 Corporate Conscience Award for Corporate Giving from the Council on Economic Priorities. The same year, the firm's two founders were honored as Vermont's Small Businesspersons of the Year.

The anti-establishment period of Cohen and Greenfield's generation provided the seeds for many of their progressive, contemporary, and sometimes zany ideas for their products. One of Ben & Jerry's new ice cream novelties is called the Peace Pop.

Cohen ran into some resistance from the board of directors on the idea, when he wanted to use a wrapper printed with educational peace-related messages. He also wanted a percentage of the profits to be distributed to groups working for peace through understanding. A similar incident occurred when competitor Pillsbury tried to coerce distributors to carry only Häagen-Dazs. Greenfield and Cohen began a full-fledged campaign against Pillsbury with a take-it-to-the-people tactic, encouraging consumers to write angry letters to Pillsbury, and printing "What's the Doughboy Afraid Of?" across their pint lids, on bumper stickers, and even trailing the message behind airplanes. Greenfield even flew to Pillsbury's Minneapolis headquarters and formed a one-man picket line.

Adding to Ben & Jerry's nonconformist image are its bizarre ice cream flavors, such as the popular White Russian and the Cherry Garcia — a mix of bing cherries and chocolate slivers. The latter flavor was suggested a few years ago by a fan of the recording group The Grateful Dead who wanted to recognize the band's lead guitarist. The company comes up with unusual flavors that large companies do not make because of the expense in changing mass-production systems over to specialty production. That is probably the best advantage for a small company. Ben & Jerry's entered the market appealing to offbeat customers and made a niche there. That niche broadened into a fairly sizeable following, and now Ben & Jerry's is the third largest producer of superpremium ice creams.

Ben & Jerry's social conscience is also evident in some of its employee benefits. The firm has a five-to-one pay scale, which means that the highest-paid person in the company cannot make more than five times what the lowest-paid employee makes. This policy places a greater value on the 200 workers at the company's Waterbury, Vermont, plant who produce more than 115,000 pints of ice cream a day and who are most responsible for its quality. Employees share in five percent of the company's pretax profits, and they each get a daily allowance of three pints of ice cream.

Cohen and Greenfield are always coming up with new products. New-product offerings in a recent year included chocolate-covered ice cream on a stick and brownie/ice cream sandwiches. The two are also constantly trying to make their products better. Says Cohen, "The commitment to quality is the whole basis for our company; certainly without it we're nothing."

Questions

1. What part of the consumer goods classification would best match Ben & Jerry's product line? Use the marketing strategy factors listed in Table 14.1 to defend your selection.

2. How would you classify Ben & Jerry's ice cream with respect to product life cycle stage? What implications does this classification have on marketing decisions made by the firm?

3. Categorize Ben & Jerry's on the following bases:
a. national brand, private brand, or generic product
b. stage of brand loyalty
c. family brand or individual brand

4. What pricing strategy is being employed for Ben & Jerry's Homemade? How is the selection of this strategy related to the price-quality relationship?

15

Distribution Strategy

Learning Goals

1. To explain the value created by the distribution function.

2. To identify the major components of a distribution strategy.

3. To outline the various types of distribution channels and discuss the factors that influence channel selection.

4. To describe how a vertical marketing system differs from a traditional distribution channel.

5. To explain the different degrees of market coverage.

6. To identify the various types of wholesaling intermediaries.

7. To discuss the role of retailing in the U.S. economy.

8. To explain the role of the physical distribution function.

Staples Inc. was a start-up firm that became a sizable business quickly. It is now a chain of 24 self-service, discount office supply stores scattered across the northeastern United States. The idea for Staples came to its founders, Leo Kahn and Tom Stemberg, when they were searching for a market that would benefit from a better developed distribution system. The pair looked at discount lingerie and deep-discount pet supplies. Kahn and Stemberg decided these markets were already highly competitive, so they turned to office supplies because no one had ever sold these items at a deep discount.

Before 1986, the distribution channel for office supplies was from their manufacturers to a limited number of national wholesalers to stationery stores to the retail customer. The wholesalers printed catalogs of 30,000 to 40,000 items. These catalogs were then imprinted with the dealers' names for local distribution. Small businesses in the area could typically buy at a 15 to 20 percent discount from the listed prices.

Kahn and Stemberg decided to go straight to the manufacturers. They asked suppliers to sell directly to the chain of discount office supply stores they were setting up. The entrepreneurs promised to keep accurate records of their customers' purchases, something upon which the manufacturers insisted. Eventually, Kahn and Stemberg lined up 150 to 200 suppliers.

Staples Inc. primarily targeted small businesses with 1 to 100 employees. Other target markets included home businesses, accountants, schools, local governments,

and hospitals. Kahn and Stemberg reasoned that once a firm had 100 office employees, it became an attractive target to the giant wholesalers. These wholesalers would assign an account representative to the firm and offer discounts on purchases. By contrast, small businesses wishing to buy office supplies would have to deal with the stationery stores. Lengthy waits for back-ordered supplies were common in this channel of distribution.

Staples is designed to stock basic office supplies, a strategy that is even reflected in the name Kahn and Stemberg choose for their chain. The stores carry substantial inventories and a variety of alternative brands. Staples' customers can also buy other products through the chain's catalog. The firm sells most office supplies at 50 percent off catalog prices. Customers who want additional service, such as de-

livery and charge accounts, are assessed a surcharge.

Most Staples outlets are in the 16,000- to 18,000-square-foot category. The stores have wide aisles and are arranged into separate departments much like a supermarket.

Staples Inc. opened the first store in May 1986 at Brighton, Massachusetts. The concept became an instant success. In 1987, its first full year of operation, Staples had sales of $40 million. Kahn and Stemberg's brainchild now has annual revenues in excess of $100 million despite the appearance of other deep-discount competitors like Office Depot and the Office Club. Even K mart has joined the list of competitors with its Office Square stores.[1]

Photo source: Courtesy of Staples, The Office Superstore.

Chapter Overview

After products are produced and priced, they must be distributed to the marketplace. All organizations perform a distribution function. Del Monte products are distributed in supermarkets and convenience stores across the United States. Public libraries use bookmobiles to distribute their services to residents in outlying areas and to others who cannot get to the library.

The distribution function is vital to the economic well-being of society because it provides the goods and services desired by the consumer. Economists often use the terms *place, time,* and *ownership utility* to describe the value of distribution. The marketer contributes to the product's value by getting it to the right place at the time the consumer wants to buy it and by providing the mechanism for transferring ownership. Firms that do not perform the distribution function effectively usually fail.

Distribution also provides employment opportunities. Salespeople, warehouse managers, truck drivers, stevedores, and forklift operators are all involved in distribution. Others service the products provided through a distribution network. Most people involved in distribution are classified as service personnel: Their role is to provide service to some other sector of the economy.

This chapter describes the two major components of an organization's distribution strategy: distribution channels and physical distribution. **Distribution channels** are the paths that goods — and title to them — follow from producer to consumer. They are the means by which all organizations distribute the goods and services they are producing and marketing.

The second major component of distribution strategy, **physical distribution**, is the actual movement of goods and services from the producer to the user. Physical distribution covers a broad range of activities. These tasks include customer service, transportation, inventory control, materials handling, order processing, and warehousing.

distribution channels
Paths that goods and services and title to them follow from producer to consumer.

physical distribution
Movement of goods from producer to user.

Distribution Channels

Distribution channels are composed of **marketing intermediaries**, the persons or firms that operate between the producer and the consumer or industrial user. The two main categories of marketing intermediaries are wholesalers and retailers.

Wholesaling intermediaries are persons or firms that sell primarily to retailers and other wholesalers or industrial users. They do not sell significant amounts to ultimate consumers. Sysco is a food-service wholesaler that buys more than 100,000 food products from manufacturers and resells them to some 150,000 restaurants, hotels, schools, hospitals, and other institutions. Sysco also distributes frozen food products to supermarkets, other retail stores, and military commissaries.

Retailers, by contrast, are persons or firms that sell goods and services to individuals for their own use rather than for resale. Retailers are the marketing intermediaries that consumers are most familiar with. The typical consumer buys food, clothing, personal-care items, furniture, and appliances from some type of retailer.

marketing intermediaries
Channel members operating between the producer and the consumer or industrial purchaser.

wholesaling intermediaries
Channel members selling primarily to retailers, other wholesalers, or industrial users.

retailers
Channel members selling goods and services to individuals for their own use rather than for resale.

Photo source: Courtesy of First Interstate Bancorp.

By installing Day & Night automated teller machines in two lodges at Mt. Bachelor ski resort in Oregon, the First Interstate Bank of Oregon creates time, place, and ownership utility for its customers. The First Interstate bank system distributes retail banking and financial services through 1,175 full-service offices and more than 1,400 automated teller machines in 21 states and the District of Columbia.

The Functions of Marketing Intermediaries

Marketing intermediaries perform various functions that assist in the operation of the distribution channel. These functions include buying, selling, storing, and transporting. Some intermediaries also sort and grade bulk products. Wholesalers of fresh produce, for example, receive bulk shipments of fruits and vegetables from growers; sort the produce according to size, color, and degree of ripeness; and then repack it in smaller quantities for their restaurant, grocery store, and other customers. Intermediaries often provide other channel members with important marketing information. Many wholesalers and retailers use scanners and computer technology to measure the movement of producers' goods.

By buying a manufacturer's output, intermediaries provide the necessary cash flow for the producer to pay workers and buy new equipment. By selling, they provide consumers or other intermediaries with want-satisfying goods and services. The buying/selling function of intermediaries brings efficiency to the distribution channel. Intermediaries facilitate the exchange process because they reduce the number of transactions needed between the producer and the consumer. If each of four manufacturers sold directly to four customers, 16 transactions would be required. With an intermediary, the number of transactions is cut to eight.

Marketing intermediaries enter a channel of distribution because they can perform some activities more efficiently or less expensively than the manufacturer or other channel members. Sometimes their efficiency wanes and they must be replaced, but someone in the channel must perform the vital distribution functions.

Types of Distribution Channels

Hundreds of channels are used to distribute the output of U.S. manufacturing and service industries. Canned food products usually pass through wholesalers and retailers to reach the consumer. Some vacuum cleaners and encyclopedias are sold directly to the consumer. No single channel is always the right one: Channel selection depends on the circumstances of the market and on consumer needs. Channels for reaching the consumer may vary over time. For example, the channel for distributing beer has changed from taverns to supermarkets. Channels shift, and effective marketers must be aware of consumer needs so they can keep their distribution methods up to date.

The primary channels of distribution are shown in Figure 15.1. The first four channels are typically used to distribute consumer goods and services, while the last two are commonly used for industrial goods and services.

Producer to Consumer   A direct channel from producer to consumer is used for most services but relatively few products. An artist who sells his or her creations at an art show is an example of this distribution channel. Other users include Avon, Fuller Brush, Electrolux, Kirby, and some encyclopedia publishers.

Producer to Retailer to Consumer   Some manufacturers distribute their products directly to retailers. The apparel industry has many producers that sell directly to retailers through their own sales forces. Some manufacturers set up retail outlets in order to maintain better control over their channels.

Producer to Wholesaler to Retailer to Consumer   The traditional channel for consumer goods, distribution to wholesalers, is used by thousands of small manufacturers that cannot afford to maintain an extensive field sales force to reach the retailing sector. Some of these manufacturers employ technical advisors to assist retailers and to secure marketing information, but they are not directly involved in the selling effort.

Producer to Wholesaler to Wholesaler to Retailer to Consumer   Several wholesalers are common in the distribution of agricultural (canned and frozen foods) and petroleum products (gasoline). An extra wholesaling level is required to divide, sort, and distribute bulky items.

Producer to Industrial User   The direct channel from producer to user is the most common approach to distributing industrial goods and services. This channel is used for nearly all industrial products except accessory equipment and operating supplies.

Producer to Wholesaler to Industrial User   The indirect channel from producer to wholesaler to user is used for some industrial items. It is also used for small accessory equipment and operating supplies that are produced in large lots but sold in small quantities.

Selecting a Distribution Channel

The selection of a distribution channel depends on several factors: the market, the product, the producer, and the competition. These factors are often interrelated.

Figure 15.1 The Primary Channels of Distribution

Consumer Goods and Services

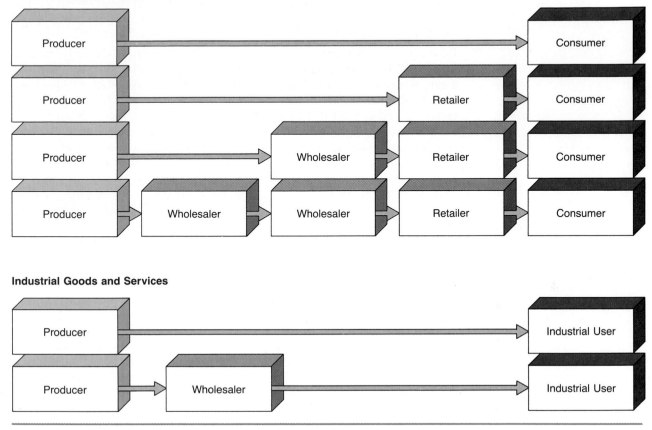

Industrial Goods and Services

Market Factors The most important consideration in choosing a distribution channel is the market segment the producer is attempting to reach. Changes in consumer buying behavior may influence a channel decision. For example, an increasing number of service firms are satisfying consumers' desire for convenience by providing home delivery. Diet-conscious shoppers can choose from an array of low-calorie, microwavable meals sold at the supermarket. But Doorstep Diets in San Diego offers the ultimate in convenience by delivering fresh, low-calorie meals directly to homes and offices. The service is especially appealing to two-income households and older people.

If the product can be marketed to more than one segment, multiple distribution channels may be required. In fact, multiple channels have become increasingly popular in recent years. Bowater Inc. uses multiple channels to distribute its stock computer paper. For years, Bowater salespeople have been selling computer paper directly to large-volume users such as corporations, banks, insurance companies, and government agencies. Today, individuals and small businesses are the fastest-growing segments for computer paper. To reach these markets, Bowater uses a variety of channels, including business forms distributors, paper merchants, office product dealers, and computer retail stores.[2]

Product Factors   In general, products that are complex, expensive, custom-made, and perishable move through shorter distribution channels. Boeing sells its 747 jet aircraft directly to British Airways and other commercial airlines. Each of the $100 million aircraft brings in about $25 million in gross profits.[3] Inexpensive and standardized products are typically sold through longer channels.

Producer Factors   Producers that offer a broad product line and have the financial and marketing resources to distribute and promote their products are more likely to use a shorter channel of distribution. American Greetings Corporation, for example, bypasses wholesaling intermediaries and sells directly to some 90,000 retail outlets worldwide. American Greetings produces 6 million greeting cards each day and also markets gift wrap and ribbon, party goods, candles, stationery, calendars, and gift items. The company has the financial resources to conduct marketing research studies and to maintain its own network of distribution centers. In addition to a large sales force, American Greetings employs 12,000 part-time merchandisers who service retail customers on a weekly basis.[4]

Competitive Factors   In choosing a distribution channel, producers must consider how well an intermediary performs the marketing functions. A producer may become less competitive when an intermediary fails to adequately promote the firm's products.

Campbell Soup Company revised its distribution channel in Japan for its Pepperidge Farm cookies because it was dissatisfied with the marketing efforts of its Japanese importer and local distributors. Cookie sales were low because the Japanese distributors did not aggressively seek new retail outlets or adequately promote the cookies. Even worse, the cookies suffered from a poor image. Consumers complained that the cookies were often stale, a problem resulting from products being stored too long in warehouses. To increase the sales of its cookies, Campbell marketers severed their relationship with the Japanese importer and distributors. Instead, they shortened the channel by selling their cookies directly to a retailer, 7-Eleven Japan, which operates 3,300 outlets in Japan. The new channel not only gives Pepperidge Farm wider exposure, but it also speeds up product delivery so Japanese consumers are assured of buying fresh cookies.[5]

Vertical Marketing Systems

In some instances, the efficiency of the distribution channel is disrupted by conflict among channel members. Conflict can occur between manufacturers and wholesaling intermediaries, such as the problems Campbell Soup had with Japanese distributors. Conflicts also develop between producers and retailers. World of Wonder Inc., marketer of Teddy Ruxpin, Lazer Tag, and other high-tech toys, alienated some of its key retail customers because it failed to deliver products when promised. By not receiving shipments of Lazer Tag guns in time for pre-Christmas selling, some retailers not only lost sales but also were left holding large inventories of the guns when they arrived after the Christmas holidays.[6]

Efforts to reduce conflict and improve the efficiency of the distribution

Firestone uses a corporate vertical marketing system in selling replacement tires it manufactures for automobiles and light trucks at 1,500 company-operated automotive service outlets as well as through independent dealers.

Photo source: Courtesy of The Firestone Tire & Rubber Company, Chicago, IL.

channel resulted in the development of vertical marketing systems. A **vertical marketing system (VMS)** is a planned distribution channel. In the past, most distribution channels were unplanned systems that changed to meet consumer needs. In recent years, vertical marketing systems have become a popular method of organizing the channel. The three types of vertical marketing systems are corporate, administered, and contractual.

vertical marketing system (VMS)
Planned distribution channel organized to reduce channel conflict and improve distribution efficiency.

Corporate VMS

A corporate vertical marketing system is one in which channel members are owned by one enterprise. AT&T selected a corporate VMS by opening 450 AT&T Phone Centers to sell its telephone products to consumers. Liz Claiborne Inc. chose a corporate system to distribute a new line of sportswear under the First Issue label. Made by Liz Claiborne, the sportswear collection is sold at company-owned First Issue retail stores. Other well-known corporate systems are Firestone and Sherwin-Williams.

Administered VMS

An administered vertical marketing system is a distribution system dominated by one channel member. This channel member, often called the **channel captain**, can be a manufacturer, a wholesaler, or a retailer. Traditionally, the channel captain has been the manufacturer that provides the promotional budget to support a brand. In recent years, however, an increasing number of retailers and wholesalers are assuming the role of channel captain.

channel captain
Channel member dominating the activities of a distribution channel.

E. & J. Gallo Winery is an example of a dominant channel member. The California wine maker exercises considerable power over company-owned and independent distributors. One independent distributor describes it this way: "I sometimes feel like an Olympic runner who gets mad at his coach. Gallo pushes so hard you end up working more than you want." Gallo believes its success in selling wine is tied directly to wholesalers' performance with retailers. It encourages distributors to hire a separate sales force to sell to and service retail customers. It requires distributors to provide exceptional customer service, from setting up floor displays to dusting bottles on store shelves. Distributors are expected to follow detailed instructions set forth in a 300-page manual that covers everything from selling techniques to how much shelf space Gallo wines should occupy. Distributors benefit from Gallo's strong brand-name recognition and aggressive promotional support. They cooperate with Gallo because of the effective working relationship. In fact, most distributors owe their success to the winery's dominance of the channel.[7]

Contractual VMS

Contractual vertical marketing systems have had the greatest impact on distribution strategy. In such a system, the members are bound by a contractual agreement. Franchises such as Burger King, Baskin Robbins, and Century 21 are contractual VMSs.

Another contractual system is the wholesaler-sponsored voluntary chain of retail stores. Under this agreement, a wholesaler provides marketing programs, merchandise selection, and other services to independent retailers that agree to purchase the wholesaler's products. McKesson Corporation, the nation's largest wholesale distributor of pharmaceuticals, established Valu-Rite, a voluntary chain of 2,500 pharmacies. McKesson provides Valu-Rite members with advertising circulars to generate store traffic and a private-label line of 170 products including vitamins, shampoos, and toothpaste.[8] Other wholesaler-sponsored chains are Sentry Hardware and IGA Food Stores. This system helps independent retailers compete with mass merchandisers and retail chains.

A third type of contractual VMS is the retail cooperative, in which retailers set up their own wholesaling operation. The retailers agree to buy a certain amount of merchandise from the wholesaling operation, but may choose a common store name and develop their own private-label line of goods. Retail cooperatives, such as Associated Grocers, are common in the grocery industry. Like the wholesaler-sponsored system, retail cooperatives help independent retailers compete with mass merchandise and large retail chains.

Market Coverage

Distribution strategy must be concerned with market coverage. There is probably only one Chevrolet dealer in your immediate area, but there may be several retail outlets that sell General Electric products. Coca-Cola can be found everywhere — in supermarkets, neighborhood convenience stores, service stations, vending machines, restaurants, and coffee shops. Different types of products require different kinds of distribution coverage. Three categories of marketing coverage exist: intensive distribution, exclusive distribution, and selective distribution.

Intensive Distribution   The **intensive distribution** strategy is used by the marketer who tries to place a product in nearly every available outlet. Tobacco products, chewing gum, newspapers, soft drinks, popular magazines, and other low-priced convenience products are available in numerous locations convenient to the purchaser. This kind of saturation market coverage requires the use of wholesalers to achieve a maximum distribution effort.

The distribution of *USA Today* illustrates the concept of intensive distribution. The national daily newspaper is sold at hundreds of newsstands, newspaper vending machines, and retail outlets throughout the country to saturate the market and provide maximum convenience for the paper's 5.5 million readers. The ultimate form of convenience is the provision of time and place utility by direct delivery to the consumer's residence.

Exclusive Distribution   The opposite of intensive distribution, **exclusive distribution** occurs when the manufacturer gives a retailer or wholesaler the exclusive right to sell its products in a specific geographic area. Automobile companies probably provide the best examples of exclusive distribution in domestic markets. Manufacturers sometimes set up effective distribution systems in foreign markets by granting resident firms the exclusive license to import or manufacture their products.

An exclusive distribution contract allows the retailer to carry an adequate inventory and provide the service facilities that might not be possible if competitive dealers existed in the area. Because the dealer has a guaranteed sales area, he or she is likely to make expensive investments in the business. In return, the manufacturer helps the dealer develop a quality image and promote its products effectively.

Selective Distribution   A degree of market coverage somewhere between intensive distribution and exclusive distribution, **selective distribution** occurs when a limited number of retailers are selected to distribute the firm's product lines. Television and electrical appliances are often handled in this manner. Manufacturers hope to develop a close working relationship with their dealers and often split advertising expenses with them. Extensive servicing and training facilities are also usually maintained by the manufacturer to help the retailer do a good job of distributing the product.

Wholesaling

Wholesaling is crucial in the distribution channel for many products, particularly consumer goods. As we explained earlier in the chapter, wholesaling intermediaries are marketing intermediaries that sell to retailers, industrial purchasers, and to other wholesalers, but do not sell directly to the ultimate consumer. The traditional customer of the wholesaling intermediary is the retailer. But some wholesaling intermediaries, referred to as **industrial distributors**, sell to industrial users. Others sell to other wholesaling intermediaries.

Wholesaling intermediaries can be classified on the basis of ownership. Some are owned by manufacturers, some by retailers, and others are independent organizations. Figure 15.2 outlines the various categories of wholesaling intermediaries.

intensive distribution
Strategy used to achieve market saturation by placing products in every available outlet.

exclusive distribution
Strategy of giving a wholesaler or retailer the exclusive right to sell a product in a specific geographic region.

selective distribution
Market coverage strategy of selecting a limited number of retailers to distribute a firm's products.

industrial distributors
Wholesaling intermediaries selling products to industrial users.

Figure 15.2   Categories of Wholesaling Intermediaries

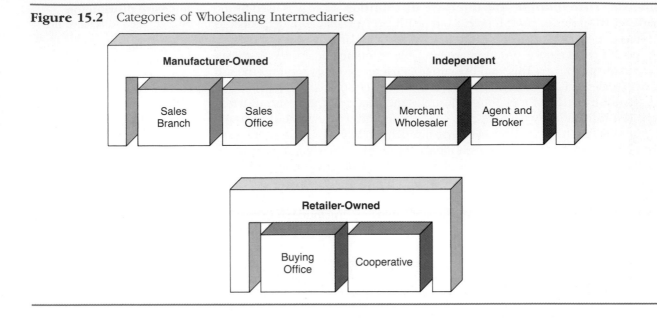

Manufacturer-Owned Wholesaling Intermediaries

Manufacturers may decide to market their products through company-owned sales branches and sales offices for a number of reasons. Producers of perishable products may operate their own distribution centers to speed the delivery of products directly to retailers. Complex products requiring installation and servicing and intensely competitive products requiring considerable promotional efforts are often distributed through company-owned channels. USG Corporation, marketers of gypsum board, acoustical ceiling tile, and other building products, established a network of 140 distribution centers to provide specialized service to construction contractors. The centers have boom-mounted trucks and other special lifting equipment to facilitate delivery of products not only to job sites but also to rooms on any level of a building under construction.[9]

sales branches

Manufacturer-owned marketing intermediaries that stock the items the firm distributes and process orders from inventory.

sales office

Manufacturer-owned office for salespeople that provides close local contacts for regular and potential customers.

Sales branches stock the products they distribute and process orders from their inventory. They are common in the chemical, petroleum products, motor vehicle, and machine and equipment industries. Snap-On Tool Corporation has 55 sales branches that warehouse hand tools and other equipment that independent dealers sell to professional mechanics. Snap-On also maintains four large distribution centers that supply products to sales branches.[10]

A **sales office** is exactly what it seems: an office for salespersons. Unlike sales branches, sales offices do not perform a storage function or warehouse any inventory. Manufacturers set up sales offices in various regions to provide a localized selling effort and to improve customer service.

Independent Wholesaling Intermediaries

Most of the wholesaling organizations in the United States are independent wholesalers. They account for about two-thirds of all wholesale trade. Independent wholesalers can be classified as either merchant wholesalers or agent wholesalers.

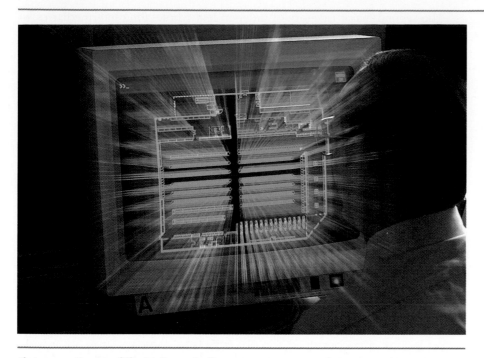

This computerized store layout is part of a store planning and development service that food wholesaler Fleming Companies provides for retail customers. As a full-function merchant wholesaler, Fleming offers retailers more than 100 services. These services are designed to help retail customers improve their competitive position, increase profits, and gain market share.

Photo source: Courtesy of Fleming Companies, Inc.

A **merchant wholesaler** takes legal title to the goods it handles. This type of independent wholesaler can be broken down by the functions it performs. A merchant wholesaler that provides a complete assortment of services for retailers or industrial buyers is referred to as a **full-function merchant wholesaler**. An example is Fleming, a food wholesaler that offers more than 100 services to its retail customers. Among these services are store planning and development, financing, advertising, counseling and training for store managers and employees, consumer-oriented nutrition and health education programs, and an insurance program. Fleming also developed computer software programs that retailers can use for direct store delivery, accounts payable, labor scheduling, and shelf labeling. To help retailers computerize their store operations, Fleming formed a special computer support department that provides retailers with consultation, installation, and training.[11]

Another type of full-function merchant wholesaler is a **rack jobber**, a person who sets up and services a particular section of a retail store, such as paperback books, magazines, toys, or records. A rack jobber supplies the racks, sets up the display, stocks the merchandise, handles the pricing, and completely services the space, which is rented from a retailer on a commission basis.

A merchant wholesaler that also takes legal title to the goods handled but provides fewer services is a **limited-function merchant wholesaler**. These wholesalers may, for example, warehouse goods but not deliver them to customers. Others may warehouse and deliver goods but not provide financing. The ultimate example of a limited-function merchant wholesaler is a **drop shipper**. This wholesaler forwards orders directly to the producer for shipment to customers. Drop shippers that operate in industries like lumber and coal never physically handle the products, although they do hold legal title.

merchant wholesaler
Independent wholesaler that takes legal title to goods.

full-function merchant wholesaler
Merchant wholesaler that performs many services in addition to taking legal title to goods.

rack jobber
Full-function merchant wholesaler that sets up and services a particular section of a retail store.

limited-function merchant wholesaler
Merchant wholesaler that takes legal title to goods but provides few services.

drop shipper
Limited-function merchant wholesaler that takes legal title to goods but never physically handles them.

agents and brokers
Independent wholesalers that never take title to goods but may or may not take possession of them.

The second major category of independent wholesaling intermediaries — **agents and brokers** — never takes title to the goods they handle, although they may or may not take possession of the goods. Agents and brokers bring buyers and sellers together and generally perform fewer services than merchant wholesalers. Boston Computer Exchange is a broker that brings together buyers and sellers of used personal computers. The firm's electronic network lists businesses and individuals that have purchased new computers and want to sell their older models, and firms that are interested in buying used models. Boston Computer Exchange receives a fee on every transaction, but it does not take title to or possession of the computers. Because most computer makers do not participate in the sale of used models, the broker serves as an important intermediary in the used personal computer market.[12]

Other examples of agent wholesalers include real estate brokers; sales agents of various types; manufacturers' agents, who sell noncompeting lines of several producers on a commission basis; commission merchants, who sell agricultural products for farmers; and auction houses.

Retailer-Owned Wholesaling Intermediaries

Some retailers have joined to form their own wholesaling organizations, either buying groups or cooperatives. The objective is to reduce costs or to provide some special service not readily available in the marketplace. To achieve cost savings through quantity purchases, independent retailers may form a buying group. Others may band together to form a cooperative, described in an earlier section as a contractual vertical marketing system.

Retailing

Retailers are the final link in the distribution channel. Because they are normally the only channel members with direct customer contact, it is essential that they operate with the times and within the environment in which they exist. Retailers are part of one of business's most dynamic settings, and special vigilance is required of them if they are to remain competitive. K mart is an example of a successful retailing company, and its successes are to be admired, but much can also be learned from the study of retailing failures.

In the early 1960s, the S. S. Kresge and W. T. Grant retailing chains were about the same size. Both faced the problem of deciding what direction to take in the years ahead. Kresge President Harry B. Cunningham decided to take his firm down the discount path and changed the name to K mart, now the second leading retailer in the United States.

Meanwhile, W. T. Grant watched and then moved to open larger stores and position itself somewhere between discounting and general merchandising. Grant's began to promote big-ticket items such as furniture and major appliances, in contrast to its traditional soft goods and clothing. It stimulated sales of the big-ticket items by issuing credit cards. The consumer's image of Grant's became confused, and the chain lost $177 million in 1975. New management reversed many of the earlier decisions, but it was too late. W. T. Grant declared bankruptcy a year later.

The Wheel of Retailing

Institutions are subject to constant change as new stores replace older establishments. This process, called the **wheel of retailing**, suggests the retail structure is continually evolving as new retailers enter the market by offering lower prices through reductions in service. Supermarkets and discount houses, for example, gained their initial market footholds through low-price, limited-service appeals. The new entries gradually add services as they grow, and they then become targets for competitive assault. Today's attractive K mart stores, for instance, offer good lighting, wide aisles, adequate paved parking, and services such as credit-card purchasing. They are unlike those early discounters that often operated from Quonset huts set up on unpaved lots in declining factory districts.

Some retailers do not survive the evolutionary processes inherent in the wheel of retailing. Robert Hall and E. J. Korvette's were two major retailers that failed to adjust to a changing marketplace and are only memories today.

wheel of retailing
Hypothesis explaining the evolution of retailing based on new types of retailers gaining competitive footholds by emphasizing low prices in exchange for limited services.

Size of the Retailing Sector

Most of the nation's 2 million retailers are small, independent stores, many of which have no paid employees. About half of all retail stores have sales of less than $100,000 each year. But some retail firms are big businesses with billions of dollars in sales.

Sears is the nation's largest retailer with sales of almost $50 billion. Each of the ten largest retailers in the United States, listed in Table 15.1, has sales exceeding $10 billion. About one-fifth of all retail stores are part of a chain, a group of two or more stores that are centrally owned and managed and handle the same product lines. The chain organization is common among shoe stores, department stores, supermarkets, and clothing stores. The Limited, The Gap, Foot Locker, and Safeway are examples of chain-store operations.

Types of Retailers

While most retailing activity is done in stores, about 10 percent of total retail sales occurs in a nonstore environment. Thus, retailers can be grouped into two broad categories: store and nonstore.

Table 15.1   The Ten Largest Retailers

Rank	Company	Sales (billions of dollars)
1	Sears, Roebuck (Chicago)	$48.4
2	K mart (Troy, Michigan)	25.6
3	Safeway Stores (Oakland, California)	18.3
4	Kroger (Cincinnati)	17.6
5	Wal-Mart Stores (Bentonville, Arkansas)	15.9
6	J. C. Penney (Dallas)	15.3
7	American Stores (Salt Lake City)	14.3
8	Federated Department Stores (Cincinnati)	11.1
9	Dayton Hudson (Minneapolis)	10.7
10	May Department Stores (St. Louis)	10.3

Source: "The 50 Largest Retailing Companies," *Fortune,* June 6, 1988, p. D29.

Table 15.2 Types of Store Retailers

Type of Retailer	Description	Examples
Variety store	Offers a variety of low-priced merchandise.	F. W. Woolworth, Ben Franklin
Department store	Offers a wide variety of merchandise sold in departmentalized sections (furniture, cosmetics, clothing) and many customer services.	Marshall Field's, J. C. Penney, Sears Roebuck
Specialty store	Offers a complete selection in a narrow range of merchandise.	Shoe stores, furriers, camera shops, jewelry stores
Convenience store	Offers staple convenience goods, long store hours, rapid checkout, adequate parking facilities, and convenient locations.	7-Eleven, Circle K, Dairy Mart, gasoline stations
Discount store	Offers a wide selection of merchandise at low prices and few services.	K mart, Target, Wal-Mart, Zayre
Off-price store	Offers designer or brand-name merchandise of many manufacturers at discount prices.	T. J. Maxx, Marshall's, Loehmann's
Factory outlet	Manufacturer-owned store selling seconds, production overruns, or discontinued lines.	Nike outlet stores
Catalog store	Sells discounted merchandise from showrooms that display samples of products detailed in catalogs mailed to consumers.	Best Products, Service Merchandise, Zales, Gordon Jewelry
Supermarket	Large, self-service store offering a wide selection of food and nonfood merchandise.	Winn-Dixie, Kroger, Lucky, Safeway, A&P, Albertson's
Hypermarket	Giant-size store (at least three times the size of the average supermarket) offering food and general merchandise at discount prices.	Hypermart USA, Bigg's, Meijer, Carrefour, Fred Meyer
Warehouse club	Large warehouse-style store that sells food and general merchandise at discount prices to people who are part of its associated club membership.	Sam's Wholesale Club, Costco

The major types of store retailers include department stores, specialty stores, variety stores, convenience stores, discount stores, off-price stores, factory outlets, catalog stores, supermarkets, hypermarkets, and warehouse clubs. These retailers are briefly described in Table 15.2. The major types of nonstore retailing are direct selling, direct-response selling, and automatic merchandising.

Direct selling involves direct contact between the sellers and the buyers. The home is the typical setting for direct-selling retailers such as Avon, Amway, Shaklee, Mary Kay Cosmetics, and Tupperware. But because women, the traditional target market of direct-selling firms, have entered the work force in record numbers, many of these retailers now sell their merchandise in offices and factories. Avon developed a special training program to instruct its 400,000 representatives how to sell makeup and jewelry to women at their place of work. Workplace sales now account for about 25 percent of total Avon sales.[13]

Direct-response retailing is conducted through mail or telephone orders of catalog merchandise or through telephone orders of merchandise on television. Mail-order selling began with a Montgomery Ward catalog in 1872. Today, mail-order houses range from Spiegel (clothing/home furnishings) to Jackson & Perkins (flowers) to L. L. Bean (primarily hunting and camping gear) to Harry and David (fruit). The fastest-growing area of direct-response retailing is home shopping, the use of cable television networks to sell merchandise through telephone orders.

Supermarkets, like many other retailers, practice scrambled merchandising to provide customers with the convenience of one-stop shopping. At Lucky Stores supermarkets, shoppers can choose from an assortment of fresh-cut flowers and plants in the stores' floral department. Shoppers can also have their prescriptions filled at in-store pharmacies.

Photo source: © 1988 William Mosgrove. All Rights Reserved.

Automatic merchandising, or the use of vending machines, is an excellent method of retailing various types of consumer goods. Candy, cigarettes, soft drinks, ice, fruit, ice cream, chewing gum, sandwiches, coffee, milk, hot chocolate, and soup are all available through vending machines. Even entertainment has been packaged for vending operations, beginning with jukeboxes and pinball machines and progressing to coin-operated video games.

How Retailers Compete

The different types of retailers compete on a variety of bases. Convenience stores and nonstore retailers focus on making the shopping experience fast and easy. Discount houses and off-price retailers attempt to compete by offering shoppers merchandise at low prices. Personalized attention and a wide variety of customer services are the keys to success of department store and specialty store retailers.

Many retailers seek to preserve or increase their sales volume by diversifying the products they offer for sale, a practice known as **scrambled merchandising**. Drugstores added soda fountains and then such items as magazines and newspapers. Now they sell cameras, small appliances, garden supplies, greeting cards, liquor, tobacco products, cosmetics, and toys. Some discount stores added pharmaceutical departments. Convenience stores such as 7-Eleven rent videotapes and sell fast food. Sears became a "financial supermarket" with its acquisition of Dean Witter Reynolds stock brokerage firm and Coldwell Banker real estate. When combined with Sears affiliate Allstate Insurance, today's Sears store is not only a retailer but a financial center as well.

scrambled merchandising
Practice of retailers carrying dissimilar product lines to appeal to consumers seeking one-stop shopping.

Planning a Retail Strategy

Retailers face a unique marketing environment because they are the channel members that have direct contact with consumers. They must develop a marketing strategy that satisfies their target market. The products offered, their prices, the store's location, the way the store is promoted, and the store's atmosphere must all work together to project an image that appeals to a well-defined market segment.

Target Market   The starting point in developing a retail strategy is to identify the target market. Discount houses and off-price retailers target price-conscious consumers. Spiegel targets upscale career women under 40 with annual incomes of $43,000. Charisma, a New York fashion retailer, targets women who wear size 14 clothing and above. GapKids targets children between the ages of 2 and 12.

Product Strategy   After identifying a target market, retailers must decide on general product categories, product lines, and the width and depth of assortment. Hypermarkets sell a wide range of merchandise, up to 70,000 different items, but the depth of assortment is very limited. Hypermarket USA's paint department, for example, sells only one color: white. Specialty retailers, on the other hand, offer a limited product line in depth. The Sock Shop in New York sells 900 styles of socks, including many one-of-a-kind items such as a pair of children's socks that plays a tune when squeezed.

The growth of specialty retailers and discount houses in recent years has forced other retailers to change their product strategy. Many department stores no longer sell toys, consumer electronics, and furniture because of increased competition from retailers known as "category killers," discount chains that sell only one category of products. Examples are Toys "R" Us (toys); The Wiz, Silo, and Best Buy Superstores (electronics); Tower Records (records); and Conrans and Home Express (home furnishings). Toys "R" Us, which offers 18,000 toys at discount prices, has captured 20 percent of the $12.5 billion toy market, and the firm's market share is expected to climb to 40 percent by 1995. Department stores and general merchandisers like K mart that do not specialize in toys and carry only 3,000 items cannot compete with Toys "R" Us. While many department stores are eliminating toys from their product mix, K mart and Service Merchandise are trimming back their toy inventories. To compete with category killers in appliances and consumer electronics, Sears decided to expand its product offerings. In addition to selling its Kenmore private label brand, Sears is now selling national brand merchandise such as Sony, Panasonic, and Pioneer electronics.[14]

Customer Service Strategy   A high level of customer service is an important competitive tool of department and specialty stores. These retailers generally offer a full complement of services, including gift wrapping, alterations, and delivery. Because services add to the retailer's operating costs, discount stores keep prices down by offering few services.

Many retailers provide services that cater to consumers' desire for convenience. A small New York retailer, Mr. Dry Clean, installed a computerized machine that allows customers to drop off and pick up their clothes 24 hours a day. The system works much like an automated teller machine. Customers pass a

Figure 15.3   Projecting a Retail Image through Pricing

Source: Courtesy of Saks Fifth Avenue.

credit card through an electronic reader that signals a robot to bring an empty bag to the machine's window. They fill the bag and write out a receipt. A day later, they can pick up their clothes by again inserting their credit card, which tells the robot which bag of clothes to bring to the window. Mr. Dry Clean does not charge customers for this added convenience.[15]

Pricing Strategy   Retailers determine the price consumers pay for goods and services. They base their prices on the cost of merchandise they purchase from other channel members. Discount retailers buy in large volume so they can offer merchandise at lower prices. Retailers' prices influence consumers' perception of the store. The $615 designer dress featured in the Saks Fifth Avenue advertisement in Figure 15.3 distinguishes Saks as an upscale fashion retailer.

Location/Distribution Strategy   Location is the primary distribution decision retailers make. Will they locate in a downtown business district, an isolated area, or a neighborhood or regional shopping center? A good location is often the difference between success and failure in retailing.

The location decision depends on the retailer's size, financial resources, product offerings, and target market. When populations shifted from urban to suburban areas in the 1950s, department stores, traditionally located in downtown districts, opened branches in suburban shopping malls to provide convenient locations for their target customers. A recent retailing trend is the specialty store shopping center. Designed to target upscale consumers, these centers consist only of specialty stores and restaurants.

Another factor in retailers' distribution strategy is making sure adequate quantities of products are available when customers want to buy. Circuit City Stores, a specialty retailer of audio and video products, operates two automated distribution centers to supply its 138 retail stores. The centers speed the delivery of products to stores and give Circuit City cost advantages over competitors, such as lower inventory requirements, less storage space and more selling space in stores, quick inventory turnaround, and less pilferage.[16]

Promotional Strategy   Retailers design advertisements and develop other promotions to communicate their store image and to provide information about their store — location, type of merchandise, prices, and store hours. Small, independent retailers with limited budgets generally place advertisements in local newspapers and send local residents mailers that announce special sales. Large retailers spend millions of dollars promoting their stores. Wal-Mart, with more than 1,000 outlets, spends about $30 million each year on advertising, mostly for television commercials. All Wal-Mart advertising, whether for clothing, electronics, or health and beauty products, focuses on a central theme — "everyday discount prices" — to project the store's image.[17]

atmospherics

Physical characteristics and amenities that attract customers and satisfy their shopping needs.

Store Atmosphere   Consumers' perception of a retailer is also shaped by **atmospherics**, the physical characteristics of a store and amenities provided by the retailer. A store's exterior should draw customers inside, and the interior should induce shoppers to make purchases. All interior elements — store layout, merchandise presentation, lighting, color scheme — should appeal to the target market. Consider the environment of WaldenKids, a chain of stores that sells children's books, educational toys, and games. Children can enter the store by crawling through a carpeted tunnel. Once inside, they are greeted by a video monitor that plays cartoon fairy tales. Painted in bright colors of blue, red, yellow, and green, the stores are equipped with stages for special events such as puppet shows and book readings. Children are encouraged to try computer games and play with toys. With each purchase, kids are given a "visa" stamp as part of a Passport to Adventure program. When they collect 12 visas, they get a free watch.[18]

Physical Distribution

Physical distribution, the second of the two major components of distribution strategy, involves the actual movement of goods from the producer to the user. This covers a broad range of activities, including customer service, transportation, warehousing, materials handling, inventory control, and order processing. Figure 15.4 shows the components of a physical distribution system.

Physical distribution is important for two reasons. First, physical distribution activities account for, on average, one-fifth the cost of a manufactured good. In the past, businesses focused on improving the efficiency of production to lower product costs. In recent years, however, managers have begun to realize that reducing the costs of physical distribution activities is another key to improving productivity and gaining significant competitive advantages. Physical distribution

Figure 15.4   Interconnecting Components of the Physical
                  Distribution System

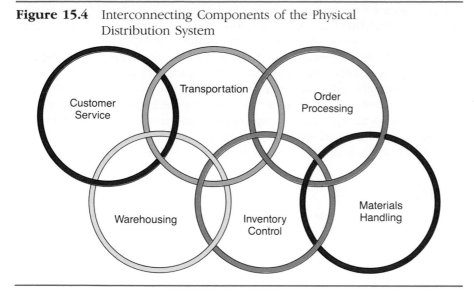

is also important because customer satisfaction, to a large extent, depends on reliable movements of goods and services.

The study of physical distribution should include all factors involved in moving goods rather than concentrating on individual aspects of the process. Because the objective of physical distribution is to provide a specified level of customer service at the lowest possible overall costs, total costs should be considered. Suboptimization can occur if individual rather than total costs are considered.

Physical distribution costs are often interrelated; a change in one element may affect other elements. Low inventory levels may reduce warehousing costs, but they can result in increases in transportation and order-processing costs. The interrelationship of these costs should be emphasized in any physical distribution strategy.

Manufacturers, wholesalers, and retailers have reduced the costs of physical distribution and improved customer service by applying computer-based electronics and automation. Computer linkups that enable channel members to share information speed up order processing and delivery and help reduce inventory on hand.

Customer Service Standards

Customer service standards involve the quality of service a firm provides for its customers. Managers frequently set quantitative guidelines for customer service. For example, a firm may stipulate that all orders be processed within 48 hours of receipt. A retailer may require that salespeople approach shoppers within two minutes.

customer service standards
Quality of service that a firm's
customers will receive.

Sometimes the customer sets the service standards and chooses suppliers that meet or exceed those standards. The University of Nebraska Medical Center in Omaha needed additional storage space for the hundreds of supplies its staff uses each day. Hospital managers considered building a new warehouse but could not justify the $500,000 construction cost. Instead, the managers developed a stockless inventory program to eliminate the need for additional storage space. They searched for a firm that could deliver medical supplies on a daily basis and meet a 98 percent "fill rate" to assure that supplies were available when needed. These standards were detailed in a contract the hospital signed with its supplier, Baxter International. Baxter's local distribution center stocks 500 of the hospital's most critical medical and surgical supplies. To ensure availability, Baxter makes daily deliveries on a just-in-time basis to the hospital. Baxter also presorts the supplies so they can be delivered directly to specific nursing stations and medical departments. Baxter has consistently exceeded the delivery standards established by the hospital.[19]

Transportation

The form of transportation used to ship products depends primarily on the kind of product, the distance, and the cost. The physical distribution manager has a number of companies and modes of transportation from which to choose.

Transportation Companies   Transportation companies can be classified into four basic types: common carriers, contract carriers, private carriers, and freight forwarders. A **common carrier** offers to perform services within a particular line of business for the general public. One example is a truckline operating in an area where general merchandise is handled. The truckline is available to serve all the people in the area who offer it general merchandise to haul. However, it may decline to handle such items as liquid petroleum gas or aviation gas. Examples of common carriers are United Airlines and Consolidated Freightways.

common carrier
Transportation firm that performs services within a particular line of business for the general public.

   Contract carriers transport goods for hire by individual contract or agreement. They do not offer to perform services for the general public; instead, they usually offer services that meet the special needs of their customers. Contract carriers are most frequently engaged in business as owner/operator motor carriers. Usually they solicit large shipments from a particular shipper to a particular recipient.

contract carriers
Transportation firms that carry goods for hire by individual contract or agreement and not for the general public.

   Private carriers transport their own property or deliver their services in their own vehicles. Amoco has its own fleet of oceangoing crude oil carriers. Hon Industries, a manufacturer of office furniture and products, maintains its own fleet of trucks to provide customers with fast delivery and reduce product damage. The Hon trucks, painted with the company name and logo, also serve as advertisements. Federal Express has a ground fleet of more than 17,000 vehicles and 145 airplanes to ensure fast, on-time delivery for its package service.

private carriers
Companies that transport their own goods in their own vehicles.

   Freight forwarders differ from the other carriers in that they do not own any of the equipment used in intercity carriage of freight. They are common carriers that lease or contract bulk space from other carriers such as the airlines and railroads and resell this space to small-volume shippers. The freight forwarder picks up the merchandise from the shipper, loads it into the equipment of whatever carrier is being used, delivers it to its destination, and takes care of all the billing involved.

freight forwarders
Common carriers that purchase bulk space from other carriers by lease or contract and resell this space to small-volume shippers.

   Freight forwarders provide shippers the advantage of better, less-expensive service, and the carriers do not have to handle many small shipments and the billing for them. A further advantage of freight forwarding is that the forwarder knows at all times where each piece of freight is while it is in transit. This intermediary saves money for everyone and makes for improved service.

Figure 15.5 Using Rail to Efficiently Transport Grain

Source: Courtesy: Norfolk Southern Corporation. Created by J. Walter Thompson Company, USA.

Modes of Transportation The five major modes of transportation are railroads, trucks, water carriers, pipelines, and air freight. The cost of using each mode is usually related to the speed at which it operates. Faster modes typically cost more than slower ones.

Railroads. About 36 percent of all domestic intercity freight is carried by the railroads, most of which are common carriers.[20] Intercity freight is measured in terms of ton-miles, the movement of one ton of freight for a distance of one mile. None of the nation's railroads is a contract carrier, and only a few (owned and operated by mining companies, lumbering operations, and very large producers like steel mills) are private carriers.

Railroads are the most efficient mode for transporting bulk commodities over long distances. For example, about 70 percent of grain is transported by rail. The Norfolk Southern advertisement in Figure 15.5 describes the efficiency of using rail to transport grain. Other types of products most often transported by rail are lumber, iron and steel, coal, automobiles, and chemicals.

Carload freight is the kind of freight railroads prefer to handle. It is provided in shipper-loaded cars to be delivered to someone who will unload the cars, which costs less because railroad personnel do not have to do the loading and unloading. Companion services to carload freight are containerization and trailer-on-flatcar (piggyback) services. Railroads also offer trainload services to shippers of bulk commodities like coal and iron ore. Some trains of this type never stop; they use continuous loading and unloading equipment.

In an effort to improve service standards and to capture more of the market, railroads are offering services such as run-through trains, which bypass congested terminals, and unit trains, which are used exclusively by a single customer that pays lower rates for each shipment.

Trucks.   Highway transportation accounts for about 25 percent of domestic freight shipping. The principal advantage of highway transportation over other modes is flexibility. A truck carrier can operate wherever there is a road, while trains depend on rails and aircraft on airports large enough to accommodate them. A number of transcontinental highway carriers move freight coast to coast. However, highway carriers are most efficient for distances up to about 300 to 400 miles. For longer distances, railroads are more advantageous.

Products most often handled by motor carriers are clothing, furniture and fixtures, food, leather and leather products, and machinery. Highway carriers are divided into common carriers, contract carriers, and private carriers.

The typical highway common carrier, with its own pickup and delivery equipment, picks up freight at the shipper's door and delivers it to a freight terminal, where it is loaded into larger trucks for delivery to a terminal in another city. There it is unloaded and delivered by smaller vehicles. Contract highway carriers can frequently offer lower rates than common carriers because they serve a limited number of customers, deal in volume shipments, and operate only when they have a profitable load. Wholesale grocery companies, supermarket chains, department stores, manufacturing firms, and mining companies all engage in private-carrier operations.

Water Carriers.   Water transportation is slow but one of the least costly of all modes of transportation. The two basic types of water carriers are the inland or barge lines and the oceangoing deepwater ships. Oceangoing ships operate on the Great Lakes, between United States port cities, and in international commerce.

Nearly 16 percent of the volume of domestic intercity freight is handled through the inland waterways of the United States. The system of waterways includes the Mississippi, Ohio, Tennessee, and other rivers; inland canals; and the Great Lakes. Much of this freight, especially on the rivers and canals, is transported on barges pushed by mammoth tugs. Great Lakes traffic is handled by specially built ships, some of which are 1,000 feet long. This low-cost type of transportation lends itself mainly to the hauling of bulky commodities such as fuel, oil and petroleum products, coal, chemicals, and minerals.

Pipelines.   Twenty-four percent of intercity freight is handled by pipelines, which convey primarily petroleum products ranging from crude oil to highly refined products and natural gas. Some successful experiments have been made in handling other bulk commodities, such as coal, this way. These commodities are ground into small pieces and mixed with water to form a slurry, which is then pumped through the pipelines. Pipelines can transport many liquids and gases more cheaply and more quickly than other modes of transportation.

Air Freight.   While still dwarfed by other transportation modes, carrying less than three-tenths of 1 percent of all freight, domestic air freight has become

Table 15.3   Comparing the Modes of Transportation

Mode	Factor					
	Speed	Dependability in Meeting Schedules	Frequency of Shipments	Availability in Different Locations	Flexibility in Handling	Cost
Rail	Average	Average	Low	Extensive	High	Medium
Water	Very slow	Average	Very low	Limited	Very high	Very low
Truck	Fast	High	High	Very extensive	Average	High
Pipeline	Slow	High	High	Very limited	Very low	Low
Air	Very fast	High	Average	Average	Low	Very high

increasingly important in recent years. Air freight is usually limited to valuable products such as furs and computers or perishable products such as flowers and live lobsters.

The certificated airlines of the United States are all common carriers. Some of them (as well as a group of carriers known as *supplemental carriers*) engage in charter work, which is a form of contract carriage. Many business organizations own or lease aircraft that are operated to transport their personnel or, in some situations, their freight; this is defined as *private carriage*.

Table 15.3 compares speed, reliable delivery, shipment frequency, location availability, handling flexibility, and cost associated with the five modes of transportation.

Warehousing

Warehousing is the physical distribution activity that involves the storage of products. The two types of warehouses are storage and distribution. A **storage warehouse** keeps products for relatively long periods of time and is used most often for products that are seasonal in supply or demand, such as farm products.

A **distribution warehouse** is used to gather and redistribute products. Distribution warehouses try to keep products for as short a time as possible. They are mainly used by manufacturers that have several small customers in various, distant locations or by firms that have several suppliers in one area.

warehousing
The storage of goods.

storage warehouse
Warehouse that stores goods for relatively long time periods.

distribution warehouse
Warehouse that stores goods for a short time; often used for gathering and redistributing products.

Materials Handling and Protective Packaging

The physical distribution activity of moving items within plants, warehouses, transportation terminals, and stores is referred to as **materials handling**. Equipment used to handle goods includes forklift trucks, conveyor belts, and trucks.

Unitization and containerization have improved materials handling in many firms. *Unitization* — combining as many packages as possible into one load that can be handled by a forklift truck — is sometimes done with steel bands or shrink packaging. *Containerization* — putting packages, usually made up of several unitized loads, into a form that is relatively easy to transfer — has significantly reduced transportation costs for many products by cutting materials handling time, theft, insurance costs, damage, and scheduling problems.

materials handling
Movement of goods within a firm's warehouse, terminal, factory, or store.

Inventory Control

inventory control
Function of controlling all costs associated with inventory.

Inventory control deals with the management of inventory costs such as storage facilities, insurance, taxes, and handling costs. Holding inventory is expensive: $1,000 of inventory held for one year can cost a company $250.

To reduce inventory costs, many firms use computerized inventory control management systems. Wetterau, a food-service wholesaler, installed on-line inventory control systems in its distribution centers to increase the efficiency of warehousing and transportation and to provide retail customers with information that helps them make buying decisions.

Another approach to controlling inventory is the just-in-time (JIT) inventory system discussed in Chapter 9. Channel members other than producers benefit from JIT. The Baxter example cited earlier reduced the University of Nebraska Medical Center's inventory by $100,000 and opened up 6,000 square feet of space the center now uses for other purposes.

Order Processing

order processing
Function of handling the preparation of an order for shipment.

The physical distribution activity of **order processing** concerns the actual preparation of an order for shipment. It also includes the receipt of orders. Lawson Products, a distributor of repair and maintenance products for large equipment, uses six facsimile machines to receive incoming orders. The machines enable Lawson to meet its objective of processing orders within 24 hours.

Order processing is closely linked to the firm's customer service standards. For Pizza Hut, fast and efficient order processing is crucial in completing pizza deliveries to homes within a half-hour. With the help of computers, Pizza Hut can process orders in just 17 seconds. Incoming calls for home delivery are received at a customer service center where order takers enter customer requests on computers and send printed instructions to a bake shop closest to each customer.[21]

Order processing and the other physical distribution activities performed by channel members ensure that customers receive goods and services at the right time and in the right place. In the next chapter, you will learn how channel members communicate information about their goods and services in order to persuade customers to buy.

Summary of Learning Goals

1.   Explain the value created by the distribution function.   The distribution function creates time, place, and ownership utility. Marketers contribute to the product's value by getting it to the right place at the time the consumer wants to buy it and by providing the mechanism for transferring ownership.

2.   Identify the major components of a distribution strategy.   The two major components of a distribution strategy are distribution channels and physical distribution. Distribution channels are the paths that goods and services and title to them follow from producer to consumer. Physical distribution involves all the activities channel members perform in moving goods and services.

3.   Outline the various types of distribution channels and discuss the factors that influence channel selection.   Distribution channels vary in length. Some channels are short, with goods and services moving directly from manufacturer to consumer. Others are longer, involving channel members such as retailers and wholesaling intermediaries. Selecting a channel depends on various factors, including the product, market, producer, and competition.

4.   Describe how a vertical marketing system differs from a traditional distribution channel.   A vertical marketing system (VMS) is a planned distribution system. It contrasts with traditional distribution channels, which were unplanned and developed over time. There are three types of vertical marketing systems. An administered VMS is dominated by one channel enterprise. A corporate VMS is owned by a single enterprise. A contractual VMS is one in which the members are bound by contractual arrangements.

5.   Explain the different degrees of market coverage.   Three categories of market coverage exist: (1) intensive distribution, in which products are placed in many outlets; (2) exclusive distribution, in which a firm has exclusive rights to sell a product in a certain geographical area; and (3) selective distribution, in which a limited number of retailers distribute a firm's products.

6.   Identify the various types of wholesaling intermediaries.   Three broad categories of wholesaling intermediaries exist. Manufacturer-owned wholesaling intermediaries consist of sales offices and sales branches. Independent wholesaling intermediaries consist of merchant wholesalers (who take title to the goods they handle) and such agents and brokers as auction houses, selling agents, manufacturers' agents, and commission merchants (who do not take title). Retailer-owned wholesaling intermediaries include retail cooperatives and buying offices.

7.   Discuss the role of retailing in the U.S. economy.   The nation's 2 million retailers sell goods and services to persons for their own use rather than for resale. Retail institutions are constantly changing. Two factors make it difficult to describe and classify them: the wheel of retailing and the trend toward scrambled merchandising. Retailers fall into two general categories: store and nonstore. Store retailers include general stores, department stores, specialty stores, convenience stores, discount houses, off-price retailers, factory outlets, catalog showrooms, supermarkets, hypermarkets, and warehouse clubs. Nonstore retailing includes direct selling, direct-response retailing, automatic merchandising, and teleshopping.

8.   Explain the role of the physical distribution function.   Physical distribution is an important part of distribution strategy. Because its objective is to maximize the level of customer service, marketers must consider total costs. The various elements in physical distribution include customer service standards, transportation, warehousing, materials handling, inventory control, and order processing.

Key Terms

distribution channels

physical distribution

marketing intermediaries

wholesaling intermediaries

retailers

vertical marketing system (VMS)

channel captain

intensive distribution

exclusive distribution

selective distribution

industrial distributors

sales branches

sales office

merchant wholesaler

full-function merchant wholesaler

rack jobber

limited-function merchant wholesaler

drop shipper

agents and brokers

wheel of retailing

scrambled merchandising

atmospherics

customer service standards

common carrier

contract carriers

private carriers

freight forwarders

warehousing

storage warehouse

distribution warehouse

materials handling

inventory control

order processing

Review Questions

1. Outline the types of utility relevant to distribution strategy.

2. Differentiate between wholesalers and retailers.

3. Draw and explain the distribution channels for consumer goods and for industrial goods and services. How does a marketer select a specific channel?

4. What is a vertical marketing system? What are the major types of vertical marketing systems?

5. Differentiate among intensive, exclusive, and selective distribution strategies. Cite examples of each.

6. Explain how independent wholesaling intermediaries differ from both: (a) manufacturer-owned wholesaling intermediaries and (b) retailer-owned wholesaling intermediaries.

7. Identify and explain an example of the wheel of retailing in operation.

8. Cite a local example (if one exists) of a variety store, department store, specialty store, convenience store, discount store, off-price store, factory outlet, catalog store, supermarket, hypermarket, warehouse club, and "category killer."

9. Why have many retailers adopted a scrambled merchandising strategy?

10. Differentiate among a common carrier, contractual carrier, private carrier, and freight forwarder. Cite examples of each.

Discussion Questions

1. The Green House of Encinitas, California, (now 50 percent owned by Mc-Cormick Co.) is a grower of fresh packaged herbs. The firm offers 19 types of herbs to retailers willing to order a minimum of 20 dozen packages. Since most of the herbs have to be used within five to seven days, The Green House uses ziplock bags for packaging. The orders are then wrapped in foam and ice packs for shipment overnight by Federal Express. Describe the importance of distribution strategy to The Green House. What other marketers face similar distribution problems?

2. Which distribution channel would you select for the following:
    a. A car seat for infants
    b. An income-tax preparation service
    c. Mack trucks
    d. Pears

3. Which types of market coverage would be best for the following products?
    a. Rolls-Royce automobiles
    b. Bubble gum
    c. Men's cologne
    d. Bulldozers and other earth-moving equipment

4. Comment on the following statement: "Hypermarkets are simply the logical extension of the scrambled merchandising concept."

5. Which transportation mode would you suggest for the following:
    a. Sheet steel
    b. Natural gas
    c. Premium electronic components
    d. Breakfast cereal

Video Case

L. L. Bean

Mention the name L. L. Bean and two images appear in most people's minds: the well-known and widely-distributed catalog of the same name and the Maine Hunting Boot. Although L. L. Bean operates manufacturing facilities and two retail stores, it relies on a relatively unusual distribution channel for its sales: direct-response retailing through mail-order purchases and/or telephone orders. Eighty-eight percent of the firm's 1988 sales of $590 million were produced through catalog sales. Retail stores, the traditional outlet for consumer purchases, accounted for only $70 million.

Leon Leonwood Bean created his first hand-made pair of hunting boots for himself. He made a few more, gave them to friends who raved about the boots' dry, lightweight comfort, and finally decided that anyone who enjoyed the outdoors should be able to acquire a pair of these boots. So, in 1912, he secured a mailing list of Maine hunting-license holders, set up shop in a basement, and prepared a three-page brochure that guaranteed "perfect satisfaction."

But the first 100 pairs of Bean's boots were far from perfect; 90 of them were returned to him after the bottoms fell off. The outdoorsman/entrepreneur had offered a 100 percent guarantee, and he was determined to live up to it. Bean borrowed the money to repair and return the boots, corrected the initial problem, and made more boots. Then he sent out more brochures.

This first experience taught Bean the value of personally testing his products, of honest advertising based on firm convictions, and of keeping the customer satisfied. He was determined to adhere to a simple business philosophy: Sell good merchandise at a reasonable price, treat customers like human beings, and they will always come back for more. The L. L. Bean Golden rule is still the guideline for the firm today.

Bean was also certain that mail-order marketing was the best way to reach his customers. The home-spun catalogs mailed to his target markets continued to prove effective and, by 1927, his operations had grown to a 25-person workforce, sales had increased to in excess of $135,000, and camping and fishing equipment had been added to the product line. "It is no longer necessary," L. L. wrote, "for you to experiment with dozens of flies to determine the few that will catch fish. We have done that for you."

Most of the profits in the early years were funneled back into advertising to stimulate further growth. Bean ran ads promoting his free catalogs; he also began collecting information for use in market segmentation by developing a coding system for evaluating responses. He then used this information to analyze his consumer base and make decisions on appropriate additions and deletions to the L. L. Bean line. This type of information aided the firm in quadrupling sales during the Great Depression. In fact, sales passed the $1 million mark in 1937.

The 1940s proved another growth decade for L. L. Bean as the firm acquired war contracts to manufacture boots and bags for the U.S. Armed Forces in addition to its thriving product line. The company's fame spread and it was the subject of major stories in mass-audience magazines like *Life* and the *Saturday Evening Post*. Bean's book, *Hunting, Fishing, and Camping*, published during this decade, became the basic handbook on those sports.

In 1945, a special retail salesroom was opened in the middle of the Freeport, Maine, factory, with a night bell outside for the convenience of sports enthusiasts passing through town late at night. Six years later, the retail store began staying open 24 hours a day, 365 days a year. In 1954, he took his wife's advice and opened a ladies' department to serve the growing number of women involved in outdoor sports. But Bean was getting older as the 1950s drew to a close and his energy and drive levels were not as high as before. The company had grown old as well: The average age of employees was over 60. Sales had stabilized between $2 and $3 million during the 1960s. Then Bean died in 1967.

Leadership passed to his grandson, Leon Gorman, who had worked at L. L. Bean since 1961. Gorman's fresh leadership, combined with growing interest in fitness and the outdoors, produced steady sales in-

Notes: Ron Zemke, *The Service Edge* (New York: NAL Books, 1989), pp. 378–381; Rebecca Fannin, "Bean's Basics," *Marketing & Media Decisions,* July 1987, p. 20; James A. Cooke, "Extending the Logistics Channel," *Traffic Management,* April 1988, pp. 69–71; Beverly Geber, "Training at L. L. Bean," *Training,* October 1988; and personal correspondence, February 23, 1989.

creases each year. This was the era of President Kennedy's promotion of physical fitness programs in the public schools and an interest in getting back to nature. Closely following this phase was the popularity of the 'preppy look' — rugby shirts, khaki-and-plaid materials, and of course the famous Maine Hunting Shoe.

While sales were climbing, Gorman was revitalizing the organization. The entire product line was critically evaluated, the advertising budget increased, mailing lists were computerized, the order-entry system was automated, and the manufacturing facilities and distribution centers were expanded. L. L. Bean also began hiring from outside the organization for the first time in its history. Improved training programs were added, and today Bean spends about $800,000 annually on training and development.

But through all the change and reorganization, the catalog has remained the mainstay of the company. It is through the catalog that Bean communicates to its customers the value and quality of its products. It is the catalog that provides time, place, and ownership utility for Bean customers with convenience services such as the toll-free telephone number for placing orders and the 100 percent return policy. The catalog permits Bean to eliminate many of the intermediaries — wholesalers and retailers — in the typical marketing channels and directly market 6,000 different items to customers in their homes. In 1988, 94 million L. L. Bean catalogs were mailed and almost 11 million packages were shipped to people who ordered from these catalogs. That same year, the firm's telephone representatives handled over eight million telephone calls involving catalog orders and customer service inquiries.

Bean's continuing reputation for superior customer service is revealed by a recent *Consumer Reports* survey of 165,000 mail-order purchasers. L. L. Bean was the top-rated company in each of its seven merchandise categories; an outstanding 99.89 percent of the 11 million packages mailed were filled correctly.

The reasons behind this superlative service are many. L. L. Bean employees who take or check customer orders over the phone are unfailingly polite. They are trained to use the customer's name, to say please and thank you, to be familiar with the products, and to be ready to answer questions about inventory or the customer's previous orders. These employees rank service quality above the number of calls they handle, giving the customer the best possible service through the use of telecommunication systems and

computers that connect the company's own telephone centers with customer records and the distribution center.

The Freeport distribution center covers 630,000 square feet. Workers who fill orders on the floor walk as many as twelve miles during a typical shift. Computers print out the order in which articles should be collected from inventory, thereby increasing warehouse efficiency by decreasing the time needed to assemble an order. The center can process more than 11 million orders a year, and it usually has them delivered anywhere in the United States and Canada within 72 hours. Although this type of response rate provides the service required to keep people coming back, Bean CEO Gorman is quick to emphasize the importance of product and service superiority: "No amount of marketing technology can overcome deficiencies in product and service."

When Gorman speaks of the future, he emphasizes the fact that his firm's distribution channel is not commonly used by U.S. marketers. After all, approximately 90 percent of all consumer purchases take place in retail stores. Even though Bean has increased its presence in traditional marketing by opening a second retail store in North Conway, New Hampshire, catalog sales will continue to be its bread and butter. Gorman explains that catalogs are in a unique position to combine research with product offerings targeted to specific markets. In his words, "Any consumer is a potential mail-order buyer if the offer is relevant to his or her lifestyle."

Questions

1. What distribution channels are used in the marketing of L. L. Bean products? Draw each channel and label all components.

2. Could L. L. Bean's method of distribution be considered a vertical marketing system? If so, what type of VMS is being used?

3. Refer to the types of retailers described in Table 15.2. Which type is most descriptive of the L. L. Bean retail stores?

4. Categorize L. L. Bean's mail-order operations on the following bases:

a. intensity of distribution coverage

b. direct selling, direct-response retailing, or automatic merchandising

5. Relate the components of the physical distribution system shown in Figure 15.4 to the L. L. Bean system. Make any assumptions necessary.

16 *Promotional Strategy*

Learning Goals

1. To list the objectives of promotion.

2. To explain the concept of a promotional mix.

3. To describe the various personal selling tasks.

4. To identify the steps in the sales process.

5. To describe the different types of advertising.

6. To identify the various advertising media.

7. To explain how sales promotion and public relations are used in promotional strategy.

8. To identify the factors that influence the selection of a promotional mix.

9. To contrast pushing and pulling promotional strategies.

When Charles and Ann Hillestad bought the house next door in order to set up a bed and breakfast inn, the couple knew little about marketing and promotion. However, the Denver attorney and his wife learned quickly, and their ten-room inn is now a widely acclaimed success.

The Queen Anne Inn is located in Denver's Clements Historic District. The inn is a renovated Victorian structure that features nineteenth-century period furnishings, original artwork, and classical music. The inn's amenities include a morning repast and afternoon tea or wine. Ann Hillestad, who quit her job to run the inn, provides a personal touch.

The Hillestads initially promoted the Queen Anne Inn through advertising. The couple used small display ads in local weeklies, radio spots, and small classified ads in the *New York Times*. While these ads failed to cover their cost, the Hillestads were shocked to see their bookings increase significantly when the *New York Times* ran a "What's Doing in Denver" story, and the paper decreed that the Queen Anne Inn was "where to stay" in the Mile High City.

As a result of this experience, Charles Hillestad became a convert to generating free publicity for his bed and breakfast. Hillestad commented: "Not having had any P.R. training, I didn't know what I wasn't supposed to do . . . so I did everything. I think that marketing is just common sense and treating people as you would want to be treated."

With a promotional budget of only $10,000, which included the cost of developing and printing 10,000 brochures, Hillestad secured 40 media stories about the Queen Anne Inn. He researched magazines at the local library and developed his press releases to meet their spe-

cific editorial needs. Many of these stories appeared in travel and leisure publications, but Hillestad also got *INC.* to write the Queen Anne Inn as a new venture story. Other articles appeared in magazines as diverse as *Elle* and the *Chief Executive*. The *Bridal Guide* ranked the Queen Anne Inn as one of the nation's 10 best wedding-night hotels.

Hillestad's public relations efforts also included nominating the Queen Anne Inn for local civic awards. He won three such awards. Hillestad also invited the mayor and the governor to a grand opening party (the mayor accepted, and so did representatives from three TV stations and several newspaper columnists). Finally, prominent guests such as visiting artists are given free lodging or discounted rates in order to generate additional publicity for the inn.

Thanks to these promotional efforts, the Queen Anne Inn's occupancy rate now exceeds that of other Denver hotels. But Charles Hillestad is quick to point out: "Meeting fascinating new people, showing off Denver to world travelers, and encouraging romance could not possibly be considered as real work."[1]

Photo source: Courtesy of Queen Anne Inn.

Chapter Overview

promotional strategy
The function of informing, persuading, and influencing a consumer decision.

This chapter completes the discussion of marketing strategy by focusing on promotion, the final marketing mix element. **Promotional strategy** is the function of informing, persuading, and influencing a consumer decision. It is as important to nonprofit organizations as it is to a profit-oriented company like Colgate-Palmolive.

Some promotional strategies are aimed at developing *primary demand,* the desire for a general product category. For example, the Wisconsin Milk Marketing Board promotes natural cheese through advertisements such as the one in Figure 16.1 without referring to any particular cheesemaker. But most promotional strategies are aimed at creating *selective demand,* the desire for a particular product. Land O' Lakes campaign — "The taste that stands above. Land O' Lakes 4-Quart Cheese" — is an example.

This chapter begins with a presentation of the objectives of promotion. Next, the components of the promotional mix — personal selling, advertising, sales promotion, and public relations — are discussed. Finally, the factors that influence marketers' decisions in selecting a promotional mix are explained.

Objectives of Promotional Strategy

Promotional strategy objectives vary among organizations. Some use promotion to expand their markets, others to hold their current positions, still others to present a corporate viewpoint on a public issue. Promotional strategies can also be used to reach selected markets. Most sources identify the specific promotional objectives or goals of providing information, differentiating the product, increasing sales, stabilizing sales, and accentuating the product's value.

An organization can have multiple promotional objectives. The National Pork Producers Council, for example, developed "The Other White Meat" promotional campaign primarily to position pork as a white meat rather than a red meat. Other goals of the campaign include increasing the sale of pork and informing consumers that pork is low in calories and cholesterol, high in nutrition, easy to prepare, and versatile. To illustrate the versatility of pork, one advertisement in the campaign features 21 different pork dishes and offers consumers a free booklet for those and other pork recipes.[2]

Providing Information

In the early days of promotional campaigns, when there was often a short supply of many items, most advertisements were designed to inform the public of a product's availability. Today, a major portion of advertising in the United States is still informational. A large section of the daily newspapers on Wednesdays and Thursdays consists of advertising that tells shoppers which products are featured by stores and at what price. Health insurance advertisements in Sunday newspaper supplements emphasize information about rising hospital costs. Industrial salespeople keep buyers aware of the latest technological advances in a particular field. Fashion retailers advertise to keep consumers abreast of current styles.

Promotional campaigns designed to inform are often aimed at specific market segments. Warner Bros. Records, for example, created a compact disc advertisement targeted at the baby-boom generation. In explaining the purpose of the

Figure 16.1   Promotional Strategy Creating Primary Demand

Source: Courtesy of Wisconsin Milk Marketing Board. Agency: Kocs, Wesson & Associates.

ad, a Warner executive said, "We believe that most boomers are unaware that our classic recordings of the 1950s, 1960s, and 1970s are on CD along with the current releases." The ad informs baby boomers that Warner releases not only contemporary recordings but also some of its best albums from previous years, including those by Fleetwood Mac, Van Morrison, ZZ Top, and The Grateful Dead, on compact discs. Included in the ad is a list of classic recordings now available on compact discs.[3]

Differentiating the Product

Marketers often develop a promotional strategy to differentiate their goods or services from those of competitors. To accomplish this, they attempt to occupy a "position" in the market that appeals to their target customers. Promotions that apply the concept of **positioning** communicate to consumers meaningful distinctions about the attributes, price, quality, or usage of a good or service.

Positioning is often used for goods or services that are not leaders in their field. The advertisement for Murphy's Oil Soap in Figure 16.2 is part of a promotional campaign The Murphy-Phoenix Company uses to differentiate its household cleaner from its much larger competition. While market leader Mr. Clean

positioning
Promotional strategy used to differentiate a good or service from those of competitors in the mind of a prospective buyer.

Figure 16.2   Using Advertising to Position a Product

and other large competitors such as Top Job are promoted as "tough on dirt" cleaners, Murphy's Oil Soap is positioned as a gentle household cleaner. The positioning strategy is carried through in other ads in the campaign, in which caretakers of churches and opera houses emphasize the soap's gentle cleaning attribute.[4]

Increasing Sales

Increasing sales volume is the most common objective of a promotional strategy. As noted earlier, some strategies concentrate on primary demand, others on selective demand. Sometimes specific audiences are targeted. In an effort to build the sales volume of its bodywear, Danskin developed an advertising campaign targeted at women age 18 to 44. Advertisements in the $3 million campaign, one of which is shown in Figure 16.3, helped boost the sales of Danskin's adult garmets by 30 percent in one year. The campaign theme — "All the World's a Stage" — communicates the message that Danskin garments can be purchased not only for exercise and dance but also as everyday apparel.[5]

Figure 16.3   Advertisement Designed to Increase Sales

Source: Courtesy of Esmark Apparel, Inc. Model: Stephanie Seymour/Elite Agency.

Stabilizing Sales

Sales stabilization is another goal of promotional strategy. Sales contests are often held during slack periods. Such contests offer prizes (such as vacation trips, color televisions, and scholarships) to sales personnel who meet certain goals. Sales promotion materials — calendars, pens, and the like — are sometimes distributed to stimulate sales during off-periods. Advertising is also often used to stabilize sales. Hotels are crowded on weekdays with business travelers, but these people go home on Friday. So many hotels promote "weekend packages" at lower rates to attract tourists and vacationers.

A stable sales pattern allows the firm to improve financial, purchasing, and market planning; to even out the production cycle; and to reduce some management and production costs. The correct use of promotional strategy can be a valuable tool in accomplishing these objectives.

Accentuating the Product's Value

Some promotional strategies are based on factors, such as warranty programs and repair services, that add to the product's value. Many Ford Motor Company advertisements promote specific car and light truck models. Some ads, however, are designed to promote Ford's 6-year, 60,000-mile powertrain warranty, while others concentrate on the Lifetime Service Guarantee offered by Ford dealers. These promotions point out greater ownership utility to buyers, thus enhancing the product's value.

The Promotional Mix

promotional mix
Firm's combination of both personal and nonpersonal selling designed to achieve promotional objectives.

Firms use various elements to achieve their promotional objectives. Promotion consists of two components: personal selling and nonpersonal selling. Personal selling is a promotional presentation made on a person-to-person basis with a potential buyer. Nonpersonal selling consists of advertising, sales promotion, and public relations. The **promotional mix** is a combination of personal selling and nonpersonal selling. Marketers attempt to develop a promotional mix that effectively and efficiently communicates their message to target customers.

Personal Selling

personal selling
Promotional presentation made on a person-to-person basis with a potential buyer.

For many companies, **personal selling** — a promotional presentation made on a person-to-person basis to a potential buyer — is the key to marketing effectiveness. The promotional strategy of Merrill Lynch, a financial services firm, focuses on its 12,000-person sales force. Selling was the original method of promotion. Today, selling employs over 6 million Americans.

The sales function of most companies is changing rapidly. In some cases, the change has been only cosmetic, such as when the title *salesperson* is changed to *account representative* but the job function remains the same. Yet, many firms are making significant changes in their sales force. Sales duties have been expanded, and in some instances, the function itself has changed. The primary trend is toward increased professionalism on the part of sales personnel. Today's salespeople act as advisors to their customers, helping them utilize more efficiently the items they buy.

Sales Tasks

A salesperson's work can vary significantly from one company or situation to another, but it usually includes three basic tasks: order processing, creative selling, and missionary selling.

order processing
Sales task of receiving and handling an order.

Order Processing   The task of **order processing** involves the receipt and handling of an order. Needs are identified and pointed out to the customer, and the order is processed. The handling of orders is especially important in satisfying customer needs. The Willamette Industries advertisement in Figure 16.4 points out that the firm's salespeople take a customer-oriented approach to order processing. They check the quality of the products their retail customers receive, know their customers' market, and ensure that products are available when customers need them.

Route sales personnel for such consumer products as bread, milk, and soft drinks are examples of order processors. They check a store's stock, report the

Figure 16.4   A Customer-Driven Approach to Order Processing

Anyone can take orders over the phone.

But when it comes to *filling* orders for wood products, that's where Willamette breaks rank.

Our salespeople know their way around the mill because they go there often. They check the quality of the

Mike Huycke, Western Lumber Sales

lumber and plywood first-hand, to make sure you're getting exactly what you've ordered.

Besides knowing their products, they also know your market. And when it's time to fill orders for your customers, the products you need are at your command.

So if you're looking for a few good men and women to do business with, call Willamette.

After all, if we only took orders, we might as well sell fast food.

Instead of wood.

Willamette Industries, Inc.
Lumber & Plywood Divisions
Western Lumber and Plywood
Albany, OR (503) 926-7771
Southern Lumber and Plywood
Ruston, LA (318) 255-6258
Atlantic Plywood
Rock Hill, SC (803) 328-3844

We don't just take orders.

Source: Courtesy of Willamette Industries, Inc., Lumber and Plywood Divisions.

inventory level to the store manager, and complete the sale. Most sales jobs have at least a minor order-processing function. It becomes the primary duty in cases where needs are readily identified and acknowledged by the customer.

Creative Selling   Sales representatives for most industrial goods and some consumer goods are involved in **creative selling**, a persuasive type of promotional presentation. Creative selling is used when the benefits of a good or service are not readily apparent and/or its purchase is being based on a careful analysis of alternatives. In new-product selling, for example, the salesperson must be very creative if initial orders are to be secured.

Missionary Selling   An indirect form of selling in which the representative markets the goodwill of a company and/or provides technical or operational assistance to the customer is called **missionary selling**. For example, many technically based organizations, such as IBM and Xerox, provide systems specialists who consult with their customers. These people are problem solvers and sometimes work on problems not directly involving their employer's product.

A person who sells a highly technical product may do 55 percent missionary selling, 40 percent creative selling, and 5 percent order processing. By contrast,

creative selling
Persuasive type of promotional presentation used when the benefits of a good or service are not readily apparent and/or when the purchase is based on a careful analysis of alternatives.

missionary selling
Indirect form of selling in which the sales representative markets the goodwill of a company and/or provides technical or operational assistance.

the job of a retail salesperson may be 70 percent order processing, 15 percent creative selling, and 15 percent missionary selling. Marketers often use these three sales tasks as a method of classifying a particular sales job. The designation is based on the primary task performed by the salesperson.

The Sales Process

Years ago, sales personnel memorized a sales talk provided by their employers. Such a **canned sales presentation** was intended to provide all the information the customer needed to make a purchase decision. The entire sales process was viewed as a situation in which the prospective customer was passive and ready to buy if the appropriate information could be identified and presented by the representative.

Contemporary selling recognizes that the interaction between buyers and sellers usually rules out canned presentations in all but the simplest of sales situations. Today's professional sales personnel typically follow a sequential pattern, but the actual presentation varies according to the circumstances. Figure 16.5 shows that seven steps can be identified in the sales process: prospecting and qualifying, the approach, the presentation, the demonstration, handling objections, the closing, and the follow-up.

Prospecting and Qualifying   In **prospecting**, salespeople identify potential customers. They may come from many sources, such as previous customers, friends, business associates, neighbors, other sales personnel, and other employees in the firm. A recent study indicated increased advertising in business publications results in more prospects for salespeople promoting industrial goods and services.[6]

In the **qualifying** process, potential customers are identified in terms of their financial ability and authority to buy. Those who lack the necessary financial resources or who are not in a position to make the purchase decision are given no further attention.

The Approach   Salespeople should carefully prepare their approach to potential customers. All available information about prospects should be collected and analyzed. Sales representatives should remember that the initial impression they give prospects often affects the prospects' future attitudes.

The Presentation   The presentation is the stage at which the salesperson transmits the promotional message. The usual method is to describe the good's or service's major features, highlight its advantages, and cite examples of consumer satisfaction.

The Demonstration   A demonstration allows the prospect to become involved in the presentation. Demonstrations reinforce the message that the salesperson has been communicating to the prospective buyer. In promoting some goods and services, the demonstration is a critical step in the sales process. Paper manufacturers, for example, produce elaborate booklets that their salespeople use to demonstrate different types of paper, paper finishes, and graphic techniques. The demonstration allows salespeople to show art directors, designers, printers, and other potential customers what different paper specimens look like when they are printed.

canned sales presentation
Memorized sales talk intended to provide all the information that the customer needs to make a purchase decision.

prospecting
The sales task of identifying potential customers.

qualifying
Sales task that enables the salesperson to concentrate on those prospects with the financial ability and authority to buy.

Figure 16.5   Steps in the Sales Process

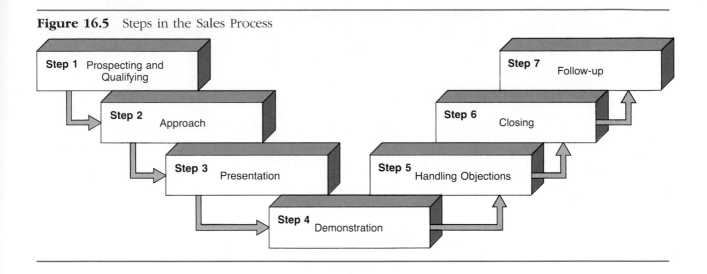

Handling Objections   Many salespeople fear objections from the prospect because they view them as a rebuke. Actually, such objections should be welcomed, because they allow the salesperson to present additional points in support of the sale and to answer questions the consumer has about the good or service.

One successful salesperson adept at turning negative questions into positive replies is Robin Milne. She likens handling objections to a judo move, a jujitsu practice of turning an opponent's energy against the opponent. Milne credits much of her selling success to her ability to make judo moves, especially since it typically takes her from 60 to 100 meetings with a client over a one- to two-year period to close a sale.[7]

The Closing   The closing is the critical point in selling — the time at which the seller actually asks the prospect to buy the product. The seller should watch for signals that the prospect is ready to buy. For example, if a couple starts discussing where their furniture would fit in a home they are inspecting, it should give the real estate agent a signal to attempt to close the sale.

Several effective closing techniques have been identified. The salesperson can ask the prospect directly or propose alternative purchases. Or the salesperson may do something that implies the sale has been completed, such as walking toward a cash register. This forces the prospect to say no if he or she does not want to complete the sale.

The Follow-Up   After-sale activities are very important in determining whether a customer will buy again later. After the prospect agrees to buy, the salesperson should complete the order processing quickly and efficiently and reassure the customer about the purchase decision. Later, the salesperson should check with the customer to determine whether the good or service is satisfactory.

Many firms employ telemarketers to conduct postsale activities. **Telemarketing** is a personal selling approach conducted entirely by telephone. Telemarketers employed by the Apple Bank for Savings in New York make follow-up calls to customers to measure their reaction to the bank's services. Telemarketers also perform other functions in the sales process. At Apple Bank,

telemarketing
Promotional presentation involving the use of the telephone.

they handle customer inquiries and help market the bank's financial services. For example, telemarketers call customers when their certificates of deposit are about to mature and suggest other savings alternatives.[8]

Advertising

advertising
Nonpersonal sales presentation usually directed at a large number of potential customers.

For many firms, advertising is the most effective type of nonpersonal promotion. **Advertising** is a paid, nonpersonal sales communication usually directed at a large number of potential buyers. Firms in the United States account for about half of worldwide advertising expenditures. U.S. marketers spend more than $100 billion each year, or about $420 for each man, woman, and child. The nation's leading advertisers are Philip Morris; Procter & Gamble; General Motors; Sears, Roebuck; and Ford Motor Company, each of which spends more than $1 billion on advertising annually.[9]

Advertising expenditures can vary considerably from industry to industry and company to company. In the nonresidential general building contracting industry, for instance, advertising spending amounts to only two-tenths of 1 percent of sales. At the other extreme is the retail mail-order house industry, which spends 14 percent of sales on advertising.

Types of Advertising

product advertising
Nonpersonal selling of a good or service.

The two basic types of advertising are product and institutional. **Product advertising** involves the selling of a good or service. Advertisements for Nike Air shoes, Marriott hotels, and Apple computers would be classified as product advertising.

institutional advertising
Promotion of a concept, idea, philosophy, or the goodwill of an industry, company, organization, or a government entity.

Institutional advertising involves the promotion of a concept, idea, or philosophy, or the goodwill of an industry, company, organization, or government entity. For example, Texas promoted tourism with the theme: "Visit a country where the natives are friendly and the language barrier is easily overcome." Institutional advertising by profit-seeking firms is called *corporate advertising*.

advocacy advertising
Advertising that supports a specific viewpoint on a public issue and is designed to influence public opinion and/or the legislative process.

A form of institutional advertising that is growing in importance, **advocacy advertising** supports a specific viewpoint on a public issue. Its purpose is to influence public opinion and/or the legislative process. Advocacy advertising is used by many nonprofit organizations. For example, advertisements by the National Rifle Association support Americans' constitutional right to keep and bear arms and speak out against the passage of gun-control laws. The Chemical Bank advertisement in Figure 16.6 is an example of a corporate advocacy advertisement. The ad expresses Chemical Bank's viewpoint concerning a current law that prohibits commercial banks from competing in the securities underwriting market. Advocacy advertising is sometimes referred to as *cause advertising*.

Advertising and the Product Life Cycle

informative advertising
Advertising approach intended to build initial demand for a good or service in the introductory phase of the product life cycle.

Product and institutional advertising can be subdivided by its purposes: to inform, persuade, or remind. **Informative advertising**, intended to build initial demand for a product, is used in the introductory phase of the product life cycle.

Figure 16.6   Example of Advocacy Advertising

> Most CFOs know just how she feels.
>
> So do shareholders and taxpayers. Lack of fair competition in the securities underwriting market is cutting us all out of hundreds of millions of dollars each year.
>
> Outdated laws prohibit commercial banks from competing in the corporate debt, equity and revenue bond markets. Consequently, last year ten firms dominated 90% of the $270 billion corporate security underwriting business and controlled 60% of the securities industry's total capital. So, they can pretty much name their own price. And we all have to pay it.
>
> By contrast, it's estimated that if commercial banks were allowed to compete, the cost of underwriting corporate debt would decline by up to 40%. In 1987 the nationwide savings on the cost of underwriting municipal revenue bonds alone would have totalled more than $200 million.
>
> Chemical Bank is already highly regarded by CFOs in areas where we're allowed to compete: private placements, swaps, municipal bonds, U.S. Government securities and foreign exchange trading. We believe that fair competition in the corporate debt and equity markets would promote the same efficient performance, innovative thinking and cost savings.
>
> We also believe that most Chief Financial Officers know just how we feel.
>
> **CHEMICALBANK**
> The bottom line is excellence.

Source: Reprinted by permission of Chemical Bank. © 1988 Chemical Bank.

When Johnson & Johnson introduced its Acuvue disposable contact lens — the nation's first disposable lens — it launched a massive advertising campaign directed at consumers and eye-care professionals to explain the health benefits of using the new product.

Persuasive advertising attempts to improve the competitive status of a product, institution, or concept. It is used in the growth and maturity stages of the product life cycle. The Kinder-Care advertisement in Figure 16.7 is an example of persuasive advertising. Since it was established in 1969, Kinder-Care used informational ads that promoted the centers' hours and programs. But now that the company has grown to almost 1,400 centers and competitors such as La Petite Academy, Children's World, and Gerber Children's Center have entered the market, Kinder-Care has shifted to a persuasive advertising approach. The theme of the campaign — "The Joys of Kinder-Care" — promotes the idea of trust, which the firm's marketing research indicated was parents' major child-care concern.[10]

One of the most popular approaches to persuasive product advertising is **comparative advertising**, which makes direct comparisons with competitive products. Numerous companies have used comparative advertising in recent years. The Pepsi Challenge is an example of comparative advertising. Pepsi-Cola ads have used blind taste tests in which a majority of consumers choose Pepsi over Coca-Cola. Although Coca-Cola still leads the soft-drink market, the Pepsi Challenge helped increase Pepsi sales considerably.

Reminder-oriented advertising, used in the late-maturity and decline stages of the product life cycle, attempts to keep a product's name in front of the consumer or to remind people of the importance of a concept or an institution. Soft drinks, beer, toothpaste, and cigarettes are products for which reminder-oriented advertising is used. The Association of Railroads used an advertisement

persuasive advertising
Advertising approach used in the growth stage of the product life cycle to improve the competitive status of a good, service, institution, or concept.

comparative advertising
Persuasive advertising approach in which direct comparisons are made with competing goods or services.

reminder-oriented advertising
Advertising approach used during the late maturity and decline stages of the product life cycle that seeks to reinforce previous promotional activity by keeping the name of the good or service in front of the public.

Figure 16.7   An Example of Persuasive Advertising

Source: Courtesy of Kinder-Care Learning Centers, Inc.

that began: "Today's railroads, America's great untapped resource." Even police cars in some areas of the United States carry reminder-oriented themes such as "We protect and serve." E. D. Bullard Company designed the poster shown in Figure 16.8 to remind workers of the importance of wearing hard hats.

Advertising Media

All marketers face the question of how to best allocate their advertising expenditures. Cost is an important consideration, but it is equally important to choose the media best suited for the job. All media have advantages and disadvantages; these are discussed in the sections that follow.

Newspapers   Newspapers, with 26 percent of total advertising volume, are the largest of the advertising media.[11] Because newspaper advertising can be tailored for individual communities, local advertising is common. Newspapers also reach nearly everyone in the community. Other advantages are that readers can refer back to them, and they can be coordinated with other advertising and merchandising efforts. In fact, advertising is considered the third most useful feature in newspapers, after national and local news. A disadvantage is the relatively short life span.

Television   Television ranks second overall to newspapers with 22 percent of all advertising volume, but it is the leader in national advertising. Television advertising can be classified as network, national, local, and cable. Television has a significant impact on potential customers despite its high cost. Mass coverage, repetition, flexibility, and prestige are other advantages. The medium's ability to reach huge audiences was demonstrated vividly by the 1989 Pepsi commercial featuring pop singer Madonna. The firm spent $5 million to beam the commer-

Figure 16.8 An Example of Reminder Advertising

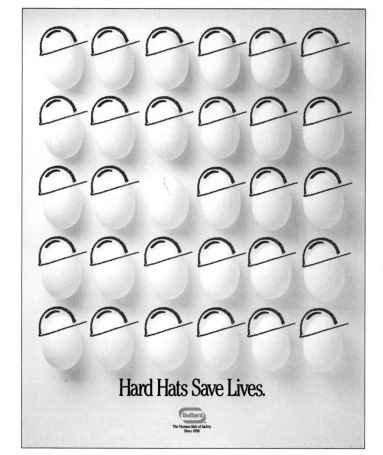

Hard Hats Save Lives.

Source: Courtesy of E. D. Bullard Company.

cial to 250 million viewers in 40 nations, from Finland to the Phillipines. (The ad was pulled two weeks after its premiere due to controversial content.) In addition to high cost, its disadvantages include the temporary nature of the message, some public distrust, and lack of selectivity in the ability to reach specific target market segments without considerable wasted coverage.

Direct Mail Direct mail is the third-leading advertising medium, with about 17 percent of total advertising expenditures. Its advantages include selectivity, intense coverage, speed, flexibility, complete information, and personalization. On the other hand, direct mail is extremely costly. It is also dependent on effective mailing lists, and it sometimes meets with consumer resistance.

Radio With 99 percent of all U.S. households owning on average five radio sets, radio is another important broadcast advertising medium. Radio, which accounts for 7 percent of total advertising volume, can be classified as network, spot, and local advertising. Advantages of radio are immediacy, low cost, targeted audience selection, flexibility, and mobility. Disadvantages include the short life span of a radio message and a highly fragmented audience.

Figure 16.9   Effective Use of Outdoor Advertising

Source: Courtesy of Michigan Department of Transportation (MDOT).

Magazines   Magazines account for about 5 percent of advertising volume. *Modern Maturity,* with almost 20 million subscribers, is the nation's largest magazine in terms of paid subscriptions. It is followed by *Reader's Digest* and *TV Guide,* each with about 17 million subscribers. Advantages of magazines include selectivity, quality reproduction, long life, and prestige. The main disadvantage of magazines is that they lack the flexibility of newspapers and broadcast media, but the appearance of local advertising in various regional editions of national news magazines suggests that this problem is being overcome.

Outdoor Advertising   Outdoor advertising, such as billboards, accounts for only 1 percent of total advertising expenditures. Its strength is in communicating simple ideas quickly. The Michigan Department of Transportation (MDOT) billboard in Figure 16.9 illustrates this concept. Other advantages are repetition and the ability to promote goods and services available for sale nearby. However, the message must be brief, and there are aesthetic considerations.

Other Media Options   Other media include advertising in movie theaters and on airline movie screens. Recently, several firms such as PepsiCo, Chrysler, and Hershey placed ads on videocassette movies. Many firms display their advertising message on trucks, while others use transit advertising. An advertising vehicle gaining in popularity is the hot-air balloon, used by organizations such as Maxwell House, Coors, Eastman Kodak, and the states of Maryland and Connecticut. These alternative media can be employed separately or in conjunction with advertising campaigns using more traditional media.

Sales Promotion

sales promotion
Form of promotion designed to increase sales through one-time selling efforts such as displays, trade shows, special events, and other methods.

Sales promotion consists of the forms of promotion other than advertising, personal selling, and public relations that increase sales through one-time selling efforts. Sales promotion was traditionally viewed as a supplement to a firm's sales or advertising efforts, but now it has become an integral part of the promotional mix. Expenditures for sales promotion total more than $100 billion each year.

Point-of-Purchase Advertising (POP)

Point-of-purchase advertising (POP) consists of displays and demonstrations promoting an item at a time and place near the location of the actual purchase decision, such as in a retail store. Video advertising on supermarket shopping carts is an example. POP can be very effective in continuing a theme developed by some other aspect of the firm's promotional strategy.

point-of-purchase advertising (POP)
Type of sales promotion that displays and demonstrates an item where the actual purchase decision is made.

Specialty Advertising

Specialty advertising is the giving away of useful merchandise such as pens, calendars, T-shirts, glassware, and pocket calculators that are imprinted with the donor's name, logo, or message. Because the items are useful and are often personalized with the recipient's name, they tend to be kept and used by the targeted audience, giving the advertiser repeated exposure. Originally designed to identify and create goodwill for advertisers, specialty advertising is now used to generate sales leads and develop traffic for stores and trade show exhibitors.

specialty advertising
Type of sales promotion that consists of giving away useful items imprinted with the donor's name, logo, or message.

Trade Shows

A **trade show** is often used to promote goods or services to resellers in the distribution channel. Retailers and wholesalers attend trade conventions and shows where manufacturers exhibit their lines. Such shows are very important in the toy, furniture, and fashion industries. They have also been used to promote the products of one nation to buyers from another.

L.A. Gear used a trade show extravaganza to let retailers know about its diversified product line. The company, which originally produced a line of teenage fashion athletic footwear, expanded its offerings to include 80 women's shoe styles, a men's and a children's line, and an apparel collection. But most retailers carry a limited number of L.A. Gear styles compared to those of nationally recognized brand names such as Nike and Reebok. To build its brand recognition among retailers, L.A. Gear designed a trade show display replicating the city of Los Angeles, complete with a Beverly Hills Hotel and a 25-foot City Hall. The display includes a stage where dancers, gymnasts, and other performers entertained retailers attending the National Shoe Fair in New York and the Super Show, the trade show of the sporting goods industry. Don Wasley, L.A. Gear's vice-president of promotion, said, "When we created this trade show booth, it was to let the retailers know we'd arrived. We wanted them to take us seriously."[12]

trade show
Type of sales promotion that uses exhibitions designed to promote goods or services to retailers, wholesalers, international buyers, and other resellers in the distribution channel.

Non tangible items (products)

Other Sales Promotion Methods

Other sales promotion techniques include samples, coupons, premiums, contests, and trading stamps. Most of these methods are used to introduce new products or encourage consumers to try a new brand.

A *sample* is a free gift of a product distributed by mail, door to door, in a demonstration, or inside packages containing other products. Samples are particularly useful in promoting new products. PepsiCo used a novel sampling promotion to boost the market share of Pepsi Cola in Brazil. Young male students wearing T-shirts with the Pepsi logo dispensed Pepsi samples from refrigerated backpacks to beachgoers sunning themselves on the beaches of Rio de Janeiro. The promotion supported PepsiCo's "Taste of a new generation" advertising campaign in Brazil, where 50 percent of the population is younger than 20.[13]

A *coupon* is an advertising clipping or package inclusion redeemable by the customer. Offering what amounts to a small price discount, it can help get a customer to try a new or different product. Many retailers, including southern supermarket giant Winn Dixie, double the face value of manufacturers' coupons. In a recent survey comparing various methods of consumer promotion, 83 percent of respondents said coupons increased the value of their shopping dollar. The respondents gave sweepstakes and other sales promotion techniques much lower ratings.[14]

A *premium* is an item given free or at a reduced cost with the purchase of another product. Premiums are most effective when they relate in some way to the purchased item. To promote its new cinnamon-and-raisin biscuits and increase overall breakfast traffic, Hardee's fast-food restaurants offered the premium of a California Raisin figurine for 99 cents with the purchase of two biscuits. Sales during the four-week promotion increased 18 percent, well above Hardee's goal of increasing sales 4.5 percent.[15] *Trading stamps* are similar to premiums in that they are redeemable for additional merchandise. Historically, they have been used to build loyalty to a certain retailer or supplier.

Contests, sweepstakes, and *games* offer cash or merchandise as prizes to participating winners. The transit poster shown in Figure 16.10 advertises an American Natural Beverage Corporation sweepstakes in which the grand prize is a 1957 Thunderbird Classic. The first person to spell "Cruisin'" by collecting specially marked bottle caps from Soho Natural Soda wins the car.

Public Relations

public relations
An organization's communications with its various publics.

Public relations is an organization's communications with its various publics, such as customers, vendors, news media, employees, stockholders, government, and the general public. Many of these communication efforts have a marketing purpose. Johnson & Johnson Health Care Company launched a five-year public relations campaign to educate the public on reducing childhood injuries. The Safe Kids program includes a free safety kit for children that contains Band-Aids and other J&J products. The firm hopes the goodwill generated by the program will not only enhance its image as a caring and concerned company but also translate into more sales. "Building our image builds our business," said a J&J executive.[16]

Public relations is often used to supplement advertising and personal selling efforts. In some cases, however, public relations is used as a dominant element in a firm's promotional campaign. For example, in addition to advertising, Paramount Pictures developed a public relations program to promote the Eddie Murphy movie "Coming to America." The program was designed to change Murphy's image and broaden his appeal beyond his hard-core, young male fans. In the movie, Murphy plays a romantic and humorous leading man, a departure from his familiar tough-guy role in previous films such as "Beverly Hills Cop" and "Trading Places." To stress the versatility of Murphy's talent, Paramount prepared publicity releases for newspapers and magazines and sent electronic press kits to television stations. These efforts resulted in extensive media coverage for the movie. For example, several magazines featured Murphy in cover stories, and radio stations gave the movie's soundtrack additional playing time.[17]

Figure 16.10 Sweepstakes Promotion for Soho Natural Soda

Source: Courtesy of American Natural Beverage Corporation, 145 6th Avenue, New York, New York 10013.

Selecting a Promotional Mix

Selecting the appropriate promotional mix is one of the toughest tasks confronting marketers, but there are some general guidelines to assist in determining the relative allocations of promotional efforts and expenditures among personal selling, advertising, sales promotion, and public relations. These guidelines might be stated as a series of four rules.

The first guideline is the decision whether to spend promotional monies on advertising or personal selling. Once this decision is made, the marketer needs to determine the level of sales promotion and public relations efforts.

A second consideration is the market served by the good or service. For instance, a drill press is sold to the industrial market, so the manufacturer's strategy must emphasize the sales force. By contrast, Scope mouthwash is sold to consumers; an effective advertising campaign is important to consumer products like Scope.

The third rule deals with the value of the product. Most companies cannot afford to emphasize personal selling in marketing a low-priced item and instead choose advertising for the promotional strategy of goods like toothpaste, cosmetics, soft drinks, and candy. Higher-priced items in both industrial and con-

Figure 16.11   Examples of Pushing and Pulling Strategies
              Pushing Strategy   Pulling Strategy

Sources: Courtesy of New Zealand Kiwifruit Authority.

sumer markets rely more on personal selling. Examples include time-share vacation condominiums and Boeing aircraft.

Finally, the marketer needs to consider the time frame involved. Advertising is usually used to precondition a person for a sales presentation. An effective and consistent advertising theme may favorably influence individuals when they are approached by a salesperson in a store. But except for self-service situations, a salesperson is typically involved in completing the actual transaction. Advertising is often used again after the sale to assure consumers of the correctness of their selection and to precondition them for repeat purchases.[18]

Alternative Promotional Strategies

The selection of a promotional mix is directly related to the promotional strategy the firm will employ. The marketer has two alternative strategies available to meet these goals: pushing strategy or pulling strategy.

A **pushing strategy** is a sales-oriented approach. The product, product line, or service is marketed to wholesalers and retailers in the marketing channels. Sales personnel explain to them why they should carry this particular item or service. The marketing intermediaries are usually offered special discounts, promotional materials, and **cooperative advertising** allowances. In the last case, the manufacturer shares the cost of local advertising of the product or line. All these strategies are designed to motivate wholesalers and retailers to "push"

pushing strategy
Sales-oriented promotional strategy designed to motivate marketing intermediaries to push the good or service to their customers.

cooperative advertising
Sharing of local advertising costs between the manufacturer and the marketing intermediary.

the product or service to their customers. The kiwifruit advertisement in Figure 16.11 is an example of a pushing strategy. In it, the New Zealand Kiwifruit Authority suggests ways retailers can merchandise the fruit so consumers will buy it.

A **pulling strategy** attempts to generate consumer demand for the product, product line, or service, primarily through advertising and sales promotion appeals. Most advertising is aimed at the ultimate consumer, who then asks the retailer for the product or service; the retailer in turn requests the item or service from the supplier. The marketer hopes that strong consumer demand will "pull" the product or service through the marketing channel by forcing marketing intermediaries to carry it. The General Foods advertisement for Maxwell House coffee in Figure 16.11 illustrates a pulling strategy. The ad announced a sales promotion that tied in with the Taste of Chicago outdoor food festival. Consumers who brought two empty coffee cans to the Maxwell House cafe at the festival received $6 worth of free food tickets. The consumer pull influenced Chicago-area retailers to prominently feature the brand at their stores. With consumers redeeming about 49,000 empty cans, the promotion was so successful it produced record sales and moved the Maxwell House brand from third place to first in the Chicago market.[19]

Most marketing situations require the use of both strategies, although the emphasis can vary. Consumer products are often heavily dependent on a pulling strategy, while most industrial products are sold through a pushing strategy.

pulling strategy
Promotional strategy utilizing advertising and sales promotion appeals to generate consumer demand for a good or service.

Summary of Learning Goals

1. List the objectives of promotion. The objectives of promotion include providing information, differentiating the good or service, increasing sales, stabilizing sales, and accentuating the value of a good or service. Organizations frequently have multiple promotional objectives.

2. Explain the concept of a promotional mix. Promotion consists of two distinct components: personal selling and nonpersonal selling, which includes advertising, sales promotion, and public relations. A promotional mix is a combination of the personal and nonpersonal elements a firm uses to achieve its promotional objectives.

3. Describe the various personal selling tasks. The three sales tasks are order processing, creative selling, and missionary selling. Order processing involves the receipt and handling of an order. Creative selling is a persuasive type of promotional presentation. It is used when the benefits of a good or service are not readily apparent and/or when its purchase is being based on a careful analysis of alternatives. Missionary selling is an indirect form of selling in which the representative markets the goodwill of a company and/or provides technical or operational assistance to the customer.

4. Identify the steps in the sales process. Personal selling is a promotional presentation made on a person-to-person basis to a potential buyer. The seven steps in the sales process are prospecting and qualifying, the approach, the presentation, the demonstration, handling objections, closing, and the follow-up.

5. Describe the different types of advertising. Product advertising involves the selling of a good or service. Institutional advertising involves the promotion of a concept, idea, or philosophy, or the goodwill of an industry, company, organization, or government entity. A special category of institutional advertising is advocacy advertising, which supports a specific viewpoint on a public issue. Both product and institutional advertising can be subclassified as informative, persuasive, and reminder-oriented. Comparative advertising is a persuasive approach that makes direct comparisons with competitive goods or services.

6. Identify the various advertising media. Newspapers are the leading advertising medium in terms of advertising revenue. They are followed by television, direct mail, radio, magazines, and outdoor advertising. Use of other media includes cinema advertising and transit advertising. Each medium has specific advantages and disadvantages.

7. Explain how sales promotion and public relations are used in promotional strategy. Sales promotion consists of the one-time supporting aspects of a firm's promotional strategy. It includes point-of-purchase advertising (POP), specialty advertising, trade shows, samples, premiums, trading stamps, and promotional contests. Public relations deals with the organization's communications with its various publics. Many of these communications have a marketing purpose.

8. Identify the factors that influence the selection of a promotional mix. The first decision necessary in the development of a promotional mix is whether to use advertising or personal selling. Sales promotion and public relations efforts are then determined. The factors that influence the selection of a promotional mix are the type of product (industrial or consumer), the value of the product, and the timing of its use.

9. Contrast pushing and pulling promotional strategies. A pushing strategy is a sales-oriented strategy designed to motivate marketing intermediaries to "push" the product to their customers. A pulling strategy utilizes advertising and sales promotion appeals to generate consumer demand for a product or product line.

Key Terms

promotional strategy	qualifying	reminder-oriented advertising
positioning	telemarketing	sales promotion
promotional mix	advertising	point-of-purchase advertising
personal selling	product advertising	specialty advertising
order processing	institutional advertising	trade show
creative selling	advocacy advertising	public relations
missionary selling	informative advertising	pushing strategy
canned sales presentation	persuasive advertising	cooperative advertising
prospecting	comparative advertising	pulling strategy

Review Questions

1. Not all promotional efforts are aimed at increasing sales. What other goals can be accomplished by promotion?

2. What promotional mix would be appropriate for the following products?
   a. Arc welder
   b. Personal computer
   c. Specialty steel products sold to manufacturers
   d. Advertising services

3. What is the primary sales task involved in the following occupations?
   a. Office supply salesperson selling to local business firms
   b. Counterperson at Burger King
   c. Representative for an outdoor advertising firm
   d. Salesperson representing Dow Chemical

4. Outline the sequence of and explain the various steps in the sales process.

5. Differentiate among product advertising, institutional advertising, and advocacy, or cause, advertising. Also explain the differences among informative, persuasive, and reminder-oriented advertising.

6. Which is the most popular advertising media in terms of total advertising volume? How do the other media rank in terms of promotional expenditures?

7. What types of sales promotion technique would you use in the following businesses?
   a. Independent insurance agency
   b. Saab dealership
   c. Pizza restaurant
   d. Hardware wholesaler

8. Explain how public relations might be used in the marketing strategy of the following:
   a. Natural gas utility
   b. Ford Motor Company
   c. Philadelphia Phillies baseball team
   d. A local McDonald's franchise

9. What variables should be considered when selecting a promotional mix?

10. Differentiate between a pushing and a pulling strategy. Under what circumstances should each be employed?

Discussion Questions

1. McGraw Hill's Laboratory of Advertising Performance reported that the average business-to-business sales call now costs $251.63, up from $229.70 two years earlier. Over the past decade, the cost of personal selling was up 160 percent, while advertising costs had increased only 88 percent. David P. Forsyth, the head of McGraw-Hill Research, commented: "This continuing increase in personal selling costs makes advertising an even more effective

tool for reaching business prospects." Why is personal selling so expensive? What can be done to moderate future cost increases? How would you allocate your promotional budget in a business-to-business marketing situation?

2. Describe the most effective salesperson you have encountered in the past year. Explain why you think this person is so effective.

3. Divide the class into three groups. Then set up a role-playing exercise in which students in Group A sell a product to someone in Group B. Group C is responsible for providing a critique of each of the sales interviews. Rotate the roles among the three groups. Continue this process for three rounds, so everyone will have a chance to play each role. Discuss what you have learned from this experience.

4. Describe the best television commercial you have seen in the past year. Discuss what made this commercial so memorable.

5. Tom Burdette's humorous radio commercials for Motel 6 end with the line: "We'll leave the light on for you." Why do you think these popular commercials were considered so effective?

Video

Stew Leonard's

Stew Leonard's retail outlet in Norwalk, Connecticut, is more than just "the world's largest dairy store." Back in 1969, it opened its doors by offering fewer than a dozen dairy items in a 17,000-square-foot store. Since then, the store has been expanded 27 times and today covers more than 100,000 square feet. Annual sales for the store, housed in an amusement park atmosphere, total more than $100 million — an amount equal to what the Food Marketing Institute estimates for a typical *ten-store* supermarket chain. Each year Stew Leonard's single store sells some 10 million quarts of milk, 8 million ears of corn, 5.6 million bananas, and more than 50 tons of Marianne Leonard's (Mrs. Stew Leonard's) meatloaf.

What makes this Connecticut store distinctive, in addition to being a cross between a huge supermarket and Disney World, is its volume — both in dollar sales and in inventory. Most supermarkets carry between 15,000 and 20,000 items in an attempt to provide everything the food and household goods shopper could want in a single location. But supermarket managers are all too aware of the 80/20 principle: 20 percent of the items in inventory will account for 80 percent of total store sales. The typical supermarket loses money on a heavy, bulky, low-margin item like sugar, but continues to stock it to be able to offer one-stop service. Not Stew Leonard's. "The world's largest dairy store" limits its stock to about 800 fast-moving, high margin items. Customers follow a winding pathway through the store's sections — bakery, dairy (milk is bottled on the premises), butcher (for meat and fish), produce, salad bar, deli with hot and cold food, and an ice cream department. Customers can do most of their food shopping there and pick up such necessities as diapers, but they must go to other stores for canned goods, spices, toothpaste, and household products. The average turnover on merchandise at Leonard's is 30 times a year, more than double that of a typical U.S. supermarket.

Notes: "They Also Serve," *Adweek's Relate,* April 24, 1989, pp. 18–19; Tom Peters, *Thriving on Chaos* (New York: Alfred A. Knopf, 1987), pp. 98–99ff; Bruce Bolger, "Unconventional Wisdom," *Incentive,* November 1988, pp. 36–40; Lisa McGurrin, "Hillbilly Music in the Frozen Peas at Stew Leonard's," *New England Business,* February 17, 1987, pp. 38–41; Stew Leonard, "Love That Customer!" *Management Review,* October 1987, pp. 36–39; and Ron Zemke, *The Service Edge* (New York: NAL Books, 1989), pp. 317–321.

In a typical week, over 100,000 shoppers will visit the Norwalk store, a total of over 5 million a year. This huge volume of sales, combined with a significant percentage of the store's own private label merchandise and direct delivery of produce from West Coast suppliers, keeps prices down and profits up so that both Leonard and his customers are happy. These factors, along with the festive atmosphere (and a free ice cream cone for each shopper) attract shoppers from as far away as New York, an hour's commute.

To serve the customer as best he can, Stew Leonard provides a feedback mechanism in the form of an easy-to-locate suggestion box. Over 100 suggestions a day are received and all are given immediate attention by management. (They are typed and distributed to each department by 10 a.m. the following day.) As a result of the suggestion box, English muffins are now stacked next to the bacon and eggs, strawberries are sold loose, and paper towels are on hand to wipe off rain-soaked shopping carts. Focus groups, where managers hear criticism and suggestions from about 20 Stew Leonard's customers, are held every three weeks. Participants are served snacks and soft drinks and are given a $20 store gift certificate for their participation. Many of their recommendations are implemented.

Stew Leonard's is a family business. All four of Stew and Marianne's children work for the store. So do over 600 full- and part-time employees. More than half of Stew Leonard's team members (Stew dislikes the term *employee*) have relatives in the store.

Many of the employees are young, over half of them under 21. Starting pay begins at $7 an hour, higher than what other retailers pay for comparable work, and the store receives 15 to 20 applicants for every opening. "We don't look for skills or knowledge," Leonard says. "We look for attitude." First, he seeks people with positive, can-do dispositions, outgoing individuals who are likely to be genuinely friendly toward fellow team members and customers. "We can teach cash register. We can't teach nice," says Stew. However, he does see to it that new employees take an in-house Dale Carnegie course stressing attitude, people skills, and customer relations.

Stew is always concerned with the selection, training, and motivation of team members because they represent a critical component of the Stew Leonard's promotional mix. Although the store does some ad-

...rtising, its greatest emphasis is on sales promotion and personal selling. Predictably, in a self-service retail store, the selling that occurs is subtle, often consisting largely of advice on locating a particular item, suggestions from bakery personnel on the use of certain products, or just a smile.

Leonard's customer relations strategy is fairly direct. "It's five times easier to keep the customer you've got than to go out and find a new one." The store's motto is chiseled on a 6,000-pound boulder at the front entrance:

Rule 1: The customer is always right.

Rule 2: If the customer is ever wrong, reread Rule 1. Pleasing customers, according to Leonard, is essential for long-term success. He reasons that since the average customer spends about $100 a week in the store, that amounts to $5,200 a year or $52,000 over the course of ten years. A single dissatisfied customer, then, represents a potential sales loss of about $50,000. This explains his comment that "When I see a frown on a customer's face, I see $50,000 about to walk out the door."

In order to determine what sells and what does not — which translates into what the customer wants and does not want — Stew Leonard's has one of the largest, most sophisticated computer systems of any single store in the world. With it, management can spot trends almost immediately from sales patterns and quickly respond with inventory changes. The high turnover rates mean that customers are buying the freshest products possible. In addition, customers almost never have to wait in checkout lines — the bane of most supermarkets. Fifty-two checkouts are available and at least 27 of them are always in operation. Any time more than three customers have to wait in a single line, additional checkouts are opened and free cookies and ice cream are passed out to those shoppers waiting in line.

In addition to this kind of service, the "come to the fair" atmosphere makes Stew Leonard's a family occasion, particularly on weekends, when the 10-acre parking lot is filled with parents and children. Both kids and adults appear to enjoy the talking cows, the two robot dogs, the "sheriff" who heads the security force, and the employees dressed as carrots walking the wide aisles singing country and western music. Among its many promotions is the $3 gift certificate given to customers who bring in a photo of themselves in some exotic locale and holding a Stew Leonard's shopping bag. These photos, which come from such unlikely spots as the Kremlin, Stonehenge, the floor of the Pacific Ocean, and the North Pole, are prominently displayed at the front of the store. Each checkout counter has a light that periodically flashes to announce a randomly-selected winner of a complimentary frozen yogurt cone. Any customer who purchases more than $100 worth of groceries receives a prize.

Behind the store is a petting zoo where children can find more than one hundred animals, including goats, chickens, geese, and cows. Inside the store, most departments are actually set out in the aisles so that, for example, shoppers feel like they are walking right into a kitchen when they enter the bakery section. This ploy works: The bakery generates 20 times the sales of the average supermarket bakery.

There are samples everywhere: lemonade, horseradish cheese, gazpacho, cupcakes, nuts, ice cream, and chocolate chip cookies. As one shopper puts it, "You come in here just for milk and you walk out with a shopping cart full of food." Leonard observes that sales increase 25 percent when he gives out samples.

For all this success, Stew has not really considered expanding his business into a chain, although a second store opens in Danbury, Connecticut, in 1990. He seems content to serve as master of ceremonies at his own store — greeting customers at the front door, serving them some of the various goods in the bakery, or stocking and adjusting displays. He seems to have as much, if not more, fun as his customers.

Questions

1. A number of promotional objectives are discussed in the chapter. Identify these objectives and explain which of them are being addressed by promotions conducted at Stew Leonard's.

2. Explain the concept of the promotional mix and describe the specific mix being used by Stew Leonard's.

3. A number of sales promotion tools are used by Stew Leonard's. Identify each tool and give an example of its use by the Norwalk retailer.

4. Identify the factors that jointly determine the most appropriate promotional mix for a firm to use. Explain how these factors were used by Stew Leonard's to determine its relatively unusual promotional mix.

Careers in Business

Advertising, marketing research, retailing, personal selling, and physical distribution management are some of the exciting, dynamic fields in marketing. Many beginning marketers start as sales personnel, then move into other positions as they gain experience; others remain part of the sales force. Retailing is another popular marketing career. Still other marketers work in advertising and marketing research.

Sales is generally considered to have the greatest potential for earnings growth. Brand or product management is next in terms of salary potential, followed by marketing research, advertising, and public relations.

Specific marketing jobs include market research analyst, public relations specialist, advertising agent, manufacturers' sales representative, wholesale trade salesperson, buyer, and operations manager.

The Bureau of Labor Statistics, which has projected the U.S. employment outlook through the year 2000, forecasts that job opportunities for wholesale trade salespeople will grow faster than the average for all occupations; opportunities for public relations specialists will grow much faster than average; and opportunities for manufacturers' sales representatives will show little change.

Marketing Research Analyst

Marketing research is one of the fastest growing fields in business. Market research analysts deal with the fascinating topic of what consumers will and will not buy. Currently, more than 30,000 marketing research analysts are employed throughout the United States.

Job Description. Marketing research analysts use a variety of techniques such as surveys, personal interviews, and test markets to assess consumer perceptions and interests. They may learn, for example, what consumers think of a company's product and how it is used in the home. These conclusions are then reported to marketing executives who use them to make product decisions. Marketing researchers work in all kinds of businesses, government, nonprofit organizations, advertising agencies, and marketing research firms.

Career Path. Entry-level jobs in marketing research usually involve clerical duties or data-collection tasks. Once the individual is established as a market

research analyst, he or she is assigned specific research projects. Advancement to supervisory positions is possible. Ultimately, the person may become director of marketing research or achieve an even higher management position.

Salary. In a recent year, analysts with a B.S. degree earned between $14,000 and $25,600; senior analysts earned between $30,000 and $35,000. The salary range of a marketing research director is between $45,000 and $65,000.

Public Relations Specialist

Public relations jobs are found in business, trade associations, government, and other entities such as colleges. The mission of the public relations specialist is to create a favorable image for his or her employer. Currently, some 87,000 public relations specialists are employed in the United States.

Job Description. Public relations specialists deal with the publics that interact with their employers. For instance, they send out press releases to newspapers, magazines, radio stations, and television news departments; produce promotional materials; and write speeches for executives.

Career Path. Trainee positions are available in public relations. Senior people are given specific responsibilities depending on their employer and the nature of the task. Supervisory positions are the next level in a public relations career.

Salary. In a recent year, starting salaries for public relations specialists with undergraduate degrees averaged $18,400. The median pay for public relations specialists as a group was $42,000.

Advertising Agent

An array of jobs are available in advertising. These include copywriter, account executive, artist, media buyer, and production coordinator. Advertising agents can be found in company advertising departments, advertising agencies, and government. More than 125,000 people are currently employed in advertising.

Job Description. The entry-level job is often in a specific activity, such as copywriting for an ad agency. Advertising copywriters sell an image of a product or service to the public. They are responsible for the written text of ads that appear in magazines and newspapers and for scripts for radio and television commercials.

Career Path. Entry-level positions are available in various phases of advertising. Success in these positions can lead to management positions. For instance, a junior copywriter might advance to senior copywriter and then to chief copyeditor. Eventually, the person might become creative director of an advertising agency.

Salary. In a recent year, advertising agencies paid the following median salaries: account executive, $28,000; copywriter, $25,000; art director, $24,000; broadcast production manager, $26,000; and media buyer, $19,000. Agency creative directors earn between $75,000 and $125,000, and executive art directors earn between $60,000 and $80,000.

Writers

Writers provide a variety of services to businesses from advertising to public relations to employee communications. Job growth is estimated to be faster than average through the year 2000. There were 214,000 writers and editors in a recent year.

Job Description. Writers gather information through interviews and library research, then use their creative abilities to produce a finished product. In some firms, they may be required to write advertisements for publications or work with printers on how a publication will look. They often work under tight deadlines and may sometimes be hired on a free-lance basis.

Career Path. In-house writers in large firms generally start with smaller projects and work their way up to larger ones. Free-lance writers tend to follow a similar path with the firms they serve. In smaller firms, a writer may plunge right in to handle all necessary projects. Advancement often means moving to larger firms or starting one's own public relations or advertising agency.

Salary. The earnings for writers varies dramatically depending on the employer. Experienced writers' earnings ranged from $20,500 to $36,500 in a recent year; beginning salaries ranged from $18,400 to $29,300.

Industrial Photographer

Photographers provide their services for a variety of purposes ranging from catalogs to employee communications.

Job Description. Photographers in private industry may work directly for a firm or on a free-lance basis. Almost half of all photographers are free-lancers. Photographers must use their imagination and technical knowledge of photography to produce good pictures. They must be able to work with models to create attractive illustrations for catalogs and similar publications. They often must meet tight deadlines for their work. In addition, free-lancers must generate more business by showing their work to prospective clients.

Career Path. In-house photographers generally begin with relatively routine work and move up with experience. Advancement often means moving to larger firms or supervising other photographers.

Salary. In a recent year, industrial photographers averaged $16,600 while photographers working for the federal government earned an average $23,900. Free-lancers' earnings vary enormously.

Manufacturers' Sales Representative

Manufacturers' sales representatives play a key role in marketing because they work with both retailers and wholesalers. This type of salesperson can be found in both consumer and industrial marketing, working with both technical and nontechnical products. Some 543,000 people are now employed as manufacturers' sales representatives.

Job Description. Manufacturers' sales representatives call upon potential customers to explain the features and benefits of their products, answer questions, and provide or arrange demonstrations. In addition to making personal contacts with potential customers, manufacturers' sales representatives also investigate customers' credit ratings, report competitive information to the home office, and complete paperwork providing information about their territories, customers, and competitors.

Career Path. Most manufacturers provide a sales training program. Such programs usually involve rotation through various parts of the company and on-the-job field experience. Successful completion of the sales training program leads to a regular sales position. Promotion to sales management positions is a typical pattern of career progression.

Salary. In a recent year, the median salary for manufacturing sales representatives was $25,600. Actual earnings are a function of such factors as the industry, the company, and the compensation system used. A sales trainee in electrical equipment and supplies averaged $36,000 in a recent year, while an experienced salesperson in glass products averaged only $24,000 in the same survey. Bonuses, incentives, and commissions typically range from 20 percent to 40 percent of total earnings.

Wholesale Trade Sales Representative

This sales representative works for wholesaling firms in marketing a line of products to retailers, commercial and industrial firms, and government. Currently, there are nearly 1.2 million wholesale trade sales representatives in the United States.

Job Description. Sales personnel for wholesaling firms make regular calls on their retail, wholesale, or organizational customers. These sellers provide many services to their buyers, including delivery and credit. Some even stock the retailer's shelves. Wholesale trade sales representatives also assist their customers with displays, inventory control, and pricing.

Career Path. Large wholesale establishments have sales trainee positions that enable applicants to observe experienced personnel and to learn specific sales tasks. Experienced sales representatives are assigned to sales territories. Promotions beyond this level are usually sales management positions.

Salary. In a recent year, the median annual salary of wholesale trade sales representatives was $25,480.

Buyer

Buyers are responsible for choosing the merchandise a store offers its customers. All retailing enterprises have a buyer or a buying function. The type of merchandise a buyer purchases is dictated by the kind of store and its clientele. Some 192,000 people are currently employed as buyers in the retail and wholesale fields, with slower than average growth forecasted through the year 2000.

Job Description. Buyers must keep pace with changing consumer needs and tastes as well as the store's competitive strategy. Buyers must also keep abreast of special discounts offered by manufacturers and the terms offered by distributors. In addition, buyers must also deal with their own store's sales personnel. Feedback from retail sales personnel helps the buyer stay attuned to consumer preferences.

Career Path. Trainees are usually called assistant buyers. They support buyers for certain merchandise lines. The step above buyer is usually merchandise manager, a person who directs several buyers.

Salary. The salary of buyers varies widely due to the incentive compensation granted by many retailing firms. The nature, size, and location of the store also affects salaries. In a recent year, the median annual earnings of buyers was $20,700 with a range from $14,600 to $29,000.

Retail Operations Manager

The operations manager is responsible for the non-merchandise-related part of retailing. Many people fail to recognize the behind-the-scenes contributions of these marketers.

Job Description. The duties of the operations manager include supervision of receiving, shipping, delivery, service, security, and inventory control departments. Experience in these areas is highly desirable for those people pursuing careers in retailing.

Career Path. The first step is to gain experience in one or more activities supervised by the operations manager. A likely stepping-stone to an operations manager position is a department head position in an area such as receiving.

Salary. Salaries of operations managers vary widely depending upon the nature, size, and location of the store. In a recent year, average salaries ranged from $20,000 to $35,000.

Chapter 17
Management
Information and
Computers

Chapter 18
Accounting

Information for Decision Making

Career Profile: Anne Thorne

Among the 99,000 people who work for Xerox is Anne Thorne. Thorne, a marketing analyst for Xerox's U.S. marketing group, where she has worked since July 1985, tracks U.S. sales of Xerox copier duplicators and printing systems. Sometimes Thorne's job takes her to various market areas, but she is usually behind a computer at her desk.

Thorne retrieves information from Xerox-operated data bases and uses it to discover what is selling where, and how well. She runs this information through a Xerox 16-8 personal computer, performing numerical computations and statistical analysis of sales figures. She uses the Xerox Star workstation 6085 to produce reports that feature graphic and tabular analysis of productivity, information on industry or area trends, statistical analysis of sales figures, and a variety of other information for use in planning.

Having three computers at her desk and analyzing markets for Xerox is not what Thorne planned when she started school. She enrolled in Monroe Community College in Rochester, New York, to learn about fashion retailing.

"She had maturity and she was very goal oriented," said John Lloyd, a business professor of Thorne's at Monroe. "She also communicated well. She seems to perceive how to deal effectively with situations and with different types of people." After earning her associate's degree at Monroe, Thorne earned a bachelor's degree in retailing and business administration at the Rochester Institute of Technology.

During college, Thorne worked in Chicago through a cooperative program at Marshall Field's, a major department store. She enjoyed the work and the environment at Field's but realized she was more interested in the computer work she had done as an undergraduate. So she returned to Rochester, earned a master's degree in marketing and computer information systems, and took a job with Xerox.

Several factors influenced her switch from retailing. One was money: The beginning salary at Xerox was higher than Thorne's other options. But more important to her was that she found her work at Xerox challenging and rewarding. "It's extremely enjoyable," Thorne said, "and that's what really counts."

Thorne says her most important skills are her computer skills and her communications skills. Her job at Xerox frequently requires her to create custom programs.

"I can program in several different languages, which I learned mostly in crash courses at RIT," she says. "I can also learn new ones pretty easily. It's simply learning how to think logically. These types of skills can be applied to any type of problem."

Despite the technical nature of her career, she says her studies of retailing still serve her.

"Being a retail major helps you. You can understand a lot about business because of the background [you now have] and it makes everything more interesting."

Thorne has found a certain outlook helpful in her career. "You have to study results. When you're in situations in business, look at what happens, and you'll start to realize some of what it takes to make it in business. Also, you have to show enthusiasm. Part of that comes from maintaining a perspective — nobody ever talks about this, but keeping a sense of humor about things is important. It makes it so much easier to get things done."

Photo source: Courtesy of Mark D. Sager.

17 Management Information and Computers

Learning Goals

1. To explain the purpose of a management information system and how it functions in a firm.

2. To describe the five generations of computers.

3. To list the major contributions and limitations of computers.

4. To distinguish between computer hardware and software.

5. To identify the components of a computer system and the functions of each.

6. To explain how binary arithmetic works and why it is appropriate for use by computers.

7. To distinguish among mainframe computers, minicomputers, and microcomputers.

8. To explain the role that computers play in business today.

9. To describe the concept of the portable office.

Summer and winter are busy seasons for Bill's Heating & Cooling Service in Overland Park, Kansas. Bill Harl installs water heaters, air conditioners, and fuel-saving devices. He travels between customers in his truck, taking messages from his wife, Judy, back at the office via two-way radio.

A few years ago, the Harls bought an Oki CDL 450 portable cellular phone from Southwestern Bell Mobile Systems in Kansas City. The investment allows Judy to leave the office for hours at a time, but still accept customer calls.

Judy says, "I'm president of the PTA at Shawnee Mission West High School and active with Girl Scouts. I can talk to customers while doing my volunteer work and driving the children around town. I go back to the office when I need to use the radio to tell Bill that a customer wants service."

Two of the Harls' three children suffer from unusual forms of cataracts. Each child has undergone two eye operations, and recovery isn't yet complete. Judy often finds herself waiting in doctor's offices — talking to customers on her cellular phone.

"People, especially first-time customers, appreciate it when you take their calls personally," says Judy. "If

they need heat, they don't want somebody to take a message and call them back in an hour." Bill says the cellular phone "speeds things up. It's like being in the office 24 hours a day. Except we're not."

The Harls had used a borrowed portable phone for two months before purchasing their Oki. The first month they used it, business revenues exceeded $6,000, Bill says. "I can't say we would have lost all that business if we didn't have a cellular

phone," Bill says. "But we would have missed getting a lot of new customers."[1]

Cellular phones are just one example of the information technology available to assist management. Others are examined in Chapter 17 and special attention is devoted to computers.

Photo source: Courtesy of Southwestern Bell Corporation.

Chapter Overview

The chief task of the manager is decision making. Managers earn their salaries by making effective decisions that allow their firms to solve problems as they occur. They also anticipate and prevent problems. Too often, managers are forced to make decisions with limited information or inadequate facts. If effective decisions are to be made, a system must be developed to ensure that information is up to date, available when needed, and in a form suitable for analysis by the decision maker.

Although noncomputerized systems for storing and retrieving management information have been developed, they are too slow, require too much storage space, and are incapable of combining separate bits of data into one meaningful bit of information in all but the smallest organizations. Today, the computer is an integral tool in processing, storing, and managing information. The tremendous speed of computers reduces the turnaround time between recognition of the need for pertinent information and its receipt, permitting significant time savings in rectifying problems and implementing solutions. In addition, the reduced size and cost of computers and the variety of software available make computers a realistic tool for even the smallest businesses.

Chapter 17 analyzes computers as a means of managing decision-oriented information and revolutionizing both business operations and our daily lives. It begins with the concept of a management information system, a brief history of computers, and a discussion of the five generations of computers. The basic types of computers and their components are discussed, and the advantages and possible problems involved with computer usage are assessed. The chapter concludes with predictions concerning the future of computers in business. The executive of the 1990s will be dependent on technology — from computers (laptops, personal computers, mainframes) to fax machines — for communications, decision making, and day-to-day office activities.

The Role of the Management Information System

The recipe for effective decisions was once given as "90 percent information and 10 percent inspiration." In order to obtain relevant information for decision making, most large- and medium-size firms establish a management information system.

◆ "What are the storage costs for Model 238?"

◆ "What is the sales potential for our brand in Portland?"

◆ "How much has Allison accomplished so far?"

◆ "How do our wage rates compare with similar firms in St. Louis?"

◆ "How many units of Model 17 are there in the Tucson warehouse?"

These are a few examples of the hundreds of questions asked every day in a business operation. An effective information system aids decision making by having answers to such questions available for the business executive. The **management information system (MIS)** is an organized method for providing past, present, and projected information on internal operations and external intelligence for use in management decision making.

Decision-related information from both secondary and primary data sources is needed for almost every company activity, whether internal or exter-

management information system (MIS)
Organized method of providing information for decision making.

Figure 17.1   Using MIS to Respond to Changing Consumer Demands

Can you spot a trend this fast?

It doesn't take very long to see the beginning of a trend on this page.

It shouldn't take very long in real life either. If pink polka-dot sweaters are flying off the shelves, the mill should know about it right away.

At IBM, we're helping make "right away" a reality.

Our quick-response information systems can link retailers to manufacturers to textile mills, making it easy for them to share critical information.

Information like what's selling and what's not.

This gives the mill and manufacturer the flexibility they need to respond quickly to the retailer's needs.

If the mill can anticipate demand it can have the right fiber on hand, the right machinery set up and the right amount made up in the right color.

The manufacturer can be prepared to produce the right goods in the right sizes and colors.

As a result, the retailer can expect a shipment of goods that customers want, thus avoiding costly stockouts and forced markdowns.

Not only does this quick-response system work in theory, it works in reality. Our POS systems, application software and EDI services are helping customers work together to work more efficiently.

No matter what you make or sell, IBM has solutions and support you can count on. To arrange for an IBM marketing representative to contact you or for literature, call 1-800-IBM-2468, ext. 32.

Don't let the latest trend in the industry pass you by. **IBM**

© IBM 1988

Source: Courtesy of International Business Machines Corporation.

nal. The latter includes information about changing consumer demands, competitors' actions, and new government regulations. If the firm knows about pending legislation, it can plan to present its viewpoint to legislators. Awareness of changing demands may result in product modifications or new marketing programs. For example, in the advertisement in Figure 17.1, IBM explains how its quick-response information systems can help retailers, clothing manufacturers, and textile mills respond to fast-changing fashion trends. Competitive moves may prompt the firm to make numerous decisions.

Many companies have designated an executive to direct their management information systems and the related computer operations. The title **CIO**, or **chief information officer**, is becoming common in corporate organizations. Like the CFO discussed in Chapter 7, the CIO reports directly to the CEO.[2]

chief information officer (CIO)
Top-management executive responsible for directing a firm's management information systems and related computer operations.

Data and Information

Vast quantities of data are collected by the various departments in the organization. The decision-making function of the MIS includes information provided by production, finance, engineering, purchasing, public affairs, accounting, marketing, and human resources departments. Such information includes data on sales, cash inflows and outflows, inventory, employees, and purchases, as well as external data in the form of government studies, economic forecasts, reports on competitive activities, and consumer surveys. But *data* and *information* are not synonymous terms. **Data** refers to statistics, opinions, facts, or predictions categorized on some basis for storage and retrieval. **Information** is data relevant to the manager in making decisions. The MIS should provide timely, accurate, and usable information for the decision maker.

In his book *Managing,* International Telephone & Telegraph Chairman Harold Geneen describes how the lack of crucial information produced a $320 million mistake for one of the world's largest corporations:

The most costly management mistake we made at ITT was in building a giant wood cellulose-processing plant in Port-Cartier, Quebec, as part of our expansion plans for Rayonier, a forest products company we acquired in 1968. . . . Millions of acres of virgin timberland — about the size of the state of Tennessee — could be leased in Quebec Province from the Canadian government for very little money, and new technology made it feasible to build a processing plant at the edge of the timberland which could convert the wood to cellulose. . . . Rayonier's plans were checked and rechecked, the risks and rewards were carefully analyzed, and we decided to go ahead. . . . What stumped us was a fundamental miscalculation made at the outset of the project: All those lovely trees out there in the wilderness of Canada's Far North grew to no more than three inches in diameter because of the extreme cold. The cost of harvesting and transporting them to the plant precluded the possibility of a profitable venture. We could not "manage" the size of the trees. Ten years after we had started, we had to abandon the project and take a loss of approximately $320 million. . . . But that $320 million loss could have been averted if someone had actually gone up and looked at those trees before we had begun.[3]

Data Base

data
Statistics, opinions, facts, or predictions categorized on some basis for storage and retrieval.

information
Data organized in some manner so it is relevant in making decisions.

data base
Integrated collection containing all of the organization's data resources.

The heart of the information system is its **data base** — a centralized, integrated collection of the organization's data resources that is designed to meet the information-processing and retrieval requirements of decision makers. It is an electronic file cabinet, capable of storing massive amounts of data and retrieving needed data within seconds. Such a system typically replaces dozens of individual data files created by different departments. For instance, separate files may have been developed for customer addresses, customer purchases, customer payments, and sales calls on customers. If a customer-firm hires a new director of purchasing, all four files must be updated. A single master data base eliminates this duplication, and a single updating corrects the entire data file.

One use of data bases is to better target direct marketing efforts. As a result, many data bases are both selective and complete. For example, Kimberly-Clark, producer of Huggies diapers, has a data base of 10 million new mothers. Similarly, a data base at RJR-Nabisco contains 30 million of the nation's 40 million smokers.[4]

Executive Information Systems

executive information system (EIS)
User-friendly computer system used by senior management.

The latest trend in management information systems is the **executive information system (EIS)**. These systems do not require executives to interface standard computers. Instead, the computers are directed to produce information by

TRW's computer center in Orange, California, houses one of the largest data bases in the United States. The data base holds credit data on 138 million consumers and 11 million business locations. From the data base, TRW furnishes more than 75 million credit reports on consumers and businesses annually. The credit data is used by financial firms in making lending decisions and in marketing products such as credit cards and equity lines of credit.

Photo source: Courtesy of TRW Inc.

a "mouse" or a simple touch of the computer screen. Executive information systems use big-screen, high-quality monitors. EIS software produces full-color displays and charts. More than one out of eight senior executives use such systems, and the percentage is expected to double in the next few years.

The value of executive information systems is illustrated by Phillips 66. The Phillips Petroleum division developed an EIS after the company laid off 40 percent of its managers in the mid-1980s. Phillips' EIS is largely credited with increasing the division's profits by $100 million in a recent year.[5]

The Role of the Computer

For the business decision maker, the computer is an amazing tool capable of quickly generating relevant information to be used in making decisions, solving problems, and taking advantage of opportunities. The tremendous speed of computers permits time savings in rectifying problems, implementing solutions, and taking advantage of business opportunities. As a result, the computer industry is now the third-largest industry in the United States; only automobiles and oil are bigger.[6]

A **computer** is an electronic machine that accepts and manipulates data to solve problems and produce information. Computers can perform mathematical computations and such logical tasks as comparisons of collected data with established standards. For example, computers help guarantee the success of Mrs. Fields cookie stores. Each store has a personal computer, for which special software was developed. The software standardizes ways of handling problems, performs 25,000 calculations, produces staffing schedules, recommends inventory, and evaluates job applicants. All of the personal computers are hooked into a mainframe in the company's home, Park City, Utah. The mainframe collects and analyzes all of the data, so a manager, for example, can review and compare the profits of all of the stores under his or her control.[7]

computer
Programmable electronic device that can store, retrieve, and process data.

A Brief History of Data Processing

The computer is less than a half-century old. The first major event that ultimately led to the computer was development of the manually operated calculator in the seventeenth century. The prototype of the modern computer grew out of the work of Charles Babbage, a British mathematician who developed the concept of the difference engine — a machine capable of adding, subtracting, multiplying, dividing, and storing intermediate results in a memory unit. During the 1880s, Herman Hollerith, a statistician from Buffalo, New York, designed the census machine to tabulate the data collected for the 1890 census. This machine used punched cards and was run by electricity.

Four Decades of Computer Evolution

The transformation of business from the manual era of pencils and mechanical tabulating machines to the computer era was accelerated by World War II. In 1944, IBM Corporation, working closely with the U.S. Navy, built the Mark I. This electromechanical computer — 50 feet long and 8 feet high — was controlled by punch cards and paper tables and could perform both arithmetic and logical problems.

In 1946, the first truly electronic computer from which current computers are derived was developed at the University of Pennsylvania. It was called ENIAC (Electronic Numerical Integrator and Computer). By using vacuum tubes rather than the Mark I's electronic relay switches, the ENIAC's calculating speed was increased 1,000 times. In 1951, the U.S. Bureau of the Census became the first organization to use a computer when Sperry's UNIVAC I was installed.

In the decades since 1944, four major evolutionary stages in computer design have occurred. These stages are frequently called generations. Many computer authorities see a fifth generation emerging in the next decade. It is discussed later in the chapter.

The First Generation

The first generation of the computer era began with the introduction of the Mark I and continued to 1959. Most first-generation computers were gigantic machines that used vacuum tubes for data storage and required huge amounts of air conditioning to offset the heat generated. For example, the ENIAC weighed 30 tons and contained 18,000 vacuum tubes, which failed an average of one every seven seconds. By today's standards, first-generation computers were slow and expensive. The ENIAC sold for $487,000 and could perform fewer than 2,000 additions per second.

Although most first-generation computers were designed for scientific uses, a growing number of business organizations recognized their potential for processing data and for such record-handling tasks as accounting, payrolls, inventory records, and consumer billing. By 1955, 244 computers were in use in the United States.

The Second Generation

transistor
Tiny device used to amplify current.

The next generation of computers began in 1959 as vacuum tubes were replaced by tiny solid-state components, such as diodes and transistors. The **transistor** amplified the electric current, which made it possible to produce computers

ENIAC, a first-generation computer, used 18,000 vacuum tubes for data storage. Although the tubes increased the computer's calculating speed, they frequently burned out in the middle of computations. They also generated warmth and light that attracted moths, which got caught inside the computer and caused short circuits. Users then had to "debug" the computer. Fixing computer problems today is still referred to as "debugging."

Photo source: Courtesy of Sperry Corporation.

that were smaller, faster, more reliable, and less expensive to manufacture and maintain. Second-generation computers, such as the IBM 1401, were the first computers that were affordable to medium and small businesses. During this period, the computer expanded its scope from a largely scientific orientation to a widely adopted business tool.

Processing speeds increased to the point where they were measured in *microseconds* (one-millionth of a second), while the relatively slow operations of input and output became a major bottleneck. As a result, high-speed card readers and printers were introduced. In addition, specialized computer programs began to be marketed to users, marking the beginning of what we know today as the software industry.

The Third Generation

The third generation traces its beginnings to 1964, when IBM announced its 360 computer system. This era was characterized by computers that were even smaller, faster, more reliable, and more versatile than their predecessors. This was made possible by the replacement of the transistor by integrated circuits. An **integrated circuit** consists of a network of dozens of tiny transistors and connections etched directly on a silicon wafer.

Faster input and output methods were developed during this era. Combining these improvements with integrated circuits resulted in smaller, faster computers requiring less electricity and capable of vastly increased processing speeds. For third-generation computers, processing speeds began to be discussed in terms of *nanoseconds* (one-billionth of a second). Storage capabilities of these computers greatly exceeded earlier machines. Remote terminals, connected to the computer but dispersed throughout the factory, office, college, and even in other cities, allowed more convenient access to the computer's vast fields of stored data.

integrated circuit
Network of transistors, circuits, and other components etched on a silicon chip.

The Fourth Generation

Many computer authorities believe the fourth generation of computer systems began during the mid-1970s as a result of developments following the 1971 introduction of Intel Corporation's integrated circuit with more than 2,000 transistors compressed on a dime-size silicon chip.

Over the next few years, silicon-wafer chips became so compact that circuits had to be squeezed into a cubic inch of space through **very large-scale integration (VLSI)**. These superchips contain the equivalent of millions of interconnected transistors and are designed to perform the arithmetic and logic functions that are the heart of any computer system. The era of the "computer on a chip" had emerged.

This breakthrough in miniaturization made personal computers a reality. Mass production of standardized **computer chips** reduced their cost to less than $10, and home computer prices plummeted. As the market grew, retail prices continued to decline and the sophistication of personal computers increased. These typewriter-size machines can easily outperform most earlier-generation computers at less than 1 percent of the cost.

Business discovered that the increased storage capacity and speed of fourth-generation computers made them useful not only in processing data for routine reports, but also for storing vast amounts of data that could be used to provide management with timely information for use in making decisions. The replacement of the term *data processing* by the broader term *management information systems* reflects a major shift in the way computers were perceived by business users.

The computer chip has made possible the creation of super computers more powerful than ever dreamed of before. Speed is now measured in *picoseconds* (one-trillionth of a second), and applications continue to grow. About 300 super computers are now operated. Each costs between $5 million and $25 million.[8] In less than a half-century, the computer has grown from a scientific curiosity to an integral part of our work, study, and play.

Advantages and Problems Associated with Computers

The rapid diffusion of computer use in virtually every phase of our lives is tangible evidence of the machine's ability to make contributions undreamed of a few decades ago. Think of the instances in which you use or observe the use of computers. These applications suggest both the important contributions of the computer and possible problems in entering and interpreting data.

Computers have five major advantages: They are fast, accurate, capable of storing large quantities of information in a small space, can make volumes of data available quickly, and can perform the mechanical, often boring, work of recording and maintaining incoming information.

As is the case with any time- or labor-saving device, there are also a number of potential problems. These pitfalls should be recognized in order to minimize the possibility of their occurrence: Computers and software customized to meet a firm's specific needs can be expensive. In addition, computers can make disastrous mistakes when programmed incorrectly, can become a management crutch rather than a tool in decision making, can be relied on too heavily, and can alienate customers by ignoring the human element.

very large-scale integrated (VLSI) circuit
Superchip created by increasing the compactness of transistors and circuits assembled on a single silicon chip.

computer chips
Thin wafers of silicon on which integrated circuits are located.

Computer technology enhances the ability of Consolidated Natural Gas Company to bring gas to consumers. The company's geologists and geophysicists use computer-generated models of the Earth's crust to analyze a wider-than-ever spectrum of data in evaluating natural-gas drilling prospects. Use of this new exploration technology contributes to the company's drilling success.

Photo source: © Gary Gladstone for Consolidated Natural Gas Company.

How Computers Work

Every computer system is made up of basic elements used in performing five functions: data input, storage of data in the computer's memory devices, control of data processing, actual processing of the data, and output of information. The terms *hardware* and *software* are applied to different elements of the system.

Hardware and Software

Computer **hardware** consists of all the tangible elements of the computer system — the input devices, the machines that store and process data and perform the required calculations, and the output devices that provide the results to the information user. Computer hardware includes all machinery and electronic gadgets that make up the computer installation.

Of equal importance in the effective use of computers is computer **software**, which consists of the instructions stored in the computer memory that tell the computer what to do. Computer languages and computer programs are both considered software.

hardware
All of the tangible elements of the computer system.

software
Programs written to tell the computer what to do.

Computer Components

Some computers need large rooms to hold all their parts. Others fit on top of a desk or in a briefcase. Regardless of size, each computer consists of two components: the central processing unit (CPU) and peripheral equipment that permits communication between the user and the computer. The CPU is the basic controller of the entire system; peripherals include auxiliary storage and the input and output devices.

Reading Data into the Computer

input

Portion of the computer system responsible for converting incoming data into a form the computer can understand.

The **input** portion of the computer is responsible for converting incoming data into a form the computer can understand. Data can be read into the computer in a number of forms: keyboard entries; punched cards; machine-readable magnetic ink characters and lines, such as the Universal Product Code on supermarket merchandise; punched-paper tapes; magnetic tapes and disks; optical character recognition formats such as the wands used by department stores to read price tags; scanning of printed material by special devices; and voice recognition by which the computer converts spoken words into electronic signals.

The Central Processing Unit

central processing unit (CPU)

Part of the computer system containing the memory, or storage unit, the arithmetic/logic unit, and the control unit.

memory unit

Part of the computer that stores information.

The **central processing unit (CPU)** controls the entire computer system by storing and processing data. The CPU is made up of three parts: the memory, or storage, unit; the arithmetic/logic unit; and the control unit.

The **memory unit** serves as the computer's filing cabinet. Stored here are data for solving a problem and instructions on how to use the data (software). The memory unit can be both internal and external. The primary storage unit, or main memory, consists of an input storage area where data is held until processing is required, a working storage space where data processing occurs, an output storage area where processed data is held until released, and a program storage area containing the processing instructions.

In addition, it is possible to increase the computer system's memory capacity through the use of external, or auxiliary, memory storage units that can be attached to the system on a permanent basis or as needed. The use of such external storage units provides added flexibility for the computer system.

arithmetic/logic unit

Part of the computer where all calculations occur.

The **arithmetic/logic unit** is the computer's adding machine, where all calculations take place. When adding, subtracting, multiplying, or dividing data is required, the necessary data moves from the memory unit to the arithmetic/logic unit. Once the calculations have been performed, the answers are transferred back to the memory unit. The arithmetic/logic unit is similar to the pocket calculator but is much faster.

control unit

Part of the computer responsible for directing the sequence of operations, interpreting coded instructions, and guiding the computer.

The **control unit** serves as the director of computer operations and is responsible for directing the sequence of operations, interpreting coded instructions, and guiding the computer. Control involves performing operations in the proper order. The computer must be guided by the software every step of the way in solving a problem or performing an assignment, such as computing the weekly payroll or printing paychecks. The control unit directs and coordinates both the input and the output elements of the computer system, moves data to and from memory, and directs the activities of the arithmetic unit. When incoming instructions are not in the proper form, an error occurs in the unit's operation.

Computer Output

output

Portion of the computer system responsible for providing processed information to the user.

The **output** devices provide processed information to the user. Often, output is in the form of a paper printout. In other cases, output is simply shown on a display screen. Output may be recorded on magnetic tapes or disks if the data is to be reused. Sometimes output even takes the form of the spoken word.

Batch Processing and On-Line Processing

Even though today's computers are remarkable in terms of storage capacity and processing speed, decisions must be made about the methods to be used in processing different types of data. In **batch processing**, data is collected for a predetermined period of time before being processed. A mail-order operation, for example, may compile orders received daily for several hours and then process all requests. A retail store utilizing numerous part-time employees may not process payrolls until noon on Fridays, when all time sheets must be submitted.

By contrast, **on-line processing** involves entering and processing each input as it is received. The term *on-line* refers to the direct linkage of the input device to the computer's central processing unit.

The Holiday Inn reservation system provides a good example of an on-line system. Holiday Inn guests can learn almost instantly whether reservations are available at a specific hotel. If reservations are made, the Holiday Inn computer records them and reduces its available room inventory immediately.

batch processing
Method in which data is collected for a predetermined period before being processed.

on-line processing
Method of computer processing in which data is entered and processed when received.

How to Talk to a Computer

One major advantage of computers is speed. The English mathematician William Shanks devoted one-third of his life to computing pi to 707 decimal places (only to make a mistake at the 528th place). Today's modern computers can duplicate Shanks' work (without error) in less than five seconds. But exactly how does this processing take place? The answer involves a special counting system called binary arithmetic.

Binary Arithmetic

The actual processing of data within the computer is much like the operation of a pocket calculator. Like most calculators, the computer can add, subtract, multiply, and divide. Calculators actually multiply by adding at incredible speeds and divide by subtracting at those speeds. Computers, being more sophisticated in design, can perform all four operations directly. Both calculators and computers use the simple yes-no system of binary arithmetic.

Binary arithmetic is a special counting system that uses two digits, 0 and 1. While decimal numbers are built on a base of 10, binary numbers are built on a base of 2. Base 10 means that when you move a digit one space to the left and add a zero, it is worth ten times as much. With binary numbers, every time a number is moved one space to the left, it is worth two times as much.

The question then arises: How do you count to two without a digit 2? To produce a 2 in binary, simply move the 1 one space to the left and add zero. Thus, 10 in binary has the same value as 2 in decimal, but it does not look the same. In converting decimal to binary numbers, 1 becomes 000001, 4 becomes 000100, 7 becomes 000111, 12 becomes 001100, 20 becomes 010100, and 33 becomes 100001.

In addition to decimal numbers, letters of the alphabet and symbols can be written in binary. The binary code for the letter A is 010001; the code for the = sign is 110000. Each digit — either a 1 or a 0 — is called a bit (for binary digit).

binary arithmetic
Counting system that uses only two digits: 0 and 1.

Home Shopping Network uses an on-line, 24-hour-a-day processing system. The data captured on-line by network operators and automated voice response units, and maintained in the company's member data base, produces consumer profiles that help HSN understand members' buying behavior, life-style, and demographic makeup. HSN uses this information to promote special products, services, and offers to specific segments of the data base. Such precision targeting is key to increasing HSN's return on investment.

Photo source: Courtesy of Home Shopping Network, Inc.

bit
A binary digit — either 0 or 1.

byte
A character of data made up of eight bits to form a number or letter of the alphabet.

megabyte
A unit containing slightly more than a million bytes.

The **bit** is the basic unit of the computer's memory. When combined in configurations of eight bits, they form bytes. A **byte** is a group of bits used to represent a single character of data — the letter P or the number 8, for example. Therefore, six bytes of memory would be required to store the word *output*. The storage capacity of a computer's memory is commonly expressed in blocks of 1,024 bytes, abbreviated by the letter *k*. A 256k computer, for example, is capable of storing 262,144 characters, and one **megabyte** of memory can store 1,048,576 characters.

Because binary consists of yes-or-no states, the computer can quickly accept incoming information simply by opening or closing an electrical circuit. A 1 is indicated when the circuit is on; a 0 is indicated when the circuit is off. For some computers, magnetizing to the left or right produces the same results.

computer program
Set of instructions that tells the computer what is to be done, how to do it, and the sequence of steps to be followed.

computer programmer
Specialist who tells the computer what to do.

Programming

The computer can do nothing toward solving a problem without a detailed set of instructions. It can follow instructions, but it cannot think. A **computer program** is a set of instructions that tells the computer what is to be done, how to do it, and the sequence of steps to be followed. The computer follows these directions until the job is completed.

The **computer programmer** — the specialist who tells the computer what to do — must analyze the problem, break it into its component parts, and outline the logical steps needed to arrive at the solution. An effective way to determine these steps is to make a **flowchart** — a pictorial description of the logical steps to be taken in solving a problem.

flowchart
Pictorial description of the logical steps to be taken in solving a problem.

Computer Languages

The programmer uses the flowchart to design the logic of programs that contain computer instructions on how to handle each step in a process. But computers do not understand English. Programmers, therefore, must write instructions to the computer in a symbolic language that it can convert into binary. Although the language of the computer is binary arithmetic, a number of programming languages have been developed to enable the programmer to communicate with the computer in English and algebraic systems. Five of the most commonly used computer languages are FORTRAN, COBOL, BASIC, Pascal, and PL/1.

Conversational Programs

Conversational programs assist the manager who does not have the necessary training in writing programs to use the computer for decision making. Advanced programming languages, such as BASIC, COBOL, FORTRAN, Pascal, and PL/1, and software packages such as *dbase* and *Excel* aid in making the computer user-friendly.

But complex underlying programs are required to permit computers to respond to commands issued in plain English. The development of more powerful chips made it possible to design such programs without exhausting the computer's capacity. The manager no longer has to type a line that reads: LIST ALL COMPANIES SALES90, FOR STATE = 'CA'.AND.SALES90 100,000. Instead, the ordinary English sentence, "Give me a list of companies with their sales in California that had 1990 sales over $100,000" is enough to obtain the requested data from the computer data base.[9]

Rather than taking their programs to the computer center, executives often use a **remote terminal** — a typewriter-like machine connected to the main computer installation by telephone lines but physically removed from the computer. The user-manager enters instructions and receives replies either on a display screen or in the form of typewritten output. In cases where the storage capacity and processing capabilities of a large computer system are not necessary, executives are likely to have access to personal computers utilizing conversational programs.

remote terminal
Machine connected to the main computer installation from a distant location.

Mainframes, Minicomputers, and Microcomputers

Twenty years ago, no size distinctions were necessary when discussing computers since only one type existed: the mainframe. The **mainframe computer** is the largest type of computer system and offers the greatest storage capacity and fastest processing speeds. In addition, mainframes are expensive, often costing millions of dollars. Increased miniaturization of computer components eventually led to development of a newer, smaller, and less expensive computer system — the minicomputer.

mainframe computer
Largest type of computer system.

By using a special software program from Baxter Healthcare Corp., this physician can get patient information from a local hospital at his office. The software helps doctors manage the clinical and financial aspects of their practice. It enables doctors and hospitals to share medical profiles, insurance information, and laboratory test results.

Photo source: Photographer: Michael Mauney. Photo courtesy of Baxter Healthcare Laboratories.

Minicomputers

minicomputer
Intermediate-size computer.

In 1965, Digital Equipment Corporation developed a smaller, less expensive computer called a minicomputer. The **minicomputer** CPU is about the size of a small file cabinet. Compared to the larger mainframe computer, the minicomputer is more compact and relatively inexpensive but has smaller storage capabilities and slower processing speeds. These smaller versions of the mainframe computer systems are often used in businesses, scientific operations, and educational institutions. In many cases, they can be connected to mainframe computers to utilize the greater capacity of these machines.

The technological evolution of the past two decades has blurred the distinctions between minicomputers and large-scale systems. Many of today's minicomputer systems possess more power and versatility than did the large-scale systems of the early 1960s. As a result, the term *minicomputer* now refers to a number of smaller, general-purpose computers.

Microcomputers

microcomputer
Desktop, limited-storage computer system.

cathode ray tube (CRT)
Visual display device that projects data onto a television-like screen.

The **microcomputer,** the smallest type of computer, is typically a desktop, limited-storage computer system that includes a **cathode ray tube (CRT)** — a visual display device that projects data onto a television-like screen — and a keyboard resembling a set of typewriter keys. Unlike mainframes and minicomputers, which are usually designed to handle the processing needs of multiple

Photo source: Courtesy of Compaq Computer Corporation and Pepsi-Cola International.

This barge transports cases of Pepsi from a bottling plant on the Chao Phaya River in Thailand to warehouses in Bangkok. Pepsi-Cola International uses Compaq personal computers to consolidate shipment and financial data from Thailand and other Far East locations at its headquarters in Somers, New York. The company previously used a mainframe system to manage global beverage sales and financial information. The power and speed of the new personal computer system enable Pepsi-Cola financial analysts and planners to respond quickly to changing market conditions. The system also consolidates financial statements, generated every four weeks, 40 percent faster than before.

users, microcomputers are single-user oriented. Most micros are self-contained units, capable of being moved to different locations.

Development of these small systems for the home, office, or classroom was made possible by the 1971 introduction of the **microprocessor**. A square silicon chip measuring one-fourth inch on a side contains the control unit and arithmetic/logic unit of the microcomputer. The several thousand electronic components that require a cabinet the size of an ordinary desk can be etched onto such a chip for as little as $10. Additional chips containing instructions and data memory are then added to convert the microprocessor into a microcomputer. Such systems, offered at relatively low prices, possess capabilities greater than those of the large computer systems costing as much as $1 million only two decades ago.

Microcomputers include personal computers for home use, personal computers for individual use in offices, and more sophisticated small-business computers. Many of them are so small and portable that they are called laptop computers. Microcomputers contain all of the functional elements found in a mainframe or minicomputer. It is estimated that personal computers used in offices will total 46 million units by the year 2000, four times the current total.[10]

Networking

Introduction of relatively low-cost microcomputers has increased the flexibility of computer use by decision makers. Not only can these smaller computers be installed in different departments or individual offices for specific computing requirements, but they can also be linked to the firm's mainframe or minicomputer that serves as the central processor for the overall MIS. A **computer network** is a system involving the interconnection of numerous computers that can function individually or communicate with each other. A sales representa-

microprocessor
One or more computer chips containing the basic arithmetic, logic, and storage elements needed for processing.

computer network
System in which numerous computers can either function individually or communicate with each other.

tive who needs product information about colors and options included in inventory arriving next week can tie into the mainframe to obtain the needed information, avoiding the time delays involved in contacting the director of purchasing and reviewing the purchase orders.

By linking microcomputers to the overall MIS, the system's data base can easily be updated as additional information becomes available. For instance, the recording of a sale on a salesperson's microcomputer can update the firm's inventory records. A comparison of actual sales of the item with forecasted sales may demonstrate a need to modify production plans. This information could be made available quickly to departments such as production, purchasing, and finance that are likely to be affected by any change in predicted sales.

Digital Equipment Corporation's computer network, called EasyNet, connects the company's 27,000 computer systems in 26 nations. The network is accessible to 75,000 of DEC's 118,000 employees and costs $40 million a year to run.[11] Similarly, Apollo Computer's network lets over 3,000 employees share computers made by nine manufacturers. Apollo's sophisticated computer network is shown in Figure 17.2.

As firms purchase additional computers for use by individual employees, control over the computers is being decentralized. A new type of executive, the network manager, has evolved. The network manager recognizes that the most efficient and effective method for supervising the computer resources of a company is to relinquish control over individual computers and focus on the networks that control them.

The lack of control and coordination can cause time-consuming and expensive problems. A lawn-equipment company allowed two of its factories to develop their own systems for tracking work orders and controlling inventory. Each factory used stand-alone IBM System/36 microcomputers, but the factories developed incompatible programs. As a result, when the CEO requested consolidated reports, the staff had to collect the data separately from each factory and combine the information by hand.[12]

How Computers Help Businesses

Federal Express provides a good illustration of how computers help businesses. The firm's 50,000 employees are served by over 30,000 computers. Federal Express's computer can trace within 30 minutes any of the nearly 800,000 packages the firm handles daily.[13]

Every area of business has felt the impact — and value — of computers. Banks, insurance companies, manufacturing firms, retailers, utilities, government agencies, airlines, accounting firms and departments, securities firms and stock exchanges, transportation companies — all have found important uses for computers. Within a business organization, virtually every department uses the computer as an indispensable tool. In thousands of offices, the computer reduces the costs and time involved in written communications.

Word Processing

word processing
Use of computers to store, retrieve, view, edit, and print text materials.

The dramatic increase in written communications coupled with rising costs create a need for more efficient methods of handling communications. Word processing provides the solution to this problem. **Word processing** is the use of

Figure 17.2   The Apollo Computer Corporate Network

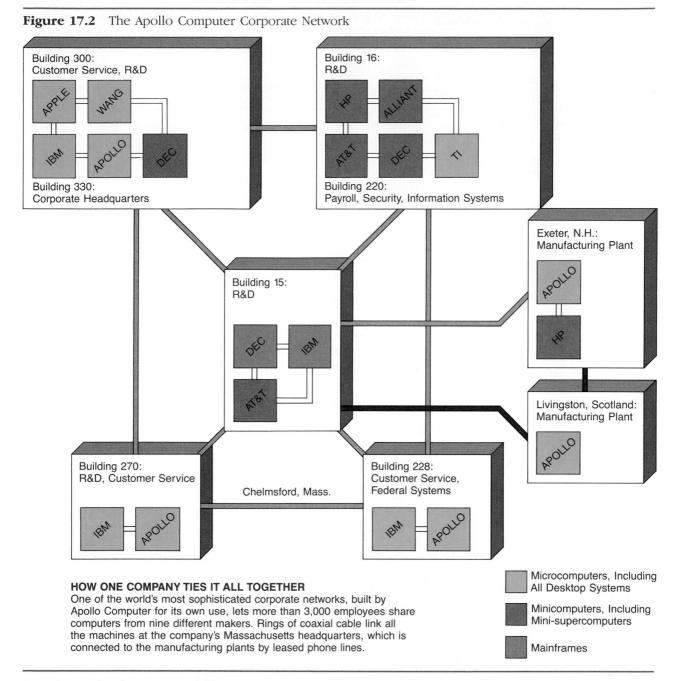

HOW ONE COMPANY TIES IT ALL TOGETHER
One of the world's most sophisticated corporate networks, built by
Apollo Computer for its own use, lets more than 3,000 employees share
computers from nine different makers. Rings of coaxial cable link all
the machines at the company's Massachusetts headquarters, which is
connected to the manufacturing plants by leased phone lines.

- Microcomputers, Including All Desktop Systems
- Minicomputers, Including Mini-supercomputers
- Mainframes

computers to store, retrieve, view, edit, and print various types of documents. By
typing information on a word processor instead of on the traditional typewriter,
the user can easily revise sentences, check spelling, correct errors, and print out
individual letters or reports as needed. Personalized letters designed to respond
to customer inquiries or to remind credit purchasers of overdue accounts can
be created by combining stored sentences and paragraphs.

Figure 17.3   How a Spreadsheet Works

Manufacturing	Fixed Costs Marketing	R&D	Fixed Cost	Per Unit Variable Cost	Sales Price	Breakeven Point in Units
$80,000	$100,000	$170,000	$350,000	$4	$8.00	87,500
$80,000	$200,000	$170,000	$450,000	$4	$8.00	112,500
$80,000	$100,000	$170,000	$350,000	$3	$6.50	100,000

Although many firms use special-purpose computers, called dedicated word processors, designed exclusively for this purpose, most microcomputers are also used as word processors. This is made possible through the use of such special software packages as *AppleWriter, WordPerfect, Microsoft Word, Multimate, XyWrite,* and *WordStar.*

Spreadsheet Analysis

spreadsheets
Special computer software permitting manipulation of decision variables to determine their impact.

The presence of a microcomputer in an executive's office is almost a guarantee that the manager uses electronic spreadsheets as decision-making aids. **Spreadsheets** are special computer software used in answering "What if?" questions. They are the computerized equivalent of an accountant's work sheet. The electronic spreadsheet, like its paper counterpart, is a grid of columns and rows that enables the manager to organize information in a standardized, easily understandable format. The most popular spreadsheets include *Lotus 1-2-3, Super-Calc,* and *Framework.*

Figure 17.3 demonstrates how a spreadsheet might be utilized in making pricing decisions concerning a proposed product. A proposed new-product entry will be marked at $8 per unit and can be produced for $4 in variable costs. Total fixed costs of $350,000 include $80,000 for such manufacturing overhead outlays as salaries, general office expenses, rent, utilities, and interest charges; $100,000 for marketing expenditures; and $170,000 for research and development on the product. The spreadsheet calculation, using the basic breakeven model introduced in Chapter 14, reveals that sales of 87,500 units are necessary to break even.

But what if the firm's marketing director persuades other members of the group to increase marketing expenditures to $200,000? As the second row in Figure 17.3 shows, the $100,000 in the marketing expenditure cell (the name of each point where the rows and columns intersect) is changed to $200,000 and the newly calculated breakeven point is 112,500 units. As soon as the figures in one or more cells are changed, the computer immediately recalculates all figures. This eliminates the tedious assignment of recalculating and revising figures by hand.

Figure 17.4   The Use of Computers in Product Design

Source: Courtesy of Prime Computer, Inc.

The final row in Figure 17.3 demonstrates the impact of a reduction in variable costs (by switching to lower-cost materials) to $3 coupled with a $1.50 reduction in the product's selling price. The new breakeven point is 100,000 units.

This relatively simple example demonstrates the ease with which a manager can use a spreadsheet to analyze alternative decisions. More complex spreadsheets may have 50 columns or more, but the spreadsheet makes new calculations as fast as the manager changes the variables.

Other Business Applications

Computers are used everywhere in business from marketing research to product design. For instance, the Contex Design System allows firms to develop bottle and carton shapes as well as alternative designs. The system can also produce planograms that show how a certain design would look on a store shelf next to competitive products.[14] The advertisement in Figure 17.4 explains how Prime Computer of Natick, Massachusetts, helped design and mass produce the molds that maintain the consistent shape and quality of the unique Perrier bottle.

Many professional sports teams also use computers in applications ranging from ticketing to improving on-the-field performance. The Dallas Cowboys coaches use computers to assess which plays would work best under certain circumstances. The computer can also answer questions like, "Who are the Redskins likely to pass to on third down and long yardage?"[15]

Computers are truly pervasive in the workplace. Even George Bush has a personal computer in the Oval Office.[16]

Computer Viruses

computer virus
Program that attaches itself to other programs and changes them or destroys the data kept on a disk.

During the past few years, a new threat to computer systems emerged in the form of the so-called computer virus. A **computer virus** is a program that secretly attaches itself to other programs and changes them or destroys the data kept on a disk. A virus can reproduce by copying itself to other programs stored on the disk. It spreads as the owner of infected software exchanges software with other users, usually by an electronic bulletin board or by trading disks. Viruses can be programmed to remain dormant for a long time, after which the infection suddenly activates itself.

Perhaps inevitably, playful and sometimes mischievous computer enthusiasts discovered ways of sending unauthorized messages through networks of computer systems. One well-known example was a West German student who sent a Christmas message over a computer network, which inadvertently spread to IBM's international network and within hours attached itself to every mailing list it encountered.

Other viruses have destroyed files of data and temporarily disabled major computing installations. When Gene Burleson, a disgruntled employee of USPA & Ira Co., a Fort Worth securities trading firm, was fired, he returned to the company and planted a program that once each month would erase all records of sales commissions. Although the company discovered the virus two days later, 168,000 records had already been lost. Burleson became the first person in the United States to be convicted of a felony for producing and releasing a computer virus.

In an age where computers are commonly linked into global networks, the threat of computer viruses is very serious. A number of "vaccine" and "inoculation" programs have been developed that are designed to detect and "cure" an infected system as well as protect the system against future infection. In addition, "safe computing" procedures have been suggested as a means of preventing the spread of viruses from one system to another.[17]

The Portable Office

As computerized and electronic equipment becomes smaller, more efficient, and less costly, small businesses and individuals are increasingly able to purchase such items. The result has been a rise in the number of people working at home, in the field, or using their cars or vans as portable offices. Such developments include laptop computers, cellular phones, electronic mail, and fax machines. These give the executive the opportunity to maximize time both inside and outside the office. In short, the separation between work and home is growing less distinct.

Laptop computers enable firms to provide better customer service. By using laptop computers, Wisconsin Bell repair supervisors can obtain necessary information from a central data base in half the time previously required. This helps business and residential customers get back on line that much sooner.

Photo source: © Mark Joseph.

Laptop computers are small, lightweight, and portable enough that they can accompany the business executive, permitting commuting time or business trips to be used more efficiently. Half the students at the Harvard Business School now take their exams on laptops rather than on paper. Laptops allow salespeople to provide up-to-date product information to clients, to enter records of sales while on calls, and to call up listings by real-estate agents. IRS field auditors are armed with laptops, as is the U.S. Defense Department, which is distributing 90,000 Zenith laptops to bases around the globe. Even the space shuttle carries two — each powerful enough to help land the craft should the on-board systems fail.[18]

The dramatic growth of the cellular phone market is another example of the new portable office. No longer a status symbol, the cellular phone is used not only by executives or salespeople conducting business from their cars, but also by a variety of organizations. For example, the Army used 12 cellular mobile phones to coordinate simulated combat situations in areas such as Weldon Spring, Missouri, where existing phone lines were inadequate. In Prince George's County, Maryland, the Clinton Volunteer Fire Department uses cellular phones to contact people inside and outside the organization to plan strategy, monitor emergency situations, and obtain information from services such as the poison control center.[19]

The latest boom in the electronics market is the fax (facsimile) machine, which enables instantaneous transmission of original material, whether documents or art, over telephone lines. In 1988, unit sales of fax machines reached 785,000, an 88 percent increase from 1987. Most of the demand came from smaller businesses, particularly as the cost of fax machines dropped. Bloomingdale's ran a newspaper ad campaign with faxed photos of clothing, and a radio station in Los Angeles takes requests by fax. Time-pressed Wall Street executives

Figure 17.5   A Fax Machine Beneficiary

IN THE NORTH SEA, YOU CAN
COUNT ON GALE-FORCE WINDS, HEAVY SEAS,
AND YOUR MURATA FAX MACHINE.

Out here, a Murata fax is used to communicate everything from production figures to drilling maps. Even letters home. Fifteen years ago Murata was a pioneer in the fax market. Today we are a leader with a complete line of compact, feature packed, easy-to-use machines. They're extraordinarily reliable, too. Which is critical, even if your office isn't in the middle of nowhere.

Call 1-800-543-INFO for the location nearest you. In Texas, (214) 392-1622.

MURATA   Determined To Be Number One.

Source: Courtesy of Murata Business Systems.

can order pizzas via Domino's fax machine and pay for them with their American Express cards. The biggest beneficiaries have been advertising agencies that have clients throughout the world. Storyboards and layouts for ads can be faxed back and forth for change and approval in a matter of seconds. Others who benefit by using fax machines are those with offices in "the middle of nowhere," as the Murata advertisement in Figure 17.5 illustrates. The only businesses suffering from the growth in the number of fax machines are messenger services and overnight or same-day shipping services.[20]

Finally, there are voice message systems and "E-Mail," an electronic mail system. These allow you to leave messages for someone at any time, whether or not the intended recipient is present. The recipient can pick up these messages at his or her convenience, eliminating telephone tag and inconvenient calls. In addition, teleconferencing has enabled companies to reduce travel expenses.

The ultimate example of the portable electronic office is that of Bernie E. Belesky, who is a marketing director for Investment Center Financial Corporation, a seller of financial services in Canada. Belesky's entire office is in his 1984 GMC van, which contains a cellular phone, a fax machine, and a laptop computer. He drives 3,700 miles a month and conducts almost all of his business from his van.[21]

What's Ahead for Computers?

Few people doubt that computer technology advances during the next quarter-century will be just as significant as thousands of others in the last 25 years. Technological developments will undoubtedly make computers faster and cheaper. In 1952, it cost $1.26 to do 100,000 multiplications on an IBM computer. Today this can be done for a penny. That same IBM computer could do about 2,000 multiplications per second in 1952. Today's computer can multiply at the rate of 2 million operations per second!

Microcomputers — small in size and inexpensive in price — are growing rapidly to service firms that cannot afford the larger installations or that do not need the capabilities of larger computers. This has resulted in less usage of **time-sharing** — the linking of several users through remote terminals (usually teletypewriters) to a large central computer. Companies whose volume of data was too small for them to own a computer used to rent processing time on a computer owned by a time-sharing company. Today, however, it is generally cheaper to own a computer than to sign up with a time-sharing outfit. General Electric, for instance, gave up on time-sharing after its $500 million business collapsed in the 1980s.[22] On the other hand, intraorganizational time-sharing, in the form of distributed data processing, has increased. In addition to being used by business firms and government agencies, intraorganizational time-sharing is often found on college campuses, where numerous buildings are linked to a central computer by input-output teletypewriters.

Software expenses often represent the chief cost of a computer facility. They are likely to decline, however, as more computer companies design and market software packages to handle more and more business tasks. Some companies are working to develop **open systems** that will rely on a common set of software that can be transferred from one brand of computer to another.[23]

In addition, new means will be found to communicate with the computer. Future users may be able to communicate directly with the computer by using special pens or voice commands. Early strides in this direction have already been made. Voice-input systems are still primitive, but they are being used for a number of business activities. Bank tellers, for example, can use a special terminal to call the computer and determine whether a check should be cashed. Some computers are also learning to talk. One developed by Bell Laboratories uses a 30,000-word dictionary to form words from special elements that are stored as fractions of syllables. The voice is not a tape recording but the result of a computer program that uses mathematical functions to represent the position of the tongue, lips, and palate in humans. The computer can also approximate the proper voice pitch, intensity, and duration for each speech sequence. Bell's talking computer is used to generate electronic speech signals that can be heard over a telephone or loudspeaker. By making direct voice contact between the user and computer possible, voice input and output systems may someday make the computer an integral tool of every manager.

The Fifth Generation

During the past quarter-century, a number of computer scientists have conducted research on **artificial intelligence**. This branch of computer science focuses on the ways humans perceive and assimilate data, reason abstractly, adapt, and communicate in an effort to produce such behavior in computers.[24]

time-sharing
Linking of several users through remote terminals to a large central computer.

open systems
Systems that will rely on a common set of software that can be transferred from one brand of computer to another.

artificial intelligence
The study of using computers to solve problems involving imagination, abstract reasoning, and common sense.

The scientists began their work recognizing the seemingly insurmountable task of giving the computer common sense — something that comes naturally to a child as young as 3 or 4 years old. Some experts are skeptical about dramatic breakthroughs in machine intelligence occurring soon.

A computer must be programmed with the most rudimentary facts that humans perceive almost from the time they are born. In addition, no computer yet has the ability to learn on its own, without human input. "Any youngster knows that if he walks off a cliff, he will fall," says Daniel Dennett, a philosophy professor at Tufts University. "But you can tell a computer all kinds of things about cliffs and the effects of gravity and it still wouldn't perceive what would happen if it walked off a cliff."[25]

Language comprehension and translation create another major problem because words in any language have multiple meanings. One early language experiment left researchers baffled when the computer referred to a "water goat." Eventually they discovered the machine was attempting to translate the term *hydraulic ram.*

However, increasingly powerful computers are making significant progress. British researchers have created a "bionic nose" capable of distinguishing subtle differences in fragrance. The invention has significant potential in such industries as food, brewing, and perfume. Similarly, computer-assisted diagnoses of diseases in a number of U.S. hospitals are so accurate that doctors can rely on the results 85 percent of the time. American Express has developed a system that simulates the thinking of company specialists in charge of unusual credit requests. The American Express computer can now decide whether to approve a $5,000 charge for an Oriental rug.[26] The advertisement in Figure 17.6 describes how engineers at Martin Marietta are using computer technologies to help robots learn from their experiences and make their own decisions.

expert systems
Programs that imitate human thinking.

There is also growing interest in **expert systems**, which are programs that imitate human thinking through a complicated series of "if . . . then" rules and can solve difficult one-of-a-kind problems. Digital Equipment Corporation's XCON, for example, checks sales orders and designs a layout of each computer order it analyzes. Previously, employees insured that each computer system on order was complete, had all the necessary components, and that the order included the correct diagram for assembly of the system.[27]

While the Japanese continue to expand their gains in today's personal computer market, Japanese government and industry have committed billions of dollars over the next decade to achieve technological leadership in the so-called fifth generation of computers.

The Japanese have the following specific targets for the 1990s:

◆ A typewriter activated by the human voice that could recognize the voice patterns of hundreds of human speakers and "understand" some 10,000 words.

◆ An optical scanner that could look at and "read" 100,000 pictures. The scanner would be able to differentiate among all the characters in the Japanese alphabet.

◆ An automatic translating machine that could translate Japanese into English, French, German, Spanish, and other major languages. Approximately 100,000 vocabulary words would be stored in this computer, which would translate with 90 percent accuracy.

Figure 17.6 Developing Machine Intelligence

Source: Courtesy of Martin Marietta Corporation.

By arranging large numbers of very large-scale integrated circuits in parallel, many computer scientists believe dramatic breakthroughs in speed and power may occur. These improved characteristics may permit the manufacture of computers able to perform humanlike reasoning: making assumptions, drawing inferences, and reaching conclusions. Dozens of U.S. firms and government agencies, from IBM to the U.S. Department of Defense, have established artificial intelligence departments. Clearly, the twenty-first century may be more amazing than the twentieth century in computer advances.

Summary of Learning Goals

1.   Explain the purpose of a management information system and how it functions in a firm.   Information is a vital element in management decisions. Effective decisions cannot be made without answers to questions about the internal operations of the firm and the external environment in which it operates. Progressive companies use a planned management information system (MIS) that provides past, present, and projected information on internal operations and external intelligence for use in making decisions. Such information systems should aid all areas of the organization — production, accounting, marketing, human resources, purchasing, engineering, and finance — in carrying out their decision-making responsibilities.

2.   Describe the five generations of computers.   The first generation of computers was characterized by the use of vacuum tubes and covered the period from 1944 to 1959. The bulky, heat-generating, vacuum-tube computers gave way to a second generation of computers that relied on smaller, less heat-generating transistors and diodes. Processing speeds of these second-generation computers greatly exceeded those of their predecessors. The third generation of computers covered the period from 1964 to the mid-1970s and witnessed the replacement of transistors with the integrated circuit. Such circuits were made up of a network of dozens of tiny transistors and connections all contained on a sliver of silicon about the size of a contact lens. In the fourth generation, very large-scale integrated (VLSI) circuits were developed, and silicon chips became so compact they had to be designed by other computers. Because millions of circuits can be located in a cubic inch of space, the fourth-generation is expected to generate breakthroughs in the science of artificial intelligence when even more powerful computers are developed.

3.   List the major contributions and limitations of computers.   In addition to speed and accuracy, computers provide many other advantages over manual methods of data processing. They can store large amounts of data in a small space, and quickly make this data available for decision makers. Also, by performing the mechanical, routine, boring work of recording and maintaining incoming information, they can free people for more challenging work.

The major limitations of computers are the costs of hardware and programming, computer mistakes caused by faulty programming, the tendency for management to use computers as a crutch rather than as a tool in decision making, and the potential for alienating customers by ignoring the human element in customer relations.

4.   Distinguish between computer hardware and software.   Computer hardware consists of all the tangible elements of the computer system. These include the input devices, the machines that store and process data and perform required calculations, and the output devices that communicate the results to the computer user.

Software consists of computer languages and programs that tell the computer what to do. The most frequently used programming languages are FORTRAN, COBOL, BASIC, Pascal, and PL/1. Special conversational programs have been developed to allow people with little or no programming training to use the computer.

5.   Identify the components of a computer system and the functions of each.   The main elements of the computer system are the central processing unit (CPU) and peripheral equipment that permits communication between the computer and the operator. The CPU consists of three parts: the memory unit, which holds the data; the arithmetic/logic unit, where calculations take place; and the control unit, which directs the sequence of operations, interprets instructions, and gives the proper commands to guide the computer. Peripheral equipment includes input devices, which feed data into the computer, and output devices, which produce the requested information. These elements represent computer hardware.

6.   Explain how binary arithmetic works and why it is appropriate for use by computers.   Binary arithmetic is a special counting system that uses two digits — 0 and 1. With binary numbers, every time a number is moved one space to the left, it is worth two times as much. The binary system, which consists of yes-no states, is appropriate for computers because electrical circuits can be opened or closed to incoming data.

7. Distinguish among mainframe computers, minicomputers, and microcomputers. The primary basis for distinction is size. Mainframes are the largest type of computer systems with the greatest storage capacity and fastest processing speeds. Minicomputers are smaller (about the size of a small filing cabinet), less powerful, and less expensive. Microcomputers, the smallest type of computers, are desktop, limited-storage systems. They consist of personal computers for home use, personal computers for individual use in offices, and small-business computers. Each type — mainframe, minicomputer, and microcomputer — contains the basic elements of any computer system.

8. Explain the role that computers play in business today. Computers are used throughout the private and public sectors. It is difficult to imagine a modern organization operating without computers. Examples of computer usage in business include word processing, spreadsheet analysis, reservation systems, banking, product design, and physical distribution.

9. Describe the concept of the portable office. Technology has provided the key to improving businesspeople's productivity both inside and outside the office setting. The separation between work and home is less distinct today than it was in an earlier era. Laptop computers, cellular telephones, electronic mail, voice message systems, and fax machines have made the contemporary office truly portable.

Key Terms

management information system (MIS)	input	remote terminal
chief information officer (CIO)	central processing unit (CPU)	mainframe computer
data	memory unit	minicomputer
information	arithmetic/logic unit	microcomputer
data base	control unit	cathode ray tube (CRT)
executive information system (EIS)	output	microprocessor
computer	batch processing	computer network
transistor	on-line processing	word processing
integrated circuit	binary arithmetic	spreadsheets
very large-scale integrated (VLSI) circuit	bit	computer virus
computer chips	byte	time-sharing
hardware	megabyte	open systems
software	computer program	artificial intelligence
	computer programmer	expert systems
	flowchart	

Review Questions

1. Explain the purpose of a management information system and its functions in an organization.

2. Distinguish between data and information.

3. Trace the major developments in the history of data processing described in this chapter. Explain the contribution each development made in leading to the computer's development.

4. What are the major contributions made by computers? What potential problems are involved with the use of computers? Suggest steps to minimize the likelihood of occurrence of each of these problems.

5. Categorize each of the following as either hardware or software and defend your choices:
   - **a.** Central processing unit (CPU)
   - **b.** Computer instruction manual
   - **c.** Line printer
   - **d.** Main memory unit
   - **e.** Keyboard input device
   - **f.** Word-processing program
   - **g.** Computer peripherals

6. What are the primary components of every computer system? What functions are performed by each component?

7. Distinguish between binary arithmetic and the decimal system. Convert the following decimal numbers to binary numbers:

   104 16 11 7 21 49 83 2

8. Differentiate among mainframe, minicomputer, and microcomputers.

9. List at least two computer applications for each of the following areas of business:
   - **a.** Physical distribution
   - **b.** Production and inventory control
   - **c.** Human resources
   - **d.** Marketing
   - **e.** Finance and accounting
   - **f.** Legal
   - **g.** Customer service

10. Explain how technology has affected the modern office.

Discussion Questions

1. Keep a diary for two or three days. Report each instance of when a computer affected your life. Discuss what you learned from the exercise.

2. There are fewer than 100,000 personal computers in the Soviet Union. Discuss how the lack of computers affects the U.S.S.R. economy and Mikhail Gorbachev's policy of *perestroika*.

3. Discuss how computers are used by your college. Suggest ways in which the college could use computers more effectively.

4. Marc Cantor was doing contract work for Seattle's Aldus Corp., a software publisher, when he accidentally acquired a disk infected with a computer virus. The Chicago-based executive ran the infected disk on his office com-

puter. Later, he reviewed a program for Aldus on the same computer, infecting the Aldus program, which Cantor sent to Seattle. Aldus then copied the infected item and inserted it in a graphics program that was distributed nationwide. This was the first time a commercial software package had been affected by a virus. Discuss what the industry can do to prevent instances of this nature.

5. An estimated 25 million fax machines will be operating in the United States in 1990, up from just 1 million in 1988. In contrast, Japanese industry already had 2.5 million fax machines by 1988. These machines now account for up to 20 percent of all telephone traffic in some sections of Japan. Discuss the rapid growth of fax technology. What will happen in the future? Why did Japan get ahead of the United States in the use of fax machines?

Video Case

White Flower Farm

Eliot Wadsworth II lives what many would consider an idyllic life. Wadsworth owns and manages White Flower Farm, a retail and catalog nursery business set on 300 acres of immaculately tended grounds, experimental gardens, commercial greenhouses, and hedgerows in Litchfield, Connecticut, about 110 miles from New York. "Right now, we've got 450,000 perennials in the fields," says Wadsworth. "And every morning I get up and run these fields with my dog, looking for things like disease problems and water problems. What a marvelous thing to be doing for a living. The idea of being paid to be out making notes in the trial gardens is indescribable."

A mail-order business is by itself difficult enough to manage. A nursery mail-order business is even more difficult. So many factors enter the success-failure equation over which the firm has little control: the weather, postal delivery problems, changing consumer tastes. In little more than a decade, Wadsworth's company has managed to create and enhance a reputation as the best, most responsible, and priciest mail-order nursery of perennial flowers, shrubs, and bulbs in the Northeast. But he is at least as proud of his computerized operations and the contributions of the White Flower Farm management information system as he is of the plants. Both are critical ingredients in the firm's success.

White Flower Farm was begun by two eccentric New York writers who went to Connecticut periodically to escape the city. They published their first catalog in 1951 and ran the business in a quiet way, almost more as a hobby than as a business, for nearly three decades. When they became too old to continue in the business, they accepted an offer in 1977 from Wadsworth, a former Wall Street investment banker. The purchase price was $750,000, an amount roughly equal to annual sales at that time. Since then, White Flower Farm sales have increased by about 10 to 15

percent a year, with current annual sales totalling about $10 million. While some sales are made to customers who visit the nursery, most of the firm's revenues are earned through mail orders. Each year the company sells about 3 million flowering bulbs and over 750,000 perennials.

Few of the nation's 500 mail-order nurseries actually grow their own plants. They simply buy them from growers, mark them up, and then resell them to customers. White Flower Farm, by contrast, is a fully integrated business. Its employees grow and pick flowers, stock the warehouse, take telephone orders, pack orders for shipment, and serve repeat customers by selling only select flowers. Over 1,000 varieties of flowers and shrubs are grown at WFF, all carefully controlled for quality. They are displayed in the company's biannual catalog called *The Garden Book*. Twice a year, this 120-page catalog is mailed free to 250,000 WFF customers who have purchased at least $20 worth of plants within the past two years. The catalog is a minor masterpiece of gardening, containing beautiful color pictures, gardening advice, and other information — all written in a patrician style and signed by the fictitious Amos Pettingill, whom many customers accept as a real person. The character was invented by WFF's original owners and carried on to Wadsworth who personally writes and edits the catalog.

When Wadsworth took over the business, it had a small staff of about twelve full-time employees. They functioned in the same informal manner as most very small businesses, getting together several times a day to talk over the latest products or pending weather concerns. As the company grew — to more than 200 employees during peak seasons — it had to become more organized. Says Wadsworth, "It's an information-intensive business. You can't walk in here and be effective shipping plants if you don't have any idea what plants are. I think that that is probably less true if you're shipping rubber boots or toothbrushes."

Wadsworth realizes that his firm's clientele expect to deal with informed company representatives when they contact WFF. Since a customer may call and ask any kind of question about horticulture, telephone operators attend regularly-scheduled briefing sessions led by the staff horticulturist so they can advise and

Notes: Nelson W. Aldrich, Jr., "Bloom Town," *New York,* June 6, 1988, pp. 41–46; John Grossman, "Cultivating Growth," *Inc.,* February 1987, pp. 89–94; Laura van Dam, "Going from Garden into the Printshop as Magazine Publisher," *New England Business,* May 6, 1985, pp. 47–51; and personal correspondence, April 25, 1989.

inform callers. Then there are the computer screens on their desks, which are linked to the WFF mainframe as part of the firm's computer network.

An early capital investment involved enhancing the firm's computers. Wadsworth wanted all available information on the computer for use by anyone who needed it. A telephone sales representative has instant access to information not just on customer orders, but also information that previously would have come only from the senior horticulturist — information on how plants grow, which grow best where, and so on. Over the years, the information system has become even more sophisticated, alerting the telephone sales representative that a phone order contains flowers in colors that will not blend well or contains a sun-loving plant amid many shade growers, or that plants are being sent to an area where they will not grow well.

The computer also helps with customer records in a business where sales are not necessarily final. Because White Flower Farm deals in live products, plant availability is never absolutely certain. The catalog may contain beautiful pictures of plants that have been ruined by a severe storm just days after the catalog was mailed. Shortages may occur for particularly popular items. Since Wadsworth refuses to risk quality problems by buying replacements at wholesale, the computer alerts the telephone spokesperson to inventory problems. It can also help a customer choose a plant on the basis of region, weather, and plant type. Finally, since all orders are computerized, the status of specific orders can be traced quickly.

Computer systems also aid nonsales operations. For instance, computers coordinate growing activities, tell where plants are located at WFF, and create cultivation and shipping schedules.

These factors explain the firm's loyal following of repeat buyers, whose average purchases of over $60 per order rank as one of the highest in the business. White Flower Farm may have already grown to its maximum size since additional growth might require that the firm compromise its standards. Wadsworth and his employees have no interest in doing that, and are content to remain a manageable size, a nursery with perhaps the loftiest reputation in the United States.

Questions

1. What are the primary purposes of the White Flower Farm management information system? How has it saved the company time, money, and customers?

2. How would a company like White Flower Farm have functioned in the days before computers?

3. Explain ways in which WFF's management information system has helped management make decisions.

4. Distinguish between computer hardware and software in the White Flower Farm management information system.

18 *Accounting*

Learning Goals

1. To explain the functions of accounting and its importance to the firm's management and to outside parties such as investors, creditors, and government agencies.

2. To distinguish between public and private accountants and to explain the role played by CPAs and CMAs.

3. To outline the steps in the accounting process.

4. To identify the accounting equation and its components and to explain the equation's relationship to double-entry bookkeeping.

5. To explain the function of the balance sheet and to identify its major components.

6. To explain the function of the income statement and to identify its major components.

7. To identify the major financial ratios used in analyzing a firm's financial strengths and weaknesses and to explain the purpose of each.

8. To explain the role of budgets in business.

Checkpoint Systems Inc., a Thorofare, New Jersey, manufacturer of electronic article surveillance (EAS) systems for retail stores and libraries, is a classic example of an entrepreneur responding to a business need. Peter Stern founded Checkpoint in 1967 to address libraries' need to reduce staggering losses from theft of books and other library materials. His special tag, attached to each book, would emit a radio signal and would be detected if not removed from the book prior to patrons leaving the library. Detection of the tag's radio signal would activate an alarm and lock the gate or turnstile to the exit.

Checkpoint's chairman, A. E. "Ted" Wolf, has guided the company to provide an integrated shoplifting prevention EAS system — Cheklink® — to retailers based on Stern's initial library application. Evolution of Cheklink addressed retailers' resistance to the difficult-to-remove, bulky, hard plastic tags. Now, Cheklink comprises a comprehensive line of small, flexible, disposable tags and pressure sensitive labels that contain a passive resonant security circuit. The system integrates the security circuit with product price and barcode information all on a single label. The Checkpoint security circuit is automatically deactivated during the barcode scanning process.

These developments have resulted in tremendous growth for Checkpoint. By the mid-1980s, Checkpoint was generating more than $16 million in sales from its library and retail markets. And, in 1988, the Cheklink integrated EAS solution for the retail market helped push sales above $40 million.

Growth brought challenge to Checkpoint, particularly in its accounting department. The company's old accounting system, although adequate for a small operation, could not accommodate the firm's rapid growth. Managers

were not being provided with decision-oriented accounting information to assist in isolating trends, making price decisions, and controlling cash flow.

Installation of a new, computer-based accounting system provided productivity benefits immediately and impacted on managerial decisions based on accounting data. For example, invoices were processed at least 13 days earlier. This improved customer service and Checkpoint received cash from sales faster. Prior to installing the computerized accounting system, the average time before Checkpoint customers paid their bills had reached an alarming 157 to 175 days. This was slashed to approximately 50 days. And, during the first year the system was implemented, the company initiated four price increases because managers iso-

lated significant negative cost/price relationships.

The growth prospects for Checkpoint Systems are excellent. The company made substantial inroads in the international marketplace in the late 1980s with 25 percent of total sales being generated outside the United States. Although libraries remain a steady market for Checkpoint, the company expects substantial growth to come from a variety of retail sectors including mass merchandisers, discount apparel, department stores, drug stores, supermarkets, music and video retailers, as well as specialty stores such as liquor stores and hardware stores. The new accounting system is designed to accommodate this growth.[1]

Photo source: Courtesy of Checkpoint Systems, Inc.

521

Chapter Overview

The stereotype of the accountant — a pale, bookish male dressed in a white shirt and narrow tie, seated behind a desk in a small office, pencil in hand, poring over invoices and making notations in a dusty ledger — describes virtually none of the million men and women in the United States who list their occupation as accountant. Accountants today are equipped with personal computers and use sophisticated computer software to perform many of their tasks.

Never before have accountants been in such demand. The U.S. Bureau of Labor Statistics reports that accounting is a fast-growing occupation, estimating that almost 400,000 new accounting jobs will be available during the 1990s.[2] The availability of jobs and the relatively high starting salaries for talented accounting graduates have lured hundreds of thousands of students into accounting classes in America's colleges and universities. Today, accounting represents almost half of all student majors in many collegiate business programs.

Accounting, like statistics, is a language of business. It is the process of measuring, interpreting, and communicating financial information to enable others inside and outside the firm to make informed decisions. Accountants gather, record, report, and interpret financial information that describes the status and operation of a firm and aids in decision making. They must accomplish three major tasks: scorekeeping, calling attention to problems and opportunities, and aiding in decision making.

This chapter explains the accounting process and discusses the development of accounting statements from financial transactions. Methods of interpreting these statements are described and the rule of budgets in planning and controlling is explained.

accounting
Measuring, interpreting, and communicating financial information for internal and external decision making.

Accounting for Whom?

Who are the interested parties — inside and outside the firm — aided by accounting? Inside the firm, managers are the major users of accounting information, which helps them plan and control both daily and long-range operations. Owners of the firm rely on accounting data to determine how well the firm is being operated. Union officials use the data in contract negotiations.

Outside the firm, potential investors use accounting information to help them decide whether to invest in the company. Bankers and other existing and potential creditors find that it helps them determine the company's credit rating and gives them insight into its financial soundness. The Internal Revenue Service and state tax officials use it to evaluate the company's tax payments for the year. Figure 18.1 identifies the major users of a firm's accounting information.

Accounting versus Bookkeeping

Too many people make the mistake of using the terms *accounting* and *bookkeeping* interchangeably. But they are not synonymous.

Bookkeeping is the chiefly clerical phase of accounting. Bookkeepers are responsible primarily for the systematic recording of company financial transactions. They provide the data that the accountant uses. Accounting is a much broader area. Accountants are responsible for developing systems to classify and summarize transactions and for interpreting financial statements.

Figure 18.1 Users of Accounting Information

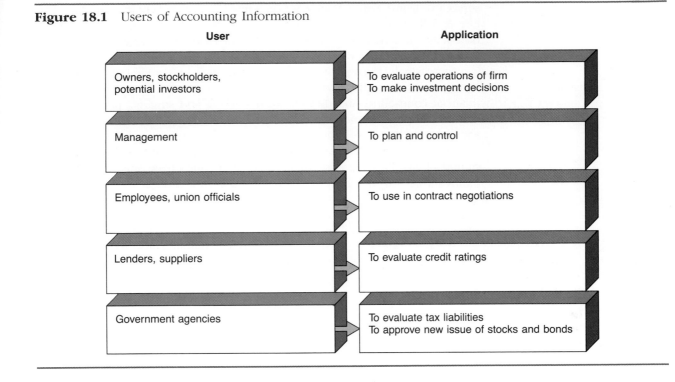

Accountants are decision makers, while bookkeepers are trained in the largely mechanical tasks of record keeping. Accountants hold positions as chief executives in many of the largest companies and in top-level government offices.

People in the Accounting Profession

The 1 million accountants in the United States are employed in a variety of areas in business firms, government agencies, and nonprofit organizations. Many are self-employed. Accountants can be classified as either public or private accountants.

Public Accountants

A **public accountant** provides accounting services to individuals or business firms for a fee. These services may include the preparation of tax statements; independent audits, or examinations, of financial records; management consulting; assistance in filing securities registration papers and loan applications; and the design of accounting systems. Since they are not employees of the firm for which they are providing services, public accountants are in a position to provide honest, unbiased advice about the firm's financial condition.

Approximately 40,000 public accounting firms exist in the United States, many of which are small one- or two-person operations. Other public accounting firms are extremely large and provide a wide range of services for their clients. The largest of these firms, the so-called Big Eight, include Arthur Ander-

public accountant
Professional who provides accounting services to other businesses and individuals.

sen & Company; Arthur Young & Company; Coopers & Lybrand; Deloitte, Haskins & Sells; Ernst & Whinney; Peat, Marwick, Mitchell & Company; Price Waterhouse; and Touche Ross & Company. Many firms whose stock is publicly traded are clients of the Big Eight.

Increasingly, large public accounting firms are becoming more involved in management consulting by designing computer systems for clients, providing financial counseling, and developing marketing and strategic planning strategies. In 1987, Arthur Andersen & Company derived 36 percent of its total worldwide revenues of $2.3 billion from management consulting services.[3]

The following examples illustrate the wide range of tax, auditing, and consulting services Touche Ross offers to clients ranging from small businesses to multinational corporations:

◆ TRETIS, a computer data base containing information on tax cases, predictions, and interpretations.

◆ World Tax Planner, an information system containing facts, figures, and analyses of tax laws and treaties in 185 countries that helps clients identify tax-saving opportunities in their operations abroad.

◆ An expert computer software program that focuses on risks in the auditing process and allocates the audit work in proportion to those risks.

◆ A computer-integrated manufacturing service that evaluates a firm's existing operations, analyzes the costs and benefits of automation, and plans and integrates automated processes.

◆ A strategic information systems planning service that provides clients with a long-range plan to meet their information systems requirements, including hardware, software, and human resources.

◆ A financial services center that advises banks, insurance firms, and other financial institutions on such transactions as mergers, acquisitions, and leveraged buyouts. The center operates a hotline 24 hours a day, 365 days a year, to answer clients' questions.

Through other specialized consulting services, Touche Ross accountants advise clients on their organizational structure; product, pricing, and distribution strategies; and employee benefits and compensation plans.[4]

The variety of services provided to client firms and the special skills required of the professional accountant are humorously depicted in Figure 18.2. This poster of the Seidman & Seidman "super accountant" was developed by the firm's marketing department for internal distribution to the firm's offices in 40 U.S. cities. The tongue-in-cheek descriptive phrases on the poster reflect the high-quality client service and performance provided by this public accounting firm.

Public accounting firms provide the greatest number of jobs for accounting graduates. Arthur Andersen, for example, plans to hire more than 9,000 college graduates a year in the 1990s.[5]

private accountant
Accounting professional employed by a government agency, nonprofit organization, or business other than a public accounting firm.

Private Accountants

An accountant who is employed by government, a nonprofit organization, or by a business other than a public accounting firm is called a **private** (or management) **accountant**. Private accountants are responsible for collecting and recording financial transactions and preparing financial statements used by the

Figure 18.2   The CPA: Super Accountant

Source: Courtesy of Seidman & Seidman.

firm's managers in decision making. In addition to preparing the financial statements, private accountants play a major role in interpreting them.

Private accountants frequently specialize in different aspects of accounting. Because of this, accountants can have various titles — cost accountant, internal auditor, or tax accountant — depending on the area in which they work. A cost accountant, for example, determines the cost of goods and services and helps set their prices. A tax accountant seeks to minimize taxes paid and is in charge of the firm's federal and state tax returns. An internal auditor examines the firm's financial practices to ensure that records are accurate and that company operations are in compliance with federal laws and regulations.

The CPA and the CMA

About 300,000 of the nation's accountants are certified public accountants. A **certified public accountant (CPA)** proves his or her skills by meeting the state's requirements for education and experience and successfully completes a number of rigorous tests in accounting theory and practice, auditing, and law. The grueling $2\frac{1}{2}$-day CPA exam, prepared by the American Institute of Certified Public Accountants, is administered twice a year nationally and each time is taken by approximately 70,000 candidates. Many of them fail on the first attempt.

certified public accountant (CPA)
Accountant who has passed a comprehensive examination covering law, accounting theory and practice, and auditing.

CPAs enjoy the same professional status within their field as attorneys and physicians do in theirs. Although the CPA certificate is not a requirement, only CPAs can officially express an opinion on whether a firm's financial statements fairly and accurately present that company's financial position. Such audits of financial records are required of most publicly held corporations and are usually required by any lending agency.

Another type of certification is granted to the **certified management accountant (CMA)**. A CMA typically works as a private accountant with management responsibilities. Certified management accountants have met certain professional and educational requirements and have also passed a series of examinations established by the National Association of Accountants. The five-part CMA examination is comparable in length and rigor to the CPA exam. Developed in 1972, the CMA certificate is now held by approximately 8,000 professionals, and the number is growing at a 10 percent annual rate. CMAs hold positions at all levels in the organization, from staff accountant to vice-president of finance.

certified management accountant (CMA)
Accountant who has met specific educational and professional requirements and has passed a series of examinations established by the National Association of Accountants.

The Accounting Process

Accounting deals with financial transactions between the firm and its employees, customers, suppliers, owners, bankers, and various government bodies. Weekly payroll checks result in cash outflows for the compensation of employees. A payment to a supplier results in the receipt of needed materials for the production process. Cash, check, and credit purchases by customers generate funds to cover the costs of operations and earn a profit. Prompt payment of bills preserves the firm's credit rating and its ability to obtain future loans. This procedural cycle used by accountants in converting individual transactions to financial statements is called the **accounting process**. As Figure 18.3 indicates, these transactions must be recorded, classified, and summarized in order to produce financial statements for the firm's management and other interested parties.

accounting process
Method of converting individual transactions to financial statements.

Accounting Journals and Ledgers

The first step in the processing of transactions by the firm is to record each of them in chronological order in a book called a **journal**. The journal can consist of a hand-prepared list or a computer printout in firms with computerized accounting systems. A sample page from a journal is shown at the top of Figure 18.4.

The accounts listed on the journal page represent sources and uses of funds by the firm. The July 5 purchase of furniture from Norway Haus cost $8,000. The firm agreed to pay $5,000 of the total cost in ten days and the remaining balance at the end of the month. The payment made to Norway Haus on July 15 reduced the cash account by $5,000. On the other hand, the July 22 payment of $1,000 on his account by Marcus Williams increased the amount of cash on hand by that amount.

In practice, the transactions work much like your checking account. Each check you write reduces your checking account balance. Conversely, each deposit you make raises the balance. The check or deposit is recorded in your checkbook for your records. The bank also keeps a record of each deposit made

journal
Accountant's book of entry listing financial transactions chronologically.

Figure 18.3 The Accounting Process

Basic Data

Transactions
Receipts, invoices, and other source documents related to each transaction are assembled to justify making an entry in the firm's accounting records.

Processing

Record
Transactions are recorded in chronological order in books called journals. Brief explanations are given for each entry.

Classify
Journal entries are transferred or posted to individual accounts kept in a ledger. All entries involving cash are brought together in the ledger's cash account; all entries involving sales are recorded in the ledger's sales account.

Summarize
All accounts in the ledger are summarized at the end of the accounting period and financial statements are prepared from these account summaries.

Financial Statements

Balance Sheet	Income Statement	Statement of Cash Flows

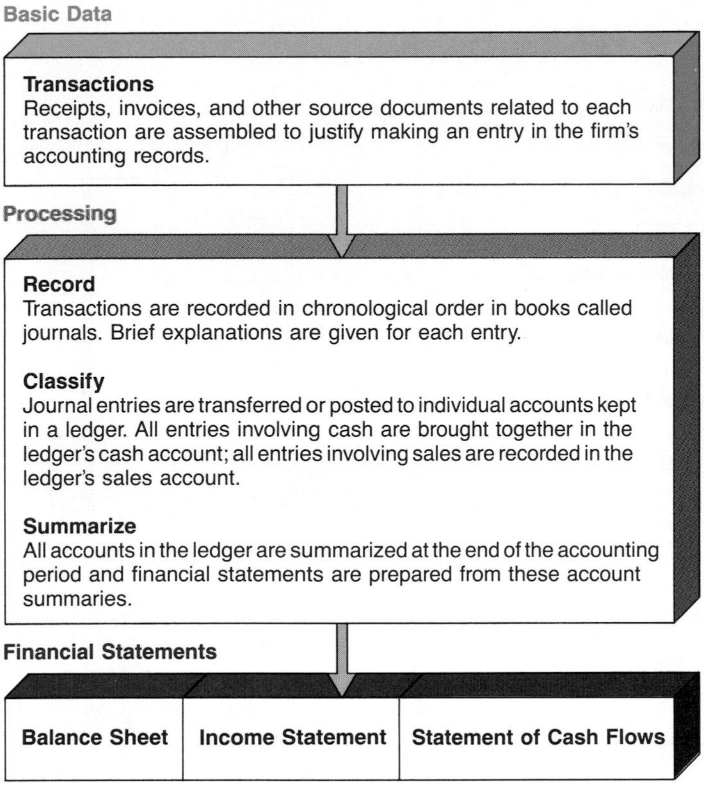

and each check written. A cash sale increases the cash account while reducing inventory. Purchases of stationery, for instance, increase the supplies account and reduce cash.

The next step involves transferring the data contained in the journal entries to individual accounts in the firm's ledger. A **ledger**, or book of account, is a specialized accounting book that contains separate accounts for such items as cash, accounts receivable, sales, inventory, and salaries. It summarizes the listing of transactions in the journal by assembling them into specific accounts.

The bottom half of Figure 18.4 shows two ledger accounts: cash and accounts receivable. The process of **posting**, or recording, the individual transactions from the general journal to specific ledger accounts is illustrated using these two accounts. At the end of the accounting period, the data in each ledger account is summarized and used as the basis for preparing the firm's accounting statements.

ledger
Accounting book with separate accounts such as cash, sales, and inventory.

posting
Recording journal entries in the appropriate ledger accounts.

Impact of the Computer on the Accounting Process

The accounting systems of thousands of firms are currently being simplified by fully automated systems developed by firms such as NCR Corporation. As cash registers are replaced with point-of-sale terminals, a number of functions are

Figure 18.4   Sample Page from an Accounting Journal and Sample Ledger Accounts

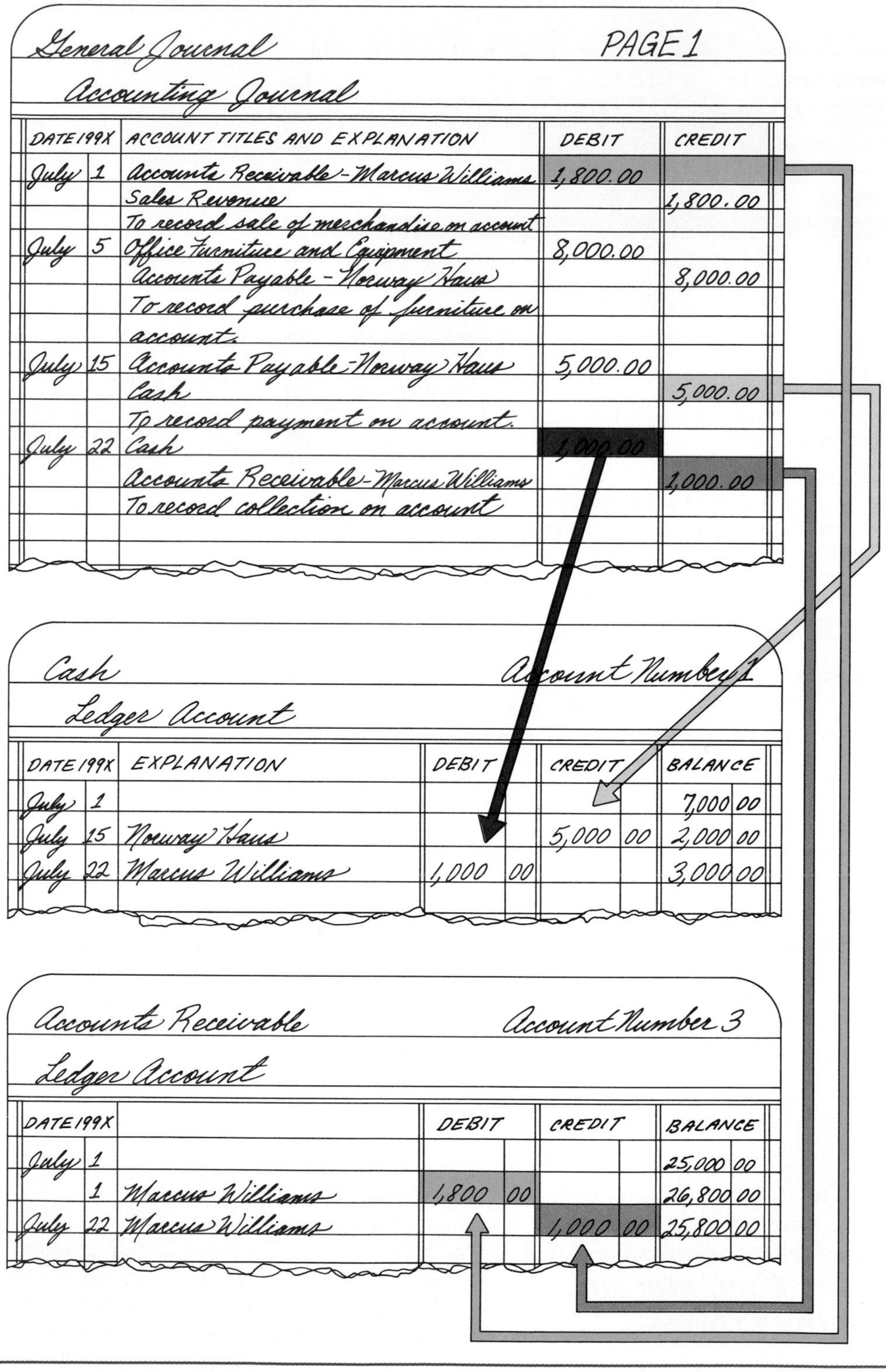

General Journal   PAGE 1

Accounting Journal

DATE 199X		ACCOUNT TITLES AND EXPLANATION	DEBIT	CREDIT
July	1	Accounts Receivable—Marcus Williams	1,800.00	
		Sales Revenue		1,800.00
		To record sale of merchandise on account		
July	5	Office Furniture and Equipment	8,000.00	
		Accounts Payable—Norway Haus		8,000.00
		To record purchase of furniture on		
		account.		
July	15	Accounts Payable—Norway Haus	5,000.00	
		Cash		5,000.00
		To record payment on account.		
July	22	Cash	1,000.00	
		Accounts Receivable—Marcus Williams		1,000.00
		To record collection on account		

Cash   *Account Number 1*

Ledger Account

DATE 199X		EXPLANATION	DEBIT		CREDIT		BALANCE	
July	1						7,000	00
July	15	Norway Haus			5,000	00	2,000	00
July	22	Marcus Williams	1,000	00			3,000	00

Accounts Receivable   *Account Number 3*

Ledger Account

DATE 199X			DEBIT		CREDIT		BALANCE	
July	1						25,000	00
	1	Marcus Williams	1,800	00			26,800	00
July	22	Marcus Williams			1,000	00	25,800	00

performed each time a sale is "rung up." Not only can such a terminal recall prices from memory and maintain a perpetual inventory count of every item in stock, but it can also perform remarkable feats for the firm's accounting system.

Each time a sale is made, the firm's computer produces a journal entry. This entry is held in storage until posted and serves as data input for developing financial statements and calculating financial ratios. This "do-it-once" approach replaces most of the traditional activities of the bookkeeper.

The Accounting Equation and Double-Entry Bookkeeping

Four fundamental terms are involved in the accounting equation: assets, equities, liabilities, and owners' equity. An **asset** is anything of value owned or leased by the business. Cash, accounts receivable and notes receivable (amounts owed to the business through credit sales), land, buildings, supplies, and marketable securities are all assets.

An **equity** is a claim against the assets of a business. The two major classifications of individuals who have equities in a firm are creditors (liability holders) and owners. A **liability** of a business is anything owed to creditors — that is, the claims of the firm's creditors. When the firm makes credit purchases for inventory, land, or machinery, the creditors' claims are shown as accounts payable or notes payable. Wages and salaries owed to employees also represent liabilities (known as wages payable). The **owners' equity** represents the proprietor's, the partners', or the stockholders' claims against the assets of the firm, or the excess of all assets over all liabilities.

$$\text{Equities} = \text{Liabilities} + \text{Owners' Equity}$$

Because equities by definition represent the total claims against assets, then assets must equal equities:

$$\text{Assets} = \text{Equities}$$

The basic **accounting equation** reflects the financial position of any firm at any point in time:

$$\text{Assets} = \text{Liabilities} + \text{Owners' Equity}$$

Double-Entry Bookkeeping

The method for maintaining the balance of the accounting equation is to use two entries for every transaction affecting the equation. This procedure, first described in a book written in 1494 by an Italian monk named Pacioli and in use since then, is called **double-entry bookkeeping**. By offsetting one side of the accounting equation with a change on the other side, the equation remains in balance. Similarly, a decrease in an account on one side of the accounting equation that is offset by an increase on the same side leaves the equation in balance.

An example from the journal shown in Figure 18.4 illustrates the use of double-entry bookkeeping. On July 5, the firm made an $8,000 office furniture

asset
Anything of value owned or leased by a business.

equity
Claim against the assets of a business.

liability
Claim of the firm's creditors.

owners' equity
Claims of the proprietor, the partners, or the stockholders against the assets of the firm; the excess of assets over liabilities.

accounting equation
Basic accounting concept that assets are equal to liabilities plus owners' equity.

double-entry bookkeeping
Process requiring two entries for every transaction, thereby keeping the accounting equation in balance.

purchase and agreed to repay Norway Haus in two installments. The accounting equation would show:

Assets	=	Liabilities	+ Owners' Equity
+$8,000	=	+$8,000	+ $0
(Office Furniture)		(Accounts Payable)	

The bookkeeping entries made to reflect transactions are referred to as debits and credits. Although these terms have become part of our language, their meaning is often misunderstood. Debits and credits do not necessarily refer to increases and decreases; they indicate in which of two columns (left or right) of the journal or ledger account an amount is to be recorded. A **debit** is a bookkeeping entry that records an increase in an asset, a decrease in a liability, or a decrease in owners' equity. A **credit** indicates a decrease in an asset, an increase in a liability, or an increase in owners' equity. As shown in Figure 18.4, debits are recorded in the left column of a journal or ledger and credits are recorded in the right column.

debit
An increase in an asset, a decrease in a liability, or a decrease in owners' equity.

credit
A decrease in an asset, an increase in a liability, or an increase in owners' equity.

Accounting Statements

The relationship expressed by the accounting equation is used to develop two primary accounting statements prepared by every business, large or small: the balance sheet and the income statement. (Many firms also prepare a third financial statement — the statement of cash flows — explained briefly later in this chapter.) These two statements reflect the current financial position of the firm and the most recent analysis of income, expenses, and profits for interested parties inside and outside the firm. They provide a fundamental basis for planning activities and are used in attracting new investors, securing borrowed funds, and preparing tax returns.

The Balance Sheet

balance sheet
Statement of a firm's financial position on a particular date.

The **balance sheet** shows the financial position of a company as of a particular date. It is like a photograph in that it captures the status of the firm's assets and equities at a moment in time.

Balance sheets should be prepared at regular intervals to provide information to management concerning the financial position of the firm. Balance sheets are provided for external users at least once a year and, more typically, quarterly. Managers are likely to receive such statements on a more frequent basis.

Figure 18.5 shows the balance sheet for The Ski Patrol, an imaginary California retailer marketing ski equipment, ski clothing, group ski tours, and ski instruction. The basic accounting equation is illustrated by the three classifications on The Ski Patrol's balance sheet. The assets total must equal the total of the firm's liabilities and the owners' equity.

Assets

The typical balance sheet classifies assets on the basis of conversion time: the ease with which they can be turned into cash. The three categories of assets are current assets, fixed assets, and intangible assets.

Figure 18.5   Balance Sheet for The Ski Patrol

The Ski Patrol
123 Main Street
Big Bear, California
09440-6725

THE SKI PATROL
Balance Sheet
as of December 31, 1990

ASSETS

Current Assets			
Cash		$ 4,000	
Marketable Securities		15,000	
Accounts Receivable	$ 79,000		
Less: Allowance for			
Doubtful Accounts	4,000	75,000	
Notes Receivable		22,000	
Inventory		56,000	
Prepaid Expenses		6,000	
Total Current Assets			$ 178,000
Fixed Assets			
Store Equipment	$ 71,000		
Less: Accumulated Depreciation	15,000	$ 56,000	
Furniture and Fixtures	$ 19,000		
Less: Accumulated Depreciation	4,000	15,000	
Total Fixed Assets			$ 71,000
Intangible Assets			
Copyrights		$ 5,000	
Total Intangible Assets			5,000
Total Assets			$ 254,000

LIABILITIES AND OWNERS' EQUITY

Current Liabilities			
Accounts Payable	$ 41,000		
Current Installments of Long-Term Debt	15,000		
Accrued Expenses	7,000		
Income Taxes Payable	6,000		
Total Current Liabilities		$ 69,000	
Long-Term Liabilities			
Long-Term Notes Payable	$ 30,000		
Total Long-Term Liabilities		30,000	
Total Liabilities		$ 99,000	
Owners' Equity			
Common Stock	$ 80,000		
Retained Earnings	75,000		
Total Owners' Equity		$ 155,000	
Total Liabilities and Owners' Equity		$ 254,000	

Current Assets   Certain items are always listed first in the asset section of the balance sheet. These **current assets** include cash and those items that can or will be converted to cash or be used within one year. Due to the ease and speed at which they can be converted to cash and the fact that they may change form several times during a typical year, current assets are frequently referred to as *liquid assets.* They are listed in order of their expected **liquidity** — the speed at which they can be converted to cash. For The Ski Patrol, the current assets include the following:

◆   Cash — funds on hand or in bank deposits that can be withdrawn immediately as needed.

current assets
Cash and other assets that can or will be converted to cash or used within one year.

liquidity
Speed at which items can be converted to cash.

◆ Marketable Securities — temporary investments of surplus funds in stocks, bonds, or other investments that can be quickly converted to cash.

◆ Accounts Receivable — credit purchases by the firm's customers. In certain cases, the amount of outstanding accounts receivable is reduced to reflect management's belief that certain of these receivables will either be partially repaid or not repaid at all. As Figure 18.5 illustrates, an allowance for doubtful accounts is included to notify interested parties of this possibility.

◆ Notes Receivable — funds owed the company as described by a written document called a *note* that specifies the amount of funds owed and the time and place of repayment.

◆ Inventory — merchandise on hand for sale by the business. For manufacturers, inventory may also consist of raw materials, component parts, and goods in process as well as finished goods ready for sale. Inventory for merchandisers such as wholesalers and retailers consists primarily of finished products offered for sale to customers.

◆ Prepaid Expenses — include services such as insurance and prepaid rent and supplies on hand that have been paid for but not used. Benefits from these services and supplies will be received during the following operating period.

fixed assets
Relatively permanent assets expected to be used for periods longer than one year.

Fixed Assets   Relatively permanent assets that are expected to be used in the operation of the firm for periods longer than one year are considered **fixed** (or plant) **assets**. Included in this category of long-term assets are land, buildings, machinery, transportation equipment, computers, and furniture and fixtures. All of these, except land, are considered depreciable assets since they wear out over time from use or age and must eventually be replaced. The cost of this wearing out of valuable assets is reflected on the balance sheet by an accounting procedure called *depreciation*. **Depreciation**, or cost recovery, is the allocation of the cost of a long-term asset over the years in which it is used to generate revenue for the firm. While no actual cash outlays are involved, charging a portion of the total cost of a machine or a piece of furniture or equipment to each of the years in which it is used results in a more accurate determination of the total costs involved in the firm's operation.

depreciation
Noncash expense involving the allocation of the cost of an asset over the years in which it is used.

intangible assets
Items of value that have no tangible physical properties.

Intangible Assets   Unlike current and fixed assets, **intangible assets** have no tangible physical properties. They include patents on inventions, designs, or processes; copyrights and trademarks protecting written or recorded materials; and goodwill. Although they are difficult to convert to cash, they frequently represent important assets for the firm. In some instances, they may be licensed for use by others or sold outright. Many of the items in the nation's toy stores, such as Pee-Wee Herman dolls, toys, and school supplies, are the result of licenses provided by copyright owners in exchange for royalty payments. As Figure 18.5 indicates, the copyrights held on The Ski Patrol's name and distinctive logo are valued at $5,000.

Liabilities

The financial obligations of the business to other businesses and individuals are called *liabilities*. Like assets, liabilities are typically listed on the balance sheet in the order in which they will come due. They are classified as either current or long-term liabilities.

Photo source: Courtesy of Reynolds Metals Company.

The fully automated equipment that packages Reynolds Metals Company's aluminum foil is one of the firm's fixed assets, while the completed product that is ready to be shipped to retailers is a current asset. An intangible asset is the well-known and well-respected Reynolds Wrap brand name.

Current Liabilities   Those claims that will be repaid within a one-year period are called **current liabilities**. For Ski Patrol, current liabilities include accounts payable, current installments of long-term debt, accrued expenses, and income taxes payable.

Accounts payable and notes payable are the liability counterparts of accounts receivable and notes receivable. Accounts payable represent credit purchases by the firm that must be repaid within a one-year period. Notes payable are loans represented by a written and signed document specifying the amount to be repaid and the time and place of repayment. In many instances, notes payable extend beyond a single year. The installments payable on the note in the current year are current liabilities and the additional funds that are payable after one year are included on the balance sheet as long-term liabilities. Accrued expenses are obligations incurred by the company for which payments have not been made. They include such items as utility services, interest on loans, labor, and taxes. Since tax payments represent a substantial accrued expense that must be paid, Ski Patrol lists the $6,000 in taxes owed as a separate item on its balance sheet.

Comparing Current Assets and Current Liabilities   Because they will require repayment within the next year, current liabilities can quickly provide a cash crisis for a business with inadequate reserves of cash or other liquid assets that can be converted to cash. Consequently, most firms closely monitor the

current liabilities
Claims of creditors that are to be repaid within one year.

working capital
Difference between current assets and current liabilities.

relationship between current assets and current liabilities. The term **working capital** refers to the difference between current assets and current liabilities. It reflects the ability of the firm to meet its short-term payment commitments. Any excess of current assets over current liabilities can provide a cushion against unexpected reductions in assets or increases in liabilities and serve as the means of financing such decisions as increasing inventory or credit sales to take advantage of unexpected situations.

long-term liabilities
Debts that come due one year or more after the date of the balance sheet.

Long-Term Liabilities   All debts that come due one year or more after the date of the balance sheet are classified as **long-term liabilities**. These include such items as bonds, long-term notes payable, mortgages, and other business loans from banks or other financial institutions that are not scheduled for repayment during the coming year.

Owners' Equity

The final major category on the firm's balance sheet is also the final component of the accounting equation. Owners' equity represents the investment in the business. It is comprised of two elements: investments made by the owners of the firm and retained earnings that are left in the business rather than distributed to the owners.

The specific listings in the owners' equity section of the balance sheet varies according to the form of business organization. Unincorporated businesses record the direct investment of the owners in a *capital account* with the name of the proprietor or partners. For partnerships, the capital account reflects the exact amount invested by each partner. Corporate investment is reflected by issuing common stock to the owners (or shareholders). In the case of Ski Patrol, the corporation was formed by issuing 80,000 shares of common stock to the firm's shareholders at a price of $1 per share. This direct investment of $80,000 is listed on the firm's balance sheet as *Common Stock.*

The profits of the corporation can be distributed to the shareholders in the form of cash dividends, or they can be retained by the corporation and reinvested in the business. Retained earnings can be used for expansion and growth and can be invested in such assets as land and buildings. Ski Patrol's retained earnings of $75,000 represent the accumulated earnings that have been left in the firm.

Unincorporated businesses do not distinguish between the initial investment of their owners and subsequent earnings retained in the business. The capital account of a proprietorship or partnership includes not only the initial direct investment but also subsequent additional investments, withdrawals, and retention of earnings. Unlike the corporate balance sheet, the owners' equity section of a proprietor's or partnership's balance sheet combines retained earnings and direct investments of owners into a single account.

The Income Statement

income statement
Financial record of revenues, expenses, and profits of a company over a period of time.

Earlier, the balance sheet was compared to a photograph in the way it reflects the financial position of the company at a specific point in time. Continuing this analogy, the **income statement** would resemble a motion picture, because it shows the income, expenses, and profits of a company over a period of time.

Figure 18.6   Income Statement for The Ski Patrol

The Ski Patrol
123 Main Street
Big Bear, California
09440-6725

THE SKI PATROL

Income Statement
For the Year Ended December 31, 1990

Revenues			
Gross Sales		$ 300,000	
Less: Sales Returns and			
Allowances		8,000	
Net Sales			$ 292,000
Costs of Goods Sold			
Beginning Inventory		$ 65,000	
Purchases during Year	$ 127,000		
Less: Purchase Discounts	4,000		
Net Purchases		123,000	
Cost of Goods Available for Sale		$ 188,000	
Less: Ending Inventory, Dec. 31		56,000	
Cost of Goods Sold			$ 132,000
Gross Profit			$ 160,000
Operating Expenses			
Selling Expenses			
Sales Salaries and Commissions	$ 51,000		
Advertising	16,000		
Depreciation: Store Equipment	5,000		
Miscellaneous Selling Expenses	3,000		
Total Selling Expenses		$ 75,000	
General and Administrative Expenses			
Office Salaries	$ 35,000		
Office Supplies	8,000		
Depreciation: Office Equipment	3,000		
Miscellaneous General Expenses	2,000		
Total General Expenses		48,000	
Total Operating Expenses			$ 123,000
Net Income Before Taxes			$ 37,000
Less: Income Taxes			7,000
Net Income			$ 30,000

The purpose of the income statement (also called an *operating statement* or a *profit and loss statement*) is to show the profitability (or unprofitability) of a firm during a period of time, usually a year, a quarter, or a month. In addition to reporting on the amount of profit or loss, it is particularly useful for enabling decision makers to focus on overall revenues and the costs involved in generating these revenues. For nonprofit organizations, this statement provides specific indications of the ability of the organization's revenues and contributions to cover the costs involved in its operation. Finally, the income statement provides much of the basic data needed to calculate numerous ratios used by management in planning and controlling the organization. Figure 18.6 shows the 1990 income statement for The Ski Patrol.

Major Components of the Income Statement

The income statement summarizes the income and expenses of the firm over a period of time. The basic format shows the deduction of costs and expenses, including taxes, from income in order to determine the net profit of the firm for that period. The equation for the income statement is:

$$\text{Revenues} - \text{Expenses} = \text{Net Profit (or Loss)}$$

Figure 18.6 may be divided into the following major sections:

	Net Sales	$292,000
Minus:	Cost of Goods Sold	− 132,000
Equals:	Gross Profit	$160,000
Minus:	Expenses	− 123,000
Equals:	Net Income before Taxes	$ 37,000
Minus:	Income Taxes	− 7,000
Equals:	Net Income	$ 30,000

revenues

Funds received from sales of products and services and from interest payments, dividends, royalties, and rents.

Revenues   For most businesses, **revenues** are generated by the sale of products or services. In addition, some firms receive additional revenues from interest earned on investments; sale of property; rents; royalties earned on patents, copyrights, or trademarks; and dividends. Nonprofit organizations may generate substantial revenues from grants and donations from individuals, businesses, and government agencies. These revenues provide the funds necessary to operate the organization and earn a profit for its owners.

Ski Patrol produces revenues by selling both products (ski equipment and clothing) and services (ski instructions and group ski tours). As Figure 18.6 indicates, total 1990 gross sales amounted to $300,000.

The gross sales figure is reduced by $8,000 as a result of a number of returns and allowances provided for Ski Patrol customers. Some reductions occur when a portion of the sales price is refunded on an item that is damaged or partially defective (a sales allowance). In other instances, returned merchandise must be subtracted from the gross sales figure to accurately reflect net sales.

Cost of Goods Sold   This section of the income statement reflects the cost of the merchandise or services that generate the firm's revenue. Since Ski Patrol is a retailer, the Cost of Goods Sold section contains a subsection called *Net Purchases.* In the case of a manufacturer, an entry labeled *Cost of Goods Manufactured* would be included in addition to purchases of raw materials and component parts. Otherwise, the income statements for manufacturers and intermediaries such as retailers and wholesalers are similar.

Cost of Goods Sold for Ski Patrol is calculated in the following manner. At the beginning of the year, total inventory of $65,000 was on hand. In addition, Ski Patrol managers purchased $127,000 in inventory during 1990 to add to the beginning inventory, but received a purchase discount of $4,000 from one firm for quantity purchases, resulting in net purchases of $123,000. When this was added to the cost of beginning inventory, the total cost of goods available for sale amounted to $188,000.

At the end of the year, $56,000 in unsold inventory was still on hand, indicating that the cost of goods sold during 1990 was $132,000 ($188,000 minus $56,000). Total *gross profit* ($292,000 net sales less $132,000 cost of goods sold) amounted to $160,000.

Figure 18.7   Example of a Selling Expense

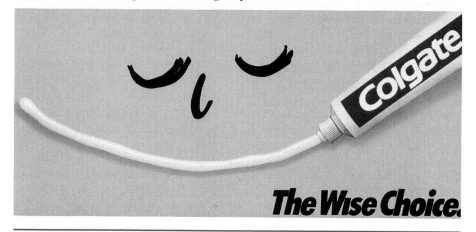

Source: Courtesy of Colgate-Palmolive Company, copyright 1988.

Operating Expenses   In addition to the costs of acquiring or producing goods to be sold, firms typically incur a number of **operating expenses** in the course of running the business. These consist of selling expenses and general expenses. **Selling expenses** are those resulting from marketing and distributing the products or services of the firm. They include salaries and commissions paid to sales personnel, advertising, sales supplies, delivery expenses, and such miscellaneous selling expenses as telephone charges, depreciation, insurance, and utilities allocated to sales. Selling expenses for Colgate-Palmolive Company include the outdoor advertisement shown in Figure 18.7 and the firm's print and television campaigns. Total selling expenses for The Ski Patrol amounted to $75,000.

    General and administrative expenses are those resulting from the overall operation of the business. They include those expense items that are not directly related to the acquisition, production, or sale of the firm's products or services. General expenses include salaries of office personnel; supplies; special services such as consulting, accounting services, or legal fees; insurance; postage; and depreciation on office equipment. In 1990, Ski Patrol incurred total general expenses of $48,000.

Net Income or Loss   Total operating expense is determined by combining selling expenses and general expenses. Ski Patrol's total operating expenses amounted to $123,000 (selling expenses of $75,000 plus $48,000 in general expenses). The firm's *net income before taxes* in 1990 amounted to $37,000 ($160,000 gross profit minus $123,000 total operating expenses). After subtracting $7,000 for taxes, the firm earned a total **net income** of $30,000 for 1990. In instances where total expenditures exceed total revenues, a net loss occurs.

    The final figure on the income statement is the well-known **bottom line** — the overall profit or loss earned by the firm. Profit or loss statistics are perhaps the most commonly quoted measures of a firm's performance. When expressed as a percentage of sales, equity, or the number of shares of stock outstanding, net income can be compared with profits of previous years and with the earnings of other firms in the industry. The bottom line permits such comparisons to be made and allows shareholders, lenders, and potential investors to make general assessments of a company's performance.

operating expenses
All business costs other than those included in the cost of goods sold.

selling expenses
Expenses incurred in marketing and distributing goods and services.

general and administrative expenses
Operational expenses not directly related to the acquisition, production, or sale of the firm's goods or services.

net income
Profit or loss incurred over a specific period; determined by subtracting all expenses from revenues.

bottom line
Overall profit or loss earned by a firm.

Statement of Cash Flows

In addition to the income statement and the balance sheet, many firms prepare a third accounting statement. Since 1987, all companies listed on organized stock exchanges have been required to prepare a statement of cash flows to include with the income statement and balance sheet as part of their annual registration information. In addition, major lenders often require it of unlisted companies. As the name indicates, the **statement of cash flows** provides investors and creditors with relevant information about a firm's cash receipts and cash payments during an accounting period. It is sometimes referred to as the "where got, where gone" statement because it presents the sources and uses of cash for the firm.[6]

> **statement of cash flows**
> Information on a firm's cash receipts and cash payments that presents the sources and uses of cash for the firm.

Proponents of the new financial statement hope its preparation and scrutiny by affected parties will prevent financial disaster for otherwise profitable firms that are forced into bankruptcy due to a lack of funds needed to continue day-to-day operations. A classic example occurred more than a decade ago with the bankruptcy of W. T. Grant. At the time it declared bankruptcy, Grant was one of the nation's largest retailers. Its annual sales had grown from $1.3 billion in 1970 to $1.8 billion in 1974. In addition, the firm had shown a net profit in every year from 1970 through 1973. However, several years of negative cash flows resulting from excessive inventories and receivables resulted in the firm's collapse and ultimate demise.

Interpreting Financial Statements

Once financial statements have been produced from the accounting data collected for a period, an accountant must interpret them. The fact that a firm earned a profit for the past year is of interest; of equal interest is the profit it should have earned. A number of techniques have been developed for interpreting financial information in order to aid management in planning and evaluating the day-to-day and ongoing operations of the company. Two commonly used techniques are percentage of net sales and ratio analysis.

Percentage of Net Sales

Figure 18.8 reveals how Ski Patrol's income statement can be converted from dollar amounts to a percentage of net sales. Cost and expense items shown in percentage form can quickly be compared with those of previous periods or with other companies in the industry. In this way, unusually high or low expenses become immediately apparent to management, and corrective action can be taken if necessary. In addition, the percentage figures assist investors and financial analysts in making such comparisons.

Ratio Analysis

A second method of interpreting financial statements, ratio analysis, is one of the most commonly used managerial planning and control tools. By comparing the company ratios to industry standards, problem areas can be pinpointed and

Figure 18.8   Percentage of Net Sales for The Ski Patrol

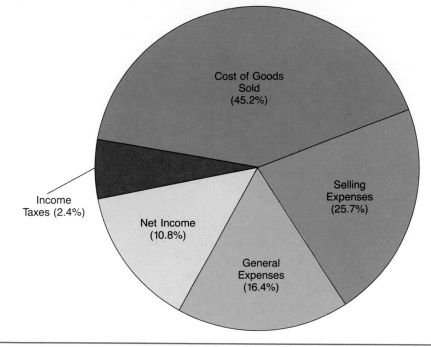

areas of excellence identified. Moreover, by comparing ratios for the current accounting period with those of previous periods, developing trends can be detected. Four categories of ratios exist; liquidity ratios, profitability ratios, activity ratios, and debt ratios.

Liquidity Ratios

A **liquidity ratio** measures a firm's ability to meet its short-term obligations. Highly liquid firms are less likely to face emergencies in raising needed funds to repay loans. On the other hand, those firms with less liquidity may be forced to use high-cost lending sources to meet their maturing obligations or face default. Two commonly used liquidity ratios are the current ratio and the acid-test ratio.

liquidity ratio
Ratio measuring a firm's ability to meet its short-term obligations.

Current Ratio   The **current ratio** compares current assets to current liabilities. It measures the company's ability to pay its current debts as they mature. The current ratio of Ski Patrol is computed as:

$$\text{Current Ratio} = \frac{\text{Current Assets}}{\text{Current Liabilities}} = \frac{\$178,000}{\$69,000} = 2.6 \text{ to } 1$$

current ratio
Ratio measuring the company's ability to pay its current debts as they mature; calculated by dividing current assets by current liabilities.

This means The Ski Patrol has $2.60 of current assets for every $1 of current liabilities. In general, a current ratio of 2 to 1 is considered to be financially satisfactory. This rule of thumb must be considered along with other factors such as the nature of the business, the season of the year, and the quality of the company's management. Ski Patrol's management and other interested parties are likely to compare this 2.6 to 1 ratio to previous operating periods and to industry averages to determine its appropriateness.

acid-test ratio
Ratio measuring the ability of a firm to meet its current debt on short notice; calculated by dividing quick assets by current liabilities.

Acid-Test Ratio   The **acid-test ratio**, or quick ratio, measures the ability of the firm to meet its current debt on short notice. It calculates quick assets against current liabilities. It does not include inventory or prepaid expenses; only cash, marketable securities, and accounts receivable — all highly liquid assets — are considered.

Ski Patrol's current balance sheet lists the following "quick" assets: cash ($4,000), marketable securities ($15,000), accounts receivable ($75,000), and current installments of notes receivable ($22,000). The firm's acid-test ratio is computed as:

$$\text{Acid-Test Ratio} = \frac{\text{Quick Assets}}{\text{Current Liabilities}} = \frac{\$116,000}{\$69,000} = 1.7 \text{ to } 1$$

Because the traditional rule of thumb for an adequate acid-test ratio is 1 to 1, Ski Patrol appears to be in a good short-term credit position. However, the same cautions as for the current ratio should be applied here. This ratio should be compared with industry averages and with previous operating periods in determining its appropriateness for The Ski Patrol.

Profitability Ratios

profitability ratio
Ratio measuring the overall financial performance of the firm.

A **profitability ratio** measures the overall financial performance of the firm. It is designed to indicate how successful a firm is in terms of its earnings as compared with its total sales or investment. Over a period of time, profitability ratios may also reveal the effectiveness of management in operating the business. Three commonly used profitability ratios are earnings per share, return on sales, and return on equity.

earnings per share
Profits earned by a corporation for each share of common stock outstanding; calculated by dividing net income after taxes by the number of common shares outstanding.

Earnings per Share   For corporations, one of the most frequently quoted and commonly watched ratios in business is **earnings per share**. This ratio indicates the amount of profits earned by a corporation for each share of common stock outstanding. Such earnings represent an important means by which a firm can continue to grow if they are reinvested in the company. They also are the basis for dividends paid to the firm's owners. Earnings per share for The Ski Patrol in 1990 are calculated as follows:

$$\text{Earnings per Share} = \frac{\text{Net Income after Taxes}}{\text{Common Shares Outstanding}} = \frac{\$30,000}{\$80,000} = \$0.375$$

The $0.375 earnings figure can be compared with earnings per share in previous years to provide some indication of Ski Patrol's performance. It can also be compared with the earnings per share of competitors in the industry to evaluate the firm's relative performance.

return on sales
Ratio measuring company profitability by comparing net income and net sales.

Return on Sales   The **return on sales** financial ratio measures company profitability by comparing net income and sales. For Ski Patrol, the ratio is computed as:

$$\text{Return on Sales} = \frac{\text{Net Income}}{\text{Net Sales}} = \frac{\$30,000}{\$292,000} = 10.3 \text{ percent}$$

This profitability ratio is a critical indicator for any profit-seeking firm. In the case of Ski Patrol, it indicates a profit of 10.3 cents was realized for every dollar of sales. Although this ratio varies widely among business firms, Ski Patrol compares very favorably with retail stores in general, which average about a 5 percent return on sales. However, it should be compared with profit forecasts, past performance, and/or more specific industry averages in determining its appropriateness.

Return on Equity   The **return on equity** focuses on the returns the firm's owners are receiving on their investment in the business. It is the ratio between net income earned by the firm and total owners' equity. Both financial statements provide data used to calculate this ratio:

$$\text{Return on Equity} = \frac{\text{Net Income}}{\text{Total Owners' Equity}} = \frac{\$30,000}{\$155,000} = 19.4 \text{ percent}$$

While Ski Patrol's return of almost 20 percent on equity appears to be satisfactory, the degree of risk present in the industry must also be considered. Stockholders use this ratio to determine whether their funds invested in the business are generating the returns they expected when they made their initial investment.

return on equity
Ratio measuring company profitability by comparing net income and total owners' equity to assess the returns owners are receiving for their overall investment.

Activity Ratios

The third category of ratios, the **activity ratio**, measures the effectiveness of the firm's use of its resources. The most frequently used activity ratio is the inventory turnover ratio.

Inventory Turnover Ratio   The **inventory turnover ratio** indicates the number of times merchandise moves through the business. It is calculated by dividing the cost of goods sold by the average amount of inventory. If the amount of inventory on hand varies considerably from month to month, all 12 of the end-of-month inventories should be totaled and divided by 12 to determine the average inventory for the year. Since The Ski Patrol's inventory is relatively constant throughout the year, average inventory is determined by adding the January 1 beginning inventory of $65,000 and the December 31 ending inventory of $56,000 (as shown on the income statement) and dividing by two. The average inventory of $60,500 is then divided into the firm's cost of goods sold using the following equation:

activity ratio
Ratio measuring the effectiveness of the firm's use of its resources.

inventory turnover ratio
Ratio measuring the number of times merchandise moves through a business; calculated by dividing the cost of goods sold by the average amount of inventory.

$$\text{Inventory Turnover Ratio} = \frac{\text{Cost of Goods Sold}}{\text{Average Inventory}} = \frac{\$132,000}{\$60,500} = 2.2 \text{ times}$$

The turnover rate can be compared with industry standards and used as a measure of efficiency. For retailers such as furniture and jewelry stores, an annual turnover rate of 1.5 times is about average. For a supermarket, however, the turnover rate is 14 to 18 times.

Debt Ratios

The final category of financial ratios, the **debt ratio**, measures the extent to which a firm relies on debt financing. Debt ratios are of particular interest to potential investors and lenders. If too much debt has been used to finance the

debt ratio
Ratio measuring the extent to which a firm relies on debt financing in its operations.

firm's operations, problems may arise in meeting future interest payments and repaying outstanding loans. In addition, both investors and lenders may prefer to deal with firms whose owners have invested enough of their own money into the firm to avoid overreliance on borrowing. The debt to owners' equity ratio provides answers to these questions.

debt to owners' equity ratio
Ratio measuring the extent to which company operations are financed by borrowed funds; calculated by dividing total liabilities by owners' equity.

Debt to Owners' Equity Ratio   The **debt to owners' equity ratio** measures the extent to which the operations of the company are financed by borrowed funds. It indicates the amount of funds contributed by creditors as compared with the total funds provided. The debt to owners' equity ratio for The Ski Patrol is computed as:

$$\text{Debt to Owners' Equity Ratio} = \frac{\text{Total Liabilities}}{\text{Owners' Equity}} = \frac{\$99,000}{\$155,000} = 0.64$$

Since a debt-to-equity ratio of greater than 1 would indicate the firm was relying more on debt financing than on owners' equity, it is clear that Ski Patrol's owners have invested considerably more than the total amount of liabilities on the firm's balance sheet. However, the specific ratio, like all of the other financial ratios discussed earlier, should be evaluated only by comparing it with average industry ratios, the ratios of other firms in the area (if such data is available), previously calculated ratios for the firm, and management expectations.

Budgeting

budget
Planning and control tool that reflects expected sales revenues, operating expenses, and cash receipts and outlays.

Although the financial statements discussed in this chapter focus on what has occurred in the past, they are the basis for planning the future. A **budget** is a financial blueprint for a future period that reflects expected sales revenues, operating expenses, and cash receipts and outlays. It is the quantification of the firm's plans for a specified future period. Since it requires management to specify expected sales, cash inflows and outflows, and costs, it serves as a planning and control tool. The budget serves as the standard with which actual performance is compared.

Budget preparation is frequently time-consuming and involves many people in various departments of the firm. The complexity of the budgeting process varies with the size and complexity of the organization. Giant corporations such as General Motors, Phillips Petroleum, and Texas Instruments tend to have more complex and sophisticated budgeting systems; their budgets serve as a means of integrating the numerous divisions of the firm in addition to being planning and control tools. But budgeting by both large and small firms is similar to household budgeting. In both instances, the purposes of the budget are to match income and expenses; to accomplish objectives; and to correctly time inflows and outflows.

Since the accounting department is the financial nerve center of the organization, it provides much of the data used in budget development. The overall master, or operating, budget is actually a composite of numerous sub-budgets for each of the departments or functional areas of the firm. These typically include the production budget, the cash budget, the capital expenditures budget, the advertising budget, and the sales budget. These budgets are typically established on an annual basis, but may be divided monthly or quarterly for

Figure 18.9 Sample Cash Budget

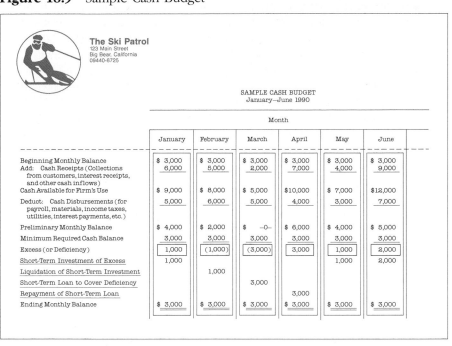

The Ski Patrol
123 Main Street
Big Bear, California
09440-6725

SAMPLE CASH BUDGET
January–June 1990

	January	February	March	April	May	June
Month						
Beginning Monthly Balance	$ 3,000	$ 3,000	$ 3,000	$ 3,000	$ 3,000	$ 3,000
Add: Cash Receipts (Collections from customers, interest receipts, and other cash inflows)	6,000	5,000	2,000	7,000	4,000	9,000
Cash Available for Firm's Use	$ 9,000	$ 8,000	$ 5,000	$10,000	$ 7,000	$12,000
Deduct: Cash Disbursements (for payroll, materials, income taxes, utilities, interest payments, etc.)	5,000	6,000	5,000	4,000	3,000	7,000
Preliminary Monthly Balance	$ 4,000	$ 2,000	$ –0–	$ 6,000	$ 4,000	$ 5,000
Minimum Required Cash Balance	3,000	3,000	3,000	3,000	3,000	3,000
Excess (or Deficiency)	1,000	(1,000)	(3,000)	3,000	1,000	2,000
Short-Term Investment of Excess	1,000				1,000	2,000
Liquidation of Short-Term Investment		1,000				
Short-Term Loan to Cover Deficiency			3,000			
Repayment of Short-Term Loan				3,000		
Ending Monthly Balance	$ 3,000	$ 3,000	$ 3,000	$ 3,000	$ 3,000	$ 3,000

control purposes. Since some activities, such as the construction of new manufacturing facilities or long-term purchasing contracts, tend to involve activities extending over several years, longer-term budgets may be used.

Figure 18.9 shows a sample cash budget for a six-month period. This company follows the common practice of establishing a minimum required cash balance each month to cover expected cash needs. The $3,000 minimum balance is determined on the basis of past experience. As the figure reveals, the cash budget identifies months in which excess funds will be invested to earn interest rather than remaining idle. The cash budget also indicates periods in which temporary loans will be required to finance operations (during March, in this example). Finally, it produces a tangible standard for comparing actual cash inflows and outflows.

Summary of Learning Goals

1. Explain the functions of accounting and its importance to the firm's management and to outside parties such as investors, creditors, and government agencies. Accounting measures, interprets, and communicates financial information to parties inside and outside the firm for effective decision making. Accountants are responsible for gathering, recording, and interpreting financial information to management. In addition, they provide financial information on the status and operation of the firm for use by such outside parties as government agencies and potential investors and lenders.

2.   Distinguish between public and private accountants and explain the roles played by CPAs and CMAs.   Public accountants are independent organizations or individuals who provide accounting services, such as tax statement preparation, management consulting, and accounting systems design, to other firms or individuals for a fee. Private, or management, accountants are responsible for collecting and recording financial transactions; preparing financial statements; and interpreting statements for managers in their own firm, nonprofit organization, or government agency.

The certified public accountant (CPA) has met state certification requirements and has passed a comprehensive examination covering law, accounting theory and practice, and auditing. CPAs are sometimes employed as private accountants but are particularly important to public accounting firms as auditors.

The certified management accountant (CMA) has passed the certification requirements of the National Association of Accountants. CMAs hold positions at all levels in the organization, from staff accountant to vice-president of finance.

3.   Outline the steps in the accounting process.   The accounting process involves the recording, classifying, and summarizing of accounting transactions and using this information to produce financial statements for the firm's management and other interested parties. Transactions are chronologically recorded in a journal, posted in ledgers, and then summarized in accounting statements.

4.   Identify the accounting equation and its components and explain the equation's relationship to double-entry bookkeeping.   Assets are things of value owned or leased and used in the business, such as cash, inventory, land, and machinery. Liabilities are claims against the assets by creditors of the firm. Owners' equity is the owners' claims against the assets. The accounting equation states that assets are equal to liabilities plus owners' equity.

Double-entry bookkeeping is the accounting practice of using two entries for every transaction. An increase in assets results in an increase in liabilities or owners' equity. As a consequence of these changes, the accounting equation remains in balance.

5.   Explain the function of the balance sheet and identify its major components.   The balance sheet shows the financial position of a company as of a particular date. The three major classifications on the balance sheet represent the components of the accounting equation: assets, liabilities, and owners' equity.

6.   Explain the function of the income statement and identify its major components.   The income statement shows the operations of a firm over a specific period. It focuses on the firm's activities — its revenues and expenditures — and the firm's profit or loss during this period. The major components of the income statement are revenues, cost of goods sold, expenses, and profits or losses.

7.   Identify the major financial ratios used in analyzing a firm's financial strengths and weaknesses and explain the purpose of each.   Liquidity ratios measure a firm's ability to meet short-term obligations. Examples are current ratios and acid-test ratios. Profitability ratios assess the overall financial performance of the firm. Earnings per share, return on sales, and return on owners' equity are examples. Activity ratios, such as inventory turnover ratio, measure how effectively a firm uses its resources. Debt ratios measure the extent to which the firm relies on debt to finance its operations, for example, the debt to owners' equity ratio. Each of these ratios assists management and others by enabling a comparison of current company financial information with that of previous years and with industry standards.

8.   Explain the role of budgets in business.   Budgets are financial guidelines for future periods reflecting expected sales revenues, operating expenses, and/or cash receipts and outlays. They represent management's expectations of future occurrences based on plans that have been made and serve as important planning and control tools by providing standards against which actual performance can be compared.

Key Terms

accounting	credit	bottom line
public accountant	balance sheet	statement of cash flows
private accountant	current assets	liquidity ratio
certified public accountant (CPA)	liquidity	current ratio
certified management accountant (CMA)	fixed assets	acid-test ratio
accounting process	depreciation	profitability ratio
journal	intangible assets	earnings per share
ledger	current liabilities	return on sales
posting	working capital	return on equity
asset	long-term liabilities	activity ratio
equity	income statement	inventory turnover ratio
liability	revenues	debt ratio
owners' equity	operating expenses	debt to owners' equity ratio
accounting equation	selling expenses	budget
double-entry bookkeeping	general and administrative expenses	
debit	net income	

Review Questions

1. Who are the major users of accounting information?

2. Distinguish between public accountants and private accountants. Why are approximately 50 percent of the nation's certified public accountants employed as private accountants?

3. Contrast the roles performed by a certified public accountant (CPA) with those of a certified management accountant (CMA).

4. Explain how journals, ledgers, and financial statements are involved with the steps in the accounting process.

5. Explain the concept of double-entry bookkeeping. How is it related to the accounting equation? What role do debits and credits play?

6. Identify the major components of the balance sheet and the income statement and explain the purpose of each component.

7. What are the major differences between the balance sheet and the income statement?

8. What are the major advantages of showing the values for the various items on a firm's income statements in percentages based upon net sales rather than showing the actual figures involved?

9. The financial ratios discussed in the chapter were divided into four basic categories. Identify these categories and describe specific ratios included in each one.

10. Explain the similarities and differences between budgeting and the development of accounting statements. What are the primary purposes of budgets?

Discussion Questions

1. Why do firms include depreciation on their accounting statements when it involves no cash outlays?

2. Identify the three types of assets and the two types of liabilities that appear on a typical balance sheet. Categorize the following account titles:
   - **a.** Adam Fielding, Capital
   - **b.** Mortgage Payable
   - **c.** Patent
   - **d.** Buildings
   - **e.** Common Stock
   - **f.** Prepaid Expenses
   - **g.** Accounts Payable
   - **h.** Marketable Securities

3. Match each of the accounts listed below with the appropriate accounting categories. Each account may be included in more than one category.
   - _____ **a.** Net Sales
   - _____ **b.** Accounts Receivable
   - _____ **c.** Copyrights
   - _____ **d.** Advertising Expenses
   - _____ **e.** Common Stock
   - _____ **f.** Equipment
   - _____ **g.** Marketable Securities
   - _____ **h.** Long-Term Notes Payable
   - _____ **i.** Salary
   - _____ **j.** Retained Earnings

   1. Current Asset
   2. Fixed Asset
   3. Intangible Asset
   4. Current Liability
   5. Long-Term Liability
   6. Owners' Equity
   7. Revenue
   8. Expense

4. Which ratio would provide information on:
   - **a.** A firm's ability to meet short-term obligations
   - **b.** A firm's ability to pay current debts
   - **c.** A firm's ability to pay current debts on short notice

d. A firm's overall financial performance

e. The amount of profits earned for each share of common stock outstanding

f. Net income compared to sales

g. Owners' equity

h. The firm's use of its resources

i. The number of times merchandise moves through the business

j. The extent to which a firm relies on financing

k. The percentage of owners' investments to debt financing

5. At the end of the year, Redmond Enterprises showed the following balances in its accounts:

Land	$ 80,000
Buildings	900,000
Inventory	100,000
Cash	10,000
Accounts Payable	90,000
Accumulated Depreciation on Buildings	586,000
Prepaid Expenses	21,000
Marketable Securities	15,000
Retained Earnings	300,000
Common Shares (80,000 shares @ $1)	80,000
Notes Payable	110,000
Equipment	120,000
Accumulated Depreciation on Equipment	80,000

a. Prepare a balance sheet for Redmond Enterprises.

b. Calculate the current ratio, acid-test ratio, and debt to owners' equity ratio. What conclusions can be drawn from these ratios?

Video Case

Springfield Remanufacturing Corp.

"We teach them about finance and accounting before they turn a wrench." A statement like this from the president and CEO of a company that remanufactures and sells diesel and gasoline engines, transmissions, and related accessories, signals a most unusual company and a unique business philosophy. The company, Springfield Remanufacturing Corporation, was generating sales of $26 million back in 1983, but was also showing a loss of $2 million annually. Its ailing parent, International Harvester (now Navistar), was warding off bankruptcy and agreed to sell SRC to Jack Stack and twelve other employees in a highly leveraged buyout.

Stack and his colleagues had their work cut out for them. Survival meant increasing sales and lowering costs because substantial new liabilities in the form of interest expenses and notes payable had become an additional burden on the new venture. Since then, an economic miracle has occurred in SRC's Springfield, Missouri, home. Within five years, sales almost doubled to $42 million, the workforce grew to 450 people, and 4,000 engines were produced monthly for customers in four industries: medium and heavy-duty trucks, agricultural equipment, heavy construction equipment, and automotive equipment. With a current growth rate approaching 40 percent a year, SRC is ranked as one of the most successful small business operations in the United States.

Central to this growth has been the open-door, open-book management style of Jack Stack, the firm's president and CEO. When Stack and his associates purchased SRC from International Harvester, 115 of the original 171 employees continued with the firm. Today, SRC is completely employee-owned through a stock ownership program (ESOP). Every year since SRC's rebirth, a portion of the company's earnings are set aside to buy some of the company's unissued stock. These purchases go into a trust fund for all full-time

Notes: D. Keith Denton, "Appealing to Their Highest Level of Intelligence," *Supervision,* August 1988, pp. 3–6; Lucien Rhodes and Patricia Amend, "The Turnaround," *Inc.,* August 1986, pp. 42–48; D. Keith Denton, "An Employee Ownership Program That Rebuilt Success," *Personnel Journal,* March 1987, pp. 114–120; Jack Stack, "Crisis Management by Committee," *Inc.,* May 1988, p. 26; and personal correspondence, February 27, 1989.

employees. Employee compensation is directly impacted by the value of corporate stock, which is in turn dependent on company profits. Because of the direct link between financial rewards and company profitability, SRC employees, encouraged by management, take an active interest in the firm's financial status. The secret has been in educating employee-owners in financial data — accounting statements, profit reports, cost control analyses, and quality measures.

Employees meet weekly to receive information on operating income, expenses, cash flows, and other relevant financial data. Employee training on how the numbers are determined and what they mean also occurs at these meetings because Stack and his management team believe that teaching employees about balance sheets, income statements, and cash flow statements is the best way to ensure the success of a company — especially an employee-owned company.

To overcome the initial lack of enthusiasm among SRC employees toward learning about financial matters, Stack emphasized his belief that business is basically a game — a game that anyone can learn to play. The first step is to teach employees the rules of the game. Next, they are given enough information to play the game, and ultimately they must have the opportunity to win or lose. At one point, Stack became so involved in this extraordinary training program that he had every worker in the plant take a series of courses covering most elements of a college business curriculum, including accounting and warehousing.

The entire SRC team — managers, supervisors, administrative personnel, and production workers — has access to the company's monthly financial reports. In small group sessions, supervisors go over the figures, encouraging questions. In addition, the cost accounting department supplies daily printouts, detailing the progress of every job in each supervisor's area. One of the most important aspects of SRC's training involves the use of the income statement. "For us," says Stack, "the income statement is the same as the daily racing form is to a guy handicapping a race, or the same as the tape is to a guy betting on the market . . . it's addictive because it's fun, it's action." The game is to beat the numbers and, in an employee-owned company, beating the numbers means more profits for everyone.

The game starts every Tuesday morning, when some 25 managers and supervisors get together in a conference room equipped with a detailed, pre-printed income statement. The first column of figures lists the income and expense figures for the previous month. The next column gives projections for the current month from the budget prepared at the start of the fiscal year. The following three columns are blank, to be filled in, one column a week, with adjusted projections based on reports given in the meeting. As Stack records the variances on a board in front of the room, the income statement produces a net operating income figure, stating the net sales needed to trigger a bonus distribution for the quarter. (Employee involvement in managerial decision making is encouraged with bonus programs that pay each employee a certain percentage of his or her salary whenever quarterly financial goals are met.) That same afternoon, the information is shared with all employees by supervisors and managers.

Employees take an active part in improving these numbers by discovering methods of meeting the goals and earning their bonuses. Mike Carrigan, an SRC vice-president, parallels these weekly updates to regular physical examinations: Employee rewards are linked directly to the health of the corporation. For example, a water pump assembler can see the impact of his efforts on costs; because each employee is aware of his or her performance standards, each can determine his or her contribution to the overall productivity of the firm. When a standard is met, rewards are given to the employee. In addition to the bonus programs, cash payments are made to employees who submit cost-saving ideas.

Decentralization of cost-control decision making is visible at SRC. For instance, first-line supervisors are actively involved in not only reducing costs in their own departments, but also in helping reduce costs in other areas, thereby affecting companywide expenses. Information is readily available, since there is one computer terminal in the plant for every three employees. Anyone can go to a terminal and secure information on incoming parts, costs, or engineering problems. Data on current labor, material and overhead costs — and comparisons with expected costs — are immediately available.

Keeping people involved is the key to winning. There are no spectators in the game of business — not at SRC. Vice-President Carrigan devised his own strategy to get everyone more involved in planning the company's future direction. He started with operating expenses. After coming up with his own projections in some 20 areas, he asked each manager and supervisor to take personal responsibility for one account and then to report back to him in a month on whether his projections were realistic. The group reconvened a month later, with each supervisor armed with information, such as tools and equipment needs of employees. They had researched past expenditures and tested the production scheduler's estimates. After studying their reports briefly, Carrigan informed them that their findings would be accepted as the budget figures for the coming fiscal year.

"You see, what happened here," says Carrigan, "is that now these people were in effect running their own small businesses. They had set their own budgets and they had to live with them. If they wanted to complain, they had to complain to themselves." More than being aware, the employees were now involved and responsible for their own future. At SRC, only the people can make the numbers work, and they are the same people who set the numbers.

Questions

1. In 1988, SRC had current assets of $13.6 million, fixed assets of $2.9 million, current liabilities of $8.4 million, long-term liabilities of $2.2 million, and stockholders' equity of $5.9 million.

 a. Calculate the current ratio and the debt to owners' equity ratio for the firm.

 b. Calculate the firm's acid-test ratio (accounts receivable amounted to $4,337,298; the cash account totalled $32,332; no marketable securities or notes receivable were on hand).

What conclusions can you make about SRC based on these ratios?

2. Two current asset accounts — accounts receivable ($4.3 million) and inventories ($8.8 million) — account for 96 percent of the firm's current assets. Explain why they represent such a large percentage of current assets. How does this fact impact cash needs for the firm?

3. The case stresses the advantages of providing SRC employees with detailed financial information. Can you think of possible drawbacks to making so much data available?

4. What are the primary advantages of permitting supervisors and employees in each department to develop their own budgets? What are the potential problems of such an approach? Does the fact that SRC is an employee-owned company reduce or eliminate these potential problems?

Careers in Business

A variety of careers exists in the fields of computers, management information systems, and accounting; and job opportunities are rapidly expanding. The Bureau of Labor Statistics forecasts that job opportunities for systems analysts, computer programmers, management accountants, and auditors will all grow much faster than the average for all occupations.

Specific jobs available in computers, management information systems, and accounting include systems analyst, computer programmer, management accountant, controller, auditor, and cost estimator.

Systems Analyst

Systems analysts are computer experts who develop the computer-based information systems required by an organization. They work in all types of business organizations, governments, and consulting and service firms. Currently, there are some 331,000 systems analysts working in the United States.

Job Description. Systems analysts determine what information is needed to solve a problem and how best to obtain it. Once management approves the recommendations, the systems analyst instructs the organization's computer programmers in how to activate the decisions.

Career Path. Trainee positions are available in this career. Trainees work under the direction of senior personnel. Additional responsibilities come with experience. Management slots in this field may come later.

Salary. In a recent year, entry-level systems analysts averaged $23,000 annually. Experienced analysts earned a median of $32,000. For analysts as a group, earnings ranged between $19,200 and $51,300 annually.

Computer Programmer

Computer programmers carry out the instructions of systems analysts. Programmers are required in computer installations in both the private and public sectors. Some 479,000 programmers are currently at work in the United States.

Job Description. Working with the systems analyst's overall plan, computer programmers write the programs that provide the required information. Once these programs are tested and verified, the program-

mer turns the program over to computer operating personnel.

Career Path. Entry-level programmers are assigned basic tasks, while experienced personnel work on more complex assignments. Advancement to supervisory positions is possible.

Salary. In a recent year, programmers' earnings ranged between $20,700 and $43,100 with a median salary of $27,000. An entry level programmer in the federal government earned, on average, $14,800.

Management Accountant

Management accountants work in business firms to provide executives with the financial information they need to make decisions. Currently, more than 900,000 accountants are employed throughout the United States. About 60 percent work in the management accounting field.

Job Description. Management accountants tend to specialize in specific areas of corporate accounting, such as cost accounting, budgeting, and corporate tax accounting. Regardless of the area, all management accounting practices are designed to provide essential information to corporate decision makers.

Career Path. Beginning accountants perform routine tasks in some aspect of management accounting. Responsibilities expand as the person acquires experience. Top positions in management accounting carry titles such as controller, treasurer, or vice-president of finance.

Salary. Entry-level salaries for accountants are among the highest available to graduates. Accounting firms, in a recent year, offered entry-level salaries of up to $30,000. Experience and performance level dictate future increases. In a recent year, chief accountants were paid up to $68,000.

Controller

Sometimes called a treasurer or vice-president of finance, the controller is the top-level executive in management accounting. Controllers are responsible for a firm's entire financial and accounting function.

Job Description. Controllers oversee corporate budgets, cash flow, payroll, accounts receivable, and accounts payable. They are responsible for the business's total flow of funds, both inward and outward. The various accounting departments, such as cost accounting, report to the controller.

Career Path. People who aspire to be controllers must have a successful career in one or more aspects of management accounting. They may then be appointed as assistant controller or division controller. These people report to the corporate controller.

Salary. Depending on the size of the company, corporate controllers earn up to $143,000 a year. Assistant controllers earn up to $70,000 a year.

Auditor

Accountants who monitor an organization's internal accounting controls are called auditors. These workers are accountants who specialize in auditing procedures in private firms, government, and nonprofit organizations.

Job Description. Auditors evaluate accounting records to determine whether monies are being handled properly and are being properly recorded by managers and employees. Audit findings are reported to higher levels of management. Consequently, auditors must be thorough and conduct comprehensive accounting reviews.

Career Path. Beginning auditors are usually assigned to largely clerical duties such as verifying the accuracy of accounting records. Experienced auditors are placed in charge of specific audits and may have several other auditors reporting to them. Management positions are also available within the auditing department. Successful auditors may also move to other areas of accounting. Many top executives began their careers in auditing.

Salary. In a recent year, the average salary for internal auditors was $30,300; for more experienced auditors, the average increased to $40,000 and more.

Cost Estimators

Cost estimators project costs and prices for a variety of businesses from construction and engineering to insurance. An accounting background is helpful. There were 157,000 cost estimators in the United States during a recent year, and job growth is projected to be as fast as the average for all occupations through 2000.

Job Description. Estimators prepare specifications for work to be performed and use past records as a guide to current costs, supplemented by changes in the prices charged by various suppliers. They often solicit bids for part or all of the work to be done. Cost estimators project completion dates in addition to prices.

Career Path. The career path varies according to the industry in which the work is performed.

Salary. Earnings vary according to experience and the industry in which the cost estimator works. In a recent year, cost estimators' salaries averaged $30,300.

Chapter 19
Money, the Banking System, and Other Financial Institutions

Chapter 20
Financial Management

Chapter 21
The Securities Market

Chapter 22
Risk Management and Insurance

Financing the Enterprise

Career Profile: *Gary Chenett*

Grand Blanc Cyclery and Vacuum, one of the largest bicycle dealers in upper Michigan, is owned and operated by Gary Chenett. He started the store 16 years ago on little more than a feeling.

"I went to buy a bike for my daughter and got treated really badly by a dealer," Chenett recalled. "He wasn't servicing the market, so I decided I would."

At the time, Chenett managed a store for a large chain of grocery stores and believed he had peaked with the company at the age of 26. So, even though he knew nothing about bicycles and less than he thought about business, he plunged into running his own shop.

After a year of struggle and learning by trial and error, Chenett realized he didn't know enough about business to succeed. So the Vietnam veteran used the GI Bill to finance his enrollment at Mott Community College. He later went to the University of Michigan–Flint. In his classes, Chenett learned the essentials of starting a business, such as the importance of a business plan and how to read a financial statement. He also learned about risk management and capitalization, both principles he later used when he moved from his original, poor location after eight years.

Once Chenett decided to move, he was frustrated by the terms of the leases being offered. So he decided to take a risk and purchase a building.

He finally found a run-down building in an outstanding location. "It was set right at an intersection that had 28,000 cars a day go by, where the strip mall I was in saw 6,000 cars on a good day," Chenett says. The building also had more than twice the square footage of his original store.

"I was after the best location, and this building had it," he says. "I didn't argue the price they wanted, because I knew in the long run, with that location, that it was worth it. So I negotiated on the terms, and I got him down from 11 percent to 8 percent interest, and got a slider built in on the mortgage payments, so I would have less to pay during the slow season.

"I assumed . . . a lot of debt, but it worked for me."

It worked in part because Chenett worked. In the beginning, he worked two jobs, three jobs, whatever he had to do to keep his business running. He was able to get credit to expand his operation in its original location because he worked hard at applying his lessons from school, writing a business plan that met with the approval of his professors, learning how to properly fill out a financial statement, and eventually diversifying his product line to make his business more stable.

"The most intimidating thing you can ever do is talk to a banker," says Chenett. "It's really tough when you know you're undercapitalized."

At one point, Chenett went to five different commercial lending officers, learning a bit from each rejection, until the fifth one agreed to do business with Chenett.

Taking calculated risks has paid off for Chenett. His cyclery is now the number one dealer in his area, even surpassing the dealer whose rudeness prompted him to enter the business. He has expanded in one of the nation's most economically depressed areas and has added treadmills, stationary bicycles, and vacuums to his retail line. The store services vacuums and small appliances as well as bicycles. Chenett is even sending an employee to school to learn VCR repair.

"Gary is an excellent example of somebody who had an idea and who wanted to accomplish something more for himself and his family," comments Paul Londrigan, one of Chenett's professors at Mott. "Most people have the opportunities but they don't take advantage of them, or they simply don't explore them further. He was willing to take risks where a lot of people might not have been."

Photo source: Courtesy of Patrick Carrington, Gary Chenett, and Raleigh Cycle Co. of America.

19

Money, the Banking System, and Other Financial Institutions

Learning Goals

1. To describe the characteristics of a good form of money and to list the functions of money.

2. To distinguish between money and near-money.

3. To identify the major categories of financial institutions and the sources and uses of their funds.

4. To explain the functions of the Federal Reserve System and the tools it uses to increase or decrease the money supply.

5. To identify the purpose and primary functions of the Federal Deposit Insurance Corporation (FDIC) and the Federal Savings and Loan Insurance Corporation (FSLIC).

6. To explain the major provisions of the Banking Act of 1980 and its impact on financial deregulation.

7. To distinguish between credit cards and debit cards.

8. To explain the role of the electronic funds transfer system (EFTS), the trend toward interstate banking, and the financial supermarkets in the current competition among financial institutions.

Like many entrepreneurs, Adam Fingersh started his small designer sweatshirt business at home, where his living-room table doubled as a workstation. The business grew, and before long Adam F. Designs cried out for an infusion of working capital. Fingersh created a business plan, approached the loan officer at his bank, offered his Apple computer as collateral, and shrewdly negotiated a set of terms. Within four months, he had not only paid off his loan but also received a revolving line of credit from the bank. An impressive small-business success story, especially considering just how small a businessman Adam Fingersh is. At 11 years old, he is only one of the young capitalists who have lined up for money at a Denver financial institution catering exclusively to children.

Step right up to the Young Americans Bank, where some of the clients stand no taller than T. Boone Pickens's belt buckle. The bank opened to a bemused titter of publicity in 1987, but it has proved to be more than a cute oddity, opening an impressive 5,000 accounts in seven months. Start-up banks typically take three years to make a profit; Young Americans, which has $1.3 million in capital, broke even in 1988. Junior partners can open a checking account with as little as $10 and take out loans. So far, the bank has lent money for everything from buying a horse to recording a record. "We get some incredibly ambitious kids here," says Leanne Cadman, Young Americans loan administrator. "They're 15, 16 years old, and they're ready to make a million dollars."

Denver cable TV magnate Bill Daniels started the bank as a way to teach money-management skills to kids. He spent two years convincing the Colorado banking board to issue a state charter and contributed $2 million of his own money toward the project. He also enlisted 20 founding sponsors, including

the Bank of Boston and Silverado Banking, which agreed to deposit $50,000 to $100,000 each for at least a year without collecting interest. The bank's data processing is being donated free of charge by the First Financial Management Corp. Deloitte Haskins and Sells, the accounting giant, is supplying audit services.... Daniels has taken special measures to make the bank user-friendly. To accommodate even the smallest of pint-size entrepreneurs, it features steps to the teller windows and multilevel loan desks.

... Daniels will use the earnings to beef up its capital base or add educational programs. Meanwhile, the customers keep coming. Cadman sees six to eight loan applicants a week—some of whom have already launched successful business ventures. Fourteen-year-old Lee Nicholson saw his snow-removal business take off after borrowing $700 for a snow blower. With a $1,500 loan, University of Colorado junior Greg Phelps began

marketing a software program for Shaklee distributors.

So far, none of the borrowers has abused the loan privileges, in part because Daniels has promised to treat junior deadbeats just like their adult counterparts. ("The kids will learn that if they default on a bicycle, we're going to repossess it.") Indeed, the only snags have been in the 18-to-22-year-old age group, where giddy checking-account customers abused their overdraft privileges. Young Americans' success has already tempted other Denver banks to go after a piece of the junior-capitalist business. Compared with third world debt and many commercial loans, kids look like a pretty safe bet.[1]

Photo source: © Carl Iwasaki.

Chapter Overview

As any business executive—from 11-year-old Adam Fingersh to 91-year-old Occidental Petroleum CEO Armand Hammer—will tell you, money is the lubricant of contemporary business. Every executive recognizes the need for adequate funds to finance the operation of the firm and to carry out the plans of management. Today's managers would agree with playwright George Bernard Shaw's contention that the *lack* of money is the root of all evil.

In analyzing the characteristics, functions, and different types of money, it is useful to begin by defining it. **Money** is anything generally accepted as a means of paying for goods and services.

Anyone asked to define *money* will probably respond something like this: "It's the coins in my pocket and the folding kind I wish I had in my wallet and whatever is currently in my checking account." And bankers would agree: These are all money.

Money is one of the most fascinating subjects for both individuals and businesspeople. Everyone seems to need it:

Money bewitches people. They fret for it, and they sweat for it. They devise most ingenious ways to get it, and most ingenious ways to get rid of it. Money is the only commodity that is good for nothing but to be gotten rid of. It will not feed you, clothe you, shelter you, or amuse you unless you spend it or invest it. It imparts value only in parting. People will do almost anything for money, and money will do almost anything for people. Money is a captivating, circulating, masquerading puzzle.[2]

This chapter analyzes the characteristics, functions, and types of money. It discusses the operations of commercial banks and other financial institutions and examines the methods used by the Federal Reserve System in regulating the U.S. financial system by controlling the money supply. Chapter 19 also describes the Federal Reserve System's activities in check processing and in protecting depositors' funds by providing insurance and evaluating banking practices. The fundamental changes that have resulted from financial deregulation are assessed, and such current developments as the growth of electronic funds transfer systems and the development of the financial supermarket are described. These sweeping changes in the structure and operations of financial institutions will have a profound effect on the financial decisions and practices of both business firms and individual households for the remaining years of the twentieth century. But the starting place for our analysis is with money.

The Characteristics and Functions of Money

Money has not always been the same to all people. Historically, objects of value were used as money. These objects can be referred to as full-bodied money, because they had utility apart from their use as money. Cattle often were used this way. A cow was valuable because it could produce milk, butter, and cheese and eventually be converted into meat and hide. Its owner could also trade the cow for other goods.

The list of products that have served as money is long, including such diverse items as wool, pepper, tea, fishhooks, tobacco, shells, feathers, salt (from

money
Anything generally accepted as a means of paying for goods and services.

Examples of old forms of money include (at left) the oldest known paper currency issued in China during the Ming Dynasty between 1368 and 1399; (top right) a silver tetradrachm used in Athens, Greece, in the fifth century B.C.; and iron bells without clappers used as bride money in Zimbabwe in the nineteenth century.

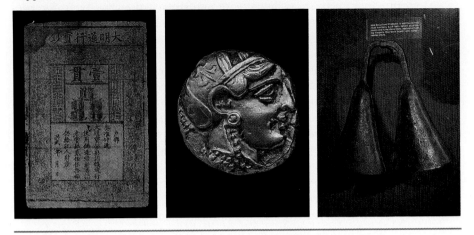

Photo source: Smithsonian Institution, National Numismatic Collection photo.

which came "salary" and "being worth one's salt"), boats, sharks' teeth, cocoa beans, wampum beads, woodpecker scalps, and precious metals. For a number of reasons, precious metals gained wide acceptance as money. As early as 2000 B.C., gold and silver were used as money, and as recently as 1933, gold coins were used as money in the United States.

What Characteristics Should Money Possess?

Most early forms of money had a number of serious disadvantages. For example, a cow is a poor form of money for an owner who wants only a loaf of bread and a bottle of wine. Exchange involving the use of money permits elaborate specialization and provides a general base for purchasing power. To perform its necessary functions, money must be divisible, portable, durable, and difficult to counterfeit — and it should have a stable value.

Divisibility   The cow owner who found that a loaf of bread cost one-fiftieth of a cow faced a major dilemma. So did the owners of most other items used as money. But gold and silver coins could be minted in different sizes with differing values in order to facilitate exchange.

Spanish gold doubloons were literally divided into pieces of eight. The dollar can be converted into pennies, nickels, dimes, and quarters. The pound of the United Kingdom is worth 100 pence. A French franc is valued at 100 centimes. The German deutsche mark can be traded for 100 pfennigs. These forms of money can easily be exchanged for goods ranging from chewing gum to a car. Today, almost all economic activity is concerned with making and spending money incomes.

Portability   The inhabitants of the little South Pacific island community of Yap chose a unique form of money — huge round stones weighing as much as 90 pounds each. Because the stone money was often placed at the door of its owner, the wealth of the inhabitant was known to every passerby. But Yap money lacked the important characteristic of portability. The process of trading the stones for needed goods and services was difficult.

Modern paper currency is lightweight, which facilitates the exchange process. United States paper money comes in denominations ranging from $1 to $100,000, although the highest denomination currently being printed is $100. Portability is an important characteristic since the typical dollar bill changes hands 400 times during its lifetime, staying in the average person's pocket or purse less than two days.

Durability   Durability is a third important characteristic of money. A monetary system using butter or cheese faces the durability problem in a matter of weeks. Although coins and paper currency wear out over time, they are replaced easily with shiny new coins and crisp new paper. U.S. dollar bills have an average life of 18 months and can be folded some 4,000 times without tearing.

Difficulty in Counterfeiting   If you hold a dollar bill to the light, you will notice small red and blue silk threads imbedded in the paper. Their purpose is to make counterfeiting difficult. Theft of currency plates from a government mint is a common plot element for espionage and mystery novels and movies because the production and distribution of counterfeit money could undermine a nation's monetary system by ruining the value of legitimate money. For this reason, all governments make counterfeiting a serious crime and take elaborate steps to prevent it.

Stability   A good money system should have a stable value. If the value of money fluctuates, people become unwilling to trade goods and services for it. Inflation is, therefore, a serious concern for governments. When people fear that money will lose much of its value, they begin to abandon it and look for safer means of storing their wealth. Where once they accepted rupees or pesos, they may now demand gold coins or they may store their wealth in the form of land, jewelry, or other physical goods. In the case of runaway inflation, where the value of money may decrease 20 percent or more in a single year, people increasingly return to a barter system, exchanging their output for the output of others.

What Are the Functions of Money?

medium of exchange
Means of facilitating exchange and eliminating the need for a barter system.

unit of account
A common denominator for measuring the value of all goods and services.

Money performs three basic functions. First, it serves primarily as a **medium of exchange** — a means of facilitating exchange and eliminating the need for a barter system. For example, rather than follow the complicated process of trading wheat directly for gasoline or clothing (the barter system), a farmer can sell the wheat and use the money from the sale to make other purchases.

Money also functions as a **unit of account** — a common denominator for measuring the value of all products and services. A new car is worth, say, $14,500; a certain cut of beef, $6 per pound; and a 40-yard-line ticket to a football game, $30. Using money as a common denominator aids in comparing widely different products and services. In the advertisement in Figure 19.1, Dollar Rent A Car uses dollar bills to communicate the value of its low-price car rental service.

Figure 19.1   Money Functioning as a Unit of Account

Source: Courtesy of Dollar Rent A Car.

Finally, money acts as a temporary **store of value** — a way of keeping accumulated wealth until it is needed to make new purchases. Wealth can also be held in the form of stocks and bonds, real estate, antiques, works of art, precious gems, or any other valuable goods. The advantage of storing value in goods other than money is that they often produce additional income in the form of dividends, interest payments, rent, or increases in value. For example, the van Gogh painting "Irises" rose in value from $47,000 in 1947 to $53.9 million in 1988. But money offers one substantial advantage as a store of value: It is highly liquid. An asset is said to be liquid if it can be obtained and disposed of quickly and easily.

A van Gogh painting may increase in value, but its owner can obtain money for it only after finding a purchaser. In order to exchange bonds for money, the owner must contact a broker and pay a commission. And the possibility always exists that the value of the bond may be less than when it was purchased. The owner can then either hold the bond until maturity (at which time the corporation or government agency that issued it will pay the total amount of the bond and interest) or sell it at a loss in order to obtain the more liquid dollars. In addition to the liquidity problem, many nonmoney stores of value involve storage and insurance costs.

There are disadvantages to holding money, particularly in inflationary times. If prices double, money that has been saved (but not in an interest-bearing

store of value
Temporary accumulation of wealth until it is needed for new purchases.

account) will buy only half as much as it would have before inflation. Its chief advantage, then, is that it is immediately available for purchasing products or paying debts.

Composition of the Money Supply

The U.S. money supply is divided into the following categories: coins, paper money, traveler's checks, demand deposits or checking accounts; NOW accounts; and credit union share draft accounts. Metal coins comprise about 3 percent of the total money supply. A recent study revealed that the average man carries $145 in his pocket — about twice as much paper money and coins as the average woman. The typical woman carries $74 in her purse. Paper money makes up 25 percent of the total money supply. These two components of the money supply are usually called **currency**.

currency
Two of the components of the money supply — coins and paper money.

Demand Deposits

demand deposits
Promises to pay immediately to the depositor any amount of money requested as long as it does not exceed the account balance.

A third component of the U.S. money supply is **demand deposits**, the technical name for checking accounts at commercial banks and savings banks. Demand deposits are considered part of the money supply because they are promises to pay immediately to the depositor any amount of money requested — as long as it does not exceed the amount in the person's checking account.

Nearly three-fourths of the dollar value of all financial transactions in the United States is conducted with checks rather than currency. Americans write and cash more than 1,000 checks a second. There are several reasons for this frequent use of checks:

1. A check is a more convenient form of payment for large or odd-numbered purchases. For example, writing a check for a $93.60 jacket is more convenient than handing the salesperson four $20s, a $10, three dollars, two quarters, and a dime.
2. Checks reduce the possibility of theft or loss of currency.
3. Checks make payment by mail easier and safer.

Though an estimated one-third of all Americans continue to deal almost exclusively in cash, checking accounts offer the advantages of convenience and safety.

Interest-Bearing Checking Accounts

negotiable order of withdrawal (NOW) account
Interest-bearing checking account offered by commercial banks, savings and loan associations, and savings banks.

share draft accounts
Interest-bearing credit union accounts that permit depositors to write drafts against them.

Certain types of checking accounts provide another benefit: they earn interest. In a move toward deregulating the banking industry during the last decade, the federal government decided to permit commercial banks, savings and loan associations, and savings banks to offer a special interest-bearing checking account called a **negotiable order of withdrawal (NOW) account**. The interest on these accounts has averaged slightly more than 5 percent annually in recent years. Depositors benefit by earning interest on deposited funds and having access to the funds when needed. Credit unions offer their members **share draft accounts**, interest-bearing accounts that permit the account holder to write drafts that are essentially checks.

In recent years, the term *M1* has been used to refer to those items considered to be money. In addition to currency and demand deposits at commercial banks, M1 includes NOW accounts, share draft accounts, and traveler's checks.

Near-Money

In addition to the money supply, a number of assets exist that are almost as liquid as checking accounts but that cannot be used directly as a medium of exchange. These are known as **near-money**. One type of near-money is the **time deposit**, a technical term for a savings account that permits a financial institution to require notice before withdrawal or to assess a penalty for early withdrawal. Government bonds and money market mutual funds are also considered near-money.

near-money
Assets almost as liquid as checking accounts but that cannot be used directly as a medium of exchange.

time deposit
Account that requires prior withdrawal notice to avoid penalty.

Money Market Mutual Funds

Money market mutual funds emerged in the high inflation years of the early 1980s. These funds sold ownership shares to investors and used this revenue to purchase short-term notes of government agencies and major corporations. During the first half of the 1980s, the number of money market mutual funds grew from 96 to almost 400 as investors chose to transfer their funds from conventional savings accounts in search of higher interest rates. The growth rate subsided during the second half of the 1980s as interest rates declined and stock prices grew to unprecedented levels. However, the stock market crash of 1987 once again prompted investors to seek safer investment outlets. These mutual funds are described in more detail in Chapter 21.

Bank Money Market Deposit Accounts

In 1982, Congress passed the Depository Institutions Act, which allows banks and savings and loan associations to offer their own money market accounts. To compete with money market mutual funds, these special deposit accounts offer highly competitive interest rates that vary with changing market conditions. The bank money market deposit accounts are insured up to $100,000 per account. However, they are not considered part of the money supply. Unlike regular checking accounts and NOW accounts, bank money market account transfers are limited to no more than six checks or automatic transactions each month.

These categories of near-monies — time deposits, government bonds, money market mutual fund shares, and bank money market deposit accounts at commercial banks and thrift institutions — are commonly referred to as *M2*.

Credit Cards

On your way to St. Mark's United Methodist Church in Lincoln, Nebraska, but short of cash? No worry: The era of "plastic money" has reached every aspect of modern society. Parishioners simply fill out a charge slip containing their Visa or MasterCard number and keep two copies: one for their records and one for the collection plate. The church then enters the card numbers on a computer termi-

United Missouri was one of the first banks in the nation to introduce the MasterCard BusinessCard. The credit card was developed in response to customer demand to control the $10 billion business travel expense industry. The BusinessCard offers company travelers acceptance of the MasterCard at millions of merchants worldwide and a reporting system that identifies business-related travel and entertainment expenses. Cardholders receive monthly reports detailing their business expenses.

Photo source: Courtesy of United Missouri Bancshares, Inc.

credit card

Plastic card used in making credit purchases; special credit arrangement between issuer, cardholder, and merchant.

nal connected to a local bank. Since St. Mark's began accepting credit-card donations, the average donation has been $75.[3]

With growing frequency, people use the **credit card** as a substitute for currency and checks. That popularity is due to the convenience of making credit-card transactions and the growing willingness of merchants throughout the world to accept credit cards in place of checks or cash. Seven of every ten U.S. households with incomes between $15,000 and $25,000 use either a Visa, MasterCard, or both. The usage rate increases to 84 percent for those in the $25,000-to-$35,000 income bracket and 88 percent for households earning between $35,000 and $50,000. In addition, cardholders may also use cards from large retailers and American Express, Diners Club, or Discover. A typical cardholder's wallet or purse contains three credit cards. In 1988, consumers owed $91 billion on their bank credit cards, roughly $1,160 per family.[4]

While the plastic card may function much like money in permitting the holder to make purchases, the monthly statement of card purchases is a tangible reminder that they are *credit* cards — not money. They merely represent a special credit arrangement between the holder and the organization issuing the card. The issuer — usually a bank — permits the cardholder to repay the outstanding balance at the end of the billing period or, in the case of bank cards and retail credit cards, to pay at least a stated minimum amount each month and pay interest on the outstanding balance until it is repaid.

The 3,000 banks and other financial institutions currently issuing Visa and MasterCards love credit cards because of their profit potential. Merchants typi-

Figure 19.2   The Operations of a Commercial Bank

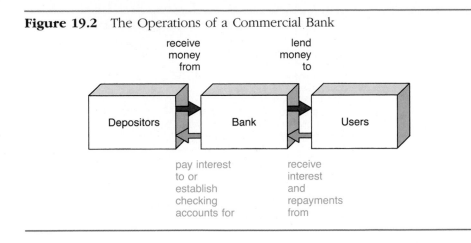

cally pay fees of 1 percent to 5 percent for credit-card sales; cardholders frequently pay an annual fee and interest charges between 17.5 percent and 20 percent on unpaid balances. As a result, credit cards can generate profits three times as high as other bank services. This profit potential prompted American Express to develop its own Optima bank card and Sears to create its Discover card.[5]

A second attraction for banks is the ability to reach cardholders outside their typical service area. Thanks in part to deregulation, banks can solicit customers virtually around the world. Citibank strengthened its ranking as the nation's largest credit-card issuer by issuing Visa and MasterCards to more than 1 million students at over 1,000 campuses nationwide in a special marketing program aimed at this high-income-potential group.[6]

Banks have discovered that few cardholders shop for credit cards. Despite its 10.92 percent rate, Arkansas Federal Savings has attracted less than $3 million in credit-card loans. Many consumers disregard interest rates because they intend to repay the balance every month, thereby avoiding interest charges. In fact, only about half do, according to Visa.[7]

The U.S. Commercial Banking System

At the heart of the U.S. banking system are the approximately 14,000 commercial banks. A **commercial bank** is a profit-making business that performs two basic functions. It holds the deposits of individuals and business firms in the form of checking or savings accounts, and its uses these funds to make loans to individuals and businesses. Figure 19.2 shows how a commercial bank performs these two functions.

Types of Commercial Banks

Most commercial banks are **state banks** — commercial banks chartered by individual states. Approximately one-third are **national banks** — commercial banks chartered by the federal government. These tend to be larger, and they hold approximately 60 percent of total commercial bank deposits. While the

commercial bank
Profit-making business that holds deposits of individuals and businesses in the form of checking or savings accounts and uses these funds to make loans to individuals and businesses.

state banks
Commercial banks chartered by individual states.

national banks
Commercial banks chartered by the federal government.

Table 19.1   The 15 Largest Commercial Banks in the United States

Rank	Company and Headquarters City	Deposits (in billions)
1	Citicorp (New York)	$103.7
2	BankAmerica Corp. (San Francisco)	72.4
3	Chase Manhattan Corp. (New York)	62.6
4	Morgan Guaranty Trust Co. (New York)	47.9
5	Manufacturers Hanover Corp. (New York)	45.5
6	Chemical Bank (New York)	39.0
7	Security Pacific Corp. (Los Angeles)	34.0
8	Wells Fargo & Co. (San Francisco)	32.7
9	Bankers Trust (New York)	31.0
10	First Chicago Corp	28.5
11	Continental Illinois Corp. (Chicago)	18.6
12	First Interstate Bank of California (Los Angeles)	17.3
13	Marine Midland Bank (Buffalo)	17.2
14	Mellon Bank (Pittsburgh)	16.9
15	Bank of New York	16.3

Source: The Rand McNally Bankers Directory, 1988 Edition.

regulations affecting state and national banks vary slightly, in practice there is little difference between the two from the viewpoint of the individual depositor or borrower.

Table 19.1 lists the 15 largest banks in the United States. New York's Citicorp is the largest, with total deposits of more than $100 billion. It is often difficult for students of business and economics to conceive of numbers of such magnitude as $1 billion. To help you understand, suppose you were given the task of *spending* $1 billion. If you spent $100,000 per day, it would take you more than 27 years!

The U.S. banking giants are dwarfed when compared with the world's largest international banks. Of the top ten banks ranked by assets, only three are not Japanese: France's Credit Agricola and Banque Nationale de Paris, and the largest U.S. bank, Citicorp. The five largest banks in the world — Dai Ichi Kangyo, Sumitomo, Fuji, Mitsubishi, and Sanwa — are all Japanese. It would take nine Citicorps to equal Sumitomo Bank in stock market value.[8]

Services Provided by Commercial Banks

"Full-service bank" is an accurate description of the typical commercial bank because of the dozens of services it offers its depositors. In addition to a variety of checking and savings accounts and personal and business loans, commercial banks typically offer bank credit cards, safe deposit boxes, tax-deferred individual retirement accounts (IRAs), discount brokerage services, wire transfers (which permit immediate movement of funds by electronic transfers to distant banks), and financial counseling. Most banks provide traveler's checks at a small fee and many of them offer overdraft checking accounts for some of their depositors. Such accounts automatically provide small loans at relatively low interest rates for depositors who write checks exceeding the balance in their account.

Customers who need to make withdrawals or deposits when the bank is closed can usually do this by using a plastic access card at the bank's **automated teller machine (ATM)**. Over 70,000 of these electronic machines are operating outside bank buildings, in freestanding kiosks, and in supermarkets, shop-

automated teller machine (ATM)
Electronic banking machine that permits customers to make cash withdrawals, deposits, and transfers on a 24-hour basis by using an access card.

Figure 19.3   Emphasizing Service Quality with Guarantee Programs

Source: Reprinted with the permission of NCNB Corporation.

ping malls, and airline terminals. Networks of interlinked systems such as MAC, CIRRUS, or TYME give users access to their hometown bank accounts from ATMs across the country.[9] Because of these and other services, commercial banks are considered the department stores of financial institutions.

The growing competition among all types of financial institutions has forced banks to become more service-oriented in seeking deposits and lending business. According to an *American Banker* survey, the primary reason people switch banks in the city — cited by 21 percent of those who switched — was poor service, particularly account-related errors.[10] To counter this, a number of banks have begun using a well-known competitive tactic: warranties. Recent National Westminster Bank USA advertisements promise $50 to customers who apply by phone for personal or car loans but do not get an answer by the end of the next business day.[11] As the advertisement in Figure 19.3 shows, North Carolina's NCNB will back its apology for any mistake on depositors' accounts with a check in the amount of $10.[12]

To make service quality a priority, 30 percent of First National Bank of Chicago's managerial bonuses are tied to whether managers meet or exceed quality-related goals. Rosemarie B. Greco, a former nun who is president of Philadelphia's Fidelity Bank, sent 25 of her managers to visit American Express, L. L. Bean, and ten other companies known for excellent customer service. Complaint-handling systems were consolidated, and management became personally involved with customer problems. Today, 87 percent of Fidelity's customers say they are satisfied or highly satisfied with service, compared with 57 percent in 1986.[13]

Just as a full-service retailer such as a department store charges higher prices to cover its services, the services of financial institutions are far from free, particularly for small depositors. Atlanta's Citizens & Southern Bank charges 75 cents per check written after the first seven each month. Mellon Bank assesses a $20 bounced-check charge and charges its depositors $10 for each stop-payment order. Although Security Pacific Bank in Los Angeles charges no fees for depositors who use the bank's own ATM, a $1 charge is levied on depositors who use other ATMs in the bank's network. In the late 1980s, New York's Goldome Bank listed some 42 customer fees, charges, or penalties that could be imposed. Such fees are designed to generate additional revenue for banks and to force all depositors to pay the cost of services rendered.

As a result of customer resentment toward these fees, banks have begun offering package deals called *bundled accounts.* In general, such accounts base charges on depositors' account balance and activity levels. For a minimum balance of $1,000 spread between any two or more accounts (including checking, savings, money market, CDs, and IRAs), participants in the ChemPlus package at New York's Chemical Bank get free checking, a 16.8 percent combined Master-Card and Visa account (free for the first year), reduced rates on loans and mortgage fees, and free 24-hour banking in a network of 18,000 ATMs around the country. "We are devouring market share with this new product," boasts one Chemical Bank official. "New Yorkers are always chasing around to get that last one-hundredth of a point interest, but we offer them free checking, loads of convenience, and a guarantee that our rates will always be near the top."[14]

Commercial banks also provide a wide range of services to meet the financial needs of the growing number of businesses engaged in international trade. A key element in Citicorp's business service package is financing trade in a variety of countries for multinational firms. The advertisement in Figure 19.4 illustrates how Citicorp's foreign exchange service, which handles more than 150 currencies, assists firms in transactions that cross national borders. Fees charged for such services produce substantial earnings for Citicorp.

Other Financial Institutions

A number of financial institutions other than commercial banks exist both as sources and users of funds. The major components of the U.S. financial system are categorized into two broad groups: deposit institutions and nondeposit institutions.

Deposit Institutions

Savings and loan associations, savings banks, and credit unions, in addition to commercial banks, are considered deposit institutions because they accept deposits from customers or members and provide some form of checking account. While each of these institutions has traditionally served specific financial needs of individuals and businesses, deregulation has blurred the distinctions among

Figure 19.4   A Bank Service for Business Customers

them. For example, at one time only commercial banks offered checking accounts. However, savings and loan associations and savings banks currently offer
interest-paying NOW accounts. Credit unions offer their own variant in the form
of share draft accounts. Although *thrifts,* as savings and loan associations and
savings banks are commonly called, have traditionally served as sources of home
mortgages, many commercial banks now compete in the home mortgage market. All of these institutions compete by offering passbook accounts, time deposits, traveler's checks, and a variety of other banking services, all at competitive
rates.

Thrifts: Savings and Loan Associations and Savings Banks   A **savings
and loan association (S&L)** is a financial institution offering both savings and
checking accounts and using most of its funds to make home mortgage loans.
Their original purpose was to encourage family thrift and home ownership, and
for years, S&Ls were permitted to pay slightly higher interest rates to savers than
could commercial banks. Deposited funds were then used to make long-term,
fixed-rate mortgages at prevailing mortgage rates. Fifteen years ago, thrifts originated 60 percent of all residential mortgages. Today, S&Ls and savings banks
hold only one-third of outstanding residential loans.[15] Approximately 44 percent
of the nation's savings and loan associations are incorporated under federal

**savings and loan
association (S&L)**
Financial institution offering
savings and checking accounts
and using most of its funds to
make home mortgage loans;
also called thrift institution.

Figure 19.5   Consumer Lending Promoted by a Savings Bank

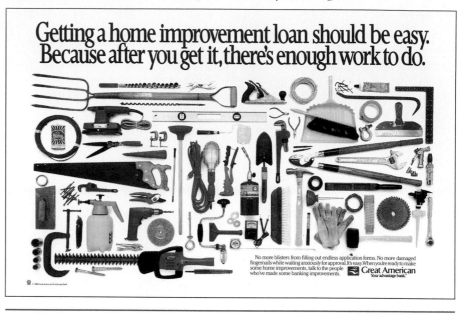

Source: Courtesy of Great American Bank/Ad Agency: Franklin and Associates, San Diego, CA.

savings banks
State-chartered banks with operations similar to savings and loan associations.

regulations and must use the word *federal* in their names. The remaining 56 percent are state chartered.

Savings banks, also known as mutual savings banks, are virtually identical to S&Ls. Their origins can be traced to the early 1800s in Boston and Philadelphia, where they were established to provide interest on savings accounts. The early U.S. banks did not provide such accounts, and the first savings banks were designed to meet the savings and borrowing needs of individual households. Their early missions are suggested by such names as Emigrant Savings Bank, Dime Savings Bank, and Seamans Bank for Savings.

The approximately 600 savings banks are concentrated in 16 states including the New England states, New York, and New Jersey. They operate much like S&Ls in offering NOW accounts and other savings accounts and in making home mortgage loans, and they have faced similar competitive pressures. Like the S&Ls, they are now permitted to make consumer and some business loans. To gain competitive advantages in loan production, Great American First Savings Bank, headquartered in San Diego, California, is developing new products and promotional strategies for its banking offices in California, Arizona, Washington, Colorado, and Montana. An aggressive promotional effort, including advertisements such as the one in Figure 19.5, is helping Great American increase its consumer loan business.

Traditionally, both S&Ls and savings banks earned money by attracting savings deposits at interest rates of perhaps 6 percent and then making home mortgages at 10 percent, generating a 4 percentage point differential to use in covering operating costs and earning a profit. As long as this spread existed between the cost of funds and the interest earned on loans, the thrifts prospered.

Rising interest rates during the early 1980s devastated the S&Ls, whose mission was to use short-term deposits to make long-term, fixed-rate mortgage loans. In 1982, for example, S&Ls were paying an average of 11.5 percent interest on their deposits while earning only 10.4 percent on their loans.

In an attempt to correct the impending disaster, Congress and many state regulatory bodies permitted S&Ls to engage in activities never before allowed. They were permitted to make commercial loans, engage in consumer leasing, provide trust services, and issue credit cards. This new freedom, combined with the removal of maximum interest levels S&Ls could pay depositors, created a monster by allowing S&Ls to raise endless amounts of money to fund disastrous investments. For example, American Diversified of Costa Mesa, California, solicited deposits by telephone, offering interest rates of more than 8.5 percent as a lure. The thrift, headed by Ranbir Sahni, a former pilot in the Indian Air Force, funneled these deposits into such risky investments as wind farms and ethanol plants. When Sahni's operation and nearby North America Savings and Loan Association were closed by federal regulators in 1988, no depositors lost money, but the federal agency guaranteeing these accounts had to come up with $1.35 billion — the largest cash payoff in U.S. banking history.[16]

Between 1980 and 1990, the number of S&Ls declined nearly 40 percent, to 3,000. Of these, approximately one-third are losing money. The number of S&Ls will continue to decline as regulatory authorities authorize the sale, merger, or liquidation of troubled thrifts. The survivors are likely to be similar to commercial banks in their operations.[17]

Credit Unions   The nation's 14,000 federally insured credit unions serve as sources of consumer loans at competitive rates for their members. A **credit union** is actually a form of savings cooperative and is typically sponsored by a company, union, or professional or religious group. The credit union pays interest to its member depositors. While credit unions tend to be relatively small, with only 30 percent having assets of $5 million or more, they exist in every state and claim nearly 52 million members. Credit unions today have outstanding loans of more than $105 billion.[18]

While credit unions have traditionally concentrated on short-term consumer loans and savings deposits, their operating flexibility has been increased as a result of deregulation. As mentioned earlier, they offer an interest-bearing checking account called a *share draft account* and can make long-term mortgage loans. Other services available to member depositors and borrowers typically include life insurance at competitive rates and financial counseling.

Nondeposit Institutions

Other sources and users of funds include insurance companies, pension funds, and consumer and commercial finance companies. An **insurance company** provides financial protection for policyholders who pay premiums. Insurance companies use the funds generated by premiums to make long-term loans to corporations and commercial real estate mortgages and to purchase government bonds. Major types of insurance companies, such as life insurance companies and property and casualty insurance companies, are discussed in detail in Chapter 22.

A **pension fund** is a large pool of money set up by a company, union, or nonprofit organization for the retirement income needs of its employees or members. According to the pension fund's rules, a member may begin to collect a monthly allotment on retirement or on reaching a certain age. Pension fund

credit union
Member-owned financial cooperative that pays interest to depositors, offers share draft accounts, and makes short-term loans and some home mortgage loans.

insurance company
Business that provides protection for policyholders in return for premium payments.

pension fund
Funds accumulated by a company, union, or nonprofit organization for the retirement income needs of its employees or members.

managers, like managers of insurance companies, are able to predict the approximate amount of money they will have to pay in benefits over a given period. Like insurance companies, pension funds invest in long-term term mortgages on commercial property, business loans, and government bonds. In addition, they often purchase common stock in major firms. When a corporation establishes a pension fund, a portion of the fund is likely to be invested in the firm's stock. Total assets of all private, state, and local government pension plans are more than $1.1 trillion.

commercial finance company
Financial institution that makes short-term loans to businesses that pledge tangible items such as inventory, machinery, or property as collateral.

consumer finance company
Financial institution that makes short-term loans to individuals, typically requiring collateral; also called personal finance or small loan company.

Consumer and commercial finance companies offer short-term loans to borrowers who pledge tangible items such as inventory, machinery, property, or accounts receivable as security against nonpayment. A **commercial finance company**, such as Commercial Credit or CIT, supplies short-term funds to businesses unable to borrow enough needed funds from banks. In some cases, these businesses cannot secure bank loans because they are relatively new and lack sufficient credit history or otherwise fail to meet the bank's lending standards. In other instances, firms may have borrowed to the limit from banks and, therefore, must turn to other sources for additional funds. Since these loans typically involve greater risks, commercial finance companies typically charge higher interest rates than commercial banks and thrift institutions. The **consumer finance company** (frequently called a *personal finance* or *small loan company*) has traditionally served a similar role for personal loans. In recent years, they have become increasingly competitive with banks and thrift institutions and are frequently able to offer more attractive loans with longer terms. Beneficial Finance and Household Finance are two major consumer finance companies. Consumer and commercial finance companies obtain their funds from the sale of bonds and from short-term loans from other firms.

The sources and uses of funds available to deposit and nondeposit institutions and the types of accounts offered to depositors are summarized in Table 19.2.

The Federal Reserve System

All deposit institutions — commercial banks, savings and loan associations, savings banks, and credit unions — use deposits as the basis of the loans they make to borrowers. Because their income is derived from loans, these financial institutions must lend at a higher interest rate than the interest rate paid to depositors. Approximately 15 percent of a commercial bank's total deposits are kept on hand at the commercial bank or at the nearest Federal Reserve District Bank to cover withdrawals; the remainder is used for loans. Other types of deposit institutions retain less in reserve because a smaller percentage of their deposits are held in accounts on which checks can be written.

The Structure of the Federal Reserve System

What would happen if all of a commercial bank's depositors decided to withdraw their funds at once? The bank would be unable to return the depositors' money — unless it could borrow the needed funds from another bank. But if the demand for currency instead of checking and savings accounts spread to other banks, the result would be a bank panic. Banks would have to close their doors (sometimes referred to as a *bank holiday*) until they could obtain loan payments

Table 19.2 Major Financial Institutions: Sources and Uses of Funds

Institution	Typical Investments	Types of Accounts Offered to Depositors	Primary Sources of Funds
Deposit Institutions			
Commercial bank	Personal loans Business loans Increasingly involved in real estate construction and home mortgage loans	Checking accounts NOW accounts Passbook savings accounts Time deposits Money market deposit accounts	Customer deposits Interest earned on loans
Savings and loan association	Bond purchases Home mortgages Construction loans	Savings accounts NOW accounts Time deposits Money market deposit accounts	Customer deposits Interest earned on loans
Savings bank	Bond purchases Home mortgages Construction loans	Savings accounts NOW accounts Time deposits Money market deposit accounts	Customer deposits Interest earned on loans
Credit union	Short-term consumer loans Increasingly involved in making longer-term mortgage loans	Share draft accounts Savings accounts Money market deposit accounts	Deposits by credit union members Interest earned on loans
Nondeposit Institutions			
Insurance company	Corporate long-term loans Mortgage of commercial real estate — major buildings/shopping centers Government bonds		Premiums paid by policyholders Earnings on investments
Pension fund	Some long-term mortgages on commercial property and business loans Government bonds Corporate securities		Contributions by member employees and employers Earnings on investments
Commercial and/or consumer finance company	Short-term loans to businesses (commercial finance companies) Individual consumer loans (consumer finance companies)		Interest earned on loans Sale of bonds Short-term borrowing from other firms

Source: Federal Reserve System.

from their borrowers. Such panics in the past resulted in the failure of numerous commercial banks and plunged the economy into major depressions.

Economic depressions occurred in the United States four times between the end of the Civil War and 1907, and most of them began with bank panics. The severe depression of 1907 prompted Congress to appoint a commission to study the banking system and to recommend changes. The commission's recommendations became the basis of the Federal Reserve Act, which President Woodrow Wilson signed in 1913.

The **Federal Reserve System** is a network of 12 district banks, controlled by a board of governors, that regulates banking in the United States. In practice, it acts as a banker's bank. The "Fed" holds the deposits of member banks, acts as a clearinghouse for checks, and regulates the commercial banking system. Figure 19.6 illustrates the regions and headquarters for each of the Federal Reserve districts.

Federal Reserve System
Network of 12 regional banks that regulates banking in the United States.

Figure 19.6   The Federal Reserve System's Districts and Headquarters

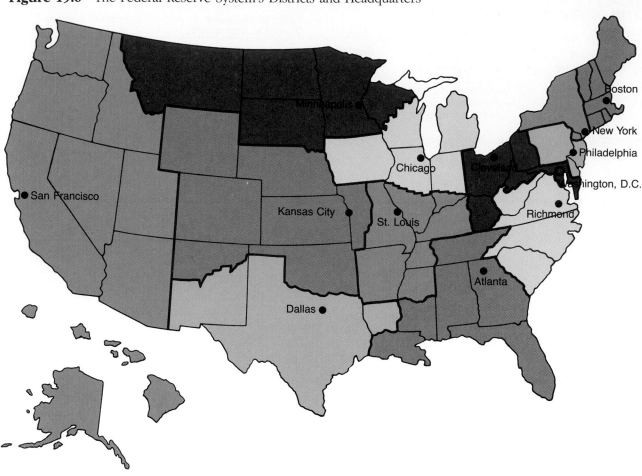

The Board of Governors of the Federal Reserve System consists of seven members appointed by the president and confirmed by the Senate. Political pressures are reduced by a 14-year term of office for each member, with one term expiring every two years.

Each of the 12 Federal Reserve district banks is managed by a president and a nine-member board of directors. Federal Reserve System member banks in a district own stock in the district bank and elect some of the board members. The other directors, of whom at least three must be businesspersons and another three must represent the general public, are appointed by the Board of Governors.

The relationship between the Washington, D.C.–based Board of Governors and the 12 district banks is analogous to that of the federal government and the 50 state governments. The Board of Governors sets the general direction for the member banks, while the district banks typically concentrate on banking issues of importance within their district.

While all national banks are required to be members of the Federal Reserve System, membership is optional for state-chartered banks. In all, there are approximately 5,800 member banks.

Control of the Money Supply: The FED's Basic Function

The most essential function of the Federal Reserve System is to control the supply of credit and money in order to promote economic growth and a stable dollar, both at home and in international markets. It performs this function through the use of three important tools: reserve requirements, open market operations, and the discount rate.

Reserve Requirements The Federal Reserve System's most powerful tool is the **reserve requirement** — the percentage of a bank's checking and savings deposits that must be kept in the bank or on deposit at the local Federal Reserve district bank. By changing the percentage of required reserves, the Federal Reserve System can affect the amount of money available for making loans. Should the Board of Governors choose to stimulate the economy by increasing the amount of funds available for borrowing, it can lower the reserve requirement.

Changing the reserve requirement is a drastic means of changing the money supply. Even a 1 percent variation in the reserve requirement means a potential fluctuation of billions of dollars in the money supply. Because of this, the board of governors would prefer to rely more often on the other two tools at its disposal — open market operations and changes in the discount rate.

reserve requirement
Percentage of a bank's checking and savings accounts that must be kept in the bank or on deposit at the local Federal Reserve district bank.

Open Market Operations A far more common method used by the Federal Reserve System to control the money supply is **open market operations** — the technique of controlling the money supply by purchasing and selling government bonds. When the Board of Governors decides to increase the money supply, it buys government bonds on the open market. The exchange of money for bonds places more money in the economy and makes it available to member banks. A decision to sell bonds serves to reduce the overall money supply.

The Federal Reserve Board often uses open market operations when small adjustments in the money supply are desired. These operations do not produce the psychological effect that often results from announcements of changes in reserve requirements. Such announcements make newspaper headlines and are widely interpreted by commercial banks, businesspeople, and the stock market as a signal by the Federal Reserve System of "tighter" or "easier" money. Over the years, open market operations have been increasingly used as a flexible means of expanding and contracting the money supply.

open market operations
Federal Reserve System method of controlling the money supply through the purchase and sale of government bonds.

The Discount Rate Earlier the Federal Reserve System was referred to as a "banker's bank." When member banks need extra money to lend, they turn to a Federal Reserve bank, presenting either IOUs drawn against themselves or promissory notes from their borrowers. The interest rate the Federal Reserve System charges on loans to member banks is called the **discount rate**.

Commercial banks choose to borrow from the Federal Reserve System when the discount rate is lower than rates charged by other sources of funds. A high discount rate may motivate bankers to reduce the number of new loans made to individuals and businesses due to higher costs of obtaining loanable funds. When the Fed raised the discount rate in 1988, the response was immediate. Stock prices plunged, interest rates moved up, and the value of the dollar increased as foreign investors gobbled up greenbacks. It was a spectacular display of power by this little-known tool.[19]

discount rate
Interest rate charged by the Federal Reserve System on loans to member banks.

Table 19.3 Tools of the Federal Reserve System

Tool	Action	Effect on Money Supply	Short-Term Impact on the Economy
Reserve requirements	Increase reserve requirements	Reduces money supply	Results in increased interest rates and a slowing of economic activity
	Decrease reserve requirements	Increases money supply	Results in reduced interest rates and an increase in economic activity
Discount rate	Increase discount rate	Reduces money supply	Results in increased interest rates and a slowing of economic activity
	Decrease discount rate	Increases money supply	Results in reduced interest rates and an increase in economic activity
Open market operations	Purchase government securities	Increases money supply	Results in reduced interest rates and an increase in economic activity
	Sell government bonds	Reduces money supply	Results in increased interest rates and a slowing of economic activity
Margin requirements	Increase margin requirements		Reduced credit purchase of securities; negative impact on securities exchanges and on securities prices.
	Reduce margin requirements		Increased credit purchase of securities; positive impact on securities exchanges and on securities prices.

The Federal Reserve banks may choose to stimulate the economy by reducing the discount rate. Because the rate is treated as a cost by commercial banks, a rate reduction encourages them to increase the number of loans to individuals and businesses.

The discount rate has been used several times in recent years in controlling the money supply, attempting to stimulate economic growth, and matching changes in discount rates made by central banks in such nations as Japan and West Germany. Like the reserve requirement, it has considerable impact on such interest-sensitive industries as automobiles and housing. Use of the discount rate also communicates to banks and to the general public the Federal Reserve Board's attitude concerning the money supply. An announcement of a reduction in the discount rate is interpreted as an indication that the Federal Reserve Board believes the money supply should be increased and credit should be expanded.

Table 19.3 shows how each of the tools of the Federal Reserve System can be used to stimulate or slow the economy.

Selective Credit Controls

selective credit controls
Federal Reserve System authority to regulate availability of credit by setting margin requirements on credit purchases of stocks and bonds and credit rules for consumer purchases.

In addition to the three general monetary controls, the Federal Reserve System also has the authority to exercise a number of **selective credit controls**. These include the power to set margin requirements on credit purchases of stocks and bonds and to set credit rules for consumer purchases. The margin requirement, discussed in detail in Chapter 21, is the percentage of the purchase price of a security that must be paid in cash by the investor. In 1929, for instance, the margin requirement was set at 10 percent and an investor could purchase $10,000 in stocks or bonds by depositing $1,000 with a stockbroker. The brokerage firm would then lend the investor the other $9,000. Today, the margin requirement is 50 percent; it has remained at this level since the late 1960s.

Although it has been a number of years since the Federal Reserve System has imposed minimum terms on loans made by financial institutions, it retains the authority to utilize its powers in this area as a means of controlling credit purchases. By establishing specific rules for minimum down-payment requirements and repayment periods for purchases of such products as automobiles, boats, or appliances, the Fed could stimulate or restrict purchases of major items that typically involve credit.

Check Processing

Check processing begins with a **check** — a piece of paper addressed to a bank or other financial institution on which is written a legal authorization to withdraw a specified amount of money from an account and to pay that amount to someone. Because $19 of every $20 of business transactions are accomplished in the form of checks, it is important to understand how checks are processed and the role played by the Federal Reserve System in the processing.

In Figure 19.7, the purchasing agent for Villa Fontana Apartments buys a $150 carpet shampoo machine from Sears. The check used to pay for the machine authorizes the Florida National Bank of Miami, where Villa Fontana has a checking account, to reduce Villa Fontana's balance by $150. This sum is to be paid to Sears to cover the cost of the machine. If both parties have checking accounts in the same bank, check processing is simple. In such a case, the bank increases Sears' balance by $150 and reduces Villa Fontana's balance by the same amount.

However, the purchase was made from a Sears catalog and involves the firm's Chicago checking account. In such a situation, the Federal Reserve System acts as a collector for intercity transactions. The Federal Reserve handles a large number of the 180 million checks written every business day. You can trace the route a check has taken by examining the endorsement stamps on the reverse side.

Reducing Float by Speeding Up Check Processing   Until recently, an average check written in the United States took $3\frac{1}{2}$ days to clear the bank. When a financial manager wrote a check to a supplier, lender, or other payee on Monday and the firm's account was not debited until Thursday, the check writer could earn interest on these funds for three days. This time period is referred to as **float**. Since an extra day of float on a $1 million payment is worth $274 if interest rates are 10 percent, many astute financial managers established checking accounts at banks in different parts of the country to take advantage of float. For example, one survey of check clearance times between cities revealed that checks drawn on banks in Grand Junction, Colorado; Midland, Texas; and Helena, Montana, generated the greatest amount of float from New York City.

In 1988, the Federal Reserve System enacted a series of rules designed to reduce float by specifying exactly when a bank, thrift, or credit union must clear a deposited check. The new regulations require next-business-day availability for cashier's checks; certified checks; local, state, and federal government checks; and checks written on other accounts at the same institution. If the checks are written on some other institution within the same metropolitan area and the same Federal Reserve check-processing region, the institution must make the funds available by the third business day after the day of the deposit. If

check
Written order to a financial institution to pay the amount specified from funds on deposit.

float
Time delay between writing a check and the transfer of funds to the recipient's account.

Figure 19.7   A Check's Journey through the Federal Reserve System

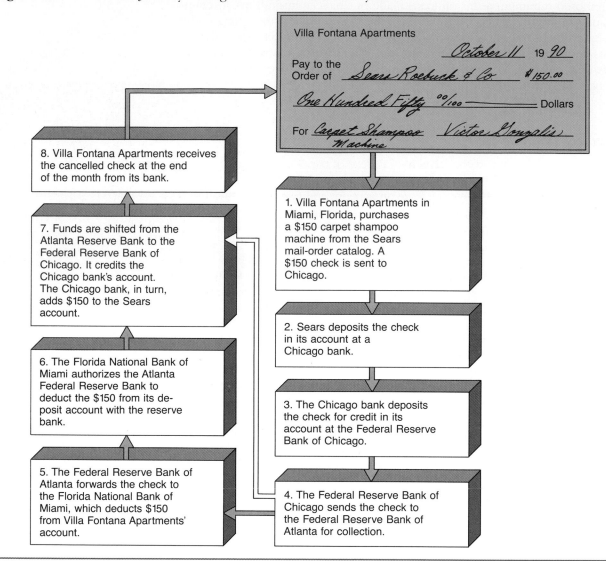

the check is written on a nonlocal institution, the funds must be made available by the seventh business day after the day of deposit. These maximum holding periods will continue to be reduced as the Fed improves the speed and efficiency of the check-clearing system.[20]

Deposit Insurance Provided by the FDIC and the FSLIC

Before 1934, bank failures were both common and catastrophic for depositors. In 1920, 30,000 commercial banks were operating in the United States; 13 years later, over half of them had failed, spreading panic and wiping out the life

When the Central Bank of New York failed in 1987, depositors (in photo at left) received the full amount of their FDIC-insured deposits. Before the Federal Deposit Insurance Corporation was formed in 1934, depositors had no protection against bank failures. Few of the people lined up at a Cleveland bank in 1933 (photo at right) got their money back when the bank failed. The Cleveland bank was one of nearly 4,000 financial institutions that failed in 1933.

Photo source: AP-Wide World Photos, Inc.

savings of millions of depositors. In the Depression year of 1933 alone, nearly 4,000 banks collapsed. Both individuals and businesses feared the loss of their deposits and looked for a means of protecting them.

The **Federal Deposit Insurance Corporation (FDIC)** began operating January 1, 1934. It insures depositors' accounts up to a maximum of $100,000 and sets requirements for sound banking practices. All commercial banks that are members of the Federal Reserve System must also subscribe to the FDIC; most other banks are FDIC members as well. In addition, deposits at savings banks and some savings and loan associations are insured by the FDIC. The **Federal Savings and Loan Insurance Corporation (FSLIC)** provides similar protection for most savings and loan associations, and the National Credit Union Administration (NCUA) insures deposits at federally chartered credit unions. All but 6 percent of the nearly 17,000 commercial banks and thrifts carry federal insurance protection for depositors. Deposits in different banks are separately insured, so there is no limit to the number of $100,000 deposits that can be fully protected in different banks in the same town or throughout the country. In addition, joint accounts opened by one person in combination with a number of other people (a spouse, a son, or a daughter) are all eligible for insurance coverage, even when opened in the same bank.

Bank Examiners

The FDIC and FSLIC have improved the stability of the commercial banking system and federally insured thrifts. The primary technique for guaranteeing the safety and soundness of commercial banks and thrifts is the use of unannounced inspections of individual banks and thrifts at least once a year by bank examiners. A **bank examiner** is a trained representative who inspects the financial records and management practices of each federally insured financial institution. Other commercial banks are inspected by examiners from the Comptroller

Federal Deposit Insurance Corporation (FDIC)
Corporation that insures bank depositors' accounts up to a maximum of $100,000 and sets requirements for sound banking practices.

Federal Savings and Loan Insurance Corporation (FSLIC)
Corporation that provides deposit insurance and establishes regulations for thrifts.

bank examiner
Representative of financial regulatory agency who conducts periodic unannounced inspections of individual financial institutions to guarantee safety and soundness.

of the Currency, the Federal Reserve System, or state regulatory authorities such as the state banking commission. These examinations are unannounced and may last from a week to several months. During the examination, the following areas are evaluated: ability of the bank's management; level of earnings and sources of earnings; adequacy of properties pledged to secure loans made by the bank; capital; and current level of liquidity.

If the bank examiners believe serious problems exist in one or more of these areas, they include the bank on a "problem list." Such banks are viewed as candidates for failure unless corrective actions are taken immediately. Needed improvements are typically discussed in the written examination report and in meetings with the bank's top management and board members. More frequent examinations are also conducted to determine whether these problems are being remedied. Should the problems uncovered during an examination require immediate action, more drastic measures can be taken. However, the problem list is confidential, and most depositors are likely to be unaware of actions taken by the FDIC or FSLIC.

What Happens When a Bank or Thrift Fails?

Even though bank and thrift failures were rare events by 1979 when only ten failed, they were running at a post-Depression high a decade later, with failures occurring daily. Almost 200 commercial banks failed in 1987, 95 of them in the depressed oil-producing states of Texas, Oklahoma, and Louisiana. That same year, the nation's 2,000 profitable S&Ls reported earnings of $6.6 billion, while the 1,000 unprofitable thrifts combined to generate losses of $13.4 billion. Some 150 of the weakest S&Ls were merged or liquidated in 1988; another 200 were closed the next year. Increased competition with other financial institutions coupled with excessive losses on business loans resulted in this disturbing number of failures among financial institutions.

At the first sign of trouble, FDIC or FSLIC regulators assess the problem and may use special loans and management assistance to remedy the situation. In 1988, to save the largest bank in Texas from closing, the FDIC granted FirstRepublic Bank an emergency loan of $1 billion. Four years earlier, the FDIC had provided $4.5 billion to prevent the collapse of Chicago's Continental Illinois National Bank. It also replaced the bank's senior directors with new management. By 1988, Continental was once again earning profits for its stockholders.[21]

If additional funding or new management appears unlikely to reverse matters, regulators attempt to negotiate a merger of the weak bank or thrift with a stronger one. Even after the FDIC emergency loan, FirstRepublic Bank continued to have problems. In 1988, the organization arranged its merger with NCNB, a highly profitable, well-managed bank headquartered in Charlotte, North Carolina. If no merger partner or outright purchaser can be found, the institution is closed.

Once the financial institution closes, federal or state officials immediately secure control of the financial records and physical facilities. Typically, authorities take control after business hours on Friday and freeze accounts. By the following Monday, they have either allowed another bank to assume control or have paid off depositors up to the $100,000 limit of the deposit insurance. Any assets held by the failed institution are sold, and proceeds are divided among creditors and holders of accounts exceeding the $100,000 insurance maximum.

The 1988 failure of North American Savings and Loan Association in Southern California illustrates these steps. After FSLIC examiners uncovered a high percentage of bad loans in the thrift's portfolio, federal regulators took over the thrift and accused management of mismanagement. The financial status of the S&L made its sale or merger with a solvent institution impossible, and North American was liquidated in 1988. Depositor Joan Steen, a Huntington Beach marketing consultant, received a notice to come to the S&L on a specific day to reclaim her deposit. Forty-five minutes after its 9 a.m. opening, she was on her way out with a check for $90,000. "I chuckled to myself about it," she says. "They were not only validating parking tickets, they were also serving coffee and doughnuts." Steen was not alone; all depositors were reimbursed.[22] In this case, and in all other failures of insured banks and thrifts, depositors have not lost a penny of their insured accounts and have received 98 percent of their uninsured deposits.

Privately Insured Thrifts

Although more than eight out of ten thrift institutions are federally insured, 30 states give thrifts the option of obtaining protection for deposit money through private, local insurance funds. These funds offer thrifts the advantage of freedom from federal regulation and less stringent requirements that enable them to grow more rapidly.

In 1985, these funds became a focus of concern when Cincinnati's Home State Savings Bank and the Old Court Savings and Loan in Baltimore faced serious financial problems that threatened their solvency. Fearing that private insurance funds would be unable to meet depositor demand, the governors of Ohio and Maryland took control of the thrifts to avoid depositor panic. Sixty-nine privately insured thrifts in Ohio were temporarily closed until the crisis eased, and Maryland's governor ordered a $1,000-a-month limit on withdrawals from the 102 thrifts in the state. Depositors in both states had reason to worry. Although total assets of the Maryland Savings-Share Insurance Corporation were $286 million, it was supposed to be providing insurance protection for $7.2 billion in deposits. Clearly, a bank panic would have brought about a system-wide collapse.

These crises have caused thousands of depositors throughout the nation to withdraw funds from privately insured institutions. As a result, many of these institutions have voluntarily sought federal deposit insurance coverage — a move that will put the guarantee of the federal government behind an increasing number of thrift institutions.

Financial Deregulation

A decade ago, the institutions that comprised the U.S. financial system were easily distinguishable. Commercial banks offered checking accounts and made short-term business and consumer loans. Savings banks and savings and loan associations were primarily in the business of making home mortgage loans and offering several types of savings accounts. Credit unions served their members with savings accounts and short-term consumer loans.

An intricate network of federal and state laws specified the types of loans and accounts each financial institution could offer, how much they could pay in the form of interest, and where they could operate. These rules were a carryover from the Great Depression years, and they produced a highly regulated industry in which specific types of financial institutions offered predetermined services in specific geographic areas.

This fragmented financial system began to unravel in the high-inflation era of the late 1970s. As investors shifted their funds from commercial banks and thrifts in search of higher interest rates offered by newly created investment outlets such as money market mutual funds, banks and thrifts suffered. Since they were operating under government-imposed interest rate ceilings, the banks and thrifts were unable to compete. During this same period, the giant broker-age firm Merrill Lynch introduced its *Cash Management Account*, which combined a money market mutual fund with a checking account, credit card, and securities account. Increasing complaints by bank and thrift management about their inability to compete for deposits resulted in deregulatory actions aimed at increasing competition among different types of financial institutions. These moves also blurred the distinctions between banks and other depository institutions.

Banking Act of 1980
Legislation deregulating financial institutions by permitting all deposit institutions to offer checking accounts; expanding services and lending powers of thrifts; and phasing out interest-rate ceilings.

This blurring began in 1981 with passage of the Depository Institution Monetary Control Act. This act, commonly known as the **Banking Act of 1980**, removed many of the barriers that had minimized direct competition among the different types of financial institutions. The act's major feature permitted all deposit institutions to offer checking accounts. Where once only commercial banks could offer them, today all deposit institutions directly compete for depositor business by offering NOW accounts and share draft accounts. A second major feature of the Banking Act of 1980 was to expand the services and lending powers of the thrifts in competing with commercial banks. Savings and loan associations and savings banks were authorized to make consumer and business loans, to issue credit cards, and to establish remote service units. Credit unions can now make mortgage loans. In addition, interest rate ceilings on all types of deposits at these financial institutions have been eliminated.

Although the Banking Act of 1980 was designed primarily to increase competition among financial institutions, it also strengthened significantly the Fed's regulatory power over nonmember deposit institutions. All such institutions — whether Federal Reserve System members or not — are required to maintain reserves against checking accounts, NOW accounts, and share draft accounts. However, these nonmember institutions are now entitled to the same discount and borrowing privileges as member banks.

FDIC-FSLIC Merger Proposals

The recent flurry of savings and loan association closings and the withdrawal of deposits from both privately insured and FSLIC-insured thrifts have resulted in suggestions that the two federal deposit-insurance organizations be merged. By 1989, the FSLIC was generating annual losses in excess of $8 billion as it attempted to aid troubled S&Ls and repay depositors at failed thrifts. An estimated $100 billion in additional funds may be required to solve the thrift crisis.

James Montgomery, head of Great Western Financial Corporation, which owns the nation's third-largest savings bank and is a profitable and strongly capitalized California institution, is one of the growing number of industry and government officials who would like to see a combination of the FSLIC, the FDIC, and the National Credit Union Share Insurance Fund, which backs credit

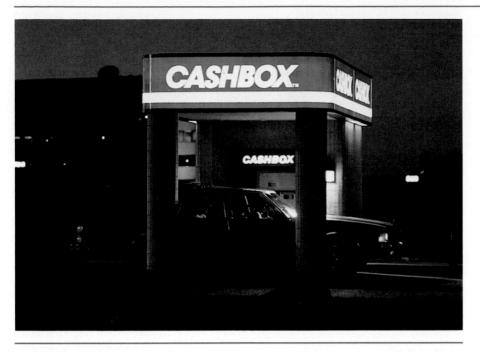

Photo source: Courtesy of Commercial Federal Corporation.

Commercial Federal Corporation, an Omaha, Nebraska–based savings and loan association, took advantage of the growth opportunities provided by deregulation of the financial industry by offering checking accounts, introducing a telephone bill-paying service, and installing Cashbox automated teller machines. In 1985, it became the first financial institution in the nation to introduce personal banking machines in branch offices. In 1987, it broadened its regional base by acquiring Empire Savings of Denver, the largest S&L in Colorado. The acquisition gave Commercial Federal access to a consumer market about twice the size of its Nebraska market.

union deposits. Not only is the FDIC in much better financial condition with almost $20 billion in cash reserves, but also its record of supervising and monitoring shaky banks is far better than the FSLIC's with the thrifts. In addition, banks are required by the FDIC to have capital assets equal to at least 6 percent of their assets — twice as much as thrifts — and to observe fairly stringent lending requirements.[23] Such a merger would also bolster depositor confidence in thrifts.

Critics of the merger proposal argue it would be unfair for the bank insurance fund to be used to bail out troubled thrifts. Moreover, the number of bank failures is also higher than at any time since the Depression, thanks to questionable third world and commercial real-estate loans. The funds required to return the thrift industry to stability may come from taxpayers. As one industry economist put it, "It is ultimately going to have to come from the taxpayer. There's no way around it."[24]

New Directions in the Banking System

The revolutionary changes in the U.S. financial system during the last decade have eroded many of the distinct characteristics of specific financial institutions. As a result of legislation permitting them to offer checking accounts and to increase their lending flexibility, savings and loan associations have moved in the direction of commercial banks. Additional developments will have a profound impact on all financial institutions in the remaining years of the twentieth century. Three major developments are electronic banking, the movement toward interstate banking, and the development of the financial supermarket.

Electronic Banking

In a single year, individuals and businesses in the United States write more than 47 billion checks. The huge cost associated with processing these checks has led companies and the banking system to explore methods to reduce the number of checks written.

The long-awaited "cashless/checkless society" may have begun in the form of the **electronic funds transfer system (EFTS)** — a computerized system for making purchases and paying bills through electronic depositing and withdrawal of funds. Some of these systems are operated by a push-button telephone, permitting the account holder to transfer funds electronically from one account to another and to pay bills. The monthly bank statement lists all telephone transactions made.

In other instances, a coded plastic **debit card** is used. Although debit cards resemble credit cards, they do not allow the holder to buy now and pay later. In fact, they require immediate payment for any cash withdrawal or purchase by deducting the amount from the individual's account.

Debit cards are access cards; they allow the cardholder to make electronic transactions and cash withdrawals from his or her account. They can be inserted into automatic teller machines to make deposits, withdraw cash, switch funds from one account to another, and pay utility bills. Automatic cash dispensers are being installed in shopping centers, major department stores, even supermarkets — wherever consumers write the greatest number of checks. The cash dispenser is connected to the bank's computer, which checks the validity of the card, reduces the cardholder's checking account total by the amount of cash requested, and provides the cash and a printed receipt — all within 20 seconds.

By 1989, U.S. retailers had replaced over 60,000 traditional cash registers with **point-of-sale (POS) terminals** linked to bank computers. By inserting the customer's debit card number into the terminal and recording the data relating to a purchase, the amount of the purchase can be transferred via computer from the customer's account to the retail store's account. Shoppers at 350 Florida Publix supermarkets and 370 Lucky Stores in California can use debit cards for grocery purchases. These cards have been tested by fast-food giants McDonald's, Wendy's, and Burger King. Preliminary results show debit-card purchases are 45 percent larger than those made with cash. The creation of regional and national networks that accept debit cards from numerous banks has led to rapid acceptance by both consumers and merchants. Gasoline marketers Exxon, Mobil, Arco, and Amoco accept debit cards at 10,000 stations.[25] Electronic banking using debit cards and point-of-sale terminals offers advantages for both businesses and consumers. Merchants can reduce their bad-check losses, banks can save on paperwork costs, and consumers can get money instantly.

To date, home banking has not lived up to expectations. When New York's Chemical Bank introduced Pronto, the nation's first major home banking system in 1983, bank officials expected 10 percent of their customers to eventually pay bills and make banking transactions from their home computers. For a $12 monthly service fee, bank customers could be linked to Pronto's computers through virtually any brand of personal computer, a modem, and an ordinary telephone.

The response to this banking innovation has been underwhelming. Today, even though 3.3 million U.S. homes are equipped with computers and modems, only 95,000 use home banking. Even though such giants as New York's Citibank

---

electronic funds transfer system (EFTS)
Computerized method for making purchases and paying bills by electronically depositing or withdrawing funds.

debit card
Coded plastic access card used to make electronic transactions.

point-of-sale (POS) terminals
Machines linked to a bank's computer that allow funds to be transferred from the purchaser's account to the seller's account when purchases are made.

and Manufacturers Hanover, Shawmut Bank in Boston, Boulevard Bank in Chicago, National City in Cleveland, First Wachovia in Winston-Salem, and United American in Memphis offer home banking, bank customers have not shown much interest in paying $8 to $15 a month for a service that requires a home computer but cannot accept deposits or dispense cash. In addition to business users, business travelers, who want the convenience of leaving bill-paying instructions with their bank, have been attracted to home banking. In 1989, Chemical Bank managers decided to cut their losses by canceling the service.[26]

The Trend toward Interstate Banking

A bank customer in Canada has the luxury of depositing money in one bank branch and withdrawing it from another branch in a distant corner of the country. This is not yet possible in the United States, where the banking system is much more fragmented than those in many other nations. In fact, many of the 14,000 U.S. commercial banks have no branches.

The Pepper-McFadden Act, passed in 1927, prohibits U.S. banks from having offices in more than one state unless authorized by state law and requires banks to adhere to the branch banking laws of the state. In some states, these laws prohibit branch banking. In 12 states, no branches are permitted even within the same city.

The Bank of California, headquartered in San Francisco, has continued to operate branches in California, Oregon, and Washington because its interstate operations were in effect before passage of the 1927 act. Currently, interstate banking is possible only if individual states invite out-of-state banks to set up branches.

While the country's 2,000 largest banks enthusiastically support interstate banking, 12,000 of the smaller banks strongly oppose any change. They fear that the nation's 12 to 15 largest banks would quickly seize control of the banking industry and eliminate small, local competition. They also fear that large, out-of-state banks would show little interest in small communities, local business, and individual borrowers and would concentrate their holdings in large cities.

Supporters of interstate banking see little risk of diminished competition and individualized service. They argue that such changes would increase competition by permitting commercial banks to do what a number of nonbank institutions are currently doing. Firms like American Express and Merrill Lynch are not subject to the same legal restrictions as banks, and they offer the equivalent of checking and savings accounts and other services on a nationwide scale. In addition, foreign banks, which are free of such restrictions, have already set up interstate operations.

Another argument for interstate banking is greater convenience for people who move to another state. In a given year, one household in six moves to a different city or state. Finally, a broader geographic service area would reduce the likelihood of bank failures sweeping across states such as Texas and Oklahoma where local banks and thrifts have little opportunity to diversify.

Interstate banking on a regional basis has already begun in several New England states and in the Southeast, Midwest, and West, where *superregionals* such as Banc One, NCNB, First Interstate, Sun Trust Banks, and PNC Financial are operating across state lines. The regional compacts were ratified by a 1985 U.S. Supreme Court ruling that sanctioned the right of groups of states to permit their banks to operate freely within a region.

Figure 19.8   Interstate Banking Resulting from Mergers

Source: Reprinted by permission of Chemical Bank. © 1988 Chemical Bank.

Banking boundaries are expanded to other states through mergers with existing banks or thrifts. A merger with American Fletcher National Bank in Indianapolis resulted in Columbus, Ohio–based Banc One expanding its operations to Indiana. As the text of the advertisement in Figure 19.8 states, Chemical Bank expanded into Texas and New Jersey as a result of mergers with banks located in those states.[27]

Financial Supermarkets

financial supermarket
Nonbank that provides financial services such as investments, loans, real estate, and insurance.

Not only are the distinctive barriers among financial institutions crumbling, but other nonfinancial operations also are joining the competitive battle. The term **financial supermarket** has been used to describe a growing number of nonbanks that act like banks by offering a wide range of financial services for their customers. Firms such as Sears, J. C. Penney, and Merrill Lynch are moving into traditional banking territory by offering consumers such one-stop financial services as investments, loans, interest-earning deposits, bill payments, real estate, and insurance.

With more than 25 million active retail accounts, Sears has a solid credit base upon which to build additional financial services. The retailing giant's Discover Card was introduced in 1985. In addition to its use as a general purpose card for shopping, travel, and entertainment, the Discover Card also permits the cardholder access to other Sears financial services ranging from a savings account at a Sears savings bank to a retirement account at Sears-owned Dean Witter. In addition, in-store financial centers enable customers to obtain insurance services from Sears' Allstate Group; real estate from Coldwell Banker; investment services from Dean Witter; and, in California, retail banking services from Sears Savings Bank. By 1993, Sears expects Discover to generate revenues of $2 billion to $3 billion. Dean Witter's 1987 revenues amounted to $4 billion, and Allstate's 1987 earnings of $963 billion accounted for 58 percent of total Sears profits. Coldwell Banker has been equally successful, and its offices broker 11 percent of U.S. residential sales.[28]

Traditional commercial banks and thrifts have responded. Banking industry representatives have sought to remove many regulations preventing them from offering such services as underwriting stocks and bonds. National ATM networks and geographic expansion through mergers have given banks a nationwide presence similar to that of the nonbank financial supermarkets. First Nationwide, which operates in 14 states, has set up over 150 kiosk-size branches in K mart aisles, where thousands of shoppers stroll past.[29] Other banks and thrifts are creating their own financial supermarkets by bringing in outside companies to help them package investment products and other new services. As kiosks staffed by people offering insurance, stocks, bonds, real estate, and even travel services begin to appear, the bank of the 1990s appears less like a mahogany- and marble-trimmed mausoleum and more like a boutique-lined shopping mall. In an era of one-stop shopping, banking services are being combined with other consumer services.

Summary of Learning Goals

1. Describe the characteristics of a good form of money and list the functions of money. In order to perform its necessary functions, money should possess the following characteristics: divisibility, portability, durability, stability, and difficulty of counterfeiting. These characteristics allow money to perform as a medium of exchange, a unit of account, and a temporary store of value.

2. Distinguish between money and near-money. Money is broadly defined as anything generally accepted as a means of paying for goods and services, such as coins, paper money, and checks. Near-money consists of assets that are almost as liquid as money but that cannot be used directly as a medium of exchange, such as time deposits, government bonds, and money market funds.

3. Identify the major categories of financial institutions and the sources and uses of their funds. The U.S. financial system consists of deposit institutions and nondeposit institutions. Deposit institutions, such as commercial banks, thrifts, and credit unions, accept deposits from customers or members and offer some form of checking account. Nondeposit institutions include insurance companies, pension funds, and finance companies and represent sources of funds for businesses and provide mortgage funds for financing commercial real estate.

4.   Explain the functions of the Federal Reserve System and the tools it uses to increase or decrease the money supply.   The regulation of the banking system is the responsibility of the Federal Reserve System through the use of reserve requirements, open market operations, and the discount rate. Increases in the reserve requirement or the discount rate have the effect of reducing the money supply, while decreases have the opposite effect. Open market operations increase the money supply by purchasing bonds and decrease the supply by selling them.

5.   Identify the purpose and primary functions of the Federal Deposit Insurance Corporation (FDIC) and the Federal Savings and Loan Insurance Corporation (FSLIC).   The Federal Deposit Insurance Corporation (FDIC) regulates the banking system, establishes rules for sound banking practices, and insures deposits up to $100,000. Savings and loan associations receive similar deposit insurance and regulations from the Federal Savings and Loan Insurance Corporation (FSLIC).

6.   Explain the major provisions of the Banking Act of 1980 and its impact on financial deregulation.   Major features of the Banking Act of 1980 include (1) permitting all deposit institutions to offer checking accounts, (2) expanding the services and lending powers of savings and loan associations and savings banks to allow them to better compete with commercial banks, (3) removing interest rate ceilings, and (4) extending the Federal Reserve System's regulatory power to nonmember financial institutions.

7.   Distinguish between credit cards and debit cards.   Credit cards function as temporary cash substitutes, but they are actually special credit arrangements between the issuer and the cardholder. Although debit cards resemble credit cards, they are access cards for making electronic transactions and cash withdrawals.

8.   Explain the role of the electronic funds transfer system (EFTS), the trend toward interstate banking, and the financial supermarkets in the current competition among financial institutions.   An electronic funds transfer system (EFTS) is a computerized system of making purchases and paying bills through electronic deposit and withdrawal of funds. It is designed to decrease paperwork involved in processing checks. As restrictive barriers on interstate banking are removed, the structure of U.S. banking will be altered radically. The current trend of bank mergers will accelerate, reducing the number of commercial banks. Financial supermarkets are nonbanks that act like banks by offering a wide range of financial services including investing, borrowing, interest-earning deposits, and insurance at a single location.

Key Terms

money

medium of exchange

unit of account

store of value

currency

demand deposits

negotiable order of withdrawal
(NOW) account

share draft accounts

near-money

time deposit

credit card

commercial bank

state banks

national banks

automated teller machine (ATM)

savings and loan association (S&L)

savings banks

credit union

insurance company

pension fund

commercial finance company

consumer finance company

Federal Reserve System

reserve requirement

open market operations

discount rate

selective credit controls

check

float

Federal Deposit Insurance
Corporation (FDIC)

Federal Savings and Loan
Insurance Corporation (FSLIC)

bank examiner

Banking Act of 1980

electronic funds transfer system
(EFTS)

debit card

point-of-sale (POS) terminals

financial supermarket

Review Questions

1. Identify the components of the U.S. money supply. What functions are performed by these components? Which money supply components are most efficient in serving as a store of value?

2. Explain the concept of near-money. Why is it not included as part of the money supply?

3. Distinguish between credit cards and debit cards. Are they part of the money supply? Why or why not?

4. Explain how the different types of financial institutions can be categorized and identify the primary sources and uses of funds available in each institution.

5. Explain the functions of the Federal Reserve System. Give an example of how each of the following tools may be used to increase the money supply or to stimulate economic activity:
   a. Open market operations
   b. Reserve requirements
   c. Discount rate
   d. Selective credit controls

6. Why was the Federal Deposit Insurance Corporation created? Explain its role in protecting the soundness of the banking system. Outline the steps that may be taken by the FDIC to assist banks with financial problems. What actions are taken in case of bank failure?

7. What are the major provisions of the Banking Act of 1980? How have they affected competition among financial institutions?

8. Outline the processing of checks by the banking system in the United States.

9. Summarize the arguments favoring and opposing interstate banking.

10. How do you explain the growth of the financial supermarket concept in recent years? What problems exist for commercial banks and thrift institutions in competing with nonbank firms offering financial services? What advantages do banks and thrifts possess over their competitors?

Discussion Questions

1. What advantages do debit cards offer banks? retail merchants? debit-card users? Why might some people choose not to use debit cards?

2. Discuss the current status of electronic banking in your community. Why do merchants prefer point-of-sale terminals over checks and traditional credit cards?

3. Explain the factors that have contributed to the current status of the S&L industry.

4. Some government officials have proposed that all commercial banks and thrift institutions be required to be FDIC-insured. Summarize the arguments favoring and opposing merger of the FDIC and FSLIC.

5. A recent listing of the ten largest banks in the world contained only one U.S. bank. Why do you think the list is dominated by Japanese banks? What factors impede the growth of U.S. banks?

Video Case

Old New York Brewing Co.

In today's corporate world, it is becoming increasingly common for executives with high-paying positions and seemingly limitless advancement opportunities to give it all up and join the ranks of the entrepreneurs. One such example is Matthew Reich, a former distribution executive for the Hearst Magazine Division and corporate loan officer for Citibank. In 1982, he shed his coat and tie and private office for a chance to do what he really wanted: open a brewery. But Reich was like almost all entrepreneurs; he had a big dream, but little cash.

In his book, *Growing a Business,* Paul Hawken describes Reich's preliminary steps to becoming an entrepreneur:

> He would have gone into the wine business, but he wanted to live and work in New York, and he decided that premium beer, as opposed to yet another winemaking operation, was a more likely venture on the East Coast. After he made this decision, he started studying beer with the same diligence he had given to wine. He took classes at the Center for Brewing Studies in San Francisco. He did research with a brewmaster. Only after two years of this informal research did he begin to gear up for the big push.

But the issue of money refused to go away. Reich was well-acquainted with the Jewish proverb, "With money in your pocket, you are wise, and you are handsome, and you sing well, too." But starting a brewery requires large amounts of money and his savings were woefully inadequate for the task. Reich had spent the previous year preparing and refining a 125-page business plan for the new venture, a plan that would aid him in the early days of the new business and would be invaluable in convincing others to supply him with needed funds.

Reich decided to skip the typical funding sources: commercial banks and other financial institutions. He remembered another saying, "If you want to know the value of money try to borrow some," and he knew that traditional lenders would base their lending decision on capacity, character, and collateral — the so-called three Cs of credit. He knew that character, or his willingness to repay the debt, would be acceptable, but he realized that capacity (ability to pay) would be a problem, as would his ability to offer sufficient collateral to support the loan. In fact, Reich considered his most valuable asset to be his Rolodex and the dozens of names of affluent acquaintances whose names and telephone numbers were listed there. He decided to take advantage of these contacts. Reich called everyone he knew personally or with whom he had previous business dealings and asked each of them to consider investing $10,000 in his planned brewery. After talking to 150 people, Reich managed to raise $220,000 in start-up funds.

Given the history of brewing in New York, Reich had to be convincing. Even though the first commercial brewery in America was housed in New York and, during its heyday, 121 breweries were operating there, the sad fact remained that no breweries had operated on Manhattan Island since Rheingold and Schaeffer closed their doors in 1976. Reich convinced his investors that this was not a lark; that a definite market and strong demand existed for specialty beers. Part of his argument was that microbreweries had become a visible component of the U.S. brewing industry, increasing in number from a dozen or so in the early 1980s to more than 75 today.

Reich's attempts to raise sufficient funds proved successful and the Old New York Brewing Company opened its doors in Utica, New York, and, under a contract with West End Brewing Company, New Amsterdam Ale and New Amsterdam Amber were brewed there for three years for resale in New York City. The beer was targeted at upper-middle class New Yorkers, appealing to their sense of civic pride and their desire for specialty beer.

Traditionally, beer contained four ingredients: malted barley, hops, yeast, and water. However, most big breweries today use less barley and add corn or rice to produce their light beers. Microbreweries like Old New York Brewing Company use only the traditional ingredients in their specialty beers. The deci-

Notes: Paul Hawken, *Growing A Business* (New York: Fireside, 1988), pp. 67, 88; Jonathan P. Hicks, "Cites High Costs and Shuts Plant," *New York Times,* December 10, 1987; Erik Larson, "The Best-Laid Plans," *Inc.,* February 1987, pp. 60–64; Frank J. Prial, "America's New Regional Brews," *New York Times Magazine,* May 15, 1988, pp. 14–16; and personal correspondence, June 13, 1989.

sion to contract production to West End Brewing Company gave Reich an edge on fixed and operating expenses and allowed him to direct New Amsterdam beer toward an elite group of clientele who could purchase the brand in a very limited number of prestigious retail outlets. At first, Reich sold the brand only to high-quality restaurants and specialty stores, delivering out of his own car. Another brewer says of Reich, "He did it with shoe leather." Reich believed that his beer was of such quality and distribution was so exclusive that he did not need to advertise or to offer buyer incentives and promotional giveaways to attract a following. He fully expected that his market would grow from repeat purchases by satisfied New Amsterdam customers and new buyers attracted by word-of-mouth. As Reich said, "What we're selling is taste, authenticity, and a traditional American product."

As the brand began to establish itself in the New York market, and sales began to pick up noticeably, Reich decided to implement his original plans to move the brewing facilities to Manhattan. This proved to be a mistake. An anguished Matthew Reich watched in horror as his brewery's profits turned to mounting losses before his eyes. "The costs of operating in New York City were heavier than we ever imagined," says Reich. He had spent over $2 million to build the Manhattan brewery, but unanticipated costs pushed the project far over the original estimates, forcing Reich to ask his fellow investors for another $2 million in funds. Those who were unwilling or unable to make the additional investment saw their percentage of ownership in the firm diminish as Reich brought in additional investors.

To generate added sales, Reich began expanding his distribution to the point where New Amsterdam beer is now sold in 600 restaurants and 500 retail stores in metropolitan New York City and in several cities outside the state. He also opened a restaurant adjacent to the brewery, called the New Amsterdam Tap Room.

The first two years of big-city operations had left Reich both disappointed and discouraged. During 1987, the brewery had lost nearly $100,000 a month. The only solution was to move the brewing operations back to Utica. Reich calculated that a return to contract brewing would save the Old New York Brewing Company $1 million a year.

Moving the brewing operations back to Utica while continuing to market New Amsterdam in New York City has proven to be one of the best decisions Reich could have made. Sales have continued to increase, taking Old New York Brewing Company from its modest beginnings a few years earlier to a stable company generating $2 million in sales (15,000 barrels of beer) in 1988. As the 10-employee company continues to master the problems encountered with soaring costs, the possibilities for satisfactory returns on investors' funds are good. As Reich says, "We are extremely optimistic about the prospects. With this move, we're back on a profitable footing."

Questions

1. Identify the primary functions of money and explain how Old New York Brewing Company uses money to perform each of these functions.

2. What are the primary characteristics of money? Explain which of these characteristics would lead investors to supply money to Matthew Reich in exchange for shares of ownership in his business venture.

3. How would Federal Reserve System rule changes designed to reduce float assist the Old New York Brewing Company in its operations? What disadvantages might result?

4. Reich's decision to build his own New York City brewery was a costly one. Do you think that his ability to raise funds from investors rather than from financial institutions may have influenced his decision?

20 *Financial Management*

Learning Goals

1. To identify the functions performed by a firm's financial manager.

2. To explain how a firm uses funds.

3. To explain how the financial manager can generate additional revenue from excess funds.

4. To compare the two major categories of sources of funds.

5. To identify the likely sources of short-term funds.

6. To list the alternative sources of long-term funds.

At 24, Stuart A. Rose showed more promise than many of the young turks on Wall Street. In three years he had completed a record number of mergers and acquisitions at Niederhoffer, Cross & Zeckhauser. "He had a way of distilling a transaction to bring out the profits," recalls his former boss, Victor Niederhoffer. Nevertheless, in 1979, when Rose asked Niederhoffer to help him start his own business, Niederhoffer said no. "It was one of the greatest blunders any executive in this business ever made," Niederhoffer concedes. "All I saw were four stores in Dayton. I didn't see the $50 million to $100 million I probably could have made."

So much for the Wall Street connections most entrepreneurs yearn for. Rose had discovered the four Rex electronics stores in Dayton when their owner hired Niederhoffer to find a buyer. By skipping meals and living in a rundown apartment, Rose had been able to save $150,000. But he needed $4.3 million. Interest rates were skyrocketing, and lenders balked at his inexperience.

Today lenders regularly knock on Rose's door. Still unassuming — he often arrives at the office with his hair still wet after a morning tennis match — Rose runs 91 stores and has easily raised more than $100 million in three stock offerings. His chain, Audio/Video Affiliates Inc., earned $7.5 million in a recent year. Revenues are approaching $250 million yearly.

The key to Rose's success: applying big-scale financial techniques to a small business. By borrowing against the stores' inventory and increasing their mortgages, he raised $2 million. A small New York investment firm, CMNY Capital Co., offered $350,000 for a 6.6% interest. And H. A. Armstrong, a finance company, lent Rose $1.5 million at 22%, or $5\frac{1}{2}$ percentage points over the prime rate. "It was truly a lever-

aged buyout. They just didn't use the term back then," says Rose.

Of his Wall Street friends Rose says, "They all thought I was out of my head." But Dayton was just for starters. As he sold stereos, televisions, and videocassette recorders, Rose kept his eye out for more stores to buy. His strategy: to dominate the market in small cities neglected by large electronics chains.

Rose found seven stores in Tampa and Des Moines in 1981 that were operated by TV & Stereo Town, a Genco Inc. subsidiary. To reach the $1.36 million purchase price, Rose once again leaned on the stores themselves. He borrowed $500,000 against Stereo Town's line of credit with Borg-Warner Acceptance Corp., got Stereo Town's owner to lend him another $500,000 and agreed to assume the stereos' accounts payable.

A year later, Rose tripled his empire by buying Kelly & Cohen, a 37-store chain, from SCOA Industries Inc. By this time, Borg-Warner had developed confidence in A/V's

cash flow, so the company stepped up with nearly all of the $3.5 million Rose needed.

Rose decided that his small-town strategy was working so well that he wanted to expand even faster. That required taking the company public. The initial public offering, at $5 per share, raised $18 million. Nearly $10 million of that went into the business. The stock has risen as high as $17\frac{3}{4}$ and has since split twice, giving Rose plenty of opportunity to return to the market for more funds. Two subsequent stock offerings raised $19 million more. Rose sold some of his shares in each and now owns just under 10% of A/V.

Rose's main concern is balancing his ambitions with the constraints of a maturing company. He wants A/V to hit $1 billion in revenues by 1991. To get there, he plans to buy or build about 35 stores every year, using cash on hand, a line of credit, and earnings.[1]

Photo source: © Bill Waugh

Chapter Overview

In order to satisfy their customers and earn profits for their owners, businesses like Audio/Video Affiliates perform two essential functions. First, they must produce a good or service — or contract with suppliers for its production. Second, they must market it to prospective customers. There is, however, a third and equally important function that must be performed. They must make sure that adequate funds are available to purchase materials and equipment, pay daily bills, cover the purchase of additional facilities, and compensate production and marketing personnel. One function of **finance** is to ensure that funds are obtained and used so the organization's objectives can be accomplished.

An organization's objectives include not only meeting expenses, but also maximizing the firm's overall value, which is often determined by the value of its common stock. More and more frequently, businesses designate a financial manager to be responsible for both meeting expenses and increasing profits for the firm's stockholders. This chapter explains why businesses need funds and how they use them; it describes how financial managers develop a plan to allocate funds; and it outlines the various types and sources of funds.

finance
Business function of effectively obtaining and using funds.

The Role of the Financial Manager

In the modern business world, effective financial decisions are increasingly becoming synonymous with organizational success. Businesses are placing greater priority on measuring and reducing the costs of conducting their business. As a result, financial managers are among the most vital people on the corporate scene. Their growing importance is reflected in the number of chief executives who were promoted from financial positions. A recent study of major corporations revealed that nearly one in three chief executives had a finance or banking background.

The **financial manager** is responsible for determining the most appropriate sources and uses of funds. In performing their jobs, financial managers continually seek to balance the risks involved with expected financial returns. *Risk* is the uncertainty of loss; *return* is the gain or loss that results from an investment over a specified period. An increase in a firm's cash on hand, for instance, reduces the risk of unexpected cash needs. But cash is not an earning asset, and the failure to invest surplus funds in an earning asset (such as marketable securities) reduces potential return, or profitability.

Similarly, the heavy reliance on borrowed funds may raise the return on the owner's or stockholders' investments. At the same time, more debt means more risk. The financial manager strives to maximize the wealth of the firm's stockholders by striking a balance between risk and profitability. This balance is called the **risk-return trade-off**. Most financial decisions involve such trade-offs.[2]

No one can always estimate risk accurately. The October 1987 stock market plunge was foreseen by almost no one in the financial world and led to losses by some of America's leading investors. One of them was Warren Buffett, the head of Berkshire Hathaway, a conglomerate that includes property and casualty insurers, a uniform manufacturer and distributor, a home furnishings retailer, and a candy maker. Just before the October 1987 crash, Buffett bought $700 million worth of Salomon Brothers Inc. stock, convertible to common stock in three years at $38 a share. On October 1, 1987, the investment bank's stock sold for

financial manager
Individual in an organization responsible for developing and implementing the firm's financial plan and for determining the most appropriate sources and uses of funds.

risk-return trade-off
Balance between the risk of an investment and its potential gain.

A major objective of Chesapeake Corporation is to improve its financial returns and generate increasing cash flow. To achieve this goal, the paper and forest products company is investing in new products, plants, and equipment, such as the 60-foot wood-treating cylinder in this photo, which can handle large volumes of wood at high speed. Such investments are needed to meet the growing demand for treated-wood products used in outdoor decks, fencing, and other applications. Chesapeake anticipates the investments will result in significant increases in sales volume and profits, thus maximizing stockholder wealth.

Photo source: Courtesy of Chesapeake Corporation.

about $33 a share; to most financial observers, the investment seemed to carry very little risk. Unfortunately, after the market crash, Salomon stock dropped to about $16 a share (the $700 million investment was worth about $685 million at the end of 1987); by early 1989, it had risen to only about $24. But while that one investment may in the long run turn out badly, Buffett's other investments for 1987 earned a total of $249 million. Berkshire Hathaway stockholders need not be too disappointed.[3]

The Financial Plan

In order to determine the best sources and uses of funds, financial managers develop the organization's **financial plan**, which indicates the funds needed by the firm for a specified period, the timing of inflows and outflows, and the most appropriate sources and uses of funds. It is based on forecasts of production costs, purchasing, and expected sales activities for the period covered. Financial managers use the forecast to determine the specific amounts and timing of expenditures and receipts. The financial plan is built on answers to three vital questions:

1. What funds does the firm require during the next period of operations?
2. How will the necessary funds be obtained?
3. When will additional funds be needed?

Some funds will be obtained through sales of the firm's products or services. But funds are needed in different amounts at different times, and the financial plan must reflect both the amount and the timing of inflows and out-

financial plan
Document that specifies the funds needed by a firm for a period of time; charts inflows and outflows; and outlines the most appropriate uses of funds.

Firms need funds to pay employees and buy raw materials used in the production of their goods and services. Miller Brewing Company uses funds to buy the barley it uses in the malting process of making beer and to pay valued employees such as maltster Lawrence Riesop. For four decades, Riesop has ensured that the barley Miller purchases is correctly malted.

Photo source: Courtesy of Philip Morris Companies.

flows of funds. Profitable firms often face a financial squeeze as a result of the need for funds when sales lag, when the volume of credit sales increases, or when customers are slow in making payments. To a considerable degree, the cash inflows and outflows are similar to those of a household whose members depend on a weekly or monthly paycheck for funds, but whose expenditures vary greatly from one pay period to the next. The financial plan should indicate when the flows of funds entering and leaving the organization will occur and in what amounts.

Why Do Organizations Need Funds?

Organizations require funds for dozens of reasons. Some funds must be held in the form of cash to meet day-to-day requirements. If the firm permits customers to make credit purchases, funds must be available to prevent cash deficiencies during the period of time between the sale and the receipt of funds. Inventory used in producing goods and services or stocked in a retail store costs money; and this money will not be recovered until the finished output is sold or the raw materials are converted into finished products and sold. Other funds requirements include making interest payments on loans; paying dividends to stockholders; and purchasing land, facilities, and equipment. The firm's financial plan will identify these specific cash needs and when these needs will occur. Comparing these needs with expected cash inflows from product sales, payments made by credit purchasers, and other sources will permit the financial manager to determine precisely what additional funds must be obtained at any given time. If inflows exceed cash needs, the financial manager will invest the surplus to earn interest. Conversely, if inflows do not meet cash needs, the financial manager will seek additional sources of funds.

Day-to-Day Business Activities

Financial managers attempt to minimize the amount of funds held in the form of cash since it does not earn interest. However, some funds must be available each day in the firm's checking account to pay bills and to meet the payroll. Periodically, larger amounts of cash must be available to pay taxes, provide stockholders with dividends (if the firm is a corporation), or make interest payments due on loans or mortgages. While the typical firm will use an interest-earning checking account for these funds, such accounts earn considerably less interest than other investments.

The general principle underlying cash management is to minimize the amount of cash required for business operations, thereby allowing a maximum amount of funds to be used in interest-producing investments. In order to minimize the firm's cash needs, the financial manager should pay bills as late as possible and collect money owed to the firm as quickly as possible. These actions lead to efficient cash management, as long as they do not damage the firm's credit rating or cost more than they save.

One of the least expensive ways for firms to manage finances themselves is by finding out where and how their cash is working for them. Banks are now selling desktop computers to larger companies, giving financial managers access to balances on bank accounts throughout the world. Excess funds that are not earning interest can be instantly moved elsewhere. Midsize companies use lockboxes, which are essentially local addresses where customers can make payments. Companies that receive large numbers of small checks can collect payments from and deposit them into banks faster, bypassing delays caused by mailing. Still another new method of managing cash is the controlled disbursement account, a system that lets a firm know how many checks in what amounts will clear what banks at what time. Firms can then keep funds invested until the minute outstanding checks clear.

All this may seem like a lot of extra work and expense, especially for smaller firms. But a recent Merrill Lynch & Company study found that companies with annual sales of as little as $2 million had an average of $40,000 in accounts that were not earning interest. With a little extra effort, these funds could be allocated to bring a greater profit to their owners.[4]

Credit Sales to Customers

In order to keep their present customers and to attract new ones, most companies find it necessary to allow their customers at least some credit purchasing. For many firms, such credit purchases — labeled **accounts receivable** on the firm's financial statements — make up 15 to 20 percent of all assets. Accounts receivable reflect customer purchases of products and services not yet paid for. Because the seller has already rendered the service or invested funds in manufacturing the goods, accounts receivable represent another need for funds.

Financial managers typically devote a great deal of attention to the efficient management of credit sales. The decision on whether to sell on credit to another firm is usually based on past dealings with that firm or on financial information

accounts receivable
Credit sales that customers have not yet paid.

Recognizing that immediate access to account information is critical in today's business world, First Alabama Bancshares Inc. offers commercial and corporate customers a direct microcomputer link to their accounts 24 hours a day. Customers use a special access code to receive information about their checking account activities and other banking transactions. The Right Call program improves the bank's service to customers by providing account information when the customer needs it and benefits the bank by reducing its cost of handling each customer call.

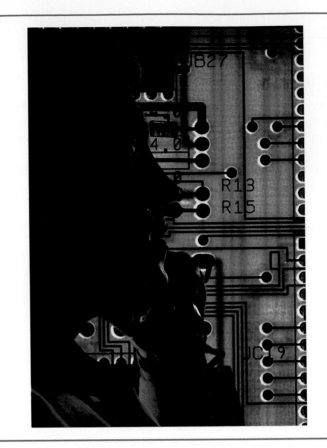

Photo source: Courtesy of First Alabama Bancshares, Inc.

provided by such credit-rating agencies as Dun & Bradstreet and Retail Credit Company. When credit sales are involved, the financial manager must balance the need for prompt collection of accounts with the need to raise sales levels.

Because long-overdue payments can disrupt a firm's financial plan, some businesspeople adopt an assertive means of dealing with customers. Helen Chen, the president of Joyce Chen Inc. which makes quality cookware, writes letters before a sale is shipped to the purchasing agent, accounts-payable manager, and the division head. She restates in these letters the agreed-upon terms of the sale and emphasizes that she expects them to be met. She occasionally mentions her policy of not filling orders before earlier ones are paid in full. With potentially risky accounts, she may even request that the customer acknowledge her letter in writing. With that attention to credit customers, Chen has had no late payments or canceled orders.[5]

Inventory

For most firms — producers, wholesalers, and retailers — inventory requires considerable investment. Most firms hold inventory in order to satisfy customer demand quickly, but it represents a major dollar investment. Cash is continuously invested in raw materials, work in process (goods in various stages of production), and finished goods inventory. Although these investments are re-

Inventory requires a considerable investment for R. R. Donnelley & Sons, the largest supplier of commercial printing services in North America. Each of Donnelley's many printing plants stocks huge paper inventories required in the production of telephone directories. Donnelley uses computerized record keeping and bar code optical scanning to improve inventory control and manufacturing throughput.

Photo source: Courtesy of R. R. Donnelley & Sons Company, Chicago, IL.

couped by the firm when the products are sold, at any time, substantial funds are tied up in unsold goods and raw materials.

The amount of money invested in inventory may vary during the year. Retail stores increase their inventory considerably just before the Christmas selling period and reduce it beginning December 26. When the next selling season approaches, inventories are again increased.

The financial manager can find ways to cut costs in a firm that requires a large inventory. The Chrysler Corporation, for example, now saves $20 million a year in carrying costs since it adopted the just-in-time inventory system. Parts are delivered to the assembly line only when they are needed and in the order they will be used. Companies can turn over inventory much faster and save money because they do not have to hold parts already purchased for long periods.[6]

Purchasing Land, Plant, and Equipment

For many companies, particularly manufacturing firms, the largest need for cash involves the purchase of the land, plant, and equipment needed to produce salable products and services. These types of purchases were referred to in Chapter 18 as *fixed assets.*

Land owned by the firm is a fixed asset with an unlimited life. Since its value does not decrease over time, the firm receives no tax benefits for income tax purposes. The term *plant* refers to buildings owned by the firm. Because buildings are likely to deteriorate over time, the owners are allowed to deduct a certain percentage of the purchase price from income each year. These deductions, commonly called *depreciation,* result in lowering the firm's taxable income. *Equipment* refers to all items used in production, from drill presses to forklift trucks, and from typewriters to computers. Because equipment is also expected to deteriorate with use and become obsolete over time, business firms are permitted to depreciate it on their tax returns, again reducing their taxable income. Because land, plant, and equipment represent major purchases, the financial manager typically plays an important role in the decision process associated with their purchase.

Servicing Debt

Kohlberg Kravis Roberts & Co.'s acquisition of RJR Nabisco for $25 billion burdened the company with a debt load of $23 billion, four times its previous level. Still other companies, such as Harcourt Brace Jovanovich, assume higher debt loads to make themselves less attractive as a takeover target.

This situation illustrates the recent phenomenon of firms having to increase their available funds in order to service debt incurred as a result of a takeover or in an attempt to avoid one. U.S. firms now have about $2 trillion of debt. Approximately 25 percent of the firms' cash flow is used just to service this debt.

Many financial experts view this trend with alarm, pointing out the inherent dangers such as the recent bankruptcy of the Revco D.S. drug chain. Its annual cash flow of $100 million was not enough to service $1 billion worth of debt resulting from a takeover.[7]

Generating Revenue from Excess Funds

At some time or another, virtually every organization will find itself with more funds than it needs to meet its day-to-day obligations. A large sale or the signing of a licensing agreement with a foreign firm may produce significant cash inflows. In such cases, the financial manager will attempt to utilize these excess funds to generate additional revenue for the firm.

Firms with substantial excess funds may decide to expand their realm of operations, to increase productive capacity, to modernize current facilities, or even to acquire other companies. For example, in 1988, Maxwell Communications Corporation, a communications conglomerate owned by British entrepreneur Robert Maxwell, purchased Macmillan Publishing for $2.6 billion, giving him a major foothold in the American publishing market. Chrysler spent $9.2 billion during a four-year period to modernize its auto manufacturing plants, some of which had been built in 1910. General Motors spent about $7 billion remodelling plants just to launch a single line of cars — the GM-10 series.[8]

As pointed out earlier, however, such uses of excess funds reduce liquidity. Capital expenditures for a new plant or the cash purchase of another firm means that the funds used for these purposes cannot easily be converted to cash should a need for additional funds arise quickly.

Once the decision is made to emphasize liquidity, a firm's financial manager has several alternatives to cash. Although interest-bearing checking accounts provide some interest, most financial managers will choose to invest the majority of a firm's excess cash in marketable securities. These are often considered near-money since they are, by definition, marketable and can easily be converted into cash. A number of different types of marketable securities are available for purchase. Three of the most common are Treasury bills, commercial paper, and certificates of deposit.

Treasury Bills   United States **Treasury bills** are issued each week on a competitive-bid basis to the highest bidder. Most are short-term U.S. Treasury borrowings with a maturity date of three, six, or twelve months. The **maturity date** is the date specified on the certificate when the principal must be repaid. The smallest denomination of a Treasury bill is usually $10,000. As issues of the U.S. government, Treasury bills are considered virtually risk-free. Because of this and their ease of resale, they are one of the most popular marketable securities.

Commercial Paper   A short-term note issued by a major corporation of very high credit standing, **commercial paper** may have a maturity of from three days to nine months. While commercial paper is riskier than a Treasury bill and does not have a well-developed secondary market for resale prior to maturity, it does pay the purchaser a higher rate of interest. The smallest denomination is normally $25,000, although most commercial paper is issued in $100,000 increments.

Certificates of Deposit   A **certificate of deposit (CD)** is a note issued by a commercial bank or a brokerage firm. The size and maturity date of a CD vary considerably and can be tailored to meet the needs of the purchaser. Large CDs in denominations of $100,000 can be purchased for periods as short as 24 hours. At the other extreme, ten-year certificates are available in denominations as low as $100 to $250. Between these two extremes are the more common CDs: 7-to-31 days, 3 months, 6 months, 18 months, and 42 months. CDs issued by banks can be redeemed before maturity, but substantial penalties are levied. Customers of brokerage firms can often avoid this penalty, since the firm may be able to arrange a resale.

Sources of Funds ✓

So far we have focused on half of the definition of finance — the reasons organizations need funds and how they use them. But of equal importance to the firm's financial plan is the choice of the best sources of needed funds. Sources represent the financial means by which the firm can accomplish its overall objectives.

Funds needed to implement the organization's financial plan come from two major sources: debt and equity. **Debt capital** represents funds obtained through borrowing. **Equity capital** consists of funds from several sources:

1. Revenues from day-to-day operations and from earnings plowed back into the firm
2. Additional contributions by the firm's owners
3. Contributions by venture capitalists, who invest in the firm in return for a share of ownership
4. Stock issues to the general investor public.

A large portion of the firm's day-to-day cash needs is generated from operating revenues. Sales, rentals, and other forms of revenue produce cash inflows that may be used to pay bills and operating expenses. In companies emphasizing growth as a major organizational objective, owners may choose to plow back earnings to finance future growth rather than withdraw profits in the form of bonuses or dividends. A growth-oriented company typically distributes less than 10 percent of its annual earnings in the form of dividends. On the other hand,

---

Treasury bills
Short-term U.S. Treasury borrowings issued each week and sold to the highest bidder; virtually risk-free and easy to resell.

maturity date
Date named on a security when the principal must be repaid.

commercial paper
Short-term note issued by a major corporation with high credit standing and backed solely by the reputation of that firm.

certificate of deposit (CD)
Short-term, high-interest note issued by a commercial bank.

debt capital
Funds obtained through borrowing.

equity capital
Funds provided by the firm's owners by plowing back earnings or making additional contributions, by contributions from venture capitalists or by stock issues to the general public.

The Southern Company electric utility system requires billions of dollars to maintain and build transmission lines, generating plants, distribution towers, substations, and other facilities needed to provide electric service to 10 million customers in the Southeast. Some of the equity capital used to finance the projects comes from Southern utility customers. But investors — the company's more than 290,000 stockholders — supply about one-third of the funds. Their purchase of new shares of common stock is essential in funding facility construction.

Photo source: Courtesy of The Southern Company.

mature companies pay out as much as 80 percent of their profits in the form of dividends to stockholders.

As pointed out earlier, cash needs vary from one time period to the next, and funds generated from daily operations may not at all times be sufficient to cover required funds. Catalog retail stores such as Best Products, Service Merchandise, Giant Stores, Vornado, Zale, and Gordon Jewelry feature a variety of products, from luggage, small appliances, and gift items to sporting equipment, toys, and jewelry. Since these products are commonly purchased as gifts, catalog retail outlets typically generate 80 percent of total annual sales during the Christmas season. A store like Service Merchandise will generate surplus cash for most of the year. But the buildup of inventory just before the Christmas season will require additional funds to finance until it is sold. As sales occur during the Christmas season, the incoming funds can be used to repay the sources of the borrowed funds. Figure 20.1 describes this annual cycle of cash needs and cash inflows for the firm.

In addition to variations in the timing of cash inflows and outflows during the year, there are other reasons for needing extra funds. Newly formed firms require substantial funds to finance purchases of equipment, train a work force, make lease payments on buildings, and purchase needed raw materials and component parts. Even established firms may not be able to generate sufficient funds from operations to cover all costs of a major expansion into new geographic areas or a significant investment in new equipment and facilities. In all of these instances, the financial manager must evaluate the merits and potential problems of seeking funds by borrowing. In borrowing, the financial manager's job is to determine the most cost-effective way to obtain funds. The alternative to borrowing is equity capital, which may be raised in several ways.

Short-Term Sources of Funds

Short-term sources of funds typically finance current needs for cash or inventory at times when cash requirements exceed available funds. These sources of funds

Figure 20.1 Seasonal Cash Inflows and Outflows for a Catalog Retailer

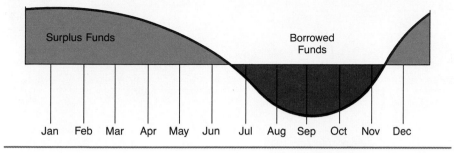

must be repaid within one year. By contrast, long-term sources of funds can be repaid over a period of one year or longer. The four major sources of short-term funds for business firms are trade credit, unsecured bank loans, commercial paper, and secured short-term loans.

Trade Credit

Most firms not only sell on credit, but they also make purchases on credit, or *open account.* These open-account purchases, called **trade credit**, represent the major source of short-term financing by most business firms.

Trade credit typically does not involve a formal contract. The purchaser who accepts shipped merchandise in effect agrees to pay the supplier for the goods. The credit terms are stated on the supplier's invoice, or bill, which accompanies the shipment.

trade credit
Short-term source of funds resulting from purchases made on credit or open account.
between people you know

Unsecured Bank Loans

A second major source of short-term funds — an **unsecured loan** from a commercial bank — accounts for much of the nation's business financing. These loans are called *unsecured* because the borrower firm is not required to pledge any assets as collateral. Commercial banks make short-term loans on the basis of previous experience in dealing with the firm and the firm's credit reputation. Loan assessments use such factors as sales, earnings, current loans outstanding, and other variables. The three types of unsecured short-term loans made by commercial banks are promissory notes, lines of credit, and revolving credit agreements.

unsecured loan
Short-term source of borrowed funds for which the borrower does not pledge any assets as collateral.

1. A **promissory note** is a traditional loan whereby the borrower signs a note that states the terms of the loan, its length, and the interest rate charged. It is to be used for a specific purpose, such as a temporary increase in inventory for the back-to-school sale season. Most promissory notes have a maturity of 30 to 90 days.

    For major business firms with high credit standings, the interest rate is at or near the **prime interest rate** — the base rate of interest charged by commercial banks for short-term loans. The prime rate shifts on the basis of availability of funds and demand for short-term funds, as well as on the basis of changes in the Federal Reserve discount rate. Each fluctuation of the

promissory note
Traditional bank loan for which the borrower signs a note that states the terms of the loan, including its date of repayment and interest rate.

prime interest rate
Base rate of interest charged by commercial banks for short-term loans.

Entrepreneurs often need substantial funds to start their ventures. This land was a research facility until a few years ago when Mack Fleming (right) realized a life-long dream and, with a partner, purchased the land to establish a tea plantation — the only one in the United States. The Charleston Tea Plantation now produces and sells American Classic tea. The partners turned to NCNB to finance the purchase of the 130-acre plantation. One division of NCNB focuses on arranging financing and providing financial guidance to firms with annual sales under $10 million. In this photo, Fleming shows an NCNB bank executive some of the tea plants brought to South Carolina more than 100 years ago from China, India, and Sri Lanka.

Photo source: Courtesy of NCNB Corporation.

line of credit
Agreement between a commercial bank and a business firm that states the amount of unsecured short-term credit the bank will make available to the borrower, provided the bank funds are available.

revolving credit agreement
Guaranteed line of credit.

prime rate makes news headlines because it indicates the relative availability of funds.

2. A **line of credit** is an agreement between a commercial bank and a business firm that states the amount of unsecured short-term credit the bank will make available to the borrower, provided the bank has enough funds available for lending. A line of credit is not a guaranteed loan. It typically represents a one-year agreement that if the bank has enough available funds, it will allow the firm to borrow the maximum stated amount of money. The presence of a line of credit speeds the borrowing process for both the bank and the borrowing firm because the bank does not have to reexamine the firm's creditworthiness each time the firm borrows money. Lines of credit are available to individuals as well as businesses.

3. A **revolving credit agreement** is simply a guaranteed line of credit. The commercial bank guarantees that the amount shown in the credit agreement will be available to the borrower. For guaranteeing availability, the bank usually charges a commitment fee that applies to the unused balance of the revolving credit agreement.

This last source of funds has been increasingly utilized in recent years, especially by small businesses. Some banks have reported as much as 40 percent increases in small-business customers using revolving credit agreements. To companies with sales of at least $200,000, Wells Fargo in California offers a revolving line of credit from $10,000 to $250,000. All the customers have to do is apply once at the bank — no more paperwork is required when the credit line changes. To raise their credit limit, customers simply call a toll-free telephone number. Funds are automatically deposited that day in the customer's account.[9]

To finance short-term borrowing needs, The Gap Inc. has unsecured revolving lines of credit with three banks. Like many other retailers, The Gap's business is seasonal, with about 40 percent of annual sales occurring in the late summer months and Christmas holiday season. Short-term borrowing helps these retailers cover seasonal inventory requirements and capital expenditures when operating cash is not available.

Photo source: Used with permission of The Gap, Inc.

Commercial Paper

As mentioned earlier, firms with excess funds often purchase commercial paper in order to earn interest. However, for major corporations attempting to raise money, it is an important source of funds.

Because commercial paper is unsecured — backed only by the reputation of the issuing firm — only very large firms with unquestioned financial stability are able to issue it. Even with large companies, some risk exists. Commercial paper is typically sold in denominations of $100,000 with a maturity of 30 to 90 days. Issuing commercial paper to raise funds is usually 1 or 2 percent cheaper than borrowing short-term funds from a bank.

Secured Short-Term Loans

As a firm continues to borrow money, it soon reaches a limit beyond which no additional unsecured loans will be made. Many companies, especially smaller ones, are unable to obtain any short-term unsecured money. For them, secured loans are the only source of short-term borrowed funds.

Secured loans require the borrower to pledge collateral such as accounts receivable or inventory. The agreement between lender and borrower lists the amount of the loan, the interest rate, due date, and pledged collateral. A copy of the agreement is filed with the state, usually at a state or county office. The filed agreement provides future lenders with information about which assets of the borrower are still free to be used as collateral.

For instance, as discussed on page 593, Stuart Rose left his job on Wall Street to start his own company. After successfully dealing in mergers and acquisitions he must have believed he knew something of finance. Intending to buy four

Figure 20.2   A Source of Financing for Small- and Mid-Size Firms

Source: Courtesy of GE Capital.

electronics stores in Dayton, Ohio, he saved $150,000 of his own but needed a total of $4.3 million. Bankers thought him inexperienced, but he managed to borrow money using the stores' inventory as collateral. Now his chain includes over 90 stores with annual revenues of about $250 million. While getting the initial funds may be difficult for the small-business person, it can pay off for all concerned.[10]

Commercial banks and commercial finance companies, such as CIT Financial Corporation and Commercial Credit Corporation, usually extend loans backed by pledges of accounts receivable or inventory. Both assets are usually highly liquid and are, therefore, an attractive form of short-term collateral. Commercial finance companies provide much of the financing for small- and medium-size firms. The advertisement in Figure 20.2 describes how GE Capital, a commercial finance company, serves the financing needs of automobile dealerships.

In 1980, C. B. Vaughan Jr., the president of a Bennington, Vermont, skiwear producer, went to banks looking for a $4 million loan to buy out a troublesome shareholder and to meet expenses in a period of poor business. The bankers refused. So Vaughan contacted Commercial Credit Business Loans, a Baltimore finance company, and arranged a secured line of credit. Now the sporting goods manufacturer has annual sales of more than $30 million and profits of more than $1 million. Interest rates for such loans, typically higher than other kinds, have declined in recent years. A few years ago, they averaged between 4 and 6 percentage points above the prime interest rate; now they are only about 1.5 to 3 points above that rate. Finance companies are not only useful for small businesses. Some have lending capacities nearly as great as banks and other commercial lending institutions. The General Electric Capital Corporation financed $544 million of an $870 million leveraged buyout of a Metromedia Inc. unit.[11]

Another means of obtaining funds, though not really a secured loan, involves using credit cards. Many small-business owners frequently use Master-Card and Visa as an alternative to bank loans and venture capital, both of which are hard to come by for startup companies. Out of a group of 83 small-business owners housed in one location in Chicago, half used credit cards to finance their companies. Some had credit lines on various credit cards totaling as much as $25,000. The 18 percent interest rates these small-business owners pay on their credit cards is about twice the prime rate, but if banks will not lend them money at the prime rate, they have limited options.[12]

Factoring

Instead of using accounts receivable as collateral for loans, some firms sell them to a **factor** — a financial institution that purchases at a discount the accounts receivable of firms such as furniture and appliance dealers, for whom credit sales are common. Selling the accounts receivable to a factor means every sale is a "cash" sale and the firm is freed from the necessity of collecting payments from customers. In many instances, sales finance companies perform the role of a factor, as do some commercial banks.

factor
Financial institution that purchases accounts receivable at a discount from retailers.
Second hand stores

Accounts receivable that are factored are sold at a discount, with the factor typically assuming all credit risks. Once the factor has purchased the accounts, customers are notified to make future payments directly to that company. Although factoring is an expensive method of raising short-term funds, it is often used in retailing because it reduces the need for major record keeping and for maintaining a collection department.

Few businesses take advantage of factors, however. A Dun & Bradstreet survey of 1,060 companies of various sizes found that only 7 percent of the businesses dealt with factoring firms. Factors make profits by paying less for accounts receivable than their face value, so businesses pay a high price for using factors. The advantage is getting cash instantly and putting it back to work earning even more money (rather than waiting much longer for accounts receivable to be paid).

Here's how factors work. David Clark, founder of a West Coast group of independent financial companies that does $200 million in business a year, typically discounts his purchases about 6 percent. That is, for each $1,000 worth of accounts receivable the seller offers, he or she is paid $940. Clark then assumes the responsibility for collecting on the accounts. If Clark receives payment on the accounts in 45 days, the seller in effect pays 4 percent a month. But over the course of a full year, the seller would pay 48 percent for being able to use cash earlier than would be possible by collecting the debt itself.[13]

Floor-Planning

Certain industries use a special type of financing called **floor-planning** — the assignment of inventory title (collateral) to financing agencies in return for short-term loans. This practice is commonly used by retailers that handle identifiable, expensive goods such as automobiles, furniture, and major appliances.

floor-planning
Assignment of inventory title (collateral) to financing agencies in return for short-term loans.

For example, an auto dealer that receives a shipment of new cars may sign an agreement with a local commercial bank or other financing agency for a loan in the amount of the shipment. Title to the cars passes to the lender, but the cars themselves (the inventory) remain with the dealer. The lender periodically checks the dealer's inventory to make sure that all the required collateral is still in the borrower's hands. As cars are sold, the dealer pays a portion of the sales price plus interest to the lender.

Some automobile manufacturers allow their own financing subsidiaries to make floor-plan loans. The local Chevrolet dealer may have the alternative of floor-planning through a local commercial bank or through General Motors Acceptance Corporation (GMAC), the financial subsidiary of General Motors.

In October 1986, GMAC, working with the First Boston Corporation, stunned the financial world by packaging its accounts receivable into publicly tradable securities. GMAC repackaged and sold $4 billion worth of loans it had recently written in $1,000 lots. The asset-backed securities had maturity dates of one to three years; for a small discount, GM acquired more capital to make more loans. Americans owe a total of $229 billion on car loans. Until the GM deal, that debt simply sat on the account books of banks and auto-company lenders; now more firms may follow in GM's footsteps and turn debt into securities.[14]

Long-Term Sources of Funds

While short-term sources of cash are satisfactory for financing current needs for cash or inventory, major purchases of land, plant, and equipment require funds for a much longer period. The business firm has three long-term financing sources available: long-term loans, bonds, and equity financing.

Long-Term Loans

Long-term loans are made by various financial institutions to business firms, primarily for purchasing machinery and equipment. They generally have maturities of five to 12 years. Although shorter maturities are available, the minimum of five years is most common. Long-term loans are made by financial institutions such as commercial banks, insurance companies, and pension funds. In some cases, equipment manufacturers may allow their customers to make credit purchases over a period of several years.

The cost of long-term loans is generally higher than that of short-term loans due to greater uncertainty about the future. Long-term financing agreements include the length of time repaying the loan, the interest rate, the timing of payments, and the dollar amount of the payments. Quarterly interest payments are normally required.

Bonds

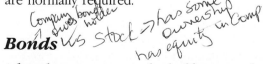

bond
Certificate of indebtedness sold to raise long-term funds for corporations or government agencies.

A **bond** represents a method of long-term borrowing by corporations or government agencies. The corporate bond is issued according to the terms of a legal contract called the *bond indenture,* which contains the provisions of the loan: amount, interest rate, and maturity date.

Bonds are typically sold in denominations of $1,000. They are purchased by commercial banks, insurance companies, pension funds, and even individuals. Like stocks, they are actively traded and can be bought and sold through any securities brokerage firm. Current market prices of bonds are quoted daily in a

Photo source: Reproduced with permission of AT&T.

Businesses often secure long-term financing to fund major projects such as constructing new plants, renovating existing ones, and purchasing equipment. In recent years, strong cash flow from operations has enabled AT&T to finance its capital expenditures programs from internally generated sources.

newspaper's financial section. Issuing bonds to raise money is generally reserved only for larger companies with regional or national reputations.

A number of different bonds are offered to meet the various needs of borrowers and lenders, and more are introduced all the time, with ever-more precise values. For instance, in February 1986, Gannett Company issued $100 million in bonds it called *step-up put bonds.* For the first five years, the buyer receives an 8.5 percent rate. After that, the buyer can either cash the bonds in or use the "put" feature: extend the bonds for another five years at 9.5 percent, which would give them an average annual interest rate of 8.98 percent.[15]

has longer term

Equity Financing ✓ *differences*

Equity funds represent ownership funds. They differ from debt in that there is no maturity date for repayment. As discussed earlier, many firms "create" needed funds by allowing earnings generated by the business to remain in the firm rather than disbursing it as dividends. However, relying completely upon plowed-back earnings may mean the postponement of important purchases for years until sufficient earnings have been accumulated. An alternative funding source for sole proprietors is to make additional investments in the business from personal funds. In the case of partnerships, the partners may choose to make additional investments. Or the partnership may choose to generate needed cash by bringing in additional partners to purchase a share in the business.

Two additional sources of equity capital are venture capital or a stock issue. Relatively new, smaller firms with strong future growth and profit prospects may be able to raise funds in the form of venture capital. In other instances, corporations may decide to offer ownership shares to the general public in the form of a stock issue.

equity funds
Funds obtained from selling stock in the company, from reinvesting company earnings, or from additional contributions by the firm's owners.

Debt vs equity interest in
specific has
repayment some ownership

venture capital
Funds invested by outside investors in new, small, or struggling businesses with potential for rapid growth in exchange for an ownership share in the business.

Attracting Venture Capital As discussed in Chapter 6, **venture capital** refers to funds for new, small, or struggling businesses with the potential for rapid growth. It is usually provided by outside investors in exchange for an ownership share in the business. The venture capitalist may be a corporation, a wealthy individual, a pension fund, or a major endowment fund. In exchange for funds, the venture capitalist receives shares of the corporation's stock at low prices and becomes a part-owner of the corporation. For taking the risks inherent in any struggling firm, the venture capitalist has the opportunity to earn substantial profit, should the firm become successful and issue shares of stock to the general public.

There are virtually hundreds of venture capitalists in the United States today. Each typically receives dozens of proposals each month from businesses seeking funds. Most applications are rejected by these investors, who seek soundly managed firms with unique products or services in a rapidly growing industry. In recent years, venture capitalists have concentrated in high-tech industries such as medical technology and robotics. Often, a venture capitalist provides a firm management assistance as well as funds.

While plenty of start-up funds are available, attracting the attention of investors can be difficult. Wesley Meador spent the better part of a year looking for $2 million in venture capital to help get his computer cable company going. Investors could not be persuaded to try the company, called Ultra Corporation, until Meador found a way to pique their interest. He added a well-known businessperson as Ultra's chairman. The presence of one of the biggest names in Silicon Valley on Meador's team was enough to bring in funds from a number of investors.

Many small businesses rely on friends and relatives for funds. James Kock left a position with the Boston Consulting Group to become his family's fifth-generation brewmaster. He produced his first batch of brew with $100,000 of his own savings and with $300,000 raised from family, friends, and BCG clients. He reached $4 million in sales in his first year. Likewise, Kevin Hay and two friends wanted to open a restaurant in Ann Arbor, Michigan, but could not find a bank willing to extend a loan. They used $28,000 in savings, and their restaurant, the Southside Grille, became enormously popular. Unfortunately for them, even success did not impress the bankers. When they wanted to open a second restaurant, they were again turned down for loans and had to turn to friends and relatives for funds.[16]

Public Sales of Stock The sale of stock, both preferred and common, to the general investor public represents a major source of equity funds for corporations. Such sales provide cash inflows for the firm and a share in ownership for

Table 20.1 How Leverage Works

ABC		XYZ	
Common stock	$ 10,000	Common stock	$100,000
Bonds (at 10% interest)	90,000	Bonds	0
	100,000		100,000
Earnings	30,000	Earnings	30,000
Less bond interest	9,000	Less bond interest	0
	21,000		30,000
Return to stockholders	$\dfrac{21,000}{\$\,10,000} = 210\%$	Return to stockholders	$\dfrac{30,000}{\$100,000} = 30\%$

the stock purchasers. **Stocks** are shares of ownership in the corporation, and stockholders are considered the real owners of the firm. However, they are not guaranteed dividend payments. Stockholders receive dividends only after a firm's bondholders are paid. Even then, dividend payments must be decided by the firm's board of directors. Since the stock of many corporations is traded on organized security exchanges, stockholders can easily sell their stock. The use of stock issues to finance corporations is an important decision and is discussed in considerable detail in the following chapter.

stocks
Shares of ownership in a corporation.

Leverage

Raising needed cash by borrowing allows the firm to benefit from the principle of **leverage** — a technique of increasing the rate of return on investment through the use of borrowed funds. Table 20.1 shows two identical firms that chose to raise money in different ways. The ABC Corporation obtained 90 percent of its funds through the issue of bonds. The XYZ Corporation raised all its needed funds through the sale of shares of stock in the firm. Each company earned $30,000. After ABC paid $9,000 in interest to bondholders, its stockholders received a 210 percent return on a $10,000 investment. However, the $30,000 earned by the XYZ Corporation represents only a 30 percent return on its stockholders' investments of $100,000.

leverage
Technique of increasing the rate of return on investment through the use of borrowed funds.

As long as earnings exceed interest payments on borrowed funds, the application of financial leverage allows a firm to increase the rate of return on a stockholder's investments. But the risk-return trade-off is present since leverage also works in reverse. If, for example, company earnings drop to $5,000, XYZ stockholders will earn a 5 percent return on their investment. But because ABC must pay its bondholders $9,000 in interest, what appears to be a $5,000 gain is actually a $4,000 loss for ABC stockholders.

Summary of Learning Goals _____

1. Identify the functions performed by a firm's financial manager.
The financial manager's major responsibility is to develop and implement a financial plan for the organization. The firm's financial plan is based on a forecast of expenditures and receipts for a specified period and reflects the timing of cash inflows and outflows. The plan includes a systematic approach to determining needed funds during the period and the most appropriate sources for obtaining them. In short, the financial manager is responsible for both raising and spending money.

2. Explain how a firm uses funds. Funds are needed for a variety of reasons. Day-to-day operating requirements call for funds to pay bills, meet payrolls, make interest payments, and pay taxes. Additional funds are tied up in accounts receivable if the firm allows customers to buy on credit. Inventory — in the form of raw materials, work in process, or finished goods — also requires considerable funds. Major purchases of land, buildings, and equipment may involve sizable outlays of funds.

3. Explain how the financial manager can generate additional revenue from excess funds. When funds on hand exceed cash needs, the financial manager may choose to make a number of investments designed to earn interest. These include the purchase of Treasury bills, commercial paper issued by major corporations, or certificates of deposit issued by commercial banks and brokerage firms. These investments generate revenue for the firm but do not tie up the funds for a long time.

4.   Compare the two major categories of sources of funds.   The two major sources of funds are debt capital and equity capital. Debt capital consists of funds obtained through borrowing. Equity capital refers to ownership funds provided by (1) revenues from day-to-day operations and plowed-back earnings, (2) additional contributions by the firm's owners, (3) contributions by venture capitalists who invest in the firm in exchange for a share of ownership, and (4) stock issues to the general public.

In contrast to equity capital, which has no maturity date, debt capital has a specific date when it must be repaid. Lenders also have a prior claim on assets and a prior claim on income paid in the form of interest. Owners have only a residual claim on assets and income after lenders have been paid. Lenders, unlike owners, have no voice in the management of the firm unless interest payments have not been made.

5.   Identify the likely sources of short-term funds.   If funds provided by day-to-day operations are inadequate to cover cash needs, the financial manager must seek short-term sources of additional funds. These include the use of trade credit provided by suppliers, unsecured bank loans, and secured short-term loans. Major corporations can also consider issuing commercial paper. Secured loans are those backed by pledges of such company assets as accounts receivable or inventory. Some firms sell their accounts receivable directly to financial institutions called *factors,* which purchase the accounts at a discount. Retailers of furniture and appliances often sell accounts receivable to factors.

6.   List the alternative sources of long-term funds.   Long-term funds may be obtained from debt capital or equity financing. Debt capital includes the use of long-term loans or the issuing of bonds. Equity capital may be obtained by additional contributions by the original owners or, in the case of a partnership, investment by new partners in exchange for a share in the firm. In some cases, new, small, and promising firms with growth and profit prospects may be able to attract funds from venture capitalists who invest in the company in exchange for ownership shares. Finally, corporations may raise equity capital by issuing stock to the general public.

Key Terms

finance	certificate of deposit (CD)	revolving credit agreement
financial manager	debt capital	factor
risk-return trade-off	equity capital	floor-planning
financial plan	trade credit	bond
accounts receivable	unsecured loan	equity funds
Treasury bills	promissory note	venture capital
maturity date	prime interest rate	stocks
commercial paper	line of credit	leverage

Review Questions

1. Explain the functions performed by the financial manager. What role does forecasting play in these functions?

2. Suppose you receive an invoice that specifies 1½ percent per month interest on unpaid balances. Relate this provision to the material in this chapter. Can an unpaid balance be considered a loan? If so, what is the annual interest rate on the invoice described above?

3. Identify the primary uses of cash in an organization.

4. Evaluate the major alternatives available to the financial manager in generating additional revenue from excess funds.

5. What role do firms like Dun & Bradstreet and Retail Credit Company play in financial management?

6. What are the primary sources for short-term financing? Distinguish between unsecured and secured loans.

7. Distinguish between debt capital and equity capital on the basis of maturity, claim on assets, claim on income, and right to a voice in management. What are the primary sources of equity capital?

8. Explain how trade credit is used in financing expenditures. Is trade credit considered short-term or long-term financing?

9. Identify the sources for long-term financing. Explain how borrowed funds produce leverage. What impact does borrowing have on a firm's financial performance?

10. Identify the basic principles underlying efficient cash management. What dangers exist if this principle is carried too far?

Discussion Questions

1. Joshua Lawson timed the opening of his Alpine Taxi/Limo in Steamboat Springs, Colorado, to coincide with the ski season. Lawson knew from the beginning that his enterprise was undercapitalized, but he hoped to cover his need for funds out of cash flow. Alpine's annual sales volume grew quickly from $80,000 to $326,000, then $675,000 and $750,000. The rapid expansion of Lawson's business involved the addition of many new services.

   Cash flow was a constant problem and remains so today. Lawson remarked: "There's a limit to bootstrapping. If you wish to remain a mom-and-pop business, bootstrapping will work, but I wanted more than that. Now I know I should have taken more time and put together more capital before jumping in feet first."

   Analyze and discuss Lawson's financial management problems. Do you agree with his views on "bootstrapping"? Why or why not?

2. Gift shops do 70 percent of their annual volume right before Christmas. Given this simple statistic, chart and then explain the cash inflows and outflows for a new gift shop. When would it be most advisable to open a new gift shop? Discuss.

3. Investigate how one of the following firms was originally financed:
   a. Federal Express
   b. Microsoft
   c. Apple Computer
   d. Food Lion
   e. Wal-Mart
   Discuss what you have learned from this exercise.

4. Houston-based Critical Industries is a distributor and manufacturer of industrial supplies and equipment. The company has expanded rapidly since federal legislation required schools to correct asbestos problems. With sales of $17.5 million, Critical needed funds for further expansion. Management decided to sell 20 percent of the firm's stock. Unfortunately, the offering came just five days before the October 19, 1987, stock market crash. As a result, the offering fell $1 million short of projection. To make up the difference, Critical Industries tightened its credit policy and hastened the collection of accounts receivable.

   Do you agree with management's approach to closing its financing gap? What other means could the company use to accomplish the same purpose?

5. Kohlberg Kravis Roberts & Co.'s acquisition of RJR Nabisco for $24.5 billion was the largest corporate takeover in history. Research and then discuss the role leverage played in this event.

Case

Mack Trucks, Inc.

Since their company's founding near the turn of the century, Mack Trucks managers have demonstrated versatility and efficiency in maintaining a lead over their competitors. Mack's truck models are industry leaders, with applications as varied as heavy hauling in the logging industry to trash collection. The company pursues a strategy of product differentiation that provides its customers with long-term benefits and unique advantages.

Mack Trucks fall into the product category called *industrial goods.* Rather than being purchased by final consumers for their own use and enjoyment, they are bought by manufacturers, utilities, government agencies, contractors, mining firms, and other companies who use them, either directly or indirectly, in producing other products or services for sale. In Chapter 14, two types of industrial products were identified: capital items and expense items. Commercial vehicles purchased from Mack Trucks, Inc., would fall into the former category. They are relatively expensive, are used for a number of years by the purchaser, and are purchased only after careful study and evaluation of alternative suppliers. The purchasers must be certain that the chosen product and supplier are capable of providing them with the product they need at the specified quantity level and the best possible price.

Commercial vehicles are Mack's sole focus. At its engineering, development, and testing center in Allentown, Pennsylvania, the finest technology and talent available are focused on creating designs aimed at improved operating efficiency and converting these designs into realities.

This continual product refinement aimed at improving operating efficiency has been in progress since the birth of Mack Trucks. English soldiers, watching the trucks in use on the battlefields of Europe during World War I, commented that the front nose of the trucks reminded them of the nose of a bulldog. They nicknamed the trucks *bulldog Mack* and it stuck.

The trucks also made short work of many difficult situations in that theater of combat, which likewise suggested the bulldog's characteristics of persistence and tenacity. Several years later, Mack Trucks management adopted the bulldog as the trademark for its trucks.

Today, the company has invested heavily in electronic technology, and the investment is beginning to pay off. Computer-controlled manufacturing centers, such as the recently completed $80 million facility in Winnsboro, South Carolina, use computer-assisted design and just-in-time inventory systems and turn out Mack trucks designed to exceed the one-million-mile mark: to be in service for at least one million miles without requiring overhaul or repair. The South Carolina facility can produce 70 vehicles a day at production costs that can make the firm's products price competitive, but also allow Mack Trucks to earn a consistent rate of return for its shareholders.

Mack's management has also concentrated on serving the firm's customers with a new order-entry system that simplifies and automates the ordering of vehicles and the scheduling of their production. In addition, the Mack warranty is unparalleled in the industry.

On the international scene, Mack has over 100 distributor locations in more than 80 countries around the globe. Its Canadian manufacturing facility can produce 26 vehicles a day, serving Canadian customers with Canadian-made products. Over 20,000 Mack trucks are currently being used in Venezuela. Also, the firm has made product modifications to enable Mack to offer Australian and New Zealand customers trucks adjusted to the unique weather and road conditions in those countries. Mack's partnership with the French company Renault has given the world its second-largest truck producer in the 15-ton capacity range.

Back in the United States, Mack's six distribution centers have automated storage and retrieval systems, and Mack's replacement parts business provides a large part of its total revenues. Another component of the company, the Mack remanufacturing centers, is devoted to overhauling and repairing Mack products and then returning them to the active market.

To be successful in serving the industrial market, a supplier must understand the unique problems of that

Notes: Kerry Hannon, "On the Road Again," *Forbes* (May 16, 1988), p. 37; Robert Wrubel, "Putting the Hammer Down," *Financial World* (October 20, 1987), pp. 25–29; Clem Morgellow, "Curcio: A New Age of Innovation," *Dun's Business Month* (November 1985), pp. 53–54; and "Mack . . . On the Move," a video produced by Mack Trucks, Inc.

market. In the case of purchasing trucks, a potential buyer is confronted with the fact that these products are extremely expensive. Financial managers must balance cash inflows and outflows as they assist other members of the management team in maximizing returns on their funds. Highly leveraged companies are especially reluctant to commit large amounts of funds to additional industrial goods purchases if they can avoid it.

Mack Trucks management has responded to these customer needs by providing options for the would-be purchaser. First of all, Mack's financing subsidiary operates 23 regional and district offices to provide customer relations services and to assist buyers in financing their Mack purchases. A second possibility for the would-be Mack Truck buyer who does not want to tie up hundreds of thousands of dollars in new transportation equipment is leasing. The Mack Leasing System was developed to offer this option to the firm's customers.

The bulldog symbol of the Mack truck has joined such familiar trademarks as the Travelers umbrella, the three-pointed star of Mercedes-Benz, and the cupped hands of Allstate Insurance as immediately recognized objects representing the values, products, and services of their owners. Mack's management believes that the firm's bulldog-like characteristics of strength, tenacity, and persistence in developing advanced products and in serving its customers will continue to make it a leader in the commercial trucking industry.

Questions

1. Explain the rationale for the creation of the Mack Leasing System. Include a discussion of the concept of leverage in your answer. Explain the potential dangers for a firm that decides to utilize the Mack Leasing System.

2. Develop an argument for use in responding to a Mack stockholder who maintains that Mack is tying too much of its own funds up in inventory by permitting the leasing of Mack trucks. What impact would the new Mack production facilities have on your response to the stockholder?

3. Why is earning a consistent rate of return for its shareholders important for a company like Mack in the long run?

4. Use concepts discussed in this chapter to explain the benefits to Mack of a joint venture with Renault in the production of certain trucks in its product line.

21 *The Securities Market*

Learning Goals

1. To distinguish between primary markets for securities and secondary markets.

2. To compare common stock, preferred stock, and bonds and to explain why investors might prefer each type of security.

3. To identify the three basic objectives of investors and the types of securities most likely to accomplish each objective.

4. To outline the steps involved in selling or purchasing a security listed on the organized securities exchanges.

5. To describe the information included in stock and bond quotations.

6. To explain the role of mutual funds in the securities field.

7. To evaluate the major features of state and federal laws designed to protect investors.

In 1980, 25-year-old Alan S. McKim launched a business that a decade later made him a multimillionaire. Clean Harbors began operating out of a trailer parked in a Boston suburb, almost within a stone's throw of the dirtiest harbor in the United States. The objectives of the environmental-services company were to transport, treat, and dispose of hazardous materials. McKim used only equity capital; his life savings of $13,000 went into the firm, which opened for business with four employees.

During the firm's first year, it secured a service contract from Texaco, its first *Fortune 500* customer, and Clean Harbors was off and running. Revenues reached $1.5 million in 1982. They almost tripled in 1984 to $4.2 million; and, by 1987, they had soared to $46.7 million. Rapidly growing companies often consume cash at a faster rate than they generate it from operating revenues. By 1987, McKim had incurred more than $11 million in long-term debt to finance his firm's growth — most of the debt was personally guaranteed by him. He continued to own 100 percent of the company, but he faced the prospect of losing his personal assets should the firm fail to generate enough revenues to cover the $11 million debt.

That same year, McKim decided to spread the risk by using other people's money. Dozens of venture capitalists had inquired about purchasing part of the company, and a number of large brokerage firms were interested in selling shares of Clean Harbors stock to investors through an *initial public offering,* or IPO. McKim's first move was a private placement sale of about 18 percent of the company to a group of Boston-based venture capital investors for $5 million. Although the sale reduced his ownership share, it infused fresh funds into the corporation. The move also made it easier for Clean Harbors to make its

second financial restructuring move in the form of an initial public offering. As McKim explained, "The [venture capital] firm helped us choose an underwriter, and they brought us credibility. Now an underwriter could say, 'Here's a company that also has recently done a private placement with a reputable firm, so they must be a *good* company.'" The fact that professional money managers had recently purchased part of the firm would also aid in attracting potential customers for the stock.

Robertson, Colman & Stephens of San Francisco, a specialist in emerging growth companies, was chosen to lead the sale to investors. After analyzing such factors as the overall stock market, the financial ratios of Clean Harbors in comparison to other firms in its industry, and general investment interest in the waste-management industry, a

tentative price of $15 per share was set for a 1.5 million-share offering. If the underwriting firm proved successful in its efforts, Clean Harbors would net about $21 million — enough to pay off all corporate debt and finance future growth.

Then disaster struck. The stock market crash on Black Monday, October 19, 1987, occurred less than five weeks before Clean Harbors' IPO. In a single day, the market value of the nation's leading stocks dropped 22.6 percent, the worst day in history for investors. The following day, Clean Harbors' management deliberated about what to do next. McKim calculated that his firm had already spent $750,000 in accounting and legal fees preparing the necessary IPO materials required by the Securities and Exchange Commission and other regulatory offices. They decided to proceed with the stock offering. Its size was reduced to 1 million shares and the offer price was slashed 40 percent to $9 per share. All other costs remained unchanged, reducing the firm's net by 60 percent to about $8 million when the offering occurred November 24, 1987. These funds, combined with the $5 million received a few months earlier from the venture capital investors, were used to remove all outstanding debt. As a result, the firm saved $1.2 million on interest expenses in 1988. Funds that would have gone to lenders were added to corporate profits.

McKim was not surprised to learn that, within four months after the IPO, his firm's shares were trading for the $15 price he had originally hoped for. Investor interest in Clean Harbors was further stimulated in August 1988 when Governor Michael Dukakis broke ground on a $6.1 billion cleanup of Boston Harbor. By 1989, the firm's stock was being bought and sold at double the price of the initial public offering.

The 1987 market crash penalized the firm severely, since it received net proceeds of only $8 per share.

However, the increase in the selling price of Clean Harbors stock still benefits its founder and other stockholders. McKim continues to own 58 percent of the company, which, at current prices, make his holdings worth nearly $100 million.[1]

Photo source: Copyright 1988 Edward Slaman.

Chapter Overview

securities
Stocks and bonds representing obligations of the issuer to provide purchasers an expected or stated return on investments.

primary market
New issues of securities sold publicly for the first time.

secondary market
Sales of previously issued shares of stocks and bonds.

The previous chapter discussed two sources of funding for long-term financial needs: debt capital and equity capital. Long-term debt capital exists in the form of corporate bonds, U.S. government bonds, and municipal bonds. Equity capital takes the form of stocks — shares of ownership in the corporation. Stocks and bonds are commonly referred to as **securities** because both represent obligations on the part of their issuers to provide purchasers with an expected or stated return on the funds invested or loaned.

Stocks and bonds are bought and sold in two marketplaces. In the **primary market**, securities are first sold to the public. The **secondary market** is the one in which previously issued securities are bought and sold.

Primary Markets

When a corporation needs capital for plant expansion, product development, acquisition of a smaller firm, or other legitimate business reasons, it may make a stock or bond offering. A stock offering gives investors the opportunity to purchase ownership shares in the firm and to take part in its future growth in exchange for current capital. In other instances, a corporation or a government agency may choose to raise funds by issuing bonds. Figure 21.1 illustrates these two methods. Similar announcements of stock and bond offerings appear daily in such business newspapers as *The Wall Street Journal* in the form of simple black-and-white announcements called *tombstones*.

The first example shows the tombstone that announced the Clean Harbors initial public offering of 1 million shares of stock. The second example summarizes supermarket giant Kroger's decision to acquire $1.25 billion in debt capital through the sale of two series of bonds: half paying $12\frac{7}{8}$ percent annual interest and due in the year 1999 and the remainder paying $13\frac{1}{8}$ percent interest and due in the year 2001. Governmental use of primary markets to generate funds ranges from the sale of U.S. Treasury bonds to finance part of the federal deficit to a bond issued by the city of Phoenix to finance additions to the city water system.

Figure 21.1   "Tombstone" Announcements of Stock and Bond Offerings

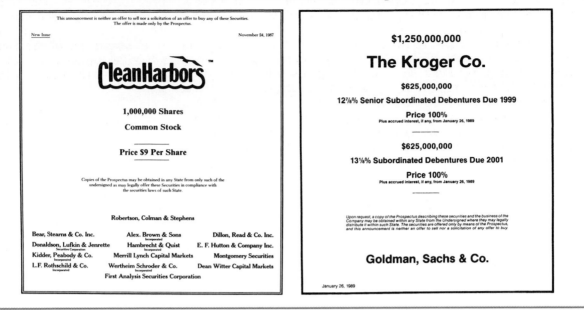

Source: Courtesy of Clean Harbors, Inc.

Although a corporation could market its stock or bond issue directly to the public, most large offerings are handled by financial specialists called investment bankers, or underwriters. An **investment banker** is a financial intermediary who specializes in selling new issues of stocks and bonds for business firms and government agencies. Well-known investment bankers include such financial specialists as Salomon Brothers, First Boston Corporation, Lazard Freres & Co., and Oppenheimer, in addition to such major securities brokerage firms as Merrill Lynch and Prudential-Bache. Investment bankers agree to acquire the total issue from the company or agency and then resell it to other investors. The investment banker underwrites the issue at a discount as compensation for services rendered. For instance, the Clean Harbors 1-million-share offering at $9 per share might be acquired by the underwriter at $8.25 per share. In addition to locating buyers for the issue, the underwriter typically advises the issuer on such subjects as general characteristics of the issue, its pricing, and the timing of the offering. Often, primary underwriters do not take complete responsibility for the public sale. Instead, they resell either all or part of the shares to other underwriters who, in turn, sell them to the public. In the example described above, the primary underwriter may acquire the issue from Clean Harbors at $8.25 per share and then sell the shares to other underwriters for $8.60. Ultimately, the public may be offered the stock at $9 per share. Figure 21.2 illustrates this process.

investment banker
Specialist in selling new issues of securities for business and government.

Secondary Markets

Daily news reports of stock and bond trading refer to the secondary markets, places where previously issued shares of stocks and bonds are traded. Such markets are convenient locations for buyers and sellers to make exchanges. The

Figure 21.2   The Role of the Investment Banker

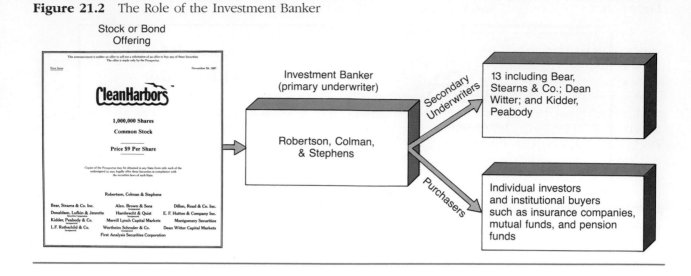

issuing corporations do not receive proceeds from such transactions, and gains and losses affect only the current and future owners of the securities. The various secondary markets are discussed later in the chapter.

Stocks

Stocks are units of ownership in a corporation. Although many corporations issue only one type of stock, two types exist: common stock and preferred stock.

Common Stock

common stock
Stock providing owners voting rights but only a residual claim to company assets.

The basic form of corporate ownership is **common stock**. Purchasers of common stock are the true owners of a corporation; in return for their investment, they expect to receive payments in the form of dividends and/or capital gains resulting from increases in the value of their stock holdings.

Holders of common stock vote on major company decisions, such as the purchase of other companies or the election of the board of directors. They benefit from company success, and they risk the loss of their investment if the company fails. Creditors and preferred stockholders are paid before common stockholders. Common stock is sold on either a par or no-par value basis. **Par value** is the value printed on the stock certificates of some companies. In some states, par value is used as the basis for paying state incorporation taxes. Because the par value is highly arbitrary, most corporations now issue no-par value stock. In either case, the total number of shares outstanding represents the total ownership of the firm, and the value of an individual stockholder's investment is

par value
Value printed on stock certificates of some companies.

based on the number of shares owned and their market price rather than on an arbitrary par value.

Sometimes confusion results over two other types of value: market value and book value. **Market value** — the price at which a stock is currently selling — is easily determined by referring to the financial page of the daily newspaper. It usually varies from day to day, depending on company earnings and investor expectations about future prospects for the firm. **Book value** is determined by subtracting the company's liabilities from its assets, minus the value of any preferred stock. When this net figure is divided by the number of shares of common stock, the book value of each share is known.

What happens when the corporation decides to raise additional long-term funds through the sale of additional stock? In most cases, current stockholders get the opportunity to purchase a proportionate share of new stock issues — their **preemptive right**. Without this right, a stockholder owning 6 percent of a company's stock would find his or her share of the company diluted to 3 percent if the company decided to double the amount of stock.

A common stock certificate for Clean Harbors is shown in Figure 21.3. Included on the certificate are the name and address of the registered owner, the number of shares represented by the certificate, the state in which the firm is incorporated, and the signatures of corporate officers.

Preferred Stock

In addition to common stock, many corporations issue **preferred stock** — stock whose owners receive preference in the payment of dividends. Also, if the company is dissolved, holders of preferred stock have a claim on the firm's assets before any claim by common stockholders.

In return for this preference, preferred stockholders usually do not have voting rights. And even when voting rights do exist, they are typically limited to such important proposals as mergers, sales of company property, and dissolution of the company itself. Although preferred stockholders are granted certain privileges over common stockholders, they are still considered owners of the firm, and their dividends are, therefore, not guaranteed.

Preferred stock can be cumulative or noncumulative. In the case of *cumulative preferred stock*, stockholders must be paid a dividend for each year before common stockholders can be paid. Suppose, for example, that RCA's board of directors decides one year to omit the $4 dividend to preferred shareholders because of poor earnings. The following year, RCA cannot pay any dividends to the common stockholders until it pays dividends of $8 to each preferred stockholder. Omitted dividends accumulate automatically and must be paid before common stockholders can receive any dividends. Owners of *noncumulative preferred stock*, on the other hand, need to be paid only the current year's dividend before common stockholders receive their dividends.

Preferred stock is often issued with a conversion privilege. This *convertible preferred stock* gives stockholders the option of having their preferred stock converted into common stock at a stated price.

Preferred stock is usually issued to attract conservative investors who want the margin of safety in having preference over common stock. Although preferred stock represents equity capital, many companies consider it a compromise between bonds and common stock.

market value
Price at which a security is currently selling.

book value
Value of stock determined by subtracting liabilities from assets, minus the value of any preferred stock.

preemptive right
Stockholders' right to purchase a proportionate amount of new issues.

preferred stock
Stock providing owners preferential dividend payment and first claim to assets after debts are paid but seldom with voting rights.

Figure 21.3   Clean Harbors Common Stock Certificate

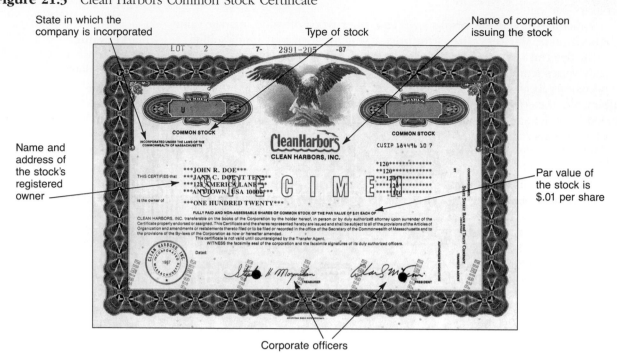

State in which the company is incorporated

Type of stock

Name of corporation issuing the stock

Name and address of the stock's registered owner

Par value of the stock is $.01 per share

Corporate officers

Source: Courtesy of Clean Harbors, Inc.

Bonds

Bondholders are creditors, not owners, of a corporation. Chapter 20 described bonds as a means of obtaining long-term debt capital for the corporation and as sources of funds for municipal, state, and federal government units. Bonds are issued in denominations of $1,000, $5,000, and even $50,000. They indicate a definite rate of interest to be paid to the bondholder and the maturity date. Because bondholders are creditors of the corporation, they have a claim on the firm's assets before any claims of preferred and common stockholders in the event of the firm's dissolution.

Types of Bonds

secured bond
Bond backed by specific pledges of company assets.

The potential bondholder has a variety of bonds from which to choose. A **secured bond** is backed by specific pledges of company assets. For instance, mortgage bonds are backed by real and personal property owned by the firm, such as machinery or furniture. Collateral trust bonds are backed by stocks and bonds of other companies owned by the borrowing firm. Railroads and airline companies, which often raise 40 to 55 percent of their long-term funds through issuing bonds, often use rolling stock (locomotives and rail cars) and airplanes as collateral. This final type of secured bond is called an *equipment trust certificate.*

Figure 21.4   A Corporate Bond

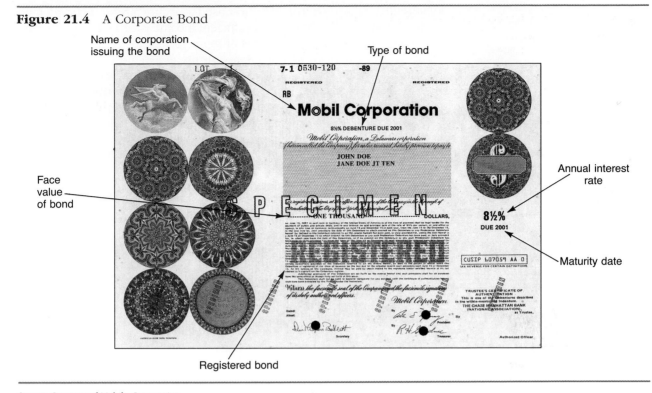

Source: Courtesy of Mobile Corporation.

Since bond purchasers are attempting to balance their financial returns with the risks involved, bonds backed by pledges of specific assets are less risky than those without such collateral. Consequently, a firm will be able to issue secured bonds at lower interest rates than would be possible if it had chosen to issue unsecured bonds.

However, a number of companies do issue these bonds. Such an unsecured bond is called a **debenture** — a bond backed only by the reputation of the issuing corporation or governmental unit. Only governments and major corporations with extremely sound financial reputations can find buyers for their debentures. American Telephone & Telegraph successfully raised billions of dollars from debentures in the past 40 years. Bond purchasers have been willing to buy AT&T unsecured bonds because of their faith in the stability of the issuing company. A Mobil Corporation debenture is shown in Figure 21.4.

A **government bond** represents funds borrowed by the U.S. government. Because they are backed by the full faith and credit of the federal government, government bonds are considered the least risky of all debt obligations. A **municipal bond** is a debt issue of a state or a political subdivision, such as a county, city, township, or village. Municipal bonds can be classified as general-obligation bonds or revenue bonds. General-obligation bonds are backed by the credit of the issuer. Revenue bonds are serviced by income produced by such revenue-generating projects as toll roads, bridges, municipal coliseums, or public utilities. Revenue bonds provide higher returns to investors than do general-obligation bonds because of the risks of default. Should the municipality fail to

debenture
Bond backed by the reputation of the issuing corporation.

government bond
Bond issued by the U.S. government.

municipal bond
Debt issue of a state or political subdivision that may be a general-obligation bond or revenue bond.

generate sufficient income from a project used to secure a revenue bond, it has no legal debt-service obligation until sufficient income is earned from the project. An important feature of both types of municipal bonds is that interest payments are usually exempt from federal income tax and, in most cases, from taxes in the state and locality in which the bonds are issued. Because of this attractive feature, these bonds can be issued at significantly lower interest rates.

convertible bond
Bond conversion option to a specific number of shares of common stock.

bond indenture
Legal contract containing all provisions of a bond.

In order to entice more speculative purchasers, convertible bonds are sometimes issued by corporations. A **convertible bond** has the option of being converted into a specific number of shares of common stock. The number of shares of stock exchanged for each bond is included in the **bond indenture** — the legal contract containing all provisions of the bond. A $1,000 bond might be convertible into 50 shares of common stock. If the common stock is selling at $18 when the bonds are issued, the conversion privilege has no value. But if the stock rises in price to $30, the value of the bond increases to $1,500. Convertible bonds offer lower interest rates than those lacking conversion provisions and, therefore, reduce the interest expenses of the issuing firm. Some bond purchasers prefer such bonds, even at lower interest rates, due to the potential of additional gains if the price of the firm's stock increases.

Rating Bonds

When most people think of investing, they immediately think of the stock market. But it is not the only investment arena available. Investors seeking safe instruments in which to put their money often choose the bond market.

A couple of factors determine the price of bonds. The first is the degree of risk: Will the company or government issuing the bond be able to pay the principal when due? Is it able to make the interest payments? Is the bond already in default? These questions indicate increasing degrees of risk for a bond.

Since the bondholder is a creditor of the company, he or she has first claim on the company's assets in the event of liquidation. For this reason, bonds are generally less risky than stocks. Still, some bonds are highly risky — especially in the recent climate of corporate takeovers. For example, Kohlberg Kravis Roberts financed much of the cost of its acquisition of RJR Nabisco by pledging the assets of the firm to lenders. Companies ranging from public utilities (Public Service Corporation of New Hampshire) to aerospace firms (LTV Corporation) have recently defaulted on bond interest payments.

In general, the level of risk is reflected in a bond's rating, provided by the two bond-rating services, Standard & Poor's (S&P) and Moody's. As Table 21.1 shows, the most risk-free bonds are rated AAA (S&P) and Aaa (Moody's), and the scale descends to the so-called *junk bonds* and then on to the most speculative issues, usually in default.

Junk bonds attract investors because of the high yields they offer in exchange for the risk involved. During the high interest rates of the early 1980s, Metropolitan Edison's BB-rated bonds, maturing in the year 2008, yielded 16.7 percent, while some companies' AAA bonds yielded only 10.7 percent. In general, the safer the bond, the higher the price and the lower the interest rate the issuer has to pay.

The second factor affecting the price of the bond is the interest rate. Other things being equal, the higher the interest rate, the higher the price at which a bond will be bought and sold. But everything else usually is not equal — the

Table 21.1 Moody's and Standard & Poor's Bond Ratings

Moody's	Interpretation	Standard & Poor's	Interpretation
Aaa	Prime quality	AAA	Bank investment
Aa	High grade	AA	quality
A	Upper medium grade	A	
Baa	Medium grade	BBB	
		BB	
Ba	Lower medium grade or speculative	B	Speculative
B	Speculative	CCC	
		CC	
Caa	From very speculative	C	
Ca	to near or in default		
C		DDD	In default (rating indicates
		DD	the relative salvage
		D	value)

bonds may not be equally risky, or one may tie up money for longer periods than the other. Consequently, investors must evaluate the trade-offs involved. Another important rule is that when interest rates go up, bond prices go down. This is because bondholders are locked into relatively lower interest rates on their money.

How Bonds Are Retired

Because bonds have a maturity date, the issuing corporation must have the necessary funds available to repay the principal when the bonds mature. The two most common methods of repayment are serial bonds and sinking-fund bonds.

In the case of a **serial bond**, a corporation simply issues a large number of bonds that mature at different dates. For example, if a corporation decides to issue $4.5 million in serial bonds for a 30-year period, the maturity dates may be established in such a manner that no bonds mature for the first 15 years. Beginning with the 16th year, $300,000 in bonds mature each year until the bonds are repaid at the end of the 30 years. Serial bonds are often issued by city governments.

A variation of the concept of serial bonds is the **sinking-fund bond**. Under this plan, the issuing corporation makes annual deposits of funds for use in redeeming the bonds when they mature. These deposits are made with a **bond trustee** — usually a major bank with the responsibility of representing bondholders. The deposits must be large enough so that with accrued interest they will be sufficient to redeem the bonds at maturity.

A **callable bond** has a provision that allows the issuing corporation to redeem it before its maturity date if a premium is paid. For instance, a 20-year bond may not be callable for the first ten years. Between 11 and 15 years it can be called at a premium of perhaps $50, and between 16 and 20 years it can be called at its face value.

Why issue callable bonds? If a corporation issues 30-year bonds paying 14 percent annual interest and interest rates decline to 10 percent, it is paying more interest than it should. In this instance, it may decide to retire the 14 percent

serial bond
Bonds issued at the same time but with different maturity dates.

sinking-fund bond
Bond whose issuer deposits funds annually for redemption payment upon maturity.

bond trustee
Financial institution or individual representing bondholders.

callable bond
Bond allowing redemption by issuer before maturity.

Figure 21.5 Types and Characteristics of Bonds

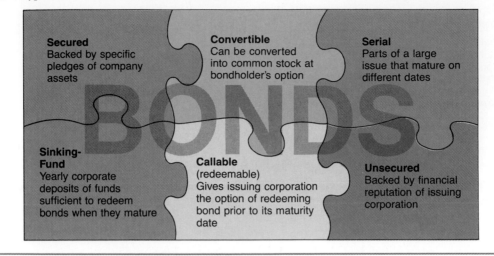

callable bonds and issue new bonds that pay a lower rate of interest. Such actions may be financially sound, even though the firm would incur additional costs in retiring the old bonds and issuing new ones. Figure 21.5 summarizes the characteristics of the most important types of bonds.

Securities Purchasers

Chapter 20 focused on why businesses and government agencies issue securities. This section discusses who purchases them and why.

Types of Investors

institutional investor
Organization that invests its own funds or funds held in trust.

Two general types of investors exist: institutional investors and individual investors. An **institutional investor** is an organization that invests its own funds or those it holds in trust for others. Included in this definition are insurance companies, nonprofit institutions such as universities and foundations, pension funds, mutual funds, and banks. Institutional investors buy and sell large quantities, often in blocks of at least 10,000 shares per transaction. Such block trading accounts for more than half of total daily volume on organized securities exchanges. Institutional investors account for approximately two-thirds of all trading volume.

Although institutional investors are the most important force in today's securities market, the impact of individual investors cannot be overlooked. Individual investors, typically purchasing in much smaller quantities than institutional investors, account for more than $2 out of every $5 involved in securities markets. Also, many of the institutional investments reflect the demands of individual investors, who have chosen to allow such institutions as mutual funds and insurance companies to make securities market investments and then to purchase shares of the institutional investors. Consequently, the investment desires of individual investors cannot be ignored by the institutions.

Characteristics of Individual Investors

The New York Stock Exchange's (NYSE) most recent survey disclosed a dramatic resurgence of share ownership in the United States during the previous decade. Today, approximately one in every four adults owns stock. Although the typical investor owns about $6,200 in stocks, one in five currently has over $25,000 in stock holdings. In addition to the nation's 40 million direct shareholders, approximately 135 million Americans own stocks indirectly through the money they save in insurance companies, savings banks, and profit and pension funds. Part of these funds is invested in public corporations.

Despite the stereotype of the investing public as affluent males, adult females account for 48 percent of all shareholders, the same percentage as adult males. (The remaining stocks are held by children.) In addition, half of all stock-holding households have annual incomes between $25,000 and $50,000. In general, both male and female shareholders are better educated than the general public. Three of every four investors have attended or graduated from college; less than 6 percent did not receive a high school diploma.

The median age of today's shareholders is 44, a record low. By contrast, the median age in 1981 was 46; in 1975, it was 53. This dramatic decline is due to the relatively young age of first-time investors. In the most recent survey, the median age of the 6.8 million adult investors who became share owners for the first time was 34 years.[2]

Investment Motivations

Why do people and institutions invest? For some investors (typically individual investors), the motive is speculation. Others seek growth, income, safety, or some combination of all three.

Speculation For some people, the motivation for purchasing stock is **speculation** — the hope of making a large profit on stocks within a short time. Speculation may take the form of high-risk stocks, such as low-priced penny stocks (so called because they sell for less than $1 per share). Shareholders hope that their $.50 stock will soar to $5, giving them ten times the amount of their purchase price in return. Penny stocks include inactive uranium mining companies, Canadian exploration companies, and numerous small oil-drilling firms. Most of them show no current profit and have little prospect of future profits.

speculation
Purchasing stocks in anticipation of making large profits quickly.

Investment In contrast to speculation, **investment** is the purchase of stocks and bonds that assure some safety for the investment and that provide satisfactory dividends and interest as payment for the risk taken. Investors may also be interested in growth — increases in the value of a stock due to the company's success. The investor's objectives include one or more of these three goals: growth in the value of the investment, income, or safety.

investment
Purchasing securities for growth in investment value or income with relative safety.

Growth. Investors who choose growth as a primary goal will select companies whose earnings have increased and are expected to continue growing faster than that of other companies. In 1940, a share of IBM could be purchased for about $.35. Today, the stock, which has split several times over the years, changes ownership at prices well over $100 per share. Growth-oriented investors are likely to own shares of companies in industries such as electronics, drugs, and energy, which typically pay only small amounts in the form of dividends. Most of their earnings are reinvested in the company to finance further growth. Investors should benefit from this growth through increases in the value of their shares.

Income.   Some investors use stocks and bonds to supplement their income. When income is the major goal, investors concentrate on the dividends of prospective companies. An investor with enough foresight to purchase 10 shares of General Motors Corporation stock in 1940 for $468 would have received dividend payments of more than $8,000 by 1990. Because dividends are paid from company earnings, investors consider the company's past record for paying dividends, its current profitability, and its prospects for future earnings. Purchasers of income stocks are likely to own shares of companies in industries such as banking, insurance, and public utilities.

Hundreds of options are available for the income-oriented investor. Over four-fifths of the companies with shares listed on the New York Stock Exchange have common stock on which dividends are currently being paid. Thirty-nine of these firms have uninterrupted records of paying annual dividends for over 100 years. Included on this list are such well-known firms as Eli Lilly, Travelers Corporation, American Express, Chase Manhattan, and Exxon. The Travelers advertisement in Figure 21.6 mentions that the financial services firm has never missed paying a dividend in more than 120 years. Both the Bank of New York and the Bank of Boston have paid annual dividends for over 200 years!

yield
Income received from securities; calculated by dividing dividends by market price.

The income received from securities is called the investor's return, or **yield**. Yield is calculated by dividing dividends by market price. It is expressed as a percentage.

Assume that a potential investor plans to purchase $2,000 in stocks. She is interested in four companies: entertainment giant Disney, selling at $68 with a $.40 annual dividend; General Electric, which pays a $1.64 annual dividend and can be purchased for about $45 per share; photography pioneer Eastman Kodak, currently priced at $50 per share and paying $2 in annual dividends; and the New York utility company Commonwealth Edison, with an annual dividend of $3 and a recent price of $33.

Using the formula for finding the yield, we see that for Disney the yield is only three-fifths of 1 percent; for General Electric, 3.6 percent; Eastman Kodak is 4 percent; and the Commonwealth Edison yield is 9.1 percent. For an investor seeking immediate income from securities, a utilities stock such as Commonwealth Edison may be appropriate.

The yield from any particular security varies with the market price and the dividend payments. Should General Electric's board of directors vote to increase the annual dividend to $1.80, the yield would rise to 4 percent for an investor who purchased the stock at $45. Also, if the market price of Commonwealth Edison rises to $50 and the dividend remains the same, the yield for a prospective investor will be 6 percent rather than 9.1 percent. Thus, even though the $3 dividend remains the same, the yield changes.

Safety.   In many cases, investors are unwilling to risk the potential reverses of common stock. Neither their blood pressure nor their bank account is able to endure fluctuations such as those that occurred in recent years. For example, in a 12-month period in 1988 and 1989, Alcoa stock prices fluctuated from 38 to 62, Philip Morris from 80 to 110, Sears from 32 to 46, and Woolworth from 37 to 60.

Figure 21.6 Firm Paying Dividends for More than a Century

Investors whose primary objective is safety for their original investments are likely to purchase high-quality bonds and preferred stocks. These securities offer substantial protection and are likely to continue paying a good return on the investment.

Most investors have more than one investment goal. Investors who emphasize safety of principal may buy preferred stocks, which can grow in market value. Those who buy growth stocks may choose stocks paying at least a 3 percent yield in order to receive some short-term return on the investment. Table 21.2 provides a useful guide for evaluating stocks and bonds in terms of the three investment objectives.

Regardless of their investment goals, individual investors are most likely to own AT&T, General Motors, IBM, or one of the seven "Baby Bells" created in

Table 21.2 Investment Objectives of Securities

Security	Investment Objective		
	Safety	Income	Growth
Bonds	Best	Very steady	Usually none
Preferred Stocks	Good	Steady	Variable
Common Stocks	Least	Variable	Best

1984 when the largest corporate breakup in U.S. history led to formation of such regional firms as Bell South, NYNEX, Bell Atlantic, and Pacific Telesis Group. The five companies most widely held by institutional investors such as mutual funds are IBM, Ford, Digital Equipment, General Electric, and Philip Morris.

Even though AT&T shocked investors with a $1.67 billion loss in 1988, the first for the communications giant in the twentieth century, it continues to have the largest number of stockholders of any corporation in the United States. For decades, its steady earnings growth and predictable dividends have attracted investors. To indicate how widely dispersed AT&T's ownership is, consider its postage bill for simply mailing dividend checks four times a year to the 2.8 million stockholders. Assuming that AT&T qualifies for the special first-class presort rate of $.21 per letter, the calculation is as follows:

$$\text{Approximately 2.8 million stockholders} \times \$.21 \text{ postage} \times \text{Four quarterly dividend payments} = \$2.4 \text{ million}$$

Secondary Markets

stock exchange
Location at which stocks and bonds are bought and sold.

Securities exchanges are the marketplaces for stocks and bonds. At a **stock exchange**, stocks and bonds are bought and sold. Although corporations' securities are traded, the corporations are not directly involved, and they receive no proceeds from the sales. The securities traded at organized exchanges have already been issued by corporations. The sales occur between individual and corporate investors.

The New York Stock Exchange (NYSE)

When investors talk about the stock market, they are usually referring to the New York Stock Exchange. Even though the Japan Stock Exchange has challenged the NYSE in recent years, the "Big Board," as it is sometimes called, is the largest and best known of all stock exchanges. Only one out of every 1,000 American corporations qualifies for listing on this exchange, but these firms account for more than 40 percent of the assets held by all U.S. companies.

A brokerage firm must be a member of the NYSE to transact business there. The exchange has 1,366 "seats"; potential members must purchase seats from current members and be approved by the exchange. Memberships have varied considerably in price, ranging from a high of $1.15 million in 1987 to a low of $17,000 in 1942.

Approximately 2,250 issues of common stock, 800 issues of preferred stock, and 3,300 bonds are listed, or traded, on the NYSE. These securities represent 86 percent of the market value of all outstanding stocks and corporate bonds in the United States. NYSE-listed stocks include such major corporations as RCA, Mobil Oil, Du Pont, Xerox, Eastman Kodak, and TWA. Such foreign stocks as Seagram Co. (Canada), KLM Royal Dutch Airlines (Netherlands), Sony (Japan), and ASA Limited (South Africa) are also listed.

The American and Regional Stock Exchanges

The American Stock Exchange (AMEX) recently slipped from being the second-largest stock exchange in the world to number five. Among U.S. securities exchanges, the AMEX is the only one besides the NYSE that is considered a national

Table 21.3 Requirements for Listing on the New York
and American Stock Exchanges

Listing Requirement	New York Stock Exchange (NYSE)	American Stock Exchange (AMEX)
Pretax earnings (previous year)	$2.5 million	$750,000
Tangible assets	$18 million	$4 million
Publicly held shares	1.1 million	500,000
Number of shareholders	2,000	1,000
Minimum market value of publicly owned shares	$18 million	$3 million

exchange. In many ways, it is virtually indistinguishable from its older, larger counterpart. The AMEX is also located in New York and has approximately 660 regular members and 160 associate members. Approximately 960 securities are traded on the AMEX, including such well-known companies as Texas Air, Hasbro, Fruit of the Loom, New York Times, and Wang Laboratories.

To be listed on the NYSE or AMEX, a firm must meet a number of rigorous requirements. Table 21.3 lists these requirements. The less stringent requirements for listing on the AMEX make it an attractive seasoning board for firms not ready to be listed on the Big Board. Its listings include the common and preferred stock of medium-size companies and a few major companies (such as Texas Air and Wang) that have chosen it over the Big Board. In addition, it lists corporate bonds and government securities.

Six regional exchanges are operating in the United States: the Boston, the Cincinnati, the Midwest (trading floor in Chicago), the Pacific (trading floor in San Francisco), the Philadelphia, and the Spokane. As the third- and fourth-largest exchanges in the world, both the Midwest and the Pacific are larger than the AMEX, though both are dwarfed by the Tokyo and New York exchanges. The total activity on the regional stock exchanges accounts for only about 10 percent of the annual dollar volume on U.S. organized exchanges.

Approximately 500 companies are listed on each of the regional exchanges. These exchanges were originally established to trade the shares of smaller firms operating within a limited geographic area. While many of the listed companies continue to be smaller corporations, the regional exchanges now also list many of the major corporations. As the volume of trading on the regional exchanges increased, larger firms decided to list their shares there. Today, about half of all the companies listed on the New York Stock Exchange are also listed on one or more regional exchanges.

Foreign Stock Exchanges

Stock exchanges are not unique to the United States. In fact, the world's oldest exchange is the Amsterdam Stock Exchange, which began operations in 1611. The London Stock Exchange, which lists more than 7,000 securities, traces its beginnings to pre-American Revolution times.

The strong Japanese economy propelled that nation's Tokyo Stock Exchange into second place in world size and importance. By 1990, Japan had boosted its share of the total value of major world markets to almost 40 percent, compared with 13.5 percent a decade earlier. Japan's Nomura Securities has a market value about four times that of American Express, while Nippon Telegraph & Telephone Co. is valued at more than the entire West German stock market.[3]

Other important foreign exchanges are located in Buenos Aires, Copenhagen, Frankfurt, Johannesburg, Milan, Montreal, Paris, Sidney, Toronto, and Zurich. Electronic connections between exchanges in different countries permit rapid exchange of information and, in some cases, allow investors to make trades on them. Major U.S. corporations are frequently listed and traded on foreign exchanges. Within a few years, computerized systems will allow investors to scan the globe on a 24-hour basis for the best stocks at the best prices and then execute trades.

Over-the-Counter Markets

over-the-counter (OTC) market
Method of trading securities not listed on national and regional exchanges through market makers who fill customers' buy and sell orders.

The investor who decides the success of MCI Communications in the long-distance telecommunications market is likely to result in continued growth will not find MCI stock listed on the New York Stock Exchange. Nor is it on the AMEX or any of the regional exchanges. MCI is one of 5,400 securities traded on the **over-the-counter (OTC) market**. At the heart of this market is the NASDAQ (National Association of Securities Dealers Automatic Quotation) system through which these securities are traded.

The OTC market, unlike the traditional exchanges, has no trading floor on which securities are bought and sold. Buyers and sellers are brought together by computer terminals, teletype, and telephone. Dealers involved in these transactions keep in regular contact with one another, and the prices of the securities they trade are established by supply and demand. They "make a market" by quoting a bid — what they will pay for a security — and an asked, or selling price. Investors who decide to purchase OTC stocks or bonds contact their brokers, who contact the dealers handling the security in order to search for the best price. When the investor and dealer agree on a price, a market is made. Over 500 market maker firms are operating, including such well-known brokerage firms as Merrill Lynch, Dean Witter, and Goldman Sachs.

The NASDAQ National Market System   The newest, most visible, and fastest-growing component of the over-the-counter market is the NASDAQ National Market System. Some 2,700 securities, accounting for 70 percent of total OTC share volume, are listed on the national market system. In a typical year, approximately 40 billion shares of NASDAQ-listed companies are traded. This volume is exceeded only by the New York and Tokyo stock exchanges and is more than ten times the annual volume on the AMEX.

All trades in the NASDAQ national market system securities are reported within a few seconds of their transaction, providing immediate access to current market systems. Also, since stockbrokers have immediate access to bid and ask prices on their automatic desktop quotation machines, the NASDAQ system is not noticeably different for them or their clients from trading in securities listed on national or regional exchanges. However, transactions involving the less actively traded OTC securities are reported less frequently, typically at the end of each trading day.

Many of the firms whose stocks are traded on over-the-counter markets have too few shares to be listed on the NYSE or AMEX. Others have too few stockholders, and still others do not have sufficient earnings to qualify for listing. Also, the

Because there are still places where you can't get something by just pushing a button, the MCI Card can be used from anywhere in the U.S., to call virtually anywhere in the world. From any phone. Push-button or rotary. **Let us show you.** 1-800-888-0800

MCI

The MCI Card.
America's Business Card.

Photo source: Courtesy of MCI Telecommunications Corporation.

The stock of most newly public firms is traded initially over the counter because the firms cannot meet the capital and operating requirements for a listing on the NYSE or AMEX. While many firms switch to an exchange when they qualify, others, such as MCI Telecommunications, prefer to continue trading their securities on the over-the-counter market even though they are eligible for a NYSE or AMEX listing.

OTC market includes the shares of most insurance companies and banks and the bonds issued by many city and state government units. A number of major corporations have chosen not to list their stocks and bonds on the national and regional exchanges. Well-known firms in the NASDAQ national market system include Apple Computer, Coors, Ben & Jerry's, Intel, LA Gear, Liz Claiborne, Mack Trucks, Spiegel, and Sun Microsystems. While NASDAQ listing requirements are considerably less stringent than those of the New York and American stock exchanges, approximately 700 NASDAQ firms meet NYSE listing requirements and 1,800 meet AMEX requirements.

How Securities Are Bought and Sold

If you decide to invest the $1,000 your grandmother presented to you as a birthday present, you first must contact a **stockbroker**, a financial intermediary who buys and sells securities for clients. If you do not already have a stockbroker, you should engage one. To find a stockbroker, look under "Stock & Bond Brokers" in the Yellow Pages of your local telephone directory. Most cities have offices of major brokerage firms and smaller firms.

Once you have contacted a broker, your next step is to discuss your investment objectives. Then you and your broker can talk about a number of stocks and bonds that appear to meet your investment goals.

For example, if Exxon common stock meets your dual goals of income and growth, the broker can determine the current market price of the stock by typing the Exxon symbol (XON) on a special desktop terminal. These devices are linked to the national exchanges in New York and the NASDAQ National Market System and can provide immediate information on current securities prices, dividends paid, recent news stories about the company, and the high and

stockbroker
Financial intermediary who buys and sells securities for clients.

Figure 21.7   How to Read a Stock Tape

AA	BJICA	KO	IBM	GE	Z
47	14¹/₂	5s38¹/₄	130 1/8	45 7/8	2s51¹/₂

How many stocks can you identify? Some of the abbreviations are easily recognizable; others offer no clue as to their identity. Under each abbreviation is shown the sales price for the stock and the number of shares involved in each transaction. Securities listed on the NYSE or AMEX are typically identified with one, two, or three letters. NASDAQ securities, such as the BJICA listing, usually have a four- or five-letter identification. Shares are traded in lots of 100; if more than 100 shares are involved, the screen will indicate the size of the transaction. The 5s shown under the symbol KO indicates that 500 shares were traded. Here is how the tape above is read:

100 shares of ALCOA at $47

100 shares of Ben & Jerry's Homemade, Inc. at $14.50

500 shares of Coca-Cola at $38.25

100 shares of International Business Machines Corp. at $130.125

100 shares of General Electric at $45.875

200 shares of Woolworth at $51.50

---

stock tapes
Continuous listings of securities transactions and their most recent market prices for national and regional exchanges and the NASDAQ system.

low prices for the year. Most of these terminals also include special **stock tapes** — continuous listings of securities transactions and their most recent market prices. Before the computerization of securities trading, these stock tapes were called *ticker tapes*. Two separate stock tapes exist for transactions on the New York and American stock exchanges. In many cities with cable television service, one channel shows the stock tape, providing maximum convenience and immediate information for the investor-viewer. Figure 21.7 shows a segment of a stock tape and explains how to read it.

Placing an Order

If you decide to purchase Exxon common stock, the broker will teletype the order to the firm's member on the floor of the New York Stock Exchange. The New York representative goes directly to the location on the floor of the exchange where Exxon is traded and attempts to make the purchase.

market order
Investor request that a stock purchase or sale be made at the current market price.

limit order
Investor request that a stock purchase or sale be made at a specified price.

round lots
Quantities of 100 shares of stock bought or sold.

Market Orders and Limit Orders   An investor request that a stock purchase or sale be made at the current market price is a **market order**. The NYSE floor member quickly makes the purchase on a "best price" basis, and the investor is notified of the purchase price within a matter of minutes. An investor request that a stock purchase or sale be made at a specified price is a **limit order**. In this case, a notation of the limit order is made at the post that handles the stock transactions, and if the price drops to the specified price, the purchase is made.

Round Lots and Odd Lots   Stock trading is conducted in quantities of 100 shares, called **round lots**. But because 100 shares of Exxon cost more than

$7,000, how can you invest your $1,000 in Exxon stock? The answer is through **odd lots** — purchases or sales of fewer than 100 shares of stock that are grouped together to make up one or more round lots. The stocks are then distributed to the various odd-lot purchasers when the transaction is completed.

Cash Accounts and Margin Accounts A basic method of purchasing securities is to pay the brokerage firm the cost of the securities and commissions charged following each purchase. A variation of this approach involves margin trading. **Margin trading** involves the purchase of securities by using funds borrowed from the brokerage firm. Under current Federal Reserve System rules, investors must pay the brokerage at least 50 percent of the security's market value. As the previous chapter pointed out, use of borrowed funds allows the borrower to use leverage. An investor with $5,000 can purchase 100 shares of a stock selling at $50 per share. But with the use of margin trading, the investor can purchase 200 shares. The brokerage firm will charge margin account customers interest on borrowed funds and will require that the stock certificates be left with the firm as collateral. While the use of margin trading increases the investor's profit potential, it also increases the size of losses should market prices decline.

Bulls and Bears The two most frequently mentioned stock market terms refer to investor attitudes. A **bull** is an investor who expects stock prices to rise. Bulls buy securities in anticipation of the increased market prices. When stock market prices continue to rise, market observers call it a *bull market*.[4]

A **bear** is an investor who expects stock prices to decline. Bears are likely to sell their securities because they expect market prices to fall. When market prices steadily decline, the market is characterized as a *bear market*.

odd lots
Quantities of less than 100 shares of stock bought or sold.

margin trading
Securities purchases made with funds borrowed from the brokerage.

bull
Investor who expects stock prices to rise along with market prices.

bear
Investor who expects stock prices to decline along with market prices.

The Cost of Trading

Buyers and sellers of securities pay commissions to brokerage firms for their services. Commission charges vary among brokerage firms, but they generally range from 1 to 2 percent of the total value of the stock transaction. A slightly higher fee is often charged when shares are traded in odd lots. The percentage charged typically declines as the dollar value of the transaction increases. Large business investors, such as insurance companies, mutual funds, and pension funds, can often negotiate major reductions in commissions because of the competition among brokerage firms for their business.

Most stockbrokers keep 43 percent of all commissions they generate for the firm. The remainder goes to the brokerage firm to cover expenses and generate profits. In 1986, the year before the stock market crash, the average broker earned $94,000. By 1988, average compensation declined one-third, to $63,000, as skittish investors temporarily reduced their securities investments to await the next bull market.[5]

Since 1975 when mandatory fixed-rate commissions were abolished, over 1,000 "discount" brokerage firms were established to compete with the traditional full-service brokerage firms. Such operations are particularly attractive to small investors, since they offer lower commissions to investors in exchange for fewer services. Discounters such as Brown & Co.; Fidelity Brokerage Services; Rose, Quick & Reilly; and Charles Schwab handle about one in ten stock trades

Figure 21.8   How to Read a Stock Quotation

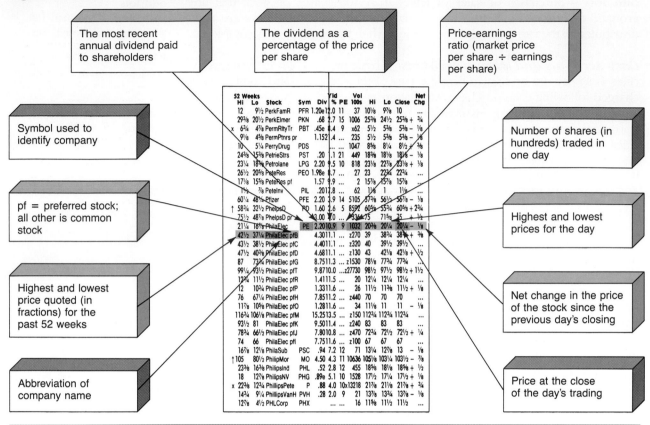

today. For the small investor, the reason to choose a discounter is simple. A full-service broker such as Prudential-Bache may charge more than $100 to buy or sell 100 shares of IBM; the commission at Brown & Co. is $33.[6] However, the discount brokers ordinarily provide no research; they simply handle purchases and sales for their clients.

Reading the Financial News

At least two or three pages of most major daily newspapers are devoted to reporting current financial news, which typically focuses on the previous day's securities transactions. Stocks and bonds traded on the NYSE and AMEX are listed alphabetically in the newspaper. Information is provided on the volume of sales and the price of each security.

Stock Quotations

To understand how to read stock quotations, focus on the stock in Figure 21.8 marked "PhilaElec" — the abbreviated name for Philadelphia Electric & Gas. The highest price paid for this utility company during the previous 52 weeks was

Figure 21.9   How to Read a Bond Quotation

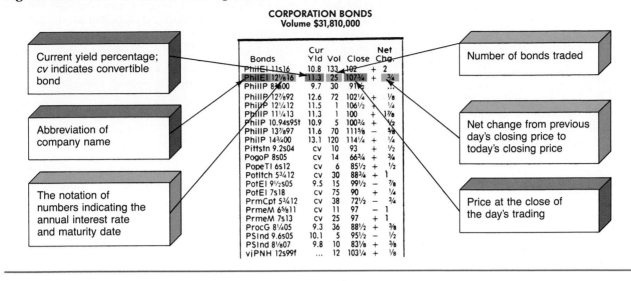

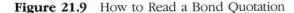

$21\frac{1}{4}$, or \$21.25 per share; the lowest price was $16\frac{7}{8}$, or \$16.875. Annual dividends paid to shareholders amount to \$2.20, which is 10.9 percent of the price per share or the yield percentage. The **price-earnings ratio** — the current market price divided by annual earnings per share — is 9. A total of 103,200 shares changed owners in the day's trading. The highest price paid for the stock that day was $20\frac{3}{8}$, or \$20.375, and the lowest price that day was $20\frac{1}{4}$, or \$20.25. When the trading stopped for the day, Philadelphia Electric & Gas was being traded for \$20.25, which amounted to $12\frac{1}{2}$ cents less than the closing price on the previous day.

Careful inspection of the sample quotation reveals additional information. All stock is common stock unless designated as preferred stock by the symbol *pf*. Additional special series preferred stock of Philadelphia Electric & Gas is designated by a capital letter following *pf*. Special information on stocks is provided at the bottom of the page. For example, a record high price for Phelps Dodge is indicated by an arrow pointing up at the far left of the listing, and the lower case letter *e* following the \$.45 dividend for Permian Basin Realty Trust indicates this is the dividend payment for the previous 12 months.

price-earnings ratio
Current market price divided by annual earnings per share.

Bond Quotations

Figure 21.9 shows a number of bond quotations. To learn how to read bond quotations, focus on the second listing for Philadelphia Electric. Most bonds are issued in denominations of \$1,000; thus, bond prices must be read differently from stock prices. Although the closing price for the Philadelphia Electric bond reads $107\frac{3}{4}$, this does not mean \$107.75. Because bond prices are quoted as a percentage of the \$1,000 price stated on the face of the bond, $107\frac{3}{4}$ means \$1,075. Similarly, the closing price of $91\frac{1}{2}$ for the first Phillips Petroleum bond listed in Figure 21.9 means \$915.

The notation "$12\frac{1}{8}$ 16" to the right of "PhilEl" indicates the bonds pay an annual interest rate of $12\frac{1}{8}$ percent and the maturity date for this issue is 2016.

Because the bond is currently selling above its original $1,000 face value, the current yield is 11.3 percent, almost a full percentage point less than the $12\frac{1}{8}$ percent stated interest rate. Bonds, such as the Pittston bond, that list the symbol *cv* instead of a yield are convertible bonds.

A total of 25 of Philadelphia Electric's bond issue maturing in 2016 were traded during the day. The closing bond price was $7.50 higher than the previous day's closing price.

Stock Averages

Dow Jones Averages
Averages based on market prices of 30 industrial, 20 transportation, and 15 utility stocks that reflect general market activity.

Standard & Poor's Index
Index based on market performance of 400 industrial, 40 financial, 40 utility, and 20 transportation stocks.

A feature of most daily newscasts is the report of current stock averages. The two most familiar stock averages are the **Dow Jones Averages** (the "Dow") and the **Standard & Poor's Index**. Both indexes have been developed to reflect the general activity of the stock market.

The Dow is actually three different indexes based on the market prices of 30 industrial, 20 transportation, and 15 utility stocks. The more broadly based Standard & Poor's Index is developed from the market performance of 400 industrial, 40 financial, 40 utilities, and 20 transportation stocks.

The most widely reported barometer of stock market activity, the Dow Jones industrial averages has been used as a general measure of changes in overall stock prices and a reflection of the U.S. economy since its appearance in 1896. The term *industrial* is a misnomer since the index is comprised of both industrial corporations such as General Motors, Union Carbide, and Boeing and such nonindustrial firms as American Express, McDonald's, and Sears.

When the Dow Jones first appeared nearly a century ago, it included such then financially sound and widely held stocks as American Cotton Oil, Distilling & Cattle Feeding, General Electric, National Lead, and Tennessee Coal and Iron. Today, only General Electric remains on the list. Table 21.4 lists the 30 corporations comprising the Dow Jones industrials and the stock trading symbol for each firm. Also shown is the method used to calculate the daily Dow Jones industrial average.

Mutual Funds

mutual funds
Financial organizations that use investors' money to acquire a portfolio of securities.

Many investors recognize that they have neither the time nor the knowledge to continually analyze stock market developments. These people often concentrate their investments in **mutual funds** — financial organizations that pool investment money from purchasers of their securities and use the money to acquire a diversified portfolio of securities. Investors who buy shares of stock in a mutual fund become part owners of a large number of companies, thereby lessening the individual risk.

Mutual funds are managed by trained, experienced professionals whose careers are based on success in analyzing the securities markets and specific industries and companies. Mutual funds attempt to accomplish for individual investors what they might do themselves, if they had the time, inclination, background, experience, and money.

Approximately 28 million people in the United States currently own shares in one or more of the 2,300 mutual funds. Mutual fund assets total more than $770 billion.

Table 21.4 The Dow Jones Industrial Average

Symbol	Stock	Price*	Symbol	Stock	Price*
ALD	Allied-Signal	$ 33.875	IP	International Paper	$ 49.5
AA	ALCOA	61.625	MCD	McDonald's	50.0
AXP	American Express	29.125	MRK	Merck	63.625
T	American Telephone & Telegraph	30.875	MMM	Minnesota Mining & Manufacturing	66.375
BS	Bethlehem Steel	25.625	NAV	Navistar	5.625
BA	Boeing Co.	63.0	MO	Philip Morris	106.125
CHV	Chevron	49.375	PA	Primerica Corp.	22.5
KO	Coca-Cola	45.75	PG	Procter & Gamble	89.625
DD	Du Pont	100.0	S	Sears, Roebuck & Co.	41.875
EK	Eastman Kodak	47.75	TX	Texaco	54.5
XON	Exxon	45.625	X	USX Corp.	31.0
GE	General Electric	46.875	UC	Union Carbide	27.5
GM	General Motors	89.5	UTX	United Technologies	44.125
GT	Goodyear	48.874	WX	Westinghouse Electric	55.0
IBM	International Business Machines Corp.	126.0	Z	Woolworth	52.875
				Total dollar value	$1,604.125
				Dow Jones Industrial Average	2,291.61

*The stock prices listed above represent the closing prices of these stocks on January 26, 1989. The Dow Jones Industrial Average is computed by adding the closing prices (on the New York Stock Exchange only) of the stocks listed above, and then dividing by a divisor (currently 0.7), which is listed below the stock tables in Section C of *The Wall Street Journal*. The divisor is used to accommodate such changes as stock splits and infrequent changes in the firms whose stocks constitute the Dow.

Just as individual investor goals differ, so do the objectives of mutual funds. Consequently, many companies operate a *family* of different mutual funds, each pursuing a different investment objective. Growth funds emphasize the purchase of growth companies. Income funds emphasize high dividends. Balanced funds diversify their holdings by purchasing all types of securities — common and preferred stocks and corporate, government, and municipal bonds. Money market funds emphasize returns to investors through investment in short-term debt instruments such as certificates of deposit, commercial paper, and Treasury bills. Specialty funds concentrate on particular industries, such as gold, real estate, health care, or banking.

The Stock Market Crash of 1987

Before Monday, October 19, 1987, the term *stock market crash* meant Black Tuesday, the day in 1929 on which the market dropped 12 percent, marking the official beginning of the worst economic catastrophe in U.S. history. The typical investor of the late 1980s believed a repeat of the crash was impossible. After all, margin requirements in 1929 promoted extreme speculation in which investors could buy stocks with only a 10 percent cash payment and manipulations of the market were widespread. Margin purchases by today's investors were still possible, but only with 50 percent cash payments. Also, numerous laws had been passed since the 1930s to regulate securities trading. By mid-1987, the Dow crossed the 2700 mark, and some forecasters believed a 4000 Dow was achievable within a few years.

Then the impossible happened. *The Wall Street Journal* headline told the story: "Stocks Plunge 508.32 Amid Panicky Selling." The end of the five-year-long bull market came when the market value of the nation's leading stocks dropped 23 percent in a single day, a far sharper decline than the 1929 crash. Investors saw $1.7 trillion stripped from their portfolios as IBM fell $33; USX Corporation nose-dived $13, to $21; and Eastman Kodak stock dropped $27.25 below its market value just 24 hours earlier. Investor confidence was shattered; these firms were supposed to represent highly secure investments that also offered stable dividends and regular growth in value.

Even though the Dow moved above the precrash average by early 1989, individual investors were slow to return to the market. The crash destroyed the idea that 1929 could never happen again. As one analyst put it, "[In 1987] everyone was counting up how rich they would be and how soon they could retire. Now, everyone is scared stiff and thinking about how to stay solvent."[7]

Searching for Causes

Like investigators who sort through the wreckage of a plane, a number of researchers — including the presidential task force referred to as the Brady Commission — have searched the ruins of the October crash for causes. So far, all cannot agree on one cause.

program trading
Computer systems programmed to buy or sell securities to take advantage of price differences that sometimes occur between stock futures and current stock prices.

A number of industry representatives, eager to locate a scapegoat, pointed the finger at **program trading**. Special computer-based systems had been developed to take advantage of the differences in price that sometimes occur between stock futures (agreements to buy or sell a stock or group of stocks within a specified period) and current stock prices. These systems created what appeared to be a type of portfolio insurance, where market players could hedge their bets with automatic buy or sell orders for stock whenever the price of that stock reached a certain level. Even though program trading was blamed by many for worsening the one-day crash, the October 19 trading volume of 604 million shares overloaded the NYSE computerized-order entry system, and program traders were not allowed to use it in the afternoon. Only about 15 percent of that day's volume involved program trading.

Many members of the financial community agree that the real cause of the crash involved a completely human flaw: greed. At the time of the crash, the price-earnings ratio for the S&P 500 was 20, at the high end of its historical range. A huge trade deficit existed and the specter of inflation appeared each month when the U.S. Treasury was forced to auction notes to cover the deficit. Professor Jeremy Siegel of the University of Pennsylvania says: "Stock prices were way too high in terms of earnings, prospective earnings, and dividends. And October 19 was just a very fast adjustment of that overvaluation."[8]

Searching for Cures

Since the crash of 1987, the major exchanges introduced circuit breakers. The idea is to halt trading temporarily after a big swing, perhaps to give investors time to think. The NYSE circuit breaker would produce a one-hour market halt if the Dow fell 250 points and a two-hour stop if it fell another 150 points. In addition, the Big Board expanded its processing system with the aim of being able to handle a daily volume of 1 billion shares by the early 1990s. Finally, it increased to $1 million the capital requirements for specialists on the floor who make a market in a particular stock, buying and selling when no one else will, in order to ensure orderly price changes.

Most observers agree that these are stopgap measures and will not prevent a repeat of the 1987 crash. Fortunately, the crash failed to usher in an economic disaster. After all, securities holdings represent only about 20 percent of household financial assets.

Yale professor Robert Shiller polled both individual and institutional investors after the crash and asked them why they sold stocks. Most said they sold because others were selling. If the crash was largely a psychological event, no method exists for predicting when and if such behavior is likely to recur. "As long as people are free to make their own decisions, you can't prevent a crash," says Shiller.[9]

Regulating Securities Transactions

Both the federal government and state governments have enacted legislation regulating the sale of securities. Early laws were passed at the state level, beginning with Kansas in 1911. While the proposed law was under consideration, one state legislator remarked that some unscrupulous securities promoters would sell stock in the "blue sky." And the name **blue-sky laws** was quickly applied to the early state laws regulating securities transactions. Eventually, every state except Nevada passed laws to protect stock purchasers.

These laws typically require that most securities sold in the state be registered with an appropriate state official, usually the secretary of state. Annual licenses are usually required for securities dealers and salespeople. But additional protection was needed for interstate sales of securities.

blue-sky laws
Early state laws regulating securities transactions.

Securities Act of 1933   The *Securities Act of 1933*, often called the Truth in Securities Act, is a federal law designed to protect investors by requiring full disclosure of relevant financial information by companies desiring to sell new stock or bond issues to the general public. This information takes two forms: a registration statement containing detailed company information that is filed with the Securities and Exchange Commission, and a condensed version of the registration statement in a booklet called a *prospectus*, which must be furnished to each purchaser.

Securities Exchange Act of 1934   One year after the passage of the Securities Act of 1933, Congress enacted the *Securities Exchange Act of 1934*. The federal law created the Securities and Exchange Commission (SEC) to regulate the national stock exchanges and established strict rules for trading on organized exchanges. A 1964 amendment extended the authority of the SEC to the over-the-counter market. All companies with securities listed on the national and regional exchanges or traded over the counter are required to file registration statements with the SEC and to update them annually. Brokerage firms, individual brokers, and dealers selling OTC stocks are regulated by the SEC, and brokers engaged in buying and selling securities are required to pass an examination.

Other Federal Legislation

The *Maloney Act of 1938*, an amendment to the Securities Exchange Act of 1934, authorized self-regulation of over-the-counter (OTC) securities operations. This led to creation of the *National Association of Securities Dealers (NASD)*, which is responsible for regulating OTC businesses. Written examinations are now re-

The National Association of Securities Dealers uses state-of-the-art computer systems to continuously monitor members' trading activities. Unusual trading patterns are automatically flagged for immediate review by analysts who investigate the causes of unusual price movements or sudden swings in volume. The automated system helps detect instances of possible insider trading, market manipulation, and other questionable trading practices. The NASD was established under the authority granted by the 1938 Maloney Act amendments to the Securities Exchange Act of 1934. As the self-regulatory organization for the over-the-counter market, NASD enforces federal and state securities laws and the ethical requirements of its own rules that obligate members to observe high standards of commercial honor.

Photo source: Courtesy of the National Association of Securities Dealers, Inc.

quired of all new brokers and dealers selling OTC securities. The *Investment Company Act of 1940* brought the mutual fund industry under SEC jurisdiction. Mutual funds are now required to register with the SEC. The state and federal laws mentioned protect investors from the securities trading abuses and stock manipulations that occurred before the 1930s.

Protecting Investors from Dealer or Broker Insolvency

In 1970, Congress enacted the Securities Investor Protection Act, which created a nonprofit corporation, the *Securities Investor Protection Corporation (SIPC)*. The SIPC is a nonprofit corporation insuring the accounts of brokerage firm clients up to $100,000 in cash in case of dealer or broker insolvency. The loss of securities is insured up to $400,000. SIPC protection is similar to the protection that the FDIC and FSLIC provide depositors, but it differs in one important respect: Both FDIC and FSLIC are federal agencies, while SIPC is a membership organization comprised of all national securities exchanges and registered brokers. Funding comes through assessments from member firms. Although the SIPC protects investors against financial disasters resulting from a brokerage's bankruptcy, it does not provide protection against market losses caused by price declines.

Protecting Investors from Insider Trading

insider trading
Illegal securities trading by persons who profit from their access to nonpublic information about a company.

Few activities can undermine public confidence in the fairness of stock trading more than **insider trading**, in which a few people with access to nonpublic information — such as a hostile takeover attempt, a pending merger, or a major oil discovery — buy stock before the public learns the story, then profit when the news is released and the stock price rises. The Securities Exchange Act of 1934 prohibits trading on the basis of inside information, but recent highly publicized incidents have led to calls for closer scrutiny by the Securities and Exchange Commission.

Perhaps the best-known incidence of insider trading involved Wall Street trader Ivan Boesky who used inside information to purchase stock in companies that were merger or acquisition targets. After his conviction, Boesky received a prison sentence and was fined $100 million in penalties and restitution. Another case involved Michael E. Milken, a securities specialist earning *$540 million* a year before being fired in 1989 as part of his employer, Drexel Burnham Lambert's, settlement with federal regulators. Still other cases included the editor of *The Wall Street Journal's* "Heard on the Street" column, who would divulge the subject of the following day's story to a friend who would buy or sell the stock in advance of the story's release; and employees of *Business Week*, who had access to a similar column before the magazine's publication.[10]

SEC analysis of stock trading patterns immediately before major announcements has uncovered a number of instances of insider trading. Suspicious activity can be investigated through analysis of transactions records. However, the SEC has been handicapped in recent years by budget cuts. The agency was aided by passage of the Insider Trading Act of 1984, which subjected insider traders to fines of up to three times their illegal gains and greatly expanded the authority of the SEC in investigating insider trading.

Summary of Learning Goals

1. Distinguish between primary markets for securities and secondary markets. The primary market is used by businesses and governmental units to sell new issues of securities. The secondary market includes transactions of previously issued securities.

2. Compare common stock, preferred stock, and bonds and explain why investors might prefer each type of security. As owners, common stockholders have voting rights, but they have only a residual claim on the firm's assets. Preferred stockholders receive preference in the payment of dividends and have first claim on the firm's assets after debts have been paid, but usually do not have voting rights. Bondholders are creditors, not owners, of a corporation, nonprofit organization, or governmental unit.

Bonds provide the most safety and common stocks the least. Bonds usually do not grow in value, but they do provide a steady income. Common stocks are likely to be purchased by investors seeking rapid growth. Many investors consider preferred stocks a compromise investment between common stock and bonds.

3. Identify the three basic objectives of investors and the types of securities most likely to accomplish each objective. The three basic objectives of investors are growth in the value of the investment, income, and safety. Bonds are relatively safe and provide a steady income. Common stocks are the most risky, but offer investment growth. Preferred stocks have limited growth opportunities, but are reasonably safe and offer a steady income.

4. Outline the steps involved in selling or purchasing a security listed on the organized securities exchanges. Securities purchases and sales are handled by a trained specialist called a stockbroker. Once the broker receives a customer's order, it is conveyed to the stock exchange through a communications terminal. The firm's floor broker executes the sale and a confirmation is communicated to the broker, who notifies the customer that the transaction has been completed.

5.   Describe the information included in stock and bond quotations. Stock quotations include the highest and lowest market price for the security during the previous 52 weeks; whether the stock is common or preferred; annual dividend; yield; price-earnings ratio; number of shares traded; high, low, and closing price for the day; and changes in closing price compared with the day before. Bond quotations include maturity date and interest rate; current yield; volume; high, low, and closing price for the day; and comparison of closing price with the previous day.

6.   Explain the role of mutual funds in the securities field. Mutual funds are professionally managed investment companies that own shares in many different companies and allow the investor to purchase their shares of the mutual fund, thereby creating a diversified investment portfolio.

7.   Evaluate the major features of state and federal laws designed to protect investors. The Securities Act of 1933, Securities Exchange Act of 1934, and individual state securities acts regulate organized securities exchanges and the over-the-counter market and protect investors by requiring disclosure of financial information from companies issuing securities. The Securities and Exchange Commission (SEC), created by the Securities Exchange Act of 1934, enforces the legislation and regulates brokers, brokerage firms, and mutual fund transactions. The Securities Investor Protection Corporation (SIPC) insures brokerage firm accounts in the event of dealer or broker insolvency. The Insider Trading Act of 1984 amended the SEC act to subject insider traders to fines as high as three times the amount of their illegal gains and greatly expanded the SEC's authority to investigate insider trading.

Key Terms

securities	convertible bond	market order
primary market	bond indenture	limit order
secondary market	serial bond	round lots
investment banker	sinking-fund bond	odd lots
common stock	bond trustee	margin trading
par value	callable bond	bull
market value	institutional investor	bear
book value	speculation	price-earnings ratio
preemptive right	investment	Dow Jones Averages
preferred stock	yield	Standard & Poor's Index
secured bond	stock exchange	mutual funds
debenture	over-the-counter (OTC) market	program trading
government bond	stockbroker	blue-sky laws
municipal bond	stock tapes	insider trading

Review Questions

1. In what ways is the secondary market different from the primary market? With which market are investment bankers involved? What role do they play in financial decisions?

2. What is common stock? Explain the alternative methods for evaluating common stock.

3. Explain the major types of bonds issued by corporations and governmental units. What are the primary methods used in retiring bonds?

4. Identify the three major goals of investors and suggest an appropriate mix of securities to achieve these goals.

5. Distinguish between the following:
   a. Market orders and limit orders
   b. Round lots and odd lots
   c. Cash accounts and margin accounts
   d. Bulls and bears

6. How does the New York Stock Exchange operate? Compare the NYSE operations with those of the over-the-counter market.

7. What are stock averages? How do they affect securities trading? Would you expect the Standard & Poor's Index of 500 stocks to be a better indicator of overall market activity than the Dow Jones Industrial Average?

8. How does an investor place an order for common stock? Should the purchase be made by margin trading? Defend your answer.

9. Discuss the purchase of shares in mutual funds as an alternative to purchasing stocks and bonds.

10. Explain the major laws affecting securities transactions. Include the primary purpose of each law and how it affects individual investors as well as the securities industry.

Discussion Questions

1. Assume you just inherited $20,000 from your aunt and her will stipulates that you must invest all the money until you complete your education. Prepare an investment plan for the $20,000 inheritance.

2. Assume you are an investment counselor who has been asked to set up general investment goals for the following individuals, each of whom has adequate current income and about $30,000 to invest. Prepare a short report outlining the proposed investment goals for each person with general suggestions of an appropriate mix of securities:
   a. 56-year-old retired Army officer
   b. 40-year-old divorced woman with two children
   c. 19-year-old college student receiving $200 weekly for the next ten years in survivors' insurance benefits
   d. 26-year-old unmarried person earning $24,000 annually

3. Discuss the events that led to the stock market crash of 1987. Include in your discussion the concept of program trading. How did the crash affect the economy, financial markets, and investor activity?

4. How do bond ratings affect bond prices? What impact does a bond rating have on its yield? How might a bond rating influence the determination of its likely purchasers?

5. A married couple in their late twenties with two small children and joint earnings of $35,000 have decided to invest in stocks that promise growth with a steady return in the form of dividends. They have narrowed the choice of stocks to five and have assembled the following data from the past three years:

Year	Company Designation	Average Price per Share	Earnings per Share	Average Dividend per Share
1988	A	$ 60	$ 5.12	$ 2.70
	B	268	13.35	10.00
	C	42	2.17	.05
	D	6	.12	.08
	E	30	3.06	1.70
1989	A	59	7.98	2.80
	B	275	15.94	10.00
	C	45	2.72	.06
	D	8	.22	.10
	E	29	3.20	1.80
1990	A	72	9.00	3.00
	B	320	17.50	10.00
	C	60	3.40	.10
	D	11	.80	.12
	E	42	3.75	2.00

Calculate the dividend yield and price-earnings ratio for each stock for each of the three years. Based on your analysis of the data and the risks and rewards involved, recommend one of the five stocks for the couple to purchase.

Case

Tyson Foods, Inc.

Although a recent Gallup Poll found that steak continues to be the most popular choice of people eating in fine restaurants, food preferences have been changing for an increasingly health- and diet-conscious population. Changes have been more noticeable on the home front, where chicken has surpassed beef as the primary source of protein in the diet of the average American. And Tyson Foods, Inc., is ready to fill this growing demand from its position as the nation's leading supplier of chicken to retail stores and food-service outlets.

Founded in the 1930s, Tyson has become the world's largest fully integrated poultry grower, processor, and marketer. Its impressive network includes 21 hatcheries, 16 feed mills, and 32 processing plants. From there, Tyson employees process 13 million chickens a week, which amounts to more than 2 billion pounds of chicken every year.

At company headquarters in Springdale, Arkansas, Tyson marketers have embarked on an aggressive product development effort. In a recent year, the number of Tyson chicken entrees doubled, with such unique varieties as Chicken Marsala and Chicken Cannelloni. In the highly competitive boneless chicken category, Tyson's Chick'n Quick dominates the industry with a 43 percent market share, more than the combined shares of the next two nationally competing brands. The firm has also expanded to meet growing demands for convenience-oriented, microwaveable food products. Still other products include Chicken Originals — fresh, marinated breast fillets — and Cornish game hens. The latter birds, complete with the Tyson name attached, are the only nationally advertised Cornish hen brand name. They dominate the market, accounting for half of all industry sales.

Tyson's management has also chosen to focus on additional markets to generate added sales above and beyond those of the retail market. Tyson's Tastybird is the leading brand found at U.S. military commissaries.

And with Americans eating almost half of their meals away from home, Tyson has sought to dominate the food-service industry as well. Eighty of the top 100 restaurant chains in the United States are served by Tyson, making it the leading poultry supplier in the food-service field. When you order chicken products at Burger King, Wendy's, and Kentucky Fried Chicken, chances are good that you are purchasing Tyson chicken.

The firm has been able to earn its leadership position in the food-service industry because of its ability to deliver quality products at competitive prices and due to its reputation as an innovator. It offers comprehensive menu-planning programs for restaurant chains and keeps them aware of the latest customer taste trends — for example, Cajun, Tex-Mex, and Light and Healthy entrees were developed in response to such trends. The firm's product-development experts even found a way to use previously unmarketable parts of the chicken, turning wing joints into Wings of Fire — fully cooked, seasoned "finger food." Also included among Tyson product offerings are Mexican foods such as tortillas, burritos, and chips.

All this growth required regular infusions of additional funds to expand capacity and improve distribution. In 1964, Tyson Foods decided to make an initial public offering by selling shares of ownership in the company to the general public. Three years later, Don Tyson became CEO of the firm following the death of his father in a railroad crossing accident.

At the time, Tyson had a major decision to make. He could sell his shares and live comfortably. After all, the firm was operating profitably and sales were continuing to increase. But Don Tyson, described as both a "good old boy" and a "financial visionary," wanted to take Tyson Foods to the top — and he has done just that. By 1989, the firm's 26,000 employees were generating sales of $2.15 billion. These figures translated into net income of $90 million for Tyson's shareholders, who held a total of 63.9 million shares. Although annual cash dividends remained tiny at four cents per share, by mid-1989, Tyson's common stock was trading on the over-the-counter market at approximately $20 per share.

Since 1984, the firm's sales have nearly tripled and net income has more than quadrupled. Total assets

Notes: "Tyson Foods to Spend About $100 Million In Move to Expand," *The Wall Street Journal,* June 14, 1989, p. C18; "Tyson to Launch Microwave Line," *Advertising Age,* July 25, 1988, p. 5; Timothy K. Smith, "Changing Tastes: By End of Year, Poultry Will Surpass Beef in U. S. Diet," *The Wall Street Journal,* September 17, 1987, p. 1; and personal correspondence, June 5, 1989.

have increased approximately 200 percent. Much of this growth has depended on the acquisition of existing companies. When Don Tyson took over the helm of Tyson Foods, he set out to generate growth through buying rather than simply building. Of the firm's 32 processing plants, 30 were acquired from other owners.

By 1989, the firm's marketing successes had created a problem. Demand was beginning to exceed the firm's capacity. In a highly controversial move, Tyson Foods made an offer to purchase Holly Farms, a major competitor based in Memphis, Tennessee. Holly's board of directors fought the acquisition attempt for months, but ultimately accepted the merger offer when Tyson agreed to pay more than $1 billion for the firm. The greatly increased capacity and expanded distribution resulting from the acquisition further solidified Tyson's position as the nation's leading chicken producer.

Tyson investors, analyzing the amazing growth of the company since 1967, have to applaud Don Tyson's decision to take over as CEO. The firm leads the Fortune 500 companies in total return to investors over the last decade, with an annual average of 46.4 percent. In 1988, Tyson was included in *Financial World's* 100 percent club — the financial magazine's list of 44 companies that have increased sales, cash flow, earnings, and book value by at least 100 percent over the

past three years without incurring excessive debt. Tyson's success speaks for itself to investors: A $1,000 investment five years ago is worth over $20,000 today. And if consumers continue to display their fondness for what they generally perceive to be a healthy white meat, Tyson's sales and profits are likely to continue to soar.

Questions

1. Relate the concept of primary and secondary securities markets to materials presented in this case.

2. Based on information in the case, calculate the following:

a. earnings per share
b. dividend yield
c. price-earnings ratio

3. A number of investment objectives for individual investors are described in the chapter. Which of these objectives are likely to be most important for a typical Tyson Foods investor? Develop a likely description of the typical Tyson investor.

4. Locate the Tyson common stock listing in the NASDAQ section of the financial section of your local newspaper. Explain each component of the listing shown for Tyson. Why do you feel that the Tyson stock is included there, instead of being listed on the American or New York Stock Exchanges?

22

Risk Management and Insurance

Learning Goals

1. To define *risk* and to distinguish between the two types of risk faced by individuals and businesses.

2. To explain each of the four methods of dealing with risk.

3. To analyze the law of large numbers and to explain how it makes insurance possible.

4. To distinguish between public and private insurance companies and to identify types of insurance provided by public insurance companies.

5. To identify the types of property and liability insurance and to describe their importance to a business.

6. To outline the various types of health insurance.

7. To explain each of the types of life insurance a firm might offer its employees.

J. L. French Corporation of Sheboygan, Wisconsin, manufactures die castings used in the automotive industry. The 500-employee firm, which has been in business for 20 years, uses the latest automated equipment and the safest manufacturing methods, but it is still plagued by high worker's compensation costs. Careless handling of large machinery and molten metal can result in serious burns, loss of fingers, and many other types of injuries. The repetitive motion of die casting and the filing and finishing of parts can cause nerve and joint damage.

In 1987, J. L. French introduced programs to reduce its worker's compensation costs, which were running $370,000 annually. Many of the injuries were not serious, but the employee still had to be taken to the hospital and treated in the emergency room. So management hired a nurse to treat minor injuries at the plant. The nurse documented each accident and any preventive action. French's insurance carrier reduced the company's worker's compensation premium by 5 percent because the nurse was hired. The company's continued efforts at accident prevention reduced its annual cost in 1988 to $186,000.

Health insurance was another cost that needed to be controlled. In 1988, J. L. French's share of its employee health insurance was $960,000. The company originally offered a conventional insurance plan and three health maintenance organizations (HMOs). In 1989, French combined some of the HMO's features with those of the conventional plan, resulting in one plan that was aimed at controlling health-care costs. Typically costs had been increasing by 24 percent per year. The HMOs did not pro-

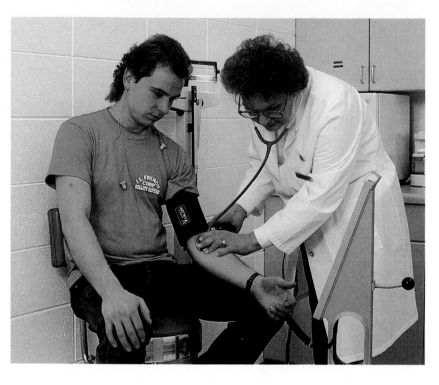

vide French with any information pertaining to expenses they incurred, so management had no way of knowing how money was spent. With the conventional plan, French receives quarterly expense reports. These reports are analyzed for higher-than-normal charges as well as repeated illnesses. Costs are controlled by working with hospitals on discount programs, giving preadmission certification for hospital stays, encouraging outpatient or home health care, and discouraging emergency room use. J. L. French also offers rewards to employees who find overcharges on their bills from the hospital. In addition, wellness programs such as quit-smoking classes are also provided by the company.

J. L. French chose a minimum premium type of policy. This offers the cost-savings advantage of a self-insured program without the risk. The company pays for each medical bill — a method similar to a self-insured plan. This allows French to benefit if management can encourage good health and responsible use of the insurance coverage. The company uses a trust arrangement, which makes insurance expense deductible as a business expense and allows the money in the trust to earn tax-free interest. This program also enhances cash flow for the Wisconsin manufacturer.[1]

Photo source: Courtesy of J. L. French Corporation of Sheboygan.

Chapter Overview

Risk is a daily fact of life for both individuals and businesses. In a recent year, 13 people died when a Delta Air Lines flight crashed soon after takeoff from the Dallas-Fort Worth Airport. In that same year, First Interstate suffered a disastrous fire at its Los Angeles office. Another fire that year at a telephone switching center in Hinsdale, Illinois, knocked out telephone service to many of Chicago's western suburbs. Major firms such as McDonald's, Spiegel, and Waste Management and hundreds of small and medium-size businesses were hampered by this outage. Meanwhile, farmers throughout the nation were losing their crops in the worst drought in years.

Businesses face these catastrophes and more. They run the risk of injury to their employees in job-related accidents, of changing consumer tastes that transform their profits into losses, of faulty products causing lawsuits and loss of business, and of employee dishonesty, as the poster in Figure 22.1 illustrates.

If managers are to carry out their responsibilities of achieving organizational objectives, they must understand the types of risks they face and develop methods for dealing with them. One important method of dealing with risk is to shift it to specialized firms called *insurance companies*. This chapter discusses the concept of insurance, the types of insurance available for various perils, and the role played by insurance in individual firms. The starting point for this discussion is to define the meaning of risk.

Defining Risk

risk
Uncertainty about loss or injury.

Risk is uncertainty about loss or injury. The business firm's list of risk-filled decisions is long. The warehouse faces the risk of fire, burglary, water damage, and physical deterioration. Accidents, judgments due to lawsuits, and nonpayment of bills by customers are other risks. Two major types of risk exist: speculative risk and pure risk.

speculative risk
Type of risk involving the chance of either profit or loss.

In the case of **speculative risk**, the firm or individual has the chance of either a profit or a loss. Purchasing shares of stock on the basis of the latest hot tip can result in profits or losses. Expansion of operations in a new market may mean higher profits or the loss of invested funds.

pure risk
Type of risk involving only the chance of loss.

With speculative risk there is a chance of profit and a chance of loss. **Pure risk** involves only the chance of loss. Automobile drivers always face the risk of accidents. If they occur, the drivers (and others) may suffer financial and physical loss. If they do not occur, however, there is no gain. Insurance is often used to protect against the financial loss resulting from pure risk.

Dealing with Risk

Because risk is an unavoidable part of business, management must find ways of dealing with it. Recognition of its presence is an important first step. Once this occurs, the manager has four methods available for dealing with it: avoiding the risk, reducing the frequency and/or severity of the risk, self-insuring against the risk, or shifting the risk to insurance companies.

Figure 22.1   The Risk of Employee Dishonesty

Source: Courtesy of United States Fidelity and Guaranty Company.

Avoiding Risk

The previous chapter described several types of investors. Some were willing to take high risks as the price for potentially high rewards, and others were not. The same is true for companies. Some firms, for example, are unwilling to risk the costs involved in developing new and untried products.

Companies unwilling to assume risk are content to produce and market products that have a stable demand and offer an adequate profit margin. This strategy ensures profitability, but it stifles innovation. Companies whose managers seek to avoid most risk are rarely leaders in the industry.

Reducing Risk

Many types of risk can be reduced or even eliminated by removing hazards. Safety programs are often developed to educate employees about potential hazards and the proper methods of performing specific tasks. Safety glasses, hard hats, and safety shoes may be required for workers performing certain activities. Danger areas within a factory may be marked with red lines or special caution signs.

Figure 22.2   Reducing Risk through Loss Control

In 1938, when a Martian invasion threatened the world,   **Allendale had been insuring planet Earth for 103 years.**

Was it really happening? Or was it a ruse? One thing was certain. The resulting mass hysteria had proven the power of radio in America.

But on that uncertain October evening back in '38 when Orson Welles' incredible broadcast shocked the world, Allendale had been a credible property

insurer for 103 years.

In a changing world where events like this shape history, this is our way of reminding you of one progressive, stable company that's been around since 1835.

Today at Allendale, we continue to shape the history of loss control with engineering, training, research

and testing, responsiveness and fairness in the way we do business.

Throughout the years we've been more than an ordinary insurance company. Commitment to our insureds goes well beyond the property coverages we provide.

After a century and a half, that part of our philosophy is not about to change. Allendale Insurance, P.O. Box 7500, Johnston, Rhode Island 02919.

Allendale Insurance/Factory Mutual System
Over 150 years of progress and stability.

Source: Reprinted with permission of Allendale Mutual Insurance Company.

Other steps can be taken to reduce risks. Guard dogs and 24-hour security patrols may minimize burglaries. Installation of fire-retardant building materials and an automatic sprinkler system can help protect a warehouse from fire. Preventive maintenance lessens the risk of defective machinery. Adequate credit checks allow managers to make careful decisions on which customers should be extended credit. All these actions can reduce the risk involved in business operations; they cannot, however, eliminate all risk.

Most major business insurers offer clients a thorough review prepared by their loss-prevention experts. These safety and health professionals evaluate customers' work environments and recommend procedures and equipment that will help firms minimize worker injuries and property losses. The Allendale Insurance advertisement in Figure 22.2 points out the firm's long history in loss control service.

Self-Insuring against Risk

self-insurance fund

An account set up to cover losses from the assumption of pure risk.

Instead of purchasing insurance against certain kinds of pure risk, some multiplant, geographically scattered firms accumulate funds to cover possible losses. A **self-insurance fund** is a special fund created by setting aside cash reserves on a periodic basis to be drawn upon only in the event of a financial loss resulting from the assumption of a pure risk. The regular payments to the fund are invested in interest-bearing securities, and losses are charged to it. Risk-reduction programs are used to minimize losses.

Before the surge in premiums for business insurance during the mid-1980s, self-insurance accounted for about 25 percent of the total insurance market. It is now about 33 percent and expanding. Hardee's Food System Inc. self-insures for losses up to $2 million. Insurance is used to cover catastrophic losses over $2 million. Hardee's also operates an effective loss-prevention program that includes nonskid floors in its restaurants.

Other firms set up their own insurance companies. This form of self-insurance is illustrated by Du Pont, which put $20 million into development of two insurance companies that cover the chemical giant and 550 other employers.[2]

The use of self-insurance may be appropriate in instances where a firm faces similar risks and the risks are spread over a broad geographic area. Self-insurance can be a realistic choice for large multiplant companies, because the likelihood of several fires in different localities is small, and the likelihood of a single fire can be calculated. For the single-plant firm, however, one fire can prove disastrous, and contributions to a reserve fund for large potential fire damage can be prohibitively high. As a result, small firms with concentrated facilities and the possibility of being forced out of business by a major fire or accident usually shift the risk to others through the purchase of insurance.

Shifting Risk to an Insurance Company

Although steps can be taken to avoid or reduce risk, the most common method of dealing with it is to shift it to others in the form of **insurance** — the process by which a firm, for a fee, agrees to pay another firm or individual a sum of money stated in a written contract when a loss occurs. In other words, the insurance company agrees to pay the insured party a predetermined sum of money as indicated in the policy in event of a loss, in exchange for the insured party's regular payment of a premium. Thus, insurance is the substitution of a small known loss — the insurance premium — for a larger unknown loss that may or may not occur. In the case of life insurance, the loss — death — is a certainty; the uncertainty is the date of occurrence. The advertisement in Figure 22.3 points out that it is important for the insurer to understand the customer's business, risk exposure, and insurance needs.

insurance
Process by which an insurer, in exchange for a fee, agrees to reimburse firms or individuals for losses up to specified limits.

Basic Insurance Concepts

The premiums accumulated by insurance companies are designed to cover eventual loss. However, as Chapter 20 indicated, these funds are carefully invested to generate additional returns for the company. The returns from insurance company investments may be utilized in reducing premiums, generating a profit for those companies organized as profit seeking, or both. Insurance companies represent a major source of long-term financing for other businesses.

Insurance companies are professional risk takers. For a fee, they accept the risk of loss or damage to businesses and individuals. Three basic principles operate in insurance: the concept of insurable interest, the concept of insurable risks, and the law of large numbers.

Figure 22.3   Shifting Risk to an Insurance Company

Source: Chubb Group of Insurance Companies.

Insurable Interest

In order to purchase insurance, an applicant must demonstrate that he or she has an **insurable interest** in the property or life insured. That is, the policyholder must stand to suffer loss, financial or otherwise, due to fire, accident, death, or lawsuit. However, for life insurance, a friend or relative may have an insurable interest even though no financial loss occurs in the event of the insured's death.

A businessperson can obtain fire insurance for property. Individuals can purchase life insurance for themselves or for members of their family. Because top managers are important assets to a firm, the corporation can purchase key executive insurance. But a businessperson cannot collect on insurance to cover damage to the property of competitors when no insurable interest exists. Nor can an individual purchase an insurance policy on the life of the president of the United States. In these two cases, an insurable interest is not present.

Insurable Risks

An **insurable risk** should meet a number of requirements in order for an insurance company to provide protection against its occurrence:

1. *The likelihood of loss should be predictable.* Insurance companies know approximately how many fires will occur each year, how many people of a

certain age will die, how many burglaries will occur, and how many traffic accidents and job-related injuries will take place. Knowledge of the numbers of such losses and of their average size allows the insurance company to determine the amount of premiums necessary to repay those companies and individuals who suffer losses.

2. *The loss should be financially measurable.* In order to determine the amount of premium income necessary to cover the costs of losses, the dollar amount of losses must be known. For this reason, life insurance policies are purchased in specific dollar amounts, which eliminates the problem of determining the value of a person's life. Many health insurance policies list the dollar value for specific medical procedures. Some policies have no schedule of benefits for such procedures but pay, say, 80 or 100 percent of the cost.

3. *The loss should be fortuitous or accidental.* Losses must happen by chance and must not be intended by the insured. The insurance company is not required to pay for damages caused by a fire if the insured is found guilty of arson. Similarly, life insurance policies typically exclude the payment of proceeds if the insured commits suicide in the first year of the policy's coverage.

4. *The risk should be spread over a wide geographic area.* An insurance company that concentrates its coverage in one geographic area risks the possibility of a major catastrophe affecting most of its policyholders. A major Louisiana hurricane, California earthquake, or Midwest tornado might bankrupt the company.

5. *The insurance company has the right to set standards for accepting risks.* The company may refuse insurance coverage to individuals with heart disease or to those in dangerous occupations, such as fire fighters, test pilots, and crop dusters. Or the company may choose to insure these people at considerably higher rates due to the greater risks involved. In the same manner, fire insurance rates may be different for residences and commercial buildings.

The Law of Large Numbers

Insurance is based on the law of averages, or statistical probability. Insurance companies have studied the occurrence of deaths, injuries, lawsuits, and all types of hazards. From their investigations they have developed the **law of large numbers** — a probability calculation of the likelihood of the occurrence of perils on which premiums are based. They also use actuarial tables to predict the number of fires, automobile accidents, plane crashes, and deaths that will occur in a given year.

The use of the law of large numbers in calculating insurance premiums can be described in the following example. A small city has 50,000 homes. Previously collected statistical data indicates the city would experience an average of 500 fires a year, with damages totaling an average of $30,000 per occurrence. What is the minimum annual premium an insurance company would charge? To simplify the calculations, assume the premiums charged would not produce profits or cover any of the insurance company's operating expenses. In total, the claims would be $15 million (500 homes damaged × $30,000). If these losses are spread over all 50,000 homes, each homeowner would be charged an annual premium of $300 ($15 million divided by 50,000 homes). In reality, the insur-

law of large numbers
The calculation of the likelihood of the occurrence of perils on which premiums are based.

Table 22.1   Mortality Table Classified by Race, Age, and Selected Ages

Vital Statistics

| | | Expectation of Life in Years | | | | Expected Deaths per 1,000 Alive at Specified Age | | | | |
| | | White | | Black | | | White | | Black | |
Age	Total	Male	Female	Male	Female	Total	Male	Female	Male	Female
At Birth	74.7	71.9	78.7	65.3	73.5	10.69	10.59	8.03	19.94	16.54
1	74.5	71.6	78.4	65.7	73.8	.70	.74	.54	1.14	.87
5	70.7	67.8	74.5	61.9	70.0	.31	.31	.24	.52	.42
10	65.8	62.9	69.6	57.0	65.1	.18	.19	.14	.29	.23
15	60.9	58.0	64.6	52.1	60.2	.59	.81	.37	.85	.34
20	56.1	53.3	59.8	47.4	55.3	1.02	1.47	.50	1.89	.61
25	51.4	48.7	54.9	42.9	50.5	1.12	1.54	.50	2.61	.94
30	46.7	44.0	50.1	38.5	45.8	1.23	1.55	.59	3.61	1.43
35	42.0	39.4	45.2	34.3	41.1	1.53	1.82	.80	4.86	1.97
40	37.3	34.7	40.4	30.2	36.6	2.12	2.46	1.25	6.70	2.91
45	32.7	30.2	35.7	26.3	32.1	3.25	3.73	2.07	9.14	4.38
50	28.3	25.8	31.1	22.5	27.9	5.25	6.15	3.46	13.13	6.65
55	24.2	21.7	26.7	19.1	24.0	8.41	10.35	5.52	18.42	10.30
60	20.3	18.0	22.6	16.0	20.3	13.12	16.49	8.80	27.16	15.81
65	16.7	14.6	18.7	13.3	17.0	19.39	24.89	13.45	36.14	20.91

Source: U.S. Bureau of the Census, *Statistical Abstract of the United States: 1988,* 108th ed. (Washington, D.C., 1987), p. 72.

ance company would set the premium at a higher figure to cover its operating expenses and to earn a reasonable return.

Table 22.1 is an actuarial table indicating life expectancies and the number of deaths per thousand persons that will occur this year by race, sex, and selected ages. For all 30-year-olds, deaths average about 1.23 per thousand, and people in this age group are expected to live about 47 more years.

No one can predict which 30-year-old per thousand will die; the insurance companies know only that an average of 1.23 per thousand will do so. Armed with this knowledge, the company can determine the size of premium necessary to pay the beneficiaries of its policies when claims arise. The longer the life expectancy, the lower the premiums. The same type of calculation is also made to determine premiums for automobile or fire insurance. The law of large numbers is the basis of all insurance premium calculations.

Matching Premiums to Different Degrees of Risk

Although the law of large numbers is used by insurance companies in designing policies, they often divide individuals and industries into different risk categories and attempt to match premiums to the risk involved. A good example is automobile insurance.

Insurance claims statistics reveal that drivers under 25 are involved in far more accidents than are older drivers. Although only one driver in five is under 25, one-third of all drivers involved in an accident are under 25. As a result, youthful drivers — especially males — pay the highest insurance premiums.[3]

The Law of Adverse Selection

The **law of adverse selection** states that persons with actual or potential health disabilities and those in dangerous occupations are more likely to purchase and renew health and life insurance policies than are others. This tendency, referred to by insurance companies as *antiselection*, can result in higher claim costs to the insurer since such policyholders are more likely than others to become ill or die. Insurance companies that fail to guard against antiselection may discover the premiums they collect are too small to cover policyholders' claims.

This is an especially serious problem for health insurers, since evidence of insurability — good health — is required only when the policy is first issued. In addition, insurance companies offering guaranteed renewable term life insurance policies face similar problems. In both cases, policyholders who develop health problems after purchasing insurance are more likely to renew these policies than are policyholders in general.

Health and life insurance companies attempt to protect themselves from the costly effects of the law of adverse selection by requiring applicants to submit detailed medical and personal histories and by submitting each application to a thorough risk-appraisal process. A risk appraiser evaluates the insurability of the applicant and makes one of three recommendations: (1) acceptance with normal premiums, (2) acceptance with higher than average premiums because of medical or occupational factors, or (3) rejection. In addition, insurance firms charge higher premiums for guaranteed renewable term insurance policies than they do for comparable nonrenewable policies.

law of adverse selection
Persons with health problems and those in dangerous occupations are more likely to purchase and renew health and life insurance policies than are others.

Confronting the AIDS Crisis

Acquired immune deficiency syndrome (AIDS) has become a worldwide health crisis since the first cases were discovered. The disease has also had a significant impact on the insurance industry. In 1986, insurers paid out $290 million to AIDS victims. By 1991, AIDS claims are expected to rise to $16 billion annually, and by 2000, AIDS could account for 20 percent of all life insurance claims.

The insurance industry has sought to protect against such claims by attempting to limit the antiselection process. In other words, the industry uses application questions and AIDS testing to sort out those who have the disease and high risk groups. Insurers point to a study showing that most AIDS claims occur within the first two years of coverage, thus illustrating the law of adverse selection. A government report showed that nearly a third of all commercial insurers considered a person's sexual orientation in issuing policies.

Numerous lawsuits and public protests resulted from the insurance industry's attempts to avoid antiselection of high-risk groups. Eighteen states prohibit insurance companies from denying AIDS benefits. AIDS testing was outlawed in the District of Columbia, where insurance companies stopped writing policies. The district has revised its law to permit the HIV Antibody Test, provided the applicant has consented. In California, the use of antibody tests is not permitted in determining eligibility for health insurance. However, such tests are allowed for life and disability income insurance applications.

While the debate continues, insurance companies have adopted a variety of responses to the AIDS crisis. New York Life funded $8.5 million to AIDS research. Guardian Life discontinued coverage for hairstylists. Provident Indemnity Life limits AIDS claims on small-business policies to $5,000 per year and

These health benefits specialists at John Hancock Financial Services discuss AIDS Case Management, a program that helps employers contain costs yet takes a compassionate approach to treating AIDS patients. Offered on a voluntary basis, the program uses a national network of registered nurses to coordinate the medical care of AIDS patients and offers inpatients the use of alternative care such as clinics, home health care agencies, and hospices. As a corporate citizen, John Hancock cosponsors an annual 10-kilometer AIDS "Walk for Life," conducts forums to educate employees on AIDS prevention, contributes to the educational programs of seven Boston health and human services organizations, and held a community forum during which experts answered teenagers' questions about AIDS.

Photo source: © Rick Friedman.

$20,000 lifetime. By contrast, Golden Rule Insurance has a policy that offers full coverage without AIDS testing, but it requires that the buyer remain free of AIDS symptoms during the first year the policy is in force. All of these responses suggest how the law of adverse selection plays a major role in today's insurance decisions.[4]

Sources of Insurance

Although the term *insurance company* is typically associated with private companies such as Prudential, John Hancock, State Farm, and Travelers, a number of public agencies also provide insurance coverage for business firms, nonprofit organizations, and individuals.

Public Insurance Companies

public insurance company
Government agency that provides specialized insurance protection for individuals and organizations.

A **public insurance company** is a government agency established at the state or federal level to provide specialized insurance protection for individuals and organizations. It provides protection in such areas as job loss (unemployment insurance), work-related injuries (workers' compensation), pension plans (social security), and specialized programs ranging from flood insurance to depositor protection at commercial banks and savings and loan associations.

unemployment insurance
State insurance program designed to assist unemployed workers.

Unemployment Insurance   Every state has an **unemployment insurance** program designed to assist unemployed workers by providing them with financial benefits, job counseling, and placement services while they are laid off or while they attempt to locate new jobs. Since the financial benefits are designed to provide temporary replacement of a part of the employee's previous earnings, they are typically paid for 26 to 39 weeks and vary in amount depending upon the worker's previous income and the state in which the worker lives. These insurance programs are funded by payroll taxes paid by employers.

Workers' Compensation   Under state law, **workers' compensation insurance** is provided by employers to guarantee payment of wages and salaries, medical care costs, and such rehabilitation services as retraining, job placement, and vocational rehabilitation to employees who are injured on the job. It exists in all 50 states and Puerto Rico. In addition, it provides benefits in the form of weekly payments or a single lump sum to the worker's spouse or children if a worker dies as a result of work-related injuries. Premiums are based on the company's payroll, and rates depend on the hazards present on the job and on the employer's safety record. Payments are usually set at a fraction of the employee's regular wage (usually one-half to two-thirds of the weekly salary). In addition, workers' compensation typically reimburses the injured worker for medical and rehabilitation expenses. A waiting period of a few days to two weeks is usually provided to discourage claims for minor accidents.

In effect, workers' compensation is a no-fault system that enables disabled workers to collect benefits regardless of fault as long as the disability is job related. In return, workers who receive these benefits give up their rights to sue their employers for injury-related negligence.

Social Security   The federal government is the largest insurer in the United States. Its social security program, officially titled **Old-Age, Survivors, Disability, and Health Insurance (OASDHI)**, grew out of the *Social Security Act of 1935*. In 1965, **Medicare**, a form of health insurance for persons 65 years or older and certain other social security recipients, was added to the OASDHI program. More than nine out of ten U.S. employees and their dependents are eligible for retirement benefits, life insurance, health insurance, and disability income insurance under this program.

The OASDHI program is funded by a tax paid by both employers and employees, based on employee earnings and paid in equal amounts. Self-employed persons pay a somewhat higher percentage of their incomes. The four types of basic benefits provided under Social Security include the following:

1. Payments for death, including a small lump-sum payment and important survivors' income payments to spouses with dependent children.
2. Income payments for disability if it is total and expected to last at least 12 months or result in death.
3. Retirement benefits, the most widely known aspect of the social security system.
4. Hospital and medical payments for eligible persons age 65 or over. These payments are made through the Medicare program.

Other Types of Public Insurance   A number of other forms of public insurance exist; some types focus on a narrow aspect of the economy, while others apply to millions of individuals and organizations. These are among the more important public insurance programs:

1. The Federal Deposit Insurance Corporation (FDIC), Federal Savings and Loan Insurance Corporation (FSLIC), and National Credit Union Administra-

workers' compensation insurance
Insurance provided by employers under state law to employees injured on the job.

Old-Age, Survivors, Disability, and Health Insurance (OASDHI)
Government insurance that is part of the Social Security program.

Medicare
Form of health insurance for persons 65 years or older and certain other social security recipients.

tion (NCUA) provide insurance protection for deposits in commercial banks, savings banks, savings and loan associations, and credit unions. They are discussed in Chapter 19.

2. The Federal Housing Administration (FHA) provides mortgage insurance to lenders as protection against possible default by home purchasers.

3. The National Flood Insurance Association provides protection against flooding and mudslides for properties located in flood-prone areas.

4. Federal crime insurance is available for owners of property located in high-crime areas who might not be able to purchase such insurance from private insurance companies.

5. The Federal Crop Insurance Corporation provides crop insurance for farmers.

6. The Pension Benefit Guaranty Corporation insures the assets of pension plans to prevent loss of retirement benefits should an employer go out of business or declare bankruptcy. This pension guarantee, created by the Employee Retirement Income Security Act of 1974 (ERISA), is discussed in Chapter 11.

Private Insurance Companies

Much of the insurance in force in the United States is provided by private insurance companies. These companies are typically categorized by ownership. Two types of private insurance companies exist: stock companies and mutual companies.

stock insurance company
Insurance company operated for profit.

Stock Companies   A **stock insurance company** is an insurance company operated for profit. Stockholders do not have to be policyholders; they invest funds in the stock company in order to receive dividends from company earnings. Profits earned by the company come from two sources: (1) insurance premiums in excess of claims and operating costs, and (2) earnings from company investments in mortgages, stocks, bonds, and real estate.

Insurance companies, whether stock or mutual companies, have the objective of minimizing the premiums necessary to cover operating expenses and to pay for personal or property losses. Accident claim data is studied in an attempt to spot problem areas and to adjust coverage costs accordingly. Such data provides expected reasons for accidents — excessive speed, alcohol consumption, equipment malfunction, and inattentiveness, among others.

The major difference between stock and mutual companies is that stockholders seek profits from stock insurance companies. Even so, there is no clear indication that the insurance premiums of stock companies are greater than those of mutual companies. Although mutual companies dominate the life insurance field, the majority of all other types of insurance is written by stock companies. The efficiency of a particular company appears to depend on its management ability.

mutual insurance company
Insurance company owned by its policyholders.

Mutual Companies   A **mutual insurance company** is a type of cooperative; it is owned by its policyholders. The mutual company is chartered by the state and governed by a board of directors elected by the policyholders. Prudential Insurance Company of America, the nation's largest insurer, is a mutual company.

These students received a share of stock in The St. Paul Companies for creating award-winning safety posters in a fire prevention program sponsored by the firm. The St. Paul Companies is a stock insurance company, so these children benefit directly from the firm's financial success. The St. Paul is the oldest business corporation in Minnesota and a leader in the property and liability insurance industry.

Photo source: Courtesy of The St. Paul Companies. Photographer: Cheryl Walsh-Bellville.

Unlike the stock company, the mutual company earns no profits for its owners. Because it is a nonprofit organization, any surplus funds remaining after operating expenses, payment of claims, and establishment of necessary reserves are returned to the policyholders in the form of dividends or premium reductions.

Mutual companies are found chiefly in the life insurance field. Although they account for slightly less than 6 percent of the 2,225 life insurance companies in the United States, they sell about half of all the life insurance in force.

Types of Insurance

Although hundreds of types of insurance policies are available for purchase by individuals and businesses, they can be conveniently divided into three broad categories: (1) property and liability insurance, (2) health insurance, and (3) life insurance.

Property and Liability Insurance

Property and liability insurance is a general category of insurance that provides protection against a number of perils. *Property losses* are financial losses resulting from interruption of business operations or physical damage to property as a result of fires, accidents, windstorms, theft, or other destructive occurrences. *Liability losses* are financial losses suffered by a business firm or individual should the firm or individual be held responsible for property damage or injuries suffered by others.

Fire Insurance

fire insurance

Insurance coverage for losses due to fire and — with extended coverage — windstorms, hail, water, riot, and smoke damage.

Fires will cause almost $6 billion in property damage this year. Many business-people and individuals purchase **fire insurance** to cover losses due to fire. Fire insurance policies are often expanded by purchasing extended coverage to encompass financial losses resulting from windstorms, hail, water, riot, and smoke damage.

Rates for fire insurance vary according to the risks involved. Homes and buildings located in cities with adequate fire protection and with records of relatively low losses from fire pay lower rates than those in rural areas and areas with high previous incidences of fire damage. Frame buildings have higher rates than brick or metal structures.

coinsurance clause

Insurance clause requiring that the insured carry fire insurance of some minimum percentage of the replacement value of the property to receive full coverage for a loss.

Because most fires result in less than total destruction, many businesspeople insure their property for less than its total value. For example, a $100,000 building may carry insurance of $80,000. Because insurance companies extend coverage on the entire building and receive premiums on only a fraction of the value of the building, they protect themselves by including a **coinsurance clause** in the policy. This clause requires that the insured carry fire insurance of some minimum percentage of the current replacement cash value of the property (usually 80 percent) in order to receive full coverage of a loss.

The coinsurance clause works this way. If the owner of a $50,000 building suffers a $20,000 fire loss, the amount the insurance company will repay depends on the value of the fire insurance policy. Should the owner have $30,000 in fire insurance, the insurance company will pay only three-fourths of the damage. Why? Because the coinsurance clause requires the owner to have a minimum of $40,000 in insurance (80 percent of the $50,000 current replacement cash value of the building), the $30,000 policy amounts to only 75 percent of the required insurance. The insurance company calculates its share of the loss as follows:

$$\frac{\text{Amount of Insurance Carried}}{\text{Amount of Insurance Required}} \times \text{Loss} = \begin{array}{c}\text{Insurance Company's Share}\\ \text{of the Loss}\end{array}$$

$$\frac{\$30,000}{\$40,000} \times \$20,000 = \$15,000$$

The remaining $5,000 of the loss must be absorbed by the insured.

Business Interruption Insurance

Fire insurance with extended benefits provisions would reimburse the owner of a factory for losses to the equipment, raw materials and inventory on hand, and smoke and water damage to the building. But if the owner is forced to close the business until repairs can be made, new raw materials ordered, and new inventory purchased or manufactured, the business will suffer a serious loss. As a

Figure 22.4   Insuring against Losses Due to Fire

Nine ways an insurance company kept an accident from becoming a disaster.

A true story.
On June 26, 1986, a company that provides gold and silver paint to chinaware manufacturers had a devastating fire. Extensive damage was done to its building, equipment and materials. Sure, the company was insured. But its insurance company did more than honor the policy.

1. They helped the business re-open quickly. Once on the scene, the claims adjuster assessed the damage and helped the owners figure out how to resume business as soon as possible.

2. They paid to erect a temporary building. Using provisions in the policy to pay for a pre-fab structure, the company was able to return to business almost as usual within two weeks.

3. They mailed a check right away. In fact, the paint company received its first check for $100,000 less than five weeks after the fire.

4. They helped dig for gold. The insurance company found that a lot of gold used in the paint was scattered under the debris. They promptly authorized a reclamation firm to recover and clean over 150 ounces of gold at a cost far below the price of the precious metal.

5. They found a way to dispose of toxic wastes. The paint company might have had a hard time finding a reliable company for such specialized work, but the insurance company found a qualified company to dispose of toxic material.

6. They gave it a personal touch. Under the company's policy, the employees were surprised to learn that they would be reimbursed for their personal belongings lost in the fire.

7. They paid to inventory the damage. Most people don't realize that taking inventory of an accident's damages is another expense. But this too was covered under the policy.

8. They took out the garbage. Under the company's policy, debris removal was covered down to the last cinder.

9. They paid the claims on time. A check arrived in September and a final check arrived in December, only five months after the fire.

In the end, the insurance company did one more thing. They wrote another policy. According to the company's owner, that second policy was his best "vote of confidence" in his insurance company.
Your insurance company does more than just sell you a policy.
For information about how we keep accidents from turning into disasters, write for our free booklet. Or call 1-800-222-1144, and ask for extension U-1.

For a free copy of *Insurance is more than a policy*, send to: Insurance Information Institute, Dept. RR, 110 William Street, NY, NY 10038.

Name

Address

City   State   Zip
No salesperson will call.   U-1

Your Insurance Company
We do a lot more than sell insurance.

Source: Courtesy of the Insurance Information Institute.

result, many businesses attempt to protect against this possibility by purchasing business interruption insurance.

Business interruption insurance, which is frequently purchased as an additional provision of a basic fire insurance policy, is designed to cover losses resulting from temporary business closings as a result of a fire or other specified property damage. This type of insurance may pay the costs of leasing equipment or temporary facilities; salaries and wages of employees; taxes; mortgage and note payments; other fixed expenses; and normal profits the owners would have earned during the reconstruction period. The paint company featured in the advertisement in Figure 22.4 had an additional provision in their basic fire insurance policy that paid the cost of erecting a temporary, prefabricated structure. The provision enabled the firm to return to business within two weeks after a fire extensively damaged its building, equipment, and materials.

A similar type of insurance aimed at insuring against loss of earning power is called **contingent business interruption insurance**. This type of policy is intended to cover the possible losses incurred by a firm should the business of a major supplier or customer be damaged by fire. Such a fire is likely to result in financial losses to the insured due to unavailable supplies or the loss of the customer's business even though the insured suffers no physical damage.

business interruption insurance
Type of insurance designed to cover losses resulting from temporary business closings.

contingent business interruption insurance
Insurance coverage for losses incurred as a result of a major supplier or customer being damaged by fire or other specified property damage.

Automobile Insurance

The National Safety Council regularly issues statements to inform the public of the risks involved in driving motor vehicles, and with good reason. Motor vehicle accidents have killed more people than all the armed forces battles since the Revolutionary War. There were 32.5 million motor vehicle accidents in a recent year. These accidents resulted in an economic loss of $76 billion.[5]

automobile insurance
Coverage for property and liability claims resulting from theft, fire, or accident.

Most **automobile insurance** includes coverage for losses due to automobile theft, fire, or collision and claims resulting from damage to the property or person of others involved in an automobile accident. The automobile owner protects against these risks through the purchase of comprehensive fire and theft, collision, and liability insurance.

Comprehensive coverage protects the insured's car against damage caused by fire, theft, hail, falling objects, and a variety of other perils. Contents of the car are also usually covered if the car is locked. In recent years, insurance companies have excluded stereo tape decks and CB radios if they are screwed in or attached to the dashboard (or issued special policies at a separate premium) due to the ease of their detachment from the car and their attractiveness to thieves.

Collision insurance pays for damage caused by collision with another vehicle or with a stationary object. Most policies list a deductible amount, ranging from $50 to $200 or $300, that the insured must pay. It is usually advisable to select a high deductible since policies with low or no deductibles charge considerably higher premiums to cover numerous minor claims. Most automobile insurance policies provide both comprehensive and collision coverage for a single premium.

Liability insurance covers both property damage and bodily injury. Bodily injury liability insurance is usually stated on the policy as $20,000/$40,000, $25,000/$50,000, $100,000/$300,000, or more. The first amount listed is the maximum amount the insurance company will pay for the injury or death of one person. The second is the maximum amount the insurance company will pay for a single accident. Property damage liability insurance covers any damage to other automobiles or property caused by the insured's automobile. Liability insurance also typically includes a medical payments endorsement, which pays hospital and doctor bills up to a specified amount for any persons injured in the insured's car.

Uninsured motorist insurance covers the policyholder who is involved in an accident with a driver who has no liability insurance and is at fault. This type of insurance also protects the insured against losses caused by hit-and-run drivers. Underinsured motorist insurance pays claims that exceed the other driver's coverage. The term *underinsured motorist insurance* is used to describe both types of coverage in some states.

no-fault insurance
State laws that require claims to be paid by the policyholder's insurance company without regard to fault and that limit the right of victims to sue.

In 1971, Massachusetts became the first state to enact a **no-fault insurance** plan — a state law requiring that claim payments by the policyholder's insurance company be made without regard to fault and limiting the right of victims to sue. Nearly half of the states and the District of Columbia now have no-fault laws.

Although the laws are not identical, all have the following features:

1. *Insurance is required for all drivers of private automobiles.* That is, all motorists must carry personal injury protection as well as liability insurance to cover medical costs resulting from accidents involving themselves and other passengers in their cars.

2. *Payments for financial losses are made, without regard to fault, to any insured driver, passenger, or pedestrian injured in an auto accident.* These payments are made by the policyholder's insurance company, not by the company of the person ruled at fault.
3. *Victims are automatically limited in their right to sue.* As a rule, lawsuits are barred except in cases where medical expenses exceed a set amount (which varies from state to state) or where the accident results in death, dismemberment, disfigurement, or certain other serious injuries.

Proponents of no-fault insurance argue that it will lead to lower premiums. To date, however, the impact of such laws upon premiums has been mixed. Although Michigan, New York, and Minnesota have enjoyed some success in modifying rate increases, Nevada repealed its 6-year-old plan after premiums rose 81 percent in two years. Pennsylvania also repealed its no-fault law after a period of rising premiums.

Burglary, Robbery, and Theft Insurance

Businesses also need insurance protection against crime. The U.S. Department of Justice reports that 99 percent of all Americans will be a theft victim at least once in their lifetime. Some 87 percent of the population will be a victim on three or more occasions. Worse yet, 83 percent of the population will become a victim of violent crime.[6]

Although burglary, robbery, and theft are all crimes, each has a different meaning, and the insurance rate for each crime is different. **Burglary insurance** provides coverage for losses due to the taking of property only by forcible entry. **Robbery insurance** provides coverage only for losses due to the unlawful taking of property from another person by force or the threat of force. **Theft insurance** gives coverage for losses due to the unlawful taking of property. Theft insurance provides the broadest coverage and is, therefore, the most expensive of all crime coverages.

burglary insurance
Insurance coverage for losses due to the taking of property by forcible entry.

robbery insurance
Insurance coverage for losses due to the unlawful taking of property from another person by force or the threat of force.

theft insurance
Insurance coverage for losses due to the unlawful taking of property.

Marine Insurance

Marine insurance is the oldest form of insurance, dating back at least 5,000 years. It is used as a means of insuring ships and their cargoes. **Ocean marine insurance** protects shippers from losses of property due to damage to a ship or its cargo while at sea or in port. **Inland marine insurance** covers losses of property due to damage while goods are being transported by truck, ship, rail, or plane. As the advertisement in Figure 22.5 illustrates, the CIGNA Companies offer a comprehensive insurance package in this field.

ocean marine insurance
Insurance that covers shippers for losses of property due to damage to a ship or its cargo while at sea or in port.

inland marine insurance
Insurance coverage for losses of property due to damage while goods are being transported by truck, ship, rail, or plane.

Fidelity, Surety, Title, and Credit Insurance

A **fidelity bond** protects employers from employees' dishonesty. Fidelity bonds are commonly used by banks, loan companies, and other businesses to cover cashiers and other employees who handle company funds. The employer is guaranteed against loss up to the amount of the policy.

A **surety bond** is designed to protect people or companies against losses resulting from nonperformance of a contract. A building contractor who agrees

fidelity bond
Bond that protects employers from employees' dishonesty.

surety bond
Bond that protects people or companies against losses resulting from nonperformance of a contract.

Figure 22.5 Insuring against Goods Damaged in Transit

Source: Courtesy of the CIGNA Companies.

to construct a new city library, for example, may be required to furnish a surety bond that the library will be erected according to specifications and completed within the time limits of the contract.

title insurance
Insurance protection for real estate purchasers against losses incurred because of a defect in title to property.

Title insurance protects real estate purchasers against losses that might be incurred because of a defect in the title to the property. It eliminates the purchaser's need to investigate legal records in order to determine the true owner of the property and the presence of any claims against it. This insurance is often purchased by a person buying a new home.

credit insurance
Insurance to protect lenders against losses caused by insolvency of customers to whom credit has been extended.

Credit insurance protects lenders against losses caused by the insolvency of customers to whom credit has been extended. Such policies do not protect against all unpaid debts because the premiums would be too expensive. Credit insurance is frequently used in international trade to cover losses for nonpayment or default for political reasons as well as the usual commercial insolvency of foreign purchasers.

Liability Insurance

liability insurance
Insurance protection for businesses and individuals against claims caused by injuries to others or damage to the property of others.

Liability insurance is designed to protect businesses and individuals against claims resulting from injuries to others or damage to the property of others. Most homeowners' insurance policies include liability coverage for claims such as those by people injured in falls or bitten by pets. Since many homeowners' policies place limits on such claims, many individuals and businesses purchase *umbrella liability insurance* to extend the amount of coverage limits to $1 million or more. The additional coverage provides a larger umbrella of protection for the business firm or individual policyholder.

To determine rates, businesses are categorized by type of activity. Between 700 and 800 general liability classifications exist, so it is important that managers verify that their operation is classified correctly.[7]

In recent years, thousands of lawsuits have been filed accusing doctors, lawyers, architects, corporate officers and board members, accountants, travel agents, ministers, and even college professors of malpractice. In order to pay the costs of such lawsuits and to provide protection against financial losses resulting from successful lawsuits, many professionals purchase *professional liability insurance.* Premiums are staggering; obstetrician-gynecologists, neurosurgeons, and orthopedic surgeons in some parts of the country pay annual malpractice premiums of $40,000 and up.

Product liability insurance is designed to protect businesses against claims for damages resulting from the use of the company's products. It covers, for example, a druggist being sued by a customer who claims a prescription was prepared improperly or a manufacturer accused of producing and selling unsafe products.

product liability insurance
Insurance protection for businesses against claims for damages resulting from the use of the company's products.

Product liability insurance has become increasingly necessary in recent years. Consider the following cases:

◆ A 41-year-old bodybuilder entered a footrace with a refrigerator strapped to his back to prove his prowess. During the race, he alleged, one of the straps came loose and the man was hurt. He sued everyone in sight, including the maker of the strap. Jury award: $1 million.

◆ Two Maryland men decided to dry their hot-air balloon in a commercial laundry drier. The drier exploded, injuring them. They won $885,000 in damages from American Laundry Machinery, which manufactured the drier.

◆ An overweight man with a history of coronary disease suffered a heart attack while trying to start a Sears lawn mower. He sued Sears, charging that too much force was required to yank the mower's pull rope. A jury in Pennsylvania awarded him $1.2 million, plus damages of $550,000 for delays in settling the claim. (Sears appealed but eventually settled out of court.)[8]

High-technology companies, particularly those in biotechnological fields, face staggering premiums for product liability insurance coverage. For 27 years, Merrill Dow Pharmaceuticals marketed Bendectin, a prescription drug designed to combat morning sickness, and an estimated 33 million pregnant women used it. Bendectin is the only drug approved in the United States for treating the nausea associated with pregnancy. Although a Food and Drug Administration review panel reported no association between Bendectin and birth defects had been demonstrated, more than 300 lawsuits were filed against the manufacturer, claiming the drug had caused birth defects. When a Washington, D.C., jury awarded $750,000 to the family of one such child, Merrill Dow Pharmaceuticals withdrew Bendectin from the market.

As a company representative remarked, "We were forced for business reasons to take a safe and effective medication off the market." Annual insurance premiums had jumped to $10 million annually, only $3 million less than income from the sale of the drug.[9]

Not only have insurance premiums soared, but in many cases companies also have been unable to secure product liability insurance coverage at any price. Coverage for the following insurance needs is difficult to obtain: pollution risks, liquor liability, day-care center coverage, medical malpractice, high-limit coverage (above $50 million) for industrial firms, asbestos removal from schools, commercial fishing boat coverage, and municipal liability.[10] The Challenger space shuttle disaster coupled with such widely publicized cases as A. H. Robbins' Dalkon shield contraceptive device, asbestos insulation manufactured by the Manville Corporation, and day-care child abuse accusations have prompted a growing number of insurance companies to cease providing such coverage. In such instances, the firm's management faces the unpleasant options of simply abandoning a promising product or offering it to the market with no insurance protection. Management at Connaught Laboratories chose to discontinue the sales of its diphtheria, whooping cough, and tetanus vaccine after liability insurance premiums skyrocketed. Rawlings Sporting Goods ended production of football helmets in 1988 because, according to the firm's CEO, ". . . the cost to insure our company against helmet-related lawsuits was more expensive than the cost of manufacturing the helmets themselves."[11] By contrast, Marine Biologicals, a Seaville, New Jersey, manufacturer of diagnostic tests for fever-causing bacteria in medical devices and injectable drugs, continued operations despite its inability to secure product liability coverage.[12] A decision to operate without insurance protection is referred to as "going naked."

Health Insurance

health insurance
Insurance designed to provide coverage for losses due to sickness or accidents.

One of every six people in the United States is hospitalized each year. Without insurance, family incomes can be cut off, a lifetime of savings can be wiped out, and a business can face the loss of a valuable employee. Because of these severe risks, over 160 million Americans have some form of employer-provided **health insurance** — insurance that provides coverage for losses due to sickness or accidents. More than $500 billion, or 11 percent of the nation's gross national product, is spent on health care annually.[13]

In 1988, Massachusetts became the first state to legislate universal health coverage for all its residents. The Massachusetts plan will be fully implemented by 1992. Senator Edward Kennedy proposed a similar employer-sponsored plan for the entire country.

Sources of Health Insurance

Most businesses and nonprofit organizations offer health and accident insurance for their employees as part of a fringe benefit package. These *group policies* are issued by private insurance companies, Blue Cross/Blue Shield, health maintenance organizations, and preferred provider organizations. These health care providers also offer similar coverage — typically with higher premiums — on an individual basis. Health insurance is also provided by the federal government through its Medicare and Medicaid programs and the disability provisions of the Social Security Act. Some 32 million people are covered by Medicare. In 1988, Medicare was extended to cover catastrophic losses that could bankrupt elderly persons.

Private Insurance Companies and Blue Cross/Blue Shield A variety of commercial insurance companies offer group health packages to employees. Provident Insurance of Chattanooga, Tennessee, is an example of such an insurer. The 78 nonprofit Blue Cross/Blue Shield plans are another option. These plans currently cover 31 percent of all U.S. households.

Figure 22.6   The Blue Cross Preferred Care Plan

Source: Courtesy of Blue Cross and Blue Shield of Alabama.

Health Maintenance Organization   A **health maintenance organiza-tion (HMO)** is a prepaid medical expense plan that provides a comprehensive set of health services and benefits to policyholders for a prepaid monthly fee. Rather than employees paying for health care services as they are administered, the HMO provides these services. It employs its own physicians and health care specialists on a salaried basis and often owns its hospitals and clinical facilities. Preventive as well as corrective medical care are emphasized as methods of minimizing health care costs.

Among the larger HMOs are Kaiser Permanente of California, Oregon, and Hawaii; the Health Insurance Plan of New York; and the Group Health Coopera-tive of Seattle. Federal law requires employers to offer such plans to employees as an alternative to a group insurance plan in areas where HMOs are available.

Preferred Provider Organization   The preferred provider organization, known as a PPO, is a relatively new source of health care coverage. The PPO organizer negotiates reduced prices from hospitals and physicians, and then offers their package to employers. Employers can pick from the list of approved health care providers, and their employees enjoy lower premiums than under conventional plans. For example, the advertisement in Figure 22.6 indicates that Blue Cross's Preferred Care plan in Alabama offers employees the choice of over 5,000 physicians and hospitals across the state.

health maintenance organization (HMO)
Prepaid medical expense plan that provides a comprehensive set of health services.

Types of Health Insurance

Sickness or accidents can prove disastrous to both the individual and the employer. Hospital costs have soared during the past 15 years to the point where a typical one-week hospital stay now costs almost $4,900.[14] Such fees escalate rapidly in instances where special facilities, such as intensive care, are required. In addition, the services of physicians and other medical specialists, coupled with expensive drugs and medication and sophisticated medical equipment, frequently result in staggering expenses.

For most households, the means of coping with this risk is securing health insurance coverage. Five major types of health insurance are available: hospitalization insurance, surgical and medical payments insurance, major medical insurance, dental insurance, and disability income insurance.

hospitalization insurance
Health insurance designed to pay for most hospital costs.

Hospitalization Insurance   Most of the costs of a hospital stay are paid for by **hospitalization insurance**. It pays the major portion of such expenses as room fees, operating room charges, and the cost of drugs and services required while the insured is in a hospital. Many hospitalization plans include a deductible provision that requires the insured to pay an initial amount; others pay a certain percentage of the total bill — typically 80 percent. Blue Cross is an example of a hospitalization plan.

surgical and medical payments insurance
Health insurance designed to pay the costs of surgery, fees of medical specialists, and physicians' care in the hospital and during recovery.

Surgical and Medical Payments Insurance   The costs of surgery, the fees of medical specialists such as anesthesiologists, and physician care in the hospital and during recovery are paid for by **surgical and medical payments insurance**. Blue Shield provides more surgical and medical payments plans than any other insurer. The typical plan specifies maximum limits for each surgical procedure covered. For instance, a policy may pay a maximum of $500 for a tonsillectomy.

major medical insurance
Insurance that protects the insured against catastrophic financial losses by covering expenses that exceed the coverage limits of basic policies.

Major Medical Insurance   Insured persons suffering a major injury or a prolonged illness may learn that their hospitalization and surgical and medical payments insurance plans typically have maximum coverage limits, normally $25,000. **Major medical insurance** is designed to protect the insured against catastrophic financial losses by covering expenses that exceed the coverage limits of the two basic medical insurance plans. Benefits typically amount to 80 percent of medical expenses up to a maximum of $250,000 — and sometimes as high as $1 million. Over 163 million Americans are currently covered by major medical insurance plans.

dental insurance
Insurance designed to pay a specified percentage of dental expenses.

Dental Insurance   One of the more recent forms of health insurance, **dental insurance**, is designed to pay a specified percentage of the insured's expenses for dental work. This type of health insurance is now frequently offered as an employee fringe benefit, and 46 percent of all Americans are currently covered by such a plan. As noted in the advertisement in Figure 22.7, Delta is the largest dental insurance plan. In order to minimize insurance premiums, many dental policies exclude such relatively expensive procedures as orthodontic care and bridgework, unless required as a result of an accident.

disability income insurance
Health insurance designed to protect against loss of income while disabled as a result of accident or illness.

Disability Income Insurance   With **disability income insurance**, the insured is protected from loss of income while disabled as a result of an accident or illness. Although this type of insurance is frequently provided as part of

Figure 22.7   Dental Insurance: An Important Aspect of Health Coverage

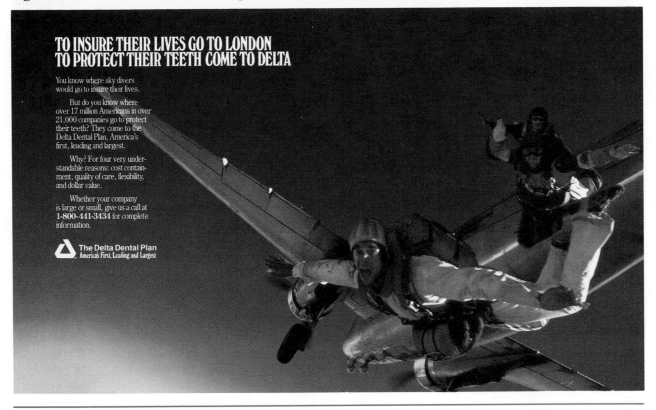

Source: Courtesy of Delta Dental Plans Association.

an employee fringe benefit program, it can also be purchased on an individual basis. After a specified waiting period, the disabled worker receives weekly or monthly payments.

Life Insurance

Life insurance is different from all the other types of insurance coverage described in this chapter. It deals with a risk that is certain — death. The only uncertainty is when it will occur. Life insurance is a common fringe benefit in most firms because its purchase provides financial protection for the family of the policyholder and, in some instances, an additional source of retirement income for employees and their families. An immediate estate is created by the purchase of a life insurance policy. Because the need for financial security is great in most households, some 154 million people — two of every three U.S. citizens — are covered by life insurance. The estimated average amount of life insurance coverage per family is $81,200.

What Is a Life Worth?   IBM Vice-President Don Estridge was killed in a Delta crash in 1985. Three years later, a federal jury in New York concluded his life was worth $7,975,000. The jury based its award on how much the man responsible for IBM's personal computer would have earned over his lifetime.[15] The Estridge case raises the complex question of how much a life is worth. This issue is directly related to how much life insurance one should carry.

Numerous methods have been devised to calculate this figure. For example, the government often uses cost-benefit analysis to determine if new regulation is justified. The cost of implementing a new regulation might be compared with the number of lives the rule would save multiplied by the presumed value of such lives. As a result, various government agencies have set values on a human life. These figures vary widely. The Department of Transportation and the Federal Aviation Administration say the figure is $1 million. The Consumer Product Safety Commission says it is $2 million. The Occupational Safety and Health Administration values human life between $2 million and $5 million. The Environmental Protection Agency has a still broader range, from $475,000 to $8.3 million.[16]

With these values in mind, it is easy to see that the average family has too little insurance to provide true financial security. While life insurance experts recommend that the average adult with family responsibility purchase insurance coverage amounting to a minimum of four to five times his or her annual salary, most people have no more than two years' protection.

Group or Individual Insurance   Life insurance policies can be purchased on an individual basis for almost any amount. Unlike property and casualty insurance, the life insurance purchases are limited only by the amount of premiums people can afford to pay, provided that purchasers qualify medically.

Most businesses purchase employee life insurance on a group basis as a company fringe benefit. Employees may be required to contribute a portion of the costs of the insurance, or the employer may pay the total cost. Company-paid premiums for over $50,000 of group life insurance must be reported as income by employees. **Group life insurance** for company employees is typically written under a single master policy, and covered employees are not normally required to undergo medical examinations. Because selling costs and administrative expenses are much lower for group insurance, this type is usually much cheaper than individual insurance.

Key Executive Insurance   The death of a sole proprietor, partner, or a key executive in a larger organization is likely to result in financial losses to the organization. **Key executive insurance** is life insurance designed to reimburse the organization for the loss of the services of an important executive and to cover the expenses of securing a qualified replacement. Such insurance may prevent the liquidation of a sole proprietorship upon the death of its owner. Although a partnership is automatically dissolved upon the death of a general partner, key executive insurance may enable the surviving partners to purchase the deceased's interest in the firm. In the case of larger organizations, key executive insurance may lessen the reduction in earning power that might result following the death of a senior executive.

The Mortality Table

The **mortality table**, discussed earlier in the chapter, is based on past experience with large numbers of policyholders. It is used to predict the number of people in each age category who will die in a given year. Once this is known, the premiums for a life insurance policy can be calculated to provide sufficient

group life insurance
Life insurance for company employees; typically written under a single master policy.

key executive insurance
Life insurance designed to compensate the organization for loss of an important executive.

mortality table
Table used to predict the number of persons in each age category who will die in a given year.

income to pay death benefits, company operating expenses, and profits (if the company is a stock company).

For example, insurance premiums for a 30-year-old black male are usually greater than for a 20-year-old black male because the number of deaths per thousand increases from 1.89 to 3.61. As the age of the insured increases, the length of expected life decreases and life insurance premiums rise.

Types of Life Insurance

The three major types of life insurance are term, whole life, and endowment. A company can choose one type or a combination of them as part of its total fringe benefit package for its employees.

In most instances, firms will provide their employees with group life insurance coverage — either free or at discount rates — in the form of **term insurance**. This type of life insurance provides protection for the individual for a specified period of years, but it has no value at the end of that period. It is "pure" insurance with no savings features. Some term policies give policyholders the right to convert to whole life insurance at a higher rate should they leave the company. Individual purchases of term insurance are most often purchased by young married couples who want protection in the early years of marriage against the possibility of an early death of one partner. Term insurance offers low-cost protection for the one or two decades before the family can develop financial security through savings and investments.

In some instances, term policies are written to provide reduced amounts of protection over the life of the policy. This type, called *decreasing term insurance,* is often appropriate for young families seeking large amounts of low-cost insurance protection for a few years and gradually reducing the amount of protection as the financial assets of the household grow and as the working members of the household are promoted to higher-paying positions.

A special form of term insurance, **credit life insurance**, is often purchased by persons buying a home or other major item. It repays the balance owed on these items if the policyholder dies, thereby protecting both the family and the lender. Credit life insurance decreases in value as the loan is repaid. In a recent year, $234 billion of credit life insurance was in force.

Whole life insurance is a combination of protection and savings. It provides protection for the individual, who pays premiums throughout a lifetime, and also builds up a cash surrender value in the policy. This **cash surrender value** is the savings portion of a life insurance policy; it can be used as collateral for a low-interest loan from the insurance company. Or it will be paid to the policyholder if the policy is canceled.

A variation of whole life insurance is *limited-payment life insurance,* for which the policyholder pays all premiums within a designated period, such as 20 to 30 years.

An **endowment policy** places more emphasis on savings than do whole life policies. The purchaser of an endowment policy gets coverage for a specific period, usually 20 years or until the age of 65. After this period, the face value of the policy is refunded to the policyholder. Endowment insurance is really forced savings.

Hybrid Forms of Life Insurance   In recent years, insurance companies have attempted to meet the needs of policyholders by developing several hybrid forms of insurance, combining characteristics of both term and whole-life poli-

term insurance
Insurance coverage protecting the individual for a specified period of years; it has no value at the end of that period.

credit life insurance
Term insurance that repays the balance owed on a house or other major purchase if the policyholder dies.

whole life insurance
Insurance providing both protection and savings for the policyholder.

cash surrender value
The savings portion of a life insurance policy.

endowment policy
Insurance that provides coverage for a specified period, after which the face value is refunded to the policyholder.

variable life insurance
Hybrid form of whole life insurance in which policyholders pay premium supplements that are invested by the insurance company.

cies. Two of the most popular new forms are variable life insurance and universal life insurance.

Variable life insurance gives policyholders the combination of a regular whole-life policy with an investment that might increase the death benefit paid to their beneficiaries. Like other types of insurance, premium payments are fixed in amount and payment dates. However, the variable life insurance policyholder earmarks a certain amount of these premium dollars for investment in a stock, bond, or money-market mutual fund. The cash value and death benefit of the policy fluctuate, depending on the yields generated by these funds. However, the policy guarantees that the death benefit will not fall below a specified minimum.

universal life insurance
Hybrid form of life insurance combining term insurance with a tax-deferred savings account.

Universal life insurance combines term insurance with a tax-deferred savings account that earns interest at bond-market rates. When the policyholder dies, the base policy amount and the accumulated earnings are paid to beneficiaries. The term *universal life* refers to the flexibility of such policies, which permit policyholders to adjust their premium payments — with limits — to meet different household needs and resources at different stages of the family life cycle. The accumulated earnings may be withdrawn by the policyholder, used to pay premiums, or left with the insurance company to generate additional earnings. The only provision is that sufficient accumulated earnings be available to meet the cost of insurance protection. This type of insurance also gives policyholders the option of increasing or reducing the amount of term insurance coverage. Unlike variable life insurance, universal life insurance policies do not have guaranteed minimum death benefits.

Which type of life insurance policy is best? Individuals must study their personal situation with the aid of a qualified insurance agent. Since most agents work on a commission basis, it is important for consumers to understand the various types of insurance and what their particular needs are. In addition to determining the appropriate type of life insurance, individuals must also decide upon both the amount and the source of such insurance coverage. Factors such as costs, the insured's age, family responsibilities, health, and future expectations must be considered. Each person must determine the proper balance between savings and protection that is best for the household. Table 22.2 shows a cost comparison of different types of life insurance policies for males offered by Nationwide Insurance.

Table 22.2   Nationwide's Premium Rates per $1,000 of Life Insurance Based on a $50,000 Policy (Nonsmoker Classification)

Male Age at Issue	Annual Premium		
	Whole Life	Variable Life	Annual Renewable Term
18	$ 9.05[1]	$ 5.28	$3.08
20	10.00	5.28	3.08
25	11.26	5.04[2]	2.72[4]
30	13.07	5.76	2.72
40	19.58	7.68	3.43
50	30.82	11.28[3]	6.48

[1]Whole life rates are based on a participating policy using male rates.
[2]Nonsmoker rates are not available until age 21.
[3]These rates reflect the minimum to keep the policy in force. In some cases, their minimum premium might not be enough to keep the policy in force for the insured's lifetime.
[4]These are first-year premiums only. The insurance goes up each year.

Source: Nationwide Insurance.

Summary of Learning Goals

1. Define *risk* and distinguish between the two types of risk faced by individuals and businesses. Risk is part of the daily life of both the individual and the business firm. It comes in different forms: property damage, dishonesty, death, injury to employees or customers, sickness, lawsuits, and nonpayment of debts. The two types of risks are speculative risk, in which the firm or individual has the chance of either a profit or a loss, and pure risk, which involves only the chance of loss.

2. Explain each of the four methods of dealing with risk. Once the presence of risk has been acknowledged, the manager has four methods available for dealing with it. Some firms may choose to avoid risk entirely; others cannot completely avoid risk, but can reduce much of the risk through risk-reduction programs designed to eliminate hazards, detect problems, and encourage employees to practice safe work procedures. Other firms may choose to self-insure by creating self-insurance funds. For many organizations and individuals, the method of dealing with risk is to shift the risk to insurance companies.

3. Analyze the law of large numbers and explain how it makes insurance possible. Insurance is based on the concepts of insurable interest, insurable risks, and the law of large numbers. Insurance companies are professional risk takers that operate by charging premiums large enough to repay insurance claims and cover operating expenses. The law of large numbers is based upon statistical probability and is used to predict the likelihood of the occurrence of perils — the number of fires, automobile accidents, earthquakes, or deaths that will occur in a given year.

4. Distinguish between public and private insurance companies and identify types of insurance provided by public insurance companies. Public insurance companies are government agencies established at the state or federal level to provide specialized insurance protection for individuals and organizations. They provide protection in such areas as unemployment insurance (job loss), workers' compensation (work-related injuries), pension plans (social security), and specialized programs ranging from flood insurance to depositor protection at commercial banks and savings and loan associations. The two basic types of private insurance companies are profit-seeking stock insurance companies and nonprofit mutual insurance companies, which are primarily involved in the life insurance field.

5. Identify the types of property and liability insurance and describe their importance to a business. Insurance can be divided into three categories: property and liability insurance, health insurance, and life insurance. Property and liability insurance provides protection against fire losses; loss of income due to fires or other property damage (business interruption insurance); automobile accident losses; and burglary, robbery, and theft losses. Other types of property and liability insurance include marine insurance; fidelity, surety, title, and credit insurance; and public liability insurance.

6. Outline the various types of health insurance. Health insurance may be provided by a number of sources: individual policies, group insurance programs offered to employees as fringe benefits, or by federal or state governments. The five major types are (1) hospitalization insurance; (2) surgical and medical payments insurance; (3) major medical insurance; (4) dental insurance; and (5) disability income insurance.

7. Explain each of the types of life insurance a firm might offer its employees. Life insurance is a common part of most employee fringe benefit programs. In addition, many organizations purchase key executive insurance to reimburse the organization for the loss of the services of an important executive and to cover the expenses involved in acquiring and training a replacement. Although life insurance can be purchased by individuals, employers who purchase on a group basis can usually secure coverage at lower rates. Three basic types of life insurance are available. Term insurance provides protection for a specific period. Whole life insurance provides a combination of protection and savings for the policyholder, who pays premiums throughout a lifetime or for a designated period. Endowment life insurance policies are a type of forced savings; they provide protection for a specified period and then return the face value of the policy to the policyholder. Two hybrid forms containing investment components are variable life and universal life insurance.

Each type of life insurance has merits and shortcomings. The choice of the best type or types must be made by the individual, who should consider factors such as age, family responsibilities, personal health, and future job expectations.

Key Terms

risk

speculative risk

pure risk

self-insurance fund

insurance

insurable interest

insurable risk

law of large numbers

law of adverse selection

public insurance company

unemployment insurance

workers' compensation insurance

Old-Age, Survivors, Disability, and Health Insurance (OASDHI)

Medicare

stock insurance company

mutual insurance company

fire insurance

coinsurance clause

business interruption insurance

contingent business interruption insurance

automobile insurance

no-fault insurance

burglary insurance

robbery insurance

theft insurance

ocean marine insurance

inland marine insurance

fidelity bond

surety bond

title insurance

credit insurance

liability insurance

product liability insurance

health insurance

health maintenance organization (HMO)

hospitalization insurance

surgical and medical payments insurance

major medical insurance

dental insurance

disability income insurance

group life insurance

key executive insurance

mortality table

term insurance

credit life insurance

whole life insurance

cash surrender value

endowment policy

variable life insurance

universal life insurance

Review Questions _____

1. Differentiate between speculative risk and pure risk.

2. Identify and give an example of each of the four methods of dealing with risk.

3. Explain the concept of self-insurance as it relates to each type of insurance. Cite an example of a firm that might be a candidate for self-insurance for each general category of insurance.

4. Outline the three basic principles of insurance. What requirements are necessary for an insurable risk?

5. Demonstrate how the law of adverse selection could affect various types of insurance.

6. Explain how each type of property and liability insurance is used in the operation of a business.

7. What are the major types of health insurance? Compare HMOs and PPOs to traditional health coverage.

8. How is life insurance different from other types of insurances? Identify and describe the four basic types of life insurance.

9. Why does group insurance cost less than individual insurance?

10. Explain the reasons for the rate differences shown in Table 22.2.

Discussion Questions _____

1. Raincheque is an insurance policy that is sold through travel agents. This unique policy insures against rainfall during vacations in the United States, Bermuda, Canada, Mexico, and the Caribbean. Premiums depend on the probability of rainfall and are set as a percentage of the expenses covered. If it rains between 9 a.m. and 5 p.m. on more than half of the days, Raincheque pays for the entire vacation. Rates range from 3 percent for Orlando and Acapulco to 4 percent in Hilton Head or Freeport, Bahamas, to 5 percent in Bermuda up to 8 percent in San Juan. Relate the Raincheque policy to the basic requirements for an insurable risk.

2. Celebrities have often been featured in commercials promoting guaranteed acceptance life insurance and supplemental health care policies targeted at the elderly. In 1988, Art Linkletter's commercial for National Home Life Assurance was ordered off the air in Washington state. Later, other states began to consider restraints on such advertising. Officials and consumer critics argue celebrities are trusted by many elderly people and many of these advertisements are misleading. Dick Marquardt, Washington's insurance commissioner, put it this way: "When the stars come out, it's a good idea to stay awake and hang on to your wallet." Argue either the pro or con viewpoint on such regulation.

3. Should insurance companies be prohibited from testing insurance applicants for AIDS? Why or why not?

4. Insurance companies typically charge higher automobile insurance rates for people under 25 than they do for older drivers. Do you think this is a fair policy? Explain. Can you think of any situations in which younger people receive more favorable insurance rates than older ones?

5. The United States faced an insurance crisis in 1985–86 when liability rates for firms and municipalities rose to unprecedented levels. Many organizations were unable to obtain liability insurance at any price. For example, the city of Lafayette, California, was refused coverage by 118 insurers. Self-insurance became an increasingly popular option. While rates dropped 40 percent by 1988, the self-insurance trend was by now well-established.

The insurance companies blamed high jury awards for the surge in premiums. It was also argued that price cutting had led to losses for the insurance companies. Their response was to raise prices and reduce coverage. But the attorney generals of 19 states later filed suit against 32 insurance companies alleging conspiracy to restrain competition and control prices during this period. Discuss the continuing effects of the insurance crisis and resulting legal cases.

Case

A. H. Robins Co.

Every profit-seeking business faces risk as it attempts to achieve a number of different objectives. Foremost among these goals is *profitability,* for profits ensure sufficient gains to provide a return for the firm's owner(s) and the means to continue the business. Other objectives may focus on growth, employee welfare, efficiency, and multinational expansion. But a variety of societal goals are always present. After all, in a very real sense society allows businesses to operate only so long as they satisfy certain obligations to the members of society. These societal commitments can be met in different ways: by providing rewarding, safe places to work for employees, by encouraging resource conservation, and by creating marketing goods and services aimed at serving the needs of consumers.

Drug manufacturers have the potential to achieve societal objectives together with their pursuit of sales, growth, and profitability. The possibility of a breakthrough leading to cures for such devastating diseases as cancer, AIDS, and even the common cold, is always present as these firms search for new products to provide for human needs. However, the process of discovering new drugs, testing them, and ultimately bringing them to market is complex and time-consuming, involving enormous resources and years of dedicated work. For one U.S. drug company, this process proved to be greatly rewarding in the case of one product, but financially destructive in the case of another.

In the United States, it usually takes from eight to ten years for a company to bring a new prescription drug from development to sale on the market. During that time, researchers face a universe of possibilities, but limited resources. They develop hundreds or even thousands of similar chemical compounds in their search for the desired product. Every possibility must be tested and evaluated, since any one might lead researchers in new directions.

Richmond, Virginia–based A. H. Robins Company, Inc., maker of such well-known products as Robitussin

cough syrup, Dimetapp cold and allergy medicine, and Chap Stick lip balm, views the world as a vast resource from which to locate new products. Company officials maintain files on research reports and patent applications filed by dozens of companies throughout the world to keep them aware of product breakthroughs that might assist Robins researchers in their own efforts. Also, Robins managers frequently license promising foreign products for sale in the United States. But to sign such licensing agreements with laboratories in other countries, Robins must be aware of current research in firms from Japan to the United Kingdom. Robins scientists and managers are actively involved in the international scientific community and they know the experts in every relevant field, from fermentation techniques to cancer chemotherapy.

Over a decade ago, Robins new-product specialists became interested in a compound developed in France by Laboratoires Lagrange. Called metoclopramide hydrochloride, its potential remained unknown for years following its development. But Robins officials believed that it offered exciting possibilities for the treatment of gastrointestinal disorders, and the company licensed the compound from Lagrange.

Then the long process of testing the drug began. Early tests were devoted to demonstrating the product's safety and effectiveness and its appropriate dosage. Researchers also needed to identify possible side effects of the drug. Exciting new possible applications for the drug were frequently discovered during the testing phase. Robins managers were particularly excited to learn that *Reglan,* the brand name they decided to use for the compound, had the potential to fill a void in the medical field. It appeared to be effective in alleviating gastrointestinal symptoms resulting from a variety of complaints, but more importantly, from cancer chemotherapy.

The final stage of testing involved clinical trials, consisting of actual administration of the drug to patients. Numerous trials were conducted in medical centers across the United States. Results such as the following were obtained:

At St. Luke's Hospital in New York City, doctors used Reglan as part of the treatment of illnesses involving

Notes: Paul M. Barrett, "Judge Clears Robins Restructuring Plan: Move May Pave Way for Firm's Takeover," *The Wall Street Journal,* July 27, 1988, p. 33; "Thousands Still Await Payment from Robins," *USA Today,* August 25, 1988, p. 3A; and "The Search," a video produced by A. H. Robins Company, Inc.

the stomach and intestines. Patients who complained of nausea, pain, and vomiting after eating were given the drug to relieve those symptoms. Reglan apparently worked by contracting and relaxing different parts of the stomach, allowing food to pass through.

At the Headache Research Foundation at the Faulkner Hospital in Boston, doctors investigated Reglan for treating nausea and vomiting caused by severe migraine headaches. Again, the drug provided positive benefits for the patients who took it.

At Brotman Medical Center in the Los Angeles suburb of Culver City, researchers used Reglan to treat the nausea that often accompanies cancer chemotherapy. Many anticancer agents have had effects severe enough to force some patients to prematurely stop treatment. In this study, no patients dropped out of treatment due to gastrointestinal side effects. Doctors hoped that these results would lead to a willingness of more patients to see their doctors soon, give patients an increased likelihood of being able to complete their treatment, and the end result would be an improvement in their survival and cure rates.

After nearly nine years of testing, Reglan was finally approved for sales in the United States by the U.S. Food and Drug Administration. The next challenge for Robins management involved marketing: Doctors had to be educated in how to use the drug. Booklets published by Robins reviewing digestive disorders and how they could be treated were distributed to physicians. Informative ads were placed in prominent medical journals. In addition, Robins sponsored nationwide symposia to explain the drug's applications in gastrointestinal disorders to the physicians who would be prescribing Reglan on a daily basis. A full profile of the drug, including possible side effects, was communicated to physicians throughout the nation.

Finally, the drug was manufactured to exacting standards. Robins took pride in producing a drug that could alleviate the pain and suffering of patients everywhere. Even today, Reglan ranks among the top 50 most frequently prescribed drugs in the United States.

But for Robins, the dramatic success of Reglan could not offset financial ruin caused by another product. As recently as 1987, Robins drug products generated worldwide sales of almost $900 million. But by then the firm had already sought protection under the federal bankruptcy laws as a result of mounting lawsuits resulting from the Robins Dalkon Shield. First marketed in 1971, the shield, an intrauterine birth control device, had been taken off the market in 1974 after a growing number of women complained of pelvic infections, sterility, and miscarriages. The number of lawsuits brought by women who suffered injuries from using the Robins IUD ultimately grew to almost 200,000. The company filed for bankruptcy in 1985, but continued to operate until 1988. That year, the firm decided to accept a merger offer from American Home Products Corporation. The merger was approved by the courts following an agreement that American Home Products Corporation set up a $2.5 billion trust for use in compensating persons injured by using the shield.

Questions

1. Every organization faces two types of risk. Identify each type and explain how they apply to events described in the case.

2. Identify the four methods of dealing with risk and illustrate how each could be used by a firm such as A. H. Robins.

3. Which of the three major types of insurance is most relevant to A. H. Robins' unfortunate experiences with the Dalkon Shield? Why do some companies decide to "go naked" rather than purchasing this type of insurance protection?

4. If a product such as the Dalkon Shield is approved for use by a government regulatory agency, should its manufacturer be held responsible for flaws or side effects not known at the time of manufacture?

Careers in Business

All businesses and many individuals require financial services. Thus, the area of finance is full of career opportunities that are not only exciting and challenging, but also provide excellent advancement possibilities.

Specific jobs in banking, finance, investments, and insurance include bank manager, bank operations officer, credit manager, securities sales worker, actuary, underwriter, claims representative, and insurance agent and broker.

The Bureau of Labor Statistics forecasts that job opportunities for bank officers and managers will grow faster than the average for all occupations and that opportunities for insurance agents and brokers will grow about as fast as the average. Job opportunities will grow much faster than average for securities and sales specialists.

Bank Manager

Bank managers administer the various activities of their units. Currently, more than 424,000 bank officers and managers are employed in the United States.

Job Description.   Bank managers are part of the executive level of the rapidly changing banking industry. They must be familiar with all banking policies, procedures, and practices, and they must keep up with the many changes that occur. Bankers must also be knowledgeable about the legal framework of their industry. The American Bankers Association offers people in the banking industry courses to help keep them current.

Career Path.   College-educated candidates usually begin in a management training program. This usually involves rotating among the various bank departments to familiarize candidates with all aspects of banking. Successful performance in a junior-level position may lead to an appointment as a bank officer or manager.

Salary.   In large banks, branch managers earn from $17,100 to $52,000, depending on the size of the branch and assets of the bank. In smaller banks, the salaries are several thousand dollars less. Managers in other bank departments earn a variety of salaries. Mortgage loan managers in small banks make an average of $36,000, for example.

Bank Operations Officer

The operations officer directs the bank's daily work flow. In smaller banks, the operations officer is the branch manager. In large banks, the operations officer handles the teller line and backroom activities and reports to the branch manager.

Job Description.   The operations officer must be thoroughly trained in bank practices and procedures in order to make decisions about daily work assignments.

Career Path.   Management trainee positions are available in the banking industry. Successful completion of such a program can lead to appointment to operations officer, a middle-management position in most banks. Effective performance at this level can lead to a senior-management appointment.

Salary.   Once the person becomes an operations officer, the salary is usually a function of the bank's size. Trainee pay ranges from $13,200 to $22,800 annually; with an MBA, trainee pay increases to $22,800 to $42,000.

Credit Manager

Credit managers play a key role on the firm's financial team because they determine whether to grant credit to customers. These people manage the firm's credit function.

Job Description.   Credit managers set overall credit policy and review the creditworthiness of customers, both businesses and individuals. They also administer the debt-collection process.

Career Path.   Credit managers usually begin as trainees in the credit department. Experienced personnel may advance to management positions in the department. Credit managers are exposed to the entire organization and may eventually reach top management.

Salary.   Depending on the industry, credit managers average $29,000 to $34,000. For larger organizations, salaries range up to $55,000.

Securities Sales Representative

Securities sales workers, also known as registered representatives, account executives, or brokers, link investors to the securities industry. Through securities salespeople, investors buy and sell stocks, bonds, shares in mutual funds, or other financial products. In a recent year, more than 195,000 securities and financial salespeople were employed in the United States.

Job Description. Securities sales representatives transmit customer orders to buy and sell securities to the market in which the trade occurs. They also offer clients a range of financial counseling services including advice on the purchase of mutual funds, annuities, life insurance, and other investments.

Career Path. Before being allowed to work with clients, securities sales reps must pass a series of examinations given by the state, the Securities and Exchange Commission, the exchange on which they will trade, and often the brokerage firm for which they will work. On-the-job training is provided to help workers pass these tests. Once fully qualified, beginning securities sales reps concentrate on building their client contacts. As they gain experience, the number and size of the accounts they handle usually increase. Some experienced reps also take on managerial duties and supervise other salespeople.

Salary. While they are being trained, beginning securities salespeople earn minimal salaries ranging between $12,000 and $16,800 annually. Experienced workers depend on commissions rather than salary. In a recent year, an average securities sales rep earned $64,000, while workers servicing institutional accounts earned $150,000.

Actuary

Actuaries provide the statistical information needed by the insurance industry.

Job Description. Actuaries gather the data needed to determine the risk of losses of various job types and perform the statistical analyses that make such data usable to the industry. They calculate the probability that people will die during the term of their life insurance policy, for example, and calculate the premium necessary for the company to profitably insure them. Some actuaries work for consulting firms or pension funds rather than insurance companies.

Career Path. Advancement in the actuarial industry depends on experience and successfully passing a series of exams given by the actuarial societies. Depending on the society, which are broken down by specialty, there are either nine or ten exams to pass, which usually take five to ten years to complete.

Salary. Average starting salaries for those not having taken their actuary exams were $19,000 to $24,000 recently. Those who had taken one exam aver-

aged $21,000 to $25,000. Associate actuaries having certificates from the Society of Actuaries earned from $32,000 to $45,000, and Fellows of the Society averaged from $44,000 to $55,000 a year.

Underwriter

Underwriters analyze the risks to which insurance applicants are exposed. In a recent year, there were 78,000 underwriters in the United States. Faster than average employment growth is expected through the year 2000.

Job Description. Underwriters use the information provided by applicants for insurance, in conjunction with statistics provided by actuaries and other specialists, to assess the risk to which the applicant is exposed. They use this information to set the terms of the policy, premiums, and so forth. The underwriter makes sure the company does not assume too much risk so it loses money but also remains competitive with other insurance firms by not turning down too many policies.

Career Path. New underwriters are generally supervised closely and required to take further courses in underwriting. They first work with routine applications and move to more demanding applications as their ability grows. This career ladder extends to supervisory positions or to top management.

Salary. In a recent year, the median salary for underwriters ranged between $21,300 and $23,600, depending on their area of insurance. Supervisors' median salaries ranged between $33,700 and $35,200.

Claims Representative

Claims representatives or claims adjusters assess insurance claims and determine how much the applicant will be paid. They study all available evidence about a loss situation and determine the insurance company's liability. Currently, about 70,000 people work as claims representatives throughout the United States.

Job Description. Most claims representatives are in property and liability insurance and tend to fall into two classes. Claims adjustors examine physical evidence of loss and witness testimony. Claims examiners investigate questionable claims and work in the field, interviewing experts and witnesses. Both groups determine the validity of a claim, whether the insurance company is liable, and how much of the loss is covered.

Career Path. Beginning claims representatives are supervised by senior-level personnel and are usually limited to small claims. As the person gains experience, he or she acquires responsibility for larger claims. Supervisory positions in the claims department head this career.

Salary.   In a recent year, the median salary of claims' representatives ranged from $19,200 to $22,500, depending on their area of insurance. The median salary of supervisors ranged between $32,300 and $41,300.

Insurance Agent/Insurance Broker

It is important to differentiate between insurance agents and brokers. An insurance agent sells insurance for a specific company. A broker is self-employed and represents several companies. Some agents and brokers specialize in certain types of insurance; others market a full line of insurance products. Recent employment figures show that more than 463,000 insurance agents and brokers are employed in the United States.

Job Description.   Both agents and brokers evaluate the financial needs of their clients and select insurance coverage that meets their needs. Insurance agents and brokers also answer questions about various types of coverage, assist clients when claims are filed, and act as liaison between the insured and the insurance company.

Career Path.   Newly hired agents typically undergo an extensive home-office training program. Afterward, they spend most of their early career establishing a clientele base. Insurance brokers undergo a similar process. Some successful agents advance to sales management positions or to head a local or regional office.

The insurance industry offers various professional certification programs. Completion of such programs is often an important stepping-stone in an insurance career.

Salary.   Agents and brokers work on a commission basis. This provides maximum incentive for effective sales performance. In a recent year, the median starting salary was $16,800. The median income for life insurance agents and brokers with five to nine years of experience was $47,000. Some successful agents and brokers earn more than $100,000 a year.

Chapter 23
Business,
Government, and
the Legal System

Chapter 24
Your Career in
Business

Additional Dimensions

Career Profile: Tony Russo

When Gainey Transportation Services, Inc., started five years ago, it had five trucks. The Grand Rapids, Michigan-based company now has 140 trucks and plans to add another 50. It also now serves major customers including Steelcase, Hayworth, Herman Miller, and White Consolidated Industries.

Parallel with Gainey's growth has been the growth of the marketing department. When Tony Russo, 27, started at Gainey, there was no marketing department. He has created all the marketing positions he's held at Gainey, including his current one—vice-president in charge of marketing.

Russo hadn't always planned to go into marketing; in fact, he wasn't even planning on college. When Russo graduated from high school, he took a job with the company his father worked for, where he started at $10 an hour as an hourly worker. During his first year, the company laid off a number of employees, including Russo.

He then turned to odd jobs and temporary positions, until he was robbed one day while making a delivery. This changed his direction. "I just decided it was ridiculous to be living the way I was, and I swallowed my pride and moved back home," he says.

It turned out to be a good move for Russo. When he moved in, he also decided to go back to school. "By going to school, Tony dis-covered he had the talent to use his head, to think, and to meet people and communicate well with them," said David Steenstra, one of Russo's professors at Davenport Business College. "He developed confidence in himself."

He did this in part through his participation in the school chapter of the Distributive Education Club of America, which organizes competitions that give students real-life business experience through tests and role playing. "In DECA, as vice-president of the chapter, I really learned a lot about how to present myself, how to motivate people and how to be involved," says Russo. "That really contributed to my personal growth and to my understanding of business."

After he graduated from Davenport, Russo started as a field dispatcher for a different Grand Rapids-based trucking company, then took a similar job with Capital Express Company. Then he met Harvey Gainey, the head of Gainey Transportation, who asked him to join the then-fledgling firm.

"Mr. Gainey was offering me less money, and no benefits, but tremendous potential for advancement," he says. "I decided I had to take a chance some time, so I went for it."

Russo joined the company as a dispatcher in January 1986 and the same year became the company's first sales representative. In 1987, as Gainey grew from a $3.2 million company to a $10.7 million company, Russo created the position of director of marketing, in charge of two salespeople. For 1989, Russo hired another sales rep and projected $22 million in sales for the company. Recently, the company hired a director of marketing, and Russo took his current position as vice-president in charge of marketing.

His responsibilities include recruiting and training new sales representatives, monitoring and evaluating the performance of the sales department, anticipating and responding to changes in the market, servicing national accounts, and developing the company's marketing plan.

His job also involves creating the company's image. "We've emphasized high service, because we feel service is the most important thing to our customers and giving them the best price is not. We want to be the Cadillac of carriers."

For Russo, developing Gainey into the Cadillac of carriers requires a lot of extra effort. He usually spends 12 to 15 weeks on the road each year. Despite this travel, he is back in school, progressing toward a bachelor's degree in business administration, with minors in communications and marketing.

Photo source: Courtesy of Tony Russo.

23

Business, Government, and the Legal System

Learning Goals

1. To explain the meaning and sources of law.

2. To describe the nature of business law.

3. To analyze the structure of the judicial system.

4. To explain how government regulates business.

5. To discuss the impact of deregulation.

6. To identify the major components of business law.

7. To outline the current status of bankruptcy law.

8. To differentiate among trademarks, patents, and copyrights.

9. To outline the effects of tax reform legislation.

In 1979, when Butch Koubek and Sam Segretto opened ZAZU Hair Design in suburban Chicago, they had no idea that a few years later they would be paired against haircare giant L'Oreal in Federal District Court. In 1985, the two entrepreneurs began selling shampoo, rinses, and other hair-care items under the ZAZU trademark. The duo's attorney, James Fitzgibbon, described the development of the trademark this way: "They wanted an unusual, memorable name, short and original. Nobody else was using anything like that for hair-care products. It's a wonderful mark."

The next year, Koubek and Segretto decided to launch a national campaign to sell ZAZU hair-care products. They bought 25,000 special bottles to package their products. They discussed an advertising campaign with *Vogue* magazine. In August 1986, a customer told Koubek and Segretto that she had seen their advertisement in *Harper's Bazaar* magazine. When they checked, they discovered the advertisement was for ZAZU by L'Oreal. Koubek and Segretto decided to sue L'Oreal for trademark infringement.

The case was heard in 1987. The attorney for ZAZU Hair Design argued that the salon had been in business for several years and was known outside the immediate area. The attorney used a local newspaper, *The Doings* of Hinsdale, Illinois, to support his claim. The salon had run full-page advertisements

ZAZU Hair Designs / 53 SOUTH WASHINGTON   SUITES 1, 2, 3 / HINSDALE, IL 60521 / (312) 325-8126

that won a Northern Illinois Newspaper Association award. The attorney pointed out that *The Doings* offered ZAZU advertising outside the immediate area because at least 4 percent of its circulation is outside the state of Illinois.

In 1988, Federal Judge Prentice Marshall found in favor of the salon. The judge awarded Koubek and Segretto $1 million to re-establish the value of the ZAZU trademark. The pair was also awarded an additional $1 million for punitive damages and $100,000 for lost compensation. In his ruling, Judge Marshall said: "Plaintiff (ZAZU) was looked upon as a nettlesome fly to be brushed aside despite the fact that it had registered the mark ZAZU in

the very industry that defendant (L'Oreal) intended to enter under that identical name." Judge Marshall also wrote that L'Oreal "regarded the plaintiff as a small-town nuisance. It acted at its peril."

Koubek summed up the partners' view this way: "I felt we were going to win all along. We knew we were right. It renewed my faith in the justice system, that it works for everyone, not just the big guys."[1]

Trademarks are just one part of the legal environment. This chapter explores a wide range of business law concepts and issues.

Photo source: Courtesy of ZAZU Hair Designs.

Chapter Overview

Business must operate within the legal framework of federal, state, and local governments, and business law is playing an increasingly important role in the private enterprise system. Executives are not expected to be attorneys, but they should be aware of the various legal requirements that can affect their management decision making.

Law consists of the standards set by government and society in the form of either legislation or custom. Arising from state and federal constitutions that originally established the forms of government, our complex body of law consists primarily of legislation and legal decisions.

The broad body of principles, regulations, rules, and customs that governs the actions of all members of society, including businesspeople, is derived from several sources. **Common law** refers to the body of law arising out of judicial decisions related to the unwritten law the United States inherited from England. This unwritten law is based on customs and court decisions of early England.

Statutory law, or written law, includes state and federal constitutions, legislative enactments, treaties of the federal government, and ordinances of towns, cities, and other local governments. Statutes must be drawn in a precise and reasonable manner in order to be constitutional (and thus enforceable), but courts are frequently called upon to interpret their intention and meaning. The court rulings often result in statutory laws being expanded, contracted, modified, or even discarded altogether.

No system of law, written or unwritten, is permanent. Laws reflect the beliefs of the people they regulate, and both courts and legislatures are aware of this fact. Laws are constantly being added, repealed, or modified to meet the requirements of society and government.

law
Standards set by government and society in the form of either legislation or custom.

common law
The body of law arising out of judicial decisions related to the unwritten law the United States inherited from England.

statutory law
Written law that includes state and federal constitutions, legislative enactments, treaties of the federal government, and ordinances of towns, cities, and other local governments.

The Nature of Business Law

In a broad sense, all law is business law because all businesses are subject to the entire body of law in the same manner as citizens are. But in a narrower sense, **business law** consists of those aspects of law that most directly and specifically influence and regulate the management of various types of business activity.

business law
Those aspects of law that most directly and specifically influence and regulate management of various types of business activity.

Types of Business Law

The term *business law* includes all law that is of concern to business, although particular areas of legal emphasis vary widely from business to business and from industry to industry. Laws affecting small firms are different from those governing large corporations. The legal interests of the automobile industry, for example, differ from those of real estate developers.

The Internal Revenue Code is an example of a law that has universal application. However, numerous federal laws regulate only one industry, such as oil and gas drilling or television communications. Federal laws regulating only the tobacco industry include the *Federal Cigarette Labeling and Advertising Act* of 1967, which requires written health warnings on cigarette packages, and the *Public Health Cigarette Smoking Act* of 1971, which prohibits tobacco advertis-

Figure 23.1 Example of a Federal Law Affecting a Specific Industry

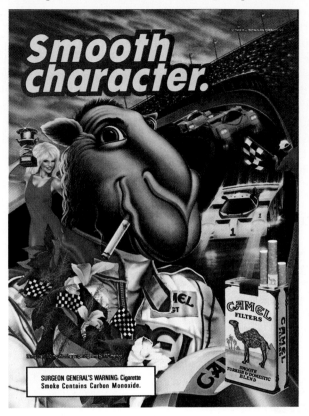

ing on radio and television. Print advertisements for cigarettes, such as the one in Figure 23.1, must include a warning that smoking may pose health risks.

State and local statutes also have varying applications. Some state laws effectively regulate all businesses operating in a particular state, regardless of the size or nature of the enterprise. Workers' compensation laws, which govern payments to workers for injuries incurred on the job, are an example. Other state laws control only certain businesses or business activities: The so-called blue laws, which regulate the extent to which businesses — particularly retailers — can operate on Sundays, are an example of this kind of narrow control.

Many local ordinances also deal with specific business activities. Here are some humorous ordinances:

◆ In Roanoke, Virginia, it is illegal to advertise on tombstones.

◆ Barbers in Waterloo, Nebraska, are not allowed to eat onions between 7 a.m. and 7 p.m.

◆ A Cold Springs, Pennsylvania, ordinance says liquor may not be sold to a married man without the written consent of his wife.

◆ Pharmacists in Trout Creek, Utah, may not sell gunpowder as a headache cure.[2]

The Importance of Business Law

No owner, manager, or employee can conduct any type of business activity without reference to some laws. All business decisions must take into account the legal consequences. Some decisions involve in-depth legal planning and review, while others need only an implied or subconscious reference to the law.

Business decision makers gain experience and expertise in applying legal standards to their decisions in much the same manner as they develop any other management skill: through constant use and refinement. When legality cannot be determined through the experience and judgment of the businessperson, other professionals (such as lawyers, government employees, and elected officials) must be consulted. Generally, the more complex the business objective, the more complex the role of law.

The Court System

judiciary
Branch of government charged with deciding disputes among parties through the application of laws.

The **judiciary**, or court system, is the branch of government charged with deciding disputes among parties through the application of laws. The judiciary is comprised of several types and levels of courts, each with specific jurisdiction. Court systems are organized at the federal, state, and local levels. Administrative agencies also have some limited judicial functions, but these agencies are more properly regarded as belonging to the executive or legislative branches of government. The structures of the state and federal court systems are shown in Figure 23.2.

Trial Courts

trial court
Court of general jurisdiction operating at both the federal and state levels.

At both the federal and state levels, the **trial court** — a court of general jurisdiction — hears a wide range of cases. Unless a case is assigned by law to another court or to an administrative agency, a court of general jurisdiction is empowered to hear it. The majority of cases, both criminal and civil, are heard by these courts. Within the federal system the trial courts are known as United States district courts, and at least one such court exists in each state. In the state court systems, the general jurisdiction courts are known as circuit courts, and in most states there is one for each county. Some states call their general jurisdiction courts by other names, such as superior courts, common pleas courts, or district courts.

The state judiciary systems also have a wide range of courts of lesser or more specific jurisdiction. These courts have limited jurisdiction in that they hear only a certain size or type of case, as set forth by statute or constitution. In most states, decisions of the lesser courts can be appealed to the general jurisdiction courts. Examples of lesser courts are probate courts (where deceased persons' estates are settled) and small claims courts (where people can represent themselves in suits involving small amounts of damage).

Appellate Courts

appellate court
Court that hears appeals from the general trial courts.

Appeals from general trial courts are heard by the **appellate court**. Both the federal and state systems have appellate courts. An appeal usually is filed when the losing party feels that the case was wrongly decided by the judge or jury.

Figure 23.2   The U.S. Judicial System

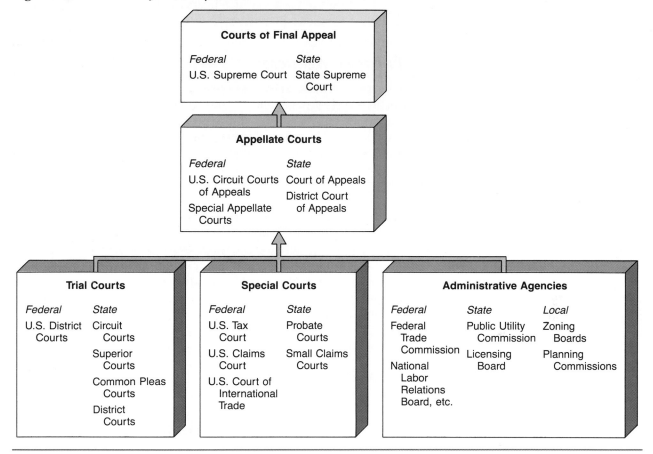

The appeals process allows a higher court to review the case and correct any lower court error complained of by the **appellant**, the party making the appeal. The federal appeals system, together with those of most states, consists of two tiers of courts. The federal courts at the intermediate level are called U.S. circuit courts of appeals, and each such court hears cases from the U.S. district courts of several states. The intermediate level of state appellate courts — if it exists — is known as the court of appeals or the district court of appeals in most states.

Appeals from the U.S. circuit courts of appeals can go to the nation's highest court, the U.S. Supreme Court. Appeals from the state courts of appeal are heard by the highest court in each state, usually called the state supreme court. In states without intermediate courts, the state supreme court hears appeals directly from the trial courts. Parties not satisfied by the verdict of a state supreme court can appeal to the U.S. Supreme Court and may be granted a hearing if grounds for such an appeal exist and if the Supreme Court considers the case significant enough to be heard. In a recent year, the Supreme Court heard 167 of the 5,268 appeals pending before it.[3]

While the great majority of cases are resolved by the system of courts described here, certain highly specialized cases require the expertise of special courts. Such cases are assigned to special courts by constitutional provision or

appellant
Party making an appeal for a higher court to review a case.

statute. Examples of specialized federal courts are the U.S. Tax Court (for tax cases) and the U.S. Court of Claims (which hears claims against the U.S. government itself). Similar specialized courts exist in many of the state court systems.

Administrative Agencies

Administrative agencies, also known as bureaus, commissions, or boards, are organized at all levels of government. Their powers and responsibilities are sometimes derived from constitutional provisions, but usually they come from state or federal statutes. An **administrative agency** decides a variety of cases. Technically, it conducts hearings or inquiries rather than trials. But the parties are often represented by attorneys, evidence and testimony are included, and the agency issues legally binding decisions based on the regulations involved.

administrative agency
Government agency empowered by state or federal statutes and constitutional provisions to hear and decide a variety of cases.

Examples of federal administrative agencies with extensive powers are the Federal Trade Commission, the National Labor Relations Board, and the Federal Energy Regulatory Commission. Examples at the state level include public utility commissions, boards that govern the licensing of various trades and professions, and other state regulatory bodies. At the city or county level are zoning boards, planning commissions, boards of appeal, and other administrative agencies concerned with similar matters.

While administrative agencies often have executive, legislative, and judicial powers, their decisions can be appealed to the courts of general jurisdiction or to specified appellate courts. Many businesses have regular contact with federal, state, and local administrative agencies even though they have almost no contact with the regular court system.

How Government Regulates Business

The legal framework influences and regulates business in many areas. Government regulates competition and competitors as well as specific business practices. The following sections outline how government regulation influences contemporary business.

Regulations Affecting Competition

Effective and ongoing competition is the cornerstone of the private enterprise economy. The *laissez-faire* ("hands off") doctrine in effect during the first hundred years of the existence of the United States was ideal for promoting the rapid growth of the nation geographically, politically, and economically.

But as the country matured, an overconcentration of economic power developed in the private enterprise system. The result was monopolization of certain basic industries. Mergers further concentrated economic power and caused problems that led to government intervention.

regulated industry
Industry in which competition is either limited or eliminated and close government control substitutes for the market controls of free competition.

Approaches to Regulating Competition   When government regulation of competition and other commercial activity came about in the late 1800s, it took two broad forms: the regulation of industry and the enactment of statutes concerning competition. In a **regulated industry**, competition is either limited or eliminated, and close government control is substituted for free competition.

Photo source: Courtesy of Georgia Power Company, Rick Ward photographer.

To meet the increasing energy demands of its electric utility customers, Georgia Power Company invests millions of dollars in massive building programs, such as the construction of this nuclear power generating plant, and in transmission and distribution facilities. Georgia Power and other public utilities are heavily regulated. The Federal Energy Regulatory Commission is the federal administrative agency responsible for developing rules that govern the energy industry. Utilities are also regulated by state agencies that deal with issues such as rate increases.

Examples of regulated industries are found in public utilities and other industries closely tied to the public interest. In these industries, competition is restricted or eliminated because it is wasteful or excessive. For example, only one electrical power company is permitted to serve a given geographical area or market. The large capital investment required to construct a pipeline or electric transmission line over great distance or to build and operate a nuclear power plant makes this type of regulation appropriate. But the lack of competition can sometimes cause deterioration in services and performance.

Statutes affecting competition and various commercial practices exist at both the state and federal levels. The first effort by the federal government to regulate competition was the *Sherman Antitrust Act* of 1890. This act, drawn in a broad and general manner, prohibits every contract or conspiracy in restraint of trade and declares illegal any action that monopolizes or attempts to monopolize any part of trade or commerce.

Additional Competitive Legislation　Another major federal statute is the *Clayton Act* of 1914, which forbids such trade restraints as tying contracts, interlocking directorates, and certain anticompetitive stock acquisitions. A **tying contract** requires a person who wishes to be the exclusive dealer for a manufacturer's products to carry other products of the manufacturer in inventory. The legality of a tying contract is based on whether it restricts competitors from major markets. In an **interlocking directorate**, competitive companies have identical or overlapping boards of directors. Under the Clayton Act, the acquisition of stock in another company is also forbidden if it lessens competition.

The act is enforced by the antitrust division of the U.S. Department of Justice. Violators are subject not only to criminal fines or imprisonment but also to civil damage suits by competitors or other parties. In some cases, the government allows the accused firm to enter into a **consent order**, under which it

tying contract
Agreement that requires a person who wishes to be the exclusive dealer for a manufacturer's product to carry other products of the manufacturer in inventory.

interlocking directorate
Situation involving identical or overlapping boards of directors for competitive companies.

consent order
Order under which an accused firm agrees voluntarily to cease conduct alleged inappropriate by the government.

agrees voluntarily to cease the conduct the government alleges is inappropriate. The *Celler-Kefauver Antimerger Act* (1950) amends the Clayton Act to include major asset purchases that decrease competition in an industry.

The Regulation of Specific Business Practices

Government also regulates specific business practices. Table 23.1 shows how selected federal laws impact different aspects of American business.

The *Federal Trade Commission Act* of 1914 set up the Federal Trade Commission (FTC) to administer various statutes applicable to business. This act bans unfair competitive practices. The powers and investigative capacities of the FTC have grown rapidly over the years. Today it is one of the primary agencies in the regulation of business. This contrasts with its original purpose of regulating competitive practices among and within businesses. The FTC can sue violators or enter into consent orders with those that agree to cease the questionable practices. The FTC is now the major regulatory and enforcement agency in the area of competitive practices. The *FTC Improvement Act* of 1980 gave Congress 90 days to veto any FTC ruling with which it disagrees.

Selected Legislation   Many of the specific business practices regulated by government are covered elsewhere in the text. But there are additional laws with which many businesspeople should be familiar. These laws include:

◆ *Pure Food and Drug Act* (1906) prohibits the adulteration and misbranding of foods and drugs. This act was strengthened by the Food, Drug, and Cosmetic Act of 1938 and by the Kefauver-Harris drug amendments of 1962. The latter resulted from the uproar over deformed babies whose handicaps were the result of their mothers taking the drug thalidomide during pregnancy.

◆ The *Robinson-Patman Act* (1936) outlaws price discrimination that is not based on cost differences or that injures competition.

◆ The *Wheeler-Lea Act* (1938) amends the Federal Trade Commission Act to further outlaw unfair or deceptive acts or practices in business. This act

Table 23.1 How Selected Laws Impact Business

Name of Law	Area of Impact
Computer Software Copyright Act	Computers and information systems
Environmental Policy Act	Environmental protection
Equal Credit Opportunity Act	Financial management
Equal Pay Act	Human resource management
Federal Reserve Act	Banking
Foreign Corrupt Practices Act	International management
Occupational Safety and Health Act	Production and operations management
Robinson-Patman Act	Pricing
Securities Act	Securities markets
Sherman Antitrust Act	Competitive prices
Small Business Act	Small business
Taft-Hartley Act	Labor-management relations
Tax Reform Act of 1986	Accounting
Uniform Commercial Code	Business transactions
Uniform Partnership Act	Business ownership form

gives the Federal Trade Commission jurisdiction over false and misleading advertising.

◆ The *Fair Packaging and Labeling Act* (1967) requires that certain kinds of information, including product identification, name and address of the producer or distributor, and quality information, be disclosed on packages or labels.

◆ The *National Environmental Policy Act* (1970) established the Environmental Protection Agency (EPA) and gave it the authority to deal with various types of pollution and those organizations causing pollution.

◆ The *Fair Debt Collections Practices Act* (1978) is aimed at prohibiting debt-collecting agencies from using harassing, deceptive, and unfair collection practices. The act — which exempts "in-house" debt-collection organizations such as banks, retailers, and attorneys — provides a maximum $1,000 civil penalty for violations. Specific prohibitions include threats of violence, obscene language, and misrepresentation of consumers' legal rights.

The 1987 federal budget reduction accord contained one amusing regulation. The congressional conferees suggested that the government would save $29 million over three years by having frozen pizza manufacturers specify on their labels whether real cheese was used in the pizzas. The reasoning went like this: Consumers would force pizza makers to switch to the real thing; thus, cheese demand would go up, and the government would not have to buy as much surplus cheese from dairy farmers.[4]

Deregulation, the movement toward eliminating legal restraints on competition in various industries, has the potential to significantly reshape the legal environment for business. The trend started with the Airline Deregulation Act, which was designed to encourage competition among airlines by allowing them to set their own rates and to add or subtract routes based on their profitability.

deregulation
Elimination of legal restraints on competition in various industries.

The Staggers Rail Act of 1980 fundamentally altered the Interstate Commerce Commission's power to regulate rail traffic. The law gave rail lines greater freedom to set rates for their freight-hauling operations, to sign long-term contracts with freight shippers, and to eliminate unprofitable routes.

The federal government also has loosened its grip on the trucking industry, enabling it to adjust its rates to meet market demand and to create new kinds of trucking services.

The Effects of Deregulation on the Business Environment

Deregulation has had a substantial impact on both legal and economic environments for business. For example, the Airline Deregulation Act has led to the merger or acquisition of several airlines. Republic Airlines was acquired by Northwest Airlines, Western Airlines by Delta, Piedmont by US Air, Air Cal by American, and so on. Furthermore, because airlines are now free to select their routes, many have pulled out of smaller markets. As a result, commuter airlines have grown significantly. Commuter airlines such as Britt, Hensen, and Horizon now serve as passenger feeders to major airlines operating out of so-called *hubs*, or major airports.

Critics of deregulation often point out the negative effects of the trend. Some fear deregulation may eventually lead to higher prices as competitors are

Deregulation of the railroad industry provided by the Staggers Rail Act of 1980 has helped railroads to improve profitability and enabled them to invest in innovative services that help them compete with other modes of freight transportation. Conrail's intermodal and double-stack services save shippers time and money by reducing the risk of damaging goods in transit and speeding up freight delivery time.

Photo source: Courtesy of Consolidated Rail Corporation.

eliminated. Others suggest safety may be sacrificed in the name of competition. While these are legitimate concerns, it is reasonable to conclude that most of the negative scenarios constructed by deregulation's critics have not occurred.

Major Components of Business Law

Most laws affect business in some manner, whether directly or indirectly. But certain laws are so vital to business enterprises that all business people must understand their role in the legal framework. The cornerstones of American business law are contract law; sales law; the Uniform Commercial Code; negotiable instruments; property law; the law of bailment; agency law; tort law; bankruptcy law; patents, trademarks, and copyrights; and tax law.

Contract Law

contract law
Legal foundation on which normal business dealings are conducted.

contract
Legally enforceable agreement between two or more parties regarding a specified act or thing.

Contract law is important because it affects most aspects of any business operation. It is the legal foundation on which normal business dealings are conducted. A **contract** is a legally enforceable agreement between two or more parties regarding a specified act or thing.

Figure 23.3   Four Requirements of a Contract

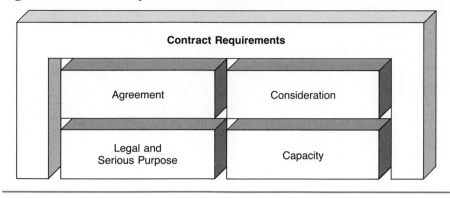

Contract Requirements

The four elements of an enforceable contract are agreement, consideration, legal and serious purpose, and capacity. These are shown in Figure 23.3

The key element in a contract is that there must be an *agreement* among the parties as to the act or thing specified. In order for such an agreement, or contract, to be valid and enforceable through the courts, **consideration** — the value or benefit that a party provides to the others with whom the contract is made — must be furnished by each party to the contract. Legal consideration for a contract exists when, for example, A agrees to work for B and B agrees to pay A a certain salary. The contract is just as valid if B actually pays A at the time A agrees to work. Similarly, valid consideration exists even if no promises are exchanged but A works for B and B pays A for the work.

In addition to consideration, an enforceable contract must involve a *legal and serious purpose*. Agreements made in a joking manner or relating to purely social matters or involving the commission of a crime are not enforceable as legal contracts. An agreement between two competitors to fix the prices for their products is not enforceable as a contract because the subject matter is illegal and because the performance of such an agreement would violate the law.

The last element of a legally enforceable contract is the capacity of each party to make the agreement. **Capacity** is the legal ability of a party to enter into agreements. The law does not permit certain persons, such as those judged to be insane, to enter into legally enforceable contracts.

Contracts are used in almost all types of business activities. Generally, they are created and executed by the firms with minimal concern on the part of the contracting parties. Examples of valid contracts are purchase agreements with suppliers, labor contracts, group insurance policies for employees, franchise agreements, and sales contracts.

consideration
The value or benefit one party provides to the others with whom a contract is made.

capacity
The legal ability of a party to enter into agreements.

Breach of Contract

Apparently, one little girl thought she had a contract with the makers of Cracker Jack. The nine-year-old sued when she failed to get a toy in her Cracker Jack box. The case was resolved when the company gave her a new box that contained a toy.

breach of contract
Violation of a valid legal agreement.

damages
Financial payments made for a loss and related suffering.

sales law
Body of law pertaining to the sale of goods or products for money or credit.

Breach of contract describes the violation of a valid contract. The injured party can go to the court system to enforce the contract provisions and, in some cases, collect **damages** — financial payment for the loss and related suffering.

Sales Law

The law of sales is an offspring of contract law. But the sales agreement, or sales transaction, is a special kind of contract that is entered into millions of times each day throughout the economic system. **Sales law** involves the sales of goods or products for money or on credit. As economic transactions, sales can be of services or real estate as well as goods, but the law of sales is concerned only with the transfer of tangible personal property. The law involved with intangible personal property and real estate will be examined later.

Sales law has evolved in a distinct manner. It goes back to ancient English law that consisted largely of the customs of merchants and included a system of merchant courts to resolve disputes. Many of these customs and practices were adopted in the United States as part of common law. Later, the Uniform Commercial Code provided uniformity in all commercial law, including sales law.

The Uniform Commercial Code

The *Uniform Commercial Code (UCC)*, drafted in 1952, is a comprehensive commercial law that has been adopted by all states except Louisiana. The UCC covers the law of sales as well as other specific areas of commercial law.

Article 2 of the UCC specifies the circumstances under which sales contracts are entered into by seller and buyer. Ordinarily such agreements are based on the express conduct of the parties. Under the UCC, enforceable sales contracts must also generally be in writing if goods worth more than $500 are involved. The formation of the sales contract is quite flexible because certain missing terms in the written contract or other ambiguities do not keep the contract from being legally enforceable. A court will look to past dealings, commercial customs, and other standards of reasonableness in evaluating the existence of a legal contract.

These variables will also be considered by a court when either the buyer or the seller seeks to enforce his or her rights against the other party where the sales contract has not been performed, has been only partially performed, or where performance has been defective or unsatisfactory. The UCC's remedies in such cases consist largely of monetary damages awarded to the injured party. The UCC defines the rights of the parties to have the contract specifically performed, to have it terminated, and to reclaim the goods or have a lien placed against them.

express warranty
Warranty with specific representations made by the seller regarding the goods.

implied warranty
Warranty legally imposed on the seller and, generally, automatically effective unless disclaimed by the seller in writing.

Warranties

Article 2 of the UCC also sets forth the law of warranty for sales transactions. There are two basic types of warranties. An **express warranty** is a specific representation made by the seller regarding the goods. An **implied warranty** is

Figure 23.4 A Whirlpool Corporation Warranty

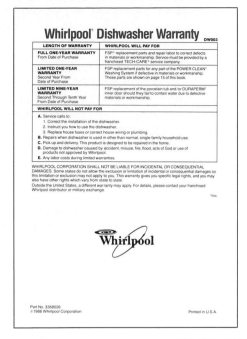

Source: Courtesy of Whirlpool Corporation.

one legally imposed on the seller. Generally, unless implied warranties are disclaimed by the seller in writing, they are automatically effective. Other provisions of Article 2 govern the rights of acceptance, rejection, and inspection of goods by the buyer; the rights of the parties during manufacture, shipment, delivery, and passing of title to goods; the legal significance of sales documents such as bills of lading; and the placing of the risk of loss in the event of destruction or damage to the goods during manufacture, shipment, or delivery. Figure 23.4 is a sample of a written warranty.

Negotiable Instruments

A **negotiable instrument** is a form of commercial paper that is transferable among individuals and businesses. The most common example of a negotiable instrument is a check; drafts, certificates of deposit, and notes are also sometimes considered negotiable instruments.

Article 3 of the UCC specifies that a negotiable instrument must be written and must also meet the following requirements:

1. Be signed by the maker or drawer.
2. Contain an unconditional promise or order to pay a certain sum in money.
3. Be payable on demand or at a definite time.
4. Be payable to order or to bearer.

negotiable instrument
Form of commercial paper that is transferable among individuals and businesses.

Types of Endorsements

endorsement
Procedure of signing a negotiable instrument that renders it transferable.

Checks and other forms of commercial paper are transferred when the payee signs the back of the instrument, a procedure known as **endorsement**. The four kinds of endorsement described by Article 3 of the UCC are shown in Figure 23.5 and include the following:

1. Blank endorsement consists only of the name of the payee. All that is required to make a blank endorsement is to sign the back of the instrument. This makes it payable to the bearer. A blank endorsement should not be used if the instrument is to be mailed.
2. Special endorsement specifies the person to whom the instrument is payable. With this kind of endorsement, only the person whose name appears after "Pay to the order of . . ." can further the negotiability of the instrument.
3. Qualified endorsement contains words stating that the endorser is not guaranteeing payment of the instrument. The qualified endorsement of "Without recourse (signed) . . ." limits the endorser's liability in the event that the instrument is not backed by the sufficient funds.
4. Restrictive endorsement limits the negotiability of the instrument. One of the most common restrictive endorsements is "For deposit only." It is useful if an instrument (usually a check) is subsequently lost or stolen, because it means the instrument can only be deposited to the indicated account; it cannot be cashed.

Property Law

property
Something for which a person or company has the unrestricted right of possession or use.

tangible personal property
Property consisting of physical things, such as goods and products.

intangible personal property
Property most often represented by a document or other written statement.

real property
Real estate.

Property law is a key feature of the private enterprise system. **Property** is something for which a person or company has the unrestricted right of possession or use. Property rights are guaranteed and protected by the U.S. Constitution.

Property can be divided into several categories. **Tangible personal property** consists of physical things such as goods and products. Every business is concerned with this kind of property, which includes equipment, supplies, and delivery vehicles.

Intangible personal property is property that is most often represented by a document or other instrument in writing, although it may be as vague and remote as a bookkeeping or computer entry. Certain intangible personal properties such as personal checks and money orders are well known. Others are less known but are important to the businesses or individuals who own and utilize them. Examples are stocks, bonds, Treasury bills, notes, letters of credit, and warehouse receipts. Mortgages are also technically intangible personal property.

The last category of property is **real property**, or real estate. Some real property customs have been formalized in statutes. There is also case law to guide real-property owners in their transactions and conduct. All firms have some concern with real estate law because of the need to own or occupy the space or building where business is conducted. The real estate needs of national chains or major manufacturing companies are indeed considerable. Some businesses are created to serve the real estate needs of others. Real estate developers, builders, contractors, brokers, mortgage companies, and architects are all concerned with various aspects of real property law.

Figure 23.5   The Four Kinds of Endorsement

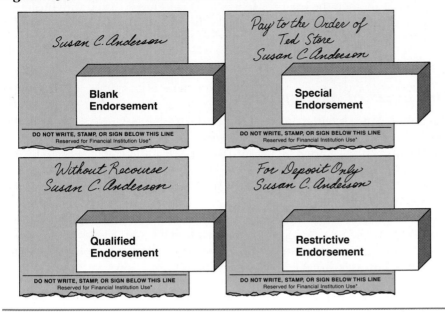

The Law of Bailment

The **law of bailment** is concerned with the surrender of personal property by one person to another when the property is to be returned at a later date. The person delivering the property is known as the *bailor*. The person receiving the property is known as the *bailee*. There are three types of bailments, and each requires a different degree of care if there is to be no liability for damage.

If the delivery of the goods is for the sole benefit of the bailor — for example, the bailee stores the bailor's property at no charge — the bailee is required to take only slight or ordinary care of the items. When the delivery is for the sole benefit of the bailee — if the bailor loans the bailee some needed property free of charge — the bailee is required to take extraordinary care of the items. When the delivery is for the mutual benefit of both parties — when the bailment is made in exchange for payment — the bailee must take only reasonable care.[5]

Rules exist for settling bailment disputes, which commonly arise in business settings such as hotels and motels, restaurants, banks, safe deposit boxes, and parking lots. The law focuses on actual delivery of the item. For example, if a patron in a restaurant hangs a coat on a hook, there has been no actual delivery to the restaurant's proprietor. Therefore, the proprietor is not liable for theft or damage. On the other hand, if the restaurant has a coat-checking room and the patron receives a claim check, the coat has been delivered and the proprietor is liable for theft of or damage to the coat.

The Law of Agency

Agency describes a legal relationship in which two parties, the principal and the agent, "agree that one will act as a representative of the other. The **principal** is the person who wishes to accomplish something, and the **agent** is the one employed to act in the principal's behalf to achieve it."[6]

law of bailment
The surrender of personal property from one person to another when the property is to be returned later.

agency
Legal relationship between two parties, principal and agent, who agree that one will act as a representative of the other.

principal
Person who is represented by an agent.

agent
Person employed to act on behalf of another individual.

While the agency relationship can be as simple as one family member acting on behalf of another, the legal concept is most closely associated with business. All types of firms conduct business affairs through a variety of agents, among them partners, directors, corporate officers, and sales personnel.

The Basis of Agency Law

The law of agency is based on common-law principles and case decisions of the state and federal courts. Relatively little agency law has been enacted into statute. The law of agency is important because the principal is generally bound by the actions of the agent.

The legal basis for holding the principal liable for acts of the agent is the Latin maxim of *respondeat superior* ("let the master answer"). In cases involving agency law, the courts must decide the rights and obligations of the various parties. Generally, the principal is held liable where an agency relationship existed and the agent had some type of authority to do the wrongful act. The agent in such cases is liable to the principal for any damages caused to that person.

The Law of Torts

tort
Civil wrong inflicted on other persons or their property.

A **tort** (French for "wrong") refers to a civil wrong inflicted on other persons or their property.[7] The law of torts is closely related to the law of agency, because the business entity, or principal, can be held liable for the torts committed by its agents in the course of business dealings. Tort law differs from both criminal and contract law. While criminal law is concerned with crimes against the state or society, tort law deals with compensating injured persons who are the victims of noncriminal wrongs.

Types of Torts

intentional tort
Civil wrong purposely inflicted on other persons or their property, such as assault, slander, or libel.

Many torts, such as assault, are intentional actions carried out by the wrongdoer. Sometimes the person can argue that while the actions were intentional, the damages were not. Examples of an **intentional tort** are slander, libel, and fraud. Businesses can become involved in such cases through the actions of both owners and employees. The supermarket clerk who roughly handles a suspected shoplifter and holds the suspect in the manager's office for questioning may be committing a tort if the conduct is excessive or otherwise unjustified. Under agency law, the store owner can be held liable for any damages or injury caused to the suspect.

negligence
A wrong based on careless rather than intentional behavior that causes injury to another person.

The other major group of torts is **negligence**. This type of tort is based on careless rather than intentional behavior that causes injury to another person. Under agency law, businesses are held liable for the negligence of their employees or agents. The delivery truck driver who kills a pedestrian while delivering goods creates tort liability for his or her employer if the accident is the result of negligence.

Product Liability

An area of tort law known as **product liability** has been developed by both statutory and case law to hold businesses liable for negligence in the design, manufacture, sale, and/or use of products. Product liability is aimed at making products safer. It encourages firms to design products with safety improvements, such as the Black & Decker iron in the advertisement in Figure 23.6.

Some states have extended the theory of tort to cover injuries caused by products regardless of whether the manufacturer is proven negligent. Under this legal concept, known as **strict product liability**, the injured party need only show "(1) that the product was defective, (2) that the defect was the proximate cause of injury, and (3) that the defect caused the product to be unreasonably dangerous."[8]

Careful supervision of employees and careful on-the-job conduct by employees are the best ways to avoid tort liability. However, with tort damages running higher and higher, most firms have turned to liability insurance for protection.

product liability
Area of tort law that holds business liable for negligence in the design, manufacture, sale, and use of products.

strict product liability
Legal concept that covers injuries caused by products regardless of whether the manufacturer is proven negligent.

Bankruptcy Law

Bankruptcy, the legal nonpayment of financial obligations, is a common occurrence in contemporary society. The term *bankruptcy* is derived from "banca rotta," or "broken bench," since creditors in medieval Venice would break up the benches of merchants who did not pay their bills.[9]

The days of debtor prisons and deportation are long past. Federal legislation passed in 1918 and revised in 1938, 1978, 1984, and 1986 provides for an orderly handling of bankruptcies by the federal court system. The bankruptcy procedure allows the individual or company to make a fresh start. Two types of bankruptcies are recognized. Under *voluntary bankruptcy*, a person or firm asks to be judged bankrupt because of an inability to pay off creditors. Under *involuntary bankruptcy*, creditors may request that a party be judged bankrupt.

bankruptcy
Legal nonpayment of financial obligations.

Major Provisions of Bankruptcy Law

Two primary options are available to individuals under bankruptcy law.[10] Chapter 13 of the bankruptcy law — the wage-earner plan — allows a person to set up a three-year debt repayment plan. Debtors often end up repaying only a portion of what they owe. The bankrupt party's current income is considered in the determination of the repayment schedule. The other alternative — Chapter 7 — is a liquidation plan under which the bankrupt person's assets are divided among creditors. Judges can now deny the use of this second alternative. The initial choice of Chapter 13 does not preclude a later switch to Chapter 7.

Under Chapter 7, certain property is exempt from the claims of creditors:

1. Home equity of $7,500.
2. Motor vehicle equity of $1,200.
3. $200 on each personal item such as household furnishings, clothes, and books, up to a maximum of $4,000.
4. $500 on personal property.

Figure 23.6   Reducing the Risk of Tort Liability by Designing Safe Products

Source: Courtesy of Black & Decker Corporation.

5. Another $400 on any other property.
6. Tools of one's trade or prescribed health items up to $750.

Husbands and wives filing jointly can double the amounts noted above. Some states set different allowances, allowing more liberal exemptions than Chapter 7 does.

A third personal bankruptcy option was added in 1986. Chapter 12 allows farmers with debts up to $1.5 million to set up a repayment plan, which had previously been denied under Chapter 13's $100,000 debt limit.

While most attention is directed toward personal bankruptcies, businesses can also go bankrupt. The specific provision under which most businesses go bankrupt is known as Chapter 11. This plan allows a firm to reorganize and develop a plan to repay its debts. More than 20,000 firms file under Chapter 11 each year.[11] The largest Chapter 11 case in history was resolved in 1988 when Texaco paid a $3 billion settlement to Pennzoil and emerged from court protection.

Trademarks, Patents, and Copyrights

A 1988 Supreme Court decision on the so-called *gray market* pointed out the important role of trademarks in commerce. Like patents and copyrights, trademarks provide legal protection for key business assets, and they are carefully

Photo source: Compliments of Blue Mountain Arts, Inc.

Entrepreneurs Susan and Stephen Schutz, founders of Blue Mountain Arts, filed a $50 million lawsuit against Hallmark Cards Inc. when Hallmark introduced its line of Personal Touch greeting cards (left in photo) similar to Blue Mountain Arts' distinctive cards (right in photo) that feature watercolor artwork and poetry in handwritten script. The lawsuit accused Hallmark of trademark infringement and resulted in a two-year legal battle. The small company was successful in protecting its card design. Under a consent order, Hallmark agreed to stop publishing its Personal Touch cards, discontinue the use of the Personal Touch name, and repurchase cards already on store shelves.

guarded by their owners. In the 1988 case, 60 luxury goods manufacturers, including Cartier, Nikon, and Charles of the Ritz, argued against Customs Service regulations that permitted discounters, such as 47th Street Photo and K mart, to buy merchandise overseas and then re-sell it in the United States without the trademark owner's authorization. This distribution is referred to as a gray market. The manufacturers are now pursuing other means such as lawsuits to keep the merchandise out.[12]

Trademark Law

A **trademark** consists of words, symbols, or other designations used by businesses to identify their products. The Lanham Act (1946) provides for federal registration of trademarks. Numerous legal battles develop over trademarks. In one 1988 case, Beretta, the Italian arms manufacturer, alleged trademark infringement against Chevrolet's Beretta and sought $250 million from General Motors. The owner of the trademark must actively protect it from generic use by the public. This is often done by advertising that something is a registered trademark. For example, the National Association of Realtors® has advertised that the term *Realtor*® is a federally registered trademark. Similarly, Triangle Publications Inc. has advertised that *TVGUIDE*® is one of its registered trademarks.

If a trademark becomes the generic term for a class of products, the registrant loses this important protection. Aspirin, nylon, kerosene, linoleum, shredded wheat, and milk of magnesia were all once the exclusive properties of their manufacturers, but they became generic terms, and now anyone can use them.

trademark
Words, symbols, or other designations used to identify a product.

Patent Law

A **patent** guarantees inventors exclusive rights to their invention for 17 years, provided the invention is accepted by the U.S. Patent Office. Copyrights and patents have a constitutional basis. The Constitution specifies that the federal

patent
Inventors' guarantee of exclusive rights to their inventions for 17 years, provided the inventions have been accepted by the U.S. Patent Office.

government has the power "to promote the progress of science and useful arts, by securing for limited times to authors and inventors the exclusive right to their respective writings and discoveries." Patent owners sometimes license the use of the patent to others for a fee.

Copyright Law

copyright
Protection of an individual's exclusive right to such materials as books, photos, and cartoons.

A **copyright** protects written material such as this textbook, designs, cartoon illustrations, photos, and so on. Copyrights are filed with the Library of Congress. Authors or their heirs hold exclusive rights to their published or unpublished works for the author's lifetime, plus 50 years. Works for hire and anonymous or pseudonymous works receive copyright protection for a period of 75 years from publication or 100 years from creation, whichever is shorter.

One of the newest areas of copyright law concerns computer software. Apple's 1988 lawsuit against Microsoft and Hewlett-Packard for alleged copyright infringement illustrates this important aspect of contemporary business law.

Tax Law

The branch of law that affects every business, employee, and consumer in the United States is tax law. Over 29 percent of the nation's gross national product, or $4,740 per capita, goes to taxes.[13] Taxes are the assessments used to raise revenue for governmental units. Federal, state, and local governments and special taxing authorities all levy taxes.

How Taxes Are Levied

Some taxes are paid by individuals and some by businesses. Both have a decided impact on contemporary business. Business taxes reduce profits, and personal taxes cut the disposable income that individuals can spend on the products of businesses. But government gets revenue from taxes and buys industry's products and services. Government also acts as a transfer agent, moving tax revenue to other consumers and transferring social security taxes from the working population to retired persons.

Taxes can be levied on several different bases: income, sales, business receipts, property, assets, and so on. The type of tax varies from one taxing authority to the other. The individual income tax is the biggest source of revenue for the federal government. Many states rely on sales taxes. In addition to a sales tax, some cities collect a tax on earnings. Many community college districts get the bulk of their revenue from real estate or property taxes. Figure 23.7 shows the breakdown of tax sources.

Tax Reform

The Internal Revenue Code of 1986, commonly called the Tax Reform Act of 1986, which lowered tax rates and limited deductions, culminated a drive to revise the tax system in order to promote economic growth, reduce tax rates, simplify tax returns, and make the tax code more equitable.[14]

Figure 23.7   Sources of Tax Revenue

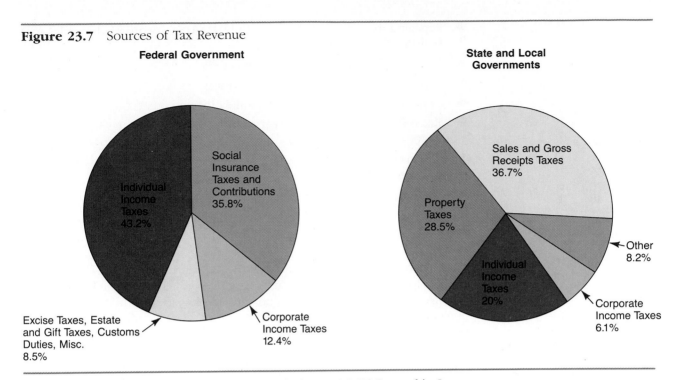

Federal Government

Individual Income Taxes 43.2%

Social Insurance Taxes and Contributions 35.8%

Corporate Income Taxes 12.4%

Excise Taxes, Estate and Gift Taxes, Customs Duties, Misc. 8.5%

State and Local Governments

Sales and Gross Receipts Taxes 36.7%

Property Taxes 28.5%

Individual Income Taxes 20%

Other 8.2%

Corporate Income Taxes 6.1%

Source: Statistical Abstract of the United States: 1988, 108th ed. (Washington, D.C.: U.S. Bureau of the Census, 1987), pp. 262, 292.

America's working poor people were the biggest beneficiaries of the revised tax code, which removed more than 6 million low-income families from the federal tax roles. The bulk of tax relief went to low- and middle-income taxpayers, while the burden was raised on upper-income individuals. Tax reform eliminated many tax shelters used by the wealthy to reduce their taxes and imposed a stiffer minimum tax on businesses and individuals.

How Tax Reform Affects Individuals   Tax rates now fall into just two brackets — 15 percent and 28 percent — but higher income individuals pay 33 percent on part of their income. Current tax law limits or eliminates many former tax deductions. The deduction for contributions to individual retirement accounts was limited; the deduction for sales taxes was dropped; the deduction for charitable contributions was limited to taxpayers who itemize; and deductions for medical expenses and union dues were restricted. Some deductions remained the same (such as the deductions for mortgage interest on first and second homes, and most state and local income and property taxes). The revised tax code also accomplished the following:

◆   Raised the personal exemption to $2,000.

◆   Raised the standard deduction for both married people and single taxpayers.

◆   Eliminated the special tax treatment of long-term capital gains. Under the new law, capital gains are taxed at the same rate as other income, with the top rate of 28 percent.

- Repealed the special deduction of up to $3,000 for married couples who both work.
- Repealed the political contributions credit.
- Repealed the income averaging provision.
- Taxed unemployment compensation as income.
- Taxed the unearned income of a minor at the parents' rate when exceeding $1,000.
- Eliminated Clifford trusts, which were used to reduce taxes on assets transferred to children.

It is estimated that individuals will lose $80 billion in tax breaks during the first five years of the tax reform (1987–1991) but will gain $200 billion from the tax rate deductions.

Corporate Tax Burden Increased   Tax reform also translated into dramatic changes for business. Corporate taxes were raised by about $120 billion over the first five years. The top corporate tax rate was lowered from 46 percent to 34 percent, but tax reform imposed a 20 percent alternative minimum tax on corporations, repealed the investment tax credit, increased levies on income earned abroad, curtailed tax-exempt bond financing, and reduced depreciation schedules.

The effects of these measures varied from industry to industry and from company to company. For many businesses, the reduction in tax rates more than offset the lost tax incentives. On the other hand, the new alternative minimum tax prevented many profitable firms from paying little or no taxes.

Industries hardest hit by tax reform are heavy manufacturing, commercial and multifamily real estate, utilities, and banking. The loss of the investment tax credit and scaled-back depreciation schedules reduced the tax breaks of capital-intensive firms that formerly received a credit for investments in plant and equipment.

In the past, the real estate industry received generous tax treatment with accelerated depreciation allowances. Tax reform cut these depreciation benefits and eliminated the capital gains tax preference. Banks, which traditionally had one of the lowest effective tax rates in the business sector, lost two tax breaks: deductions for loan-loss reserves and carrying costs on the purchase of municipal bonds.

Industries benefiting the most from tax reform are those that do not invest heavily in plant and equipment. They include retailers, wholesalers, publishing firms, electronics firms, many consumer-products companies, and service firms.

Small business benefited from the 1986 tax legislation, which continued to allow lower rates for small businesses. Income up to $50,000 is taxed at a 15 percent rate; income between $50,000 and $75,000 at a 25 percent rate; and income over $75,000 at the top 34 percent rate. Small businesses, however, now have less incentive to incorporate. Sole proprietorships and partnerships will benefit as a result of the drop in individual rates. Many small firms now choose to be taxed as an S corporation in which income or losses flow through to the owners' tax returns. In the past, a corporation with substantial taxable income would not benefit from S corporation status because the income could be taxed at the highest maximum individual rate of 50 percent.

Although the tax reform bill is designed to spur economic growth, its long-term effects are difficult to assess. Opponents argue that the $120 billion increase in corporate taxes could slow business investment needed to raise American industry's efficiency and productivity. Supporters of tax reform disagree. They claim tax reform will force businesses to make decisions based on the marketplace rather than on tax codes. More efficient business investment decisions based on making money rather than on offsetting taxes, they say, will lead to a stronger and more productive economy in the long run.

Tax law is just part of the legal environment in which a firm must operate. While businesspeople are not expected to be attorneys, they should have a general awareness of the basic legal concepts outlined here, as well as specific knowledge of the area of law that affects their specific activities or operations. Questions should be referred to the firm's legal counsel.

Summary of Learning Goals

1. Explain the meaning and sources of law. Law consists of the standards set by government and society in the form of either legislation or custom. The primary sources of law are common law, statutory law, and court decisions. Common law refers to the legal concepts arising out of judicial decisions related to the unwritten law the United States inherited from England. Statutory law refers to written laws such as the U.S. Constitution, state laws, and local ordinances. Court rulings on statutory enactments are another important source of law.

2. Describe the nature of business law. Business law consists of those aspects of law that most directly and specifically influence and regulate the management of various types of business activity. Managers must take into account the legal consequences of their business decisions if they are to be successful. In some cases, it is necessary for executives to consult an attorney when making a decision with legal implications.

3. Analyze the structure of the judicial system. The judiciary, or court system, is charged with deciding disputes among parties through the application of laws. Both state and federal court systems include trial courts (courts of general jurisdiction), special courts, and administrative agencies. There are also appellate courts and courts of final appeal.

4. Explain how government regulates business. Government regulates competition and competitors as well as specific business practices. Government regulation of competition became necessary in the late 1800s, when mergers and monopolization began to cause problems in certain industries. This regulation took two broad forms: regulation of industry and enactment of statutes concerning competition. The first act regulating competition was the Sherman Antitrust Act of 1890. Since then, many more acts have been drafted to further regulate this area. Specific business practices are also regulated by government. The laws affect nearly all facets of business, including business ownership forms, small business, human resource management, labor-management relations, marketing, production and operations management, computers and information systems, accounting, banking, financial management, securities markets, international management, business transactions, competitive practices, and the environment.

5.   Discuss the impact of deregulation.   Deregulation, or the elimination of legal restraints on competition, began with the Airline Deregulation Act of 1978. Since then, the railroad, trucking, banking, and other industries have also experienced deregulation. This trend has had a significant impact on both the legal and economic environment for business. In the air travel industry, for example, it has led to the consolidation of many major carriers, as well as the growth of commuter lines designed to serve smaller markets.

6.   Identify the major components of business law.   Contract law is the legal foundation on which normal business dealings are constructed. The elements of enforceable contracts are agreement, consideration, legality and seriousness of the agreement, and the parties' capacity to make the agreement.

Sales law is an offspring of contract law. It involves the sale of goods or products for money or on credit. The Uniform Commercial Code (UCC) provides the basis of much of sales law in the United States.

Negotiable instruments are forms of commercial paper that are transferable among individuals and businesses. Article 3 of the UCC gives specifications for negotiable instruments and describes the four basic kinds of endorsements: blank endorsement, special endorsement, qualified endorsement, and restrictive endorsement.

Property law is a key feature of the legal system. Property can be divided into three categories: tangible personal property, intangible personal property, and real property.

When someone gives another person property to hold, it is covered under the law of bailment. The bailee is the person holding the item, whereas the bailor is the person who delivers the property.

Agency law is based primarily on common-law principles. An agency is a relationship in which two parties (the principal and the agent) agree that one will act as a representative of the other. The principal in any agency relationship is responsible for the actions of the agent.

Tort law deals with compensating injured persons who are the victims of noncriminal wrongs. It is closely related to the law of agency. The three major areas of this law are intentional tort, negligence, and product liability.

7.   Outline the current status of bankruptcy law.   Bankruptcy law provides for an orderly handling of bankruptcies by the federal court system. Two types of bankruptcies are recognized: voluntary and involuntary. For personal bankruptcies, the available options are: Under Chapter 13, the bankrupt person may set up a repayment plan provided debts do not exceed $100,000. Chapter 7 is a liquidation plan that divides a person's assets among his or her creditors. Farmers with debts as high as $1.5 million can set up a repayment plan under Chapter 12. For business bankruptcies, the relevant provision of the bankruptcy law is Chapter 11.

8.   Differentiate among trademarks, patents, and copyrights.   Trademarks are words, symbols, or other designations used to identify products. They can be registered with the federal government, but their owners must actively protect them. Patents guarantee inventors exclusive rights to their inventions for a period of 17 years. Copyrights give exclusive rights to a published or unpublished work to an author or the author's heirs during the author's lifetime and for a period of 50 years after the author's death.

9. Outline the effects of tax reform legislation. The tax reform legislation passed in 1986 was designed to promote economic growth, reduce tax rates, simplify tax returns, and make the tax code more equitable. In effect, tax reform reduced tax rates for most people by offsetting the cuts with the elimination or limitation of numerous deductions.

The impact on business was varied. Corporate tax rates went down, but business tax collections went up because of other changes in the tax code such as reduced depreciation schedules. In general, capital-intensive industries pay more, and other industries pay less under the 1986 legislation.

Key Terms

law	contract law	real property
common law	contract	law of bailment
statutory law	consideration	agency
business law	capacity	principal
judiciary	breach of contract	agent
trial court	damages	tort
appellate court	sales law	intentional tort
appellant	express warranty	negligence
administrative agency	implied warranty	product liability
regulated industry	negotiable instrument	strict product liability
tying contract	endorsement	bankruptcy
interlocking directorate	property	trademark
consent order	tangible personal property	patent
deregulation	intangible personal property	copyright

Review Questions

1. Identify the sources of law. Which sources are the most important today?

2. What should a businessperson know about business law?

3. Outline the organization of the U.S. courts system. Cover all three levels — trial courts, appellate courts, and courts of final appeal — for both federal and state judiciaries.

4. Explain the role of the administrative agency in the legal system.

5. How does government regulate both competition and specific business practices?

6. What are the advantages and disadvantages of deregulation?

7. Explain the role of the Uniform Commercial Code (UCC) in business law.

8. Outline the major chapters of bankruptcy law.

9. How might trademark, patent, and copyright law affect a computer manufacturer?

10. Explain how the Tax Reform Act of 1986 affected business firms and the general public.

Discussion Questions

1. Michigan has some 33 pages of laws covering dry-cleaning establishments. These laws cover washers, tumblers, scouring tables, drains, scubbing tubs, and floors. What does this example suggest about the American legal system for business?

2. A Massachusetts high school teacher, Bob Anastas, founded SADD (Students Against Drunk Driving) after two of his students were killed in two separate driving accidents. Today, there are some 8,000 SADD chapters in the nation's high schools. One of SADD's programs is the distribution of the "Contract for Life" reprinted here. Does this form meet the four requirements for a contract? Discuss.

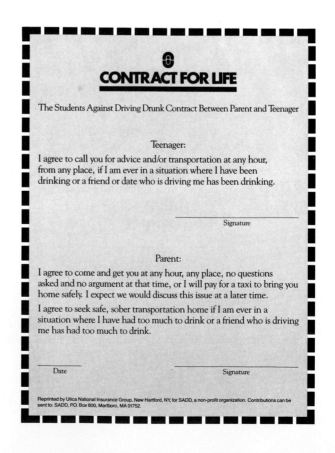

3. A representative of organized crime has just taken out a contract on a rival gangster. The hit man was offered $10,000 to complete the contract. Under a strict legal interpretation, is this a valid contract? Why or why not?

4. A driver for a local delivery firm became intoxicated over a long lunch with a friend at a local pub. The driver then struck another truck as he left the pub's parking lot. Is the delivery firm responsible for the actions of its driver? Discuss the legal concepts involved here.

5. Various sources have noted that the United States has become a litigation-prone society. Part of the blame is sometimes assigned to *contingency fees*, a system whereby attorneys collect a percentage of any settlement or damage award. These fees can run as high as a third of any monies collected. Proponents of this system argue that it makes legal services available to the poor since they could not afford an attorney's hourly fee. Critics argue that high contingency fees encourage litigation. What is your opinion on this issue?

Case

...ta Air Lines, Inc.

Delta Air Lines celebrated its sixtieth birthday in 1989. The giant air carrier traces its beginnings to 1929 when it first offered air transportation to daring travelers between Dallas and Jackson, Mississippi. By the 1940s, Delta had grown to the recognized leader in passenger service in the Southeast. Year by year it offered faster speeds and such innovations as two-way radios and registered nurses as flight attendants. It also introduced the first aircraft large enough for a passenger to actually stand up in.

The real potential of passenger air service began to be realized during World War II. The contributions of aviation to the war and the marked increase in the number of people who had actually flown established air travel as an important part of modern life. The introduction of the 21-seat DC-3 to the Delta fleet offered new standards of passenger service and comfort. Both Delta and the entire airline industry were beginning to fulfill their promise.

The period following the end of the war in 1945 formed a new chapter in the evolution of the airline industry. Instead of competing for mail and limited passenger routes, airlines began competing for passengers, cargo, and access to new markets. Delta continued to grow during this period, and by 1953, it ranked as the fifth largest airline in the United States. At that time, it was serving 59 U.S. cities and a few Caribbean destinations and flying a 10,000-mile route system. Its fleet of airlines featured pressurized cabins, air conditioning, and champagne service.

The 1960s saw the arrival of the jet age. Flying became easier, more comfortable, and more convenient. There were more places to fly to and more carriers serving those places. Under the regulatory umbrella of the Civil Aeronautics Board (CAB), the 36 U.S. carriers enjoyed a period of prosperity that extended until 1978.

Prior to 1978, the CAB approved fare requests and determined which airlines would fly which routes.

Notes: Louis E. Boone and James C. Johnson, "The Impact of Airline Deregulation on Rates and Services," *Journal of Applied Business Research,* Fall 1989; Scott Ticer, "Why the Folks at Delta Are Walking on Air," *Business Week,* August 1, 1988, pp. 92–93; "Delta Airlines," *Advertising Age,* September 28, 1988, p. 63; and Dan Koeppel, "American's No-Nonsense Marketers," *Adweek's Marketing Week,* June 5, 1989, pp. 18–24.

The Airline Deregulation Act of 1978 changed all that. The new law, passed during an era that saw moves to deregulate financial institutions, rail carriers, motor transportation, and water transportation, granted considerable freedom to commercial airlines in setting fares and choosing new routes. It also made it easier for new carriers to enter the industry and abolished the CAB.

Within a few months following deregulation, the number of air carriers mushroomed to as many as 198. Some new carriers, such as People Express, decided to compete on the basis of price. Others chose to match the price of their closest competitors, but to emphasize service, on-time arrivals and departures, and the number of cities they served. The increased competition in the years since deregulation has seen the demise of airlines (such as People Express), the mergers of dozens of air carriers with the so-called mega-carriers, and the difficulty of remaining profitable on the part of the surviving carriers. So many airlines have gone out of business or merged with other carriers that today only a few dozen remain, and only nine of those can be considered mega-carriers (major national airlines).

Delta participated in this merger wave by acquiring Western Airlines in December, 1986. The Western acquisition and internal growth made Delta the nation's third largest carrier in terms of passenger miles with a 13.4 percent share of the U.S. market. It trailed only American Airlines and United Airlines in the industry rankings.

Deregulation has produced opportunities as well as challenges for Delta management. The company has responded to recent growth by automating as many of its functions as possible. In the old days, reservation systems depended on chalkboards, teletypes, and volumes of printed flight information. Seating was available on a first-come-first-served basis. Today's information systems make scheduling, routing, cost management, and time management more efficient. And technology has made possible the development of new aircraft that operate with greater fuel efficiency while simultaneously providing better operational features for improved customer service.

One of Delta's moves aimed at maintaining a competitive edge was the development of a new 42-acre maintenance facility in Atlanta. This facility, located near the company's Atlanta headquarters, is responsible for jobs as varied as applying new paint and repairing carpets to performing a 10,000 worker-hour maintenance check on each plane before it is returned to service. The facility has more than 50 repair shops that specialize in repairs, from rebuilding seats to testing radar.

Delta's employees are all rigorously trained and evaluated. Flight attendants receive training at Delta's own school, and pilots in training must serve 12 years with the company before they earn the rank of captain. Pilots are trained, retrained, and tested at the Delta facility that is one of the industry's largest flight simulation centers. Each simulator costs as much as $6 million and emulates virtually every situation that could be encountered in an actual flight.

Delta's success is due in a large part to people. The firm benefits from a no-layoff policy and from a policy of promoting from within. Other than professionals with specialized skills, every Delta employee starts at an entry-level position. In addition, each employee is taught to perform at least two or three related functions, thereby producing increased flexibility.

Few of Delta's original employees could have envisioned today's modern company, with airplanes that seat 400 passengers and fly at speeds of 500 miles per hour to every corner of the globe. Nor could those early workers imagine an industry with 400 million passengers a year on 6 million scheduled flights. They would have laughed at the old joke that says that anyone who dies in the Southeast and goes to heaven will have to change planes in Atlanta. They also would not be surprised to learn that Delta has managed to maintain its commitment to providing the best possible service to customers. That's one aspect of the company that hasn't changed much over the decades.

Questions

1. In what ways is the airline industry different today as a result of deregulation? Which of the changes that have occurred in airline industry operations in recent years would have occurred regardless of deregulation?

2. In what ways has Delta benefited from deregulation?

3. Summarize the logic behind the decision to deregulate the airline industry. Are these arguments also valid explanations for deregulation moves in the banking industry?

24 *Your Career in Business*

Learning Goals

1. To explain the concept of an occupational cluster and how it helps one establish a career in business.

2. To describe the challenges facing nontraditional students seeking a business career.

3. To discuss why self-assessment is vital for career development.

4. To list the steps in the job search process.

5. To outline the special problems of women choosing business careers.

6. To explain how women can overcome career barriers.

A surprising list of products Americans enjoy today have their roots in Chinese culture. Included in this list are items as diverse as fireworks, precious Ming Dynasty jade sculptures, pottery, and Chinese checkers. But few Americans have assimilated Chinese culture with as much success as Virginia Kamsky, head of Kamsky Associates, Inc.

The company's abbreviation, KAI, means *open door* in Chinese — and it could not be more appropriate for this consulting firm. KAI negotiates contracts and joint ventures for a variety of Western firms seeking business ventures in the People's Republic of China. When it began in 1980, KAI's annual overhead was $35,000. Today, it is double that amount. In fact, Kamsky's company was responsible for negotiating more than $1 billion of these contracts in a recent year.

Those numbers look good on the books, and it was a book that first got Kamsky interested in China. Kamsky, now in her mid-thirties, was 10 years old when she read Pearl Buck's *The Good Earth*. Since then, China has fascinated her. She became fluent in Chinese during her senior year in high school, which she spent in Taiwan, and then matriculated in Princeton University, where she studied Japanese and classical Chinese, intending to be an academic.

Her career as a scholar never got started, though. With guidance from the chairman of her department, Kamsky took some classes at Princeton's Woodrow Wilson School of Public and International Affairs and found macroeconomics as fascinating as China itself.

Despite the frenzied pace of her business (she manages 30 employees, all of whom must speak Chinese fluently), Kamsky has no complaints. She recently remarked: "I love what I do. . . . Sure, it's not always easy. It can be scary. It can

be lonely. But the rewards are immeasurable."

After four years with Chase Manhattan's international division, where she spent a year as the only female banking officer in Japan, Kamsky struck out on her own when a bank customer asked her to leave Chase for his firm. She had met a number of high-level government officials and businesspeople when she worked for Chase, and they served her well. When China opened its doors to trade in 1980, KAI was one of only 20 firms allowed to do business in the country; the others were giant firms such as General Electric and Mobil.

The road to success has been filled with barriers, all of which Kamsky has leaped over. She frequently is the only woman present in a room when making presentations and negotiating deals. She works 16-hour days, rarely sleeps more than 5 hours a day, and keeps a Telex in her Park Avenue apartment, so she will not miss any requests for action. She takes no vacations and she is highly organized (she can pack for a three-week trip in four minutes). She does not expect to marry or have a family, but she does spend time with her sisters and their families. Kamsky's motto is perhaps provided by, fittingly enough, a fortune cookie: "In order to conduct an orchestra, you must turn your back on the crowd."[1]

Photo source: Copyright 1989 Steven Begleiter.

Chapter Overview

entry-level job
First permanent employment
after leaving school.

Selecting a career is probably the most important decision you will ever make. It is important to know the best way to approach career decisions and how to prepare for your first **entry-level job** — that is, your first permanent employment after leaving school.

First, you should become aware of employment projections and trends. The Bureau of Labor Statistics has developed three sets of job projections based on high, moderate, and low growth in economic activity. The moderate projection is that the U.S. labor force will grow by 21 million people during 1986–2000. The average annual job growth of 1.3 percent during this period contrasts with a 2.2 percent rate in the previous 14-year period.[2]

Various projections are presented in this chapter, in addition to discussions of important topics such as occupational clusters, nontraditional students, self-assessment, job search guidelines, resumés, personal interviews, and women in business.

The Occupational Cluster

In an employment area where the supply of workers exceeds the demand, many qualified individuals will still be able to obtain employment, but some will have to accept alternative jobs. Therefore, students should select and prepare for a group of related jobs — an **occupational cluster** — to maximize their employment opportunities.

occupational cluster
Group of related jobs.

The notion of an occupational cluster is not difficult to understand. Changes in technology and demand for goods and services make it difficult to forecast employment opportunities in specific jobs. A significant portion of the nation's future labor force will work in jobs relating to products and services not yet in existence.

Because each entry-level job requires specific skills and knowledge, students are wise to select a primary job interest. But they should also acquire the broad base of knowledge and skills associated with an overall occupational cluster. This kind of preparation allows for greater flexibility in seeking entry-level jobs.

The Bureau of Labor Statistics has identified 18 occupational clusters, including managerial and management-related occupations, marketing and sales, administrative support occupations, service occupations, production, and transportation and materials handling.[3]

Career Preparation

In most colleges, the business curriculum is organized around the key courses of accounting, business law, computers, economics, finance, management, marketing, and statistics. These courses deal with the common knowledge required in any meaningful entry-level business position. Students then acquire more specialized knowledge by taking advanced classes in each area.

Many students underestimate the difficulty of finding a desirable job, but thorough preparation can improve one's prospects. Besides academic prepara-

A summer internship at Procter & Gamble helped Vincent Clark land a job with the consumer goods firm after he graduated from college. During the internship, Clark gained experience selling paper products. After graduation, he joined P&G as a sales representative with a starting salary of about $25,000.

Photo source: © Junebug Clark 1989.

tion, students should try to gain related experiences, either through a job or participation in campus organizations. Cooperative education programs, internships, or work-study programs can give a student "hands-on" experience while he or she pursues an education. The importance of acquiring work experience is well illustrated by the fact that 70 percent of McDonald's senior management started with the firm by flipping hamburgers.[4]

Thorough preparation, along with a positive attitude, provides the initial flexibility needed for many kinds of business jobs. More knowledge can be acquired at any time by anyone valuing personal and professional improvement. Many business jobs are in high demand, but individuals with a good understanding of the workplace can gain entry-level employment in several areas.

The Nontraditional Student

Any college instructor can recount how college students have changed over the years. Most may remember when colleges and universities served a market of primarily 18- to 22-year-olds. It was this age group that once sought the entry-level jobs described earlier.

But times have changed. At the College of DuPage, in Glen Ellyn, Illinois, the average age of the student population is 30.9 years.[5] Clearly, America's collegiate student body is aging. This is the most distinguishing feature of the group referred to as nontraditional students.

Who Are the Nontraditional Students?

nontraditional student
Any student who does not fall into the 18-to-22-year-old age group.

The term **nontraditional student** can be defined as any student who does not fit into the 18-to-22-year-old age group (the "traditional" clients of higher education). To some, the term is already inaccurate, since older students have become the norm on many campuses. In any case, nontraditional students have two other characteristics: they work, either full-time or part-time; and college is often only one of their daily responsibilities. Many are married, and many, regardless of marital status, have children.

Most nontraditional students come from one of the following groups:

displaced homemaker
Homemaker who returns to school or takes a job because of divorce, widowhood, or economic reasons.

technologically displaced worker
Worker whose job is lost due to automation or industrial decline.

1. The **displaced homemaker** — a full-time homemaker who returns to school or joins the work force because of divorce, widowhood, or economic reasons.
2. The military service veteran — another major segment of nontraditional students, many of whom lack practical job skills.
3. The **technologically displaced worker** — one whose job was lost to automation or to the decline of the industry in which he or she was previously employed.
4. The older full-time employee — one who seeks additional education to enhance career prospects or for personal satisfaction.

Problems and Advantages of Nontraditional Students

All nontraditional students have two primary disadvantages as they seek career opportunities in business: their unfamiliarity with the fields in which they are attempting to secure skills, and the burden of their other responsibilities. A textile worker seeking to become a computer analyst, for example, has to adopt a whole new set of behaviors. This switch is often difficult for older students.

Going to college part-time, usually on weekends or in the evening, is exhausting. Most nontraditional students juggle the responsibilities of work, school, and maintaining a household. Some must also attend to a spouse or children. Studying may have to be accomplished at odd times: during meals, at coffee breaks, while commuting, or late at night, while the rest of the family sleeps.

But nontraditional students have one extremely important advantage: They have experience, even if it is in an unrelated field. Technologically displaced workers and returning students know how businesses operate. Displaced homemakers possess human relations skills from managing a household and from previous school, church, or community activities. And veterans can describe organizational foul-ups by the hour.

Nontraditional students need to take inventory of their personal accomplishments. They might list them in one column on a sheet of paper. Then, in a

Many colleges cater to the special needs of nontraditional students. The College of DuPage allows older students to design their curriculum around work, family, and other outside commitments. The college's Older Adult Institute is designed for persons 55 years and older and is especially helpful for people seeking skills that will prepare them for a new career.

Photo source: Courtesy of College of DuPage.

second column, they should try to relate these experiences to business-related work activities. This analysis will point up an individual's strengths and weaknesses. The weaknesses may be remedied with courses at a local college. The strengths can be featured in the resumé.

Like traditional students, older students need to look at employment trends and how to organize a job search. These topics are explored in the following sections.

Employment Trends

While the U.S. labor force is expected to grow by 19 percent between 1986–2000, it is important to look at where that growth will occur. Industry projections show that virtually all of the job growth is expected to be in wholesale and retail trade with about 4.9 million new jobs added to the labor force.

The composition of the labor force is also changing. Over 90 percent of the job growth in this period will come from women and minorities. For example, jobs for African-Americans are expected to expand 23 percent compared to the national average of 19 percent. Women in the labor force are expected to increase 25 percent. Employment for Asian and other race categories (American Indians, Alaskan Natives, Asians, and Pacific Islanders) is expected to jump 70 percent. The biggest job growth will come from Hispanics with a 74 percent increase.

College students should also study employment trends for specific occupations. From now until the year 2000, some of the business-related occupations with the largest growth will be retail sales personnel, general managers and top executives, accountants and auditors, computer programmers, computer systems analysts, first-line clerical supervisors and managers, and attorneys.[6]

Figure 24.1   Jobs Providing Personal and Financial Satisfaction

Self-Assessment for Career Development

In order to succeed in a job, a person should enjoy and value the tasks required by that job. It makes sense, then, for most people to select a line of work that provides such satisfaction. In addition to personal satisfaction, another consideration for many others is financial reward, as the advertisement in Figure 24.1 illustrates.

In addition to analyzing the demand for employment, people must understand themselves. The process of doing so will enhance their career development. The procedure used for this self-assessment can vary. But regardless of the format selected, it involves answering some tough questions:

1.   What motivates me to do something?
2.   What type of life-style do I want?
3.   What do I want to be doing in five years? in 10 years? in 20 years?
4.   What do I like and dislike?
5.   What do I fear?
6.   What personal values do I hold?
7.   What is my honest opinion of myself?

Finally, people must understand the job requirements if they are to do well in any job. The goal of career development, in fact, is to match individuals with compatible jobs. There are numerous sources of career information to assist students. Some of these are outlined in the section that follows.

Most people need help in both self-assessment and job analysis. College students can find considerable information and personal assistance in their school library, at their counseling center, and at career guidance or placement offices. During recent years, there has been a major trend toward career education. Most schools now have materials explaining how to analyze strengths and weaknesses, personal value structures, and job interests.

Job Search Guidelines

Lee Iacocca advises students as follows: "One of the toughest hurdles you'll ever overcome is landing your first job. That can be a confusing and frustrating experience. It will take work and determination on your part. But if you believe in yourself and trust your best instincts, you'll succeed."[7] Iacocca's comments are supported by a popular job guide that equates a student's job search to the work required in a 3-credit-hour course.[8]

What is the best way to find the right job for you? While there is no single approach, there are some general principles to follow.

The job search process is hard work. Good entry-level positions are highly sought after, and you must expect competition; thus, the best first step is to locate available positions that interest you. Then, be resourceful! Your success depends on gathering as much information as possible. Register at your school's placement office. Establish a placement, or credentials, file including letters of recommendation and supporting personal information. Become familiar with how the placement office conveys employment information. Most placement offices send out a monthly list of new job vacancies, so be sure your name and address are on their mailing list. If possible, visit the placement office regularly to check out new job information. Try to meet all the people who work in the office. They can prove invaluable in your job search.

Preparing Your Job Placement Materials

Most placement or credentials files include the following information: (1) letters of recommendation from people who know you — instructors, employers and others; (2) transcripts of academic work to date; (3) a personal data form reporting factual information; and (4) a statement of career goals. The placement office will provide special forms to be used in developing your placement file. These forms should be completed neatly and accurately. Employers are extremely interested in your ability to communicate in writing. The written narrative in your file should be clear, logical, and creative. Give yourself ample time to write several drafts and to polish the final copy. Be sure to prepare the best possible set of credentials. Let other people read and critique your work. Keep a copy of the final file for later use in preparing similar information for other employment sources. Check back with the placement office to make sure your file is in order.

Letters of reference are very important. Be selective in securing recommendations and try to include a business instructor in your list of references. The people you ask for recommendations (instructors, former employers, and community leaders) should know you, including your strengths and your career goals.

Always ask people personally if they will write a letter of recommendation for you. Be prepared to give them a brief outline of your academic preparation along with information concerning your entry-level preferences and your career objectives. This will help them prepare the letter and may enable them to respond quickly. But remember that these people are usually busy. Allow them adequate time to prepare their reference letters, then follow up on missing ones.

Finding Employment Sources

The next step — the process of identifying job openings — involves seeking out additional job sources, such as educational placement offices and private and public employment agencies.

Educational Placement Offices   Your school placement office is a good place to begin. If you have completed formal academic course work with more than one college or university, check with each of them about setting up a placement file. Some colleges have a reciprocity agreement that permits a student who has completed course work at several schools to establish a file with each placement office.

Private Employment Agencies   Another useful source to consider are the private employment agencies. These firms, which often specialize in certain types of jobs, perform several services for both employers and job candidates that are not provided elsewhere. For example, some private agencies interview, test, and screen job applicants.

Many agencies have established good relationships with employers looking for particular types of workers. They also can offer candidates valuable counseling on how to market skills to employers.

Private employment agencies usually charge the prospective employer a fee for finding a suitable employee. In some cases, the job seeker is expected to pay a fee. Be sure you understand the terms of any agreement you sign with a private employment agency.

Do not assume that the agency's terms will be the same in all areas. Since employment agencies are regulated by state and local governments, fees and fee regulations vary a great deal across the country. In New York City, for example, virtually all the fees for professional and clerical jobs are paid by the company at a fee structure of 1 percent per thousand dollars of yearly income. Similarly, the Robert Half agency, which deals in accounting, finance, and data-processing jobs, has a nationwide policy that all fees are employer paid. But, in Denver, the Snelling & Snelling agency reports that only 25 percent of its jobs are employer paid because of a stagnant local economy.

State Employment Offices   Still another source of job leads are the employment offices in your state. However, in many states, these public agencies process unemployment compensation along with other related work. Because of this mix of duties, some people view state employment agencies as providing services for semiskilled or unskilled workers. But these agencies also list jobs in many professional categories.

Other Sources   A variety of other sources can help in identifying job openings. They include (1) newspaper employment advertisements (the Sunday edition of

Figure 24.2   Identifying Firms that Match Personal Qualities

metropolitan newspapers is often a rich source of job leads); (2) trade journals or magazines; (3) college instructors and administrators; (4) community organizations, such as the local chamber of commerce; and (5) family and friends.

Another approach is to identify all the organizations where you think you might like to work. Many business firms place advertisements in career publications that designate the type of employees they are seeking. The Pepsi-Cola Company advertisement in Figure 24.2, for example, shows that the company is interested in people who are independent and have an entrepreneurial spirit. Mail a letter of inquiry and your resumé to those companies. If possible, direct your mailing to a specific person who has the authority to hire new employees (such as "Director of Personnel"). The letter should ask briefly about employment opportunities in a particular line of work. It should also ask for a personal interview.

Writing a Resumé

Regardless of how you identify job openings, you must learn how to develop and use a **resumé**, a written summary of your personal, educational, and professional achievements. The resumé is a very personal document covering your educational background, work experience, career preference, major interests, and other personal information. It should also include such basic information as your address and telephone number.

resumé
Written summary of personal, educational, and professional achievements.

The primary purpose of a job resumé is to highlight your qualifications. The traditional wisdom regarding the preparation of a resumé for someone seeking an entry-level job was to limit it to one page. However, Marilyn Moats Kennedy, a career planning consultant based in Wilmette, Illinois, now says many companies are seeking longer resumés from their applicants.[9] Regardless of whether a one-page or longer resumé is used, an attractive layout facilitates the employer's review of your qualifications. Figure 24.3 illustrates traditional one-page resumés using chronological, functional, and targeted formats.

There are several acceptable ways of preparing a resumé. Some use narrative sentences to explain job duties and career goals; others are in outline form. If the job resumé is being sent with the credentials file, the resumé can be quite short. Remember, too, that it should be designed around your own needs and objectives.

Studying Employment Opportunities

You should carefully study the various employment opportunities you have found. Obviously, some opportunities will be preferable to others, but you should consider a variety of factors when assessing each job possibility: (1) the actual job responsibilities, (2) industry characteristics, (3) the nature of the company, (4) geographical location, (5) salary and advancement opportunities, and (6) the job's contribution to your long-run career objectives.

Too many graduates consider only the most striking features of a job, perhaps the location or the salary. However, a comprehensive review of job openings should provide a balanced perspective of the overall employment opportunity, including long-run as well as short-run factors.

A number of information sources are useful in rating job prospects. Annual reports, financial summaries, and other data can usually be obtained from libraries, stockbrokers, and placement offices. In addition, a placement office or employment agency may be familiar with the companies on your list. If possible, try to visit each of these companies for firsthand impressions. Ask friends and associates what they know about any companies you are studying.

The Personal Interview

The initial objective of a job search is to obtain an appointment for an interview with prospective employers. Once this has been accomplished, you should begin planning for the interview. You will want to enter the interview equipped with a good understanding of the company, its industry, and its competition. Preparation includes obtaining the following essential information about the company:

1. How was the company founded?
2. What is its current position in the industry?
3. What is its financial status?
4. In which markets does it compete?
5. How is the firm organized?
6. Who are its competitors?
7. How many people does it employ?
8. Where are its plants and offices located?

Figure 24.3 Three Types of Resumé Formats

Chronological Format: Presents work experience and education in reverse time sequences and lists responsibilities and achievements under each category.

Sally Winter

Campus address (until 6/1/90)	Home Address
Elm Street Apartments #2B	123 Front Street
College Town, Ohio 44042	Teaneck, NJ 07666
Phone: (614) 555-1648	Phone: (201) 555-4995

EDUCATION   B.A. in Economics, Ohio State University, 1990 Cum laude—3.3 overall GPA—3.6 GPA in major

WORK EXPERIENCE

Paid for 70 percent of my college expenses through the following part-time and summer jobs:

<u>Legal Secretary</u>, Smith, Lee & Jones, Attorneys at Law, New York, NY—Summer, 1989
- Took dictation and transcribed tapes of legal proceedings
- Typed contracts and other legal documents
- Reorganized client files for easier access
- Answered the phone and screened calls for the partners

<u>Sales Clerk</u>, College Varsity Shop, College Town, Ohio— 1987-1989 academic years
- Helped customers with buying decisions
- Arranged stock and helped with window displays
- Assisted in year-end inventories
- Took over responsibilities of store manager when she was on vacation or ill

<u>Assistant Manager</u>, Treasure Place Gift Shop, Teaneck, NJ—summers and Christmas vacations—1987-1988
- Supervised two sales clerks
- Helped select merchandise at trade shows
- Handled daily accounting
- Worked comfortably under pressure during busy seasons

CAMPUS ACTIVITIES
- Elected captain of the women's varsity tennis team for two years
- Worked as a reporter and night editor on campus newspaper for two years
- Elected historian for Mortar Board chapter, a senior women's honorary

PERSONAL INTERESTS
- Collecting antique clocks, listening to jazz, swimming

REFERENCES AVAILABLE ON REQUEST

(continued)

Source: Adapted from C. Randall Powell, "Secrets of a Selling Resumé," *The Honda How to Get a Job Guide.* A special edition created by the staff of *Business Week's Guide to Careers,* © McGraw-Hill, 1985, pp. 6–7.

Figure 24.3　Three Types of Resumé Formats (*continued*)

Functional Format: Experience explained under major skill headings; degrees, job titles, employers, and dates are listed separately.

Sally Winter

Campus address (until 6/1/90)　　　　　　　Home Address
Elm Street Apartments #2B　　　　　　　　123 Front Street
College Town, Ohio 44042　　　　　　　　　Teaneck, NJ 07666
Phone: (614) 555-1648　　　　　　　　　　Phone: (201) 555-4995

Job Objective:　　　To work as a sales representative for a firm that markets
　　　　　　　　　　office products or services

Education:　　　　　B.A. in Economics, Ohio State University, 1990
　　　　　　　　　　Cum laude

Sales:　　　　　　　• Worked 10–15 hours per week in sportswear store as a sales
　　　　　　　　　　　clerk for two years
　　　　　　　　　　• Acted as assistant manager in my parents' gift store.
　　　　　　　　　　　Purchased merchandise at trade shows. Handled preferred
　　　　　　　　　　　customers in my parents' absence
　　　　　　　　　　• Interacted with office products and service sales
　　　　　　　　　　　representatives who called on my boss when I worked in a
　　　　　　　　　　　law office

Communications:　　• Worked as a reporter and night editor for two years on
　　　　　　　　　　　college newspaper
　　　　　　　　　　• Excelled academically in six writing and public speaking
　　　　　　　　　　　courses

Organization:　　　• Managed time effectively while working part-time, going to
　　　　　　　　　　　school full-time (earned a 3.3 overall GPA and a 3.6 GPA in
　　　　　　　　　　　my major)
　　　　　　　　　　• Worked in a gift shop during hectic seasonal rush periods
　　　　　　　　　　　—and enjoyed it
　　　　　　　　　　• Handled a variety of office tasks as a secretary in a law firm
　　　　　　　　　　　where I also became familiar with a range of office products
　　　　　　　　　　　and services

Work experience:
　　College Varsity Shop, College Town, Ohio—1987-1989 academic years
　　Treasure Place Gift Shop, Teaneck, NJ—summers and Christmas vacations—
　　　　1987-1988
　　Smith, Lee & Jones, Attorneys at Law, New York, NY—Summer, 1989

Personal Interests:　Collecting antique clocks, listening to jazz, swimming

References Available on Request

Figure 24.3   Three Types of Resumé Formats (*continued*)

Targeted Format: Focuses on capabilities and accomplishments that are targeted specifically
at a particular job or field.

Sally Winter

Campus address (until 6/1/90)	Home Address
Elm Street Apartments #2B	123 Front Street
College Town, Ohio 44042	Teaneck, NJ 07666
Phone: (614) 555-1648	Phone: (201) 555-4995

JOB TARGET   To work as a sales representative for a firm that markets
                     office products or services

EDUCATION   B.A. in Economics, Ohio State University, 1990
                     Cum laude

CAPABILITIES   • Assist customers in a helpful and pleasant manner
                     • Explain the pros and cons of a product, keeping the
                       customer's needs in mind
                     • Clinch a sales deal in a short amount of time
                     • Speak with ease in front of an audience
                     • Make a thorough inventory
                     • Handle basic accounting procedures
                     • Write effective reports using good grammar, spelling, and
                       punctuation
                     • Supervise sales personnel
                     • Make "cold calls" on potential clients

ACHIEVEMENTS   • Maintained a 3.3 overall GPA and a 3.6 GPA in my major
                       while holding a 10—15 hour-a-week job
                     • Assisted in the design and implementation of a store
                       display window that won a local merchants' association
                       award
                     • Helped lead the tennis team into regional championships
                       during two successive years as team captain

WORK HISTORY   • Sales Clerk, College Varsity Shop, College Town,
                       Ohio—1987-1989 academic years
                     • Assistant Manager, Treasure Place Gift Shop, Teaneck,
                       NJ—summers and Christmas vacations—1987-1988
                     • Legal Secretary, Smith, Lee & Jones, Attorneys at Law, New
                       York, NY—Summer, 1989

PERSONAL INTERESTS
                     • Collecting antique clocks, listening to jazz, swimming

REFERENCES AVAILABLE ON REQUEST

This information is useful in several ways. First, it helps instill in you a feeling of confidence during the personal interview. Second, it can keep you from making an unwise employment decision. Third, it can impress interviewers, who often try to determine how much applicants know about the company as a way of assessing their interest level. Candidates who do not make the effort to obtain such information are often eliminated from further consideration. Victoria Coleman, a psychologist and career counselor, put it this way:

A lot of people do not prepare for the interview. If I could give one piece of advice it would be: prepare. Know what you have to offer the organization. Second, you must have interviewed the corporation — that doesn't mean a personal interview; you could have gotten the annual report — so that when you walk in, you know how you could fit in the organization. If you don't know anything about the organization, how do you know if it's even appropriate for you to be there.[10]

Where do you get this preinterview information? First, your school placement office or employment agency should have information on prospective employers. Business instructors at your school may also provide tips. Your school or community library should have various references to help you investigate a firm or you can write directly to a company. Many firms publish career brochures as well as annual reports.

Finally, ask friends and relatives for input. Often they, or someone they know, may have had experience with the company.

There are two main reasons for poor performance in an interview. Interviewers report that many students fail due to ineffective communication, either because of inadequate preparation for the interview or a lack of confidence. Remember that the interviewer will first determine whether you can communicate effectively. You should be specific in answering and asking questions and should clearly and positively express your concerns. The questions interviewers ask most often include the following:

◆ What are your short-term and long-term career objectives?

◆ What do you see yourself doing five years from now?

◆ What are your greatest strengths?

◆ What are your weaknesses?

◆ How do you think you can contribute to this company?

◆ What were your best, worst, and favorite subjects in school?

◆ If you could have any job, which one would you choose?

It is important to know who is doing the interviewing. Most people who conduct initial employment interviews work in the firm's personnel division. They are in a staff position, which means that they can make recommendations to other managers about which individuals should be employed. Line managers get involved in interviewing later in the hiring process. In many instances, the decision is made by personnel people and the immediate supervisor of the prospective employee. In other cases, it is made entirely by the immediate supervisor. Rarely does the personnel department have sole hiring authority.

Job applicants also need to know how interviews are conducted. Interviewers use a number of techniques to elicit information. If you are interested in a job as a supervisor, for example, the company will want to know how you cope

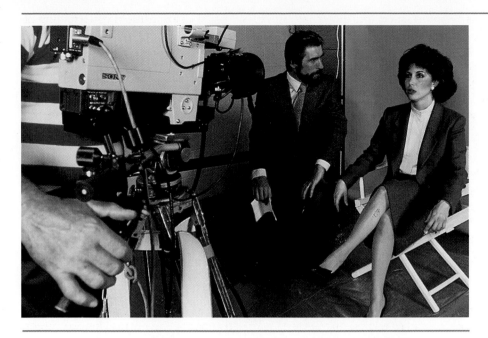

Photo source: © Alan D. Levenson 1989.

Some firms use videotaped interviews to screen job candidates. Applicants are requested to attend a videotaping session during which they respond to a list of questions prepared by the employer. The videotapes are viewed by several executives involved in the hiring process. Candidates showing the most potential are then invited to an in-depth personal interview.

with conflict. To find out, it may put pressure on you by creating a crisis situation, the **stress interview**. The interview may begin with a harsh criticism of your academic record or lack of practical experience. You may also be faced with a series of rapid-fire questions about how you would handle a hypothetical situation. It is important to retain your composure and communicate in a clear and precise manner.

Another, more common technique is for the interviewer not to talk much during the interview. This type of **open-ended interview** is designed to study your thought processes. The open-ended interview forces you to talk about yourself and your goals. If you appear unorganized, the interviewer may eliminate you as a possible employee. When faced with this type of situation, be sure to express your thoughts clearly and keep the conversation on target. Talk for about ten minutes, then ask some specific questions of the interviewer. Listen carefully to the responses. Remember that if you are prepared for a job interview, it will involve a mutual exchange of information.

If the initial interview is satisfactory, you will probably be invited to come back for another interview. Sometimes you will also be asked to take a battery of intelligence tests or aptitude tests. Most students do very well on these tests, because they have had plenty of practice in college!

The Employment Decision

By this time, the company knows a lot about you from your placement file, resumé, and initial interview. You should also know a lot about the company. The primary purpose of this interview is to determine whether you can work effectively with your potential superior and with your peers.

If you create a positive impression during your second or later interview, you may be offered a job. Again, your decision to accept the offer should depend

stress interview
Interview that creates a crisis situation in order to determine how that person copes with conflict.

open-ended interview
Interview designed to force applicants to talk about themselves and their goals.

Linda Kostic is manager of a building-materials store owned by Payless Cashways. At one time, the Kansas City–based chain of 168 stores in the Midwest and Southwest was operated entirely by men. That changed when David Stanley joined the firm as CEO and began hiring women for jobs traditionally held by men. As a result of Stanley's strong support of women in a male-dominated industry, slightly more than one-third of Payless's 13,000 employees are women, and seven of the firm's 49 top management positions are held by women.

on the closeness of the match between career opportunities and career objectives. If there appears to be a good match, your work is just beginning.

Make the best entry-level job decision you can; then get on with your career plan. Learn your job responsibilities as quickly and thoroughly as possible; then start looking for other ways to improve your performance and that of your company. Remember, your first promotion is just around the corner, so be sure not to miss the opportunity in your lifelong career development plan.

Women in Business

Women now account for 44.4 percent of the U.S. labor force.[11] However, while the number of employed women has increased substantially over the years, women are only now opening doors to executive suites.

Moving Away from Traditional Career Fields

Traditionally, women held teaching, nursing, and secretarial positions. While many probably exhibited an aptitude for such careers, others selected them because of societal and family pressure, poor career advice, and bias in other fields. The situation has changed considerably, with women entering fields that once were closed to them.

For instance, the number of women in field selling more than doubled in the 1980s. According to William O'Connell of Personnel Corp. of America, a human resource consulting firm, women are attracted to the equitable compen-

Table 24.1   Percentage of Selected Occupations Held by Women

Occupation	Percentage of Labor Force
Managerial and professional	43.4
Technical, sales, and administrative support	64.7
Service occupations	60.7
Precision production, craft, and repair	8.6
Operators, fabricators, and laborers	25.4
Farming, forestry, and fishing	15.9

Source: Statistical Abstract of the United States: 1988, 108th ed. (Washington, D.C.: U.S. Bureau of the Census, 1987), pp. 376–377.

sation system of field selling. O'Connell explains: "Performance in sales is quantitatively measured, whereas in office jobs it's qualitatively measured."[12] Examples of firms with significant increases in female sales personnel include McCormick & Co., which nearly doubled the level in three years; American National Insurance, which doubled in five years; and Dow Chemical, up 50 percent over five years.[13] The percentage of jobs in selected occupational groups is outlined in Table 24.1.

Today, women work in virtually all industries and career fields. Many have moved into middle management, and it is reasonable to anticipate that some of these people will progress to the top spots in their organizations as they acquire the relevant experience. This growth is likely to accelerate in the future. Nearly half of all business graduates are now female, up from less than 10 percent in the early 1970s.[14] Still, even today, women face a variety of career obstacles that cannot be overlooked if contemporary business is to reach its goal of career opportunity based solely on merit.

Special Career Problems Facing Women

What are some of the special problems that confront women who choose a business career? Women often lack the sort of career development model that is common for men. Young women entering industry today often represent their family's first generation of female businesspeople. They may lack the career perspectives that business executives provide their sons. Once employed, they sometimes lack peers on which to base a career development pattern. In the past, women tended to enter business with educational backgrounds in such nonbusiness areas as elementary education and home economics. They lacked business-oriented associations from their college days. Finally, the limited number of female executives provide few career models for young women advancing in a company, so businesswomen break new ground at each stage of their careers.

Male co-workers can also create special problems for female executives. Unaccustomed to working with women of equal or higher managerial rank, men are sometimes ill at ease in such situations. Some may disregard or circumvent directives or suggestions by female executives.

Married women face the dilemma created by a spouse's career aspirations and traditional family responsibilities. This problem should become easier to solve as more husbands and wives consider both careers in making their job decisions. While such situations can force difficult choices, successful executives do cope with the problems and go on to pursue their own professional goals. Success in any field has always required hard work and tough decisions, and contemporary businesswomen are proving they can and will make the sacrifices necessary to succeed.

Overcoming Career Barriers to Women

The career barriers cited above can be overcome. Most women are optimistic about their future, and their job progress justifies this favorable view. Two techniques women use to overcome career barriers have long been used by men: networking and the mentor system.

Networking   One of the major reasons women have been treated like outsiders in the world of business is their lack of professional contacts. They have simply not known the people who make the decisions. But networking may eventually help to change that situation. **Networking** refers to the development and use of contacts to get ahead in business. Job leads, information and advice about business deals, and interdepartmental information are all passed on through an informal network of co-workers.

networking
Development and use of contacts to get ahead in business.

In order to develop an effective networking system, women must be willing to provide information even when they gain nothing for themselves in return. Like their male counterparts, not all women are willing to do so. Networking may also break down because of the scarcity of women in high executive positions. No matter how willing women are to share information with each other and to help each other, without political clout they may not be very effective.

To solve this problem, women may have to turn to men who are well entrenched in the corporate power structure as their networking sources. In order to be effective, male-female networking must break down traditional barriers. Men are used to talking to other men about business, but some may be unwilling to do the same with women.

mentor system
Counseling or advising relationship between an aspiring employee and a higher-ranking executive.

The Mentor System   The **mentor system** refers to a counseling or advising relationship between an aspiring lower-level employee and a higher-ranking executive. It takes the concept of networking one step further by providing a promising but inexperienced person with a kind of advisor, a senior executive in the company who teaches a protegé about business and business politics.

A Final Note . . . the Authors' View

We believe that choosing a career is the most important, and often the toughest, decision you will ever have to make. There is little room for error; your future happiness depends on a wise, thoughtfully considered choice.

Do not procrastinate or trust others to make this decision for you. Follow the steps outlined here or in other sources, and make your own decision. Your instructors, parents, friends, and advisors will be willing to help in a multitude of ways. But in the end, the bottom line is that it is your own decision.

We hope this textbook has opened a panorama of business- and management-oriented careers for you. But whatever your decision, be sure it is right for you. As the old saying goes, "You pass this way only once." Enjoy!

Summary of Learning Goals

1.   Explain the concept of an occupational cluster and how it helps one establish a career in business.   When approaching a career in business, students should become aware of projected employment trends and should prepare for a group of related jobs — an occupational cluster — that offer good employment and career opportunities. A good business background along with a positive attitude will pave the way for many entry-level jobs. Students should also acquire business-related experience either through part- or full-time employment, cooperative education programs, or participation in campus activities.

2.   Describe the challenges facing nontraditional students seeking a business career.   Nontraditional students are any students who do not fall into the 18-to-22-year-old age group, the traditional clients of higher education. Many nontraditional students are displaced homemakers, veterans, technologically displaced workers, and full-time employed persons seeking education for career enhancement or personal satisfaction. All face two primary problems: the challenge of adopting new, unfamiliar behaviors and balancing their school responsibilities with their other responsibilities.

3.   Discuss why self-assessment is vital for career development.   Besides analyzing the demand for people in certain areas, students should learn about themselves. Help is available from school libraries, counseling centers, and career guidance or placement offices. Motivations, life-style preferences, career ambitions, and personal tastes and values need to be critically assessed. A person must enjoy and value the tasks required by a job if they are to be successful.

4.   List the steps in the job search process.   The steps in the job search process are as follows:

1. Prepare placement materials.
2. Find employment sources.
3. Prepare a resumé.
4. Study employment opportunities.
5. Prepare for the personal interview.
6. Make the employment decision.

5.   Outline the special problems of women choosing business careers.
Women have a number of problems in pursuing a business career:

1. Women lack the kinds of career development models that have been common for men.
2. They are sometimes discriminated against by male co-workers.
3. Married women are caught in the dilemma of allocating priorities among their spouse's career aspirations, family responsibilities, and their own career goals.

6.   Explain how women can overcome career barriers.   Women are overcoming former career barriers with two useful techniques: networking and the mentor system. Networking is the development and use of contacts to get ahead in business. The mentor system refers to a counseling or advising relationship between an aspiring employee and a higher-ranked executive.

Key Terms

entry-level job

occupational cluster

nontraditional student

displaced homemaker

technologically displaced worker

resumé

stress interview

open-ended interview

networking

mentor system

Review Questions

1. Why is the concept of an occupational cluster so important in career planning?

2. Discuss how nontraditional students should prepare for a career in business.

3. Trace the major employment trends outlined in the chapter. Do you expect these trends to affect your own personal situation? Why or why not?

4. What is meant by self-assessment? How would you respond to the self-assessment question outlined in Chapter 24?

5. Discuss how a student should approach each of the steps in the job search process.

6. Identify and discuss the various employment sources.

7. Differentiate among chronological, functional, and targeted resumés.

8. Explain the various types of personal interviews.

9. Explain how networking can assist women in overcoming employment barriers.

10. Describe how the mentor system works. Why is this concept so important to businesswomen?

Discussion Questions

1. An annual survey of first-year college students found that 76 percent of 210,000 respondents thought financial success was an "essential" or "very important" goal in their lives. By contrast, only 39 percent of the students rated "a meaningful philosophy of life" as equally important, the lowest figure ever in the 22-year history of the survey.

    How would you have evaluated these two goals? What are the implications of this research for career preparation?

2. A recent study by the University of Chicago reported that college graduates now earn a 55 percent premium over high-school graduates during the early years of their careers. This differential was up sharply from the 27 percent posted five years earlier. Researchers suggest the increase may represent the demand for more educated workers in a service-oriented economy. Do you agree with this conclusion? Why or why not?

3. Construct your own resumé following the procedure outlined in this chapter. Ask your instructor, friends, relatives, and associates to criticize it. What did you learn from this exercise?

4. Discuss how you would answer each of the questions interviewers most often ask.

5. "My philosophy of life is that if we make up our mind what we are going to make of our lives, then work hard toward that goal, we never lose — somehow we win out."

Ronald Reagan
(from a 1942 letter to a young fan)

Relate former President Reagan's comment to the content of Chapter 24.

Case

Mary Kay Cosmetics

If any one image stands out in the public's mind when the name Mary Kay Cosmetics is mentioned, it is likely to be the pink Cadillac. Thousands of these distinctively colored luxury autos have been awarded to extremely successful sales representatives of this Dallas–based firm. Pink is the theme color of the firm's founder Mary Kay Ash, who over the past quarter-century has built a tiny company into the second-largest direct-selling cosmetics company in the United States (after Avon). Ash began her business back in 1963 with a $5,000 investment and a team of ten saleswomen, following her retirement from a successful career in direct sales. Her cosmetic lines were based originally upon a formula for softening animal hides. Since then, Mary Kay Cosmetics has grown to include a sales force of over 200,000 representatives and yearly sales of more than $300 million.

In starting her cosmetics business, Ash sought to provide women with the kind of opportunities she thought were being denied to them in the early 1960s: the challenge of a meaningful career, high income, personal growth, and independence. She and her son, now Mary Kay president, Richard Rogers, began by focusing on their managerial strengths. Mary Kay chose to concentrate on creating a sales organization; Richard worked on marketing and finance. Both of them agreed that the new company would manufacture and distribute a complete line of skin-, body-, and hair-care products, cosmetics, toiletries, and fragrances. They also agreed that they would not use the typical manufacturer to retail store marketing channel, but would go directly to the homes of their customers. The key to marketing success would involve the abilities and efforts of highly trained *beauty consultants:* the sales representatives who go directly into customers' homes and offer skin-care classes to introduce people to new products and concepts.

Notes: "Beauty Bash," *USA Today,* August 1, 1988, p. 82; Kim Wright Wiley, "Cold Cream and Hard Cash," *Savvy,* June 1985; R. Bruce Holmgren, "Mary Kay Cosmetics Mechanizes Line in Two Stages," *Packaging,* March 1987, pp. 45–47; and Jill A. Fraser, "Behind Closed Doors: Can Public Firms That Go Private Handle Their New Freedom?" *Working Woman,* March 1986, pp. 56–58.

The approach proved highly successful. To finance the growth of the firm, Ash decided to sell ownership shares and become a publicly-traded corporation. By 1986, Mary Kay Cosmetics had cornered a 9 percent share of the total skin-care market, with Estee Lauder's Clinique as its major competitor. After being a publicly-held company for years, Mary Kay and her son bought back all outstanding shares in 1985, returning the firm to family ownership and control.

The number of women in the workforce has grown substantially since the early years of Ash's firm. However, she continues to believe strongly that her firm provides outstanding opportunities and role models for women. Her firm offers sales representatives flexibility in determining their own work schedules, fulfilling work, the opportunity to meet many people on a day-to-day basis, and good income. Indeed, a recent *Wall Street Journal* report revealed that more female Mary Kay Cosmetics representatives earn over $50,000 a year than do women in any other major U.S. company. If saleswomen advance to the position of national sales directors, they can expect to average $150,000 in annual earnings.

Mary Kay Cosmetics sales representatives begin their careers as independent beauty consultants. President Richard Rogers insists that every member of the corporate staff, in fact every job in the company, is geared to supporting the careers of consultants. If they succeed, the entire company succeeds. The training that accompanies the early months as a beauty consultant is designed to impart product knowledge and selling skills. It also contributes to building confidence, self-esteem, and a sense of leadership that transfers into other areas of a person's life. In return for this commitment, the sales representatives set their own career goals, grow professionally at their own pace, get to travel, and can plan their own time to make room for family and personal lives. With dedication and hard work, sales representatives have the opportunity to advance to positions of sales director and even national sales director.

Along the way, Mary Kay sales representatives are rewarded for their efforts. The company holds seminars, attended by thousands of Mary Kay consultants, at which it recognizes outstanding achievements. The

1988 Mary Kay seminar in Dallas extended over 13 days. During the gala event, $6 million in sales incentives were distributed. They ranged from the famous pink Cadillacs and trips to Europe to diamond rings and mink coats.

And everywhere was the tiny symbol that Mary Kay Ash had chosen almost 30 years earlier to reflect the goals of her firm: the bumblebee. As any aerodynamics engineer will explain, the bumblebee can't fly — its wings are too small to lift its body. But since none of the engineers bothered to tell the bumblebee, it flies anyway.

Mary Kay Cosmetics is flying, too. The company tries to set itself apart from other cosmetic companies by being aware of its customers' special needs, demonstrating a concern for individual life-styles, developing advanced products, and assuring the highest possible standards of quality. This commitment and devotion have carried it through more than a quarter-century as a recognized leader in the skin-care field.

Questions

1. Compare the three types of resumés. Which of the three would be most appropriate for use in evaluating a prospective Mary Kay Cosmetics employee?

2. Relate the materials in this case to the steps in the human resource planning process shown in Figure 11.2 on page 314. How would a company like Mary Kay Cosmetics go about recruiting qualified personnel?

3. A number of special career problems facing women were discussed in the chapter. Are such problems likely to be more or less prevelant in positions involving personal selling and customer service? How could Mary Kay employees seeking promotion to a position such as sales director utilize networking and the mentor system?

4. Why does Mary Kay Cosmetics categorize new sales representatives as independent beauty consultants rather than regular company employees? Is this practice used in other industries? What are the disadvantages of this approach?

Careers in Business

Careers in the areas of business, government, and the legal system include lobbyist, attorney, legal assistant, health and regulatory inspector, college recruiter, and employment counselor. Most of the careers were discussed in earlier sections, but they are worth repeating here.

Lobbyist

Large firms with important interests in local, state, or federal law hire lobbyists to represent their positions. Lobbyists are typically attorneys or have backgrounds in public relations.

Job Description. Lobbyists must monitor legal developments and legislative developments that affect their clients. Therefore, most of their work is done when the relevant legislative body is in session. They must keep legislators up-to-date on their clients' interests and needs and provide them with the information to justify positions, such as studies and research reports. They have formal and informal contact with legislators and work to build relationships with those most important to their clients' interests.

Career Path. Many lobbyists start with a public relations firm, which handles the public affairs of a number of firms. Others are attorneys with law firms that represent clients with interests in pending legislation. They begin by doing research or handling smaller issues. With experience, they take on larger and more important clients. Top lobbyists often start their own firms.

Salary. Earnings vary widely according to the size and number of clients.

Corporate Attorney

Businesses have many legal needs that are primarily filled by in-house or hired attorneys specializing in corporate law. In a recent year, 527,000 lawyers were in the work force, with much faster than average growth forecast until the year 2000.

Job Description. Depending on the size of the firm, the corporate attorney may be a generalist or a specialist in a type of law, such as tax law or labor law. The corporate attorney meets with top officials of the firm to discuss strategy and give legal advice. A great deal of time is spent preparing for negotiations or trials.

Career Path. New law school graduates do research for experienced attorneys and handle small cases. As they gain experience, they take on increased responsibility. With a firm, advancement into top management is sometimes the final career step.

Salary. Size of the company and location play a role in determining salaries. A corporate attorney with three years' experience in Atlanta could make as little as $26,000 in a recent year, while his counterpart in San Francisco made as much as $58,000. General counsels for large corporations can make more than three times as much as the average private sector salary in a law firm. The average salary for a corporate attorney in a recent year was $101,000.

Legal Assistant

Legal assistants, or paralegals, work with attorneys in providing legal services to individuals and businesses, including many small businesses. Currently, about 45,000 people are employed as legal assistants throughout the United States.

Job Description. Paralegals are supervised by an attorney. Most of their work involves legal research, but they also file court papers, help develop legal arguments, and assist with affidavits. Legal assistants working directly for firms assist attorneys with their specific areas of responsibility, such as financing.

Career Path. Beginning paralegals are given routine tasks and are closely monitored. As they acquire experience, they are assigned more challenging responsibilities. Opportunity for advancement is limited. However, some paralegals achieve management positions.

Salary. The average starting salary for legal assistants, in a recent year, was $17,200. Their average salary was $22,000.

Health and Regulatory Inspectors

As government employees, health and regulatory inspectors are responsible for implementing the rules and regulations established by Congress, federal agencies, or state and local governments. Recently, 125,000 people were employed as health and regulatory inspectors.

Job Description. Health inspectors work in the area of consumer safety, food, agricultural quarantine, and environmental health. Regulatory inspectors work in the areas of immigration; customs; postal service; aviation safety; railroads; motor vehicles; occupational safety and health; mines; wage-hour compliance; and alcohol, tobacco, and firearms. For example, agricultural quarantine officers inspect shipments and people entering the country in order to protect U.S. farming industries. Immigration inspectors examine those seeking to enter the United States. They process immigrant and temporary residence applications and examine visitors to the United States. Customs inspectors enforce the various laws and taxes dealing with exports and imports.

Career Path. A qualifying civil-service exam administered by federal, state, or local authorities is required. Successful candidates receive on-the-job training. A career ladder with regular promotions is available to all employees.

Salary. Entry-level salaries vary according to the activity involved. For example, in a recent year, customs inspectors averaged $24,635; food inspectors, $21,711; and aviation inspectors, $43,030. The national median salary is $23,700; the federal average is $28,900.

College Recruiter

College recruiters visit college campuses to search for qualified job applicants.

Job Description. Recruiters travel to colleges and universities throughout the nation with a list of job openings and the qualifications needed for each job. Recruiters talk with students about job openings, analyze their resumes, interview those who seem qualified, and arrange for further interviews at the company's home office for promising candidates.

Salary. Salaries vary widely depending on the size and location of the firm and its type of business. The median salary in a recent year was $26,500.

Employment Counselor

State employment offices employ the bulk of the nation's employment counselors. These people evaluate and attempt to place job applicants.

Job Description. Employment counselors use interviews and various tests to assess a person's capabilities for the job market. They then try to match these people to available jobs. Sometimes employment counselors get involved in career planning/counseling. They may also work with other agencies or educational institutions to improve a person's job skills.

Career Path. Most beginning counselors undergo a training period before taking on a caseload of job applicants. Supervisory and management positions are also available.

Salary. In a recent year, employment counselors with a state agency earned an average of $17,000, while those in private industry earned an average of $20,000.

Notes

Chapter 1

1. M. Sharon Murphy, "Service is Jewel in Emerald's Crown," *Journal-American,* August 4, 1988, p. C1.
2. Wood quote from Sears, Roebuck and Co. *1987 Annual Report,* p. 24.
3. The term *land* is sometimes substituted for *natural resources* in the economics literature.
4. Charles Wolf, "America's 'Decline': Illusion and Reality," *The Wall Street Journal,* May 12, 1988, p. 22.
5. Robert J. Samuelson, "Productivity Bounces Back," *Newsweek,* August 22, 1988, p. 50.
6. "Madison Avenue Moscow Style," *U.S. News & World Report,* January 16, 1989, p. 19.
7. Shawn Tully, "Europe Goes Wild Over Privatization," *Fortune,* March 2, 1987, pp. 68–69; and "Prof: Private Corporations Should Run Prisons," *Marketing News,* March 14, 1988, p. 43.

Chapter 2

1. Joseph P. Shapiro, Robert F. Black, Patrick Barry, and Alice Z. Cunlo, "When Companies Play Nanny," *U.S. News & World Report,* September 19, 1988, pp. 43–45; additional information provided by Loretta M. Kollar, director of the Excel-Nyloncraft Learning Center, January 4, 1989.
2. Reported in *The Wall Street Journal,* July 10, 1979.
3. Gene R. Laczniak and Jacob Naor, "Global Ethics: Wrestling with the Corporate Conscience," *Business,* July–September 1985, p. 7.
4. This study is discussed by Max Ways in "Business Faces Growing Pressure to Behave Better," *Fortune,* May 1974, p. 310.
5. Alan L. Otten, "Ethics on the Job," *The Wall Street Journal,* July 14, 1986, p. 19.
6. Nancy Jeffrey, "Preparing for the Worst," *The Wall Street Journal,* December 7, 1987, p. 29.
7. Chris Welles, "What Led Beech-Nut Down the Road to Disgrace," *Business Week,* February 22, 1988, pp. 124–128.
8. Rick Wartzman, "Nature or Nurture? Study Blames Ethical Lapses on Corporate Goals," *The Wall Street Journal,* October 9, 1987, p. 27.
9. Todd Barrett, "Business Ethics for Sale," *Newsweek,* May 9, 1988, p. 56.
10. John Goodwin Tower, "Ethics in American Business: A National Opinion Survey," Touche Ross, *Ethics in American Business: A Special Report,* pp. 68–70.
11. Tower, *Ethics in American Business: A Special Report,* p. 19.
12. Gregory L. Miles, "Information Thieves Are Now Corporate Enemy No. 1," *Business Week,* May 5, 1988, pp. 120–125.
13. Daniel Seligman, "The Case of the Ethical Ketchup," *Fortune,* February 16, 1987, p. 28.
14. Kerry Elizabeth Knobelsdorff, "More Shoppers Weight Ethics," *Christian Science Monitor,* July 10, 1987.
15. Joan O'C. Hamilton, Emily T. Smith, Paul Angiolillo, and Reginald Rhein, "'No Smoking' Sweeps America," *Business Week,* July 27, 1987, pp. 40–52.
16. Nancy Seufert, "All Fired Up Over Smoking," *Time,* April 18, 1988, pp. 64–75, and "Company Policy: If You Light Up, You're Fired," *Journal American,* January 21, 1987, p. A5.
17. John Hoerr, "Privacy," *Business Week,* March 28, 1988, pp. 61–65.
18. Joseph J. Kane, "A Big Stink on the Pigeon," *Time,* June 6, 1988, p. 22.
19. Denise Grady, "Something Fishy about Acid Rain," *Time,* May 9, 1988, p. 61.
20. Denise M. Topolnicki, "Overextended Family," *Savvy,* July 1988, pp. 24–25.
21. Karen Blumenthal, "Job-Training Effort," *The Wall Street Journal,* February 9, 1987, pp. 1, 15.
22. Alex Beam, "Why Few Ghetto Factories Are Making It," *Business Week,* February 16, 1987, pp. 86–89.
23. Nancy J. Perry, "The Education Crisis: What Business Can Do," *Fortune,* July 4, 1988, pp. 71–81.
24. Ed Magnuson, "The Pentagon up for Sale," *Time,* June 27, 1988, pp. 16–18.
25. Gloria Borger, "The Enemy Within," *U.S. News & World Report,* July 4, 1988, pp. 16–26.
26. Cathy Trost, "Labor Letter," *The Wall Street Journal,* July 19, 1988, p. 1.
27. U.S. Equal Employment Opportunity Commission, *Affirmative Action and Equal Employment: A Guidebook for Employers* (Washington, D.C.: U.S. Government Office, 1974).
28. Quotation in Carrie Gottlieb, "Hiring the Handicapped," *Fortune,* September 26, 1988, p. 11. See also Roger Ricklefs, "Faced with Shortages of Unskilled Labor, Employers Hire More Retarded Workers," *The Wall Street Journal,* October 21, 1986, p. 39.
29. "The Birth of a Saleswoman," *U.S. News & World Report,* February 6, 1989, p. 40.
30. This section draws from Daniel Seligman, "Harassment II," *Fortune,* August 1, 1988, p. 251; Joseph Pereira, "Women Allege Sexist Atmosphere in Offices Constitutes Harassment," *The Wall Street Journal,* February 10, 1988, p. 23; Amy Saltzman, "Hands Off at the Office," *U.S. News & World Report,* August 1, 1988, pp. 56–58, and Robert L. Simison and Cathy Trost, "Abusive Acts: Sexual Harassment at Work Is a Cause for Growing Concern," *The Wall Street Journal,* June 24, 1986, p. 1.
31. Betsy Freeman, "Breaking the Code," *Savvy,* June 1988, pp. 55–56, 94.
32. "Fair-Pay Drive by Women Hits a Legal Detour," *U.S. News & World Report,* September 15, 1985, p. 31.
33. "Battle of the Sexes Over 'Comparable Worth,'" *U.S. News & World Report,* February 20, 1984, pp. 73–74. See also "Why Can't a Woman's Pay be More Like a Man's?" *Business Week,* January 28, 1985, pp. 82–83; and Mariam Rosen, "Comparable Worth: New Management Bugaloo," *Dun's Business Month,* February 1985, p. 52.
34. This section is based on John D. Williams "Businessmen to Seek End to Greenmail, Golden Parachutes," *The Wall Street Journal,* January 24, 1985, p. 26; "The Bigger Splash from Saul Steinberg's Dive into Disney," *The Economist,* July 16, 1984, p. 69; Andrew Kirtzman, "Disney's Buyout of Steinberg Sparks Lawsuit, Investigations: Analysts Rush to Condemn," *Variety,* June 20, 1984, p. 30.
35. "How the Market is Rigged Against You," *U.S. News & World Report,* December 1, 1986, pp. 44–51.
36. "Who Made the Most — And Why," *Business Week,* May 2, 1988, pp. 50–56.
37. Graef S. Crystal, "The Wacky, Wacky World of CEO Pay," *Fortune,* June 6, 1988, pp. 68–78.

Chapter 3

1. Stuart Gannes, "America's Fastest Growing Companies," *Fortune,* May 23, 1988, pp. 28–40; and Christopher Knowlton, "What America Makes Best," *Fortune,* March 28, 1988, pp. 40–54.
2. "U.S. Debt Rose at Slower Pace in First Quarter," *The Wall Street Journal,* June 8, 1988, p. 52.
3. "Budget Deficit Grew 6.3% in First 8 Months of U.S. Fiscal Year," *The Wall Street Journal,* June 22, 1988, p. 54.
4. "How Much is $2,000,000,000,000?" *U.S. News & World Report,* September 1, 1985, p. 33.
5. "U.S. Debt Rose at Slower Pace in First Quarter."
6. "Budget Deficit Grew 6.3% in First 8 Months of U.S. Fiscal Year"; "Fiscal 1989 Budget, Without New Taxes, Is Cleared by Senate," *The Wall Street Journal,* June 7, 1988, p. 74.
7. Bruce Nussbaum, "Needed: Human Capital," *Business Week,* September 19, 1988, p. 101.
8. "Deficit Fallout: Dangers for Business, Workers," *U.S. News & World Report,* February 11, 1985, p. 30.
9. Mitchell Locin, "Trade law gets Reagan signature," *Chicago Tribune,* August 24, 1988, sec. 3, pp. 1, 6.
10. Ibid.
11. Ibid.
12. OECD *Economic Outlook,* December 1987 (Paris: Organization for Economic Cooperation and Development).
13. Annetta Miller, "Burgers: The Heat Is On," *Newsweek,* June 16, 1988, p. 53.
14. "Will the U.S. Stay Number One?" *U.S. News & World Report,* February 2, 1987, pp. 18–22.
15. "What America Makes Best."
16. Trowbridge quote in "What America Makes Best," p. 40.
17. "Will the U.S. Stay Number One?"
18. "Unleashing Workers, *U.S. News & World Report,* August 24, 1987, p. 44.
19. "What America Makes Best."
20. Bro Uttal, "Companies That Serve You Best," *Fortune,* December 7, 1987, pp. 98–116.
21. Sharon Hanes Brown, "Capitalizing on Customer Complaints," *Sky,* pp. 118–122; Uttal, "Companies That Serve You Worst," *Fortune,* December 7, 1987. p. 116.
22. Laura A. Walbert, "Service is our most important product," *Forbes,* April 6, 1987, pp. 48–50.
23. "Companies That Serve You Best."

24. "America's Blue Collars Get Down to Business," *U.S. News & World Report,* February 2, 1988, pp. 52–53.
25. Karen Pennar, "The Productivity Paradox," *Business Week,* June 6, 1988, pp. 100–102.
26. David Carey, "The World Class Mill," *Financial World,* March 8, 1988, p. 30.
27. "The Productivity Paradox"; data on service sector productivity from Maureen F. Allyn, "Rising Factory Productivity Is Giving the Expansion Room to Run," The Fortune Forecast in *Fortune,* August 1, 1988, pp. 25–26.
28. "Productivity Paradox."
29. Otis Port, "How the New Math of Productivity Adds Up," *Business Week,* June 6, 1988, pp. 103–114.
30. Simon Ramo, "How to Revive U.S. High Tech," *Fortune,* May 9, 1988, pp. 124–133.
31. Information on dropouts/near illiterates and Frito/Lay recruiting from Aaron Bernstein, "Help Wanted," *Business Week,* August 10, 1987, pp. 48–53.
32. Michael Broday, "Helping Workers to Work Smarter," *Fortune,* June 8, 1987, pp. 86–88.
33. Anne Lowrey Bailey, "Chrysler's Iacocca, Class of '45, Brings Verve to Lehigh U. Fund-Raising Drive," *The Chronicle of Higher Education,* December 2, 1987, pp. 1, 30.
34. "Helping Workers to Work Smarter."
35. Ibid.
36. Kenneth Labich, "The Innovators," *Fortune,* June 6, 1988, pp. 50–64.
37. Barbara Rudolph, "Eyes on the Prize," *Time,* March 21, 1988, pp. 50–51.
38. Stephen Kindel, "What's Wrong with Corporate R&D," *Financial World,* January 26, 1988, pp. 25–30.
39. "Eyes on the Prize."
40. Stuart Gannes, "The Good News About U.S. R&D," *Fortune,* February 1, 1988, pp. 48–56.
41. Quigg quote from "Eyes on the Prize."
42. Charles P. Alexander, "The Declining Dollar: Not a Simple Cure," *Time,* November 16, 1987, p. 57.

Chapter 4

1. Sylvia Nogaki, "Going Global," *The Seattle Times/Seattle Post Intelligencer,* January 17, 1988, pp. B1, B7.
2. Lester Thurow, "A Surge in Inequality," *Scientific American,* May 1987, p. 33.
3. "The 100 Largest U.S. Multinationals," *Forbes,* July 25, 1988.
4. Karen Elliot House, "The '90s & Beyond: For All Its Difficulties U.S. Stands to Retain Its Global Leadership," *The Wall Street Journal,* January 23, 1989, p. A6.
5. Exchange rates from *Chicago Tribune,* January 8, 1989, sec. 12, p. 29.
6. Exchange rates from *Chicago Tribune,* January 27, 1985, sec. 12, p. 26.
7. Tim Carrington, "Vital Parts: Military's Dependence on Foreign Suppliers Causes Rising Concern," *The Wall Street Journal,* March 24, 1988, p. 1.
8. These examples are from Christopher Knowlton, "The New Export Entrepreneurs," *Fortune,* June 6, 1988, pp. 98, 102.
9. Stewart Toy, Neil Gross, James B. Treece, "The Americanization of Honda," *Business Week,* April 25, 1988, pp. 90–92, 94, 96.
10. "Avon Adds China to its List of Foreign Markets," *Marketing News,* October 25, 1982, p. 1; "Avon is Calling in China," *Seattle Times,* September 23, 1982, p. A2.
11. Jason Zweig, "It Was a Matter of Economics," *Forbes,* February 22, 1988, pp. 106, 108.
12. Steven Koepp, "Good News in Trade — But Beware," *Time,* September 26, 1988, pp. 59; and Clemons P. Wack, Robert F. Black, William J. Cook, Peter Dworkin, Mike Tharp, Pamela Sherrid, David Lawday, Dusko Dudo, David Bartal, "Business Without Borders," *U.S. News & World Report,* June 20, 1988, p. 49.
13. International Trade Administration, July 9, 1985.
14. John Bussey, "For What It's Worth, Japan's Auto Makers Are Buying American," *The Wall Street Journal,* March 7, 1988, p. 12.
15. Mary L. Nowicki, "Countertrade," *Monsanto Magazine,* November 2, 1988, pp. 24–27.
16. Alyssa A. Lappen, "Worldwide Connections," *Forbes,* July 27, 1988, pp. 78–82.
17. CPC International *1987 Annual Report,* pp. 14–15.
18. The Procter & Gamble Company *1988 Annual Report,* pp. 15, 19.
19. Peter Behr, "Donut Company Discovers Junk-Food Hole in the Market in Japan," *The Seattle Times,* December 25, 1984, p. G3.
20. Janice Simpson, "Remember Metric? Shift by U.S. Proves an Impossible Feat," *The Wall Street Journal,* July 2, 1987, pp. 1, 10.

21. Edward A. Finn, Jr., "Sons of Smoot-Harley," *Forbes,* February 6, 1989, p. 38.
22. Mary H. Cooper, "Trade Systems May Grapple with Admitting Soviets," *Journal-American,* September 14, 1986, p. D7.
23. Charles Alexander, "A Freeze Play at the Banks," *Time,* September 13, 1982, pp. 72–73.
24. Fredrick Painton, "Toward Real Community?" *Time,* April 18, 1988, pp. 54–55.
25. Susan Lee, "An Impossible Dream?" *Forbes,* July 25, 1988, pp. 78–83.
26. "Getting Ready for the Great North American Shakeout," *Business Week,* April 4, 1988, pp. 44–46.
27. Finn, "Sons of Smoot-Harley," p. 40.
28. Richard I. Kirkland, Jr., "Outsiders Guide to Europe in 1992," *Fortune,* October 24, 1988, p. 126.
29. Kevin Manly, "No Food, No Fuel, and No Fun," *USA Today,* November 16, 1988, pp. B1–B2.
30. "Losing Ground," *Time,* May 9, 1988, p. 63; and David Wessel, "Despite Fallen Dollar, Americans Continue to Snap Up Imports," *The Wall Street Journal,* February 9, 1988, p. 1.
31. "Vital Statistics," *U.S. News & World Report,* February 1, 1988, p. 73.
32. "Losing Ground," pp. 62–63.
33. Steven Golob, "No Ebb Tide for Imports," *Nation's Business,* September, 1988, p. 18.
34. John Motavalli, "Selling to the Marx Brothers," *Adweek Special Report,* December 5, 1988, pp. 16–19.
35. John Heins, "A Mixed Blessing," *Forbes,* February 22, 1988, pp. 63–65.
36. Brian Dumaine, "Japan's Next Punch in U.S. Markets," *Fortune,* September 26, 1988, p. 146.

Chapter 5

1. Based on Steven Flax, "The Ultimate Incentive," *INC.,* May 1988, pp. 147–148.
2. Earl C. Gottschalk, Jr., "Public Limited Partnership Sales Are Expected to Slump," *The Wall Street Journal,* January 4, 1988, p. 24B; Alan Murray and Monica Langley, "Relatively New Form of Business Structure Is Causing Controversy," *The Wall Street Journal,* June 30, 1987, pp. 1, 19; and Lisa Gubernick, "A little Problem," *Forbes,* December 1, 1986, p. 201.
3. Charles P. Alexander, "A Handshake for All Seasons," *Time,* May 11, 1987, p. 54.
4. Lawrence J. Tell, "Finley Kumble: The Bigger They Are, The Harder . . . ," *Business Week,* May 2, 1988, pp. 94–95.
5. U.S. Bureau of the Census, *Statistical Abstract of the United States: 1988,* 108th edition (Washington D.C.: U.S. Government Printing Office, 1987), p. 495.
6. The Small Business Administration.
7. Dayton Hudson Corporation, *1987 Annual Report,* p. 14.
8. Elliott D. Lee, "Takeover Pace Is Seen Picking Up in 1988," *The Wall Street Journal,* January 4, 1988, pp. 8B, 19B.
9. Christopher Power and Mark Maremont, "The Top 200 Deals," *Business Week,* April 15, 1988, pp. 47–54.
10. Judith H. Dobrzynski, "Learning from the Mangled Mergers of the Past," *Business Week,* March 21, 1988, p. 126.
11. John Byrne, "Who Made the Most — and Why," *Business Week,* May 2, 1988, p. 50.
12. Icahn quote is from "Icahn on Icahn" *Fortune,* February 29, 1988, pp. 54–58.
13. CBS Inc. *Annual Reports,* 1986 and 1987.
14. Ellyn E. Spragins, "When Power Investors Call the Shots," *Business Week,* June 20, 1988, pp. 126–130.
15. Carol J. Loomis, "Buyout Kings," *Fortune,* July 4, 1988, pp. 52–60, and Bill Powell and Carolyn Friday, "Deal of the Century," *Newsweek,* December 12, 1988, pp. 40–44.
16. "Engineer Your Own LBD," *U.S. News & World Report,* January 30, 1989, pp. 74, 76.
17. Vittoria quote is from Chuck Hawkins, "Is Avis Moving into the Passing Lane?" *Business Week,* May 9, 1988, pp. 100, 105.
18. Blue Diamond Growers, *Protecting Your Food Supply,* pp. 4–5.
19. Blue Diamond Growers, *Annual Report 1986–1987,* and *Almond Facts.*
20. Corie Brown, "Why Farm Co-ops Need Extra Seed Money," *Business Week,* March 21, 1988, p. 96.

Chapter 6

1. Larry Hicks, "A Small Firm Takes Tentative Wing," *Sacramento Bee,* August 7, 1988, pp. E1, E4; and personal correspondence with John Stoll, January 1989.

2. The data in this section is from Janice Castro, "Big vs. Small," *Time*, September 5, 1988, p. 49; "USA Snapshots," *USA Today*, June 15, 1988, p. B1; and "The Job Machine," a supplement to *U.S. News & World Report*, September 28, 1987, pp. A24–A25.
3. Leon Winer, "Many Students Seek the Skills Successful Entrepreneurs Need," *Marketing News*, July 18, 1986, p. 30.
4. Mindy Pantiel, "The Sky's the Limit," *Entrepreneur*, February 1989, pp. 12–13.
5. Buck Brown, "Market Niche: Teaching Entrepreneurship," *The Wall Street Journal*, September 14, 1988, p. 37.
6. "Center for Entrepreneurial Leadership," *Enterprise*, Spring 1988, p. 6.
7. James F. DeCarlo and Paul R. Lyons, "Toward a Contingency Theory of Entrepreneurship," *Journal of Small Business Management*, July 1980, pp. 37–42.
8. "The Entrepreneurial Personality," *INC.*, August 1988, p. 18.
9. Golisano's quote from *INC.*, April 1988, p. 128.
10. Ellen Graham, "The Entrepreneurial Mystique," *The Wall Street Journal*, May 20, 1985.
11. U.S. Bureau of the Census, *Statistical Abstract of the United States: 1988*, 108th ed. (Washington, D.C.: U.S. Government Printing Office, 1987), p. 517.
12. "Small Business Is Defined and Defended," *CPA Client Bulletin*, April 1980, p. 1.
13. These features were suggested in *Meeting the Special Problems of Small Business* (New York: Committee for Economic Development, 1947), p. 14.
14. Miriam Horn, "Happiness in the Hills," *U.S. News & World Report*, December 12, 1988, pp. 83–84.
15. Stephen D. Solomon, "The INC. 100," *INC.*, May 1988, p. 120.
16. Bureau of Labor Statistics, *Employment and Earnings*, January 1985.
17. "When Job Training Will be a Lifelong Process," *U.S. News & World Report*, May 9, 1983, p. A25.
18. "Grocery Express Flirts with Success as Service," *Arkansas Democrat*, October 3, 1988, p. 5C; and Kathy Rebello, "Fax Rings Dinner Bell with Delivery Service," *USA Today*, December 21, 1988, p. 1B.
19. Paulette Thomas, "Against Sizeable Odds, a Small Firm Is Poised to Run a Space Station," *The Wall Street Journal*, March 11, 1988, pp. 1, 10.
20. Pam McClintock, "The Kid Rep Doesn't Kid Around," *Sales & Marketing Management*, June 1988, p. 16. Reprinted from *The Washington Times*.
21. Frederick Waugh, "Anatomy of a Start-Up: Frulait's Makers Eye Expansion With Yogurt-Juice Drink," *Adweek's Marketing Week*, February 29, 1988, p. 2.
22. Doug Margeson, "The Class Reunion," *Journal-American*, May 17, 1988, p. D1.
23. The data in this section is from Buck Brown, "Business Failure Rates Aren't So Bad after All," *The Wall Street Journal*, May 20, 1988, p. 29; and "Business Failures," *The Wall Street Journal*, March 3, 1988, p. 19. (Data from Dun & Bradstreet Corp.)
24. Interagency Study of Small Business Financing, 1982.
25. Debra Prinzing, "Nona Brazier: Recycling Champion," *Woman Inc.*, December 5, 1988, pp. 1, 10.
26. Maria Henson, "Law Attacks Sex Barriers," *Arkansas Gazette*, December 11, 1988, pp. 1B, 2B; the data in this section is from "Fast Forward," *The Conference Board*, October 1987, p. 3; and "Women-Owned Companies," *INC.*, January 1987, p. 11.
27. Jay Finegan, "Sisterhood is Powerful," *INC.*, December 1988, p. 19; and Henson, "Law Attacks Sex Barriers."
28. Kevin D. Thompson, "Starting Over," *Black Enterprise*, August 1988, p. 58.
29. *The State of Small Business: A Report to the President*, transmitted to Congress, May 1985, p. 347.
30. Jack Wynn, "Where the Money Is," *Nation's Business*, October 1988, p. 79.
31. David L. Birch, "Trading Places," *INC.*, April 1988, p. 42.
32. Charles R. Kuehl and Peggy A. Lamburg, *Small Business* (Hinsdale, Ill.: The Dryden Press, 1987), p. 432.
33. Eugene Carlson, "Webegone Agency," *The Wall Street Journal Reports*, June 10, 1988, p. 19R; C. Michael Gooden, "Bad Machine," *INC.*, June 1988, p. 34; and Kevin D. Thompson, "Starting Over."
34. Richard W. Anderson, "Bringing Top-Line Computer Gear to the Sticks," *Business Week*, May 23, 1988, pp. 123–124.
35. These statistics are from Jeffrey Cohen, "Franchising and Its Discontents," *Adweek Special Report*, August 1, 1988, p. M.R.C. 10; and "Franchisors Expected to Prosper in U.S. and Abroad in '88," *Marketing News*, May 23, 1988, p. 5.
36. "Franchises Expected to Prosper in the U.S. and Abroad in '88," pp. 5, 7.
37. Meg Whittemore, "International Franchising," *INC.*, April 1988, p. 120.

38. "New Franchisees for Less Than $100,000," *Changing Times*, September 1987, p. 84.
39. Jim Osterman, "'Subway Sandwiches': Franchises on a Roll," *Adweek's Marketing Week*, February 15, 1988, p. 61.
40. "Franchises Expected to Prosper in U.S. and Abroad in '88," p. 7.
41. Thomas G. Marx, "Distribution Efficiency in Franchising," *MSU Business Topics*, Winter 1980, p. 51.
42. These examples are from Roland Addison's, "Success: A Long-Term Proposition," *Nation's Business*, October 1988, p. 69; Jim Osterman, "'Subway Sandwiches': Franchises on a Roll"; and Sanford L. Jacobs, "To Buy or Not to Buy," *The Wall Street Journal*, June 10, 1988, p. 26R.
43. Paul Plawin, "Franchiser: Buying a Piece of the Action," *Changing Times*, September 1988, p. 81.
44. *Ibid*, p. 82.

Chapter 7
1. Katherine M. Hafner and Richard Brandt, "Steve Jobs: Can He Do It Again?" *Business Week*, October 24, 1988, pp. 74–78, 80 (Jobs quote on p. 80), and John Schwartz, Michael Rogers, and Richard Sandzer, "Steve Jobs Comes Back," *Newsweek*, October 24, 1988, pp. 46–51.
2. Clemons P. Work, Betty Brophy, Andrea Gabor, Robert F. Black, Mike Thorp, and Alice Z. Cuneo, "The 21st Century Executive," *U.S. News & World Report*, March 7, 1988, p. 51.
3. Kenneth Labich, "The Seven Keys to Business Leadership," *Fortune*, October 24, 1988, p. 59.
4. Laurie Baum, "Korea's Latest Export: Management Style," *Business Week*, January 19, 1987, p. 66.
5. Peter Nulty, "What a Difference Owner-Bosses Make," *Fortune*, April 25, 1988, pp. 97–98.
6. Frank Gibney Jr., "Southwest's Friendly Skies," *Newsweek*, May 30, 1988, p. 49.
7. Carol Hymowitz, "Five Main Reasons Why Managers Fail," *The Wall Street Journal*, May 2, 1988, p. 31.
8. Penny Moser, "The McDonald's Mystique," *Fortune*, July 4, 1988, p. 113.
9. *Moore Financial Group Annual Report 1987*.
10. Kenneth Labich, "Big Changes at Big Brown," *Fortune*, January 18, 1988, p. 56.
11. Arie P. DeGeus, "Planning as Learning," *Harvard Business Review*, March–April 1988, p. 70.
12. The Bush Industries examples in this section are from James Cook, "A Better Mousetrap," *Forbes*, March 7, 1988, pp. 96, 98.
13. Kenneth Labich, "The Seven Keys to Business Leadership."
14. George Garties, "Fire-Swept First Interstate Banked on Disaster Plan," *Journal-American*, June 6, 1988, C3.
15. Andrew Feinberg, "He Dares to Delegate," *Success*, June 1988, pp. 34–38. Quote from p. 37.
16. Kerry Hannon, "The King of Ketchup," *Forbes*, March 21, 1988, pp. 58–59, 62, 65.
17. Kenneth Labich, "Big Changes at Big Brown," p. 58.
18. Terrence E. Deal and Allan A. Kennedy, *Corporate Cultures: The Rites and Rituals of Corporate Life* (Reading, Mass.: Addison-Wesley, 1982), chap. 6.
19. Dillard B. Tinsley, "Understanding Business Customers Means Learning About Its 'Culture,'" *Marketing News*, March 14, 1988, p. 15.
20. John A. Byrne, "The Rebel Shaking Up Exxon," *Business Week*, July 18, 1988, pp. 104–107, 110–111.
21. Matthew Schifrin, "Horatio Alger Kim," *Forbes*, October 17, 1988, pp. 94, 96. Quotes from p. 96.
22. Lee Iacocca with William Novak, *Iacocca: An Autobiography* (New York: Bantam Books, 1984), p. 52.
23. Zachary Schiller, "Can Bridgestone Make the Climb," *Business Week*, February 27, 1989, pp. 78–79; Laura R. Walbert, "The Liquidator," *Forbes*, May 5, 1986, p. 62; and Ralph E. Winter, "Firestone's Restructuring Bid Works Well — to a Point," *The Wall Street Journal*, January 14, 1987, p. 6. Ross quote from Winter, p. 6.
24. These guidelines are suggested in Larry D. Alexander, "Effective Time Management Techniques," *Personnel Journal*, August 1981, pp. 637–640; and "How to Stop Wasting Time — Experts' Advice," *U.S. News & World Report*, January 25, 1982, pp. 51–52. The examples of how selected CEOs approach time management are from Ford S. Worthy, "How CEOs Manage Their Time," *Fortune*, January 18, 1988, pp. 88–89, 92, 96–97.

Chapter 8
1. Information gathered from a telephone interview with Wendy Lewis, Director of Human Resources, Chicago Cubs.

2. Lee Iacocca with William Novak, *Iacocca: An Autobiography* (New York: Bantom Books, 1984), p. 153.
3. Geoff Lewis, Arne R. Field, John J. Keller, and John W. Verity, "Big Changes at Big Blue," *Business Week,* February 15, 1988, pp. 92–98. Akers quote from p. 93.
4. The above material and quotes are from Alfred D. Chandler, Jr., "Origins of the Organization Chart," *Harvard Business Review,* March–April 1988, pp. 156–157. McCallum quote from p. 156. Ford quote from p. 157.
5. Quinn's estimate and the Franklin Mint example are from Jeremy Main, "The Winning Organization," *Fortune,* September 26, 1988, pp. 50–52, 56, 60.
6. "Translating Bureaucratise," *U.S. News & World Report,* October 3, 1977, p. 26.
7. Thomas Moore, "Goodbye, Corporate Staff," *Fortune,* December 21, 1987, p. 76.
8. Larry Reibstein, "IBM's Plan to Decentralize May Set a Trend — but Imitation has a Price," *The Wall Street Journal,* February 19, 1988, p. 17.
9. C. Northcote Parkinson, *Parkinson's Law and Other Studies in Administration* (Boston: Houghton Mifflin, 1957), pp. 2–11.
10. Moore, p. 65.
11. Keith Davis, *Human Behavior at Work* (New York: McGraw-Hill, 1976), pp. 268–270.
12. Anne B. Fisher, "The Downside of Downsizing," *Fortune,* May 23, 1988, pp. 42, 46.
13. Gifford Pinchot III, *Intrapreneuring* (New York: Harper & Row, 1985), p. ix.
14. Ronald Alsop, "Consumer — Product Giants Relying on 'Intrapreneurs' in New Ventures," *The Wall Street Journal,* April 22, 1988, p. 25.
15. Main, p. 6.
16. Fisher, p. 42.
17. Peter F. Drucker, "The Coming of the New Organization," *Harvard Business Review,* January–February 1988, p. 48.
18. Fisher, p. 46.

Chapter 9

1. Paragraphs 1 and 2 and Packer quotations from Joel Dreyfuss, "Victories in the Quality Crusade," *Fortune,* October 10, 1988, pp. 80, 82.
2. Resa W. King, "UPS Gets a Big Package — of Computers," *Business Week,* July 25, 1988, p. 66A.
3. Quoted in John Holusha, "An Assembly-Line Revolution," *New York Times,* September 3, 1985, p. D1.
4. Ibid., p. D4.
5. "First a Vision, Now the Payoff," *General Motors Public Interest Report,* May 16, 1988, pp. 2–6.
6. Gene Bylinsky, "Invasion of the Service Robots," *Fortune,* September 14, 1987, p. 84.
7. Ralph E. Winter, "Upgrading of Factories Replaces the Concept of Total Automation," *The Wall Street Journal,* November 30, 1987, p. 1.
8. Bill Saporito, "IBM's No-Hands Assembly Line," *Fortune,* September 15, 1987, p. 105.
9. Robert Kreitner, *Management* (Boston: Houghton Mifflin, 1983), p. D4.
10. Russell Mitchell, "Boldly Going Where No Robot Has Gone Before," *Business Week,* December 22, 1986, p. 45.
11. Bylinsky, "Invasion of the Service Robots," pp. 81–88.
12. William D. Marbach, "A Small World Grows Tinier," *Newsweek,* November 30, 1987, p. 65.
13. Ralph King, Jr., "Made in the U.S.A." *Forbes,* May 16, 1988, pp. 108–112. See also Suzanne Loeffelholz, "CAD/CAM Comes of Age," *Financial World,* October 8, 1988, pp. 38–39.
14. Carey W. English, "Factories That Turn Nuts into Bolts," *U.S. News & World Report,* July 14, 1986, pp. 44–45; and Bill Saporito, "The Smokestacks Won't Tumble," *Fortune,* February 2, 1987, pp. 30–32.
15. William G. Wild, Jr., and Otis Port, "This Video 'Game' is Saving Manufacturers Millions," *Business Week,* August 17, 1987, pp. 82–84.
16. Alex Taylor III, "Lee Iacocca's Production Whiz," *Fortune,* June 22, 1987, pp. 36–44.
17. Kenneth Labich, "The Innovators," *Fortune,* June 6, 1988, pp. 50–64. See also Michael Hiestand, "Brave New World of Design," *Adweek's Marketing Week,* October 24, 1988, pp. 30, 34.
18. John Bussey and Douglas R. Sease, "Manufacturers Strive to Slice Time Needed to Develop Products," *The Wall Street Journal,* February 23, 1988, p. 1; and Christopher Know Hon, "What America Makes Best," *Fortune,* March 28, 1988, pp. 40–54.
19. Cynthia F. Mitchell, "Some Firms Resume Manufacturing in U.S. after Foreign Fiascoes," *The Wall Street Journal,* October 14, 1986, pp. 1, 29.
20. Eugene Carlson, "What's a Toyota Plant Worth to Kentucky? Possibly Plenty," *The Wall Street Journal,* June 9, 1987, p. 37.
21. John A. Byrne, "Culture Shock at Xerox," *Business Week,* June 22, 1987, pp. 106–110.
22. Raab quote is from Stephen Kindel, "Ample Rewards," *Financial World,* June 14, 1988, p. 23.
23. Steven P. Galante, "Small Manufacturers Shifting to 'Just-in-Time' Techniques," *The Wall Street Journal,* December 21, 1987, p. 25; and Ralph E. Winter, "Upgrading of Factories Replaces the Concept of Total Automation," *The Wall Street Journal,* November 30, 1987, pp. 1, 8.
24. Harold C. Livesay, *American Made* (Boston: Little, Brown, 1979), pp. 20–21.
25. Richard B. Chase and Nicholas J. Aquilano, *Production and Operations Management: A Life Cycle Approach* (Homewood, Ill.: Richard D. Irwin, 1981), p. 516.
26. John Hillkirk, "The Man Japanese Firms Follow," *USA Today,* May 23, 1988, p. 7B.
27. *Corning Glass Works 1987 Annual Report,* p. 38.
28. "The New Industrial Revolution," *Business Week,* May 11, 1981, p. 98.

Chapter 10

1. Joshua Hyatt, "A Self-Managing Restaurant," *Inc.,* February 1989, p. 66. Reprinted by permission.
2. Daniel Machalaba, "Up to Speed: United Parcel Service Gets Deliveries Done By Driving Its Workers," *The Wall Street Journal,* April 22, 1986, p. 1.
3. Stuart Chase, *Men at Work* (New York: Harcourt, Brace & World, 1941), pp. 21–22.
4. Abraham H. Maslow, "A Theory of Human Motivation," *Psychological Review,* July 1943, pp. 370–396.
5. Ibid., pp. 294, 382.
6. Robert Louis Stevenson, *Familiar Studies of Men and Books* (1882).
7. Jeffrey Rothfeder, "Memo to Workers: Don't Phone Home," *Business Week,* January 25, 1988), p. 90.
8. Hay El Nasser, "Video Terminals Watch Workers," *USA Today,* July 7, 1986, p. 6B.
9. Ibid.
10. Douglas McGregor, *The Human Side of Enterprise* (New York: McGraw-Hill, 1960), pp. 33–34, 47–48.
11. Stan Luxenberg, "Lifetime Employment, U.S. Style," *New York Times,* April 17, 1983.
12. James R. Norman, "A New Union Carbide Is Slowly Starting to Gel," *Business Week,* April 8, 1988, pp. 68–69.
13. "Labor Letter," *The Wall Street Journal,* May 27, 1986, p. 1.
14. Bill Saporito, "The Revolt Against 'Working Smarter,'" *Fortune,* July 21, 1986, pp. 58–65.
15. Bradley A. Stertz, "Management Lesson for Today: How Not to Make Workers Loyal," *The Wall Street Journal,* May 19, 1988, p. 22.
16. Frederick Herzberg, *Work and the Nature of Man* (Cleveland: World Publishing, 1966).
17. Beth Brophy, "Nice Guys (and Workshops) Finish First," *U.S. News & World Report,* August 22, 1988, p. 44.
18. "A Raise in Every Paycheck," *Inc.,* February 1984, pp. 110–114.
19. Brophy, "Nice Guys (and Workshops) Finish First."
20. Brian Dumaine, "Cool Cures for Burnout," *Fortune,* June 20, 1988, pp. 78–84.
21. Peter Drucker, *The Practice of Management* (New York: Harper & Bros., 1954), pp. 128–129.
22. Charles R. Walker and Robert Guest, *Man on the Assembly Line* (Cambridge, Mass.: Harvard University Press, 1952), p. 19.
23. Jeremy Main, "Work Won't Be the Same Again," *Fortune,* June 28, 1982, p. 58.
24. "The ABCs of QWL at GM," *Nation's Business,* May 1983, p. 30.
25. "Flexible Hours Help a Hospital Counter a National Nursing Shortage," *The Wall Street Journal,* January 23, 1987, p. 1.
26. "Flex-Time Isn't a Cure-all, But Many Workers and Firms Love It," *The Wall Street Journal,* March 15, 1988, p. 1.
27. Joe L. Welch and David Gordon, "Assessing the Impact of Flexitime on Productivity," *Business Horizons,* December 1980, pp. 61–65.
28. Mark Memmott, "4-Day Workweek Still Rare," *USA Today,* August 11, 1986, p. 4B.
29. Bob Cohn, "A Glimpse of the 'Flex' Future," *Newsweek,* August 1, 1988, p. 38, and Amy Saltzman, "One Job, Two Contented Workers," *U.S. News & World Report,* November 14, 1988, pp. 74, 76.
30. John Hillkirk, "Commuting by Computer," *USA Today,* July 15, 1988,

p. 7B; Clark Ansberry, "When Employees Work at Home, Management Problems Often Arise," *The Wall Street Journal,* April 20, 1987, p. 25.

31. Susan Lee and Stuart Flack, "Hi Ho, Silver," *Forbes,* March 9, 1987, pp. 90–98.

Chapter 11

1. Hastings quotation from Bruce G. Posner, "Right from the Start," *Inc,* August 1988, p. 96. See also Nancy J. Perry, "Here Come Richer, Riskier Pay Plans," *Fortune,* December 19, 1988, p. 51.
2. "Human Resource Managers Grow in Corporate Stature," *The Wall Street Journal,* October 18, 1988, p. 1.
3. Brian Dumaine, "The New Art of Hiring Smart," *Fortune,* August 17, 1987, pp. 78–79.
4. "The New Headhunters," *Business Week,* February 6, 1989, p. 65.
5. Marisa Manley, "Employment Lines," *Inc,* June 1988, p. 132.
6. "Bias Suit Settlement," *USA Today,* January 11, 1989, p. B1.
7. Malcolm S. Forbes, "How Not to Turn Down Job Applicants," *Forbes,* June 15, 1977, p. 22.
8. Dumaine, "The New Art of Hiring Smart."
9. "Ban on Lie Detector Use Now in Effect," *Mobile Register,* December 28, 1988, p. 7A; Albert R. Karr, "Law Limiting Use of Lie Detectors Is Seen Having Widespread Effect," *The Wall Street Journal,* July 1, 1988, p. 19.
10. Leonor Cervera, "First Impressions Count," *USA Today,* September 19, 1988, p. B1.
11. Theodore T. Pettus, *One on One: Win the Interview, Win the Job* (New York: Random House, 1981). See also Dumaine, "The New Art of Hiring Smart."
12. Alix M. Freedman, "Harmful Habit: Cigarette Smoking Is Growing Hazardous to Careers in Business," *The Wall Street Journal,* April 23, 1987, pp. 1, 27.
13. This cost estimate is from William L. Weis, "Can You Afford to Hire Smokers?" *Personnel Administrator,* May 1981, pp. 71–78; also see Patrick Fleenor, David L. Kurtz, and Louis E. Boone, "Where There's Smoke You May Be Fired," *Journal of Applied Business Research,* Spring 1988, p. 82.
14. Joel Dressang and Mark Memmott, "Firms Moving to Remove Smokers," *USA Today,* February 11, 1987, p. 5B; "Most Companies Now Have Smoking Policies," *Business,* April–June 1988, p. 61.
15. Winifred Yu, "Firms Tighten Resume Checks of Applicants," *The Wall Street Journal,* August 20, 1985, p. 31.
16. "Firm Says 5% of Doctors Lied in Recruiting Efforts," *The Wall Street Journal,* February 11, 1988, p. 39.
17. Roger Ricklefs, "Health Costs Spur Small Firms to Screen New Workers," *The Wall Street Journal,* January 3, 1989, p. B2.
18. Andrew Kupfer, "Is Drug Testing Good or Bad?" *Fortune,* December 19, 1988, pp. 133–140.
19. Ricklefs, "Health Costs Spur Small Firms to Screen New Workers."
20. Michael Waldholz, "Drug Testing in the Workplace: Whose Rights Take Precedence?" *The Wall Street Journal,* November 11, 1986, p. 39.
21. "AIDS: Where Insurers Are Showing Little Mercy," *Business Week,* November 21, 1988.
22. *Arline v School Board of Nassau County — U.S. Supreme Court, 1987; Vincent Chalk v Orange County Superintendent of Schools — U.S. Court of Appeals, 9th Circuit, 1988.* See also Roger Ricklefs, "Victims of AIDS-Related Discrimination Are Fighting Back — and Getting Results," *The Wall Street Journal,* July 15, 1988, p. 19.
23. "Labor Letter," *The Wall Street Journal,* November 22, 1988, p. 1.
24. "Motorola Sends Its Work Force Back to School," *Business Week,* June 6, 1988, p. 80.
25. "Who Gets Training?" *The Wall Street Journal,* July 17, 1987, p. 23.
26. Roger Ricklefs, "Firms Turn to Videos to Teach Workers," *The Wall Street Journal,* December 6, 1988, p. B2; "Videos Are Starring in More and More Training Programs," *Business Week,* September 7, 1987, p. 108; and Al Urbanski, "Electronic Training May Be in Your Future," *Sales & Marketing Management,* March 1988, pp. 46–48.
27. James Braham, "Cultivating Tomorrow's Execs," *Industry Week,* July 27, 1987, pp. 34–38; and Judith H. Dobrzymaki, "GE's Training Camp: An 'Outward Bound' for Managers," *Business Week,* December 14, 1987, p. 98.
28. Richard L. Daft, *Management* (Hinsdale, Ill.: Dryden Press, 1988), p. 702.
29. Lisa R. Sheeran and Donna Fenn, "The Mentor System," *Inc,* June 1987, p. 140.
30. Walter Kiechel, III, "How to Appraise Performance," *Fortune,* October 12, 1987, pp. 239–240.
31. "Labor Letter," *The Wall Street Journal,* October 15, 1985.

32. Andrew Kupfer, "Is Drug Testing Good or Bad?" *Fortune,* December 19, 1988, p. 138.
33. *1988 AMS Smoking Policies Survey* (Trevose, Pa.: Administrative Management Society, 1988). See also Cheryl L. Lockett, *Smoking in the Workplace* (Fort Washington, Pa.: LRP Publications, 1988).
34. Gregory Stricharchuk, "Fired Employees Turn the Reason for Dismissal into a Legal Weapon," *The Wall Street Journal,* October 2, 1986, p. 33.
35. Everett T. Suters, "The Toughest Job Around," *Inc,* October 1986, pp. 138–140.
36. Beth Brophy and Maureen Walsh, "Thanks for the Bonus, But Where's My Raise?" *U.S. News & World Report,* July 20, 1987, p. 43.
37. "Getting Ready for a Competitive Age," *Southern Highlights,* Winter 1988, p. 17; "Commissions Catch on at Department Stores," *Adweek's Marketing Week,* February 1, 1988, p. 5.
38. Michael Schroeder, "Watching the Bottom Line Instead of the Clock," *Business Week,* November 17, 1988, pp. 134, 136.
39. Perry, "Here Come Richer, Riskier Pay Plans," pp. 52–53.
40. Steven Waldman and Betsy Roberts, "Grading 'Merit Pay,'" *Newsweek,* November 14, 1988, pp. 45–46; Paul Plawin, "Bonuses for the Best," *Changing Times,* August 1988, p. 75.
41. Jacob M. Schlesinger, "GM's New Compensation Plan Reflects General Trend Tying Pay to Performance," *The Wall Street Journal,* January 26, 1988, p. 39; "It Often Doesn't Pay to Give Cash Bonuses," *The Wall Street Journal,* August 17, 1987, p. 23; and "Hawaii's the Word," *USA Today,* January 20, 1988, p. B2.
42. Perry, "Here Come Richer, Riskier Pay Plans," p. 58.
43. Jolie Solomon, "Pay Equity Gets a Tryout in Canada — And U.S. Firms Are Watching Closely," *The Wall Street Journal,* December 28, 1988, p. B1.
44. Kathy Rebello and John Hillkirk, "Sabbaticals at Core of Apple Perks," *USA Today,* June 10, 1988, p. B1; and William Dunn, "Sabbaticals Aim to Cool Job Burnout," *USA Today,* July 25, 1986, p. B1.
45. Bob Cohn, "A Glimpse of the 'Flex' Future," *Newsweek,* August 1, 1988, p. 39.
46. Earl Ubell, "Is Your Job Killing You?" *Parade Magazine,* January 8, 1989, p. 4–7.
47. "OSHA Awakens From Its Six-Year Slumber," *Business Week,* August 10, 1987, p. 27.
48. Anthony Ramirez, "Making Better Use of Older Workers," *Fortune,* January 30, 1989, pp. 179–187.
49. "Labor Letter," *The Wall Street Journal,* July 19, 1988, p. 1; Kenneth E. Newgren, C. E. Kellogg, and William Gardner, "Corporate Responses to Dual-Career Couples: A Decade of Transformation," *Arkansas Business & Economic Review,* Summer 1988, pp. 85–96; and "Home Is Where the Heart Is," *Time,* October 3, 1988, pp. 46–53.
50. Jolie Solomon, "The Future Look of Employee Benefits," *The Wall Street Journal,* September 7, 1988, p. 29.

Chapter 12

1. Quotation from Christopher S. Eklund, "How A&P Fattens Profits By Sharing Them," *Business Week,* December 22, 1986, p. 44. See also John Hoerr, "Is Timework a Management Plot? Mostly Not," *Business Week,* February 20, 1989, p. 70.
2. "Blue Collars in the Boardroom: Putting Business First," *Business Week,* December 14, 1988, p. 126.
3. Quoted in Campbell R. McConnell, *Economics* (New York: McGraw-Hill, 1975), p. 754.
4. Matt Yancey, "Labor Groups Lost 62,000 Members," *Mobile Press Register,* January 23, 1988, p. 8C.
5. Jacob M. Schlesinger, "Plant-Level Talks Rise Quickly in Importance: Big Issue: Work Rules," *The Wall Street Journal,* March 11, 1987, p. 1.
6. Kenneth B. Noble, "Teamsters Gain a Readmittance to AFL-CIO," *New York Times,* October 25, 1987, p. 1; and "The AFL-CIO: A Tougher Team with the Teamsters," *Business Week,* November 9, 1987, p. 110.
7. Robert J. Samuelson, "Minimum-Wage Politicking," *Newsweek,* July 6, 1988, p. 54.
8. Robert Townsend, *Up the Organization* (New York: Alfred A. Knopf, Inc., 1970), p. 93.
9. "A Silver Bullet for the Union Drive at Coors?" *Business Week,* July 11, 1988, pp. 61–62.
10. Janet Quist, "The Plant-Closing Bill," *Nation's Cities Weekly,* August 8, 1988, p. 1; Alan Murray, "Business Is Worried That Bill on Plant Closings Presages More Laws Mandating Worker Benefits," *The Wall Street Journal,* August 17, 1987, p. 44; and Monica Langley and Walter S. Mossberg, "Trade Bill, Vulnerable to a Veto, Goes to Reagan after Senate Vote," *The Wall Street Journal,* April 28, 1988, p. 3.

11. David Kirkpatrick, "What Givebacks Can Get You," *Fortune*, November 24, 1986, p. 64.
12. Alex Kotlowitz, "Job of Shop Steward Has New Frustrations in Era of Payroll Cuts," *The Wall Street Journal*, April 1, 1987, pp. 1, 23.
13. "The Secondary Boycott Gets a Second Wind," *Business Week*, June 27, 1988, p. 82; "Labor's Boardroom Guerrilla," *Time*, June 20, 1988, p. 50; and "Labor Letter," *The Wall Street Journal*, July 12, 1988, p. 1.
14. "The Strikers Strike Out," *U.S. News & World Report*, October 26, 1987, pp. 41–42.
15. Larry Weisman, "A Year after Strike, NFL Sees No Gain," *USA Today*, September 22, 1988, pp. C1, C2.
16. Larry Reibstein, "More Firms Use Peer Review Panel to Resolve Employees' Grievances," *The Wall Street Journal*, December 3, 1986, p. 29.
17. Richard M. Hodgetts, *Management: Theory, Process, and Practice* (Philadelphia: W. B. Saunders, 1979), pp. 334–335.
18. Ralph King, Jr., "Fair — To Whom?" *Forbes*, November 28, 1988, p. 116.
19. Personal correspondence from W. E. Whalley, IBM manager of information activities, July 7, 1983.
20. "When Workers Get in the Takeover Game," *U.S. News & World Report*, June 8, 1987, p. 48. See also Joseph R. Blasi, *Employee Ownership: Revolution or Ripoff?* (New York: Ballinger, 1988).
21. David Kirkpatrick, "How the Workers Run Avis Better," *Fortune*, December 5, 1988, pp. 103–114.
22. Nelson W. Aldrich, Jr., "ESOP's Rising Stock," *INC.*, April 1985, p. 59. See also "They Own the Place," *Time*, February 6, 1989, pp. 50–51.
23. Daniel Forbes, "With Its Image at an All-Time Low, Labor Turns to Madison Avenue," *Adweek's Marketing Week*, August 1, 1988, pp. 30, 32.
24. "For American Business, a New World of Workers," *Business Week*, September 19, 1988, pp. 112–113.
25. "Unions' Popularity Grows among Health-Care Workers," *The Wall Street Journal*, February 3, 1987, p. 1.

Chapter 13
1. Christine Donahue, "Former Beatrice Executive Develops Microwaveable Entrees for Kids," *Adweek's Marketing Week*, August 8, 1988, p. 17.
2. Richard B. Bagozzi, "Marketing as an Organizational System of Exchange," *Journal of Marketing*, October 1974, p. 77. Further work by Bagozzi on this subject appears in "Marketing as Exchange," *Journal of Marketing*, October 1975, pp. 32–39, and "Marketing as Exchange: A Theory of Transactions in the Marketplace," *American Behavioral Scientist*, March–April 1978, pp. 535–536.
3. General Electric *1952 Annual Report*, p. 21.
4. Matthew Grimm, "A Truly Interactive Printer," *Adweek's Marketing Week*, August 29, 1988, p. 41.
5. Mary-Paige Royer, "Please Give Generously, Okay?" *American Demographics*, June 1988, pp. 35–37, 58, 60.
6. "Selling of Self," *Marketing News*, August 15, 1987, pp. 4, 11.
7. Janet Meyers, "States Lure Foreign Tourists," *Advertising Age*, March 14, 1988, p. 38.
8. Amy Zipkin, "Car Lovers Take a Shine to Beauty Treatment," *Advertising Age*, May 16, 1988, pp. S-12–S-13.
9. Len Strazewski, "Path Clear for Roadway Expansion," *Advertising Age*, June 20, 1988, pp. S-9–S-10.
10. "Telemarketing Firms Barred from New York," *Marketing News*, October 24, 1988, p. 5.
11. Otis Port, Katherine M. Hafner, and Robert Block, "TV That Lets the Viewer Call the Shots," *Business Week*, May 2, 1988, pp. 100–104.
12. James F. Engel, Roger D. Blackwell, and Paul W. Miniard, *Consumer Behavior*, 5th ed. (Hinsdale, Ill.: The Dryden Press, 1986), p. 5.
13. Patricia Winters, "Using Pop Psychology?" *Advertising Age*, June 6, 1988, p. 70.
14. Ronald Alsop, "Advertisers Put Consumers on the Couch," *The Wall Street Journal*, May 13, 1988, p. 19.
15. Pete Engardio, Walecia Konrad, Ronald Grover, Jo Ellen Davis, and Lois Therrien, "Fast Times on *Avenida Madison*," *Business Week*, June 6, 1988, pp. 62–67.
16. David Kiley, "At Long Last, Detroit Gives Consumers the Right of Way," *Adweek's Marketing Week*, June 6, 1988, pp. 26–28.
17. Horst H. Stipp, "Children as Consumers," *American Demographics*, February 1988, pp. 27–32; Joe Agnew, "Children Come of Age as Consumers," *Marketing News*, December 4, 1987, pp. 8–9; and Laurie Freeman, "Colgate Makes Play for Kids' Market," *Advertising Age*, September 12, 1988, p. 24. Quote is from Ellen Graham, "As Kids Gain Power of Purse, Marketing Takes Aim at Them," *The Wall Street Journal*, January 19, 1988, pp. 1, 23.

18. Ira Teinowitz, "Heileman Focuses on Regional Brands," *Advertising Age*, May 2, 1988, p. 81; and Christine Donahue, "Campbell Soup May Restructure in Favor of Regional Marketing," *Adweek's Marketing Week*, May 4, 1987, pp. 1, 8.
19. Aimee Stern, "Tired of Playing Mind Games," *Adweek's Marketing Week*, July 13, 1987, pp. 1, 6.
20. Michael Hiestand, "Value Judgment Cures Hospital's Image," *Adweek's Marketing Week*, February 29, 1988, p. 50.
21. David Martindale, "Segmenting the Market," *Adweek*, September 12, 1988, p. F.P. 76.

Chapter 14
1. Kirk Jackson, "It's in the Cards for L'Image," *Black Enterprise*, August, 1988, p. 33; Personal Correspondence, October 19, 1988; and press releases provided by The Blaine Group, Inc.
2. Resa King, Keith Hammonds, and Ted Holden, "Will $4 Perfume Do the Trick for Bic?" *Business Week*, June 20, 1988, pp. 89, 92.
3. Michael Kaplan, "Lea & Perrins' Steve Silk," *Adweek's Marketing Week*, August 1, 1988, pp. M.R.C. 34–36.
4. Patricia Strnad, "Goodyear Rides with Awareness Effort," *Advertising Age*, September 12, 1988, pp. 36, 88.
5. See William Lazer, Mushtaq Lugmani, and Zahir Quraeshi, "Product Rejuvenation Strategies," *Business Horizons*, November–December 1984, pp. 21–28; and E. Stewart DeBruicker and Gregory L. Summe, "Make Sure Your Customers Keep Coming Back," *Harvard Business Review*, January–February 1985, pp. 92–98.
6. Steve Weiner and Janis Bultman, "Calling Betty Crocker," *Forbes*, August 8, 1988, pp. 88–89.
7. Joshua Hyatt, "Too Hot to Handle," *INC.*, March 1987, pp. 52–58.
8. "AMA Names 10 Best New Products of 1987," *Marketing News*, March 28, 1988, p. 1.
9. Paul B. Brown, "The Eternal Second Act," *INC.*, June 1988, pp. 119–120.
10. "How a Move to Pink Put 7Up in the Black," *Adweek's Marketing Week*, May 16, 1988, pp. 66–67.
11. Hyatt, "Too Hot to Handle."
12. Leslie Brennan, "Quick Study," *Sales & Marketing Management*, March 1988, p. 50–53.
13. "Name That Brand," *Fortune*, July 4, 1988, p. 9.
14. Alice Z. Cuneo, "AIDS Prompts Ayds Move," *Advertising Age*, May 30, 1988, p. 66.
15. Robert Johnson, "Naming a New Product Is Tough when the Best Names Are Taken," *The Wall Street Journal*, January 19, 1988, p. 31; and John Schwartz, "What Really Is in a Name?" *Newsweek*, November 30, 1987, p. 55.
16. "Generic Items Continue Slide," *Advertising Age*, January 22, 1988, p. 38.
17. "With a Dated Image, Gillette Stayed Cool," *Adweek's Marketing Week*, June 13, 1988, pp. 61–62.
18. Quote and example from Michael Hiestand, "Food Companies Offer Healthful Fare to Kids Toting Lunch Boxes," *Adweek's Marketing Week*, September 5, 1988, pp. 32–34.
19. Len Strazewski, "Wands Trace Path from Store to Shelf," *Advertising Age*, August 24, 1987, pp. S-11–S-12.
20. Christopher W. L. Hart, "The Power of Unconditional Service Guarantees," *Harvard Business Review*, July–August 1988, pp. 54–62.
21. Michael Hiestand, "Traditional Staples Shake Primitive Packaging," *Adweek's Marketing Week*, May 2, 1988, pp. 1, 4.
22. Carolyn Lochhead, "The Lodging Industry Giants Build to Woo Budget Travelers," *Insight*, June 6, 1988, pp. 40–42.
23. John Hillkirk and Mark Lewyn, "Getting to the Core of a Macintosh's Cost," *USA Today*, June 16, 1988, p. 7B.
24. John Birmingham, "How Bausch & Lomb Keeps Ray-Ban in the Limelight," *Adweek's Marketing Week*, July 4, 1988, pp. 27–28.
25. "The Customer Is Always Right," *Time*, March 7, 1988, p. 57.

Chapter 15
1. Todd Krasnow, "The Toys 'R' Us of Office Supplies," *Adweek's Marketing Week*, August 15, 1988, pp. 44–45.
2. Bowater, Inc., *1987 Annual Report*, pp. 8–9.
3. Richard Meyer, "Instrument Landing?" *Financial World*, August 23, 1988, pp. 18–19.
4. American Greetings Corporation, *1988 Annual Report*, pp. 8, 12.
5. Ted Holden, "Campbell's Taste of the Japanese Market is Mm-Mm Good," *Business Week*, March 28, 1988, p. 42.

6. Carrie Dolan, "Yesterday's Marvel, Worlds of Wonder Inc. Is in Worlds of Trouble," *The Wall Street Journal*, October 28, 1987, pp. 1, 20.
7. Distributor quote and example is from Jaclyn Fierman, "How Gallo Crushes the Competition," *Fortune*, September 1, 1986, pp. 25–31.
8. McKesson Corporation, *1987 Annual Report*, p. 12.
9. USG Corporation, *1987 Annual Report*, p. 10.
10. Snap-On Tools Corporation, *1987 Annual Report*, p. 16.
11. Fleming Companies, *1987 Annual Report*, p. 10.
12. Susan M. Gelfond, "Old PCs Don't Die, They Just Go Back to Market," *Business Week*, August 29, 1988, p. 52.
13. John Birmingham, "The New American Office Party, Minus the Lamp Shade," *Adweek's Marketing Week*, June 13, 1988, pp. 28, 32.
14. Joseph Pereira, "Toys 'R' Us, Big Kid on the Block, Won't Stop Growing," *The Wall Street Journal*, August 11, 1988, p. 6; and David Kiley, "Invasion of the Category Killers," *Adweek's Marketing Week*, February 29, 1988, p. 5.
15. Susan Dillingham, "Automated Drop-off for Dry Cleaning," *Insight*, August 29, 1988, p. 46.
16. Jeffrey A. Tannenbaum, "Circuit City Stores Wins Praise of Analysts as Competition Grows during a Shake-Out," *The Wall Street Journal*, June 24, 1987, p. 51.
17. Laurie Freeman, "Wal-Mart Adds Midwest Stores," *Advertising Age*, August 17, 1987, p. 26S.
18. Russell Mitchell and Kevin Kelly, "Waldenbooks Tries Hooking Young Bookworms," *Business Week*, May 11, 1987, p. 48.
19. Baxter Travenol Laboratories, Inc., *1987 Annual Report*, p. 15.
20. The percentages of intercity freight reported for the various transportation modes are from the U.S. Bureau of the Census, *Statistical Abstract of the United States: 1988*, 108th ed. (Washington, D.C.: U.S. Government Printing Office, 1987), p. 570.
21. "Mr. Winchester Orders Pizza," *Fortune*, November 24, 1986, pp. 134–137.

Chapter 16
1. Lynn Coleman, "Hotelier Uses 'Audacious PR' to Capture Media Attention," *Marketing News*, July 4, 1988, pp. 1–2.
2. "Pork Producers Extend Campaign," *Marketing News*, February 29, 1988, p. 19.
3. Matthew Grimm, "Time to Trade in those LPs," *Adweek's Marketing Week*, July 25, 1988, p. 4.
4. Paul B. Brown, "The Put-Up-Or-Shut-Up Strategy," *INC.*, July 1988, p. 113.
5. Robert T. Grieves, "Stretching the Image," *Forbes*, April 18, 1988, p. 99.
6. "Study: Increase Business Ads to Increase Sales," *Marketing News*, March 14, 1988, p. 13.
7. Dyan Machan, "The Life of a Saleswoman," *Forbes*, February 2, 1988, pp. 116–118.
8. Apple Bank for Savings, *1987 Annual Report*, p. 8.
9. "The Top 50 Advertisers," *Adweek's Marketing Week*, August 1, 1988, p. M.R.C. 22.
10. Patricia Winters, "Kinder-Care Plan Is Kid Stuff," *Advertising Age*, June 13, 1988, p. 10.
11. U.S. Bureau of the Census, *Statistical Abstract of the United States, 1988*, 108th ed. (Washington, D.C.: U.S. Government Printing Office, 1987) p. 530.
12. Shelly Garcia, "L.A. Gear Shoots Beyond Its Glitter Image," *Adweek's Marketing Week*, June 13, 1988, pp. 18–19.
13. Tania Anderson, "Pepsi Rescues Parched Beachgoers," *Advertising Age*, May 2, 1988, p. S-9.
14. Scott Hume, "Coupons Score with Consumers," *Advertising Age*, February 15, 1988, p. 40.
15. "Raisin Expectations," *Adweek's Marketing Week*, April 11, 1988, p. 7.
16. "Good Will, Good Sales," *Adweek's Marketing Week*, May 23, 1988, p. 49.
17. Laura Landro, "Paramount's Marketers Try for a 'New' Eddie Murphy," *The Wall Street Journal*, July 7, 1988, p. 25.
18. This rule is noted in Harold C. Cash and W. J. E. Crissy, "The Salesman's Role in Marketing," *Psychology of Marketing Vol. 12* (Personnel Development Associates).
19. "GF's Taste of Success," *Adweek's Marketing Week*, April 11, 1988, p. 5.

Chapter 17
1. Abridged from Jeff Dunlap, "Bill and Judy Harl: Cellular Provides Portable Office," Southwestern Bell Corp's *Update*, No. 2, 1988, p. 36.

2. CIOs are discussed in John J. Donovan, "Beyond Chief Information Officer to Network Manager," *Harvard Business Review*, September–October 1988, pp. 134–140.
3. Harold Geneen with Alvin Moscow, *Managing* (New York: Doubleday, 1984), pp. 118–119.
4. Michael Finley, "Data-base Marketing Alters Landscape," *Marketing News*, November 7, 1988, p. 1.
5. William M. Bulkeley, "Special Systems Make Computing Less Traumatic for Top Executives," *The Wall Street Journal*, June 20, 1988, p. 21; and Susan M. Gelfond, "The Computer Age Dawns in the Corner Office," *Business Week*, June 27, 1988, pp. 84, 86.
6. Stuart Gannes, "Tremors from the Computer Quake," *Fortune*, August 1, 1988, p. 43.
7. "Techniques: Insuring Quality with Computers," *Success*, September 1988, p. 35; and Ron Richman, "Mrs. Fields' Secret Ingredient," *INC.*, October 1987, pp. 65–67, 70, 72.
8. Philip Elmer-DeWitt, "Fast and Smart," *Time*, March 28, 1988, p. 55.
9. "News/Trends," *Fortune*, October 28, 1985, p. 10.
10. Joel Dreyfuss, "Catching the Computer Wave," *Fortune*, September 26, 1988, p. 78.
11. Leslie Helm, "How the Leader in Networking Practices What it Preaches," *Business Week*, May 16, 1988, p. 96.
12. Donovan, "Beyond Chief Information Officer," p. 135.
13. Kate Bollen, "On the Rise," *Fortune*, December 7, 1987, p. 170.
14. John S. Blyth, "Concern that Computers Will Make Design a Commodity Is Groundless," *Marketing News*, November 7, 1988, p. 16.
15. David Coursey, "Cowboys Use Computers to Field Winning Team," *USA Today*, June 8, 1987, p. 10E.
16. John Hillkirk, "White House Capitalizes on Computers' Versatility," *USA Today*, June 8, 1987, p. 3E; personal correspondence, April 28, 1989.
17. "Is Your Computer Safe?" *Business Week*, August 1, 1988, pp. 64, 70; Philip Elmer-DeWitt, "Invasion of the Data Snatchers," *Time*, September 26, 1988, pp. 61–67.
18. Michael Brody, "Laptop Computers Stand Tall at Last," *Fortune*, March 28, 1988, p. 109.
19. "When the Going Gets Tough . . . the Tough Get Cellular," *SBC Update*, No. 3, 1988, pp. 42–43; Jeff Dunlap, "Cellular Phones Sweeping the Nation," *SBC Update #2*, 1988, pp. 33–34, 39.
20. "Fax Fixation," *Advertising Age*, August 15, 1988, pp. 3–4; Susan Gelfond, "It's a Fax, Fax, Fax, Fax World," *Business Week*, March 21, 1988, p. 136.
21. Geoff Lewis, Jeffrey Rothfelder, Resa W. King, Mark Maremont, and Jane Peterson, "The Portable Executive," *Business Week*, October 10, 1988, pp. 102–112.
22. Alyssa A. Lappen, "Messenger of the Gods," *Forbes*, March 21, 1988, p. 150.
23. "Getting Computers to Dance to the Same Music," *Business Week*, May 23, 1988.
24. Marguerite Zientara, "What's Past Is Prologue: A Glimpse into the Future," *Computer World*, November 30, 1981, p. 31.
25. Stanley N. Wellborn, "Machines That Think," *U.S. News & World Report*, December 5, 1983, p. 62.
26. Eugene Linden, "Putting Knowledge to Work," *Time*, March 28, 1988, p. 60.
27. Dorothy Leonard-Barton and John J. Sviokla, "Putting Expert Systems to Work," *Harvard Business Review*, March–April 1988, p. 92.

Chapter 18
1. Charles R. Elrick, "Turnkey Accounting Systems," *ICP INTERFACE Administrative & Accounting*, Autumn 1983, pp. 29–30.
2. U.S. Department of Labor, Bureau of Labor Statistics, *Occupational Outlook Quarterly*, Spring 1988, p. 17.
3. Arthur Andersen & Company, *1987 Message for Our People*, p. 26.
4. Touche Ross & Company, *The Competitive Edge (1987)*, pp. 8–11, 16–17, 23.
5. Arthur Andersen & Company, *1987 Message for Our People*, p. 8.
6. Benton E. Gup and Michael T. Dugan, "The Cash Flow Statement: The Tip of an Iceberg," *Business Horizons*, November–December 1988, pp. 47–50.

Chapter 19
1. "Seed Money for Small Fry" by Annetta Miller with Carolyn Friday. *Newsweek*, March 28, 1988. Copyright © 1988 Newsweek, Inc. All rights reserved. Reprinted by permission. See also Joshua Levine, "How

Much Is That 'Ferrari' in the Window?" *Adweek's Marketing Week,* July 11, 1988, pp. 3, 4.

2. Quoted in Campbell R. McConnell, *Economics* (New York: McGraw-Hill, 1987), p. 335.

3. "Heaven Express?" *Fortune,* October 24, 1988, pp. 9, 12.

4. Lori Kesler, "Charge!" *Southwestern Bell Corporation Update,* December 1988, p. 52.

5. "Is MasterCard Mastering the Possibilities?" *Business Week,* October 10, 1988, p. 123; Barbara Marsh, "American Express Chases After the Fast-Food Market," *The Wall Street Journal,* April 5, 1989, p. B1.

6. Robert E. Taylor, "Parents Would Have Appreciated Some Card Burning by Protesters," *The Wall Street Journal,* May 6, 1988, p. 23.

7. Jeff Bailey, "Major Credit-Card Issuers Tighten Grip on Market Despite High Interest Charges," *The Wall Street Journal,* July 29, 1988, p. 19; John R. Dorfman, "As Credit-Card Disclosure Bill Advances, Consumer Groups Assail it as Too Weak," *The Wall Street Journal,* February 17, 1988, p. 31.

8. "The World's Top 50 Banks: It's Official — Japan Is Way Out Front," *Business Week,* June 27, 1988, pp. 76–77.

9. Augustin Hedberg, "Ways to Get the Most from Your Bank," *Money,* March 1988, p. 113; "ATMs Not the Time Savers Some Bankers Expected," *Marketing News,* March 28, 1988, p. 8.

10. John Hillkirk, "Smart Firms Sell Quality to Clients," *USA Today,* June 6, 1988, p. B1.

11. Judith Graham, "Bank Guarantees," *Advertising Age,* February 15, 1988, p. 82.

12. Ronald Alsop, "Banks Aim New Image Ads at Consumers," *The Wall Street Journal,* October 11, 1988, p. B1.

13. Patricia Sellers, "How to Handle Customers' Gripes," *Fortune,* October 24, 1988, p. 92.

14. Hedberg, "Ways to Get the Most from Your Bank," p. 111.

15. Vicky Cahan, "It May Be Time for S&Ls to Just Fade Away," *Business Week,* June 1, 1987, p. 52.

16. "Going for Broke," *Newsweek,* June 20, 1988, pp. 40–41; "The Man in the Muddle," *U.S. News & World Report,* December 12, 1988, pp. 67, 69.

17. Barbara Rudolph, "Finally, the Bill Has Come Due," *Time,* February 20, 1989, pp. 68–73; Dennis Cauchon and Wendell Cochran, "The S&L Mess," *USA Today,* February 13, 1989, pp. A1, A2; and "Bush's Sweet and Sour S&L Recipe," *U.S. News & World Report,* February 20, 1989, pp. 49–51.

18. *1988 Midyear Statistics for Federally Insured Credit Unions* (Washington, D.C.: National Credit Union Administration, 1988).

19. Manuel Schiffres, "The Federal Reserve Walks Quietly, But It Affects the Economy with a Big Stick," *Changing Times,* December 1988, p. 16.

20. Joel Dresang and Harriet C. Johnson, "Not All Endorse the Changes," *USA Today,* September 1, 1988, pp. B1, B2; Deborah Rankin, "The Dreaded Check-Clearing Bottleneck," *New York Times,* March 6, 1988, p. F9.

21. "Continental Illinois Tries to Leave Its Past Behind," *Business Week,* December 5, 1988, p. 160.

22. "Going for Broke," *Newsweek,* June 20, 1988, p. 40.

23. Gary Hector, "How to Rescue the S&L Industry," *Fortune,* December 19, 1988, p. 146.

24. "Going for Broke," p. 41. See also Dave Skidmore, "Savings and Loans: An Industry Under Siege," *Mobile Press Register,* February 5, 1989, p. D1.

25. Dennis Cauchon, "Our ATM Cards Are in the Express Line," *USA Today,* October 20, 1988, p. B1; Ronit Addis, "Will Greenbacks Become Museum Pieces?" *Forbes,* May 30, 1988, pp. 262, 264.

26. "Back to the Velvet-Roped Lines," *Time,* January 9, 1989, p. 49; and "Home Banking is Here — If You Want It," *Business Week,* February 29, 1988, pp. 108–109.

27. Gary Hector, "How Banking Will Shake Out," *Fortune,* April 25, 1988, pp. 207–224; John Helyar, "Multistate Banks Rile Many Consumers," *The Wall Street Journal,* April 20, 1988, p. 25; and "Two California Banks Riding Different Waves," *Business Week,* May 9, 1988, pp. 127–130.

28. "Plodding Along in Financial Services," *Fortune,* December 5, 1988, p. 84.

29. "A Bank Line That's Getting a Lot Longer," *Business Week,* March 28, 1988, pp. 80–81; Gary Hector, "The Money Game Will Get Brutal," *Fortune,* February 2, 1987, pp. 42–44; and "Are Banks Obsolete?" *Business Week,* April 6, 1987, pp. 74–82.

Chapter 20

1. "How Big-League Techniques Paid Off for Stuart Rose" by Dan Cook. Reprinted from November 3, 1986 issue of *Business Week* by special permission, copyright © 1986 by McGraw-Hill, Inc.

2. J. Fred Weston and Eugene F. Brigham, *Essentials of Managerial Finance,* 9th ed. (Hinsdale, Ill.: The Dryden Press, 1990).

3. Carol J. Loomis, "The Inside Story of Warren Buffett," *Fortune,* April 11, 1988, pp. 26–34.

4. Stuart Weiss, "Making the Most of the Cash on Hand," *Business Week,* November 3, 1986, pp. 112–116.

5. "Making Them Pay," *INC.,* April 1988, p. 128.

6. Alex Taylor III, "Lee Iacocca's Production Whiz," *Fortune,* June 22, 1987, pp. 36–44.

7. Ibid.

8. Rick Gladstone, "Deals Leave Companies Strapped with Debt," *Mobile Press Register,* December 25, 1988, pp. 1-E, 2-E.

9. Sarah Bartlett, "It Will Get a Bit Easier to Find Startup Cash," *Business Week,* November 3, 1986, pp. 100–104.

10. Dan Cook, "How Big-League Techniques Paid Off for Stuart Rose," *Business Week,* November 3, 1986, p. 124.

11. Gary Weiss, "Who Says Banks Are Your Only Finance Option?" *Business Week,* November 3, 1986, p. 96.

12. "Companies Stay Afloat by Using Credit Cards," *The Wall Street Journal,* May 20, 1988, p. 29.

13. Robert A. Mamis, "Factors to Consider," *INC.,* October 1986, pp. 131–136.

14. Kenneth R. Sheets, "GM's Newest Product," *U.S. News & World Report,* October 27, 1986, pp. 39–40.

15. Ellyn E. Spragins, "The Feast of Funding That Awaits Corporate Borrowers," *Business Week,* November 3, 1986, pp. 91–96.

16. Bartlett, "It Will Get a Bit Easier to Find Startup Cash"; and Jonathan B. Levine, "Turning Points in the Lives of Companies," *Business Week,* November 3, 1986, pp. 116–117.

Chapter 21

1. The Clean Harbors initial public offering is described in Robert A. Mamis, "Going Public," *INC.,* October 1988, pp. 52–62. McKim quotation is from p. 53.

2. Data from *Fact Book* (New York: New York Stock Exchange, 1989).

3. Peter Gumbel, "Japan Stock Market Overtakes the U.S. As World's Largest," *The Wall Street Journal,* April 13, 1987, p. 12.

4. Rick Gladstone, "Origin of Bull, Bear as Market Symbols Unclear," Bellevue, Washington, *Journal-American,* May 2, 1988, p. C3.

5. Daniel Kadlec, "Brokers: Less Luxury, More Worry," *USA Today,* December 5, 1988, pp. B1–B2.

6. William Giese, "When Discounts Don't Count," *Changing Times,* February 1989, pp. 50–55. See also "For Discount Brokers, the Crash Still Isn't Over," *Business Week,* December 5, 1988, pp. 154–155.

7. Jack Egan, "A Crashing Anniversary," *U.S. News & World Report,* October 17, 1988, p. 56.

8. "Did the Crash Make a Dent?" *Business Week,* October 17, 1988, p. 90.

9. "Did the Crash Make a Dent?" p. 90. See also William E. Sheeline, "Why the Crash Left Few Traces," *Fortune,* October 24, 1988, pp. 81–84.

10. Chris Welles, "Drexel's Deal with the Feds: How Much Will It Hurt?" *Business Week,* February 6, 1989, p. 36; "Insider Trading: Business as Usual," *Business Week,* August 27, 1987, pp. 20–21.

Chapter 22

1. (Source for opening vignette to come)

2. Christopher Ferrill, Resa King, and Joan O'C. Hamilton, "The Crisis Is Over — But Insurance Will Never Be the Same," *Business Week,* May 25, 1987, p. 122; "The Surge in Self-Insurance," *Newsweek,* March 7, 1988, pp. 74–75.

3. Statistics Department, National Safety Council.

4. George Melloan, "Insurers Try to Cope with AIDS Test Barriers," *The Wall Street Journal,* May 31, 1988, p. 25; Tamar Jacoby, "Who Will Pay the AIDS Bill?" *Newsweek,* April 11, 1988, p. 71; and Joan O'C. Hamilton, "Insurers Pass the Buck on AIDS Patients," *Business Week,* March 28, 1988, p. 27.

5. Insurance Information Institute, *1986–1987 Property/Casualty Fact Book,* p. 75.

6. "The Odds of Being a Crime Victim," *The Wall Street Journal,* July 15, 1988, p. 29.

7. "Controlling Insurance Costs," *INC.,* April 1988, p. 128.

8. "A World without Insurance?" *Forbes,* July 15, 1985, p. 40. Reprinted by permission.

9. Jane E. Brody, "Shadow of Doubt Wipes Out Bendectin," *New York Times,* June 19, 1983.

10. Insurance Information Institute data reported in David B. Hilder, "Small Firms Face Sharp Cost Hikes for Insurance — If They Can Get It," *The*

Wall Street Journal, August 8, 1985. See also "The Insurance Crisis That Could Cripple Day Care," *Business Week,* June 17, 1985, pp. 114, 116.

11. Stephen Engelberg, "Maker of Vaccine Quits the Market," *New York Times,* December 2, 1984; Bob McCoy, "Keeping Score," *The Sporting News,* October 24, 1988, p. 11.

12. Kathleen Day, "Biotechnology Companies Meet Insurance Reluctance," *Los Angeles Times,* May 28, 1985; and "A Vaccine Crisis Lands in Congress," *Fortune,* April 19, 1985, p. 238.

13. These statistics are from "Forgotten Patients," *Newsweek,* August 22, 1988, p. 52; and Janice Castro, "Cultural Condition," *Time,* February 1, 1988, p. 42.

14. Castro, "Cultural Condition," p. 42.

15. "The Price of a Life," *Time,* April 4, 1988, p. 61.

16. Steven Waldman, "Putting a Price Tag on Life," *Newsweek,* January 11, 1988, p. 40.

Chapter 23

1. Ann Hamman, "Local Salon Wins $2.1 Million Suit," *The Doings,* September 21, 1988, p. 5.

2. Dick Hyman, *The Trenton Pickle Ordinance* (New York: Viking Penguin, Inc., 1976).

3. Telephone interview, July 20, 1988.

4. Jacob V. Lamar, Jr., "Turkey and Trimmings," *Time,* November 30, 1987, p. 15.

5. Donald W. Moffat, ed., *Concise Desk Book of Personal Finance* (Englewood Cliffs, N. J.: Prentice-Hall, 1975), pp. 35–36.

6. Rate Howell, John R. Allison, and N. T. Henley, *Business Law,* 4th Alternate ed. (Hinsdale, Ill.: The Dryden Press, 1989), p. 326.

7. Ibid, p. 110.

8. Ibid, p. 404.

9. Reported in "Was the Chrysler Bailout Worth It?" *Business Week,* May 20, 1985, p. 23. This article is a book review of Robert B. Reich and John D. Donahue, *New Deals: The Chrysler Revival and the American System* (New York: Times Books, 1985).

10. Some of the information here and in the sections that follow is based on Robert A. Bennett, "Who Pays for Bankruptcy?" *New York Times,* June 3, 1983; U.S. Bureau of the Census, *Statistical Abstract of the United States: 1982–1983,* 103rd ed. (Washington, D.C.: U.S. Government Printing Office, 1982), p. 533; and Jane Bryant Quinn, "A Bankruptcy Report Card," *Newsweek,* November 18, 1982, p. 65.

11. Elliott D. Lee, "Bankruptcy Lawyers Gain Status, Wider Role in Corporate Strategy," *The Wall Street Journal,* July 9, 1987, p. 31.

12. Paula Dwyer and Amy Dunkin, "A Red-Letter Day for Gray Marketers," *Business Week,* June 13, 1988, p. 30.

13. *Statistical Abstract of the United States: 1988,* 108th ed. (Washington, D.C.: U.S. Bureau of the Census, 1987), p. 810.

14. This section is based on "Most Businesses Face Higher Taxes, Repeal of Reagan-Created Incentives for Investment," *The Wall Street Journal,* August 18, 1986, p. 8; "House Approves Historic Overhaul of Tax System That Would Slash Rates for Individuals and Business," *The Wall Street Journal,* September 26, 1986, pp. 3, 13; and "Tax Reform — At Last," *Business Week,* September 1, 1986, pp. 54–60.

Chapter 24

1. Based on Susan Hazen-Hammond, "One Smart Cookie," *Business Week Careers,* June 1988, pp. 14–18.

2. Ronald E. Kutscher, "An Overview of the Year 2000," *Occupational Outlook Quarterly,* Spring 1988, pp. 4, 6.

3. Martha C. White, "The 1988–89 Job Outlook in Brief," *Occupational Outlook Quarterly,* Spring 1988, p. 10.

4. Janet Bodnar, "Your Brilliant Career," *Changing Times,* November 1987, p. 29.

5. *Challenge to Change* (Glen Ellyn, Ill.: College of DuPage).

6. This section is based on Kutscher, pp. 4, 6, 8.

7. Lee A. Iacocca quote from *Business Week Careers,* June 1988, special advertising section.

8. Christopher Billy and Mark Geoffrey, eds., *Peterson's Business and Management Jobs: 1988* (Princeton, N.J.: Peterson's Guides, 1988), p. 14.

9. Marilyn Moats Kennedy, "The New Look in Resumés," *The Honda How to Get A Job Guide.* A special edition created by the staff of *Business Week's Careers,* a McGraw-Hill Publication, 1987 edition, p. 10.

10. Neil Steinberg, "Strategies for Successful Job Hunting," *Chicago Sun-Times,* January 1988, pp. 14–15.

11. *Statistical Abstract of the United States: 1988,* 108th ed. (Washington, D.C.: U.S. Bureau of the Census, 1987), p. 376.

12. "'Pink Ghetto' in Sales for Women," *Sales & Marketing Management,* July 1988, p. 80.

13. *The Wall Street Journal,* March 29, 1988, p. 1.

14. Elizabeth Greene, "Business Is Most Popular Major, but Many Recruiters Stress Liberal Arts," *The Chronicle of Higher Education,* November 11, 1987, p. A38.

15. "Siren Call of the Classroom," *Time,* January 25, 1988, p. 27.

16. *The Wall Street Journal,* March 22, 1988, p. 1.

17. "Fan Values 1942 Letter," *The Seattle Times,* November 30, 1080, p. A-2.

Dictionary of Business Terms

absolute advantage: situation in which a country has a monopolistic position in the marketing of a good or produces it at the lowest cost (p. 86)

accessory equipment: capital item, such as a typewriter, that is less expensive and shorter-lived than an installation (p. 398)

accountability: liability of subordinates to accomplish duties for which they have the necessary authority and responsibility (p. 201)

accounting: measuring, interpreting, and communicating financial information for internal and external decision making (p. 522)

accounting equation: basic accounting concept that assets are equal to liabilities plus owners' equity (p. 529)

accounting process: method of converting individual transactions to financial statements (p. 526)

accounts receivable: credit sales that customers have not yet paid (p. 597)

acid rain: rain with high levels of acid that many blame for the death of forests and lakes (p. 36)

acid-test ratio: ratio measuring the ability of a firm to meet its current debt on short notice; calculated by dividing quick assets by current liabilities (p. 540)

acquisition: one firm acquiring the property and assuming the obligations of another firm (p. 124)

Active Corps of Executives (ACE): SBA program using volunteer consultants who assist people in small business (p. 152)

activity ratio: ratio measuring the effectiveness of the firm's use of its resources (p. 541)

administrative agency: governmental agency empowered by state or federal statutes and constitutional provisions to hear and decide a variety of cases (p. 695)

advertising: nonpersonal sales presentation usually directed at a large number of potential customers (p. 468)

advocacy advertising: advertising that supports a specific viewpoint on a public issue and is designed to influence public opinion and/or the legislative process (p. 468)

affirmative action program: program set up by businesses to increase opportunities for women and minorities (p. 42)

agency: legal relationship between two parties, principal and agent, who agree that one will act as a representative of the other (p. 705)

agency shop: employment policy not requiring union membership, but nonunion members pay a fee equal to union dues (p. 339)

agent: person employed to act on behalf of another individual (p. 705)

agents and brokers: independent wholesalers that never take title to goods but may or may not take possession of them (p. 440)

alien corporation: firm organized in one country but operating in another (p. 120)

American Federation of Labor (AFL): national union made up of affiliated individual craft unions (p. 333)

analytic system: system of reducing raw materials into component parts (p. 225)

antiselection: tendency for persons with actual or potential health disabilities and those in dangerous occupations to purchase and renew health and life insurance policies (p. 661)

antitrust laws: laws that prohibit attempts to monopolize or dominate a particular market (p. 6)

appellate court: court that hears appeals from the general trial courts (p. 694)

appellant: party making an appeal for a higher court to review a case (p. 695)

apprenticeship training: program wherein an employee learns job tasks by serving as an assistant to a trained worker for a relatively long time (p. 306)

arbitration: process of bringing an impartial third party into a union-management dispute to render a legally binding decision (p. 346)

arithmetic/logic unit: part of the computer where all calculations occur (p. 498)

artificial intelligence: the study of using computers to solve problems involving imagination, abstract reasoning, and common sense (p. 511)

assembly line: manufacturing technique wherein the product passes through several workstations, each with a specific task (p. 224)

assessment center: method for training managers and identifying employees with management potential (p. 308)

asset: anything of value owned or leased by a business (p. 529)

atmospherics: physical characteristics and amenities that attract customers and satisfy their shopping needs (p. 446)

authority: power to act and make decisions in carrying out assignments (p. 201)

autocratic leader: one who makes decisions without consulting others (p. 184)

automated teller machine (ATM): electronic banking machine that permits customers to make cash withdrawals, deposits, and transfers on a 24-hour basis by using an access card (p. 564)

automatic merchandising: use of vending machines to retail various types of consumer goods (p. 443)

automation: replacement of a person by a machine in a work environment (p. 71)

automobile insurance: coverage for property and liability claims resulting from theft, fire, or accident (p. 668)

bailee: person receiving property under the law of bailment (p. 705)

bailor: person delivering property under the law of bailment (p. 705)

balance of payments: flow of money into or out of a country (p. 83)

balance of payments deficit: a net outflow of money from the country (p. 83)

balance of payments surplus: a net inflow of money from abroad (p. 83)

balance of trade: relationship between a country's exports and imports (p. 82)

balance sheet: statement of a firm's financial position on a particular date (p. 530)

bank examiner: representative of a financial regulatory agency who conducts periodic unannounced inspections of individual financial institutions to guarantee safety and soundness (p. 577)

bank holiday: situation in which banks must close their doors until they can obtain loan payments from their borrowers (p. 570)

Banking Act of 1980: legislation deregulating financial institutions by permitting all deposit institutions to offer checking accounts; expanding services and lending powers to thrifts; and phasing out interest-rate ceilings (p. 580)

bankruptcy: legal nonpayment of financial obligations (p. 707)

bargaining zone: the range of collective bargaining before a union will strike or management will close the plant (p. 342)

batch processing: method in which data is collected for a predetermined period before being processed (p. 499)

bear: investor who expects stock prices to decline along with market prices (p. 637)

bear market: market characterized by stock prices that steadily decline (p. 637)

bet-your-company culture: type of corporate culture characteristic of high-stakes firms (p. 182)

bill of materials: detailed listing of all parts and materials needed to produce a product or service (p. 242)

binary arithmetic: counting system that uses only two digits: 0 and 1 (p. 499)

bit: a binary digit — either 0 or 1 (p. 500)

blue sky laws: early state laws regulating securities transactions (p. 643)

board of directors: governing body of a corporation elected by the stockholders (p. 122)

bond: certificate of indebtedness sold to raise long-term funds for corporations or government agencies (p. 608)

bond indenture: legal contract containing all provisions of a bond (p. 626)

bond trustee: financial institution or individual representing bondholders (p. 627)

bonus: an addition to a salary or wage based on productivity or for exceptional performance (p. 315)

bookkeeping: chiefly clerical phase of accounting (p. 522)

book value: value of stock determined by subtracting liabilities from assets, minus the value of any preferred stock (p. 623)

bottom line: overall profit or loss earned by a firm (p. 537)

boycott: attempt to keep people from purchasing goods or services from a company (p. 340)

brand: name, term, sign, symbol, or design used to identify the goods or services of a firm (p. 408)

brand insistence: stage of brand acceptance at which the consumer will accept no substitute for the preferred brand (p. 410)

brand name: words or letters that identify the firm's offerings (p. 408)

brand preference: stage of brand acceptance in which the consumer selects one brand over competitive brands based on previous experience with it (p. 410)

brand recognition: stage of brand acceptance in which the consumer is aware of the brand but does not prefer it to competing brands (p. 410)

breach of contract: violation of a valid legal agreement (p. 702)

breakeven analysis: method of determining the minimum sales volume needed to cover all costs at a certain price level (p. 417)

breakeven point: level of sales that will cover all the company's costs, both fixed and variable (p. 417)

budget: planning and control tool that reflects expected sales revenues, operating expenses, and cash receipts and outlays (p. 542)

bull: investor who expects stock prices to rise along with market prices (p. 637)

bull market: market characterized by stock prices that continue to rise (p. 637)

bundled accounts: package deals offered by banks that base charges on depositors' account balance and activity level (p. 566)

burglary insurance: insurance coverage for losses due to the taking of property by forcible entry (p. 669)

burnout: employee condition whose symptoms include low morale and fatigue (p. 276)

business: all profit-seeking activities and enterprises that provide goods and services necessary to an economic system (p. 4)

business ethics: the businessperson's standards of conduct and moral values (p. 29)

business incubator: common facility that houses start-up firms (p. 138)

business interruption insurance: type of insurance designed to cover losses resulting from temporary business closings (p. 667)

business law: those aspects of law that most directly and specifically influence and regulate management of various types of business activity (p. 692)

buyer's market: market situation characterized by adequate or even excess supplies (p. 371)

byte: a character of data made up of eight bits to form a number or letter of the alphabet (p. 500)

callable bond: bond allowing redemption by issuer before maturity (p. 627)

canned sales presentation: memorized sales talk intended to provide all the information the customer needs to make a purchase decision (p. 466)

capacity: legal ability of a party to enter into agreements (p. 701)

capital: funds that finance the operation of a business (p. 7)

capitalism: economic system founded on the principle that competition among businesses best serves society (p. 5)

capital items: relatively expensive long-lived industrial products used in producing other goods for resale (p. 398)

cartel: monopolistic organization of foreign firms (p. 96)

cash surrender value: the savings portion of a life insurance policy (p. 677)

cathode ray tube (CRT): visual display device that projects data onto a television-like screen (p. 502)

cause advertising: *see* advocacy advertising (p. 468)

Celler-Kefauver Antimerger Act: federal statute that amended the Clayton Act to include major asset purchases that decrease competition in an industry in its general prohibition of trade restraints (p. 698)

centralization: managerial practice of dispersing little authority to subordinates (p. 205)

central processing unit (CPU): part of the computer system containing the memory, or storage unit, the arithmetic/logic unit, and the control unit (p. 498)

certificate of deposit (CD): short-term, high-interest note issued by a commercial bank (p. 601)

certified management accountant (CMA): accountant who has met specific educational and professional requirements and has passed a series of examinations established by the National Association of Accountants (p. 526)

certified public accountant (CPA): accountant who has passed a comprehensive examination covering law, accounting theory and practice, and auditing (p. 525)

chain of command: established authority and responsibility relationships (p. 207)

change agents: managers who seek to revitalize established concerns in order to keep their competitiveness in the modern marketplace (p. 140)

channel captain: channel member dominating the activities of a distribution channel (p. 435)

check: written order to a financial institution to pay the amount specified from funds on deposit (p. 575)

chief executive officer (CEO): top position in the managerial hierarchy; responsible for overall direction of the firm (p. 169)

chief operating officer (COO): person responsible for the daily operations of the firm (p. 169)

chief financial officer (CFO): top executive responsible for the financial affairs of the firm (p. 169)

chief information officer (CIO): top management executive responsible for directing a firm's management information system and related computer operations (p. 491)

classic entrepreneurs: those who identify a business opportunity and allocate their available resources to tap that market (p. 139)

classroom training: program that uses classroom techniques to teach employees difficult, high-skill jobs (p. 306)

Clayton Act: federal statute that forbids trade restraints such as tying contracts, interlocking directorates, and certain anticompetitive stock acquisitions (p. 697)

close corporation: corporation owned by relatively few stockholders who control and manage its activities (p. 121)

closed shop: illegal employment policy of refusing to hire nonunion workers (p. 338)

coalition bargaining: negotiations between a coalition of several unions representing the employees of one company (p. 342)

coinsurance clause: insurance clause requiring that the insured carry fire insurance of some minimum percentage of the replacement value of the property to receive full coverage for a loss (p. 666)

collective bargaining: negotiation between management and union representatives concerning wages and working conditions (p. 341)

commercial bank: profit-making business that holds deposits of individuals and businesses in the form of checking or savings accounts and uses these funds to make loans to individuals and businesses (p. 563)

commercial finance company: financial institution that makes short-term loans to businesses that pledge tangible items such as inventory, machinery, or property as collateral (p. 570)

commercial paper: short-term note issued by a major corporation with high credit standing and backed solely by the reputation of that firm (p. 601)

committee organization: organizational structure wherein authority and responsibility are jointly held by a group of individuals (p. 209)

common carrier: transportation firm that performs services within a particular line of business for the general public (p. 448)

common law: body of law arising out of judicial decisions related to the unwritten law the United States inherited from England (p. 692)

common market: form of economic integration that maintains a customs union and seeks to bring other trade rules into agreement (p. 97)

Common Market: the European Economic Community (p. 97)

common stock: stock whose owners have only a residual claim to the firm's assets but who have voting rights in the corporation (p. 122)

communism: economic theory, developed by Karl Marx, under which private property is eliminated and goods are owned in common (p. 14)

comparable worth: equal pay for jobs requiring similar levels of education, training, and skills (p. 46); also, the philosophy of compensation equity for men and women in similar positions (p. 316)

comparative advantage: a country's ability to supply a particular item more efficiently and at a lower cost than it can supply other products (p. 86)

comparative advertising: persuasive advertising approach in which direct comparisons are made with competing goods or services (p. 469)

competition: battle among businesses for consumer acceptance (p. 4)

component parts and materials: finished industrial goods that become part of a final product (p. 398)

compressed workweek: scheduling work so workers spend fewer days on the job, but work approximately the same number of hours (p. 283)

compulsory arbitration: arbitration to which both union and management representatives must submit as required by a third party (p. 346)

computer: programmable electronic device that can store, retrieve, and process data (p. 493)

computer-aided design (CAD): interaction between a designer and a computer resulting in a product, building, or part that meets predetermined specifications (p. 228)

computer-aided manufacturing (CAM): computer analysis of a CAD to determine steps in producing the design, and electronic transmission of instructions to production equipment used in producing the part or product (p. 228)

computer chips: thin wafers of silicon on which integrated circuits are located (p. 496)

computer network: system in which numerous computers can either function individually or communicate with each other (p. 503)

computer program: set of instructions that tells the computer what is to be done, how to do it, and the sequence of steps to be followed (p. 500)

computer programmer: specialist who tells the computer what to do (p. 500)

computer virus: program that attaches itself to other programs and changes them or destroys the data kept on a disk (p. 508)

concept testing: marketing research designed to solicit initial consumer reaction to a new-product idea before the product is developed (p. 406)

conceptual skills: ability to view the organization as a unified whole and to understand how each part relates to other parts (p. 172)

conglomerate merger: merger of unrelated firms (p. 125)

Congress of Industrial Organizations (CIO): national union made up of affiliated individual industrial unions (p. 334)

consent order: order under which an accused firm agrees voluntarily to cease conduct alleged inappropriate by the government (p. 697)

conservation: preservation of declining energy resources (p. 38)

consideration: the value or benefit one party provides to the others with whom a contract is made (p. 701)

consumer behavior: the acts of individuals in obtaining and using economic goods and services, including the decision processes that precede and determine these acts (p. 378)

consumer finance company: financial institution that makes short-term loans to individuals, typically requiring collateral; also called personal finance or small loan company (p. 570)

consumer goods: goods and services purchased by the ultimate consumer for his or her own use (p. 377)

consumerism: public demand for business to consider consumer wants and needs in making its decisions (p. 39)

containerization: practice of putting packages, usually made up of several unitized loads, into a form that is relatively easy to transfer.

contests: sales promotion method offering cash or merchandise as prizes to participating winners (p. 474)

contingency planning: planning to deal with crises such as fires, explosions, product tamperings, gas leaks, and product failure (p. 179)

contingency theory: theory that leadership styles should reflect the specific details of the managerial situation (p. 184)

contingent business interruption insurance: insurance coverage for losses incurred as a result of a major supplier or customer being damaged by fire or other specified property damage (p. 667)

continuous process: manufacturing operation with long production runs lasting months or years (p. 225)

contract: legally enforceable agreement between two or more parties regarding a specified act or thing (p. 700)

contract carriers: transportation firms that carry goods for hire by individual contract or agreement and not for the general public (p. 448)

contract law: legal foundation on which normal business dealings are conducted (p. 700)

controlling: evaluating the organization's performance to determine whether it is accomplishing its objectives (p. 181)

control unit: part of the computer responsible for directing the sequence of operations, interpreting coded instructions, and guiding the computer (p. 498)

convenience goods: products that consumers seek to purchase frequently, immediately, and with a minimum of effort (p. 396)

convertible bond: bond conversion option to a specific number of shares of common stock (p. 626)

convertible preferred stock: stock that gives stockholders the option of having their preferred stock converted into common stock at a stated price (p. 623)

cooling-off period: government-enforced 80-day suspension of a threatened strike (p. 340)

cooperative: organization that is operated collectively by the owners (p. 128)

cooperative advertising: sharing of local advertising costs between the manufacturer and the marketing intermediary (p. 476)

copyright: protection of an individual's exclusive right to such materials as books, photos, and cartoons (p. 710)

corporate advertising: institutional advertising by profit-seeking firms (p. 468)

corporate citizenship: management's consideration of the social and economic effects of its decision making; used interchangeably with social responsibility (p. 28)

corporate culture: an organization's inner values, beliefs, rituals, norms, and philosophies (p. 182)

corporation: a legal entity with authority to act and have liability separate and apart from its owners (p. 117)

cost-of-living escalator clause (COLA): clause in a bargaining agreement that protects real income by adjusting wages to reflect consumer price index changes (p. 343)

cost-push inflation: inflation resulting from a significant increase in a production cost passed on to consumers (p. 58)

countertrade: international bartering agreement (p. 88)

coupon: sales promotion method that uses advertising clippings or package inclusions offering a small discount on the purchase price of a product (p. 474)

craft union: labor union consisting of skilled workers in a specific craft or trade (p. 332)

creative selling: persuasive type of promotional presentation used when the benefits of a good or service are not readily apparent and/or when the purchase is based on a careful analysis of alternatives (p. 465)

credit: a bookkeeping entry recording a decrease in an asset, an increase in a liability, or an increase in owners' equity (p. 530)

credit card: plastic card used in making credit purchases; special credit arrangement between issuer, cardholder, and merchant (p. 562)

credit insurance: insurance to protect lenders against losses caused by insolvency of customers to whom credit has been extended (p. 670)

credit life insurance: term insurance that repays the balance owed on a house or other major purchase if the policyholder dies (p. 677)

credit union: member-owned financial cooperative that pays interest to depositors, offers share draft accounts, and makes short-term loans and some home mortgage loans (p. 569)

crisis manager: person who directs a firm's contingency planning (p. 179)

critical path: sequence of operations in PERT diagram requiring the longest time for completion (p. 243)

cumulative preferred stock: stock that requires owners receive dividends for each year before dividends can be paid to common stockholders (p. 623)

cumulative voting: practice of enabling stockholders to combine their votes in electing directors (p. 123)

currency: two of the components of the money supply — coins and paper money (p. 560)

current assets: cash and other assets that can or will be converted to cash or used within one year (p. 531)

current liabilities: claims of creditors that are to be repaid within one year (p. 533)

current ratio: ratio measuring the company's ability to pay its current debts as they mature; calculated by dividing current assets by current liabilities (p. 539)

customer-oriented layout: service facility design that promotes interaction between the organization's services and the customers (p. 236)

customer service: aspect of competitive strategy that refers to how a firm treats its customers (p. 69)

customer service standards: quality of service that a firm's customers will receive (p. 447)

customs union: form of economic integration within which a free trade area is established for member nations and a uniform tariff is imposed on trade with nonmember nations (p. 97)

cyclical unemployment: joblessness because of reduced economic activity (p. 59)

damages: financial payments made for a loss and related suffering (p. 702)

data: statistics, opinions, facts, or predictions categorized on some basis for storage and retrieval (p. 492)

data base: integrated collection containing all of the organization's data resources (p. 492)

debenture: bond backed by the reputation of the issuing corporation (p. 625)

debit: a bookkeeping entry recording an increase in an asset, a decrease in a liability, or a decrease in owners' equity (p. 530)

debit card: coded plastic access card used to make electronic transactions (p. 582)

debt capital: funds obtained through borrowing (p. 601)

debt ratio: ratio measuring the extent to which a firm relies on debt financing in its operations (p. 541)

debt to owners' equity ratio: ratio measuring the extent to which company operations are financed by borrowed funds; calculated by dividing total liabilities by owners' equity (p. 542)

decentralization: decision to disperse substantial amounts of authority to subordinates (p. 205)

decision making: process of choosing among alternatives (p. 186)

decreasing term insurance: term life insurance policy written to provide reduced amounts of protection over the life of the policy (p. 677)

delegation: act of assigning part of a manager's activities to subordinates (p. 201)

demand: schedule showing what consumers will buy at various price levels (p. 9)

demand curve: schedule showing the relationship between different prices and the quantity demanded at each price (p. 60)

demand deposits: promises to pay immediately to the depositor any amounts of money requested as long as it does not exceed the account balance (p. 560)

demand-pull inflation: inflation resulting from too much money in circulation relative to the goods and services available (p. 58)

democratic leader: one who involves subordinates in making decisions (p. 184)

dental insurance: insurance designed to pay a specified percentage of dental expenses (p. 674)

departmentalization: subdivision of work activities into units within the organization (p. 200)

depreciation: noncash expense involving the allocation of the cost of an asset over the years in which it is used (p. 532)

deregulation: elimination of legal restraints on competition in various industries (p. 699)

devaluation: reduction in value of a country's currency (p. 84)

direct exporting: seeking to export business (p. 87)

directing: guiding and motivating subordinates to accomplish organizational objectives (p. 181)

direct-response retailing: conducted through mail or telephone orders of catalog merchandise or through telephone orders of merchandise on television (p. 442)

direct selling: direct contact between the sellers and the buyers (p. 442)

disability income insurance: health insurance designed to protect against loss of income while disabled as a result of accident or illness (p. 674)

discount rate: interest rate charged by the Federal Reserve System on loans to member banks (p. 573)

discouraged workers: people who give up searching for jobs (p. 58)

dispatching: phase of production control that instructs each department on what work is to be done and the time allowed for its completion (p. 244)

displaced homemaker: homemaker who returns to school or takes a job because of divorce, widowhood, or economic reasons (p. 724)

dissatisfiers: maintenance factors that are absent or inadequate (p. 274)

distribution channels: paths that goods and services and title to them follow from producer to consumer (p. 430)

distribution strategy: element of marketing decision making involving the physical distribution of goods and the selection of distribution channels (p. 375)

distribution warehouse: warehouse that stores goods for a short time; often used for gathering and redistributing products (p. 451)

divestiture: the selling off of a corporation's divisions or units (p. 126)

dividends: payments to stockholders from a corporation's earnings (p. 119)

domestic corporation: firm doing business in the state in which it is incorporated (p. 120)

double-entry bookkeeping: process requiring two entries for every transaction, thereby keeping the accounting equation in balance (p. 529)

Dow Jones Averages: averages based on market prices of 30 industrial, 20 transportation, and 15 utility stocks that reflect general market activity (p. 640)

drop shipper: limited-function merchant wholesaler that takes legal title to goods but never physically handles them (p. 439)

dumping: selling goods abroad at a price lower than that charged in the domestic market (p. 97)

earnings per share: profits earned by a corporation for each share of common stock outstanding; calculated by dividing net income after taxes by the number of common shares outstanding (p. 540)

ecology: relationship between people and their environment (p. 35)

economics: the science of allocating scarce resources (p. 58)

8 (a) Program: SBA program that allows companies owned by "socially and economically disadvantaged individuals" to negotiate government contracts outside the standard competitive bidding procedure (p. 152)

electronic funds transfer system (EFTS): computerized method for making purchases and paying bills by electronically depositing or withdrawing funds (p. 582)

embargo: ban on certain imported or exported products (p. 93)

employee benefits: employee rewards such as pension plans, insurance, sick-leave pay, and tuition reimbursement given at all or part of the expense of the company (p. 317)

Employee Retirement Income Security Act (ERISA): federal law establishing minimum standards for employee participation in private pension plans and providing protection for participants in the event of failure of a private pension plan (p. 318)

employers' associations: cooperative efforts by employers to present a united front in dealing with labor unions (p. 349)

employment at will: right of employers to retain or dismiss personnel as they wish (p. 311)

endorsement: procedure of signing a negotiable instrument that renders it transferable (p. 704)

endowment policy: insurance that provides coverage for a specified period, after which the face value is refunded to the policyholder (p. 677)

energy crisis: the world's diminished ability to provide for future energy needs (p. 37)

entrepreneur: a risk taker in the private enterprise system (pp. 5, 138)

entrepreneurship: taking risks to set up and operate a business (p. 7)

entry-level job: first permanent employment after leaving school (p. 722)

environmental impact study: analysis of the impact of a proposed plant location on the quality of life in a specific area (p. 235)

Environmental Protection Agency (EPA): federal agency with primary authority for dealing with various types of pollution (p. 36)

Equal Employment Opportunity Commission (EEOC): federal commission created to increase job opportunities for women and minorities and help eliminate job discrimination (p. 41)

equilibrium price: price at which quantity supplied is equal to quantity demanded (p. 61)

equipment: all items used in production (p. 599)

equipment trust certificate: type of secured bond that pledges company assets (p. 624)

equity: claim against the assets of a business (p. 529)

equity capital: funds provided by the firm's owners by plowing back earnings or by making additional contributions, by contributions from venture capitalists or by stock issues to the general public (p. 601)

equity funds: funds obtained from selling stock in the company, from reinvesting company earnings, or from additional contributions by the firm's owners (p. 609)

esteem needs: desire for accomplishment, a feeling of achievement, and the respect of others (p. 269)

exchange: process by which two or more parties give something of value to one another to satisfy felt needs (p. 368)

exchange control: allocation, expansion, or restriction of foreign exchange according to existing national policy (p. 94)

exchange rate: rate at which a country's currency can be exchanged for other currencies or gold (p. 84)

exclusive distribution: strategy of giving a wholesaler or retailer the exclusive right to sell a product in a specific geographic region (p. 437)

executive information system (EIS): user-friendly computer system used by senior management (p. 492)

expense items: industrial products that are less costly than capital items, consumed within one year of their purchase (p. 398)

expert systems: programs that imitate human thinking (p. 512)

exporting: selling domestic goods abroad (p. 82)

Export Trading Companies Act (1982): legislation designed to encourage export trading companies (p. 96)

export trading company: any type of organization that seeks to expand exports (p. 96)

express warranty: warranty with specific representations made by the seller regarding the goods (p. 702)

external data: data generated outside the organization (p. 382)

factor: financial institution that purchases accounts receivable at a discount from retailers (p. 607)

factors of production: basic inputs into the private enterprise system, including natural resources, labor, capital, and entrepreneurship (p. 7)

Fair Debt Collections Practices Act: federal law aimed at prohibiting debt-collecting agencies from using harassing, deceptive, and unfair collection practices (p. 699)

Fair Labor Standards Act: federal law that sets a minimum wage and maximum basic hours for workers employed in industries engaged in interstate commerce (p. 337)

Fair Packaging and Labeling Act (1966): federal law that requires certain kinds of information on packages or labels, including product identification, name and address of the producer or distributor, and quality information (p. 412)

family brand: brand name used for several related products or entire product mix (p. 410)

featherbedding: paying workers for work not done (p. 340)

Federal Cigarette Labeling and Advertising Act: federal law requiring written health warnings on cigarette packages (p. 692)

Federal Deposit Insurance Corporation (FDIC): corporation that insures bank depositors' accounts up to a maximum of $100,000 and sets requirements for sound banking practices (p. 577)

Federal Reserve System: network of 12 regional banks that regulates banking in the United States (p. 571)

Federal Savings and Loan Insurance Corporation (FSLIC): corporation that provides deposit insurance and establishes regulations for thrifts (p. 577)

Federal Trade Commission Act: federal law that set up the Federal Trade Commission (FTC) as a federal agency and gave it administrative powers to ban unfair competitive practices among businesses (p. 698)

federation: association comprised of numerous national unions; serves a mediation and political function (p. 336)

fidelity bond: bond that protects employers from employees' dishonesty (p. 669)

finance: the business function of effectively obtaining and using funds (p. 594)

financial manager: individual in an organization responsible for developing and implementing the firm's financial plan and for determining the most appropriate sources and uses of funds (p. 594)

financial plan: document that specifies the funds needed by a firm for a period of time, times inflows and outflows, and outlines the most appropriate uses of funds (p. 595)

financial supermarket: nonbank that provides financial services such as investments, loans, real estate, and insurance (p. 584)

fire insurance: insurance coverage for losses due to fire and — with extended coverage — windstorms, hail, water, riot, and smoke damage (p. 666)

fiscal policy: governmental actions concerning revenues and expenditures (p. 59)

fixed assets: relatively permanent assets expected to be used for periods longer than one year (p. 532)

fixed costs: costs that remain stable regardless of the production level achieved (p. 417)

fixed exchange rates: exchange rates fixed by government policy (p. 84)

fixed-position layout: manufacturing facility design that locates the product in a fixed position, with workers, materials, and machines transported to and from it (p. 236)

flexible benefit plans: system of flexible benefits in which employees are provided with specific dollar amounts of benefits and are allowed to select areas of coverage (p. 318)

flexible manufacturing system (FMS): state-of-the-art facility that allows production methods to be modified quickly when different products are manufactured (p. 228)

flextime: work-scheduling system that allows employees to set work hours within constraints specified by the firm (p. 281)

float: time delay between writing a check and the transfer of funds to the recipient's account (p. 575)

floating exchange rates: exchange rates that vary according to market conditions (p. 84)

floor-planning: assignment of inventory title (collateral) to financing agencies in return for short-term loans (p. 607)

flowchart: pictorial description of the logical steps to be taken in solving a problem (p. 501)

follow-up: phase of production control that spots production problems and informs management of needed adjustments (p. 244)

foreign corporation: firm doing business in a state other than the one in which it is incorporated (p. 120)

Foreign Corrupt Practices Act (1978): legislation that prohibits bribery of foreigners by American firms to secure sales (p. 96)

form utility: utility created through the conversion of raw materials and other inputs into finished goods and services (p. 222)

franchisee: small-business person who is allowed to sell the products or service of a supplier in exchange for some payment (p. 154)

franchising: contractual agreement that sets the methods a dealer can use to produce and market a supplier's goods or service (p. 153)

franchisor: supplier of a franchise that provides various services in exchange for a payment by the franchisee (p. 154)

free-rein leader: one who believes in minimal supervision and who leaves most decisions to subordinates (p. 184)

free trade area: form of economic integration within which participants agree to allow trading among themselves without tariffs or trade restrictions (p. 97)

freight forwarders: common carriers that purchase bulk space from other carriers by lease or contract and resell this space to small-volume shippers (p. 448)

frictional unemployment: people who are temporarily not working but are searching for jobs (p. 58)

friendship, commerce, and navigation (FCN) treaties: agreements with other nations that include many aspects of international business relations (p. 96)

FTC Improvement Act: federal statute giving Congress 90 days to veto any FTC ruling with which it disagrees (p. 698)

full-function merchant wholesaler: merchant wholesaler that performs many services in addition to taking legal title to goods (p. 439)

gain sharing: incentive compensation program in which employee pay is based on predetermined productivity increases (p. 314)

games: sales promotion method offering cash or merchandise as prizes to participating winners (p. 474)

General Agreement on Tariffs and Trade (GATT): international trade accord that has sponsored a series of negotiations on tariffs and trade restrictions (p. 94)

general and administrative expenses: operational expenses not directly related to the acquisition, production, or sale of the firm's goods or services (p. 537)

general partnership: partnership in which all partners are liable for the business's debts (p. 115)

generic product: nonbranded item with plain packaging and little or no advertising support (p. 410)

givebacks: wage and employee benefit concessions by union members to assist employer in remaining competitive (p. 344)

glasnost: policy of open communication in the Soviet Union (p. 15)

golden parachute: executive severance package available to those who lose their jobs through acquisition or merger (p. 125)

government bond: bond issued by the U.S. government (p. 25)

grapevine: informal network of communication found in most organizations (p. 212)

great man theory: leadership theory that says only an exceptional person will achieve a prominent leadership position (p. 183)

greenhouse effect: warming of the Earth's temperature as carbon dioxide collects in the atmosphere (p. 36)

greenmail: situation in which a wealthy investor buys a significant portion of a cash-rich but minimally profitable (or unprofitable) firm and then hints of intentions to take over (p. 47)

grievance: employee or union complaint that management is violating some provision of the union contract (p. 346)

gross national product (GNP): sum of all goods and services produced in an economy during a year (p. 7)

group life insurance: life insurance for company employees; typically written under a single master policy (p. 676)

hardware: all of the tangible elements of the computer system (p. 497)

Hawthorne effect: phenomenon in which subjects become more productive because they feel important and appreciated (p. 266)

Hawthorne studies: investigations that revealed money and job security are not the only sources of employee motivation; led to human relations approach to employee motivation (p. 266)

health insurance: insurance designed to provide coverage for losses due to sickness or accidents (p. 672)

health maintenance organization (HMO): prepaid medical expense plan that provides a comprehensive set of health services (p. 673)

hierarchy of organizational objectives: levels of objectives that progress from the overall objectives to the specific objectives for each employee (p. 200)

hiring from within: organizational policy of first considering a firm's own employees to fill job vacancies (p. 297)

horizontal merger: merger between firms in the same industry (p. 125)

hospitalization insurance: health insurance designed to pay for most hospital costs (p. 674)

human relations: study of how organizations manage and interact with employees to improve effectiveness of the firm and the employees (p. 264)

human relations skills: ability to work with and through people (p. 172)

human resource forecast: determining personnel needs in terms of numbers of individuals and their required skills (p. 294)

human resource management: process of acquiring, training, developing, motivating, and appraising a sufficient quantity of qualified employees to perform necessary activities; and developing activities and an organizational climate conducive to maximum efficiency and worker satisfaction (p. 292)

human resource manager: specialist responsible for performing human resource management (p. 292)

human resource planning: developing a comprehensive strategy for meeting future human resource needs (p. 294)

idea marketing: marketing efforts designed to promote a cause or social issue (p. 373)

implied warranty: warranty legally imposed on the seller and, generally, automatically effective unless disclaimed by the seller in writing (p. 702)

importing: buying foreign goods and raw materials (p. 82)

import quota: limitation on the number of products in certain categories that can be imported (p. 93)

incentive compensation: addition to a salary or wage given for exceptional performance (p. 313)

income statement: financial record of revenues, expenses, and profits of a company over a period of time (p. 534)

indirect exporting: exporting products that are part of another good that is exported (p. 87)

individual branding: giving each product in a line its own brand name (p. 411)

industrial distributors: wholesaling intermediaries selling products to industrial users (p. 437)

industrial goods: goods purchased to be used directly or indirectly in the production of other goods for resale (p. 378)

industrial park: planned commercial site that provides necessary zoning, land, shipping facilities, and waste disposal outlets (p. 235)

Industrial Revolution: shift to a factory system of manufacturing that began in England about 1750 (p. 11)

industrial union: labor union consisting of all workers in a specific industry, regardless of occupation or skill level (p. 332)

industrywide bargaining: single national union engages in collective bargaining with several employers in a particular industry (p. 342)

inflation: situation in which there are rising prices or decreased purchasing power of the nation's currency (p. 58)

informal organization: self-grouping of employees who possess informal communication channels (p. 211)

information: data organized in some manner so it is relevant in making decisions (p. 492)

informative advertising: advertising approach intended to build initial demand for a good or service in the introductory phase of the product life cycle (p. 468)

injunction: court order prohibiting some practice (p. 349)

inland marine insurance: insurance coverage for losses of property due to damage while goods are being transported by truck, ship, rail, or plane (p. 662)

input: portion of the computer system responsible for converting incoming data into a form the computer can understand (p. 498)

insider trading: illegal securities trading by persons who profit from their access to nonpublic information about a company (p. 664)

installations: expensive and long-lived major capital items such as a new factory or heavy machinery (p. 398)

institutional advertising: promotion of a concept, idea, philosophy, or the goodwill of an industry, company, organization, or a government entity (p. 468)

institutional investor: organization that invests its own funds or funds held in trust (p. 628)

insurable interest: insurance concept wherein the policyholder must stand to suffer loss (p. 658)

insurable risk: requirements that a risk must meet in order for the insurer to provide protection against its occurrence (p. 658)

insurance: process by which an insurer, in exchange for a fee, agrees to reimburse firms or individuals for losses up to specified limits (p. 657)

insurance company: business that provides protection for policyholders; premium payments are used to make long-term loans to corporations and commercial real-estate mortgages and to purchase government bonds (p. 569)

intangible assets: items of value that have no tangible physical properties (p. 532)

intangible personal property: property most often represented by a document or other written statement (p. 704)

integrated circuit: network of transistors, circuits, and other components etched on a silicon chip (p. 495)

intensive distribution: strategy used to achieve market saturation by placing products in every available outlet (p. 437)

intentional tort: civil wrong purposely inflicted on other persons or their property, such as assault, slander, or libel (p. 706)

interlocking directorate: situation involving identical or overlapping boards of directors for competitive companies (p. 697)

intermittent process: manufacturing operation with short production runs allowing machines to be shut down or changed to make different products (p. 226)

internal data: data generated within the organization (p. 382)

International Monetary Fund (IMF): organization that lends foreign exchange to countries requiring assistance in international trade (p. 97)

international union: national union with membership outside the United States (p. 335)

intrapreneur: entrepreneurial type manager operating within a corporate structure (p. 214)

inventory control: balancing costs of holding raw materials, work in progress, and inventory with costs involved in ordering them (pp. 239, 452)

inventory turnover ratio: ratio measuring the number of times merchandise moves through a business; calculated by dividing the cost of goods sold by the average amount of inventory (p. 541)

investment: purchasing securities for growth in investment value or income with relative safety (p. 629)

investment banker: specialist in selling new issues of securities for business and government (p. 621)

Investment Company Act of 1940: federal law that brought the mutual fund industry under the jurisdiction of the Securities and Exchange Commission in order to protect investors from possible trading abuses and stock manipulation (p. 644)

invisible hand of competition: Adam Smith's description of how competition regulates the private enterprise system (p. 6)

involuntary bankruptcy: situation in which creditors may request that a party be judged bankrupt (p. 707)

job analysis: identification of job characteristics and requirements of personnel for that particular job (p. 294)

job description: defines job objectives, work to be performed, responsibilities involved, skill requirements, working conditions, and the relationship of the job to other jobs (p. 294)

job enlargement: increasing the number of tasks a worker performs; may or may not be job enriching (p. 280)

job enrichment: redesigning work giving employees more authority in planning their work, deciding how it is to be done, and allowing them to learn related skills or to trade jobs (p. 280)

job evaluation: determination of wage level for a job based on skill requirements, education requirements, responsibilities, and physical requirements (p. 312)

job-order production: intermittent production that occurs in response to a specific customer order (p. 226)

job rotation: familiarization of junior executives with the various operations and contributions of each department through temporary assignments in those departments (p. 308)

job sharing: division of one job assignment between two or more employees (p. 283)

job specification: written description of the qualifications required for a particular job (p. 294)

Job Training Partnership Act: federal program designed to increase the skills of the hard-core unemployed (p. 37)

joint venture: partnership formed for a specific undertaking (p. 115); sharing of a foreign operation's costs, risks, and management with a foreign firm or government (p. 88)

journal: accountant's book of entry listing financial transactions chronologically (p. 526)

judiciary: branch of government charged with deciding disputes among parties through the application of laws (p. 694)

jurisdictional strikes: strikes resulting from disputes between two unions seeking jurisdiction over a group of workers (p. 338)

just-in-time (JIT) inventory system: system designed to minimize inventory at production facilities (p. 240)

key executive insurance: life insurance designed to compensate the organization for loss of an important executive (p. 676)

labor: the human resources of businesses (p. 7)

labor union: group of workers united by common goals such as wages, hours, and working conditions (p. 332)

Landrum-Griffin Act: federal law requiring regularly scheduled elections of union officers by secret ballot and increased regulation of the handling of union funds (p. 340)

law: standards set by government and society in the form of either legislation or custom (p. 692)

law of adverse selection: persons with health problems and those in dangerous occupations are more likely to purchase and renew health and life insurance policies than are others (p. 661)

law of bailment: the surrender of personal property from one person to another when the property is to be returned later (p. 705)

law of large numbers: calculation on which premiums are based of the likelihood of the occurrence of perils (p. 659)

law of supply and demand: economic law stating that market price is determined by the intersection of the supply and demand curves (p. 9)

layoff: temporary separation due to business decline (p. 310)

leadership: motivating or causing others to perform activities designed to achieve specific objectives (p. 183)

leadership style: way in which a leader uses available power to direct others (p. 184)

ledger: accounting book with separate accounts such as cash, sales, and inventory (p. 527)

leverage: technique of increasing the rate of return on investment through the use of borrowed funds (p. 611)

leveraged buyout (LBO): use of borrowed money to purchase a company or division (p. 126)

liability: claim of the firm's creditors (p. 529)

liability insurance: insurance protection for businesses and individuals against claims caused by injuries to others or damage to the property of others (p. 670)

liability losses: financial losses suffered by a business firm or individual should the firm or individual be held responsible for property damage or injuries suffered by others (p. 666)

limited-function merchant wholesaler: merchant wholesaler that takes legal title to goods but provides few services (p. 439)

limited partnership: partnership composed of one or more general partners and one or more partners with limited liability (p. 115)

limited-payment life insurance: variation of whole life insurance for which the policyholder pays all premiums within a designated period (p. 677)

limit order: investor request that a stock purchase or sale be made at a specified price (p. 636)

line-and-staff organization: organizational structure that combines the direct flow of authority with staff departments that support the line departments (p. 208)

line manager: manager of such functions as production, marketing, and finance (p. 208)

line of credit: agreement between a commercial bank and a business firm that states the amount of unsecured short-term credit the bank will make available to the borrower, as long as the bank funds are available (p. 604)

line organization: organizational structure based on a direct flow of authority from the chief executive to subordinates (p. 207)

liquid assets: another phrase for current assets (p. 531)

liquidity: speed at which items can be converted to cash (p. 531)

liquidity ratio: ratio measuring a firm's ability to meet its short-term obligations (p. 539)

local union: branch of a national union representing members in a specific area (p. 334)

lockout: management's closing of a firm to bring pressure on union members (p. 348)

long-term liabilities: debts that come due one year or more after the date of the balance sheet (p. 534)

lot-order production: intermittent production that occurs in response to inventory needs (p. 226)

macroeconomics: study of the overall operation of an economy (p. 58)

Magnuson-Moss Warranty Act (1975): federal legislation that authorized the Federal Trade Commission to establish warranty rules for any product covered by a written warranty and costing $15 or more (p. 412)

mainframe computer: largest type of computer system (p. 501)

maintenance factors: job-related factors (job security, salary) that are not strong motivators, but must be present to prevent worker dissatisfaction (p. 274)

major medical insurance: insurance that protects the insured against catastrophic financial losses by covering expenses that exceed the coverage limits of basic policies (p. 674)

make, buy, or lease decision: whether to manufacture, purchase, or lease a needed product, component, or material (p. 236)

Maloney Act of 1938: amendment to the Securities Exchange Act of 1934; authorized self-regulation of over-the-counter securities operations (p. 643)

managed trade agreement: negotiated limit on imports (p. 93)

management: achievement of organizational objectives through people and other resources (p. 168)

management by objectives (MBO): program designed to improve employee motivation through participation in goal setting and by informing employees in advance of the factors used in performance evaluations (p. 277)

management development program: training designed to improve skills and broaden the knowledge of managers and potential managers (p. 307)

management information system (MIS): organized method of providing information for decision making (p. 490)

management pyramid: managerial hierarchy of an organization (p. 169)

manufacturing resource planning (MRP II): integration of planning data from individual departments resulting in a master business plan (p. 241)

margin trading: securities purchases made with funds borrowed from the brokerage (p. 637)

market: people with the authority, financial ability, and willingness to purchase goods and services (p. 377)

marketing: planning and executing the conception, pricing, promotion, and distribution of ideas, goods, and services to create exchanges that satisfy individual and organizational objectives (p. 368)

marketing concept: organizationwide consumer orientation with the objective of achieving long-run success (p. 371)

marketing intermediaries: channel members operating between the producer and the consumer or industrial purchaser (p. 430)

marketing mix: combination of a firm's product, pricing, distribution, and promotional strategies focused on selected consumer segments (p. 374)

marketing research: information function that links the marketer to the marketplace (p. 382)

market order: investor request that a stock purchase or sale be made at the current market price (p. 636)

market segmentation: process of dividing the total market into several relatively homogeneous groups (p. 384)

market share: percentage of a market controlled by a certain company, good, or service (p. 414)

market value: price at which a security is currently selling (p. 623)

mass production: manufacture of products in large quantities as a result of standardization, specialized labor, and mechanization (p. 222)

master limited partnership: limited partnership that is publicly traded and functions like a corporation (p. 115)

materials handling: movement of goods within a firm's warehouse, terminal, factory, or store (p. 451)

materials requirement planning (MRP): computer-based production planning system for ensuring needed parts and materials are available at the right time and place in the correct amounts (p. 241)

matrix organization: structure in which specialists from different parts of the organization are brought together to work on specific projects (p. 210)

maturity date: date named on a security when the principal must be repaid (p. 601)

mechanization: use of machines to perform work previously performed by humans (p. 223)

mediation: process of settling union-management disputes through recommendations of an impartial third party (p. 345)

Medicare: form of health insurance for persons 65 years or older and certain other social security recipients (p. 663)

medium of exchange: means of facilitating exchange and eliminating the need for a barter system (p. 558)

megabyte: unit containing slightly more than a million bytes (p. 500)

memory unit: part of the computer that stores information (p. 498)

mentor: senior employee who acts as a sponsor and teacher to a younger, less-experienced employee (p. 308)

mentor system: counseling or advising relationship between an aspiring person and a higher-ranking executive (p. 738)

merchant wholesaler: independent wholesaler that takes legal title to goods (p. 439)

merger: two or more firms that combine to form one company (p. 124)

microcomputer: desktop, limited-storage computer system (p. 502)

microeconomics: study of a firm's economic activities (p. 58)

microprocessor: one or more computer chips containing the basic arithmetic, logic, and storage elements needed for processing (p. 503)

microsecond: one-millionth of a second (p. 495)

middle management: managers responsible for developing detailed plans and procedures to implement plans of top management (p. 170)

minicomputer: intermediate-size computer (p. 502)

missionary selling: indirect form of selling in which the sales representative markets the goodwill of a company and/or provides technical or operational assistance (p. 465)

mixed economy: economic system having a mix of government ownership and private enterprise (p. 17)

monetary policy: governmental policies and actions concerning regulation of the nation's money supply (p. 59)

money: anything generally accepted as a means of paying for goods and services (p. 556)

monopolistic competition: situation in which a large number of competing firms sell goods and services that can be distinguished from each other (p. 9)

monopoly: market situation in which there are no direct competitors (p. 9)

morale: mental attitude of employees toward their employer and/or job (p. 276)

mortality table: table used to predict the number of persons in each age category who will die in a given year (p. 676)

motivational factors: job-centered factors (recognition, responsibility) that are strong sources of employee motivation (p. 274)

motive: inner state that directs individuals toward the goal of satisfying a felt need (p. 266)

multinational corporation: corporation that operates production and marketing facilities on an international level (p. 90)

multiplant single-employer agreements: collective bargaining results that apply to all plants owned by the employer (p. 342)

municipal bond: debt issue of a state or political subdivision that may be a general-obligation bond or revenue bond (p. 625)

mutual funds: financial organizations that use investors' money to acquire a portfolio of securities (p. 640)

mutual insurance company: insurance company owned by its policyholders (p. 664)

nanosecond: one-billionth of a second (p. 495)

National Association of Securities Dealers (NASD): association created by the Maloney Act of 1938; responsible for regulating over-the-counter securities operations (p. 643)

national banks: commercial banks chartered by the federal government (p. 563)

national brand: brand that is offered and promoted by a goods or services producer (p. 410)

National Environmental Policy Act: federal statute that established the Environmental Protection Agency and gave it the authority to deal with various types of pollution (p. 699)

National Labor Relations Board (NLRB): federal agency that supervises union elections and prohibits unfair labor practices on the part of management (p. 337)

national union: labor organization comprised of numerous local chapters (p. 334)

natural resources: everything useful as a productive input in its natural state (p. 7)

near-money: assets almost as liquid as checking accounts but that cannot be used directly as a medium of exchange (p. 561)

need: lack of something useful; discrepancy between a desired state and the actual state (p. 266)

negligence: wrong based on careless rather than intentional behavior that causes injury to another person (p. 706)

negotiable instrument: form of commercial paper that is transferable among individuals and businesses (p. 703)

negotiable order of withdrawal (NOW) account: interest-bearing checking account offered by commercial banks, savings and loan associations, and savings banks (p. 560)

net income: profit or loss incurred over a specific period; determined by subtracting all expenses from revenues (p. 537)

networking: development and use of contacts to get ahead in business (p. 738)

no-fault insurance: state laws that require claims to be paid by the policyholder's insurance company without regard to fault and that limit the right of victims to sue (p. 668)

noncumulative preferred stock: stock that requires owners receive only the current year's dividend before common stockholders receive their dividends (p. 623)

nonprogrammed decision: decision involving complex, important, and nonroutine problems or opportunities (p. 186)

nontraditional student: any student who does not fall into the 18-to-22-year-old age group (p. 724)

Norris-La Guardia Act: federal legislation that protects unions by reducing mangement's ability to obtain injunctions halting union activities (p. 337)

note: document that describes the amount of funds owed and the time and place of repayment (p. 532)

objectives: guideposts in defining what the organization should achieve in areas such as profitability, customer service, and social responsibility (p. 173)

occupational cluster: group of related jobs (p. 722)

Occupational Safety and Health Administration (OSHA): federal agency created to assure safe and healthful working conditions (p. 320)

ocean marine insurance: insurance that covers shippers for losses of property due to damage to a ship or its cargo while at sea or in port (p. 669)

odd lots: quantities of less than 100 shares of stock bought or sold (p. 637)

odd pricing: practice of using uneven prices, such as $1.11, in the belief that odd prices are psychologically more attractive to consumers than even ones (p. 420)

Office of the CEO concept: organizational structure whereby the duties of the chief executive are shared among two or more executives (p. 209)

Old-Age, Survivors, Disability, and Health Insurance (OASDHI): government insurance that is part of the Social Security program (p. 663)

oligopoly: market having few sellers and substantial entry restrictions (p. 9)

on-line processing: method of scheduling computer processing in which data is entered and processed when received (p. 499)

on-the-job training: training employees for job tasks by allowing them to perform them under the guidance of an experienced employee (p. 306)

open-ended interview: interview designed to force applicants to talk about themselves and their goals (p. 735)

open market operations: Federal Reserve System method of controlling the money supply through the purchase and sale of government bonds (p. 573)

open shop: employment policy making union membership voluntary for all employees (p. 339)

open systems: systems that will rely on a common set of software that can be transferred from one brand of computer to another (p. 511)

operating expenses: all business costs other than those included in the cost of goods sold (p. 537)

operational plans: work standards that implement tactical plans (p. 178)

orderly marketing agreement: negotiated limit on imports (p. 93)

order processing: sales task of receiving and handling an order; function of handling the preparation of an order for shipment (pp. 452, 464)

organization: structured grouping of people working together to accomplish objectives (p. 198)

organization chart: diagram showing the division of work, chain of command, and departmentalization of an organization (p. 202)

organization marketing: marketing efforts designed to influence others to accept the goals of, receive the services of, or contribute in some way to an organization (p. 373)

organizing: process of blending human and material resources through the design of a formal structure of tasks and authority (p. 179)

output: portion of the computer system responsible for providing processed information to the user (p. 498)

outside directors: members of the board who are not employed by the organization (p. 122)

outsourcing: contracting all or part of a firm's production to overseas suppliers (pp. 65, 88)

over-the-counter (OTC) market: method of trading securities not listed on national and regional exchanges through market makers who fill customers' buy and sell orders (p. 634)

owners' equity: claims of the proprietor, the partners, or the stockholders against the assets of the firm; the excess of assets over liabilities (p. 529)

ownership utility: utility created by arranging for transfer of ownership at the time of purchase (p. 369)

parent company: corporation that owns all or a majority of another corporation's stock (called a subsidiary) (p. 123)

Parkinson's law: theory stating that work expands to fill the time available to complete it (p. 206)

partnership: two or more persons who operate a business as co-owners (p. 114)

par value: value printed on stock certificates of some companies (p. 622)

patent: inventors' guarantee of exclusive rights to their inventions for 17 years, provided the inventions have been accepted by the U.S. Patent Office (p. 709)

pay for knowledge: incentive compensation system in which employee salaries or wages increase with the number of tasks they are capable of performing (p. 315)

peer-review boards: committees consisting of peer workers and management representatives with the power to make binding resolutions of disputes involving promotion decisions, dismissals, and other disciplinary actions (p. 350)

penetration pricing: strategy of pricing a new product relatively low compared to similar goods in the hope that it will secure wide market acceptance that will allow the company to raise the price (p. 419)

pension fund: funds accumulated by a company, union, or nonprofit organization for the retirement income needs of its employees or members (p. 569)

perestroika: policy to restructure the Soviet economy (p. 15)

performance appraisal: defining acceptable employee performance levels, evaluating them, then comparing actual and desired performance to aid in determining training, compensation, promotion, transfers, or terminations (p. 308)

perpetual inventory: continuously updated listing of items in inventory (p. 239)

personal selling: promotional presentation made on a person-to-person basis with a potential buyer (p. 464)

person marketing: marketing efforts designed to cultivate the attention, interest, and preference of a target market toward a person (p. 373)

persuasive advertising: advertising approach used in the growth state of the product life cycle to improve the competitive status of a good, service, institution, or concept (p. 469)

PERT (Program Evaluation and Review Technique): scheduling technique for minimizing production delays by coordinating all aspects of the process (p. 243)

physical distribution: movement of goods from producer to user (p. 430)

physiological needs: primary human needs for food, shelter, and clothing that must be satisfied before higher-order needs can be considered (p. 267)

picketing: workers marching at a plant entrance protesting against some management practice (p. 348)

picosecond: one-trillionth of a second (p. 496)

piece wage: employee compensation based on productivity (p. 312)

place marketing: marketing efforts designed to attract people to a particular geographical area (p. 373)

place utility: utility created by making goods and services available where the consumer wants to purchase them (p. 369)

planning: anticipating the future and determining the best courses of action to achieve organizational objectives (p. 176)

plant: building owned by a firm (p. 599)

Plant-Closing Notification Act of 1988: federal legislation aimed at assisting employees and cities by requiring employers to give 60 days' notice before a plant closing or mass layoff (p. 341)

platinum handcuffs: benefits to reward employees for staying on past a certain age or period of service (p. 322)

point-of-purchase advertising (POP): type of sales promotion that displays and demonstrates an item at a time and place close to where the actual purchase decision is made (p. 473)

point-of-sale (POS) terminals: machines linked to a bank's computer that allow funds to be transferred from the purchaser's account to the seller's account when purchases are made (p. 582)

poison pill: takeover deterrent whereby stockholders are allowed to buy additional shares below market value (p. 125)

pollution: the tainting or destroying of a natural environment (p. 35)

positioning: promotional strategy used to differentiate a good or service from those of competitors in the mind of a prospective buyer (p. 461)

posting: recording journal entries in the appropriate ledger accounts (p. 527)

power: ability of one person to influence the behavior of another (p. 184)

preemptive right: stockholders' right to purchase a proportionate amount of new issues (p. 623)

preferred stock: stock that has the first claim to the corporation's assets after all debts have been paid (p. 122); provides owners with preferential dividend payment but seldom with voting rights (p. 623)

premium: sales promotion method offering a small gift to the consumer in return for buying a product (p. 474)

price: exchange value of a good or service (p. 396)

price-earnings ratio: current market price divided by annual earnings per share (p. 639)

pricing strategy: element of marketing decision making that deals with methods of setting profitable and justifiable prices (p. 375)

primary boycott: boycott in which union members are told not to patronize a specific firm (p. 340)

primary demand: desire for a general product category (p. 460)

primary market: new issues of securities sold publicly for the first time (p. 620)

prime interest rate: lowest rate of interest charged by commercial banks for short-term loans to major businesses with high credit standings (p. 603)

principal: person who is represented by an agent (p. 705)

private accountant: accounting professional employed by a government agency, nonprofit organization, or business other than a public accounting firm; also called management accountant (p. 524)

private brand: brand name owned by a wholesaler or retailer (p. 410)

private carriers: companies that transport their own goods in their own vehicles (p. 448)

private enterprise system: economic system in which success or failure is determined by how well firms match and counter the offerings of competitors (p. 4)

private property: property that can be owned, used, bought, sold, and bequeathed under the private enterprise system (p. 6)

privatization: trend to substitute private ownership for public ownership in a mixed economy (p. 17)

process culture: type of corporate culture involving relatively low-risk, slow feedback firms; emphasizes procedures (p. 182)

process layout: manufacturing facility design suited to the production of a variety of nonstandard products in relatively small batches (p. 236)

product: bundle of physical, service, and symbolic attributes designed to satisfy consumer wants (p. 396)

product advertising: nonpersonal selling of a good or service (p. 468)

production: use of people and machinery to convert materials into finished products or services (p. 222)

production and operations management: managing people and machinery used in converting materials and resources into finished products and services (p. 230)

production control: well-defined set of procedures for coordinating people, materials, and machinery to provide maximum production efficiency (p. 242)

production era: early part of the twentieth century, when business managers concentrated almost solely on the firm's production tasks (p. 12)

production planning: phase of production control that determines the amount of resources needed to produce a certain amount of goods or services (p. 242)

productivity: measure of the efficiency of production (pp. 8, 70)

product launch: stage at which the product is made generally available in the marketplace (p. 408)

product layout: manufacturing facility design that accommodates a few products in relatively large quantities (p. 236)

product liability: area of tort law that holds business liable for negligence in the design, manufacture, sale, and use of products (p. 707)

product liability insurance: insurance protection for businesses against claims for damages resulting from the use of the company's products (p. 671)

product life cycle: four stages through which a successful product passes: introduction, growth, maturity, and decline (p. 401)

product line: series of related goods offered by a firm (p. 400)

product line pricing: offering merchandise at a limited number of prices instead of pricing each item individually (p. 419)

product mix: assortment of products offered by a firm (p. 400)

product strategy: element of marketing decision making that deals with developing goods and services, package design, trademarks, warranties, and product life cycles (p. 375)

professional liability insurance: coverage that provides protection against financial losses resulting from successful malpractice lawsuits and to cover the costs of such lawsuits (p. 671)

profitability ratio: ratio measuring the overall financial performance of the firm (p. 540)

profit maximization: pricing strategy whereby management sets increasing levels of profitability as its objective (p. 414)

profits: difference between a company's revenues (receipts) and expenses (expenditures) (p. 4)

profit sharing: percentage of company profits distributed to employees involved in producing those profits (p. 313)

programmed decision: decision involving routine, recurring problems for which well-established solutions exist (p. 186)

program trading: computer systems programmed to buy or sell securities to take advantage of price differences that sometimes occur between stock futures and current stock prices (p. 642)

promissory note: traditional bank loan for which the borrower signs a note that states the terms of the loan, including its date of repayment and interest rate (p. 604)

promotion: increase in authority, responsibility, and salary (p. 310)

promotional mix: firm's combination of both personal and nonpersonal selling designed to achieve promotional objectives (p. 464)

promotional strategy: element of marketing decision making involving the blending of personal selling, advertising, and sales promotion tools to produce effective communication between the firm and the marketplace (p. 375); the function of informing, persuading, and influencing a consumer decision (p. 460)

property: something for which people have the unrestricted right of possession or use (p. 704)

property losses: financial losses resulting from interruption of business operations or physical damage to property as a result of fires, accidents, windstorms, theft, or other destructive occurrences (p. 665)

prospecting: sales task of identifying potential customers (p. 466)

protective tariff: tax designed to raise the retail price of imported goods to the level of goods produced domestically (p. 93)

proxy: authorization by stockholders for someone else to vote their shares (p. 122)

proxy fight: situation where both management and an outside party seek control of a firm through solicitation of proxies (p. 125)

public accountant: professional who provides accounting services to other businesses and individuals (p. 523)

Public Health Cigarette Smoking Act: federal law that prohibits tobacco advertising on radio and television (p. 692)

public insurance company: government agency that provides specialized insurance protection for individuals and organizations (p. 662)

public ownership: enterprise owned and operated by a governmental unit (p. 128)

public relations: an organization's communications with its various publics (p. 474)

pulling strategy: promotional strategy utilizing advertising and sales promotion appeals to generate consumer demand for a good or service as a means of exerting pressure on channel members to handle it (p. 477)

pure competition: situation in which the firms in an industry are so small that none individually influences market prices (p. 9)

Pure Food and Drug Act: federal law prohibiting the adulteration and misbranding of foods and drugs (p. 698)

pure risk: type of risk involving only the chance of loss (p. 654)

pushing strategy: sales-oriented promotional strategy designed to motivate marketing intermediaries to push the good or service to their customers (p. 476)

qualifying: sales task that enables the salesperson to concentrate on those prospects with the financial ability and authority to buy (p. 466)

quality circle: group of employees from the same work area who meet regularly to define, analyze, and solve quality and related problems in their area (p. 247)

quality control: measurement of products and services against established quality standards (p. 245)

quality of work life (QWL): program permitting employee participation in job design and the overall work environment decisions, includes job enrichment, flexible work schedules, and Theory Z management (p. 279)

rack jobber: full-function wholesaler that sets up and services a particular section of a retail store (p. 439)

raw materials: farm and natural products used in producing final goods (p. 398)

real gross national product: inflation-discounted gross national product data (p. 8)

real property: real estate (p. 704)

recycling: reprocessing of used materials for reuse (p. 35)

regulated industry: industry in which competition is either limited or eliminated and close government control substitutes for the market controls of free competition (p. 696)

reminder-oriented advertising: advertising approach used during the late maturity and decline stages of the product life cycle that seeks to reinforce previous promotional activity by keeping the name of the good or service in front of the public (p. 469)

remote terminal: machine connected to the main computer installation from a distant location (p. 501)

research and development: scientific process of developing new commercial products (p. 73)

reserve requirement: percentage of a bank's checking and savings accounts that must be kept in the bank or on deposit at the local Federal Reserve district bank (p. 573)

responsibility: obligation of a subordinate to perform assigned duties (p. 201)

resumé: written summary of one's personal, educational, and professional achievements (p. 729)

retailers: channel members selling goods and services to individuals for their own use rather than for resale (p. 430)

return on equity: ratio measuring company profitability by comparing net income and total owners' equity to assess the returns owners are receiving for their overall investment (p. 541)

return on sales: ratio measuring company profitability by comparing net income and net sales (p. 540)

revaluation: upward adjustment in the value of a nation's currency (p. 84)

revenues: funds received from sales of products and services and from interest payments, dividends, royalties, and rents (p. 536)

revenue tariff: tax designed to raise funds for the government (p. 93)

revolving credit agreement: guaranteed line of credit (p. 604)

right-to-work laws: state laws prohibiting compulsory union membership (p. 339)

risk: uncertainty about loss or injury (p. 654)

risk-return trade-off: balance between the risk of an investment and its potential gain (p. 594)

robbery insurance: insurance coverage for losses due to the unlawful taking of property from another person by force or the threat of force (p. 669)

Robinson-Patman Act: federal statute outlawing price discrimination that is not based on quality or quantity differences and that injures competition (p. 698)

robot: reprogrammable machine capable of performing numerous programmed tasks by manipulating materials and tools (p. 227)

round lots: quantities of 100 shares of stock bought or sold (p. 636)

routing: phase of production control that determines the sequence of work throughout the facility (p. 242)

safety needs: second level of human needs including job security, protection from physical harm, and avoidance of the unexpected (p. 268)

salary: employee compensation calculated weekly, monthly, or annually (p. 312)

sales branches: manufacturer-owned marketing intermediaries that stock the items the firm distributes and process orders from inventory (p. 438)

sales law: body of law pertaining to the sale of goods or products for money or credit (p. 702)

sales maximization: strategy under which management sets an acceptable minimum level of profitability and then tries to maximize sales (p. 414)

sales office: manufacturer-owned office for salespeople that provides close local contacts for regular and potential customers (p. 438)

sales promotion: form of promotion designed to increase sales through one-time selling efforts such as displays, trade shows, special events, and other methods (p. 472)

sample: type of sales promotion that uses distribution of free product gifts to gain public acceptance and future sales (p. 473)

savings and loan association (S&L): financial institution offering savings and checking accounts and using most of its funds to make home mortgage loans; also called thrift institution (p. 567)

savings banks: state-chartered banks operating similar to savings and loan associations (p. 568)

scheduling: phase of production control that develops timetables specifying how long each operation in the production process takes (p. 243)

scientific management: management approach to increase efficiency through scientific analysis of the jobs of individual workers, careful selection and training, and improved supervision (p. 264)

S corporations: corporations that are taxed as a partnership while maintaining the advantages of a corporation (p. 119)

scrambled merchandising: practice of retailers carrying dissimilar product lines to appeal to consumers seeking one-stop shopping (p. 443)

seasonal unemployment: joblessness of workers due to the seasonal hiring practices of their industry (p. 59)

secondary boycott: boycott or work stoppage intended to force an employer to cease dealing in the product of another firm (p. 340)

secondary market: sales of previously issued shares of stocks and bonds (p. 620)

secured bond: bond backed by specific pledges of company assets (p. 624)

securities: stocks and bonds representing obligations of the issuer to provide purchasers an expected or stated return on investments (p. 620)

Securities Act of 1933: federal law designed to protect investors by requiring full disclosure of relevant financial information from companies desiring to sell new stock or bond issues to the general public; also known as the Truth in Securities Act (p. 643)

Securities Exchange Act of 1934: federal law that created the Securities and Exchange Commission (SEC) to regulate the national stock exchanges (p. 643)

Securities Investor Protection Corporation (SIPC): nonprofit corporation that insures the accounts of individual investors to a maximum of $100,000 in cash losses and another $400,000 in securities in the event of dealer or broker insolvency (p. 644)

selective credit controls: Federal Reserve System's authority to regulate availability of credit by setting margin requirements on credit purchases or stocks and bonds and credit rules for consumer purchases (p. 574)

selective demand: desire for a particular product (p. 460)

selective distribution: market coverage strategy of selecting a limited number of retailers to distribute a firm's products (p. 437)

self-actualization needs: needs for fulfillment, for realizing one's potential, and for totally using one's talents and capabilities (p. 269)

self-insurance fund: an account set up to cover losses from the assumption of pure risk (p. 656)

seller's market: market situation characterized by shortages (p. 371)

selling expenses: expenses incurred in marketing and distributing goods and services (p. 537)

seniority: length of employment in a particular job, department, or company (p. 310)

separation: resignation, retirement, layoff, or termination of an employee (p. 310)

serial bond: bonds issued at the same time but with different maturity dates (p. 627)

Service Corps of Retired Executives (SCORE): SBA program using retired executives as consultants to assist small businesses (p. 152)

services: intangible tasks that satisfy both business and consumer needs (p. 66)

set-aside program: legislation that specifies only small businesses are eligible for certain government contracts (p. 152)

share draft accounts: interest-bearing credit union accounts that permit depositors to write drafts against them (p. 560)

shark repellent: provision that requires that a large majority of stockholders approve any takeover (p. 125)

Sherman Antitrust Act: federal antitrust legislation that prohibits every contract or conspiracy in restraint of trade and declares illegal any action that monopolizes or attempts to monopolize any part of trade or commerce (p. 697)

shopping goods: products purchased only after the consumer has compared competing goods in competing stores on price, quality, style, and color bases (p. 396)

shop steward: local union member responsible for representing other union members on the job on a daily basis (p. 346)

single-plant single-employer agreements: subject of most collective bargaining (p. 342)

sinking-fund bond: bond whose issuer deposits funds annually for redemption payment upon maturity (p. 627)

skimming pricing: strategy of setting the price of a new product relatively high compared to similar goods and then gradually lowering it (p. 418)

small business: business that is independently owned and operated, does not dominate its field, and meets a variety of size standards (p. 141)

Small Business Administration (SBA): principal government agency concerned with small U.S. firms (p. 151)

Small Business Development Centers (SBDC): centers using faculty and others to assist small business through research and consulting activities (p. 153)

Small Business Export Expansion Act: law providing SBA loan guarantees for up to 90 percent of bank loans of less than $500,000 to assist small businesses in developing international markets (p. 152)

Small Business Institute (SBI): SBA program that uses business students as consultants to small businesses (p. 152)

Small Business Investment Company (SBIC): federally funded investment group that makes loans to small businesses (p. 152)

Small Business Trade and Competitiveness Act: law designed to assist the small-business exporter hurt by foreign trade (p. 152)

social audit: formal examination of a firm's social responsibility programs (p. 32)

social (belongingness) needs: desire to be accepted by members of the family, other individuals, and groups (p. 268)

socialism: economic system that advocates government ownership and operation of all basic industries (p. 16)

social responsibility: management philosophies, policies, procedures, and actions that have the advancement of society's welfare as one of their primary objectives (p. 28); also management's consideration of the social and economic effects of its decisions (p. 33)

software: programs written to tell the computer what to do (p. 497)

sole proprietorship: ownership (and usually operation) of an organization by one person (p. 112)

span of management: optimal number of subordinates a manager can effectively supervise (p. 203)

specialization: dividing work into its simplest components to permit concentration in performing each task (p. 223)

specialty advertising: type of sales promotion that consists of giving away useful items imprinted with the donor's name, logo, or message (p. 473)

specialty goods: products perceived to be so desirable that the buyer is willing to make a special effort to obtain them (p. 397)

speculation: purchasing stocks in anticipation of making large profits quickly (p. 629)

speculative risk: type of risk involving the chance of either profit or loss (p. 654)

spreadsheets: special computer software permitting manipulation of decision variables to determine their impact (p. 506)

staff manager: manager who provides information, advice, or technical assistance to the line managers (p. 208)

Standard & Poor's Index: index based on market performance of 400 industrial, 40 financial, 40 utility, and 20 transportation stocks (p. 640)

standardization: production of uniform and interchangeable goods and parts (p. 224)

state banks: commercial banks chartered by individual states (p. 563)

statement of cash flows: information on a firm's cash receipts and cash payments that presents the sources and uses of cash for the firm (p. 538)

statistical process control (SPC): process of gathering, plotting, and analyzing data to pinpoint problem areas (p. 245)

statutory law: written law that includes state and federal constitutions, legislative enactments, treaties of the federal government, and ordinances of towns, cities, and other local governments (p. 692)

stockbroker: financial intermediary who buys and sells securities for clients (p. 635)

stock exchange: location at which stocks and bonds are bought and sold (p. 632)

stockholders: people who acquire the shares of, and therefore own, a corporation (p. 121)

stock insurance company: insurance company operated for profit (p. 664)

stocks: shares of ownership in a corporation (p. 611)

stock tapes: continuous listings of securities transactions and their most recent market prices for national and regional exchanges and the NASDAQ system (p. 636)

storage warehouse: warehouse that stores goods for relatively long time periods (p. 451)

store of value: temporary accumulation of wealth until it is needed for new purchases (p. 559)

strategic planning: process of setting organizational objectives, then determining overall strategy and resource allocations necessary to reach the objectives (p. 177)

stress interview: interview that creates a crisis situation in order to determine how that person copes with conflict (p. 735)

strict product liability: legal concept that covers injuries caused by products regardless of whether the manufacturer is proven negligent (p. 707)

strike: employees' temporary work stoppage until a dispute is settled or contract signed (p. 348)

strikebreaker: nonunion worker hired to replace a striking worker (p. 348)

structural unemployment: joblessness of people who lack necessary skills for employment or whose skills are no longer demanded (p. 59)

structured interview: prepared set of questions is asked of a job candidate (p. 301)

Subchapter S corporations: former name for S corporations (p. 119)

Subchapter S Revision Act of 1982: legislation that raised the maximum number of shareholders in an S corporation and changed the rules for converting an S corporation to regular corporation (p. 119)

subsidiary: corporation with all or a majority of its stock owned by another corporation (p. 123)

supervisory management: people directly responsible for details of assigning workers to specific jobs and evaluating performance (p. 170)

supplemental carriers: common carriers that engage in charter work (p. 451)

supplies: expense items needed in the firm's daily operation but not part of the final product (p. 399)

supply: schedule of what sellers will offer in the market at various price levels (p. 9)

supply curve: schedule that shows the relationship between different prices and the quantity supplied at each price (p. 60)

surety bond: bond that protects people or companies against losses resulting from nonperformance of a contract (p. 669)

surgical and medical payments insurance: health insurance designed to pay the costs of surgery, fees of medical specialists, and physicians' care in the hospital and during recovery (p. 674)

sweepstakes: sales promotion method offering cash or merchandise as prizes to participating winners (p. 474)

synthetic system: system that combines raw materials or parts into a finished product or changes them into completely different products (p. 225)

tactical planning: planning for the short-term implementation of current activities and the resource allocation for these activities (p. 177)

Taft-Hartley Act: federal law designed to balance the power of unions and management by prohibiting a number of unfair union practices (p. 338)

tangible personal property: physical things, such as goods and products (p. 704)

target market: group of consumers toward which a firm decides to direct its marketing efforts (p. 374)

target return goal: pricing strategy whereby the desired profitability is stated in terms of particular goals, such as a 10 percent return on sales (p. 414)

tariff: tax levied against imported products (p. 93)

technical skills: ability to understand and use techniques, knowledge, and tools of a specific discipline or department (p. 171)

technologically displaced worker: worker whose job is lost due to automation or industrial decline (p. 724)

telecommuting: working at home on a terminal hooked to a central computer (p. 283)

telemarketing: promotional presentation involving the use of the telephone (p. 467)

tender offer: when someone offers to buy all or a portion of a firm's stock at a premium over its current price (p. 125)

termination: permanent separation resulting from poor job performance, repeated rule violations, excessive absenteeism, elimination of job, or company closing (p. 310)

term insurance: insurance coverage protecting the individual for a specified period of years; it has no value at the end of that period (p. 677)

test marketing: stage in the new-product development process in which the product is sold in a limited area (p. 407)

theft insurance: insurance coverage for losses due to the unlawful taking of property (p. 669)

Theory X: managerial assumption that employees dislike work and must be coerced, controlled, or threatened to motivate them to work (p. 270)

Theory Y: managerial assumption that workers like work and, under proper conditions, accept and seek out responsibilities to fulfill their social, esteem, and self-actualization needs (p. 271)

Theory Z: management approach emphasizing employee participation as the key to increased productivity and improved quality of work life (p. 272)

therblig: smallest possible time-and-motion unit for a given task (p. 223)

thrifts: common name for savings and loan associations and savings banks (p. 567)

ticker tapes: continuous listings of securities transactions and their most recent market prices; replaced by computerized stock tapes (p. 636)

time deposit: account that requires prior withdrawal notice to avoid penalty (p. 561)

time management: process of allocating one's time effectively (p. 187)

time-sharing: linking of several users through remote terminals to a large central computer (p. 511)

time utility: utility created by making products and services available when the consumer wants to purchase them (p. 368)

time wage: employee compensation based on hours worked (p. 312)

title insurance: insurance protection for real estate purchaser against losses incurred because of a defect in title to property (p. 670)

tombstones: announcements of stock and bond offerings appearing in business newspapers (p. 620)

top management: managers who develop long-range plans and interact with the government and the community (p. 169)

tort: civil wrong inflicted on other persons or their property (p. 706)

tough-guy macho culture: type of corporate culture typical of high-risk industries; demands immediate results and rewards aggressive, individualistic members (p. 182)

trade credit: short-term source of funds from making purchases on credit or open account (p. 603)

trade deficit: unfavorable balance of trade (p. 65)

trademark: brand that has been given legal protection exclusive to its owner (p. 408); words, symbols, or other designations used to identify a product (p. 709)

trade show: type of sales promotion that uses exhibitions designed to promote goods or services to retailers, wholesalers, international buyers, and other resellers in the distribution channel (p. 473)

trade surplus: favorable balance of trade (p. 82)

trade war: situation in which protectionist trade policies of a nation cause trading partners to initiate reciprocal restrictions (p. 93)

trading stamps: sales promotion method offering stamps that are redeemable for additional merchandise (p. 474)

transfer: lateral change of position with about the same authority, responsibility, and salary (p. 310)

transistor: tiny device used to amplify current (p. 494)

Treasury bills: short-term U.S. Treasury borrowings issued each week and sold to the highest bidder; virtually risk-free and easy to resell (p. 601)

trial court: court of general jurisdiction operating at both the federal and state levels (p. 694)

tying contract: agreement that requires a person who wishes to be the exclusive dealer for a manufacturer's product to carry other products of the manufacturer in inventory (p. 697)

umbrella liability insurance: insurance that extends the amount of coverage limits to $1 million or more (p. 670)

unemployment: joblessness of people who are looking for work (p. 58)

unemployment insurance: state insurance program designed to assist unemployed workers (p. 662)

unfriendly merger: unsolicited and unwanted merger offer (p. 125)

Uniform Commercial Code (UCC): comprehensive commercial law (adopted by all states except Louisiana) that covers sales as well as other specific areas of commercial law (p. 702)

Uniform Limited Partnership Act: legislation that spells out the requirements for a limited partnership (p. 115)

Uniform Partnership Act: legislation regulating the partnership form of business ownership (p. 114)

union shop: employment policy requiring nonunion workers to join the union within a specified period (p. 339)

unitization: practice of combining as many packages as possible into one load that can be handled by a forklift truck (p. 443)

unit of account: common denominator for measuring the value of all goods and services (p. 558)

universal life insurance: hybrid form of life insurance combining term insurance with a tax-deferred savings account (p. 678)

Universal Product Code (UPC): bar code read by optical scanners, which print the item and the price on a receipt (p. 412)

unsecured loan: short-term source of funds from a loan for which the borrower does not pledge any assets as collateral (p. 603)

Uruguay Round: current round of trade talks centered in Montreal (p. 94)

utility: want-satisfying power of a product or service (p. 222)

variable costs: costs that change with the level of production, such as labor and raw materials (p. 417)

variable life insurance: hybrid form of whole life insurance in which policyholders pay premium supplements that are invested by the insurance company (p. 678)

venture capital: funds invested by outside investors in new, small, or struggling businesses with potential for rapid growth in exchange for an ownership share in the business (p. 610)

venture capitalist: private individual or business organization that invests in promising new businesses (p. 147)

vertical marketing system (VMS): planned distribution channel organized to reduce channel conflict and improve distribution efficiency (p. 434)

vertical merger: merger that occurs between firms at different levels in the production and marketing process (p. 124)

very large-scale integrated (VLSI) circuit: superchip created by increasing the compactness of transistors and circuits assembled on a single silicon chip (p. 496)

vestibule school: facsimiles of actual work areas where employees learn jobs using equipment similar to that on the job (p. 306)

voluntary arbitration: arbitration in which both union and management representatives decide to present their unresolved issues to an impartial third party (p. 346)

voluntary bankruptcy: situation in which a person or firm asks to be judged bankrupt because of an inability to pay off creditors (p. 707)

wage and salary administration: development and implementation of an employee compensation system (p. 311)

wages: employee compensation based on hours worked or on productivity (p. 311)

Wagner Act: federal law legalizing collective bargaining and requiring employers to bargain with the elected representatives of their employees; also known as the National Labor Relations Act (p. 337)

warehousing: the storage of goods (p. 451)

warranty: firm's promise to repair, replace, or refund the purchase price of a good or service if it proves unsatisfactory (p. 412)

Webb-Pomerene Export Act (1918): Law exempting antitrust legislation for U.S. firms acting together to develop export markets (p. 96)

Wheeler-Lea Act: federal law that both amends the Federal Trade Commission Act to further outlaw unfair or deceptive acts and practices in business and gives the FTC jurisdiction over false and misleading advertising (p. 698)

wheel of retailing: hypothesis explaining the evolution of retailing based on new types of retailers gaining competitive footholds by emphasizing low prices in exchange for limited services (p. 441)

white knight: friendly takeover whereby the acquired firm remains independent and keeps its existing management (p. 125)

whole life insurance: insurance providing both protection and savings for the policyholder (p. 677)

wholesaling intermediaries: channel members selling primarily to retailers, other wholesalers, or industrial users (p. 430)

Women's Business Ownership Act of 1988: law amending the Equal Credit Opportunity Act of 1974 to ban discrimination in business loans (p. 149)

word processing: use of computers to store, retrieve, view, edit, and print text materials (p. 504)

worker buyout: financial incentive designed to encourage older employees to voluntarily retire (p. 321)

workers' compensation insurance: insurance provided by employers under state law to employees injured on the job (p. 663)

work hard/play hard culture: type of corporate culture common in sales-oriented firms; frequently uses rallies, contests, and special promotions (p. 182)

working capital: difference between current assets and current liabilities (p. 534)

World Bank: organization that funds long-term economic development projects (p. 97)

yield: income received from securities; calculated by dividing dividends by market price (p. 630)

Name and Company Index

Subject Index

L.L. Bean, Inc.

1912 – 1920

Entrepreneur Leon Leonwood Bean launches a mail-order business in 1912 to sell his Maine Hunting Shoe. He mails a brochure to Maine hunting license holders from out of state and sets up shop in the basement of his brother's haberdashery store on Main St. in Freeport, Maine. When 90 of the first 100 pairs of boots sold are returned because they fell apart, L.L. refunds the purchase price, beginning the company's long tradition of a 100% money-back guarantee. L.L. borrows money, buys rubber from U.S. Rubber Co., improves the boot's rubber bottom, and mails more brochures. As demand for the boots grows, L.L. moves to a larger facility in 1917; he also begins selling hand-knit stockings and hunting apparel.

To keep his feet dry on hunting trips, L.L. Bean fashioned his Maine Hunting Shoe by stitching the tops of traditional leather hunting boots to the bottoms of rubber galoshes. Today, the boot is still the company's core product.

1941 – 1950

In 1941, L.L. travels to Washington, D.C., to help design boots the company makes for the Armed Forces during World War II. In 1945, he sets up a special retail salesroom in the middle of the factory. The *Saturday Evening Post* runs a feature article on the company in 1946 and the publicity results in 19,000 catalog inquiries. By 1950, sales reach $1.8 million.

L.L. Bean moved his boot manufacturing and mail-order business to the top two floors of this building in 1917, current site of the company's retail store.

1921 – 1940

By 1924, the company has 25 employees and sales of $135,000. L.L. begins advertising in outdoor magazines to promote his catalog. In 1927, he adds fishing and camping gear to the product mix. The business is incorporated in 1934. Sales pass $1 million in 1937.

1951 – 1960

In 1951, the retail store is opened 24 hours a day, 365 days a year. Recognizing the growing importance of women in the outdoor marketplace, L.L. adds a ladies' department to the store in 1954. The company buys the Small-Abbott moccasin factory in 1956 so that hand-sewn footwear can be manufactured in-house. Sales level off at $2 million during the late fifties.

1961 – 1969

Leon A. Gorman, L.L.'s grandson, joins the firm in 1961. During the mid-sixties he initiates changes to revitalize growth. The company updates products to appeal to the recreation-boom customers of the mid-sixties, improves catalogs to make ordering easier, sends summer and Christmas catalogs in addition to the spring and fall issues, increases advertising, and builds the mailing list. In 1967, L.L. Bean dies at the age of 94, and Gorman becomes president. NBC's Huntley-Brinkley evening news telecast devotes 8 minutes to L.L.'s death. The company receives 50,000 letters of condolence, and most include requests for catalogs. Sales reach $4.75 million and

L.L. Bean points out features of his Maine Hunting Shoe to a customer. The company's success is based on L.L.'s business philosophy: "Sell good merchandise at a reasonable profit, treat your customers like human beings, and they'll always come back for more."